Readings in
Distributed Artificial Intelligence

Edited by

Alan H. Bond

Concurrent Computation Program
California Institute of Technology

and

Les Gasser

University of Southern California

MORGAN KAUFMANN PUBLISHERS, INC.
SAN MATEO, CALIFORNIA

Editor   *Bruce Spatz*
Production Manager   *Shirley Jowell*
Design   *Beverly Kennon-Kelley*
Composition and Typesetting   *Arthur Ogawa and Carol Edwards-Atwood*
Pasteup and Cover Design   *Irene Imfeld*
Cover Illustration   *Jo Jackson*
Copy Editor   *Lyn Dupré*
Research Assistant   *Pamela Ellis*

Library of Congress Cataloging-in-Publication Data

Readings in distributed artificial intelligence

    Bibliography: p.
    Includes index.
    1. Distributed artificial intelligence.   2. Problem
solving–Data processing.   I. Bond, Alan H.   II. Gasser
Leslie George, 1949–
Q337.R42   1988   006.3   88-13475
ISBN 0-934613-63-X   CIP

Morgan Kaufmann Publishers, Inc.
2929 Campus Drive, San Mateo, California 94403
© 1988 by Morgan Kaufmann Publishers, Inc.
All rights reserved.
Printed in the United States of America

93 92 91 90 89 5 4 3 2 1

Dedication

We dedicate this book to two people: Elihu M. Gerson, sociologist and founder of the Tremont Research Institute, San Francisco, and Victor R. Lesser, Professor of Computer Science at the University of Massachusetts. Their deep, long term interest in basic research problems of order, representation, coordination, and distributed problem solving, their commitment to clear ideas and high-quality research, their contagious enthusiasm and encouragement, their perseverence, and their patience as educators and colleagues have greatly inspired us and will continue to enrich the work of those who work in this challenging, fascinating, and growing research arena.

Contents

Preface   xi

Acknowledgments   xv

I   Orientation   1

1   An Analysis of Problems and Research in DAI   3
   1.1   Introduction 3
   1.2   Description, Decomposition, Distribution, and Allocation of Tasks 10
   1.3   Interaction, Language, and Communication 16
   1.4   Coherence and Coordination 19
   1.5   Modeling Other Agents and Organized Activity 25
   1.6   Interagent Disparities: Uncertainty and Conflict 29
   1.7   Tools for Distributed Artificial Intelligence 33
   1.8   Open Problems 35

2   A Subject-Indexed Bibliography of Distributed Artificial Intelligence   37
   Bibliography 42

II   Basic DAI Problems and Approaches   57

3   Distribution and Task Allocation   59
   Introduction 59
      3.1   Frameworks for Cooperation in Distributed Problem Solving 61
         R. G. Smith, R. Davis
      3.2   Network Structures for Distributed Situation Assessment 71
         R. Wesson, F. Hayes-Roth, J. W. Burge, C. Stasz, C. A. Sunshine
      3.3   Architectures for Distributed Air-Traffic Control 90
         R. Steeb, S. Cammarata, F. Hayes-Roth, P. Thorndyke, R. Wesson
      3.4   Strategies of Cooperation in Distributed Problem Solving 102
         S. Cammarata, D. McArthur, R. Steeb
      3.5   Parallelism in Artificial Intelligence Problem Solving: A Case Study of Hearsay II 106
         R. D. Fennell, V. R. Lesser
      3.6   Distributed Interpretation: A Model and Experiment 120
         V. R. Lesser, L. D. Erman
      3.7   An Organizational View of Distributed Systems 140
         M. Fox
      3.8   Modeling Coordination in Organizations and Markets 151
         T. W. Malone

4   Coherence and Coordination   159
   4.1   Reasoning about Agents' Knowledge and Behavior 159

4.1.1 BEINGs: Knowledge as Interacting Experts 161
    D. B. Lenat

4.1.2 Elements of a Plan-Based Theory of Speech Acts 169
    P. R. Cohen, C. R. Perrault

4.1.3 Synchronization of Multi-Agent Plans 187
    J. S. Rosenschein

4.1.4 Knowledge Preconditions for Actions and Plans 192
    L. Morgenstern

4.1.5 Communication and Interaction in Multi-Agent Planning 200
    M. P. Georgeff

4.1.6 A Theory of Action for MultiAgent Planning 205
    M. P. Georgeff

4.1.7 The Representation of Events in Multiagent Domains 210
    M. P. Georgeff

4.1.8 An Implementation of a Multi-Agent Plan Synchronizer 216
    C. Stuart

4.1.9 Cooperation Without Communication 220
    M. R. Genesereth, M. L. Ginsberg, J. S. Rosenchein

4.1.10 Deals Among Rational Agents 227
    J. S. Rosenschein, M. R. Ginsburg

4.2 Reasoning about Collective Processes 235

4.2.1 Strategies for Distributed Decisionmaking 236
    R. R. Tenney, N. R. Sandells

4.2.2 Interacting Plans 248
    B. Bruce, D. Newman

4.2.3 Coherent Cooperation Among Communicating Problem Solvers 268
    E. H. Durfee, V. R. Lesser, D. D. Corkill

4.2.4 Using Partial Global Plans to Coordinate Distributed Problem Solvers . . 285
    E. H. Durfee, V. R. Lesser

4.3 Achieving Coherence by Resolving Disparities and Uncertainty 294

4.3.1 Functionally Accurate, Cooperative Distributed Systems 295
    V. R. Lesser, D. D. Corkill

4.3.2 The Scientific Community Metaphor 311
    W. A. Kornfeld, C. E. Hewitt

4.3.3 Offices Are Open Systems 321
    C. Hewitt

5 Interaction Languages, Structures and Protocols   **331**
Introduction 331

5.1 Negotiation as a Metaphor for Distributed Problem Solving 333
    R. Davis, R. G. Smith

5.2 The Contract Net Protocol: High-Level Communication and Control in a Distributed Problem
    Solver 357
    R. G. Smith

5.3 Multistage Negotiation in Distributed Planning 367
    S. E. Conry, R. A. Meyer, V. R. Lesser

5.4 Dialogue-Games: Metacommunication Structures for Natural Language Interaction 385
    J. A. Levin, J. A. Moore

5.5 Concurrent Programming Using Actors: Exploiting Large-Scale Parallelism 398
    G. Agha, C. Hewitt

5.6 Control of Processes by Communication over Ports as a Paradigm for Distributed
    Knowledge-Based System Design 408
    A. S. Cromarty

III   Implementation Frameworks and DAI Applications   **421**

6   Implementation Languages and Systems   **423**
Introduction 423
   6.1   An Object-Oriented Approach to Knowledge Systems 425
        M. Tokoro, Y. Ishikawa
   6.2   Object-Oriented Concurrent Programming in ABCL/1 434
        A. Yonezawa, J-P. Briot, E. Shibayama
   6.3   Implementing Distributed AI Systems Using MACE 445
        L. Gasser, C. Braganza, N. Herman
   6.4   A Software and Hardware Environment for Developing AI Applications on Parallel Processors . . 451
        R. Bisiani
   6.5   ABE: A Cooperative Operating System and Development Environment 457
        F. Hayes-Roth, L. D. Erman, S. Fouse, J. S. Lark, J. Davidson
   6.6   Modeling and Diagnosing Problem-Solving System Behavior 490
        E. Hudlicka, V. Lesser

7   Blackboard Structures   **503**
Introduction 503
   7.1   A Blackboard Architecture for Control 505
        B. Hayes-Roth
   7.2   Achieving Flexibility, Efficiency, and Generality in Blackboard Architectures 541
        D. D. Corkill, D. Q. Gallagher, P. M. Johnson
   7.3   COPS: A System for Constructing Multiple Blackboards 547
        L. V. Leao, S. N. Talukdar
   7.4   Transactional Blackboards 557
        J. R. Ensor, J. D. Gabbe

8   Example Applications of DAI   **563**
Introduction 563
   8.1   An Intelligent System for Document Retrieval in Distributed Office Environments 565
        U. Mukhopadhyay, L. M. Stephens, M. N. Huhns, R. D. Bonnell
   8.2   Supporting Organizational Problem Solving with a Work Station 578
        G. Barber
   8.3   Providing Intelligent Assistance in Distributed Office Environments . . . 590
        S. Nirenburg, V. Lesser
   8.4   Knowledge-Based Support of Cooperative Activities 599
        W. B. Croft, L. S. Lefkowitz
   8.5   An Architecture for Control and Communications in Distributed Artificial Intelligence Systems . 606
        J.-Y. D. Yang, M. N. Huhns, L. M. Stephens
   8.6   An Examination of Distributed Planning in the World of Air Traffic Control 617
        N. V. Findler, R. Lo

Index   **629**

Preface

During the past several years, there has been a strong revival of interest in Distributed Artificial Intelligence (DAI), with a recognition that the core problems are quite profound and impact many areas interesting to others both in AI and in related disciplines. Many recent developments encourage this conclusion:

- The spread of concurrent and distributed computing
- Deeper integration of computing into the lives of people, which has led to increasing collaborations among large collections of interacting people and large groups of interacting machines
- Growing interest in integrating research in AI, cognitive science, and the like with the construction and use of open distributed systems

DAI promises to provide stimulating challenges for years to come. At this time there are few clear organizing frameworks with which to compare and relate research in DAI. Eight DAI workshops have been held, and reports on these workshops do provide useful scope and overviews of topics of interest to DAI researchers. Until recently, however, the only survey available was Jeff Rosenschein's [Rosenschein85a] (Decker and Lesser and Corkill published surveys of distributed problem solving in 1987 [Decker87b; Lesser87]). In our opinion, there has been too little articulation of basic problems and methods that might begin to unify the field, to provide both research focus for other researchers, and to present students with an integrating perspective.

Over several years of teaching courses and seminars in DAI, we have begun to identify a set of the most central and helpful papers on DAI research. These papers cover the range of topics treated in the contemporary DAI literature. They form a core set of readings to which we most often refer, and provide graduate students with manageable but comprehensive access to the key ideas in the field. In developing our own research, building on the results in these papers, we have asked ourselves what problems of DAI are basic ones? As practitioners, what techniques and insights do we have to guide us in solving them? When we teach graduate students, to what basic history, perspectives, and prior research would we like to expose them?

This book is an attempt to provide answers for these questions. As we have used and thought about these materials and talked with other researchers, we have begun to generate a coherent set of research problems that we feel DAI research must address. We have begun to use these problems as a way of organizing our conceptions. With a focus on problems, rather than topics, we reveal some surprising gaps in DAI research. For example, there has been virtually no DAI research on collective learning. Almost no one in DAI has examined automated problem description, construction, and decomposition strategies. Perhaps the most glaring oversight has been the lack of strong attention to a set of core problems, research methods, and clear evaluation criteria in DAI research. (This may not be surprising, given the relative dearth of attention to these topics in AI, and, especially with respect to methods, in computer science in general). We remember Mike Genesereth making a plea for stronger methods and evaluations at the 1985 DAI workshop [Gasser87b], and to date, (with certain particular exceptions) the gap seems to remain.

Another purpose of this book is to provide some new and possibly challenging perspectives in studying the problems of Distributed AI. We hope that the survey that introduces this book will illuminate some of the conceptual assumptions often made in contemporary DAI research, and open some new avenues for addressing DAI problems. For example, we have reconceived "distribution" along dimensions of time, semantics, and logical dependency, as well as the more common spatial conception, in part because we feel that it better unifies the problems of decomposition and allocation with those of reconciling disparities in view. Also, based on alternative social perspectives, we have suggested that "organization" in DAI systems can be treated as an emergent property of interaction, not just as a structural condition, as is usually the case in DAI research. There are others, but we will leave them for the body of the book.

How to Use This Book

We have intended *Readings in Distributed Artificial Intelligence* to be useful to new students of DAI, to practitioners who wish to review techniques and knowledge for solving particular problems, and to researchers who need a compendium of perspectives and results. It is difficult to satisfy the organizational demands of such a wide audience, so herewith we present some strategies for exploring the DAI terrain.

Readers new to Distributed AI might begin by perusing the Contents and the categories in the Subject-Indexed Bibliography to get an intuitive feel for the kinds of topics of interest in DAI circles. A good next step would be reading Lesser and Corkill's "Functionally Accurate, Cooperative Distributed Systems," followed by reading the survey in Chapter 1. Other good introductory papers include those by Davis and Smith [Davis83], Lesser and Erman [Lesser80a], and Rosenschein [Rosenschein82]. The structure of the survey closely matches the chapter organization of the book, so it should be a simple matter to move from review topics to other papers that seem interesting.

Practitioners interested in how DAI systems have been built might first concentrate on Section 7 of the Survey, and Chapters 6, 7, and 8 of the book, which discuss specialized tools and applications of DAI. Other papers in the book that deal with implemented systems, and that might be of interest to practitioners include [Cromarty86; Davis83; Durfee87d; Fennell77; Gasser87c; Lenat75; Lesser80a; Smith80]. The survey will provide approaches to the problems that have needed to be addressed in virtually all real DAI systems. These problems and the approaches presented (augmented by more detailed knowledge found in the relevant book sections) can be used as an organizing framework for thinking through and possibly organizing the design and construction process.

To use the book for a course in Distributed AI, we suggest introducing material in the order we have recommended earlier for readers new to DAI, and then covering chapters in the order they have been presented in the book. An alternative might be to cover all the papers related to each core DAI research project or stream as a group, in chronological order, followed by Chapters 6, 7, and 8. The survey in Chapter 1 provides an organizing framework for the ideas in the diverse streams of research. Using this approach, papers could be grouped as follows:

- Papers about the Distributed Vehicle Monitoring Testbed (DVMT) and its predecessors, by Corkill, Durfee, Erman, Fennell, Hudlicka, and Lesser [Fennell77; Lesser80a; Durfee87d; Durfee87c; Lesser81; Hudlicka87].
- Papers on actors and open systems, by Agha, Kornfeld, and Hewitt [Agha85; Kornfeld81b; Hewitt86].
- Papers on the Contract Net by Davis and Smith [Davis83; Smith80; Smith81b].
- Papers on Rand research in Air-Traffic Control (ATC) by Cammarata, Hayes-Roth, McArthur, Steeb, Thorndyke, and Wesson [Cammarata83; Steeb81].
- Papers on reasoning about action and planning by Georgeff, Morgenstern, and Stuart [Georgeff83; Georgeff84; Georgeff86a; Morgenstern87; Stuart85].
- Papers on game-theoretic models of interaction by Genesereth, Ginsburg, and Rosenschein [Rosenschein85b; Rosenschein86].

Other papers cover other diverse topics such as natural language and DAI [Cohen79; Bruce78; Levin77]; distributed decision making [Tenney81a]; human organizations, social metaphors, and DAI [Fox81; Malone87a]; and so on.

Most of the papers in this book will presume some significant prior knowledge of Artificial Intelligence, and some also presume knowledge of logic and discrete mathematics. At USC, we teach most of the material as a second tier course in a graduate AI curriculum, following up a graduate introduction to AI. But in seminar courses, some advanced undergraduates have been comfortable discussing many of the papers.

We assume that researchers somewhat familiar with the field will be able to use the Survey to gain an organizing perspective to a set of research problems, which can be fleshed out further by reading particularly interesting papers that appear in the book. The Subject-Indexed Bibliography can be used as a guide to other research.

Acknowledgements

This book has been in many ways a collaborative (if not always highly coordinated!) effort, resting on the thoughts and efforts of numerous friends and colleagues. It wouldn't have been possible for us to complete it without the generous assistance we received from many people. We are most grateful, of course, to the authors of the articles reprinted here for the stimulation and quality of their research and for the generous permission to reprint their work. We are also especially grateful for the critical comments, suggestions, and encouragement we received from Dan Corkill, Ed Durfee, Mike Georgeff, Nava Herman, Carl Hewitt, Vic Lesser, Joseph Pasquale, and Randy Steeb who read and discussed with us various materials and drafts. Conversations with Yigal Arens, Salah Bendifallah, Dave Billstrom, Carl Braganza, Joe Brandenburg, Phil Cohen, Mike DeBellis, Elihu Gerson, Randy Hill, Julia Hough, Rick Hull, Dean Jacobs, John Lieb, Tom Malone, Jeff Rosenschein, Nick Rouquette, Walt Scacchi, Leigh Star, members of the USC DAI Group and students in the DAI courses at USC also helped clarify for us many of the issues presented in the book, though in some cases they may not have realized it. N.S. Sridharan has been an ardent supporter of Distributed AI for years, and also provided great encouragement.

We are especially grateful for the generous support of Charles Bishop, Dave Billstrom, and others at Intel Scientific Computers, Inc., as well as the ATT Foundation, and the USC/UCLA Institute for Manufacturing and Automation Research. Geoffrey Fox of the California Institute of Technology provided moral, intellectual, and financial support. SRI International provided a congenial workplace in Menlo Park during the early writing phases in the summer of 1987, and we are especially grateful to Mike Georgeff there. The Tremont Research

Institute, San Francisco, also has provided unflagging support, workspace, and sustinence at various points.

At Morgan Kaufmann, we thank Bruce Spatz, Jennifer Ballentine, Shirley Jowell, and Mike Morgan for infectious enthusiasm for the book throughout, for much hard work putting it together, and for helping us find our way through the publishing maze. Erica Goebel and Irene Imfeld helped with the cover concept and execution, Jo Jackson provided the cover illustration, Lyn Dupré meticulously copy-edited the manuscript, and Art Ogawa performed LaTeX miracles for formatting, indexing, and typesetting.

Of course, responsibility for the selection, perspectives and criticisms presented within ultimately lie with us, and blame for any misjudgements or factual errors cannot be laid at the doorstep of those mentioned above.

Alan H. Bond and Les Gasser
Los Angeles, California
June, 1988

Acknowledgments

The editor would like to thank the publishers and authors for permission to reprint copyrighted material in this volume.

Gul Agha and Carl E. Hewitt, "Concurrent Programming Using Actors: Exploiting Large-Scale Parallelism," *Proceedings of the 5th Conference on Foundations of Software Technology and Theoretical Computer Science*, 1985. © 1985, Springer-Verlag. All rights reserved. Reprinted with permission of the publisher and the authors.

Gul Agha, "An Overview of Actor Languages," *SIGPLAN Notices 21*(10):58–67, 1986. © 1986, ACM. All rights reserved. Reprinted with permission of the publisher and the author.

Gerald R. Barber, "Supporting Organizational Problem Solving with a Work Station," *ACM Transactions on Office Information Systems 1*:45–67, 1983. © 1983, ACM. All rights reserved. Reprinted with permission of the publisher and the author.

Roberto Bisiani, "A Software and Hardware Environment for Developing AI Applications on Parallel Processors," *Proceedings AAAI-86*, pp. 742–747, 1986. © 1986, AAAI. All rights reserved. Reprinted with permission of the publisher and the author.

Bertram Bruce and Denis Newman, "Interacting plans," *Cognitive Science*, pp. 195–233, 1978. © 1978, Ablex Publishing Corp. All rights reserved. Reprinted with permission of the publisher and the authors.

Stephanie Cammarata, David McArthur, and Randall Steeb, "Strategies of Cooperation in Distributed Problem Solving," *Proceedings of the 1983 International Joint Conference on Artificial Intelligence*, pp. 767–770, 1983. © 1983, used by permission of the International Joint Conferences on Artificial Intelligence, Inc. All rights reserved. Reprinted with permission of the publisher and the authors.

P. Cohen and R. Perrault, "Elements of a plan-based theory of speech acts," *Cognitive Science 3*:177–212, 1979. © 1987, Ablex Publishing Corp. All rights reserved. Reprinted with permission of the publisher and the authors.

S. Conry, R. Meyer, and V. Lesser, "Multistage Negotiations in Distributed Planning," *COINS TR86-87*, pp. 1–17. © 1986, University of Massachusetts. All rights reserved. Reprinted with permission of the publisher and the authors.

Daniel D. Corkill, Kevin Q. Gallagher, and Philip M. Johnson, "Achieving Flexibility, Efficiency, and Generality in Blackboard Architectures," *Proceedings AAAI-87*, pp. 18–23, 1987. © 1987, AAAI. All rights reserved. Reprinted with permission of the publisher and the authors.

W. Bruce Croft and Lawrence S. Lefkowitz, "Knowledge-Based Support of Cooperative Activities," © 1988, IEEE. Reprinted, with permission of publisher and authors, from *Proceedings of the 21st Annual Hawaii International Conference on System Sciences*, Vol III, pp. 312–318, 1988. All rights reserved.

Andrew S. Cromarty, "Control of Processes by Communication over Ports as a Paradigm for Distributed Knowledge-Based System Design," in Kerschberg (ed.), *Expert Database Systems*, pp. 91-103, 1987. © 1987, Benjamin/Cummings Publishing Company, Inc.. All rights reserved. Reprinted with permission of the publisher and the author.

Randall Davis and Reid G. Smith, "Negotiation as a metaphor for distributed problem solving," *Artificial Intelligence 20*:63–109, 1983. © 1983, North Holland. All rights reserved. Reprinted with permission of the publisher and the authors.

Edmund H. Durfee and Victor R. Lesser, "Using Partial Global Plans to Coordinate Distributed Problem Solvers," *Proceedings of the 1987 International Joint Conference on Artificial Intelligence*, pp. 875–883, 1987. © 1987, used by permission of the International Joint Conferences on Artificial Intelligence, Inc. All rights reserved. Reprinted with permission of the publisher and the authors.

Edmund H. Durfee, Victor R. Lesser, and Daniel D. Corkill, "Coherent Cooperation Among Communicating Problem Solvers," © 1987, IEEE. Reprinted, with permission, from *IEEE Transactions on Computers C-36*:1275–1291, 1987. All rights reserved.

J. Robert Ensor and John D. Gabbe, "Transactional Blackboards," *Proceedings of the 1985 International Joint Conference on Artificial Intelligence*, pp. 340–344, 1985. © 1985, used by permission of the International Joint Conferences on Artificial Intelligence, Inc. All rights reserved. Reprinted with permission of the publisher and the authors.

Richard D. Fennell and Victor R. Lesser, "Parallelism in Artificial Intelligence Problem Solving: A Case Study of

Part I

Orientation

Chapter 1

An Analysis of Problems and Research in DAI

1.1 Introduction

Most artificial intelligence (AI) research investigates how a single agent can exhibit intelligent behavior such as solving problems using heuristic or knowledge-based methods, planning, understanding and generating natural language, perception and learning. Several recent developments have together provoked interest in concurrency and distribution in AI: the development of powerful concurrent computers, the proliferation of multinode computer networks, and the recognition that much human problem solving and activity involves groups of people. *Distributed Artificial Intelligence* (DAI) is the subfield of AI concerned with concurrency in AI computations, at many levels.

1.1.1 What is DAI?

Initially, on the basis of the historical interests of researchers in DAI [Davis80; Davis82; Fehling83; Smith85b; Gasser87b; Sridharan87], we shall divide the world of DAI into two primary arenas. Research in *Distributed Problem Solving* (DPS) considers how the work of solving a particular problem can be divided among a number of modules, or "nodes," that cooperate at the level of dividing and sharing knowledge about the problem and about the developing solution [Lesser87; Smith81b]. In a second arena, which we shall call *Multiagent* (MA) systems, research is concerned with coordinating intelligent behavior among a collection of (possibly pre-existing) autonomous intelligent "agents"[1] how they can coordinate their

knowledge, goals, skills, and plans jointly to take action or to solve problems. The agents in a multiagent system may be working toward a single global goal, or toward separate individual goals that interact. Like modules in a DPS system, agents in a multiagent system must share knowledge about problems and solutions. But they must also reason about the *processes of coordination among the agents*. In multiagent systems, the task of coordination can be quite difficult, for there may be situations (in so-called *open systems*) where there is no possibility for global control, globally consistent knowledge, globally shared goals or global success criteria, or even a global representation of a system [Hewitt85; Hewitt86].

Research in a third arena, related to DAI, which we shall call *Parallel AI* (PAI), is concerned with developing parallel computer architectures, languages, and algorithms for AI. These are primarily directed toward solving the performance problems of AI systems, and not toward conceptual advances in understanding the nature of reasoning and intelligent behavior among multiple agents. Earlier, Parallel AI was not highly differentiated as a subdiscipline separate from DAI (cf. [Davis80; Davis82; Fehling83]). However, for the most part, we shall be only minimally concerned with Parallel AI in this survey (and in the book as a whole), consistent with more recent specializations in the field. We shall focus on approaches to the problems of distributing and coordinating knowledge and action in distributed problem-solving and multiagent systems, and this research is what we shall term "DAI." It is important

---

[1] For most of this survey, we will rely on a simple and intuitive notion of an *agent* as a computational process with a single locus of control and/or "intention". This view, however, is actually very problematic: agents may be implemented using concurrent subprocesses [Agha86a; Gasser87d], they may have multiple and conflicting goals, and the nature and reality of the concepts "goal" and "intention" are unclear (cf. [Cohen87a; Suchman87]). The process of defining the boundaries of what comprises an agent interacting with a world is also fraught with difficulties, from the standpoint of epistemology, of social psychology, and, we think, of computer science. See, for example, [Bentley54; Dewey16; Mead34]

to note, however, that developments in concurrent languages and architectures may have profound impacts on DAI system architectures, reliability, knowledge representation, and so on.

Another dimension for differentiating systems with different types of concurrency is how much of the reasoning about problem solving and coordination is done by system developers, and how much is done by the system itself; that is, how adaptive can the system itself be to changes in the problem or in the context? Parallel AI systems may be able to adapt to temporal uncertainty (e.g., indeterminate computation speeds), but not to alternative solution paths or to the loss of problem-solving knowledge. A DPS system may be adaptive to uncertainty in problem-solving knowledge [Lesser81], but not to alternative problem contexts or to changing problem-solving roles for modules. A multiagent system may be able to form and restructure coordination frameworks based on emerging contexts and changing problem-solving roles without the intervention of a programmer.

Research in Distributed AI promises to have wide-ranging impacts in cognitive science (e.g., mental models, social cognition), distributed systems (reasoning about knowledge and actions in distributed systems, architectural and language support for Distributed AI), human-computer interaction (task allocation, intelligent interfaces, dialogue coherence, speech acts), basic AI research (problem representations, epistemology, joint concept formation, collaborative reasoning and problem solving), and the engineering of AI systems ("cooperating expert systems," distributed sensing and data fusion, cooperating robots, collaborative design problem solving, etc.). But research into DAI is also attractive for more fundamental reasons: to coordinate their actions, intelligent agents need to represent and reason about the knowledge, actions, and plans of other agents. Distributed AI research can help us to improve our techniques for representing and using knowledge about beliefs, action, plans, goals, and so on [Davis80]. Moreover, other investigators have suggested that DAI may draw from and contribute to other disciplines, both absorbing and providing theoretical and methodological foundations [Chandrasekn81; Lesser83; Wesson81]. "Fields of study heretofore ignored by AI — organization theory, sociology, and economics, to name a few — can contribute to the study of DAI. Presumably, DAI will advance these fields as well by providing a modeling technology suitable for precise specification and implementation of theories of organizational behavior" ([Wesson81], pg. 18).

A Methodological Note

From a methodological perspective, virtually all extant research in DAI has focused on how a collection of agents can interact to solve a single common "global" problem, such as designing a very large scale integrated circuit (VLSI) chip, devising a globally consistent interpretation of geographically distributed sensor data, or constructing a globally coherent plan

for several agents. The range of problems and the objects of study appropriate to DAI research are actually much wider than this, and a larger conceptual frame should be brought to bear in analyzing the difficulties and possibilities of DAI. There are three classes of objects of study for DAI, all of which comprise coordinated aggregates of intelligent agents. A *natural systems* approach to Distributed AI would study the strategies and representations that people use to coordinate their activities, in much the same way that cognitive scientists investigate individual cognition in people. This approach would, of course, include computer modeling and simulation of the coordination activities of people. An *engineering-science* perspective on Distributed AI would investigate how to build functioning, automated, coordinated problem solvers for specific applications. In many cases, the problems of coordination would be simplified (over those in multiperson aggregates) by using standard communication protocols and by relying upon global viewpoints. A *person-machine coordination* approach would be useful in analyzing and developing collections of people and machines working together in coordinated ways. Within this approach, research in DAI is already seeding research and practice in the areas of computer-supported cooperative work and office automation [Barber80; Barber82; Barber83; de Jong88; Croft88; Fikes82; Hewitt86; Nirenburg86].

In each case, it may be tempting to carve away the study and understanding of people interacting. But this approach can pose diffculties. In analyzing person-machine coordination[Gasser84; Gasser86; Suchman87]. Complete analysis of engineered DAI systems may also demand consideration of which conflicts are to be settled by people "outside" the system, and which are handled "autonomously" by the system itself. The nature of the boundaries dividing "the system" from "the environment" are analytically problematic.

The survey presented here is organized around a set of basic questions for DAI, that is applicable to all these approaches. Nonetheless, the primary focus of this survey and and of this book is distributed *artificially* intelligent systems. We shall examine what is currently known and what is not known about answers to these questions. In this way, we hope to allow scientists and engineers to appreciate the open problems and the currently accepted wisdom in the field.

Historical Antecedents of Distributed AI

Distribution and parallelism have historically been important themes in artificial intelligence. The conceptual basis for concurrent processes underlying artificial intelligence has been well established and motivated by many, from the inception of AI in the early fifties, up to and including Minsky's vision of the mind as a society of cooperating agents [Minsky79; Minsky80; Minsky86] and Arbib's conception of the brain's information processing as a collection of concurrent "schemas" [Arbib85; Arbib88]. During the fifties, there were two main approaches to AI — heuristic search using list processing methods on the one hand and neural net modeling on the other. Neural models reached conceptualized forms in Selfridge's Pandemonium [Selfridge59] and Rosenblatt's Perceptron [Rosenblatt62]. The computational structures used were layers of "neurons," the processes they modeled were usually pattern recognition tasks, and the main programming method was synaptic learning. There were some theoretical results in learning theorems. Hybrid analog and digital nets were explored in probability state variable (PSV) systems [Lee63]. Feedback in neural nets was investigated by Aleksander [Aleksander75], who also generalized the systems to networks of RAM memory elements. Unfortunately, the lack of sufficiently powerful programming or learning methods, theoretical intractability, but principally implementation difficulties, made such work difficult. It has been taken up anew in the present implementationally more fortunate era, as *Parallel Distributed Processing* [McClelland87] and *Connectionism* [Feldman82].

Over time, serial list processing problem-solving methods were generalized into quasi-parallel symbol processing models, which began with the pattern-directed control of PLANNER [Hewitt71], and with the production system approach of Newell and Simon [Newell72] in the late sixties. The pattern-directed approach of Hewitt allowed separate processes, triggered associatively off a global database of symbolic structures. The parallelism was motivated by the advantages of separating knowledge from inference, and of modularizing knowledge into identifiable and meaningful parts. Each part had a specified problem-solving method and also a specification (in the form of a symbolic pattern) of the problems to which it was applicable.

Processes could not communicate easily or retain failure information in the Planner model, and it was this observation that led to its generalization in Conniver [Sussman72]. In Conniver, processes could suspend themselves and be reactivated. Each concurrent process was seen as an expert on some small area of activity. Conniver was not widely used or developed (like many experimental systems in AI), but it influenced later systems.

The production-system approach of Newell and Simon took a different tack. Here, the units of processing, production rules, did not correspond so well to units of knowledge. Rather they corresponded to primitive symbol-manipulation processes from which active data structures or higher-level processes could be built. The left-hand side of a production rule was a conjunction of primitive tests, and the right-hand side was a sequence of primitive actions. The rules operated "in parallel" in the sense in that they associatively monitored a common database and fired when a successful match became possible. Production systems were intended to facilitate the discovery of new representational structures for psychological modeling. Unfortunately, in spite of the development of several different basic production-rule architectures by Newell, the representation of many existing AI systems, and the development of novel AI systems in production system form, the approach has not directly yielded the intended insights, although it has been influential in many other ways.

Blackboard systems evolved from the production-system approach. In a blackboard system, a set of processes, typically called *knowledge sources* (KSs) share a common database or *blackboard* of symbolic structures, often called (and indeed denoting) *hypotheses*. Each KS is an expert in some area, and may find a hypothesis it can work on, solve that hypothesis, create new hypotheses, and modify other existing hypotheses. The set of processes thus cooperates by sharing the common blackboard, rather like a group of human experts, each endowed with expertise and a piece of chalk, and using a common chalkboard. Conventional blackboard systems, exemplified by HEARSAY-II and its descendents [Erman80; Hayes-Roth85; Nii86b; Nii86a], were not truly parallel, since they ran on serial machines, and since they incorporated schedulers that ensured sequential invocation of knowledge sources to maintain blackboard and knowledge-source consistency. However, they can be called quasiparallel, since the best conceptual model of their operation is quite parallel, and since they rely upon semantically distributed conceptions of knowledge.

These three architectures are precursors, but not exemplars, of contemporary DAI. In post-HEARSAY research, Lesser and Erman suggested dividing the interpretation problem among *several* HEARSAY-like blackboard systems, and they studied several possible task-decomposition regimes [Lesser80a]. By the late 1970s, work on Actors and on the PUP6, Contract Net, DVMT, and Rand air-traffic control (ATC) systems had begun, and the first phase of research into DAI as we now know it was in full swing [Corkill79; Davis80; Hewitt77a; Lenat75; Smith79; Lesser81; Steeb81].

In the current AI research that is explicitly concerned with concurrent models of intelligent behavior, there are two main currents. *Distributed Artificial Intelligence* research addresses the problems of designing and analyzing large-grained coordinated intelligent systems. *Connectionism* research is devoted to explaining higher mental functions and higher-level reasoning processes by reference to highly parallel collections of processes made up of very simple computing elements. This book will not cover research in fine-grained Distributed AI or Connectionism. For an introduction to the latter, see [Feldman82; McClelland87].

1.1.2 Exemplary Systems

In this section, we give a brief overview of several exemplary DAI systems, so that the reader can gain some basic and intuitive familiarity with standard DAI concepts and experience. We shall draw on the ideas embodied in these systems to illustrate many of the problems and solution strategies of DAI, and to set the stage for more complete definitions of some concepts later. We illustrate three approaches here: a collection of *blackboard-based* problem solvers called the *Distributed Ve-hicle Monitoring Testbed* (DVMT); a system called the *Contract Net* which exploits flexible distributed task-allocation; and an approach to multiagent computation and reasoning in *open systems* based on the *actor model*. These approaches differ along dimensions of flexibility, adaptability, and degree of as-sumed prior organization among computing agents.

The Distributed Vehicle Monitoring Testbed (DVMT)

The DVMT is a major ongoing project at the University of Massachusetts at Amherst [Lesser81; Corkill82; Lesser83; Durfee87a; Durfee87d; Durfee87e]. This system provides an example application in which both perception and knowledge are distributed. The DVMT uses a collection of identical, blackboard-based systems (see Chapter 7) to solve problems of monitoring and of interpreting data from a set of sensors at spatially distributed locations, covering a region. Data (which may be noisy or redundant) from some subset of the sensors are routed to each problem-solving node. The nodes then cooperate to construct a global picture of vehicle traffic across the whole sensor net.

In the DVMT experiments, problem-solving performance, or *coherence*, has been calculated in terms of the efficiency of the system measured by simulated clock time to solution. For each experiment, an optimal solution time is calculated, based on each node having complete global data at all times and always making the correct choice. When sensor regions overlap, or when signals are noisy, the nodes may have incomplete or inconsistent data, and performance can degrade due to redundant or misguided work. The research goal is to achieve performance as close to the optimal level as possible, with incomplete or noisy data. To gain efficiency, researchers at the University of Massachusetts at Amherst have found that they need to enhance both *metalevel control* among nodes and *local control* within nodes. That is, individual nodes should have knowledge about their own problem-solving behavior and about the behavior of other nodes and of the system as a whole.

Three kinds of metalevel control have been explored:

1. *Exchanging metalevel information*: one node explains its actions to another by exchanging information about how or why it has acted, abstractions of its state, or high-level solutions it has generated.
2. *Planning*: a node creates a plan for its activity, which can be communicated to other nodes. Ultimately, the nodes build and exchange *partial global plans* that are shared, partially complete views of joint problem-solving activities, giving each node greater insight into the roles and intentions of its collaborators.
3. *Organization*: Some organization can be impressed upon the system in the form of *problem-solving roles* for each node. In the DVMT, a role is a restriction on the

capability or focus of a node, such that the node does *not* perform certain actions or look at certain areas of data. This restriction yields a division of responsibility and hence a division of labor among the nodes.

For different problems or different states of problem solv-ing, different node organizations may be needed. Hence, the DVMT experiments have begun to address the problem of *or-ganization self-design* [Corkill82]. For each new problem, the system needs ways of recognizing and creating the appropriate set of roles. The DVMT project has begun (essentially experi-mental) research into *organizational knowledge*; namely, how to associate a particular collection of roles with a particular type of problem and level of performance.

Making a transition from one role organization to another in the course of problem solving requires recognizing and characterizing problem-solving situations, and instantiating new organizational forms in a decentralized manner. As a part of organizational self-design, a group of problem-solving nodes must be able to diagnose and observe its own behavior, in order to tell how well it is working, so that it can know when to adapt and how to adapt, and so that it can recognize when certain sensors or problem solvers are disabled. Toward this end, the DVMT experiments have investigated how to model and diagnose system behavior, using expected problem-solving trajectories as a basis for reasoning.

The project's principal contributions to the DAI field in-clude

The study of interaction among complex individual problem solvers, each of which is a powerful Hearsay-like system.

Investigations of the *functionally accurate, coopera-tive* (FA/C) systems, that converge on solutions despite incomplete and possibly inconsistent data, as distinct from systems which maintain complete global consis-tency. The DVMT system is designed to converge on the best acceptable answer, even though it consists of a set of asynchronous evocations of possibly inconsistent knowledge sources.

Enhancements to the sophistication of local control in blackboard systems (e.g., integrated goal-directed and data-directed control).

Mechanisms for *metalevel control* through communica-tion, individual and joint planning, and organizational roles.

Approaches to *organization self-design*.

Preliminary studies of how to abstract, model, and diagnose distributed-system behavior.

Careful, thoughtful experimental methodologies and controlled experiments to test the performance of con-trol enhancements.

The Contract Net

The Contract Net was a distributed problem-solving system designed by Randall Davis and Reid Smith [Davis83; Smith80; Smith81a; Smith81b]. The primary goal of this system was opportunistic, adaptive task allocation among a collection of problem solvers, using a framework called "negotiation," based on task announcements, bids, and awarded "contracts." The basic architecture comprised nodes with *manager* and *worker* roles; any node could be at any one time both a manager and a worker for different tasks. A manager for a task

> Decomposed its task into subtasks. Task decomposition was given, that is, the task was described in a way that made it already decomposable.
> Constructed task announcements for each subtask and distributed them either by broadcasting to all nodes or by focused addressing to a selected subset of nodes.
> Selected the most appropriate bid and allocated the subtask to that bidder.
> Monitored progress on the contract, possibly requesting information, interim reports and so on, and was free to reallocate the subtask if the contractor failed to complete that subtask in a timely manner.
> Integrated the partial results produced by its contractors into a complete solution at its level of decomposition.

Worker processes that received task announcements evaluated their own eligibility and returned bids to do the subtask if interested. They then performed subtasks allocated to them, provided interim reports on progress, partial results, and so on, and reported results, produced from performing subtasks, to the manager of the subtask.

The Contract Net Protocol (CNP) was designed to solve the problem of *opportunistic connection* between managers and workers. Nodes could exchange procedures and data to augment their capabilities during problem solving, to provide incrementally better fit of workers to tasks. However, the Contract Net included no general *problem-solving protocol*; issues such as metalevel control or measures of *global coherence*[2] were outside the scope of the protocol. What coherence existed was a product of eligibility and mutual-selection criteria, which were purely local. Because of this, the Contract Net could deal reasonably well with the kind of problems that are easily decomposable into independent subproblems, and where the mix of subproblems matched the availability of worker nodes. If decomposition was difficult, or if there was interaction between subtasks, the Contract Net did not work well. There was no provision for lateral communication between subtasks or for global optimization via changes in roles, and there were few mechanisms for explicit reasoning about the global effects of local decisions or of possible

harmful interactions among nodes. Davis and Smith applied a Contract Net implementation called CNET to the n-queens problem (treated as distributed search) and to a distributed sensor net task [Davis83]. Other researchers have extended the Contract Net framework to real-time task scheduling and to manufacturing control [Parunak87; Ramamritham85].

Some major innovations of the Contract Net project were the following

> The study of distributed task allocation, by a process of mutual selection and agreement. This scheme is different from a manager-centered invocation (e.g., procedure calls) or worker-centered invocation (e.g., data-driven computations) in that it relies on mutual selection by both manager and worker processes.
> A differentiation between task sharing and result sharing, where task sharing is sharing the labor on tasks to be done, and result sharing is combining partial results from several agents into an aggregated solution.
> Control based on mutual commitments, or "contracts," among agents.
> The design of a communication protocol for a specific style of interaction, termed "negotiation".

Actors and Open Systems

The study of Actors and Open Systems has been an important sustained research project at the Massachusetts Institute of Technology (MIT) since 1973, lead principally by Carl Hewitt [Agha86a; Agha86b; Clinger81; Hewitt77a; Hewitt77b; Hewitt84a; Hewitt86]. Hewitt raised a broad research question in his early Actors work [Hewitt77a]: What should be the communication mechanisms and conventions of civilized discourse for effective problem solving by a society of experts? Newell had pointed out that, in conventional single-agent problem-solving paradigms, a problem-solving agent "appears to be wandering over a goal net much as an explorer wanders over the countryside, having a single context and taking it with him wherever he goes." The single-agent view leads researchers to focus on the internal processes of search, or on reasoning processes with a single locus of control and focus of attention. This, too, has led to preoccupations with organizational mechanisms, such as goal stacks and agendas for making control decisions and for changing contexts.

Hewitt's basic insight was that, rather than viewing a control structure as a sequence of choices made by a single decision maker in a web of choice points, it could instead be seen as a pattern of messages passing among a collection of computational agents he called "actors." Using this model, the structure of control immediately became parallel, making the actors concept a convenient opportunity to exploit the growing interest in parallel computer architectures.

Kornfeld and Hewitt also suggested the scientific community as a model of problem solving. Problem solving could

---

[2] Coherence is discussed in Section 4 of this survey.

then mimic how scientists build, communicate, test, and revise theories. (Lenat had by this time already called for problem solving via a "committee of experts" and had constructed his prototype PUP-6 system [Lenat75].) Recognizing that the actual work of scientists has much in common with other human work (cf. [Latour87]), Hewitt has since expanded his view to draw upon and develop theories of problem solving work in many human organizations [Hewitt86].

An actor system comprises two parts: the actors, which are the only computational entities; and an operating system, which creates and destroys actors, and passes messages (actually other actors) among them using the universal communication mechanism called *actor transmission*.

The definition of each actor also comprises two parts: a *script*, which defines the behaviors of an actor upon receipt of a message; and a finite set of *acquaintances*, which are the other actors known to the actor. Events in the actor model consist solely of the arrival of actor messages; the internal state of an actor is invisible outside of that actor. When a message arrives, an actor may take three types of actions: it may change its local state (if it does, it is called a *serialized actor*, because its state depends on the order in which messages are received), it may create new actors, or it may send messages to other actors.

Actor models face (as do other DAI approaches) the issues of coherence: the actor community must not degenerate into a society of bureaucrats that sends many messages but makes little progress. Issues of actor design, decisions on granularity of data and control representations, composition of actors into larger communities, constraints on actor behaviors, achievement of higher-level performance goals with only local knowledge, and so on, which are characteristic of other DAI approaches, still appear in actor systems and have yet to be addressed comprehensively. In addition, realistic actor communities depend on a comprehensive *message-delivery (addressing) layer*, which presents difficulties in a large, dynamic, possibly open system.

Hewitt and his associates are also interested in actors as an underlying model for *due-process reasoning* in *open systems* [Gerson86; Hewitt84a; Hewitt85; Hewitt86]. Hewitt notes that many real-world distributed systems (e.g., office work, interbank transactions, large distributed databases such as a group of libraries) exhibit characteristics of (1) mutual inconsistency in knowledge or belief; (2) bounded influence or "arms-length relationships" among components; (3) asynchronous operation; (4) concurrency; and (5) decentralized control. He calls these systems *open systems*. Reasoning and coordinated action in open systems depend on using debate and negotiation to mediate among "microtheories": internally consistent but globally inconsistent sets of facts or beliefs.

The main features of Actor systems are the following:

The ability for a society of experts or actors to achieve intelligent behavior
A theory of computation that supports fine-grained and naturally concurrent computation

Control structures as patterns of messages rather than as sequential choice among alternatives
Nonserialized actors, as opposed to serialized actors, having a local state that persists on reinvocation

Open Systems are systems that have the following features:

they are composed of independently developed parts in continuous evolution
they are concurrent and asynchronous, and they have decentralized control based on debate and negotiation
they exhibit many local inconsistencies
they consist of agents with bounded knowledge and bounded influence
they have no fixed global boundaries visible to the agents constituting the system

1.1.3 Rationales for Distributed AI

Elements of an intelligent system are distributed if there is some *distance*[3] between them, and if some significant cost and/or some intermediary process is entailed in connecting them. There are many reasons for distributing intelligence. These include classical reasons for distributing any program or system, and reasons particular to Distributed AI systems. In some domains where AI is being applied, (e.g., distributed sensing, medical diagnosis, air-traffic control), knowledge or activity is inherently distributed. The distribution can arise because of geographic distribution coupled with processing or data bandwidth limitations, because of the natural functional distribution in a problem, or because of a desire to distribute control (e.g., for fail-soft degradation), or for modular knowledge acquisition, etc. In other domains, we may expect to simplify the development and evolution of intelligent systems by building them as collections of separate but interacting parts. Typical rationales for distributing an AI system include the following:

Adaptability: Logical, semantic, temporal, and spatial distribution allows a DAI system to provide alternative perspectives on emerging situations, and potentially greater adaptive power.
Cost: A distributed system may hold the promise of being cost-effective, since it could involve a large number of simple computer systems of low unit cost. If communication costs are high, however, centralized intelligence with distributed perception or sensing may be more expensive than distributed intelligence.

---

[3] We mean a *conceptual distance*, with respect to some conceptual frame, such as time, space, semantics, etc. — see later in this section.

Development and Management: If an intelligent system can be built in a distributed way, each part could be developed separately by a specialist in a particular type of knowledge or domain. A distributed intelligent system may be extensible [Rosenschein85a].

Efficiency or Speed: Concurrency may increase the speed of computation and reasoning (but concurrency must be traded off against the overhead of problem-dependent coordination).

History: We might already have an historical basis for a distributed system. This basis could be a collection of existing resources, such as a network of control computers on an aircraft, or a collection of workstations and people in an office or industrial environment. It also could be an existing set of facilities or software processes (e.g., expert systems) that we would like to integrate.

Isolation/Autonomy: For protection and for local control, parts of a system may be separated and isolated from one another; this approach is sometimes termed "arms-length relationships."

Naturalness: Some problems are better described as collections of separate agents; there is a "better fit" to a problem or domain because elements are "naturally" distributed along some of the axes of distribution discussed above [Rosenschein85a].

Reliability: Distributed AI systems may be more reliable than are centralized systems because they provide redundancy, cross-checking, and triangulation of results [Mason88].

Resource limitations: Individual computational agents have bounded rationality, bounded resources for problem solving, and possibly bounded influence, necessitating cooperation and coordination to solve large problems.

Specialization: Knowledge or action may be collected in specialized, bounded contexts, for purposes of control, extensibility, comprehensibility, and so on.

Distributed AI systems present quite difficult problems of analysis and development, in part because the following aspects can be independently distributed:

Action-in-the-world: Simultaneous actions may take place at different physical locales, or actions may occur at different points in time.

Focus of Attention: Different agents may focus on different aspects of the world.

Authority: Different agents may have different levels of authority or responsibility for different aspects of a situation.

Credibility: The support for some conclusion may be distributed, or different agents may be differentially trustworthy or credible.

Interpretations: Events and objects may mean different things to different agents.

Knowledge: Different agents may have different knowledge, or no agent may hold a complete representation of some important collection of knowledge, a situation, or a problem.

Perception: Different agents may perceive different events or objects, giving them partial or incommensurate views.

Reliability: Different agents may be differentially reliable, and overall system reliability may be contingent on some collection of subsystems.

Resources: Different agents may have different resources or levels of resources.

Value: Different agents may place different values on resources and on the outcomes of actions.

Work: Different agents may perform different parts of a task.

We can define the conceptual "distances" that define distribution (and that describe *how* the aspects listed above can be distributed) in several ways:

Computation cost: The cost of using knowledge or drawing on a specialized skill (measured in time, space, or other resources) may vary depending on its location, so cost of use is a way of defining a distribution.

Spatial distance: The spatial location of processes, knowledge, sensor input, and action effectors defines an axis of distribution. Both physical and human information processing depend upon sensing, input, transduction, etc. of data. These processes occur at spatially distributed locations, at different times, and on different and therefore distributed devices. There is a cost, often a large cost, involved in moving these input data to a single central point in the system for processing. Similarly, the *actions* taken by an intelligent system typically are taken on distributed systems, on distributed knowledge-bases, and on spatially distributed actuators.

Temporal distance: Events and knowledge may be temporally distributed, in that they may appear or become inaccessible through time. Some knowledge may not be available at a given time, because it has not yet been produced or derived. Whether knowledge can be precompiled and stored or must be deduced is a matter affecting temporal distribution and the utility of the knowledge; storage is one intermediary that makes knowledge accessible through time. Deduced knowledge is "less local" both temporally and in terms of costs and resources required. Thus, the form and content of existing knowledge bases affect choices about distribution. Especially in real-time systems, there may be costs for waiting or for rushing to attain temporal coordination.

Logical or Deductive distance: The degree of logical dependency between items of knowledge (i.e., the need to rely on intermediary deductive processes to make some new knowledge accessible) is a basis for distribution or aggregation. Logical dependency is often exploited in parallelizing production systems, for example. **Semantic Distance:** People cluster knowledge into specializations pertaining to the conventionalized and practical uses of knowledge. Thus, there may be one knowledge cluster for homeopathic medicine and another for scientific medicine, or one for plumbing and another for carpentry, the two being different and incompatible knowledge and representations. Knowledge is sometimes sparse between conventional knowledge clusters; *translation processes* provide intermediaries. The clustering of knowledge items and their access and use within a set or language of knowledge-description expressions may be a cause for distribution.

1.1.4 Basic Problems of Distributed AI

The basic questions that Distributed AI must address are the following:

> How to formulate, describe, decompose, and allocate problems and synthesize results among a group of intelligent agents
>
> How to enable agents to communicate and interact: what communication languages or protocols to use, what and when to communicate, etc.
>
> How to ensure that agents act coherently in making decisions or taking action, accommodating the global effects of local decisions and avoiding harmful interactions
>
> How to enable individual agents to represent and reason about the actions, plans, and knowledge of other agents in order to coordinate with them; how to reason about the state of the coordinated process (e.g., initiation and termination)
>
> How to recognize and reconcile disparate viewpoints and conflicting intentions among a collection of agents trying to coordinate their actions; how to synthesize views and results

Each of these problems appears in some form in all DAI application domains, although some of them (e.g., some problems of disparate reference frames) can be "designed out" in some engineered DAI systems. The solutions to these problems partly depend on features of particular application domains, and part of the task of DAI research involves determining what the domain-dependent features are and how they affect the answers to these questions. Ultimately, we would like to understand how a DAI system can reason about solving many of these problems itself, because one goal of a multiagent system is adaptive self-configuration.

In the remainder of this survey, we consider each of these problems in greater detail, and discuss tools and languages for constructing DAI systems.

1.2 Description, Decomposition, Distribution, and Allocation of Tasks

Chandrasekaran ([Chandrasekn81] pg. 1) observes that "Social organizations from honeybee colonies to a modern corporation, from bureaucracies to medical communities, from committees to representative democracies, are living examples of distributed information processing embodying a variety of strategies of decomposition and coordination." When work is to be done by a collection of agents in some coordinated fashion, it is important to answer the question of division of labor and organization: *which agent does what task, when?* A distribution of tasks among agents requires that the tasks be *formulated* and *described* in ways that account for their distribution or allow them to be distributed. Tasks that require more resources or knowledge than is possessed by one agent must be *decomposed* so that they can be accomplished. Tasks must be *allocated*: assigned to particular agents that will actually perform them. All these activities are deeply interdependent. The languages and concepts used for task description and formulation will affect how tasks can be decomposed into parts, and what dependencies explicitly exist among tasks; the same task described from different perspectives may require different partitioning and different skills. Choices of decomposition affect how tasks can be allocated, because the skills and knowledge of agents who will perform tasks must eventually match the task requirements [Lesser80a]. Task decomposition is affected by dependence among tasks, by exchange of messages, by adjacency requirements and by dynamically changing patterns of dependency. Decomposition decisions may need to be revised with contextual changes. Resources available for allocation may affect distribution and aggregation choices. Finally, the work of making these decisions is itself a task that autonomous (collections of) agents must address; in the extreme, they will need to reason about their representations and formulations of problems and the decomposition/allocation processes they use. In multiagent systems in particular, agents may need to negotiate over the appropriate formulation of problems and over appropriate responsibility for the description, decomposition, and allocation decisions, in order to form and maintain problem-solving alliances. In such cases (i.e. those without a global view), problems may be *constructed rather than decomposed*. Agents need to make decisions about problem descriptions, about the appropriate boundaries for problem *elaborations*, and about the *aggregation and combination of tasks into clusters*. A complete treatment of these problems for DPS and MA systems would need to treat each of these activities as potentially dynamic tasks that themselves have to be allocated and settled by collections of agents.

There has been remarkably little work in DAI that addresses automated problem formulation and decomposition. Correspondingly greater effort has been put into flexible task-allocation mechanisms that are used *after* a problem has been described and decomposed into subproblems. The Contract Net and its successors all have addressed flexible opportunistic *allocation* of tasks; decompositions were provided by programmers. Similarly, in the DVMT the descriptions, partitioned knowledge for data interpretation, and regional responsibilities (input data), have been generated by designers; the system itself makes semiautonomous opportunistic allocation decisions about which nodes perform which particular aggregation tasks. Actor systems, too, have thus far treated allocation decisions as dynamic, but have not so treated description or decomposition decisions (see e.g., [Kornfeld81b]).

1.2.1 Description

Decomposition choices are critically dependent on how a problem is described, because it is the collection of attributes and descriptive categories for stating the problem that provides a language for expressing interproblem and interagent dependencies. In real settings, formulation of problems requires some *representation* for the problem, as well as decisions on the boundaries of the problem and on what is known and unknown [Gasser88a]. In a conventional DPS system, many of these activities are carried out by designers; in MA systems, they may well be done by the agents themselves. This approach may require the effort of elaborating a problem description to cover all aspects of distribution and allocation; all problem-description knowledge may not be available to one agent, and, especially in a dynamic setting, a problem description may be collaboratively (and even dynamically) constructed. Although there is little extant research in this area in DAI (but see [Hinke88]), some relevant research has occurred in knowledge-acquisition systems [Lefkowitz87]. We regard this area as a fruitful one for further research.

1.2.2 Decomposition

The problem of task decomposition can be seen from several perspectives. In typical decomposition processes, a single "supertask" is decomposed into smaller subtasks, each of which requires less knowledge, or fewer resources. In general, there should be a choice among alternative task decompositions, depending on the ability of agents actually to perform tasks. Alternative decompositions are sometimes conventionally obtained by alternative problem-reduction operators, corresponding to an OR branch in a goal graph. Further types of decomposition can be obtained by transformation of problem representation [Amarel68; Simon69]. There is, however,

more than this to the problem of task decomposition. Most decomposition processes flow directly from the descriptions of available operators for problem-solving, indicating that they actually depend on designers' forethought in operator construction and description. Key research questions include how we construct or select a set of operators for the task set to be produced, and how we construct and decompose problems so as to minimize the costs of knowledge distribution and resource distribution.

The decomposition problem for multiple agents is more complex because of the need to match resources and capabilities of different agents with appropriate tasks; there must be sufficiency of knowledge, resources, and control in the overall system to bring about an effective solution [Lesser80a]. This means that any decomposition regime will need to account for the capabilities and resources of agents, and hence to make decisions about alternative types and granularity of decompositions. Subtask aggregation, coalescing several tasks into one, larger-grained unit, is one method of varying the granularity of tasks distributed to agents. It also becomes important in MA systems wherein multiple agents working without centralized control must aggregate their efforts for greater capability [Agha86a; Gasser87d], rather than decomposing a global problem.

Difficult problems of decomposition arise because of dependencies among subproblems and among the decisions and actions of separate agents. Conflicts over incompatible actions and shared resources may place ordering constraints on activities, restricting decomposition choices and forcing a need to consider decomposition in a *temporal* (or other resource) dimension as well as the more usual dimensions of knowledge, location or abstraction dimensions. When plans are generated independently by several agents, there may be problems in reconciling the subplans produced by each agent to reduce dependencies and conflicts [Cammarata83; Durfee87a; Durfee87c; Georgeff83; Steeb81]. In some circumstances, the issue of *redundancy* enters the decomposition problem. Choices about redundancy are related to the tradeoffs between efficiency and reliability; redundancy should be eliminated to improve efficiency, but may be necessary for reliability.

In summary, intelligent approaches to task decomposition need to consider the representation of tasks, several dimensions of decomposition, available operators that can be applied to perform subtasks, available resources, and dependencies among tasks.

Decision Bases

Several researchers have given their own views of the basis for problem decomposition. In their study of distributed-interpretation problem solving, Lesser and Erman [Lesser80a] argued for three dimensions of problem decomposition. Problems could be decomposed along lines of location (e.g., spatial, temporal, logical), by information level or degree of abstraction, and by what they called "interest areas," which included the given partitioning of skills among knowledge sources. This work was the distribution basis for later experiments using the DVMT [Lesser83]. Rand researchers investigating air-traffic control (a domain in which geographic distribution is inherent) [Steeb81] proposed several bases for reasoning about how to decompose problems. These included solving the total problem from several different perspectives at once, solving geographically local problems locally, decomposing problems by spatial clustering, decomposing problems by functional clustering (e.g., stage of flight), and decomposing problems hierarchically, with one agent producing an abstract plan, and several low-level agents doing local plan refinement. But what general basis do we have for making decisions on how to decompose tasks? The basis of all task-decomposition approaches is to find dependencies and logical groupings in problem tasks and knowledge. Several bases for cleaving dependencies and for decomposing tasks have appeared in the literature:

Abstraction level: Numerous researchers have used abstraction levels as a basis for decomposition [Sacerdoti77; Erman75; Erman80; Lesser83; Wesson81]. Decomposition of the problem into abstraction levels provides a simple task-decomposition basis: level-specific tasks are generated. Abstraction levels become a way of defining particular functional groups. Gomez and Chandrasekaran [Gomez81] studied distributed medical problem solving, and suggested that specialists be hierarchically organized, by reference to abstractions of medical knowledge. Finally, Wesson [Wesson81], in an empirical study, found that hierarchical organization worked better than did freely ("anarchic") communicating committees, in message-puzzle tasks; Benda et al. found that hierarchically controlled organizations worked more efficiently than did fully negotiated ones for certain problem-solving tasks, although they did not study the effects of uncertainty or dynamism in the problem domain [Benda85]. From a task-aggregation perspective, levels in hierarchies should be formed when global coordination can be improved using data abstracted for a lower level. However, extracting this information in the case of a particular problem is difficult. Although it is tempting to think we may be able to rely on decomposition by abstraction level as a potential for automated problem decomposition, there remains the great difficulty of how to define, recognize, or to construct these different abstraction levels in a problem.

Availability of coordination: A problem can be decomposed when appropriate control mechanisms for that decomposition can be provided, decompositions should make successful control possible and control choice explicit or easy. When control decisions are distributed, some control over the processing may lost, depending on the degree of communication, certainty, relative authority, and reliability of processes. It may be difficult to detect failure (cf. [Halpern87]), and it is usually impossible to detect deadlock, without a global picture.

Control dependencies: Tasks can be decomposed to reduce control dependencies. Along with bounded resources, individual agents may may have limited control (power or authority) over each other's actions. Hewitt terms this "bounded influence" [Hewitt84a]. In the DVMT, the degree of interagent control can be set by varying how important a node rates internally versus externally generated tasks [Lesser83].

Data dependencies: Relative data dependencies among the tasks along axes of semantics, logical dependencies (cf. [deKleer86; Doyle79]), or temporal dependence can serve as a basis for decomposition choices. Tasks related by strong or numerous knowledge-production and knowledge-consumption relationships may be grouped together.

Data partitioning: Tasks can be decomposed by taking account of natural or dependency-related partitions in input data. For example, in distributed sensor networks, spatial distribution of input data provides a natural basis for decomposition of tasks. Lesser and Erman [Lesser80a] describe the relation between data and time or space as a "location" dimension. It is also related to resource minimization and to product/function dimensions.

Functional/product division: Malone suggests (by analogy to human organizations) decomposing problems along either functional or product dimensions. *Functional decomposition* refers to grouping the classes of generic tasks needed to produce any product into individual clusters by task type. *Product decomposition* means grouping all tasks related to one product into one cluster, and dividing along multiple product lines [Malone87a; Malone88a]. Functional and product decompositions, respectively, correspond to the Rand functional and spatial dimensions for ATC problem solving, and to the abstraction level or interest area versus location dimensions of Lesser and Erman. Malone also provides a structural analysis of proposed theoretical benefits of different decompositions.

Interaction levels: Structurally, greater numbers of subtasks and a greater degree of interaction among subtasks may require more intermediate control tasks. This is the classic *span of control problem* (cf. [Fox81; Malone87a; Malone88a]). For example, Wesson et al. suggest that greater interaction among subproblems will increase the need for authority (and hierarchy) [Wesson81] because, as the need for a global picture increases, so does the need for an integrator node to be able to assert conclusions or policies to a subtask node. The span of control is related to uncertainty, to resources, and to bounded rationality of the agents.

Need for redundancy: If redundancy is needed for reliability or uncertainty reduction, tasks can be decomposed into redundant subtasks. For example, Wesson et al. [Wesson81] suggest that, if redundancy of control is necessary (e.g., for reinforcement or reduction of control uncertainty), additional control tasks should be generated and some subtasks should be assigned to more than one controlling task. However, redundant tasks require methods for discriminating redundant results [Durfee87d]. Subtasks may also be generated that treat the same problem from different perspectives, and this too requires discrimination and integration of the results [Steeb81].

Resource minimization: Tasks can be decomposed by reviewing their resource requirements and finding ways to minimize resource use: for example, by exploiting locality in parts of problems. Rand researchers, for example, suggest that local problems be solved locally to minimize uncertainty, and communication and coordination costs [Steeb84; Steeb86].

Uncertainty: Greater uncertainty in a task or its components may require spawning redundant subtasks that address a problem from different perspectives [Kornfeld81b; Lesser81]. Moreover, additional articulation work [Bendif87; Gasser86] in the form of control or coordination tasks (e.g., communication) may be necessary [Lesser83; Durfee87d].

Uniqueness avoidance: Davis and Smith [Davis83] pointed out the problem of *unique nodes*. Any agent that has unique data, or a unique process, produces a form of centralization of control and resources, which can create potential bottlenecks. They suggested dividing up a unique node functionally, or distributing it redundantly.

Methods for Solving Decomposition Problems

General classes of solutions have been proposed for the problem of task decomposition, although there appear to be few principles, methods, or experimentally validated techniques, for automatic decomposition of tasks by a DAI system. There are some theoretical approaches: decomposition to achieve deadlock avoidance, for example, and heuristic approaches: using models of agents, reliability, and so on. Some classes of solution are as follows:

Pick tasks that are inherently decomposable: In this approach, the given representation of the task contains its decomposition. The description of the states, of the space of states, and of the operators, leads to a natural decomposition, using the selector operations of the data structure. An example is the n-queens problem used in the Contract Net work. Here, the state is given by a data structure, which is essentially a tree of subproblem descriptions.

Decomposition by a programmer: This typical programming approach is used, for example, in the DVMT and in HEARSAY-II. It is useful because there seem to be few known principles or methods for automatically decomposing tasks. The problem is intimately tied up with the representation of the task; in most systems, decompositions possibilities are already built into programmer-generated action descriptions.

Hierarchical planning: A hierarchical planner does genuine task decomposition. It generates tasks that are goals to work on. However, this provides only a partial solution, because the decomposition depends on the prior descriptions of the available execution operators, which are usually static. This approach thus produces limits to reconfiguration. See, for example, Corkill's distributed hierarchical planner [Corkill79].

Load balancing: Load balancing gives good examples of choices of decompositions, and some guidance. Load balancing has been explored mainly for the case of large numerical computations on parallel computer architectures [Fox88]. A very large set of numerical tasks, numbering in the tens of thousands, is partitioned into subsets, by an allocation to processors that optimizes communication and computation load. Currently, optimization methods such as simulated annealing are used. Common dynamic load-balancing techniques such as bidding schemes [Malone88b; Parunak87; Ramamritham85], typically rely on predefined decompositions and on tasks of fixed grain size, and provide less insight into task decomposition methods.

Minimally connected subgraphs: If a problem can be described as a collection of interdependent elements, using a graph structure, then a decomposition algorithm can identify minimally connected subgraphs. Again, decomposition is built into the problem description. The difficulty is identifying the graph from the problem. For example, Levin and Moore [Levin77] observed that problems are solved by interaction with other agents. Describing the required pattern of interaction can give a dynamic pattern of decomposition in terms of interaction requirements. Davis and Smith regard problem decomposition as the creation of the map of subproblems, and believe this should be part of a DPS system's task [Davis83]. Once this map is created, the locality of action and information represented in the subproblem map allow for decomposition. Similarly, Pavlin, Hudlicka, and Lesser use dynamic problem-solution graphs to represent problem-solving activity and propose that information so gained be used as a basis for organization self-design [Pavlin84; Hudlicka86b; Hudlicka86a; Hudlicka87].

Subtask aggregation: Tasks can be decomposed also by *aggregating* collections of known operators to fit the requirements of subparts of a larger task. This approach requires manipulation of subsets of tasks and operators, and the ability to structurally aggregate a collection of operators. Structural aggregation or composition of operators has been addressed in systems of actors and in the MACE testbed [Agha86a; de Jong88; Gasser87d].

1.2.3 Task and Resource Allocation

The problem of allocating particular tasks to particular agents is the problem of assigning responsibility for a particular activity. Task allocation is a metaproblem that may be addressed statically by a designer; for example, by establishing a collection of specialized agents with predetermined roles. If we conceive of task allocation as a kind of *articulation work* [Bendif87; Gasser86] to be done dynamically by a collection of agents themselves, using techniques such as contracting [Malone83; Malone88a; Smith81b; Smith81a; Parunak87] and organization self-design [Corkill82; Lesser83], it is just another task, and can, like other tasks, also be allocated recursively [Bond88a]. Decisions on when and how to reallocate tasks, when to make organizational transitions or to redesign the organization, depend upon knowledge linking performance to task allocations and on how available are slack resources for redesign [Gasser88b; Gasser88a; Pasquale88; Rosenschein83; Wesson81].

There are several choices of what aspects of a problem or task to provide in order to allocate responsibility for accomplishing that task to a particular agent. A task to be done can be completely or partially constructed by the agent itself, it can be assimilated via interaction with a "controlling" agent, or it can be given by a designer and embedded in the structure of the agent. For example, a task can be allocated by sending to an agent an entire problem description, a solution method, and a control trigger, which the agent simply enacts. Alternatively, an agent can be provided with data to which it can apply methods it already has, or it can receive methods to apply to data it already has. (These last two options, along with a task-allocation message that serves as a control trigger, are provided in the Contract Net.) Finally, an individual agent may receive only a control or responsibility "trigger," while gathering for itself its problems, its data and knowledge, and its solution methods. This range of choices indicates that we need some basis for deciding what level of responsibility and choice to give to agents. Dynamic task allocation of any type requires reliable communication, coordination overhead, or redundancy. Durfee, Lesser, and Corkill [Durfee87d] noted that dynamic task passing (as in the Contract Net) may be a problem where there are error-prone channels, because of the mutual agreement required. Research in "reasoning about knowledge" [Halpern86a; Halpern86b; Halpern87] and common-knowledge protocols promise to help address this problem.

Bases for Making Task-Allocation Decisions

In the literature, there are several bases for choosing which agent should get which tasks of a collection:

Bottleneck avoidance: Allocation decision should avoid bottlenecks by overloading particular unique or critical resources [Davis83].

Fit to specification: Tasks should be allocated to those available agents that provide the best fit to the task specification [Davis83; Smith81a].

Knowledge dependency: Task coordination and precedence constraints affect allocation decisions when a node cannot work until another has finished its task [Durfee87d]. Task precedences are one type of task interdependency. With adequate interaction capability, tasks addressing matters of consistency, definition, or direction should be left to the node with the most global view [Cammarata83; Wesson81].

Overlap in roles: Durfee and his colleagues [Durfee87d] noted that nodes should have overlapping responsibility to achieve flexibility and coherence. The Rand group [Steeb81] also noted that overlap would alleviate hand-off problems between clusters of problem solvers. Mechanisms of specifying "interest areas", a node's responsibilities in a partial solution space, can be used to control overlap and redundancy in nodes [Lesser80a; Durfee87d].

Uncertainty avoidance, and reliability: Tasks whose results or completion are uncertain should be allocated redundantly, to reduce the uncertainty and to improve reliability [Lesser83].

Resource consumption: From one perspective, tasks should be allocated such that their use of critical resources is lowest. Pasquale, for example, suggests allocating tasks such that times to complete are minimized (when completion time is the critical success criterion) [Pasquale88]. Similarly, highly interdependent tasks should be allocated to agents in similar regions (e.g., spatial or semantic regions) to minimize critical communication and synchronization costs [Lesser80a; Steeb81; Steeb84; Steeb86]. From another perspective, resource slack can be a useful indicator for allocation decisions. In the Rand air-traffic control work [Steeb81], the investigators developed a strategy for exploiting slack resources by choosing the agent with greatest resource slack as a manager for centralized planning and organization tasks.

Urgency: Redundant allocation of urgent tasks may occur dynamically, and may be related to the breakdown of authority under load. For example, Wesson et al. suggest a strategy of *constructive usurpation*: in a busy system, when an agent with authority for a task will not do that task due to load, any agent that can perform the task should, because results are more important than protocols [Wesson81]. Wesson et al. also suggest that allocation decisions should be decentralized when busy, and centralized when resources are slack, noting that allocation is itself work that consumes scarce resources. Anticipatory self-allocation may also be useful; if an agent has not received a specific request to do some task, but knows that performing that task will be useful, it may anticipate requests if the system is not busy [Wesson81]. This approach requires global knowledge and coordination to avoid redundancy.

Mechanisms for Making Task-Allocation Decisions

Task allocation can be approached with a number of mechanisms, which range from planned allocation to opportunistic, marketlike strategies. The following are typical mechanisms for making allocation decisions:

Market mechanisms: Tasks can be allocated without explicit planning using various market mechanisms, wherein available tasks are matched with available agents by generalized agreement and possibly by mutual selection [Fox79; Smith80]. Underlying mechanisms for matching and decision making include "pricing" tasks according to their criticality or urgency [Malone83; Gasser87a; Kurose85; Malone87a]. Agents may use self-selection from a global or regional agenda of tasks, based on fit and task prices [Gasser87a].

Markets need policies and protocols through which agents communicate their intentions for doing particular tasks [Davis83; Smith80; Smith81a; Malone88b], and reach agreement using negotiation and conflict resolution when there is contention for tasks or when certain important tasks are overlooked [Durfee87d; Durfee87e]. Mutual agreement is reached when agents make a decision based on the best fit between the task and the agent. This is the method used in the Contract Net system [Davis83]. Fit can be assessed via pattern match (cf. Planner [Hewitt71]), possibilities lists (cf. Conniver [Sussman72]), metarules and metalevel control (cf. [Hayes-Roth85; Erman80], or transfer by discussion [Lenat75].

Multiagent planning: A planner or collection of planners can combine the work of task decomposition and task allocation by treating agents as specialized resources and objects that interact and depend upon one another. Multiagent planning can be done using a single centralized planner with global plan synchronization and conflict elimination [Georgeff83; Georgeff84; Georgeff87c; Pednault87; Stuart85], or with distributed planners that make joint multiagent plans [Corkill79; Durfee86; Durfee87a; Durfee87c]. Conflicts in task allocations can be resolved by allowing agents with related interests to exchange and elaborate proposed activities, using techniques termed *partial global planning* [Durfee86; Durfee87a; Durfee87c] and *negotiation* [Benda85; Conry86].

Organizational roles: Organizational roles are predetermined or slowly changing policies for assigning task responsibilities to agents. An agent cannot accept tasks that do not meet its role in the organization, and perhaps cannot be presented with such tasks from other agents, assuming role knowledge is disseminated.

Recursive allocation: We can link recursive allocation to subproblem decomposition, by letting agents that are handling problems do the work of allocating their subproblems. This mechanism is employed in the Contract Net [Davis83], where allocation work itself is decentralized. Policies for allocation (organizational design) also can be accomplished by recursive global reassignment. With a view of its subordinates' load and tasks, an agent can reassign responsibilities; this can be done recursively [Wesson81].

Voting: At least one project has explored voting as a task-allocation mechanism. Rand air-traffic control agents allocated centralized planning tasks to one central agent chosen opportunistically by the set of agents, which voted using common evaluative conventions [Steeb81].

Allocating Resources

Resources are the products that are consumed to accomplish problem-solving work. Resource allocation is a subproblem of task allocation in a DPS or MA system. Allocating resources to tasks is a way of prioritizing the tasks, because tasks without resources cannot run [Kornfeld81b]. Some typical resources that are allocatable in DAI systems include processing time and communication bandwidth. For example, in some air-traffic control problems, it is necessary to restrict some communication to allow important collaborators to interact [Steeb81]. Resource-bounded reasoning is important in any real system, and recent research has begun to address tradeoffs in resource allocation and real-time performance, using a reasoned approach to reducing search complexity termed "approximate processing" (see, e.g., [Lesser88]). Temporal resource allocation is the problem of doing the most pressing or critical activities first. For example, Wesson et al. suggested pursuing less important activities in less dynamic situations (e.g., looking for global obstacles in a robot-control system when the system is not busy). "Less important" work may be work that an agent knows another agent may do, here redundancy reduction provides a means for temporal resource allocation [Wesson81].

Representation has impacts on reasoning about resource allocations. Agents using logic-based representations of action and belief based on possible-worlds semantics have had theoretical difficulty with resource allocation and resource-bounded reasoning partially due to the problem of *logical omniscience*. In short, it is difficult to avoid concluding that an agent believes the deductive closure of its explicitly declared knowledge (which may be infinite), yet this is impossible in any resource-bounded system. Konolige has presented a logic-based approach to resource-bounded reasoning in [Konolige86].

Several important approaches are resource allocation using specialist "sponsor" agents [Kornfeld81b; de Jong88] that allocate fixed portions of resources in a manner analogous to research sponsors, resource allocation based on the criticality of tasks [Lesser88], and resource allocation via resource pricing [Chandrasekn81; Kurose85]. Distributed resource allocation can be done by recursive allocation of resource-allocation tasks to subagents, and by decentralized bidding schemes where tasks bid for resources, thereby changing prices. There is much more room for interaction between researchers in DAI and those in economics, on the subject of resource-allocation mechanisms and policies.

1.3 Interaction, Language, and Communication

Interaction is important as a basic concept in DAI because it is the processes of interaction that make it possible for several intelligent agents to combine their efforts. Problems of different agents may exhibit mutual dependency, so agents must interact to solve them. We shall use *interaction* to mean some type of collective action in an MA or DPS system, wherein one agent takes an action or makes a decision that has been influenced by the presence or knowledge of another agent. Whereas knowledge, perception, goals, actions, and so on may or may not be distributed, interaction is inherently distributed, and interaction is inherently dependent upon the coordinated action of at least two agents. We are ultimately interested in two kinds of interaction: *nonroutine interactions*, in which the actual terms and conditions of interaction are uncertain and are under development, and *routine interaction*, wherein individual acts (which are part of interactions) are carried out under particular expectations of future actions of other agents' actions and belief states. In natural systems, there is no "pure" interaction of either type; there is a constant motion between the problem solving (nonroutine) and routine, with one predominating in a given situation. Both types of interaction critically depend on agents' *models of one another*, for example, to formulate expectations, etc.

Interactions may occur through explicit linguistic actions and through other actions in the world. They involve reactions of one agent to some representation of another agent it holds (part of the interpretive context) [Mead34]. Ideally, each interaction in a DAI system would cause revisions in each agent's model of the other, it seems that this is a requirement of adaptive communication, but it is rarely seen in existing DAI systems.

A *rational action* is an action that an agent takes in response to goals it has, in the belief that the action will satisfy the goal. A communication exists only when the *intention to communicate* exists, because knowledge of this intention to communicate provides additional information for both the sender and the receiver. One model of communication is that *A communicates with B* when *A acts upon B* with linguistic actions (manifesting the intention to communicate) and *B reacts to A* (accomplishing the communication). Agents may be able to communicate meaningfully in order to structure their coordination, but coordinated interaction does not necessarily require communication. Agents may coordinate their actions based on models they have of each other, without interaction (except the prior interaction or design necessary to set up the models). For example, Axelrod, Rosenschein and Genesereth, and Tenney and Sandell have studied how cooperation can occur without explicit communication [Axelrod84; Rosenschein86; Tenney81a].

1.3.1 Interaction

Several dimensions of multiagent interaction are important for viewing organized aggregates. These include *among whom* the interaction takes place; *when* the interaction occurs (this matters because of the possible temporal/causal relationships among new knowledge and beliefs across agents); *what is the content* of the interaction or communication (e.g., results to be shared or tasks to be assigned); *how the interaction is accomplished* (e.g., what processes are involved or what resources are utilized); *why* the action occurs (what goals have driven the action); and *what the basis of commonality is* (is there a common language, shared interpretive context, or reference?).

Since action in the systems we consider is generally goal-directed, many interactions are derived from goals, and thus each action is traceable to some outcome or performance criteria (i.e., "did the [inter]action achieve the goal?"). For analysis, individual actions and patterns of action, communication, and interaction can be linked to questions such as, *What are the varieties of possible interactions? What are the interactions that obtain in a given situation? Why are these the interactions, rather than others? What is the result of this pattern of interactions? What patterns of interaction can exist?* These questions become more central as we try to conceptualize and describe frameworks for coordination, such as organizations. One perspective on describing an organization is its *pattern of activity* (e.g., its patterns of interaction). Since organized interactions are at some level routine and predictable, they form patterns that provide the basis for expectations about the behaviors of other agents. (Organized actions, of course, may be subject to revision or reinforcement.)

The routinization, conventionalization, and codification of interaction patterns (whether done by designers or the agents themselves) result in a language system (cf. the discussion of the origins of the PUP6 communication protocols in [Lenat75;

Lenat87]). Typically, tokens from a conventionalized dictionary are composed into messages, which are exchanged by agents. Automated language systems usually have grammatical constraints and internal semantic relations encoded into programs for generating or interpreting communications. The relation of the message to the communication environment is usually called the *pragmatics* of the language utterances.

Considering communication in the context of cooperating agents leads to further issues. Communication is often an extended series of exchanges with a common purpose, a dialogue, which may have conventions of form and mechanism. Another issue is the sharing of knowledge to form the commonality upon which communication and cooperation may proceed. We can ask what language and communication mechanisms maintain this commonality. For example, how can the alignments of meaning be maintained among agents in dynamic worlds, where each agent has incomplete knowledge (cf. [Winograd86])? This makes us concerned with the effect and role of knowledge of other agents in communication and language. By conceiving communication and interaction in a framework of goals for utterances, knowledge of participants,. and planned actions to change that knowledge, we can synthesize a unified description of action and communication where communications are treated as actions, usually called *speech acts* [Austin62; Cohen79].

Reasoning about Languages

When we work with distributed agents, we need to design and understand the language used for interaction, communication, and organization. This means that we need to know what knowledge to represent for communicating, and how to represent it in an interaction language. For example, agents may need to communicate about their mutual beliefs, their knowledge of each other, or their current goals, etc. Communicating agents in general will have disparate knowledge, so the language system may have to allow for differences in knowledge, in order for communication and cooperation to succeed, in spite of disparate knowledge, to allow communication about disparity, and so on. One topic that has attracted the attention of linguists is that of disparate references, that is, two agents may refer to the same object using different terms and from different viewpoints [Walker78].

Typical DAI systems have employed inflexible, predesigned communication languages. For more adaptive DAI systems, we need more flexible approaches based on linguistic knowledge. Some of these approaches may come from research on dialogue structures and on speech-act theory.

Context and Speech Acts

In terms of simply making other agents aware of data (such as observations, results etc.), different kinds of information may be appropriate for different agents. Also, different levels of abstraction may be appropriate. Criteria are thus needed for deciding what types of information to represent and how to represent them. The communication of goals is often needed for cooperation [Durfee87d]. Awareness of other agents goals is needed, and also the ability to allocate a goal from one agent to another (the latter is sometimes called *goal induction*) [Cohen79; Rosenschein82; Wilensky84].

It may be necessary to keep track of other agents' states in order to know with which one to communicate. This requirement leads to issues of how accurate models of other agents need to be to allow effective communication, and, of course, to cost tradeoffs in deciding whether to communicate more abstractly and to spend resources on inferring meanings, or to spend resources maintaining more precise models of other agents and of their communication requirements [Lesser83; Durfee87d; Durfee87e; Wesson81]. In a completely decentralized system, bounded influence (the limitations of control over other agents' actions and knowledge) is a problem [Hewitt85; Hewitt86].

Since awareness of other agents is crucial to cooperation, information must be continually communicated and updated. However, this requirement may impose a formidable burden on communication resources, so communication, in terms of both destination and content, must be selective. In the DVMT, for example, communicating the wrong or redundant information can lead to harmfully *distracting* an agent from useful tasks. Selecting the proper information to communicate is difficult. To combat specificity problems such as these, manager nodes in the Contract Net can employ focused addressing to limit interaction to agents known to be relevant, thus reducing communication loads. Conversely, where there are similar agents working on related problems, the optimal communication level may involve some duplication of effort by the agents.

To capture the structure of larger interaction patterns, we need knowledge representations for the description and realization of dialogues [Grosz85; Grosz86; Grosz87]. We also need to identify and represent the speech acts involved in interaction, which will include indirect actions, such as inferring the plans of other agents. Intentional, language-based interactions include the communication of beliefs and goals. Some interactional goals include understanding and influencing the beliefs and actions of other agents.

Using Fixed Interaction Languages

Standard conventions about the representations of knowledge held by other agents can directly lead to interaction languages. For example, the PUP6 system used standard message types related to the standard structure of agents. Since each agent had identical parts, queries were restricted to the values of those parts. [Lenat75; Lenat87]. Similarly, the Contract Net Protocol [Smith80] introduced a common internode language, which consisted of structured message types, such as task announcements, bid messages, and award messages. The Contract Net used a framelike structure for messages, with different frames for each type of message. The message types were specialized to the types of information needed to solve the contract net's primary problem, marketlike task allocation. There were no messages, for example, that could directly handle control, reorganization, or focusing information. Virtually all DAI systems have used standard interaction languages put in place by designers. The DVMT employs some levels of reasoning about communication activities, primarily concerning what information to communicate (based on knowledge of interest areas of other nodes) and when to communicate it. Communication is handled by separate send and receive knowledge sources in each node, whose activities can be planned and prioritized like those of any other knowledge source.

Different choices of what to communicate to another agent have been studied in the DVMT project. This has been done manually for each experiment, and there have been no experiments with automatic or programmed criteria. Agents could communicate (1) sensor data for the distributed sensor sector allocated to them, which is usually relevant to agents allocated to spatially adjacent sectors; (2) interpreted data at more abstract and more condensed levels; (3) goals, communicating current goals and allocating goals to each other by mutual agreement, and (4) plans for their own activity, to improve network awareness.

The Rand air-traffic control work [Steeb81] worked with the notion of *information-distribution policies*. These were characterized along four binary dimensions: (1) selective or broadcast communication (2) unsolicited or on-demand communication (3) acknowledged or unacknowledged communication, and (4) single-transmission or repeated-transmission communication. The Contract Net used targeted broadcasting for announcing contracts. This approach answered the question of whom to communicate with by keeping relevance criteria that were applied to each task description to determine the "mailing list" for broadcasting. The DVMT project studied the interesting and important case where there are similar agents working on related problems, with duplication of effort.

Interaction Protocols and Dialogues

The individual message types used in the Contract Net combined with their expected responses yield a protocol for interaction that spans more than one interaction. A *contract* here is an agreement relating to any task to be allocated, so this protocol is of quite general applicability. This interaction regime elegantly provides for two-way transfer of information, with the potential for complex information transferred in both directions, for local evaluation in the context of individual knowledge sources, and for symmetric mutual selection of control points.

Levin and Moore [Levin77] introduced the notion of a *dialogue game*, which gives a way of initiating an interaction of a specified type, and of controlling it with a partially ordered set of subgoals. The participants in the dialogue game take roles and attempt to achieve the goals in the given (partial) temporal order. Levin and Moore are thus distinguishing between the function and the topic of a dialogue. Interaction types observed in naturally occurring dialogues, in which one person interacts with another for some purpose, include *Helping*, *Action-seeking*, *Information-seeking*, *Information-probing*, *Instructing*, and *Griping*, for example. The speaker and hearer in such a dialogue ordinarily hold multiple goals, which are related in highly constrained ways. Persons cooperate in dialogues only if both hold goals that are subserved by the cooperation. In the dialogue-games model, interaction proceeds at two levels. At one level, interaction decides whether to *enter* a given dialogue game, which roles are to be taken by the participants, and when to terminate. At the second level, the dialogue game is entered and the interaction is controlled by the speaker and hearer taking their agreed roles to solve the set of goals defined by the game, and instantiated by the current context. Dialogue games shed light on comprehension issues in natural language. A goal-oriented view of language limits the explosion of inferences by giving a focus, favoring inferences that look for goals. The dialogue-games model also provides a theory of the indirect uses of language. Other multisentential knowledge representations for the description of naturally occurring dialogue include "rules" (Labov and Fanshel) and "sequences" [Sacks74].

Planning Communications

Communication between problem-solving agents may originate as part of a procedurally constructed dialogue such as the Contract Net Protocol [Smith80], or they may be treated as planned activities, akin to *speech acts*. Austin introduced speech acts as requests, assertions, suggestions, warnings, and so on [Austin62]. Searle tried to specify necessary and sufficient conditions for the successful performance of speech acts, involving the intentions of the participants. To satisfy their own goals, people often *plan* their speech acts to affect their listeners beliefs, goals and emotional states. Cohen and Perrault [Cohen79] have developed a *plan-based theory of speech acts*, which has been further extended into a deep theory of the relationships among belief, intention, and rational communication by Cohen and Levesque [Cohen87a; Cohen87b].

Speech acts can be modeled as operators in a planning system. Operators for requesting and informing can be defined such that *compositional adequacy* is achieved; that is, requests to inform, requests to request and so on can be used consistently. Rosenschein used Cohen and Perrault's [Cohen79] operators as the basis of a multiagent plan-synchronization regime [Rosenschein82], but neither Rosenschein nor Cohen and Perrault were able to handle goal induction adequately.

Both projects used the predicate CAUSE-TO-WANT as a basis, assuming that, when one agent received a request from another, a CAUSE-TO-WANT condition would be conditionally generated, and it would immediately imply cooperation and the successful induction of a goal of doing the requested action. The DVMT uses specialized communication knowledge sources for sending and receiving messages from other problem solvers [Lesser83]. In this way, the same control regimes can be applied to communications reasoning as are applied to other problem-solving activities [Durfee87e].

1.4 Coherence and Coordination

Coherence and coordination are concepts widely used in analyzing and describing DAI systems, but they are seldom clearly defined or differentiated. We shall use the term *coherence* in discussing properties of the total DAI system (or of some region within it), and the term *coordination* in discussing particular patterns of activity and interaction among agents. "Coherence" will refer to how well the system behaves as a unit, along some dimension of evaluation. We can evaluate coherence by examining several dimensions of a system's behavior:

Solution Quality: This is the system's ability to reach satisfactory solutions, and the quality of the solutions it produces.

Efficiency: This is the system's overall efficiency in achieving some end.

Clarity: This is the conceptual clarity of the system's actions, and the usefulness of its representation. Can the system's behavior be described and represented so that an outside system observer can understand it? In a well-structured, describable system, self-representation can be used for internal communication, reorganization, fault diagnosis, preformance analysis, etc.

Graceful Degradation: This is how gracefully the system degrades in the presence of failure or uncertainty—what is its behavior at the limits of its environment, specification, or self-description?

Coordination, on the other hand, is a property of interaction among some set of agents performing some collective activity. The degree of coordination exhibited among a collection of agents is the extent to which they can avoid "extraneous" activity (e.g., the indirect activity of synchronizing and aligning their tasks) in achieving their primary ends. We call this extraneous activity *articulation work*, following [Bendif87; Gasser84; Gasser86; Gerson86; Strauss85]. Effective coordination implies some degree of mutual predictability and lack of conflict; the more unexpected conflict must be ironed out, the less well coordinated are the agents. We do not explicitly consider *cooperation* as a separate concept here, because we

(and other investigators) see it as a special case of coordination among nonantagonistic actors [Axelrod84; Rosenschein85b]. Coordination does not necessarily imply cooperation, since antagonists can be coordinated, for example, in legal proceedings. Coordination and coherence are partially related—better coordination may lead to greater efficiency coherence, through reduction of articulation work. However, good local decisions do not necessarily add up to good global behavior, because good local decisions may have unfortunate global effects.

Most DAI researchers have been interested in a system's coherence as measured by its efficiency. From this perspective, incoherence can result from conflict over resources, from one agent unwittingly (or maliciously) undoing the results of another, and from duplicate actions being carried out redundantly [Davis83; Lesser83]. For example, duplication of task announcements is possible in the Contract Net, where it can be limited by using *focused addressing* (sending announcements to only those nodes with known interests), but this requires models of other agents and more certainty about the world.

Inordinate problem or interaction *complexity* may also reduce coherence. Fox defined complexity as excessive demands on rationality [Fox81]. He identified information, task, and coordination complexity. When task requirements exceed current resource capacity bounds, the need to make resource-allocation choices adds additional work and uncertainty, which may lead to incoherence or to lack of coordination.

The primary difficulty in establishing coherence and coordination is the attempt to achieve them *without centralized control or viewpoints*. Achieving global or regional coherence with only local control is probably the primary problem to which DAI researchers have addressed themselves, to date. This problem is also important in distributed computing systems of all types (see, e.g., [Huberman88b; Pasquale88]). From a DAI perspective, the problem is rich because agents must reason about the intentions and knowledge states of other agents and, in DPS systems, about the overall goals of problem solving, generally under conditions of disparate knowledge and/or representations [Lesser83; Hewitt86].

Lesser and Corkill [Lesser87] have suggested that solution coherent behavior in a DPS system requires the achievement of three conditions: *coverage* — each necessary portion of the overall problem must be included in the activities of at least one node; *connectivity* — nodes must interact in a manner that permits the covering activities to be developed and integrated into an overall solution; and *capability* — coverage and connectivity must be achievable within the communication- and computation-resource limitations of the network (cf. [Lesser80a]). Other forms of coherence may be more difficult to link to specific system attributes for design purposes. Lesser and Erman introduced the concept of *distraction*, meaning the degree to which a node's focus can be shifted based on interactions with other nodes. *Positive* distraction shifts a node to tasks more globally useful, whereas *negative* distraction introduces redundant or diversionary effort. Much more research is needed to understand how to achieve coherence, especially with only local control, but several approaches have been advanced in the current literature.

1.4.1 Organization

An *organization* can provide a framework of constraints and expectations about the behavior of agents (e.g., a set of "roles") that focuses the decision making and action of particular agents. Corkill, Durfee, and Lesser have suggested that organization can be seen as a long term, strategic load-balancing technique, which can improve efficiency coherence [Corkill82; Durfee87d]. The organization of a collection of agents can be revised to accomplish by default what focused addressing or direct load balancing would accomplish by direct action [Durfee87d]. There is general agreement that no organization structure is appropriate in all situations; this was pointed out long ago by contingency theorists of human organizations (see, e.g., [Galbraith73; Lawrence69; Perrow67; Thompson67]). Fox [Fox79; Fox81] developed a taxonomy of how organizational types evolve as an organization grows, becomes more complex, and encompasses more diverse activities. According to Fox, as organizations grow, they produce multiple products. Since agents compete for resources in multiple-product organizations, they are often reorganized into a multidivisional hierarchy, comprising a division for each product, with some strategic control level over them. With further development, a collective organization emerges, where the hierarchy is split into separate organizations that cooperate to achieve a shared goal—rather like shared, long-term contracts. The next development in the reduction of control and information flow in organizations is a competitive organizational system. We lack concrete theories of organizational performance, but Malone in particular has begun to study the comparative information-processing performance of rigid organization structures [Malone87a; Malone88a]. However, there is still meager insight linking attributes of situations and problems to organizational design. What little DAI-related research exists primarily focuses on structural models of organization (cf. [Pattison87; Malone88a; Malone88b]), a view considered problematic by some investigators (see, e.g., [Gasser88a; Strauss78]).

Centralized and hierarchical organization: Typical hierarchical organizations associate greater control with a more global viewpoint. Nodes with more global information guide nodes with less global information as decision-making data flow "upward" in progressively more abstracted forms, and control flows "downward." Chandrasekaran [Chandrasekn81] notes that the simplest hierarchy is two levels, wherein one agent at the top level has complete information and all authority to control problem-solving agents at a second level. In such a "centralized" organization, coherence is achieved by limiting decision making and by centralizing all decisions in one agent, at the possible expense of solution quality in a dynamic

environment [Steeb81]. For example, coherence was generally assumed by the Rand team to be difficult to achieve in the ATC problem, so they opted for the conservative solution of complete decision-making centralization [Steeb81].

Organization as authority structure: Authority structures are one way of reducing coordination work. When one node has authority over another, the latter must accept a goal or result. Solution coherence may be increased or decreased depending on the accuracy of the global view provided by the authoritative node and on the need for global coordination for higher quality [Wesson81]. Lowering the coupling and interdependencies among agents can reduce the need for authority structures among nodes by reducing conflict among nodes and hence reducing the need to resolve it with authority [Wesson81]. Authority structuring can improve coherence if it is coupled with information about which nodes have the most accurate views of a situation [Durfee87d]. The most accurate nodes should be allowed to guide the less-informed ones.

Marketlike organization: Numerous authors have proposed that distributed computer systems be organized as markets, and have studied the performance of these systems under various (usually closed world) market assumptions (e.g., [Kurose85; Malone88b; Ramamritham85; Sproull78]). Competitive, marketlike organizations have been proposed to organize DAI systems as well [Davis83; Fox81; Kornfeld81b; Smith80; Parunak87; Stefik88]. For example, the Contract Net architecture supports a market in both tasks and processing resources, through competitive bidding, whereas Kornfeld and Hewitt and later Hewitt alone have suggested competitive schemes for generating and settling problems, rather than task allocations [Kornfeld81b; Hewitt85; Hewitt86]. Most research has considered mechanisms for implementing marketlike organizations, while relatively little DAI research has gone into understanding local decision-making policies and market rules that produce coherent system performance. The emergence and reconfiguration of market structures has received virtually no attention in DAI, and merits more research.

Organization as a community with rules of behavior: An organization may be construed as a set of locally interpreted *rules of behavior*, rather than as an externally defined structure. For example, in Lenat's PUP6 system, knowledge was organized as a community of interacting agents ("beings"), in contrast to a set of hierarchically organized structures [Lenat75]. A beings system was a "flat" organization of specialists, including a "chooser" specialist for conflict resolutions. The entire community had an imposed constraint that each agent had to be represented using the same standard structure. The rules of behavior were derived from the common structure of agents. Agents could interact only by making queries about particular aspects of other agents' predefined structure. Hewitt later urged the search for "rules of civilized discourse" among agents [Hewitt77a] in his quest for concepts underlying decentralized control. As has been pointed out for both human and automated systems, however, inconsistent local interpretations can a render global conception of rules problematic (cf. [Gasser88a; Gerson86; Lesser83; Manning77; Winograd86]).

1.4.2 Increased Localization

Two extreme coordination regimes are (1) predefine a fully partitioned set of actions for each node with full synchronization, making problem-solving completely routine, and (2) broadcast all state changes, so every agent has complete awareness of the network conditions, allowing it to make fully informed local decisions [Durfee87d]. In most DAI systems, and in particular in open systems, neither of these extremes apply. Both are useful only if bandwidth is available, if the situation does not change faster than the synchronization, communication, or decision making works, if there is no uncertainty in the task structure, and if the system scale is kept within resource limits. Two mechanisms have been suggested for improving localization:

Specialization: Specialization can improve performance by reducing and focusing the responsibilities of a node, and hence reducing its local decision-making overhead [Durfee87d].

Reducing dependencies: Coordination and coherence can be increased if local dependency among nodes can be reduced so that there is less possibility for harmful interaction and correspondingly lower computation or communication overhead. This could be achieved by good task decomposition, but it is not obvious how to connect problem characteristics with decision dependencies. Interagent dependencies can also be reduced by increasing the supply of resources [Fox81], because agents will have less contention over the resources that are available.

1.4.3 Increased Local Capability

Increased coordination and coherence should result from making each agent more capable locally (e.g., giving it better problem-solving knowledge, better internal control, or greater resources), and from making it evaluate each of its potential actions in the light of how that action will affect network problem solving [Durfee87d]. Nodes can get closer to optimality overall by making their local decisions less redundant and/or less disruptive of the work of other nodes. *Local planning* is one way to improve local capability. Plans (sequences or conditional partial orderings of activities) can give a node the ability to reason about what it is and will be doing, and thus to know whether or not to send or accept certain temporally constrained data [Durfee87d]. Local planning gives a node greater

control over its own processing, reducing local redundancy and extraneous work. This occurs by (1) packaging common sequences of activities into macro-operators, and (2) using goals to focus on specific, highly rated tasks and on planning methods for achieving them [Corkill83].

Increased local capability must be balanced against local overhead costs and alternative strategies, such as increased communication. Experimental results on coherence [Durfee87d] indicate that, as a node becomes less certain about what and where to communicate, the computational overhead for planning and metalevel communication becomes more acceptable. This is more true when planning becomes relatively inexpensive compared to problem-solving activities.

1.4.4 Planning

We can achieve greater coordination by aligning behavior of agents toward common goals, with explicit divisions of labor. Techniques such as centralized planning for multiple agents, plan reconciliation, distributed planning, organizational analysis, and appropriate control transfers (e.g., focus of attention strategies based on reasoning about the state of local problem solving [Lesser83]) are ways of helping to align the activities of agents by assigning tasks after reasoning through the consequences of doing those tasks in particular orders. For the activities of several agents to be aligned using planning, interactions in the plans of different agents must be controlled. Plan interactions may involve incompatible states, incompatible orders of steps, or incompatible use of resources. Plan synchronization can be performed at several points. It can be done during problem decomposition [Corkill79]. It can be done during plan construction, by building smoothly interacting plans hierarchically [Corkill79], by aligning partial plans incrementally [Durfee87c], or by reasoning about interactions and dependencies as a part of planning [Rosenschein82]. It can also be done after plan construction [Georgeff83]. The control of plan interactions can be done using *multiagent planning*, wherein a single agent generates plans for multiple agents [Georgeff83; Steeb81], or using *distributed planning* and dividing up the planning activities as well [Corkill79; Durfee87c; Hayes-Roth79a; Hayes-Roth85].

Multiagent planning: Generating multiagent plans requires reasoning about how actions of different agents may interfere with one another, and thus requires explicit representations for parallel actions. Structures and state-based representations of parallel activity based on logical formalisms have been proposed by [Allen84; Backstrom88a; Dean87; Georgeff84; Georgeff86a; Georgeff87b; Georgeff87a]. The frame problem is of paramount importance. Techniques under investigation for handling it include localized, *event-based* (rather than *state-based*) action representations [Lansky85; Lansky87a;

Lansky87b], the use of indexical logical operators such as fluents [Georgeff87b; Georgeff87a], and the treatment of multiagent plans using single-agent frameworks [Pednault87]. One approach to multiagent planning, developed by Georgeff, is to insert communication acts into single agent plans, so that agents can avoid harmful interactions. In Georgeff's work, actions are microsequences of states. Plan reconciliation is achieved in three stages by a single global agent. First, an interaction analysis is performed, to determine where plans interact. Next, a safety analysis determines where plans have potential conflicts. Finally, unsafe state sequences are coalesced into critical regions, and conventional synchronization mechanisms based on communication acts are applied. The communication acts concern properties of actions, resources, and physical constraints at the time of execution of the plan [Georgeff83].

Distributed planning: In distributed planning, a single plan is produced by the cooperation of several agents. Each agent produces a subplan, but there may be conflicts among subplans that need to be reconciled. One hierarchical approach, developed by Corkill, is to synchronize levels of planning in all the agents, communicating shared variables between goals and resolving conflicts at each level before refining plans to lower levels [Corkill79].

Mutual plan construction is not well understood. It is confounded by disparities in goals and intentions, as well as disparities in world knowledge. All the problems of multiagent planning exist, along with the problems of inconsistent world views due to distribution. Durfee and Durfee and Lesser have originated the idea of *partial global planning* as a mechanism to enable communicating problem solvers to construct mutually coherent plans incrementally [Durfee87a; Durfee87c]. Added benefits may accrue by using multiple perspectives in the planning process at different levels of abstraction, as Hayes-Roth has suggested in work on the OPM system (cf. [Hayes-Roth85]).

1.4.5 Increasing Contextual Awareness

Coherence and coordination can be improved by giving nodes greater knowledge about the context in which they are making decisions — greater knowledge of the goals, plans, and activities of other agents, deeper knowledge of the problem domain (which is the context for individual domain-dependent decisions), and greater temporal context (e.g., greater lookahead or history). Tenney and Sandell have done extensive characterization and theoretical analysis of coordination possibilities of agents with various levels of contextual awareness, ranging from no communication and purely local knowledge, to abstracted global or regional network models [Tenney81a]. Several mechanisms for increasing contextual awareness are as follows:

Network views: Each node can be given a general view of network responsibilities to guide its problem-solving and communication decisions; that is, it can be informed of its place in an organization. Note that it is not enough to *establish* roles. They must be communicated and widely known to affect local decisions. Three representation options are to encode responsibilities in network-centered models [Pattison87], in task-centered models [Durfee87c] or in agent-centered models [Gasser87d].

Extrapolation, prediction, and modeling of others: Making predictions and generating expectations of other agents' behavior are powerful approaches to coordination. For example, Ginsberg suggests using assumptions of common rationality as a basis for techniques that allow rationally coordinated decisions [Ginsberg87]. Wesson et al. suggest communicating information about how data will change, along with the data themselves [Wesson81]. Durfee, Lesser, and Corkill suggest exchanging plans to allow nodes greater access to the anticipated future behaviors of others [Durfee87d; Durfee87c]. In speech act related research, Cohen and Perrault [Cohen79] develop belief models of other agents (useful information about the belief context of other agents' actions) as a foundation for coordinated communication activities. Rosenschein [Rosenschein82] and Morgenstern use belief and knowledge models to generate workable multiagent plans. (See also Section 5 of this survey.)

Bruce and Newman [Bruce78] distinguish between single actor plans and *interacting plans* in their work on understanding stories about coordinated actions. The motivation for their research was the analysis and representation of narrative text. Analysis of narratives should explicate interactions among plans, and is important to DAI from the standpoint of representing and reasoning about the plans and intentions of other agents. In the Bruce and Newman framework, an understander must reason about how agents represent the plans and beliefs of others. Beliefs about plans determine actions. Actions include the perceptions of each other's plans. The example they use — the Hansel and Gretel story — illustrates these points. Analysis of stories proceeds in terms of actions connected through goals, effects and enabling conditions. An actor can interpret the actions of another in terms of goals, and change his or her actions accordingly. Deception and differing beliefs are a common feature of stories. Representation of interacting plans involves showing how the beliefs and plans of one character are embedded in the beliefs and plans of another. The scheme provides for the representation of intentions and the effects of actions. The authors show that a single actor plan can be modified by the needs of cooperative interaction with others, and that cooperative interactive episodes can be transformed and used deceptively by one party in achieving his or her own covert goals.

1.4.6 Managing Communication

Agents can improve both coordination and coherence by managing what, how, and when they communicate with one another. Communication may provide agents with the knowledge to place their actions in the context of what other agents are doing, and may help to synchronize actions [Georgeff83; Rosenschein82; Stuart85]. It may also provide information generated elsewhere that will improve the quality of an agent's local decision making. Wesson et al. derived two basic motivators for communication: agents sharing time-varying information about the external world they are sensing, and agents sharing time-varying information about their own internal states of processing [Wesson81]. Knowing when something has changed sufficiently to notify another agent is tricky; if the world did not change, or was in a steady state, no messages would need to be exchanged (but no action could take place). Wesson et al. suggest that, if a widely held tentative conclusion is found to be incorrect, other agents should be notified immediately of the fact (to save redundant computation) [Wesson81].

Three characteristics of domain-level communicated information relate communication and coherence: relevance, timeliness, and completeness [Durfee87d]. *Relevance* is the amount of information in the message consistent with the global solution. *Timeliness* measures the extent to which a message will influence the current activity of the receiving node. The timeliness of a message varies with the state of a node. A message that will have no effect should not be sent. *Completeness* is the fraction of a complete solution the message represents. More complete messages reduce redundancy—they are more discriminatory in Wesson et al.'s [Wesson81] sense, because more complete messages can be combined with known, reliable beliefs in fewer ways. With greater awareness of the global situation, and with classification of messages on these dimensions, a node can make better decisions about what to send and what not to send to increase coherence (i.e. to reduce negative distraction and to increase positive distraction). Nodes must also know what to listen to and what to ignore. Knowing what *not* to communicate also is important for coordination and coherence. Explicit communication is not always necessary for synchronization, as it may be accomplished by using agent models and reasoning about the activities of others, for example, under assumptions of common knowledge and rationality [Rosenschein86; Tenney81a]. There is always a tradeoff between the need for reliable and timely information and the costs of communication and computation. Equally important, however, communicating obsolete or uncertain information may negatively distract an agent, if the new information is less useful than what the agent already has [Lesser83].

For communication that aids coherence and improves coordination, agents should exchange only highly *diagnostic* data — data that are consistent with the smallest number of current hypotheses or decision alternatives, and so will have the great-est discriminating effect. Exchanging one of these data can discriminate multiple hypotheses, killing many birds with one stone [Wesson81]. Durfee et al. believe that messages should contain less detailed information about domain-specific actions, and more detailed information about plans for problem-solving activities. Messages should contain metalevel information, rather than domain-level data such as partial solutions [Durfee87d]. In addition, metalevel information specifically intended to enhance coherence can enable nodes to make more informed communication decisions [Durfee87e].

1.4.7 Managing Resource Use

Regulating the use of consumable resources in a DAI system is a method of encouraging coherence and coordination. Allocating resources is one mechanism for focusing the attention of a community of agents, either through market mechanisms or through explicit control policies (cf. [Kornfeld81b]). Coherence and coordination can be improved if the agents with the most accurate, global, or discriminating viewpoints are allocated adequate resources [Steeb81; Steeb84]. Allowing slack resources at critical coordination points in the problem-solving process can also improve coordination and coherence by reducing the overhead of decision making about contentions over scarce resources.

Knowledge resources such as domain-level problem knowledge or capability, and decision-making resources such as the degree of freedom of choice, can also be a factor in achieving coherence. For example, allowing greater (or less) freedom of choice for each participant (effectively making each participant less [or more] certain of the future commitments of others) is one way to make coordination easier (or more tightly constrained) by controlling "slack" in a decision-making process [Chandrasekn81; Fox81]. For actions that are mutually constraining, agents can improve coordination by allowing other agents maximum freedom of choice—for example by using *least commitment* strategies or by relaxing quality requirements. Chandrasekaran [Chandrasekn81] suggests a benevolent *principle of least commitment* as a coherence device; each agent makes only conservative changes to allow other agents greatest information and freedom for their own decisions. Some commitment is unavoidable at each choice, but proper choices can provide useful islands of certainty, rather than overly constraining obstacles. In a related strategy for coherence called *local relaxation* [Chandrasekn81], each agent's results or commitments may be relaxed to become consistent with those of that agent's local neighbors (cf. [Goldstein75; Sycara85a].

1.4.8 Managing Uncertainty

Both Galbraith's and Perrow's contingency theories of (human) organization note that organizational structure is related to the uncertainty and diversity of the task environment of the organization [Galbraith73; Perrow67]. Uncertainty, in this context, can be defined as the difference between the information available and the information necessary to make the best decision. Fox [Fox81] discusses several types of uncertainty not exploited in contingency theory, including *information uncertainty* (uncertainty of the correctness of data), *decision algorithm uncertainty* (uncertainty due to lack of knowledge of outcomes of decision), *environmental uncertainty* (poor estimation of changing environment), and *behavioral uncertainty* (individual agents may not deliver on their commitments).

The quality of knowledge among nodes in a network affects the amount of uncertainty and error (in data and communications) that can be accommodated [Lesser83] for a given level of solution quality. Solution coherence is thus related to knowledge and data uncertainties. Formal progress is being made (see, e.g., [Halpern86a; Halpern87]), with respect to the problems of how common knowledge can be guaranteed in the face of particular communication failures.

Conversely, degrees of coherence and coordination can be controlled by management of degree of uncertainty willingly tolerated. As agents become less certain about the place of their actions in a global picture, they have a harder time making local decisions with better global effects. Manipulating the quality and certainty of interim solutions may be one way of achieving real-time performance [Lesser88].

1.4.9 Pluralism

Kornfeld and Hewitt [Kornfeld81b] base their "scientific community metaphor" on the idea that the success (i.e., quality and robustness, or the solution coherence) of scientific research depends critically on the concurrency and diversity of the scientific community. For this reason, they feel that parallelism is fundamental to the design and implementation of expert systems, independently of technological pressures for parallelism. The language ETHER was designed by Kornfeld for creating highly parallel problem-solving systems. (The correspondence of ETHER to the scientific community is not direct, but is only seen at a high level of abstraction.) More recently, Hewitt has called for reasoning based on "due processes," that incorporate multiple conflicting points of view for problem solving [Hewitt86].

Coordination has been conceptualized as a problem of aligning activity from multiple perspectives in [Bond88a; Gasser84; Gasser86]. Misalignment across perspectives results in "disarticulation" in a lattice of activity, and serves as an indicator of how and where perspectives must be integrated to achieve coordination. Other researchers have suggested using uncorrelated perspectives to help stabilize control through redundancy. Fox, among others, has also noted that function or product decomposition in an organization will give a beneficial mesh effect [Fox81]. Redundancy of decisions from

disparate perspectives has been explored as a stabilizing organizational principle in the Rand ATC work and in the DVMT [Durfee87d]. In particular, the functionally accurate, cooperative (FA/C) framework of Lesser and Corkill [Lesser81] relies strongly on the reconciliation of multiple competing hypothetical explanations for phenomena, and on combining evidence from multiple points of view.

1.4.10 Abstraction and Metalevels

Abstraction is a powerful device for enhancing coherence and coordination in DAI system design. Nodes are most likely to need communicate with other nodes that are semantically closer, with respect to the nodes' mutual problem. Data abstraction can lead to a relaxation of this rule, as it and globality go hand in hand — abstraction increases the semantic scope of data. Abstracted data are potentially more applicable to a wider variety of cases, and hence are semantically more global. In the distributed sensor net examples of the DVMT and of Wesson's group, there is a strong relationship between knowledge that is problem specific (in a semantic sense) and geographic location. This relationship allows these researchers to assert that nodes are more likely to need to communicate with other nodes that are working with geographically similar information [Lesser83; Wesson81]. Thus, communication channels and decisions (resources) can be structured along two dimensions: problem locality, and data abstraction. This insight gives guidelines for resource allocation and organizational structures that will lead to more coherent systems. Abstraction also is used centrally in the Contract Net. Task abstraction enables a node to compare and select tasks within a common framework, and bid abstraction enables a manager to compare and select bids.

Metalevel information should allow a node to reason about the past, current, and future activity of another node [Durfee87d]. For example, abstracted blackboard information can help in making high-level focusing and control decisions that depend on results from past activities. There is some evidence to indicate that nodes that work with redundant data perform better when they exchange metalevel information about the goals and plans of other nodes, because that allows them to avoid redundant work. Metalevel information enables agents to assess more accurately the effects of communications on the activities of other nodes [Durfee87d]. The abstractions afforded in metalevel communication serve two useful purposes — fewer messages need to be exchanged, (communication reduction) and computation to interpret all the messages and predict future actions in other nodes is reduced (increasing computational coherence). With no overlap, metalevel communication is unnecessary [Durfee87d]. With moderate overlap, it is sufficient to exchange enough information to avoid immediate redundancy. With high overlap, enough metalevel information must be exchanged to prevent future redundancy.

Metalevel information can nearly halve the time necessary to generate a solution in highly overlapping environments [Durfee87d]. DVMT experiments with exchanging metalevel information are interesting because they indicate that to achieve reliability via redundancy, metalevel reasoning may be important for focusing. Of course, if global performance is at a premium, metalevel communication will help, but it also will increase communication load. Moreover, obsolete metalevel information can be dramatically counterproductive where there is high overlap.

1.4.11 Adaptation

Adaptation can improve coherence and coordination over time, by allowing agents to reconfigure their styles of processing and interaction to conform best to the requirements of changing problem situaitons. Locally, when a node's activities are controlled by local planning, replanning in response to new contingencies can be an important adaptive strategy. It requires interleaving of planning and execution. An approach to locally reactive replanning in a DPS system has been presented in [Durfee86].

Organizations of agents can also be adapted, by the roles, knowledge, and activities of agents being changed to conform to new problem situations. Fox [Fox81] points out that *organizational adaptability* is important for efficiency because programmed organizational responses will not be appropriate in environments where uncertainty is high. Organizational adaptation is critically dependent on identifying dysfunctional organizational aspects, projecting new organizational forms with better performance, and having mechanisms for making transitions among organizations. These, in turn, depend heavily on representations of organization and organized activity, about which we have few insights (see also Section 5 of this survey). Several DAI systems have explicitly addressed explicit organizational reconfiguration. At one extreme, the Contract Net of Davis and Smith performed dynamic organizational reconfiguration, to suit the opportunistically generated requirements of an unfolding problem, but there was little persistence of organizational form [Davis83]. Rand ATC researchers examined several strategies for replacing a centralized controller using voting and shared convention schemes [Cammarata83; Steeb81; Steeb84]. Adaptation in the form of organization self-design has been a longstanding goal of the DVMT project. Corkill suggested underlying representational mechanisms for reconfigurable organizations of problem solvers in the DVMT [Corkill82]; Pattison et al. developed a high-level language for specifying organization; and Corkill, Hudlicka, Lesser and Pavlin developed schemes for reasoning about the adequacy of problem-solving behavior in the DVMT [Hudlicka86a; Hudlicka87; Pavlin83; Pavlin84]. To date, however, these have not been combined into a complete organization self-design system. Finally, Gasser and his colleagues believe that adaptability requires complex reasoning

about organization. They have begun to study representations for organized activity that allow for flexible reconfiguration, based on conceptualizing "organization" as locally held collections of expectations about the knowledge and action of other agents, rather than as role restrictions or as fixed interaction structures [Gasser88a].

Unfortunately, there has been little research on learning and adaptation in DAI systems (but see [Huhns87b]). Even with the adaptive regimes already known, there is virtually no opportunity for incorporating performance feedback to tune organizational forms for greater coherence. Collaborative and distributed learning approaches provide a fruitful area for further research.

1.5 Modeling Other Agents and Organized Activity

In early DAI research, Wesson et al. reported that "One of the most important principles we devised involved the use of models to simulate and predict other nodes' activities" ([Wesson81] pg. 14). Meaningful interaction between two agents requires that they have at least implicit knowledge of each other, such as the knowledge encoded in a communication protocol or language. Meaningful communication through language is impossible without some agreement on the intended effects of an utterance. One agent must know what reaction to expect on receipt of a message it sends, to plan communication intelligently. From this perspective, even a typewriter has encoded a model of its user—the shape and structure of its keyboard.

Coordination, which is important for avoiding harmful interactions and because local decisions have global effects, is possible only when some agent has some expectation about the character of the interaction (this agent may be a designer). This expectation may be implicit, but it also may require reasoning. If one aim of DPS and MA systems is decentralized control, then, to make local decisions in varying circumstances, individual agents must be able to reason about their effects on other agents, and about possible undesirable impediments. Durfee, Lesser, and Corkill [Durfee87d; Durfee87e] use the term *network awareness* to describe the knowledge that individual nodes use for coordinating with other nodes. One example is the need for adaptation. To allocate tasks adaptively, even a central controller (manager) needs to know (or learn) what potential task-performing agents can do.

Finally, an agent must be able to reason about its own activities for purposes of control and coordination with other agents. In this respect, an agent must *objectify* itself (incompletely) to see where it fits in a coordinated process, or what the outcomes of its own actions are. Indeed, sociologists and social psychologists in the *symbolic interactionist* tradition have proposed that the primary mechanism for creating organized societies of individuals is the ability of the individual to generate and use internal models of other agents and of him- or herself to reflect on actions and their effects [Abraham82; Blumer69; Cooley64; Mead34].

Restrictions in agents' roles or interactions, using, for example, organizational roles or fixed communication protocols, can limit what agents need to know explicitly about other agents. For example, the Contract Net protocol [Smith80] limits what an agent needs to know to the eligibilities of other agents for a proposed subtask, the addresses of other agents for communication, the contracts that have been assigned, and (sometimes) the state of processing of other agents (e.g., finished or not).

1.5.1 Rationales for Agent Modeling

There are several general reasons for modeling other agents. First, models are useful for predicting the requirements and effects of events not directly sensible (e.g., because they are in the future or are elsewhere in a system). For example, Wesson et al. believe that agents in a distributed sensor network should represent and predict changes to the belief systems of their relevant neighbors. The benefit is that frequent data reporting can be replaced by a system that reports only data that it knows are relevant and/or needed for predicted future actions. This improves coherence (less communication work, less filtering of unneeded data) at the expense of maintaining and using the belief model [Wesson81]. This predictive approach has also been employed in the DVMT. The implications of increasing predictive power are that each node moves more toward being a universal node, with a more complete global simulation of the system in which it resides (including the other agents), which it builds over time. There is, of course, a tradeoff here, based on resource constraints. Two problems come to mind: (1) how to generalize situations and expectations into routine patterns and thus to develop general skills for prediction (and to reduce individual processing load for individual cases), and (2) which prior predictive information to delete or overlook (as new predictions enter the picture).

Prediction can be useful for reducing communications, because only necessary data need to be communicated [Wesson81; Cohen79; Cohen87b; Cohen87a]. Wesson et al. [Wesson81] provide a limited example of how modeling the world and other agents using their *process assembly network* (PAN) concept would reduce communications significantly, by allowing nodes autonomously to maintain predictions about upcoming events. These predictions reduce the necessity of sharing conforming information, and leave communication channels free for sharing surprising, unpredictable information. Moreover, it is possible to coordinate without communication (except the communication necessary to set up the models!) by using explicit models of values and possible choices of other agents, as Rosenschein et al. have investigated [Rosenschein85a; Rosenschein86]

Agent models may also prove useful for evaluating the credibility, usefulness, reliability, or timeliness of data. Durfee

et al. suggest that, to deal with new information that is potentially distracting, nodes must have knowledge about other nodes' activities, to decide, for example, whether information received from them is believable or timely enough to be acted on [Durfee87d].

Agent models may improve efficiency by focusing activity or by directing search. As indicated earlier, knowledge of the data and resource requirements of other agents may prevent unnecessary communication, and may engender early communication of important data. Agent models also aid in thinking about where to get particular information and about how available that information is [Huhns87b; Davis83]. Overhead and bidding delays can be reduced through use of *focused addressing*. Focused addressing can be implemented directly through the use of models of agent capabilities and resources, or indirectly through the use of metalevel communication, organization structuring, and plans [Durfee87d; Durfee87e]. In the Contract Net, for example, nodes could use focused addressing to announce tasks to agents they knew had appropriate capabilities [Davis83; Smith80].

1.5.2 What Knowledge of Other Agents Must be Represented?

Existing DAI research provides some guidance about what kinds of knowledge about other agents can be useful. As we have reiterated throughout this survey, much of this knowledge is needed in *any* DAI system, although it is often implicit in the system, and may be known explicitly to only the designers.

Knowledge of agent capabilities: Capability knowledge is necessary for allocation decisions, performance assessment, and feasibility analysis, as well as for agents to know what results they may be able to provide for other agents (cf. [Davis83; Smith81a; Durfee87d; Durfee87e; Durfee87a; Lenat75]).

Knowledge of agent resources and demands: Real-time constraints (or other resource constraints) may require that nodes model the temporal or resource behavior of other nodes to know what to send those nodes and when to expect answers [Durfee87d; Durfee87e; Wesson81]. For example, Wesson et al. suggest the following communication heuristics:

> If a node is known to be very busy, (assuming single priority messages) don't send it a message. It won't process the message before the world has updated itself, and the message will just add to communication overhead. [Wesson81]

> If a node is known to have inadequate resources send it aggregated information which will enable it to focus on types of tasks which involve making

important conclusions and exploiting its important local data, rather than on global and less important tasks (such as building a global obstacle map, which someone else could do). [Wesson81]

A variant of this second heuristic has been examined in the DVMT, in experiments designed to test the performance of the system in response to varying levels of abstraction in exchanged information.

Knowledge of responsibilities: Assigned responsibilities provide a way of reducing task-allocation overhead, and have been exploited in the Rand ATC experiments [Cammarata83; Steeb86] and as organization structuring in the DVMT. Responsibility assignments must be communicated and known, to have effects on adaptive decentralized task allocation.

Knowledge of solution progress: Knowledge of an agent's processing state is not only important to detect deadlock and liveness, but also to predict whether it will be useful to exchange any information with that agent. If an agent is known to be running behind, then newly generated information may be out of date before it is useful to the agent.

Knowledge for communicating: Communication knowledge falls into two classes: knowledge of channels, languages, protocols, and so on, and knowledge about what information it will be useful to communicate. For example, the actor systems at the Massachusetts Institute of Technology have explicit models of other agents that are typically limited to the location or name of each agent. These limited models require an underlying operating system that keeps track of the locations of all agents, and takes responsibility for delivering messages. Although any two automated agents typically use common language and protocol knowledge for communication, the extent to which this knowledge must be (or is actually) "common" or "shared" among certain (e.g., human) agents is not settled [Winograd86].

Knowledge of beliefs, goals, plans, and actions: Coordination requires at a minimum some knowledge of the *actions* of other agents, and the ability to reason about the effects of those actions [Cohen79; Georgeff83; Georgeff84; Georgeff87c; Fikes71; Schank77; Wilensky84]. Being able to anticipate or explain actions requires further reference to knowledge of the plans, goals, and beliefs of agents that have led to actions, and the causal relations among these, as well as knowledge about how they will evolve. For Bruce and Newman [Bruce78], a representation of a social episode includes a representation of each character's *role*. A role is the set of actions the character expects to perform, and the intentions that can reasonably be inferred from these actions, given the assumption that the characters are cooperating. In the Rand ATC work [Steeb81],

each agent (airplane) needs to know the plans of other airplanes as well as their speeds, headings, fuel levels, destinations and emergency statuses. Bruce and Newman's representation scheme [Bruce78] allows representation of causal relationships among states, enabling actions etc. Changing the actions of other agents may also require providing justifications, and meaningful justifications can be generated only by using knowledge of the other agent's beliefs, goals, and so on. (or the *assumption* of common beliefs). For reasoned communication and for synchronization of plans, detailed knowledge of the beliefs and goals of other agents is necessary and has been discussed in the framework of several domains [Bruce78; Cohen79; Cohen87a; Cohen87b; Levin77; Rosenschein82].

The completeness of models of other agents is a difficult issue. More complete models of the beliefs of other agents may be ineffective, because they may require that an agent duplicate the processing of another node. This is a matter of computation versus communication, as well as problem-solving speed requirements and efficiencies [Durfee87d; Durfee87e]. Moreover, some belief models may require large amounts of processing. Virtually all working DAI systems use abstracted and heuristic models of other agents rather than precise propositional models of belief, such as those described by Konolige, Cohen, Halpern, Levesque, and Perrault [Cohen79; Cohen87a; Cohen87b; Halpern86a; Halpern86b; Konolige86], which are largely used for theoretical and analytical purposes. With better understanding and better algorithms, these more formal approaches may become more widely used for implementation.

1.5.3 How Should Knowledge of Other Agents be Organized?

Knowledge of other agents can be organized relative to tasks, actions, and processes that are occurring, relative to the agents being modeled, or using multiple perspective representations. For example, in the Contract Net, knowledge of task assignments and processing state is organized relative to tasks. The DVMT organizes knowledge of task assignments relative to goals of the processing being done, so it is easy to retrieve information about how goals are being accomplished. In the MACE DAI testbed, each agent has an associative database of knowledge of other agents from which knowledge can be retrieved relative to tasks, goals, plans, skills, organizational roles, or agents, allowing for flexible and multidimensional modeling [Gasser87c; Gasser87d].

1.5.4 Problem-Solving Process Knowledge

Process knowledge includes knowledge of problem-solving roles, roles in the multiagent process, (e.g., constraints on an individual's potential activities as in a DVMT "organization"), knowledge of states and interactions (e.g., termination), and knowledge of behavior (how the world and beliefs will change). Process knowledge is important for and related to the *predictive knowledge* mentioned earlier. Wesson et al. in fact have suggested that the important aspects to model about other agents are those that will *change*, and that these can be recognized by modeling the world and looking for things that will force changes, such as obstacles or the arrival of new relevant information [Wesson81]. To do this, they proposed using "active hypotheses" that could update themselves along with the expected trajectories of change in the world, and periodically could check their conditions with respect to conditions in the real world. Thus, messages should contain not just static data, but also dynamic procedures for changing that data over time, allowing agents to reduce communication. These dynamic procedures are in effect transportable process models of aspects of other agents or of the world.

Scripts are well known AI techniques for representing processes involving several agents [Schank77]. Scripts encode knowledge of the agents involved, of their respective roles, and of the temporal precedence of actions. Strangely, there has been little application of scriptlike structures in DAI research.

Representing Control Knowledge

By *control knowledge*, we mean knowledge that informs decisions about what actions to take next. In general, control knowledge makes reference to some aspect of the process state, and thus the state of the problem solving or mutual activity must be represented (possibly in abstracted form) to reason about control. Control knowledge and process representation are deeply intertwined. Given this definition, it is also clear that the distinction between control knowledge and other types of knowledge is sometimes difficult to recognize; domain-specific problem data may influence control decisions. Lesser and Corkill mention two kinds of control knowledge in a DPS system: control within an agent (local control), and control of interactions among agents for coherence and coordination (network control). They note that there must be an intimate relation between local control and network control if we hope to achieve truly distributed control; the global network performance must be derived from local control decisions. Internal control knowledge in the DVMT is represented in the form of "interest areas," that specify the type of tasks a node considers relevant to its interests.

Some representations of processes can encode control knowledge. If processes are represented as sequences of state changes, with control points and correctness criteria, the control points allow synchronization and the ability to express dependencies among agents (or between an agent and its environment) [Georgeff83]. Some explicit representations of control knowledge are found in global-memory blackboard systems in the form of scheduling tables and of explicit *control blackboards* [Erman80; Lesser83; Hayes-Roth79a; Hayes-Roth79b; Hayes-Roth85; Nii86b; Nii86a]. In these systems,

control is opportunistically linked to the system state as represented on the control blackboard or in scheduling rules.

1.5.5 Organizational Knowledge

By *organizational knowledge*, we mean one of four types of knowledge: (1) general principles of organization (to be used by self-designing and organizationally adaptive systems), (2) knowledge of the organizational method used in the system, (3) a set of default expectations about actions and beliefs of others, or (4) a structural view of relationships among nodes, such as communication structure, authority, knowledge, etc.

Representing Organizational Knowledge

There are several approaches to representing organizational knowledge:

Representation by the use of a particular architecture: Languages and shells that reflect particular architectures encode some implicit knowledge about the possible forms of interaction among problem solvers, the possible roles each problem solver shall play, and how the roles and interaction can be modified. They include (1) the Contract Net Protocol, which organizes problem solvers into a strict virtual hierarchy—there is no lateral communication among several workers on related subtasks, and no preemption; (2) blackboard shells such as Erasmus [Jagannathan87a], GBB [Corkill87; Corkill87] and BB1 [Johnson86; Hayes-Roth85; Hayes-Roth86], which organize interaction among expert knowledge sources sequentially, incorporate fixed problem-solving roles and fixed communication paths, but allow temporal and control reconfiguration, using opportunism and control metaknowledge; and (3) concurrent object-oriented languages that provide maximally flexible interaction but no structure (see Section 7).

Representations for organization and interaction: Organizations are represented primarily in three ways. First, organizations are commonly seen as structural entities, and are represented with graphs delineating functional roles or products connected in relationships of authority, communication, control, and information flow [Malone84; Malone87a; Malone87b; Malone88a; Pattison87]. Functional roles may be described constructively by listing the capabilities of agents, by specifying constraints on the activities of agents [Lesser83; Pattison87] or by recording the eligibility criteria for tasks [Davis83]. Second, organizations can be represented as collections of tasks or actions in network, plan, and process models, such as Wesson et al.'s PAN, Gasser's production lattices, Bruce and Newman's social episodes, and the DVMT's problem-solution graphs, etc. [Bruce78; Corkill79;

Durfee87d; Durfee87c; Gasser84; Gasser86; Gasser88b; Gasser88a; Wesson81]. Third, organizations may also be described as collections of expectations, commitments, and/or behavioral defaults among agents [Barber80; Barber83; Fikes82; Gasser87d; Gasser88b; Gasser88a]. Finally, organizations may be represented as implicit knowledge encoded in agents' internal structures and capabilities, such as the agent structures found in [Agha85; Davis81; Davis83; Durfee87d; Erman75; Hewitt77a; Lenat75].

Existing DAI systems have used several particular representation techniques:

Some projects have used delineated, fixed (but changeable) *roles and communication patterns* to represent organizations. For example, the EFIGE language represents particular organizations in the DVMT, by establishing fixed roles and communication patterns. In the DVMT, each agent has facilities for solving all problems; "roles" are actually static restrictions on the agents' capabilities and on data to which agents will respond.

MACE *acquaintance databases* contain models of other agents used in reasoning about interaction, and represent both implicit (goals and skills of agents) and explicit (named roles) organizational knowledge.

The ICE problem-solving system uses localized *production-lattice models* [Gasser86; Gasser88b; Gasser88a] that encode expectations of multiagent interactions and that are used for default reasoning about the actions of other agents. Organizations are defined as hierarchically abstracted networks of settled and unsettled issues relating to the "basic organizational question:" *Who does what, when?* Temporary settlements provide expectations and default contexts for local decisions and action, but can be revised (with the right knowledge) to provide flexible organization.

Partial global plans (PGPs) [Durfee87a; Durfee87d; Durfee87e] are representations of aggregated local plans of agents, with conflicts removed. They provide incrementally global or regional views of planned activity, enabling agents to allocate resources selectively.

Process assembly networks (PANs), introduced by Wesson, et al., are actually graphs of how the problem-solving processes will assemble partial results into global solutions, and are similar to the problem-solution graphs of Hudlicka et al. [Hudlicka86a; Hudlicka86b]. Like PGPs and production lattices, PANs enable agents to relate their planned local actions to the actions of other agents.

Problem-solution graphs (PSGs) represent the actual set of steps that need to be taken (or that have been taken) by a set of agents to solve a particular problem, and can be seen as a goal network for the problem [Pavlin83; Pavlin84; Hudlicka86a; Hudlicka86b]. PSGs may be generated statically or dynamically. In Pavlin and Hudlicka's work, actual PSGs were matched against optimal

ones to generate knowledge for analyzing performance, and for diagnosing and repairing failures of problem-solving systems.

1.6   Interagent Disparities: Uncertainty and Conflict

Intelligent problem-solving agents must objectify portions of their world to reason about them. This objectification process is always subject to problems of abstraction and incompleteness, in part because no object or process can be fully described. Thus, intelligent agents have to be able to cope with problems of disparity and uncertainty between their objectified representations and the affairs to which the representations refer. Sometimes, these states of affairs involve other agents in the world; when agents act in coordinated ways, they (or some designer) must objectify one another into representations, and they must at some level align these representations to coordinate. This is a difficult conceptual problem, in general, because "alignment" does *not* mean that agents must have identical or "shared" representations, but rather that the representations must allow them to act so as to accomplish their individual ends. Establishing standard or common representations, such as standard communication protocols or information exchange regimes (cf. [Durfee87a; Durfee87d; Durfee87e; Smith80]), seems to be a reliable solution, but it critically depends on the agents having compatible ways of *interpreting* those protocols [Winograd86]. For example, in the DVMT, network nodes may compete or conflict because they must *locally interpret* the network goals [Durfee87d; Durfee87e]. It is the differing local interpretations which lead to competition or conflict (in the DVMT these are manifested as distraction, extraneous processing, or redundancy). As Hewitt has pointed out [Hewitt86], establishing a notion of semantics of an action as "effects on future behavior," rather than as changes in state, eases the conceptual problem; Agha has developed such a semantics for concurrent ACTOR systems [Agha86a].

Nonetheless, in many extant DPS systems, this is not a problem, because common interpretive frameworks and standard protocols are designed in. These systems still face problems of disparity, uncertainty, and conflict among agents, their beliefs, and the actual behaviors of the worlds they reason about. Agents may have knowledge bases in which beliefs are relatively *incomplete* (one knowledge base contains some belief that another does not contain), *logically inconsistent*, *confidence inconsistent* (two knowledge bases represent similar beliefs at different confidence levels), or *incompatible* (two knowldege bases use different representations). Incomplete viewpoints are evident in the DVMT (where each node has only partial information about global state), in the Contract Net (where each node has only partial information about potential contractors—those which are submitting bids) and in the Rand ATC systems [Steeb81] where each airplane has an incomplete viewpoint of the total system airspace or plans of other airplanes. Incompatible viewpoints are rarely found in working DAI systems, largely because designers have installed common representational mechanisms in agents. For example, Lenat insisted on a common structure for all his agents in the PUP6 system, in order to combat the problems of representational incompatibility [Lenat75]. Inconsistent viewpoints are found, for example, in the plan conflicts studied by Georgeff and other investigators [Georgeff83; Konolige80]. Inconsistencies in viewpoints in the Rand ATC [Steeb81] work were not explored—agents could have different and incompatible assumptions about one another's plans. Several researchers (e.g., [Gerson86; Hewitt85; Hewitt86; Lenat87]), have proposed that *all* large-scale description systems have inherent inconsistencies, and distributed systems must be made to reason with *local consistency* only.

Any disparity can lead to interagent goal conflict. An example of a goal conflict can be given for the Rand ATC system. The central (controlling or leader) airplane may have an incomplete world view in having positions and routes for all airplanes except one. It may then generate a route plan for itself, based on this world view. Another airplane, unknown to the central airplane, may have a disparate world view, possibly consisting of positions of other airplanes, but no knowledge of any route plans except its own. This may lead it to generate subgoals incompatible with those of other airplanes, because its resulting route plan may be in conflict with that of the central airplane. The Contract Net work on distributed sensing gives another clear illustration of disparity in goals and priorities, in this case for manager and worker nodes. A manager is interested in placing contracts with workers distributed in space over the monitoring region, to cover all subregions. A worker, on the other hand, is interested in bidding for contracts with managers whose communication distance is small, to preserve response time. This disparity can lead to global incoherence without effective policies for mediating the disparity.

Not all disparities must cause conflict. Indeed, there must be something different in agents' knowledge or structure to avoid duplication of work. If nodes have identical (i.e., overlapping or redundant) data, they must know which data are relevant to them, and which to another node, so as to avoid duplication [Lesser83]. In essence, the problem is to keep the boundaries straight, and to allow and manage *appropriate differences* among agents.

A situation in which many agents pursue duplicate, variant, different, and even conflicting activities can be healthy. The disparities can serve much like variety in a gene pool. Several authors have remarked on the potential benefits of alternative solution approaches. The use of alternative solution approaches has been a theme in literature on the fault tolerance of software in general. In the Rand ATC [Steeb81] plan-centered organization, alternative solution plans submitted by every airplane are merged (resolving their disparities by unspecified methods) to create the best overall plan. Similar merging occurs among partial global plans in the DVMT [Durfee87a; Durfee87d; Durfee87e]. Gasser [Gasser86] and Bond and Gasser [Bond88a] have argued for multiple perspectives in organizational description, and for elucidating organizational problems from an examination of disparities among different perspectives. In research on scientific problem solving, it has been argued—for example by Karl Popper [Popper59]—that it is essential for scientific progress that scientists hold conflicting explanations of phenomena. A set of conflicting explanations promotes a natural-selection mechanism for theories. Kornfeld and Hewitt suggest that the scientific community is a useful metaphor for organizing multiagent problem solvers [Kornfeld81b]. From their perspective, scientific research has three basic types of agent: (1) *proposers* that put new theories, goals and techniques forward for critical assessment, and which also adjust theories to deal with anomalies pointed out by skeptics; (2) *proponents* that try to substantiate new proposals; and (3) *skeptics* that test proposals and attempt to establish inconsistency, anomalies, falsehood, and so on. These agents exchange two types of messages: (1) conjectures that account for observations, and (2) refutations that undermine conjectures. New proposals are often based on commonsense knowledge, and sometimes on metaphor. Kornfeld and Hewitt's view is based on Popper's [Popper59] notion of *falsificationism*: No theory can be confirmed, but agents may believe a theory and rely on it because many agents have worked on it and none have overturned it (or at least overturning arguments have been successfully combatted or discredited). Adjustment of theories is an effort to protect a core of fundamental concepts that motivate work (Kuhn's "paradigm" [Kuhn70]).

1.6.1 Representing and Recognizing Disparities

Agents can recognize disparities through processes of objectifying beliefs (fixing them by representing them), and then comparing the representations. A prerequisite for reasoning about belief disparities among agents, then, is the ability to represent other agents' beliefs. A similar prerequisite for reasoning about disparities in an agent's model of the world is the ability to create alternative models of the world — namely those produced, for example, by some sensing or execution monitoring component. Recognizing disparities requires representational compatibility. Two beliefs (or states) that are representationally indistinguishable are not disparate [Rosenschein87a].

Bruce and Newman [Bruce78] developed a *mutual belief space* mechanism for reasoning about disparate beliefs among agents. Each actor has a *belief space*, which includes (possibly nested) propositional beliefs of the forms: (bel P (bel Q R)) (meaning P believes that Q believes R). Nested beliefs may lead to arbitrary recursive levels, and so Bruce and Newman suggest dividing beliefs into two classes: those that are held commonly, and those that are disparate or incomplete. The mutual belief space is convenient, to avoid explicit representation of infinitely nested beliefs. The mutual belief space is used to represent the beliefs active in a cooperative interactive episode, i.e., social episode.

More recently, a number of researchers have used the paradigm of "reasoning about knowledge" to address problems of synchronization and control among concurrent processes, and specifically the notion of "common knowledge," which describes propositions that each agent knows, and that each agent knows every other agent knows (hence common knowledge is a closed-world notion, since it requires complete knowledge of the agent population). Halpern and Moses have shown the impossibility of achieving common knowledge unless communication is guaranteed and communication delay is finite [Halpern84]. Their framework presumes common interpretive bases for representational structures, i.e., that a proposition refers to the same thing no matter which agent holds it.

Additional representational research on the multiple belief spaces and the problems of common knowledge can be found in [Ballim86a; Ballim86b; Halpern84; Halpern86b; Konolige82; Konolige86; Wilks83; Wilks87]

1.6.2 Reconciling Disparities

To resolve disparities, agents must have some basis on which they agree. Therefore, in open systems, not all disparities can be resolved. One way of establishing a basis is to use a central or global controller that has decision making authority. In the Rand ATC work, conflict resolution was assumed to be so difficult that negotiating a solution would be insurmountable in real time. This led Steeb et al. to use cooperation regimes relying on centralized authority [Steeb81].

Given that some workable interactional bases exist (which, in multiagent systems, may have to be settled over long ranges of time, with negotiations at multiple levels of knowledge), useful conflict resolution methods include those based on power, where one agent can influence or dominate another, and those based on agreed conflict-resolution strategies, such as priorities set by convention, or mediation procedures. Potential methods for conflict resolution include the following:

Abstraction of common frameworks: Any object or entity can be described to arbitrary levels of detail. Adding detail by *elaboration* or removing it by *abstraction and generalization* are two ways of realigning the representations of objects to make them compatible. Generalization is commonly used in machine learning systems for just this purpose. Finally, *translating* disparate representations into a common and comparable representation provides a basis for recognizing and removing conflicts. Approaches to natural language understanding, generation, and translation have relied on internal representations, so that several disparate output sentences could be generated from the same internal representation, and so that several input sentences could be represented using the same framework. In DAI, for example, common internode languages and interaction protocols such as the Contract Net Protocol [Smith80] or partial global plans [Durfee87a; Durfee87c] are common frameworks that have been abstracted by designers, into which possibly disparate views of situations, skills, goals, or plans can be fit for reconciliation.

Achievement of common knowledge: For disparities that result from incomplete knowledge, the problem becomes one of identifying and communicating the appropriate knowledge to resolve the incompleteness. This may require reasoning about the knowledge state of separate agents; discussion of techniques and problems can be found in [Halpern84; Halpern86a; Halpern86b]. Achieving common knowledge among agents can be impossible in the face of communiction unreliability, as Halpern and Moses have illustrated [Halpern84].

Assumption surfacing: Agents can sometimes reconcile inconsistent propositions by backtracking through the assumptions on which the propositions rest to discover whether the roots of disparity lie in the assumptions. Disparities can be resolved at any point along this chain of support. This approach, of course, requires that an agent has (or can construct) knowledge of the supporting assumptions and their relationships. This capability is easiest to ensure in a system where shared and comparable knowledge representations are assumed, which is normally the case in DAI research. This assumption of sharing, however, has been challenged as impossible and unrealistic (see e.g., [Gerson86; Hewitt86; Suchman87; Winograd86]). Assumption surfacing is an underlying technique found in many forms of argumentation and negotiation [Sycara85a; Sycara85b] and has been suggested as an organizational conflict resolution scheme by Mason and Mitroff [Mason69; Mason81]. It is the basis for the truth maintenance systems of Doyle and DeKleer [Doyle79; deKleer86], and it is sometimes use as a basis of belief revision. Distributed belief revision has been studied by Pearl [Pearl87]. Temporal- and recency-based approaches to resolving assumption conflicts are discussed in [Borchardt87].

Authority and knowledgeable mediation: Authority, possibly coupled with higher-level knowledge, can be used to to resolve conflicts. This approach was used in HEARSAY-II [Erman80], where two KSs might set conflicting goals to solve the same problem. This conflict is then resolved by heuristic knowledge in the blackboard scheduler. Higher-level knowledge can be centralized, as in HEARSAY-II, or distributed, as in the Rand ATC case. In the latter, all airplanes could simultaneously and independently compute ratings of which goal to solve, using conventionalized priorities. Similar shared conventions were used by airplanes in electing a new central planner. We view both centralized and decentralized conflict-resolution strategies of this sort as mediation by higher authority, because decision making rules are unchangeable by the agents whose conflicts are being resolved. It is important to note that, in general, rules and conventions are notoriously subject to local reinterpretation [Manning77]; in closed DAI systems this may not be the case, because reinterpretive capacity has been limited by design.

Constraint resolution: Agents can resolve conflicts and disparities that arise because of conflicting constraints by relaxing those constraints, or by reformulating a problem to eliminate them. Constraint relaxation requires prioritization of constraints. This process was elucidated by Goldstein in a scheduling system that made use of preferences [Goldstein75]; weaker preferences were relaxed first. More recently, Fox and other researchers have studied constraints in scheduling for manufacturing [Fox84; Sathi86].

Evidential reasoning and argumentation: It may be possible to formulate arguments in support of a particular perspective, by sharing evidence. Evidence, methods, and so on may have to be justified recursively. Hewitt and Kornfeld discuss argumentation as a basic method for organizing problem solving in [Kornfeld81a]. Modes of argumentation are discussed in [Alvarado86; Carbonell81; Gerson86; Hewitt86; Sycara85a; Sycara85b; Willer81]. Evidential reasoning is quite familiar in AI, particularly in the contexts of justifying conclusions made by knowldge-based systems to human users. Lesser and Corkill's *functionally accurate, cooperative* (FA/C) processing [Lesser81], applied in the DVMT, supports convergence despite conflicting hypotheses by building evidence to strengthen the most favorable hypotheses. Related work on distributed evidential reasoning can be found in [Geffner87; Pearl82].

Goal priority conventions: Setting priorities on goals provides a way to reason about the effects of particular disparities, and to make choices about which disparities are important enough to resolve. For example, conventions set by experiment designers are used in the DVMT to deal with the disparity between the world views of two agents. A node distinguishes between internally and externally directed processes, and there is a (manually set) table of priorities for goals from different sources. Thus, an agent has preset priorities on all goals and can resolve conflicts. Similar mechanisms are incorporated in blackboard systems of many kinds through the use of scheduling metarules and scheduling knowledge sources. These mechanisms encode knowledge about settling conflicts over which knowledge source should be activated [Hayes-Roth85; Erman80; Nii86b; Nii86a] at a given time. Such mechanisms are typically called "conflict resolution mechanisms" for rule based systems.

Integration without conflict: For resolving conflicts of incompleteness, a simple approach is to integrate new knowledge by simple incorporation. This approach presumes common, compatible representations and mechanisms for adding

new knowledge, and may require consistency-checking. Many DAI information exchange schemes use this method, including most of those discussed in work on common knowledge [Halpern86b].

Negotiation: Negotiation often is proposed in DAI research as a conflict-resolution and information-exchange scheme. Many negotiation models fall short of providing detailed descriptions of the boundaries and assumptions of the processes of negotiations, and most make simple and computationally useful assumptions of negotiation procedures (e.g., what the bases—such as protocol or language—are). Discussions of varieties and models of negotiations can be found in [Strauss78; Pruitt81; Willer81]. Typically, negotiation involves some *context*, some (disparate) sets of *goals*, some (disparate) *information or knowledge*, and some *procedure or protocol*. Negotiations depend on bases, and in general may shift to multiple levels of meta-negotiations, and to negotiating over assumptions. Little DAI research has investigated the variety of negotiations. Several researchers have pointed out the need for negotiated approaches to accomplish flexible coordination [Davis83; Durfee87a; Durfee87c; Gasser86; Gasser88a; Hewitt85; Hewitt86; Sycara87]. Recently, there has been a resurgence of interest in topics in negotiation, including [Durfee87a; Durfee87c; Conry86]. Foundations for conflict resolution at various levels in negotiations may include all of the mechanisms discussed here. In addition, much more work needs to be done on control structures and flexible protocols for negotiation, especially those that treat negotiation as another type of goal-directed activity.

Levin and Moore's work on information-seeking, information-probing, instructing and griping "dialogue games" [Levin77] explicitly considers the context of negotiations. Dialogue games can represent negotiation over determining whether interaction should occur and and can treat negotiations over the roles of the dialogue participants as a stage of the interaction.

Davis and Smith [Davis83] viewed task distribution as an interactive process, treating it as a form of contract negotiation. In the Contract Net, "negotiation" referred to the two way transfer of information, after which each party evaluated the information from its own perspective, Final agreement was achieved by mutual selection of a result (an allocation). As a basic framework for negotiation, the contract net was weak, as it incorporated no developed discussion of the nature of negotiation, such as finding original common basis for interaction, judging credibilities, weighing of priorities, or compromising. This negotiation framework has been extended in new domains by Parunak and Ramamritham et al. [Parunak87; Ramamritham85].

Development of alternative representations: Seeing the problem in a new way, by adding previously unknown knowledge, or by changing the representational schema, may reconcile disparities. Also, exploring another (OR) branch of a goal graph may provide an alternative subproblem or operator description.

Standardization: The repeated renegotiation of similar alternatives over time, and the recognition of common requirements and routine behaviors, can lead to *standardization* as a basic mechanism for conflict avoidance. Over time, conflicts are resolved by common mechanisms which are incorporated into standards and are disseminated among agents (or designed into systems). Agents can avoid some conflicts by adhering to standards, but standards may impede adaptation [Durfee87d; Durfee87e; Lesser83], and they may be subject to local interpretation (cf. [Manning77]).

1.7 Tools for Distributed Artificial Intelligence

DAI researchers have built a variety of software tools that enable them to express solutions to the basic questions of DAI and to experiment with different approaches in different domains. There are several reasons why we are concerned with the particular tools currently being used. First, research tools help to verify theoretical insights through hard, real-world experimentation. Experimental studies have proven useful in some cases because of the difficulty of constructing complete theoretical analyses, and because some research issues (e.g., performance of problem-specific architectures) cannot practically be theoretically modeled due to their complexity. But in a more positive sense, experimentation is a useful way of generating new ideas and sometimes surprising results.

Some tools are designed to express ideas important to the domain. The actor languages of Hewitt, Agha, and others (e.g., [Agha85; Kornfeld79; Kornfeld81b; Theriault83]) are in part designed to capture the requirements of *open systems*. The MACE language includes explicit constructs for representing one agent's knowledge of the skills, roles, plans, and so on of other agents, to allow for reasoning about interaction. The blackboard system shells GBB and BB1 support the requirements of opportunistic problem solving and integrated control knowledge [Corkill86; Hayes-Roth85]

The tools we survey here have each been driven by several of the following goals:

> To design and implement distributed object-oriented languages
>
> To provide high-level environments for experimentation and simulation
>
> To provide high-level knowledge representation scheme for representing world models, knowledge of other agents, control knowledge, etc.
>
> To provide a reusable shell for a particular problem-solving architecture
>
> To provide a framework for integrating heterogeneous subsystems or different problem-solving architectures

> To provide development tools for constructing large-scale DAI systems, for experimentation or for applications

Many of the DAI tools described in this section are implemented on serial machines. Often, tools designed for research experimentation simulate the concurrent communications and processing of a distributed system. Several of the tools are actually implemented on parallel architectures. Actor implementations exist for a network of LISP machines, and the highly concurrent Jellybean machine is now under development at Massachusetts Institute of Technology. In the DVMT, a simulator written in LISP simulates the concurrent execution of several DVMT nodes. The simulator itself is then distributed among a network of computers, providing a *distributed simulation of a distributed problem-solving system* [Durfee84a]. The University of Southern California MACE system is implemented on a heterogeneous network of parallel and sequential machines, including LISP machines and a 16-processor Intel Hypercube.

There are basically four kinds of tools for DAI experimentation and development: integrative systems; experimental testbeds; distributed, object-oriented languages; and paradigm-specific shells.

1.7.1 Integrative Systems

Integrative systems provide the framework to combine a variety of paradigm-specific tools and methods into a useful whole. ABE [Hayes-Roth88] is designed to be a framework for integrating a number of heterogeneous, independently developed problem-solving paradigms and software tools. It provides for several different subsystems, each possibly using a different method, to constitute a DAI system and to communicate. ABE is the glue that holds other systems together. It provides a window-based and menu based front-end, and interfacing software.

AGORA [Bisiani87] is designed to be an opaque, high-level operating system. Constructed for projects in speech understanding, it has been designed so that heterogeneous hardware systems could be integrated under a common operating system. In AGORA, the user-software layer describes data structures and processes, and the operating system distributes these onto the appropriate portions of the distributed hardware.

MACE [Gasser87d; Gasser87c] is a generic testbed for building DAI systems of varying levels of granularity. MACE allows integration of different problem-solving and communication structures by supplying programmers with a collection of facilities (e.g., pattern matchers, remote demons) and system agents (e.g., allocators, user interfaces, command interpreters, dictionaries) and allowing arbitrary message formats and interpretations, using a user-supplied "engine" for each agent.

1.7.2 Experimental Testbeds

Several systems have been tailored for controlled experiments, requiring them to support both *measurement* and *monitoring*. They may also need to support *simulation*, if experiments must be exactly repeatable. Experimental testbeds for DAI research provide parameterization of control variables and experimental conditions. The DVMT and MACE systems are explicitly tailored for controlled, parameterized experimentation using simulation and instrumentation.

1.7.3 Distributed, Object-Oriented Languages

The family of languages that is becoming known as *distributed, object-oriented languages* (DOO languages) is a natural framework for implementing truly concurrent DAI systems. These languages typically describe data and procedural abstractions in objects, and allow for interobject interaction using message communication. Language processors and underlying kernels implement allocation, load-balancing, addressing and message-routing schemes invisible to programmers. Synchronization primitives may be included as language constructs, or may be left for the programmer to implement using messages.

A family of actor languages [Agha85] has been designed at Massachusetts Institute of Technology. The actor languages ETHER, PLASMA, ACT, ACT1, and ACT3 have been research attempts to implement systems for experimental programming using actors, and to our knowledge have not been applied to serious application developments. ABCL/1 [Yonezawa86] is in part an attempt to make actorlike languages more computationally practical, given current technology. As a consequence, not all activity is concurrent in ABCL/1. The basic objects are serial at some medium grain of system granularity.

Although ACTORS provide an elegant computational model, actor-based systems appear to have some important practical limitations under current technology. In any actor system, many messages are sent, and many new actors are spawned, necessitating large and dynamic routing tables and large amounts of overhead. Dynamic load balancing involves moving actors and forwarding messages, adding more overhead. These problems force the question of whether the level of concurrency (virtually *total* in pure actor systems) is appropriate for current hardware technology. The answer of ABCL/1, MACE, and ORIENT84/K seems to be that we probably need to introduce larger granularity to build large-grain DAI systems with practical performance.

Of the other DOO languages, both OIL [Cohen85] and ORIENT84 [Tokoro84] are attempts to integrate logic programming and object-oriented programming in languages for message-passing distributed systems. VULCAN employs "logical concurrent objects" [Huberman88b]. MACE is most similar to ABCL/1, with the added capability that programmers

can describe message formats and interpretations (i.e., messages need not be patterns). ABCL/1 provides synchronization, while MACE relies on program-level synchronization using messages.

1.7.4 Blackboard Systems

Blackboard systems provide a central data structure called a *blackboard*, which is often divided into regions or *levels*. A collection of independent processes called *knowledge sources* may read and write one or more levels, under the supervision of a *control system*, which may be a synchronous global scheduler, a system of concurrency locks, or a collection of integrated control-knowledge sources [Hayes-Roth85; Fennell77]. In the latter case, the blackboard is used for both problem solving and control. Several DAI systems surveyed in this book have incorporated blackboard architectures (e.g., [Hayes-Roth85; Corkill86; Hayes-Roth79a; Lesser83; Yang85]). Numerous specialized blackboard systems have been built, and the BB1 [Hayes-Roth85] and GBB [Corkill86] systems are high-level domain-independent blackboard shells.

Some of the key issues that blackboard-based systems must address include indexing schemes for retrieving knowledge from levels, granularity of representations, synchronization and conflict resolution among knowledge sources, and granularity of actions of the knowledge sources.

1.7.5 Remaining Problems

Several problems remain for the next generation of tools, languages and systems for DAI:

> *Facilities to represent knowledge of other agents and of the world of the agent:* Currently two languages have simple mechanisms to this—the actor languages and MACE. Actor languages have rather simple models of other agents: references to an actors *acquaintances*. MACE provides for more complex models that can include representations of the beliefs, plans, goals, locations, and organizational roles of agents. The DVMT incorporates models of other agents—the plans and activities of other nodes. However, in the DVMT there are no explicit language constructs for building this knowledge of other agents; it is simply programmed in.
>
> *Support for multigrain problem solving:* How to decide about *granularity* of agents in a DAI system is an important issue related to the basic problems of task decomposition and task allocation. Languages and testbeds ought to accommodate agents of varying granularity for experimental purposes.
>
> *Integration of knowledge-base access with DAI:* The blackboard shells GBB and BB1 incorporate high-level

knowledge-structuring and knowledge-access mechanisms, and pattern-directed retrieval of data. MACE provides associative databases within agents. In general, however, the problem of giving agents access to large and possibly shared knowledge bases is difficult.

- *Better development environments:* Understanding the operation of a concurrent system is extremely difficult; for large-scale experimental DAI systems with changing requirements and architectures, the problems of debugging, development, and evaluation are complex. We need more automated (and knowledge-based) support for modeling, analyzing, and controlling the execution of concurrent DAI systems, including tools and support for profiling, tracing, and debugging systems of agents with conflicting behaviors and disparate world views.

1.8 Open Problems

In this survey, we have outlined a number of considerations in current DAI systems and research. We believe that some of the more interesing open problems and avenues for research in DAI include the following:

- More research needs to be done on linking theoretical results in distributed computing systems to DAI problems and approaches (e.g., fairness and starvation in market-based system organizations).
- We need more study of how to generalize and extend existing problem solvers and approaches to new domains — this study is just beginning (cf. Parunak's and Ramamrithm et al.'s extensions of the Contract Net framework [Parunak87; Ramamritham85]).
- There has been very little research into the knowledge and structures required for automated task or problem description and decomposition. These will be necessary if agents in DAI systems are to begin jointly to construct and recognize their own problems. This knowledge would be useful, for example, for self-diagnosis, organizational self-design, adaptive control, and automated learning and discovery.

- There are interesting possibilities for research in collaborative and pluralistic learning among collections of agents, including the use of multiple perspectives to refine concepts, refinement of the organizational knowledge and behavior of agents, and so on.
- We can envision greater connection with economic approaches to coherent behavior, resource allocation, and task distribution than has been exploited in contemporary DAI research.
- Large collections of intelligent agents, person-machine collaborative systems, or any group of agents without global perspectives in design or knowledge, will be subject to the problems of *open systems*. Generating new knowledge and solving problems using varieties of disparity resolution approaches, such as *due process*, deserve greater attention.
- The problems of building and diagnosing the behavior of collections of automated intelligent agents need greater attention. Most researchers with experience in experimental DAI projects, and especially with those that involve actual concurrency (versus simulation) can attest to the great difficulty of understanding and modeling the actual behavior of such systems. We need better models, abstraction mechanisms, and representations for concurrent activity.
- Much greater attention should be focused on the problems of method in DAI. The usefulness of metaphors, methods, and models from other fields, such as sociology or economics, needs to be examined carefully. The assumptions underlying the perspectives and methods we use and those we import need careful articulation and criticism. The research we do needs to include clear and carefully used criteria for evaluation, and tests that employ them.

Research on many of these open problems will interlock, and progress on one will often aid progress on the others. Research progress will be inherently dependent on integrating multiple perspectives and new ideas from other disciplines as "close" as distributed computing and possibly as "distant" as history. We echo the voices of a number of our colleagues when we express the exciting potential for interaction between researchers and research results in DAI and in cognate fields.

Chapter 2

A Subject-Indexed Bibliography
of
Distributed Artificial Intelligence

It is impossible to draw clear boundaries on the literature of a field, especially one as broad and interdisciplinary as Distributed AI. The total published literature in DAI now exceeds 500 papers, of which only 40 or so key papers could be included in this book. This bibliography has been designed to support the reader in pursuing his or her interest in DAI by reading further papers.

Due to limitations of space, we selected for this bibliography about 300 papers which were relatively recent and relatively accessible. We left out some older papers which for the most part have been superseded. We also excluded extremely recent papers on new ideas that have not yet been adequately explored or evaluated. We have to overlook numerous papers on the fringes of DAI, and papers in other related areas that, even though important, only contribute indirectly to DAI. We have included a limited selection of works from related disciplines, but unfortunately we could not reference many sources in subject areas such as small-group theory, organization theory, economics, and game theory, that would provide important new possibilities. We urge the reader to seek these references by studying the bibliographies of papers included in the book.

We limited our selection to papers published in journals and conferences, or at least in established report series from major universities. We also have tried to maintain an international balance by mentioning papers from other countries that might be less accessible from the United States. Unfortunately, several important entries in the DAI canon are virtually or completely inaccessible; we included some of these for historical accuracy and information. Perhaps the most notable is the often cited *Proceedings of the 1985 Workshop on Distributed Artificial Intelligence*, held at Sea Ranch, CA, which has not been available (although many papers from this workshop have been published elsewhere subsequently; e.g., see [Huhns87a]).

The subject index is intended to guide the reader in navigating the broad ocean of DAI. We have adopted a medium-grained subject-description index with about 50 categories. Finer distinctions are made in our survey and the reader can be guided by them in making his or her own further distinctions. Each index category lists five to twenty papers to consult. The set of papers in each category covers most of the currently available research on relevant, concepts, mechanisms and systems. Papers in particular application domains have been grouped under the index categories *air traffic control domains*, *design domains*, *distributed sensing and interpretation domains*, *manufacturing domains*, *office information systems*, *robot domains*, and *miscellaneous domains*.

Actors

[Agha85] [Agha86a] [Agha86b] [Clinger81] [de Jong88] [Garner87] [Hewitt77a] [Hewitt77b] [Hewitt80] [Hewitt84a] [Hewitt85] [Hewitt86] [Kornfeld81b] [Lieberman83] [Theriault83] [Yonezawa86]

Air-traffic control (ATC) domains

[Cammarata83] [Findler86] [McArthur82b] [Steeb81] [Steeb84] [Steeb86] [Thorndyke81]

Articulation work

[Bendif87] [Gasser84] [Gasser86] [Gerson86] [Hewitt86] [Strauss85]

Belief modeling

[Ballim86a] [Ballim86b] [Bruce78] [Carbonell81] [Cohen79] [Cohen87a] [Cohen87b] [Cohen87a] [deKleer86] [Konolige82] [Konolige86] [Pearl87] [Pollack87] [Sproull81] [Sycara85a] [Sycara85b] [Vilain88] [Wilks87]

Blackboard systems

[Corkill86] [Corkill87] [Cullingford81] [Ensor85] [Ensor86] [Elfes86] [Erman75] [Erman80] [Fennell77] [Fox81] [Gomez81] [Hayes-Roth79a] [Hayes-Roth79b] [Hayes-Roth85] [Hayes-Roth86] [Jagannathan87a] [Jones86] [Leao86] [Lesser80a] [Lesser82] [Lesser83] [Nii86b] [Nii86a] [Yang85]

Centralized control

[Ackland85] [Cammarata83] [Cullingford81] [Georgeff83] [Georgeff84] [Georgeff87d] [Hayes-Roth79a] [Hayes-Roth79b] [Konolige80] [Konolige82] [Lansky85] [Lenat75] [Pednault87] [Steeb81] [Steeb84] [Steeb86] [Stuart85] [Wood83]

Coherence

[Corkill83] [Davis83] [Durfee85] [Durfee87d] [Durfee87e] [Gasser87d] [Genesereth84] [Lesser83] [Rosenschein85b] [Rosenschein87b] [Sacks74]

Contract net

[Davis83] [Parunak87] [Ramamritham85] [Smith79] [Smith80] [Smith81a] [Smith81b] [Stankovic85]

Cooperation

[Axelrod84] [Axelrod86] [Backstrom88a] [Benda85] [Cammarata83] [Davis81] [Durfee85] [Durfee87a] [Durfee87b] [Durfee87c] [Durfee87d] [Durfee87e] [Erman75] [Erman80] [Fikes82] [Genesereth84] [Harmon84] [Rosenschein86] [Smith81b] [Steeb81] [Steeb86] [Steels79] [Werner87] [Zachary88]

Coordination

[Abraham82] [Axelrod84] [Axelrod86] [Becker86] [Backstrom88b] [Corkill83] [Davis81] [Durfee87a] [Durfee87b] [Durfee87c] [Gasser86] [Gasser88b] [Gasser88a] [Harmon84] [Harmon86] [Hewitt77b] [Hewitt83] [Lansky87b] [Malone87a] [Malone88a] [Mead34] [Moses86] [Rosenschein82] [Rosenschein86] [Schank77] [Strauss78] [Strauss85] [Stuart85] [Tenney79] [Tenney81a] [Tenney81b] [Winograd86]

Design domains

[Ackland85] [Ensor85] [Ensor86] [Lenat75] [Verrilli87] [Yang85]

Distributed control

[Brooks82] [Cammarata83] [Corkill79] [Cromarty86] [Davis83] [Elfes86] [Ferber88a] [Findler87] [Huhns83] [Lesser80a] [Lesser81] [Lesser87] [Minsky86] [Steeb81] [Steeb86] [Tenney79] [Tenney81a] [Tenney81b] [Yang85]

Distributed expert systems

[Ackland85] [Blelloch86] [Cromarty86] [Huhns83] [Leao86] [MacIntosh87a] [MacIntosh87b] [Mukhopadhyay86] [Silverman86] [Sowizral84] [Thorndyke81]

Distributed knowledge and knowledge representation

[Appelt80] [Axelrod86] [Blelloch86] [Borchardt87] [Brooks82] [Cammarata83] [Carley86] [Corkill79] [Cullingford81] [de Jong88] [Doyle79] [Fahlman83] [Genesereth84] [Georgeff83] [Georgeff84] [Gomez81] [Green87] [Halpern86b] [Halpern86a] [Halpern84] [Hayes-Roth79a] [Hewitt77a] [Hewitt84a] [Hewitt85] [Konolige80] [Kornfeld81b] [Konolige82] [Lenat75] [Lesser80a] [Lesser81] [Lesser83] [Lieberman86] [Mason88] [Minsky80] [Pearl87] [Rieger81] [Smith79] [Steeb81] [Steeb84] [Steeb86] [Steels79] [Vilain88] [Wesson81]

Distributed planning

[Backstrom88b] [Backstrom88c] [Backstrom88a] [Conry86] [Corkill79] [Dean87] [Durfee86] [Durfee87a] [Durfee87b] [Durfee87c] [Findler86] [Georgeff87c] [Hayes-Roth79a] [Hayes-Roth79b] [Koo87] [Lansky87b] [Lesser81] [Morgenstern87] [Rosenschein82] [Shaw85] [Shaw87]

[Steeb81] [Steeb84] [Steeb86] [Stuart85] [Thorndyke81] [Yang85]

Distributed problem solving

[Cammarata83] [Corkill82] [Corkill83] [Davis83] [Decker87b] [Dietrich86a] [Durfee85] [Durfee86] [Durfee87a] [Durfee87b] [Durfee87c] [Durfee87d] [Durfee87e] [Erman75] [Erman80] [Fennell77] [Filman84] [Green87] [Haase86] [Hsu87] [Kornfeld81a] [Kornfeld81b] [Leao86] [Lenat75] [Lesser81] [Lesser83] [Lesser87] [Mazer86] [Mazer87a] [McArthur82b] [Nii86c] [Smith81a] [Smith81b] [Steeb81] [Steeb84] [Steeb86] [Verrilli87] [Wilensky84] [Zachary88]

Distributed sensing and interpretation domains

[Brown86] [Corkill82] [Corkill83] [Davis83] [Durfee85] [Durfee86] [Durfee87a] [Durfee87b] [Durfee87c] [Durfee87d] [Durfee87e] [Erman75] [Erman80] [Hudlicka84] [Hudlicka86a] [Lesser83] [Lesser88] [Schoen86] [Smith80] [Smith81a] [Wesson81]

Distributed vehicle monitoring testbed

[Corkill82] [Corkill83] [Durfee85] [Durfee86] [Durfee87a] [Durfee87b] [Durfee87c] [Durfee87d] [Durfee87e] [Hudlicka84] [Hudlicka86a] [Hudlicka86b] [Hudlicka87] [Lesser83] [Lesser88]

Experimental research

[Brooks82] [Brown86] [Cammarata83] [Corkill83] [Durfee84a] [Durfee84b] [Durfee85] [Durfee87d] [Gasser87d] [Gasser87c] [Hayes-Roth79a] [Hayes-Roth79b] [Lenat75] [Lesser80a] [Lesser83] [Pavlin83] [Steeb81] [Steeb84] [Steeb86] [Wesson81] [Yang85]

Formal approaches, theories, and methods

[Agha86a] [Appelt80] [Backstrom88c] [Clinger81] [Cohen79] [Cohen87b] [Cohen87a] [Genesereth84] [Georgeff83] [Georgeff84] [Georgeff86a] [Georgeff86b] [Georgeff87c] [Georgeff87b] [Georgeff87a] [Ginsberg87] [Hewitt77a] [Hewitt77b] [Hewitt84a] [Huberman88a] [Konolige80] [Konolige82] [Lansky85] [Lansky87a] [Lansky87b] [Rosenschein85a] [Rosenschein87a] [Shaw87] [Stuart85] [Stuart87] [Tenney79] [Tenney81a] [Tenney81b] [Waldinger77] [Werner87]

Functionally accurate, cooperative systems

[Conry86] [Decker87b] [Lesser81] [Lesser83] [Lesser87] [Lesser88]

Hardware architectures

[Billstrom87] [Bisiani86] [Bisiani87] [Casais88] [Durfee84a] [Durfee84b] [Hayes-Roth88] [Fennell77] [Hewitt80] [Hewitt84b] [Hewitt84a] [Kornfeld81b] [Lesser83] [Lieberman86] [McArthur82b]

Hierarchical control

[Cammarata83] [Chandrasekn81] [Davis81] [Findler87] [Fox79] [Fox81] [Malone87a] [Malone88a] [Steeb81] [Steeb84] [Steeb86]

Manufacturing domains

[Findler87] [Fox84] [Gasser87a] [Maimon85] [Parunak87] [Sathi85] [Sathi86] [Shaw85] [Shaw87]

Markets

[Davis83] [Drexler88] [Kurose85] [Malone83] [Malone87a] [Malone87b] [Miller88a] [Miller88b] [Parunak87] [Ramamritham85] [Smith79] [Smith80] [Smith81a] [Smith81b] [Stankovic85]

Metalevel knowledge and control

[Corkill82] [Corkill83] [Durfee85] [Durfee86] [Durfee87d] [Durfee87e] [Hayes-Roth85] [Hudlicka84] [Lesser83] [Rosenschein83] [Yang85]

Miscellaneous domains

[Borchardt87] [Brooks82] [Bruce78] [Conry86] [Doran87] [Fox79] [Gomez81] [Hayes-Roth79a] [Hayes-Roth79b] [Johnson86] [Minsky79] [Minsky80] [Sycara85a] [Sycara85b]

Modeling other agents

[Bruce78] [Cohen79] [Cohen87a] [Cohen87b] [Cohen87a] [Corkill79] [Davis81] [deKleer86] [Doyle79] [Durfee87a] [Gasser87d] [Gasser87c] [Gasser88a] [Ginsberg87]

[Konolige82] [Konolige86] [Lenat75] [Mead34] [Pollack87] [Rosenschein82] [Rosenschein83] [Rosenschein85a] [Rosenschein85b] [Rosenschein87b] [Rosenschein86] [Schank77] [Steeb81] [Steeb84] [Steeb86] [Sycara85a] [Sycara85b] [Thorndyke81] [Wilensky84] [Wilks83] [Wilks87] [Winograd86] [Wood83]

Multiagent planning

[Appelt80] [Backstrom88c] [Backstrom88a] [Bruce78] [Croft87] [Davis81] [Durfee86] [Durfee87a] [Durfee87b] [Durfee87c] [Georgeff83] [Georgeff84] [Hayes-Roth79a] [Hayes-Roth79b] [Konolige80] [Konolige82] [Koo87] [Lansky85] [Morgenstern86] [Morgenstern87] [Pednault87] [Steeb81] [Steeb84] [Steeb86] [Stuart85] [Werner87] [Wood83]

Multiple–perspective reasoning

[Bond88a] [Cammarata83] [Carbonell81] [deKleer86] [Dietrich86b] [Durfee87a] [Durfee87c] [Gerson86] [Hewitt83] [Hewitt84a] [Hewitt84a] [Hewitt85] [Hewitt86] [Johnson86] [Kornfeld79] [Kornfeld81a] [Kornfeld81b] [Kornfeld82] [Nirenburg86] [Smith85a] [Sycara85a] [Sycara85b]

Natural language and DAI

[Appelt81] [Cohen79] [Cohen87a] [Cohen87b] [Cohen87a] [Cullingford81] [Cullingford84] [Erman75] [Erman80] [Grosz85] [Grosz86] [Grosz87] [Rieger81] [Sacerdoti78] [Sacks74] [Small82]

Negotiation

[Alvarado86] [Carbonell81] [Conry86] [Davis83] [Doyle79] [Durfee87a] [Durfee87c] [Gerson86] [Goldstein75] [Hewitt86] [Kornfeld81b] [Lee88] [Lesser83] [Levin77] [Pruitt81] [Rosenschein85b] [Rosenschein87b] [Shaw87] [Smith79] [Smith80] [Rosenschein85b] [Strauss78] [Sycara85a] [Sycara85b] [Willer81]

Observing, modeling, and describing distributed–system behavior

[Geffner87] [Huberman88b] [Hudlicka84] [Hudlicka86a] [Hudlicka86b] [Hudlicka87] [Lesser80b] [Lesser81] [Lesser83] [Miller88b] [Pattison87] [Pavlin83] [Pavlin84]

Office information systems

[Barber80] [Barber82] [Barber83] [Croft87] [de Jong88] [Fikes80] [Fikes82] [Fox84] [Gasser86] [Gerson86] [Hewitt86] [Ho86] [Huhns83] [Koo87] [Mazer86] [Mazer87a] [Mazer88] [Mukhopadhyay86] [Nirenburg86] [Sathi85] [Sathi86] [Woo86]

Open systems

[Dietrich86b] [Fikes80] [Gerson86] [Hewitt83] [Hewitt84a] [Hewitt84a] [Hewitt85] [Hewitt86] [Huberman88b] [Huberman88a] [Miller88a] [Miller88b]

Organizational structures, policies, and architectures

[Axelrod86] [Benda85] [Bond88a] [Cammarata83] [Corkill82] [Corkill83] [Davis83] [de Jong88] [Durfee87a] [Durfee87b] [Durfee87c] [Findler87] [Fox79] [Fox81] [Gasser86] [Gasser88a] [Hudlicka87] [Kornfeld81b] [Lesser80a] [Lesser83] [Malone83] [Malone84] [Malone87a] [Malone88a] [McArthur82b] [Miller88a] [Pavlin83] [Pavlin84] [Pattison87] [Reddy82] [Rosenschein82] [Sathi85] [Smith81b] [Steeb81] [Steeb84] [Steeb86] [Stuart85] [Tenney79] [Tenney81a] [Tenney81b] [Wesson81]

Person–machine cooperation

[Barber82] [Barber83] [Borchardt87] [Chang87] [Croft87] [Fikes80] [Fikes82] [Goodson83] [Hewitt86] [Mazer86] [Mazer87a] [Mazer87b] [Nirenburg86] [Oberquelle83] [Suchman87] [Woo86]

Rationality

[Cohen79] [Cohen87a] [Cohen87b] [Genesereth84] [Ginsberg87] [Rosenschein85a] [Rosenschein87b]

Real time and time dependence

[Elfes86] [Green87] [Lesser88] [Ramamritham85] [Schoen86] [Stankovic85] [Tenney79] [Tenney81a] [Tenney81b] [Wood83]

Reasoning about action

[Allen84] [Backstrom88b] [Backstrom88c] [Backstrom88a] [Barber80] [Croft87] [Dean87] [Georgeff83] [Georgeff84] [Georgeff86a] [Georgeff86b] [Georgeff87a] [Georgeff87b]

[Georgeff87c] [Hayes-Roth86] [Hewitt83] [Konolige82] [Lansky85] [Mazer88] [McDermott78] [Morgenstern86] [Morgenstern87] [Pednault87] [Sathi85] [Schank77] [Stuart85] [Stuart87]

Reasoning about communication

[Appelt81] [Cammarata83] [Cohen79] [Cohen87b] [Cohen87a] [Cromarty86] [Cohen87b] [Davis83] [Durfee87e] [Genesereth84] [Gordon71] [Grosz85] [Grosz86] [Grosz87] [Koo87] [Lesser80a] [Lesser83] [Levin77] [Rosenschein86] [Rosenschein87b] [Sacks74] [Smith80] [Smith81b]

Reasoning about knowledge

[Halpern84] [Halpern86a] [Halpern86b] [Halpern87] [Konolige86] [Rosenschein87a]

Representing action structures

[Backstrom88a] [Backstrom88b] [Backstrom88c] [Dean87] [Durfee87a] [Durfee87c] [Gasser86] [Gasser88a] [Hudlicka84] [Hudlicka86a] [Hudlicka86b] [Hudlicka87] [Pavlin83] [Pavlin84] [Sathi85] [Wesson81]

Resolving disparities

[Deen87] [deKleer86] [Doyle79] [Durfee84a] [Durfee84b] [Durfee85] [Durfee86] [Durfee87a] [Durfee87b] [Durfee87c] [Durfee87d] [Durfee87e] [Erman75] [Erman80] [Fennell77] [Genesereth84] [Halpern84] [Hayes-Roth79a] [Hewitt84a] [Hewitt85] [Holzner83] [Koo87] [Kornfeld81b] [Lenat87] [Lesser81] [Manning77] [Mason88] [Moses86] [Pearl82] [Rosenschein83] [Rosenschein85a] [Rosenschein85b] [Rosenschein86] [Steels79] [Stuart85] [Suchman87] [Tenney79] [Tenney81a] [Tenney81b] [Vilain88] [Wilensky84] [Wilks83] [Winograd86]

Resource allocation

[Barber82] [Barber83] [Davis81] [Davis83] [Hayes-Roth79a] [Hayes-Roth79b] [Kornfeld79] [Kornfeld81b] [Kornfeld82] [Lesser83] [Parunak87] [Ramamritham85] [Smith79] [Smith80] [Smith81a] [Smith81b] [Stankovic85]

Robot domains

[Elfes86] [Gasser87a] [Georgeff86b] [Harmon84] [Harmon86] [Maimon85]

Simulation

[Durfee84a] [Durfee84b] [Fennell77] [Fox84] [Hayes-Roth79a] [Lesser80b] [Lesser83] [Lieberman83] [MacIntosh87a] [MacIntosh87b] [McArthur82a] [Reddy82] [Wood83]

Social metaphors

[Carley86] [Chandrasekn81] [Chang87] [Fikes82] [Fox79] [Fox81] [Gasser86] [Hewitt77a] [Hewitt85] [Ho86] [Holzner83] [Kornfeld81b] [Latour87] [Lesser83] [Malone88a] [Minsky79] [Minsky86] [Sproull81] [Steels79] [Sycara85a] [Sycara85b] [Wesson81] [Woolgar85]

Social–science background

[Abraham82] [Becker86] [Bentley54] [Blumer69] [Cooley64] [Dewey16] [Gerson86] [Hall82] [Kurose85] [Latour87] [Lawrence69] [Manning77] [Marshak72] [Mead34] [Parsons60] [Pruitt81] [Shibutani86] [Strauss78] [Thompson67] [Willer81]

Surveys, collections and bibliographies

[Abram84] [Bond88b] [Chandrasekn81] [Davis80] [Davis82] [Decker87b] [Fehling83] [Ferber88b] [Filman84] [Gasser87b] [Gasser88b] [Gasser88d] [Gasser88c] [Georgeff87c] [Halpern86a] [Hewitt84b] [Huhns87a] [Jagannathan87b] [Lesser81] [Lesser87] [Nii86b] [Nii86a] [Rosenschein85a] [Smith85b] [Sridharan87] [Veach86] [Zachary88]

Systems (by name)

AF [Green87],
APIARY [Lieberman83] [Hewitt80],
CADRE [Ackland85] [Ensor85] [Ensor86],
CALLISTO [Sathi85] [Sathi86],
CAOS [Brown86] [Schoen86],
CIS [Blelloch86],
CONTRACT NET [Davis83] [Smith81a] and see CNET section,
DESCANT [Decker87a],
DVMT [Lesser83] and see DVMT section,
FACILITY ADVISOR [Silverman86],
HEARSAY-II [Erman75] [Erman80] [Fennell77] [Lesser80a] [Fox81],
ISIS [Fox84],
MINDS system [Mukhopadhyay86] [Huhns83],
OPM [Hayes-Roth79a] [Hayes-Roth79b] [Hayes-Roth85],

PERSUADER [Sycara85a] [Sycara85b],
POLIGON [Rice86],
POLYMER [Croft87],
PRESSURE [Gasser87a],
PUP6 [Lenat75] [Lenat87],
SPRING [Ramamritham85] [Stankovic85],
YAMS [Parunak87]

Task allocation

[Cammarata83] [Corkill79] [Cullingford81] [Davis83]
[Durfee87a] [Durfee87c] [Gasser87a] [McArthur82b]
[Malone87b] [Parunak87] [Ramamritham85] [Shaw85]
[Shen85] [Smith79] [Smith81a] [Smith81b] [Stankovic85]
[Steeb81] [Steeb84] [Steeb86] [Thorndyke81] [Wesson81]

Task decomposition

[Chandrasekn82] [Fahlman83] [Hinke88] [Lesser80a]
[Smith85a] [Wesson81] [Yang85]

Tools

Integrative systems
ABE [Hayes-Roth88],
AGORA [Bisiani86] [Bisiani87],
MACE [Gasser87d] [Gasser87c]
Concurrent, Distributed and Object-oriented languages
[Casais88] [Arbib85] [Arbib88] [Casais88],
CCLISP [Billstrom87],
OIL [Cohen85],
ORIENT84/K [Tokoro84] ,
ROSS [McArthur82a]
Actor languages
[Agha86a] [Garner87],
ABCL/1 [Yonezawa86],
ACT2 [Theriault83],
ACT3 [Agha85],
APIARY [Hewitt80],
ETHER [Kornfeld81b] [Kornfeld79] [Kornfeld82],
PLASMA [Hewitt77a]
UBIK [de Jong88]
Experimental Testbeds
[Yeung86],
AF [Green87],
APIARY [Lieberman83],
CAOS [Schoen86],
CNET [Smith81a],
DVMT [Durfee84a] [Durfee84b],
MACE [Gasser87d] [Gasser87c],
POLIGON [Nii86c] [Rice86],
SIMULACT [MacIntosh87a] [MacIntosh87b]

Parallel production systems and Blackboard languages
BB [Hayes-Roth86],
Blackboard shells [Jones86] [Hayes-Roth85],
CAGE [Aiello86] [Nii86c],
COPS [Leao86],
ERASMUS [Jagannathan87a],
FACILITY ADVISOR [Silverman86],
GBB [Corkill86] [Corkill87],
HEARSAY-III [Balzer80] [Erman81]
Performance and modeling tools
[Pavlin83] [Pavlin84],
EFIGE [Pattison87],
GEM specification framework [Lansky87b]
Miscellaneous
CALLISTO [Sathi85] [Sathi86],
PCS [Chang87]

Bibliography

[Abraham82] M. Francis Abraham. *Modern Sociological Theory*. Oxford University Press, 1982.

[Abram84] J.M. Abram, C.Y. Chong, M.R. Fehling, J.S. Rosenschein, and E. Tse. *Distributed Decisionmaking Environments*. Technical Report RADC-TR-84-132, Rome Air Development Center, Griffiss AFB, NY, 13441, July 1984. Distributed AI Section reprinted as an appendix to Jeffrey S. Rosenschein, *Rational Interaction: Cooperation Among Intelligent Agents*, PhD thesis, Department of Computer Science, Stanford University, Stanford, CA., October, 1985.

[Ackland85] B. Ackland, A. Dickinson, R. Ensor, J. Gabbe, P. Kollaritch, T. London, C. Poierier, P. Subrahmanyam, and H. Watanabe. CADRE—A System of Cooperating VLSI Design Experts. In *Proceedings of ICCD-85*, 1985.

[Agha85] Gul Agha and Carl E. Hewitt. *Concurrent Programming Using Actors: Exploiting Large-Scale Parallelism*. AI Memo 865, Massachusetts Institute of Technology, 1985.

[Agha86a] Gul Agha. *Actors: A Model of Concurrent Computation in Distributed Systems*. MIT Press, Cambridge, MA, 1986.

[Agha86b] Gul Agha. An Overview of Actor Languages. *SIGPLAN Notices*, 21(10):58–67, 1986.

[Aiello86] Nelleke Aiello. *User-Directed Control of Parallelism; The CAGE System*. Technical Report KSL 86-31, Knowledge Systems Laboratry, Stanford University, Stanford, CA, April 1986.

[Aleksander75] I. Aleksander. Action-Oriented Learning Networks. *Kybernetes*, 4:39–44, 1975.

[Allen84] James F. Allen. Towards a General Theory of Action and Time. *Artificial Intelligence*, 23(2):123–154, 1984.

[Alvarado86] Sergio J. Alvarado, Michael G. Dyer, and Margot Flowers.   Editorial Comprehension in OpEd Through Argument Units. In *Proceedings of 1986 Conference of the American Association for Artificial Intelligence*, pages 250–256, Philadelphia, PA, August 1986.

[Amarel68] Saul Amarel. On Representations of Problems of Reasoning About Actions. In D. Michie, editor, *Machine Intelligence 3*, pages 131–171, 1968.

[Appelt80] Douglas E. Appelt. A Planner for Reasoning About Knowledge and Action. In *Proceedings of 1980 Conference of the American Association for Artificial Intelligence*, pages 131–133, 1980.

[Appelt81] Douglas E. Appelt. *Planning Natural Language Utterances to Satisfy Multiple Goals*. PhD thesis, Stanford University, 1981.

[Arbib85] Michael A. Arbib. Brain Theory and Cooperative Computation. *Human Neurobiology*, 4:201–218, 1985.

[Arbib88] Michael A. Arbib. *The Metaphorical Brain 2: An Introduction to Schema Theory and Neural Networks*. Wiley-Interscience, 1988. In press.

[Austin62] J. L. Austin. *How to do things with words*. Harvard University Press, 1962.

[Axelrod84] Robert Axelrod. *The Evolution of Cooperation*. Basic Books, 1984.

[Axelrod86] Robert Axelrod. An Evolutionary Approach to Norms. *American Political Science Review*, 80, December 1986. Also in *Proceedings of the 1988 Spring Symposium on Parallel Models of Intelligence: How Can Slow Components Think So Fast?*, Computer Science Department, Stanford University, Stanford, CA., March, 1986, pages 10–52.

[Backstrom88a] Christer Backstrom. A Representation of Coordinated Actions. In *Proceedings of the First Scandinavian Conference on Artificial Intelligence*, pages 193–207, International Organisations Services B.V., Van Diemenstraat 94, 1013CN, Amsterdam, Netherlands, March 1988.

[Backstrom88b] Christer Backstrom. *A Representation of Coordinated Actions Characterized by Interval Valued Conditions*. Technical Report LiTH-IDA-R-88-06, Department of Computer and Information Science, Linkoping University, Linkoping Sweden, 1988.

[Backstrom88c] Christer Backstrom. *Keeping and Forcing: How to Represent Cooperating Actions*. Technical Report LiTH-IDA-R-88-05, Department of Computer and Information Science, Linkoping University, Linkoping Sweden, 1988.

[Ballim86a] Afzal Ballim. *Generating Points of View*. Technical Report MCCS-86-68, Computing Research Laboratory, New Mexico State University, Las Cruces, NM, 1986.

[Ballim86b] Afzal Ballim. *The Subjective Ascription of Belief to Agents*. Technical Report MCCS-86-74, Computing Research Laboratory, New Mexico State University, Las Cruces, NM, 1986.

[Balzer80] Robert Balzer, Lee Erman, Philip London, and Chuck Williams. HEARSAY-III: A Domain-Independent Framework for Expert Systems. In *Proceedings of 1980 Conference of the American Association for Artificial Intelligence*, pages 108–110, 1980.

[Barber80] Gerald R. Barber. Reasoning About Change in Knowledgeable Office Systems. In *Proceedings of 1980 Conference of the American Association for Artificial Intelligence*, pages 199–201, 1980.

[Barber82] Gerald R. Barber. *Office Semantics*. PhD thesis, EE-CS Department, Massachusetts Institute of Technology, Cambridge, MA, February 1982.

[Barber83] Gerald R. Barber. Supporting Organizational Problem Solving with a Work Station. *ACM Transactions on Office Information Systems*, 1:45–67, 1983. Earlier Version was Massachusetts Institute of Technology Artificial Intelligence Laboratory AI Memo 681, July, 1982.

[Becker86] Howard Becker. *Doing Things Together*. Northwestern University Press, Evanston, Illinois, 1986.

[Benda85] M. Benda, V. Jagannathan, and R. Dodhiawalla. *On Optimal Cooperation of Knowledge Sources*. Technical Report BCS-G2010-28, Boeing AI Center, Boeing Computer Services, Bellevue, WA, August 1985.

[Bendif87] Salah Bendifallah and Walter S. Scacchi. Understanding Software Maintenance Work. *IEEE Transactions on Software Engineering*, SE-13(3):311–323, March 1987.

[Bentley54] Arthur F. Bentley. *Inquiry into Inquiries*. Beacon Press, Boston, MA, 1954.

[Billstrom87] David Billstrom, Joseph Brandenburg, and John Teeter.   CCLISP on the iPSC Concurrent Computer. In *Proceedings of the 1987 International Joint Conference on Artificial Intelligence*, 1987.

[Bisiani86] Roberto Bisiani. A Software and Hardware Environment for Developing AI Applications on Parallel Processors. In *Proceedings of 1986 Conference of the American Association for Artificial Intelligence*, pages 742–747, 1986.

[Bisiani87] R. Bisiani, F. Alleva, A. Forin, R. Lerner, and M. Bauer. The Architecture of the AGORA Environment. In Michael N. Huhns, editor, *Distributed Artificial Intelligence*, pages 99–118, Pitman Publishing/Morgan Kaufmann Publishers, San Mateo, CA, 1987.

[Blelloch86] Guy E. Blelloch. CIS: A Massively Concurrent Rule Based System. In *Proceedings of 1986 Conference of the American Association for Artificial Intelligence*, pages 735–741, August 1986.

[Blumer69] Herbert Blumer. *Symbolic Interactionism*. Prentice Hall, Englewood Cliffs, NJ, 1969.

[Bond88a] Alan H. Bond and Les Gasser. *Organizational Analysis of Distributed Artificial Intelligence Systems*. Technical Report CRI-88-43, Computer Research Institute, University of Southern California, Los Angeles, CA, July 1988.

[Bond88b] Alan H. Bond and Les Gasser. *Readings in Distributed Artificial Intelligence*. Morgan Kaufmann Publishers, San Mateo, CA, 1988.

[Borchardt87] Gary C. Borchardt. Incremental Inference: Getting Multiple Agents to Agree on What to Do Next. In *Proceedings of 1987 Conference of American Association for Artificial Intelligence*, pages 334–339, August 1987.

[Brooks82] Richard Samuel Brooks. *Experiments in Distributed Problem Solving with Iterative Refinement*. PhD thesis, Department of Computer and Information Science, University of Massachusetts, Amherst, MA, 1982.

[Brown86] Harold Brown, Eric Schoen, and Bruce Delagi. *An Experiment in Knowledge Based Signal Understanding Using Parallel Architectures*. Technical Report STAN-CS-86-1136, Computer Science Department, Stanford University, Stanford, CA, October 1986.

[Bruce78] Bertram Bruce and Denis Newman. Interacting Plans. *Cognitive Science*, 2(3):195–233, 1978.

[Cammarata83] Stephanie Cammarata, David McArthur, and Randall Steeb. Strategies of Cooperation in Distributed Problem Solving. In *Proceedings of the 1983 International Joint Conference on Artificial Intelligence*, pages 767–770, 1983.

[Carbonell81] Jaime G. Carbonell. *Subjective Understanding: Computer Models of Belief Systems*. UMI Research Press, Ann Arbor, MI, 1981.

[Carley86] Kathleen Carley. Knowledge Acquisition as a Social Phenomenon. *Instructional Science*, 14:381–438, 1986.

[Casais88] Eduardo Casais. An Object Oriented System Implementing KNOs. In *Proceedings of the Conference on Office Information Systems*, pages 284–290, ACM Press, New York, March 1988.

[Chandrasekn81] B. Chandrasekaran. Natural and Social System Metaphors for Distributed Problem Solving: Introduction to the Issue. *IEEE Transactions on Systems, Man and Cybernetics*, SMC-11(1):1–5, January 1981.

[Chandrasekn82] B. Chandrasekaran. Decomposition of Domain Knowledge into Knowledge Sources: the MDX Approach. In *Proceedings of the Fourth National Conference of the Canadian Society for Computational Studies of Intelligence*, Saskatchewan, May 1982.

[Chang87] Ernest Chang. Participant Systems. In Michael N. Huhns, editor, *Distributed Artificial Intelligence*, pages 311–340, Pitman Publishing/Morgan Kauf-

mann Publishers, San Mateo, CA, 1987.

[Clinger81] William D. Clinger. *Foundations of Actor Semantics*. Technical Report AI-TR-633, Artificial Intelligence Laboratory, Massachusetts Institute of Technology, Cambridge, MA, May 1981.

[Cohen79] Philip R. Cohen and C. Raymond Perrault. Elements of a Plan-Based Theory of Speech Acts. *Cognitive Science*, 3(3):177–212, 1979.

[Cohen85] Shimon Cohen, John Conery, Al Davis, and Shane Robison. *OIL Programming Language Reference Manual*. Schlumberger Palo Alto Reseach Center, Palo Alto, California, 94304, 1985.

[Cohen87a] Philip R. Cohen and Hector J. Levesque. Intention =Choice + Commitment. In *Proceedings of 1987 Conference of American Association for Artificial Intelligence*, pages 410–415, 1987.

[Cohen87b] Philip R. Cohen and Hector J. Levesque. *Persistence, Intention, and Commitment*. Technical Report CSLI-87-88, Center for the Study of Language and Information, Stanford University, Stanford, CA, March 1987.

[Conry86] Susan E. Conry, Robert A. Meyer, and Victor R. Lesser. *Multistage Negotiation in Distributed Planning*. Technical Report 86–67, Department of Computer and Information Science, University of Massachusetts, Amherst, MA, December 1986.

[Cooley64] Charles H. Cooley. *Human Nature and the Social Order*. Schocken Press, New York, 1964.

[Corkill79] Daniel D. Corkill. Hierarchical Planning in a Distributed Environment. In *Proceedings of the 1979 International Joint Conference on Artificial Intelligence*, pages 168–175, 1979.

[Corkill82] Daniel D. Corkill. *A Framework for Organizational Self-Design in Distributed Problem Solving Networks*. PhD thesis, Department of Computer and Information Science, University of Massachusetts, Amherst, MA, December 1982. Also University of Massachusetts Department of Computer and Information Science Technical Report COINS-TR-82-33.

[Corkill83] Daniel D. Corkill and Victor R. Lesser. The Use of Meta-Level Control for Coordination in a Distributed Problem Solving Network. In *Proceedings of the 1983 International Joint Conference on Artificial Intelligence*, pages 748–756, August 1983. Also appeared in Benjamin W. Wah and G.-J. Li, editors, *Computer Architectures for Artificial Intelligence Applications*, IEEE Computer Society Press, pages 507–515, 1986.

[Corkill86] Daniel D. Corkill, Kevin Q. Gallagher, and Kelly E. Murray. GBB: A Generic Blackboard Development System. In *Proceedings of 1986 Conference of the American Association for Artificial Intelligence*, pages 1008–1014, August 1986.

[Corkill87] Daniel D. Corkill, Kevin Q. Gallagher, and Philip M. Johnson. Achieving Flexibility, Efficiency, and

Generality in Blackboard Architectures. In *Proceedings of 1987 Conference of American Association for Artificial Intelligence*, pages 18–23, 1987.

[Croft87] W. Bruce Croft and Lawrence S. Lefkowitz. Knowledge-Based Support of Cooperative Activities. In *Proceedings of the 21st Annual Hawaii International Conference on System Science*, vol. III, pages 312-318, 1988.

[Croft88] W. Bruce Croft and Lawrence S. Lefkowitz. Using a Planner to Support Office Work. In *Proceedings of the Conference on Office Information Systems*, pages 55–62, ACM Press, New York, March 1988.

[Cromarty86] Andrew S. Cromarty. *Control of Processes by Communication over Ports as a Paradigm for Distributed Knowledge-Based System Design*. Benjamin/Cummings Publishing Company, Inc., 1987.

[Cullingford81] Richard E. Cullingford. Integrating Knowledge Sources for Computer Understanding Tasks. *IEEE Transactions on Systems, Man and Cybernetics*, SMC-11(1):52–60, January 1981.

[Cullingford84] Richard E. Cullingford and Michael J. Pazzani. Word-Meaning Selection in Multiprocess Language Understanding Programs. *IEEE Transactions on Pattern Analysis and Machine Intelligence*, PAMI-6(4):493–509, July 1984.

[Davis80] Randall Davis. Report on the Workshop on Distributed AI. *SIGART Newsletter*, 73:42–52, October 1980.

[Davis81] Randall Davis. *A Model For Planning in a Multi-Agent Environment: Steps Toward Principles For Teamwork*. Technical Report AI Working Paper 217, Artificial Intelligence Laboratory, Massachusetts Institute of Technology, Cambridge, MA, June 1981.

[Davis82] Randall Davis. Report on the Second Workshop on Distributed AI. *SIGART Newsletter*, 80:13–23, April 1982.

[Davis83] Randall Davis and Reid G. Smith. Negotiation as a Metaphor for Distributed Problem Solving. *Artificial Intelligence*, 20(1):63–109, 1983.

[de Jong88] Peter de Jong. The UBIK Configurator. In *Proceedings of the Conference on Office Information Systems*, pages 309–315, ACM Press, New York, March 1988.

[Dean87] Thomas L. Dean. Intractability and Time-Dependent Planning. In Michael P. Georgeff and Amy L. Lansky, editors, *Reasoning About Actions and Plans: Proceedings of the 1986 Workshop*, pages 245–266, Morgan Kaufmann Publishers, San Mateo, CA, 1987.

[Decker87a] Keith S. Decker. *Descant: A Distributed Expert System Control Architecture for Non-Decomposable Tasks*. Technical Report 87-CRD-030, GE Corporate Research and Development, April 1987.

[Decker87b] Keith S. Decker. Distributed Problem-Solving Techniques: A Survey. *IEEE Transactions on*

Systems, Man and Cybernetics, SMC-17:729–740, 1987.

[Deen87] S.M. Deen, R.R. Amin, and M.C. Taylor. Data Integration in Distributed Databases. *IEEE Transactions on Software Engineering*, SE-13(7):860–864, July 1987.

[deKleer86] Johan de Kleer. An Assumption Based Truth Maintenance System. *Artificial Intelligence*, 28(2): 127–162, March 1986.

[Dewey16] John Dewey. *Essays in Experimental Logic*. Dover Publications, New York, 1916.

[Dietrich86a] Eric Dietrich and Chris Fields. *Creative Problem-Solving Using Wanton Inference: It Takes at Least Two to Tango*. Technical Report MCCS-86-70, Computing Research Laboratory, New Mexico State University, Las Cruces, NM, 1986.

[Dietrich86b] Eric Dietrich and Chris Fields. *Problem Solving in Multiple Task Environments*. Technical Report MCCS-87-84, Computing Research Laboratory, New Mexico State University, Las Cruces, NM, 1986.

[Doran87] Jim Doran. *Distributed Artificial Intelligence and the Modeling of Sociocultural Systems*. Technical Report CSM-87, Department of Computer Science, University of Essex, United Kingdom, 1987.

[Doyle79] Jon Doyle. A Truth Maintenance System. *Artificial Intelligence*, 12(3):231–272, 1979.

[Drexler88] K. Eric Drexler. Incentive Engineering for Computational Resource Management. In Bernardo Huberman, editor, *The Ecology of Computation*, Elsevier Science Publishers/North Holland, 1988.

[Durfee84a] Edmund H. Durfee. *A Parallel Simulation of a Distributed Problem Solving Network*. Technical Report COINS-TR-84-19, Department of Computer and Information Science, University of Massachusetts, Amherst, MA, 1984.

[Durfee84b] Edmund H. Durfee, Daniel D. Corkill, and Victor R. Lesser. Distributing A Distributed Problem Solving Network Simulator. In *Proceedings of the 5th Real Time Systems Symposium*, pages 237–246, December 1984.

[Durfee85] Edmund H. Durfee, Victor R. Lesser, and Daniel D. Corkill. Increasing Coherence in a Distributed Problem Solving Network. In *Proceedings of the 1985 International Joint Conference on Artificial Intelligence*, pages 1025–1030, 1985.

[Durfee86] Edmund H. Durfee. Incremental Planning to Control a Blackboard-Based Problem-Solver. In *Proceedings of 1986 Conference of the American Association for Artificial Intelligence*, pages 58–64, 1986.

[Durfee87a] Edmund H. Durfee. *A Unified Approach to Dynamic Coordination: Planning Actions and Interactions in a Distributed Problem Solving Network*. PhD thesis, Department of Computer and Information Science, University of Massachusetts, Amherst,

MA, September 1987. Also University of Massachusetts Department of Computer and Information Science Technical Report COINS-TR-87-84.

[Durfee87b] Edmund H. Durfee and Victor R. Lesser. *Planning Coordinated Actions in Dynamic Domains.* Technical Report COINS-TR-87-130, Department of Computer and Information Science, University of Massachusetts, Amherst, MA, December 1987.

[Durfee87c] Edmund H. Durfee and Victor R. Lesser. Using Partial Global Plans to Coordinate Distributed Problem Solvers. In *Proceedings of the 1987 International Joint Conference on Artificial Intelligence,* pages 875–883, 1987.

[Durfee87d] Edmund H. Durfee, Victor R. Lesser, and Daniel D. Corkill. Coherent Cooperation Among Communicating Problem Solvers. *IEEE Transactions on Computers,* C-36:1275–1291, 1987.

[Durfee87e] Edmund H. Durfee, Victor R. Lesser, and Daniel D. Corkill. Cooperation Through Communication in a Distributed Problem Solving Network. In Michael N. Huhns, editor, *Distributed Artificial Intelligence,* pages 29–58, Pitman Publishing/Morgan Kaufmann Publishers, San Mateo, CA, 1987.

[Elfes86] Alberto Elfes. A Distributed Control Architecture for an Autonomous Mobile Robot. *International Journal for AI in Engineering,* 1(2):99–109, 1986.

[Ensor85] J. Robert Ensor and John D. Gabbe. Transactional Blackboards. In *Proceedings of the 1985 International Joint Conference on Artificial Intelligence,* pages 340–344, August 1985.

[Ensor86] J. Robert Ensor and John D. Gabbe. Transactional Blackboards. *International Journal for Artificial Intelligence in Engineering,* 1(2):80–84, 1986.

[Erman75] Lee D. Erman and Victor R. Lesser. A Multi-Level Organization for Problem Solving Using Many, Diverse, Cooperating Sources of Knowledge. In *Proceedings of the 1975 International Joint Conference on Artificial Intelligence,* pages 483–490, 1975.

[Erman80] Lee D. Erman, Frederick A. Hayes-Roth, Victor R. Lesser, and D. Raj Reddy. The Hearsay-II Speech-Understanding System: Integrating Knowledge to Resolve Uncertainty. *Computing Surveys,* 12(2):213–253, June 1980.

[Erman81] Lee D. Erman, Philip E. London, and Stephen F. Fickas. The Design and an Example Use of Hearsay-III. In *Proceedings of the 1981 International Joint Conference on Artificial Intelligence,* pages 409–415, 1981.

[Fahlman83] Scott E. Fahlman and Geoffrey E. Hinton and Terrence J. Sejnowski. Massively Parallel Architectures for AI: Netl, Thistle and Boltzmann Machines. In *Proceedings of 1983 Conference of the American Association for Artificial Intelligence,* pages 109–113, 1983.

[Fehling83] Michael Fehling and Lee Erman. Report on the Third Annual Workshop on Distributed Artificial Intelligence. *SIGART Newsletter,* 84:3–12, April 1983.

[Feldman82] Jerome A. Feldman and Dana H. Ballard. Connectionist Models and their Properties. *Cognitive Science,* 6(3):205–254, 1982.

[Fennell77] Richard D. Fennell and Victor R. Lesser. Parallelism in Artificial Intelligence Problem Solving: A Case Study of Hearsay II. *IEEE Transactions on Computers,* C-26(2):98–111, 1977.

[Ferber88a] Jacques Ferber. *Des Objets aux Agents: Une Architecture Stratifiee.* Technical Report Laboratoire Formes et Intelligence Artificielle Report 88-18, CNRS Lab, Universite Pierre et Marie Curie, 4 Place Jussieu, 75252 Paris, France, 1988.

[Ferber88b] Jacques Ferber. *Introduction a l'Intelligence Artificielle Distribuee.* Technical Report Laboratoire Formes et Intelligence Artificielle Report 88-17, CNRS Lab, Universite Pierre et Marie Curie, 4 Place Jussieu, 75252 Paris, France, 1988.

[Fikes71] Richard E. Fikes and Nils J. Nilsson. STRIPS: A New Approach to the Application of Theorem Proving to Problem Solving. *Artificial Intelligence,* 3(3-4):189–208, 1971.

[Fikes80] Richard E. Fikes and D. Austin Henderson Jr. On Supporting the Use of Procedures in Office Work. In *Proceedings of 1980 Conference of the American Association for Artificial Intelligence,* pages 202–207, 1980.

[Fikes82] Richard E. Fikes. A Commitment-Based Framework for Describing Informal Cooperative Work. *Cognitive Science,* 6(4):331–347, 1982.

[Filman84] Robert E. Filman and Daniel P. Friedman. *Coordinated Computing: Tools and Techniques for Distributed Software.* McGraw Hill, New York, 1984.

[Findler86] Nicholas V. Findler and Ron Lo. An Examination of Distributed Planning in the World of Air Traffic Control. *Journal of Parallel and Distributed Computing,* 3:411–431, 1986.

[Findler87] Nicholas V. Findler and Ji Gao. Dynamic Hierarchical Control for Distributed Problem Solving. *Data and Knowledge Engineering,* 2:285–301, 1987.

[Fox79] Mark S. Fox. *Organization Structuring: Designing Large Complex Software.* Technical Report CMU-CS-79-155, Department of Computer Science, Carnegie Mellon University, Pittsburgh, PA, December 1979.

[Fox81] Mark S. Fox. An Organizational View of Distributed Systems. *IEEE Transactions on Systems, Man and Cybernetics,* SMC-11:70–80, 1981.

[Fox84] Mark S. Fox and Stephen F. Smith. ISIS — a Knowledge-Based System for Factory Scheduling. *Expert Systems,* 1(1):25–49, July 1984.

[Fox88] Geoffrey C. Fox, Mark A. Johnson, Gregory A. Lyzenga, Steve W. Otto, John K. Salmon, and David

W. Walker. *Solving Problems on Concurrent Processors, Volume 1: General Techniques and Regular Problems*. Prentice Hall, Englewood Cliffs, NJ, 1988.

[Galbraith73] Jay Galbraith. *Designing Complex Organizations*. Addison Wesley, Reading, MA, 1973.

[Garner87] B.J. Garner, C. Chong, A. Jiramahasuwan, D. Lui, D. Lukose, and E. Tsui. *Actor Implementations in Cybernetic Reasoning Systems*. Technical Report 87-9, Xerox Artificial Intelligence Laboratory, Division of Computing and Mathematics, Deakin University, Victoria 3217, Australia, August 1987.

[Gasser84] Les Gasser. *The Social Dynamics of Routine Computer Use in Complex Organizations*. PhD thesis, Department of Computer Science, University of California, Irvine, Irvine, CA. 92717, February 1984.

[Gasser86] Les Gasser. The Integration of Computing and Routine Work. *ACM Transactions on Office Information Systems*, 4(3):205–225, July 1986.

[Gasser87a] Les Gasser. PRESSURE: An Adaptive, Distributed, Multi-Robot Task Allocation System. In *Proceedings of the SME Conference on AI in Manufacturing, Long Beach, California*, October 1987.

[Gasser87b] Les Gasser. Report on the 1985 Workshop on Distributed Artificial Intelligence. *AI Magazine*, 8(2):91–97, Summer 1987.

[Gasser87c] Les Gasser, Carl Braganza, and Nava Herman. Implementing Distributed Artificial Intelligence Systems Using MACE. In *Proceedings of the Third IEEE Conference on Artificial Intelligence Applications*, pages 315–320, 1987.

[Gasser87d] Les Gasser, Carl Braganza, and Nava Herman. MACE: A Flexible Testbed for Distributed AI Research. In Michael N. Huhns, editor, *Distributed Artificial Intelligence*, pages 119–152, Pitman Publishing/Morgan Kaufmann Publishers, San Mateo, CA, 1987.

[Gasser88a] Les Gasser. Distribution and Coordination of Tasks Among Intelligent Agents. In *Proceedings of the First Scandinavian Conference on Artificial Intelligence*, pages 177–192, International Organisations Services B.V., Van Diemenstraat 94, 1013CN, Amsterdam, Netherlands, March 1988.

[Gasser88b] Les Gasser. Large Scale Concurrent Computing in Artificial Intelligence Research. In *Proceedings of the Third Conference on Hypercube Concurrent Computers and Applications*, ACM Press, New York, January 1988.

[Gasser88c] Les Gasser. Report on the 1988 Distributed AI Workshop. *AI Magazine*, 1988. in press.

[Gasser88d] Les Gasser, editor. *Collected Draft Papers from the 1988 Distributed AI Workshop*. Technical Report CRI-88-41, Computer Research Institute, University of Southern California, Los Angeles, CA,

June 1988.

[Geffner87] Hector Geffner and Judea Pearl. Distributed Diagnosis of Systems with Multiple Faults. In *Proceedings of the Third IEEE Conference on Artificial Intelligence Applications*, pages 156–162, IEEE Press, 1987.

[Genesereth84] Michael R. Genesereth, Matthew L. Ginsberg, and Jeffrey S. Rosenschein. *Cooperation without Communication*. Technical Report HPP-84-36, Stanford Heuristic Programming Project, Stanford University, Stanford, CA, September 1984.

[Georgeff83] Michael P. Georgeff. Communication and Interaction in MultiAgent Planning. In *Proceedings of 1983 Conference of the American Association for Artificial Intelligence*, pages 125–129, 1983.

[Georgeff84] Michael P. Georgeff. A Theory of Action for MultiAgent Planning. In *Proceedings of 1984 Conference of the American Association for Artificial Intelligence*, pages 121–125, 1984.

[Georgeff86a] Michael P. Georgeff. The Representation of Events in Multi-Agent Domains. In *Proceedings of 1986 Conference of the American Association for Artificial Intelligence*, pages 70–75, 1986.

[Georgeff86b] Michael P. Georgeff, Amy L. Lansky, and Marcel J. Schoppers. *Reasoning and Planning in Dynamic Domains: An Experiment with a Mobile Robot*. Technical Report, SRI International, Menlo Park, CA, 1986.

[Georgeff87a] Michael P. Georgeff. Actions, Processes, and Causality. In Michael P. Georgeff and Amy L. Lansky, editors, *Reasoning About Actions and Plans: Proceedings of the 1986 Workshop*, pages 99–122, Morgan Kaufmann Publishers, San Mateo, CA, 1987.

[Georgeff87b] Michael P. Georgeff. *Many Agents are Better Than One*. Technical Report 417, SRI International, Menlo Park, CA, March 1987. An earlier version appears in *The Frame Problem in Artificial Intelligence: Proceedings of the 1987 Workshop*, Morgan Kaufmann Publishers, 1987.

[Georgeff87c] Michael P. Georgeff. Planning. *Annual Reviews of Computer Science*, 2:359–400, 1987.

[Georgeff87d] Michael P. Georgeff and Amy L. Lansky. Reactive Reasoning and Planning. In *Proceedings of 1987 Conference of American Association for Artificial Intelligence*, pages 677–682, August 1987.

[Gerson86] Elihu M. Gerson and Susan Leigh Star. Analyzing Due Process in the Workplace. *ACM Transactions on Office Information Systems*, 4(3):257–270, July 1986.

[Ginsberg87] Matthew L. Ginsberg. Decision Procedures. In Michael N. Huhns, editor, *Distributed Artificial Intelligence*, pages 3–28, Pitman Publishing/Morgan Kaufmann Publishers, San Mateo, CA, 1987.

[Goldstein75] Ira Goldstein. Bargaining Between Goals. In

Proceedings of the 1975 International Joint Conference on Artificial Intelligence, pages 175–180, Tbilisi, USSR, August 1975.

[Gomez81] Fernando Gomez and B. Chandrasekaran. Knowledge Organization and Distribution for Medical Diagnosis. *IEEE Transactions on Systems, Man and Cybernetics*, SMC-11(1):34–42, 1981.

[Goodson83] J. Goodson, W. Zachary, J. Deimler, J. Stokes, and W. Weiland. Distributed Intelligence Systems: AI Approaches to Cooperative Man Machine Problem Solving in C3I. In *Proceedings of the AIAA Computers in Aerospace IV Conference*, pages 1–8, Hartford, CT, October 1983.

[Gordon71] D. Gordon and G. Lakoff. Conversational Postulates. In *Papers from the 7th Meeting of the Chicago Linguistic Society*, page , 1971.

[Green87] Peter Green. AF: A Framework for Real Time Distributed Cooperative Problem Solving. In Michael N. Huhns, editor, *Distributed Artificial Intelligence*, pages 153–176, Pitman Publishing/Morgan Kaufmann Publishers, San Mateo, CA, 1987.

[Grosz85] Barabara J. Grosz and Candace L. Sidner. Discourse Structure and the Proper Treatment of Interruptions. In *Proceedings of the 1985 International Joint Conference on Artificial Intelligence*, pages 832–839, 1985.

[Grosz86] Barbara J. Grosz and Candace L. Sidner. Attention, Intentions and the Structure of Discourse. *Computational Linguistics*, 12:175–204, 1986.

[Grosz87] Barbara J. Grosz and Candace L. Sidner. *Plans for Discourse*. Technical Report TR-11-87, Center for Research in Computing Technology, Harvard University, 1987.

[Haase86] Ken Haase. *Cauldrons: An Abstraction for Concurrent Problem-Solving*. Technical Report AIM-673, Artificial Intelligence Laboratory, Massachusetts Institute of Technology, Cambridge, MA, September 1986.

[Hall82] Richard H. Hall. *Organizations: Structure and Process*. Prentice-Hall, Englewood Cliffs, NJ, 1982.

[Halpern84] Joseph Y. Halpern and Yoram Moses. Knowledge and Common Knowledge in a Distributed Environment. In *Proceedings of the Third ACM Conference on Principles of Distributed Computing*, pages 50–61, 1984.

[Halpern86a] Joseph Y. Halpern. Reasoning About Knowledge: An Overview. In *Proceedings of the 1986 Conference on Theoretical Aspects fo Reasoning About Knowledge*, pages 1–17, Morgan Kaufmann Publishers, San Mateo, CA, 1986. Also Technical Report RJ-5001 (52251), IBM Almaden Research Center, San Jose, CA. January, 1986.

[Halpern86b] Joseph Y. Halpern. *Theoretical Aspects of Reasoning About Knowledge: Proceedings of the 1986 Conference*. Morgan Kaufmann Publishers, San Mateo, CA, 1986.

[Halpern87] Joseph Y. Halpern. Using Reasoning About Knowledge to Analyze Distributed Systems. In J.F. Traub, editor, *Annual Review of Computer Science*, Annual Reviews, Inc., 1987. Also Research Report RJ5522, IBM Research Laboratory, Almaden CA.

[Harmon84] S.Y. Harmon, D.W. Gage, W.A. Aviles, and G.L. Bianchini. Coordination of Intelligent Subsystems in Complex Robots. In *Proceedings of the First Conference on AI Applications*, pages 64–69, December 1984.

[Harmon86] S.Y. Harmon, W.A. Aviles, and D.W. Gage. A Technique for Coordinating Autonomous Robots. In *Proceedings of the IEEE International Conference on Robotics and Automation*, pages 2029–2034, April 1986.

[Hayes-Roth79a] Barbara Hayes-Roth and Frederick A. Hayes-Roth. A Cognitive Model of Planning. *Cognitive Science*, 3(4):275–310, 1979.

[Hayes-Roth79b] Barbara Hayes-Roth and Frederick A. Hayes-Roth. Modeling Planning as an Incremental Opportunistic Process. In *Proceedings of the 1979 International Joint Conference on Artificial Intelligence*, pages 375–383, 1979.

[Hayes-Roth85] Barabara Hayes-Roth. A Blackboard Architecture for Control. *Artificial Intelligence Journal*, 26:251–321, 1985.

[Hayes-Roth86] Barbara Hayes-Roth, Alan Garvey, M. Vaughan Johnson Jr., and Michael Hewett. *A Layered Environment for Reasoning About Action*. Technical Report KSL 86-38, Computer Science Department, Stanford University, 1986.

[Hayes-Roth88] Frederick A. Hayes-Roth, Lee D. Erman, Scott Fouse, Jay S. Lark, James Davidson. ABE: A Cooperative Operating System and Development Environment. *AI Tools and Techniques*, ed. Mark Richer, ABLEX 1988.

[Hewitt71] Carl E. Hewitt. *Description and Theoretical Analysis (Using Schemata) of PLANNER: A Language for Proving Theorems and Manipulating Models in a Robot*. PhD thesis, Massachusetts Institute of Technology, 1971. Report Number AI-TR-258, Massachusetts Institute of Technology Artificial Intelligence Laboratory.

[Hewitt77a] Carl E. Hewitt. Viewing Control Structures as Patterns of Passing Messages. *Artificial Intelligence*, 8(3):323–364, 1977.

[Hewitt77b] Carl E. Hewitt and Henry Baker. Laws for Communicating Parallel Processes. In *Information Processing 77*, Elsevier Science Publishers, Amsterdam, 1977.

[Hewitt80] Carl E. Hewitt. The Apiary Network Architecture for Knowledgeable Systems. In *Proceedings of 1980 Conference of the American Association for Artificial*

Intelligence, pages 107–117, 1980.

[Hewitt83] Carl E. Hewitt and Peter de Jong. Analyzing the Roles of Descriptions and Actions in Open Systems. In *Proceedings of 1983 Conference of the American Association for Artificial Intelligence*, pages 162–166, 1983.

[Hewitt84a] Carl E. Hewitt and Peter de Jong. Open Systems. In *On Conceptual Modeling*, pages 147–164, Springer Verlag, New York, 1984.

[Hewitt84b] Carl E. Hewitt and Henry Lieberman. Design Issues in Parallel Architectures for Artificial Intelligence. In *Proceedings of COMPCON S'84*, pages 418–423, 1984. Also Massachusetts Institute of Technology Artificial Intelligence Laboratory AI Memo 750 Cambridge, MA., November, 1983.

[Hewitt85] Carl E. Hewitt. The Challenge of Open Systems. *Byte*, 10(4):223–242, April 1985.

[Hewitt86] Carl E. Hewitt. Offices are Open Systems. *ACM Transactions on Office Information Systems*, 4(3):271–287, 1986. Also in Huberman, B.A. *The Ecology of Computation*, Elsevier Science Publishers/North Holland, Amsterdam, 1988.

[Hinke88] Thomas Hinke. Distributed Problem Elaboration: An Investigation in the Domain of Distributed Query Formulation. USC DAI Group Resarch Note 45, Department of Computer Science, University of Southern California (in preparation), 1988.

[Ho86] Cheng-Seen Ho, Yang-Chang Hong, and Te-Son Kuo. A Society Model for Office Information Systems. *ACM Transactions of Office Information Systems*, 4(2):104–131, April 1986.

[Holzner83] Burkhart Holzner. Social Processes and Knowledge Synthesis. In Spencer A. Ward and Linda J. Reed, editors, *Knowledge Structure and Use: Implications for Synthesis and Interpretation*, pages 187–227, Temple University Press, Philadelphia, PA, 1983.

[Hsu87] Ching-Chi Hsu, Shao-Ming Wu, and Jan-Jan Wu. A Distributed Approach for Inferring Production Systems. In *Proceedings of the 1987 International Joint Conference on Artificial Intelligence*, pages 62–67, August 1987.

[Huberman88a] Bernardo A. Huberman and Tadd Hogg. The Behavior of Computational Ecologies. In Bernardo A. Huberman, editor, *The Ecology of Computation*, Elsevier Science Publishers/North Holland, Amsterdam, 1988.

[Huberman88b] Bernardo Huberman, editor. *The Ecology of Computation*. Elsevier Science Publishers/North Holland, Amsterdam, 1988.

[Hudlicka84] Eva Hudlicka and Victor R. Lesser. Meta-Level Control Through Fault Detection and Diagnosis. In *Proceedings of 1984 Conference of the American Association for Artificial Intelligence*, pages 153–161, 1984.

[Hudlicka86a] Eva Hudlicka. *Diagnosing Problem Solving System Behavior*. PhD thesis, Department of Computer and Information Science, University of Massachusetts, Amherst, MA, February 1986. Also University of Massachusetts Department of Computer and Information Science Technical Report COINS-TR-86-03.

[Hudlicka86b] Eva Hudlicka, Victor R. Lesser, Jasmina Pavlin, and Anil Rewari. *Design of a Distributed Diagnosis System*. Technical Report COINS-TR-86-63, Department of Computer and Information Science, University of Massachusetts, Amherst, MA, December 1986.

[Hudlicka87] Eva Hudlicka and Victor R. Lesser. Modeling and Diagnosing Problem Solving System Behavior. *IEEE Transactions on Systems, Man, and Cybernetics*, SMC-17(3):407–419, May/June 1987.

[Huhns83] Michael N. Huhns, Larry M. Stephens, and Ronald D. Bonnell. Control and Cooperation in Distributed Expert Systems. In *Proceedings of the IEEE Southeastcon*, pages 241–245, Orlando, FL, April 1983.

[Huhns87a] Michael N. Huhns, editor. *Distributed Artificial Intelligence*. Pitman Publishing/Morgan Kaufmann Publishers, San Mateo, CA, 1987.

[Huhns87b] Michael N. Huhns, Uttam Mukhopadhyay, Larry M. Stephens, and Ronald D. Bonnell. DAI For Document Retrieval: the MINDS Project. In Michael N. Huhns, editor, *Distributed Artificial Intelligence*, pages 249–284, Pitman Publishing/Morgan Kaufmann Publishers, San Mateo, CA, 1987.

[Jagannathan87a] V. Jagannathan, L.S. Baum, and R.T. Dodhiawala. Designing a Distributed Blackboard System with Erasmus. July 1987. Draft Paper, Boeing AI Center, Boeing Computer Services, Bellevue, WA. Also in *Proceedings of the Blackboard Systems Workshop*, 1987.

[Jagannathan87b] V. Jagannathan and R. Dodhiawalla. Distributed Artificial Intelligence: An Annotated Bibliography. In Michael N. Huhns, editor, *Distributed Artificial Intelligence*, pages 341–390, Pitman Publishing/Morgan Kaufmann Publishers, San Mateo, CA, 1987.

[Johnson86] M. Vaughan Johnson and Barbara Hayes-Roth. Integrating Diverse Reasoning Methods in the BB1 Blackboard Control Architecture. In *Proceedings of 1986 Conference of the American Association for Artificial Intelligence*, pages 30–35, August 1986.

[Jones86] J. Jones and M. Millington. An Edinburgh Prolog Blackboard Shell. In *Blackboard Systems, Theory and Practice*, Addison Wesley, 1986.

[Konolige80] Kurt Konolige and Nils J. Nilsson. Multiple-Agent Planning Systems. In *Proceedings of 1980 Conference of the American Association for Artificial Intelligence*, pages 138–142, 1980.

[Konolige82] Kurt Konolige. A First-Order Formalization of Knowledge and Action for a Multi-Agent Planning System. In *Machine Intelligence 10*, Ellis Horwood, 82.

[Konolige86] Kurt Konolige. *A Deduction Model of Belief*. Pitman Publishers/Morgan Kaufmann Publishers, San Mateo, CA, 1986.

[Koo87] Charles C. Koo. *A Distributed Model for Performance Systems: Synchronizing Plans among Intelligent Agents Via Communication*. PhD thesis, Stanford University, Stanford, CA, November 1987.

[Kornfeld79] William A. Kornfeld. ETHER: A Parallel Problem-Solving System. In *Proceedings of the 1979 International Joint Conference on Artificial Intelligence*, pages 490–492, August 1979.

[Kornfeld81a] William A. Kornfeld. *The Use of Parallelism to Implement Heuristic Search*. Technical Report AI Memo 627, Artificial Intelligence Laboratory, Massachusetts Institute of Technology, Cambridge, MA, March 1981.

[Kornfeld81b] William A. Kornfeld and Carl E. Hewitt. The Scientific Community Metaphor. *IEEE Transactions on Systems, Man and Cybernetics*, SMC-11(1):24–33, January 1981.

[Kornfeld82] William A. Kornfeld. *Concepts in Parallel Problem-Solving*. PhD thesis, EE-CS Department, Massachusetts Institute of Technology, Cambridge, MA, February 1982.

[Kuhn70] Thomas Kuhn. *The Structure of Scientific Revolutions*. University of Chicago Press, Chicago, IL, 1970.

[Kurose85] J.F. Kurose, M. Schwartz, and Y. Yemini. A Microeconomic Approach to Optimization of Channel Access Policies in Multiaccess Networks. In *Proceedings of the Fifth International Symposium on Distributed Computing Systems*, pages 70–80, May 1985.

[Lansky85] Amy L. Lansky. *Behavioral Specification and Planning for Multiagent Domains*. Technical Report 360, SRI International, Menlo Park, CA, 1985.

[Lansky87a] Amy L. Lansky. A Representation of Parallel Activity Based on Events, Structure, and Causality. In Michael P. Georgeff and Amy L. Lansky, editors, *Reasoning About Actions and Plans: Proceedings of the 1986 Workshop*, Morgan Kaufmann Publishers, San Mateo, CA, 1987. Also Technical Report 401, SRI International, Menlo Park, CA., December, 1986.

[Lansky87b] Amy L. Lansky and Dan Fogelsong. Localized Representation and Planning Methods for Parallel Domains. In *Proceedings of 1987 Conference of American Association for Artificial Intelligence*, pages 240–245, August 1987.

[Latour87] Bruno Latour. *Science in Action*. Harvard University Press, Cambridge, MA, 1987.

[Lawrence69] Paul R. Lawrence and Jay W. Lorsch. *Organization and Environment*. Richard D. Irwin, Homewood, IL, 1969.

[Leao86] Luis V. Leao and Sarosh N. Talukdar. An Environment for Rule-Based Blackboards and Distributed Problem Solving. *International Journal for Artificial Intelligence in Engineering*, 1(2):70–79, 1986.

[Lee63] B.J. Lee, L.O. Gilstrap Jr. and B.F. Snyder, and M.J. Pedelty. *Theory of Probability State Variable Systems Volume 1: Summary and Conclusions*. Technical Report ASD-TDR-63-664, Vol No.1, AF Avionics Laboratory, Wright-Patterson Air Force Base, Ohio, 1963.

[Lee88] Sukhan H. Lee and Yeong-Gil Shin. *Multi-Agent Cooperative Problem-Solving and Learning with Axiom-Based Reasoning*. Technical Report CRI-88-13, Department of EE-Systems, University of Southern California, 1988.

[Lefkowitz87] Lawrence S. Lefkowitz. *Knowledge Acquisition Through Anticipation of Modifications*. PhD thesis, Department of Computer and Information Science, University of Massachusetts, Amherst, MA, September 1987.

[Lenat75] Douglas B. Lenat. BEINGs: Knowledge as Interacting Experts. In *Proceedings of the 1975 International Joint Conference on Artificial Intelligence*, pages 126–133, 1975.

[Lenat87] Douglas B. Lenat and Edward A. Feigenbaum. On the Thresholds of Knowledge. In *Proceedings of the 1987 International Joint Conference on Artificial Intelligence*, August 1987. Also in *Proceedings of the Workshop on the Foundations of Artificial Intelligence*, Massachusetts Institute of Technology, June, 1987.

[Lesser80a] Victor R. Lesser and Lee D. Erman. Distributed Interpretation: A Model and Experiment. *IEEE Transactions on Computers*, C-29(12):1144–1163, December 1980.

[Lesser80b] Victor R. Lesser, Scott Reed, and Jasmina Pavlin. Quantifying and Simulating the Behavior of Knowledge-Based Interpretation Systems. In *Proceedings of 1980 Conference of the American Association for Artificial Intelligence*, pages 111–115, 1980.

[Lesser81] Victor R. Lesser and Daniel D. Corkill. Functionally Accurate, Cooperative Distributed Systems. *IEEE Transactions on Systems, Man and Cybernetics*, SMC-11(1):81–96, January 1981.

[Lesser82] Victor R. Lesser, Daniel D. Corkill, and Eva Hudlicka. Unifying Data-directed and Goal-directed Control: An Example and Experiments. In *Proceedings of 1982 Conference of the American Association for Artificial Intelligence*, pages 143–147, 1982.

[Lesser83] Victor R. Lesser and Daniel D. Corkill. The Distributed Vehicle Monitoring Testbed: A Tool For Investigating Distributed Problem Solving Networks. *AI Magazine*, 15–33, Fall 1983.

[Lesser87] Victor R. Lesser and Daniel D. Corkill. Distributed Problem Solving. In Stuart C. Shapiro, editor, *Encyclopedia of Artificial Intelligence*, pages 245–251, John Wiley and Sons, New York, 1987.

[Lesser88] Victor R. Lesser, Jasmina Pavlin, and Edmund H. Durfee. Approximate Processing in Real Time Problem Solving. *AI Magazine*, 9(1):49–61, Spring 1988.

[Levin77] James A. Levin and James A. Moore. Dialogue-Games: Metacommunication Structures for Natural Language Interaction. *Cognitive Science*, 1:395–420, 77.

[Lieberman83] Henry Lieberman. An Object-oriented Simulator for the Apiary. In *Proceedings of 1983 Conference of the American Association for Artificial Intelligence*, 1983.

[Lieberman86] Henry Lieberman. Delegation and Inheritance: Two Mechanisms for Sharing Knowledge in Object-Oriented Systems. In *ACM Conference on Object-Oriented Systems and Languagesd Langes*, 1986.

[MacIntosh87a] Douglas J. MacIntosh and Susan E. Conry. A Distributed Development Environment for Distributed Expert Systems. In *Proceedings of the 1987 Confeence on Expert Systems in Government*, IEEE Computer Society Press, 1987.

[MacIntosh87b] Douglas J. MacIntosh and Susan E. Conry. SIMULACT: A Generic Tool for Simulating Distributed Systems. In *Proceedings of the 1987 Eastern Simulation Conference*, 1987.

[Maimon85] Oded Z. Maimon. A Multi-Robot Control Experimental System with Random Parts Arrival. In *Proceedings of the IEEE International Conference on Robotics*, pages 895–899, IEEE, 1985.

[Malone83] Thomas W. Malone, Richard E. Fikes, and M.T. Howard. *Enterprise: A Market-Like Task Scheduler for Distributed Computing Environments*. Technical Report CISR-WP-111, Center for Information Systems Research, Sloan School, Massachusetts Institute of Technology, Cambridge, MA, October 1983.

[Malone84] Thomas W. Malone and Stephen A. Smith. Tradeoffs in Designing Organizations: Implications for New Forms of Human Organizations and Computer Systems. Sloan Working Paper 1541-84, Sloan School of Management, Massachusetts Institute of Technology, March 1984.

[Malone87a] Thomas W. Malone. Modeling Coordination in Organizations and Markets. *Management Science*, 33(10):1317–1332, 1987.

[Malone87b] Thomas W. Malone, Richard E. Fikes, Kenneth R. Grant, and Michael T. Howard. Market-Like Load Sharing in Distributed Computing Environments. April 1987. Working Paper 1785-86, Sloan School, Massachusetts Institute of Technology, Cambridge, MA.

[Malone88a] Thomas W. Malone. Organizing Information Processing Systems: Parallels Between Human Organizations and Computer Systems. In W. Zachary, S. Robertson, and J. Black, editors, *Cognition, Cooperation and Computation*, Ablex Publishing Corporation, Norwood, NJ, 1988.

[Malone88b] Thomas W. Malone, Richard E. Fikes, Kenneth R. Grant, and M. T. Howard. Enterprise: A Market-Like Task Scheduler for Distributed Computing Environments. In Bernardo A. Huberman, editor, *The Ecology of Computing*, Elsevier Science Publishers/North Holland, 1988.

[Manning77] Peter K. Manning. Rules in an Organizational Context. In J. Kenneth Benson, editor, *Organizational Analysis: Critique and Innovation*, pages 46–63, Sage Publications, Beverly Hills, CA, 1977.

[Marshak72] J. Marshak and R. Radner. *Economic Theory of Teams*. Yale University Press, 1972.

[Mason69] Richard O. Mason. A Dialectical Approach to Strategic Planning. *Management Science*, 15:B-403–B-414, 1969.

[Mason81] Richard O. Mason and Ian I. Mitroff. *Challenging Strategic Planning Assumptions*. John Wiley, 1981.

[Mason88] C. Mason, R. Johnson, R. Searfus, D. Lager, and T. Canales. A Seismic Event Analyzer for Nuclear Test Ban Treaty Verification. In *Proceedings of the Third International Conference on Applications of Artificial Intelligence in Engineering*, August 1988.

[Mazer86] Murray S. Mazer. Exploring the Link Between Office Information Systems and Distributed Problem-Solving Systems. In Frederick H. Lochovsky, editor, *Office and Database Systems Research '86*, Computer Systems Research Institute, University of Toronto, Toronto, July 1986. Technical Report Number CSRI-183.

[Mazer87a] Murray S. Mazer. Exploring the Use of Distributed Problem-Solving in Office Support Systems. In *Proceedings of the IEEE Computer Sociery Symposium on Office Automation*, pages 217–225, Gaithersburg, MD, April 1987.

[Mazer87b] Murray S. Mazer and Carson C. Woo. The Role of Representative Agents in Coordinating Distributed Problem Solving. In Frederick H. Lochovshy, editor, *Office and Database Systems Research '87*, pages 70–78, Technical Report CSRI-195, Computer Systems Research Institute, University of Toronto,, Toronto, ON., Canada, July 1987.

[Mazer88] Murray S. Mazer. Problems in Modeling Tasks and Task Views. In *Proceedings of the Conference on Office Information Systems*, pages 38–45, ACM Press, New York, March 1988.

[McArthur82a] David McArthur and Philip Klahr. *The ROSS Language Manual*. Technical Report N-1854-AF, Rand Corporation, Santa Monica, CA, September 1982.

[McArthur82b] David McArthur, Randall Steeb, and Stephanie Cammarata. A Framework for Distributed Problem Solving. In *Proceedings of 1982 Conference of the American Association for Artificial Intelligence*, pages 181–184, 1982.

[McClelland87] James L. McClelland, David E Rumelhart, and the PDP Research Group. *Parallel Distributed Processing: Explorations in the Microstructure of Cognition (2 Volumes)*. MIT Press, Cambridge, MA, 1987.

[McDermott78] Drew V. McDermott. Planning and Acting. *Cognitive Science*, 2(2):71–109, 1978.

[Mead34] George Herbert Mead. *Mind, Self, and Society*. University of Chicago Press, Chicago, 1934.

[Miller88a] Mark S. Miller and K. Eric Drexler. Comparative Ecology: A Computational Perspective. In Bernardo Huberman, editor, *The Ecology of Computation*, Elsevier Science Publishers/North Holland, 1988.

[Miller88b] Mark S. Miller and K. Eric Drexler. Markets and Computation: Agoric Open Systems. In Bernardo Huberman, editor, *The Ecology of Computation*, Elsevier Science Publishers/North Holland, 1988.

[Minsky79] Marvin Minsky. The Society Theory of Thinking. In *Artificial Intelligence: an MIT Perspective*, pages 423–450, MIT Press, Cambridge, MA, 1979.

[Minsky80] Marvin Minsky. K-Lines: A Theory of Memory. *Cognitive Science*, 4(2):117–133, 1980.

[Minsky86] Marvin Minsky. *The Society of Mind*. Simon and Schuster, New York, 1986.

[Morgenstern86] Leora Morgenstern. A First Order Theory of Planning, Knowledge, and Action. In Joseph Y. Halpern, editor, *Proceedings of the 1986 Conference on Reasoning About Knowledge*, pages 99–114, Morgan Kaufmann Publishers, San Mateo, CA, March 1986.

[Morgenstern87] Leora Morgenstern. Knowledge Preconditions for Actions and Plans. In *Proceedings of the 1987 International Joint Conference on Artificial Intelligence*, pages 867–874, 1987.

[Moses86] Yoram Moses and Mark R. Tuttle. Programming Simultaneous Actions Using Common Knowledge: Preliminary Version. In *Proceedings of the Symposium on the Foundations of Computer Science*, pages 208–221, 1986.

[Mukhopadhyay86] Uttam Mukhopadhyay, Larry Stephens, Michael Huhns, and Ronald Bonnell. An Intelligent System for Document Retrieval in Distributed Office Environments. *Journal of the American Society for Information Science*, 37:123–135, 1986.

[Newell72] Allen Newell and Herbert A. Simon. *Human Problem Solving*. Prentice Hall, Englewood Cliffs, NJ, 1972.

[Nii86a] H. Penny Nii. Blackboard Systems: Blackboard Application Systems, Blackboard Systems from a Knowledge Engineering Perspective. *AI Magazine*, 7(3):82–106, August (Conference edition) 1986.

[Nii86b] H. Penny Nii. Blackboard Systems: The Blackboard Model of Problem Solving and the Evolution of Blackboard Architectures. *AI Magazine*, 7(2):38–53, Summer 1986.

[Nii86c] H. Penny Nii. CAGE and POLIGON: Two Frameworks for Blackboard-Based Concurrent Problem-Solving. In *Proceedings of the DARPA Expert Systems Workshop*, Pacific Grove, CA, April 1986. Also Stanford Knowledge Systems Lab Report KSL-86-41, April, 1986.

[Nirenburg86] Sergei Nirenburg and Victor R. Lesser. Providing Intelligent Assistance in Distributed Office Environments. In *Proceedings of the ACM Conference on Office Information Systems*, pages 104–112, 1986.

[Oberquelle83] Horst Oberquelle, Ingbert Kupka, and Susanne Maass. A View of Human-Machine Communication and Co-operation. *International Journal of Man-Machine Studies*, 309–333, 1983.

[Parsons60] Talcot Parsons. *Structure and Process in Modern Society*. Free Press, New York, 1960.

[Parunak87] H. Van Dyke Parunak. Manufacturing Experience with the Contract Net. In Michael N. Huhns, editor, *Distributed Artificial Intelligence*, pages 285–310, Pitman Publishing/Morgan Kaufmann Publishers, San Mateo, CA, 1987.

[Pasquale88] Joseph C. Pasquale. *Intelligent Decentralized Control in Large Distributed Computer Systems*. PhD thesis, Department of Electrical Engineering and Computer Science, University of California, Berkeley, Berkeley, CA, April 1988. Also Technical Report 88-422, Department of EECS, U.C. Berkeley.

[Pattison87] H. Edward Pattison, Daniel D. Corkill, and Victor R. Lesser. Instantiating Descriptions of Organization Structures. In Michael N. Huhns, editor, *Distributed Artificial Intelligence*, pages 59–96, Pitman Publishing/Morgan Kaufmann Publishers, San Mateo, CA, 1987.

[Pavlin83] Jasmina Pavlin. Predicting the Performance of Distributed Knowledge-Based Systems: A Modeling Approach. In *Proceedings of 1983 Conference of the American Association for Artificial Intelligence*, pages 314–319, 1983.

[Pavlin84] Jasmina Pavlin and Daniel D. Corkill. Selective Abstraction of AI System Activity. In *Proceedings of 1984 Conference of the American Association for Artificial Intelligence*, pages 264–268, 1984.

[Pearl82] Judea Pearl. Reverend Bayes on Inference Engines: A Distributed Hierarchical Approach. In *Proceedings of 1982 Conference of the American Association for Artificial Intelligence*, pages 133–136, 1982.

[Pearl87] Judea Pearl. Distributed Revision of Composite Beliefs. *Artificial Intelligence*, 33(2):173–215, 1987.

[Pednault87] Edwin P.D. Pednault. Formulating Multiagent Dynamic-World Problems in the Classical Planning

Framework. In Michael P. Georgeff and Amy L. Lansky, editors, *Reasoning About Actions and Plans: Proceedings of the 1986 Workshop*, pages 47–82, Morgan Kaufmann Publishers, San Mateo, CA, 1987.

[Perrow67] Charles Perrow. A Framework for Comparative Organizational Analysis. *American Sociological Review*, 32(2):194–208, April 1967.

[Pollack87] Martha E. Pollack. A Model of Plan Inference that Distinguishes Between the Beliefs of Actors and Observers. In Michael P. Georgeff and Amy L. Lansky, editors, *Reasoning About Actions and Plans: Proceedings of the 1986 Workshop*, pages 279–296, Morgan Kaufmann Publishers, San Mateo, CA, 1987.

[Popper59] Karl R. Popper. *The Logic of Scientific Discovery*. Harper and Row, New York, 1959.

[Pruitt81] Dean G. Pruitt. *Negotiation Behavior*. Academic Press, 1981.

[Ramamritham85] Krithivasan Ramamritham and John A. Stankovic. Distributed Task Scheduling in Hard Real-Time Distributed System. *IEEE Software*, 7:65–75, 1985.

[Reddy82] Y.V. Reddy and Mark S. Fox. Knowledge Representation in Organization Modeling and Simulation: A Detailed Example. In *Proceedings of the Thirteenth Annual Pittsburgh Conference, Modeling and Simulation*, pages 685–691, 1982.

[Rice86] James P. Rice. *Poligon: A System for Parallel Problem Solving*. Technical Report KSL-86-19, Knowledge Systems Laboratory, Stanford University, Stanford, CA, April 1986. Also in *Proceedings of the DARPA Workshop on Expert Systems Technology Base*, Asilomar, April, 1986.

[Rieger81] Chuck Rieger and Steve Small. Toward a Theory of Distributed Word Expert Natural Language Parsing. *IEEE Transactions on Systems, Man and Cybernetics*, SMC-11(1):43–51, January 1981.

[Rosenblatt62] F. Rosenblatt. *Principles of Neurodynamics and the Theory of Brain Mechanisms*. Spartan Books, Washington, D.C., 1962.

[Rosenschein82] Jeffrey S. Rosenschein. Synchronization of Multi-Agent Plans. In *Proceedings of 1982 Conference of the American Association for Artificial Intelligence*, pages 115–119, 1982.

[Rosenschein83] Jeffrey S. Rosenschein and Vineet Singh. *The Utility of Meta-level Effort*. Technical Report HPP-83-20, Stanford Heuristic Programming Project, Stanford University, Stanford, CA, March 1983.

[Rosenschein85a] Jeffrey S. Rosenschein. *Rational Interaction: Cooperation Among Intelligent Agents*. PhD thesis, Computer Science Department, Stanford University, Stanford, CA, October 1985.

[Rosenschein85b] Jeffrey S. Rosenschein and Michael R. Genesereth. Deals Among Rational Agents. In *Proceedings of the 1985 International Joint Conference on Artificial Intelligence*, pages 91–99, August 1985.

[Rosenschein86] Jeffrey S. Rosenschein, M. Ginsburg, and Michael R. Genesereth. Cooperation Without Communication. In *Proceedings of 1986 Conference of the American Association for Artificial Intelligence*, pages 51–57, 1986.

[Rosenschein87a] Stanley J. Rosenschein. *Formal Theories of Knowledge in AI and Robotics*. Technical Report CSLI-87-84, Center for the Study of Language and Information, Stanford, CA, 1987.

[Rosenschein87b] Jeffrey S. Rosenschein and Michael R. Genesereth. Communication and Cooperation Among Logic-Based Agents. In *Proceedings of the Sixth Phoenix Conference on Computers and Communications*, pages 594–600, February 1987.

[Sacerdoti77] Earl D. Sacerdoti. *A Structure for Plans and Behavior*. Elsevier, New York, 1977.

[Sacerdoti78] Earl D. Sacerdoti. What Language Understanding Research Suggests About Distributed Artificial Intelligence. In *Proceedings of the 1978 DARPA Distributed Sensor Nets Workshop*, pages 8–11, Defense Advanced Research Projects Agency, 1978. Published by the Department of Computer Science, Carnegie MEllon University, Pittsburgh, PA.

[Sacks74] H. Sacks, E.A. Schegloff, and G. Jefferson. A Simplest Semantics for the Organization of Turn-Taking in Conversation. *Language*, 50:696–735, 1974.

[Sathi85] Arvind Sathi, Mark S. Fox, and Michael Greenberg. *Representation of Activity Knowledge for Project Management*. Technical Report, Carnegie Mellon University, 1985.

[Sathi86] Arvind Sathi, Thomas E. Morton, and Steven F. Roth. Callisto: An Intelligent Project Management System. *AI Magazine*, Winter:34–52, 1986.

[Schank77] Roger C. Schank and Robert P. Abelson. *Scripts, Plans, Goals and Understanding: An Inquiry into Human Knowledge Structures*. Lawrence Earlbaum Associates, Hillsdale, NJ, 1977.

[Schoen86] Eric Schoen. *The CAOS System*. Technical Report STAN-CS-86-1125, Computer Science Department, Stanford University, Stanford, CA, March 1986.

[Selfridge59] Oliver G. Selfridge. Pandemonium: A Paradigm for Learning. In D. Blake and A. Uttley, editors, *Proceedings of the Symposium on Mechanisation of Thought Processes*, pages 511–529, Her Majesty's Stationery Office, London, 1959.

[Shaw85] Michael J-P. Shaw and Andrew B. Whinston. Automatic Planning and Flexible Scheduling: A Knowledge-Based Approach. In *Proceedings of the IEEE International Conference on Robotics*, pages 890–894, IEEE, 1985.

[Shaw87] Michael J-P. Shaw. Distributed Planning in Cellular Flexible Manufacturing Systems. *INFOR*, 25(1):13–25, 1987.

[Shen85] C-C. Shen and W-H. Tsai. A Graph Matching Approach to Optimal Task Assignment in Distributed Computing Systems Using a Minimax Criterion. *IEEE Transactions on Computers*, C-34(3), March 1985.

[Shibutani86] Tamotsu Shibutani. *Social Processes*. University of California Press, Berkeley, CA, 1986.

[Silverman86] Barry G. Silverman. The Facility Advisor: A Distributed Expert System Testbed. In *Proceedings of the 1986 Conference on Expert Systems in Government*, IEEE Computer Society Press, 1986.

[Simon69] Herbert A. Simon. *The Sciences of the Artificial*. MIT Press, Cambridge, MA, 1969.

[Small82] Steve Small and Chuck Reiger. Parsing and Comprehending with Word Experts (A Theory and its Realization). In Wendy G. Lehnert and Martin H. Ringle, editors, *Strategies for Natural Language Processing*, Lawrence Earlbaum, Hillsdale NJ, 1982.

[Smith79] Reid G. Smith. A Framework for Distributed Problem Solving. In *Proceedings of the 1979 International Joint Conference on Artificial Intelligence*, pages 836–841, 1979.

[Smith80] Reid G. Smith. The Contract Net Protocol: High-Level Communication and Control in a Distributed Problem Solver. *IEEE Transactions on Computers*, C-29(12):1104–1113, December 1980.

[Smith81a] Reid G. Smith. *A Framework for Distributed Problem Solving*. UMI Research Press, 1981.

[Smith81b] Reid G. Smith and Randall Davis. Frameworks for Cooperation in Distributed Problem Solving. *IEEE Transactions on Systems, Man and Cybernetics*, SMC-11(1):61–70, 1981.

[Smith85a] Stephen F. Smith and Peng Si Ow. *The Use of Multiple Problem Decompositions In Time Constrained Planning Tasks*. Technical Report CMU-RI-TR-85-11, Carnegie-Mellon University, 1985.

[Smith85b] Reid G. Smith. Report on the 1984 Distributed Artificial Intelligence Workshop. *AI Magazine*, 6(3): 234–243, 1985.

[Sowizral84] Henry Sowizral. Experiences With Distributed Heuristic Agents in ROSIE. In *Proceedings of the International Conference on Systems, Man, and Cybernetics*, pages 355–358, January 1984.

[Sproull78] Robert F. Sproull and Dan Cohen. High-level Protocols. *Proceedings of the IEEE*, 66:1371–1386, 1978.

[Sproull81] Lee S. Sproull. Beliefs in Organizations. In Paul C. Nystrom and William H. Starbuck, editors, *Handbook of Organization Design*, chapter 9, pages 203–224, Oxford University Press, 1981.

[Sridharan87] N.S. Sridharan. Report on the 1986 Workshop on Distributed Artificial Intelligence. *AI Magazine*, 8(3):75–85, Fall 1987.

[Stankovic85] John A. Stankovic, Krithivasan Ramamritham, and Sheng-Chang Cheng. Evaluation of a Flexible Task Scheduling Algorithm for Distributed Hard Real-Time Systems. *IEEE Transactions on Computers*, C-34:1130–1143, 1985.

[Steeb81] Randall Steeb, Stephanie Cammarata, Frederick A. Hayes-Roth, Perry W. Thorndyke, and Robert B. Wesson. *Architectures for Distributed Intelligence for Air Fleet Control*. Technical Report R-2728-ARPA, Rand Corporation, Santa Monica, CA, 1981.

[Steeb84] Randall Steeb, David McArthur, Stephanie Cammarata, Sanjai Narain, and William Giarla. *Distributed Problem Solving for Air Fleet Control: Framework and Implementations*. Technical Report N-2139-ARPA, Rand Corporation, Santa Monica, CA, 1984.

[Steeb86] Randall Steeb, Stephanie Cammarata, Sanjai Narain, Jeff Rothenberg, and William Giarla. *Cooperative Intelligence for Remotely Piloted Vehicle Fleet Control*. Technical Report R-3408-ARPA, Rand Corporation, Santa Monica, CA, October 1986.

[Steels79] Luc Steels. *Reasoning Modeled as a Society of Communicating Experts*. Technical Report AI-TR-542, Artificial Intelligence Laboratory, Massachusetts Institute of Technology, Cambridge, MA, June 1979.

[Stefik88] Mark J. Stefik. The Next Knowledge Medium. In *The Ecology of Computation*, pages 315–342, North-Holland, New York, 1988.

[Strauss78] Anselm L. Strauss. *Negotiations: Varieties, Contexts, Processes and Social Order*. Jossey-Bass, San Francisco, 1978.

[Strauss85] Anselm L. Strauss, Shizuko Fagerhaugh, Barbara Suczek, and Carolyn Wiener. *The Social Organization of Medical Work*. University of Chicago Press, Chicago, IL, 1985.

[Stuart85] Christopher J. Stuart. An Implementation of a Multi-Agent Plan Synchronizer. In *Proceedings of the 1985 International Joint Conference on Artificial Intelligence*, pages 1031–1033, 1985.

[Stuart87] Christopher J. Stuart. Branching Regular Expressions and Multi-Agent Plans. In Michael P. Georgeff and Amy L. Lansky, editors, *Reasoning About Actions and Plans: Proceedings of the 1986 Workshop*, pages 161–188, Morgan Kaufmann Publishers, San Mateo, CA, 1987.

[Suchman87] Lucy Suchman. *Plans and Situated Actions: The Problem of Human-Machine Communication*. Cambridge University Press, New York, 1987.

[Sussman72] Gerald Sussman and Drew V. McDermott. *CONNIVER Reference Manual*. Technical Report AI Memo 259, Artificial Intelligence Laboratory Massachusetts Institute of Technology, 1972.

[Sycara85a] Katia P. Sycara. Arguments of Persuasion in Labor Mediation. In *Proceedings of the 1985 Inter-*

national Joint Conference on Artificial Intelligence, 1985.

[Sycara85b] Katia P. Sycara. Persuasive Argumentation in Resolution of Collective Bargaining Impasses. In *Proceedings of the Cognitive Science Society Conference*, pages 356–360, 1985.

[Sycara87] Ekaterini P. Sycara. *Resolving Adversarial Conflicts: An Approach Integrating Case-Based and Analytical Methods*. PhD thesis, School of Information and Computer Science, Georgia Institute of Technology, 1987. Also Technical Report GIT-ICS-87-26, Georgia Institute of Technology.

[Tenney79] Robert R. Tenney. *Distributed Decisionmaking Using A Distributed Model*. PhD thesis, Massachusetts Institute of Technology, Cambridge, MA, June 1979. Available as Technical Report LIDS-TD-938, Laboratory for Information and Decision Systems, Massachusetts Institute of Technology.

[Tenney81a] Robert R. Tenney and Nils R. Sandell Jr. Strategies for Distributed Decisionmaking. *IEEE Transactions on Systems, Man and Cybernetics*, SMC-11(8):527–538, 1981.

[Tenney81b] Robert R. Tenney and Nils R. Sandell Jr. Structures for Distributed Decisionmaking. *IEEE Transactions on Systems, Man and Cybernetics*, SMC-11(8):517–526, 1981.

[Theriault83] Daniel G. Theriault. *Issues in the Design and Implementation of ACT2*. Technical Report AI-TR-728, Artificial Intelligence Laboratory, Massachusetts Institute of Technology, Cambridge, MA, June 1983.

[Thompson67] James D. Thompson. *Organizations in Action*. McGraw Hill, New York, 1967.

[Thorndyke81] Perry W. Thorndyke, Dave McArthur, and Stephanie Cammarata. Autopilot: A Distributed Planner for Air Fleet Control. In *Proceedings of the 1983 International Joint Conference on Artificial Intelligence*, pages 171–177, 1981.

[Tokoro84] M. Tokoro and Y. Ishikawa. An Object-Oriented Approach to Knowledge Systems. In *Proceeedings of the International Conference on Fifth Generation Computer Systems*, pages 623–631, 1984.

[Veach86] Glenn Veach. *An Annotated Bibliography of Systems and Theory for Distributed Artificial Intelligence*. Technical Report TR-86-16, Computer Science Department, University of Kansas, 1986.

[Verrilli87] R.J. Verrrilli, K.L. Meunier, J.R. Dixon, and K.M. Simmons. Iterative Respecification Management: A Model For Problem Solving Networks in Mechanical Design. In *Proceedings of the ASME Computers in Engineering Conference*, August 1987.

[Vilain88] Mark Vilain. Heterogeneous Concurrency in a Parallel Truth Maintenance System. In *Proceedings of the 1988 Spring Symposium on Parallel Models of Intelligence: How Can Slow Components Think So Fast?*, pages 237–242, Computer Science Department, Stanford University, Stanford, CA, March 1988.

[Waldinger77] Richard Waldinger. Achieving Several Goals Simultaneously. In *Machine Intelligence 8*, pages 94–136, Ellis Horwood, 1977.

[Walker78] Donald E. Walker, editor. *Understanding Spoken Language*. North Holland, New York, 1978.

[Werner87] Eric Werner. Toward a Theory of Communication and Cooperation for Multiagent Planning. Working Paper, Department of Computer Science, Bowdoin College, Brunswick, Maine, 1987.

[Wesson81] Robert B. Wesson, Frederick A. Hayes-Roth, John W. Burge, Cathleen Stasz, and Carl A. Sunshine. Network Structures for Distributed Situation Assessment. *IEEE Transactions on Systems, Man and Cybernetics*, SMC-11(1):5–23, January 1981.

[Wilensky84] Robert Wilensky. *Planning and Understanding*. Addison-Wesley, 1984.

[Wilks83] Yorick Wilks and Janusz Bien. Beliefs, Points of View, and Multiple Environments. *Cognitive Science*, 7:95–119, 1983.

[Wilks87] Yorick Wilks and Afzal Ballim. Multiple Agents and the Heuristic Ascription of Belief. In *Proceedings of the 1987 International Joint Conference on Artificial Intelligence*, pages 118–124, August 1987.

[Willer81] David Willer and Bo Anderson. *Networks, Exchange, and Coercion*. Elsevier North Holland, New York, 1981.

[Winograd86] Terry Winograd and Fernando Flores. *Understanding Computers and Cognition*. Ablex, Norwood, NJ, 1986.

[Woo86] Carson C. Woo and Frederick H. Lochovsky. Supporting Distributed Office Problem Solving in Organizations. *ACM Transactions on Office Automation*, 4(3):185–204, July 1986.

[Wood83] Sharon Wood. Dynamic World Simulation for Planning with Multiple Agents. In *Proceedings of the 1983 International Joint Conference on Artificial Intelligence*, pages 69–71, 1983.

[Woolgar85] Steve Woolgar. Why Not a Sociology of Intelligent Machines? The Case of Sociology and Artificial Intelligence. *Sociology*, 19(4):557–572, November 1985.

[Yang85] Ju-Yuan D. Yang, Michael N. Huhns, and Larry M. Stephens. An Architecture for Control and Communications in Distributed Artificial Intelligence Systems. *IEEE Transactions on Systems, Man and Cybernetics*, SMC-15:316–326, 1985.

[Yeung86] Dit-Yan Yeung. Using CNET on the iPSC. USC DAI Group Research Note 20, Department of Computer Science, University of Southern California, Los Angeles, CA, 1986.

[Yonezawa86] Akinori Yonezawa, Jean-Pierre Briot, and Etsuya Shibayama. Object-Oriented Concurrent

Programming in ABCL/1. In *Proceedings of the 1986 Conference on Object-Oriented Programming Systems and Languages*, pages 258–268, 1986.

[Zachary88] W. Zachary, S. Robertson, and J. Black, editors. *Cognition, Computation, and Cooperation*. Ablex Publishing Corporation, Norwood, NJ, 1988.

Part II

Basic DAI Problems and Approaches

Chapter 3

Distribution and Task Allocation

The papers in this section treat various aspects of distributing control and problem-solving behavior among agents or nodes. A number of these papers investigate strategies for cooperation and organizational topologies — different ways of dividing the labor of problem solving. Taken together, these papers give us a good introduction to a wide array of distribution regimes (see also Chapter 1, Section 2). In general, they also provide insight into other aspects such as coordination and cooperation among problem solvers. Reid Smith and Randall Davis discuss two types of cooperation in distributed problem solving, which they call *task sharing* and *result sharing*. Task sharing cooperation is exemplified in their Contract Net in which problem-solving nodes opportunistically decompose tasks and share the work of getting subtasks done. In result sharing, each node works on some aspect of a problem and shares portions of its results with the other agents. Result sharing is a more implicit kind of cooperation that is useful when subproblem decomposition is difficult and/or when it leads to extensive interactions among subproblems. Both types of cooperation can achieve stability and fault tolerance if agents overlap tasks and cross check results.

Robert Wesson and coworkers studied two different distribution and task allocation organizations in the context of situation assessment using an automated distributed sensor network. They used an interesting synthetic game-like environment called the "message puzzle task" in which portions of messages move around screen that resembles a crossword puzzle. After investigating human performance, Wesson et al. studied several automated problem-solving organizations using task representations called *process assembly networks*. The organizations studied included a flat, non-hierarchical

("anarchic") organization of cooperating experts, and a two-level hierarchical organization.

Randall Steeb and coworkers present six different organizations for the problem of air-traffic control in their first paper, the core of a somewhat longer technical report. This domain exhibits the special requirements of critical real-time control, and unreliable and limited communication. By studying the distribution of the same processes in the six different organizations, the processes' different strengths and weaknesses were revealed. In the second paper on Rand air traffic control research, Cammarata et al. discuss several cooperation strategies as well as empirical studies of one simple type of organization based on completely centralized control. Three different methods of mutually choosing the central decision making aircraft were quantitatively compared.

The next several papers involve problem solving among somewhat more tightly coupled nodes. Richard Fennell and Victor Lesser discuss the mechanisms necessary for implementing a knowledge-based problem solving system with a blackboard architecture, such as HEARSAY-II, in a multiprocessing environment. The HEARSAY-II organization is extremely modular and involves dynamic redistribution of tasks that use some global and some local data. Fennell and Lesser focus on the mechanisms necessary for distributing control among a collection of knowedge sources that share a common resource—the blackboard. They report on simulation experiments that allowed them to characterize the multiprocessing performance of their mechanisms on speech understanding tasks.

In their classic paper from post-HEARSAY-II research, Victor Lesser and Lee Erman investigate the possibilities for distributing tasks in interpretation problem-solving. Distributed interpretation involves deciding how to interpret signal data using a collection of cooperating but geographically distributed nodes, and how to decompose a given interpretation technique for distribution. Most interpretation techniques use a problem-solving paradigm of searching for an overall solution the incrementally aggregating partial solutions. Lesser and Erman investigate the distribution of interpretation work over a network of HEARSAY-II blackboard systems. They envisioned an application domain that involved mobile processors equipped with sensing devices, interacting through a packet-radio communication network. The distribution was studied and evaluated using simulation experiments. This work was the direct precursor of the DVMT experiments run by Lesser and his colleagues through the 1980's (see also Chapter 4, Section 2, and Chapters 7 and 8).

Drawing upon conceptions from studies of human organizations, Mark Fox discusses distributed systems as organizations. Taking an information processing view of organization largely derived from the work of Herbert Simon and the "Carnegie School," Fox treats distributed systems as problem-solving organizations that have particular task decompositions and control regimes, resulting from the distribution of sets of tasks. He develops a very insightful scheme of organizational description, starting from Simon's notion of bounded rational-

ity, and using the dimensions of complexity and uncertainty reduction. Fox's work provides insight into the representation of organizational knowledge for DAI systems, as well as alternative perspectives on task allocation (see Chapter 1, Sections 2 and 5).

Finally, Tom Malone has made an attempt to describe the information processing and robustness properties of four organizational structures. The forms are derived from various mixes of product and functional decomposition, and hierarchical and market structures. Malone believes his four generic distributions model information processing pathways of both human organizations and distributed computer systems, treated as hierarchies and markets. He is interested in coordination structures to support organizations and particularly in evaluating the structures in terms of cost and fault tolerance. Like Fox's earlier paper, Malone's approaches provide some groundwork for representing and reasoning about organizational knowledge, which may be useful for organizational adaptation (see Chapter 1, Sections 1, 4, and 5).

The structural and information processing views of organizations expressed by Fox and Malone seem natural for mapping to distributed AI systems with fairly rigid structures. As we begin to explore more dynamic environments and more reconfigurable problem-solving architectures, other organizational models will undoubtedly emerge.

Frameworks for Cooperation in Distributed Problem Solving

REID G. SMITH, MEMBER, IEEE, AND RANDALL DAVIS

Abstract—Two forms of cooperation in distributed problem solving are considered: *task-sharing* and *result-sharing*. In the former, nodes assist each other by sharing the computational load for the execution of subtasks of the overall problem. In the latter, nodes assist each other by sharing partial results which are based on somewhat different perspectives on the overall problem. Different perspectives arise because the nodes use different knowledge sources (KS's) (e.g., syntax versus acoustics in the case of a speech-understanding system) or different data (e.g., data that is sensed at different locations in the case of a distributed sensing system). Particular attention is given to control and to internode communication for the two forms of cooperation. For each, the basic methodology is presented and systems in which it has been used are described. The two forms are then compared and the types of applications for which they are suitable are considered.

I. DISTRIBUTED PROBLEM SOLVING

DISTRIBUTED problem solving is the cooperative solution of problems by a decentralized and loosely coupled collection of knowledge sources (KS's) (procedures, sets of rules, etc.), located in a number of distinct processor nodes. The KS's *cooperate* in the sense that no one of them has sufficient information to solve the entire problem; mutual sharing of information is necessary to allow the group as a whole to produce an answer. By *decentralized* we mean that both control and data are logically and often geographically distributed; there is neither global control nor global data storage. Loosely coupled means that individual KS's spend the great percentage of their time in computation rather than communication.

Distributed problem solvers offer advantages of speed, reliability, extensibility, the ability to handle applications with a natural spatial distribution, and the ability to tolerate uncertain data and knowledge. Because such systems are highly modular they also offer conceptual clarity and simplicity of design.

Although much work has been done in distributed processing, most of the applications have not addressed issues that are important for the design of artificial intelligence (AI) problem solvers. For example, the bulk of the

Manuscript received January 28, 1980, revised September 1, 1980. This work was supported by the Department of National Defence of Canada, Research and Development Branch, and by the Advanced Research Projects Agency of the United States Department of Defense under Office of Naval Research Contract N00014-75-C-0643.

R. G. Smith is with the Defence Research Establishment Atlantic, Dartmouth, NS, Canada, B2Y 3Z7.

R. Davis is with the Artificial Intelligence Laboratory, Massachusetts Institute Of Technology, Cambridge, MA 02139.

processing is usually done at a central site with remote processors limited to basic data collection (e.g., credit card verification). While it is common to distribute data and processing, it is not common to distribute control, and the processors do not cooperate in a substantive manner.

Researchers in the area of distributed processing have not taken problem solving as their primary focus. It has generally been assumed, for example, that a well-defined and *a priori* partitioned problem exists and that the major concerns lie in an optimal static distribution of tasks, methods for interconnecting processor nodes, resource allocation, and prevention of deadlock. Complete knowledge of timing and precedence relations between tasks has generally been assumed, and the major reason for distribution has been taken to be load balancing (see for example [1], [3]). Distributed problem solving, on the other hand, includes as part of its basic task the partitioning of a problem.

Perhaps the most important distinction between distributed problem solving and distributed processing systems can be found by examining the origin of the systems and the motivations for interconnecting machines. Distributed processing systems often have their origin in an attempt to synthesize a network of machines capable of carrying out a number of widely disparate tasks. Typically, several distinct applications are envisioned, with each application concentrated at a single node (as for example in a three-node system intended to do payroll, order entry, and process control). The aim is to find a way to reconcile any conflicts and disadvantages arising from the desire to carry out disparate tasks, in order to gain the benefits of using multiple machines (sharing of data bases, graceful degradation, etc.). Unfortunately, the conflicts that arise are often not simply technical (e.g., word sizes and data base formats) but include sociological and political problems as well [6]. The attempt to synthesize a number of disparate tasks leads to a concern with issues such as access control and protection, and results in viewing cooperation as a form of *compromise* between potentially conflicting perspectives and desires at the level of system design and configuration.

In distributed problem solving, on the other hand, a single task is envisioned for the system, and the resources to be applied have no other predefined roles to carry out. A system is constructed *de novo*, and as a result the hardware and software can be chosen with one aim in mind: the selection that leads to the most effective environment for cooperative behavior. This also means that cooperation is viewed in terms of benevolent problem-solving behavior; that is, how can systems that are perfectly willing to accommodate one another act so as to be an effective team? Our concerns are thus with developing frameworks for *cooperative behavior between willing entities*, rather than frameworks for enforcing cooperation as a form of compromise between potentially incompatible entities.

This leads us to investigate the structure of interactions between cooperating nodes. We are primarily concerned with the *content* of the information to be communicated between nodes and the *use* of the information by a node for cooperative problem solving. We are less concerned with the specific *form* in which the communication is effected.

In this paper two forms of cooperation in distributed problem solving are considered: *task-sharing* and *result-sharing*. In the former, nodes assist each other by sharing the computational load for the execution of subtasks of the overall problem. In the latter, nodes assist each other by sharing partial results which are based on somewhat different perspectives on the overall problem. Different perspectives arise because the nodes use different KS's (e.g., syntax versus acoustics in the case of a speech-understanding system) or different data (e.g., data that is sensed at different locations in the case of a distributed sensing system).

For each form, the basic methodology is presented, and systems in which it has been used are described. The utility of the two forms is examined, and their complementary nature is discussed.

The physical architecture of the problem solver is not of primary interest here. It is assumed to be a network of loosely coupled, asynchronous nodes. Each node contains a number of distinct KS's. The nodes are interconnected so that each node can communicate with every other node by sending messages. No memory is shared by the nodes.

II. Cooperating Experts

A familiar metaphor for a problem solver operating in a distributed processor is a group of human experts experienced at working together, trying to complete a large task. This metaphor has been used in several AI systems [10]–[12], [18]. Of primary interest to us in examining the operation of a group of human experts is the way in which they interact to solve the overall problem, the manner in which the workload is distributed among them, and how results are integrated for communication outside the group.

It is assumed that no one expert is in total control of the others, although one expert may be ultimately responsible for communicating the solution of the top-level problem to the customer outside the group. In such a situation each expert may spend most of his time working alone on various subtasks that have been partitioned from the main task, pausing occasionally to interact with other members of the group. These interactions generally involve requests for assistance on subtasks or the exchange of results.

Individual experts can assist each other in at least two ways. First, they can divide the workload among themselves, and each node can independently solve some subproblems of the overall problem. We call this *task-sharing* (as in [11] and [18]). In this mode of cooperation, we are primarily concerned with the way in which experts decide who will perform which task. We postulate that one interesting method of effecting this agreement is via negotiation.

An expert (E1) may request assistance because he encounters a task too large to handle alone, or a task for which he has no expertise. If the task is too large, he will first partition it into manageable subtasks, and then attempt to find other experts who have the appropriate skills to handle the new tasks. If the original task is beyond his expertise, he immediately attempts to find another more appropriate expert to handle it.

In either case, if E1 knows which other experts have the necessary expertise, he can notify them directly. If he does not know anyone in particular who may be able to assist him (or if the task requires no special expertise), then he can simply describe the task to the entire group.

If another expert (E2) believes he is capable of carrying out the task that E1 described, he informs E1 of his availability and perhaps indicates any especially relevant skills he may have. E1 may discover several such volunteers and can choose from among them. The chosen volunteer then requests additional details from E1, and the two engage in further direct communication for the duration of the task.

Those with tasks to be executed and those capable of executing the tasks thus engage each other in a simple form of negotiation to distribute the workload. They form subgroups dynamically as they progress towards a solution.[1]

When subproblems cannot be solved by independent experts working alone, a second form of cooperation is appropriate. In this form, the experts periodically report to each other the partial results they have obtained during execution of individual tasks. We call this *result-sharing* (as, for example, in [12] and [13]). It is assumed in this mode of cooperation that problem partitioning has been effected *a priori* and that individual experts work on subproblems that have some degree of commonality (e.g., interpreting data from overlapping portions of an image).

An expert (E1) reports a partial result for his subproblem to his neighbors (E2 and E3) when that result may have some bearing on the processing being done by them. (For example, a partial result may be the best result that E1 can derive using only the data and knowledge available to him.) E2 and E3 attempt 1) to use E1's result to confirm or deny competing results for their subproblems, or 2) to

---

[1]Subgroups offer two advantages. First, communication among the members does not needlessly distract the entire group. This is important because communication itself can be a major source of distraction and difficulty in large groups (see, for example, [9]). Thus one of the major purposes of organization is to reduce the amount of communication that is needed. Second, the subgroup members may be able to communicate with each other in a language that is more efficient for their purpose than the language in use by the entire group.

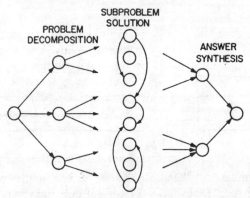

Fig. 1. Phases of distributed problem solving.

aggregate partial results of their own with E1's result to produce a result that is relevant to E1's subproblem as well as their own, or 3) to use E1's result to indicate alternative lines of attack that they might take to solve their own subproblems.

III. A Perspective On Distributed Problem Solving

In this section we present a model for the phases that a distributed problem solver passes through as it solves a problem (Fig. 1). The model offers a framework in which to anchor the two forms of cooperation that are the primary focus of this paper. It enables us to see the utility of the two forms, the types of problems for which they are best suited, and the way in which they are complementary.[2]

In the first phase, the problem is decomposed into subproblems. As Fig. 1 shows, the decomposition process may involve a hierarchy of partitionings. In addition, the process may itself be distributed in order to avoid bottlenecks. Decomposition proceeds until kernel (nondecomposable) subproblems are generated. Consider as an example a simple distributed sensing system (DSS). In the problem decomposition phase, the subproblems of detecting objects in specific portions of the overall area of interest are defined and distributed among the available sensors.

The second phase involves solution of the kernel subproblems. As shown in the figure, this may necessitate communication and cooperation among the nodes attempting to solve the individual subproblems. In the DSS example, communication is required in the subproblem solution phase 1) if objects can move from one area to another so that it is helpful for sensors to inform their neighbors of the movement of objects they have detected, or 2) if it is difficult for a single sensor to reliably detect objects without assistance from other sensors.

Answer synthesis is performed in the third phase; that is, integration of subproblem results to achieve a solution to the overall problem. Like problem decomposition, answer synthesis may be hierarchical and distributed. In the DSS

example, the answer synthesis phase involves generation of a map of the objects in the overall area of interest.

For any given problem, the three phases may vary in complexity and importance. Some phases may either be missing or trivial. For example, in the traffic-light control problem considered in [13], the problem decomposition phase involves no computation. Traffic-light controllers are simply placed at each intersection. For a DSS, the problem decomposition is suggested directly by the spatial distribution of the problem.[3]

There is also no answer synthesis phase for traffic-light control. The solution to a kernel subproblem is a smooth flow of traffic through the associated intersection. There is no need to synthesize an overall map of the traffic. Thus the solution to the overall problem *is* the solution to the kernel subproblems. (This is generally true of control problems; note that it does not mean, however, that communication among the nodes solving individual subproblems is not required.)

Many search problems (like symbolic integration [16]) also involve a minimal answer synthesis phase. Once the problem has been decomposed into kernel subproblems and they have been solved, the only answer synthesis required is recapitulation of the list of steps that have been followed to obtain the solution. However, for some problems the answer synthesis phase is the dominant phase. An example is the CONGEN program [4]. CONGEN is used in molecular structure elucidation. It generates all structural isomers that are both consistent with a given chemical formula and that include structural fragments known to be present in the substance (superatoms). In the problem decomposition phase, CONGEN generates all structures that are consistent with the data (by first generating intermediate structures, then decomposing those structures, and so on until only structures that contain atoms or superatoms remain). At this point, the superatoms (like the atoms) are considered by name and valence only. In the answer synthesis phase, the superatoms are replaced by the actual structural fragments they represent and are embedded in the generated structures. Because embedding can often be done in many ways, a sizable portion of the overall computation is accounted for by this phase.

IV. Caveats For Cooperation

One of the main aims in adopting a distributed approach is to achieve high-speed problem solving. In order to do this, situations in which processors "get in each other's way" must be avoided. This obviously depends on the problem itself (e.g., there are problems for which data or computation cannot be partitioned into enough mostly independent pieces to occupy all of the processors). Performance also depends, however, on the *problem-solving architecture*. It is therefore appropriate to consider frameworks for cooperation.

---

[2]It will be apparent that the model is also applicable to centralized problem solving. The distinct phases, however, are more obvious in a distributed problem solver, primarily because communication and cooperation must be dealt with explicitly in this case.

[3]Note that the problem solver must still implement even an obvious decomposition. Nodes must still come to an agreement as to which node is to handle which portion of the overall area.

It is common in AI problem solvers to partition expertise into domain-specific KS's, each of which is expert in a particular part of the overall problem. KS's are typically formed empirically, based on examination of different types of knowledge that can be brought to bear on a particular problem. In a speech-understanding problem, for example, knowledge is available from the speech signal itself, from the syntax of the utterances, and from the semantics of the task domain [7]. The decisions about which KS's are to be formed is often made in concert with the formation of a hierarchy of levels of data abstraction for a problem. For example, the levels used in the hierarchy of the HEARSAY-II speech-understanding system were parametric, segmental, phonetic, surface-phonemic, syllabic, lexical, phrasal, and conceptual [7]. KS's are typically chosen to handle data at one level of abstraction or to bridge two levels (see, for example, [7] and [15]).

Interactions among the KS's in a distributed processor are more expensive than in a uniprocessor because communication in a distributed architecture is generally much slower than computation. The framework for cooperation must therefore minimize communication among processors. Otherwise, the available communication channels may be saturated so that nodes are forced to remain idle while messages are transmitted.[4]

As a simple example of the difficulty that excessive communication can cause, consider a distributed processor with 100 nodes that are interconnected with a single broadcast communication channel. Assume that each of the nodes operates at 10^8 instructions per second; the computation and communication load is shared equally by all nodes, and the problem-solving architecture is such that one bit must be communicated by each node for every ten instructions that it executes. With these parameters it is readily shown that the communications channel must have a bandwidth of at least 1 Gbit/s (even ignoring the effect of contention for the channel) [18]. With a smaller bandwidth, processors are forced to stand idle waiting for messages.

There are, of course, many architectures that do not lead to channel bandwidths of the same magnitude. However, the point remains that special attention must be paid to internode communication and control in distributed problem solving if large numbers of fast processors are to be connected.

The framework for cooperation must also distribute the processing load among the nodes in order to avoid computation and communication bottlenecks. Otherwise, overall performance may be limited by concentration of disproportionate amounts of computation or communication at a small number of processors. It is also the case that the *control* of processing must itself be distributed. Otherwise, requests for decisions about what to do next could in time

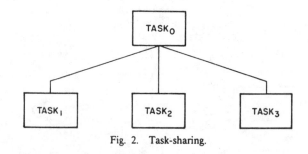

Fig. 2.   Task-sharing.

accumulate at a "controller" node faster than they could be processed.[5] Distribution of control does, however, lead to difficulties in achieving globally coherent behavior since control decisions are made by individual nodes without the benefit of an overall view of the problem. We will illustrate this problem in Section VII.

V.   TASK-SHARING

Task-sharing is a form of cooperation in which individual nodes assist each other by sharing the computational load for the execution of subtasks of the overall problem. Control in systems that use task-sharing is typically goal-directed; that is, the processing done by individual nodes is directed to achieve subgoals whose results can be integrated to solve the overall problem.

Task-sharing is shown schematically in Fig. 2. The individual nodes are represented by the tasks in whose execution they are engaged.

The key issue to be resolved in task-sharing is how tasks are to be distributed among the processor nodes. There must be a means whereby nodes with tasks to be executed can find the most appropriate idle nodes to execute those tasks. We call this the *connection problem*. Solving the connection problem is crucial to maintaining the focus of the problem solver. This is especially true in AI applications because they do not generally have well-defined algorithms for their solution. The most appropriate KS to invoke for the execution of any given task generally cannot be identified *a priori*, and there are usually far too many possibilities to try all of them.

In the remainder of this section, we consider negotiation as a mechanism that can be used to structure node interactions and solve the connection problem in task-shared systems. Negotiation is suggested by the observation that the connection problem can also be viewed from the perspective of an idle node. It must find another node with an appropriate task that is available for execution. In order to maximize system concurrency, both nodes with tasks to be executed and nodes ready to execute tasks can proceed simultaneously, engaging each other in a process that resembles contract negotiation to solve the connection problem.

In the contract net approach to negotiation [18], [19], a contract is an explicit agreement between a node that

---

[4]The focus here is on speed but the other reasons for adopting a distributed approach are also relevant—for example, reliability (i.e., the capability to recover from the failure of individual components, with graceful degradation in performance) and extensibility (i.e., the capability to alter the number of processors applied to a problem).

[5]Such a node would also be a hazard to reliability since its failure would result in total failure of the system.

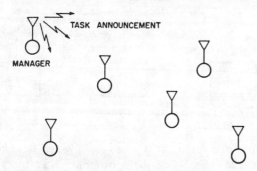

Fig. 3. Sending a task announcement.

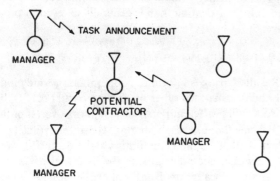

Fig. 4. Receiving task announcements.

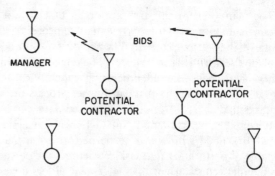

Fig. 5. Bidding.

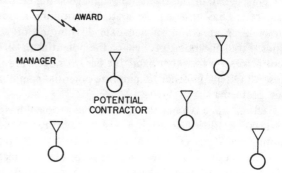

Fig. 6. Making an award.

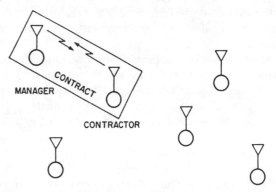

Fig. 7. Manager–contractor linkage.

generates a task (the manager) and a node willing to execute the task (the contractor). The manager is responsible for monitoring the execution of a task and processing the results of its execution. The contractor is responsible for the actual execution of the task. Individual nodes are not designated *a priori* as manager or contractor; these are only roles, and any node can take on either role dynamically during the course of problem solving. Nodes are therefore not statically tied to a control hierarchy.

A contract is established by a process of local mutual selection based on a two-way transfer of information. In brief, the manager for a task advertises the existence of the task to other nodes with a task announcement message (Fig. 3). Available nodes (potential contractors) evaluate task announcements made by several managers (Fig. 4) and submit bids on those for which they are suited (Fig. 5). An individual manager evaluates the bids and awards contracts for execution of the task to the nodes it determines to be most appropriate (Fig. 6). Manager and contractor are thus linked by a contract (Fig. 7) and communicate privately while the contract is being executed.

The negotiation process may then recur. A contractor may further partition a task and award contracts to other nodes. It is then the manager for those contracts. This leads to the hierarchical control structure that is typical of task-sharing. Control is distributed because processing and communication are not focused at particular nodes, but rather every node is capable of accepting and assigning tasks. This avoids bottlenecks that could degrade performance. It also enhances reliability and permits graceful degradation of performance in the case of individual node

failures. There are no nodes whose failure can completely block the contract negotiation process.

We have only briefly sketched the negotiation process. Several complications arise in its implementation, and a number of extensions to the basic method exist that enable efficient handling of specialized interactions where the full complexity is not required (e.g., when simple requests for information are made). See [19] for a full treatment.

The following is an example of negotiation for a task that involves gathering of sensed data and extraction of signal features. It is taken from a simulation of a distributed sensing system (DSS) [17]. The sensing problem is partitioned into a number of tasks. We will consider one of these tasks, the *signal* task, that arises during the initialization phase of DSS operation.[6]

[6]The DSS in general is an example of a system that uses both task-sharing and result-sharing. Task-sharing is used to initialize the system (the problem decomposition phase of Fig. 1).

The managers for this task are nodes that do not have sensing capabilities but do have extensive processing capabilities. They attempt to find a set of sensor nodes to provide them with signal features. The sensor nodes, on the other hand, have limited processing capabilities and attempt to find managers that can further process the signal features they extract from the raw sensed data.

Recall that we view node interaction as an agreement between a node with a task to be performed and a node capable of performing that task. Sometimes the perspective on the ideal character of that agreement differs depending on the point of view of the participant. For example, from the perspective of the *signal* task managers, the best set of contractors has an adequate spatial distribution about the surrounding area and an adequate distribution of sensor types. From the point of view of the potential *signal* task contractors, on the other hand, the best managers are those closest to them, in order to minimize potential communication problems.

Each message type in the contract net protocol has slots for task-specific information. The slots have been chosen to capture the types of information that are usefully passed between nodes to determine appropriate connections without excessive communication. For example, *signal* task announcements include the following slots.

1) A *task abstraction* slot is filled with the task type and the position of the manager. This enables a potential contractor to determine the manager to which it should respond.

2) The *eligibility specification* slot contents indicate that bidders must have sensing capabilities and must be located in the same area as the manager. This reduces extraneous message traffic and bid processing by explicitly specifying the attributes of a contractor that are deemed essential by the manager.

3) The *bid specification* slot contents indicate that a bidder must specify its position and the name and type of each of its sensors. This reduces the length of bid messages by specifying the information that a manager needs to select a suitable set of contractors.

The potential contractors listen to the task announcements from the various managers. If eligible, they respond to the nearest manager with a bid that contains the information specified in the task announcement. The managers use this information to select a set of bidders and then award *signal* contracts. The award messages specify the sensors that a contractor must use to provide signal-feature data to its manager.

Use of the contract net protocol in a DSS makes it possible for the sensor system to be configured dynamically, taking into account such factors as the number of sensor and processor nodes available, their locations, and the ease with which communication can be established.

Negotiation offers a more powerful mechanism for *connection* than is available in current problem-solving systems. The connection that is effected with the contract net protocol is an extension to the *pattern-directed invocation* used in many AI programming languages (see [5] for an

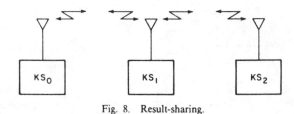

Fig. 8. Result-sharing.

in-depth discussion). It is most useful when tasks require specialized KS's, when the appropriate KS's for a given task are not known *a priori* and when the tasks are large enough to justify a more substantial transfer of information before invocation than is generally allowed in problem solvers.

VI. RESULT-SHARING

Result-sharing is a form of cooperation in which individual nodes assist each other by sharing partial results, based on somewhat different perspectives on the overall problem. In systems that use result-sharing, control is typically data-directed; that is, the computation done at any instant by an individual node depends on the data that it has available, either locally or from remote nodes. An explicit hierarchy of task–subtask relationships does not exist between individual nodes. Result-sharing is shown schematically in Fig. 8. The individual nodes are represented by KS's.

A simple example of the use of result-sharing is the development of consistent labelings for "blocks world" images [20]. A blocks world image is a line drawing that shows the edges of a collection of simple objects (e.g., cubes, wedges, and pyramids) in a scene. Each image is represented as a graph with nodes that correspond to the vertices of the objects in the image and arcs that correspond to the edges that connect the vertices. The goal is to establish a correspondence between nodes and arcs in the graph and actual objects.

A physically realizable vertex can be given a set of *a priori* possible labels based on the number of lines that meet at the vertex and the angles between the lines (e.g., "L," "T," "ARROW," and "FORK") [20]. A vertex is further specialized by the character of the lines that compose it (e.g., a line can define a convex boundary between surfaces of an object, a boundary between light and shadow, and so on). These labelings are established by examining the vertices in isolation. Ambiguity arises because generally more than one label is possible for each vertex. However, the number of possible labels can be reduced (often to a single label) by considering the constraints imposed by the interactions between vertices that share edges in an object. Very few of the large number of combinatorially possible vertex types can share an edge in a physically realizable object. Thus the key to achieving consistent image labeling is to compare the label set of each vertex with those of its neighbors and discard inconsistent labels.

If we partition the problem so that a processor node is responsible for one vertex in the image, then the basic

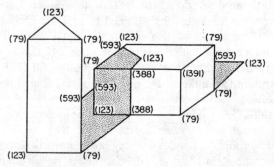

Fig. 9. Sample blocks world problem (from [21]).

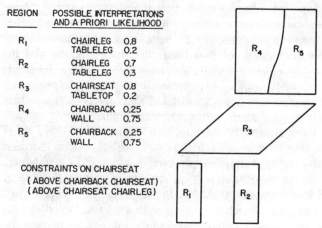

REGION	POSSIBLE INTERPRETATIONS AND A PRIORI LIKELIHOOD	
R₁	CHAIRLEG	0.8
	TABLELEG	0.2
R₂	CHAIRLEG	0.7
	TABLELEG	0.3
R₃	CHAIRSEAT	0.8
	TABLETOP	0.2
R₄	CHAIRBACK	0.25
	WALL	0.75
R₅	CHAIRBACK	0.25
	WALL	0.75

CONSTRAINTS ON CHAIRSEAT
(ABOVE CHAIRBACK CHAIRSEAT)
(ABOVE CHAIRSEAT CHAIRLEG)

Fig. 10. MSYS: sample problem.

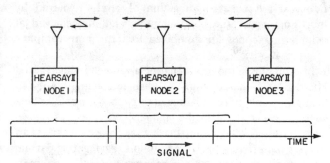

Fig. 11. Distributed interpretation: segmentation.

result-sharing process is evident. Nodes communicate their local label sets to their neighbors. Each node uses these remote label sets together with consistency conditions to prune its own label set. It then transmits the new label set to its neighbors. The process continues until unique labels have been established for all nodes or no further pruning is possible. (This process of iterative refinement of label sets is called *relaxation*, *constraint propagation*, or *range restriction*.)[7]

Fig. 9 shows a simple image considered by Waltz. The numbers shown in parentheses beside each vertex indicate the number of *a priori* labelings possible for that vertex, in the absence of any intervertex constraints.[8]

In addition to the ambiguity that arises in images from the blocks world, real images also suffer from ambiguity that arises as a result of noisy data and inaccurate feature detectors. The image is again considered to be a graph, but in this case the nodes correspond to small regions of the image [2], [22]. Examples of labels in this context are line segments with specified orientation, or objects (e.g., doors, chairs, and wastebaskets).

As with the blocks world problem, the aim is to establish unique labels for each node by considering contextual information from adjacent nodes. In this case, no absolute constraints are possible. Instead, the constraints (or *compatibilities* as they have also been called) express a degree of certainty that the labels associated with neighboring nodes are consistent (e.g., a line segment with a particular orientation detected at one node has a high degree of compatibility with another line segment with the same orientation detected at an adjacent node).

The method is initialized by associating a set of labels with each node on the basis of local feature detection. A numerical certainty measure is also assigned to each label. As before, nodes then communicate their local label sets to their neighbors. Instead of pruning its label set, each node uses these remote label sets to update the certainty measures associated with the labels in its own label set. The

updating is done on the basis of the interactions among labels described above, and strengthens or weakens the certainty measure for each label.[9] This process continues until unique labels have been established for all nodes (i.e., one label at each node has a large certainty measure with respect to those associated with the other labels for that node) or no further updating is possible.

Fig. 10 shows a sample collection of regions of the type considered by MSYS [2]. For each region, possible interpretations and their *a priori* likelihoods are shown. Also shown are the constraints placed on any region that is to be interpreted as a "chairseat." These constraints increase the certainty that the collection of regions should be interpreted as a chair.

Lesser and Erman [14] have experimented with distribution of the HEARSAY-II speech-understanding system [12]. Distribution has been effected by partitioning each utterance into segments overlapping in time and assigning each segment to a node. Fig. 11 shows the style of segmentation that has been implemented.

Each node attempts to develop an interpretation for the data to which it has access. It does this by creating partial interpretations or hypotheses and testing them for plausibility at each stage of the processing. (This is the classic AI paradigm of hypothesize and test.) A solution is constructed through the incremental aggregation of mutually constraining or reinforcing partial solutions while inconsistent partial solutions die out. Tentative decisions are

---

[7]Whereas a high-level protocol has been developed to facilitate task-sharing [19], no analogous protocol has emerged from research on result-sharing. We are presently examining the structure of communication for result-sharing with a view to extending the contract net protocol to better incorporate it.

[8]Waltz actually solved this problem using a centralized algorithm that considered only one vertex at a time. The algorithm required 80 iterations to produce a unique labeling for this image.

[9]Examples of updating algorithms are given in [23].

made on the basis of partial information and then reevaluated when further information becomes available (either in the form of more data or in the form of partial interpretations received from other nodes). Constraint in the speech-understanding domain is offered by the need for consistency of interpretation of the overlapping segments and by the syntactic and semantic constraints that one part of an utterance may place on another part.

The methods used by distributed HEARSAY-II are quite similar to those used by the image labeling systems. Successive refinement of hypotheses is effected in a manner similar to the updating of label sets. However, the image labeling systems achieve cooperation solely by mutual constraint or restriction on the results achieved by individual nodes. Distributed HEARSAY-II takes a more general approach. It achieves cooperation by both mutual restriction and by mutual aggregation of results achieved by individual nodes (i.e., partial interpretations achieved at neighboring nodes are combined to form more complete interpretations).[10]

In initial tests, the result-sharing approach in distributed HEARSAY-II has demonstrated an interesting ability to deal with ambiguity and uncertainty in data and knowledge. In a variation on the standard *search versus knowledge* trade-off, the result-sharing approach suggests an *aggregation versus knowledge* trade-off: aggregating partial, inexact solutions can at times be much easier than attempting to produce a single, complete and exact solution, and may in fact result in almost no loss of accuracy.

VII. TASK-SHARING AND RESULT-SHARING: A COMPARISON

Task-sharing is used to organize problem decomposition through formation of *explicit* task–subtask connections between nodes. The resultant hierarchy is also useful as a means of structuring answer synthesis. Task-sharing assumes that kernel subproblems can be solved by individual nodes working independently with minimal internode communication and that the major concern is efficient matching of nodes and tasks for high-speed problem solving. It is most useful for problem domains in which it is appropriate to define a hierarchy of tasks (e.g., heuristic search) or levels of data abstraction (e.g., audio or video signal interpretation). Such problems lend themselves to decomposition into a set of relatively independent subtasks

with little need for global information or synchronization. Individual subtasks can be assigned to separate processor nodes; these nodes can then execute the subtasks with little need for communication with other nodes. If this is the case, then task-sharing is a sufficiently powerful form of cooperation to handle all three phases of distributed problem solving.

Result-sharing is used to facilitate subproblem solution when kernel subproblems are such that they cannot be solved by individual nodes working independently without significant communication with other nodes. Result-sharing offers no mechanism for problem decomposition. Hence it can only be used alone as a form of cooperation for problems in which problem decomposition and distribution of subproblems to individual nodes are handled by an agent external to the distributed problem solver. Result-sharing does offer a minimal mechanism for answer synthesis. It is useful in this regard to the extent that the same result-sharing mechanism can be used for overall answer synthesis as well as subproblem solution.[11]

Result-sharing is most useful in problem domains in which 1) results achieved by one node influence or constrain those that can be achieved by another node (i.e., the results are relevant to each other), 2) sharing of results drives the system to converge to a solution to the problem (i.e., results received from remote nodes do not cause oscillation), and 3) sharing of results drives the system to a *correct* solution to the problem.

Minimization of internode communication is important for both the task-sharing and result-sharing forms of cooperation because of the computation/communication speed imbalance in distributed processors. The contract net protocol uses mechanisms like the eligibility specification slot in task announcements to reduce extraneous bid messages, while distributed HEARSAY-II uses a range of interesting mechanisms to limit the number of hypotheses communicated between nodes. One strategy, for example, is to only consider transmission of results for which no further refinement or extension is possible through local processing. (This type of result has been called "locally complete" [14].)

It has previously been stated [13] that the major advantage of result-sharing is its tolerance to uncertainty. However, it is interesting to note that task-sharing can also be used to achieve tolerance to uncertainty. Consider, for example, an application in which three nodes are trying to achieve a consistent interpretation of data that is taken from overlapping portions of an image. In a result-sharing approach they attempt to achieve consensus by communicating partial interpretations of the data. In a task-sharing approach, the three nodes each process their own part of

---

[10] Nodes in a result-sharing system are faced with a connection problem analogous to that described for task-sharing systems. In the result-sharing case, a node must select, from among all results generated, the particular results to be transmitted, as well as the other nodes to which they are to be transmitted. Similarly, upon receipt of a result, a node must decide whether or not to accept it, and what action to take based on the received result. Furthermore, we cannot generally assume that a node will communicate only with its neighbors. This would preclude the possibility of solving problems that involve *nonlocal interactions* between subproblems (e.g., although shadow regions in blocks world images may not be adjacent, they must be consistent with respect to their relation to the source of illumination). The problem is that we must distinguish between physical adjacency in the communication network and causal or *information-impact* adjacency.

[11] There still remain the problems of deciding when to terminate problem solving activity and deciding which node will communicate the answer to the customer outside the group. In the distributed HEARSAY-II system, all nodes will eventually derive an interpretation for the whole utterance. This may be acceptable for a three node system, but will lead to an unacceptable amount of communication for a larger system.

the data but then, instead of communicating their partial interpretations directly to each other, they communicate them to a fourth node (a manager in contract net terms) that has the task of sorting out the inconsistencies. This node periodically retasks the three other nodes, using the most current data and partial interpretations.[12]

This brief example does bring out a major difference between the two approaches, namely, that result-sharing is a more *implicit* form of cooperation than task-sharing. Cooperation and convergence are achieved by careful design of individual KS's so that they can make meaningful use of results received from remote KS's. Task-sharing, on the other hand, makes the cooperation explicit by setting up formal lines of communication and inserting nodes whose specific task is to integrate the partial interpretations from the nodes that operate on the actual data.

The example also illustrates one of the major unsolved problems in distributed problem solving—how to achieve coherent behavior with a system in which control is distributed among a number of autonomous nodes. When the number of tasks or results that could be processed exceeds the number of available nodes, then nodes with tasks or results to share must compete for the attention and resources of the group.

In the case of task sharing, mechanisms must be designed that give some assurance that individual subproblems are actually processed, that processors do not get in each other's way in trying to solve identical subproblems while other subproblems are inadvertently ignored. In addition, it is very important that the subproblems that eventually lead to solutions be processed in preference to subproblems that do not lead to solutions. We have suggested negotiation as a mechanism for dealing with these difficulties and have designed the contract net protocol with them in mind [19]. However, it is apparent that much work remains to be done.

In the case of result sharing, there must be some assurance that nodes influence each other in such a way as to converge to a correct solution. Just as partial results received from a remote node can suggest fruitful new lines of attack for a problem, they can also be distracting. In recent work on result sharing systems, it has been seen that certainty measures generated at different nodes can be particularly difficult to integrate. In distributed HEARSAY-II, for example, it was found that certainty measures used in a centralized approach are not necessarily appropriate for a distributed formulation. The effect was that remotely generated results sometimes caused nodes to pursue lines of attack that were not as fruitful as the ones they had been pursuing before receipt of those results. Some evidence of this phenomenon can be inferred from the experiments that were performed in which some results

were lost in transmission. In some cases, system performance actually improved, an indication that nodes sometimes distract their neighbors. Once again, much work remains to be done in this area.

VIII. CONCLUSION

Two complementary forms of cooperation in distributed problem solving have been discussed: task-sharing and result-sharing. These forms are useful for different types of problem and for different phases of distributed problem solving. Task-sharing is useful in the problem decomposition and answer synthesis phases of distributed problem solving. It assumes that subproblem solution can be achieved with minimal communication between nodes. Result-sharing is useful in the subproblem solution phase when kernel subproblems cannot be solved by nodes working independently without communication with other nodes. It is also helpful to some extent in the answer synthesis phase—in particular, for problems in which the answer synthesis phase is essentially a continuation of the subproblem solution phase. We eventually expect to see systems in which both forms of cooperation are used, drawing upon their individual strengths to attack problems for which neither form is sufficiently powerful by itself.

ACKNOWLEDGMENT

These ideas have evolved as a result of many discussions with our colleagues. The contributions of Victor Lesser, Rick Hayes-Roth, and Steve Zucker have been particularly helpful.

REFERENCES

[1] J. L. Baer, "A survey of some theoretical aspects of multiprocessing," *Comput. Surveys*, vol. 5, pp. 31–80, Mar. 1973.

[2] H. G. Barrow and J. M. Tenenbaum, "MSYS: A system for reasoning about scenes," SRI International, Menlo Park, CA, SRI AIC TN 121, Apr. 1976.

[3] E. K. Bowdon, Sr., and W. J. Barr, "Cost effective priority assignment in network computers," in *FJCC Proc.*, vol. 41. Montvale, NJ: AFIPS Press, 1972, pp. 755–763.

[4] R. E. Carhart, D. H. Smith, H. Brown, and C. Djerassi, "Applications of artificial intelligence for chemical inference—XVII: An approach to computer-assisted elucidation of molecular structure," *J. Amer. Chem. Soc.*, vol. 97, pp. 5755–5762, Oct. 1, 1975.

[5] R. Davis and R. G. Smith, "Negotiation as a metaphor for distributed problem solving," in preparation.

[6] C. R. D'Olivera, *An Analysis Of Computer Decentralization*, Massachusetts Inst. Technol., Cambridge, MIT LCS-TM-90, Oct. 1977.

[7] L. D. Erman and V. R. Lesser, "A multi-level organization for problem solving using many, diverse, cooperating sources of knowledge," in *Proc. 4th Int. Joint Conf. Artificial Intelligence*, Sept. 1975, pp. 483–490.

[8] M. S. Fox, "An organizational view of distributed systems," *IEEE Trans. Syst. Man, Cybern.*, vol. SMC-11, pp. 70–80, Jan. 1981, this issue.

[9] J. R. Galbraith, "Organizational design: An information processing view," in *Organizational Psychology*, 2nd ed., D. A. Kolb *et al.*, Eds. Englewood Cliffs, NJ: Prentice-Hall, 1974, pp. 313–322.

[10] C. Hewitt, "Viewing control structures as patterns of passing messages," *Artificial Intelligence*, vol. 8, pp. 323–364, 1977.

---

[12] In organization theoretic terms, the fourth node carries out an "integrating role." Hierarchical control of this type is a standard mechanism used by human organizations to deal with uncertainty [9], [8]. In the contract net approach, the managers for tasks are in the best position to perform such duties.

[11] D. B. Lenat, "Beings: Knowledge as interacting experts," in *Proc. 4th Int. Joint Conf. Artificial Intelligence*, Sept. 1975, pp. 126–133.

[12] V. R. Lesser, R. D. Fennell, L. D. Erman, and D. R. Reddy, "Organization of the HEARSAY II speech understanding system," *IEEE Trans. Acoust., Speech, Signal Processing*, vol. ASSP-23, pp. 11–24, Feb. 1975.

[13] V. R. Lesser *et al.*, "Working papers in distributed computation I: Cooperative distributed problem solving," Dep. Comput. and Inform. Sci., Univ. of Massachusetts, Amherst, July 1979.

[14] V. R. Lesser and L. D. Erman, "Distributed interpretation: A model and experiment, *IEEE Trans. Comput.*, vol. C-29, pp. 1144–1163, Dec. 1980.

[15] H. P. Nii and E. A. Feigenbaum, "Rule-based understanding of signals," in *Pattern-Directed Inference Systems*, D. A. Waterman and F. Hayes-Roth, Eds. New York: Academic, 1978, pp. 483–501.

[16] N. J. Nilsson, *Problem Solving Methods In Artificial Intelligence*. New York: McGraw-Hill, 1971.

[17] R. G. Smith and R. Davis, "Applications of the contract net framework: Distributed sensing," *Proc. ARPA Distributed Sensor Net Symp.*, pp. 12–20, Dec. 1978.

[18] R. G. Smith, "A framework for problem solving in a distributed processing environment," Dep. Comput. Sci., Stanford Univ., Stanford, CA, STAN-CS-78-700 (HPP-78-28) Dec. 1978.

[19] ____, "The contract net protocol: High-level communication and control in a distributed problem solver," *IEEE Trans. Comput.*, vol. C-29, pp. 1104–1113, Dec. 1980.

[20] D. L. Waltz, "Generating semantic descriptions from drawings of scenes with shadows," Massachusetts Inst. Technol., Cambridge, MIT AI-TR-271, Nov. 1972.

[21] P. H. Winston, *Artificial Intelligence*. Reading, MA: Addison-Wesley, 1977.

[22] S. W. Zucker, R. A. Hummel, and A. Rosenfeld, "An application of relaxation labelling to line and curve enhancement," *IEEE Trans. Comput.*, vol. C-26, pp. 394–403, Apr. 1977.

[23] S. W. Zucker, Y. G. Leclerc, and J. L. Mohammed, "Continuous relaxation and local maxima selection," Dep. Elec. Eng., McGill Univ., Rep. 78-15R, Dec. 1978.

Network Structures for Distributed Situation Assessment

ROBERT WESSON, FREDERICK HAYES-ROTH, JOHN W. BURGE, CATHLEEN STASZ,
AND CARL A. SUNSHINE

Abstract—A new approach to situation assessment is an automated distributed sensor network (DSN) consisting of many "intelligent" sensor devices that can pool their knowledge to achieve an accurate overall assessment of a situation. Laboratory experiments were conducted to investigate potential DSN organizations and to ascertain some general design principles. These experiments have been performed with a network of "sensor nodes," each of whom sees only a small portion of the entire environment and attempts to identify the environmental mobile entities as quickly as possible. To do this, they must cooperatively communicate their hypotheses and data, using a limited number of messages. Two general DSN organizations were tested. The first was hierarchical. The second was an "anarchic committee" whose nodes could each send messages to one, some, or all other nodes. The performance of the committee organization consistently surpassed the hierarchical one. This lent support to the contention that DSN architectures need to emphasize cooperative aspects of problem-solving. A machine-based simulation of such a network that achieved performance levels comparable to that of the human committee DSN organization was also constructed and tested. Because most situation assessment communications concern hypothesis updating and revision, minimizing communication requirements through the concept of active "hypothesis processes," which are responsible for predicting their own evolution over time, is suggested.

Manuscript received January 24, 1980; revised August 26, 1980.

R. Wesson, F. Hayes-Roth, and C. Stasz are with The Rand Corporation, 1700 Main Street, Santa Monica, CA 90406.

J. W. Burge was with The Rand Corporation, Santa Monica, CA. He is now with Operating Systems, Inc., Woodland Hills, CA 91364.

C. A. Sunshine was with The Rand Corporation, Santa Monica, CA. He is now with the Information Science Institute, University of Southern California, Marina Del Rey, CA 90291.

I. INTRODUCTION

SITUATION ASSESSMENT (SA) involves acquiring, organizing, and abstracting information about the environment which may either correlate well with our expectations or serve to create new ones. Large-scale SA usually involves a network of information producers and consumers handling information which varies by locale, amount of aggregation, and level of abstraction. Timely situation assessments in current military environments require systems that can process more of this information faster than ever before.

New information processing technologies suggest automating more of the SA task. Advances in microprocessors, packet-switching radio communications, sensors, and artificial intelligence methods for automated problem-solving, all combine to form the foundations of a highly automated, low-cost, intelligent, distributed sensor network (DSN) (see Fig. 1). A DSN consisting of inexpensive intelligent nodes scattered across a battlefield is expected to be useful in acquiring noisy intelligence data, processing it to reduce uncertainty and produce higher level interpretations, and transmitting this abstracted information quickly to the commanders who require it. The development of distributed sensor networks is proceeding rapidly, both for this problem area (see especially [1] and [2]) and other related ones, such as traffic control [3] and industrial control [4].

The research reported here addresses the basic question, "What computer network organizational structures are best suited to the situation assessment task?" In attempting to characterize suitable structures for a DSN, we have been influenced by several general hardware trends: processing power is increasing at the same rapid rate that hardware costs are decreasing; communication capabilities are also becoming better and less costly, but significantly more slowly than computational power; and low-cost and low-power sensors are likely to remain moderately unreliable. We have attempted to keep our research sensitive to the foregoing relationships among DSN elements while remaining unrestricted by specific current hardware designs and constraints.

We previously described two structures that seemed appropriate for SA tasks [5]. One, a committee structure, facilitates communication and reorganization, while another one, more strictly hierarchical, presumably fosters the apprehension of a superior global problem perspective. To compare these structures we performed research based upon a simplified SA task. This experimental task was created by converting many of the elements of a battlefield SA task into more familiar information processing problems. Specifically, messages (moving words and phrases) move in a snake-like manner through a field sparsely littered with obstructions before stopping at their final destinations. From a DSN perspective the words represent moving platforms that emit spectral signals. The task is to identify incoming platforms as quickly as possible before they reach their destinations. Each member of the organization is limited in his field of view, so cooperation is imperative for the organization to perform its mission well.

In these experiments the committee organization consistently outperformed the hierarchical one. Our analysis of the results leads us to believe that DSN designers should

Fig. 1. Distributed sensor network.

emphasize cooperative aspects of problem-solving rather than issues like subgoaling or problem reduction. Communication requirements can be reduced if passive data hypotheses are replaced by active hypothesis processes that predict their own evolution over time. We describe a process assembly network (PAN) that enables nodes to represent and predict the "belief systems" of its relevant neighbors. By doing so, it replaces the typically frequent data reporting task with a system in which only the unexpected needs to be reported.

We have performed both man–machine and machine-only experiments to compare alternative organizations. The next section expands the preceding description of the laboratory task and the two organizations tested. It describes the experiments we performed and their results. Integrated with previous work from organization theory, our laboratory experiences refined our thoughts about DSN designs—Section III explicates them in general terms. Then, turning specifically to machine-based DSN structures, we end with a section about pure machine DSN's. We describe a set of experiments in which a computer program performed the message puzzle task (MPT), and suggest better and more complex designs for eventual implementation. This paper ends with an appendix containing some "heuristics of cooperation" identified during our studies.

II. Bringing Distributed Situation Assessment into The Laboratory

The question, "Which organizational structures are best suited to SA tasks?" is too general and abstract to address directly. To start with, the notion of "organizational structure" must be clarified. The following broad questions touch only a few of its aspects which we could examine.

- *Control hierarchies*: How many levels of managerial authority should the SA structure have?
- *Hypothesis formulation and sharing*: Who should construct the more abstract or more aggregated world views? How is formulation of high-level interpretations related to structure? Who should communicate them out of the network?

- *Communication*: What is the most efficient communication network structure? Who needs to talk to whom?
- *Raw data acquisition and sharing*: Should the nodes that acquire raw data send it to a higher level for further processing or deal with it directly?
- *Adaptation to environmental changes*: Which structures most readily adjust to rapid external changes? Within a structure, what constitutes an effective change?

Next, what is a representative situation assessment task suitable for laboratory experimentation? We required a problem in which confusing, perishable, and componential information could be aggregated to interpret and explain high-level events. Military battlefield environments, like many other environments faced by organizations, are too complex and ill-defined to support this type of laboratory analysis, so we needed to construct a reduced domain which captured the essence of the generic case. Our requirements for this task included:

- a battlefield-like scenario consisting of objects moving around both individually and in formation, because the problem should support typical kinds of actions, such as concealment and cover, coordinated attacks, and feints;
- multiple sensors, each of which can see some, but not all, of the low-level activities, because reported data must contain errors and permit incompleteness;
- perishable data, in the sense that information value depends critically on timely processing;
- limited communication among processors so that the communication–computation trade-off could be investigated;
- a rich data environment, because enough information must be present in the data to allow the system to overcome the above limitations and achieve a solution.

We designed an experimental task manifesting these characteristics and used it to study the organizational facets outlined above. This task has formed the foundation for all of our experimental work in this area.

The Message Puzzle Task

The testbed designed for these experiments is a game-like environment with multiple players cooperating at a task. It is called the message puzzle task (MPT) because messages consisting of words and phrases move about in a puzzle-like two-dimensional grid. A group of players, each of whom can see only a small portion of the grid, must communicate among themselves and identify the moving items as quickly and accurately as possible. Fig. 2 represents this task pictorially. All of our experimental tasks used 15×15 puzzle boards, divided up into nine overlapping views. Each view measures approximately 6×6 squares in size.

This task, although apparently quite simple, requires very sophisticated information processing capabilities and cooperative strategies. To interpret the data in their own view and other data received over the message channels,

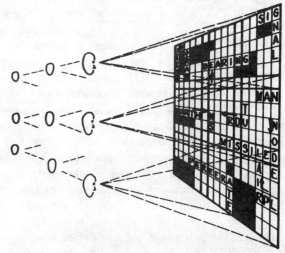

Fig. 2. Message puzzle task (MPT).

the players need to

- autocorrelate successive sensor reports, using past letter and word motions to achieve a current understanding of the contents of their portion of the grid;
- filter out noise and modify their reports of raw data accordingly;
- infer or detect terrain features (black squares blocking motion);
- send or request raw data such as complete views, the locations of black squares, and the like;
- hypothesize and extrapolate tracks or unit identities to match their own sensor reports with those of adjacent nodes;
- send or request hypotheses of the above;
- maintain a time history of hypotheses in order to assist future hypothesis generation;
- predict future behaviors of elements;
- hand off tracking, hypothesizing, and guessing responsibilities to other nodes;
- assign or request processing resources and task responsibilities.

The MPT has the most important characteristics of typical situation assessment tasks: information exists and must be processed at multiple levels of abstraction; elements in the world are constantly moving or changing; no single individual can solve the task alone, so cooperation is required for success; the many constraints present in the data and its motion allow effective processing in the context of perishable and errorful data; and the communication channels between individual nodes are severely limited relative to the processing capability of each node.

Organizations Tested

Within this task environment we tested two very different organizational structures as candidates for similar tasks. The first organization we chose to study was a "flat" non-hierarchical organization. In the artificial intelligence (AI) literature this type of structure is commonly known as the "cooperating experts" paradigm. Perhaps the best-known AI work of this type is exemplified by the Hearsay-II speech understanding system [7]. Organizational theory uses the term "type X" organizations to denote this class [6], and points to crisis management teams and small research and development firms with loose management styles as examples. In general, organizations of "cooperating experts" are composed of specialists with little or no hierarchical structure. Such organizations solve problems by sharing individual perspectives, which refine and ultimately integrate local interpretations into a unified group consensus. Subtasking, reporting requirements, and resource allocation decisions are generally not specified *a priori*. The organization forms behavior and communication patterns dynamically in response to the environment and changes the patterns in a data-directed way.

In direct contrast to the "cooperating experts" paradigm lies the very hierarchical "theory Y" or "perceptual cone" organizations. The former name comes from organizational theory [6] which points to large established steady-state firms as an example. The latter term comes from early AI work in pattern recognition [8]. Organizations of this class are assembled as strict hierarchies of abstraction levels. At each level individual elements receive reports from the levels below them, integrate the reports according to their special skills and position in the hierarchy, and report upward abstracted versions of their results. The highest level of the network may repeatedly order its subordinates to adjust some previous reports in accordance with its own global perspectives, or it can report the overall interpretation it has formed. As each node has precisely specified input/output (I/O) activity and task requirements, this type of organization is generally found in domains requiring routine, but complex, information processing. The "cooperating experts" organizations tend to be favored in less complex, but more uncertain or rapidly changing, environments.

The MPT domain clearly involves complex and routine information processing. Letters must always be tracked and combined together into fragments which must then be used to generate word and phrasal guesses. On the other hand, it is also a highly uncertain and rapidly changing environment in which noisy data and node failures occur unpredictably.

Since our MPT, and the full SA task, exhibit features which suggest that each organizational structure might be suitable, we tested both. The first structure became known as the anarchic committee (AC) to reflect the absence of overt governmental structure and the tendency for this organization to spawn many overlapping committees to perform specific tasks. The second structure was tested in the form of a dynamic hierarchical cone (DHC). The DHC is a "perceptual cone" organization, modified to be more responsive to either a spatially unbalanced or rapidly changing data flow. We have described both organizations in a previous paper [5]. Thus our treatment here will be brief.

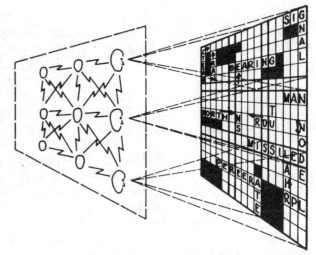

Fig. 3. Anarchic committee (AC).

Illustrated in Fig. 3, the AC consists of the nine nodes shown in Fig. 2 and a fully interconnected communications network. It is designed to exhibit minimal organizational constraints. Message passing, for example, is especially simple, since complete simultaneous broadcasting is provided. Each node can communicate with any other node. Messages sent to "all" are delivered to all nine nodes. Additionally, the structure imposes no natural authority decomposition. We assumed that cooperation would occur via the formation of geographic committees sharing data on particular words and phrases. Coordination between these mutually supportive committees was expected to be limited and, at best, *ad hoc*.

The DHC, on the other hand, was expected to coordinate its elements much more easily, by virtue of its structure. As shown in Fig. 4, two levels of "manager" nodes were added to the basic nine positions from the AC. Conceptually "above" the nine low-level (LL) nodes were three middle-level (ML) nodes. Above the ML was a single high-level (HL) node. Communication was restricted to flow between adjacent layers, but not within a layer. Each of the nine LL nodes had the same view of the puzzle as in the AC, but they could only communicate directly with the three ML nodes. The single "top" level node could only communicate with the middle levels. All four higher level nodes received no message data reports of their own, but had to rely on reports from low-level ones.

There is a natural allocation of authority in this structure. ML nodes were expected to function as "middle managers," carrying out the instructions of the HL one who presumably would acquire the most global perspective. The LL nodes were expected to function as intelligent sensors, preprocessing data for subsequent integration by their ML managers. The assignment of low-level nodes to middle-level managers was left open, allowing the managers to establish whatever scope of responsibility and reporting structures seemed appropriate, and to reconfigure them as events unfolded.

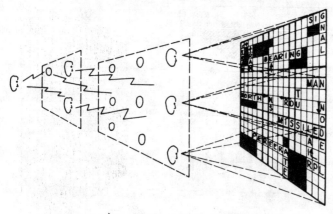

Fig. 4.   Dynamic hierarchical cone (DHC).

Communication restrictions were imposed on both organizations. Each node could generate a prespecified number of messages per unit time. Message reception and processing was limited only by the nodes' abilities to process the incoming data. Other than these, no *a priori* restrictions were placed on nodes' utilization of communication resources.

Human-Based Network Experiments

Apparatus, Subjects, and Procedure: A major goal of the initial experiments, in which human players acted as nodes, was to capture information on the activity of nodes in a form suitable for analysis. This led us from the start to consider a computer-based testbed that could provide better tools for each node to perform its task, and, at the same time, could record traces and performance data automatically. In the system that resulted, each node is provided with a cathode-ray tube (CRT) terminal. Using this terminal, he may send messages to other nodes (with the constraints of the problem), make official reports of puzzle entities to an outside "controller," and display his current view of the grid (if he has one).

Using this testbed and the organizations described above, we conducted a series of informal experiments. These experiments were not designed with strict experimental controls to permit formal hypothesis testing. Rather, they were undertaken to develop familiarity with the limitations imposed by each of the organizational structures and to derive heuristics for use by a computer program that would support properly controlled experiments. Six separate trials or "problems" were run. Three trials employed the AC organizational structure, and three employed the DHC structure. A different puzzle was used in each case.

Prior to each trial, subjects met to receive node assignments (i.e., node position) and to develop standard problem-solving strategies and procedures. These standards covered both low-level conventions for formatting messages (e.g., "In messages, indicate that a word was already officially guessed by marking it 'g!'"), and higher level strategies (e.g., "To reduce repetitious official guesses, send formal hypotheses for external communication to HL who

alone would report them"). Nodes also exchanged information about how they approached their individual problem-solving tasks, such as methods for tracking word or letter motions. These planning meetings lasted about 30 min. The subjects then performed the task. The total time for each problem was about 1 h. A short debriefing followed, in which subjects provided general impressions of the exercise, their problem-solving heuristics, and new ideas for improving procedures in the future. They also completed a short post-experiment questionnaire.

Experimental Analysis and Results: The first two problem-solving sessions were treated as practice sessions to gain experience with each organizational structure. The last four were analyzed and compared, first in terms of absolute problem-solving performance (accuracy and timeliness of guesses), and later in more detailed ways. This analysis resulted in the conclusions and somewhat weaker conjectures reported at the end of this section.

Since each problem used a different puzzle, we cannot assess the reliability of observed differences between problems. Differences could be due, in part, to puzzle difficulty and node variability as well as to organizational structure. Recognizing this limitation, it seemed reasonable to compare actual node performance with some global performance criterion for that particular problem. Therefore, for each problem we computed benchmark performance by a hypothetical "global node." By assumption, a global node can see the whole puzzle grid without errors, and has a list of rules or heuristics for formulating hypotheses and official reports. For each successive round (one data update every few minutes) a scorer applied these rules to the current view to determine which words the global node would report.

Performance results are presented in Fig. 5. Each graph displays the cumulative percent of correct reports by the global and actual nodes at each round. The hatched area between the curves indicates the extent to which the actual performance falls short of the global criteria. Overall, it appears that AC performs better than DHC. It more nearly achieves the global benchmark reporting levels in all cases.

To understand the organizational dynamics which lead to good performance, we conducted further analyses of the problem-solving traces. These analyses focused on three general conjectures.

1) AC communicated more efficiently than DHC, using fewer messages to achieve comparable performance.
2) AC promoted faster communication than DHC, with nodes responding to request for information more quickly.
3) Higher level, more abstract information—such as phrase and theme hypotheses—was shared and understood more often in the AC structure.

The first conjecture was clearly true. DHC teams used about twice as many messages as AC teams per problem.

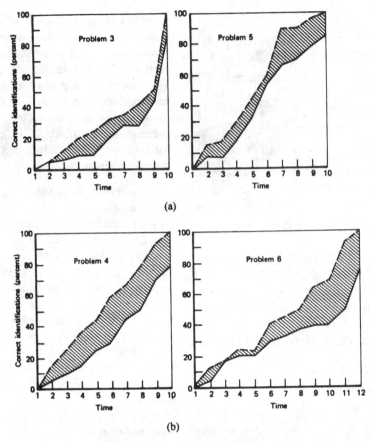

Fig. 5. Overall performance: Problems 3–6. (a) Anarchic committee. (b)
Dynamic hierarchical cone.

This happened primarily because of differences in self-monitoring and task apportionment communications. The authority structure used in DHC problems stimulated many more reports and requests about node activity (e.g., "busy or idle now?"). Upper level managers used this information to redistribute task responsibilities, such as assigning LL nodes to managers. The basic communication constraints of the DHC furthermore generated many more messages because of the need for messages to be relayed through the hierarchy. Messages were also repeated much more frequently in the DHC. Three times as many repeats were evident in DHC problems (21 repetitions) than in AC problems (7 repetitions), indicating widespread dissatisfaction with the greater delays in DHC processing (see below).

This thought leads to the second conjecture—that the AC communicated information faster. In the dynamic MPT situation, speed of communication is essential. Since words overlap viewing areas and views change with every round, information in this task is highly perishable. By the time the information is received, it may be obsolete. On the average, time to respond to requests in AC problems was about 1 min, as compared to 3–4 min in DHC problems. Distinguishing between LL nodes and ML managers in the DHC, we found that the response delay for managers is much higher, reflecting the difficulty of their task. ML managers receive requests for information from many independent nodes. If they know the information, they can respond immediately. If not, they must make inquiries and wait for replies before responding to the original message. They must also remember who requested which information. In short, bottlenecks at the middle level caused significant delays in information exchange.

The third conjecture concerns levels of abstraction in the MPT. Higher level solutions, such as phrases and theme, are more difficult than simple single-word identifications. Since phrases overlap between areas, a single node can never see a complete one. Thus higher level solutions require a more global perspective of the puzzle than is obtained by viewing a single area.

Comparing the higher level solution capabilities of AC and DHC structures, we note that the AC identified 83 percent of the possible phrases, while the DHC identified only 62 percent. Furthermore, comparing the actual time of reporting with the best possible time (using the global node criteria) reveals that the AC identified phrases earlier than the DHC: the average time beyond optimal for reporting phrases was 1.2 rounds in the AC, as compared to 2.6 rounds in the DHC. Finally, while the AC identified all but one phrase before the final round, the DHC did not identify any phrases until the final round. These results thus tend to support the following general conclusion. In the MPT domain the committee structure performs best, reporting more information faster while using fewer communicating resources to do so.

III. IMPROVED CONJECTURES ON DISTRIBUTED ARTIFICIAL INTELLIGENCE

The fact that the AC performed so consistently better than the DHC indicates that the AC structure manifests some especially appropriate properties for the SA task, or the DHC structure has some especially bad properties for it, or perhaps both. We think the third answer is most probable. We note emphatically that we do not think that committees should replace existing hierarchical organizations, nor that all networks should have fully connected broadcast communication channels. Our work is too limited for that sort of generalization. We do think, however, that we have explored in the laboratory a relevant portion of the range of DSN design choices, and that our results, suitably aided by our now improved conjectures, can provide a valuable basis for improved conjectures about DSN designs.

Task Decomposition

How should an organization subdivide situation assessment problems? Our best recommendation remains the same as the hypothesis with which we began this research: activities should be divided among multiple cooperating knowledge sources or specialists producing competing and ultimately cooperating hypotheses. Since communication constraints limit and delay data dissemination, and processing constraints limit the effectiveness of centralized problem-solving, decomposing the overall SA task into pieces assignable to the distributed elements seems most desirable. Assuming we know the knowledge source (KS) set necessary to solve this problem centrally, the question then becomes how to endow a network of processing elements with the initial specialists, interconnections, and additional specialists required for data and hypothesis sharing to achieve good overall problem-solving performance.

Natural geographic boundaries (such as sensor or communication limits) provide one way to organize processors. However, such a separation necessarily limits the system's capability to achieve global coordination of information gathering, organizing, and reduction activities. The trade-off here is between a rapid, local, data-directed processing and a (usually less responsive) global, goal-directed one. Traditional wisdom suggests that complex low-level data processing, such as the conversion of raw signal spectral data into power spectra, should occur near the sensor reporting the data, while higher level inferences, such as platform identification, may require a more global perspective utilizing multiple sensor data. The low-level processing should be geographically assigned to sensor/low-level processor nodes; the higher level inferences may be released from this proximity-based restriction if communications are accurate and swift enough.

If not constrained by geography, the choice between a "cooperating experts" or hierarchical approach becomes clearer. Because of its sheer size, of course, a DSN will undoubtedly require some hierarchical levels of processing abstraction to coordinate information gathering, inference, hypothesizing, and control. However, we feel that since the upper levels must frequently communicate with the lower ones, and since this may be difficult given the differences in types of data and processing for each, the number of such levels that are physically distinguished should be minimized.

Our experiments lacked the detail necessary to contribute much to the question of how many such levels a DSN should contain. The MPT focused mainly on two abstraction levels—letters and words. Phrases and themes were infrequent and occasionally obvious in the context of a few words.

We did demonstrate quite vividly how *not* to create a task hierarchy, though. Levels in hierarchies should be formed when global coordination can be improved using data abstracted from a lower level. The essential requirement is that either the abstracted data are reduced in complexity or the level being created is given additional resources sufficient for the integration task. Neither condition existed in our MPT, and the middle-level nodes dealt with information too complex for the tools provided to them. On the other hand, many environments faced by distributed organizations do exhibit the property of "natural abstraction levels." The signal processing environment seems to. The common abstractions found useful in other AI-based signal processing tasks seem intuitive and appropriate: signal → spectral line groups → platforms and tracks → groups. Yet, even there, in the higher levels of abstraction (platforms, for example), very low-level and complex data relationships (such as consistencies between the presence and absence of specific spectral lines) may depress the complexity-reducing effect of the abstraction process.

Integration

Integration denotes the degree and type of internode coupling required to solve a decomposed SA task. What information must they share? How often? How can they reduce integration requirements to increase their own autonomy and thus decrease the waiting caused by subtask interdependencies? In a well-integrated organization subtasking occurs smoothly with a minimum amount of communication.

One method of achieving integration is the use of *protocols*. Communication protocols ("If I don't report a platform's position, that means I don't know it..."), authority protocols ("...so don't ask me for it."), tasking protocols ("When you see the platform I've been telling you about, take over tracking and notify me.")—all of these can reduce the need to coordinate during the problem-solving process itself. They do require extensive coordination at some point, though, either by system designers during conception or during periods of network inactivity. Furthermore, if critical data are filtered by the use of an inappropriate protocol, performance may suffer, yet no individual may perceive any difficulties. Thus, while protocols serve a valuable function by encoding routine interactions, they must allow flexibility for rapidly changing environments.

A more important integration technique uses *expectations* to reduce communication and coordination needs. Human behavior exemplifies this technique. Particularly in specialty domains, linguistic patterns evolve that support tersely informative exchanges. Witness the cryptic voice communication between pilots, which can usually be understood only by the participants. This use of linguistic expectations provides a basis for detailed models of communication partners.

From a system design perspective we need to specify how to generate, encode, maintain, and verify such assumptions, expectations, and predictions. For a DSN node to model its neighbors in comparable ways, it will require knowledge about their processing states, pending hypotheses, incoming data which may be useful to itself, etc. In the absence of full communication, one method may be for each node to contain executable simulations of neighboring processors, so that what communication does exist can be used to generate and maintain a consistent picture of what the neighbor might know. The cost/benefit of maintaining such a simulation of neighboring belief systems depends on the relationship between the parameters of communication, such as cost and availability, and those of computation, such as the ability to update and store alternate world states as often as necessary.

Even with modeling, communication is expected to be quite precious in a DSN. Maximizing the usefulness of shared data is of utmost importance. Hence a principal question arises about *what* to communicate when candidate hypotheses or data items exceed channel capacity. Sharing a certain but obvious hypothesis is fruitless; likewise, telling a neighbor something you have little faith in may lead to unproductive inferences or effective deception. Nodes need to evaluate how their hypotheses could benefit or confuse their collaborators to decide whether or not to communicate them. With limited communication, this evaluation may be largely guesswork. It can be improved significantly by maintaining predictive models of neighboring nodes as mentioned above. Nonetheless, uncertainty about how valuable a particular hypothesis is likely to be to neighbors, coupled with instances where specific poorly supported hypotheses allow key processing decisions for neighboring nodes, confuse this issue and make it dependent on specifics of the dynamic environment.

Authority

Subtasking and integration require distributed authority in the network. Which nodes can perform task assignment? How many nodes should be controlled by one higher level one? How centralized should decisionmaking be?

An immediate conclusion from the MPT experiments is that while centralized authority in the AC was absent by design, it was also absent in the DHC. Middle-level nodes, because of their processing and communications overload, were unable to exercise their implicit authority and ineffectively delegated it downward. For the same reasons, they were unable to provide the higher level node with enough timely and correctly aggregated information to support his exercise of global judgment. Therefore, another conclusion from our experience (relevant once again to human organizations) tells us to give the nodes exercising any control enough excess information processing and communication resources (i.e., enough power) to wield their authority successfully.

Monitoring is an important function of authority. However, the implicit authority structure of the DHC also contributed to its problem with excessive self-monitoring. Human experience verifies that, generally speaking, as the number of levels and individuals in authority increases, so does internal monitoring. To a certain point this is good, since it supports a network's global perspective and overall coordination. Beyond that point it simply consumes resources while dragging down overall performance. The line between useful and excessive control messages in a dynamic distributed intelligence network is not precise. Some functions are clearly valuable—knowing if neighboring nodes have failed, for example, is essential for the proper control of both global and individual behaviors. Other communications may be useful in some contexts but simply excess baggage in different situations. The contract net concept of Smith and Davis [2] may provide a valuable framework for the dynamic assignment and exercise of authority, but when small, simple tasks are being negotiated, the administrative overhead of proposal, bid, acceptance, and assignment may prove excessively costly.

Another important duty of authority in a network is the optimal use of resources. This may mean reassigning tasks from overloaded nodes to less inundated ones. It may mean monitoring the problem-solving activity to detect nodes that are pursuing local hypotheses known to be false from a more global viewpoint. It may mean resolving conflicts, both of resources or of inferences. In order to perform this overseer role, a higher level node must receive regular information from below. If the higher level node is also integrating individual lower level views, upward reports must communicate not only abstracted data but also process state information. Accomplishing this cheaply may require regular status reports.

A final note on authority. A network with a committee structure similar to our AC seems to require very little authority assignment. Much, if not most, of problem-solving is dictated by localized conditions. Nodes tend to correlate incoming data autonomously, communicating across sensor boundaries to neighbors to resolve ambiguity. Relatively few nodes must cooperate to achieve the detection, classification, and tracking of targets. Many complex existing networks share these characteristics (e.g., the discrete address beacon system (DABS) sensor net [10], and indeed the entire modern air traffic control network). It may be that a network can neglect making authority explicit because it has sufficient resources at each node to obviate the need for extensive cooperation. If that is true, then the real question for the design of a DSN is whether hardware costs are sufficiently low compared to the pay-off of intelligent cooperative software to warrant a similar solution here.

Communication Pathways

Several suggestions made previously concern network communications: hypotheses expected to be especially useful to others should be transmitted; their transmission could occur at abstraction levels which reduce actual data transfer to a minimum; higher level nodes will likely require regular reports from their subordinates for resource allocation and contention-resolving purposes. These ideas mainly concern the "what" of communication. In this section we address other aspects such as the "how" and "to whom" questions.

Channel Capacity: We begin by noting that in our MPT the primary determinant of performance differences was the structure of communication partners. DHC members, especially the low-level ones, were disallowed contact with their neighbors who had access to the essential data. To be sure, they could share through intermediaries, but this was clearly a poor substitute. The middle-level nodes, moreover, were inundated by communications requests they had neither the channel capacity nor time to handle. And the highest level node received too little information to be of service to the network at all. All of these phenomena were caused by inappropriate communications pathways for this problem.

Heading the list of deficiencies is the limitation on low-level data sharing. Abstracting data in this domain yielded little compression or reduction; too much higher level processing depended on cues in the raw data. This phenomenon may occur in many other situation assessment domains as well.[1] Our recommendation for the DSN is to facilitate low-level data sharing among nodes doing initial signal processing and cross correlation, allowing especially for the upward transfer of those data expected to be highly diagnostic.[2]

Allowing direct data sharing at the lowest level would have greatly improved the DHC's performance. Giving the middle-level nodes additional channel capacity to handle the incoming data flows and attendant outgoing report requirements would have also improved their performance. The levels of hierarchy in a network typically compromise between too much centralization (the extreme being centralized problem-solving with multiple sensors feeding a single integrator) and not enough (so that integration nodes

have too little scope or support from below to form much of a global perspective at all). Whatever the choice for a node's span of purview and control, it must be provided the communication capacity necessary to carry out its designed function. Conversely, a fixed capacity greatly constrains the feasible span-of-control for DSN hierarchies.

That capacity may vary greatly across levels in the network, affecting the individual choices for processor and communication channel design in a variety of ways. One network design may stress the uniformity of hardware to facilitate adaptivity to change. In a uniform system each node would be a generalist with all of the capabilities of another node. The replacement of failed nodes, for example, would be simplified, and network interconnections themselves would be standardized. However, this design must incorporate maximum expected channel capacity everywhere to preclude communication bottlenecks. This restriction is mitigated by natural levels of knowledge abstraction in many domains. In such multilevel systems, moving up a level in the network hierarchy simultaneously reduces information complexity while increasing its scope. This can result in a constant channel capacity requirement throughout the network.

Network Interconnections: Situation assessment tasks typically require localized coordination among neighbors with shared boundaries. The frequency of distant communication is usually much lower. This was certainly true in our laboratory model, and we expect it to be true in the DSN case as well. The network design for communications interconnections should exploit this fact.

The need for longer range data-sharing increases with data abstraction. This need does not necessarily require direct physical connections between all nodes which share such hypotheses. Virtual connections, such as those provided by packet radio switching networks [12], could suffice. These have the additional benefit of automatic adaptivity to changes in physical communication pathways. Broadcasting, either directly or via store-and-forward, will also work, provided each node can simply and quickly discriminate between those messages useful to it and those to be ignored or forwarded. This is a complex question, since the usefulness of information in highly dynamic environments generally cannot be determined at the time it is generated or transmitted. Heuristics found useful in the MPT environment included ignoring messages from far away; stacking messages of a general nature after those requesting immediate, simple, and precise action; and ignoring messages until local autocorrelation and hypothesis formulation is complete. (See the Appendix for these heuristics and more.)

Communicate or Compute?: This question poses a classic trade-off. Should nodes share information frequently and extensively, or reserve their communication resources while exploiting the data on hand? Each approach involves some risk: not communicating may generate much analysis obviated by the diagnostic data conveniently available elsewhere; talking too much may clog channels and waste time. How should a node decide what to do?

---

[1] A vivid example comes from the Mayaguez incident when the President received first-hand reports directly from observers at the scene of the action.

[2] This term was used by Hayes-Roth [11] to describe information which greatly limits the number of interpretations or hypotheses which are consistent with it. A diagnostic spectral line, for example, is one which uniquely determines a particular platform type. Its occurrence with a reasonable certainty allows all competing platform hypotheses and their attendant emitter and spectral signature interpretations to be immediately dropped.

One solution involves using a little communication to possibly save a lot of computing. When starting a complex computational task which might be obviated with new data, a node should announce its intentions and pause for any preferred help. This device can reduce processing needs greatly, especially in networks where sensor fields of view overlap significantly and redundant processing might frequently occur without such coordination. A more generally applicable heuristic suggests delaying communication until currently available data have been integrated with existing known hypotheses. New data may produce new hypotheses or, more typically, reconfirm previously transmitted ones.

The answer ultimately depends on the relative benefits and costs between talking and thinking, of course, and our experiments touch only a small area in this space. Further experimental work with specific network parameters and alternative heuristic strategies is needed to identify a good general technique for DSN's.

IV. MACHINE STRUCTURES FOR DISTRIBUTED SITUATION ASSESSMENT

We now turn to the question of whether the preceding ideas can be implemented on a network of computer, rather than human, nodes. After all, human beings have a lengthy history of group problem-solving skills that are still poorly understood. Was it presumptuous to assume that we could transfer the heuristics of cooperation garnered from our experimental subjects to a purely machine-based organization?

The answer is to be found in this section about the construction of a set of cooperative computer programs that solve the MPT. Taking the best aspects of the two human structures as our guide, we compared the performance of both communicating and noncommunicating network structures with a uniprocessor design employing the same heuristics. The first section below traces the design, implementation, and results of these experiments.

The difficulty of transferring human expertise to machine nodes made us look for simple and usable principles of cooperative behavior that could somehow guide the overall design process. One of the most important principles we devised involved the use of models to simulate and predict other nodes' activities. After explaining this principle in the second section below, we outline a network design based on it—the processor assembly network (PAN). It is as yet unimplemented and tested, and we provide more questions than answers about its potential. Nonetheless, it appears to be an important contender for the design of networks which manifest distributed intelligence.

Experiments with Machine Networks

Our basic motivations for building a machine network should be obvious. We wanted to see how difficult it would be to transfer the heuristics of cooperation to a machine; we wanted a more controlled environment within which to

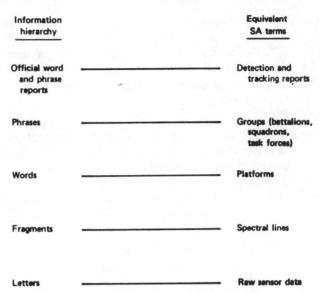

Fig. 6. Information hierarchy for model DSN.

compare structures; and we needed a mechanism for developing more formal procedures for storing and sharing knowledge in a DSN task.

We continued to use the message puzzle task as our domain. However, because it was merely a symbolic stand-in for more general situation assessment problems, we discuss our design here in the more general terminology of sensing and tracking objects moving through space (platforms). The information hierarchy on the left-hand side of Fig. 6 was used in constructing data structures in our programs; the equivalent SA terms used in this paper are on the right. Note that the information hierarchy resembles other signals interpretation decompositions quite closely [9].

Program Structure: Our basic approach was to construct a global problem-solver (which could see the whole puzzle each round) using the "cooperating experts" paradigm from artificial intelligence [7]. This global program, extended with communication capabilities, formed the kernel of each node in a simulation of a sensor network. We simulated multiple processors by using the classic approach of time-slicing among processes, which requires no further comment here. However, the technique of cooperating experts within a single process being less well-known does require explanation.

As in Hearsay-II [7] and HASP [9], each node kept a global data structure called a *blackboard* upon which information at different levels of abstraction was posted. Referring back to Fig. 6, this information consisted of raw sensor input data and more abstract and less certain *hypotheses* about the specific spectral lines, platforms, and platform groups which might be deduced from that data. Information on the blackboard came primarily from code modules called knowledge sources (KS's) which resided at the node. Other nodes' information could, however, be posted on the blackboard by communication modules.

The KS's operated by taking as input hypotheses and data from the blackboard and posting new ones there. We can trace their operation by tracing the conversion of initial sensor data to a final report. At the close of each round any data that has not been accounted for will be used by a KS specialist to spawn a series of possible spectral line combinations which it knows are plausible explanations for that new information. When this occurs another KS responsible for converting spectral line hypotheses into platform hypotheses "wakes up" and posts its best guesses about platforms that might be generating those lines. As time goes by and new data come in, the confidences of these various hypotheses change as one begins to stand out as the best explanation of the input stream. After a certain point a hypothesis becomes good enough to share with other nodes in the system—a KS that "knows" about such criteria determines this and passes the hypothesis to the communication module. Later, perhaps as confirming information from a neighbor arrives, the confidence in a hypothesis becomes so high that it is officially reported outside the network. When that happens, the initially competing hypotheses have been pruned away by a system of cooperating KS experts.

Communication restrictions were relaxed from those in the human experiments. Each node could communicate with any other node in the network, as well as with the outside world (via sensor data and official reports). The communication medium was perfect and instantaneous. Three types of information could be shared—low-level (LL) sensor reports, intermediate-level (IL) spectral line combination hypotheses, and high-level (HL) platform hypotheses.

Tests Performed and Results: Three basic structures were tested using this network simulation.

- *A global centralized node*: This structure can also be viewed as a two-level hierarchy if one limited the operation of all lower level nodes to the rote acquisition and retransmission of raw sensor data. This structure provided a benchmark against which to evaluate the network structures below, since we thought that, given enough processing power, a centralized algorithm would necessarily display the best possible problem-solving capabilities within a fixed set of KS modules.
- *A unilevel network of noncommunicating nodes*: Simply reducing the field of view of the global node above and creating a network simulation based on it allowed us to observe how performance was affected by strict decomposition with no communication or coordination.
- *A unilevel network of communicating nodes*: This structure—basically the AC—was expected to perform better than the network of mute nodes but worse than the global node.

We did not test a DHC-like structure, partly because of its poor performance during the human tests, and partly because computer resource and time limitations made it impossible to add more nodes and the considerably more

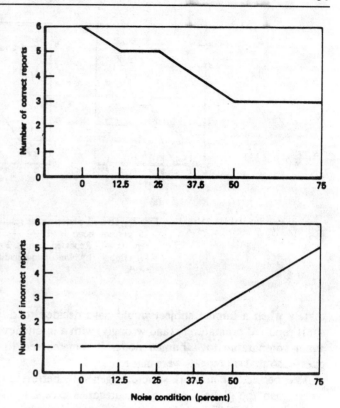

Fig. 7. Effect of noise on performance of machine global node.

complex "heuristics of management" which would have been required.

These limitations forced us to make simplifications even in what was implemented. The 15×15 square board used in the human experiments was reduced to 9×9 in size. Each node thus had a 3×3 view instead of 5×5. The dictionary used was, of course, greatly reduced from that present in people's heads. We attempted to keep the discrimination problem intact in such a reduced dictionary by biasing each puzzle's dictionary with those words especially similar to the correct ones. For example, if "man" were correct, then the dictionary might include "may," "many," "me," "my," "human," and others designed to propogate competing hypotheses for as long as possible.

Numerous different puzzles and degrees of noise injection were tried. Noise, here as in the human experiments, meant that some characters changed into their nearest neighbors—e.g., a "c" might be incorrectly sensed as a "b" or "d." A parameter determined the percentage of noisy incoming characters for each run. Generally, performance degraded gracefully up to about 50 percent noise, at which point it dropped off severely. See Fig. 7 for the results from a single puzzle in six noise conditions of 0–75 percent. At all noise levels, results were remarkably consistent across puzzles, enabling us to exemplify general results with the performance graphs in Fig. 8.

The global node eventually produced human-like performance patterns (see Fig. 8(a)).[3] It made reports approxi-

---

[3] The heuristic nature of the program, coupled with the fuzziness of what "good performance" in this task is, made it necessary to balance or "fine-tune" reporting criteria. We choose human performance as our standard.

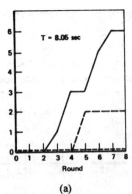 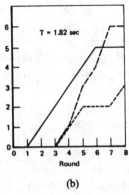 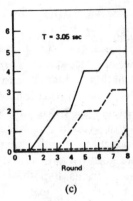

Fig. 8. Overall performance results of machine structures: Problem 3, 25 percent noise level. ——— Correct reports. — — — Incorrect reports. ---- Repeated reports. T = total solution time for slowest node. (a) Global. (b) Noncommunicating network. (c) Communicating network.

mately when a human subject would have decided to do so; it reported prematurely (and wrongly) with a frequency again comparable to a human node; it remembered its guesses so that no repeats were made.

As expected, the network structures generally performed worse than the global node in all categories except total solution time. Working alone, the global node required significantly more time to solve a problem, taking between three and ten times longer than the slowest of the network nodes for each round. It also produced significantly fewer wrong and repeated reports than either of the network structures.

However, graphs of correct reports are remarkably similar for all structures. The global node performed marginally better than the networks more often than not, but we were surprised to see a network structure outperform the global node even once. Perhaps the limited information available to each network node reduced the number of possible explanations at some points and thus actually improved reporting performance.

Another anomaly is the marginal difference that communication made among network nodes. Although sharing reported hypotheses did decrease the frequency of repeated reports, it did very little to improve overall performance. Yet, communicating cost a great deal—not only in execution time and space but also in the inordinate amount of time required to design and implement the required modules of code. This effect can be partially explained by noticing that the first node in the path of a fragment entering from the outside was generally able to report it—quickly, correctly, and autonomously. A domain with more interdependencies among the sensed elements would presumably require much more data and hypothesis sharing than this one did.

A number of other deficiencies, both in the chosen simplified domain and in our implementation, should be noted here. We hasten to point out, for example, that time-sliced simulation of parallelism is not a replacement for a real network of intercommunicating processors. We

did some sensitivity testing by varying node activation sequences and found our results to be robust over such changes. However, asynchronous nodes with imperfect time-delayed communication links may produce very different behavior from that observed here.

Another deficiency stems from the simplistic design of our problem-solving algorithm. The MPT did not seem to require, nor did we attempt to create for it, any model-driven or "look-for" KS modules. As previously explained, KS's refined data in a bottom-up fashion: sensor data → hypotheses → reports. Higher level hypotheses were never used to direct the acquisition of new lower level data, to "look-for" certain key confirming sequences. Were processing and sensing resources to be limited, as would of course be the case in a real-world DSN, such intelligent directing of the internal problem-solving process would become essential.

The Process Assembly Network

Recall that minimizing communication bandwidth requirements is a primary goal of our design efforts. During our construction of the machine network we were able to greatly reduce message traffic over that of the human networks by exploiting the machine's advantages. The machine nodes never had to ask for repeats or clarifications because they had perfect memory and communication. They never entered into dialogues in which a node requested data from another which then responded because a protocol required nodes to share overlapping information with appropriate neighbors automatically. No general requests for assistance ("Anyone know a five-letter word beginning with c-h-o?" or "Help! I'm overloaded!") were required because each node shared identical problem-solving knowledge and unlimited processing power.

The fact that our machine network achieved human levels of performance with such reduced communication loading prompted us to analyze the factors which motivate communication in a distributed intelligence network. Among the reasons nodes talk to one another are the following:

1) to share raw local information that might have more global implications;

2) to update others' knowledge with newly arrived local information;

3) to direct the acquisition, processing, and transmission of another node's information based upon local needs;

4) to subdivide and share the overall task load in a balanced way;

5) to share processing and reporting intentions to prevent redundant activities;

6) to share high-level inferences or hypotheses which may redirect or obviate the need for others' processing activities;

7) to predict where, what, and when new information will arrive to confirm or disconfirm existing hypotheses.

From all of these reasons can be derived two basic communication requirements.

- Nodes must share time-varying information about the external world they are sensing.
- Nodes must share time-varying information about their own internal states of processing.

This seemingly simple observation explains why communication requirements in our machine structure were so small. Implicit in the communication processing was the knowledge of what type of information would be forthcoming from other nodes, when it would be prompted, and how transmitted information would be used. In short, the nodes in our network implicitly shared models of each other's behavior.

This may not be possible, of course, with more complex systems performing more complex tasks. Moreover, the real world does not accommodate us by dividing itself into rounds that make update messages well-structured and convenient. It is continuously changing, presenting new aspects of its objects to us all the time, and knowing when something has changed sufficiently to tell another about it may be difficult indeed. If the world were steady-state, messages would not be required at all (at least, after some initialization)!

In that truism lies the key to a promising new concept in distributed problem-solving. The world is not static, so why should the hypotheses to explain it be? What if hypotheses were somehow *active* themselves and could evolve over time in lock-step with the changing reality they purport to model? If the messages that nodes transmit contain both static data and dynamic procedures or models for changing that information over time, would not the need for frequent updating messages go away?

These questions have prompted us to construct a generically different network structure. Christened the "process assembly network" (PAN) because of its similarity to Hebb's postulated organization of the human brain [13], the design is based upon the concept of a "hypothesis process" as the basic system component. Although still unimplemented, here is how it would work.

For the purpose of explanation, assume a completely interconnected network of processors and sensors. When a new target is sensed, a hypothesis about it (classification, velocity vector, intentions, etc.) is formed and assigned to an available processor. This hypothesis is very different from those we have already seen, however, because it contains not only descriptive information about the target but also processing information about routine expected changes it should undergo as the situation unfolds. As before, the formation of this hypothesis process may prompt the creation of higher level ones doing aggregation over space or more refined situation assessment. Also as before, incoming information from the sensors will tend to confirm or discredit the hypothesis as a valid explanation for what is observed.

The advantage of the hypothesis process in this situation is that once transmitted to each of these related entities— the lower level information producers feeding it and the higher level consumers using it—no further *routine* communication need take place. Each network element will contain models of the other elements relevant to its activities and can thereby autonomously produce accurate expectations of their capabilities and needs. Only when nonroutine surprising information arrives should a message be sent to revise neighbors' models of what you know.

An example comparing our AC-like network with a PAN design should clarify this concept. Fig. 9 shows a typical tracking task required of a distributed sensor network. Three sensors, S_1–S_3, have been deployed to protect three targets, T_1–T_3. Two groups of two attackers enter and form together into a V-wave, which then proceeds as a single unit toward target T_3. We first describe how the traditional AC-like network would react to this situation, then how a PAN would do so.

At time t in the traditional network, S_1 and S_2 would independently detect the incoming attackers and begin tracking. Each would notify its neighbors of the track initiation and current location of the attackers—two messages to each of two nodes equals eight messages in all. At $t+1$, S_1 and S_2 would again notify their neighbors of the attackers they could see—16 messages in all now. At $t+2$, another 16 messages would circulate, and at $t+3$, S_3 would begin sharing its detection data, and the total number of messages per unit time would rise to 24. In all, 64 messages were exchanged in this simple example, each containing updated track information.

A PAN structure would not necessarily pair processors directly with sensors as above, but let us assume that it would, for simplicity's sake. It would thus begin at time t by creating hypothesis processes about the individual attackers detected and higher level aggregation hypotheses about the two-attacker groups traveling together. S_1 and S_2 would each transmit models of expected flightpaths to their neighbors, enabling them to predict the targets' locations at any point in time. In particular, they can know when to

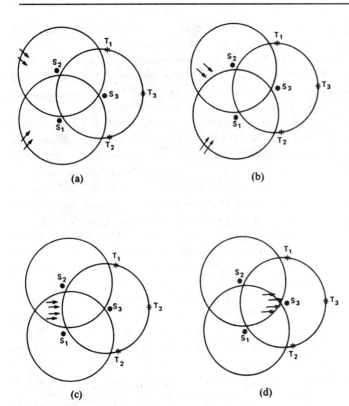

Fig. 9. DSN tracking task. (a) Time$=t$. (b) Time$=t+1$. (c) Time$=t+2$. (d) Time$=t+3$.

upcoming events. These predictions reduce the necessity to share conforming information, and leave the communication channels free for the transmission of surprising unpredictable information. When messages of this type are used to revise and refine existing models, the PAN should evolve toward a steady-state operation with minimal communication requirements.

Naturally the PAN design is preferable to the more traditional approach only if certain conditions are satisfied. Computational requirements are very great. Because each node must be able to model its associates, each node must therefore be a "generalist" with a full complement of problem-solving capabilities. This alone suggests that specialization may not be possible in a PAN, either in hardware or in software. As in any other distributed intelligence (DI) network, the PAN requires modules of domain expertise to transform incoming sensor signals into meaningful abstract reports. Unfortunately, it has the added requirement that these modules must be communicable among nodes, for they form the basis for the hypothesis process concept. We expect that a PAN implementation may employ coded references to common procedures with the hypothesis processes in order to reduce the sheer volume of material transmitted. Nonetheless, a "language" of hypothesis processes would be required in a PAN where none was overtly necessary before. Finally, the predictions that PAN relies on so heavily must be matched against sensor data with some regularity; knowing how often and how well this matching process must be performed is still a poorly understood problem of artificial intelligence.

The basic virtue of the PAN remains its ability to perform distributed situation assessment with minimal communications. In an environment where communications are limited, either by technology or design (a quiet sensor net is less likely to be detected and jammed than a noisy one, for example), the PAN structure provides a promising design alternative. We have set forth only a superficial description of how it might function. Major questions remain about its efficacy as an implementable high-performance network structure for tasks of this nature.

expect the targets to penetrate their detection fields and the targets' parameters of motion when that occurs. S_3 can immediately infer that S_1 targets may be headed toward target T_1, that S_2 targets may be attacking T_2, and can begin directing defensive forces accordingly. A total of four complex messages containing the hypothesis process models of aggregated target behavior have been transmitted.

At $t+1$, the targets are still traveling as expected, and no messages are exchanged. By $t+2$, however, both S_1 and S_2 notice the formation of the V-wave, and the new group direction of travel. Since each contains a model of the others' knowledge and processing state, a preestablished protocol to prevent redundancy selects S_1 to report this surprising development to S_3; S_2 knows that S_1 will do so and keeps silent. Another message is thus transmitted. At $t+3$, the network's expectations are met as S_3 finally verifies what it has been told and marshalls defensive forces firmly around T_3. In all, five messages were exchanged.

This example illustrates the PAN's basic design principle: additional computation (in the form of complicated hypothesis processes which must be constantly maintained) can be used to reduce communication needs. To perform this feat, the PAN relies upon two kinds of computation models that stem directly from our previous observations of information that nodes must share. Models of the sensed world and models of each other combine, enabling each PAN node to autonomously maintain predictions about

Finally, Distributed Artificial Intelligence

The study of DSN's is merely the beginning of an entirely new field: distributed artificial intelligence (DAI). Where artificial intelligence to this point has studied and attempted to duplicate individual problem-solving methods, DAI transcends the limits of the individual and enters an entirely new dimension. Fields of study heretofore ignored by AI—organizational theory, sociology, and economics, to name a few—can contribute to the study of DAI. Presumably, DAI will advance these fields as well by providing a modeling technology suitable for precise specification and implementation of theories of organizational behavior.

Thus DSN studies appear to herald a new and exciting direction in artificial intelligence. We expect cooperative problem-solving to become a central focus of future AI research, partly because of the trend toward system architectures that exploit multiple microprocessors, partly because distributed problem-solving is naturally implemented as a system of cooperating experts, and partly because organizational theory is likely to benefit from computational approaches as much as cognitive psychological theory did from computational attempts to model the individual mind.

APPENDIX

HEURISTICS FOR DISTRIBUTED SITUATION ASSESSMENT

This appendix lists some of the heuristics needed to perform the distributed situation assessment task. As in the body of this paper, these rules are expressed in more general terms than the experimental MPT domain from which they were derived. For instance, the objects under surveillance are referred to as "platforms," although they could in actuality be anything from personnel to cruise missiles. Refer to Fig. 6 for other equivalences used here.

In general, the model DSN of this appendix receives raw sensor data at various low-level nodes and transmits reports or declarations of platform motion out of the network. Nodes are arranged at various levels of authority and capability, with superior nodes generally integrating and abstracting the data they receive from lower level nodes. The communication bandwidth is quite limited for the amount of information which might be shared.

Problem-solving in this hypothetical DSN proceeds neither top-down nor bottom-up. Rather, both procedures are represented in the heuristics below. Platform hypotheses, which contain both classification and tracking information, are created to account for multiple sensor reports. Recognizable spectral lines generate the platform hypotheses bottom-up, while existing hypotheses seek confirming or disconfirming information in a top-down fashion. Platform hypotheses near one another may suggest a group hypothesis. Either of these hypothesis types may be reported or declared whenever its confidence increases sufficiently.

Heuristics of various types which embody this problem-solving technique appear below. Overall, they create or refine hypotheses for interpreting the data, or they direct the communication of information and tasks. The heuristics can be classified according to which tasks they support. The tasks include the incorporation of data into hypotheses, the identification of hypothesized objects, the allocation and conservation of resources, and so on. To avoid a complex naming scheme, heuristics have been cataloged by their most important function. The following table shows the number of heuristics with specific functions, and the heuristics follow in the same order.

Sensor data	
Identification	1
Platform hypothesis	
Formation	2
Sensor data	
Incorporation	5
Scheduling	2
Motion	4
Identification	12
Communication	1
Deletion	1
Groups of platforms	
Identification	1
Motion	1
Sensor failure	3
Communication	
General	4
Conservation	8
Scheduling	3
Task allocation	9

The heuristics below are set forth using the following format.

Goal:	what the heuristic attempts to accomplish.
Condition:	characteristics of the world which must be true before the heuristic can be applied.
Action:	what to do when the conditions are satisfied.
Reason:	why this heuristic works and any beneficial side effects.

Sensor Data Identification

Goal:	identify spectral data.
Condition:	the data come from the edge of a sensor's region.
Action:	request identification at that location from other sensors.
Reason:	sensor distortions, increasing with distance, may be resolved by pooling reports.

Platform Hypothesis Formation

Goal:	create a platform hypothesis.
Condition:	processing of preexisting platform hypothesis is complete and some spectral data remains unattributed to any extant hypothesis.
Action:	create a new hypothesis for each local grouping of data.
Reason:	such spectral data may have been produced by hitherto undetected platform(s).

Goal:	fractionate the platform hypothesis.
Condition:	the tracks of the spectral lines in a hypothesis form subgroups with separable tracks.
Action:	form new hypotheses, one for each group, and delete the old composite hypothesis.
Reason:	there seems to be multiple platforms, not one as previously hypothesized.

Platform Hypothesis Sensor Data Incorporation

Goal:	assign new spectral line data to an existing platform hypothesis.
Condition:	there is an unassigned spectral line and there is an existing hypothesis "near" the signal source, and that hypothesis contains that spectral line.
Action:	assign the spectral line to the hypothesis and adjust the hypothesis position estimate to reflect the position of the new spectral line.
Reason:	spectral lines follow the platform motion.

Goal:	assign new spectral line data to an existing platform hypothesis.
Condition:	there is an unassigned spectral line and there is an existing hypothesis "near" the signal source, and that hypothesis contains a spectral line very similar to the one observed.
Action:	assign the spectral line to the hypothesis, adjust the expected spectral line slightly to reflect the new observation, and adjust the hypothesis position estimate to reflect the new spectral line.
Reason:	noise may change the spectral line characteristics slightly.

Goal:	assign new spectral line data to an existing platform hypothesis.
Condition:	there are no unassigned spectral lines in the hypothesis' region to match the predicted spectral lines, and there is a nearby platform whose spectral lines may mask the predicted spectral lines.
Action:	credit the hypothesis with the missing line.
Reason:	spectral lines may mask each other.

Goal:	assign spectral lines to platform hypotheses.
Condition:	the region may be partitioned into disjoint clusters of spatially proximate sensor reports.
Action:	consider each such subregion separately.
Reason:	helps to control combinatorial search problems.

Goal:	assign new spectral line data to an existing platform hypothesis.
Condition:	the platform is entering the sensor's region.
Action:	incorporate into the hypothesis spectral line data arising from the edge of the sensor field nearest the platform.
Reason:	such data are likely to arise from the incoming platform(s).

Platform Hypothesis Sensor Data Scheduling

Goal:	schedule what to do next.
Condition:	there are unassigned spectral data.
Action:	assign new spectral line data to platform hypotheses known to the individual node prior to transmitting them or requesting related information.

Reason:	it may obviate some communication needs.
Goal:	account for spectral data.
Condition:	always.
Action:	assign spectral data to existing platform hypotheses before forming new hypotheses.
Reason:	helps prevent formation of ephemeral spurious hypotheses ("ghosts") and makes more data available for testing existing hypotheses.

Platform Hypothesis Motion

Goal:	predict position of platform hypothesis.
Condition:	there is an established direction of motion for the hypothesis.
Action:	predict spectral lines will move according to the direction of motion.
Reason:	platforms generally move in continuous trajectories.

Goal:	predict position of platform hypothesis.
Condition:	there is an obstacle nearby and a hypothesized platform is moving toward it.
Action:	remove obstacle location from the set of possible positions and expect a change in the direction of motion.
Reason:	platforms avoid obstacles.

Goal:	identify constraints on platform motion.
Condition:	the motion is near the boundaries of your sensor region.
Action:	request obstacle location from adjacent nodes.
Reason:	the motion of a platform near the boundary of a region can be influenced by obstacles just outside the region.

Goal:	assist other nodes.
Condition:	you have noticed global obstacle patterns.
Action:	inform all nodes.
Reason:	it may constrain their hypotheses.

Platform Hypothesis Identification

Goal:	platform identification.
Condition:	not all its spectral lines are identified.
Action:	obtain the best partial matches from the set of platform signatures.
Reason:	an informed guess is often better than no identification at all.

Goal:	platform identification.
Condition:	its spectral lines match a platform signature (S1), and its spectral lines are also a subset of some other platform signature (S2).
Action:	insure that the additional lines in S2 are not present in the data.
Reason:	competing identifications must be isolated and disconfirmed.

Goal:	platform identification.

Condition: not all its spectral lines are identified, and a group-type is known.

Action: obtain the best partial matches from the set of platform signatures in the group-type.

Reason: the search for partial matches will be faster, and the resulting set of possible identifications will be smaller.

Goal: platform identification.

Condition: the location of the hypothesized platform is also in the region of another sensor.

Action: request data on the platform hypothesis from the other sensor.

Reason: pooled data will lead to more accurate identification.

Goal: assign responsibility for platform identification.

Condition: information is needed from just one node.

Action: assign responsibility to that node.

Reason: reduces command redundancy and communication requirements.

Goal: declare an identification of a platform.

Condition: a platform has been identified and you do not have the authority to declare identifications.

Action: notify your superior of the declaration.

Reason: it will be passed to someone with the required authority.

Goal: make an identification of a platform.

Condition: a platform has been identified and the message system is very busy.

Action: declare the identification yourself, rather than sending it to a superior.

Reason: it is more important to declare identifications than to adhere strictly to communication protocols.

Goal: assist other sensors.

Condition: you intend to declare an identification.

Action: before doing so, broadcast the identity and track.

Reason: helps to prevent duplicate declarations by others.

Goal: assist other sensors and nodes.

Condition: a declaration is found to be incorrect.

Action: broadcast a correction immediately.

Reason: other sensors and nodes may be wasting resources and making errors as a result of believing the incorrect hypothesis.

Goal: assist other nodes.

Condition: you intend to cite a platform whose identity has been declared.

Action: also restate the node that identified the platform previously.

Reason: reminds nodes of platform's overall processing status.

Goal: unify global activity.

Condition: you are the superior node.

Action: require all declarations to be made by you.

Reason: most efficient way to keep the whole system informed of declarations.

Goal: inform subordinates of platform declarations and conserve messages.

Condition: there are several identifications pending formal declaration.

Action: collect them into one message and broadcast it.

Reason: this information is not urgent and can be packed for efficiency.

Platform Hypothesis Communication

Goal: assist adjacent nodes.

Condition: an hypothesized platform is about to leave your region.

Action: send all information about it to the sensor whose region it is entering.

Reason: that sensor will best be able to monitor and track it.

Platform Hypothesis Deletion

Goal: disconfirm a platform hypothesis.

Condition: many of its predicted spectral lines are disconfirmed.

Action: delete the hypothesis.

Reason: lack of supporting data.

Groups of Platforms Identification

Goal: group-destination identification.

Condition: several platforms have been tracked.

Action: find a common pattern of motion and extrapolate it.

Reason: platforms are likely to travel in groups with a common purpose.

Groups of Platforms Motion

Goal: understand platform or group movement.

Condition: the processor is not busy.

Action: obtain positions of obstacles from other sensors and look for global patterns.

Reason: avoiding obstacles is a constraint on platform movement.

Sensor Failure

Goal: assist node with hardware problems.

Condition: a hardware problem has just arisen in some node.

Action: send the node a map of obstacles in and around its region.

Reason: its own processing capacity is better spent on reestablishing hypotheses than on such subsidiary tasks.

Goal: recover from a hardware error.
Condition: you have just recovered from a hardware error.
Action: broadcast your spectral line data immediately upon getting it.
Reason: you may go down again, but others may be able to use the data.

Goal: assist a node with hardware problems.
Condition: the node has just come back up.
Action: send the node copies of hypotheses in its region and such other useful information as global patterns.
Reason: help the node to reestablish its knowledge base.

Communication

Goal: obtain information.
Condition: you do not have the information and you suspect that another node does.
Action: send a request for that information to the other node.
Reason: you may get a reply containing the information.

Goal: compute a value.
Condition: you are busy.
Action: broadcast the problem, with a request for answers.
Reason: some idle node may solve it for you.

Goal: assist a node.
Condition: the node has made a request.
Action: respond in a timely manner.
Reason: data and results are perishable.

Goal: obtain a response from a node.
Condition: the request was sent a long time ago and an answer is still needed.
Action: repeat the request.
Reason: the node may have ignored, or not received, the request.

Communication Conservation

Goal: conserve message capacity.
Condition: a message is not intended for only one node, and broadcasting is possible.
Action: broadcast it.
Reason: saves processing associated with multiple message addressing and routing.

Goal: conserve processing capacity.
Condition: there is a message relating to distant events.
Action: ignore it.
Reason: those events will probably not affect you soon.

Goal: conserve message capacity.
Condition: there is a message to be sent and it is to be broadcast widely by your superior and you have more than one superior.
Action: send it to only one superior.
Reason: it will be broadcast with less redundancy.

Goal: conserve global processing and message capacity.
Condition: you are responding to a broadcast request.
Action: send a copy of your reply to all other original addressees.
Reason: obviate others' superfluous processing and messages.

Goal: conserve messages.
Condition: there are several messages to send and communication capacity is scarce.
Action: send to the union of the addressees a message that composes all the messages, preceding each with its specific addressee's name.
Reason: decoding packed messages is less costly than sending many independent messages.

Goal: conserve processing and message capacity.
Condition: you are very busy.
Action: do not attempt to integrate data that other sensors can also process and do not send detailed status reports to your superior.
Reason: these are less important parts of your task.

Goal: conserve messages.
Condition: you are preparing a message for a node who is known to be very busy.
Action: delete the message.
Reason: the busy node will not have time to process it.

Goal: conserve processing and message capacity.
Condition: system organization is hierarchical.
Action: do not reconfigure authority structures dynamically.
Reason: such reorganization cuts into subordinates' capacity to handle essential task activities.

Communication Scheduling

Goal: schedule.
Condition: there are many unprocessed messages.
Action: process them.
Reason: other processing would probably benefit.

Goal: schedule.
Condition: there are few unprocessed messages and there are data to process.
Action: process data.
Reason: improving hypothesis is probably more valuable.

Goal: process a message.
Condition: always.
Action: respond as quickly as possible.
Reason: a late answer may be valueless, in which case the effort expended on it would be wasted.

Task Allocation

Goal: assist in the allocation of responsibility.
Condition: action has just commenced, the processor is not busy, and there has been no message from your superior asking that raw data not be sent.
Action: send the superior the entire set of spectral lines and positions.
Reason: the superior may have sufficient resources to develop a detailed understanding of its large region.

Goal: assist in the allocation of responsibility.
Condition: action has just commenced, the processor is busy or there has been a message from your superior asking that raw data not be sent.
Action: send the superior the number of data reports and identify all of your busy borders.
Reason: the superior may be able to derive a general understanding of its region even from such abstractions.

Goal: assist in allocating responsibility.
Condition: you are short of messages or processing capacity.
Action: inform your superior.
Reason: your superior may be able to lighten your load.

Goal: allocate responsibility.
Condition: action has just commenced.
Action: assign some subordinates to two or more superiors.
Reason: provides redundancy of command and supports communication over borders between adjacent command regions.

Goal: allocate responsibility.
Condition: always.
Action: request business status from subordinates and reallocate so that business is evenly distributed.
Reason: greater overall throughput and reduced bottlenecks.

Goal: allocate responsibility.
Condition: a sensor's region is inactive.
Action: deallocate all responsibility for this region.
Reason: nothing is going on there.

Goal: assist in reallocation.
Condition: you are idle.
Action: report to superior.
Reason: allows him to understand workloads.

Goal: assist in reallocation.
Condition: you are busy.

Action: report to superior.
Reason: allows him to understand workloads.

Goal: assist a very busy subordinate.
Condition: you have an idle subordinate.
Action: send the busy node's data to the idle node for processing and tell the idle node what to do with them.
Reason: share tasks over available resources.

ACKNOWLEDGMENT

Other Rand staff members provided valuable assistance during this project. Norm Shapiro provided gems of insight when we first grappled with the task of characterizing distributed situation assessment. We must also mention and thank the volunteers who formed the pool of human DSN nodes, as their participation assured us of firsthand experience with the subject of this paper: Patricia Aicher, Robert Anderson, Monti Callero, Stephanie Cammarata, Nancy Daniel, William Faught, R. Stockton Gaines, William Giarla, Dan Gorlin, Barbara Hayes-Roth, Philip Klahr, Walter Matyskiela, Doris McClure, Ralph Strauch, and Perry Thorndyke.

REFERENCES

[1] R. Lacoss and R. Walton, "Strawman design for a DSN to detect and track low-flying aircraft," in *Proc. Distributed Sensor Nets Conf.*, Carnegie-Mellon Univ., Pittsburgh, PA, Dec. 1978, pp. 41–52.

[2] R. Smith and R. Davis, "Distributed problem solving: The contract net approach," in *Proc. Second Nat. Conf. of Canad. Soc. for Computational Studies of Intelligence*, Toronto, ON, Canada, July 1978, pp. 278–287.

[3] L. Sanderson and J. Lord, "Microcomputers promise less stop, more go," *IEEE Spectrum*, pp. 30–35, Nov. 1978.

[4] S. Kahne, I. Lefkowitz, and C. Rose, "Automatic control by distributed intelligence," *Scient. Am.*, vol. 240, no. 6, pp. 78–90, June 1979.

[5] F. Hayes-Roth and R. Wesson, "Distributed intelligence for situation assessment," Rand Corp., Santa Monica, CA, Rep. N-1447-ARPA, Jan. 1980.

[6] P. R. Lawrence and J. W. Lorsch, *Organization and Environment.* Boston, MA: Harvard Univ., 1967.

[7] L. D. Erman, F. Hayes-Roth, V. R. Lesser, and D. R. Reddy, "The Hearsay-II speech understanding system: Integrating knowledge to resolve uncertainty," Carnegie-Mellon Univ., Pittsburgh, PA, Tech Rep. CMU-CS-79-156, in press.

[8] L. Uhr, *Pattern Recognition, Learning and Thought.* Englewood Cliffs, NJ: Prentice-Hall, 1973.

[9] H. P. Nii and E. A. Feigenbaum, "Rule-based understanding of signals," in *Pattern-Directed Inference System*, D. A. Waterman and F. Hayes-Roth, Eds. New York: Academic, 1978, pp. 483–501.

[10] C. M. Applewhite, "Distributed computer architecture for the discrete address beacon system," in *Proc. 1st Int. Conf. on Distributed Computer Systems*, Huntsville, AL, Oct. 1–5, 1979, pp. 480–489.

[11] F. Hayes-Roth, "The role of partial and best matches," in *Pattern-Directed Inference Systems*, D. A. Waterman and F. Hayes-Roth, Eds. New York: Academic, 1978.

[12] R. E. Kahn, "The organization of computer resources into a packet radio network," *IEEE Trans. Commun.*, vol. COM-25, no. 1, pp. 169–178, Jan. 1977.

[13] D. O. Hebb, *The Organization of Behavior.* New York: Wiley, 1979.

Distributed Intelligence for Air Fleet Control

Randall Steeb, Stephanie Cammarata,
Frederick A. Hayes-Roth, Perry W. Thorndyke,
Robert B. Wesson

October 1981

Prepared for the
Defense Advanced Research Projects Agency

III. ARCHITECTURES FOR DISTRIBUTED AIR TRAFFIC CONTROL

In this section, we propose six distinct organizations, or architectures, of multiple processors for cooperative planning. Each provides a complete structure for sensing situational conditions, sharing information, recognizing problems, planning cooperatively, and coordinating execution. After describing the structure and characteristics of the six architectures, we illustrate their application in several typical ATC environments.

The architectures, summarized in Fig. 2, use three distinct distribution methods. The first exploits a natural association of processors to the objects they control or the data they gather. These individual-planning methods are based on objects that develop plans for themselves and coordinate with the plans of others. The second type of distribution takes advantage of clusters suggested by the planning environment, such as groups of aircraft in high-density regions or aircraft clustered during approach to an airport. The third type of distribution focuses on decomposition of the solution process, rather than the environment, to distribute planning effort. Here a complete solution must be found by one of the processors. The processors search different options by starting at different points or by using different information.

The object-centered autonomous and object-centered cooperative architectures are variants of a one-processor-per-vehicle design. This one-to-one design is important because it has an increasing number of applications to onboard processing. Collision avoidance systems, cruise missile guidance systems, and automated landing systems all demonstrate the advantages of providing sensing, processing, and planning capabilities in the controlled vehicle. The autonomous and cooperative variants of the object-centered structure reflect different styles of distributing planning functions among the controlled vehicles. The autonomous structure relies on each processor's own sensing and inference for information-gathering—planning and plan execution occur without communication among processors. In the cooperative structure, aircraft communicate to exchange data and collaborate during planning.

The space-centered and function-centered architectures derive from situations with natural, stable groupings of objects, most of which occur along either regional or functional lines. In a regional grouping, a processor controls all objects within a specified spatial region. Current enroute control of civilian air traffic utilizes a space-centered architecture. In a functional grouping, each processor controls all objects engaged in a particular type of activity. Distribution by function frequently occurs in terminal control areas, where different controllers handle approaches, landings, and overflights.

The final two architectures, plan-centered and hierarchical, address problems requiring a global solution—that is, one that considers all aircraft. A problem requires a global solution (rather than a combination of local partial solutions) if interactions affect all objects in the airspace, or if environmental dynamics preclude stable groupings. The plan-centered structure assigns to each processor a different

portion of the search space or a different approach to the problem. The processors work silently until one arrives at a solution. This type of organization is exemplified by oil exploration and drilling. The hierarchical approach attempts to achieve a global solution by decreasing the problem into high-level decisionmaking and low-level sensing and problem-solving. The high-level processors rely on global data aggregation and extensive communication. Low-level processors execute plans, monitor plan execution, and perform local replanning. We describe each of these architectures and distribution methods in more detail below.

OBJECT-CENTERED AUTONOMOUS ARCHITECTURE

The object-centered autonomous architecture is a communication-free organization in which each aircraft performs all situation assessment, conflict recognition, planning, and control functions autonomously. Figure 3 illustrates a possible event sequencing among three aircraft using the object-centered autonomous architecture. In this case, planning is reactive and incremental, and preplanned protocols are used for resolving conflicts. Natural organizations that exemplify this type of autonomous planning and control include joggers, who avoid collisions by independent prediction and response, and automobile traffic at unregulated intersections.

Figure 4 shows the organization of activities for each aircraft in this architecture. This diagram is a variant of the problem-solving kernel shown in Fig. 1. The major difference is the absence of the communicator module. The inability to communicate places a greater burden on the sensor to infer the plans of others from sensed locations, altitudes, and headings. Since these estimates can be incorrect and uncertain, plan evaluations can only be tentative and must be frequent. Replanning may be required.

For example, suppose that a slow propeller craft in level flight is potentially in conflict with an ascending jet, as shown in Fig. 3. Each aircraft may sense the other and use trajectory projection to predict the time and location of the conflict. Each aircraft may use its plan generator to synthesize possible maneuvers for avoiding the other. The plan generator posts the selected action in the world model for the evaluator to test using a fast-time simulation. The simulation returns the predicted conflicts and expected effects on fuel and schedule. If the expected performance is acceptable, the controller executes the plan. If the expected performance is unacceptable, the plan generator produces a different action sequence, using information about why the previous actions failed.

Since this architecture allows consideration of only single-aircraft actions, problems may arise when actions selected independently by the aircraft are incompatible or inefficient. Incompatibility results, for example, if both aircraft decide to detour in the same direction. The ability of the system to iterate safely to a conclusion depends to a large extent on tracking delays and sensor accuracy (Andrews and Hollister, 1980) or on a complete set of "rules of the road." Efficiency problems result if both aircraft maneuver when only one needs to, or if the aircraft use overly conservative separation requirements and resolution lead times. The aircraft need such "cushions" only when they have incomplete data regarding the intentions of other aircraft.

Individual Planning

Object-Centered Autonomous — Each onboard processor solves its own problem through silent planning

Object-Centered Cooperative — Each onboard processor solves local problem through cooperative planning

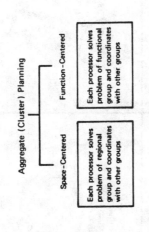

Aggregate (Cluster) Planning

Space-Centered — Each processor solves problem of regional group and coordinates with other groups

Function-Centered — Each processor solves problem of functional group and coordinates with other groups

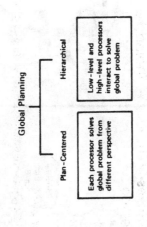

Global Planning

Plan-Centered — Each processor solves global problem from different perspective

Hierarchical — Low-level and high-level processors interact to solve global problem

Fig. 2 — Architectures for distributed planning

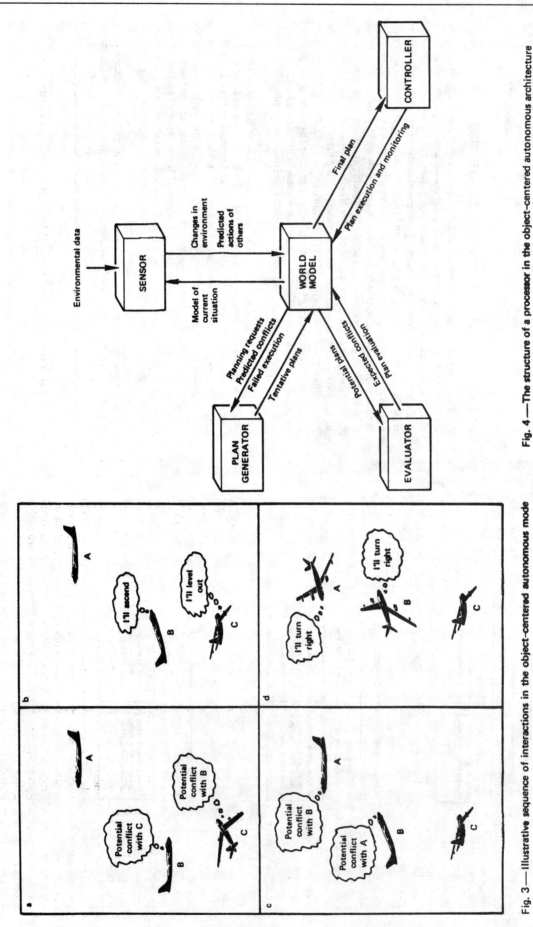

Fig. 4 —The structure of a processor in the object–centered autonomous architecture

Fig. 3 —Illustrative sequence of interactions in the object–centered autonomous mode

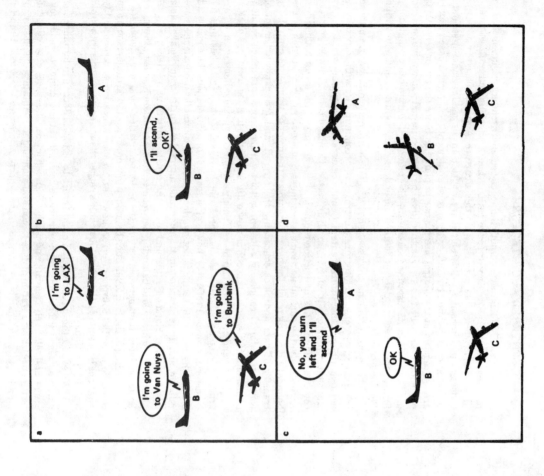

Fig. 5 — Illustrative sequence of interactions in the object-centered cooperative mode

OBJECT-CENTERED COOPERATIVE ARCHITECTURE

The object-centered cooperative architecture also has a processor associated with each aircraft, but the aircraft communicate to plan collaboratively. Figure 5 illustrates how neighboring aircraft might plan cooperatively to resolve conflicts. In this case, new plans are developed and agreed upon prior to execution.

The processing capabilities associated with each aircraft processor now expand to include communication procedures, as shown in Fig. 6. If communication costs are low, knowledge that might have been derived through inference can instead be obtained though communication with the aircraft in question, as shown by the activities of the communicator.

Decisions about whether to communicate or to perform computations locally depend on the expected value of the information and the relative cost of obtaining it by either method. Unfortunately, accurate computation of communication cost requires that the sender have accurate knowledge of the recipient's goals, world model, and pending activities. In general, communication is more desirable than local inferencing only if (1) the information changes the current situation assessment of the recipient, (2) the new situation assessment leads to a different action than was originally planned, and (3) the expected value of the new action is greater than the expected value of the previously pending action plus the cost of transmission (Marschak, 1973).

The planning process changes dramatically with the addition of communications. In the example of the slow propeller craft conflicting with an ascending jet (illustrated in Fig. 5), a new set of options emerges. The propeller plane may generate and evaluate maneuvers for itself, for the jet, or both. If the fast-time simulation in the evaluator indicates that a slight change in the jet's trajectory results in the least overall fuel usage and the greatest safety, the propeller aircraft can request such an action via message-passing.

This architecture can support either iterative local planning or asynchronous cooperative planning. Potentially conflicting aircraft exchange goals and constraints and then formulate, send, revise, and receive partial plans until a global solution is achieved. In this way, aircraft plan in parallel, occasionally sharing information to focus their efforts and prune unpromising alternatives. Since plans are shared, processors may use accurate plans of others in their fast-time lookahead. The frequent short-distance communications used in the object-centered cooperative architecture favor the use of a flexible local-area network in which the aircraft use broadcast transmissions to locate other aircraft and point-to-point transmissions to make the data transfers (Clark, Pogram, and Reed, 1978).

The inherent redundancy of the object-centered cooperative architecture should make it relatively immune to losses of individual processors or breaks in communication links. Loss of a processor or communication link for some interval can be detected by the other aircraft through monitoring of communication exchanges or from inference following unexpected behavior. The other aircraft should be able to make plans that accommodate the degraded performance of that processor. Needed data may be requested from other aircraft or obtained from the degraded aircraft by rerouting transmissions through links that are still secure. Simple data inaccuracies may be recognized and treated through comparison of redundant data structures onboard each aircraft.

On the other hand, the object-centered cooperative architecture is not suited to long-range strategic planning or complex multi-aircraft interactions because of its small scope of view. This architecture appears most effective in situations having range-limited communications and time-stressed decisionmaking. It minimizes long-distance communications, each aircraft has maximum autonomy to respond to unforeseen conditions, and planning loads are evenly distributed throughout the group.

SPACE-CENTERED ARCHITECTURE

Current ATC facilities exemplify the space-centered architecture, in which each processor controls a region of space rather than a particular aircraft. Figure 7 illustrates a typical interaction within this structure. A ground-based or airborne processor monitors and controls all aircraft within an assigned region. Sensor data collected by individual aircraft or by special equipment (e.g., ground-based radar) are aggregated at the control site for use in planning. Since the sector center has plans for all aircraft, this architecture (like the object-centered cooperative one) can use the plans in its fast-time look-ahead. The planning program can plan globally for the entire sector, or it can define independent conflict clusters and plan within these separately.

The communications processes, shown in Fig. 8, are quite different from those of the object-centered architecture. Control centers communicate with both individual aircraft and other control centers. Control centers receive sensor data from and transmit commands to aircraft in their sector. Communication between centers consists of data, plans, and action requests about activity at the sector boundaries. Accordingly, the communication system must contain rules for prediction of the boundary crossing point, for bargaining about the point of transfer of control, for transfer of data and plans concerning the aircraft, and for acknowledgment of control transfer. Occasionally, adjacent sectors will also coordinate to achieve flow management (i.e., delay takeoffs or slow outbound flights to smooth out load peaks).

This hand-off process can be extremely complex. Typically, handoffs are governed by preplanned protocols that prescribe locations, altitudes, and bearings for transfer of control. Preferably, however, a transfer of control should be considered only if the receiving sector is not overloaded, if the communication channels are reliable, and if the information-transfer time interval is shorter than the allowable decision time. Hand-off rates and locations can be varied, using iterative local planning to achieve load balancing between sectors. For example, where there are large load variations between sectors, the sector boundaries could move dynamically according to the load level. Such boundary movements could be cumbersome and could be potential sources of error, however, so such allocation of responsibility might be best suited to long-term load shifts rather than to environments with rapid load fluctuations.

We expect the space-centered architecture to be most effective in terminal and enroute areas with reliable, high-bandwidth communications, complete radar coverage, and relatively constant and predictable load levels. The space-centered architecture uses centralization of data fusion and planning to facilitate problem-solving on a larger scale than is performed in the object-centered architectures. Unfortu-

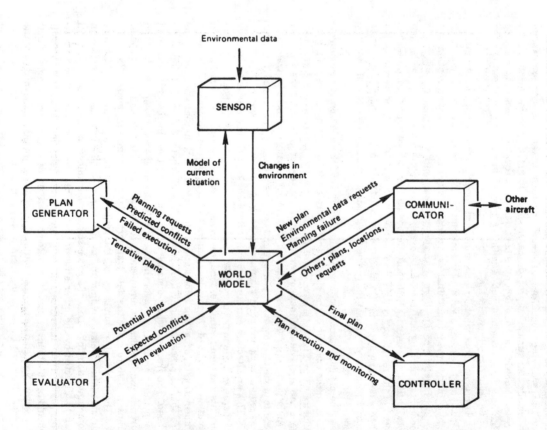

Fig. 6—The structure of a processor in the object-centered cooperative architecture

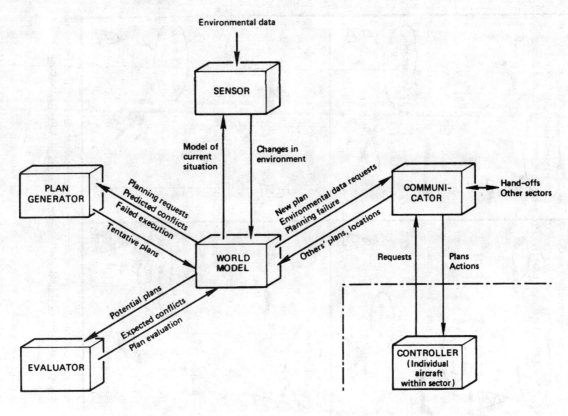

Fig. 8 —The structure of a processor in the space–centered architecture

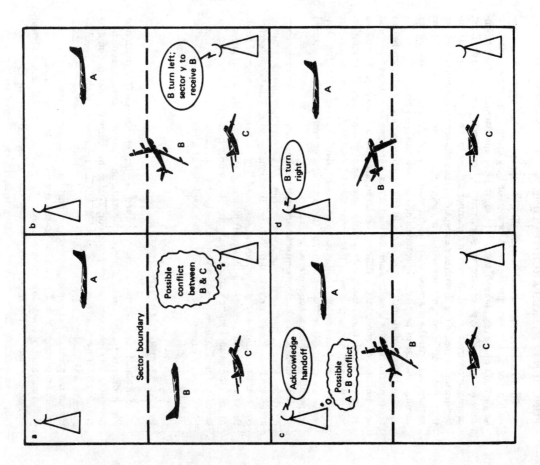

Fig. 7 —Illustrative sequence of interactions in the space–centered mode

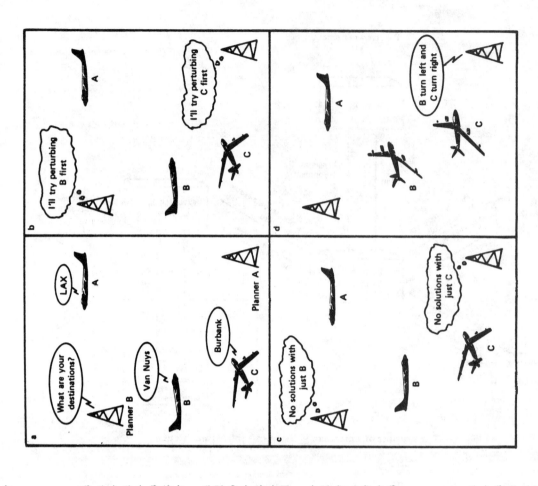

Fig. 9 — Illustrative sequence of interactions in the plan-centered mode

natly, the architecture must be supported by extensive processing and communications networking capabilities, and it is vulnerable to communication system or processor losses.

FUNCTION-CENTERED ARCHITECTURE

The function-centered architecture, like the space-centered approach, assigns multiple objects to each processor. A processor may control all aircraft within a single flight phase (e.g., takeoff, transition, enroute, or approach) or may be responsible for a specific type of aircraft (e.g., private, commercial, or military). Each processor controls several aircraft in a manner similar to the space-centered architecture illustrated in Fig. 8, with one exception: Hand-offs occur between processors that control different functions within a geographic region rather than different regions. As with the space-centered architecture, cooperation is achieved either through the use of preplanned protocols or iterative local planning.

Assignment of aircraft to processors in the function-centered architecture can occur on the basis of time, location, or load. Thus, allocation of responsibility and coordination of effort in the function-centered architecture may be difficult to achieve and maintain. Also, the geographic overlap of groups controlled by different processors means that some inter-processor interactions will involve aircraft conflict resolution, and some will involve control hand-off. As a result, the function-centered architecture shares many of the problems of both the object-centered cooperative and the space-centered structures.

Nevertheless, the function-centered architecture seems well suited to the coordination of traffic near terminals, since current ATC operations in the terminal areas tend to cluster aircraft into natural functional groups. This architecture concentrates data fusion and planning responsibility at a small number of sites, thus facilitating long-range multi-aircraft planning. However, it is not as applicable to communications-limited situations, since it requires high-bandwidth, long-distance communications. It is also vulnerable to communication and processor losses because of its concentration of data and knowledge at a few sites.

PLAN-CENTERED ARCHITECTURE

The plan-centered architecture, portrayed in a terminal-area ATC situation in Fig. 9, distributes the planning process by assigning different approaches or portions of the search space to each processor. This architecture is suited to domains characterized by relatively simple problem-solving requirements and a problem space in which solutions are very sparse. In such cases, each processor can attack the entire problem but can explore only a portion of the entire search space. All processors attempt to find a solution to the overall problem using simultaneous global planning, but they do so independently. An illustrative ATC situation, shown in Fig. 9, would be the impending convergence of several aircraft in a highly congested airspace. Each processor, acting independently, would seek a unique resolution to the conflict by electing, for example, to alter the routes of a different subset of conflicting aircraft.

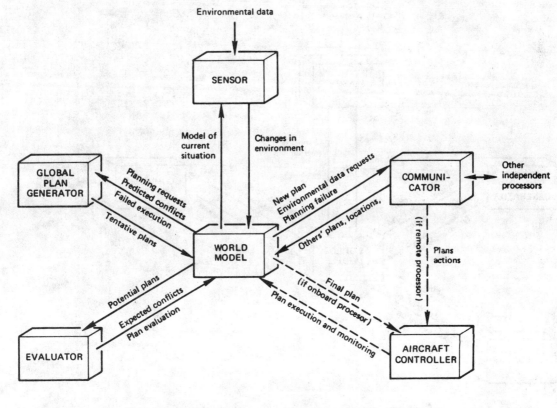

Fig. 10 —The structure of a processor in the plan–centered architecture

Figure 10 presents the structure of a plan-centered node. In performing simultaneous global planning, each processor requires accurate knowledge of the locations and intentions of all aircraft. Thus, processors exchange data via communication to perform situation assessment. No cooperative planning takes place, however, and the amended plans are transmitted only if a processor discovers a suitable global solution.

The relatively high overhead incurred by extensive knowledge distribution makes this architecture suitable only for complex, high-density ATC situations. The plan-centered architecture also appears appropriate in situations with frequent processor losses, since each processor essentially acts as a redundant element.

HIERARCHICAL ARCHITECTURE

Some problems are inherently hierarchical in structure. In a hierarchical architecture, lower-level nodes gather information and/or control objects directly. They pass abstracted and aggregated information up the hierarchy to supervisory nodes, which both direct their subordinates' behavior and report to their own supervisors. A high-level decisionmaker postulates and evaluates strategic plans. A hierarchical architecture most closely resembles the structure of a centralized problem-solver, in that the upper-level nodes have approximately global perspectives on the problem.

Cockpit display of traffic information (CDTI) scenarios postulated by Lincoln Laboratory (Andrews and Hollister, 1980) and by NASA-Ames Research Center (Kreifeldt et al., 1976) exemplify hierarchical ATC operations. In these proposed systems, the ground control center acts as the high-level supervisory controller, while the CDTI-equipped aircraft perform self-separation and short-time-horizon route planning.

The local and supervisory nodes in the hierarchical architecture are shown in Figs. 11 and 12. The local processor functions similarly to a processor in the object-centered cooperative structure. Instead of communicating only with other equivalent processors, however, the local processor communicates with the supervisor. The local processor senses and aggregates data locally, performs local planning, sends abstracted data to the supervisor, and executes commanded actions. The supervisor node, much like a space- or function-centered node, collects and processes the data sent from the local processors, performs long-range planning, and sends commands back to the local nodes.

This hierarchical architecture entails high overhead in communications. To solve a problem, information and requests must always be passed up the hierarchy to centralized decisionmakers (Parnas, 1974). Furthermore, information exchanged among low-level nodes must often be routed through intermediate-level "managers," thus increasing communication time and communication loads (Wesson et al., 1980). The hierarchical architecture appears most appropriate for applications with natural levels of abstractions (such as flow control and separation assurance in terminal-area ATC), high-bandwidth and relatively error-free communications, and a reliable supervisory processor.

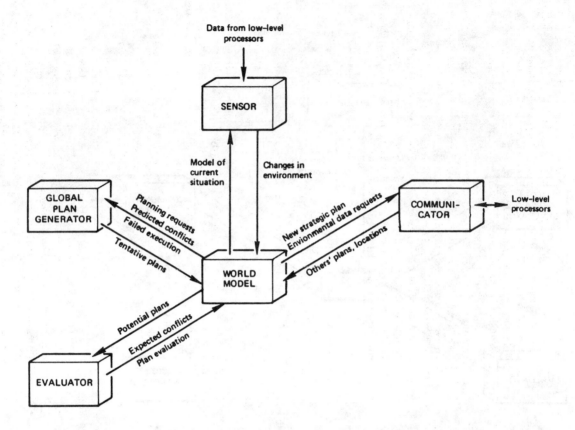

Fig. 12 — The structure of a supervisory or high-level processor in the hierarchical architecture

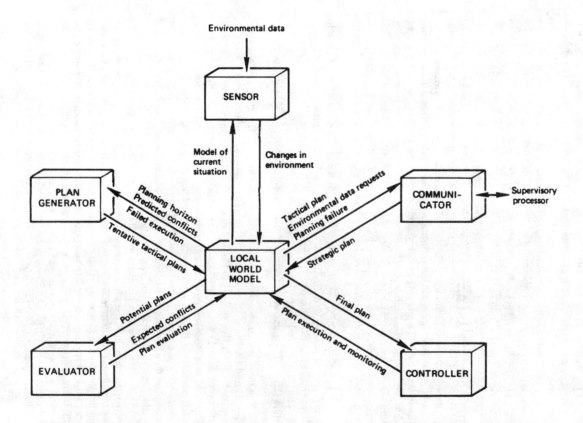

Fig. 11 — The structure of a local or low-level processor in the hierarchical architecture

IV. ENVIRONMENTAL INFLUENCES ON COOPERATIVE PROBLEM-SOLVING

In Section III we examined general relationships between distributed problem-solving architectures and the task environment. In this section, we consider potential task environments in more detail. In developing each of the architectures, we made certain assumptions about the characteristics of the task and the processors cooperating to perform the task. In reality, a variety of environmental constraints may confront designers of distributed systems. Therefore, we must evaluate the utility of the different architectures and problem-solving methods under a variety of environmental conditions.

Our investigations of air fleet control revealed eight important environmental attributes:

1. *Environmental uncertainty*—the prior uncertainty of environmental conditions, aircraft locations, and aircraft intentions.
2. *Environmental dynamics*—the variability of environmental conditions over time.
3. *Communication constraints*—the range, noise level, and bandwidth limitations of available communications.
4. *Degree of clustering*—the extent of functional grouping of the processors.
5. *Time stress*—the time available for decisionmaking.
6. *Option multiplicity*—the number of planning options available to each processor.
7. *Density of the solution space*—the ratio of acceptable, conflict-free plans to the number of potential plans.
8. *Situational complexity*—the number of elements necessary for problem representation.

We shall describe each of these environmental conditions and how they influence the choice of cooperative problem-solving architectures and methods.

ENVIRONMENTAL UNCERTAINTY

The world model may not contain accurate or certain knowledge of crucial environmental states—traffic, weather, terrain, etc.—that the plan generator and evaluator use in formulating plans. Such situations occur, for example, in general aviation in mountainous areas. Methods to deal with this problem include the following:

1. *Data pooling.* Processors may integrate sensor data at designated nodes to reduce data uncertainty. If situation assessment requires aggregation of data from most or all possible sources, a hierarchical structure may be optimal. Unfortunately, a hierarchical structure may result in complex and time-consuming calculations, since complete situation assessment en-tails continuous updating of airspace conditions and aircraft locations in a large region.

2. *Data quality evaluation.* The representation of world knowledge should incorporate certainty levels that reflect sensor accuracy, channel quality, recency of sensor reports, and reliability of the knowledge aggregation method. These values should be revised in successive situation updates and used to guide the search for either robust plans or alternative plans to implement in the event of possible environmental changes.

3. *Expansion of the planning function to include data-gathering options.* When possible, the planning choices should include the option of delaying actions and gathering further data. This requires the use of an information value model that weighs the usefulness of the information against the time delays and costs involved in obtaining it.

4. *Reduction of look-ahead horizons.* The conflict-detection and plan-evaluation routines of the evaluator must make shorter projections into the future. Because of the cascading of uncertainties with time, problem recognition, planning, and evaluation based on short projections may be more effective than those based on long projections.

ENVIRONMENTAL DYNAMICS

Task conditions (e.g. geographic region, data links, traffic loads) may vary with time. This problem is closely related to that of environmental uncertainty, particularly if the dynamics of the environment are unpredictable. Induced architectural refinements include:

1. *Transitions among architectures.* Distribution schemes relying on stationary communication links, standard protocols, or predictable sector loadings may become handicapped in dynamic environments. Such schemes include the space-centered, function-centered, and hierarchical architectures. The more flexible architectures should be invoked to distribute planning and control dynamically as demanded by the changing situation.

2. *Maintenance of belief or confidence estimates.* Situation assessments should have associated confidence and perishability estimates. To monitor the accuracy of these beliefs, the system should maintain data dependencies between linked beliefs, as is done in Hearsay-II (Erman et al., 1980).

3. *Dynamic communications addressing.* The architecture must support continuous communication between the nodes. Communication demands between nodes may be unpredictable, as well as non-uniformly distributed in time. This may require use of broadcasts to locate nodes and point-to-point communications to pass messages.

4. *Increased inference capabilities.* The situation assessment and planning mechanisms may have to rely on inexact pattern-matches to recognize conditions in the unpredictable environment. This may require inference systems that can partially match situation descriptions to rule antecedents (Hayes-Roth, 1978).

COMMUNICATION CONSTRAINTS

The communication links between aircraft may be degraded as a result of bandwidth limitations, environmental interference (e.g., mountains, weather), or range limitations. These problems could be alleviated by the adoption of additional types of sophistication:

1. *Increase in local area networks.* Each separable cluster of aircraft may have to rely more on specialized local area networks than on long-distance communications to remote processing centers. Clark, Pogram, and Reed (1978) discuss the advantages of such local-area networks in geographically limited communication tasks.

2. *Network flexibility.* Because of the possibility of blockages or losses, the networks must have alternative pathways for transmission. ARPANET-like protocols may be used to check link conditions and specify back-up routings (Kahn et al., 1978). Network flexibility may also be increased by multi-hop routing, i.e., routing the data in several hops through the fleet members. This may reduce the individual link distances and link data rates, as compared to direct broadcast communications, but at the same time it may increase the time delays. Variable network geometries based on packet radio techniques, for example, timeshare digital radio frequencies and are organized so that messages reach their destinations through varying, irregular pathways. Unfortunately, systems with many store-and-forward relay nodes can experience high levels of contention and queuing during peak loading periods (Martin, 1977).

3. *Shift to autonomous problem-solving.* Communication range constraints may force a change from global updating of situation estimates and exhaustive search by each node to a less data-intensive strategy. Local data-sensing, planning, and execution should decrease the amount of long-range high-bandwidth data exchange. This type of organization is found in the object-centered cooperative architecture. In extreme situations, requirements for radio silence may dictate the use of the object-centered autonomous architecture.

DEGREE OF CLUSTERING

The form of distribution of planning and control depends strongly on the dispersion of aircraft and the location of objects in the environment. When aircraft group naturally into clusters, with virtually all interactions within the clusters, each group of aircraft may be handled separately. The organization of aircraft into clusters significantly reduces the computation required to detect conflicts. (Calculations illustrating this reduction from an exponential problem to a nearly linear problem are presented in the Appendix.) Other changes that may be induced by clustering are:

1. *Knowledge distribution by specialization.* Communication, data fusion, planning, and control may be replicated only within each specific group. This minimizes unnecessary knowledge replication across all processors.

2. *Local area networks.* If the environmental situation is stationary over time, each cluster may require its own local communication network. This circumvents the need for establishing costly, time-consuming procedures for coordinating with other groups.

TIME STRESS

The time available for decisionmaking depends on aircraft speed, communication constraints, and sensor ranges. In both enroute and terminal-area control situations, problems arise that require resolution within a few seconds. Time stress may require that the architecture have the following characteristics:

1. *High communication channel throughput.* Transmission time in the architectures relying on communications may be reduced through use of very high channel frequencies (Kahn et al., 1978), and response time may be improved by the use of frequency-division multiple-access (FDMA) techniques, in which each link uses a different channel. This avoids the data queues present in single-channel time-division multiple-access (TDMA) systems (Martin, 1977).

2. *Extensive knowledge distribution.* The inclusion of comprehensive knowledge bases in each node processor can reduce the need for interrogating other nodes. Of course, the most critical knowledge may be temporally variable and local in influence. Such information cannot be preloaded into the knowledge bases.

3. *Emphasis on heuristic planning techniques over exhaustive search.* Heuristic planning techniques such as condition-action rules (Newell and Simon, 1972), opportunistic planning (Hayes-Roth and Hayes-Roth, 1978), and simulation-based look-ahead planning (Wesson, 1977) may provide rapid-response capabilities by relaxing the requirement for optimality.

OPTION MULTIPLICITY

The number of possible actions open to each aircraft increases with the number of maneuver options, the sensing range, and the physical extent of the available airspace. The complexity of the planning problem suggests the following problem-solving approaches:

1. *Heuristic planning techniques.* Complete and exhaustive search for optimal routes may be too time-consuming. Heuristic search methods can prune from consideration many planning options, thereby minimizing the number of options to be evaluated in computationally expensive fast-time simulation algorithms.

2. *Planning distribution.* Distributing the planning tasks among a large number of parallel processors can exploit the availability of multiple systems. Each processor might adopt a different solution strategy or take responsibility for a different function or geographic area. The most extreme examples of this approach are the object-centered autonomous and

plan-centered architectures, in which completely disjoint sets of options are considered by each processor.

DENSITY OF THE SOLUTION SPACE

There may be very few conflict-free solutions in a high-density ATC airspace, because of the large number of routing constraints. The following problem-solving approaches are favored in this situation:

1. *Emphasis on deep search.* Determining one of a very few solutions is similar to finding the optimal solution. The planning program must examine virtually all possible options or use a highly discriminating evaluation function to prune non-optimal paths. Such an evaluation function requires extensive simulation-based look-ahead capabilities.

2. *Global view.* Unless the problem can be decomposed into almost completely independent subproblems, the complete problem must be solved. If the complete problem is confronted, information and knowledge must be concentrated at a single processing center. Alternatively, the overall problem may be distributed by assigning individual branches of the search tree to different processing nodes, as in the plan-centered approach.

SITUATIONAL COMPLEXITY

Situational complexity is a function of the number of elements that must be represented—aircraft, navigational aids, terrain obstacles, weather conditions, airfields, etc.—and the amount of conflict between the goals of the participants. Both factors increase the demands on data fusion, problem recognition, planning, and bargaining. High situational complexity suggests the following architectural features:

1. *Data distribution.* The communication of sensor data may be limited to those nodes requesting such data. The recipient nodes may be those closest to or most affected by the object under surveillance. Limiting the dissemination of situation data reduces the communication requirements and processing demands.

2. *Designation of an arbitrator.* If the different processing nodes have very different goals, they may have to bargain for scarce resources such as space and fuel. Unstructured bargaining requires communication of candidate plans, pairwise comparisons between all competing plans, and transmission of evaluations between all affected processing nodes. Designation of one processor as an arbitrator for each conflict reduces the maximum number of communication links from $N \cdot T(N-1)/2$ to $(N-1)$.

STRATEGIES OF COOPERATION IN DISTRIBUTED PROBLEM SOLVING†

Stephanie Cammarata, David McArthur, Randall Steeb

Rand Corporation
1700 Main Street
Santa Monica, California 90406
USA

ABSTRACT

Distributed Artificial Intelligence is concerned with problem solving in which groups solve tasks. In this paper we describe strategies of cooperation that groups require to solve shared tasks effectively. We discuss such strategies in the context of a specific group problem solving application: collision avoidance in air traffic control. Experimental findings with four distinct air-traffic control systems, each implementing a different cooperative strategy, are mentioned.

I. INTRODUCTION

Distributed Artificial Intelligence is concerned with problem solving in which groups solve tasks. Through systems like STRIPS [4], ABSTRIPS [9], BUILD [3], and NOAH [10], we now have some understanding of how a single agent can solve problems. Unfortunately, recent work suggests that the representations of knowledge [5], [1] and planning expertise [8] required of agents in distributed or group problem solving is quite different than that required of single agent problem solvers.

In this paper we focus on one particularly important but little understood topic: The kinds of *strategies of cooperation* that groups require to solve shared tasks effectively. We begin with a discussion of the difficulties facing distributed problem-solving groups. From this analysis we infer a set of requirements on the information-distribution and organizational policies such groups require. We then discuss a set of distributed problem solvers that we have developed in the domain of air traffic control. We concentrate on the particular cooperative strategies they embed, how they are implemented, and how they successfully overcome some of the obstacles that make it difficult to coordinate groups of agents.

II. DISTRIBUTED PROBLEM SOLVING DIFFICULTIES

To understand the difficulties facing groups solving problems it helps to note some important characteristics of distributed problems. The following traits are true of a wide variety of group situations:

- Most situations consist of a collection of agents, each with various *skills*, including sensing, communication (often over limited- bandwidth channels), planning, and acting.
- The group as a whole has a set of assigned *tasks*. As in single agent problem-solving situations, these tasks may need to be decomposed into subtasks, not all of which may be logically independent. The group must somehow assign subtasks to appropriate agents.
- Typically each agent has only *limited knowledge*. An agent may be subject to several kinds of limitations: limited knowledge of the environment (e.g., because of restricted sensing horizons), limited knowledge of the tasks of the group, or limited knowledge of the intentions of other agents.
- There are often shared *limited resources* with which each agent can attack tasks. For example, if the agents are in a blocksworld environment, the shared resources are the blocks out of which their constructions must be made.
- Agents typically have differing *appropriateness* for a given task. The appropriateness of an agent for a task is a function of how well the agent's skills match the expertise

required to do the task, the extent to which its limited knowledge is adequate for the task, and current processing resources of the agent.

Several kinds of distributed problem-solving difficulties follow from this characterization. First, there are difficulties with *optimal task assignment*. Many mappings of decomposed subtasks to agents are possible, but, because agents have differing appropriateness with respect to a given task, only a few agents will be acceptable for any task. In many distributed problems it is crucial for agents to adopt the right *role*. In addition to insuring that any given task is assigned to an appropriate agent, the group has to achieve *task coverage*. All subtasks should be assigned to some agent (complete role assignment) and multiple unnecessary agents should not be assigned a task (consistent role assignment). The limited knowledge of agents compounds the difficulty of optimal task assignment and task coverage. Incomplete knowledge prevents consistent and complete role assignment because no one agent may have a global knowledge of all the roles or subtasks that need to be assigned. Optimal task assignment is also threatened since agents may not know about tasks for which they are the most appropriate.

Second, *task coordination problems* arise because tasks assigned to agents may not be independent. For example, if two blocksworld agents are each to build towers (as subtasks of a larger task), the plan that one agent produces might negatively interact with the plan of another if both intended to use the same block. While single-agent problem solvers have difficulties in handling non-independent tasks or subgoals, these difficulties multiply for distributed problem solvers. Again, limited knowledge is the reason. If two agents have only local knowledge—if they know only the local environment, know only their tasks and intentions—then they will not know of, or be able to prevent, negative interactions between their roles and those of other agents.

In summary, a main challenge to distributed problem solving is that the solutions which a distributed agent produces must not only be locally acceptable, achieving the assigned tasks, but also they must be interfaced correctly with the actions of other agents solving dependent tasks. The solutions must not only be reasonable with respect to the local task, they must be *globally coherent* and this global coherence must be achieved by *local computation alone*.

III. STRATEGIES FOR COOPERATION

How can groups achieve global coherence in the face of limited knowledge and the requirement that all computation be local? Broadly, the key to coherent distributed problem solving lies in the fact that while distributed agents have greater difficulties in solving a given task, they have potentially more options as well. For example, a distributed agent may plan or act, but he may also request others to do so. In short, much of the power of distributed problem solving comes through cooperation and communication.

Although communication between agents provides the basis for effective cooperative problem solving, it is just another problem-solving tool that may be used poorly or effectively. If the tool is used poorly then group problem-solving performance may be worse than individual problem-solving performance. Considerable expertise is required to use communication effectively. We refer to such expertise as *cooperative strategies*. Our main theoretical and empirical goals have been to understand two distinct classes of such strategies: *organizational policies* and *information-distribution policies*.

† The work reported here was supported by Contract MDA903-82-C-0061 from the Information Processing Technology Office of the Defense Advanced Projects Agency (DOD).

A. Organizational Policies

Organizational policies dictate how a larger task should be decomposed into smaller (sub)tasks which can be assigned to individual agents. Typically a given organizational policy assigns specific roles to each of the agents in a group. Such a policy is useful if for some tasks the resulting division of labor enables agents to work independently. For example, the corporate hierarchy is an organizational policy that is particularly effective if the corporate task can be decomposed in such a way that an agent at one level can work independently of others at that level, reporting results only to his immediate superior who takes care of any necessary interfacing.

Organizational policies not only define a task decomposition but prescribe communication paths among agents. They turn a random collection of agents into a network that is fixed, at least for a given task. In the corporate hierarchy, again, the arcs between agents usually indicate which pairs are permitted to talk to one another, and, in addition, determine the nature of the messages that are allowed. Such communication restrictions will be beneficial if they encourage only those agents who should communicate to do so; in particular, agents that have dependent tasks or who may share resources. In general, organizational policies strongly direct and constrain the behavior of distributed agents. If those constraints are appropriate to the task at hand, then the organization is effective, otherwise its performance may be sub-optimal.

In our distributed problem-solving systems and others [11],[2] groups begin by establishing an organizational policy. To do so, the agents must not only know which policy is appropriate to the current circumstances, but also must know *techniques by which a group can implement the chosen policy in a distributed fashion.* Briefly, any distributed method of implementing an organizational policy must answer a variety of questions, including:

- When does organization structuring take place?
- How is the assignment of roles specified by the policy made to agents? In other words, how is the agent who is most appropriate found for a given task found?
- Are agents "externally-directed" or "data-directed" [7]? That is, does an agent arrive at its roles by being told them or is information relayed, allowing it to make the assignment of roles itself?
- When an agent is requested by another to conform to a role, or take on another subtask for that agent, does the first agent have a right to negotiate? How does an agent weigh the value of competing tasks?

Smith [11] has proposed the contract net as a formalism for implementing organizational policies in a distributed fashion. In Section V.B., we discuss how some organizational policies were imposed in distributed air-traffic control.

B. Information-distribution Policies

An information-distribution policy addresses the nature of communication between cooperating agents. Decisions about how agents communicate with each other are, first of all, constrained by the choice of organizational policy, since that policy decides the network of permissible communicators. However, within these constraints, a great number of lower level decisions must be made about how and when communications should occur. Briefly:

- *Broadcast or selective communication.* Are agents discriminating about who they talk to? If so what criteria are used to select recipients?
- *Unsolicited or on-demand communication.* Assuming you know who you want to communicate with, do you do so only if information is requested, or do you infer the informational needs of other agents and transmit data accordingly?
- *Acknowledged or unacknowledge communication.* Do you indicate that you have received information?
- *Single-transmission or repeated-transmission communication.* Is a piece of information only sent once, or can it be repeated? How frequently? Lesser and Erman [6] refer to a repeated-transmission policy as murmuring.

Poor decisions at this level result, at best, in the highly inefficient use of limited-bandwidth channels. At worst, such choices endanger global coherence by preventing agents whose tasks may interact from talking to one another. The goal of information-distribution policies is to minimize these possibilities. As with organizational policies, the utility of communication policies

depends on current conditions. These include the bandwidth of the communication channel, the reliability of the channel, the load of the channel, the maximum acceptable information turn-around time, and the relative cost (and time) of computation versus communication.

IV. DISTRIBUTED PROBLEM SOLVING IN AIR-TRAFFIC CONTROL

Problem solving in air-traffic control may be distributed in several ways. Elsewhere [12] we discuss a variety of architectures of distribution. Currently we have implemented only *object-centered* systems, where one agent is associated with each aircraft. In our air-traffic control task, aircraft enter a rectangular (14 x 23 mile) airspace at any time, either at one of 10 infixes on the borders of the airspace, or from one of two airports. The main goal of the agent associated with each aircraft is to traverse the airspace to an assigned destination--either a boundary outfix, or an airport. Each aircraft has only a limited sensory horizon, hence its knowledge of the world is never complete and it must continually gather information as it moves through the airspace. Information may be accumulated either by sensing or communication. Agents are allowed to communicate over a limited bandwidth channel to other aircraft for purposes of exchanging information and instructions.

Distributed ATC is a group problem not only because agents may help one another gather information but also because the goals of one agent may interact with those of another. Goal interactions come in the form of shared conflicts. A conflict between two or more agents arises when, according to their current plans, the two will violate minimum separation requirements at some point in the future. When shared conflicts arise, agents must negotiate to solve them. In a crowded airspace, such goal conflicts can get particularly complex, and involve several aircraft, thus necessitating a high degree of group cooperation.

In terms of the vocabulary developed in Section II, the detection and resolution of conflicts are the main distributed problem-solving *tasks.* These tasks may be decomposed into several *subtasks* or distinct *roles.* Agents may gather information about a shared conflict, evaluate or interpret the information, develop a plan to avoid a projected conflict, or execute such a plan. Agents may be more or less *appropriate* for such roles depending on their current processing load (Are they currently involved in helping resolve other conflicts?), their state of knowledge (Do they know a lot about the intentions of other agents in the conflict?), or their spatial constraints (Can they see many nearby aircraft? Do they have much excess fuel?).

The issue of *optimal task assignment* arises because a group of aircraft may fail to assign the agent that is the most appropriate to each role in a conflict-task if some of the conflictees do not know about a shared conflict. In addition, care must be taken that a complete and consistent set of roles is assigned. Some role inconsistencies can be fatal. For example, two agents would be adopting inconsistent roles if one decides to move left to avoid a head-on collision with the second while the second decides to jog right. Severe *task coordination problems* also threaten to arise in distributed ATC. The action of moving to avoid one conflict may create or worsen other conflicts (negative task interactions) or lessen other conflicts (positive task interactions). Both forms of interaction are caused by the fact that while several agents may be dealing with different conflict-tasks, they are nevertheless exploiting shared limited spatial resources.

V. FOUR DISTRIBUTED PROBLEM SOLVERS FOR AIR TRAFFIC CONTROL

We now outline the cooperative strategies embedded in four distinct ATC systems. All four systems are implemented in our framework for constructing distributed agents [8]. This in turn is implemented in INTERLISP- D, running on Xerox Dolphins.

A. Information-distribution Policies in ATC

The information-distribution policy common to all four systems prescribes that information should be sent to other aircraft selectively (no broadcasting), without waiting for a request, without expecting an acknowledgement, and without repeating the information a second time. These choices are reasonable since we assume in all systems that communication is error-free. When we add noise to the communication channel, we envision adopting a policy that injects some needed redundancy or safety into communication: for example a policy that includes murmuring [6]. We also assumed a constant effective communication bandwidth for all four systems. Each aircraft was allowed to send a maximum of 5 messages per 15 seconds of time.

B. Organizational Policies in ATC

The organizational policy embedded in three of the four systems may be characterized as *task centralization*, and the fourth system adheres to a policy of *task sharing*. Under *task centralization*, the agents involved in any given conflict task will choose one of their number to play most of the roles. In particular one agent will perform the evaluation role (do all the evaluation of the potential conflict between aircraft), the plan-fixing role (attempt to devise a plan-fix to dissolve the entire conflict) and the actor role (act on the new plan). The selected agent is required to modify only his plan to resolve the conflict, thus the remaining agents perform no planning or actions. Instead these conflictees, having agreed on the choice of a replanner, adopt passive information-gathering roles, merely sending their intentions (plan) to the selected agent. The policy of task centralization, whatever its shortcomings, is worth considering because it enjoys many of the advantages of centralized, single-agent problem solving that it is meant to mimic. Specifically, by centralizing most task roles in a single agent the group has to worry less about negative task interactions such as the threat of two aircraft acting in an inconsistent fashion, noted above.

Although three of our four systems embed a task centralization policy, they differ in how they measure and choose the agent who is the most appropriate for the several centralized roles.

Selection by shared convention. Here each aircraft uses only directly sensed information about the other aircraft (position, heading, and speed) to decide who should plan and who should transmit its current route. The aircraft silently use a common set of conventions for this decision, minimizing communications. Figure 1 shows a prototypic sequence of tasks and communications between two aircraft under this policy.

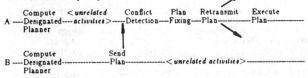

Figure 1. Prototypic task sequence under Shared Convention policy.

Time lines for tasks executed by aircraft A and B. Solid lines indicate communications.

Because of the limited criteria used, the aircraft selected as the replanner is not likely to be the most appropriate. This version mainly serves as a benchmark against which to judge the utility of more intelligent methods of selection which are also more costly in terms of computation and communication.

Selection of the least spatially constrained agent. Here each aircraft in a potential conflict transmits its *constraint factor* to the other aircraft. The constraint factor is an aggregation of such considerations as the number of other nearby aircraft, fuel remaining, distance from destination, and message load. Figure 2 gives an idea of the standard sequence of tasks and communications under this policy.

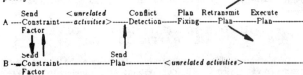

Figure 2. Prototypic task sequence under Least Constrained policy.

This method of selection maintains that the agent that is the most appropriate is the one with the most degrees of freedom for modifying its plan. It is a more complex selection than the shared convention, and should result in more effective replanner choices, although at some additional cost in initial communications.

Selection of the most knowledgeable, least committed agent. As above, aircraft share *constraint factors* with the other conflictees, but here they are computed differently. This method of selection maintains that the best agent to replan is the one who knows the

most about other agents' intentions, because, in replanning, a well informed agent can explicitly take account of possible interactions between his intentions and those of other agents. More globally coherent plan-fixes should therefore result. In addition, this method also says that agents whose intentions are known by others should not replan. If such an agent does modify its plan, it will have violated the expectations of cooperating agents, making their knowledge incorrect and in turn making cooperation difficult. Thus, this policy implements a common adage of cooperation: Don't do the unexpected.

In spite of their simplicity, task centralization policies are often ineffective. Although the agent selected to perform the centralized roles may be *overall* the best, that agent is rarely the best for *each* of the centralized roles. For example, we still might want to assign the actor role to the agent in a conflict set who is least constrained in the sense defined above. However, that agent might not be the best in the set for fixing his plan — for making a modification to the plan and evaluating the implications of such a change. Presumably the best agent for this role is the (possibly distinct) member of the conflict set that knows most about the environment and intentions of aircraft neighboring the one whose plan is to be fixed. This aircraft is in the best position to determine that any changed plan is not only locally reasonable, solving the conflict, but that it is globally reasonable, not creating new conflicts with other aircraft.

Our *task sharing* policy attempts to avoid such problems by evaluating agents' qualifications with respect to each of the roles associated with a conflict. While in centralized policies a single negotiation determines an overall replanner, in the task sharing policy two rounds of negotiation are necessary, one to determine the plan-fixer and one to determine the actor. Figure 3 gives a detailed description of a prototypical sequence of tasks and communications showing how such a policy is implemented in a distributed fashion.

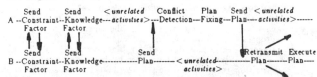

Figure 3. Prototypic task sequence under Task Sharing policy.

Performance of groups working under a task sharing policy is potentially superior to groups working under a policy of centralization because in the former the group attempts to optimize on each role. However, in practice this policy has several possible drawbacks. It is communication intensive and may be inappropriate when communication channels are unreliable or costly. Moreover, it risks potential negative interactions, because several agents have to coordinate intimately to achieve a solution.

VI. EXPERIMENTAL STUDIES

We are conducting a series of rudimentary experimental studies on the four policies outlined above. We report here on results pertaining to only the three task centralization policies, since data collection for the task sharing policy is not yet complete. All three variants were tested on eight distributed scenarios. Each scenario stipulated (i) how many aircraft would enter the airspace in the session, (ii) when and where they would enter, and (iii) where they would exit. This control over the parameters of distributed problem-solving situations allowed us to isolate situation features that uncovered the strengths and weaknesses in performance of our policies. In particular, the scenarios varied considerably in task density, time stress, and task difficulty.

We examined three performance indices when comparing the systems: communication load, processing time, and task effectiveness. Task effectiveness was indicated by two distinct factors: separation errors (more important) and fuel usage (less important). A summary of the main results is given in Table 1.

VII. DISCUSSION OF RESULTS

Examining the individual scenarios, we found the *Shared convention* policy, relying on essentially arbitrary assignment of planning responsibility, performed well only in low complexity, low difficulty tasks. It minimized communications and responded rapidly compared to the other policies but quickly foundered in 3- and 4-body conflicts.

	Shared Convention	Least Constrained	Most Knowledgeable
Communications (i)	10.9	28.6	28.2
Processing time (ii)	1265	1726	1651
Separation errors (iii)	4.3	1.4	2.3
Fuel usage (iv)	96	108	101

(i) *Communication load* = Mean messages sent per aircraft while flying from infix to outfix

(ii) *Processing time* = mean Xerox 1100 cpu seconds per aircraft while flying

(iii) *Separation errors* = Mean number of near misses or collisions for all aircraft in a scenario

(iv) *Fuel usage* = Mean number of fuel units used for all aircraft

Figure 1. Performance measures of three organizational policies (statistics averaged across 8 scenarios)

The *Least Constrained* policy performed best overall. It did particularly well with high complexity, high difficulty tasks. In such cases the planning aircraft tended to be located at the edge of the fray, able to find more viable solutions than those aircraft in the interior. The policy was time and communication intensive, however, largely because of the high number of messages needed to cooperatively determine the replanner and to maintain consistency after replanning. In any of the three systems, when a replanner is successful it must send *data retransmission messages* to all aircraft to which it had previously sent its intentions. The number of data retransmissions was especially high under the *Least Constrained* policy.

The *Most Knowledgeable* policy was intermediate in performance. It performed best in tasks of low complexity and high difficulty, that is, tasks with primarily 2- and 3-body interactions but having few potential solutions. In complex multi-aircraft situations, if the wrong aircraft was chosen for planning, the effect was often catastrophic. This is because the aircraft that then received replan requests tended to have little knowledge about the routes of other aircraft. By design of the policy, this knowledge was typically concentrated in the initially selected planner.

When successful, the *Most Knowledgeable* policy's performance was in some ways better than that of the *Least Constrained* policy. In particular, when an agent found a solution to a local conflict-task under the *Most Knowledgeable* policy its solution was likely to be more globally coherent than under other policies, since the replanning agent was selected partially because of his wide knowledge of other aircraft's plans. This knowledge allowed the agent to more effectively replan without incurring new conflicts. In addition, a successful replanning agent under a *Most Knowledgeable* policy generally needed to issue less data retransmission messages than under the other policies, since it was selected to replan partially because its intentions were known to fewer others (i.e., it was the less committed agent). We had initially anticipated minimizing data retransmissions would be very important for guaranteeing globally coherent performance. We envisioned situations where one retransmission would cause the receiving agent to re-evaluate, possibly finding new conflicts, causing more replanning, further data retransmissions, and so on in a vicious propagation of changes. This did not happen as much as we had expected under the the *Least Constrained* policy, although a few instances were observed.

Another expectation that did not arise was a wide variation in processing times among the aircraft under the *Most Knowledgeable* policy. This policy should tend to bias replanning in the favor of a few agents. If an agent is the replanner once, it gains new knowledge of other's plans making it an even better choice as replanner for later conflict-tasks. We anticipated that this concentration would skew the processing times compared to a more uniform distribution of responsibilities under the other policies. This would have been a disadvantage in a truly distributed system, as some agents would be quiescent much of the time. The expected variation in times did not evidence itself, however, except in the relatively easy scenarios.

VII.   CONCLUSIONS

Distributed problem solving is an enigma. Potentially, a group of agents should be able to solve problems more effectively than the same agents working individually. In practice, however, groups often work ineffectively and their joint productivity is less than the sum of the productivities expected of each member. Our aim is to discover the elusive cooperative strategies that enable groups to reach optimum productivity. On the theoretical side we are developing concepts that allow us to simply and formally describe various cooperative strategies. On the empirical side, we are testing such strategies by imposing them on groups and observing the resulting group performance. Both phases are necessary. The theoretical investigations are valuable because most problem solving models presently available describe only the information processing of single agent problem solvers, not distributed problem solvers. The empirical work is necessary because many of the behavioral properties of complex cooperative strategies are not apparent without observing how they actually perform in real or simulated settings.

REFERENCES

[1] Appelt, D. E., Planning Natural-language utterances to satisfy multiple goals, Technical Note 259, SRI International, 1982.

[2] Davis, R., Smith, R.G., Negotiation as a metaphor for distributed problem solving, Memo 624, MIT Artificial Intelligence Lab, 1981.

[3] Fahlman, S., A planning system for robot construction tasks, *Artificial Intelligence*, 5, (1), 1974, 1-49.

[4] Fikes, R.E., Nilsson, N.J., Strips: A new approach to the application of theorem proving to problem solving, *Artificial Intelligence*, 2, (2), 1971, 189-208.

[5] Konolige, K., A first order formalization of knowledge and action for a multi-agent planning system, *Machine Intelligence* 10, 1981.

[6] Lesser, V. R., Reed, S., Pavlin, J., Quantifying and Simulating the behavior of knowledge-based interpretation systems, *Proceedings of the First Annual National Conference on Artificial Intelligence*, Stanford University, 1980, 111-115.

[7] Lesser, V., A high-level simulation testbed for cooperative problem solving, COINS Technical Report 81-16, University of Massachusetts, Amherst, MA, 1981.

[8] McArthur, D., Steeb, R., and Cammarata, S., A framework for distributed problem solving, *Proceedings of the National Conference on Artificial Intelligence*, Pittsburg, PA, 1982, 181-184.

[9] Sacerdoti, E., Planning in a hierarchy of abstraction spaces. *Artificial Intelligence*, 5, (2), 115-135, 1974.

[10] Sacerdoti, E., A structure for plans and behavior. New York: Elsevier North-Holland, 1977.

[11] Smith, R.G., A framework for problem solving in a distributed processing environment, STAN-CS-78-700, Stanford University, 1978.

[12] Steeb, R., Cammarata, S., Hayes-Roth, F.A., Thorndyke, P.W., Wesson, R.B., Distributed intelligence for air fleet control, R-2728-ARPA, The Rand Corporation, 1981.

Parallelism in Artificial Intelligence Problem Solving:

A Case Study of Hearsay II

RICHARD D. FENNELL AND VICTOR R. LESSER

Abstract—The Hearsay II speech-understanding system (HSII) (Lesser *et al.* [11], Fennell [9], and Erman and Lesser [6]) is an implementation of a knowledge-based multiprocessing artificial intelligence (AI) problem-solving organization. HSII is intended to represent a problem-solving organization which is applicable for implementation in a parallel hardware environment such as C.mmp (Bell *et al.* [2]). The primary characteristics of this organization include: 1) multiple, diverse, independent and asynchronously executing knowledge sources (KS's), 2) cooperating (in terms of control) via a generalized form of the hypothesize-and-test paradigm involving the data-directed invocation of KS processes, and 3) communicating (in terms of data) via a shared blackboard-like data base in which the current data state is held in a homogeneous, multidimensional, directed-graph structure. The object of this paper is to explore several of the ramifications of such a problem-solving organization by examining the mechanisms and policies underlying HSII which are necessary for supporting its organization as a multiprocessing system. In addition, a multiprocessor simulation study is presented which details the effects of actually implementing such a parallel organization for use in a particular application area, that of speech understanding.

Index Terms—Artificial intelligence (AI) problem solving, data-directed control, multiprocessors, parallelism, speech understanding, synchronization, system organization.

Manuscript received September 5, 1975; revised August 27, 1976. This research was supported by the Defense Advanced Research Projects Agency under Contract F44620-73-C-0074 and monitored by the Air Force Office of Scientific Research.

R. D. Fennell was with the Department of Computer Science, Carnegie-Mellon University, Pittsburgh, PA 15213. He is now with the Federal Judicial Center, Washington, DC 20005.

V. R. Lesser is with the Department of Computer Science, Carnegie-Mellon University, Pittsburgh, PA 15213.

INTRODUCTION

MANY artificial intelligence (AI) problem-solving tasks require large amounts of processing power because of the size of the search space that needs to be examined during the course of problem solution. This is especially true for tasks that involve the interpretation of real-world perceptual data which is generally very noisy (e.g., speech and image understanding systems). For example, a speech-understanding system capable of reliably understanding connected speech involving a large vocabulary is likely to require from 10 to 100 million instructions per second (mips) of computing power, if the recognition is to be performed in real time.[1] Recent trends in technology suggest that this computing power can be economically obtained through a closely coupled network of asynchronous "simple" processors (involving perhaps 10 to 100 of these processors), (Bell *et al.* [3], and Heart *et al.* [10]). The major problem (from the problem-solving point of view) with this network multiprocessor approach for generating computing power is in specifying the various problem-solving algorithms in such a way as to exhibit a structure appropriate for exploiting the parallelism available in the multiprocessor network.

The Hearsay II speech-understanding system (HSII) (Lesser *et al.* [11], Fennell [9], and Erman and Lesser [6]) currently under development at Carnegie-Mellon University represents a problem-solving organization that can effectively exploit a multiprocessor system. HSII has been designed as an AI system organization suitable for expressing knowledge-based problem-solving strategies in which appropriately organized subject-matter knowledge may be represented as knowledge sources capable of contributing their knowledge in a parallel data-directed fashion. A *knowledge source* (KS) may be described as an agent that embodies the knowledge of a particular aspect of a problem domain and is useful in solving a problem from that domain by performing actions based upon its knowledge so as to further the progress of the overall solution. The HSII system organization allows these various independent and diverse sources of knowledge to be specified and their interactions coordinated so they might cooperate with one another (perhaps asynchronously and in parallel) to effect a problem solution. As an example of the decomposition of a task domain into KS's, in the speech task domain there might be distinct KS's to deal with acoustic, phonetic, lexical, syntactic, and semantic information. While the speech task is the first test of the multiprocessing problem-solving organization of HSII, it is believed that the system organization provided by HSII is capable of supporting other knowledge-based AI problem-solving strategies (Erman and Lesser [6]), as might be found in vision, robotics, chess, natural language understanding, and protocol analysis. In fact, work is under way which further tests the applicability of the HSII organization for the analysis of natural scenes (Ohlander [13]) and as a model for human reading (Rumelhart [17]).

The rest of this paper will explore several of the ramifications of such an organization by examining the mechanisms and policies underlying HSII which are necessary for supporting its organization as a multiprocessing problem-solving system. First, an abstract description of a class of problem-solving systems is given using the production system model of Newell [12]. Then, the HSII organization is described in terms of this model. The various decisions made during the course of design necessitated

the introduction of various multiprocessing mechanisms (e.g., mechanisms for maintaining data localization and data integrity), and these mechanisms are discussed. Finally, a simulation study is presented which details the effects of actually implementing such a problem-solving organization in a multiprocessor environment.

THE MODEL

An Abstract Model for Problem Solving

In the abstract, the problem-solving organization underlying HSII may be modeled in terms of a "production system," (Newell [12]). A *production system* is a scheme for specifying an information processing system in which the control structure of the system is defined by operations on a set of *productions* of the form $P \rightarrow A$, which operate from and on a collection of data structures. P represents a logical antecedent, called a *precondition*, which may or may not be satisfied by the information encoded within the dynamically current set of data structures. If P is found to be satisfied by some data structure, then the associated *action A* is executed, which presumably will have some altering effect upon the data base such that some other (or the same) precondition becomes satisfied. This paradigm for sequencing of the actions can be thought of as a data-directed control structure, since the satisfaction of the precondition is dependent upon the dynamic state of the data structure. Productions are executed as long as their antecedent preconditions are satisfied, and the process halts either when no precondition is found to be satisfied or when an action executes a stop operation (thereby signalling problem solution or failure, in the case of problem-solving systems).

The HSII Organization: A Production System Approach

The HSII system organization, which can be characterized as a "parallel" production system, has a centralized data base which represents the dynamic problem solution state. This data base, which is called the *blackboard*, is a multidimensional data structure, the fundamental data element of which is called a *node*. For example, the dimensions of the HSII speech-understanding system data base are informational level (e.g., phonetic, surface-phonemic, syllabic, lexical, and phrasal levels), utterance time (speech time measured from the beginning of the input utterance), and data alternatives (where multiple nodes are permitted to exist simultaneously at the same level and utterance time). The blackboard is readable and writable by any precondition or KS process (where a KS process is the embodiment of a production action, to use the terminology of production systems). Preconditions are procedurally oriented and may specify arbitrarily complex tests to be performed on the data structure in order to decide precondition satisfaction. In order to avoid executing these precondition tests unnecessarily often, they

---

[1] The Hearsay I (Reddy *et al.* [14]–[16] and Erman [5]) and Dragon (Baker [1]) speech-understanding systems require approximately 10 to 20 mips of computing power for real-time recognition when handling small vocabularies.

in turn have *pre-preconditions* which are essentially monitors on relevant primitive data base events (e.g., monitoring for a change to a given field of a given node in the data base, or a given field of any node in the data base). Whenever any of these primitive events occurs, those preconditions monitoring such events become schedulable and, when executed, test for full precondition satisfaction. Testing for precondition satisfaction is not presumed to be an instantaneous or even an indivisible operation, and several such precondition tests may proceed concurrently.

The KS processes representing the production actions are also procedurally oriented and may specify arbitrarily complex sequences of operations to be performed upon the data structure. The overall effect of any given KS process is usually either to hypothesize new data which are to be added to the data base or to verify (and perhaps modify) data previously placed in the data base. This follows the general *hypothesize-and-test* problem-solving paradigm wherein hypotheses representing partial problem solutions are generated and then tested for validity; this cycle continues until the verification phase certifies the completion of processing (and either the problem is solved or failure is indicated). The execution of a KS process is usually temporally disjoint from the satisfaction of its precondition; the execution of any given KS process is not presumed to be indivisible; and the concurrent execution of multiple KS processes is permitted. In addition, a precondition process may invoke multiple instantiations of a KS to work on the different parts of the blackboard which independently satisfy the precondition's pattern. Thus, the independent data-directed nature of precondition evaluation and KS execution can potentially generate a significant amount of parallel activity throught the concurrent execution of different preconditions, different KS's, and multiple instantiations of a single KS.

The basic structure and components of the HSII organization may be depicted as shown in the message transaction diagram of Fig. 1. The diagram indicates the paths of active information flow between the various components of the problem-solving system as solid arrows; paths indicating control activity are shown as broken arrows. The major components of the diagram include a passive global data structure (the *blackboard*) which contains the current state of the problem solution. Access to the blackboard is conceptually centralized in the *blackboard handler* module,[2] whose primary function is to accept and honor requests from the active processing elements to read and write parts of the blackboard. The active processing elements which generate these data access requests consist of *KS processes* and their associated *preconditions*. Preconditions are activated by a *blackboard monitoring mechanism* which monitors the various write-actions of

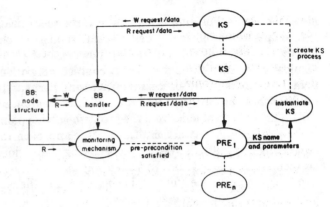

Fig. 1.   Simplified HSII system organization.

the blackboard handler; whenever an event occurs which is of interest to a particular precondition process, that precondition becomes schedulable.[3] If, upon further examination of the blackboard, the precondition finds itself "satisfied," the precondition may request a process instantiation of its associated KS to be established, passing the details of how the precondition was satisfied as parameters to this instantiation of the KS. Once instantiated, the KS process can respond to the blackboard data condition which was detected by its precondition, possibly requesting further modifications be made to the blackboard, perhaps thereby triggering further preconditions to respond to the latest modifications. This particular characterization of the HSII organization, while overly simplified, shows the data-driven nature of the KS activations and interactions. A more complete message transaction diagram for HSII will be presented in a subsequent section.

HEARSAY II MULTIPROCESSING MECHANISMS

In order to adapt the HSII organization to a multiprocessing environment, mechanisms must be provided to support the individual localized executions of the various active and ready processes and to keep the processes from interfering with one another, either directly or indirectly. On the other hand, mechanisms must also be provided so that the various active processes may communicate with one another so as to achieve the desired process cooperation. Since the constituent KS's are assumed to be independently developed and are not to presume the explicit existence of other KS's, communication among these KS's must necessarily be indirect. The desire for a modular KS structure arises from the fact that usually many different people are involved in the implementation of the set of KS's, and, for purposes of experimentation and KS performance analysis, the system should be able to be reconfigured easily using alternative subsets of KS's. Communication among KS's takes two primary forms: data base monitoring for collecting pertinent data event information for future use (*local contexts* and precondition activation),

---

[2] The blackboard handler module could be implemented either as a procedure which is called as a subroutine (with appropriate protected critical sections) from precondition and KS processes, or as a process which contains a queue of requests for blackboard operations sent by precondition and KS processes. In the implementation discussed in this paper, the former method is used.

[3] During the period between when the precondition process is first scheduled and the time it is executed, the monitoring for relevant data base events continues. Thus, a precondition process, when finally executed, may check more than one part of the data base for satisfaction.

and data base monitoring for detecting the occurrence of data events which violate prior data assumptions (*tags* and *messages*). The following paragraphs discuss these forms of data-base monitoring and their relationship to the data-access synchronization mechanisms required in a multiprocess system organization.

Local Contexts

Interprocess communication (and interference) among KS's and their associated preconditions occurs mainly via the global data base, as a result of the design decisions involved in trying to maintain process independence. It is therefore not surprising that the mechanisms necessary to bring about the desired process cooperation and independence are based on global data-base considerations. The global data base (the *blackboard*) is intended to contain only dynamically current information. Since preconditions (being data-directed) are to be tested for satisfaction upon the occurrence of relevant data-base changes (which are historical *data events*), and since neither precondition testing nor action execution (nor the sequential combination of the two) is assumed to be an indivisible operation, localized data bases must be provided for each process unit (precondition or action) that needs to remember relevant historical data events. These localized data bases, called *local contexts* in HSII, which record the changes to the blackboard since the precondition process was last executed or since the KS process was created, provide personalized operating environments for the various precondition and KS processes. A local context preserves only those data events[4] and state changes relevant to its owner. The creation time of the local context (i.e., the time from which it begins collecting data events) is also dependent upon the context owner. Any given local context is built up incrementally: when a modification occurs to the global data base, the resulting data event is distributed to the various local contexts interested in such events. Thus, the various local contexts retain a history of relevant data events, while the global data base contains only the most current information.

Data Integrity

Since precondition and KS processes are not guaranteed to be executed uninterruptedly, these processes often need to assure the integrity of various assumptions they are making about the contents of the data base;[5] should these assumptions become violated due to the actions of an in-tervening process, the further computation of the assuming process may have to be altered (or terminated). One way to approach the problem of data integrity is to guarantee the validity of data assumptions by disallowing intervening processes the ability to modify (or perhaps even to examine) critical data. The HSII system provides two forms of locking primitives, *node-* and *region-locking*, which can be used to guarantee exclusive access to the desired data. Node-locking guarantees exclusive access to an explicitly specified node in the blackboard, whereas region-locking guarantees exclusive access to a collection of nodes that are specified implicitly based on a set of node characteristics. In the current implementation of HSII, the region characteristics are specified by a particular information level and time period of a node. If the blackboard is considered as a two-dimensional structure with coordinates of information level and time, then region-locking permits the locking of an arbitrary rectangular area in the blackboard. Region-locking has the additional property of preventing the creation of any new node that would be placed in the blackboard area specified by the region by other than the process which had requested the region-lock. Additional locking flexibility is introduced by allowing processes to request read-only access to nodes or regions (called *node-* or *region-examining*); this reduces possible contention by permitting multiple readers of a given node to coexist, while excluding any writers of that node until all readers are finished. The system also provides a "super lock," which allows an arbitrary group of nodes and regions to be locked at the same time. A predefined linear ordering strategy for nonpreemptive data-access allocation (Coffman *et al.* [4]) is applied by the "super lock" primitive to the desired node- and region-locks so as to avoid the possibility of data-base deadlock.

The technique of guaranteeing data integrity through exclusive access is applicable only if all the nodes and regions to be accessed and modified are known ahead of time and thus are able to be locked simultaneously. The sequential acquisition of exclusive access to nodes and region, without intervening unlocks, can result in the possibility of deadlock. In the HSII blackboard, nodes are interconnected to form a directed graph structure; because it is possible to establish an arbitrarily complex interconnection structure, it is often very difficult for a KS process to anticipate the sequence of nodes it will desire to access or modify. Thus, the mechanisms of exclusive access cannot always be used to guarantee data integrity in a system with a complex data structure and a set of unknown processes. Furthermore, even if the KS can anticipate the area in the blackboard within which it will work and thereby request exclusive access to this area, the area may be very large, leading to a significant decrease in potential parallel activity by other processes waiting for this locked area to become available.

An alternative approach to guaranteeing data integrity is to provide a means by which a process (precondition or KS) may place data assumptions about the particular state of a node or group of nodes in the data base (the action of

---

[4] The information which defines a data event consists of the locus of the event (i.e., a data node name and a field name within that node) and the old value of the field (the new value being stored in the global data base).

[5] There are two different forms of data integrity that need to be differentiated: syntactic (system) and semantic (user). For example, a syntactic consistency requirement associated with a list structure is that each element of the list contains a pointer to another valid list element; whereas, a semantic consistency requirement, which relates to how the list structure is interpreted by a KS, could be that the values associated with adjacent list elements are always less than 100 apart. Both types of data integrity are dealt with in this paper, but the main focus of the discussion in this section is on semantic consistency.

putting these assumptions in the blackboards is called *tagging*). If these assumptions are invalidated by a subsequent blackboard modification operation of another process, then a *message* indicating this violation is sent to the process making the assumption. In the meantime, the assuming process can proceed without obstructing other processes, until such time as it intends to modify the data base (since data-base modification is the only way one process can affect the execution of another). The process must then acquire exclusive access to the parts of the data base involved in its prior assumptions (which parts will have been previously *tagged* in the data base, thereby defining a *critical data set*) and check to see whether the assumptions have been violated (in which case, messages indicating those violations would have been sent to the process). If a violation has occurred, the assuming process may wish to take alternative action; otherwise, the intended data base modifications may be made as if the process had had exclusive access throughout its computation. This tagging mechanism can also be used to signal the KS process that the initial conditions in the blackboard (i.e., the precondition pattern) that caused the precondition to invoke it have been modified; this is accomplished by having the precondition tag these initial conditions on behalf of the KS process prior to the instantiation of the KS.

Thus, the HSII organization provides mechanisms to accomplish two forms of data integrity assurance: the various data-base locking mechanisms described previously provide several ways to acquire exclusive or read-only data access; and the data-tagging facility allows data assumptions to be placed in the data base without interfering with any process' ability to access or modify that area of the data base (with data invalidation warning messages being sent by data-base monitors whenever the assumptions are violated).

To provide a basis for the discussion in the subsequent sections of this paper, Fig. 2, depicting the various components of the HSII organizational structure, is offered. The diagram is a more detailed version of the message transaction model presented previously. The new components of this diagram are primarily a result of addressing multiprocessing considerations. As in the earlier, more simplified organizational diagram, the dynamically current state of the problem solution is contained in the *blackboard*. The blackboard not only contains data *nodes*, but also records data-monitoring information (*tags*) and data-access synchronization information (*locks*). Access to the blackboard is conceptually centralized in three modules. As before, the *blackboard handler* module accepts read and write data-access requests from the active processing elements (the *KS processes* and their *precondition processes*). A *lock handler* coordinates node- and region-lock requests from the KS processes and preconditions, with the ability to block the progress of the requesting process until the synchronization request may be satisfied. A *monitoring mechanism* is responsible for accepting *data-tagging* requests from the KS process and

preconditions, and for sending *messages* to the tagging processes whenever a tagged data field is modified. It is also the responsibility of the monitoring mechanism to distribute *data events* to the various *local contexts* of the KS processes and preconditions, as well as to activate precondition processes whenever sufficient data events of interest to those preconditions have occurred in the blackboard.

Associated with each active processing element is a local data structure, the *local context*, which records data events that have occurred in the blackboard and are of interest to that particular process. The local contexts may be read by their associated processes in order to find out which data nodes have been modified recently and what the previous values of particular data fields were. The local contexts are automatically maintained by the blackboard monitoring mechanism.

Upon being activated and satisfied, precondition processes may instantiate a KS (thereby creating a *KS process*), passing along the reasons for this instantiation as parameters to the new KS process and at the same time establishing the appropriate data-monitoring connections necessary for the new process. The *scheduler* retains the actual control over allocating hardware processing capability to those KS processes and precondition processes which can best serve to promote the progress of the problem solution.[6]

EXPERIMENTS WITH AN IMPLEMENTATION

The preceding sections of this paper have presented the mechanisms necessary for implementing a knowledge-based problem-solving system such as HSII in a multiprocessing environment. The present sections will discuss the various experiments that have been performed in an attempt to characterize the multiprocessing performance of the HSII organization in the speech-understanding task.

HSII Multiprocess Performance Analysis through Simulation

In order to gain insight into the various efficiency issues involving multiprocess problem-solving organizations, a simulation model was incorporated within the uniprocessor version of the HSII speech-understanding system.[7]

---

[6] One way a scheduler might help in reducing (or eliminating) global data-base access interference is to schedule to run concurrently only processes whose global data demands are disjoint. Such a scheduling policy could even be used to supplant an explicit locking scheme, since the global data-base locking would be effectively handled by the scheduler (albeit probably on a fairly gross level). Of course, other factors may rule out such an approach to data-access synchronization, such as an inability to make maximal use of the available processing resources if only data-disjoint processes are permitted to run concurrently, or the inability to know in advance the precise blackboard demands of each KS instantiation. Nonetheless, the information relating to the locality of KS data references is useful in scheduling processes so as to avoid excessive data-access interference (thereby improving the effective parallelism of the system).

[7] This system was programmed on the DECsystem-10 computer in an Algol-like language, SAIL (Swinehart and Sproull [18]), using SAIL's multiprocessing facilities (Feldman *et al.* [8]).

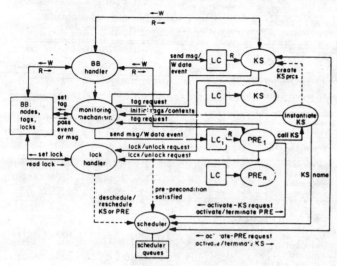

Fig. 2.   HSII system organization.

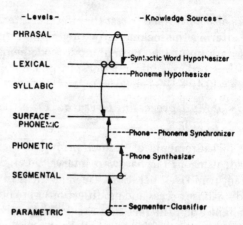

Fig. 3.   Simplified HSII, KS, and information level configuration.

The HSII problem-solving organization was not itself modeled and simulated, but rather the actual HSII implementation (which is a multiprocessing organization even when executing on a uniprocessor) was modified to permit the simulation of a closely coupled multiprocessor hardware environment.

There were four primary objectives of the simulation experiments: 1) to measure the software overheads involved in the design and execution of a complicated, data-directed multiprocess(or) control structure, 2) to determine whether there really exists a significant amount of parallel activity in the speech-understanding task, 3) to understand how the various forms of interprocess communication and interference, especially that from data-access synchronization in the blackboard, affect the amount of effective parallelism realized, and 4) to gain insight into the design of an appropriate scheduling algorithm for a multiprocess problem-solving structure. Certainly, any results presented will reflect the detailed efficiencies and inefficiencies of the particular system implementation being measured, but hopefully the organization of HSII is sufficiently general that the various statements will have a wider quantitative applicability for those considering similar multiprocess control structures.

The HSII Speech Understanding System: The Simulation Configuration

The configuration of the HSII speech-understanding system, upon which the following simulation results were based, consists of eight generic KS's that operate on a blackboard containing six information levels. The KS's used in the simulation were as follows: the *segment classifier*, the *phone synthesizer* (consisting of two KS's), the *phoneme hypothesizer*, the *phone-phoneme synchronizer* (consisting of three KS's), and the *rating policy module* (see Fig. 3). These KS's are activated by half a dozen permanently instantiated precondition processes which are continuously monitoring the blackboard data base for

events and data patterns relevant to their associated KS's. Due to the excessive cost of the simulation effort (and due to the limited stages of development of some available KS's), this configuration represents only a subset of a more complete system which currently contains approximately 15 KS's. Lesser *et al.* [11] contains a more detailed description of the blackboard and the various KS's for the more complete HSII speech-understanding system.

Simulation Mechanisms and Simulation Experiments

The various multiprocessor simulation results were obtained by modifying the flow of control through the usual HSII multiprocessing organization to allow simulation scheduling points every time a running process could interact in any way with some other concurrently executing process. Such points include blackboard data base accesses and data-base access synchronization points (including attempts to acquire data-base resources, both at the system and user levels, and any resulting points of process suspension due to the unavailability of the requested resource, as well as the subsequent points of process wake-up for retrying the access request). Simulation scheduling points were also inserted whenever a data modification warning message (triggered by modifying a tagged data field) was to be sent, as well as whenever a process attempted to receive such a message. The scheduling mechanism itself was also modified to allow for the simulated scheduling of multiple processing units, while maintaining the state information associated with each processor being simulated (such as the processor clock time of that simulated processor and the state of the particular process being run on that processor). The simulation runs were performed so as to keep the processor clock-time of each processor being simulated in step with one another (the simulation being *event-driven*, rather than *sampled*), thereby allowing for the accurate measurement and comparison of concurrent events across processors. Most of the results presented here were achieved by using a single set of KS's (as described above), with a single speech-data input utterance, keeping the data-base locking structure and scheduling algorithms essentially fixed, while varying the number of simulated (identical) processors. Several runs were also performed to test the effects of altering the KS set, altering the locking structure, and altering the mode of data input (the normal input mode being a utterance-time-ordered introduction of input data which simulates real-time speech input).

Measures of Multiprocessing Overhead: Primitive Operation Timings

Time measurements of various primitive operations were made using a 10-μs hardware interval timer. Some of the timed primitive operations (such as those involving simple data-base access and modification) were not especially reliant upon the fact that the problem-solving organization involved multiple parallel processes, whereas others (such as those involving process instantiation and process synchronization) were directly related to the multiprocess aspects of the organization (and might even be taken in part as overhead when compared to alternative single-process system organizations). The times for the various system operations, as shown in Table I, should be read as relative values, comparing the multiprocess-oriented operations with the data-accessing operations to get a relative feel for the overheads involved in supporting and maintaining the multiprocess organization of HSII. Keep in mind that such time measurements are highly dependent on the particular implementation and can change fairly radically when implemented differently.

Table I gives timing statistics relating to the costs involved in maintaining the shared blackboard data base. Two sets of statistics are given, one set showing the operation times without the influence of data-access synchronization (blackboard locking) and one set with the locking structures in effect. These two sets of times give a quantitative feeling for the cost of data-access synchronization mechanisms in this particular implementation of HSII. The figures given include the average runtime cost per operation, the number of calls (in this particular timing run) to each operation (thereby showing the relative frequencies of operation usage), and the percentage of the overall run time consumed by each operation. With respect to the individual entries, *create.node* is a composite operation (involving many field-writes and various local context updates) for creating blackboard nodes. The *read.node.field* and *write.node.field* operations are used in accessing the individual fields of a node. Note that included in any given field-read or field-write operation is the cost of perhaps tagging (or untagging) that particular field (or its node). The various functions of the blackboard monitoring mechanism are contained within the field-write operations. Thus, also included in the field-write operation is the cost of distributing the data event resulting from the write operation to all relevant precondition and KS process local contexts, as well as the cost of sending tag messages to all processes which may have tagged the field being modified; these additional costs are also accounted for independently in the *send.msgs.and.events* and *notify.sset* table entries. Field-write operations are also responsible for evaluating

TABLE I
Primitive Operation Times

	% total runtime w/o lock	% total runtime w/ lock	mean time (ms) w/o lock	mean time (ms) w/ lock	number of calls w/o lock	number of calls w/ lock
Blackboard Accessing:						
create.node	6.96	4.15	35.81	50.77	287	287
read.node.field	5.06	15.68	0.31	2.03	23577	25279
write.node.field	14.13	7.75	13.96	18.44	1493	1476
Process Handling:						
invoke.ks	5.29	2.30	22.64	23.64	345	342
create.ks.prcs	0.75	0.31	3.21	3.22	345	342
ks.cleanup	8.20	5.24	35.06	53.94	345	342
invoke.pre	0.10	1.04	10.41	10.59	14	14
create.pre.prcs	0.42	0.40	8.53	19.57	72	72
Local Context Maintenance:						
transfer.tags	7.12	2.99	9.12	9.17	1152	1149
delete.all.tags	0.52	0.22	2.01	2.03	383	380
notify.sset	6.52	3.01	2.63	2.92	3665	3626
send.msgs.and.events	4.04	2.12	3.68	4.68	1021	1594
receive.msg	0.36	0.15	1.00	1.01	531	530
read.cset.or.sset	0.11	0.05	0.84	0.84	192	192
Data Access Synchronization:						
lock! (overhead)	---	7.78	---	57.47	---	476
unlock! (overhead)	---	3.22	---	23.78	---	476
lock.node	---	2.32	---	2.94	---	2770
exam.node	---	9.34	---	2.40	---	13675
lock.rgn	---	0.11	---	1.77	---	227
write.access.chk	---	0.41	---	0.98	---	1470
read.access.chk	---	14.45	---	1.60	---	31761

any pre-preconditions associated with the field being modified and activating any precondition whose pre-precondition is satisfied. Included in the cost of reading a data field (e.g., *read.node.field*) is the cost of verifying the access right of the calling process to the node being read (which could involve a temporary-locking operation[8] the cost of which is also given independently in the *lock.node* table entry); this access-right checking cost is also separately accounted for by the *read.access.chk* operation. It should be noted that because most of the mechanisms required to implement a data-directed control structure are embedded in the blackboard write operations, the time to execute a write operation is significantly more expensive than a read operation. However, the actual cost in terms of total runtime of implementing a data-directed control structure is comparatively small in the HSII speech-understanding system, because the frequency of read operations is much higher than that of write operations. If this relative frequency for read and write operations holds for other task domains (e.g., vision, robotics), then a data-directed control structure (which is a very general and modular type of sequencing paradigm) seems to be a very reasonable framework within which to implement such tasks.

Table I also relates the costs of process handling within HSII. Process invocation and process creation are separated (the former being a request from a precondition or KS process to the scheduler to perform the latter), and the costs are accounted separately, as in *invoke.ks* and *crea-*

---

[8] If a process has not previously locked the node to which it desires access and the process does not have any other node locked, then the system will temporarily lock the node for the duration of the single read or write operation, without the process having explicitly to request access to the node. This locking operation is required in order to guarantee the internal consistency of the list data structure of a node.

te.ks.prcs. Ks.cleanup is the cost of terminating a KS process; preconditions never get terminated. The cost of initializing and terminating a KS process (i.e., *invoke.ks* and *ks.cleanup*) is due to the overheads involved in maintaining local contexts, locking structures, and database monitoring (tagging), all of which are necessitated by the multiprocess nature of the HSII organization. However, in a relative sense, this is not expensive, since the total overhead associated with process-handling amounts to only about 9 percent of the overall execution time.

Additionally, local context maintenance costs are given in Table I, since they are also a cost of having asynchronous parallel processes. While individual tag creation and deletion is handled by the primitive field-read and field-write operations, tags may be transferred from a precondition to the KS it has invoked via *transfer.tags* and destroyed at termination of a process via *delete.all.tags*. As noted above, *send.msg.and.events* and *notify.sset* are suboperations of the field-write operations and represent the cost of distributing data-event notifications to all relevant local contexts. *Receive.msg* is the operation used by precondition or KS processes to receive a tagging message (or perhaps wait for one, if one does not yet exist); and *read.cset.or.sset* is the operation for retrieving the information from a local context.

Finally, Table I gives the costs associated with the data-access synchronization mechanism. *Lock!* and *unlock!* represent the overhead costs of locking and unlocking a group of nodes specified by the process requesting access rights. These two operations are among the most complex routines in the HSII operating system, the complexity arising from having to coordinate the allocation of database resources by two independent access allocation schemes (node-locking and region-locking). This coordination is necessary in order to avoid any possibility of data base deadlock by maintaining a homogeneous linear ordering among all data resources (nodes and regions). The costs of *lock!* and *unlock!* do not include the time spent in performing the actual primitive locking operations. The primitive lock costs are given by *lock.node* (lock a node for exclusive access), *exam.node* (lock a node for read-only access), and *lock.rgn* (lock a region for exclusive access). The access-checking operations (*write.access.chk* and *read.access.chk*) are used by the blackboard accessing routines discussed above.

These timing statistics can be used to determine the amount of system overhead incurred in running precondition and KS processes under the HSII operating system. The following summary statistics are offered, given as percentages of the total execution time, the percentages being calculated so as to avoid overlapping between categories (e.g., blackboard access synchronization costs are factored out of blackboard reading costs):

Blackboard reading	16 percent
Blackboard writing	4 percent
Internal computations of processes	34 percent
Local context maintenance	10 percent
Blackboard access synchronization	27 percent
Process handling	9 percent

Another way of viewing these figures is that approximately half of the execution time involves multiprocessor overheads (i.e., local context maintenance, blackboard access synchronization, and process handling). Based on the assumption that this multiprocess overhead is independent of the parallelism factor achieved,[9] then a parallelism factor of 2 or greater is required in order to recover the multiprocess overhead.

Effective Parallelism and Processor Utilization

Several experiments were run to measure the parallelism achieved using varying numbers of identical processors. Each of these experiments was run with the KS set described previously, using the same input data (introduced into the data base in such a manner as to simulate real-time speech input), the same blackboard locking structure, and the same scheduling algorithm, while varying the number of (identical) processors. An example of the output by the simulation, for the case of eight processors, is displayed in Fig. 4. To comment on these activity plots, the "# runnable processes" plot gives the number of processes either running or ready to run at each simulation scheduling point; the "# running processes" plot gives the number of actively executing processes at each scheduling point; the "# ready processes" plot shows the number of processes awaiting assignment to a processor at each scheduling point; and the "# suspended processes" plot gives the number of processes blocked from executing because of data-access interference or because they are waiting on the receipt of a tagging message.

Referring to Fig. 4(c), notice the spiked nature of the ready-processes plot. This is a result of delaying the execution of a precondition (due to the limited processing power available) beyond the point in time at which its pre-precondition is first satisfied: the longer a precondition is delayed, the more data events it is likely to accumulate in the meantime, and the more KS processes it is likely to instantiate once it does get executed; hence the spiked nature of the resultant ready-processes plots for configurations of few processors. As parallel processing power increases, preconditions can more often be run as soon as their pre-preconditions are intitially satisfied, and the spiking phenomenon subsides.

As an example of how these activity plots have been used in upgrading the performance of the implementation, compare Fig. 5 to Fig. 4(c). Fig. 5 depicts the process activity under the control of an earlier scheduler which did not attempt to perform load balancing with respect to ready preconditions; and as a result of not increasing the

[9] This assumption, based on timing statistics from a series of runs with different numbers of processors, seems valid except for the cost of context swapping and process suspension, which depends upon the amount of data-base interference and the number of processors.

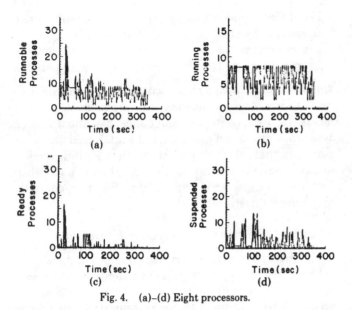

Fig. 4.   (a)–(d) Eight processors.

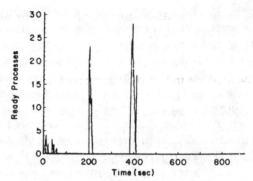

Fig. 5.   Eight processors: Old scheduling strategy.

relative scheduling priority of preconditions as they received more and more data events, the activity spike phenomenon referred to above became predominant, to the extent of reducing process activity to a synchronous system while the long-time waiting precondition instantiates a great many KS processes all at once. Fig. 4(c) shows the activity on the same number of processors, but using a somewhat more intelligent scheduling algorithm, with a resulting reduction in the observed spiking phenomena. This improved scheduling strategy is the one used for all plots presented herein.

In addition to the plots described above, various other measures were made to allow an explicit determination of processor utilization and effective parallelism for varying numbers of processors. Referring to Table II, one can get a feeling for the activity generated by employing increasing numbers of processors. All simulations represented in Table II were run for equivalent amounts of processing effort with respect to the results created in the blackboard by the KS activity. The final clock time of the multiprocessor configuration being simulated is given in simulated real-time seconds, and the accumulated processor idle and lost times are also given. *Idle time* is attributed to a processor when it has no process assigned to it and there are no ready processes to be run; *lost time* is attributed when the process on a processor is suspended for any reason and there are no ready processes which could be swapped in to replace the suspended process. Processor utilization (calculated using the final clock time and processor idle and lost times) is given in Table II; Fig. 6 shows the corresponding effective parallelism (speed-up), based on the processor utilization factors of Table II.

The speed-up for this particular selection of KS's is appreciable up to four processors, but drops off substantially as one approaches sixteen processors. In fact, a rather distressing feature of this effective parallelism plot is that the speed-up actually decreases slightly in going from eight processors to a sixteen-processor configuration (from a

TABLE II
Processor Utilization

number of prcrs (all times in secs)	1	2	4	8	16	32 (special*)
KS instantiations	355	401	423	421	415	434
PRE activations	82	126	173	213	200	229
multiprcr clock time	1076	634	389	350	351	43
total idle time	9	15	37	380	2608	867
total lost time	0	5	34	900	1546	0
avg cxt swaps	0	309	942	368	9	0
avg prcr utilization	99%	98%	95%	54%	26%	37%
effective # prcrs	0.99	1.96	3.80	4.32	4.16	11.84
utilization speed-up	1.00	1.98	3.84	4.36	4.20	11.96

* The 32-processor column represents an experiment which was run under special conditions, to be explained below, and should not be compared directly to the other columns of the table.

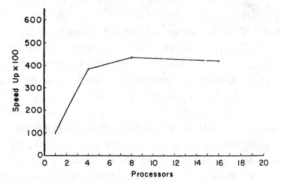

Fig. 6.   Effective parallelism according to processor utilization.

speed-up of 4.36 over the uniprocessor case, down to 4.20). This may be explained by noting that both the eight- and sixteen-processor runs had approximately equal final clock times; but in the sixteen-processor case, the number of runnable processes never exceeded sixteen processes, so any ready process could always be accommodated immediately. As a result, the number of KS instantiations and precondition activations fell off a bit from the eight-processor case, because the preconditions were more likely to be fully satisfied the first time they were activated (since all ready-processes, KS processes in particular, could be executed immediately and complete their intended actions sooner, so that when a precondition came to be activated, it would more likely find its full data pattern to be satisfied); thus, preconditions would not often be aborted, having to be retested upon receiving a subsequent data event. However, running fewer preconditions resulted in much more idle time for the sixteen-processor configuration (the increase in lost time indicated in Table II is an artifact of having too many processors available, since suspended processes would tend to remain on otherwise idle processors rather than being swapped off the processor—note the rather dramatic decrease in context swaps indicated by Table II for the sixteen-processor case). The result is a lower proportionate utilization of the processor configuration, and hence a decrease in the effective parallelism from the eight-processor configuration to the sixteen-processor configuration.

Due to the limited state of development of the total set of KS's, the set of KS's used in the simulation was necessarily restricted;[10] so the fact that these plots indicate that not more than about four to eight processors are being effectively utilized is not to say that the full HSII speech-understanding system needs only eight processors. One might ask that if only 4.16 processors of the sixteen-processor configuration are being totally utilized (see Table II), what is the maximum potential effective parallelism, given this set of KS's? To answer this question, an experiment was performed in which effectively infinite processing power was provided to this KS set and all data-access interference was eliminated (by removing the locking structure overheads and blocking actions); the scheduling algorithm was kept unchanged, as was the input data, although the input data stream was entered so as to be instantaneously available in its entirety (rather than being introduced in a simulated real-time, "left-to-right" manner). The results of this experiment are summarized by the 32-processor column of Table II (32 processors was an effective infinite computing resource in this case, since eight of the processors were never used during the simulation). Notice that no lost time was attributed to the run, due to the absence of locking interference; and the resultant processor utilization was 37% of 32 processors, or 11.84 totally utilized processors. Thus, data-base interference caused by particular data-base accessing patterns and associated locking structures of the KS set used in the experiment significantly affected processor utilization; if the use of the locking structures could be accomplished in a more noninterfering manner, the speed-up indicated by the eight- or sixteen-processor configurations could be increased substantially. The next section will analyze in detail the exact causes for this data base interference, and propose changes to the KS locking structure so as to reduce potential interference.

Table III presents some other system configurations to show effective processor utilizations under varying con-

[10] The particular set of KS's chosen for use in the simulation experiments happened to be an effectively bottom-up speech recognition system. It is expected that as top-down KS's are added, the system will work in a more combined top-down and bottom-up fashion thereby increasing the potential parallelism (since the top-down KS's will presumably not interfere with the execution of the bottom-up KS's as much as additional competing bottom-up KS's would).

TABLE III
System Configuration Variations

experiment description	multiprcr clock	total idle	total lost	% util	effective # prcrs
8 KS's, 6 PRE's 16 prcrs, w/ lock l-to-r input	351	2608	1546	26%	4.16
8 KS's, 6PRE's 32 prcrs, w/o lock instantaneous input	43	867	0	37%	11.84
9 KS's, 7 PRE's 16 prcrs, w/ lock l-to-r input	148	854	726	33%	5.28
9 KS's, 7 PRE's 16 prcrs, w/ lock instantaneous input	155	839	784	35%	5.60
9 KS's, 7 PRE's 32 prcrs, w/o lock instantaneous input	13	226	0	46%	14.72

ditions. The first row repeats the statistics of the sixteen-processor case of Table 2; the second row is a summary of the 32-processor case of Table II, as described above. Three further data points are offered to indicate the effects of increasing the size of the KS set. The last three rows of Table III involve experiments using an expanded KS set consisting of the KS's of all the previous runs plus the *Syntactic Word Hypothesizer* and its precondition. Simulations were performed to evaluate the effects of this expanded KS set on a sixteen-processor configuration with the locking structure in effect, presenting the input data in the usual "left-to-right" manner, as well as in the instantaneous manner used in the infinite-processor test. Comparing the results (in Table III) to the original sixteen-processor run, the "left-to-right" input scheme achieved a processor utilization of 33 percent, up 7 percent from the smaller KS set case; and by presenting all input data simultaneously, the utilization rose to 35 percent. The fifth row of Table III represents the results of providing effectively infinite computing power (only 25 processors were ever used during the run) to the expanded KS set and eliminating all data access interference, in the same manner as for the experiment of the second row. In this "optimal" situation for the expanded KS set, processor utilization was measured at 46%, or 14.72 totally utilized processors. Again, it may be noted that a more effective (less interfering) use of the locking structures can result in substantial increases in processor utilization and effective parallelism.

The addition of the syntactic word hypothesizer was able to achieve the increases in utilization noted in Table III because it operates on information levels that are used by only one other KS (the phoneme hypothesizer) in the basic KS set; hence, the process interference introduced by adding this KS was minimal. Unfortunately, the development of KS's at an information levels which more directly conflict with those of existing KS's has been limited, so direct experimentation on the interfering effects of such KS's could not be performed; but based on the observations comparing the 32-processor without-lock experiments to the original sixteen-processor with-lock runs, substantial interference due to ineffective use of the locking structure would be expected in such cases of adding "competing" KS's. One mitigating circumstance which could alleviate such interference was noted in the "instantaneous" input case of the expanded KS set case, as compared to the "left-to-right" input case: if process activity can be spread across the utterance-time dimension of the blackboard, process interference would decrease— but interference due to data-access synchronization interference can easily overwhelm this improvement.

Execution Interference Analysis

As previously described, there are two methods in the HSII system for preserving data integrity: 1) guaranteeing exclusive access through the use of node- and region-locking primitives, and 2) placing data assumptions in the blackboard, through tagging primitives, which when violated cause a signal to be sent to the process making the assumption. There is an interesting balance in terms of execution overhead and execution interference between these two techniques. The region-locking technique is least costly in terms of execution overhead and is the easiest to embed in a program but causes the most execution interference. This is in contrast to the use of tagging which is the most costly in terms of execution overhead and is the most difficult to embed in a program but causes the least execution interference.[11] Both these methods were used for guaranteeing data integrity in the precondition and KS set that was used in the simulation experiments.

In structuring each KS so as to preserve its data integrity, no *a priori* assumptions were made about the non-modifiability of any blackboard data that KS used in its processing (i.e., it was assumed that any blackboard information that the KS read could perhaps be modified by some other concurrent KS). This self-contained approach to the design of a KS's locking and tagging structure is required if the modularity of the system, with respect to deletion or addition of KS's, is to be preserved.

The KS's that were used in the simulation experiments were not originally designed so that they could be interrupted at arbitrary points in their processing, and consequently they lacked the appropriate locking and tagging structure to guarantee data integrity in a multiprocess(or) environment. The addition, as an afterthought, of the appropriate locking and tagging structure to these KS's was sometimes quite difficult. This was an especially serious problem when an attempt was made to put tagging

primitives into KS's which had internal backtracking control structures for searching the node graph structure in the blackboard. This difficulty arises because previously made data assumptions (tags in the blackboard) associated with a partial path (sequence of nodes in the blackboard) must be removed upon discovering that the path cannot be successfully completed. Thus, most of the KS's in the experiment did not use tagging as a method of guaranteeing integrity, but rather used a combination of node- and region-locking. However, preconditions, which have a much simpler structure and generally do not write in the blackboard, were modified to use the tagging mechanism. In addition, to further simplify KS locking structures, region-locking was used wherever possible. This excessive use of region-locking was mainly responsible for the significant amount of interference among processes which caused the effective processor utilization to go from an optimal 12 to a realized 4 (see Table II).

Table IV contains the simulation results relating to the data-access interference experienced by precondition and KS processes, for varying numbers of processors. This table is an extension of Table II, which was discussed in the previous section (i.e., the underlying simulation runs were the same for both tables). Execution interference was measured by recording the amount of process suspension (also called *descheduling*), which results from processes being temporarily blocked in their attempts to gain access to some part of the blackboard data base.[12] As might be expected, as process activity increases with increasing numbers of processors, the possibility of execution interference increases (see table entries on "deschedules/ primitive lock"). This phenomenon stops at eight processors because in these simulation experiments there were rarely more than eight processes executing at any given moment. At the same time, with more and more processing power available, the likelihood of suspended processes being unblocked and becoming available for further processing increases as the number of processors increases (see table entries on "deschedule duration"). This phenomenon is also indicated by the significant decrease in processor context swaps per deschedule (i.e., with more processors, it becomes less likely that when a process is suspended there will be another process ready to execute).

The major conclusion that can be drawn from this table is that the decrease in processor utilization caused by the locking structure is not due to the high rate of data-access interference (i.e., at most only 6 percent of the primitive

---

[11] An alternative approach to these two methods for maintaining data integrity which was not explored in the simulations is the following paradigm: 1) accumulate the critical data set without the use of tagging or locking; 2) lock the critical data set, perhaps by using a single region-lock which encloses the entire critical data set; and 3) always reverify that the critical data set meets the necessary assumptions before performing the desired modifications. This alternative approach can potentially lead to less interference and lower system overhead for maintaining data integrity than the other two approaches if the following conditions are met: 1) the KS examines a large number of nodes before finally determining the small number of them that meet the desired criteria (i.e., the critical data set); and 2) the cost of reverifying this small critical set is much less costly than the initial search to construct it.

[12] The number of deschedules attributed to a process is also related to the granularity of the process-blocking mechanism. For example, processes could be blocked upon trying to gain access to a region and then relegated to waiting in a set of processes which are waiting on *any* region at that information level in the blackboard; or the wait set could be divided according to the individual regions being waited upon. While it is more expensive in the former strategy to determine whether, upon receiving an unlock wake-up signal for the wait set, which particular members of the wait set are really reschedulable, this strategy does have the advantage of causing fewer context swaps. Both strategies were tried and it was found that the more complex strategy led to higher throughput. The simpler strategy resulted in a significant number of unnecessary context swaps because the average number of suspended processes waiting at the same level was quite large.

TABLE IV
Data-Access Characteristics

number of prcrs (all times in secs)	1	2	4	8	16
avg BB accesses/KS	54.4	52.8	54.5	53.9	56.4
avg BB accesses/PRE	96.7	68.7	55.7	48.2	51.1
avg prim locks/KS	27.9	27.4	28.0	25.7	26.9
avg prim locks/PRE	96.7	68.7	55.7	48.2	51.1
avg dsched/prim lock(KS)	0	0.020	0.060	0.055	0.053
avg dsched/prim lock(PRE)	0	0.009	0.026	0.045	0.040
avg dsched duration/KS	0	5.08	5.69	1.75	1.90
avg dsched duration/PRE	0	3.95	1.91	1.35	1.86
avg cxt swaps	0	309	942	368	9
avg cxt swaps/dsched	0	1.03	0.97	0.75	0.01

locks result in deschedules) but rather from the long duration over which descheduled processes are blocked. This deschedule duration, in the optimal case of 16 processors, where processes do not have to wait for an available processor, is approximately 2 s, which is very close to the average run time of a KS. This long duration occurs because the KS locking structures typically involve executing region-locks at the beginning of the KS execution. The region-locks define the entire blackboard area (and perhaps even more) that the KS will either examine or modify during its entire execution. The locks are then released only at the termination of the KS execution. Thus, if data-access interference (i.e., a primitive lock deschedule) occurred because of a previously executed region-lock, the suspended process would very likely not be unblocked until the KS executing the region-lock had completed its processing.

Another important point that can be drawn from these simulation studies is that the self-contained approach used to develop KS locking structures, which makes no assumptions about the nature of processing of other KS's in the system, may lead to a significant amount of unnecessary interference. This unnecessary interference occurs because of the way in which KS processes actually cooperate indirectly through the blackboard. The majority of modifications that KS's make to the blackboard occur through the addition of new independent nodes rather than by modifying or deleting existing structures. Thus, most KS changes to the blackboard do not directly interfere with the concurrent processing of other KS's. In addition, due to the data-directed, incremental and error-correcting nature of KS processing, these new additions to the blackboard are eventually processed and the appropriate blackboard structure generated based on this new information. The data from the simulations run without locking confirm these observations since approximately the same results were produced as the system with locking. Thus, it seems that making some assumptions about the basic nature of KS processing can significantly reduce process interference and the overhead required to maintain data integrity. It should be pointed out that it is not being claimed that all explicit synchronization code embedded in a KS for guaranteeing data integrity can

be removed; but there is the feeling the self-correcting nature of information flow in the system will make the majority of this code unnecessary. Besides, there is still a need for temporary locks on nodes when reading and writing in order to guarantee the internal consistency of the node data structure, as well as a need for region-locking so as to avoid the creation of duplicate copies of the same node.

Finally, it is once again stated that the results presented here are derived from a rather limited selection of KS processes. However, it is hoped that the system organization (including the data-base design) is of sufficiently general character that these particular results at least give a feeling for the results that might be expected using a different set of KS processes to solve the same or different problems.

SUMMARY AND CONCLUSIONS

This paper has presented an organization for a knowledge-based AI problem-solving system which is designed to take maximum advantage of any separability of the processing or data components available within that organization. KS's are intended to be largely independent and capable of asynchronous execution in the form of KS processes. Overall system control is distributed and primarily data-directed, being based on events occurring in a globally shared blackboard data base. The intercommunication (and interdependence) of the various KS processes is minimized by making the blackboard data base the primary means of communication, thereby exhibiting an indirection with respect to communication similar to the indirect data-directed form of process control. Such a problem-solving organization is believed to be particularly amenable to implementation in the hardware environment of a network of closely coupled asynchronous processors which share a common memory. The HSII, which has been developed using the techniques for system organization described here, has provided a context for evaluating the multiprocessing aspects of this system architecture.

In specifying the blackboard as the primary means of interprocess communication, particular attention was paid to resolving the data-access synchronization problems and data-integrity issues arising from the asynchronous data-access patterns possible from the various independently executing parallel KS processes. A nonpreemptive data-access allocation scheme was devised in which the units of allocation could be linearly ordered and hence allocated according to that ordering so as to avoid data deadlocks. The particular units of data allocation (locking) were chosen as being either blackboard nodes (node-locking) or abstract regions in the blackboard (region-locking). The region-locking mechanism views the potential blackboard as an abstract data space in which access rights to abstract regions could be granted without regard to the actual data content of these regions.

Another area of concern relating to the use of a shared blackboard-like data facility has to do with the assumptions made by the various executing KS's concerning issues of data integrity and localized data contexts. Since the blackboard is intended to represent only the most current global status of the problem solution state, mechanisms were introduced to allow individual KS's to retain recent histories (in the form of local contexts) of modifications made to the dynamic blackboard structure. Local contexts provide KS's with the ability to create a local data state which reflects the net effects of data events which have occurred in the data base since the time of the KS's activation. Combined with the blackboard data-tagging capabilities, local contexts also provide a means by which KS's can execute quite independently of any other concurrently executing KS's (and without interfering with the execution progress of any of these processes).

In an attempt to improve the problem-solving efficiency of a multiprocessor implementation of the system by increasing the amount of potential parallelism from KS activity, the logical functions of precondition evaluation and KS execution were split into separate processing entities. A precondition process is responsible for monitoring and accumulating blackboard data events which might be of interest to the KS associated with the precondition; and when the appropriate data conditions for the activation of the KS exist in the blackboard, the precondition instantiates a KS process, giving to the new process the data context in which the precondition was satisfied. The activation of the precondition itself is also data-directed, being based on monitoring for primitive blackboard modifications.

In order to indicate the nature of the performance of the HSII organization when run in a closely coupled multiprocessor environment, a simulation system was embedded into the multiprocess implementation of HSII on the DEC system-10. Given the knowledge-based decomposition of a problem-solving organization as prescribed by the HSII structure, effective parallelism factors of four to six were realized even with a relatively small set of precondition and KS processes, with indications that up to fourteen processors could be totally utilized, given appropriate usage (or structuring) of the data-access synchronization mechanisms. Experiments thus far have indicated that careful use of the locking structure is required in order to approach the optimal utilization of any given processor configuration. An extended use of noninterfering tagging seems to be indicated, along with a reduction in the use of region-locking (perhaps substituting region-examining or node-locking wherever possible). In addition, it is felt that the basic self-correcting nature of information flow in the HSII system, may obviate the need for most uses of explicit synchronization techniques to maintain data integrity. Studies are under way to determine whether other types of symbol manipulation problems can be structured for a multiprocessor without a major use of explicit synchronization techniques by employing such a self-correcting information flow paradigm as is used in HSII. Measurements were also made of various system level primitive operations which indicate that overhead to support the multiprocessing aspects is approximately 100 percent; thus, with a parallelism factor of 2 or greater the multiprocess overheads can be recovered. While all these results are based on a small set of KS's in the particular task domain of speech understanding, they seem to indicate that the HSII organization is indeed applicable for efficient use in a closely coupled multiprocessor environment.

ACKNOWLEDGMENT

We wish to acknowledge the contributions of the following people: L. Erman for his major role in the design and development of HSII, R. Reddy for many of the basic ideas which have led to the uniprocessor version of the problem-solving organization described here, and G. Gill for his untiring efforts in systems implementation.

REFERENCES

[1] J. K. Baker, "The DRAGON system—An overview," in *Proc. IEEE Symp. Speech Recognition*, Carnegie-Mellon Univ., Pittsburgh, PA, Apr. 1974, pp. 22–26; also in *IEEE Trans. Acoustics, Speech, and Signal Processing*, vol. ASSP-23, pp. 24–29, Feb. 1975.

[2] C. G. Bell *et al.*, "C.mmp: The CMU multi-mini-processor computer," Comp. Sci. Dep., Carnegie-Mellon Univ., Pittsburgh, PA, Tech. Rep., 1971.

[3] C. G. Bell, R. C. Chen, S. H. Fuller, J. Grason, S. Rege, and D. P. Siewiorek, "The architecture and application of computer modules: A set of components for digital systems design," presented at the *COMPCON 73*, San Francisco, CA, 1973.

[4] E. G. Coffman, M. J. Elphick, and A. Shoshani, "System deadlocks," *Comput. Surv.*, vol. 3, pp. 67–78, 1971.

[5] L. D. Erman, "An environment and system for machine understanding of connected speech," Ph.D. dissertation, Comp. Sci. Dep., Stanford Univ., Stanford, CA; also, Comp. Sci. Dep., Carnegie-Mellon Univ., Pittsburgh, PA, Tech. Rep., 1974.

[6] L. D. Erman, and V. R. Lesser, "A multi-level organization for problem solving using many, diverse, cooperating sources of knowledge," in *Proc. 4th Int. Joint Conf. on Artificial Intelligence*, Tiblesi, Georgia, USSR, pp. 483–490, 1975.

[7] L. D. Erman, R. D. Fennell, V. R. Lesser, and D. R. Reddy, "System organizations for speech understanding: Implications of network and multiprocessor computer architectures for AI," *IEEE Trans. Comput.*, vol. C-25, pp. 414–421, Apr. 1976.

[8] J. A. Feldman *et al.*, "Recent developments in sail—An Algol-based language for artificial intelligence," *Proc. FJCC*, 1972.

[9] R. D. Fennell, "Multiprocess software architecture for AI problem solving," Ph.D. dissertation, Comp. Sci. Dep., Carnegie-Mellon Univ., Pittsburgh, PA, Tech. Rep., 1975.

[10] F. E. Heart, S. M. Ornstein, W. R. Crowler, and W. B. Barker. "A new minicomputer/multiprocessor for the ARPA network," in *Proc. AFIPS*, NDD42, pp. 529–537, 1973.

[11] V. R. Lesser, R. D. Fennell, L. D. Erman, and D. R. Reddy, "Organization of the Hearsay II speech understanding system," in *Proc. IEEE Symp. Speech Recognition*, Carnegie-Mellon Univ., Pittsburgh, PA, Apr. 1974; also in *IEEE Trans. Acoustics, Speech, and Signal Processing*, vol. ASSP-23, pp. 11–23, Feb. 1975.

[12] A. Newell, "Production systems: Models of control structures," in *Visual Information Processing*, W. C. Chase, Ed. New York: Academic Press, 1973, pp. 463–526.

[13] R. B. Ohlander, "Analysis of natural scenes," Ph.D. dissertation, Comp. Sci. Dep., Carnegie-Mellon Univ., Pittsburgh, PA, Tech. Rep., 1975.

[14] D. R. Reddy, "Eyes and ears for computers," Comp. Sci. Dep., Carnegie-Mellon Univ., Pittsburgh, PA, Tech. Rep., Keynote Speech presented at Conf. on Cognitive Processes and Artificial Intelligence, Hamburg, Apr. 1973.

[15] D. R. Reddy, L. D. Erman, and R. B. Neely, "A model and a system for machine recognition of speech," *IEEE Trans. Audio and Electroacoust.*, vol. AU-21, pp. 229–238, June 1973.

[16] D. R. Reddy, L. D. Erman, R. D. Fennell, and R. B. Neely, "The HEARSAY speech understanding system: An example of the recognition process," in *Proc. 3rd Int. Joint Conf. on Artificial Intelligence*, Stanford, CA, pp. 185–193; also in *IEEE Trans. Comput.*, vol. C-25, pp. 422–431, Apr. 1976.

[17] D. E. Rumelhart, "Towards an interactive model of reading," Center for Human Information Processing, Univ. of California at San Diego, La Jolla, CA, Tech. Rep. 56, Mar. 1976.

[18] D. Swinehart and R. Sproull, "SAIL," Stanford AI Proj. Operating Note 57.2, Comp. Sci. Dep., Stanford Univ., Stanford, CA, 1971.

Richard D. Fennell was born in Pittsburgh, PA, on June 1, 1947. He received the B.S. degree in physics from Rensselaer Polytechnic Institute, Troy, NY, in 1969, and the Ph.D. degree in computer science from Carnegie-Mellon University, Pittsburgh, PA, in 1975.

He is currently with the Federal Judicial Center, Washington, DC, serving as Chief of Software Systems Research and Development. He is also a Consulting Research Computer Scientist at Carnegie-Mellon University. Dr. Fennell was the President of APL Software Systems, Inc., and a software consultant for Digital Equipment Corporation, Maynard, MA. He is a member of Sigma Pi Sigma.

Victor R. Lesser was born in New York, NY, on November 21, 1944. He received the A.B. degree in mathematics from Cornell University, Ithaca, NY, in 1966, and the M.S. and Ph.D. degrees from Stanford University, Stanford, CA, in 1969 and 1972, respectively.

He was a Research Associate in the Computer Science Department at Carnegie-Mellon University, Pittsburgh, PA, from 1972 to 1974. He currently holds the position of Research Computer Scientist there. In addition to work on system organizations for speech understanding, his research interests include computer architecture, particularly multiprocessor systems and microprogramming.

Distributed Interpretation: A Model and Experiment

VICTOR R. LESSER AND LEE D. ERMAN

Abstract—The range of application areas to which distributed processing has been applied effectively is limited. In order to extend this range, new models for organizing distributed systems must be developed.

We present a new model in which the distributed system is able to function effectively even though processing nodes have inconsistent and incomplete views of the databases necessary for their computations. This model differs from conventional approaches in its emphasis on dealing with distribution-caused uncertainty and errors in control, data, and algorithm as an integral part of the network problem-solving process.

We will show how this new model can be applied to the problem of distributed interpretation. Experimental results with an actual interpretation system support these ideas.

Index Terms—Cooperative problem solving, distributed artificial intelligence, distributed interpretation, distributed processing, knowledge-based interpretation system.

Manuscript received January 10, 1980; revised July 9, 1980. This work was supported in part by the Defense Advanced Research Projects Agency (DARPA) under Contract F44620-73-C-0074 to Carnegie-Mellon University, Pittsburgh, PA, the National Science Foundation under Grant MCS78-04212 to the University of Massachusetts, Amherst, and DARPA under Contract DAHC 1572-C-0308 to the University of Southern California, Marina del Rey. The views and conclusions contained in this document are the authors' and should not be interpreted as representing the official opinion or policy of DARPA, the U.S. Government, or any other person or agency connected with them. An expanded version of this paper appeared in *Proc. 1st Int. Conf. on Distributed Comput. Syst.*, Huntsville, AL, October 1979, under the title "An Experiment in Distributed Interpretation."

V. R. Lesser is with the Department of Computer and Information Science, University of Massachusetts, Amherst, MA 01003.

L. D. Erman is with the Information Sciences Institute, University of Southern California, Marina del Rey, CA 90291.

I. INTRODUCTION

AN interpretation system accepts a set of signals from some environment and produces higher level descriptions of objects and events in the environment. Speech and image understanding, medical diagnosis, determination of molecular structure, and geological surveying are problems that have been pursued with interpretation systems. A *distributed* interpretation system may be needed for applications in which sensors for collecting the environmental data are widely distributed, interpretation requires data from at least several of the sensors, and communication of all sensory data to a centralized site is undesirable. Sensor networks (composed of low-power radar, acoustic, or optical detectors, seismometers, hydrophones, etc.), network (automotive) traffic control, inventory control (e.g., car rentals), power network grids, and tasks using mobile robots are examples of potential applications for distributed interpretation. In these applications, an architecture that locates processing capability at the sensor sites and requires only limited communication among the processors is especially advantageous and is, perhaps, the only way to meet the demands of real-time response, limited communication bandwidth, and reliability.

Two major questions arise in the distributed interpretation task: how to interpret the signal data and how to decompose a given interpretation technique for distribution. Some interpretation algorithms and control structures cannot be replicated or partitioned on the basis of the distribution of the sensory data without requiring unacceptably large amounts of interprocessor communication to maintain completeness and consistency among the local databases. In such a case, it is necessary to modify the algorithm and control structure to operate on local databases that are incomplete and possibly inconsistent. For some interpretation techniques, such modifications might be difficult or impossible.

Knowledge-based artificial intelligence (AI) interpretation systems developed recently for speech, image, and signal interpretation applications have structures that seem to make them suitable for decomposition in distributed environments where local databases are incomplete and possibly inconsistent. Examples of these systems include Hearsay-II [6], HARPY [18], MSYS [1], SIAP [3], CRYSALIS [4], and VISIONS [10]. These interpretation techniques use the problem-solving paradigm of searching for an overall solution by the *incremental aggregation of partial solutions*. In this paradigm, errors and uncertainty from input data and incomplete or incorrect knowledge are handled as an *integral* part of the interpretation process. This is in contrast to more conventional problem-solving techniques, in which errors are fatal or are handled as exceptional conditions, requiring additional processing outside the normal problem-solving strategy.

We hypothesize that these knowledge-based AI systems can handle the additional uncertainty introduced by a distributed decomposition without extensive modification.[1] Preliminary work in testing this hypothesis with respect to synchronization has been encouraging. Experiments with a multiprocessor implementation of the Hearsay-II speech-understanding system have shown that eliminating explicit synchronization results in increased parallelism without a decrease in problem-solving accuracy [7]. Similarly, a class of iterative refinement methods (although not knowledge-based) for solving partial differential equations has been decomposed for multiprocessor implementation so as to avoid most explicit synchronization, thus allowing for increased speed-up due to parallel processing [2]. This decomposition is accomplished by allowing each point in the differential grid to be calculated

from values of its neighboring points that are not necessarily the most up-to-date.

While such AI systems provide a promising basis for distributed problem solving, none has yet been built for a fully distributed environment; centralized global knowledge or global control has been used in existing interpretation systems to coordinate various system modules. In this report, we describe an experiment in the complete decomposition of an existing knowledge-based interpretation model—Hearsay-II [5], [15]. Although Hearsay-II was developed in the context of speech understanding [14], [6], its basic structure has been applied to a range of interpretation tasks, including multisensor signal interpretation [19], protein-crystallographic analysis [4], and image understanding [10].

This report concentrates on applying the Hearsay-II architecture to the distributed interpretation problem, where each processor can be mobile, has a set of (possibly nonuniform) sensing devices, and interacts with nearby processors through a packet-radio communication network [13]. Processors communicate among themselves to generate a consistent interpretation of "what is happening" in the environment being sensed.

Section II presents a brief overview of the Hearsay-II model of knowledge-based AI interpretation, followed by a description of the Hearsay-II architecture. This section presents mechanisms for handling uncertainty as an integral part of the problem-solving process. Section III outlines several possible directions for designing a distributed Hearsay-II architecture, with Section IV presenting the particular organization we feel most appropriate.

Section V describes the details of a distributed Hearsay-II speech-understanding system based on this organization. Each node is a functionally complete Hearsay-II system with access to one segment of the speech input data of the utterance. The nodes cooperatively generate an interpretation of the entire utterance by communicating partial, tentative interpretations based on their local views. Section VI presents experimental performance of this distributed speech-understanding system and compares it to that of the centralized system. This includes comparisons of several internode communication strategies, as well as the effects of communication errors. We discuss here and in Section VII how the Hearsay-II mechanisms are able to resolve successfully with low-internode communication the uncertainty introduced by the distribution of the system.

Our goal is not to prove that one *should* design a distributed speech-understanding system, but rather to point out some of the issues involved in designing a distributed interpretation system dealing with incomplete and inconsistent local data as an integral part of its processing. We are using the Hearsay-II speech-understanding system because it has a structure that we feel is appropriate and because it is a large, knowledge-based interpretation system to which we have access. There are serious problems with using this system for experimentation.

1) Because of several considerations discussed in Sections V-B and VI-A, networks are limited to about three nodes.
2) Because of the costs of the network simulation, only a

limited number of experimental runs could be done and with relatively simple test data and communication policies.

3) There is probably no practical need for distributing a single-speaker speech-understanding system.

We feel that these limitations are sufficiently outweighed by the advantages of experimentation with a *real* system to make the effort worthwhile and the results, while not conclusive, indicative.

II. OVERVIEW OF HEARSAY-II: A SYSTEM THAT HANDLES UNCERTAINTY

A. The Model

We will take, as the competence goal of an interpretation system, the construction of the most credible complete interpretation of the input data.[2] In Hearsay-II, an interpretation is constructed by combining partial interpretations derived from diverse knowledge. Each area of knowledge is represented by an independent module called a "knowledge source" (*KS*). In the application of Hearsay-II to speech understanding, for example, these *KS*'s cover such knowledge areas as acoustics, phonetics, syntax, and semantics. The Hearsay-II architecture is designed to permit cooperative and competitive problem solving among the *KS*'s in order to resolve the uncertainty caused by noise and incompleteness in the input data and inaccurate processing by the *KS*'s.

The interaction of *KS*'s is based on an iterative data-directed form of the hypothesize-and-test paradigm. In this paradigm, an iteration involves the creation of an hypothesis, one possible interpretation of some part of the solution, followed by test(s) of its plausibility. When performing these actions, *KS*'s use *a priori* knowledge about the problem, as well as previously generated hypotheses that form a context for applying the knowledge. When a *KS* creates an hypothesis from previously created hypotheses, the *KS* extends the existing (partial) interpretation with more information, thereby reducing the uncertainty of the interpretation. The processing is terminated when a consistent hypothesis is generated that satisfies the requirements of a complete solution.

A *KS* often generates incorrect hypotheses because its knowledge or its input data, including previously generated hypotheses, contains errors or is incomplete. Thus, if *KS*'s were to generate only a single hypothesis for each specific part of the problem, the problem-solving process would often terminate with an inaccurate interpretation or with a partial interpretation that could not be extended because of its inconsistency. In order to avoid this problem, *KS*'s, in general, create several *alternative* hypotheses for each part of the problem. The *KS* associates with each hypothesis a *credibility* rating, which is its estimate of the likelihood that the hypothesis is correct. The lower the credibility of the alternatives, the greater the number that must be generated to produce the same likelihood that a correct one is included.

[2] In general, some applications might not contain a notion of a complete or spanning interpretation, but rather are interested in successive partial interpretations. Nothing in the discussion that follows is actually specific to complete interpretations, but we adopt that notion because of our involvement with the speech-understanding task and the interpretation of individual single-sentence utterances.

The set of all possible partial interpretations defines the problem-solving search space. The more alternative hypotheses generated, the larger the fraction of the space actually searched. Since each partial interpretation can give rise to multiple extensions, the possibility of a combinatoric explosion exists. At each step in the search, a subset of the existing partial interpretations is selected for extension; the resulting extended partial interpretations then compete for selection with those previously generated. The selection of the subset of hypotheses to extend is called the *focus-of-control* (or focus-of-attention) problem. An integral part of effective focus-of-control is the problem-solving system's ability to focus quickly on information that constrains the search, in order to contain combinatoric explosions. This is called an *opportunistic* and *asynchronous* style of problem solving. It can be implemented through the Hearsay-II formulation of the hypothesize-and-test paradigm, in which promising tentative decisions are made (despite incomplete information or knowledge), then reevaluated later in the light of new information. Focus-of-control is discussed further below; it is also discussed more extensively in [11].

Three requirements must be met for the effective operation of this general approach to problem solving.

1) *Sufficiency of Knowledge:* The knowledge can generate some sequence of partial interpretations that culminates in a correct complete interpretation.

2) *Sufficiency of Credibility Evaluation:* The credibility function rates the correct complete interpretation higher than any incorrect complete intepretation generated.

3) *Sufficiency of Control Strategy:* The focus-of-control strategy can find a correct complete interpretation within the bounds of computing resources allocated to the task.

Increasing the constraint of knowledge, the discrimination power of the credibility evaluation or the selectivity of the control strategy beyond that which is minimally sufficient to meet these criteria will, in general, decrease the amount of computing resources needed for the interpretation. Also, these three aspects of the problem solving are not independent; within limits, the same performance can be achieved by trading off the uncertainty resolving power of one aspect for that of another.

B. The Architecture

Fig. 1 shows a simplified schematic of the centralized Hearsay-II architecture. The major data structures are the shared global database (called the *blackboard*), focus-of-control database, and scheduling queues.

The blackboard is partitioned into distinct information levels, each used to hold a different kind of representation of the problem space. The major units on the blackboard are the hypotheses. Relationships among hypotheses at different levels are represented by a graph structure. The sequence of levels on the blackboard forms a loose hierarchical structure in which the elements at each level can be described approximately as abstractions of elements at the next lower level. For example, in speech understanding an utterance can be represented as a signal or as sequences of phones, syllables, words, phrases, or concepts; in image understanding, typical levels might in-

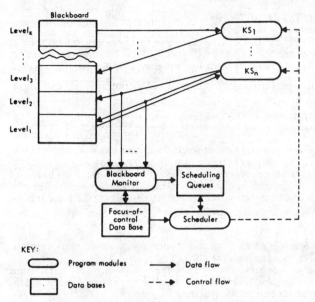

KEY:
- ⬭ Program modules
- ▭ Data bases
- → Data flow
- --→ Control flow

Fig. 1. Schematic of the (centralized) Hearsay-II architecture.

clude picture points, line segments, areas, surfaces, and objects; levels in an aircraft-tracking radar system might include signals, signal groups, vehicles, area maps, and overall area maps (see [21]). The set of possible hypotheses at a level forms a problem space for KS's operating at that level. A partial interpretation (i.e., a group of hypotheses) at one level can be used within the opportunistic strategy to constrain the search at another level. For example, a KS can create a phrase hypothesis as an abstraction of a sequence of word hypotheses. Similarly, another KS can use the phrase hypothesis to predict (i.e., constrain) the set of possible word hypotheses that might follow the phrase.

In order to implement the data-directed activation of KS's, each KS has two components: a pattern and an action. Whenever the pattern is matched by some hypothesis structure on the blackboard, an activation of the KS is created. If the KS activation is selected eventually by the scheduler, its action is executed in the context of the matched structure. For example, the pattern of a KS might be the creation of a new syllable hypothesis and its action might be to use that syllable hypothesis and, possibly, other adjacent syllable hypotheses to create new word hypotheses.

KS activity and hence, the search process, is managed by the scheduler using the focus-of-control database and the scheduling queues. At any point, the *scheduling queues* contain the pending KS activations. The scheduler calculates a priority for each waiting activation and selects for execution the one with the highest priority. The priority calculation attempts to estimate the impact of the information to be generated by an activation on the current state of the problem solving. From the problem-solving viewpoint, the impact of some information is a measure of the degree to which it reduces the uncertainty of the interpretation or, alternatively, the degree to which it reduces the number of competing interpretations. This measure changes as the problem solving progresses; thus, the timeliness of creation of the information affects its impact. For example, if two pieces of information can lead to the same hypothesis, the creation of the first of them may have

high impact, but the creation of the second will have little, other than adding confirmation to the hypothesis. Lesser *et al.* [16] describe a formal model for this kind of problem-solving activity.

Several dimensions can be used to estimate the impact of information, including the following:

1) The *credibility* of some information is a measure of the system's confidence in the information; the more credible the information, the higher its expected impact.

2) The *scope* of some information is a measure of the amount of the total problem solution that it describes. Scope is related to the level of abstraction (e.g., in speech understanding, a word has larger scope than a syllable) and to the size (e.g., a two-second phrase has larger scope than a one-second phrase). The larger the scope, the greater the impact because a larger portion of the complete interpretation, and hence, more constraint is specified.

3) The *diagnosticity* of some information is a measure of how much competing information can be resolved by the information [12]. For example, if one part of the current partial solution has high credibility while another part has only low credibility, a moderately credible piece of information in the former area will have low diagnosticity, but a moderately credible piece in the latter area will have high diagnosticity and, hence, greater impact.

The *focus-of-control* database contains meta-information about the state of the system's problem-solving activity. The meta-information is used to estimate the impact of information, based on its credibility, scope, and diagnosticity. Meta-information includes such things as the current best hypotheses on the blackboard and how much time has elapsed since these hypotheses were generated or combined with others. (This latter kind of information allows the system to recognize a state of stagnation in part of the problem solving, and then to cause the reappraisal of the impact of the current best hypotheses.) The focus-of-control database is updated by the blackboard monitor based on the generation and modification of hypotheses on the blackboard by KS's.

The blackboard monitor is also used to implement the data-directed activation of KS's. At system initialization, each KS declares hypothesis characteristics relevant to it. When an hypothesis is created or modified so as to match those characteristics, the blackboard monitor creates an activation record for the KS on that hypothesis and places it in the scheduling queues.

III. Issues in Distributing Hearsay-II

Fig. 2 presents a number of dimensions of decomposition of Hearsay-II for a distributed environment and several options for each dimension. From this table and the overview above, it can be seen that the characteristics of the Hearsay-II organization appear to make it suitable for a distribution along several dimensions.

1) *Information* might be distributed: The blackboard database is multidimensional (with the information levels forming one dimension). Each KS activation generally accesses only a small localized subspace within the blackboard.

2) *Processing* might be distributed: Knowledge is encapsulated in *KS* modules that are largely independent, anonymous, and capable of asynchronous execution.

3) *Control* might be distributed: *KS* activation is based on the generation and modification of hypotheses on the blackboard (data-directed control). To the extent that these hypotheses can be distributed, control of *KS* activation can also be distributed. The data-directed form of the hypothesize-and-test paradigm permits *KS*'s to exchange partial results in a cooperative fashion.

Given these possibilities, it would appear that the Hearsay-II organization could be decomposed easily for a distributed environment so as to emulate efficiently and exactly the processing that occurs in the centralized version of the organization. In fact, a shared-memory multiprocessor implementation, using explicit synchronization techniques to maintain data integrity and distributed along the processing and control dimensions, achieved significant parallelism—a speedup factor of six [7]. However, the following characteristics of Hearsay-II introduce a number of difficulties for such a straightforward emulation in a distributed environment:

1) the scheduler, which requires a global view of the pending *KS* instantiations (scheduling queues) and the focus-of-control database, is centralized,

2) the blackboard monitor, which updates the focus-of-control database and scheduling queues when a specific type of blackboard change occurs, is centralized, and

3) the patterns of *KS* access to the blackboard overlap, prohibiting the construction of compartmentalized subspaces of the blackboard accessed exclusively by small groups of *KS*'s.

Because there are many *KS* executions, each accessing the blackboard frequently, an extensive amount of interprocessor communication would be required to emulate exactly a centralized view of the blackboard, scheduling queues, and focus-of-control database. The dynamic information in these data structures controls the degree and nature of *KS* cooperation and is essential to the effective implementation of the hypothesize-and-test problem-solving strategy.

Given that the communication and synchronization costs of emulating perfectly the centralized views are too high, one is led to their approximation. The amount and range of internode communication can be reduced, leading to inconsistency and incompleteness of the local views and thus, unnecessary, redundant, and incorrect processing. Experiments with the shared-memory multiprocessor Hearsay-II speech-understanding system described above demonstrated that the system could operate in such an environment [7]. In these experiments, the explicit synchronization was eliminated without degrading accuracy as measured at the end of processing, with an attendant increase in the speedup factor from 6–15 because of the reduction in interprocess interference.

The explanation for this phenomenon is that the asynchronous, data-directed control can apply knowledge to correct certain types of internal errors. Consider the normal activity sequence of a *KS*, which involves first examining the blackboard and then creating new hypotheses on the basis of the examined hypotheses. If the set of relevant hypotheses changes

** INFORMATION **
Distribution of the blackboard:
     The blackboard is distributed across the nodes with no duplication of information.
     The blackboard is distributed with possible duplication of information; synchronization techniques are used to insure consistency.
     The blackboard is distributed with possible duplications and inconsistencies.
Transmission of hypotheses:
     Hypotheses are not transmitted beyond the node in which they are created.
     Hypotheses may be transmitted directly to a subset of nodes.
     Hypotheses may be transmitted directly to all nodes.
  In addition, the transmission and reception of hypotheses can be filtered based on characteristics of the hypotheses, e.g., type of hypothesis (information level), credibility rating, and location of the "event" the hypothesis describes.

** PROCESSING **
Distribution of KS's:
     Each node has only one *KS*.
     Each node has a subset of *KS*'s. The selection might depend on factors such as the type of sensors at the node, the node's physical location, and the input/output characteristics of the *KS*'s.
     Each node has all *KS*'s.
Access to the blackboard by KS's:
     A *KS* activation can access only the blackboard in its local node.
     A *KS* activation can access blackboards in a subset of nodes.
     A *KS* activation can access blackboards in any node in the network.

** CONTROL **
Distribution of KS activation:
     A change to an hypothesis activites *KS*'s only within the local node.
     A change activates *KS*'s in a subset of nodes.
     A change activates *KS*'s in any node.
Distribution of scheduling and focus-of-control:
     Each node does its own scheduling, based on local information.
     Each subset of nodes has a scheduler.
     A single, distributed database is used for scheduling.

Fig. 2.   Dimensions of decomposition for Hearsay-II.

after the *KS* looks at them and before it modifies the blackboard, the modification is inconsistent or incomplete with respect to the current state of the blackboard; however, because of the data-directed nature of *KS* activation, the intervening changes will trigger the same *KS* to recalculate its modifications and, perhaps, generate new alternative hypotheses that are more consistent and/or complete. In addition, other types of inconsistency can be resolved because a complete solution is pieced together from mutually constraining information; thus, additional *KS* processing will usually produce lower credibility ratings for an incorrect hypothesis and its extensions, lessening the likelihood that these incorrect hypotheses will be considered further. This process occurs whether the incorrect hypothesis resulted from a synchronization error, from a mistake in the knowledge used by the *KS*, or from erroneous data. Thus, this self-correcting nature of information flow among *KS*'s, created through the use of the incremental data-directed hypothesize-and-test paradigm, in many cases obviates the need for explicit use of synchronization.

The key issue is whether a distributed decomposition of a Hearsay-II-like system can be designed that can deal with the errors introduced by the approximate emulation well enough to maintain satisfaction of the sufficiency criteria of Section II-A. In the distributed system, internode communication becomes part of the "computing resources" that must be limited for effective system performance.

IV. A Network of Hearsay-II Systems

A primary goal of our decomposition design is to minimize internode communication relative to intranode processing. Because of this and the relatively fine granularity of KS activity within a Hearsay-II system, a node must be able to complete a number of KS executions in a self-directed way, i.e., without internode communication. Thus, each node in the network must contain KS's, a scheduler and focus-of-control database for selecting the next KS activation to execute at each step, a blackboard for KS communication, and a blackboard monitor for KS activation. Therefore, each node is an architecturally complete Hearsay-II system.

There are dual points from which to view the distribution of the dynamic information (i.e., partial interpretations and meta-information) in the network:

1) A virtual global database represents all the system's information; the local databases at each node contain the node's partial view of the virtual global database, perhaps with some inconsistencies (because of limited internode communication and synchronization).

2) Each node has its own databases; the union of these across all the nodes, with any inconsistencies, represents the total system interpretation.

The first viewpoint corresponds to the way most distributed computing systems are considered—a centralized system is *decomposed*, with each piece (node) in the decomposition viewed as a part of the whole system. From the second viewpoint, the distributed system is *synthesized* from systems operating at each node. The second approach shifts the view from that of a system distributed over a network to that of a network of cooperating systems, each able to perform significant, local, self-directed processing. Another way of distinguishing these viewpoints is that the first considers each node from the context of the whole system, while the second considers the system from the context of the individual node. When considering any particular design choice, one or the other of these viewpoints might be more appropriate. From either viewpoint, the major design decisions are the selection and focusing of knowledge sources at each node and the choice of mechanisms and policies for internode communication to permit effective cooperative problem solving. We will now describe some possibilities for each of these areas.

A. Intranode Considerations—Selection and Focusing of KS's

Intranode processing can be maximized relative to internode communication if KS activity is such that the inputs needed by KS actions are available on the node's blackboard. Thus, the selection of KS's for each node and the focusing of their activity on particular portions of the problem greatly affects this goal.

The blackboard in a Hearsay-II system is described along several dimensions. One of these is *information level;* this dimension has discrete points, each corresponding to a different way of representing the situation being interpreted. A KS typically works with a small number of information levels by noticing one or more hypotheses (called the "stimulus") at one

or two levels and by creating new hypotheses or modifying existing ones (the KS's "response") at one or two levels. For a collection of KS's to be connected across levels, then, it must be that any level used by some KS as its stimulus is used by some KS as its response. There are also KS's that are transducers between the system (i.e., the blackboard) and the external world. For the purposes of this discussion, we will think of an input transducer as having no blackboard stimulus and an output transducer as having no blackboard response. In a network of Hearsay-II systems, if a particular node has a KS which is level-disconnected on its stimulus or response side, that node is forced to communicate with other nodes to supply the missing stimulus or to provide a use for the "extra" response. Since a primary goal is to maximize intranode processing relative to internode communication, the selection of KS's for each node should maximize the level connectivity. Likewise, transducer KS's should be selected for their appropriateness to the particular types of sensors (and effectors) at the node.

In addition to the information level, there is an orthogonal dimension (or set of dimensions) for locating hypotheses in the blackboard—this is the *location* of the event which the hypothesis describes. For signal interpretation tasks this usually represents a physical location. In speech understanding, for example, most hypotheses (phones, syllables, words, phrases, etc.) can be located as segments on the dimension of time within the utterance. For image understanding, objects (at any of the levels) can be located in the two or three dimensions of the image space. For radar tracking of aircraft, signals and objects can be located in the three-dimensional world. In general, hypotheses closer in the location dimension are more likely to be relevant to each other and to be needed jointly for further KS activity. For example, a word hypothesis is likely to be created from adjacent syllable hypotheses, an object from surfaces near each other, and a signal group from signals detected nearby. Thus, a node should attempt to acquire for its local blackboard all of the hypotheses at a given level within a contiguous segment in the location dimension(s).

All levels in the system taken together with the full extent of the location dimension(s) define a node's largest possible scope. The term *area-of-interest* will be used to denote, for each node, that portion of the maximum scope representable within the node's local blackboard.

The levels in the area-of-interest are the union of the stimulus and response levels of the KS's in the node—any other levels would be useless to the node.[3] A node's area-of-interest at the information level(s) to which the sensory data is transduced should cover in the location dimensions at least the area covered by the node's sensors; otherwise, some of the sensory data would be lost, since the only direct action the transducer KS can take is to create hypotheses on the local blackboard about the data.[4] At the other levels, the location segment

---

[3] In Section IV-D2), we will show one use for representing hypotheses which cannot be processed by local KS's, in particular, for allowing a node to act as a store-and-forward message handler.

[4] Of course, the transducer could use the sensory information to modify hypotheses about adjacent areas, but this would represent the sensory information only indirectly.

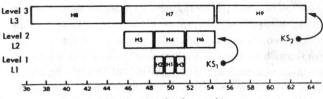

Fig. 3. Simple example of area-of-interest.

should probably include at least the projection of the location segment at the transduction level, since it is reasonable to create higher level hypotheses about the locations covered by the node's sensors. In addition, the location segment should also likely be extended somewhat beyond the range of the local sensors; this is to allow the node to acquire information from neighboring nodes to use as context for *KS* processing. Finally, this context extension should probably be larger at higher information levels because the size of hypotheses [i.e., their length in the location dimension (s)] tend to be larger at the higher levels; e.g., words are usually bigger than syllables, objects are usually bigger than surfaces, and area maps larger than aircraft.

As an aid to understanding the notion of area-of-interest, let us consider a simple example of bottom-up processing at a single node of a network operating in a one-dimensional location space. The node has three information levels, labeled $L1$, $L2$, and $L3$ and two knowledge sources, $KS1$ and $KS2$ (see Fig. 3). Hypotheses on $L1$ are uniformly one unit long in the location dimension and are contiguous and nonoverlapping. The sensor associated with the node produces a single hypothesis on $L1$, called $H1$, at location 50.[5] Knowledge source $KS1$ in the node can take three contiguous hypotheses on $L1$–call them $H2$, $H1$, and $H3$–and produce $H4$ as an abstraction of them on $L2$. Likewise, knowledge source $KS2$ produces hypotheses on $L3$ from triples of hypotheses on $L2$.

In order for $KS1$ to operate, the node must receive hypotheses $H2$ and $H3$ as messages from some other nodes because its local sensor can generate only $H1$. Likewise, for $KS2$ to operate, the $H5$ and $H6$ hypotheses must be received on $L2$. The scope required to be representable on $L2$ is larger than on $L1$. If processing were to continue similarly above $L3$, $L3$'s scope would have to be larger still. Thus, the location dimension of the area-of-interest expands at higher levels. The lateral communication (e.g., $H2$ and $H3$, and $H5$ and $H6$) forms a context for processing and provides a connectivity in the location dimension (*lateral connectivity*), similar to the connectivity in the information-level dimension.

The particular scope of the area-of-interest is dependent on the information required by the *KS*'s. In this simple example, $KS2$ is able to create hypotheses on $L3$ based solely on the information on $L2$. If $KS2$ required information about an $L2$ hypothesis that is not represented in the abstraction on $L2$, it will want to look at the $L1$ substructure of the hypothesis. If the information needed is about $H4$, $KS2$ can access it on the node's blackboard directly, looking at hypotheses $H2$, $H1$, and

$H3$. If, however, $KS2$ needs to look at the substructure of $H5$ or $H6$, there is a problem because the $L1$ representations of those hypotheses are not on the node's blackboard. One solution is to have $KS2$ do the best it can without the information, thus requiring no additional internode communication, but introducing additional uncertainty in the problem solving. Another solution to this problem is to extend the node's area-of-interest on $L1$ in order to represent the needed information. This extension can be handled in several ways.

1) *A priori* analysis of $KS2$ indicates that the $L1$ information is likely to be needed. Thus, the scope of the node's area-of-interest on $L1$ is permanently specified to be 46–54, and the node gathers all $L1$ information that it receives. If the needed information is less than the full scope, the expansion of the area can be limited. For example, if information about just boundaries of the $L2$ hypotheses is needed, the scope could be specified as 48–52, rather than 46–54.

2) Each node that transmits $L2$ hypotheses knows that some of the corresponding $L1$ information is likely to be needed; it therefore transmits the relevant $L1$ information whenever it transmits an $L2$ hypothesis. Thus, the scope of the receiving node's area-of-interest on $L1$ dynamically expands in response to the reception of $L2$ hypotheses.

3) When $KS2$ discovers the need for the $L1$ information, it expands the scope of the node's area-of-interest so that it is capable of representing the needed information if it is received. $KS2$ then processes as best it can without the information, perhaps creating no $L3$ hypothesis. If the needed $L1$ information is subsequently received, $KS2$ can be retriggered to reevaluate the earlier action and perform corrective modification if needed.[6]

The suggestions here for defining the area-of-interest of a node are only one possible set of guidelines; others could be used. The area can also be adjusted dynamically to adapt to changing conditions, such as movements of the node or its sensors or changes in demands on the node's processing or memory capacity. What is important is that each node has an area-of-interest that defines its blackboard and thereby puts bounds on the area in which local processing can occur and on what information is important for it to receive. As suggested by the example in this section, the particular sections of the area-of-interest from which information needs to be transmitted and received are task-specific, depending upon the specific requirements of the *KS*'s and their selection and focusing in the network.

B. Network Configurations

Within the guidelines developed so far, a variety of organizational structures can be implemented in the network, depending on the selection and focusing of *KS*'s in each node. For example, if all nodes contain the same set of *KS*'s and levels,

---

[5] In general, multiple, alternative, competing hypotheses could be produced throughout this example, but we will not consider them here.

[6] There are a variety of approaches for acquiring the needed information which involve more explicit communication among nodes. For example, attached to each transmitted hypothesis is the name of the sender so that later point-to-point communication might be established. Even though the basic approach to internode communication developed here is based on a more implicit communication approach (similar to the way *KS*'s communicate through the blackboard), we briefly discuss some of these more explicit approaches in Section IV-D2).

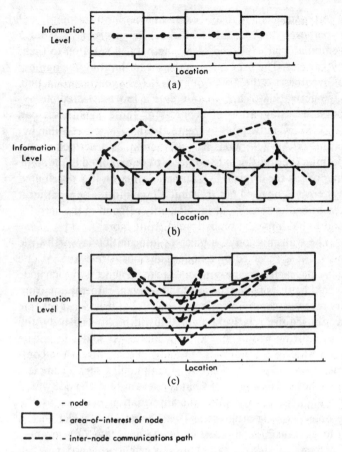

Fig. 4.   Schematics of some network configurations. (a) Schematic of a "flat" configuration. (b) Schematic of an overlapping hierarchical configuration. (c) Schematic of a matrix configuration.

the network structure is "flat" and information flow is essentially lateral. This is the simple structure of the system used for the experiments described in the rest of the report. Fig. 4(a) represents such a flat configuration.

More complex processing organizations occur where there is a nonuniform distribution of KS's and levels across the nodes. Fig. 4(b) shows an overlapping hierarchical structure. Fig. 4(c) shows the implementation of what is called a "matrix" configuration in organizational structuring (see, for example, [9]). In this configuration, each of a set of general-purpose nodes (at the higher levels) makes use of information from lower level specialists.

Fig. 4 shows simplified schematics of the configurations indicating the levels in each node's area-of-interest, its approximate position in a one-dimensional location scheme, and the internode communication paths. This figure does not indicate the intensity of communication from what sections in an area-of-interest information is being transmitted, whether the paths are bidirectional, or the actual shape of the area-of-interest—varying these parameters leads to greater varieties of network configurations.

The emphasis throughout this report is on the flow of information among nodes, with each node cooperating but having control autonomy. Within this paradigm, various control relationships can be synthesized implicitly by establishing particular information flow paths, resulting in appropriate data-directed activity of nodes. A more explicit imple-

mentation of control relationships can be integrated with information flow through the use of a mechanism in Hearsay-II called a *processing goal* [15]. This is an information structure a KS creates on the blackboard as an active request for information of a particular type. KS's that can produce such information may then respond to the goal in the same way they would to the creation of a relevant hypothesis. When a goal is transmitted between nodes, as with any other hypothesis, the same kind of request–response activity can occur. A more extended version of this notion, involving a two-way dialogue, is the central idea in the contract net formalism for resource allocation in a distributed environment [21], [22].

C. Internode Communication—Mechanism

In a Hearsay-II system, all inter-KS communication is handled indirectly via the creation, modification, and inspection of hypotheses on the blackboard. This same mechanism may be used for internode communication. Consider a Hearsay-II system operating at one node in a network, with its area-of-interest defining the scope of its blackboard and hence the possible areas of attention of its KS's. Now consider adding to that node a transducer KS with access to a communication medium (e.g., packet radio) for receiving messages from other nodes describing their hypotheses; if this *RECEIVE KS* modifies its node's blackboard to reflect those messages, other KS's in the node can use this information. Likewise, a *TRANSMIT KS* can select hypotheses on the blackboard and transmit them for reception by other nodes. Fig. 5 shows a network of such systems.

The decision to use the blackboard as the sole means of KS interaction in Hearsay-II was made to provide uniformity and to keep KS's relatively independent of each other. The same advantages accrue by using the blackboard for internode communication. A KS is triggered by and uses information on the blackboard independent of what other KS created it; thus, information placed on the blackboard by the *RECEIVE KS* is automatically usable by the other KS's, indistinguishably from locally generated information. Likewise, each KS posts its results on the blackboard without concern for what other KS's might use it; thus, the information to be transmitted by the *TRANSMIT KS* is already available on the blackboard.

A node could transmit, in addition to hypotheses, waiting KS activation records from its scheduling queues, in order for them to be executed at another node. If a node receiving such an activation record has both the KS and blackboard data needed for executing the activation, the data-directed nature of KS activation would have already created an equivalent activation locally. If either the KS or data are not present, the activation could not be executed by the receiving node. Thus, it is redundant or useless to share the scheduling queues.[7]

KS's in Hearsay-II interact asynchronously. That is, a KS

---

[7] We are assuming here that the environment for KS execution (i.e., the KS itself and the relevant blackboard data) is not transmitted. One could consider transmitting such information with KS activations for internode load balancing. One could also consider transmitting activations and the node's priority evaluation of them in order to influence the scheduling decisions of other nodes.

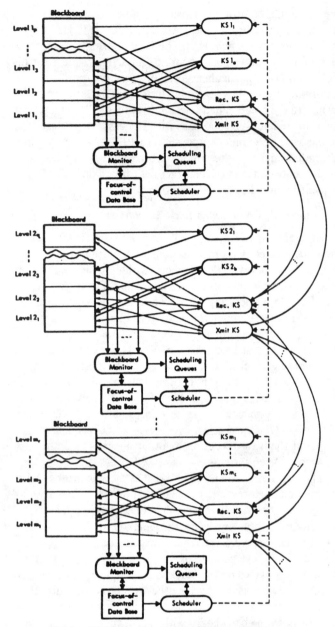

Fig. 5. Schematic of a network of Hearsay-II systems.

triggers whenever an event occurs of interest to it and, when executed, makes use of whatever relevant information is available on the blackboard to make the best statement it can about the situation. Such asynchronous intranode operation naturally allows *KS*'s to handle asynchronous internode communication without modification.

D. Internode Communication—Policies

The ability to run asynchronously eliminates the need for communication costs of synchronization and simplifies the interaction mechanisms. There is still a need to reduce the amount of internode communication while providing each node with the information needed from other nodes (i.e., guaranteeing level and lateral connectivity of *KS* processing). Internode communication can be reduced by limiting the amount of information transmitted, the set of nodes to which any particular message is transmitted, and the distance the message is transmitted.

A centralized Hearsay-II system must limit the number of hypotheses created on its blackboard, in order to avoid a combinatorial explosion of *KS* activity in reaction to these hypotheses. The primary mechanism for limiting the number of hypotheses is the structuring of a *KS* as a generator function. One activation of a *KS* can create a few most credible hypotheses. Stagnation of progress of those hypotheses can trigger new activations to create alternative, less credible hypotheses. Asynchronous *KS* interaction, as described above, permits the additional hypotheses to be exploited in the same manner as the original hypotheses. Similarly, in a distributed system a node need not transmit all its information; rather it can select its "best" and subsequently respond to the need for additional information by transmitting more.

The transmission of a piece of information is worthwhile only if it is received by a node that finds it relevant. At one extreme, each transmission could go to all nodes and each node would be responsible for selecting relevant information from its received communications—this global broadcast scheme would require relatively high bandwidth. Alternatively, the transmitting node could know which other nodes might be interested in the information and, thereby, direct the communication explicitly. The cost of maintaining such a complete distributed knowledge of what is relevant.to each node would be high, especially since the information changes as the problem solving progresses. The scheme we consider here is a local transmission based on local knowledge of relevance. Each message is transmitted to a few neighboring nodes. When a node receives information relevant to it, it incorporates the information into its problem-solving state. This action may, in turn, trigger the node to retransmit the information (perhaps modified by its knowledge) on the basis of its local knowledge of relevance.

The transmission of a limited subset of a node's information to a limited subset of other nodes leads to an incremental transmission of information with problem-solving processing at each step, similar to the relaxation paradigm [20]. This transmission scheme results in what can be thought of as a "spreading excitation" of important news through the network. As in relaxation, the propagation of a piece of information dies out as it reaches nodes that find it irrelevant or unimportant.

Local knowledge-based processing at each step of the transmission can serve to correct errors in the information, including errors introduced by the communication process itself. Since communication is incremental, this error correction capability can serve to limit the propagation of errors, as opposed to a global broadcast scheme, which propagates them widely. One drawback of the incremental transmission strategy is the increase in the time needed to communicate important information across the net, because each local step adds some delay. However, a node's information is generally most directly relevant to nodes nearby, and the information contained in these neighboring nodes is generally more constraining (i.e., error-correcting) than that of nodes farther away. Another drawback is the possibility that the transmission of important information will die out because the local measures of importance may be incorrect. This danger is reduced because of the correlation between the proximity of nodes and their measures of relevance. It can be reduced further by increasing the richness of connectivity of the internode communication paths, at the cost of additional communication.

In order for one node to have information relevant to another, their areas-of-interest must overlap, since each node's area-of-interest defines what is of interest to it. Thus, the selection of areas-of-interest also constrains the potential internode communication patterns. The criteria for selecting the area-of-interest given in Section IV-A led us to place the center of the node's area at the location of the node's sensors. Thus, geographically proximate nodes—i.e., those with sensors proximate in the location dimension—have more overlap in their areas than nodes that are further apart, and therefore have more to communicate.

The incremental communication strategy is also more economical, since communication between nodes is generally less costly the closer they are. This is certainly true if the communication medium is hard-wired lines. It is also true for radio; in fact, as the distance that messages need travel is reduced, the power requirement is reduced (and with it the cost of hardware). Also, the same broadcast channel can be used simultaneously in different parts of the network with less interference.

In order to implement such an incremental communication system, three policies must be specified:

1) the *RECEIVE KS*'s integration of received information onto the blackboard,

2) the *TRANSMIT KS*'s selection of information to transmit, and

3) the determination of which nodes will communicate.

At the heart of these different policies are measures of the relevance (i.e., expected impact) of information for the processing at individual nodes. As described in Section II-B, estimating impact is an important part of the focus-of-control issue for the centralized problem-solving system and meta-information (called the "focus-of-control database") plays a key role in this estimation. Because this meta-information attempts to measure the current state of progress in the problem-solving system, it requires a global view of the problem-solving database (the blackboard). In attempting to develop mechanisms to distribute the meta-information among the nodes, there is s tradeoff between the accuracy and scope of this information on one hand and the cost of acquiring it on the other. The more accurate and globally representative this meta-information, the better the estimate of the relevance of local processing to other nodes. Better estimation leads to lower transmission bandwidth requirements, less redundant processing, and more responsiveness of the system to new, important information. However, the cost of acquiring the more accurate meta-information has its own attendant bandwidth and processing costs that can possibly outweigh the advantages of better local estimates. This tradeoff is classic to all resource-allocation problems, i.e., the cost of doing the allocation (in terms of processing and information acquisition necessary to support it) versus the resources saved by doing it.

1) *The Basic Policy:* The basic policy for communication to be considered is for a node

a) to accept any received information that is representable within its area-of-interest and to integrate that information onto its blackboard as if it were generated by local *KS*'s (and, hence, update its meta-information accordingly),

b) to select for transmission those hypotheses whose estimated impact is highest and that have not been transmitted previously, and

c) to broadcast them to all nodes that can receive the communication directly.

This policy is simple in that communication is not directed to specific receiving nodes, no distinction is made between locally generated and externally received hypotheses, and the mechanism already used to control local activity is also used to select hypotheses to be transmitted.

This policy leads to the same kind of generator behavior that is produced in the local *KS* activity: high-impact hypotheses (locally decided) are transmitted initially. If, after a time, no higher impact hypotheses arrive on the node's blackboard (either generated locally or received from some other node) that subsume or compete with these transmitted hypotheses, the stagnation mechanism will cause other, previously lower rated hypotheses now to be rated high impact and, hence, transmitted.

Since a node's meta-information is strongly dependent on those hypotheses judged high impact, and since it is those hypotheses that are transmitted, a receiving node, by incorporating those hypotheses and modifying its meta-information accordingly, will implicitly incorporate a large part of the sender's relevant meta-information. Thus, the meta-information will also be "relaxed" across the network.

We will now discuss some variants of this basic policy. These respond to particular characteristics of the problem-solving task and the communication channels.

2) *Variants:* If the reliability of the problem-solving processing is such that most hypotheses of small scope are incorrect and if most of the small-scope hypotheses can be refuted by additional processing within the creating node, then it may be better to transmit only hypotheses for which the node has exhausted all of its possible local processing and which come through that processing with a high-impact measure. This strategy, called *locally complete,* can 1) reduce the communication bandwidth needed, since fewer hypotheses need to be sent (just those that survive unrefuted), 2) reduce the processing requirements of the receiving nodes, since they will have fewer hypotheses to incorporate and judge, 3) avoid redundant communication in the case that two nodes have a large area-of-interest overlap, and 4) increase the relevance of transmitted hypotheses because their scopes are larger (due to the additional processing) and are, thus, more likely to overlap areas-of-interest of other nodes. The potential disadvantage is a loss of timeliness—the earlier transmission might provide significant constraint for the receiving node.

A technique we call *murmuring* can be used to improve the reliability of communication. In this technique, a node retransmits high-impact hypotheses. A simple approach is to murmur periodically, independent of other communication. A more efficient approach is to murmur high-impact hypotheses unless the node receives or generates higher impact hypotheses. The stagnation measures (see Section II-B) can be used to implement this strategy. Murmuring is a knowledge-based technique which can be used to correct for lost communications due to intermittent channel or node failures and to bring up-to-date new or moving nodes, thereby gaining some measure of dynamic network configuration. This mechanism has the advantage of preserving anonymity of communication and requires no explicit handshaking or acknowledgment.

The mechanisms described so far involve the acquisition by each node of a model of the processing state of other nodes implicitly through the problem-solving information received by the node. Such implicit mechanisms are simple, but may not be efficient enough for some cases. For example, the assumption that nodes that can communicate directly have overlapping areas-of-interest is needed to guarantee that relevant and needed information is propagated throughout the network; if, however, there are discontinuities or insufficient redundancy in these overlaps, a more explicit mechanism is needed to guarantee a rich enough connectivity to handle the problem-solving.

One way to handle such problems is for a node to transmit a description of its area-of-interest, explictly indicating what kinds of information it needs and what kinds it can produce, i.e., its *input/output (I/O) characteristics*. Each node receiving this message responds with a reply containing its I/O characteristics. If the initiating node is unsatisfied with the richness of the neighborhood connectivity implied by the responses, it can transmit another message, indicating which of its I/O requirements are not sufficiently satisfied and requesting its neighbors to ask their neighbors, in turn, to fulfill them. The initiating node can continue expanding the area of its request until all of its requirements are met or until it decides to give up. Subsequently, the intermediate neighbors will act as store-and-forward message processors supporting the desired connectivity. This provides a mechanism for generating explicit communication paths between nodes that have no direct communication capabilities. This may be necessary for some of the more complex network configurations, e.g., as in Fig. 4(c), in which overlapping areas-of-interest do not necessarily imply the geographic proximity of the nodes.

This process can be viewed as the dynamic increase of the area-of-interest of each intermediate node so that it can accept the kind of information it is requested to forward. Even though the intermediate node might do no local problem-solving processing on this information, once it has accepted it, the normal criteria for transmission will handle the forwarding function.

Modification of a node's area-of-interest in response to explicit meta-information can also be used for resource allocation. For example, if a node has completed all possible processing within its area-of-interest and does not expect any new tasks to appear within that area-of-interest for some time, it may be worthwhile for it to advertise for new work, using a mechanism similar to that used for insuring connectivity. Conversely, if a node finds the demands on its local processing power too great, it might shrink its area-of-interest, thereby reducing the domain of its activity. If there is sufficient overlap

of areas-of-interest, this action results in just a reduction of redundancy; if the overlap is not sufficient, a renegotiation, using the I/O characteristics, is needed to assure coverage of the whole problem.

It may be useful to transmit other meta-information with hypotheses: for example, the name and location of the sending node, the time the hypothesis was generated, the amount of computing effort expended on the hypothesis, and the number of nodes that previously processed the hypothesis. The receiving node can augment its meta-information with this information.

Fig. 6 summarizes the design decisions we have made along each of the dimensions of Fig. 2.

V. THE EXPERIMENT

An experiment was performed to determine how the problem-solving behavior of such a network of Hearsay-II systems compares to a centralized system. The aspects of behavior studied include the accuracy of the interpretation, time required, amount of internode communication, and robustness in the face of communication errors. This experiment was a simulation only in part, since it used an actual interpretation system analyzing real data, i.e., the Hearsay-II speech-understanding system [6].

A. Simulating a Network

The simulation aspects of the experiment involved emulating a distributed network of nodes with a broadcast communication structure. This was accomplished by developing a multijob coordination facility for the Decsystem TOPS-10 operating system. This facility coordinates communication and concurrency among a collection of independent jobs, each running a Hearsay-II speech-understanding system. The network communication structure is simulated by a shared file that holds a record of each transmission in the network and additional information, such as when and by which node it was generated and which nodes have read it. All jobs can access this file through an internode communication handler added to the basic Hearsay-II system. The simulation of concurrency among the jobs is accomplished by keeping the jobs' clock-times in step; each time a job makes a request to transmit or receive internode communication, it is suspended if its local processor time is no longer the smallest. In this way, the simulation of concurrency is event-driven rather than sampled; this permits accurate measurement and comparison of concurrent events across simulated nodes.

B. Selection of KS's and Areas-of-Interest

A major design decision in the decomposition of a system is the selection and focusing of KS processing at each node. In the case of the distributed Hearsay-II speech-understanding system, the decision was to allocate all the KS's to each node. The area-of-interest for each node has all the information levels, but is restricted to a statically assigned segment of the location dimension, i.e., to a segment of the speech signal. Two aspects of the particular blackboard structure and KS configuration of the Hearsay-II system used in this experiment motivate this design.

Distribution of the blackboard:
  The scope of a node's local blackboard defines its area-of-interest.
Transmission of hypotheses:
  A node transmits hypotheses to a local subset of nodes.

** PROCESSING **
Distribution of KS's:
  Each node has a subset of *KS*'s.
Access to the blackboard by KS's:
  A KS activation can access only the blackboard in its local node.

** CONTROL **
Distribution of KS activation:
  A change to an hypothesis activates *KS*'s only within the local node.
Distribution of scheduling and focus-of-control:
  Each node does its own scheduling, based on local information.

Fig. 6.   Design decisions for a network of Hearsay-II systems.

The first aspect concerns how hypotheses are located on the blackboard. The information levels of the Hearsay-II speech-understanding system are shown in Fig. 7. The position of an hypothesis on the location dimension is defined by its time segment within the spoken utterance. For example, a hypothesis might be that the word "today" occurred at the word level from ms 100 to ms 600 in the utterance. One can think of each node as having a microphone sensor which acquires its input from a segment of the utterance. As discussed in Section IV-A, it is natural to define a node's area-of-interest as being centered, in the location dimension, over its sensor's area. *Thus we are led to a one-dimensional network with each node listening to some portion of the utterance and with the portions overlapping.*

The second aspect concerns the propagation of information across levels of the blackboard. *KS* processing in this version of the Hearsay-II speech system (see Figs. 7 and 8) is bottom-up and pipelined (without feedback) until the word level is reached; i.e., all segments are created, then all syllables, then a selection of words. Additionally, the context of hypotheses required for *KS*'s operating at these levels is highly localized in terms of position within the utterance—i.e., in the location dimension. Thus, by choosing the areas-of-interest to have sufficient size and overlap in the location dimension, it is possible to guarantee that all bottom-up processing to the word level can be accomplished with no internode communication—i.e., there is no need for communication to maintain lateral connectivity for this processing—at the cost of possible redundant processing. The "sufficient" size and overlap criteria must be such that all possible valid hypotheses at these levels can be hypothesized because their time regions lie totally within at least one node.

Above the word level, the more incremental, data-directed form of processing occurs, in which the context of hypotheses required for *KS* processing cannot be localized in the time dimension. In particular, phrase hypotheses must be transmitted among nodes.

Additionally, *KS* processing at the phrase level often requires the detailed characteristics of the underlying word support for the phrase abstractions. As discussed in the example in Section IV-D.1, there are a number of possible approaches to providing the appropriate information to a node. The approach taken here is to transmit explicitly with each phrase hypothesis the name, rating, and time region charac-

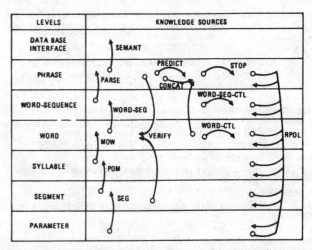

Fig. 7.   Levels and knowledge sources of the speech-understanding system. Each *KS* is indicated by one or two vertical arcs, with the circled end indicating the level of its input and the pointed end indicating the level of its output.

teristics of each word contained in its underlying word support. However, there is still a limitation on the scope of a node's area-of-interest at the phrase level, since local *KS* processing at that level can merge disjoint phrase hypotheses into an enlarged phrase hypothesis only if their juncture at the segment level is contained in the area-of-interest of the node. This requirement must be met in order for the *KS*'s to ascertain that particular acoustic phenomena occur at the juncture. This implies that a received phrase hypothesis should be discarded if it does not overlap the node's area-of-interest at the segment level.

C. Communication Strategy

The previous section defines the type of information to transmit (phrase hypotheses and their underlying word support) as well as the policy for its reception (i.e., ignore all received hypotheses that do not overlap the area-of-interest). What remain to be described of the communications strategy are the mechanisms for determining which phrase hypotheses should be transferred and to which nodes they should be sent. Three policies were explored for selecting hypotheses to transmit.

The first policy, called "full transmission," is to have no selection criteria and to transmit each phrase hypothesis as soon as it is created. This policy provides a benchmark for the other policies and simulates a nonsynchronized, centralized blackboard at the phrase level.

The second policy, called "dynamic thresholding," corresponds to the basic policy presented in Section IV-D.1 and uses the local focus-of-control database as a basis for evaluating the importance of a locally generated phrase hypothesis. The focus-of-control database keeps track of the best phrase hypothesis created (or received) for each time area of the utterance. The criterion for "best" hypothesis is constantly reevaluated on the basis of whether a hypothesis has been successfully extended into an enlarged hypothesis—if not, its rating is decreased, possibly resulting in the choice of another hypothesis to replace it as the best in the area. The criterion for transmission using this policy is straightforward: transmit a hypothesis when it becomes the best in its area.

Signal Acquisition, Parameter Extraction, Segmentation, and Labeling:
    SEG: Digitizes the signal, measures parameters, and produces a labeled segmentation.
Word Spotting:
    POM: Creates syllable-class hypotheses from segments.
    MOW: Creates word hypotheses from syllable classes.
    WORD-CTL: Controls the number of word hypotheses that MOW creates.
Phrase-Island Generation:
    WORD-SEQ: Creates word-sequence hypotheses that represent potential phrases, from word hypotheses and weak grammatical knowledge.
    WORD-SEQ-CTL: Control the number of hypotheses that WORD-SEQ creates.
    PARSE: Attempts to parse a word-sequence and, if successful, creates a phrase hypothesis from it.
Phrase Extending:
    PREDICT: Predicts all possible words that might syntactically precede or follow a given phrase.
    VERIFY: Rates the consistency between segment hypotheses and a contiguous word-phrase pair.
    CONCAT: Creates a phrase hypothesis from a verified, contiguous word-phrase pair.
Rating, Halting, and Interpretation:
    RPOL: Rates the credibility of each new or modified hypothesis, using information placed on the hypothesis by other *KS*'s.
    STOP: Decides to halt processing (detects a complete sentence with a sufficiently high rating, or notes the system has exhausted its available resources), and selects the best phrase hypothesis (or a set of complementary phrase hypotheses) as the output.
    SEMANT: Generates an unambiguous interpretation for the information-retrieval system which the user has queried.

Fig. 8.   The speech-understanding *KS*'s.

The third policy investigated, called "locally complete," is to transmit an hypothesis if there is no more local *KS* processing that can be performed on the hypothesis. This condition is recognized when the acoustic region of an hypothesis "almost" covers the node's acoustic area-of-interest. This policy implements a simplified version of the locally complete strategy presented in Section IV-D.1. This version is simplified since the impact of a locally complete hypothesis is never explicitly evaluated. Rather, the successful extension of a phrase hypothesis to the boundaries of the node's area-of-interest is taken as an implicit indication that the hypothesis is important and should be transmitted. Additionally, in order to minimize the number of hypotheses transmitted, none of the intermediate phrase hypotheses used in the construction of a locally complete hypothesis are transmitted.

Due to the static allocation of the areas-of-interest and the small number of nodes (a maximum of three), a fully connected communication configuration was chosen. Thus, we are not able to test more complicated and selective communication strategies in which a limited subset of nodes receives each transmission. In this broadcast strategy, all nodes receive the message, the sender does not receive a positive acknowledgment that the message has been received correctly, and the receiver does not know the identity of the sender.

VI. RESULTS

There are two main purposes for gathering experimental data on the performance of a network of Hearsay-II systems. The first is to provide empirical evidence for the assertion that the additional uncertainty introduced by distribution can be handled within the basic, uncertainty-resolving mechanisms of the Hearsay-II architecture. The second is to see if there are

dynamic interaction phenomena among the nodes that we had not anticipated from our static analysis, particularly phenomena dealing with communication bandwidth and overall performance.

A. Network versus Centralized

The most important experimental results come from comparing the performance of a three-node Hearsay-II system with that of the centralized version. Given the requirements described in Section V-B and the lengths of the utterances in the test data, three nodes is about the maximum that can be used. Both systems were configured with the same task language (called "*S*5"), which has a 250-word vocabulary and a very simple grammar.[8] We chose for test data a set of ten utterances that had been understood correctly by the centralized system.

The nodes in the network were configured with extensive overlap between their areas-of-interest (see Section V-B). Fig. 9 shows the ten sentences and the areas-of-interest for each of them. The locally complete strategy (see Section V-C) was used for internode communication.

The network system correctly understood all ten of the utterances. Thus, the uncertainty introduced by this distribution of the problem solving was handled by the basic Hearsay-II architecture without the need for additional mechanisms. This basic result has been substantiated by consistently correct interpretations in several additional experiments with, in turn, 1) decreased area-of-interest overlaps, 2) less-constraining grammar, 3) alternative communication policies (Section VI-B), and 4) two-node configuration.

Fig. 10 is a summary of the execution costs for running these ten utterances on the network system relative to the costs on the centralized system. The summary is along two dimensions: the processing time and the number of phrase hypotheses generated and transmitted. As described in Section V-B, the selection of areas-of-interest for these experiments has led to a configuration in which all bottom-up processing through the word level can be accomplished with no internode communication. Since the purpose of these experiments is to investigate internode cooperation, as opposed to task-specific parallelism, the times reported are of the processing after that bottom-up phase has completed. Note that the results of the bottom-up phase are used throughout the subsequent processing—in particular, the segment and word hypotheses within a node are constantly used by the node while investigating the extension of phrase hypotheses. The rationale of the distributed design is to avoid the transmission of the word and segment hypotheses to a central site. When reporting processing time in the network case, the time given is the maximum time over the three nodes, which is an estimate of the clock time of the simulated network.

For the network system, three counts of phrase hypotheses are used. First, is the number of phrase hypotheses **generated locally** by each node, summed over the three nodes. This measures the amount of search more directly than does pro-

---

[8] The Hearsay-II speech-understanding system is configurable with a varying range of task languages. The use here of a simple language reduced the amount of computing resources required for the experimental runs.

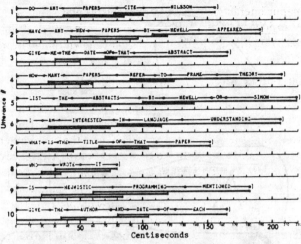

Fig. 9.   The test utterances and areas-of-interest.

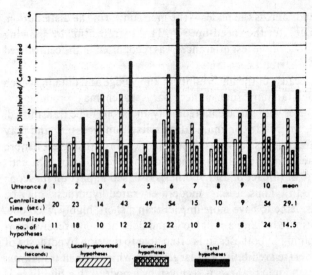

Fig. 10.   Performance of the centralized system versus the network system using the locally-complete transmission strategy.

cessing time. Next, is the number of these hypotheses that were selected by the locally complete strategy for **transmission**. This is a measure of the channel costs for communication. Finally, there is the **total number** of phrase hypotheses that occurred; this is the sum over the three nodes of the number of hypotheses created locally by the node and the number of received hypotheses accepted by the node and placed on its blackboard.[9] For each of these three measures, Fig. 10 gives the ratio of that number to the number of hypotheses created in the centralized system.

The major conclusions that can be drawn from the summary statistics in Fig. 10 are as follows:

1) Effective cooperation was achieved among the nodes even though only 44 percent of the locally generated hypotheses were transmitted. This represents 77 percent of the number of hypotheses created in the centralized runs.

2) There was a slight speedup of 10 percent in performing the interpretation above the word level with three nodes. Thus, the interpretation took 2.7 ($=3 \times 0.9$) times as much processing as compared to the centralized version. (Recall that the times reported are of the high-level, highly cooperative processing only. If the bottom-up processing is included, which accounts for about half the time in the centralized system, there is an overall speedup of about 60 percent for the three-node configuration over the centralized version).

We classify the increase in the total amount of high-level processing into three areas: communication, incomplete information for knowledge application, and incomplete meta-information for focusing.

Communication costs include deciding which hypotheses to transmit and accept as well as the physical act of message passing. Also, the receiving node must merge accepted hypotheses into its blackboard structure. These sending and receiving functions account for about six percent of the processing time. To reduce the size of each message, the grammatical structure of the phrase hypothesis is not transmitted; rather, the receiving node recomputes that structure when

needed, thus trading off additional processing for reduced communication bandwidth. None of these processing costs occurs in the centralized system.

Incomplete information makes it more costly to process hypotheses. For example, in the centralized system the *PREDICT KS* uses the heuristic of attempting to extend first in the direction with the fewer number of predicted words (i.e., either at the beginning or end of the phrase). In the distributed system, this heuristic often cannot be exploited because the preferred direction would carry the prediction outside the node's area-of-interest. The inability to predict in the direction of greater constraint leads to more word verification processing. A more subtle effect of a node's limited area-of-interest is a shift in the distribution of the length of phrase hypotheses towards hypotheses having fewer words. In general, shorter phrase hypotheses have less grammatical constraint on the number of words they predict, leading to additional word verification. These effects showed up as a doubling of the number of words predicted per phrase hypothesis.

Incomplete meta-information can lead to redundant search and unnecessary search (i.e., with a low likelihood of a correct solution), which reduce the potential speed-up benefits of a parallel search. *Redundant search* occurs because there is no centralized scheduler to coordinate the search of nodes with overlapping areas-of-interest. *Unnecessary search* occurs because the search paradigm is opportunistic across the length of the utterance, i.e., working out from a few islands of reliability discovered in the data. These islands are not, in general, distributed uniformly among the nodes in the network. This leads to cases in which a particular node can do little effective processing until it receives constraining information, i.e., a reliable island, from another node. Likewise, after a node has fully explored all of its reliable islands, it may have little effective processing to do. The processing occurring before the node receives a reliable island and the processing after it has fully exploited all of its reliable islands is, from a global view, unnecessary. Thus, the opportunistic scheduling partially sequentializes the search. The effect this has on the parallel speed-up in a network system depends on the distribution of

[9] This third number may be more or less than the sum of the other two because a transmitted hypothesis is accepted by a receiving node only if it overlaps the node's area-of-interest. Thus, an hypothesis transmitted in a three-node network might be accepted by zero, one, or two nodes.

islands across the nodes—the more uniform the distribution, the greater the speed-up. Fig. 11 illustrates this by showing how one of the test utterances was recognized in the centralized and distributed systems.

Because of the uncertainty in knowledge and data in speech understanding, such unnecessary search may produce hypotheses with sufficient credibility and scope to be transmitted. This internode communication is itself unnecessary and may distract nodes doing productive work, thus causing even more unnecessary search. This distraction occurs because the estimate of impact of an hypothesis is based in part on its scope (length). Thus, a long, moderately rated hypothesis may be considered to have more impact than a short, highly rated one. If a node lacking a reliable island does not soon receive constraining hypotheses, it is often able to develop hypotheses of moderate credibility and large scope which it then transmits. If such an hypothesis is received by a node with a highly reliable island before it has been able to develop that island fully, the node may switch its attention to the longer, received hypothesis, thus delaying, perhaps indefinitely, the useful processing of the shorter, highly credible island. The recognition trace of the utterance shown in Fig. 12 shows the results of such distraction.

This method of estimating impact for focusing decisions is reasonable in a centralized system in which all the input data are received together. In such a system, the development of hypotheses is implicitly more synchronized—the higher rated island would have been extended before the lower rated hypothesis would have been developed. A possible solution to this problem in the network system is to normalize the estimate of impact of received hypotheses according to the scope of the largest locally generated ones.[10]

Five utterances were also run using a more complex (i.e., less constraining) grammar, called "S15." Again, all five were recognized by both the centralized and three-node configurations, adding credence to our hypothesis that the accuracy of the problem solving can be maintained within the distributed configuration. In these runs, the overall speedup increased to 30 percent from the 10 percent of the simpler grammar, indicating more parallelism in the larger search space. The fraction of hypotheses transmitted remained similar to the fraction in the simpler grammar runs.

B. Transmission Policies

The network data in the previous section were generated using the locally complete transmission policy. Fig. 13 presents experimental comparisons of that policy with those of dynamic thresholding and full transmission. (See Section V-C for descriptions of these policies.) The utterances used were the first five of the ten used in the previous section; the same areas-of-interest were used. All five utterances were correctly understood under all three transmission policies.

On the basis of both processing time and number of hypotheses transmitted, locally complete is more efficient than the dynamic thresholding, which in turn is better than the full

---

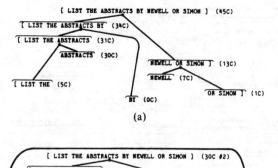

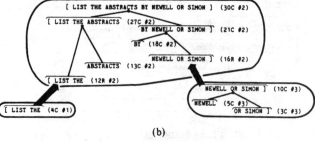

Fig. 11. Recognition process for those partial interpretations of utterance #5 that led to the correct overall interpretation. Joined lines indicate intranode hypothesis creation. Arrows show internode communication of an hypothesis. Numbers in parentheses indicate network processing time in seconds when the hypothesis was created (C) or received as a message (R). In the multinode case, a second number indicates the node number (e.g., #2 for node two). (a) In the centralized system. (b) In the three-node configuration.

transmission. It thus appears that the timeliness advantage of the dynamic thresholding policy is dominated by the reductions in redundant processing and distracting communication of the locally complete. In some experiments with a more complex grammar, the differential between the two selective policies was reduced—our conjecture is that the extra timeliness of the dynamic thresholding policy becomes more important as the complexity of the search increases.

C. Communication with Errors

In order to assess the robustness of the network system with respect to communication errors, experiments were run in which messages received by a node are randomly discarded with a specified probability. This serves to model communication systems with good error detection but poor correction capabilities, e.g., packet radio. Selection at the receiving end allows for cases in which a broadcast message is received successfully by some nodes but not others.

Two characteristics of the network system should make it robust in the face of communication errors. First, there are redundancies that can recreate the information in lost messages; and second, the system can exploit the recreated information even though it arrives later than would have the original, lost communication. There are several ways of recreating the lost information.

1) The overlapping of areas-of-interest leads to the possibility of creating redundant information directly.

2) The transmission policy can introduce redundant communications. For example, the dynamic threshold policy (and the full transmission policy) can produce a sequence of messages representing the stages of development of a partial solution. Each message in the sequence subsumes the information in the previous messages. This redundancy does not exist in the

---

[10] It might be desirable to expand such differential treatment of received hypotheses, e.g., to use meta-information about the transmitting node for evaluating the received hypothesis.

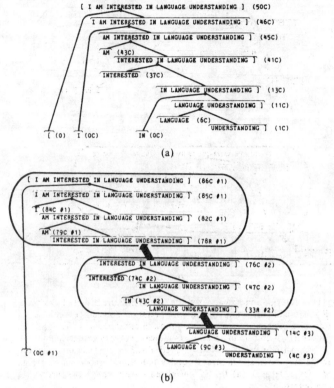

Fig. 12. Recognition process for those partial interpretations of utterance #6 that led to the correct overall interpretation. (a) In the centralized system. (b) In the three-node configuration.

locally complete policy, which transmits only the final message in that sequence; it is for this reason that dynamic threshold was used for this experiment. Other mechanisms, such as murmuring (Section IV-D), can be used for additional explicit redundant communication—we have not explored them in these experiments.

3) The broadcasting of messages makes it possible that messages might be lost to one node, but received by another. The node that correctly receives the information might operate on it and subsequently broadcast a message based on information in the original message. The rebroadcast may be received by the node that lost the original version. This propagation of information among the nodes thus implicitly creates redundant communication paths.

4) The method of building an interpretation by incremental aggregation of partial interpretations makes it possible to derive a correct interpretation in multiple ways. This kind of behavior has been observed in the centralized version of the Hearsay-II speech-understanding system—for example, cases have occurred in which a complete interpretation could not be constructed from one correct island of reliability because of KS errors, but could be derived from another. Because a particular message may not be crucial for all ways of deriving a correct interpretation, its loss does not preclude a correct interpretation.

These experiments used the same data as those in Section VI-B. The dynamic threshold transmission policy was used, to provide more redundancy in communication than the locally complete. Fig. 14 shows the performance with 0, 25, 35, and 50 percent of the messages discarded. One utterance of the five was not correctly recognized (i.e., no complete interpretation

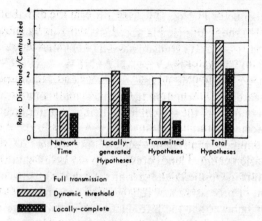

Fig. 13. Performance comparisons of the three transmission policies (means of utterances 1–5).

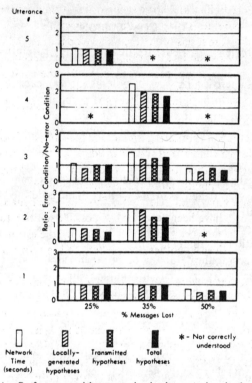

Fig. 14. Performance with communication losses (using the dynamic threshold transmission policy).

was constructed in the maximum allocated processing time) in the 25 and 35 percent cases, and three were missed in the 50 percent case. There are several interesting points about the statistics. For example, the execution times for some runs was decreased *because of* the errorful communication channel. This occurred when messages, discarded due to the simulated communication failures, happened to be either incorrect or redundant. Other runs, as expected, required additional processing time and communication to recreate the nonredundant information lost due to communication failure.

Several runs were not correctly recognized because a message was lost which contained the first or last word in the utterance.[11] Information about these extreme areas is contained in only a single node and is, thus, especially difficult to recreate

[11] Because of the randomness of message lossage, this happened to occur in utterance #2 in the 25 percent error case but not in the 35 percent case.

in another node. The loss of this information is not always fatal. Fig. 15(b) shows an example where first-word information was lost on two separate transmissions (([+HAVE+ANY from node 1 to 2 and [+HAVE+ANY+NEW+PAPERS+BY from node 1 to 3). The system, however, was resilient enough to recreate the information through a roundabout path. Fig. 15(a) is a trace of the system recognizing the utterance when this information was not lost.

In summary, the system's performance with a faulty communication channel lends credence to our belief that the architecture is resilient and permits a tradeoff between the amount of processing and reliability of communication. We further believe that the introduction of a knowledge-based murmuring scheme would correct most of the incorrect runs without increasing communication costs significantly.

VII. Conclusions

Let us review our model for distributed interpretation systems.[12]

1) There is a network of systems (nodes), each of which is able to perform significant local processing in a self-directed way. For example, if a node does not receive a particular piece of information in a given amount of time, it is able to continue processing using whatever information is currently available to it.

2) The parts of the problem a node is responsible for working on is called its *area-of-interest* and is defined by the information it needs and produces. In general, areas-of-interest of the nodes overlap. The local database of a node (i.e., what information it actually has) may be incomplete or inconsistent with respect to the databases of the other nodes. Nodes resolve the uncertainty in their information through an iterative, asynchronous exchange of partial, tentative results at various levels of abstraction.

3) Control of cooperation among the nodes is decentralized and implicit in the autonomous behaviors of the individual nodes. Each node uses its local estimate of the state of problem solving in the network to control its processing (i.e., what new information to generate) and transmissions to other nodes.

This model differs from conventional approaches to distributed system design in its emphasis on dealing with uncertainty and error in control, data, and algorithms caused by the distribution as an integral part of the network problem-solving process. An attractive structure for accomplishing this is an opportunistic problem-solving structure and, in particular, one which has implicit (data-directed) information flow and control flow.

The conventional approach to the design of distributed systems is to overlay some basic, centralized problem-solving strategy with new mechanisms to handle the uncertainty and errors introduced by the distribution. It is our hypothesis that this conventional approach limits both the type of systems that can be distributed effectively and the environments in which

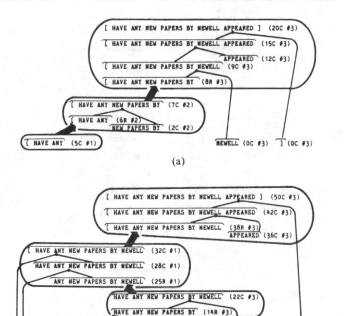

(a)

(b)

Fig. 15. Trace of utterance #2 processing with and without messages discarded, showing those partial interpretations that led to the correct overall interpretation. (a) With no messages discarded. (b) With 35 percent of the messages discarded.

they can operate. We feel the key to the design of distributed systems is to incorporate mechanisms for dealing with uncertainty and error as an integral part of the problem-solving approach.

The Hearsay-II architecture appears to be a good one for such an integrated approach. The processing can be partitioned or replicated naturally among network nodes because it is already decomposed into independent, self-directed modules (i.e., the *KS*'s), which interact anonymously and are limited in the scope of the data they need and produce. Issues involved in the distribution of the control and data structures of Hearsay-II can be dealt with effectively because of the mechanisms already in the system for resolving uncertainty caused by incomplete or incorrect data and *KS* processing. Let us review these mechanisms and their impact on the ease of system distribution.[13]

Mechanism 1: **Opportunistic nature of information gathering**—Problem-solving is viewed as an incremental, opportunistic, and asynchronous process in which decisions, if they look promising, can be made with incomplete information and later reevaluated in the light of new information.

Impact 1: **Reduced need for synchronization**—Because of this style of problem solving, a node does not have an *a priori* order for processing information and can exploit incomplete

---

[12] Smith and Davis [23] compare this model with the contract net model. Fox [8] discusses distributed problem-solving models from the viewpoint of organizational theory.

[13] Not all these mechanisms were exploited in the distributed Hearsay-II speech-understanding system described in the previous section. In general, the possibility for exploiting a particular mechanism is dependent on the specifics of the problem-solving application being distributed.

local information. Thus, the processing order within nodes and the transmission of information among nodes does not need to be synchronized.

Mechanism 2: **Use of abstract information**—Because the problem-solving database is structured as a loose hierarchy of increasingly more abstract problem representations, an abstract representation of one aspect of the solution can be used to constrain analysis of other aspects of the problem.

Impact 2: **Reduced internode communication bandwidth**—The ability to use abstract information permits nodes to cooperate by using messages with high information content; thus, the communication bandwidth needed for effective cooperation is reduced.

Mechanism 3: **Incremental aggregation**—A solution is constructed through the incremental piecing together of mutually contraining and consistent information; incorrect partial solutions naturally die out as a result of this process.

Impact 3: **Automatic error detection**—This method of problem solving allows a distributed system to detect and reduce the impact of incorrect decisions caused by incomplete and inconsistent local databases and communication losses.

Mechanism 4: **Problem solving as a search process**—Because of uncertainty in data and *KS* processing, many alternative partial solutions need to be examined in the process of constructing a complete and consistent solution; in this search process, the more uncertainty there exists, the larger the number of alternatives that, in general, have to be explored.

Impact 4: **Internode parallelism**—The requirement that many alternative partial solutions need to be examined generates the possibility that this search can be carried out in parallel by different nodes. The asynchronous nature of information gathering introduces the possibility for additional parallelism, since different aspects of the problem and different information levels can be worked on independently. Further, the introduction of additional uncertainty through incomplete and inconsistent local databases can be traded off against more search—to the degree that this extra search can be done in parallel and does not itself generate proportionally more internode communication, internode bandwidth can be lowered without significant degradation in system response time.

Mechanism 5: **Functionally-accurate definition of solution**—Due to the opportunistic nature of processing and the existence of diverse and overlapping *KS*'s, the correct solution may be derivable in different ways, i.e., using different ordering sequences for incrementally constructing the solution components or using different solution components. Because a solution is based on a set of mutually constraining pieces of information, it is also possible for a correct solution to incorporate information that is correct but not considered very likely, or to use incorrect information that is considered very likely.

Impact 5: **Self-correcting**—Because there are multiple paths from which a solution can be derived, it is possible to correct for what would be considered fatal errors in a conventional distributed problem-solving system. Additionally, system reliability can be varied without modifying the basic problem-solving structure, through the appropriate selection and focusing of local node processing. For example, it is pos-

sible to improve reliability by enlarging the overlap among nodes' areas-of-interest, thus increasing the likelihood of generating redundant information. This increases the number of alternative ways that a solution can be derived.

Within the basic distributed problem-solving structure defined by these mechanisms, several other mechanisms have been incorporated or proposed to handle issues specific to a distributed environment.

1) To limit internode communication, an incremental transmission mechanism (with processing at each step) has been developed in which only a limited subset of a node's information is transmitted and to only a limited subset of nodes. A node acts as a generator, which transmits only a few most credible pieces of information and which can subsequently respond to stagnation of progress by producing alternative information. As part of this approach, two policies ("dynamic thresholding" and "locally complete") have been developed for controlling the generator function.

2) To increase network reliability, a knowledge-based mechanism called "murmuring" has been proposed. Here, a node retransmits high-impact information if during a specified time interval it neither receives nor generates higher impact information. Murmuring can be used to correct for lost communications due to intermittent channel or node failures and to bring new or moving nodes up-to-date.

3) To guarantee the appropriate communication connectivity among nodes, a decentralized mechanism for constructing a communication network has been developed. Using this mechanism, which relies on descriptions of the I/O characteristics of each node, nodes act as store-and-forward message processors to provide needed connectivity. A similar mechanism can be used for dynamic allocation of processing tasks among nodes.

4) To provide more sensitive implicit internode control while still retaining decentralization, each node may transmit explicitly its local control information ("meta-information"). Nodes can, thus, determine more directly the state of processing in other nodes.

The experiments described here explore these mechanisms in only a limited way. A number of issues need to be resolved in order to gain an understanding of the more general applicability of this approach.

Distributed Focus of Control:

1) How to coordinate in a decentralized and implicit way the activity of nodes that have overlapping (i.e., redundant) information, so as to control redundant computation, and

2) How to decide locally that a node is performing unnecessary computation and how to select the aspects of the problem on which it should instead focus its attention. This is the problem of dynamic allocation of information and processing capabilities of the network.[14]

Self-correcting Computational Structure:

1) What and how much uncertainty (errors) can be

---

[14] This issue is related to the classical allocation problem in networks: how to decide if the cost of accessing a distant database is too expensive and whether, instead, the processing should be moved closer to the data or the data moved closer to the processor.

handled using these types of computational structures, and what is the cost in processing and communication to resolve the various types of errors.

Task Characteristics and the Selection of an Appropriate Network Configuration:

1) What characteristics of a task can be used to select a network configuration appropriate for it? When can implicit control and information flow structures be used? Similarly, when should flat, hierarchical, or matrix configurations, or mixtures of them, be used? Candidate characteristics include the patterns of *KS* interaction, the type, spatial distribution, and degree of uncertainty in information, interdependencies of partial interpretations, size of the search space, desired reliability, accuracy, responsiveness and throughput, and available computing resources.

The Hearsay-II speech-understanding system, with only minor changes, performs well as a cooperating network, even though each node has a limited view of the input data. In the experiment with communication losses, system performance degrades gracefully with as much as 50 percent of the messages lost; this experiment also indicates that the system can often compensate automatically for the lost messages by performing additional computation. These results support our general model of distributed systems design. They also indicate that the Hearsay-II architecture is a good one to use as a basis for this approach.

Acknowledgment

The authors wish to thank J. Adams for his help with the programming of the multinode simulation. Also, helpful comments on various drafts of this report were generously given by J. Barnett, D. Corkill, R. Davis, A. Hanson, R. Hayes-Roth, J. Pavlin, D. Schwabe, and Y. Yemini.

References

[1] H. G. Barrow and J. M. Tennenbaum, "MSYS: A system for reasoning about scenes," SRI Int., AI Center, Menlo Park, CA, Tech. Rep. 121, Apr. 1976.
[2] G. M. Baudet, "Asynchronous iterative methods for multiprocessors," Comput. Sci. Dep., Carnegie-Mellon Univ., Pittsburgh, PA, Tech. Rep., Nov. 1976.
[3] R. J. Drazovich and S. Brooks, "Surveillance integration automation project (SIAP)," in *Distributed Sensor Nets Workshop*. Pittsburgh, PA: Carnegie-Mellon Univ., Dec. 1978, pp. 119-121.
[4] R. S. Engelmore and H. P. Nii, "A knowledge-based system for the interpretation of protein X-ray crystallographic data," Comput. Sci. Dep. Standard Univ., Stanford, CA, Tech. Rep. Stan-CS-77-589, 1977.
[5] L. D. Erman and V. R. Lesser, "A multilevel organization for problem solving using many diverse cooperating sources of knowledge," in *Proc. 4th Int. Joint Conf. on Artificial Intell.*, Tbilisi, USSR, 1975, pp. 483-490.
[6] L. D. Erman, F. Hayes-Roth, V. R. Lesser, and D. R. Reddy, "The Hearsay-II speech-understanding system: Integrating knowledge to resolve uncertainty," *Comput. Surveys*, vol. 12, pp. 213-253, June 1980.
[7] R. D. Fennell and V. R. Lesser, "Parallelism in AI problem-solving: A case study of Hearsay-II," *IEEE Trans. Comput.* vol. C-26, pp. 98-111, Feb. 1977.
[8] M. S. Fox, "An organizational view of distributed systems," in *Proc. Int. Conf. on Syst. and Cybern.* Denver, CO, Oct. 1979, pp. 354-359.
[9] J. Galbraith, *Designing Complex Organizations*. Addison-Wesley, 1973.
[10] A. R. Hanson and E. M. Riseman, "VISIONS: A computer system for interpreting scenes," in *Computer Vision Systems*, A. Hanson and E. Riseman, Eds. New York; Academic, 1978, pp. 303-333.
[11] F. Hayes-Roth and V. R. Lesser, "Focus of attention in the Hearsay-II speech-understanding system," in *Proc. 5th Int. Joint Conf. on Artificial Intell.*, Cambridge, MA, 1977, pp. 27-35.
[12] F. Hayes-Roth, "The role of partial and best matches in knowledge systems," in *Pattern-Directed Inference Systems*, D. A. Waterman and F. Hayes-Roth, Eds. New York: Academic, 1978.
[13] R. E. Kahn, S. A. Gronemeyer, J. Burchfiel, and R. C. Kunzelman, "Advances in packet radio technology," *Proc. IEEE*, vol. 66, pp. 1468-1496, Nov. 1978.
[14] V. R. Lesser, R. D. Fennell, L. D. Erman, and D. R. Reddy, "Organization of the Hearsay-II speech understanding system," *IEEE Trans. Acoust., Speech, Signal Processing*, vol. 23, pp. 11-23, 1975.
[15] V. R. Lesser and L. D. Erman, "A retrospective view of the Hearsay-II architecture," in *Proc. 5th Int. Joint Conf. on Artificial Intell.*, Cambridge, MA, 1977, pp. 790-800.
[16] V. R. Lesser, J. Pavlin, and S. Reed, "Quantifying and simulating the behavior of knowledge-based interpretation systems," in *Proc. 1st Nat. Conf. on Artificial Intell.*, Stanford, CA, Aug. 1980, pp. 111-115.
[17] V. R. Lesser and D. D. Corkill, "Functionally accurate cooperative distributed systems," *IEEE Trans. Syst. Man Cybern.*, 1981, to be published. (This is an expanded version of "Cooperative distributed problem solving: A new approach for structuring distributed systems," Comput. and Inform. Sci. Dep., Univ. of Massachusetts, Tech. Rep. COINS 78-7, May 1978.)
[18] B. T. Lowerre and R. Reddy, "The HARPY speech understanding system," in *Trends in Speech Recognition*, W. A. Lea, Ed. Englewood Cliffs, NJ: Prentice-Hall, 1980, ch. 15.
[19] H. P. Nii and E. A. Feigenbaum, "Rule-based understanding of signals," in *Pattern-Directed Inference Systems*, D. A. Waterman and F. Hayes-Roth, Eds. New York: Academic, 1978.
[20] A. Rosenfeld, R. A. Hummel, and S. W. Zucker, "Scene labeling by relaxation operators," *IEEE Trans. Syst., Man, Cybern.*, vol. SMC-6, 1976.
[21] R. G. Smith and R. Davis, "Distributed problem solving: The contract net approach," in *Proc. 2nd Nat. Conf. of Canadian Soc. for Computational Studies of Intell.*, Toronto, Canada, July 1978, pp. 278-287.
[22] R. G. Smith, "The contract net protocol: High-level communication and control in a distributed problem solver," in *Proc. 1st Int. Conf. on Distributed Comput. Syst.* Huntsville, AL, Oct. 1979, pp. 185-192.
[23] R. G. Smith and R. Davis, "Cooperation in distributed problem solving," in *Proc. Int. Conf. on Syst. and Cybern.*, Denver, CO, Oct. 1979, pp. 366-371.

Victor R. Lesser was born in New York City, on November 21, 1944. He received the A.B. degree in mathematics from Cornell University, Ithaca, NY, in 1966 and the M.S. and Ph.D. degrees in computer science from Stanford University, Stanford, CA, in 1969 and 1972, respectively.

From 1972 to 1977 he was a Research Computer Scientist in the Computer Science Department at Carnegie-Mellon University, Pittsburgh, PA. While there, he was a principal on the Hearsay-II Speech-Understanding Project and was also on the initial design team for the CM* multiprocessor architecture. Since 1977 he has been on the faculty of the Computer and Information Sciences Department of the University of Massachusetts, Amherst, MA where he currently holds the position of Associate Professor. His current research interests focus on system architectures for distributed problem solving and knowledge-based artificial intelligence.

Lee D. Erman was born in Chicago, IL, in 1944. He received the B.S. in mathematics from the University of Michigan, Ann Arbor, in 1966 and the M.S. and Ph.D. degrees in computer science from Stanford University, Stanford, CA, in 1968 and 1974, respectively.

From 1971 to 1978 he was on the faculty of the Carnegie-Mellon University Computer Science Department as Research Associate, Research Computer Scientist, and Assistant Professor. He was a principal designer, implementor, and manager of the Hearsay speech understanding research. Since 1978 he has been on the Research Staff of Information Sciences Institute (ISI) of the University of Southern California, Los Angeles, where he is doing research on converting informal specifications of systems to high-level, formal specifications and on the architectures of systems for implementing knowledge-based systems. His major interests are in knowledge-based artificial intelligence systems in er-

rorful domains, and the tailoring of computer systems for specialized tasks.

Dr. Erman is currently Chairman of the Association for Computing Machinery's. Special Interest Group on Artificial Intelligence (SIGART). He is also on the Editorial Board of the journal *Artificial Intelligence* and the Executive Council of the American Association for Artificial Intelligence.

An Organizational View of Distributed Systems

MARK S. FOX, MEMBER, IEEE

Abstract— The relationship between organization theory and distributed systems is studied. By viewing distributed systems as analogous to *human organizations*, concepts and theories germane to the management science field of organization theory can be applied. Task *complexity, uncertainty*, coupled with *resource constraints* are shown to be important factors in deciding how a system is to be distributed.

I. Introduction

DISTRIBUTED SYSTEMS are difficult to design. At least two approaches should be taken to alleviate this problem. We should build more distributed systems (learning by doing) and draw upon ideas from other fields (e.g., biology, management science) that have considerable experience with their own distributed systems (learning by analogy). This paper is an example of the latter. By viewing distributed systems as being analogous to human organizations, concepts and theories germane to the management science field of organization theory can be applied.

To begin our discussion, a distributed system is defined as a particular organization— task decomposition and control regime— resulting from the distribution of a set of tasks over a set of logically or physically disjoint processing elements. Research in distributed systems has focused on analyzing classes of systems. Systems where multiple tasks exist but share the same goal have been termed *teams* [1].

Team tasks where the data (resource) are (initially) physically distributed, e.g., weather monitoring, have come under the study of *distributed sensor nets* [2]. Team tasks that require the sharing of data (raw or processed) have been termed *cooperative* [3]. Tasks where control is hierarchical are called *organizations* [4]. Though a variety of structural forms have been distinguished, there is a paucity of knowledge available to guide system design. Moreover, the design of a distributed system's hardware often precedes the organizational analysis, resulting in inadequate architectures. The major problem with designing distributed systems is deciding how the task should be decomposed and the control regime to be used, and this choice of organization is determined by features of the task (domain) and some measurement criteria.

Economics and management science have had a history of designing and analyzing distributed systems, i.e., human organizations. Beginning with Adam Smith's theory of labor division [5], through the more current organizational work of March and Simon [4], Galbraith [6], and Williamson [7], much research has centered around constructing distributed systems that best suit a particular task. Given the existence of this body of knowledge, can it be applied to distributed systems design in the computer sciences? Or, stated another way, is the distributed computer systems– human organization metaphor valid? Distributed systems

Manuscript received December 5, 1979; revised September 10, 1980 and September 25, 1980. This work was supported in part by the Defense Advanced Research Projects Agency (DOD), Arpa Order 3597, monitored by the Air Force Avionics Laboratory Contract 533615-78-C-1551 and in part by a National Research Council of Canada Post-Graduate Scholarship.

The author is with The Robotics Institute and Department of Computer Science, Carnegie-Mellon University, Pittsburgh PA, 15213.

face the problem of allocating tasks, resources, and information to a set of processors. These are precisely the problems of human organizations. Hence it appears valid at the macro level, but does it hold at the micro level, i.e., does the computer processor share characteristics with the human mind? Simon's theory of *bounded rationality* seems applicable here:

> The capacity of the human mind for formulating and solving complex problems is very small compared with the size of the problems whose solution is required for objectively rational behavior in the real world—or even for a reasonable approximation to such objective rationality [8].

The human mind's processing capacity is limited. This result is what Simon calls *bounded rationality*. Bounded rationality implies that both the information a person can absorb and the detail of control he may wield is limited. As tasks grow larger and more complex, means must be found to effectively limit the increase of information a person sees and the complexity of control. Bounded rationality is a prime factor in the evolution of multiperson organizations from an unregimented group to more structured alternatives.

A computer processor also has a limited processing capacity. A processor can execute only a limited number of instructions per second. This limits the amount of information a processor may process and the amount of control it may exercise within a given time period. Hence, programmed systems, whether centralized or distributed, may exhibit symptoms similar to the bounded rationality exhibited by humans when capacities are exceeded. The metaphor appears viable.

The purpose of this paper is to attempt a technology transfer from the field of organization theory; to transfer both descriptive and analytical information to aid in the analysis and design of distributed systems. Fig. 1 depicts the overall approach to be taken in analyzing such systems. The design of a distributed system (organization) requires the selection of an organizational structure, i.e., processes (modules) and communication paths, and a control regime. The efficacy of a selected organization is dependent upon complexity and uncertainty features of the task. Determining how uncertainty and complexity affects the organization requires measurement techniques, for example, transaction analysis. Finally, the measurement cannot be interpreted without some reference criteria called organizational goals.

The following sections elucidate the levels in Fig. 1. First, the Hearsay-II speech understanding system architecture which will be used as an example throughout the paper is described. Next, the analysis of organization theory is begun by surveying the set of organization structures and control found in the literature. The requirements for a theory of organization analysis are then described, followed by an analysis of two task features, uncertainty and complexity, which affect the organization (level 2). For most task features, an analysis technique is outlined (level 3) and an organizational solution specified (level 1).

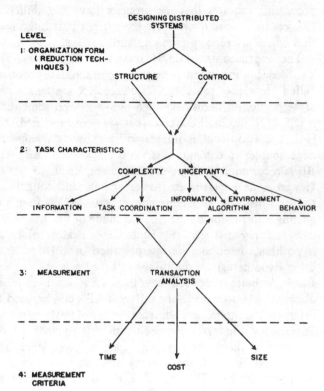

Fig. 1.   Organization analysis.

II.   AN EXAMPLE: HEARSAY-II

Throughout this paper, organization theoretic concepts will be introduced. To aid the reader in interpreting their applicability, we apply and contrast these ideas with the architecture of the Hearsay-II speech understanding system. The reader should refer to the following description throughout the rest of the paper.

Hearsay-II [9], [10] is a system designed to understand connected speech.[1] Utterances, without artificially introduced pauses between words, are spoken to the system. Hearsay-II must interpret, understand, and reply to the utterance. The current version of Hearsay-II retrieves and answers questions about abstracts stored in its data base [11].

The process of understanding utterances requires the application of many sources of knowledge: acoustic, syllabic, lexical, prosodic, syntactic, semantic, pragmatic, etc. Each source of knowledge can be used to interpret the utterance at its own particular level of representation. Each source of knowledge only partially represents the knowledge a human brings to bear when parsing speech. These sources represent the state of the art of our knowledge of the speech understanding process. Because of the incompleteness of the knowledge, the understanding process is saturated with error. Thus speech understanding is a search in a large space of possible interpretations for the utterance that best fits the input data, i.e., the speech waveform.

The design of a speech understanding system must allow the integration of sources of knowledge in such a way that they may gracefully interact. The errorfulness of the

---

[1]See [30] for a good introduction to the problem.

processing requires that the program have the ability to redirect its attention whenever the current best interpretation of the utterance proves implausible.

The approach taken in Hearsay-II is as follows. The knowledge in the system is represented in separate processes called knowledge sources (KS's). Each KS contains a separate portion of knowledge such as syntax and semantics: SASS [12]; lexical:POMOW [13]; semantics: SEMANT [14]. The knowledge is integrated by allowing the knowledge sources to communicate via a blackboard (BB). The BB is a common dynamic data structure. Each KS can be viewed as an expert in its particular field and contributes to the "discussion" among the experts by reading and writing information on the BB. The mode of BB interaction is *hypothesize and test* [15]. Each KS can either place an hypothesis, describing its interpretation of BB data (i.e., other hypotheses), on the BB, or test (i.e., accept or reject) BB hypotheses produced by other KS's. As mentioned above, the knowledge in the different KS's can be used to interpret the utterance at different levels of representation. Specifically, the levels of representation (knowledge) form a hierarchy. Each level is built upon a lower level. The lexical level is built upon the syllabic, and the syntactic upon the lexical. The job of a KS is to construct an interpretation (hypothesis) at its level of expertise by postulating (or testing) hypotheses constructed from hypotheses at a lower level or by elaborating hypotheses from a higher level.

The processing of the system is data-directed. It is directed by the current state of the BB data.[2] Each KS can view BB hypotheses at its level(s) of expertise. Whenever a change is made to an hypothesis or the BB by a KS, other KS's react through further hypothesization and testing. At any time there are many possible KS's capable of executing. The choice of which KS to execute is controlled by policy modules and the scheduler. Together they provide a focus of control (FOCUS) mechanism [16] capable of directing the system's attention to the currently best hypotheses, or redirecting the system when the current hypothesis proves unfruitful.

Fig. 2 shows the organization of the Hearsay-II system. Fig. 3 shows the blackboard hypotheses for interpreting the utterance "Tell me about beef." Initially, the segmentation KS segments the speech input and places on the BB hypotheses for all possible labels of the sound in each segment. The syllable KS (MOW) looks at the label hypotheses and transforms them to syllables. The lexical KS (POM) transforms syllable hypotheses to words and the syntax and semantics KS (SASS) transforms words to phrases. SASS also predicts, top down, missing words which causes the lower level KS's to attempt to verify the predictions. At any time over 100 possible KS executions are queued. FOCUS chooses the best KS to work on the more highly rated hypotheses.

---

[2]Each hypotheses is rated. It is a function of the ratings of the hypotheses it is constructed from and the knowledge used in the construction.

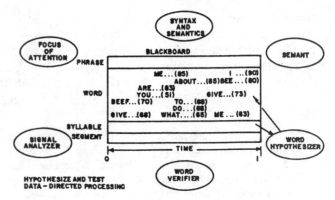

Fig. 2.   Hearsay-II architecture.

III.   ORGANIZATIONAL STRUCTURE AND CONTROL

An organization was defined as a composition of structure and control regime. The set of possible structures range from strict hierarchies to heterarchies. Possible control regimes range from an employment relation where people (processes) are directly controlled by others via agreed upon commands, to a price system where services are contracted. In the following, a variety of organizations found in the organizational literature are defined and related to the Hearsay-II architecture.

The simplest organization is the single person. The person performs all tasks, reacting to information and the environment when necessary. A single-person organization suffices as long as the person has the resources to achieve the goal. *If Hearsay-II had only a single KS, it could be viewed as a single-person organization.*

As the task requires more resources (mental or physical), the size of the organization increases, requiring more complex control and an increase in information processing capabilities. Organizational forms such as a group result. A group allows the cooperative coordination of individual members to achieve a shared goal. The task is divided up and subtasks are allocated to members who are best able to execute them. Coordination in a group is achieved through mutually agreed upon decisions. To achieve this type of coordination, group members must share all available information. They must understand it and be able to communicate their views. Finally, they must arrive at a decision that satisfies all. Each step in the coordination problem is a series of transactions. *In its simplest interpretation, Hearsay-II is a group. Though all KS's are theoretically independent, their tasks are well integrated for achieving the problem of understanding speech. The PUP6 system [17] is another example of a group organization.*

As the size of the group increases, collective decision-making becomes costly. The cost of information distribution and communication required to converge to a common decision increases. Hence a simple hierarchy evolves. A simple hierarchy has two levels. The top level contains a single decisionmaker who coordinates the efforts of the persons on the lower level. Complete information must be made available only to that person, and he must have the authority to effect changes in the organization's behavior.

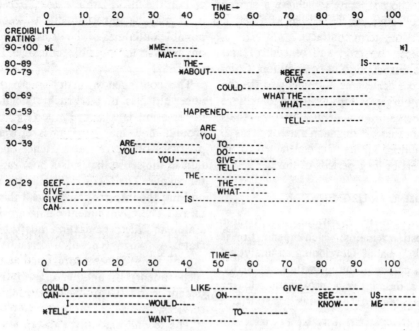

Fig. 3. Hearsay-II blackboard.

Proper coordination, implying employment and authority relations, and distribution of information, is required for the organization to be effective. *The final version of Hearsay-II fits this definition. The FOCUS KS made overall scheduling and directional decisions. (Also see SU/P[18], a derivative of Hearsay-II.)*

As the size of the single product organization grows, groups and simple hierarchies fail due to bounded rationality. The decisionmaker is unable to process all information (saturation). A uniform hierarchy results. Multiple levels of management are created to insure proper and centralized decisionmaking. Each level of the hierarchy acts as a filter on the information and decisions that are propagated up the hierarchy. Decisions are made at the lowest level in the hierarchy that has both the information to make the best decision and the authority to execute it. *Such an organization could be constructed with a hierarchy of Hearsay-II's. Each subsystem is a separate Hearsay-II system with a manager (focus) and employees (the rest of the KS's). Such a structure can be found in [19].*

As the uniform hierarchy increases in size and the number of products, powers of control are impaired, resulting in transactional diseconomies. With multiple products being produced, competition for the same resources arises among units. The problem of allocating resources so that enough are available to produce the products on schedule is quite complex.

One approach to reducing these effects is the multidivisional hierarchy. The organization is split along product lines. Each division is in full control of the tactics involved in producing their product. Hence control is situated locally where the information that enables control is available. Strategic control is vested in an elite staff assigned to a general office. The general office is concerned with strategic planning, appraisal and control including resource allocation. *If one viewed the interpretation of each area of the utterance time line as a separate "product," then the distributed Hearsay-II system [20] closely approximates this structure. Distributed Hearsay-II differs from a multidivisional hierarchy in that there is no strategic planning KS.*

As the organization grows, so does the coordination problem and the amount of the information to be processed. A significant step towards solving the problem is the price system. A number of disjoint organizations are available to produce a product or supply a service. Actions are initiated after the successful negotiation of a contract. This system eliminates all forms of control between units. All communication is contained in a contract to purchase some product or service. Control is exerted through the price of the product. Price (should) reflects the marginal cost of the product. The assumption is that through marginal pricing of goods, all resources will be utilized without waste. If a product is priced too high, it will not be purchased, if too low, the unit supplying it will go bankrupt. *Communication and control in Hearsay-II is noncontractual. The system was designed so that KS's share the same goal and blackboard communication process. Contracting assumes that a set of independent processes exists. Once processes enter into a contract, an organization is instantiated. Hence, contracting can be viewed as the dynamic creation of a system architecture. One could interpret a pre-Hearsay-II architecture as a heterarchy of unrelated KS's. A focus-like KS would let contracts to other KS's to do various speech understanding functions, with the resulting postcontractual architecture being similar to the Hearsay-II architecture.*

With the introduction of the price (or market) system, an organization does not have to create a new unit for each new function but can contract for the function in the marketplace. The next step in the evolution of an organization is a collective organization. The hierarchy is split into separate organizations who cooperate to achieve a shared goal. In one sense a collective can be viewed as a set of organizations that share long-term contracts.

The next step in successive reduction of control and information flow is the introduction of competition. Competing approaches to goal achievement are allowed (in the marketplace) with many organizations available to achieve any goal. Hence each organization peruses its own goals which correspond to another organization's needs. This is the general market situation. Services are contracted for in the marketplace for short or long periods of time.

IV. Choosing an Organization

The previous section presented a variety of possible organizations. The question remains: which organization is best suited for the task at hand? Developing an analytical theory of organization choice is the ultimate goal. Sadly, none exists yet,[3] but a descriptive approximation to the analytical theory can be sketched. It contains three parts:

1) a delineation of diagnostic features of a task,
2) a set of organizational structures and control regimes that can cope with these features, and
3) a way of measuring how well the organization performs.

In the descriptive theories developed by organization theory, two features have received major attention. The first is complexity. Complexity is defined as excessive demands on rationality. That is, task requirements exceed current bounds on computational capacity. For example, a manager receives more information than he or she can possibly read, or must coordinate more workers than he possibly can. Three types of complexity are described in the following sections: information, task, and coordination.

The second feature is uncertainty. Galbraith [6] in his explication of the contingency theory[4] approach to organization, states that organization structure is dependent upon uncertainty and diversity of task. Uncertainty is defined as the difference between information available and the information necessary to make the best decision. Variation in organizational structure results from diverse attempts in reducing uncertainty.

Contingency theory design strategies are based on the manifestation of uncertain information. We depart from the contingency view by defining three additional types of uncertainty. First, uncertainty can manifest itself in information. This means that the correctness of the information can be represented by a certainty measure;[5] the organization may not fully believe the information (stimuli) it perceives. For example, the correctness of a survey of consumer desires concerning a product the company produces is always under scrutiny. The second manifestation of uncertainty is found in the algorithm. No matter how

certain the information a decision is based on, the decision itself may be uncertain due to knowledge lacking in the possible outcomes of the decision. Optimal decisions based on analysis of possible outcomes have been extensively studied [1].

The contingency theory interpretation of information uncertainty is that at each state in the organization all information is assumed true (e.g., how much material is around, how many machines broken, etc.) but is a poor predictor of future states. Hence the information is uncertain in the sense that it is a poor estimator of environmental change. The focus is actually the changing environment and not the information. We call this environmental uncertainty. The environment changes over time (from state to state), and the organization must adapt to these changes in state. A fourth type of uncertainty commonly found in organizations is behavioral uncertainty. An employee, unit (department), or another organizations cannot always be depended on to produce the contracted for products or services.

The second part of the theory would associate organization structures and control regimes that can adequately cope with the complexity and uncertainty features of the task. Such associations are described in the next two sections.

Finally, the theory requires a way of measuring how well an organization performs its task. The task goal provides the measurement criteria. Goals such as minimizing resource consumption, maximizing production, minimizing quality, etc., are commonly found in business organizations. These are analogous to reducing time and space, increasing processing power, and producing results of higher certainty (validity) in distributed systems. One measurement technique that has experienced renewed interest in management science is transaction analysis [7]. Transactions take on a rather broad definition. They encompass normal contractual agreements, communication of information, monitoring, delegation and control, and most other activities that require interaction among participants within an organization or market. The handling of transactions requires the consumption of resources. Hence transactions are too complex when they require more resources than are available (bounded rationality); complexity reduction becomes the problem of minimizing resource consumption. The distributed system analog is that processing is resource limited. Memory, cycles, and bandwidth are limited. Hence transactions among processes have to be well-structured to minimize resource consumption. Transactions can also be characterized by the assumed differences in information, motivation, and behavior amongst the parties of the transaction. By detailing the transactions among organization participants, the efficacy of alternative organizational structures can be measured.

In the next two sections, the second part of the theory—associating structure and control with task features—is elaborated. A variety of complexity and uncertainty types and organizations for reducing their effects are described. Where possible, a transactional approach for measuring

---

[3]Systems science [31], computer science [32], [33] artificial intelligence [22], [34], and decision theory [1] have done some work towards this ideal.

[4]Contingency theory has two premises: 1) there is no best way to organize, and 2) all ways of organizing are not equally effective.

[5]Lesser et al. [34] propose a measure called reliability.

uncertainty and complexity is defined. And the suggested organizations are interpreted in the Hearsay-II architectural framework.

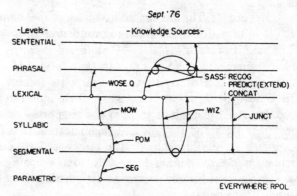

Fig. 4. Levels of representation.

V. Complexity Reduction Techniques

A. Information Complexity

Bounded rationality limits the amount of information a human or processor may process within a given time period (or other resource constraint). Information becomes too complex when it requires more processing than available in order to be properly analyzed and understood. Ways must be found to reduce the complexity of information so that humans and processors can be more effective.

Recognizing information complexity requires the characterizing of information flow as transactions. For each communication channel the average number of transactions and processing per transaction must be compiled and compared to the processing power of the receiving person (or module).

How is the information complexity reduced? By abstraction and omission. Abstraction is attained by use of several levels of representation. A purchasing manager does not care how much material is used every minute in a department, or how it is used. He is interested only in gross usage of materials. Material/minute is a detail that can be abstracted into material/day or material/week, while its usage can be ignored completely, since the former is actually an abstraction of it. A second approach to information reduction is computer-based summarization techniques. Whether statistical or graphical in nature, information can be reduced to a few meaningful parameters.

Information complexity, due to a processor's bounded rationality, also exists in distributed systems. Accordingly, similar techniques have been used. Examples of these techniques can be found in the Hearsay-II and Baseball [21] systems. In Hearsay-II information is represented at many levels (Fig. 4). Each level is an abstraction of the lower levels. A KS that makes a decision at the syntax level only uses information at the syntax and lexical levels, without going into the more detailed levels. To do so would require a greater information processing capacity and the ability to interpret information at those levels. To analyze information complexity, each hypothesis would be considered a transaction. Then knowing the average number of hypotheses at each level, the average number of hypotheses produced by a KS, and the average number of resources consumed by a KS when processing a hypothesis, complexity limitations can be calculated. (See [22] for more detail.) The concept of omission requires that a module's task be analyzed to deduce what information must be communicated, and what should be stored or hidden locally and communicated on demand.

B. Task Complexity

Task complexity is concerned with the volume of actions (disjoint or coupled) necessary to accomplish a task. When

volume exceeds a manager's ability to grasp the task's "gestalt," then this complexity must be reduced. The solution to this problem is the division of labor [5]. This requires the partitioning of resources (men and materials; modules and computer resources) into units. Each unit is assigned a specific task related to the organizational goal. The manager delegates jobs to these units, viewing them as primitives[6] in the organizational plan. Each unit then interprets the control instructions and expands upon them to control the primitives within the unit.

The encapsulation of both mechanism and information is primary to the proper structuring of an organization. It is necessitated by bounded rationality. The following describes the characteristics of units that satisfy the constraints imposed by bounded rationality.

1) View the numerous actions (programs) contained in a unit as a single action (abstraction).
2) Control units as if they were primitive actions (planning in abstraction spaces).
3) Delegate authority. Commands to a unit are elaborated by and within the unit.
4) Reduce information flow. Information within a unit can be summarized by the unit.
5) Hide detail. Information and control not needed by other units is hidden within the unit.

Interpreting the above constraints in the design of distributed systems requires that

1) the products of the process must be well defined;
2) the interaction between processes must be minimal (near decomposability);
3) the effects of a process upon other processes must be understood;
4) clear lines of authority must be recognized;
5) clear lines of information flow must be recognized.

The first interprocess constraint is a minimum requirement. We must know what a process produces before it can be used. The second reduces the control complexity of the organization which may reduce its effectiveness. The third is necessary so that one process's action will not undermine

---

[6]Viewing units as primitives is another example of an abstraction. In this case it is program abstraction as opposed to information abstraction.

another process's. The last two points insure proper control and the information upon which to base that control.

The architecture of Hearsay-II conforms to many of these requirements. A KS is a unit that can be viewed as a single action. In Hearsay-II stimulus-response frames are used to describe the effect of a KS as a single action to the scheduler. A KS hides its algorithm and temporary results from other KS's and restricts its communication to a few hypotheses on the blackboard. The blackboard structure mechanism clearly defines how KS's communicate and how they interact (simply posting an hypothesis may cause another KS to react).

C. Coordination Complexity

Task and coordination complexity are strongly linked. Once a task has been decomposed to a point where it is comprehensible, coordination must be considered. If the units cooperate in the completion of a task, then, there is usually resource dependence between them, i.e., information, partial products, etc. The actions of each unit must be coordinated so that each produces the proper resource at the proper time.

At present there are few heuristics that guide the division process so that coordination complexity is reduced. One of these is the definition of near decomposability of a system [23] which implicitly appears in the contingency theory approach to design: construct the units so that the interaction between units is minimal.

Analyzing coordination complexity is similar to analyzing information complexity. The set of transactions necessary to carry out a task are quantified and compared to the controlling person or module's limited resources.

It has been thought that task size (space and time) can be overcome by adding more processors and memory. Such simplistic views ignore the problem of dependence in task decomposition. Empirical and analytical results on multiprocessor systems such as C.mmp [24] and CM* [25] have shown that linear speedups are not always attainable [26], [27]. In some problem situations there is an upper bound on the effect of added resources. Conversely, linear speedups can be obtained if algorithms and information storage are carefully analyzed and properly structured. Consequently, greater attention to task decomposition in program organizations and problem solving must be paid.

Following is a set of organizational substructures that reduce the complexity of coordination.

1) Slack Resources: One aspect of coordination complexity is the coordination of coupled tasks. Tasks are coupled when the input of one depends on the output of another. Tasks are tightly coupled when state changes in one task immediately affect the state of another task. To reduce the tightness of the coupling, slack resources are introduced. Buffer inventories are inserted between coupled tasks so that if one task has something go wrong with it, the other tasks are not immediately affected.

Two interpretations of slack in distributed systems are 1) the replication of tasks (processes, modules) on alternate processors in case of a processor failure, and 2) the replace-

ment of procedure calls by message queues. Requests and messages to a task are placed in a queue to reduce the synchronization (tight coupling) of tasks.

Slack has also been used extensively in computer hardware. The reliability of hardware has been extended by the duplication of functional units. Space vehicles, for example, duplicate essential units. Slack appears in a number of ways in Hearsay-II. KS's can be duplicated on many processors so that the same task can be carried in parallel. Secondly, the creation and placement of multiple hypotheses on the blackboard can be viewed as creating a buffer inventory. A KS has many hypotheses to work on and can continue processing without being aware of what another KS is doing or is not doing.

2) Function Versus Product Division: The coupling of tasks can also be reduced by proper decomposition. Organization theory distinguishes between two types of organization partitioning. The first is a product or self-contained division. This division requires that units be centered around the product that is to be produced by the organization. The second type is a functional division. A functional division orients the units to the functions necessary to produce the products (e.g., purchasing, marketing, materials, etc.). Why do we have these alternate forms of division? Depending on characteristics of the problem being solved by the organization (e.g., producing a plane), one division reduces complexity while the other increases complexity. An important measure of complexity is the amount of coordination. Any division of a problem assumes that there is greater interaction within a unit than between units (interaction locality). A system that exhibits interaction locality is called a nearly decomposable system [23]. When interaction locality no longer exists, the coordination of units becomes too complex.

An example of the division methodology is the restructuring of an operating system. The creation of scheduler, memory manager, I/O controller, and file manager modules is a functional decomposition. Each job interacts with the modules and indirectly with the other jobs. Thus coordination between jobs is important and time-consuming. If the machine was restricted to Basic and APL programming, the generality would not be necessary. The operating system could be divided into two modules, an APL module and a Basic module. Each would contain a memory manager, file manager, etc., plus certain physical resources such as disk, a portion or main memory, etc. Coordination would concern resources shared by both modules only. Economy of specialization and reduced coordination is achieved. Hearsay-II is a functional decomposition. Each KS embodies a function required for each level of speech analysis.

3) Contracting: In an organization there may exist functions that are too costly to carry out. This cost may be due to

• lack of experience within the organization,
• small usage, hence economy of size is not afforded,
• coordination problems,
• information processing problems.

It is simpler for the organization to contract for this service in the marketplace, hence information is reduced to a single price, control to contractual terms. Conditions exist under which contracting is not achievable; this is usually due to the idiosyncratic nature of the job. Williamson views most positions in organizations as being idiosyncratic. Though a position may be characterized by a general job classification, the organization, methods of communication, people interacted with, on the job learning, etc., make positions idiosyncratic. A primary consequence is that the cost of replacing a person is not negligible, nor is the service easily contracted for in the marketplace.

It is unclear how transaction analysis would detect situations where contracting is applicable. A simple approach would be to tag all transactions (communication, control, resources, etc.) with the task that produces and consumes them. Tasks whose transaction costs exceed some function of the market cost for the same product or service should be contracted.

The problem of market versus hierarchical organizations is important when more than one task is competing for the same resources (element, memory, etc.). Hence ownership (employment contract) of a processor and associated process by one task is uneconomical if it is under-utilized while external demand is high. Greater utilization is afforded when the element is a free agent, able to contract services to many different tasks.

D. The Complexity Shift

It is clear that complexity has a definite effect on organization structure. The cause of the transition from single person to group to simple hierarchy was ascribed to capacity excesses stemming from bounded rationality. As tasks become larger, processing capacities are exceeded, requiring task decomposition and allocation. Groups fail when information sharing exceeds capacity (resources), and decisionmaking and coordination becomes too complex. Simple and uniform hierarchies utilizing information reduction techniques and authority relations appear. Uniform hierarchies usually suffice until the organization grows to a point of producing multiple products. As a result, interaction among modules reaches a thrashing level. This is due to competition among organization participants (departments, people, modules) for other participant's attention (e.g., competition among different products for the same resources). The multidivision hierarchy deals with this problem by decomposing the organization along product lines so that key departments (modules) are duplicated for each product division. The next step in reducing information and control complexity is to contract for products and services in the marketplace. Information is reduced to a single variable: price.

VI. UNCERTAINTY REDUCTION TECHNIQUES

In the contingency theory approach to organization structuring, uncertainty has been recognized as a primary factor in choosing an appropriate organization [6]. Trans-

action analysis [7] also focuses on uncertainty in transactions as a cause of organizational change. The emphasis in the former is information uncertainty, while in the latter it is behavioral uncertainty. Because of the fuzziness of the definition of these two types, Section IV introduced four types of uncertainty: information, algorithm, environment, and behavior. A detailed discussion of each of the uncertainty types and their effects can be found in [22], [10]. In following, we analyze how uncertainty affects the structure of organizations.

Information uncertainty can be reduced using verification techniques such as synthesis or prediction. To reduce or recover from algorithm uncertainty distributed systems must maintain multiple approaches to achieving a task, e.g., multiple hypotheses in Hearsay-II and relaxation techniques [37], or formulate new programs of action: data gathered, programs constructed and executed, results evaluated and program repaired (feedback). Some work in the latter approach has been done in artificial intelligence [38], but much research remains.

It is often the case that the existence of information, algorithm, and/or environment uncertainty results in behavioral uncertainty such as opportunism. Opportunism occurs when a party in a transaction takes advantage by making self-disbelieved threats or promises, or withholds information. The opportunistic party secures a contract that is less favorable to the other party than might be obtained otherwise. The following are factors that lead to behavioral uncertainty.

Information impactedness [7] is a differential of information between parties of a transaction. Impactedness may be due to bounded rationality considerations because of the amount of information, unavailability of information due to one party's inability to communicate, or a party's deliberate hiding of information. Impactedness would be of little concern if the cost of achieving parity was not prohibitive in most cases. Information impactedness is a recurring condition for opportunistic behavior.

Small numbers is a market condition where the number of market participants is small, circumventing the marginal pricing behavior of competition. Contracting under a small numbers condition may result in opportunistic behavior due to participant's lack of competitive pressure.

First-mover opportunity occurs when a person or organization has idiosyncratic knowledge of a particular function, which is unattainable (due to cost and information impactedness) by other market participants. As a result, a small numbers market condition results, enabling opportunistic behavior. A first-mover condition can appear when a person in an organization attains idiosyncratic knowledge of his particular job, or an initial contractor attains idiosyncratic knowledge of the contracted job. In subsequent contracting for the same or similar job, or searches for new personnel, the previous person or contractor has a considerable advantage due to their superior (idiosyncratic) knowledge.

Whenever uncertainty is manifest, programmed organizational responses will not be appropriate. An organization must quickly adapt to unanticipated situations. The question is, "What organizational structures facilitate the adaptation process?" In contrast to complexity, uncertainty, especially environmental and behavioral, appears to shift organization structure in the opposite direction, from heterarchy to hierarchy.

The smooth operation of markets requires marginal pricing, little uncertainty, and no opportunistic bargaining in small-number situations. Market uncertainty may invalidate contracts before they expire: materials may not be available, prices increase, a strike occurs, etc. Insuring uncertain events requires complex contingent contracts, but at some point accounting for all possible contingences becomes too costly. Bounded rationality also limits contingent contracts. Contract writers cannot foresee all possible contingencies or assimilate the necessary information to do so. Hence uncertainty in market environments must be small.

Reducing information to a single signal, price, results in information impactedness which opens the door for opportunistic behavior. Opportunism will succeed only if a small-numbers bargaining situation obtains. Barring that, competition among market participants should attenuate opportunistic behavior since no advantage can be attained.

Long-term contracts in the marketplace are not feasible due to uncertainty and bounded rationality. Under such conditions it is better to make spot (short-term) contracts. Spot contracting allows organizations to sequentially adapt to changing environments. This reduces the information and certainty required in writing a contract. A problem immediately occurs negating the satisfiability of spot contracting. That is, the initial contractor obtains first-mover advantages resulting in small-numbers bargaining.

As uncertainty increases in the marketplace, bounded rationality reduces the market's ability to contract accordingly, and as opportunism appears in first-mover advantages, an alternate form of organization must appear. Such a form is the collective organization. Market participants are integrated into a single organization to cooperate in achieving a single goal. Hence bargaining costs are lowered and idiosyncratic tasks are undertaken without risk of exploitation. A collective approach allows greater adaptability to uncertain environments since formal contracts do not exist and the collective jointly decides in a sequential fashion how best to adapt to the current situation. Opportunism does not appear since it is a joint venture. Information impactness is reduced by sharing information among the group.

The transition from the market (as typified in the above structures) to a hierarchical organization has been called vertical integration. Vertical integration is the process of adding to a hierarchical organization a product or service that was originally contracted for in the market. Uncertainty, information impactness, opportunism, etc., are the attributes in the market that have to be considered when analyzing the cost of contracting versus integrating into the firm.

As uncertainty increases, the transition from a heterarchy to a hierarchy becomes preferable. The attributes of a hierarchy that support this are [7, p. 40] as follows.

1) In circumstances where complex contingent claims contracts are infeasible and sequential spot markets are hazardous, internal organization facilitates adaptive sequential decisionmaking, thereby economizing on bounded rationality.

2) Faced with present or prospective small-numbers exchange relations, internal organization serves to attenuate opportunism.

3) Convergent expectations are promoted, which reduces uncertainty.

4) Conditions of information impactedness are more easily overcome and, when they appear, are less likely to give rise to strategic behavior.

5) A more satisfying trading atmosphere sometimes occurs.

More importantly, hierarchies are not bound to particular courses of action. Due to the employment relation employees have with the firm and the firm's ability to control resource allocation, unexpected situations can be dynamically adapted to: employees assigned new tasks and resources assigned to different products. This flexibility is not typically available in contracted relations. Finally, the type of hierarchy created is dependent upon size and number of products produced, which in turn determines the organization's complexity.

The problem of behavioral uncertainty has not been considered in computer systems. Such a problem can occur in hierarchical organizations but is more prevalent in market situations. The question can be asked whether distributed systems will ever be organized as markets. Such a possibility is near.

Recent work has demonstrated the feasibility of computer networks supporting a market organization. For example, assume that each host on an ARPANET-like network is a separate organization offering services and products to other hosts. Each host has a software package that allows it to decide what services to acquire and sell under a variety of conditions. In their discussion of high-level protocols for networks, Sproull and Cohen [28] describe a network plotter protocol (NPP), a language for describing graphics plotting tasks which allows market participants to communicate about plotting tasks. The work of Smith [29] defines a protocol for contracting among modules. Hence the mode of market interaction, contracting and bargaining, and the language for describing the task, NPP, have been created for the task of contracting for plotter printings by market participants. In a commercial network (nonsubsidized), the price hosts charge for their services must reflect the costs of maintaining them, and if the same service is provided by more than one host (e.g., color graphics output, Illiac-4-like services), competition may occur. Hence the equivalent of a market organization will result. Problems of complexity and uncertainty can arise, requiring the application of the reduction techniques described in the previous sections.

Reduced communication in markets (i.e., price) implies reduced information inviting information impactedness conditions. If modules can be hard-wired to share the same goal, then opportunistic advantages due to an information imbalance will not occur, but when modules have the freedom to choose when and where to do processing, methods of prerating module performance (e.g., similar to a credit agency) and monitoring of module performance are required to reduce opportunistic behavior. Transaction analysis suggests the latter can be too costly in the market, hence requiring the integration of a market function into an organization.

VII. CONCLUSION

Early computer programs bore little resemblance to human organizations, but as the problems attacked grew in size, resource limitations appeared and prevented the success of programmed solutions. Resource limitations can be viewed as the cause of bounded rationality whose effects appear in programs as in businesses. One can view the work in artificial intelligence as attempts circumvent resource limitations. Hence it is not surprising to find programs that (attempt to) exhibit "intelligence" that also display characteristics of human organizations. Systems such as Hearsay-II have shown trends that reflect human organizations and human problem solving methods (also see [17], [35], [3]). These trends have resulted in modules that contain problem solving characteristics similar to humans.

In this survey of organization theory ideas, we have found that some of the solutions to organizational problems have already been discovered and used in computer systems, and some have not. What organization theory does contribute is another way of looking at distributed systems. That complexity and uncertainty are two important factors in deciding how to structure an organization. It appears that complexity and uncertainty are two opposing forces; complexity forcing a distribution of task ultimately resulting in a heterarchical structure; uncertainty pushing in the opposite direction, vertically integrating tasks into a more hierarchical structure (Fig. 5). By utilizing this view, the distributed system designer has an organization tool kit that contains structures and control regimes that reduce the effect of the particular factor. It also provides a pointer to transaction analysis—which at this time is still poorly developed—as a tool for recognizing these factors.

An important view underlying this paper is that modules, processes, and tasks act like humans in an organization. Consequently, the problem of motivation, a cause of behavioral uncertainty, must be considered. Little attention has been paid to motivation in computer programs, but the advent of the module approach to constructing complex programs and the limitations on resources (e.g., processors) will necessitate a module's ability to decide when and what problems to work on. Once self-motivation appears in a module, goal conflicts will follow.

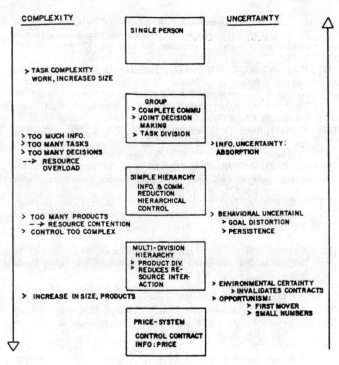

Fig. 5.   Organization structure continuum.

This paper lays part of the groundwork for constructing a theory of distributed system organization design. The approaches described by organization theory are interesting and useful but not rigorous. Better methods of measuring complexity and uncertainty must be found. Whether these measures will be derived from organization theory, system science, or computer science remains to be seen.

ACKNOWLEDGMENT

The author wishes to thank Herb Simon for his introduction to and guidance in organization theory. I would also like to thank Victor Lesser, Karsten Schwans, Reid Smith, Dan Corkhill, Raul Medina-Mora, Rich Korf, B. Chandrasekaran, and the referees for their comments on various aspects of this work.

REFERENCES

[1] J. Marschak and R. Radner, *Economic Theory of Teams* New Haven, CT: Yale Univ. Press, 1972.
[2] DSN, *Distributed Sensor Nets*, Workshop Proc. Comput. Sci. Dep., Carnegie-Mellon Univ., Pittsburgh, PA, Dec. 1978.
[3] V. R. Lesser and D. D. Corkhill, "Cooperative distributed problem-solving: A new approach for structuring distributed systems," Tech. Rep., Dep. Comput. Inform. Sci., Univ. Massachusetts at Amherst, Amherst, MA.
[4] J. G. March, H. A. Simon, and H. Guetzkow, *Organizations*. New York: Wiley, 1958.
[5] A. Smith, *Wealth of Nations*, 1776.
[6] J. Galbraith, *Designing Complex Organizations*. Reading, MA: Addison-Wesley, 1973.
[7] O. E. Williamson, *Markets and Hierarchies: A Transactional and Antitrust Analysis of the Firm*. New York: Free Press, 1975.
[8] H. A. Simon, *Models of Man*. New York: Wiley, 1957.
[9] L. D. Erman, and V. R. Lesser, "The Hearsay-II system: A tutorial," in *Trends in Speech Recognition*, W. A. Lea, Ed. Englewood Cliffs, NJ: Prentice-Hall, 1979.

[10] L. D. Erman, F. Hayes-Roth, V. R. Lesser, and D. R. Reddy, "The Hearsay-II speech understanding system: Integrating knowledge to resolve uncertainty," Computing Surveys, vol. 12, pp. 213–254, 1980.

[11] F. Hayes-Roth, G. Gill, and D. J. Mostow, "Discourse analysis and task performance in the Hearsay-II speech understanding system," in Speech Understanding Systems: Summary of Results of the Five-Year Research Effort, Dep. Comput. Sci., Carnegie-Mellon Univ., Pittsburgh, PA, 1977.

[12] F. Hayes-Roth, D. J. Mostow, and M. S. Fox, "Understanding speech in the Hearsay-II system," in Speech Communication with Computers, L. Bolc, Ed. Berlin: Springer-Verlag, 1978.

[13] A. R. Smith, "Word hypothesization in the Hearsay-II speech system," in Proc. 1976 IEEE Int. Conf. Acoustics, Speech, and Signal Processing, pp. 578–581, 1976.

[14] M. S. Fox and D. J. Mostow, "Maximal consistent interpretations of errorful data in hierarchically modelled domains," presented at the 5th Int. Joint Conf. Artificial Intelligence, Cambridge, MA, 1977.

[15] A. Newell, "Heuristic programming: Ill-structured problems," in Progress in Operations Research 3, J. Aronofsky, Ed. New York: Wiley, 1969, pp. 360–414.

[16] F. Hayes-Roth and V. R. Lesser, "Focus of attention in a distributed logic speech understanding system," in Proc. 1976 IEEE Int. Conf. Acoustics, Speech, and Signal Processing, 1976, pp. 416–420.

[17] D. Lenat, "Beings: Knowledge as interacting experts," in Proc. 4th Int. Joint Conf. Artificial Intelligence, 1975.

[18] P. Nii and E. Feigenbaum, "Rule based understanding of signals," in Pattern-Directed Inference Systems, D. Waterman and F. Hayes-Roth, Eds. New York: Academic, 1977.

[19] M. S. Fox, "Knowledge structuring: Knowledge accommodation and discovery using specialization and planning," Ph.D. thesis, Comput. Sci. Dep., Carnegie-Mellon Univ., Pittsburgh, PA (to appear, 1980).

[20] V. R. Lesser and L. D. Erman, "An experiment in distributed interpretation," in Proc. 1st Int. Conf. Distributed Computing Systems, 1979, pp. 553–571.

[21] E. Soloway and E. Riseman, "Levels of pattern description in learning," presented at the Int. Joint Conf. Artificial Intelligence, Cambridge, MA, Aug. 1977.

[22] M. S. Fox, "Organization structuring: Designing large, complex software," Comput. Sci. Dep., Carnegie-Mellon Univ., Pittsburgh, PA, Tech. Rep. 1979.

[23] H. A. Simon, "The architecture of complexity," Proc. Amer. Phil. Soc., vol. 106, pp. 467–487, 1962. (Also in Simon 1968.)

[24] S. H. Fuller and S. P. Harbison, "The C.mmp multiprocessor," Comput. Sci. Dep., Carnegie-Mellon Univ., Pittsburgh, PA, Tech. Rep. 1978.

[25] R. Swan, S. H. Fuller, and D. P. Siewiorek, "Cm*: A modular, multi-processor," in Proc. Nat. Computer Conf., 1977.

[26] P. Oleinick and S. H. Fuller, "The implementation and evaluation of a parallel algorithm on C.mmp." Comput. Sci. Dep., Carnegie-Mellon Univ., Pittsburgh, PA, Tech. Rep. 1978.

[27] L. Raskin, "Performance evaluation of multiple processor systems," Ph.D. thesis, Comput. Sci. Dep., Carnegie-Mellon Univ., Pittsburgh, PA, Tech. Rep., 1978.

[28] R. F. Sproull, and D. Cohen, "High-level protocols," Proc. IEEE, vol. 66, Nov. 1978.

[29] R. G. Smith, "A framework for problem solving in a distributed environment," Ph.D. thesis, Comput. Sci. Dep., Stanford Univ., Stanford, CA, Memo HPP-78-28, 1978.

[30] D. R. Reddy, "Speech recognition by machine: A review," Proc. IEEE, vol. 64, 1976.

[31] M. D. Mesarovic, D. Macko, and Y. Takahara, Theory of Hierarchical Multi-level Systems. New York: Academic, 1970.

[32] P. N. Chanon, "On a measure of program structure," Ph.D. thesis, Comput. Sci. Dep., Carnegie-Mellon Univ., Pittsburgh, PA, 1974.

[33] C. L. McClure, "A model for program complexity analysis," in Proc. 3rd Int. Conf. Software Engineering, 1978.

[34] V. R. Lesser, S. Reed, and J. Pavlin, "Quantifying and simulating the behavior of knowledge-based interpretation systems," in Proc. 1st Annu. Nat. Conf. Artificial Intelligence, pp. 111–115.

[35] C. Hewitt, "The ACTOR formalism," in Proc. 3rd Int. Joint Conf. Artificial Intelligence, 1973.

[36] B. Chandrasekaran, F. Gomez, S. Mittal, and J. Smith, "An approach to medical diagnosis based on conceptual structures," in Proc. 6th Int. Joint Conf. Artificial Intelligence, 1979, pp. 134–142.

[37] S. W. Zucker, "Relaxation labelling and the reduction of local ambiguities," in Pattern Recognition and Artificial Intelligence, C. H. Chen, Ed. New York: Academic, 1976.

[38] G. Sussman, A Computational Model of Skill Acquisition. New York: American Elsevier, 1975.

MODELING COORDINATION IN ORGANIZATIONS AND MARKETS*

THOMAS W. MALONE

Sloan School of Management, Massachusetts Institute of Technology, Cambridge, Massachusetts 02139

This paper describes a simple set of coordination structures that model certain kinds of information processing involved in organizations and markets. Four generic coordination structures are defined: product hierarchies, functional hierarchies, centralized markets, and decentralized markets. Then tradeoffs among these structures are analyzed in terms of production costs, coordination costs, and vulnerability costs. This model is unusual in that it includes detailed definitions of the structures at a micro-level and mathematical derivations of comparisons among them at a macro-level. In the final section of the paper, several connections are made between these formal results and previous work on organizational design.
(ORGANIZATIONAL STRUCTURE; ORGANIZATION DESIGN; COORDINATION; INFORMATION PROCESSING)

Human organizations and markets are possibly the most complex entities on our planet. Their complexity can be viewed from many different perspectives, each emphasizing some factors and neglecting others. This paper emphasizes one perspective: analyzing these structures in terms of the information processing involved in coordination. This perspective appears particularly promising for understanding how information technology may affect organizational structure, and because they are likely to be directly affected by information technology.

We first develop detailed definitions of several structures that represent common ways of coordinating human activity—various forms of markets and hierarchies. These definitions are based on micro-level assumptions about how tasks are selected and assigned. Then we analyze and compare these structures in terms of macro-level characteristics such as production costs and coordination costs. In the final section of the paper, we suggest some connections between these formal models and previous generalizations about organizational design. Clearly there are many important aspects of human organizations and markets that are not captured by these simple coordination structures. However, we have been surprised at the range of issues this simple coordination approach helps illuminate (e.g., see Malone and Smith 1984; Malone 1986; Malone, Yates, and Benjamin 1987; Crowston, Malone, and Lin in press).

The formal models draw heavily on work by Baligh and Richartz (1967), Baligh and Damon (1980), and Baligh and Burton (1981, 1984). The models also draw implicitly on analogies between the information processing done by people and the information processing done by computers (see Malone and Smith 1984; Malone in press). While people and computers differ in many ways, this "cognitive" approach has been useful in many of the social sciences (e.g., March and Simon, 1958; Norman 1981) and appears to have unrealized potential for analyzing human organizations.

Background

There is a large body of literature about organizational design, and since there are already a number of integrative summaries of this work (e.g., Mintzberg 1979; Galbraith 1977; Hax and Majluf 1981), we will only briefly review here several of the formal mathematical models that bear most directly on the questions with which we are concerned.

Our central problem was formulated in very general mathematical terms by Marschak and Radner (1972). In their formulation of "team theory," each member of a group of *actors* has some initial information about the world and some ability to control certain actions in the world. A team also has some shared *payoff function* that determines, for a given state of the world, the value team members attach to the results of the different possible actions. Since, in general, the team members who must take actions do not possess all the relevant information about the world, there must be some *information structure* that determines how members perceive and communicate information, and there must also be some *decision function* that determines how members decide what actions to take based on the information they receive. The goal of an organizational designer may be thought of as choosing an information structure and a decision function that maximize the *net payoff* to the team members, i.e., the gross payoff less the cost of communicating and deciding.

Unfortunately for our purposes, the range of possible formal assumptions and parameter values that can be used within Marschak and Radner's general framework leads to a multitude of highly conditional results. Almost all the Marschak and Radner theorems depend on the assumption that the payoffs are determined by a quadratic function of the action variables. While this is, of course, a very general mathematical formulation, it is not at all clear what substantive processes in the real world can be represented in this manner or how to interpret the results.

Other theorists have used somewhat more easily interpretable models of the relationship between payoffs and coordination. For example, Jonscher (1982) and Beckman (1982) model the efficiency of production processes as simple functions of the amount of coordination resources applied to them. Burton and Obel (1984) assume that the coordination process in organizations is in some ways similar to iteratively approximating the solution of an optimization problem. Accordingly, they formulate linear programming problems and iterative solution methods that correspond to various organizational forms (e.g., grouping by product or function) and various control mechanisms (e.g., budgets vs. internal prices). Then they use the solutions that would result from a few iteration steps to model the efficiency of the different organizational structures. Mackenzie (1986a, b) describes a detailed set of models and methodologies for studying and representing the tasks, structures, and coordination methods of specific organizations. For instance, he shows how a sequence of tasks can be represented as a process and how tasks and coordinating processes can be analyzed at a series of different levels of abstraction.

The modeling approach we emphasize views each activity as a task that must be performed by some processor (either a person or a machine) and the performance of which requires some amount of time. This view, therefore, highlights the importance of assigning tasks to processors as one of the fundamental components of coordination and it highlights delay time and processing capacity as important components of overall output or cost. Several previous theorists have analyzed organizational coordination from this general point of view. For example, Kochen and Deutsch (1980) analyze queuing delays for tasks in evaluating the desirability of various kinds of decentralization in service organizations.

Perhaps the most extensive analyses of these issues is the work on vertical market structures by Baligh and Richartz (1967). Baligh and Richartz assume that a commodity-like product is being exchanged between a number of buyers and sellers in a market. Their analyses emphasize the conditions under which there are incentives for various numbers of middlemen to enter the market. They analyze a variety of factors including

* Accepted by Richard M. Burton; received August 27, 1986. This paper has been with the author 2 months for 1 revision.

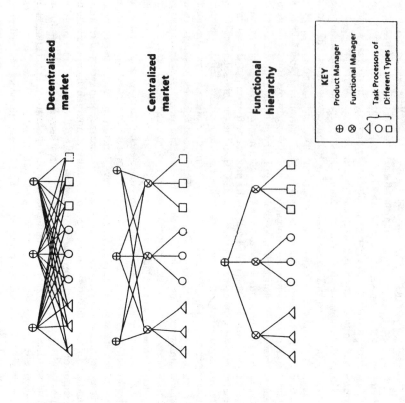

FIGURE 1. Alternative Coordination Structures.

KEY
⊕ Product Manager
⊗ Functional Manager
△ ○ □ Task Processors of Different Types

Product hierarchy

Decentralized market

Centralized market

Functional hierarchy

queuing delays, costs for exchanging messages, rebate strategies, and inventory carrying costs. In the next section, we describe how our models build on certain aspects of theirs.

Model

We define a *coordination structure* as a pattern of *decision-making and communication* among a set of *actors* who perform *tasks* in order to achieve *goals* (cf., Baligh and Damon 1980; Baligh and Burton 1981; Baligh 1986). For example, a coordination structure used by an automobile manufacturing company might be thought of as having a set of goals (e.g., producing several different lines of automobiles) and a set of actors, or "processors," (people and machines) to perform the tasks (e.g., engineering, manufacturing, and sales) necessary for achieving those goals. The various forms of markets analyzed by Baligh and Richartz (1967) can also be viewed as coordination structures with goals (e.g., satisfying consumer demands), actors (e.g., buyers, sellers, and middlemen), and tasks (e.g., filling orders). For the sake of concreteness, we will usually refer to "goals" as "products."

We will focus here on three kinds of costs for these coordination structures: *production costs, coordination costs,* and *vulnerability costs.* We include in production costs the costs of production capacity and the costs of delays in processing tasks. We include in coordination costs the costs of maintaining communication links (or "channels") between actors and the costs of exchanging "messages" along these links. By vulnerability costs, we mean the unavoidable costs of a changed situation that are incurred before the organization can adapt to a new situation. We model these costs in terms of the expected costs that result when actors fail to perform their tasks (e.g., when actors fail to fill orders or make decisions).

Our analysis of production and coordination costs is quite similar to that by Baligh and Richartz (1967), though our detailed assumptions differ in a few cases. We have extended Baligh and Richartz's analysis in two ways. First, they did not analyze vulnerability costs at all, and that constitutes an important part of our analysis. Second, they explicitly analyzed only market structures. We extend their analyses to include two coordination structures that resemble those found in hierarchical organizations.

Figure 1 shows the coordination structures we consider: product hierarchies, functional hierarchies, decentralized markets, and centralized markets. The lines and symbols in the figure summarize the patterns of decision-making, communication, and task processing described in the next section. More detailed formal descriptions of each structure are provided by Malone (1986) using a framework adapted from Baligh and Damon (1980) and Baligh and Burton (1981, 1984). While there are certainly many other possible coordination structures, these four represent a wide range of patterns that seem to be common in collective human activity. The extent to which these structures reflect the processes in real organizations and markets is, of course, an empirical question. However, we have attempted to define formal structures that capture the essence of some of the intuitive ways people use these terms.

Alternative Coordination Structures

Product Hierarchy. In a product hierarchy, there are separate divisions for different product lines. We use the term "product hierarchy" here, even though the groupings are sometimes made along other "mission-oriented" lines such as geographical regions or market segments. Each division has a manager (whom we will call a "product manager") and its own separate departments for different functions such as marketing, manufacturing, and engineering. General Motors was one of the earliest and best known examples of this general form with its separate divisions for Chevrolet, Pontiac, Cadillac, and other product lines (see Chandler 1962). This form is sometimes called the "multi-divisional" form (Chandler 1962) or the "M-form" (Williamson 1975).

We represent this form by the following coordination structure: Each division has a product manager and a specialized processor (e.g., a department) for each different type of task. The product manager decides what tasks need to be done to produce a product (or, more generally, to achieve some goal). As each task arises, the product manager assigns it to the processor for that type of task. For example, if General Motors used this structure for coordinating engineering tasks, the general manager of the Chevrolet division would expect all new Chevrolet models to be designed by the engineering department in the Chevrolet division. (We will use General Motors as a source of examples throughout this section. Here, and in the rest of this section, *these examples are hypothetical illustrations only, not actual descriptions of General Motors. General Motors* is an attractive choice for illustration because the names of its product divisions are household words for most readers.)

We assume that one "message" is required to assign a task to a processor, and that one "message" is required to notify the product manager that the task is complete. This

just an individual task processor, the processing of the entire organization may be disrupted. For instance if the vice-president in charge of all manufacturing performed very poorly, the manufacturing of all products could be excessively costly or delayed and these effects would be felt throughout the organization.

Markets. So far we have considered two hierarchical structures for coordinating task assignments. One of the important insights from the literature of organizational theory and economics (e.g., see Williamson 1975) is that the same tasks can, in principle, be coordinated by either a market or a hierarchy. For example, General Motors does not need to make all the components that go into its finished products. Instead of manufacturing its own tires, for instance, it can purchase tires from other suppliers. When it does this, it is using a market to coordinate the same activities (i.e., tire production) that would otherwise have been coordinated by hierarchical management structures within General Motors.

If General Motors used an extreme form of this coordination structure, the vice-president in charge of the Chevrolet division might have only a small staff and all the basic tasks of product design, manufacturing, and sales would be performed by outside suppliers. This form of subcontracting as a coordination structure is already common in some industries (e.g., construction).

Decentralized Market. We distinguish here between two kinds of markets: decentralized and centralized. In the "pure form" of a decentralized market, all buyers are in contact with all possible suppliers and they each make their own decisions about which transactions to accept. This is the case Baligh and Richartz (1967) analyze as a market without middlemen.

In defining the coordination structure to represent this kind of market, we assume that the suppliers are task processors for various types of tasks and that there are "buyers" for each type of product to be produced (or for each overall goal of the structure). The buyers thus play the role of "product managers." We assume, like Baligh and Richartz (1967, Chapter 2), that each buyer has a communication link with each potential supplier and that all buyers exchange messages with all suppliers. Baligh and Richartz assume that each supplier receives "orders" randomly from different buyers (pp. 113–114). With our model of task processing, it seems more plausible to assume that, if buyers exchange messages with all suppliers, buyers will know enough to choose the "best" supplier and will not just send their orders to a random supplier. Therefore, we depart from Baligh and Richartz by assuming that tasks are not randomly assigned to suppliers, but instead are sent to the "best" supplier (e.g., the supplier who can start processing the order soonest). We model this process as one in which buyers send some form of "request for bids" messages to all suppliers of the appropriate type and then select a supplier from among all the "bids" received. If there are *m* suppliers, this requires 2*m* messages per task. Two additional messages are also used: one to assign the task to the "best" bidder, and one to notify the buyer that the task is complete.

We assume that when a processor fails in a decentralized market, the task it was to have performed is reassigned to another processor of the same type. For example, if one independent dealer for General Motors cars failed to achieve a satisfactory sales volume, that dealer's contract might be terminated and another dealer selected.

Centralized Market. In a centralized market, buyers do not need to contact all possible sellers because a broker is already in contact with the possible sellers. This centralization of decision-making means that substantially fewer connections and messages are required compared to a decentralized market. One of the best known examples of a centralized market is the stock market. People who want to buy a particular

means that there must be communication links between each of the product managers and their own processors, but not with any of the other divisions. We further assume that when a processor fails, the product division in which the failure occurs is disrupted, but the other divisions are not affected. For example, a major mechanical failure at a factory that produced only Chevrolets would not have any direct effect on the other divisions. A failure by the Cadillac marketing department to correctly predict what their customers would want in next year's models would not necessarily affect the other divisions, either.

Since the "product hierarchy" coordination structure does not include any interactions between the divisions, it could also be used to model a holding company or, indeed, a set of separate companies that do not share any resources.

Functional Hierarchy. In a functional hierarchy, a number of processors of similar types are pooled in functional departments and shared among products. This sharing of processors may reduce duplication of effort and may allow processing loads to be balanced over all products. For example, General Motors might need less manufacturing capacity if instead of providing enough capacity in each division to meet peak demands it had a central manufacturing department and balanced heavy demands for one product against lighter demands for other products. (The functional hierarchy is also sometimes called the "unitary" form or "U-form" (Williamson 1975).)

In the coordination structure we use to represent this organizational form, processors of the same type are grouped into functional departments, each of which has a "functional manager." There is also an "executive office" that decides what tasks need to be done to produce all the products of the organization (or, more generally, to achieve all the overall goals of the structure). The executive office, therefore, plays the role of the "product manager" for all products. Assigning tasks in this structure is somewhat more complicated than for the product hierarchy because an extra layer of management is involved (cf., Burton and Obel 1984, Chapter 4). We assume that whenever a task of a certain type needs to be done, the executive office delegates the task to the functional manager of the appropriate type who, in turn, assigns the task to one of the processors in the functional manager's department. In order to make this assignment intelligently, the functional manager needs to keep track of the loads and capabilities of the processors in the department. For example, if General Motors used this coordination structure for the product hierarchy, a central manufacturing department would manage all the manufacturing plants. The vice-president of manufacturing and his or her staff would be responsible for coordinating the sharing of these facilities to produce all the different kinds of cars for all the different product lines.

In defining this coordination structure, we assume that four messages are required to assign a task: one to delegate the task to the appropriate functional manager, one to assign it to a processor, and two to notify the functional manager and the executive office, respectively, that the task is complete. In order to exchange these messages, the executive office must have a communication link to each functional manager, and each of the functional managers must have a link to the processors in their department.

When an individual task processor fails in this structure, the tasks it would have performed are delayed until they can be reassigned to another processor in the same department. For example, if General Motors had a single centralized sales and distribution department for all its products, it could shift car allocations from poorly performing dealerships to more successful ones. If GM had a pure product hierarchy, on the other hand, it would be difficult to shift sales volume of Cadillacs into dealerships that handled only Chevrolets.

There is another kind of failure, however, to which the functional hierarchy is much more vulnerable. When a functional manager or the executive office fails, instead of

stock do not need to contact all the owners of shares of that stock; they only need to contact a broker who is also in contact with people who want to sell the stock.

Our model for this coordination structure resembles Baligh and Richartz's model of a market with a "middleman as a pure coordinator" (1967, pp. 123–126). In addition to the buyers and suppliers present in a decentralized market, we assume that there is also a "broker" (or middleman) for each type of task processor. Each broker coordinates all the task processors of a given type and thus plays the role of a "functional manager." Like Baligh and Richartz, we assume that (1) the broker has a communication link to each buyer and each supplier of the appropriate type and (2) tasks are assigned to the "best" available supplier. We also assume that four messages are required to assign tasks in this structure: one from the buyer to notify the broker that the task needs to be done, one from the broker to assign the task to a processor, and two to notify the broker and the buyer, respectively, that the task is complete.

The centralized market and the functional hierarchy structures are thus quite similar in the patterns of messages they use. We assume that they are also similar in their responses to failures of processors. Both can often reassign tasks when a task processor fails, and in both cases, the production of all products is disrupted when one of the central schedulers (i.e., a broker or a functional manager) fails. The difference between the two structures is that in the centralized market, one of the general contractors can fail without disrupting the production of the other products, but in the functional hierarchy, if the executive office fails, the production of all products is disrupted.

Tradeoffs among Coordination Structures

Now that we have distinguished among these generic coordination structures, one of the most important questions we can ask is what are the relative advantages of each. In particular, we will focus on the tradeoffs between *efficiency* and *flexibility* in the different structures. We will view efficiency as being composed of two elements: *production costs* and *coordination costs*. Coordination costs are also a component of flexibility, since the amount of re-coordination necessary to adapt to new situations helps determine how flexible a structure is. The other component of flexibility we consider is *vulnerability costs*, or the unavoidable costs of a changed situation that are incurred before the organization can adapt to the new situation.

As shown in Table 1, we can compare the different coordination structures on the dimensions of production costs, coordination costs, and vulnerability costs. All the dimensions shown in the chart are represented as costs, so in every column low is "good" and high is "bad". The comparisons apply only within columns, not between rows. Primes are used to indicate indeterminate comparisons. For example, H' is more than L, but it may be either more or less than $H+$ or $H-$. In the next two sections, we present justification for these comparisons, first informally, and then formally.

Informal Justifications for Coordination Structure Comparisons

The key assumptions necessary to compare the different coordination structures are summarized in Table 2. We compare the structures separately for each of the dimensions analyzed: production costs, coordination costs, and vulnerability costs.

Production Costs

Our primary assumption about production costs is that they are proportional to the amount of processing capacity in the organization and the average delay in processing tasks. We assume that tasks of a given type arrive at random times and that processing each task takes a random amount of time. We also assume that processing capacity for a given organizational form is chosen to minimize the total costs of capacity and delay time.

The product hierarchy has the highest average delay in processing tasks because it uses processors that are not shared. The decentralized market, centralized market, and functional hierarchy all have a somewhat lower average delay time because they are able to take advantage of the "load leveling" that occurs when tasks are shared among a number of similar processors. For example, processors that would otherwise be idle can take on "overflow" tasks from busy processors thus reducing the overall average delay.

Coordination Costs

Our primary assumption about coordination costs is that they are proportional to the number of connections between agents and the number of messages necessary to assign tasks. Table 2 summarizes our assumptions about the number of connections and messages required.

The product hierarchy requires the least number of connections since each processor must only be connected to its division manager. This form also requires the least number of messages for task assignment since each task is simply assigned to the processor of the appropriate type in the division in which the task originates.

TABLE 1

Tradeoffs Among Alternative Coordination Structures

Coordination Structure	Evaluation Criteria			
	Efficiency		Flexibility	Vulnerability Costs
	Production Costs	Coordination Costs		
Product hierarchy	H	L	L	H'
Functional hierarchy	L	M−	M−	H+
Centralized market	L	M+	M+	H−
Decentralized market	L	H	H	L

Note. L = Low costs ("good").
M = Medium costs
H = High costs ("bad").
Comparisons apply only within columns, not between rows.

TABLE 2

Definition of Alternative Coordination Structures

Coordination Structure	Processors Shared Among Products	No. of Connections Required Between Actors[a,b]	No. of Messages Required to Assign a Task[a]	Results of Failure of		
				Task Processor	Functional Manager	Product Manager
Product hierarchy	No	m	2	1 product disrupted	—	1 product disrupted
Decentralized market	Yes	mn	2m + 2	Task reassigned	—	1 product disrupted
Centralized market	Yes	m + n	4	Task reassigned	All products disrupted	1 product disrupted
Functional hierarchy	Yes	m	4	Task reassigned	All products disrupted	All products disrupted

[a] m = Number of task processors of functional type being analyzed; n = number of products.
[b] Number required per functional type.

TABLE 3
Symbol Table

Variable	Definition
Total Costs	
$P_{PH}, P_{FH}, P_{CM}, P_{DM}$	= production costs per task for the various organizational forms
$C_{PH}, C_{FH}, C_{CM}, C_{DM}$	= coordination costs per task for the various organizational forms
$V_{PH}, V_{FH}, V_{CM}, V_{DM}$	= vulnerability costs per task for the various organizational forms
Component Costs	
c_C	= cost of production capacity (cost per unit of processing capacity capable of processing 1 task per time unit)
c_D	= cost of delay (or waiting) for tasks to be processed (cost of delay of 1 task for 1 time unit)
c_L	= cost of maintaining a connection (or link) between processors (cost per time unit)
c_M	= cost of sending a message (cost per message)
c_T	= cost of reassigning a task to another processor (average cost attributed to this function per reassignment)
c_P	= cost of disrupting production of 1 product (average cost per disruption)
c_A	= cost of disrupting production of all products (average cost per disruption)
Probabilities	
p_T	= probability of task processor failure (per time unit)
p_F	= probability of failure of a functional manager or broker (per time unit)
p_P	= probability of failure of a product manager or buyer (per time unit)
p_E	= probability of failure of an executive office (per time unit)
Other quantities	
m	= number of processors of this type for all products combined
n	= number of products
k	= number of functions
λ	= number of tasks per time unit of this type for each product
μ	= average processing rate of each processor

TABLE 4
Evaluation Criteria for Alternative Coordination Structures

Coordination Structures	Production Costs	Coordination Costs	Vulnerability Costs
Product hierarchy	$2m(c_D c_C \lambda)^{1/2} + m\lambda c_C$	$mc_L + 2m\lambda c_M$	$mp_T c_P + np_P c_P$
Functional hierarchy	$2m(c_D c_C \lambda)^{1/2}$	$(m+1)c_L + 4m\lambda c_M$	$mp_T c_T + p_F c_A + p_E c_A$
Centralized market	$2m(c_D c_C \lambda)^{1/2}$	$(m+n)c_L + 4m\lambda c_M$	$mp_T c_T + p_F c_A + np_P c_P$
Decentralized market	$2m(c_D c_C \lambda)^{1/2}$	$mnc_L + (2m+2)m\lambda c_M$	$mp_T c_T + np_P c_P$

The centralized market and functional hierarchy require more connections since the functional managers (or brokers) must be connected not only to the processors they supervise, but also to the product managers (or clients) who originate tasks. These two forms also require more scheduling messages since an extra layer of management is involved in assigning tasks to the proper processor.

The decentralized market requires the most connections of all because it requires each buyer to be connected to all possible suppliers. This form also requires the most messages since assigning each task requires sending "requests for bids" to all possible processors of the appropriate type and then receiving bids in return.

Vulnerability Costs

Our primary assumption about vulnerability costs is that they are proportional to the expected costs due to failures of task processors and managers. We assume that both processors and managers sometimes fail (i.e., with probabilities greater than 0). Our assumptions about the consequences of different kinds of failures in different organizational forms are summarized in Table 2. We assume that when a task processor fails in a market or in a functional hierarchy, the task can be reassigned to another processor of the same type. When a task processor fails in a product hierarchy, however, there is no other processor of the same type available, so the entire production of the product in question is disrupted. The entire production of a product is also disrupted if the product manager fails, or, in the case of the market, if the client who supervises that product fails. Finally, the production of all products is disrupted if a centralized market broker, or a functional manager, or an executive office fails.

We assume that the cost of delaying a task in order to reassign it is less than the cost of disrupting all the production for a given type of product and that this cost is, in turn, less than the cost of disrupting the production of all products.

Given these assumptions, the decentralized market is the least vulnerable to component failure since if one processor fails, the task is only delayed until it can be transferred to another processor. The centralized market and functional hierarchy are more vulnerable since not only can tasks be delayed by the failure of individual processors, but also the entire system will be disrupted if a centralized functional manager or broker fails. The functional hierarchy is somewhat more vulnerable than the centralized market because the functional hierarchy can also be completely disrupted if the executive office fails. The product hierarchy is more vulnerable than the decentralized market because when a processor fails, tasks cannot be easily transferred to another similar processor. Whether the product hierarchy is more or less vulnerable than the functional hierarchy and the centralized market cannot be determined from our assumptions alone. It depends on the relative sizes of costs and probabilities for failures of product managers and functional managers.

Formal Justifications for Coordination Structure Comparisons

The bases for the qualitative comparisons of coordination structures in Table 1 are summarized in Tables 3 and 4 and explained below. Table 3 lists the variables used in this section and Table 4 shows the values for production costs, coordination costs, and vulnerability costs in the different organizational forms. The following abbreviations are used: *PH* for product hierarchy, *FH* for functional hierarchy, *CM* for centralized market, and *DM* for decentralized market. We let m be the number of processors of the functional type being analyzed, n be the number of products, and k be the number of functions. In all cases, we assume that

(A0) Costs not explicitly modeled are the same in all organizational forms.

Production Costs

For all coordination structures, we make the following assumptions:

(A1) Tasks of a given type are generated randomly according to a Poisson process that is the same for each product and has arrival rate $m\lambda$ for the system as a whole.

(A2) Individual tasks are assigned to the first available processor of the appropriate type and are processed, in the order of arrival, at a rate μ on each processor. The processing times are exponentially distributed.

(A3) Production costs are proportional to the amount of processing capacity in the organization and the amount of time that tasks are delayed.

(A4) The processing capacity μ of each processor is chosen to minimize total production costs.

We let c_C be the cost of a unit of processing capacity (measured in dollars per time unit per unit of processing capacity; where a unit of processing capacity can process one task per time unit). We also let c_D be the cost of delay for tasks that have been generated but not yet completed (measured in dollars per task per unit of time task remains uncompleted). With these assumptions, the total production costs per unit of time are $P = m\mu c_C + Ac_D$ where A is the average number of uncompleted tasks in the system at any given time. In this and the other cost expressions, we are concerned only with relative costs of different organizational forms, so by assumption A0, we may omit all other (constant) costs. When tasks are not shared among processors, the tasks arrive randomly at each processor with arrival rate λ. The processing characteristics in this case are the same as the market without middlemen analyzed by Baligh and Richartz (1967). They show (pp. 113–118) that the capacity that minimizes this cost is $\mu^* = (c_D\lambda/c_C)^{1/2} + \lambda$ and that total production costs are then $P = 2m(\lambda c_D c_C)^{1/2} + m\lambda c_C$.

When tasks are shared among the processors, we have the case that Baligh and Richartz analyze as a market with a "middleman as pure coordinator". In this case, orders are assigned to the best processor, and the system behaves as if the processors were m servers for the overall queue of tasks. Baligh and Richartz show (pp. 123–125) that the optimal capacity, in this case, is $\mu^* = (c_D\lambda/c_C)^{1/2}$ and the total production costs are $P = 2m(\lambda c_D c_C)^{1/2}$. The latter result holds exactly only in the limit as m becomes large.

These two production cost results are the basis for the production cost expressions in Table 4: Product hierarchies have processors with separate streams of tasks; the other organizational forms are able to share tasks among processors.

Comparisons. Using the expressions for production costs P shown in Table 4, it is clear that $P_{PH} > P_{FH} = P_{CM} = P_{DM}$ as reflected in Table 1.

Coordination Costs

Assumptions. We make the following assumption about coordination costs:

(A5) Coordination costs are proportional to the number of communication paths (or links) between actors and the number of messages sent over these links.

We let c_L be the cost per time unit of maintaining a link and c_M be the cost of sending a message.

Comparisons. Using assumption A5 and the values given in Table 2 for the number of messages and links in the different organizational forms, it is a simple matter to calculate the costs shown in Table 4. If $n > 1$ and $m \geq 1$, then the following inequalities for coordination costs, C, follow immediately: $C_{PH} < C_{FH} < C_{CM} < C_{DM}$.

Vulnerability Costs

Assumptions. We make the following assumptions about vulnerability costs:

(A6) Vulnerability costs are proportional to the costs of reassigning tasks and the costs of disrupting products due to the failures of processors or managers.

(A7) Processors and managers sometimes fail (i.e., with probability greater than 0), and they do so independently at constant rates according to a Poisson process.

(A8) Product managers that manage more than one product (i.e., with centralized product decisions) fail at least as often as other product and functional managers.

(A9) The cost of reassigning the tasks from one processor to another processor is less than the cost of disrupting a product.

(A10) The cost of disrupting one product is less than the cost of disrupting all products.

We let p_T, p_F, and p_P be the failure rates of task processors, functional managers, and product managers, respectively, and we let p_E be the failure rate for executive offices. According to assumptions A7 and A8, $p_T, p_F, p_P > 0$, and $p_E \geq p_F, p_P$. We let c_T be the expected cost of reassigning the tasks from a failed processor to another processor, c_P be

the expected cost of having the production of one product disrupted, and c_A be the expected cost of having all the products disrupted. From assumptions A8 and A9, we know that $c_T < c_P < c_A$.

Comparisons. Given these assumptions, the expressions for failure costs F in Table 4, and the following inequalities all follow immediately: $F_{DM} < F_{CM} < F_{FH}$, and $F_{DM} < F_{PH}$.

Alternative Assumptions

Production Costs. Malone and Smith (1984) examine the consequences of removing the assumption that in all organizational forms, processing capacity is optimally chosen to minimize total production costs. They assume instead that all organizational forms have the same processing capacity. This alternative assumption does not change our results.

Malone and Smith (1984) also analyzed alternative forms of functional hierarchies and centralized markets that include one large scale processor for a function instead of several small scale processors. The large scale organizational forms have lower production costs, but higher vulnerability costs, than their small scale counterparts.

Coordination Costs. Malone (1986) considers several alternative sets of assumptions about coordination costs. The most important of these alternatives involves the role of prices in the decentralized market. In its "pure" form, this structure requires connections and messages between all possible buyers and all possible suppliers. One might argue that in a market with a functioning price mechanism, buyers would only need to contact a few potential suppliers, since most suppliers would have approximately the same price anyway. Malone (1986) shows, however, that as long as the number of suppliers contacted by buyers is, on the average, at least two, this organizational form still has the highest coordination costs of all the forms considered.

Malone (1986) also considers the fixed costs of keeping coordinating processors (i.e., managers, brokers, and clients) in a structure. Introducing these costs into the models does not lead to results that directly contradict the main results in Table 1, but, depending on the size of the fixed costs, it does render some of the comparisons indeterminate. It seems plausible to assume that, in the long run, the number of messages to be processed will be the major determiner of the number of coordinating processors needed. Accordingly, the main results presented here ignore the fixed costs of coordinating processors and focus on the costs of maintaining communication links and the variable costs of processing messages.

Malone and Smith (1984) consider only the message processing costs of coordination and ignore the costs of communication links. With this assumption, functional hierarchies cannot be distinguished from centralized markets in terms of coordination costs.

Vulnerability Costs. Malone and Smith (1984) ignore the possibility of failures of "product coordinators" (e.g., product managers) and the "executive office." When these possibilities are ignored, we cannot distinguish between functional hierarchies and centralized markets in terms of vulnerability costs.

Size of the Structure

The tradeoffs shown in Table 1 assume that the size of the structure being modeled is fixed, that is, that the number of processors, the number of products, and the total number of managers generating tasks are all constant. As the number of processors increases, the relative rankings of the alternative coordination structures do not change on any of the evaluation criteria. However, the values change much faster for some structures and criteria than for others. Thus simply changing the size of the structure,

TABLE 6

Rates of Change of Evaluation Criteria as Size of Structure Increases

Coordination Structures	Production Costs		Coordination Costs		Vulnerability Costs	
	$\dfrac{\delta}{\delta m}$	$\dfrac{\delta}{\delta n}$	$\dfrac{\delta}{\delta m}$	$\dfrac{\delta}{\delta n}$	$\dfrac{\delta}{\delta m}$	$\dfrac{\delta}{\delta n}$
Product hierarchy	$2(c_P c_C)^{1/2} + \lambda c_C$	0	$c_L + 2\lambda c_M$	0	$p_T c_P$	$p_P c_P$
Functional hierarchy	$2(c_P c_C)^{1/2}$	0	$c_L + 4\lambda c_M$	0	$p_T c_T$	0
Centralized market	$2(c_P c_C)^{1/2}$	0	$c_L + 4\lambda c_M$	c_L	$p_T c_T$	$p_P c_P$
Decentralized market	$2(c_P c_C)^{1/2}$	0	$mc_L + 2\lambda c_M(2m+1)$	mc_L	$p_T c_T$	$p_P c_P$

even without changing any other parameter values, may change the relative importance of different criteria and therefore change the "optimal" coordination structure. The relative rates of change for the different criteria are summarized in Table 5. The different numbers of pluses in the table represent the different rates of change. For example, as the size of an organization increases, vulnerability costs increase more rapidly for product hierarchies than for the other forms, and coordination costs increase most rapidly for decentralized markets.

To justify the results in Table 5, we assume that

(A11) As the size of the organization increases, the number of products n and the number of processors m increase.

To determine the effect of these increases on the different kinds of costs, we examine the partial derivatives with respect to m and n. Table 6 shows these partial derivatives. The assignment of varying numbers of pluses for the values in Table 5 all follow immediately from the relative sizes of the partial derivatives in Table 6.

Discussion

We have now analyzed four generic coordination structures that are intended to capture some of the intuitive ways people describe different kinds of organizations and markets. These definitions suggest many empirical questions about how coordination actually occurs in real organizations and markets. At a micro-level, questions of the following sort arise: What actors are involved in deciding which tasks to do and who will do them? What information do they communicate in order to make these decisions? How do they make decisions using this information? Our models are obviously extreme simplifications of the complexities that occur at this level, but this general approach may help suggest and organize micro-level empirical observations (e.g., see Crowston, Malone, and Lin, in press).

Regardless of the detailed validity of the micro-level models, our results also suggest and help organize macro-level hypotheses about the relative advantages of different kinds of structures. For instance, one simple test of how well our formal definitions match the terms people use intuitively is whether our results correspond to previous generalizations about organizational design. Certainly, the qualitative comparisons shown in Table 1 do not begin to include all the factors discussed by organizational design theorists (e.g., Mintzberg 1979; Galbraith 1977; March and Simon 1958; Gulick and Urwick 1937; and Hax and Majluf 1981). However, in the cases where our model addresses issues considered previously, the comparisons in the table do appear to be consistent with previous work. Three examples are summarized below.

Tradeoffs between production costs and coordination costs. March and Simon (1958, p. 29) summarize the problem of departmentalization as a tradeoff between self-containment and skill specialization: "[Functional] departmentalization generally takes greater advantage of the potentialities for economy through specialization than

does [product] departmentalization; [product] departmentalization leads to greater self-containment and lower coordination costs. . . ."[1] Table 1 reflects this tradeoff with the "economies of specialization" in functional hierarchies being represented as lower production costs, and the advantages of self-containment in product hierarchies being represented as lower coordination costs.

Organizational structure and flexibility. It is commonly claimed that product hierarchies are more flexible in rapidly changing environments than functional hierarchies (e.g., Galbraith 1973, pp. 113–116; Mintzberg 1979, p. 415; Ansoff and Brandenburg 1971, p. 722). Our model reflects this but goes on to suggest an important distinction between two kinds of flexibility: *adaptability* and *vulnerability*. According to our model, product hierarchies are indeed more *adaptable*, in the sense that their coordination costs for re-coordinating in new environments are less than for functional hierarchies.

But our models suggest that product hierarchies are not necessarily less *vulnerable*, in the sense of the losses suffered when unexpected changes occur. For example, Mintzberg, quoting Weick, observes that: ". . . the [product hierarchy] spreads its risk. ' . . . if there is a breakdown in one portion of a loosely coupled system then this breakdown is sealed off and does not affect other portions of the organization' (Weick 1976, p. 7). In contrast, one broken link in the operating chain of the functional structure brings the entire system to a grinding halt" (Mintzberg 1979, p. 415).

Table 1 suggests, however, that the overall vulnerabilities of the product and functional hierarchies may not necessarily be different. While a failure in one product division may, indeed, be limited in its effect to that division, the failure of a single processor may bring the entire division to a halt. The failure of an equivalent processor in a functional hierarchy, on the other hand, might be less costly since other processors of the same type are pooled in a central department and shifting tasks between them is presumably easier than shifting tasks between product divisions. The real vulnerability of the functional hierarchy is to failures of the functional managers themselves, because a failure there does indeed disrupt the entire organization. Without more information about the relative frequency and costs of these two kinds of failures, however, we cannot say *a priori* whether the product or functional hierarchy is more vulnerable.

Comparison between markets and hierarchies. There is a growing body of literature concerned with the relative advantages of markets and hierarchies as coordination structures (e.g., Coase 1937; Williamson 1975, 1981). As Williamson (1981, p. 558) summarizes, ". . . trade-offs between production cost economies (in which the market

[1] We have substituted "functional" and "product" for the terms used in the original: "process" and "purpose," respectively.

TABLE 5

Changes in Costs as Size of Structure Increases

	Production Costs	Coordination Costs	Vulnerability Costs
Product hierarchy	+	+	+++
Functional hierarchy	+	++	++
Centralized market	+	+++	++
Decentralized market	+	++++	++

Note: Different numbers of pluses indicate relative rates of change (more pluses mean faster change).

may be presumed to enjoy certain advantages) and governance cost economies (in which the advantages may shift to internal organization) need to be recognized." Table 1 reflects this result in the following way: Separate firms that "make" products internally are represented by the separate divisions of a product hierarchy. Separate firms that pool their demands and "buy" products in a market are represented by either the centralized or decentralized markets. As the table shows the market structures have lower production costs, but higher coordination costs.

Conclusion

In this paper, we have defined and mathematically analyzed four generic coordination structures. The models are unusual in the degree to which they (a) link micro- and macro-level hypotheses, (b) are formal and mathematical, (c) integrate organizational and market models, and (d) include measures of vulnerability costs along with production and coordination costs.

The models are also interesting because of the surprising range of questions they help illuminate. For instance, elsewhere (e.g., Malone and Smith 1984; Malone 1986; Malone, Yates and Benjamin, in press; Crowston, Malone, and Lin, in press) we have suggested how the models can be used to (a) help understand major changes that have occurred in the structure of American businesses during the last century, (b) make speculative predictions about the possible consequences that the widespread use of information technology may have for organizational structures, and (c) help analyze and predict design options for computer processing networks.[2]

[2] This research was supported, in part, by the Center for Information Systems Research and the Management in the 1990s Research Program at MIT; by Citibank, N.A.; by the Xerox Corporation Palo Alto Research Center; and by National Science Foundation Grant No. SES-8213169.
The author would especially like to thank John Little, Michael Cohen, and three anonymous referees of a previous paper for helpful comments.

References

ANSOFF, H. I. AND R. G. BRANDENBURG, "A Language for Organization Design. Parts I and II," *Management Sci.*, 17 (1971), B-705 to B-731.

BALIGH, H. H., "Decision Rules and Transactions, Organizations and Markets," *Management Sci.*, 32 (1986), 1480–1491.

—— AND R. M. BURTON, "Describing and Designing Organizational Structures and Processes," *Internat. J. Policy Analysis and Information Systems*, 5 (1981), 251–266.

—— AND ——, "The Process of Designing Organization Structures and Their Information Substructures," In S. K. Chang (Ed.), *Management and Office Information Systems*, Plenum Press, New York, 1984, 3–26.

—— AND W. W. DAMON, "Foundations for a systematic process of organization structure design," *J. Information and Optimization Sci.*, 1 (1980), 133–165.

—— AND L. RICHARTZ, *Vertical Market Structures*, Allyn and Bacon, Boston, 1967.

BECKMANN, M. J., "A Production Function for Organizations Doing Case Work," *Management Sci.*, 28, 10 (October 1982), 1159–1165.

BURTON, R. M. AND B. OBEL, *Designing Efficient Organizations: Modelling and Experimentation*, Elsevier Science Publishers B. V., Amsterdam, 1984.

CHANDLER, A. D. JR., *Strategy and Structure: Chapters in the History of the American Industrial Enterprise.* MIT Press, Cambridge, Mass., 1962.

COASE, R. H., "The Nature of the Firm," *Economics N.S.* (1937).

CROWSTON, K., T. W. MALONE AND F. LIN, "Cognitive Science and Organizational Design: A Case Study of Computer Conferencing," *Human-Computer Interaction*, in press.

GALBRAITH, J., *Organization Design*, Addison-Wesley, Reading, Mass., 1977.

GULICK, L. AND L. URWICK (Eds.), *Papers on the Science of Administration*, Institute of Public Administration, Columbia University, New York, 1937.

HAX, A. AND N. MAJLUF, "Organizational Design: A Survey and an Approach," *Oper. Res.*, 29, 3 (May–June 1981).

JONSCHER, C., *Productivity Change and the Growth of Information Processing Requirements in the Economy: Theory and Empirical Analysis*, Unpublished draft, Cambridge, Mass., 1982.

KOCHEN, M. AND K. W. DEUTSCH, *Decentralization*, Oelgeschlager, Gunn & Hain, Cambridge, Mass., 1980.

MACKENZIE, K. D., *Organizational Design: The Organizational Audit and Analysis Technology*, Ablex, Norwood, N.J., 1986a.

——, "Virtual Positions and Power," *Management Sci.*, 32 (1986b), 622–642.

MALONE, T. W., "A Formal Model of Organizational Structure and its Use in Predicting Effects of Information Technology," Sloan School of Management Working Paper No. 1849-86, Massachusetts Institute of Technology, Cambridge, MA. August 1986.

——, "Organizing Information Processing Systems: Parallels Between Human Organizations and Computer Systems." In W. Zachary, S. Robertson and J. Black (Eds.), *Cognition, Computation, and Cooperation*, Ablex Publishing Corp., Norwood, N.J., in press.

—— AND S. SMITH, "Tradeoffs in Designing Organizations: Implications for New Forms of Human Organizations and Computer Systems," Center for Information Systems Research, Working paper No. 112, Sloan WP #1541-84, Sloan School of Management, MIT, Cambridge, Mass., 1984.

—— J. YATES AND R. I. BENJAMIN, "Electronic Markets and Electronic Hierarchies," *Comm. ACM*, 30 (1987), 484–497.

MARCH, J. G. AND H. A. SIMON, *Organizations*, Wiley, New York, 1958.

MARSCHAK, J. AND R. RADNER, *Economic Theory of Teams*, Yale University Press, New Haven, Conn., 1972.

MINTZBERG, H., *The Structuring of Organizations*, Prentice-Hall, Englewood Cliffs, N.J., 1979.

WILLIAMSON, O. E., *Markets and Hierarchies*, Free Press, New York, 1975.

——, "The Economics of Organization: The Transaction Cost Approach," *Amer. J. Sociology*, 87 (1981), 548–575.

Chapter 4

Coherence and Coordination

We have divided our treatment of coherence and coordination into three sections. In the first, we have included papers on representing and reasoning about individual agents and coordination among them, and in the second we have placed papers on representing and reasoning about collections of intelligent agents. In the third section we have included papers on the driving issue of the description, use, and resolution of disparities among agents and knowledge.

4.1 Reasoning about Agents' Knowledge and Behavior

Agents must reason about the knowledge and behavior of others to coordinate. The papers in this section deal with a number of issues in modeling other agents. One of the key approaches is the use of common assumptions about other agents exemplified in the work of Michael Genesereth, Matthew Ginsburg, Douglas Lenat, and Jeffrey Rosenschein. Another approach is the explicit modeling of beliefs, and the links between beliefs, action, and communication explored in papers by Philip Cohen, Hector Levesque, Leora Morgenstern, amd Jeffrey Rosenschein. Representing the projected behavior of agents using action structures becomes important for planning, and also forms a basis for reasoning about organization. Michael Georgeff's papers present several approaches to reasoning about actions and interactions in multiagent planning, using knowledge of the planned actions of other agents. Section 5 of Chapter 1 gives an overview of issues in modeling knowledge of other agents, their activities, and organizations of agents.

Douglas Lenat's very original concept of Beings demonstrated in his PUP6 system is one of the few to explore the advantages of uniformity of structure for aiding modeling of and interaction with other agents. By giving each agent a standard structure, any other agent can always interrogate that agent to find representations of its knowledge and behavior by asking questions about known structural attributes. PUP6 was one of the first AI systems structured as a collection of high-level cooperating experts, and it was designed to mimic dialogues among human expert program designers.

In coordinating with other agents, the use of communication actions is a part of planning and action. Communication actions such as requesting and informing were first explored by the philosopher J.L. Austin with his notion of "speech acts," which were further developed by John Searle. Philip Cohen and Raymond Perrault suggested that a formal theory of speech acts must involve representations agents' beliefs, goals and emotional states, as well as representations of their plans and intentions. By including these concepts, Cohen and Perrault achieve satisfying formal definitions of communication actions, which can be composed into higher level structures and plans. Their work provides a foundation for using knowledge of belief and action for communication, opening the way to more flexible interaction regimes in DAI systems. Interaction regimes based on speech act models grounded in plans and beliefs will more closely unify theories of coordination and communication. Jeffrey Rosenschein's paper begins to make this connection clear, by building upon Cohen and Perrault's work. Rosenschein's paper concerns multiagent planning — the ways one agent can construct a plan to be executed jointly by several other agents. Actions often have to be executed by different agents but in a specified sequence, and this paper outlines mechanisms for maintaining the execution sequence. These include the use in plans of communication acts to find out current goals and facts and to induce other agents to perform desired actions. See Chapter 1, Section 3, for discussion of other issues relating interaction and coordination.

Leora Morgenstern presents a formal theory of action that is general enough to represent multiagent plans and partially-specified plans. A main focus of this work was a core problem arising in flexible and cooperative planning — how an agent can reason (1) that it knows how to perform an action, and (2) whether it can successfully complete an underspecified plan. An agent may reason that it can perform an action when it knows it has help, and Morgensterns framework provides a representation strong enough to reason about such situations. An agent's ability to reason using knowledge of itself and its place in a problem-solving framework, sometimes called *reflection*, is an important aspect of coordination, and is also treated in papers by Ed Durfee and Victor Lesser in Chapter 4, Section 2, by Gerald Barber, in Chapter 8, and by Eva Hudlicka and Victor Lesser in Chapter 6.

Michael Georgeff's 1983 paper develops another approach to multiagent plans, namely how to synthesize them from a collection of single agent plans. This involves analyzing interactions (to detect harmful interactions and to avoid them) as well as to make allowance for dynamic synchronization of the individual plans. This paper integrates approaches to conflict resolution, coordination through planning and action, and communication in a simple framework. Georgeff's 1984 paper presents a formal theory of action suitable for reasoning about interaction in multiagent environments. It uses a formal process model to represent the behaviors of agents, their parallel composition, and the ways their actions may interfere. His 1986 paper extends his formal theory of action to model events as well as actions. Taken together, these papers give a good introduction the necessities and theoretical techniques for reasoning about actions and plans, which Georgeff and others have continued to refine.

Christopher Stuart reports on an implemented multiagent synchronizer. It uses a more mainstream (computer science) theoretical treatment. Agents are non-deterministic finite automata. A plan synchronizer reasons about synchronization using a propositional temporal logic, and realized using a modification of Hoare's CSP mechanism.

Michael Genesereth, Matthew Ginsberg and Jeffrey Rosenschein use a game-theoretic notion of rationality to explore how rational agents can cooperate without ever needing to communicate. Their paper also illustrates a method of reasoning about the beliefs of other agents using payoff matrices, rather than explicit logic-based belief models, and integrates this representation with an explicit coordination framework. Their approach depends upon the strong assumption of shared views of a situation, namely that each agent accurately knows the payoffs of particular actions to both itself and the other agent, and it is difficult to see how this can be achieved without some prior communication. However, when in situations where automated agents are designed with specific goals in mind, their approach provides a very useful technique for coordination.

Jeffrey Rosenschein and Michael Genesereth's paper generalizes their previous work on rational agents that cooperate without communication to include some communication that resolves conflicts. Agents can make deals and are able to cooperate more easily than in the communication-free case.

BEINGS: KNOWLEDGE AS INTERACTING EXPERTS

Douglas B. Lenat
Artificial Intelligence Laboratory
Stanford University, Stanford, California

Abstract

Knowledge may be organized as a community of interacting modules. Each module is granted a complex structure, to simulate a particular expert in some small domain. An extended analogy is drawn to a group of cooperating human specialists. Based on this, an internal constraint is imposed on the modules: Their structure must be standard over the entire community. Some advantages of a uniform formalism are thereby preserved. An experimental community was implemented for the task domain of automatic programming. It has managed to synthesize a few inductive inference LISP programs, nonformally, from specific restricted dialogues with a human user.

1. Experts and Beings

Consider an interdisciplinary enterprise, attempted by a community of human experts who are specialists in -- and only in -- their own fields. What modes of interactions will be productive? The dominant paradigm might well settle into *questioning and answering* each other. Instead of a chairman, suppose the group adopts rules for gaining the floor, what a speaker may do, and how to resolve disputes. When a topic is being considered, one or two experts might recognize it and speak up. In the course of their exposition they might need to call on other specialists. This might be by name, by specialty, or simply by posing a new sub-question and hoping someone could recognize his own relevance and volunteer a suggestion. Such transfers would be more common at the beginning, when the task is (by assumption) too general for any one member to comprehend. As the questions focus on more specific issues, single individuals should be able to supply complete solutions. If the task is to construct something, then the activities of the experts should not be strictly verbal. Often, one will recognize his relevance to the current situation and ask to *do* something: clarify or modify or (rarely) create.

What would it mean to *simulate* the above activity? Imagine several little programs, each one modelling a different expert. What should each program, called a *Being*, be capable of? It must possess a corpus of specific facts and strategies for its designated speciality. It must interact via questioning and answering other Beings. Each Being should be able to recognize when it is relevant. It must set up and alter structures, just as the human specialists do.

Let us return to our meeting of human experts. To be more concrete, suppose their task is to design and code a large computer program: a concept formation system[2]. Experts who will be useful include scientific programmers, non-programming psychologists, system hackers, and management personnel. What happens in the ensuing session? When an expert participates, he will either be aiding a colleague in some difficulty or else transferring a tiny, customized bit of his expertise (facts about his field) into a programmed function which can do something. The final code reflects the members' knowledge, in that sense. One way the session might proceed is for the specialists to actually *do* the concept formation task. As they become familiar with what part of their own expertise is being called upon, and in what ways, they can begin to isolate it. When it is clear

precisely what each is doing, they can take their extracted bits of knowledge, organize them, formalize them, and program them. (A conscious effort along these lines was made in [8], where experts gradually replaced themselves by programs. Instead of discussing how to write a speech program, they *did* speech recognition, until each one could introspect sufficiently into his own activities to formalize them.) For our task, one expects the psychologists to dominate the early discussions, later yielding to programmers. The project sponsor might be passive, submitting a single specification order for the program, or active, participating in the work as a (somewhat privileged) member of the team. This individual is the one who wants the final product, hence will be called the *user*.

How could Beings do this? There would be some little program containing information about CONCEPT-FORMATION (much more than would be used in writing any single concept formation program), another Being who knows how to manage a group to WRITE-PROGRAMS, and many lower-level specialists, for example INFO-OBTAINER, TEST, MODIFY-DATA-STRUCTURE, UNTIL-LOOP, VISUAL-PERCEPTION, AVOID-CONTRADICTION, PROPOSE-PLAUSIBLE-NAME. Like the human specialists, the Beings would contain far too much information, far too inefficiently represented, to be able to say "we ourselves constitute the desired program!" They would have to discuss, and perhaps carry out, the concept formation task. They would write specialized versions of themselves, programs which could do exactly what the Beings did to carry out the task, no more nor less (although they would hopefully take much less time, be more customized). This activity is referred to in the sequel as *automatic programming*. Some Beings (e.g., TEST) may have several distinct, streamlined fractions of themselves in the final program. Beings (e.g., PROPOSE-PLAUSIBLE-NAME) which only aided other Beings may not have *any* correlates in the final synthesized code.

An experimental system, PUP6, was designed and partially implemented. PUP6 synthesized a concept formation program (similar to [7]), but the user, who is human, must come up with certain specific answers to some of the Beings' critical queries. A grammatical inference program and a simple property list maintenance routine were also generated. A few new Beings had to be added to PUP6 to synthesize them.

The next section illustrates how the experts might have cooperated on the task of writing the concept formation program. Section 3 describes the program they produced. Next comes the Being hypothesis: complex but standard anatomy. Later sections explain this, both theoretically and by examining the behavior of the actual PUP6 pool of 100 Beings. The appendix exhibits a typical Being.

2. Experts Interacting

The input/output behavior of the desired concept formation program is specified in this section, and we eavesdrop on a simulated group of specialists as they get to work on writing it. As the presentation of the experts' activities becomes more specific, the reader's currently vague conception of Beings will be made less amorphous (because Beings are constrained to carry on approximately the same discussion as the experts below do).

Externally, the concept formation task can be specified as follows: pictures of structures (built out of simple geometrical shapes) will be presented one after another. For each such scene, the concept formation program, call it CF, must guess its name. The presenter will then reveal the correct name of the structure. CF must quickly learn to identify simple structures (ARCH, TOWER), and must never make the same mistake twice in a row. Assume, as given, a process which extracts a description of a visual scene.

Our group of experts are given this specification for CF. Assume that the user (the financial sponsor) is available for resolving important questions, via messenger, and he may in fact ask questions of the group. Whenever an expert speaks, almost all the others in the room hear him. Usually only a few can benefit from what he says, and fewer still care to react. The conversation in the room might go something like the following (the suggestive names of the experts are of course coincidental):

GENL-MANAGER: Can anybody here figure out what to do, what the user's saying? (waves the input/output specifications in the air)

PGM-MANAGER: I can. He wants a computer program to be written. If somebody will explain the task "con-cept-for-ma-tion" to me a little more clearly, I'll delegate it properly.

PSYCH: Permit me to assist you. I know all about concept formation. In fact, my master's thesis...

PGM-MANAGER: Wait, the user must be told that we'll be able to handle the job for him.

MESSENGER: Here, I can take that message. Go on with your work.

PGM-MANAGER: We need a name for this program. Somebody get one, please.

NAMER: How about "CONCEPT"? Maybe just "CF". Let's ask the user to decide.

MESSENGER: (panting) I just came back from there! Alright, I'm going... User says to call it "CF".

PGM-MANAGER: Now then, I have four people in mind, one of whom must take over now in an important way. Each of them always wants to do something different.

CHOOSER: Give me their names and I'll choose the best one for you.

PGM-MANAGER: They are INFO-OBTAINER, INFO-USER, PGMMER, and ANALYST.

CHOOSER: You four experts each must justify to me why you should take control now.

     INFO-OBTAINER: We already have some unused information, so I guess I can wait.

     INFO-USER: Let me have the floor! I know what to do with the user's specification.

     PGMMER: Well, I suppose I could set up some "empty" top-level function, er...

     ANALYST: Marginal profits accruing from my working at this point in time do not warrant...

CHOOSER: Okay, INFO-USER, you seem to be the only relevant expert.

INFO-USER: First thing is for PSYCH to tell us how to actually *do* concept formation.

PSYCH: There are several decisions to be made, depending on what your independent variables and your experimental setup are. For example, are we studying one individual, or must our program adapt to simulate many different subjects? Must stimulus items be just classified, or classified and ordered, or classified and ordered and metrized? Are the scenes left in view indefinitely, or just the current scene, or is even that one just flashed before the subject for a limited time? May the subject make written notes? Can he learn from positive instances of the concepts? from negative instances? Is there to be any positive transfer effect...?

DEFER: Hold on here; we can't swamp the user with lots of unnecessary questions. Let's go through each one and see if it can wait. Consider the decision about the task being classificatory, comparative, or metrical. What is the first situation where that decision really matters?

WHEN-NEXT: This involves a list of alternatives. Who knows about that?

ALTERNATIVES: I know a few tricks here. If all the alternative sequences of activities have the same initial subsequence, then do that common subsequence before making the decision.

UTILIZE: In this case, all three begin by partitioning a domain of elements.

DEFER: Temporarily, replace the task CF by the task of partitioning a domain. (*The user is informed of this.*) Now consider the decision about subject-specific behavior being required.

PSYCH: This involves periodically inputting a description of the human subject.

CODER: That would mean adjusting the algorithms based on a vector of parameters.

WHEN-NEXT: This would probably affect the entire code.

DEFER: I can't defer this decision. Someone resolve it.

RESOLVE: Ask the user about it.

ASK-USER: Phrase this as a yes/no question. Explain each alternative to the user.

MESSENGER: That's my job... <*types on teletype*> User says no, don't simulate different people.

DEFER: The next decision...

     Eleven decisions are ultimately proposed by PSYCH, and all but one are deferred.

INFO-USER: I have no objections now if someone wants the floor.

PGM-MANAGER: Do any of the other three experts I mentioned earlier want to speak now?

PGMMER: Yes. I think that the top-level function CF can now be coded.

CODER: Give me the arguments and the body of the code.

PGMMER: There are no known arguments. The body is a call on *PARTITION-DOMAIN*.

CODER: Okay. I will precede that with a call to an *INITIALIZE* function, and follow it with a call to a *FINALIZE* function, which are both defined as NIL for now. Is *PARTITION-DOMAIN* simple enough to be composed right now and filled in here?

MATHEMATICIAN: No way. Any realizate...

CODER: Uh, thanks. There. The function CF is defined as: (LAMBDA () (INITIALIZE) (PARTITION-DOMAIN) (FINALIZE)).

ANALYST: Remind me to examine the initialization and finalization functions at the end of our task. If either function is still null, it will be deleted.

WARNER: I have just put that note into the code for CF, as a comment of type "demon"

PGMMER: Can someone advise me of what else to do to finish defining this function?

PGM-MANAGER: Each function should have a proper name. Show the user the names you have picked, and let him choose other ones if he prefers.

MESSENGER: Okay... The user agrees to all 3 names.

INFO-USER: Somebody, please tell the group how to *do* partitioning of a space of examples.

A complete script, like the above, was constructed by hand. In the sequel, this will be referred to as the *protocol*. In all, 87 different experts were called for: 17 specifically dealing with inductive inference tasks, and 70 dealing with programming, managing workers, and communicating with the user. Near the end of the protocol, the user is asked which of the three types of concept formation CF is supposed to do. He responds "*CLASSIFICATORY only*", and the experts discover that they are finished. All the newly created code is dumped out onto a fresh file: After hundreds of pages, a concept formation program meeting the user's specifications had been written. The next section will describe that program in detail.

3. The Program the Experts Wrote

One of the experts at the simulated meeting must have read P. Winston's dissertation[7], because CF, the synthesized concept formation program, was remarkably similar to the one therein described. CF has a much simpler graph-matching algorithm, and relations on relations are stored in a different way than simple relations on objects. Since CF was later synthesized by PUP6, the programmed pool of Beings, it is worth detailing here.

CF repeatedly scans a scene and tries to name it. As a first step, the scene is broken into a set of objects and a set of features (relations on those objects). CF maintains a model for each differently-named scene it has encountered. A model contains a description of the objects one expects in such a structure, a set of features which *must* be present in any scene having this name, a set of features which *must not* be present if the scene is to have this name, and a set of features which *may* be present or absent. Thus a model is an archetypical scene plus a name. For example, part of a scene might be described as:

```
OBJECTS     a,b,c,d
RELATIONS   (Green a) (Blue c) (Touches c d)
            (Supports a c) (Supports b c)
```
CF's current model for an arch might be:
```
NAME      Arch
OBJECTS   a,b,c
MUST      (Supports a c) (Supports b c)
MUSTNOT   (Touches a b)
MAY       (Green a) (Wedge c) (Prism a) (Block b)
          (Parallel a b) (Red a) (Red b)
```

Each time it is confronted by a new scene, CF must scan its models until it finds one which matches it. A model is said to match a scene if all the MUST features associated with that model are observed in the scene, and all the MUSTNOT features are absent from the scene. CF informs the user of this guess, and accepts the proper name. If it guessed incorrectly, CF modifies its models. The wrong-guess model may have features added to its MUST or MUSTNOT sets. This is sufficient to prevent CF from making the same wrong guess twice in succession. The correct-name model may have to be modified or (if it's a new name) created and inserted into the list of models, to ensure that CF will eventually learn that concept. A *concept* here simply means a model; i.e., all scenes having a given name.

Suppose that the target program reads in the above scene fragment and tries to match it to the above ARCH model. The MUST relations should all be present. Yes, the scene does contain (SUPPORTS a c) and (SUPPORTS b c). Next, the MUSTNOT relations must be absent from the scene. Sure enough, (TOUCHES a b) isn't there. So the model and scene are consistent, and the program announces that its guess is ARCH. If the user verifies this guess, then the MAY set of the ARCH model is augmented with the relations (BLUE c) and (TOUCHES c d), and the OBJECTS set is augmented with "d."

If the user denies that the scene is an arch, CF sees if there are any relations in the ARCH model's MAY set which do not occur in the scene. If so, one of them (e.g., (PARALLEL a b)) will be transferred from the MAY to the MUST set. If no such feature existed, the program would look for a feature present in the scene but not mentioned in any set of the ARCH model (e.g., (TOUCHES c d)), and insert it into the MUSTNOT set. In either case, the user would be asked what the true name was, and that model would have its MAY set augmented by any new features in the scene and by any features on the true-name model's MUST or MUSTNOT sets which contradicted the scene.

4. Anatomy of Synergetic Cooperation

Consider the birth of one small idea necessary in the writing of CF (e.g., that of classifying a model's features into three categories (MUST, MUSTNOT, MAY)). No single specialist at the meeting could have had this idea by himself. How do intellects mesh, effectively communicate, and unite their powers? A tentative mechanism, which barely scratches the surface of this mystery, will be hypothesized. The Beings in PUP6 embody this concept, and are able to reproduce both the experts' discussion and the final CF program.

Viewing the group of experts as a single entity, what makes it productive? The members must be very different in abilities, in order to handle such a complex task, yet similar in basic cognitive structure (in the anatomy of their minds) to permit facile communications to flow. For example, each specialist knows how to direct a programmer to do some of the things he can do, but the specific facts each expert has under this category must be quite unique. Similarly, each member may have a set of strategies for recognizing his own relevance to a proposed question, but the *contents* of that knowledge varies from individual to individual. The hypothesis is that all the experts can be said to consist of categorized information, where the set of categories is fairly standard, and indicates the *types* of questions any expert can be expected to answer. An expert is considered *equivalent* to his answers to several standard questions. Each expert has the same mental "parts", it is only the values stored in these parts, their contents, which distinguish him as an individual.

Armed with this dubious view of intelligence, let us return to the design of Beings. Each Being shall have many parts, each possessing a name (a question it deals with) and a value (a procedure capable of answering that question). Henceforth, "*part*" will be used in this technical sense. When a Being asks a question, it is really just one part who is asking. In fact, it must be that the *value* subpart of some part can't answer *his* question without further assistance. He may not know enough to call on specific other Beings (so he lets anyone respond who feels relevant), but he should *always* specify what Being *part* the question should be answered by. By analogy with the experts, each Being will have the same "universal" set of types of parts (will answer the same kinds of queries), and this uniformity should permit painless intercommunication. Since the paradigm of the meeting is questioning and answering, the names of the parts should cover all the types of questions one expert wants to ask another. Each part of each Being will have implicit access to this list: it may ask only these types of questions. Each Being should *not* have access to the list of all Beings in the system: requests should be phrased in terms of what is wanted; rarely is the name of the answerer specified in advance. (By analogy: the human speaker is not aware of precisely who is in the room; when he feels inadequate, he asks for help and hopes someone responds). Another point is that Beings are not a recursive concept (like ACTORs[3] are): a part of a Being is a brief collection of knowledge (usually procedural), not another Being; a collection of Beings (also called a community, a pool, the system, or a group) is also not itself a Being. There are no *structured* clusters of Beings.

Once again: the concept of a pool of Beings is that many entities coexist, each having a complex structure, but that structure does not vary from Being to Being. This idea has analogues in many fields: transactional analysis in psychology, anatomy in medicine, modular design in architchture.

How can we test out this idea? We must build a pool of Beings, a modular program which will interact with a human user and generate the CF program. Recasting the idea into operational terms, we arrive at this procedure for writing a pool of Beings:

(1) Study the task which the pool is to do. See what kinds of questions are asked by simulated experts.

(2) Distill this into a core of simple questions, Q, in such a way that each inter-expert question or transfer of control can be rephrased in terms of Q. The size of Q is very important. If Q is too large, addition of new Beings will demand either great effort or great intelligence (an example of a system like this is ACTORS). If Q is too small, all the non-uniformity is simply pushed down into the values of one or two general catchall questions (all first-order logical languages do this).

(3) List all the Beings who will be present in the pool, and fill in their parts. The time to encode knowledge into many simple representation schemes is proportional to the square of (occasionally exponential in) the amount of interrelated knowledge (e.g., consider the frame problem). The filling in of a new Being is *independent* of the number of Beings already in the pool, because Beings can communicate via nondeterministic goal mechanisms, and not have to know the names of the Beings who will answer their queries. This filling in is *linear* in the number of Being parts listed in Q; all parts of all Beings must be (at least, should be) filled in.

(4) The human user interacts with the completed Being community, until the desired task is complete.

Section 5 clarifies the effects of constraining that Q be constant (over all the Beings in the system). Theoretical aspects of Being systems follow, in section 6. Next comes an evaluation of PUP6's behavior. The uses and the problems with Beings are summed up in the final section.

5. Internal Details of Beings

A set of 29 ubiquitous questions were chosen, representing everything one expert might want to ask another. At least, they naturally encompass those questions which were asked during the simulated meeting, hence should be sufficient for generating CF. Q, this universal set of Being parts, is listed in Appendix 1. The reader is urged to glance at this now, and refer to it whenever a Being part is specifically mentioned.

Each of the 100 Beings in PUP6 should have had a value for each part (in reality, only 40% of these 2900 slots were filled in; only 30% were actually necessary to generate CF). A value for a part is simply a LISP program which can answer that question, often by asking questions of the same Being, of other Beings, and of the user. A part may also assert some fact, create or modify some structure (including demons, Beings, and parts of Beings). Appendix 1 shows the values stored under each part for the typical Being named "INFO-OBTAINER".

The set of parts breaks into three rough categories: (1) those parts which are useful in deciding which Being gets control, (2) those which are used once the Being gains control, and (3) those useful only to answer the user's questions and keep him oriented. The next section describes categories 1 and 2; the section after that explicates the third category of Being parts.

5.1. Control in the PUP6 System

At the humans' meeting, only one expert spoke at a time; in the Beings community, only one Being has control at any given moment. He uses his parts to do things (ask, create, modify), and yields control either voluntarily or through interruption.

In slightly more procedural terms, the scenario is as

follows. One part of a Being senses its relevance (often the IDEN or EFFECTS parts, which are united with all such parts to form a large production system[5]). If more than one Being wants control at any time, a special Being, CHOOSER, seizes control momentarily. He asks each competing Being to evaluate its WHEN part, to see how seriously it needs to go immediately. If some Beings are still tied for first place, he asks them to evaluate their COMPLEXITY parts, to see which is the simplest. If any *still* tie for top, one is randomly chosen. In any case, the winner is then passed control. Once in control, a Being arranges some of its parts in some order and evaluates them. For example, the ARGS part might be first; if it asks for some arguments which no Being has supplied, then the whole Being might decide to fail. Some parts, when evaluated, might create a new Being, might ask questions which require this whole process to repeat recursively, etc. This "asking" really means broadcasting a request to one or two parts of every Being; for example "Is there a known fast way of gronking toves?" would be asked as a search for a Being whose COMPLEXITY part indicated speed, and whose EFFECTS part contained a production with a template matching "gronking toves". A list of the responders would be returned. (Incidentally, GERUND would recognize this, but later give up when no one could recognize "gronk toves".) The questioner might pose some new questions directly to these Beings, might turn control over to them directly, etc. One way or another, the Being eventually relinquishes control. If it had no direct successor in mind, all the Beings are asked if they want to take over. There will always be *some* Being who will take over; the general management types of Beings are always able -- but reluctant -- to do so.

How does each Being decide which parts to evaluate, and in which order, once it gains control? The answer might seem to be difficult or tedious for whoever writes Beings, since it might vary from Being to Being. In fact, it doesn't! The commitment to a universal set of Being parts is inefficient in some ways (each Being *needed* only a third of all the parts) but allows for some simplifications right here. What parts should be evaluated, and in what order, when a Being gains control? This decision depends primarily on the *types* of parts present in the Being, not on their *values*. But every Being has the same anatomy, so one single algorithm can assemble any Being's parts into an executable LISP function. Moreover, this assembly can be done when the system is first loaded (or when a new Being is first created), and need only be redone for a Being when the values of its parts change. Such changes are rare: experts are not often open-minded. The precise algorithm is sketched in the box below. The parts useful here include ARGS, DEMONS, META-CODE, COMMENTS, ARG-CHECK, and REQUISITES.

Assembling a Being into an executable function
When a Being B first gains control, its EXPLICIT-ARGS are bound. The IMPLICIT-ARGS are initialized, the name B is pushed onto the Being control stack, and any newly-activated DEMONS are so tagged. The Being who called B should have explained his reasons by assigning some phrase to the variable BECAUSE. This reason is now stored as a special sub-part of the WHY part of B. BECAUSE is rebound periodically in the META-CODE and COMMENTS parts, to keep current the explanation of each call that B makes. Each ARG-CHECK predicate is evaluated. If any returns NIL, the entire Being reports that it has failed; otherwise, the PRE-REQUISITES are examined. Effort is expended to make them true, if they are currently not satisfied. Each COMMENT is evaluated, then the CO-REQUISITES, META-CODE, and the current demons are executed in pseudo-parallel. Each POST-REQUISITE is then examined, and an effort made to satisfy it. The newly-activated demons are exorcized, B is

> popped from the Being control stack, and the value computed by the META-CODE is returned. Some heuristics were devised to take advantage of the fact that the Beings often didn't need many of the standard parts. For example, INFO-OBTAINER has no new demons or co-requisites, so no parallel processing need be simulated.

5.2. Keeping the User Informed

In the earlier conversation excerpts, the simulated human user had no trouble whatever understanding what the simulated experts asked him. In the actual programmed PUP6 system, the human who was sitting at the teletype quite *rarely* understood what was wanted by the Beings. He frequently had to interrupt them and ask them questions about who was in control, why, what he was trying to do, what had recently transpired, etc. These ideally can be phrased as simple retrievals and EVALs of active Beings' parts. The Being parts most often called for by the user are the simple one-line "orientation" templates. These include WHAT, HOW, WHY, and AFFECTS. For theoretical reasons explained later, the synthesized program, CF, was written as a pool of Beings itself (by PUP6, but not during the protocol. Actually, a fortuitous "bug" in PUP6 created this intriguing situation.) Although its question-answering ability is inferior to PUP6, the fact that it has *any* such power was surprising to the author. In other words, one can interrupt the target program as it is running and ask questions. Any Being on the control stack will provide fully instantiated answers to any of its 29 allowable queries (its parts); all other Beings will provide only hypothetical answers. As an example, consider this actual excerpt of a human using the CF program synthesized by PUP6. (Some liberty has been taken with the English; e.g., the user really types *WHAT?*, not *What are you doing?*) "???" simply means "guess the name of the scene with these objects and relations". CF types in *italics*, the user in **boldface**.

> *CF: Ready to accept brand new scene.*
> **User: (??? (A B) (Block A) (Wedge B) (Touches A B))**
> *CF: Not an Arch. Not a Tower. Might be a Row.*
> *My guess is Row. What is it Really?*
> **User: Nothing**
> *CF: Transfer from the May to the Must set of the*
> *Row model, the feature: (Block B)*
> *CF: Ready to accept brand new scene.*

Here is the *same* excerpt, but with the user interrupting occasionally. "U:" signifies he has interrupted, and "OK." signifies "Go back to work now, CF."

> **U: What are you doing?**
> *CF: Divide a domain into subdomains,*
> *using specialized version of PARTITION-DOMAIN.*
> **How?**
> *CF: By building up the partition gradually,*
> *by adding one <scene, name> pair.* **OK.**
> *CF: Ready to accept brand new scene.*
> **User: (??? (A B) (Block A) (Wedge B) (Touches A B))**
> **U: What are you doing?**
> *CF: Break OBJECTS piece off input scene to examine.*
> **What code is the current Being going to execute?**
> *CF: The meta-code is (CADR arg1). Evals to (A B).* **OK.**
> *CF: Not an Arch.* **U: Why?**
> *CF: The ARCH MUST-relation (SUPPORTS A B)*
> *is contradicted in the SCENE.* **OK.**
> *CF: Not a Tower. Might be a Row. My guess is Row.*
> *What is it really?* **U: Why are you asking?**
> *CF: I must resolve it now, but can't, so I ask User.*
> **OK. What you wanted is: Nothing**
> **U: What are you doing now?**
> *CF: Go through space of concept names, and make user*

aware of changes. **What Beings might this affect?**
> *CF: MESSAGE is possibly called; some version of TEST*
> *is possibly called.* **OK.**
> *CF: Transfer from the May to the Must set of the*
> *Row model, the feature: (Block B)* **U: Why?**
> *CF: Change model of ROW until it contradicts*
> *the previous inputted Scene.* **OK.**
> *CF: Ready to accept brand new scene.*

6. Theory of Pure Beings Systems

We now discuss the constraints each Being, and each group of Beings, must conform to. Hopefully, ideas will be separated from implementation details, prejudices from plausible features.

It would be aesthetically pleasing to restrict all entities in the system to be Beings. However, this would cause an infinite regress, as each part of each Being would have parts which had parts... To stop this, one can assert that at some finite level, all constructs are primitive. ACTORs, for example, set this level to zero; Beings set it to one. ACTORs themselves are primitive, but only *parts* of Beings can be. For this reason, Beings can not be viewed as a convergent recursive definition, as can ACTORs.

Suppose it were decreed that the only autonomous entities possessing control abilities were Beings. In particular, we forbid any plain *functions* to exist. In the case of an automatic programming task, the Beings would have to write new Beings, not new LISP functions. The target program would thus itself be a community of Beings. In order to fill in all the parts, a vast amount of superfluous information would be collected. These supplementary facts can be viewed as a standardized, organized body of *documentation*, a formatted system of comments tacked onto each Being produced.

Which Beings would write the new Beings? Looking back at our interdisciplinary experts, we see that each expert is responsible for distilling his own essential contribution, which is then encoded by a programmer. Perhaps each Being should be able to direct construction of new, specialized Beings which relate to it. If no Being relates to a task, then it can't be coded; if several respond, they should cooperate. This ability is in reality the SPECIALIZATIONS part of each Being (see Appendix 1). The Being which actually does the creation (CODER) in the experimental system is almost trivial, getting very precise instructions from other Beings.

Since the pool must communicate with the user, some Beings must translate quasi-English phrases into calls on Beings. Drawing again on our experts analogy, we require that each Being recognize his own relevance. So translation is merely the act of asking the whole pool "Who can recognize this...", collecting the responders, having *them* decide who should take control, and letting the winner do the translation. Most communication is done as if it, too, were such a translation activity.

One bias is the rejection of debugging as a fundamental programming tool. It is felt to be worth the extra effort to make the system's internal model of the current partial target program *correct*. Debugging demands detective work, examing one's earlier efforts for flaws, for details which have been overlooked. Any tireless system should not ignore details, but rather defer them, asserting a warning to this effect when it does so. Procrastination is quite valuable; in PUP6, much effort is spent deferring any unresolvable decision. Undeferrable unresolvable decisions must cause a backtrack point to be reluctantly set up. Another prejudice is that most carelessness bugs can be eliminated by this deferral, feed-forward, and precise record-keeping. Humans depend on their adaptability to compensate for limitations in their brain hardware, but there is no need for an *automatic* programming system to do so. These biasses are not inherent in the Beings formulation, but only in the design of the PUP6 system (and in the mind of the author).

To clarify what Beings are and are not, they are contrasted with some other ideas. FRAMES[4] are sufficiently amorphous to subsume Beings. In philosophy, FRAMES are meant to model perception, and intentionally rely on implicit default values; Beings intentionally avoid making decisions by default. This is also the difference between HACKER and PUP6. Since PUP6 writes structured programs, it should be distinguished from macro expansion. Macro procedures expand mechanically: expand(sequence m_1 m_2) = (sequence expand(m_1) expand(m_2))). Beings could use information gleaned during expansion of m_1 to improve the way m_2 was handled. ACTORs[3], unlike Beings, have no fixed structure imposed, and do not broadcast their messages (they specify who gets each message, by name, to a bureaucracy).

Beings subsume (inefficiently) many popular AI features; the demonstration will be brief: A *demon* could be replaced by a Being whose ARG-CHECK predicate was the triggering predicate, whose WHEN part was high enough to ensure frequent attention, and whose META-CODE part was the body of the demon. An *assertion* in an associative data network could be a Being with only an IDEN part filled in; when it recognizes its relevance, a fully instantiated assertion is returned. A *function* is equivalent to a Being with only a META-CODE, ARGS, and EVAL-ARGS parts; one knows almost nothing about it before executing it. The inefficiencies should be clear: whenever a Being throws a question open to the floor, "Who can...", it takes an amount of time proportional to the number of Beings in the system. One would introduce this huge time factor by replacing any of the above mechanisms by Beings.

The *number* of Being parts seems to indicate the balance between uniformity and structure in the community. This was touched on as point (2) of Section 4. A small universal set of Being parts is necessary to preserve some of the advantages of uniformity (easy addition of knowledge to the system, easy inter-Being communication). This demands that the number of parts of each Being be, say, under 100. But it is the complex structure of a Being which makes complex behaviors feasable, including flexible communication as well as viable final products. So each Being should have many parts, say at least ten. This range, $10 \leq ||Q|| \leq 100$, is wide for the domain of automatic programming. In other domains, it may be narrow or disappear altogether; this would indicate that Beings could *not* be used effectively for those tasks.

7. Experimental Results

Two of the most significant questions for automatic programming systems are what programs are synthesized, and what kinds of things the user must tell the system.

7.1. Character of the Dialogue between User and PUP6

By lumping all the parts of the PUP6 system together conceptually, the interaction is seen as a *dialogue* between a human user and an automatic programming system. The level of detail maintained in the earlier polylogue (discussions among the experts) obscured what the human actually saw and responded. Below is the same excerpt as was presented in Section 2, but as the *user* sitting at a teletype actually saw it. These were the initial few lines of an actual 300-page long dialogue. In section 2, this excerpt was presented the way experts (the same way the PUP6 Beings) discussed it.

PUP: I want any task.
USER: Write a program which does concept formation
PUP: I am about to write a program for the task:
    specialized kind of CONCEPT-FORMATION.
PUP: Give me a proper name for this program.
    (I suggest CF or CONCEPT)
USER: CF
PUP: Must CF mimic different human subjects?
USER: NO
PUP: I am temporarily replacing the task "specialized kind of CONCEPT-FORMATION" by the simpler task "specialized kind of PARTITION-A-DOMAIN".

From the above, one gets the true impression that the dialogue was fairly tedious: choosing names and resolving design decisions *was* the user's main role. There were, in sum, about 300 such responses involved in generating CF. 13 crucial responses were also necessary, where the user supplies needed information that was not explicitly requested by the Beings. A few of these key lines are: *Write a program which does concept formation; An "element of the domain of stimuli" is a static scene; The guessing process is one of searching, not computing; Terminate the loop iff any model feature is incompatible with the scene's features.*

The translation mechanism is simply the IDEN parts of all the Beings. Each such part contains a few productions, which are united with those of the other Beings into one large production system. The left side of a production is a template which is matched against the given phrase. The right side is a small program to be executed in case the phrase is recognized. Generally, that program simply says to translate some subphrase of the phrase, and then (probably) pass control to the Being which this is in the IDEN part of. While not up to the "state of the art" in natural language processing, this is both adequate and faithful to the spirit of distributing problems over all the Beings, by making them *parts*, so it is each Being's duty to know a little about them.

During the course of the dialogue, PUP6 originates the idea of a MUST/MUSTNOT/MAY structuring of each model's features. Here is how the user sees that portion of the synthesis. Notice that only the first user comment is other than a simple choice.
PUP: How do we know when to terminate this loop?
USER: Terminate iff any feature in model-features is incompatible with scene-features
PUP: PUP wants USER to type in name for specialized version of CONTRADICTS
USER: Call it IMPOSS
PUP: Move cursor to IMPOSS type of CONTRADICTS. I can no longer defer this decision: A: Contradiction arises from features who have probability=1 of occurring. B: Contradiction arises from features who have probability=0 of occurring. C: Contradiction arises from features who have probability>0&<1 of occurring Please type some of: A,B,C; or type: Defer, ?, or Details.
USER: A, B, and C are all relevant.
PUP: I recommend that each model's features be structured (along 1 dimension) into these 3 pieces: PRESENT, which will hold features whose occurrence should have probability=1; ABSENT, which will hold features whose occurrence should have probability=0; and EITHER, which will hold features whose occurrence should have any other probability. Please type back YES, NO, UNSURE, DETAILS, and/or 3 new names.
USER: YES. Call them MUST-BE-PRESENT, MUSTNOT-BE-PRESENT, MAY-BE-PRESENT.
PUP: Too long. Nicknamed Must, Mustnot, May.
PUP: Located 3 references to model's features in code generated so far. In each case, the reference has been replaced by "(APPEND Must Mustnot May)".

This is PUP6 at its best: making just the "right" inference at the "right" time. The hundreds of inter-Being transfers are masked; the system appears to type out just what is necessary. The next few paragraphs dispell this false illusion; there is no mystery to PUP6's doing the right things, and any *typical* dialogue excerpt would be boringly verbose.

Because of its genesis from a single "experts meeting" protocol, the PUP6 pool of Beings was (i) easily able to reproduce that "proper" dialogue, but (ii) incapable of widely varied dialogues with the user. Two assumptions implicit in using the simulated experts' discussion as a literal model turned out to be serious: the abilities of any actual user of PUP6 must coincide with those of the user who was simulated in the protocol, and the order of and wording of the actual user's comments must closely adhere to those of the user in the protocol. Such difficulties must be overcome in any system designed for wide usership, but were considered ignorable in the specific automatic code generation task at hand.

Also as a result of this approach to system specification, each Being had only those parts specified which it actually would need in the ensuing dialogue. Part of the difficulty with new dialogues stemmed from this minimal completion. In the protocol, when a decision was made by experts, the knowledge necessary to follow the *other* alternative branch was not used, nor were such superfluous facts supplied to the Beings in PUP6. Thus the user of PUP6 must almost always resolve each choice the way the simulated (protocol) user did. It is felt that if all the parts of all the Beings had been faithfully filled in, this problem would have subsided. Basically, the difficulty is one of modelling all the possibly relevant knowledge an expert has, rather than (as was done) just capturing enough of his knowledge to do a few given tasks.

While all the Beings' interactions were invisible to the user, the system still swamped him with data about what was going on. For example, most of the entities he was asked to name were never referred to again by name. The converse problem existed as well: it was necessary to include a Being which simulated forgetfulness, to prevent, e.g., anaphora spanning minutes of real time. Orienting the user was not solved satisfactorally. Pointers into a graph of generated code were simulated, but often a user wished to refer to a piece of code not by name or by pointing, but by some brief meaningful (to him only!) phrase.

7.2. The Range of Programs Synthesized by PUP6

The system, PUP6, did eventually synthesize CF, the target concept formation program. PUP6 was 200 pages of INTERLISP[6], CF was 30 pages long (6 pages when coded by hand during the protocol). CF was generated in 60 cpu minutes (compiled, PDP-10 TENEX). The dialogue consisted of 300K characters typed by PUP6, and 4K by the user. It occupied 300 pages, and five hours of real time.

Despite the lack of dialogue flexibility, it *was* felt that most of the Beings could be useful in generating other programs. For this reason, two additional target programs were specified. They were synthesized with little change to PUP6, but only by someone familiar with the system.

The second target program, GI, is a grammatical inference program, which accepts strings labelled LEGAL, ILLEGAL, or ??. In the latter case, GI must guess the legality. Internally, potential sets of rules are maintained. Of the original pool, 49 out of the 87 Beings were used in synthesizing both targets. Four totally new Beings had to be added, related to formal grammars and rules. Unfortunately, the addition of *any* new Beings demands that the user be acquainted with the format conventions of PUP6. The GI program generated was 20 pages long; a hand-coded version was one-fifth that size.

PL was the final target program attempted, a simple property list manipulator. It repeatedly accepts requests from the user to insert, inspect, or delete some record(s). Any unspecified fields are treated as don't-cares, so a simple pattern-matcher had to be synthesized. Two Beings had to be *added* to PUP6. The important piece of data is that about half of the original PUP6 pool of Beings were actually used in *all three* target-synthesizing dialogues.

As proposed in Section 6, the Beings generate other Beings, never plain functions. This explains the huge increases in target code lengths in the PUP6 versions compared to the versions produced by hand when simulating the experts (who wrote the target programs as functions). CF was a pool of 56 brand new Beings, GI 37, and PL 24. As with PUP6, one can interrupt the target programs as they are running and ask questions. Any Being on the control stack will provide fully instantiated answers to any of its 29 allowable queries (its parts); all other Beings will provide only hypothetical answers. Recall the excerpt from CF itself running, found in section 5.2.

Some of the difficulties stem from the nature of the task. In any long dialogue, the user often forgets, changes his mind, errs, etc. A very sophisticated user model would be necessary to accomodate this errorful process in a non-debugging system. Without such abilities, the system itself may be led into error. While most bugs *are* avoidable by careful record-keeping, it proved unrealistic to make no provision for debugging a new thirty-page program. When a few errors did occur in CF, PUP6 itself had to be altered.

8. Conclusions

8.1. About PUP6

What have we learned from this experimental study? The overall feasability of Beings was demonstrated, but the difficulties of communicating with the user made the system almost impossible to work with. The set of questions the user was expected to want to ask is the same as the set that one Being can ask another: the Being parts. When the "nice" user interrupts, his questions are translated trivially into a simple retrieval. Real users are seldom nice; the Beings generally misunderstood what users asked.

To modify PUP6 to synthesize new programs, it was necessary to add a few general-purpose programming and communication Beings, plus add several Beings specific to the new program's domain, plus generalize a few existing Beings' parts. The dialogue to produce the new program may be poorly suited to that domain, since most of the recognized phrases stem from a single (CF-producing) protocol.

To improve PUP6's performance, one could add some debugging specialist Beings, some dialogue specialists, some sophisticated user psychology experts (why is the user asking me that question, what needn't I tell him, how should I direct his attention), some Beings whose task is to aid the untrained user in inserting new domain-specific Beings, and perhaps a whole library of varied specialist Beings.

8.2. About Beings

The performance of the Beings representation itself in PUP6 is mixed. Two advantages were hoped for by using a uniform set of Being parts. Addition of new Beings to the pool was not easy (for untrained users) but communication among Beings *was* easy (fast, natural). Two advantages were hoped for by keeping the Beings highly structured. The interactions (especially with the user) were brittle, but the complex tasks put to the pool *were* successfully completed.

The crippling problems are seen to be with user-system communication, not with the Beings ideas themselves. Sophisticated, bug-free programs *were* generated, after hours of fairly high level dialogue with an active user, after tens of thousands of messages passed among the Beings. Part of this success is attributed to distributing the responsibility for writing code and for recognizing relevance, to a hundred entities, rather than having a few central monitors worry about everything. The standardization of parts made filling in the Beings' contents fairly painless.

What *are* Beings good for? For which tasks won't the problems encountered in PUP6 recur? The idea of a fixed set of parts (which distinguishes them from ACTORs) is useful if the mass of knowledge is too huge for one individual to keep "on top" of. It then should be organized in a very uniform way (to simplify preparing it for storage), yet it must also be highly structured (to speed up retrieval).

For these reasons, the author is currently investigating, as a potential task domain, "research in elementary number theory". This has the added benefit of isolating the problems in representation research from the staggering complexities of natural language handling. Beings are big and slow, but valuable for organizing knowledge in ways meaningful to how it will be used. In the future Automated Mathematician system, Beings will be one -- but not the only -- internal mechanism for representing and manipulating knowledge.

References

[1] Green, Waldinger, Barstow, Elschlager, Lenat, McCune, Shaw, and Steinberg, *Progress Report on Program-Understanding Systems*, Memo AIM-240, Stanford Artificial Intelligence Laboratory, August, 1974.

[2] Hempel, Carl G., *Fundamentals of Concept Formation in Empirical Science*, Chicago: U. Chicago, 1952.

[3] Hewitt, Carl, *A Universal Modular ACTOR Formalism for Artificial Intelligence*, Third International Joint Conference on Artificial Intelligence, 1973, pp. 235-245.

[4] Minsky, Marvin, *Frames*, in (P. Winston, ed.) *Psychology of Computer Vision*, New York: McGraw Hill, 1975.

[5] Newell, A., *Production Systems: Models of Control Structures*, in (W. Chase, ed.), *Visual Information Processing*, New York: Academic Press, 1973.

[6] Teitelman, Warren, *INTERLISP Reference Manual*, XEROX PARC, Palo Alto, Ca., 1974.

[7] Winston, Patrick, *Learning Structural Descriptions from Examples*, MIT Project MAC, TR-231, September, 1970.

[8] Woods, W.A., and Makhoul, J., *Mechanical Inference Problems in Continuous Speech Understanding*, Third IJCAI, 1973, pp. 200-207.

Many hours of creative discussions were quite important. In particular, the author acknowledges C. Green, R. Waldinger, D. Shaw, and E. Sacerdoti. Computer time was generously provided by the Artificial Intelligence Center of SRI.

Appendix 1: A Typical Being

We consider INFO-OBTAINER, a Being which is independent of task domain. Below is listed, for each part, its abbreviated name (in bold), an English question that it might (try to) answer, and the stored program which should try to answer it (often a simple template or a constant). The percentages given indicate how many of the (ultimately 100) Beings in PUP6 actually used that part during the synthesis of one of the three target programs.

WHAT What do you do? Summarize your basic idea.   82%
   (OBTAIN SOME INFORMATION WHICH CAN BE USED)
WHY Justification? Summarize your motivation.   77%
   (PUP HAS NO MORE INFO THAT IT CAN USE TO PROGRESS)
HOW Global strategy? Summarize your method.   72%
   (OBTAIN NEW FACTS ABOUT OLD INFO, OR BRAND NEW INFO)
IDEN Do you recognize: "Find out more about frob gyrnation"?   (if I see either phrase:
   (INFO-OBTAINER any1) or (FIND OUT MORE ABOUT any1),
   then I return: (INFO-OBTAINER (TRANSLATE any1)))   54%
EXPLICIT-ARGS What argument(s) do you take? (U)   63%
EVAL-ARGS Which are quoted, not evaluated? NIL   4%
IMPLICIT-ARGS What local variables are needed? NIL 11%
WHEN When should you take control (justify your answer)?
   ((if T then add in -10 because
   (I AM EXPONENTIALLY-GROWING, GENERALLY UNDESIRABLE))   19%
   (if New-Info-List then add in (Plus 100 (Length New-Info-List))
   because (WE SHOULD WORK ON UNASSIMILATED NEW
   INFORMATION IF THERE IS ANY)))
REQUISITES What must you ensure is true just before
   (pre) and after (post) you go? NIL   10%
DEMONS What demons should you activate while you're
   in control? NIL   7%
META-CODE What happens when you are in control?   70%
   (DO (CHOOSE-FROM ((GET-NEW-INFORMATION U)
                    (TRANSLATE U)
                    (ANALYZE-IMPLICATIONS U)
                    (EXTRACT-RELEVANT-SUBSET U)))
   BECAUSE (WE CAN ONLY TRY TO OBTAIN USABLE
         INFO IN ONE WAY AT A TIME))
COMMENTS Do you have any special hints for filling
   in undefined subparts of this Being? NIL   16%
STRUCTURE Viewing this Being as a data structure,
   what can you do to it? NIL   4%
MAIN-EFFECTS Can you cause this goal to occur:
   "Usable information exists"?   27%
   ((to get (NEW INFORMATION any1) or to get
     (USABLE INFORMATION any1), do (INFO-OBTAINER any1)))
AFFECTS What other Beings might you call on directly?   14%
   ((CHOOSE-FROM is called)
   (call on some Being who can satisfy the goal:
     (AWARE USER (ABOUT TO OBTAIN USABLE INFO))
   (GET-NEW-INFORMATION possibly is called)
   (TRANSLATE possibly is called)
   (ANALYZE-IMPLICATIONS possibly is called)
   (EXTRACT-RELEVANT-SUBSET possibly is called))
GENERALIZATIONS What Beings are more general than
   you? (WRITE-PROGRAM SERVE-THE-USER)   27%
ALTERNATIVES What Beings are similar to you, to try
   in case you fail?   16%   (USE-INFORMATION, OPTIMIZE,
   FIX-INCORRECT-PIECE, and FILL-IN-UNDEFINED-SECTION)
ENCODABLE Any special constraints on what order
   the parts should be evalled in? NIL   9%
COMPLEXITY-VECTOR How costly are you?   92%
   (.5 .5 .9 .5 .1)

A vector of utility measures. The first component says that INFO-OBTAINER is of average difficulty to call. Next, there exists a .5 chance that some descendant will call it again. Next: this activity almost always succeeds. The time/space used in allowing this Being to try is typical. Finally, there is no good reason for inhibiting it ever. In general, each component can be a *program*, not just a constant. These weights, like the contents of all the parts of all the Beings initially in the experimental PUP6 system, were decided upon and inserted by hand.

Elements of a Plan-Based Theory of Speech Acts*

PHILIP R. COHEN

Bolt Beranek and Newman Inc.

AND

C. RAYMOND PERRAULT

University of Toronto

This paper explores the truism that people think about what they say. It proposes that, to satisfy their own goals, people often plan their speech acts to affect their listeners' beliefs, goals, and emotional states. Such language use can be modelled by viewing speech acts as operators in a planning system, thus allowing both physical and speech acts to be integrated into plans.

Methodological issues of how speech acts should be defined in a plan-based theory are illustrated by defining operators for requesting and informing. Plans containing those operators are presented and comparisons are drawn with Searle's formulation. The operators are shown to be inadequate since they cannot be composed to form questions (requests to inform) and multiparty requests (requests to request). By refining the operator definitions and by identifying some of the side effects of requesting, compositional adequacy is achieved. The solution leads to a metatheoretical principle for modelling speech acts as planning operators.

1. INTRODUCTION

The Sphinx once challenged a particularly tasty-looking student of language to solve the riddle: "How is saying 'My toe is turning blue,' as a request to get off my toe, similar to slamming a door in someone's face?" The poor student stammered that in both cases, when the agents are trying to communicate something, they have analogous intentions. "Yes indeed" countered the Sphinx, "but what are those intentions?" Hearing no reply, the monster promptly devoured the poor student and sat back smugly to wait for the next oral exam.

Contemporary philosophers have been girding up for the next trek to Giza. According to Grice (1957)[1], the slamming of a door communicates the slammer's anger only when the intended observer of that act realizes that the slammer wanted both to slam the door in his face and for the observer to believe that to be his intention. That is, the slammer intended the observer to recognize his intentions. Slamming caused by an accidental shove or by natural means is not a communicative act. Similarly, saying "My toe is turning blue" only communicates that the hearer is to get off the speaker's toe when the hearer has understood the speaker's intention to use that utterance to produce that effect.

Austin (1962) has claimed that speakers do not simply produce sentences that are true or false, but rather perform speech actions such as requests, assertions, suggestions, warnings, etc. Searle (1969) has adapted Grice's (1957) recognition of intention analysis to his effort to specify the necessary and sufficient conditions on the successful performance of speech acts. Though Searle's landmark work has led to a resurgence of interest in the study of the pragmatics of language, the intentional basis of communicative acts requires further elaboration and formalization; one must state for any communicative act, precisely which intentions are involved and on what basis a speaker expects and intends those intentions to be recognized.

The Sphinx demands a competence theory of speech act communication—a theory that formally models the possible intentions underlying speech acts. This paper presents the beginnings of such a theory by treating intentions as plans and by showing how plans can link speech acts with nonlinguistic behavior. In addition, an adequacy test for plan-based speech act theories is proposed and applied.

1.1 A Plan-based Theory of Speech Acts

Problem solving involves pursuing a goal state by performing a sequence of actions from an initial state. A human problem-solver can be regarded as "executing" a *plan* that prespecifies the sequence of actions to be taken. People can construct, execute, simulate, and debug plans, and in addition, can sometimes infer the plans of other agents from their behavior. Such plans often involve the communication of beliefs, desires and emotional states for the purpose of influencing the mental states and actions of others. Furthermore, when trying to communicate, people expect and want others to recognize their plans and may attempt to facilitate that recognition.

Formal descriptions of plans typically treat actions as *operators*, which are defined in terms of applicability conditions, called *preconditions, effects* that will be obtained when the corresponding actions are executed, and *bodies* that describe the means by which the effects are achieved. Since operators are repre-

*The research described herein was supported primarily by the National Research Council of Canada, and also by the National Institute of Education under Contract US-NIE-C-400-76-0116, the Department of Computer Science of the University of Toronto, and by a summer graduate student associateship (1975) to Cohen from the International Business Machines Corporation.

[1]See also (Strawson, 1964; Schiffer, 1972)

sentations, their preconditions, effects, and bodies are evaluated relative to the problem-solver's model of the world. We hypothesize that people maintain, as part of their models of the world, symbolic descriptions of the world models of other people. Our plan-based approach will regard speech acts as operators whose effects are primarily on the models that speakers and hearers maintain of each other.[2]

Any account of speech acts should answer questions such as:

—Under what circumstances can an observer believe that a speaker has sincerely and successfully performed a particular speech act in producing an utterance for a hearer? (The observer could also be the hearer or speaker.)

—What changes does the successful performance of a speech act make to the speaker's model of the hearer, and to the hearer's model of the speaker?

—How is the meaning (sense/reference) of an utterance x related to the acts that can be performed in uttering x?

To achieve these ends, a theory of speech acts based on plans should specify at least the following:

—A planning system: a formal language for describing states of the world, a language for describing operators, a set of plan construction inferences, a specification of legal plan structures. Semantics for the formal languages should also be given.

—Definitions of speech acts as operators in the planning system. What are their effects? When are they applicable? How can they be realized in words?

As an illustration of this approach, this paper presents a simple planning system, defines the speech acts of requesting and informing as operators within that system, and develops plans containing direct requests, informs and questions (which are requests to inform). We do not, however, discuss how those speech acts can be realized in words.

We argue that a plan-based theory, unlike other proposed theories of speech acts, provides formal adequacy criteria for speech act definitions: given an initial set of beliefs and goals, the speech act operator definitions and plan construction inferences should lead to the generation of plans for those speech acts that a person could issue appropriately under the same circumstances.[3] This adequacy criterion should be used in judging whether speech act definitions pass certain tests, in particular, the test of compositionality. For instance, since a speaker can request that a hearer do some arbitrary action, the operator definitions should show how a speaker can request a hearer to perform a speech act. Similarly, since one can inform a hearer that an action was done, the definitions should capture a speaker's informing a hearer that a speech act was performed. We show how a number of previous formulations of requesting and informing are

compositionally inadequate, and then develop definitions of informing that can be composed into questions.

Another goal of this research is to develop metatheoretical principles that state how to formulate speech act definitions to pass these adequacy tests. This paper proposes such a principle and shows how its application leads to compositionally adequate definitions for multiparty requests (as in "Ask Tom to open the door").

To simplify our problems in the early stages of theory construction, several restrictions on the communication situation that we are trying to model have been imposed:

—Any agent's model of another will be defined in terms of "facts" that the first believes the second believes, and goals that the first believes the second is attempting to achieve. We are not attempting to model obligations, feelings, etc.

—The only speech acts we try to model are requests, informs, and questions since they appear to be definable solely in terms of beliefs and goals. Requesting and informing are prototypical members of Searle's (1976) "directive" and "representative" classes, respectively, and are interesting since they have a wide range of syntactic realizations, and account for a large proportion of everyday utterances.

—We have limited ourselves to studying "instrumental dialogues"—conversations in which it is reasonable to assume that the utterances are planned and that the topic of discourse remains fixed. Typically, such dialogues arise in situations in which the conversants are cooperating to achieve some task-related goal (Deutsch, 1974), for example, the purchasing of some item. The value of studying such conversations relative to the structure of a task is that the conversants' plans can be more easily formalized.

1.2   A Competence Theory of Speech Acts

At least two interdependent aspects of a plan-based theory should be examined—the plans themselves, and the methods by which a person could construct or recognize those plans. This paper will be concerned with theories of the first aspect, which we shall term *competence* theories, analogous to competence theories of grammar (Chomsky, 1965). A plan-based competence theory of speech acts describes the *set of possible plans* underlying the use of particular kinds of speech acts, and thus states the conditions under which speech acts of those types are appropriate. Such descriptions are presented here in the form of a set of operator definitions (akin to grammatical "productions") and a specification of the ways in which plans are created from those operators.

The study of the second aspect aims for a *process* theory, which concerns *how* an ideal speaker/hearer chooses one (or perhaps more than one) plan out of the set of possible plans. Such a theory would characterize how a speaker decides what speech act to perform and how a hearer identifies what speech act was performed by recognizing the plan(s) in which that utterance was to play a part.

By separating out these two kinds of theoretical endeavors we are not claiming that one can study speech act competence totally divorced from issues of processing. On the contrary, we believe that for a (careful) speaker to issue a particular speech act appropriately, she must determine that the hearer's speech

---

[2]This approach was inspired by Bruce and Schmidt (1974) and Bruce (1975). This paper can be viewed as supplying methodological foundations for the analyses of speech acts and their patterned use that they present.

[3]Though this could perhaps be an empirical criterion, it will be used intuitively here.

describe language use in terms of a person's beliefs about the world. Accordingly, AGT1's model of AGT2 should be based on "believe" as described, for example, in Hintikka (1962; 1969). Various versions of the concept "know" can then be defined to be agreements between one person's beliefs and another's.

Our initial competence theory has been embodied in a computer program (Cohen, 1978) that can construct most of the plans presented here. Programs often point out weaknesses, inconsistencies, and incorrect assumptions in the statement of the competence theory, and can provide an operational base from which to propose process theories. However, we make no claims that computational models of plan construction and recognition are cognitive process theories; such claims would require empirical validation. Moreover, it is unclear whether there could be just one process theory of intentional behavior since each individual might use a different method. A more reasonable goal, then, is to construct computational models of speech act use for which one could argue that a person could employ such methods and converse successfully.

2.1 Belief

Apart from simply distinguishing AGT1's beliefs from his beliefs about AGT2's beliefs, AGT1's belief representation ought to allow him to represent the fact that AGT2 knows *whether* some proposition P is true, without AGT1's having to know which of P or ~ P it is that AGT2 believes. A belief representation should also distinguish between situations like the following:

1. AGT2 believes that the train leaves from gate 8.
2. AGT2 believes that the train has a departure gate.
3. AGT2 knows what the departure gate is for the train.

Thus, case 3 allows AGT1 to believe *that* AGT2 knows what the departure gate is without AGT1's actually knowing which gate AGT2 thinks that is. This distinction will be useful for the planning of questions and will be discussed further in section 6.

Following Hintikka (1969), belief is interpreted as a model operator A BELIEVE(P), where A is the believing agent, and P the believed proposition.[5] This allows for an elegant, albeit too strong, axiomatization and semantics for BELIEVE. We shall point out uses of various formal properties of BELIEVE as the need arises.

A natural question to ask is how many levels of belief embedding are needed by an agent capable of participating in a dialogue? Obviously, to be able to deal with a disagreement, AGT1 needs two levels (AGT1 BELIEVE and

[5]The following axiom schemata will be assumed:

B.1 $aBELIEVE$(all axioms of the predicate calculus)
B.2 $aBELIEVE(P) => aBELIEVE(aBELIEVE(P))$
B.3 $aBELIEVE(P)$ OR $aBELIEVE(Q) => aBELIEVE(P$ OR $Q)$
B.4 $aBELIEVE(P\&Q) <=>aBELIEVE(P)$ & $aBELIEVE(Q)$
B.5 $aBELIEVE(P) => \sim aBELIEVE(\sim P)$
B.6 $aBELIEVE(P => Q) => (aBELIEVE(P) => aBELIEVE(Q))$
B.7 $\exists x \, aBELIEVE(P(x)) => aBELIEVE(\exists x \, P(x))$
B.8 all agents believe that all agents believe B.1 to B.7

These axioms unfortunately characterize an idealized "believer" who can make all possible deductions from his beliefs, and doesn't maintain contradictory beliefs. However, we shall weaken the usual possible worlds semantics of BELIEVE in which the axioms are satisfied in a model consisting of a *universe* U, a subset A of U of *agents*, a set of *possible worlds* W, and *initial world* WO in W, a *relation* R on the cross-product $A \times W \times W$, and for each world w and predicate P, a subset Pw of U called the *extension* of P in w. The truth functional connectives *and*, *or*, *not*, and $=>$ have their usual interpretations in all possible worlds. $aBELIEVE(P)$ is true in world w if P is true in all worlds w1 such that R(a', w,w1), where a' is the interpretation of a in w. $\exists x \, P(x)$ is true in world w if there is some individual i in U such that P(x) is true in w when all free occurrences of x in P are interpreted as i.

---

act recognition process(es) will correctly classify her utterance. Thus, a competence theory would state the conditions under which a speaker can make that determination—conditions that involve the speaker's beliefs about the hearer's beliefs, goals, and inferential processes.

1.3 Outline of the Paper

The thread of the paper is the successive refinement of speech act definitions to meet the adequacy criteria. First, we introduce in sections 2 and 3 the tools needed to construct plans: the formal language for describing beliefs and goals, the form of operator definitions, and a set of plan construction inferences.

As background material, section 4 summarizes Austin's and Searle's accounts of speech acts. Then, Searle's definitions of the speech acts of requesting and informing are reformulated as planning operators in section 5 and plans linking those speech acts to beliefs and goals are given. These initial operator definitions are shown to be compositionally inadequate and hence are recast in section 6 to allow for the planning of questions. Section 7 shows how the definitions are again inadequate for modelling plans for composed requests. After both revising the preconditions of requests and identifying their side effects, compositional adequacy for multiparty requests is achieved. The solution leads to a metatheoretical "point of view" principle for use in formulating future speech act definitions within this planning system. Finally, section 8 discusses the limitations of the formalism and ways in which the approach might be extended to handle indirect speech acts.

2. ON MODELS OF OTHERS

In this section, we present criteria that an account of one agent's (AGT1) model of another's (AGT2's) beliefs and goals ought to satisfy.[4] A theory of speech acts need not be concerned with what is actually true in the real world; it should

[4]The representations used by Meehan (1976), and Schank and Abelson (1977) do not, in a principled way, maintain the distinctions mentioned here for belief or want.

operators in that plan. An operator will be regarded as transforming the planner's model of the world, the *propositions* that the planner believes, in correspondence with the changes to the real world made by the operator's associated action.[9] An operator is *applicable* to a model of the world in which that operator's *preconditions* hold. Operators can be defined in terms of others, as stated in their *bodies* (Sacerdoti, 1975). The changes that an operator makes to the world model in which it is evaluated to produce a new world model are called that operator's *effects*.

We shall view plans for an arbitrary agent S to be constructed using (at least) the following heuristic principles of purposeful behavior:

At the time of S's planning:

1. S should not introduce in the plan actions whose effects S believes are (or will be) true at the time the action is initiated.

2. If E is a goal, an operator A that achieves E can be inserted into the plan.

3. If an operator is not applicable in the planner's belief model, all the preconditions of that operator that are not already true can be added to the plan.

The previous two inferences reflect an agent's reasoning "in order to do this I must achieve that."

4. If the planner needs to know the truth-value of some proposition, and does not, the planner can create a goal that it know whether that proposition is true or false.

5. If the planner needs to know the value of some description before planning can continue, the planner can create a goal that it find out what the value is.

The previous two inferences imply that the planner does not have to create an entire plan before executing part of it.

6. Everyone expects everyone else to act this way.

Since agents can sometimes recognize the plans and goals of others, and can adopt others' goals (or their negations) as their own, those agents can plan to facilitate or block someone else's plans. Bruce and Newman (1978) and Carbonell (1978) discuss these issues at length.

The process of planning to achieve a goal is essentially a search through this space of inferences to find a temporal sequence of operators such that the first operator in the sequence is applicable in the planner's current world model and the last produces a world model in which the goal is true. A new world model is obtained by the execution of each operator.

3.1 The Form of Operators

Early approaches to problem-solving based on first order logic (Green, 1969; McCarthy & Hayes, 1969) have emphasized the construction of provably correct

[9]We are bypassing the fact that people need to observe the success or failure of their actions before being able to accurately update their beliefs. The formalism thus only deals with operators and models of the world rather than actions and the real world. Operators names will be capitalized while their corresponding actions will be referred to in lower case.

AGT1 BELIEVE AGT2 BELIEVE). If AGT1 successfully lied to AGT2, he would have to be able to believe some proposition P, while believing that AGT2 believes that AGT1 believes P is false (i.e., AGT1 BELIEVE AGT2 BELIEVE AGT1 BELIEVE (~ P)). Hence, AGT1 would need at least three levels. However, there does not seem to be any bound on the possible embeddings of BELIEVE. If AGT2 believes AGT1 has lied, he would need four levels. Furthermore, Lewis (1969) and Schiffer (1972) have shown the ubiquity of *mutual belief* in communication and face-to-face situations—a concept that requires an infinite conjunction of beliefs.[6] Cohen (1978) shows how a computer program that plans speech acts can represent beliefs about mutual beliefs finitely.

2.2 Want

Any representation of AGT2's goals (wants) must distinguish such information from: AGT2's beliefs, AGT1's beliefs and goals, and (recursively) from AGT2's model of someone else's beliefs and goals. The representation for WANT must also allow for different scopes of quantifiers. For example, it should distinguish between the readings of "AGT2 wants to take a train" as "There is a specific train that AGT2 wants to take." or as "AGT2 wants to take any train." Finally, it should allow arbitrary embeddings with BELIEVE. Wants of beliefs (as in "AGT1 WANTS AGT2 BELIEVE P") become the reasons for AGT1's telling P to AGT2, while beliefs of wants (i.e., AGT1 BELIEVES AGT1 WANTS P) will be the way to represent AGT1's goals P.[7] In modelling planning behavior, we are not concerned with goals that the agent does not think he has, nor are we concerned with the subtleties of "wish," "hope," "desire," and "intend" as these words are used in English. The formal semantics of WANT, however, are problematic.

3. MODELS OF PLANS

In most models of planning (e.g., Fikes & Nilsson, 1971; Newell & Simon, 1963), real world actions are represented by *operators* that are organized into plans.[8] To execute a plan, one performs the actions corresponding to the

[6]Lewis (1969) and Schiffer (1972) talk only about mutual or common knowledge, but the extension to mutual belief is obvious.

[7]This also allows a third place to vary quantifier scope, namely:

$$\exists x \; aBELIEVE \; aWANT \; P(x)$$
$$aBELIEVE \; \exists x \; aWANT \; P(x),$$
$$aBELIEVE \; aWANT \; \exists x P(x)$$

[8]One usually generalizes operators to *operator schemata* in correspondence with *types of* actions; operator instances are then formed by giving values to the parameters of an operator schema. Since only operator instances are contained in plans we will not distinguish between the operator schema and its instances unless necessary. The same schema/instance, type/token distinction applies as well to speech acts modelled as planning operators.

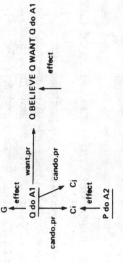

S BELIEVE S WANT:

Figure 1. A schematic of S's plan to achieve G.

This diagram illustrates the building block of plans—given goal G, S applies an inference of type 2 and selects operator A1, whose agent is Q as a producer of that effect. That operator is applicable when preconditions Ci and Cj hold and when agent Q wants to perform A1. Type 3 inferences allow each of the preconditions to be achieved by other actions (e.g., A2), which may be performed by another agent (e.g., P). This chaining of operators continues until all preconditions are satisfied. Plan diagrams are thus read from "top" to "bottom".

To indicate that this schematic is part of agent S's plan, the plan components are "embedded" in what S BELIEVE S WANTs. The truth or falsity of preconditions is evaluated with respect to S's beliefs. For example, verifying the WANT.PR of operator A1 (i.e., Q BELIEVE Q WANT Q do A1) would involve establishing that S BELIEVE Q BELIEVE Q WANT Q do A1. If Q is the same person as S (i.e., S is planning her own action A1) then this condition is trivially true since A1 is already part of S's plan, and since for all agents R, we assume that if R BELIEVE (P) then R BELIEVE R BELIEVE (P). However, if Q is not the same as S, the WANT.PR also needs to be achieved, leading, as we shall see, to S's planning a speech act.

4. SPEECH ACTS

4.1 Austin's Performatives

Austin (1962) notes a peculiar class of declarative utterances, which he termed *performatives*, that do not state facts but rather constitute the performance of an action. For instance saying, "I hereby suggest you leave" is an act of suggesting. Unlike the usual declaratives, such sentences are not true or false, but rather are subject to the same kinds of failures ("infelicities") as nonlinguistic actions—such as being applied in the wrong circumstances or being performed insincerely.

Generalizing further, Austin claims that in uttering any sentence, one performs three types of speech acts: the *locutionary*, *illocutionary*, and *perlocution-*

plans. Such approaches formalize the changes an action makes to the state of the world model by treating an operator as a predicate of one whose arguments is a *state variable*, which ranges over states of the world model. Unfortunately, to be able to reason about what is true in the world after an action is executed, one must give axiom schemata that describe which aspects of the state of the world are *not* changed by each operator. For instance, calling someone on the telephone does not change the height of the Eiffel Tower. This thorny "frame problem" (McCarthy & Hayes, 1969) occurs because individual states of the world are not related to one another *a priori*.

To overcome this problem, Fikes and Nilsson (1971) in their STRIPS planning system assume that all aspects of the world stay constant except as described by the operator's effects and logical entailments of those effects. Such an assumption is not formalized in the reasoning system, making it difficult to prove the correctness of the resulting plans. Nevertheless, it has become the standard assumption upon which to build problem-solvers. We too shall make it and thus shall describe an operator's effects by the propositions that are to be added to the model of the world.[10]

All operator schemata will have two kinds of preconditions—"cando" and "want" preconditions. The former, referred to as CANDO.PRs, indicate proposition schemata that, when instantiated with the parameter values of an operator instance, yield propositions that must be true in the world model for that operator instance to be applicable. We do not discuss how they can be proven true. The "want" precondition, henceforth WANT.PR, formalizes a principle of intentional behavior—the agent of an action has to want to do that action. The following example serves to illustrate the form of such definitions.

MOVE(AGT,SOURCE,DESTINATION)

CANDO.PR:	LOC(AGT,SOURCE)
WANT.PR:	AGT BELIEVE AGT WANT move-instance
EFFECT:	LOC(AGT, DESTINATION)

The parameters of an operator scheme are stated in the first line of the definitions and it is assumed that values of these parameters satisfy the appropriate selectional restrictions, (here, a person, and two locations, respectively). The WANT.PR uses a parameter "move-instance" that will be filled by any instance of the MOVE operator schema that is currently being planned, executed, or recognized. The CANDO.PR states that before an agent can move from the SOURCE location, he must be located there. The EFFECT of the MOVE indicates that the agent's new location is the DESTINATION.

S's plan to achieve goal G is pictured schematically in Figure 1 (P and Q are arbitrary agents, A1 and A2 are arbitrary actions). Instead of indicating the entire state of the planner's beliefs after each operator, those propositions that are effects of an operator and are preconditions of some other operator in the plan are presented.

[10]Those propositions that need to be deleted (or somehow made "invisible" in the *current* worldmodel) will not be discussed here.

ary acts. A speaker performs a *locutionary* act by making noises that are the uttering of words in language satisfying its vocabulary and grammar, and by the uttering of sentences with definite meaning (though perhaps having more than one). Such acts are used in the performance of *illocutionary acts* which are those acts performed *in* making utterances. For instance, stating, requesting, warning, ordering, apologizing, are claimed to be different types of illocutionary acts, each of which is said to have a unique *illocutionary force* that somehow characterizes the nature of the act. Each illocutionary act contains *propositional content* that specifies what is being requested, warned about, ordered, etc.

New distinctions, however, bring new problems. Frequently, when performative verbs are not used, the utterance's illocutionary force is not directly interpretable from its content. For example, to understand the force of the utterance ''The door,'' the hearer may need to use his beliefs that the door is currently closed, that the speaker has two arm-loads of groceries, and that he wants to be on the other side of the door in determining that the speaker has requested that the door be opened. Furthermore, a speaker may appear to be performing one illocutionary act, and actually may be trying to use it to do something else. Thus, ''We have to get up early tomorrow'' may simply be an assertion but when said at a party, may be intended as an excuse to the host for leaving, *and* may be intended as a request that the hearer leave. Such *indirect speech acts* (Gordon & Lakoff, 1971; Searle, 1975) are the touchstone of any theory of speech acts.

The last major kind of act identified by Austin is the *perlocutionary act*— the act performed *by* making an utterance. For instance, with the illocutionary act of asserting something, I may *convince* my audience of the truth of the corresponding proposition (or *insult* or *frighten* them). Perlocutionary acts produce *perlocutionary effects*: convincing produces belief and frightening produces fear. While a speaker often has performed illocutionary acts with the goal of achieving certain perlocutionary effects, the actual securing of those effects is beyond his control. Thus, it is entirely possible for a speaker to make an assertion, and for the audience to recognize the force of the utterance as an assertion and yet not be convinced.

4.2 Speech Acts à la Searle

Searle (1969) presents a formulation of the structure of illocutionary acts (henceforth referred to simply as speech acts) by suggesting a number of necessary and sufficient conditions on their successful performance. He goes on to state rules corresponding to these conditions, for a speaker's using any ''indicator of illocutionary force'' to perform a particular speech act.

As an example, let us consider Searle's conditions for a speaker S, in uttering T, to request that some hearer H do action A. The conditions are grouped as follows:

Normal Input/Output Conditions. These include such conditions as: H is not deaf and S is not mute, joking, or acting.

Propositional Content Conditions. Literal speech acts only use propositions of certain forms. The restrictions on these forms are stated in the *propositional content conditions*. For a request, the proposition must predicate a future act of H.

Preparatory Condition. A preparatory condition states what must be true in the world for a speaker to felicitously issue the speech act. For a request, the preparatory conditions include:

—H is able to do A.
—S believes H is able to do A.
—It is not obvious to S and H that H will do A in the normal course of events (the ''non-obviousness'' condition).

Searle claims the non-obviousness condition is not peculiar to illocutionary acts. This paper will support his claim by showing how the condition can be applied more generally to rational, intentional behavior.

Sincerity Condition. A *sincerity condition* distinguishes a sincere performance of the speech act from an insincere one. In the case of a request, S must want H to do A; for a promise, S must intend to do the promised action; for an assertion, S must believe what he is asserting.

Essential Condition. An *essential condition* specifies what S was trying to do. For a request, the act is an attempt to get H to do A.

Force Condition (our terminology). The purpose of the *force condition* is to require that the speaker utter a speech act only if he intends to communicate that he is performing that act. ''Intending to communicate'' involves having certain intentions regarding how the hearer will recognize the force of the utterance. The basic idea is that it is intended that the hearer recognize that the speaker is trying to bring about the satisfaction of the essential condition. For a request this amounts to the speaker's wanting the hearer to realize that the speaker intends for him to do A.

5. A FIRST REFORMULATION OF SEARLE'S CONDITIONS

Searle (1969) unfortunately does not supply justifications for the adequacy of his definitions for various kinds of speech acts. A primary goal of this paper is to show how a plan-based theory provides the basis for such adequacy criteria by allowing one to see clearly how changes in speech act definitions affect the plans that can be generated.

A second, more specific point of this formulation exercise is to show which of Searle's conditions are better regarded as pertaining to more general aspects of intentional behavior than to particular speech acts. In this spirit, we show how the sincerity condition, which we shall argue is a misnomer, and the propositional content and "non-obviousness" conditions arise during the course of act planning. Concerning the remaining conditions, we assume the "normal input/output conditions," but have chosen not to deal with the force condition until we have a better understanding of the plans for speech acts and how they can be recognized. The remaining conditions, the preparatory and essential conditions, will be mapped into the formalism as the preconditions and effects of speech act operators.

5.1 First Definition of REQUEST

Searle claims the preparatory conditions are required for the "happy" performance of the speech act—where "happy" is taken to be synonymous with Austin's use of "felicitous." Austin was careful to distinguish among infelicities, in particular, misapplications (performing the act in the wrong circumstances), and flaws (incorrectly performing the act). We take Searle's preparatory conditions as conditions guaranteeing applicability rather than successful performance, allowing them to be formalized as preconditions. Thus if an operator's preconditions are not satisfied when it is performed, then the operator was "misapplied." Before expressing preconditions in a formalism, a systematic "point of view" must be adopted. Since the applicability conditions affect the planning of that speech act, the preconditions are stated as conditions on the speaker's beliefs and goals. Correspondingly, the effects describe changes to the hearer's mental state.[11] We establish a *point-of-view principle*, that is intended to be a guideline for constructing speech act definitions in *this* planning system—namely: preconditions begin with "speaker believe" and effects with "hearer believe."

Let us consider Searle's preparatory conditions for a request: H is able to do ACT, and S believes H is able to do ACT. From our discussion of "belief," it should be clear what H can *in fact* do, i.e., what the real world is like is not essential to the success of a request. What may be relevant is that S and/or H thinks H can do ACT. To formalize "is able to do A," we propose a predicate CANDO (Q,ACT) that is true if the CANDO.PR's of ACT are true (with person Q bound to the agent role of ACT).[12]

The essential condition, which is modeled as the EFFECT of a REQUEST, is based on a separation of the illocutionary act from its perlocutionary effect. Speakers, we claim, cannot influence their hearers' beliefs and goals directly. The EFFECTs of REQUEST are modeled so that the hearer's actually wanting to do ACT is not essential to the successful completion of the speech act. Thus, the EFFECT is stated as the hearer's believing the speaker wants him to do the act. For important reasons, to be discussed in section 5.7, this formulation of the essential condition will prove to be a major stumbling block.

The operator REQUEST from SPEAKER to HEARER to do action ACT, which represents a literal request, can now be defined as:

REQUEST(SPEAKER,HEARER,ACT)

CANDO.PR: SPEAKER BELIEVE HEARER CANDO ACT
            AND
            SPEAKER BELIEVE
            HEARER BELIEVE HEARER CANDO ACT
WANT.PR: SPEAKER BELIEVE SPEAKER WANT request-instance
EFFECT: HEARER BELIEVE
            SPEAKER BELIEVE SPEAKER WANT ACT

5.2 Mediating Acts and Perlocutionary Effects

To bridge the gap between REQUESTs and the perlocutionary effect for which they are planned, a mediating step named CAUSE-TO-WANT is posited, that models what it takes to get someone to want to do something. Our current analysis of this "act" trivializes the process it is intended to model by proposing that to get someone to want to do something, one need only get that person to know that you want them to do it.

The definition of an agent's (AGT1) causing another agent (AGT) to want to do ACT is:

CAUSE-TO-WANT (AGT1,AGT,ACT)
CANDO.PR: AGT BELIEVE
            AGT1 BELIEVE AGT 1 WANT ACT
EFFECT: AGT BELIEVE AGT WANT ACT

The plan for a REQUEST is now straightforward. REQUEST supplies the necessary precondition for CAUSE-TO-WANT (as will other act combinations). When the WANT.PR of some action that the speaker is planning for someone else to perform, is not believed to be true, the speaker plans a REQUEST. For example, assume a situation in which there are two agents, SYSTEM[13](S) and JOHN, who are located inside a room (i.e., they are at location INROOM), and we wish the SYSTEM to plan a REQUEST of JOHN to leave the room by moving himself to location

---

[11] This does not violate our modelling just one person's view since a speaker, after having issued a speech act, will update his beliefs to include the effects of that speech act, which are defined in terms of the hearer's beliefs.

[12] This should be weakened to "... are true or are easily achievable"—i.e. if Q can plan to make them true.

[13] The agent who creates plans will often be referred to as "SYSTEM," which should be read as "planning system."

do the action being requested, independently of the request. If that were obvious to the speaker, the request would be pointless. However, as Searle noted, the non-obviousness condition applies more generally to rational, intentional behavior than to speech acts alone. In our formalism, it is the WANT.PR of the act being requested (goal "++" in Figure 2). If the planning system believed the WANT.PR were already true, i.e., if it believed that John already wanted to leave the room, then the plan would proceed no further; no REQUEST would take place.

Searle's "sincerity" condition, stated that the speaker had to want the requested act to be performed. The sincerity condition in the plan of Figure 2 is the goal labeled "+." The speaker's wanting the hearer to move is the reason for planning a REQUEST.

Notice also that the propositional content of the REQUEST, a future act to be performed by the hearer, is determined by prior planning—i.e., by a combination of that act's WANT.PR, the mediating act CAUSE-TO-WANT, and by the EFFECT of a REQUEST. Searle's propositional content condition thus seems to be a function of the essential condition (which is approximated by the EFFECTs of the speech act operator), as Searle claimed. So far, we have factored out those aspects of a request that Searle suggested were eliminable. Future revisions will depart more significantly.

5.4   Definition of INFORM

The speech act of informing is represented by the operator INFORM, which is defined as a speaker's stating a proposition to a hearer for the purpose of getting the hearer to believe that the speaker believes that proposition to be true. Such acts will usually be planned on the basis of wanting the hearer to believe that proposition. For a SPEAKER to INFORM a HEARER that proposition PROP is true, we have:

INFORM(SPEAKER, HEARER, PROP)

CANDO.PR:	SPEAKER BELIEVE PROP
WANT.PR:	SPEAKER BELIEVE
	SPEAKER WANT inform-instance
EFFECT:	HEARER BELIEVE
	SPEAKER BELIEVE PROP

The CANDO.PR simply states that the only applicability condition to INFORMing someone that proposition PROP is true is that the speaker believes PROP.[14] The EFFECT of an INFORM is to communicate what the speaker believes. This allows for the hearer to refuse to believe the proposition without

[14]Other preconditions to the INFORM act could be added—for instance, to talk to someone one must have a communication link (Schank & Abelson, 1977); which may require telephoning or going to that person's location, etc. However, such preconditions would apply to any speech act, and hence probably belong on the locutionary act of making noises to someone.

OUTROOM, the plan would be as in Figure 2. Notice that the WANT.PR of the REQUEST itself, namely

        S BELIEVE
        S WANT
               REQUEST(S,JOHN,MOVE(JOHN,INROOM,OUTROOM))

is trivially true since that particular REQUEST is already part of S's plan. The CANDO.PR's of the REQUEST are true if S believes JOHN is located INROOM and if it believes JOHN thinks so too. Thus, once the planner chooses someone else, say H, to do some action that it believes H does not yet want to do, a directive act (REQUEST) may be planned.

5.3   Comparison with Searle's Conditions for a REQUEST

Searle's "non-obviousness" condition for the successful performance of a request stated that it should not be obvious to the speaker that the hearer is about to

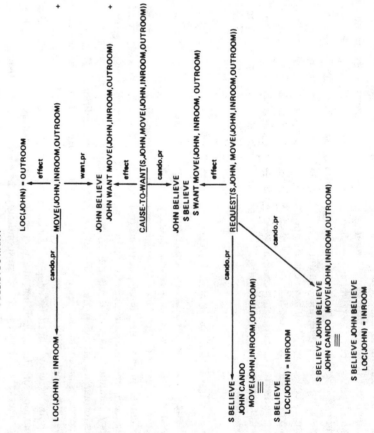

Figure 2.   A plan for a REQUEST.

invalidating the speaker's action as an INFORM. Therefore, an intermediate "act," termed CONVINCE, is necessary to get the hearer to believe the proposition.

For a person AGT 1 to CONVINCE another person AGT that proposition PROP is true, we define:

```
CONVINCE(AGT1, AGT, PROP)
CANDO.PR:     AGT BELIEVE
              AGT1 BELIEVE PROP

EFFECT:       AGT BELIEVE PROP
```

This operator says that for AGT 1 to convince AGT of the truth of PROP AGT need only believe that AGT1 thinks PROP is true. Though this may be a necessary prerequisite to getting someone to believe something, it is clearly not sufficient. For a more sophisticated precondition of CONVINCE, one might state that before AGT will be convinced, she needs to know the justifications for AGT1's belief, which may require that AGT believe (or be CONVINCE of) the justifications for believing those justifications, etc. Such a chain of reasons for believing might be terminated by mutual beliefs that people are expected to have or by a belief AGT believes AGT1 already has. Ideally, a good model of CONVINCE would allow one to plan persuasive arguments.[15]

5.5 Planning INFORM Speech Acts

The planning of INFORM speech acts now becomes a simple matter. For any proposition PROP, S's plan to achieve the goal H BELIEVE PROP would be that of Figure 3. Notice that it is unnecessary to state as a precondition to inform, that the hearer H does not already believe PROP. Again, this non-obviousness condition that can be eliminated by viewing speech acts in a planning context.

What would be Searle's sincerity condition for the INFORM above (S BELIEVE PROP) turns out to be a precondition for the speech act rather than a reason for planning the act as we had for REQUEST's sincerity condition, (i.e., SPEAKER BELIEVE SPEAKER WANT HEARER do ACT). If we were to use REQUEST as a model, the sincerity condition for an INFORM would be SPEAKER BELIEVE SPEAKER WANT HEARER BELIEVE PROP. One may then question whether Searle's sincerity condition is a consistent naming of distinctive features of various kinds of speech acts. Insincerity is a matter of falsely claiming to be in a psychological state, which for this model is either belief or want. By this definition, both conditions, SPEAKER BELIEVE PROP

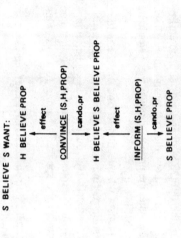

Figure 3. A plan for an INFORM.

and SPEAKER BELIEVE SPEAKER WANT HEARER BELIEVE PROP, are subject to insincerity.

5.6 Planning an INFORM of a WANT

As stated earlier, there are other ways to satisfy the precondition to CAUSE-TO-WANT. Since REQUEST was taken as a prototypical directive act, all members of that class share the same EFFECT (Searle's (1976) "illocutionary point"). However, issuing an INFORM of a WANT, as in "I want you to do X," also achieves it. Another plan to get John to move appears in Figure 4.

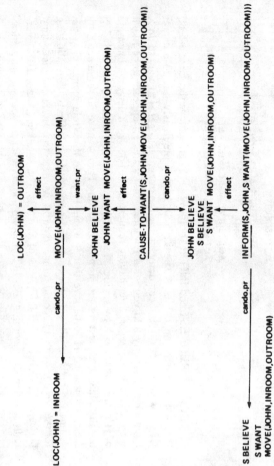

Figure 4. A plan for an INFORM of a WANT.

[15] Without a specification of the justifications for a belief, this operator allows one to become convinced of the truth of one's own lie. That is, after speaker S lies to hearer H that P is true, and receives H's acknowledgment indicating H has been convinced, S can decide to believe P because he thinks H thinks so. Further research needs to be done on CONVINCE and BELIEVE to eliminate such bizarre behavior.

The initial stages of this plan are identical to that of Figure 2 through the CANDO.PR of CAUSE-TO-WANT. This precondition is achieved by an INFORM whose propositional content is S WANT MOVE (JOHN, INROOM, OUTROOM). In this instance, the planning system does not need to proceed through CONVINCE since an INFORM of a WANT produces the necessary effects. Testing the CANDO.PR of INFORM determines if the system believes this proposition, which it does since the MOVE by John is already one of its goals. The WANT.PR of INFORM is trivially true, as before, and thus the plan is complete.

5.7 REQUEST vs. INFORM of WANT

Searle claimed that the conditions he provided were necessary and jointly sufficient for the successful and nondefective performance of various illocutionary acts. Any behavior satisfying such a set of conditions was then said to be a particular illocutionary act. Thus, if two utterances have the same illocutionary force, they should be equivalent in terms of the conditions on their use. We believe that the two utterances "please open the door" and "I want you to open the door (please)" can have the same force as directives, differing only in their politeness. That is, they both can be planned for the same reasons. However, our treatment does not equate the literal speech acts that could realize them when they should be equated. The condition on REQUEST that distinguishes the two cases is the precondition SPEAKER BELIEVE HEARER BELIEVE HEARER CANDO ACT. Since there is no corresponding precondition in the plan for the INFORM of a WANT, there is no reason to check the hearer's beliefs.

In order to force an equivalence between a REQUEST and an INFORM of a WANT, various actions need to be redefined. We shall remove the above condition as a CANDO.PR from REQUEST and add it as a new CANDO.PR to CAUSE-TO-WANT. In other words, the new definition of CAUSE-TO-WANT would say that you can get a person to decide to want to do some action if she believes you want her to do it and if she believes she can do it. With these changes, both ways of getting someone to want to do some action would involve her believing she is able to do it. More formally, we now define:

REQUEST (SPEAKER, HEARER, ACT)

CANDO.PR:	SPEAKER BELIEVE HEARER CANDO ACT
WANT.PR:	SPEAKER BELIEVE SPEAKER WANT request-instance
EFFECT:	HEARER BELIEVE
	SPEAKER BELIEVE SPEAKER WANT ACT

and

CAUSE-TO-WANT (AGT1, AGT, ACT)

CANDO.PR:	AGT BELIEVE
	AGT1 BELIEVE AGT1 WANT ACT
	AND
	AGT BELIEVE AGT CANDO ACT
EFFECT:	AGT BELIEVE AGT WANT ACT

Though REQUEST and INFORM of a WANT can achieve the same effect, they are not interchangeable. A speaker (S), having previously said to a hearer (H) "I want you to do X," can deny having the intention to get H to want to do X by saying "I simply told you what I wanted, that's all." It appears to be much more difficult, however, after having requested H to do X, to deny the intention of H's wanting to do X by saying "I simply requested you to do X, that's all." S usually plans a request for the purpose of getting H to want to do some act X by means of getting H to believe that S wants H to do it. While maintaining the distinction between illocutionary acts and perlocutionary effects, thus allowing for the possibility that H could refuse to do X, we need to capture this distinction between REQUEST and INFORM of WANT. The solution (Allen, 1979; Perrault & Allen, forthcoming) lies in formulating speech act bodies as plans achieving the perlocutionary effect—plans that a hearer is intended to recognize.

In the next two sections, we investigate the compositional adequacy of these operator definitions via the planning of REQUESTs that a hearer perform REQUEST or INFORM speech acts.

6. COMPOSITIONAL ADEQUACY: QUESTIONS

We are in agreement with many others, in proposing that questions be treated as requests for information. In terms of speech act operators, the questioner is performing a REQUEST that the hearer perform an INFORM. That is, the REQUEST leads to the satisfaction of INFORM's "want precondition." However, for a wh-question, the INFORM operator as defined earlier cannot be used since the questioner does not know the full proposition of which he is to be informed. If he did know what the proposition was there would be no need to ask; he need only decide to believe it.

Intuitively, one plans a wh-question to find out the value of some expression and a yes/no question to find out whether some proposition is true. Such questions are planned, respectively, on the basis of believing that the hearer knows what the value of that expression is or that the hearer knows whether the proposition is true, without the speaker's having to know what the hearer believes.

Earlier we stated that a person's (AGT1) belief representation should represent cases like the following distinctly:

1. AGT2 believes the Cannonball Express departs at 8 p.m.
2. AGT2 believes the Cannonball Express has a departure time.
3. AGT2 knows what the departure time for the Cannonball Express is.

Case 1 can be represented by a proposition that contains no variables. Case 2 can be represented by a belief of a quantified proposition—i.e.,

AGT2 BELIEVE

∃x (the y : DEPARTURE-TIME(CANNONBALL-EXPRESS,y)) = x

However, Case 3 can be approximated by a *quantified belief*, namely,

AGT2 BELIEVE

(the y : DEPARTURE-TIME(CANNONBALL-EXPRESS,y)) = x),

where "the y : P(y)," often written "iy P(y)," is the logical description operator read "the y which is P." This formula is best paraphrased as "there is something which AGT2 believes to be the departure time for the Cannonball Express."[16] Typical circumstances in which AGT1 might acquire such quantified beliefs are by understanding a definite description uttered by AGT2 referentially (Donnellan, 1966). Thus, if AGT2 says "the pilot of TWA 461 on July 4," AGT1 might infer that AGT2 knows who that pilot is.

Quantified beliefs often become goals when a planner needs to know the values of the parameters of an operator and when these parameters occur in that operator's preconditions.[17] We show how, when a quantified belief is a goal for AGT, AGT can plan a wh-question.

6.1 Planning Wh-Questions

First, a new operator, INFORMREF, and its associated mediating act CONVINCEREF, are needed.[18]

INFORMREF(SPEAKER,HEARER, λxDx) (i.e., D is a predicate of one argument)

CANDO.PR: ∃y SPEAKER BELIEVE (ixDx) = y
WANT.PR: SPEAKER BELIEVE SPEAKER WANT informref-instance
EFFECT: ∃y HEARER BELIEVE SPEAKER BELIEVE (ixDx) = y

Thus, before a speaker will inform a hearer of the value of some description, there must be some individual that the speaker believes is the value of the description, and the speaker must want to say what it is. The effect of performing this act is that there is then some individual that the hearer thinks the speaker believes to be the value of the description. As usual, we need a mediating act to model the hearer's then believing that individual to be the value of the description. To this end, we define AGT1's convincing AGT of the referent of the description as:

CONVINCEREF(AGT1,AGT, λxDx)

CANDO.PR: ∃y AGT BELIEVE AGT1 BELIEVE (ixDx) = y
EFFECT: ∃y AGT BELIEVE (ixDx) = y

Using these operators, if the planning system wants to know where Mary is and believes that Joe knows where she is, it can create the plan underlying the question "Where is Mary?" as is shown in Figure 5. After the system plans for Joe to tell it Mary's location, on the basis of believing that he knows where she is, it must get Joe to want to perform this act. In the usual fashion, this leads to a REQUEST and hence the construction of a question. The precondition to

S BELIEVE S WANT:

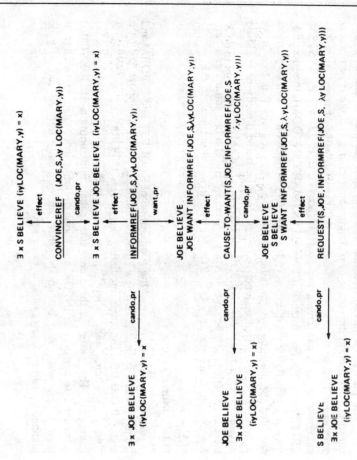

Figure 5. A plan for a wh-question.

[16] Another conjunction can be added to the representation of (3) as suggested by Allen (1979) to refine our representations of "AGT2's knowing what the value of the description is," namely:

∃x [(the y: D(y) = x & AGT2 BELIEVE ((the y: D(y)) = x)]

We shall, however, use the simpler quantified belief formulation.

[17] We would prefer to formalize declaratively that "the agent of an action must know the values of the parameters of the action." One way of doing this is suggested by Moore (1979).

[18] In Cohen (1978) we achieved the same effect by parameterizing INFORM and CONVINCE so that different sets of preconditions and effects were used if the original goal was a quantified belief. In addition, Cohen (1978) did not use descriptions. We believe the formulation that follows, due to J. Allen, is clearer. The actual names for these acts were suggested by W. Woods.

CAUSE-TO-WANT, namely, JOE BELIEVE JOE BELIEVE JOE CANDO the INFORMREF is actually:

$$\text{JOE BELIEVE}$$
$$\exists y \text{ JOE BELIEVE}$$
$$ixLOC(MARY,x) = y$$

which is implied by

$$\exists y \text{ JOE BELIEVE } ixLOC(MARY,x) = y$$

that was asserted, for this example, to be one of the planning system's beliefs. Notice, that the planning of this question depends upon the system's having chosen Joe to tell the answer, and upon its having chosen itself to get Joe to want to perform the INFORM. Section 7 discusses what happens when different decisions are made.

6.2 Plans for Yes/No Questions

To plan a yes/no question about some proposition P, one should think that the hearer knows whether P is true or false (or, at least "might know"). An approximate representation of AGT2's knowing whether P is true or false is OR (AGT2 BELIEVE P, AGT2 BELIEVE ~ P).[19] Such goals are often created, as modelled by our type 4 inference, when a planner does not know the truth-value of P. Typical circumstances in which an agent may acquire such disjunctive beliefs about another are telephone conversations, in which AGT1 believes that there are certain objects in AGT2's view. AGT1 then probably believes that AGT2 knows whether certain visually derivable (or easily computable) properties of those objects are true, such as whether object A is on top of object B.

To accommodate yes/no questions into the planning system, a third INFORM, called INFORMIF, and its associated mediating act CONVINCEIF are defined as follows:

INFORMIF(SPEAKER,HEARER,P)

CANDO.PR: OR(SPEAKER BELIEVE P, SPEAKER BELIEVE ~ P)

EFFECT: OR(HEARER BELIEVE SPEAKER BELIEVE P,
         HEARER BELIEVE SPEAKER BELIEVE ~ P)

WANT.PR: SPEAKER BELIEVE SPEAKER WANT informif-instance

CONVINCEIF(AGT,AGT1,P)

CANDO.PR: OR(AGT BELIEVE AGT1 BELIEVE P,
         AGT BELIEVE AGT1 BELIEVE ~ P)

EFFECT: OR(AGT BELIEVE P, AGT BELIEVE ~ P)

[19] Allen (1979) also points out that another conjunct can be added to the representation of "knowing whether" as a disjunctive belief, to obtain (P & AGT2 BELIEVE (P)) OR (~ P & AGT2 BELIEVE (~ P)).

The plan for a yes/no question to Joe is now parallel to that of a wh-question.[20] That is, in the course of planning some other act, if the system wants proposition P to be true or to be false, and if the truth-value of proposition P is unknown to it, it can create the goal OR(SYSTEM BELIEVE P, SYSTEM BELIEVE ~ P). For instance if P were LOC(MARY,INROOM), the illocutionary acts underlying the question to Joe "Is Mary in the room?" can be planned provided the planning system believes that Joe either believes P is true or he believes P is false. That disjunctive belief could be stated directly or could be inferred from a belief like ∃y JOE BELIEVE(ixLOC(MARY,x)) = y—i.e., there is something Joe believes is Mary's location. But if it had some idea where Joe thought Mary was, say OUTROOM, then it would not need to ask.

6.3 Summary

A plan for a question required the composition of REQUEST and INFORM and led to the development of two new kinds of informing speech acts, INFORMREF and INFORMIF, and their mediating acts. The INFORMREF acts lead to "what," "when," and "where" questions while INFORMIF results in a yes/no question.[21] The reason for these new acts is that, in planning a REQUEST that someone else perform an INFORM act, one only has incomplete knowledge of their beliefs and goals; but an INFORM, as originally defined can only be planned when one knows what is to be said.

7. COMPOSITIONAL ADEQUACY AND THE POINT OF VIEW PRINCIPLE

Earlier, a guiding "Point of View Principle" (POVP) for defining speech acts as planning operators was proposed: the preconditions of the operator should be stated from the speaker's point of view, i.e., in terms of the speaker beliefs; the effects should be stated from the hearer's point of view. We now wish to judge the adequacy of speech act definitions formulated along these lines. The test case

[20] Searle (1969) suggested there were different speech acts for real and teacher-student (or exam) questions, where in the latter case, the questioner just wants to know what the student thinks is the answer. Since teacher-student questions seem to have similar conditions on their appropriateness as real questions, save the questioner's intention to be convinced, we have good reason for factoring the mediating acts out of each of the three INFORM act types. This leaves the INFORM acts neutral with respect to what kind of question they are contained in. In general, if the perlocutionary effects of an INFORM were incorporated into the act's definition, then we would need two new primitive teacher-student question speech acts. For now, we opt for the former.

[21] The language for stating operators needs to be extended to account for "which," "how," and "why" questions. For instance, "why" and "how" questions involve quantifying over actions and/or plans.

will be the composing of REQUESTs, i.e., the planning of a REQUEST that some third party himself perform a REQUEST. For instance, the utterance ''Ask Tom to tell you where the key is'' is an example of such a third party request.

The current definitions of speech acts will be shown to be compositionally inadequate since they force speakers to have unnecessary knowledge about intermediaries' beliefs. Achieving compositional adequacy, however, requires more than a simple restatement of the point of view principle; the side effects of speech act operators also must be considered.

Our scrutiny will be focused upon the seemingly innocent precondition to REQUEST, SPEAKER BELIEVER HEARER CANDO ACT whose form depended on the POVP. The goal is to show how the POVP leads us astray and how a formulation of that precondition according to a new POVP that suggests a more neutral point of view for speech act definitions sets us back on course. From here on, the two versions of the precondition will be referred to as the ''speaker-based'' and ''neutral'' versions.

7.1 Plans for Multiparty Speech Acts

Multiparty speech acts can arise in conversations where communication is somehow restricted so as to pass through intermediaries.[22] The planning system, since it is recursive, can generate plans for such speech acts using any number of intermediaries provided that appropriate decisions are made as to who will perform what action.

Let us suppose that the planning system wants to know where a particular key is and that it must communicate through John. We shall use the speaker-based precondition on REQUEST for this example, and for readability, the following abbreviations:

SYSTEM—S	TOM—T	JOHN—J
BELIEVE—B	WANT—W	LOC(KEY23,y)—D(y)

Figure 6 shows the plan for the specific three-party speech act underlying ''Ask Tom to tell me where the key is.''

S develops the plan in the following fashion: T is chosen to tell S the key's location since, we shall assume, he is believed to know where it is. Since T is not believed to already want to tell, and since S cannot communicate directly with T (but T can communicate with S), J is chosen to be the one to talk T into telling. Since J is not believed to already want to do that, S plans a REQUEST that J perform a REQUEST, namely REQUEST(S,J,REQUEST (J,T,INFORMREF (T,S,λyLOC (KEY23,y)))). J, then, is an intermediary who is just expected to do what he is asked; his status will be discussed soon.

[22]For instance, in the Stanford Research Institute Computer-based Consultant research (Deutsch, 1974) communication between an expert and an apprentice was constrained in this way. The apprentice typically issued such speech acts, while the expert did not.

The preconditions that need to be satisfied in this plan are:

S BELIEVE:

(P1) $\exists y$ T BELIEVE $[\iota x \iota LOC(KEY23,x)=y]$
(P2) T BELIEVE (P1) (implied by P1)
(P3) J BELIEVE (P1)
(P4) J BELIEVE J BELIEVE (P1) (implied by P1)
(P5) S BELIEVE J BELIEVE (P1) (implied by P3)

S BELIEVE S WANT:

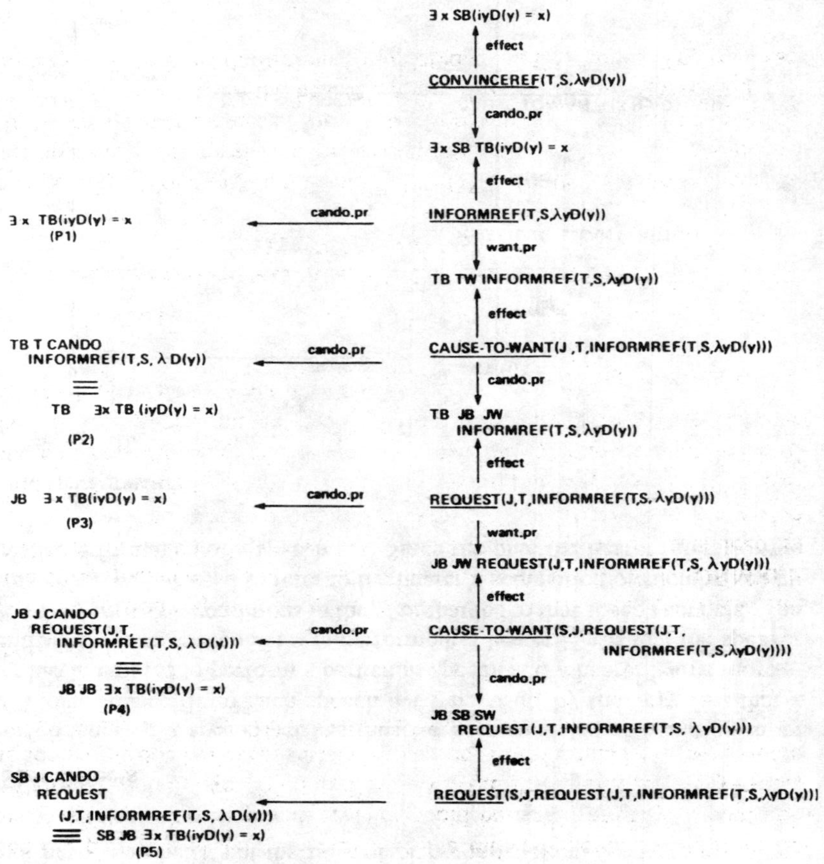

$\exists x$ SB(ιyD(y) = x)
   ↑ effect
CONVINCEREF(T,S,λyD(y))
   ↑ cando.pr
$\exists x$ SB TB(ιyD(y) = x
   ↑ effect
INFORMREF(T,S,λyD(y))
   ↑ want.pr
TB TW INFORMREF(T,S,λyD(y))
   ↑ effect
CAUSE-TO-WANT(J,T,INFORMREF(T,S,λyD(y)))
   ↑ cando.pr
TB JB JW INFORMREF(T,S,λyD(y))
   ↑ effect
REQUEST(J,T,INFORMREF(T,S,λyD(y)))
   ↑ want.pr
JB JW REQUEST(J,T,INFORMREF(T,S,λyD(y))
   ↑ effect
CAUSE-TO-WANT(S,J,REQUEST(J,T,INFORMREF(T,S,λyD(y))))
   ↑ cando.pr
JB SB SW REQUEST (J,T,INFORMREF(T,S, λyD(y)))
   ↑ effect
REQUEST(S,J,REQUEST(J,T,INFORMREF(T,S,λyD(y)))

$\exists x$ TB(ιyD(y) = x)   (P1)   —cando.pr→

TB T CANDO INFORMREF(T,S, λ D(y))   ≡   TB $\exists x$ TB (ιyD(y) = x)   (P2)

$\exists x$ TB(ιyD(y) = x)   (P3)   —cando.pr→

JB J CANDO REQUEST(J,T, INFORMREF(T,S, λ D(y)))   ≡   JB JB $\exists x$ TB(ιyD(y) = x)   (P4)

SB J CANDO REQUEST (J,T,INFORMREF(T,S, λ D(y)))   ≡   SB JB $\exists x$ TB(ιyD(y) = x)   (P5)

Figure 6. A plan for a third party REQUEST.

While the plan appears to be straightforward, precondition P3 is clearly unnecessary—S ought to be able to plan this particular speech act without having any *prior* knowledge of the intermediary's beliefs. This prior knowledge requirement comes about because precondition P5 is constructed by composing

REQUEST's precondition schema with precondition P3, and P3 is similarly constructed from P1.

The problem can be eliminated by reformulating REQUEST's precondition as HEARER CANDO ACT. Consider a general plan for three-party REQUESTs, as in Figure 7. T's INFORMREF has been generalized to "ACT(T)" whose precondition is "P."

Conditions P3 and P5 are the same as P1, and thus the preconditions to the REQUESTs in the plan, are independent of the speaker's beliefs; they depend only on *the planner's* beliefs. While the use of the neutral precondition eliminates prior knowledge requirements for REQUESTs *per se*, condition P4 still requires, as a precondition to CAUSE-TO-WANT, that the planner have some knowledge of the intermediary's beliefs. The next section shows why the planner need not have such beliefs at the time of plan construction.

7.2 Side Effects

The performance of a speech act has thus far been modeled as resulting in an EFFECT that is specific to each speech act type. But, by the very fact that a speaker has attempted to perform a particular speech act, a hearer learns more—on identifying which speech act was performed, a hearer learns that the speaker believed the various preconditions in the *plan* that led to that speech act held. The term *side effect* will be used to refer to the hearer's acquisition of such beliefs by way of the performance of a speech act. Since the plan the hearer infers for the

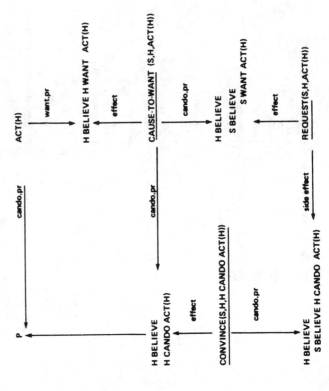

Figure 8. A REQUEST with side effects.

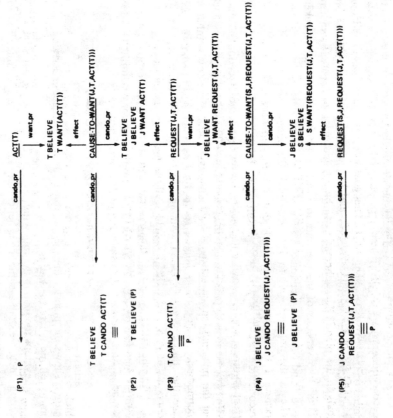

Figure 7. A third party REQUEST using the "neutral" precondition.

The preconditions that have to be satisfied in S's plan are:

S BELIEVE:

(P1) P (also P3 and P5)
(P2) T BELIEVE (P)
(P4) J BELIEVE (P)

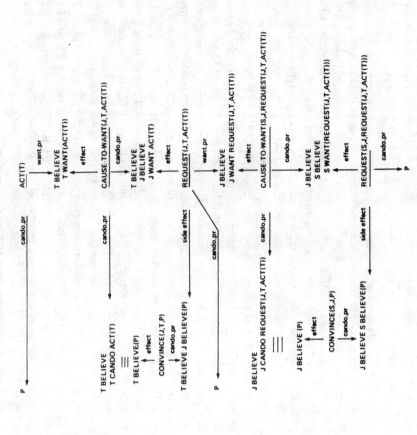

Figure 9.   A third party REQUEST using the "neutral" precondition and side effects.

speaker depends upon his beliefs about the speaker's beliefs and goals, the side effects of a speech act cannot be specified in advance. However, the hearer is minimally entitled to believe the speaker thought her speech act's preconditions held (Bruce, 1975; Bruce & Schmidt, 1974).[23] Furthermore, not only do hearers make such assumptions about speakers' beliefs, but speakers know that and often depend on those assumptions for the success of their plans. Figure 8 is a schematic of a simple plan by S to REQUEST H to do action ACT that illustrates this situation.

The minimal side effect is that the hearer believes the speaker believes the precondition of the REQUEST holds, i.e., that HEARER BELIEVE SPEAKER BELIEVE HEARER CANDO ACT. This goal satisfies, via a CONVINCE, the CANDO.PR of CAUSE-TO-WANT, and hence the REQUEST achieves two goals in the plan.[24] The schematic can be applied twice in Figure 7 to obtain Figure 9.

After the side effects of J's REQUEST to T take hold, T would think J believes the preconditions to J's REQUEST (P) obtain. We claim that it is because T thinks that J believes P that T comes to believe P. In this way, precondition (P2) is satisfied as a result of J's REQUEST. Naturally, the side effect argument applies equally to J as the hearer of S's REQUEST. That is, J comes to believe P (precondition (P4)) because he thinks S believes P. S's belief that the preconditions to action A hold thus gets "passed" down the line of intermediaries, whatever its length, to the final agent of A. In this way S can issue the third party REQUEST without having any prior knowledge of J's beliefs about P; S's REQUEST provides all the necessary information!

An interesting aspect of this transmission is that, while J may come to believe P and, by making a REQUEST to T, transmit this belief, T's belief that P may be of little use to T. Consider Figure 9 again. Suppose P were

$$\exists y \ T \ BELIEVE \ (ixLOC(KEY23,x)) = y$$

which we are loosely paraphrasing as T knows where the key is. S's REQUEST conveys S's belief that T knows where the key is. Though J, to decide to perform his REQUEST, need only think that T knows where the key is, T actually has to know where it is before he can do A.[25] J's conveying his belief does no good

[23]The hearer may in fact believe those preconditions are false.

[24]The simple backward-chaining planning algorithm described in Cohen (1978) could not easily construct this plan since it ignores intermediate states of the world model that would be created after each operator's execution (i.e., after S's, and J's, REQUESTs).

[25]T cannot obtain that information from believing P since

$$\exists y \ T \ BELIEVE \ \exists y \ T \ BELIEVE \ ixLOC(KEY23,x) = y \ \text{cannot be inferred from}$$
$$T \ BELIEVE \ \exists y \ T \ BELIEVE \ ixLOC(KEY23,x) = y, \ \text{by B.2 and B.7 (footnote 5).}$$

since he has supplied information for a CONVINCE, but T needs information sufficient for a CONVINCEWH. A planning system has to be able to realize this and to plan, by making the same choices as before, the additional REQUEST that John perform an INFORM, e.g., "Tell Tom that the key is in the closet."[26]

7.3   A New Point-of-View Principle

In addition to considering side effects for speech acts, we are led to propose a new point-of-view principle:

The "Cando" preconditions and effects of speech acts should be defined in a way that does not depend on who the speaker of that speech act is. That is, no CANDO.OR or EFFECT should be stated as a proposition beginning with "SPEAKER BELIEVE."

[26]The side effects again figure in this additional three-party REQUEST—John comes to believe that the key is in the closet by believing that S thinks so.

If CONVINCE can be defined so that AGT1 cannot be convinced by AGT2 that AGT1 believes something, then J could not CONVINCE T that $\exists y \ T \ BELIEVE \ ixLOC(KEY23,x) = y$ on the basis of T's thinking that J believes it.

The CANDO.PRs of speech acts defined according to this principle not only resolve our difficulties with composite speech acts, but they also behave as desired for the usual noncomposite cases since preconditions now depend only on the *planner's* beliefs, and the planner is often the speaker. Thus speech act operator definitions are intimately bound to the form of the planning system.

The only result the new principle has on the form of the EFFECTs of speech acts is to make clear whose beliefs should be updated with those EFFECTs. After successfully executing a speech act to H, the speaker can update his model of H with the speech act's EFFECTs. But, for a composite speech act *ultimately* directed to H, the initial planner must observe or assume the success of the rest of the multiparty plan in order to conclude that the EFFECTs of the final speech act to H hold.

While the new principle guarantees that the EFFECTs of speech acts are independent of the use of intermediaries, hearers have every right to believe that the speakers of those speech acts believe that the preconditions hold. Because side effects are stated in terms of the hearer's beliefs about the speaker's beliefs, intermediaries are vulnerable to a charge of insincerity if they brazenly execute the speech acts they were requested to perform. It is to avoid such a charge, and thus make intermediaries "responsible for" the speech acts they execute, that we place the condition on CAUSE-TO-WANT stating that AGT BELIEVE AGT CANDO ACT.

Finally, to complete the reexamination of speech act definitions we point out that the WANT.PR also has a SPEAKER BELIEVE on it. One cannot, in the spirit of "housecleaning," remove the SPEAKER BELIEVE SPEAKER WANT from the WANT.PR of speech acts since a speaker's goal cannot be characterized independently of the speaker's beliefs, unless one is willing to model someone's "unconscious" goals. We are not.[27]

7.4 New Definitions of REQUEST and INFORM

Using this principle, REQUEST is redefined as:

REQUEST(SPEAKER,HEARER,ACT)

CANDO.PR:	HEARER CANDO ACT
WANT.PR:	SPEAKER BELIEVE
	SPEAKER WANT request-instance
EFFECT:	HEARER BELIEVE
	SPEAKER BELIEVE SPEAKER WANT ACT

The principle applied to the definition of the operator INFORM results in a CANDO.PR stated as PROP rather than as SPEAKER BELIEVE PROP.[28] Such a change allows one to plan to request an intermediary, say a child, to tell

someone else that the key is in the closet without the planner's having to believe, at the time of planning, that the child thinks so. The new definition of INFORM then becomes:

INFORM(SPEAKER,HEARER,PROP)

CANDO.PR:	PROP
WANT.PR:	SPEAKER BELIEVE
	SPEAKER WANT inform-instance
EFFECT:	HEARER BELIEVE
	SPEAKER BELIEVE PROP

Regarding the other informing speech acts, the principle cannot be used to justify the deleting of the SPEAKER BELIEVE from the CANDO.PR of INFORMREF and INFORMIF since the highest elements of those conditions are "∃" and "OR", respectively. Intuitively speaking, this is a sensible result since a speaker SP cannot plan for an intermediary, INT, to tell H whether P is true, or what the value of description D is unless INT is believed to have that information.

7.5 Summary

The appropriate planning of composite speech acts has turned out to be a powerful test of the adequacy of speech act definitions. To meet its demands on the planning of questions and multiparty speech acts, two new speech acts, INFORMREF and INFORMIF have been defined, and the preconditions to REQUEST and INFORM have been reformulated according to a point-of-view principle. Since these last two speech acts were taken to be prototypes of Searle's (1976) "directive" and "representative" classes, the principle will find wide application.

A side effect of direct requests was identified and used in planning multiparty speech acts. Side effects, however, cannot be calculated until the hearer has recognized the speaker's plan and thus has classified the observed utterance as a particular speech act type. Thus the minimal side effect formulation given here should be further justified on the basis of what a hearer needs to assume about the speaker's beliefs in order to identify an utterances's illocutionary force.

There may be other ways to meet compositional adequacy. For instance, one could state explicitly that an action's preconditions should be true at the time the action is to be done (Bruce, 1975). For our multiparty REQUESTS, such an approach (using a speaker-based precondition) produces preconditions like: S believes J will believe P will be true when ACT is to be done, which seems reasonable. However, the minimal side effect of S's REQUEST then becomes: J now believes that (before that REQUEST) S *expected* J to believe that P would be true when ACT is done (where "now" is just after the REQUEST was made). As yet, we do not have an analogue of CONVINCE that would allow J to then come to believe that P would be true. Again, if REQUEST is defined using the neutral precondition, this problem does not arise.

---

[27] The fact that a WANT.PR is found on *every* intentional act makes us suspect that it belongs on some single "element" that is present for *every* act.

[28] Of course, what must be satisfied in any plan for INFORM is that the planner believe PROP.

representative classes, have been examined here, but the approach can be extended to other members of those classes (Bruce, 1975) and perhaps to the commissive class that includes promises. However, in order to model promises and warnings, a better understanding of the concepts of benefit and obligation is necessary.

Finally, we have so far discussed how a planning system can select illocutionary force and propositional content of a speech act, but not how utterances realizing it can be constructed nor how illocutionary acts can be identified from utterances. Extending the plan-based approach to the first area means investigating the extent of "pragmatic influence" of linguistic processing. An important subproblem here is the planning of referring expressions involved in performing illocutionary acts (Perrault & Cohen, forthcoming; Searle, 1969). Regarding speech act identification, the acid-test of a plan-based approach is its treatment of indirect speech acts (Searle, 1975). Gordon and Lakoff (1971) proposed "conversational postulates" to account for the relation between the direct or literal and the indirect illocutionary forces of an utterance. But, as Morgan (1977) notes, by calling them "postulates," one implies they cannot be explained by some other independently motivated analysis.

We suggest that the relation between direct and indirect readings can be largely accounted for by considering the relationship between actions, their preconditions, effects, and bodies, and by modelling how language users can recognize plans, which may include speech acts, being executed by others. The ability to recognize plans is seemingly required in order to be *helpful*, independent of the use of indirect speech acts. For instance, hearers often understand a speaker's utterance literally but go beyond it, inferring the speaker's plans and then performing acts that would enable the speaker's higher level goals to be fulfilled. Indirect speech acts arise because speakers can intend hearers to perform helpful inferential processing and they intend for hearers to know this. Allen (1979) and Perrault and Allen (forthcoming) formalize this process of intended plan-recognition (and thus Searle's force condition) extending our plan-based approach to the interpretation of indirect speech acts.

8. CONCLUDING REMARKS

It has been argued that a theory of speech acts can be obtained by modelling them in a planning system as operators defined, at least, in terms of the speakers' and hearers' beliefs, and goals. Thus, speech acts are treated in the same way as physical acts, allowing both to be integrated into plans. Such an approach suggests new areas for application. It may provide a more systematic basis for studying real dialogues arising in the course of a task—a basis that would facilitate the tracking of conversants' beliefs and intentions as dialogue and task proceed. A similar analysis of characters' plans has also been shown (Bruce & Newman, 1978) to be essential to a satisfactory description of narrative. Finally, Allen (1979) and Cohen (1978) have suggested how computer conversants might plan their speech acts and recognize those of their users.

Given this range of application, the methodological issues of how speech acts should be modelled in a planning system become important. Specifically, a plan-based competence theory, given configurations of beliefs and goals, speech act operators, and plan construction inferences should generate plans for all and only those speech acts that are appropriate in those configurations. This paper developed tests that showed how various definitions of the speech acts of requesting and informing were inadequate, especially to the demand that they generate appropriate plans when composed with other speech acts to form questions and multiparty requests.

To resolve the difficulties, two "views" of INFORM to be used in constructing questions were defined, allowing the questioner to have incomplete knowledge of the hearer's beliefs. After revising both the form of speech act preconditions and identifying some speech act side effects, compositional adequacy for multiparty REQUESTS was achieved. The solution led to a metatheoretical "point-of-view" principle for use in defining future speech acts as operators within this planning system.

Our approach has both assumed certain idealized properties of speaker/hearers, and has been restricted in its scope. The preconditions and effects of our operators are stated in the language of logic, not because of any desire to perform logically valid inferences, but because the conditions in the plans should have well-defined semantics. While this has been partially realized through the adoption of the possible-worlds semantics for belief, the semantics is too strong to be a faithful model of human beliefs. For instance, it leads here to requiring a questioner to have very strong, though incomplete, knowledge of the hearer's beliefs. To reflect human beliefs more accurately, one needs to model (at least): degrees of belief, justifications, the failure to make deductions, inductive leaps, and knowing what/who/where something is. These refinements, though needed by a theory of speech acts, are outside its scope. Finally, the semantics for WANT and for actions are lacking (but see Moore (1979) for an interesting approach to the latter).

Only two kinds of speech acts, prototypes of Searle's (1976) directive and

ACKNOWLEDGMENTS

We would like to thank Marilyn Adams, James Allen, Ron Brachman, Chip Bruce, Sharon Oviatt, Bill Woods and the referees for their comments, and Brenda Starr, Jill O'Brien, and Beverly Tobiason for their tireless assistance in the paper's preparation. Special thanks are extended to Brenda Starr for her invaluable editorial help.

Sacerdoti, E. D. A structure for plans and behavior. Ph.D. Thesis, Technical Note 109, Artificial Intelligence Center, Stanford Research Institute, Menlo Park, California, August 1975.

Schank, R., & Abelson, R. Scripts, plans, goals, and understanding. Hillsdale, N.J.: Lawrence Erlbaum Associates, 1977.

Schiffer, S. Meaning. Oxford: Oxford University Press, 1972.

Searle, J. R. A taxonomy of illocutionary acts. In K. Gunderson (Ed.), Language mind and knowledge, University of Minnesota Press, 1976.

Searle, J. R. Indirect speech acts. In P. Cole & J. L. Morgan (Eds.), Syntax and semantics, (Vol. 3), Speech acts. New York: Academic Press, 1975.

Searle, J. R. Speech acts: An essay in the philosophy of language. Cambridge: Cambridge University Press, 1969.

Strawson, P. F. Intention and convention in speech acts. In The Philosophical Review, v: lxxiii, 1964. Reprinted in Logico-linguistic papers, London: Methuen & Co., 1971.

REFERENCES

Allen, J. A plan-based approach to speech act recognition. Ph.D. Thesis, Technical Report No. 131/79, Dept. of Computer Science, University of Toronto, January, 1979.

Austin, J. L. How to do things with words. J. O. Urmson (Ed.), Oxford University Press, 1962.

Bruce, B. Belief systems and language understanding. Report No. 2973, Bolt Beranek and Newman, Inc. January, 1975.

Bruce, B., & Newman, D. Interacting plans. Cognitive Science, 1978, 2, 195–233.

Bruce, B., & Schmidt, C. F. Episode understanding and belief guided parsing. Presented at the Association for Computational Linguistics Meeting at Amherst, Massachusetts (July 26–27, 1974).

Carbonell, J. G. Jr. POLITICS: Automated ideological reasoning. Cognitive Science, 1978, 2, 27–51.

Chomsky, N. Aspects of the theory of syntax. Cambridge, Mass. MIT Press, 1965.

Cohen, P. R. On knowing what to say: Planning speech acts. Ph.D. Thesis, Technical Report No. 118, Department of Computer Science, University of Toronto, January 1978.

Deutsch, B. G. The structure of task-oriented dialogues. In L. D. Erman (Ed.), Proceedings of the IEEE symposium on speech recognition. Pittsburgh, PA: Carnegie-Mellon University, 1974.

Donnellan, K. Reference and definite description. In The Philosophical Review, v. 75, 1960, 281–304. Reprinted in Steinberg & Jacobovits (Eds.), Semantics, Cambridge University Press, 1966.

Fikes, R., & Nilsson, N. J. STRIPS: A new approach to the application of theorem proving to problem solving. Artificial Intelligence, 1971, 2, 189–208.

Gordon, D., & Lakoff, G. Conversational postulates. Papers from the Seventh Regional Meeting, Chicago Linguistic Society, 1971, 63–84.

Green, C. Application of theorem-proving techniques to problem-solving. In D. E. Walker & L. M. Norton (Eds.), Proceedings of the international joint conference on artificial intelligence. Washington, D.C., May 1969.

Grice, H. P. Meaning. In The Philosophical Review, 1957, 66, 377–388. Reprinted in D. A. Steinberg & L. A. Jacobovits (Eds.), Semantics: An interdisciplinary reader in philosophy, linguistics, and psychology. New York: Cambridge University Press, 1971.

Hintikka, J. Knowledge and belief. Ithaca: Cornell University Press, 1962.

Hintikka, J. Semantics for propositional attitudes. In J. W. Davis et al. (Eds.), Philosophical logic. Dordrecht-Holland: D. Reidel Publishing Co., 1969. Reprinted in L. Linsky (Ed.), Reference and modality. New York: Oxford University Press, 1971.

Lewis, D. K. Convention: A philosophical study. Cambridge, Mass: Harvard University Press, 1969.

McCarthy, J., & Hayes, P. J. Some Philosophical Problems from the Standpoint of Artificial Intelligence. In B. Meltzer & D. Michie (Eds.) Machine intelligence 4, New York: American Elsevier, 1969.

Meehan, J. R. Tale-spin, an interactive program that writes stories. In Proceedings of the fifth international joint conference on artificial intelligence. Cambridge, Mass., 91–98.

Moore, R. C. Reasoning about knowledge and action. Ph.D. Thesis, Artificial Intelligence Laboratory, Department of Electrical Engineering and Computer Science, Massachusetts Institute of Technology, February, 1979.

Morgan, J. Conversational postulates revisited. Language, 1977, 277–284.

Newell, A., & Simon, H. A. GPS, A program that simulates human thought. In E. A. Feigenbaum & J. Feldman (Eds.), Computers and thought. New York: McGraw Hill, 1963.

Perrault, C. R., & Allen, J. F. A plan-based analysis of indirect speech acts. Forthcoming.

Perrault, C. R., & Cohen, P. R. Inaccurate Reference. Proceedings of the workshop on computational aspects of linguistic structure and discourse setting, Joshi, A. K., Sag, I. A., & Webber, B. L. (Eds.), Cambridge University Press, forthcoming.

Synchronization of Multi-Agent Plans

Jeffrey S. Rosenschein
Computer Science Department
Stanford University
Stanford, California 94305

Abstract

Consider an intelligent agent constructing a plan to be executed by several other agents; correct plan execution will often require that actions be taken in a specific sequence. Therefore, the planner cannot simply tell each agent what action to perform; explicit mechanisms must exist for maintaining the execution sequence. This paper outlines such mechanisms. A framework for multiple-agent planning is developed, consisting of several parts. First, a formalism is adopted for representing knowledge about other agents' beliefs and goals, and is extended to allow representation of their capabilities. Communication primitives are defined that allow selective acceptance of goals and facts, and an explicit means of inducing an agent to perform an act is introduced. Finally, the ordering mechanisms (consisting of sequencing operators and a planning heuristic) are presented, along with a specific example of their use.

Introduction

In recent years there has been growing interest in *distributed artificial intelligence* systems, collections of intelligent agents cooperating to solve goals. The motivation for a distributed approach to problem solving is two-fold: increased efficiency and increased capabilities. Certain tasks, such as sensing and control of air or ship traffic, have an inherently distributed nature and so lend themselves to a distributed solution [1] [2]. Even non-sensory tasks may be inherently distributed; the knowledge required to carry out these tasks might be split among several machines. Again, distributed problem solving is a natural way to proceed.

There exist two major paradigms for distributed artificial intelligence systems. The first paradigm is *planning for multiple agents*, where a single intelligent agent constructs a plan to be carried out by a group of agents, and then hands out the pieces of the plan to the relevant individuals. Randy Davis calls this paradigm "distributing the solution" [3]. The second paradigm is *distributed problem solving*, where a group of intelligent agents together construct, and possibly execute, the final plan.

This paper is concerned with the first paradigm, that of planning for multiple agents; in particular, we examine the problem of achieving synchrony among a group of agents who will be carrying out a centrally-produced plan. Imagine, for example, intelligent agents (located on various computers) that can construct and execute plans in the operating systems domain as well as communicate with each other (this is the domain being explored by the Stanford Intelligent Agents project). A user might tell the agent at Stanford that he wants a file X at MIT to be printed at CMU; the Stanford agent will construct a complete plan to accomplish this goal (containing certain actions to be taken by the MIT and CMU agents), and then tell MIT and CMU what to do. The plan might involve MIT sending the file to CMU, and CMU's printing it, but the Stanford agent must ensure that these two actions occur in this order and are not reversed. One solution is for MIT to send file X to CMU, and then notify CMU that it has been sent; CMU waits for this notification, and then prints the file.

We present a method that formalizes the above solution, and thus can be used to maintain an ordering of actions performed by various agents. As a framework for the multiple-agent planning system, a formalism is adopted for representing beliefs and goals of agents, as well as their capabilities; primitives for inter-agent communication are defined. A planning heuristic for multi-agent synchrony is presented, along with its requisite operators. Finally, the example above is presented in greater detail.

The Multi-Agent Formalism

Beliefs and Goals

To construct plans for other agents, the planner must be able to represent and reason about their beliefs and goals. Though several alternatives are possible (such as "possible-worlds" formalisms [4] [5] [6] [7]), we choose the FACT and GOAL list formalism of Konolige and Nilsson [8]. In this approach, each agent has a FACT list that contains items that it believes, including the beliefs and goals of other agents (these last two are specified through the use of a metalanguage); the GOAL list contains the current goals of the agent. As an example, if A0 believes that A1 believes A1 has file FOO, and A0 also believes that A1 has the goal of deleting that file, the following items appear in A0's data base:

$$\text{FACT(A1,'EXIST(FOO,A1)')}$$
$$\text{GOAL(A1,'DELETED(FOO)')}$$

All planning will make use of STRIPS-like operators [9]. We allow instantiated operators to appear explicitly on any agent's GOAL list, rather than limiting this list to state descriptions. We differentiate between the two types of goals by calling the latter "operator-goals" and the former "state-goals".

Capabilities

Previous work on multiple agents has assumed that all agents have identical capabilities, that is, that all agents have access to the identical operators. When agents are planning for differing operating system environments, this is clearly not the case. For example, an agent located on one machine may be able to run TEX on a file, while the agent on another machine that lacks TEX will not. We introduce the predicate HASCAP(agent,operator) to represent the capability of *agent* to carry out *operator*. Generality is provided by the use of partially instantiated operators in the HASCAP predicate. For example, if agent A0 believes that agent A1 can, in general, DELETE files, the following would appear in A0's data base:

$$\text{HASCAP(A1,DELETE(A1,file))}$$

We use the standard convention that the free variable "file" is universally quantified. HASCAP is also defined over more complex operator combinations; for example, the following axiom holds:

$$\text{HASCAP(agent,AND(operator1,operator2))} \rightleftarrows$$
$$\text{HASCAP(agent,operator1)} \wedge \text{HASCAP(agent,operator2)}$$

WILL-PERFORM as a Precondition

Cohen and Perrault [10] recognized the usefulness of making an agent's "wanting" to use an operator an explicit precondition of that operator. In this manner, one can get an agent to perform some action by making the action's preconditions true, including the precondition of making the agent "want" to carry out the action. We adopt a similar strategy recast into a more general form, and introduce the predicate WILL-PERFORM(agent,operator) to signify that *agent* will perform *operator*. WILL-PERFORM appears as an explicit precondition of all operators that do not occur spontaneously; so, for A0 to get A1 to apply the operator OP, A0 needs to make sure WILL-PERFORM(A1,OP) is true. The following axiom says that if an agent has the capability to perform an act and has the desire to perform the act, then he will perform it:

$$\text{HASCAP(agent,oper)} \wedge \text{GOAL(agent,oper)} \supset$$
$$\text{WILL-PERFORM(agent,oper)}$$

Since the fact that this axiom is universally known is also known, the following axiom actually appears in every agent's data base:

$$\text{FACT(x,'HASCAP(agent,oper)} \wedge \text{GOAL(agent,oper)} \supset$$
$$\text{WILL-PERFORM(agent,oper)')}$$

This axiomatization of WILL-PERFORM models an agent's using an operator as an act of volition; if involuntary performance of acts is possible, WILL-PERFORM(agent,operator) could be made true without the agent actually possessing the operator as a goal. Other axioms would be introduced to model these cases.

An agent can apply an operator once WILL-PERFORM(agent,operator) becomes true; he will not necessarily check the truth of the operator's other preconditions or try to make them true. Given these assumptions, it is essential for the planner to ensure that WILL-PERFORM's brother preconditions are true before WILL-PERFORM itself becomes true. Achieving this ordering of preconditions is identical to achieving synchrony, and will be discussed in further detail below.

Communication Primitives

To integrate planning and communication, we need to adopt a coherent theory of planning communication acts themselves. The work of Cohen and Perrault sheds considerable light on this issue, and we use several of their communication operators (with modification) in the work that follows. For simplicity, the initiator of a communication act will be called the "speaker," and the receiver will be called the "hearer."

We use four communication operators: REQUEST, CAUSE-TO-WANT, INFORM, and CONVINCE. REQUEST and INFORM are illocutionary acts, that is, they model the speaker's communication act, but not the effect that act has on the hearer. CAUSE-TO-WANT and CONVINCE are perlocutionary acts, that is, they model the effects of communication acts. For example, the speaker might REQUEST some act of a hearer, but this will not directly cause the hearer to adopt that act as a goal; before the hearer adopts the goal, a CAUSE-TO-WANT must occur. This decoupling of the communication act from its effect allows for natural modeling of goal or fact refusal by the hearer (as contrasted with Konolige and Nilsson's single-step "asktoachieve" and "tell" operators). While Cohen and Perrault make CAUSE-TO-WANT and CONVINCE trivially triggered by REQUEST and INFORM respectively, we introduce the predicates ACCEPT and BE-SWAYED as explicit preconditions on the former operators. The communication operators are defined as follows:

REQUEST(x,y,act) -- x requests y to adopt act as a goal
P: WILL-PERFORM(x,REQUEST(x,y,act))
A: FACT(y,'GOAL(x,act)')

The effect of REQUEST is to let y know that x has "act" as a goal; x need not believe *a priori* that y can satisfy "act."

CAUSE-TO-WANT(x,y,act)--x causes y to adopt act as a goal
P: FACT(y,'GOAL(x,act)') ∧ FACT(y,'HASCAP(y,act)') ∧ ACCEPT(x,y,act) ∧ HASCAP(y,CAUSE-TO-WANT(x,y,act))
A: GOAL(y,act)

CAUSE-TO-WANT causes y to adopt x's goal as its own, but only if y believes he has the capability to satisfy the goal and the ACCEPT predicate is true.

INFORM(x,y,prop) -- x informs y of prop
P: prop ; WILL-PERFORM(x,INFORM(x,y,prop))
A: FACT(y,'FACT(x,prop)')

INFORM should only take place if prop is true; its effect is to let y know that x believes prop. The ";" appearing in INFORM's precondition list means that the item appearing before it should be satisfied before the item following it.

CONVINCE(x,y,prop) -- x convinces y to believe prop
P: FACT(y,'FACT(x,prop)') ∧ BE-SWAYED(x,y,prop) ∧ HASCAP(y,CONVINCE(x,y,prop))
A: FACT(y,prop)
D: FACT(y,NEGATE(prop))

CONVINCE causes y to adopt x's belief as its own, but only if BE-SWAYED is true; any contradictory belief is discarded. NEGATE is a function over strings such that NEGATE('x') gives the string '¬x'. Also, note the absence of WILL-PERFORM as a precondition of CAUSE-TO-WANT and CONVINCE; these operators will be applied when their preconditions are true, without any agent explicitly "wanting" them.

Agents' data bases contain axioms involving the ACCEPT and BE-SWAYED predicates; these axioms specify conditions under which the hearer will accept the speaker's facts or goals. For example, if agents A0 and A1 are in a master-slave relationship, we might have the following three axioms to indicate A1's subservience to A0's dictates:

MASTER(A0,A1)

MASTER(x,y) ⊃ ACCEPT(x,y,act)

MASTER(x,y) ⊃ BE-SWAYED(x,y,prop)

Other axioms might model A1's willingness to ACCEPT requests if his machine's load is low, or if he owes A0 a favor; he might BE-SWAYED by A0 if he knows A0 to be reliable, or to have particularly good information about this kind of fact (e.g. A0 will know best whether a file exists on his own machine).

Ordered Preconditions

As explained above, the planner expects to make WILL-PERFORM(agent,operator) true in order to get *agent* to perform *operator*; once this predicate is true, the operator can be applied at any time. WILL-PERFORM will not be made true, however, until *agent* accepts the operator-goal *operator* (because of the above axiomatization of WILL-PERFORM). Thus, all other preconditions of *operator* should be true before the operator itself is adopted as a goal. Satisfaction of this principle will guarrantee multi-agent synchrony.

In general, an operator-goal should not be adopted by an agent until he *knows* that the other preconditions of the operator have been satisfied. To accomplish this, we introduce the predicates WAITING and HAS-DONE, and the operators PAUSE and WHEN-GET, defined as follows:

PAUSE(agent,precond,aim) -- agent decides to wait until precond is satisfied before adopting aim
P: WILL-PERFORM(agent,PAUSE(agent,precond,aim))
A: FACT(agent,'WAITING(precond,aim)')

WHEN-GET(agent,precond,aim) -- agent adopts aim when he knows that precond is satisfied
P: FACT(agent,'WAITING(precond,aim)') ∧ FACT(agent,precond) ∧ HASCAP(agent,WHEN-GET(agent,precond,aim))
A: GOAL(agent,aim)
D: FACT(agent,'WAITING(precond,aim)')

So, for example, to get agent A1 to wait until agent A0 has done act G before himself doing act H, we would pass the following operator-goal to A1:

PAUSE(A1,HAS-DONE(A0,G),H).

This causes A1 to place WAITING(HAS-DONE(A0,G),H) in its data base. When A1 finds out (or more usually, is told) that A0 HAS-DONE G, WHEN-GET is triggered and A1 adopts H as a goal.

Note that the variable "precond" can actually be a conjunction of items; only when all the items are believed by the agent will WHEN-GET be triggered, since

FACT(agent,prop1) ∧ FACT(agent,prop2) ⇄
FACT(agent,AND(prop1,prop2)).

Our planner employs the following heuristic to guarantee multi-agent synchrony: assume there is an operator OP with preconditions P1 through PN (some J element subset "S" of which is not already true in the initial state), and WILL-PERFORM. The planner wants agent A0 to apply OP. Expansion of the plan on P1 through PN occurs before expansion of WILL-PERFORM; assume that the elements of S are made true by agents A1 through AJ, using operators O1 through OJ respectively. Then, instead of directly inducing OP's WILL-PERFORM operator-goal through a REQUEST and CAUSE-TO-WANT, the planner satisfies it through the PAUSE and WHEN-GET operators, whose "precond" variables are instantiated as the conjunction of J elements of the form HAS-DONE(Ai,Oi), where "i" ranges from 1 to J. Satisfaction of WHEN-GET's second FACT precondition is accomplished by INFORMs and CONVINCEs of the agents satisfying S, each of whom sends their own "HAS-DONE(Ai,Oi)" message. Finally, the planner must direct each of these agents to first apply Oi, and then inform A0 that they have done so (with a HAS-DONE message).

An Example

A person using an Intelligent Agent at Stanford [ST] would like file REP.PRESS at MIT to be printed on the Dover printer at CMU. The agent at Stanford knows about the following two operators (in addition to the communication operators, PAUSE and WHEN-GET operators explained above):

    DOVER(agent,file) -- agent prints file on the Dover
    P: EXIST(file,agent);
           WILL-PERFORM(agent,DOVER(agent,file))
    A: D-PRINTED(file,agent)

    FTP-SEND(x,y,file) -- x sends file to y
    P: EXIST(file,x) ; WILL-PERFORM(x,FTP-SEND(x,y,file))
    A: EXIST(file,y)

The following items appear on the Stanford agent's FACT list (in addition to the HASCAP and WILL-PERFORM axioms listed above):

(1) FACT(x,'HASCAP(CMU,DOVER(CMU,file))')
(2) FACT(x,'HASCAP(MIT,FTP-SEND(MIT,CMU,file))')
(3) FACT(x,'HASCAP(CMU,PAUSE(CMU,precond,aim))')
(4) FACT(x,'HASCAP(CMU,WHEN-GET(CMU,precond,aim))')
(5) FACT(z,'HASCAP(x,REQUEST(x,y,act))')
(6) FACT(z,'HASCAP(y,CAUSE-TO-WANT(x,y,act))')
(7) FACT(z,'HASCAP(x,INFORM(x,y,prop))')
(8) FACT(z,'HASCAP(y,CONVINCE(x,y,prop))')
(9) EXIST(REP.PRESS,MIT)
(10) FACT(x,'MASTER(ST,CMU)')
(11) FACT(x,'MASTER(ST,MIT)')
(12) FACT(x,'BE-SWAYED(MIT,CMU,prop)')
(13) FACT(z,'MASTER(x,y) ⊃ ACCEPT(x,y,act)')
(14) FACT(z,'MASTER(x,y) ⊃ BE-SWAYED(x,y,prop)')

Axioms 1 through 8 list capabilities of the agents involved (actually, knowledge about these capabilities), with 5-8 stating that all agents have the basic communication primitives. Axioms 10 through 14 enlighten us about the hierarchy of control among the agents. Note that by the semantics of FACT, the axiom FACT(x,prop) in an agent's data base implies that prop is also in

his data base (i.e. if an agent knows that everyone knows prop, then he knows prop).

Figure 1 gives the expanded plan that ST constructs to fulfill the user's goal (the communication acts are represented schematically). It involves getting MIT to first send the file to CMU and then inform CMU that the file has been sent. In turn, CMU is told to wait until notified that MIT has carried out the FTP-SEND, and then to DOVER the file.

Construction of the plan proceeds as follows: working backwards from the D-PRINTED goal, ST chooses the DOVER operator to achieve it. Since the operator's preconditions are ordered, ST expands the first precondition (EXIST) before the second (WILL-PERFORM). The WILL-PERFORM in Figure 1's left branch does not trigger the planning heuristic, since its brother precondition "EXIST(REP.PRESS,MIT)" is true in the initial state. However, the WILL-PERFORM in the right branch does trigger the heuristic, since its brother precondition, "EXIST(REP.PRESS,CMU)" is not initially true. Thus, the goal "DOVER(CMU,REP.PRESS)" is not passed to CMU by a REQUEST and CAUSE-TO-WANT from ST. Instead, ST plans for CMU to get this goal through the PAUSE and WHEN-GET operators; both of these operators' *aim* variables are instantiated to "DOVER(CMU,REP.PRESS)", while their *precond* variables have "HAS-DONE(MIT,FTP-SEND(MIT,CMU,REP.PRESS))" as an instantiation. WHEN-GET's second FACT precondition is thus satisfied by a message from MIT, "HAS-DONE(MIT,FTP-SEND(MIT,CMU,REP.PRESS))". In turn, MIT is instructed to send this message to CMU after it has, in fact, done the FTP-SEND.

Acknowledgments

The issues presented in this paper have been greatly clarified through many useful discussions with Mike Genesereth. This research is supported by ONR Contract #N00014-81-K-0303.

REFERENCES

[1] Davis, R. and R. G. Smith, "Negotiation as a Metaphor for Distributed Problem Solving," Artificial Intelligence Laboratory Memo No. 624, Massachusetts Institute of Technology, Cambridge, MA (May 1981).

[2] Steeb, R., S. Cammarata, F. A. Hayes-Roth, P. W. Thorndyke and R. B. Wesson, "Distributed Intelligence for Air Fleet Control," R-2728-ARPA, Rand Corporation, Santa Monica, CA (October 1981).

[3]   Davis, R., "A Model for Planning in a Multi-Agent Environment: Steps Toward Principles for Teamwork," A.I. Working Paper, Massachusetts Institute of Technology, Cambridge, MA (June 1981).

[4]   Moore, R. C., "Reasoning About Knowledge and Action," in *Proc. IJCAI-5*, Cambridge, Massachusetts, August, 1977, pp. 223-227.

[5]   Moore, R. C., "Reasoning About Knowledge and Action," Artificial Intelligence Center Technical Note 191, SRI International, Menlo Park, California (1980).

[6]   Appelt, D., *Planning Natural Language Utterances to Satisfy Multiple Goals*, Ph.D. thesis, Stanford University, December 1981.

[7]   Appelt, D. E., "A Planner for Reasoning about Knowledge and Action," *Proc. of the First Annual Conference of the American Association for Artificial Intelligence*, Stanford, California, August, 1980, pp. 131-133.

[8]   Konolige, K. and N. J. Nilsson, "Multiple-Agent Planning Systems," *Proc. of the First Annual Conference of the American Association for Artificial Intelligence*, Stanford, California, August, 1980, pp. 138-141.

[9]   Nilsson, N. J.,   *Principles of Artificial Intelligence*, (Menlo Park: Tioga Publishing Co., 1980).

[10]   Cohen, P. R. and C. R. Perrault, "Elements of a Plan-Based Theory of Speech Acts," *Cognitive Science, 3* (3), pp. 177-212 (1979).

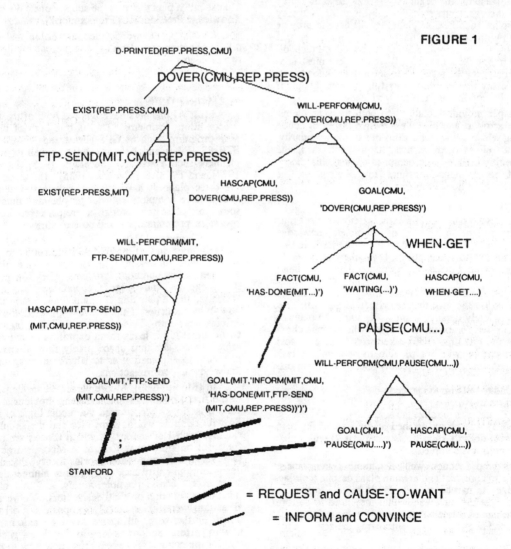

FIGURE 1

Knowledge Preconditions for Actions and Plans

Leora Morgenstern
New York University
Department of Computer Science
New York, N.Y. 10012
(212) 781-6539
morgenst@nyu.csd2.edu.arpa

Abstract

Agents who operate in complex environments must often construct plans on the basis of incomplete knowledge. In such situations, the successful agent must incorporate into his plans actions which obtain information. These plans are intrinsically sketchy to begin with and become more specified as the agent proceeds through his plan. A theory which allows for such flexible planning will have to provide solutions to two problems: (1) how can an agent reason that he knows how to perform an action? (Knowledge Preconditions Problem for Actions) and (2) if an agent must construct an underspecified plan due to incomplete knowledge, when can we say that he can successfully execute his plan? (Knowledge Preconditions Problem for Plans)

This paper provides solutions to both these problems. We develop a robust and highly expressive theory of action and planning which allows for actions of varying granularity, primitive as well as complex acts, multi-agent plans, and partially specified plans. We demonstrate that this theory lends itself in a natural manner to solutions to the Knowledge Preconditions Problems.

1. Introduction

An agent who operates in a complex environment must often construct plans on the basis of incomplete knowledge. Agents frequently don't know detailed procedures for the tasks they set out to accomplish. They likewise generally fail to keep up with a piece of information that is constantly changing, such as the location of a moving object. These gaps in knowledge mean that an agent may not have enough information to do the task that he wishes to perform, or to draw up completely detailed plans as he starts the planning process. Consider, for example, an agent who enters a chemistry lab for the first time and is asked to neutralize an acid. It is likely that he will not be able to perform the task. Moreover, he cannot even completely specify a simple plan such as:

1) ask a friend to tell him the procedure P
2) friend tells him P
3) perform P, that is, neutralize the acid.

Both 2) and 3) will be unspecified at the start of the plan, since the agent doesn't know P. In particular 2) will remain unspecified until it is completed.

Agents who function well in complex environments must be able to construct and execute plans despite their lack of knowledge. In particular, they should be able to successfully plan to get the information that they need to perform specific actions. An intelligent agent, for example, should realize that the above plan for neutralizing the acid is a reasonable one, while a plan such as

1) swim the English Channel
2) neutralize the acid

makes no sense at all.

A theory that allows for such flexible planning will have to provide solutions to at least two problems. Firstly, it must explain under what circumstances an agent knows how to perform an action. We call this the Knowledge Preconditions Problem for Actions. Secondly, even if an agent does not know how to perform an action, it must explain how he can execute a plan that gets the action done. We call this the Knowledge Preconditions Problem for Plans.

In this paper, we develop a flexible and expressive theory of action and planning, and present solutions to these two problems.

2. Previous Work

Most AI planners have ignored both of the Knowledge Preconditions Problems. This is true both of classic planning programs such as GPS [Ernst and Newell 1969] and STRIPS [Fikes and Nilsson 1971] as well as more recent planners such as NOAH [Sacerdoti 1975], Non-Lin [Tate 1977], and TWEAK [Chapman 1985]. The theories underlying these planners have all implicitly assumed that agents always have complete knowledge; planning thus reduces to some sort of search through a pre-packaged list of action operators, pre-conditions, and post-conditions.

McCarthy and Hayes [1969] were the first to argue that an agent does in fact reason about his ability to perform an action, thus addressing themselves to the first of the Knowledge Preconditions Problems. They suggested writing down explicit knowledge precondition axioms for each action, so that a planning program could reason that it knew how to do an action if the relevant knowledge precondition axioms were true. This proposal, however, fails on at least two counts: (1) it leads to an explosion of axioms, a large search space, and thus unacceptably slow proofs, and (2) it provides no explanation as to why or how agents come to know how to perform actions.

In [Moore 1980], Moore presented an elegant solution to the first Knowledge Preconditions Problem for a limited class of actions. Moore used the modal logic of knowledge S4 with possible worlds semantics and the simple situation calculus model of actions, in which actions are regarded as functions on situations. Central to Moore's argument were two concepts from possible worlds theory: that of the rigid designator, an entity such as a name or number denoting the same object across possible worlds, and that of the rigid function, a function on rigid designators. Moore argued that all actions were (axiomatically composed out of) rigid functions. Furthermore, all agents knew all axioms and knew how to perform actions as long as they knew rigid designators for the actions. An agent thus knew how to perform an action if he knew rigid designators for the parameters of the action.

Unfortunately, Moore's system is insufficiently general for the following reasons: (1) The S4 model entails that all agents know all axioms and that they thus have the same procedural knowledge; this reduces the entire Knowledge Preconditions Problem to a toy problem, (2) the first order modal logic that Moore uses is severely inexpressive, and does not allow us to express an agent's partial knowledge, (3) the McCarthy-Hayes situation calculus that Moore uses is too rigid to serve as the basis for a flexible theory of planning.

Since the first two objections follow from Moore's use of a modal logic of knowledge, and the third objection follows from Moore's use of the McCarthy-Hayes model of action, it makes sense to develop a theory which avoids both. We will build our theory upon a first order logic of knowledge, in which knowledge is represented as a relation on strings, and integrate it with an expressive, set-theoretic model of action. The resulting theory will lend itself in a natural manner to solutions to both of the Knowledge Preconditions Problems.

This paper extends the work of [Morgenstern 1986a] in which we first addressed the problem of constructing a first order logic of knowledge and action. There, we focussed upon developing a first-order logic of knowledge which avoids paradox and obeys the classical inference rules, and which could be integrated with various models of action. In this paper, we construct a detailed theory of action and planning and present our solution to the Knowledge Preconditions Problems within that context.

3. The Logical Language

We will be using a language L, which is an instance of the first order predicate calculus. L' s symbols consist of the logical symbols, such as $\lor$, $\neg$, and $\exists$, constants, variables, predicates, and functions. We will feel free to substitute the English equivalents for logical symbols when it improves legibility. Constants are numbers or begin with an upper case letter. Predicates begin with upper case; functions and variables begin with lower case. Predicates and constants, functions and variables, will be disambiguated by context. In our axioms and definitions, variables will be assumed to be universally quantified unless otherwise specified.

Our logic is sorted; sorts are distinguished by their first letter(s). Some of the more commonly used sorts are s, ranging over situations, i, ranging over intervals, a, ranging over agents, act, ranging over actions, str, ranging over strings. Other sorts will be introduced as needed, and will be understood from context.

The quotation construct is an important feature of L. We assume a meta-function of L, G, which maps distinct expressions of L into distinct numbers. G is invertible; the analogue of G^{-1} in L is g^{-1}. In the proper context, a number of L is said to 'stand for' the expression of L which maps into it. When used in this way, numbers are known as strings. A string is written as the expression it represents, surrounded by quotation marks. For example, the string 'At(John,NYC,S3)' represents the expression At(John,NYC,S3). Strings thus provide us with a way of talking *about* expression of L within L.

Various predicates of L take strings as their arguments; the most important of these are the predicates True and Know. Know takes three arguments: an agent, a string representing a sentence, and a situation. For example, to say that John knows something that Bill doesn't know, we write:

$\exists$ p (Know(John,p,S5) & $\neg$ Know(Bill,p,S5))

Note that by using strings, we are effectively quantifying over sentences while remaining in a first order language; we can use this trick to 'quantify' over functions and predicates by quantifying over strings which represent them. Note also the ease with which we can express partial knowledge.

Achieving full expressivity in languages with quotation can be complicated since the quoted constructs are opaque. For example to state the principle of positive introspection, that if an agent knows something, he knows that he knows it, we cannot simply say:

$\forall$ a,p,s Know(a,p,s) => Know(a,'Know(a,p,s)',s)

This would mean that all agents always know the string 'Know(a,p,s)'. If we try to substitute values for a,p, and s, we will not be able to substitute the values within the quoted context: a string is a constant. To solve this problem, we introduce some syntactic abbreviations: a name-of-operator, @, where @ applied to an object yields the name of that object, ! !, where ! ! applied to a string variable yields the string the variable stands for, and ˆ ˆ, where ˆ ˆ applied to a string variable yields the string the variable stands for, stripped of surrounding quotes. (*) As an example of their use, we now write the principle of positive introspection correctly:

$\forall$ a,p,s Know(a,p,s) => Know(a,'Know(@a,!p!,@s)',s)

Our axioms on Know correspond closely to the standard S4 axiomatization of knowledge. We assume veridicality, positive introspection, and consequential closure. We do not, however, assume necessitation: agents are required to know all logical axioms and axioms on knowledge, but not all axioms about the world.

4. Theory of Action

4.1. Requirements

Underlying every theory of action is an explicit or implicit ontology of action. The ontology of action that we choose will be determined by the set of requirements that are placed upon the theory. These requirements, in turn, are determined by the problems that our theory seeks to solve. Below, we briefly list the more salient requirements which we place upon our theory:

[1] **Fidelity of Temporal Representation:** A theory of action must be able to talk about both instants of time and intervals of time. Actions take place over intervals of time; facts may be true over instants or intervals. Instants are necessary so that we can describe what it true at a particular moment. Time intervals are necessary so that we can describe how the world changes over time.

[2] **Granularity:** The theory should be able to view actions with varying degrees of granularity. That is, the term 'action' should encompass broadly general as well as detailed descriptions of actions. For example, both driving a car and driving a red Alfa Romeo with the roof down on a hot summer's day should be considered actions. This is especially important for the purposes of planning. At the start of the planning process, agents often think in general terms, about coarse-grained actions. However, these coarse-grained actions may become transformed into increasingly finer grained actions as the planning process continues and plan refinement occurs.

[3] **Interval Dependent Actions:** There are many actions whose very descriptions depend on the time during which

----

(*) These operators are defined in terms of standard features of L such as concat. For further details, see [Morgenstern 1986b].

they take place, such as going to the top of the tallest building in New York. The values of descriptions such as 'the tallest building in New York' change with time. We wish to have a theory which allows us to describe actions in this manner.

[4] Composability: Most actions are formed by composing simpler actions in various ways. For example, the action of making blackberry jam can be thought of as a sequence of the action of crushing blackberries, mixing with sugar and pectin, bringing to a hard boil, and pouring into Mason jars. Our theory should provide a mechanism for composing simple actions to form complex actions, using the standard operators of a concurrent programming language, such as sequences, conditionals, while loops, and concurrency.

[5] Multiple Agents: Many of the actions we are interested in, such as communicative actions, are *interagent actions*, which involve at least two agents. Our theory must therefore be flexible enough to describe how multiple agents act and interact. In particular, we should be able to talk about agents acting simultaneously. We should also be able to talk about individual plans which are constructed out of actions done by many agents.

4.2. Choosing an Ontology

There are two major questions which must be addressed when choosing an ontology:
1) What are actions? and
2) How can we describe actions?

Mainstream AI research has provided us with two answers for each of these two questions.

1)   Actions have been *regarded* as

    a)   functions on states, or

    b)   sets of intervals.

2)   Actions have been *described* using

    c)   functional descriptions such as put-on(a,b), or

    d)   set theoretic descriptions of the form $\{i \mid \phi(i) \}$ where $\phi(i)$ is a well formed formula free only in i.

It is important to realize that these approaches can be combined in a variety of ways. Three of the four possible combinations are coherent and have in fact been incorporated into AI theories. McCarthy and Hayes [1969] have regarded actions as functions on states and have used functions to describe these actions. Both McDermott [1982] and Allen [1984] have argued that actions are sets of intervals. However, Allen uses functional descriptions, while McDermott makes use of the set theoretic description of actions.

These approaches can be contrasted in different ways. There is a clear advantage to approach b) over approach a) : that of *ontological realism*. There are many actions, such as running around the block or waiting on the corner, which do not seem to involve a state change, and which are not the null action.

Each of approaches c) and d), however, has some advantage over its rival. It is clear that d) is more expressive than c). There are many actions, such as our example of driving a red Alfa Romeo with the roof down which cannot be described in any natural manner using functional descriptions. However, it is easy to describe such an action using a set theoretic description:

$\{i \mid \exists$ a,c Alfa-Romeo(c) and Red(c) and Down(roof(c),i) and Drives(a,c,i) $\}$

If an action cannot be described using function descriptions, we say that it is *composite*.
In point of fact, however, no researcher using approach d)

has utilized its expressive potential in any systematic manner. Moreover, approach c) has an important advantage over approach d) : it is less cumbersome and easier to use for those actions which are functionally describable, such as driving a car (drive(c)) or putting one block on another (put-on(x,y)).

We aim to construct a theory which maximizes ontological realism, expressivity, and ease of use. With these ends in mind, we will regard actions as sets of intervals. To achieve expressivity, we will describe actions using set theoretic descriptions. We will show in a systematic manner how we can exploit the notation's expressive potential. To maximize ease of use, we will identify those classes of actions which are functionally describable, and use functional descriptions for these actions whenever possible.

4.3. Presentation of Theory

We now present a theory of action which satisfies the requirements discussed in section 4.1. The basic building block of our theory is the situation or state. States are ordered by the < relation, indicating precedence in time. (*) An interval is defined as a set of contiguous instants, all of which are linearly ordered. It is determined by its beginning and end points; these points name the interval. Thus, the interval starting at S11 and ending at S25 is denoted [S11,S25]. Intervals in general are closed.

We define actions and events as sets of intervals, intuitively those in which the action or event takes place. Actions are those events in which the performing agent is not specified.

We place in L a set of action functions, such as put-on(bl1,bl2), dial(x) and drive(c). These functions map their arguments onto sets of intervals, or actions. We can associate in a natural manner an n+2-place predicate with each n-place action function. The extra arguments are used for the agent performing the action, and the interval during which the action is performed. For example, we associate with the action functions above the predicates: Puts-on(a,bl1,bl2,i), Dials(a,x,i) and Drives(a,c,i). We call these predicates *action predicates*.

Actions are introduced using these action predicates. Since an action is a class, it must be of the form $\{i \mid \phi(i)\}$, where ϕ is a wff free only in i. If Act = $\{i \mid \phi (i)\}$, we call ϕ the descriptive wff of Act. $\phi(i)$ must contain an action predicate.

We can achieve our second requirement, varying granularity of action, by expanding or restricting ϕ in a systematic manner. We give some examples of this below:

(1) $\{i \mid \exists$ a Puts-on(a,Bl1,Bl2,i)$\}$ - the act of putting block Bl1 on block Bl2

(2) $\{i \mid \exists$ a,bl1,bl2 Puts-on(a,bl1,bl2,i)$\}$ - the act of putting one block on another

(3) $\{i \mid \exists$ a,bl1,bl2 Red(bl1) and Puts-on(a,bl1,bl2,i)$\}$ - the act of putting a red block on some other block

(4) $\{i \mid \exists$ a,bl1,bl2 Equal(bl1,favorite-block(Mary)) and Equal(bl2,favorite-block(Jane)) and
       Puts-on(a,bl1,bl2,i)$\}$ - the act of putting Mary's favorite block on Jane's favorite block.

It will be noted that only some of these actions are functionally describable. (1), (2), and (4) are: their func-

----

(*) If this order is total, we have linear time; if it is partial, we have branching time. Neither assumption is crucial for the work done in this paper.

tional descriptions are, respectively: put-on(Bl1,Bl2), put-on(bl1,bl2) and put-on(favorite-block(Mary),favorite-block(Jane)). There is, however, no way to produce a functional description for (3), unless we are willing to create functions such as put-red-block-on on the fly.

In general, we can show that an action Act = {i | φ(i) } is functionally describable if φ(i) is one of the following forms:

[1] φ contains no quantified variables, other than the variable representing the performing agent(s).

[2] φ contains quantified variables; these are all existentially quantified. Furthermore, φ does not contain any predicates involving these variables other than the action predicate(s) or the predicate Equal.

Functionally describable actions can further be subdivided into deterministic and non-deterministic actions. An action is said to be deterministic if all the arguments of its functional description evaluate to constants; otherwise it is non-deterministic. (1) and (4) are deterministic; (2) is not. We furthermore say that all composite actions are non-deterministic.

We close this section by giving two more examples of actions:

(5) {i | ∃ a,bl1,bl2 Smallest-block(bl1,i) and Largest-block(bl2,i) and Puts-on(a,bl1,bl2,i)} - the act of placing the smallest block on the largest block

Note that this is an example of an interval dependent action.

(6) {i} - the set of all intervals. We will call this the null action, Null.

We can easily define such programming language operators as sequence(act1,act2), cond(p,act1,act2), while(p,act) and concurrent(act1,act2) using standard set theoretic notation. In particular, we can recursively define while loops in terms of sequences, conditionals, and the null act: While(p,act) = cond(p,sequence(act,while(p,act)),Null). (see [Moore 1980].) We say that sequence, cond, while, and concurrent are action functions.

4.4. Events

Events are sets of intervals; intuitively, those intervals in which some agent performs an action. Every action is an event; thus, examples (1) - (6) above are all events. However, the following are also events:

(7) {i | ∃ a,bl1,bl2 Child(a) and Puts-on(a,bl1,bl2,i)} - the event of a child placing one block on another

(8) {i | ∃ bl1,bl2 Puts-on(Bill,bl1,bl2,i)} - the event of Bill placing one block on another

These are not actions because the performing agent is in some way restricted.

If the performing agent in deterministically specified, we can express an event as do(a,act), where a is the performing agent, act is the action, and do is the function mapping agents and actions onto events. For example, (8) can be expressed as do(Bill,put-on(bl1,bl2)).

We introduce the predicates on events R and Occur. If Ev is an event R(Ev,S1,S2) is true if S2 is the result of Ev1's occurrence in S1. Occur(Ev,S1,S2) is true if Ev occurs between S1 and S2. The two predicates are equivalent in a model of linear time. Note that the predicate R, while superficially similar to the Result predicate of the situation calculus, can in fact be defined in terms of our interval based ontology:

Def. R(ev,s1,s2) iff [s1,s2] ∈ ev

In a model of branching time, in which only some states are actualized, or *real states*, we define:

Def. Occur(ev,s1,s2) iff R(ev,s1,s2) and Real-state(s1) and Real-state(s2).

5. Solution to the Knowledge Preconditions Problem for Actions

Our solution is based upon five general observations about actions, the agents who perform them, and the knowledge these agents possess:

[1] Agents need to have explicit procedural knowledge for the actions they perform. Agents often don't have the knowledge they need, and thus are not able to perform the actions. If an agent does not know the explicit procedure for making a souffle, he will not be able to do it.

[2] All agents in a community know how to perform some basic actions. This assumption is a necessary precondition for meaningful teaching to occur.

[3] An agent needs more than procedural knowledge in order to perform an action. He also needs to know definite descriptions for the parameters of the action he is performing. For example, even if an agent knows how to dial a phone number, he will not be able to perform the action Dial(telno(Mary)) if he doesn't know what Mary's number is. This observation has been the major focus of Moore's research on the Knowledge Preconditions Problem for Actions.

[4] Action descriptions make a difference. The same action can be described in a number of different ways; an agent may be able to reason that he knows how to perform the action in only one of its guises. For example, an agent might know how to perform sequence(beat-eggs,fry-eggs), but not how to perform make-omelette; he might know how to perform Dial(460-7100) but not Dial(telno(Courant)).

[5] An agent knows how to compose his knowledge. If an agent knows how to perform two actions, for example, he will generally know how to perform a sequence of those actions.

Our solution to the Knowledge Preconditions Problem for Actions will synthesize and formalize these notions. We present our solution in two stages, first giving the solution for functionally describable actions, and then giving the solution for composite actions.

5.1. Solution for Functionally Describable Actions

5.1.1. Deterministic actions

5.1.1.1. Primitive Actions:

We begin by designating a class of action functions as *primitive*. This class will include such simple action types as move, put-on and dial. In general, an action is primitive if it cannot be further decomposed into simpler actions. The intuitive idea is that all agents know the basic procedures for these simple, non-decomposable acts.

As mentioned, an agent needs to know more than the basic procedure in order to do an action; he must also know definite descriptions for the parameters of the action functions. We say that an agent knows a definite description for a parameter if he knows some *standard identifier* e.g., a constant, for the parameter. So, if f(arg1...argn) is an action, f is primitive, and an agent knows standard identifiers for each of arg1...argn, he *knows how to perform* those actions. This principle is expressed in Axiom 1. Note that Stidstr is a predicate that ranges over strings; it is *true* of a string iff the string is the quoted form of a standard identifier of *L*.

Axiom 1:

Knows-how-to-perform(a,'@f(@arg1,...,@argn)',s)
  if
  primitive-action(f) and
  ∃ p1 (Stidstr(p1) and Know(a,'equal(^p1^,@arg1,@s)',s)
  and ... and
    ∃ pn (Stidstr(pn) and Know(a,'Equal(^pn^,@argn,@s)',s)

For example, if put-on is a primitive action, then A knows how to perform put-on(favorite-block(Mary),favorite-block(Jane)) if he knows standard identifiers for those blocks.

Note that the argument to the Knows-how-to-perform predicate is the *string* representing the action description in question. This is important so that the predicate can be opaque with respect to action descriptions: otherwise the predicate would be true or false of all action descriptions which evaluated to the same action. If an agent knows how to perform an action description Act1, and Act1 and Act2 designate the same action, he will be able to perform Act2 only if he knows they designate the same action.

Axiom 2 :

Knows-how-to-peform(a,'@f(@arg1,...,@argn)',s) if
  ∃ f†,arg1†,...,argm†
  (Know(a,'@f(@arg1,...,@argn)
       =@f†(@arg1†,...,@argm†)',s)
    and
  Knows-how-to-perform(a,'@f†(@arg1†,...,@argm†)',s))

5.1.1.2. Complex Actions

Actions that are composed out of simple actions using our four composition operators are designated as complex actions. The knowledge preconditions for complex acts depend in a straightforward manner on the knowledge preconditions for simpler actions.

Sequence: An agent knows how to perform a sequence of two actions if he knows how to perform the first, and knows that as a result of performing the first, he will know how to perform the second.

Axiom 3:

Knows-how-to-perform(a,'sequence(@act1,@act2)',s1) if
  Knows-how-to-perform(a,'@act1',s1) and
  R(Do(a,act1),s1,s2) =>
    Knows-how-to-perform(a,'@act2',s)

Conditionals: An agent knows how to perform cond(p,act1,act2) if he knows p and knows how to perform act1 or he knows that p is false and he knows how to perform act2.

Axiom 4:

Knows-how-to-perform(a,'cond(^p^,@act1,@act2)',s) if
  Know(a,p,s) and Knows-how-to-perform(a,'@act1',s) or
  Know(a,'¬ ^p^',s) and Knows-how-to-perform(a,'@act2',s)

While Loops: Since while loops are defined in terms of conditionals and sequences (4.3), the knowledge precondition axiom for loops is straightforward:

Axiom 5:

Knows-how-to-perform(a,'while(^p^,@act)',s) if
  Knows-how-to-perform
  (a,'cond(^p^,sequence(@act,while(^p^,@act),Null))',s)

Concurrency: An agent who knows how to perform concurrent(act1,act2) must know how to perform each of act1 and act2. In addition, the intersection of the two actions must be feasible, and the agent must have sufficient resources for both actions.

Axiom 6:

Knows-how-to-perform('concurrent(@act1,@act2)',s) if
 Knows-how-to-perform(a,'@act1',s) and
 Knows-how-to-perform(a,'@act2',s) and
 Feasible(do(a,concurrent(act1,act2))) and
 Resource-compatible(a,act1,act2,s)

The predicates Feasible and Resource-compatible are discussed in [Morgenstern 1987].

5.1.2. Non-deterministic Functionally Describable Actions

A non-deterministic functionally describable action is always of the form f(arg1...argn) where at least one of the arg_i does not evaluate to a constant. An example is put-on(bl1,bl2). Intuitively, an agent knows how to perform an action of this sort if he knows how to perform at least one deterministic instantiation of the action. So, for example, if Bl72 and Bl8 are blocks, and an agent knows how to perform put-on(Bl72,Bl8), he also knows how to perform put-on(bl1,bl2). The same is true if he knows how to perform put-on(Bl72,favorite-block(Jane)). This intuition is justified by the set theoretic structure of non-deterministic functionally describable actions, which, we will remember, is {i | ∃ a [∃ arg1] ... [∃ argn] act-pred(a,arg1,...,argn,i)}. The 'existential generalization' is true as long as we can find some values to satisfy it.

To formalize this rule, we need only add

Axiom 7:

Assume one of arg1 ... argn does not evaluate to a definite description. Suppose further that ∃ x1 ... xn, such that each xi is a deterministic instantiation of arg1 ... argn, and that
Knows-how-to-perform(a,'@f(@x1,...,@xn)',s)
Then, Knows-how-to-perform(a,'@f(@arg1,...,@argn)',s)

This axiom, together with Axiom 1, will achieve the desired result.

5.2. Composite Actions

A composite action can be characterized in terms of its descriptive function φ. The following is true of φ:

(i)   φ begins with a subexpression of the form '∃ a'
(ii) φ contains other quantified variables besides a
(iii) φ contains non-action predicates involving at least some of these variables.

Although in theory, φ's quantifiers may be either universal or existential, in practice most composite actions of interest contain only existential variables. We can identify the following form as being of particular interest to us:

(●) {I | ∃ a [∃ arg1] ... [∃ argn] P1(arg1,...,argn) conj. P2(arg1,...,argn) conj. ... conj. Pm(arg1,...,argn) and Action-pred(a,arg1,...,argn,i) }
    where each Pi is a predicate of 1 through n arguments, and each conj. stands either for ∨ or &.

The expression
P1(arg1,...,argn) conj. ... conj. Pm(arg1,...,argn)
is called the *restriction* of φ.

If an action is of this form, we say it is an REQ (restricted existentially quantified) action. Thus, for instance, example (3) of Section 4.3 and the action of driving a Red Alfa Romeo with the roof down (Section 4.2) are both examples of REQ actions.

Intuitively, an agent a knows how to perform an REQ action if there exist some constants C1 ... Cn satisfying the restriction, for which he knows how to perform the associated action $\{i \mid \phi / a, C1...Cn, i \}$. Suppose, for example, that Act is example (3) of section 4.3:

$\{i \mid \exists a, bl1, bl2 \ Red(bl1) \ and \ Puts-on(a, bl1, bl2, i)\}$

If there is some constant value for bl1, say Bl55, such that
(i) Red(Bl55) and
(ii) Knows-how-to-perform(a,'$\{i \mid \exists a, bl2 \ Puts-on(a, Bl55, bl2, i)\}$',s),
we say that a knows-how-to-perform Act as well. We formalize this notion in the following axiom:

Axiom 8:

Let act be of the form described in (●), an REQ action.
Suppose that there exist n strings, str1 ... strn,
such that Stidstr(str1) and ... and Stidstr(strn).
Suppose further that Pi(g^{-1}(^str^)) for each i in a through n;
that is, that for each i, the predicate Pi of (●),
is true of the constant denoted by the standard identifier stri.
Then,
  if Knows-how-to-perform
    (a,'$\{i \mid Act-pred(a, \hat{}str1\hat{}, ..., \hat{}strn\hat{}, i)\}$',s},
  then Knows-how-to-perform(a,'@act',s)

We defer for the present those composite actions which contain universal quantifiers. These cases will be considered in future research.

6. Solution to the Knowledge Preconditions Problem for Plans

6.1. The Concept of a Plan

Standard AI planning research [Fikes and Nilsson 1971, Sacerdoti 1975] has regarded plans as sequences of actions that are performed by a single agent. (*) This planning paradigm, while adequate for simple single-agent toy domains like the blocks world, is nonetheless inadequate for more robust planning systems for at least two reasons:

(1) Planning may involve interactions between two or more agents. Consider even a simple plan such as my getting to the airport: it consists of my hailing a taxi, the driver driving to the airport, and my paying the taxi. The taxi driver's action is an essential part of my plan.

(2) Constructs other than sequence, such as concurrency, are widely used in real life plans. An army general's plan to attack a city might consist of his attacking the city's eastern front, while his colonel attacks the city's western front.

(*) It is a common misconception that NOAH allows for concurrent and multi-agent plans. In fact, NOAH simply allows for the representation of unordered actions during the intermediate stages of planning. This is not the same as representing concurrency: the final output of NOAH is always an ordered sequence of actions. Moreover, NOAH has no explicit representation for the actions of other agents (although this could conceivably be built in). Since in any case, NOAH cannot handle concurrency, general multi-agent planning is clearly impossible.

These observations lead us to define a plan as any structure of events constructed with our standard event operators of sequence, conditionals, while loops, and concurrency. For example, we can express the general's plan, above, as:

concurrent(do(General,attack(eastern-front(City))),
    do(ColonelX,attack(western-front(City))))

Note that this notation permits a particularly flexible kind of plan construction in which the planner need not even fully specify all the agents who will be performing the actions. For example, if the general is simply planning for *one* of his colonels to attack the city's western front, he might construct his plan as:

concurrent(do(General,attack(eastern-front(City))),
    $\{i \mid \exists a \ Colonel(a) \ and \ Under-command(a, General)$
        $and \ Attacks(a, western-front(City), i)\}$)

We introduce the function actors, which applied to a plan, yields the set of actors involved in the plan, and the function actions, which applied to a plan, yields the set of actions involved in the plan.

6.2. Plan Execution

To solve the second of the Knowledge Precondition Problems, we must explain under what circumstances an agent can successfully execute a plan. Intuitively, an agent can execute a plan if he can in some sense 'make sure' that all the events in the plan get done. More precisely, we can say that an agent can execute a plan if he knows that he will be able to perform all the actions in the plan for which he is the actor, and he can predict that the other events in the plan will take place at their proper time. In the taxi plan above, for example, I can successfully execute the plan if I know that I will be able to perform the actions of hailing a taxi and paying the driver, and I can predict that the taxi driver will indeed drive me to the airport.

This section is devoted to formalizing this seemingly simple concept. We will begin by examining how agents can execute simple single-agent plans and subsequently extend our analysis to more complex plans.

We first define the concept of a simple plan. We introduce the predicate Simple-plan, which is true of plans consisting of events done by a single agent. Thus, for example, Simple-plan(do(A,drive(car)),do(A,park(car)))   is   true; Simple-plan(do(A,drive(car)),do(B,park(car))) is false. A plan that is a simple plan can always be re-written as a single event. If Pln is a simple plan, we write ev(Pln) to denote the single event associated with this plan. Note that for simple plans, the function actors evaluates to a singleton.

If P is a simple plan, and A is the performing agent in this plan, A can execute P if he knows he is able to perform the action construct associated with P. We say that an agent is able to perform an act if he knows how to perform it and if the physical preconditions are satisfied. (**)

Def. Can-Perform(a,'@act',s) iff
    Knows-how-to-perform(a,'@act',s) and
    Physprecondsat(a,act,s)

(**) In our full theory [Morgenstern 1987] we say that an agent is able to perform an action if he knows how to perform it, if the physical preconditions are satisfied, and if certain social protocols are satisfied. These protocols are an important part of our theory of communication. We omit this condition here for simplicity.

Axiom 9:

```
actors(pln) = {a} =>
  Can-execute-plan(a,pln,s) iff
    Know(a,'Can-Perform(@a,@action(@pln),@s)',s)
```

If A is not the performing agent for a simple plan, we say that A can execute the plan if he can predict its occurrence.

Axiom 10:

```
Simple-plan(pln) and actors(pln) ≠ {a} =>
  Can-execute-plan(a,pln,s) <=>
    Know(a,'∃ s2 Occur(ev(@pln),@s,s2)',s)
```

6.2.1. Complex Plans

If a plan is not simple, we say that it is complex. A complex plan must always be constructed via our four compositional operators. The knowledge preconditions for complex plans turn out to be considerably more difficult to state than the knowledge preconditions for complex actions.

Sequences: Our first attempt at a knowledge precondition axiom for plan sequences might parallel the axiom for action sequences:

(wrong axiom :)

```
Can-execute-plan(a,seq(pln1,pln2),s) if
  Can-execute-plan(a,pln1,s) and
  R(pln1,s1,s2) => Can-execute-plan(a,pln2,s2)
```

This axiom, however, places overly strong demands on the knowledge of the executing agent. Suppose Jones, a dying man, constructs the plan

```
        sequence(Do(Jones,
                sequence(write(Will),die)),
                Do(Smith,execute(Will)))
```

Jones can conceivably execute the plan if he knows he can write a will, knows he will die, and can trust his attorney Smith. However, if we accept the above axiom attempt, Jones will not be able to execute the plan because once he is dead he does not know that Smith will execute the will. Clearly, what is important here is that Jones know what is going on at the beginning of the plan. Once he leaves the picture, we do not care what he knows. (*)

It turns out to be impossible to formalize the Can-execute-plan axiom for plan sequences in terms of the Can-execute-plan axioms for simple plans. We must in fact introduce a level of indirection, via the predicate Control. An agent is said to control a plan if he can perform the action(s) associated with it, or if the plan will occur. (**) The axioms on Control are self-explanatory:

```
Controls(a,pln,s) if
  actors(pln) = {a} and Can-Perform(a,'action(@a,@pln)',s)
```

(*) The slightly unusual case of a dying man is only one of the more salient examples of a basic truth: agents often lose information after they construct a plan; they are nonetheless capable of executing the plan. Consider, for example, a busy executive who plans a conference in detail, convinces herself that the plan will work, delegates the plan to a secretary, and then proceeds to forget the details of the plan. At the time she delegates the plan, it makes sense to say that she can execute the plan.

(**) This use of control is unintuitive in some cases; for example, I control the plan in which humans land on Mars, if it will occur.

```
Controls(a,pln,s) if
  ¬ a ∈ actors(pln) and ∃ st occur(pln,s,st)
```

```
Controls(a,sequence(pln1,pln2),s1) iff
  Controls(a,pln1,s) and
  R(pln1,s1) => Controls(a,pln2,s2)
```

```
Controls(a,cond(p,pln1,pln2),s) iff
  p => Controls(a,pln1,s)  and
  ¬ p => Controls(a,pln2,s)
```

```
Controls(a,while(p,pln),s) iff
  Controls(a,
    cond(p,sequence(p,pln,while(p,pln)),Null),s)
```

```
Controls(a,concurrent(pln1,pln2),s) iff
  Controls(a,pln1,s) and Controls(a,pln2,s)
```

We now say that an agent can execute a sequence of two plans if he knows that he can control the first and he knows that as a result of the first plan he will control the second.

Axiom 11:

```
Can-execute-plan(a,sequence(pln1,pln2),s1) iff
  Know(a,'Controls(@a,@pln1,@s)',s1) and
  Know(a,'R(@pln1,@s1,s2)
    => Controls(@a,@pln2,s2)',s1)
```

In the Jones-Smith example, above, Jones can execute his plan because at the beginning he knows that Smith will execute his will.

Conditionals: As with sequences, it is easy to overstate the knowledge preconditions for conditional plans. We might say that an agent can execute cond(p,pln1,pln2) if he knows p and can-execute pln1 or he knows that p is false and can execute pln2. It turns out, however, that an agent can often successfully execute a plan without knowledge of the crucial condition. Consider Smith's plan to play the stock market by listening to the advice of his stockbroker Brown. Smith knows that Brown is watching out for the earnings report of IBM. Smith can construct the following plan:

```
cond(Favorable(earnings-rept(IBM)),
    sequence(do(Brown,tell(Smith,'Buy')),
        do(Smith,buy-shares(IBM))),
    sequence(do(Brown,tell(Smith,'Sell')),
        do(Smith,sell-shares(IBM))))
```

Smith can execute this plan even though he doesn't at the start know anything about IBM's earnings. Intuitively, this is true because he is not involved in the first part of the plan. It is *Brown* who must know IBM's earnings. More precisely, Smith's actions at the beginning of the plan (here Null) are not affected by the conditions of the plan.

We thus say that an agent executing a conditional plan is required to know the condition only if his actions at the beginning of the plan would be affected by the condition. We introduce the function first-action(a,pln) which returns the actions done by a during the first part of pln.

Axiom 12:

```
Can-execute-plan(a,cond(p,pln1,pln2),s) iff
  (first-action(a,pln1) ≠ first-action(a,pln2))
    => p => Know(a,p,s) and
      ¬ p => Know(a,'¬ ^p^',s) and
  (p and Can-execute-plan(a,pln1,s))
      or
  (¬ p and Can-execute-plan(a,pln2,s))
```

While Loops: Since while loops are defined in terms of sequence and conditionals, our axiom for while loops is simply:

Axiom 13:
Can-execute-plan(a,while(p,pln),s) iff
 Can-execute-plan
   (a,cond(p,sequence(pln,while(p,pln)),Null),s)

Concurrency: We say that an agent can execute a plan consisting of two concurrent plans if he can execute each plan. In addition, he must know that they are physically feasible, and that there are sufficient resources available.

Axiom 14:

Can-execute-plan(a,concurrent(pln1,pln2),s) iff
Can-execute-plan(a,pln1,s) and
Can-execute-plan(a,pln2,s) and
Know(a,'Physically-feasible(concurrent(@pln1,@pln2))',s)
   and
Know(a,'∀ a1 ∈ actors(concurrent(@pln1,@pln2))
 (Resource-compatible
   (a1,action(@pln1),action(@pln2)),@s)',s)

6.3. Example

We now demonstrate how our theory works in practice. We consider again the case introduced in Section 1. An agent A, entering a chemistry lab for the first time, is asked to neutralize an acid; he has no idea how to perform the procedure. We assume that A knows that some agent B knows how to neutralize the acid, and that A and B are cooperative agents. For the purposes of this brief paper, we furthermore assume that the following is true of our planning domain:
1) all communicative acts are primitive
2) friendly agents wish to do what they're asked to do
3) if an agent wishes to do an act and he can, then he will
4) friendly agents are constrained to tell the truth.
Finally, we assume that the physical preconditions for the actions here are satisfied. (These assumptions are dropped in [Morgenstern 1987], where an isomorphic problem is worked out in detail.) We can then show that A can successfully execute the following plan. The actions introduced below should be self-explanatory.

The plan consists of a sequence of three steps:

sequence
{Step 1} do(A,request-act(B,
   '{i∃ p Procedure-string(p) and
    Tells(B,A,
     'do(A,neutralize-acid) = do(A,ˆpˆ)',i)}')

{Step 2} {i∃ p Procedure-string(p) and
    Tells(B,A,'do(A,neutralize-acid)= do(A,ˆpˆ)',i)}

{Step 3} {i∃ p Procedure-string(p) and
    do(A,ˆpˆ)=do(A,neutralize-acid)
    and Does(A,ˆpˆ,i)}
Equivalently, do(A,neutralize acid)

Since communicative acts are primitive, A knows that he automatically knows enough to ask B to perform the requested action. In addition, the physical preconditions for this action are satisfied. Thus, A knows that he is able to perform the action of the first step in this plan. Moreover, since A and B are friendly, A knows that B will perform the favor that he has requested, telling him how to neutralize the acid, if B possibly can. In point of fact, since B knows how to neutralize the acid, he can tell A how to perform the

action. Thus, A can predict the occurrence of the second step. Once B tells A the procedure, A will know what the procedure is. So A can predict that he will be able to perform the act of neutralizing the acid. A can thus reason that he can successfully execute the plan consisting of the sequence of Step1, Step2, and Step3.

7. Conclusion

We have constructed a highly flexible model of action and planning, and have demonstrated that it is well suited for partially specified plans and for multi-agent interactions. We have presented solutions to both of the Knowledge Preconditions Problems within that context, explaining how agents can reason about their ability to perform actions and execute plans.

This paper represents the second stage of a three-stage research effort to develop a robust logic of knowledge, action, and communication. In a future paper, we present a logic of communication based upon an Austinian model of speech acts [Austin 1962], and discuss how we can integrate this theory with our solutions to the Knowledge Preconditions Problems.

Acknowledgements: This research was supported in part by NSF grant DCR-8603758. Thanks to Ernie Davis for many helpful ideas, suggestions, and discussions.

BIBLIOGRAPHY

Allen, James: 'Toward a General Theory of Action and Time', *Artificial Intelligence*, Vol. 23, No.2, 1984

Austin, J.L.: *How to Do Things With Words*, Harvard University Press, Cambridge, 1962

Chapman, David: *Planning for Conjunctive Goals*, MIT TR 83-85, 1985

Ernst, G. and Newell, Allan: *GPS: A Case Study in Generality and Problem Solving*, Academic Press, New York, 1969

Fikes, R.E. and Nils Nilsson: 'STRIPS: a New Approach to the Application of Theorem Proving to Problem Solving,' *Artificial Intelligence*, Vol 2, 1971

McCarthy, John and Patrick Hayes: 'Some Philosophical Problems from the Standpoint of Artificial Intelligence' in Bernard Meltzer, ed: *Machine Intelligence 4*, 1969

McDermott, Drew: 'A Temporal Logic for Reasoning About Processes and Plans,' *Cognitive Science*, 1982

Moore, Robert: *Reasoning About Knowledge and Action*, SRI Technical Note 191, 1980

Morgenstern, Leora: 'A First Order Theory of Planning, Knowledge, and Action', *Proceedings of the Conference on Theoretical Aspects of Reasoning About Knowledge*, Morgan Kaufmann, Los Altos, 1986

Morgenstern, Leora: *Foundations of a Logic of Knowledge, Action, and Communication*, forthcoming NYU Ph.D. thesis, 1987

Morgenstern, Leora: 'Preliminary Studies for a First Order Logic of Knowledge and Action,' NYU Technical Report 262, 1986

Sacerdoti, Earl: *A Structure for Plans and Behavior*, American Elsevier, New York 1977

Tate, Austin: 'Generating Project Networks', *Proceedings, Fifth International Conference on Artificial Intelligence*, 1977

COMMUNICATION AND INTERACTION IN MULTI-AGENT PLANNING*

Michael Georgeff

Artificial Intelligence Center,
SRI International,
333 Ravenswood Ave.,
Menlo Park, CA., 94025.

Abstract

A method for synthesizing multi-agent plans from simpler single-agent plans is described. The idea is to insert communication acts into the single-agent plans so that agents can synchronize activities and avoid harmful interactions. Unlike most previous planning systems, actions are represented by *sequences* of states, rather than as simple state change operators. This allows the expression of more complex kinds of interaction than would otherwise be possible. An efficient method of interaction and safety analysis is then developed and used to identify critical regions in the plans. An essential feature of the method is that the analysis is performed without generating all possible interleavings of the plans, thus avoiding a combinatorial explosion. Finally, communication primitives are inserted into the plans and a supervisor process created to handle synchronization.*

§1 Introduction

One of the things robots and other agents need to be able to do is to organize their activities so that they can co-operate with one another and avoid conflicts. For example, we might want two robots to co-operate in building a component, one holding some part while the other attaches some other part to it, or we might want each to pursue different goals, making sure that they both don't attempt to use the same resource at the same time. One way to organize such robots is to carefully time each of their activities in such a way that this sort of co-operation and conflict avoidance is guaranteed. However, in many real-world situations, it is not possible to time events with enough accuracy to enable this approach to work, and some run-time synchronization of activities is needed. Further, because these robots like to be as autonomous as possible, pursuing their own goals at their own speed, we should not impose ordering constraints on their activities unless it is absolutely necessary. Such synchronization can only be achieved by getting the robots (or some observers) to talk to each other or to some supervising agent.

This paper describes a relatively simple method for achieving this synchronization, given that the plans of the individual robots have already been constructed. The method also extends to single-agent planning, where one tries to achieve subgoals separately and defers decisions as to how these subplans will finally be interleaved (e.g., as in NOAH [Sacerdoti 77]). Note that we are not concerned with some of the more problematic issues in multi-agent planning, such as questions of belief or persuasion (e.g., [Konolige 82]). Similarly, the type of communication act that is involved is particularly simple, and provides no information other than synchronizing advice (cf. [Appelt 82]).

Most approaches to planning view actions (or events) as a mapping from an old situation into a new situation (e.g., [McCarthy 68, Sacerdoti 77]). However, in cases where multiple agents can interact with one another, this approach fails to adequately represent some important features of actions and events (e.g., see [Allen 81, McDermott 82]). For example, consider the action of tightening a nut with a spanner. To represent this action by the changes that it brings about misses the fact that a particular tool was utilized *during* the performance of the action. And, of course, this sort of information is critical in allocating resource usage and preventing conflicts. Wilkins [Wilkins 82] recognized this problem with the STRIPS formulation, and extended the representation of actions to include a description of the resources used during the action. However, these resources are limited to being objects, and one cannot specify such properties of an action (or action instance) as "I will always remain to the north of the building", which might help other agents in planning to avoid a potentially harmful interaction.

In this paper we show how representing actions as *sequences* of states allows us to take account of both co-operative and harmful interactions between multiple agents. We assume that the duration of an action is not fixed, and that we can only know that an action has been completed by asking the agent that performed the action (or some observer of the action). This does not mean to say that we cannot take into account the expected duration times of actions, but rather that we are concerned with problems where this information is not *sufficient* for forming an adequate plan. For example, if some part in a machine fails, then knowing that delivery of a new part takes about 24 hours can help in planning the repair, but a *good* plan will probably want a local supervisor or agent to be notified on delivery of the part.

*This research was supported in part by ONR contract N000014-80-C-0296 and in part by AFOSR contract F49620-79-C-0188.

§2 Formalizing the Problem

We consider an action to be a *sequence* $S_1, S_2, \ldots S_n$ of sets of states, intuitively those states over which the action takes place.* The *domain* of the action is the initial set of states S_1, and the *range* is the final set of states S_n. The intermediate sets of states $S_2, \ldots S_{n-1}$ are called the *moments* of the action.

A *planning problem* P consists of a set of states, S; a designated set of initial states, I, in S; a set of primitive actions, A, which can be performed by the various agents operating in the domain; and a set of goal states, G, in S. For any given planning problem, a *single-agent [unconditional] plan* P is a description of a sequence of actions $a_1, a_2, \ldots a_n$ from A such that

i. a_1 is applicable to all initial states I (i.e., the domain of a_1 contains I)

ii. for all $i, 1 < i \leq n$, the action a_i is applicable to all states in the range of a_{i-1}

iii. a_n achieves the goal G (i.e., the range of a_n is contained in G).

A *multi-agent plan* for a problem P is a collection of plans for subproblems of P which are synchronized to be applicable to all initial states I and to achieve the goal G.

We will describe the problem domain using a predicate-calculus-like representation and assume that all actions satisfy the so-called "STRIPS assumption" [Nilsson 80]. Under the STRIPS assumption, all conditions that cannot be proved [under some suitable restriction] to have changed by the performance of an action are assumed to remain unchanged.

Further, we are only concerned with problems in which the components of a world state involving distinct agents are sufficiently decoupled to permit us to assume that the effects of actions of one agent are largely independent of any other. Although violation of this restriction would not affect the validity of any solutions obtained, we would then be less certain of finding solutions, even if they existed.

The representation of actions that we will use is a generalization of the standard STRIPS representation. Each action description contains a *pre-condition* and a *post-condition*, denoting the domain and range of the action. In addition, we need to represent what happens *during* the action. This is achieved by specifying an *unordered* set of conditions to denote the moments (intermediate state sets) of the action. We will call these conditions the *during* conditions of the action. Again, under the STRIPS assumption, all other conditions are assumed to remain unchanged during the performance of the action, unless it can be proved otherwise.

For example, here is a possible description for the blocks world action that places one block on another:

```
puton(x,y)
    pre:      holding(x) and clear(y)
    during:   { holding(x) and clear(y) }
    post:     clear(x) and handempty and on(x,y)
```

---

*More generally, an action may be a *set* of such sequences. While this generalization can easily be accommodated within the formalism, it needlessly complicates our exposition.

In the above problem domain, we could assume also that there was a *static domain constraint* [Rosenschein 82] saying that holding(x) always implies clear(x).

§3 The Method

Let us assume that, given a planning problem, we have decomposed the original goal into appropriate subgoals. Without loss of generality, we will only consider decomposition into *two* subgoals. Also assume that we have separately generated plans for solving each of these subgoals (using some simple search technique, for example). Our problem now is to combine the two plans into a multi-agent plan that avoids conflicts and allows as many actions to proceed in parallel as possible.

The first thing we have to work out is the manner in which individual actions may interact with one another. Then we need to determine which of the feasible situations are "unsafe" (i.e., could lead us into deadlock) and finally we need to insert synchronization primitives into the two subplans (single-agent plans) so that these unsafe situations can be avoided.

3.1 Interaction Analysis

Our first task is to establish which situations occurring in the two single-agent plans are incompatible with one another. For example, if, in one single-agent plan, a situation occurs where block A is on top of block B, and, in the other single-agent plan, a situation occurs where block B is required to be clear, then these two situations are clearly incompatible. Similarly, if one agent expects a component of some assembly to be held by some other agent, and that other agent is not holding it, then the situations are again incompatible. We will now make this notion a little more precise.

Consider two (single-agent) plans P and Q, and let p and q be some state descriptions occurring at some point in the action sequences for P and Q, respectively. We will denote by $<p, q>$ the situation (set of states) where both p and q hold. If p and q are contradictory (i.e., we can prove that p and q cannot both be true at the same time), then of course $<p, q>$ will denote the empty set and we will say that $<p, q>$ is *unsatisfiable*. Otherwise, we will say that $<p, q>$ is *satisfiable*.

Now consider what happens when we try to execute actions in parallel. Let us begin by describing the sequence of state sets defining an action by a *sequence* of conditions. Then, given two actions $a = p_1, p_2, \ldots p_m$ and $b = q_1, q_2, \ldots q_n$, what can we say about the way they can be executed?

Assume we are in some situation $<p_i, q_j>$. To establish feasibility and safety, we need to know what are the possible successor situations. Say that, at this given instant, action a continues next, while action b remains at its current point of execution. Then, clearly, in the next situation p_{i+1} will hold. But will q_j also hold in this new situation? In the general case, we would need to use the properties of the problem domain to determine what in fact does happen next. However, under the STRIPS assumption, we are guaranteed that q_j holds in this new situation, provided $<p_{i+1}, q_j>$ is satisfiable. Similarly, if action b proceeds before action a, then p_i will continue to hold in the new situation, provided again that this new situation is satisfiable. Thus the possible successors of the situation $<p_i, q_j>$ are just $<p_{i+1}, q_j>$ and $<p_i, q_{j+1}>$.

The STRIPS assumption is thus seen to be very important, because it allows us to determine the manner in which actions can be interleaved solely on the basis of satisfiability of the pairwise combination of the conditions defining the actions. If this were not the case, we would have to examine every possible interleaving of the actions, inferring as we went just what the successor situations were and whether or not they were satisfiable. Even without taking into account the cost of performing the necessary inferences, the complexity of this process is of order $(n + m)!/(n! \ m!)$, compared with a complexity of order $n \times m$ if we make the STRIPS assumption (and thus need only examine all possible pairs of conditions). Furthermore, in the general case it would not be possible to specify the during conditions as an unordered set — we would have to specify the actual order in which these conditions occur during the performance of the action. This complicates the representation of actions and, in any case, may not be information that we can readily provide.

We are now in a position to determine how actions as a whole can be safely executed. Consider two plans $P = a_1, a_2, \ldots a_m$ and $Q = b_1, b_2, \ldots b_n$, and assume actions a_i and b_j are next to be executed.

One possibility is that actions a_i and b_j can be executed in parallel. Because we have no control over the rates of the actions, all interleavings of the actions must therefore be possible. Under the STRIPS assumption, this will be the case if, and only if, all situations $<p, q>$ are satisfiable, where p and q are any condition defining the actions a_i and b_j, respectively. Such actions will be said to *commute*.

Alternatively, action a_i could be executed while b_j is suspended (or vice versa). For this to be possible, we require that the preconditions of b_j be satisfied on termination of some action that follows a_i in plan P. We will in fact impose somewhat stronger restrictions than this, and require that the preconditions of b_j be satisfied on termination of a_i itself.* This amounts to assuming that the preconditions for one of the actions appearing in one of the plans are unlikely to be achieved by the other plan (or that, in worlds where interactions are rare, so is serendipity). It is clear that, for actions satisfying the STRIPS assumption, and under the restriction given above, action a_i can be executed while b_j is suspended if, and only if, (1) the situation consisting of the preconditions of both actions is satisfiable and (2) the situation consisting of the postcondition of a_i and the precondition of b_j is satisfiable. If actions a_i and b_j have this property, we will say that a_i has *precedence* over b_j.

Note that it is possible for both actions to have precedence over each other, meaning that either can be executed while the other is suspended. Also, neither action may have precedence over the other, in which case neither can be executed. In the latter case, we will say that the actions *conflict*.

---

*This is simply a restriction on the *solutions* we allow, and simplifies the analysis. The fact that one of the plans might fortuitously achieve the preconditions for one or more actions in the other plan does not *invalidate* any solution we might obtain — it just means that the solution we obtain will not make constructive use of that fact.

In problem domains that are best described by predicate calculus or some parameterized form of action description, the above conditions need to be determined for the *instances* of the actions that occur in the particular plans under consideration. However, in many cases these conditions can be established for the primitive actions, irrespective of the particular instance. For example, in the blocks world, **handempty** conflicts with **holding(x)**, irrespective of the value of **x**. Furthermore, one can often establish relatively simple *isolation conditions* under which classes of actions will or will not commute irrespective of the particular instance. Thus although the deductions necessary for determining satisfaction of situations may be time consuming, much of the analysis can be done *once only* for any given problem domain.

3.2 Safety Analysis

We can now use these properties to set up the safety conditions for individual actions. Consider two plans $P = a_1, a_2, \ldots a_m$ and $Q = b_1, b_2, \ldots b_n$. Let $begin(a)$ denote the beginning of an action a and $end(a)$ the termination of the action. Let the initial conditions of the plans P and Q be denoted by $end(a_0)$ and $end(b_0)$, respectively. For each pair of actions a_i and b_j occurring in P and Q we then have the following:

i.   If a_i and b_j do not commute, then $<begin(a_i), begin(b_j)>$ is unsafe.

ii. If a_i does not have precedence over b_j, then $<begin(a_i), end(b_{j-1})>$ is unsafe.

The set of all such unsafe situations is called the *interaction set*.

However, we still need to determine whether these unsafe situations give rise to other unsafe situations — that is, we must determine which of all the possible situations occurring in the execution of the plans P and Q could result in deadlock. The rules that govern the safety of a given situation s are as follows:

i.   If $s = <begin(a_i), begin(b_j)>$, then s is unsafe if either successor situations are unsafe.

ii. If $s = <begin(a_i), end(b_j)>$, then s is unsafe if $<end(a_i), end(b_j)>$ is unsafe.

iii. If $s = <end(a_i), end(b_j)>$, then s is unsafe if both successor situations are unsafe.

iv. Together with those situations occurring in the interaction set, these are all the unsafe situations.

Unfortunately, to use these rules to determine which of all feasible situations are unsafe requires the examination of all possible interleavings of the actions comprising the plans, and the complexity of this process increases exponentially with the number of actions involved. However, in the kinds of problem domain that we are considering, actions rarely interact with each other, and as a result long subsequences of actions often commute. The following theorem, which is not difficult to prove, allows us to make use of this fact.

Commutativity Theorem. *Let $a_1, a_2, \ldots a_m$ be a [consecutive] subsequence of actions in a plan P and $b_1, b_2, \ldots b_n$ be a subsequence of actions in a plan Q. If all the actions a_i, $1 \leq i \leq m$, commute with the actions b_j, $1 \leq j \leq n$, then all possible situations occurring in all possible interleavings of these sequences will be unsafe if, and only if, the situations $<end(a_m), begin(b_1)>$ and $<begin(a_1), end(b_n)>$ are unsafe. Further, all situations occurring in all interleavings of these sequences will be safe if, and only if, $<end(a_m), end(b_n)>$ is safe.*

This theorem means that, if any two subsequences of actions commute with each other, then we need only consider those situations that occur on the "boundaries" of the sequences. Exactly what states within those boundaries are safe and unsafe depends only on the safety or otherwise of the boundary states, and this can be determined in a straightforward manner. As commutativity is common when interactions are rare, this result allows us to avoid the exploration of a very large number of interleavings and to substantially reduce the complexity of the problem. In particular, actions that commute with all actions in the other plan can simply be removed from consideration.

We will now use these results as a basis for our method of safety analysis. Assume we have constructed two single-agent plans and have performed the interaction analysis. All references to actions that commute with the other plan in its entirety (i.e., which do not appear in the interaction set) are removed from the plans, and the beginning and termination points of the remaining actions are explicitly represented. We will say that the resulting plans are *simplified*. Then, beginning with the initial situation, the conditions of safety given above are applied recursively to determine all situations that are feasible yet unsafe. However, whenever we reach a situation where following subsequences of actions commute, we use the commutativity theorem to avoid the explicit exploration of all possible interleavings of these subsequences.[*]

3.3 Interaction Resolution

The set of unsafe situations is next analyzed to identify contiguous sequences of unsafe situations. These represent *critical regions* in the single-agent plans. Once these critical regions have been determined, standard operating-system methods can be used to enforce synchronization of the actions in the plans so that conflicting critical regions will not both be entered at the same time.

We will use CSP primitives [Hoare 1978] for handling this synchronization. A program in that formalism is a collection of sequential processes each of which can include interprocess communication operations. Syntactically, an interprocess communication operation names the source or destination process and gives the information to be transmitted. In Hoare's notation, the operation "send *s* to process P" is written

P!s

and the operation "receive *s* from process P" is

P?s

---

[*]In fact, the analysis of safety can be further simplified. These details need not concern us here, our intention being primarily to establish the importance of the STRIPS assumption and the commutativity theorem to avoid a combinatorial explosion.

Semantically, when a process reaches a communication operation, it waits for the corresponding process to reach the matching communication operation. At that point the operation is performed and both processes resume their execution.

The synchronization is achieved as follows. At the beginning and end of each critical region R we set up a communication command to a supervisor S, respectively S!begin-R and S!end-R. The supervisor then ensures that no critical regions are allowed to progress at the same time. Placing the communication commands in the original single-agent plans is clearly straightforward. So all we now have to do is construct the scheduler, which is a standard operating-systems problem.

3.4 Example

We will consider an example where two robots are required to place some metal stock in a lathe, one making a bolt and the other a nut. Only one robot can use the lathe at a time.

We will not formally provide the details of the actions and the problem domain, but only sufficient to give the idea behind the analysis and the solution. The fact that the lathe can only be used by one robot at a time is represented as a static constraint on the problem domain.

The actions are informally as follows:

a1m: agent 1 moves to the lathe
a2m: agent 2 moves to the lathe
a1p: agent 1 places metal stock in lathe
a2p: agent 2 places metal stock in lathe
a1b: agent 1 makes a bolt
a2n: agent 2 makes a nut
a1f: agent 1 moves to end
a2f: agent 2 moves to end

The preconditions and during conditions for actions **a1b** and **a2n** include the constraint that the lathe must be in the possession of the appropriate agent, as do the postconditions and during conditions for actions **a1p** and **a2p**.

Assume that a simple planner produces the following single-agent plans:

a1m → a1p → a1b → a1f
a2m → a2p → a2n → a2f

The following precedence and commutativity properties can then be established:

i.   actions **a1b** and **a2n** conflict with one another

ii.   actions **a1p** and **a2p** each have precedence over the other, but do not commute.

iii. action **a1b** has precedence over **a2p**, but not vice versa.

iv.   action **a2n** has precedence over **a1p**, but not vice versa.

We now proceed to determine the unsafe situations. First, the interaction set is determined to be:

$<begin(a1b), begin(a2n)>$ $<begin(a1b), end(a2p)>$
$<end(a1p), begin(a2n)>$ $<begin(a1p), begin(a2p)>$
$<begin(a1b), begin(a2p)>$ $<end(a1p), end(a2p)>$
$<begin(a1p), begin(a2n)>$ $<begin(a1p), end(a2p)>$

We next form the simplified solutions:

begin(a1p) → end(a1p) → begin(a1b) → end(a1b)
begin(a2p) → end(a2p) → begin(a2n) → end(a2n)

Then we perform the safety analysis, which, in this case, returns the set of unsafe situations unchanged from the interaction set. On concatenating consecutive elements, we get only two critical regions: **begin(a1p) → end(a1b)** conflicts with **begin(a2p) → end(a2n)**.

Finally we insert CSP commands into the original plans:

Solution for agent 1 (P)

a1m → S!begin(a1p) → a1p → a1b → S!end(a1b)
→ a1f

Solution for agent 2 (Q)

a2m → S!begin(a2p) → a2p → a2n → S!end(a2n)
→ a2f

Solution for the synchronizer (S)*

```
[   not N ; P?begin(a1p)  →  M := true
 [] not M ; Q?begin(a2p)  →  N := true
 [] true ; P?end(a1b)     →  M := false
 [] true ; Q?end(a2n)     →  N := false]
```

Both M and N are initially set to "false".

The solution obtained is, of course, the obvious one. Both agents must advise the supervisor that they wish to put stock in the lathe, and can only proceed to do so when given permission. Both agents must also advise the supervisor when they have finished with the lathe. On his part, the supervisor makes sure that only one agent at a time is putting stock into the lathe and using it. Notice that the synchronizer allows *any* interleaving or parallel execution of the single-agent plans that does not lead to deadlock. Further, the synchronizer allows the plans to be continually executed, which is useful for production-line planning.

Although the problem described above involved the avoidance of harmful interactions (mutual exclusion), the method can equally well be applied to problems that require co-operation between agents. The reason is that unless the actions are synchronized to provide the required co-operation, situations will arise which are unsatisfiable. For example, if two agents are required to co-operate to paint a block of wood, one holding the piece and the other painting it, then any situation where one agent was painting the wood while the other was *not* holding it would be unsatisfiable.

The multi-agent plan synthesizer described in this paper has been used to solve a number of tasks involving both co-operation and interaction avoidance. These problems include two arms working co-operatively to bolt subassemblies together, some typical blocks world problems requiring "non-linear" solutions, and various "readers and writers" problems.

---

*The form "[] <guard> → <command>" is a *guarded command* (see [Hoare 78]), and the command following the symbol "→" can only be executed if the execution of the guard (i.e. the boolean expression and the input command preceding "→") does not fail.

§4 Conclusions

We have presented a simple and efficient technique for forming flexible multi-agent plans from simpler single-agent plans. The critical features of the approach are that

i. actions are represented as sequences of states, thus allowing the expression of more complex kinds of interaction than would be possible if simple state change operators were used, and

ii. the STRIPS assumption and commutativity conditions are used to avoid the explicit generation of all possible interleavings of the actions comprising the plans, thus avoiding a combinatorial explosion.

While the approach does not guarantee solutions to some classes of problem involving complex interactions between single-agent plans, it has wide applicability in many real-world settings, such as in automated factories and co-operative robot assembly tasks. Future work will extend the formalism to include conditional plans and hierarchical planning techniques.

Acknowledgments

The author wishes to thank Peter Cheeseman for his critical reading of this paper.

References

[1]   Allen, J.F., "A General Model of Action and Time", University of Rochester, Comp. Sci. Report TR 97, 1981.

[2]   Appelt, D. "Planning Natural Language Utterances", in *Research on Distributed Artificial Intelligence*, Interim Report, AI Center, SRI International, Menlo Park, Ca., 1982.

[3]   Hoare, C.A.R., "Communicating Sequential Processes", *Comm. ACM*, Vol. 21, pp 666-677, 1978.

[4]   Konolige, K. "A First Order Formalization of Knowledge and Action for a Multiagent Planning System", in *Research on Distributed Artificial Intelligence*, 1982.

[5]   McCarthy, J., in Minsky (ed.) *Programs with Common Sense*, MIT Press, Cambridge, Mass., 1968.

[6]   McDermott, D., "A Temporal Logic for Reasoning about Processes and Plans", Yale University Comp. Sci. Research Report 196, 1981.

[7]   Nilsson, N.J. *Principles of Artificial Intelligence*, Tioga Press, Palo Alto, Ca., 1980.

[8]   Rosenschein, S. "Plan Synthesis: A Logical Perspective" Multiagent Planning System", Proc. IJCAI-81, Vancouver, Canada, pp. 331-337, 1981.

[9]   Sacerdoti, E.D. *A Structure for Plans and Behaviour*, Elsevier, North Holland, New York, 1977.

[10] Wilkins, D.E., "Parallelism in Planning and Problem Solving: Reasoning about Resources", Tech Note 258, AI Center, SRI International, Menlo Park, Ca., 1982.

A Theory of Action for MultiAgent Planning

Michael Georgeff
Artificial Intelligence Center
SRI International
333 Ravenswood Ave.
Menlo Park, California 94025.

Abstract

A theory of action suitable for reasoning about events in multiagent or dynamically changing environments is presented. A device called a process model is used to represent the observable behavior of an agent in performing an action. This model is more general than previous models of action, allowing sequencing, selection, nondeterminism, iteration, and parallelism to be represented. It is shown how this model can be utilized in synthesizing plans and reasoning about concurrency. In particular, conditions are derived for determining whether or not concurrent actions are free from mutual interference. It is also indicated how this theory provides a basis for understanding and reasoning about action sentences in both natural and programming languages.

1. Introduction

If intelligent agents are to act rationally, they need to be able to reason about the effects of their actions. Furthermore, if the environment is dynamic, or includes other agents, they need to reason about the interaction between their actions and events in the environment, and must be able to synchronize their activities to achieve their goals.

Most previous work in action planning has assumed a single agent acting in a static world. In such cases, it is sufficient to represent actions as state change operators (e.g., [4], [9]). However, as in the study of the semantics of programming languages, the interpretation of actions as functions or relations breaks down when multiple actions can be performed concurrently. The problem is that, to reason about the effects of concurrent actions, we need to know *how* the actions are performed, not just their final effects.

Some attempts have recently been made to provide a better underlying theory for actions. McDermott [10] considers an action or event to be a set of sequences of states, and describes a temporal logic for reasoning about such actions and events. Allen [1] also considers an action to be a set of sequences of states, and specifies an action by giving the relationships among the intervals over which the action's conditions and effects are assumed to hold. However, while it is possible to state arbitrary properties of actions and events, it is not obvious how one could use these logics

in synthesizing or verifying multiagent plans. [1]

In a previous paper [5], we proposed a method for forming synchronized plans that allowed multiple agents to achieve multiple goals, given a simple model of the manner in which the actions of one agent interact with those of other agents. In this paper, we propose a more general model of action, and show how it can be used in the synthesis or verification of multiagent plans and concurrent programs.

2. Process Models and Actions

Agents are machines or beings that act in a world. We distinguish between the internal workings of an agent and the external world that affects, and is affected by, that agent. All that can be observed is the external world. At any given instant, the world is in a particular *world state*, which can be described by specifying conditions that are true of that state.

Let us assume that the world develops through time by undergoing discrete changes of state. Some of these changes are caused by agents acting in the world; others occur "naturally," perhaps as a result of previous state changes. Actions and events are considered to be composed of primitive objects called *atomic transitions*. An atomic transition is a relation on the set of world states. Any sequence of states resulting from the application of some specified atomic transitions will be called an *event*. Note that we do not require that atomic transitions be deterministic, but we do require that they terminate.

An *action* is a class of events; viewed intuitively, those that result from the activity of some agent or agents in accomplishing some goal (including the achievement of desired conditions, the maintenance of desired invariants, the prevention of other events, etc.)

In carrying out or performing an action, an agent forces some sequence of atomic transitions in the world. For every action the agent is capable of performing, there will correspond some internal structure that specifies just how and under what conditions these atomic transitions are to be made.

---

[1] Allen [2] proposes a method for forming multiagent plans that is based on his representation of actions. However, he does not use the temporal logic directly, and actions are restricted to a particularly simple form (e.g., they do not include conditionals).

Usually we do not have access to this internal structure. However, since we are interested only in the *observable* behavior of the agent, we do not need to know the internal processes that govern the agent's actions. Thus, to reason about how the agent acts in the world and how these actions interact with events in the world, we need only an abstract model that explains the observable behavior of the agent.

We shall specify the class of possible and observable behaviors of an agent when it performs an action by means of a device called a *process model*. A process model consists of a number of internal states called *control points*. At any moment in time, *execution* can be at any one of these control points. Associated with each control point is a *correctness condition* that specifies the allowable states of the world at that control point.

The manner in which the device performs an action is described by a partial function, called the *process control function*, which, for a given control point and given atomic transition, determines the next control point. A process model can thus be viewed as a finite-state transition graph whose nodes are control points and whose arcs are labeled with atomic transitions.

A process model for an action stands in the same relationship to the internal workings of an agent and events in the external world as a grammar for a natural language bears to the internal linguistic structures of a speaker and the language that is spoken. That is, it models the observable behavior of the agent, without our claiming that the agent actually possesses or uses such a model to generate behaviors.

3. Formal Definition

A *process model* describes an action open to an agent. Formally, a process model is a seven-tuple $A = \langle S, F, C, \delta, P, c_I, c_F \rangle$ where

- S is a set of *world states*
- $F : S X S$ is a set of *atomic transitions*
- C is a set of *control points*
- $\delta : C X F \to C$ is a *process control function*
- $P : C \to 2^S$ associates subsets of S with each control point; values of this function are called *correctness conditions*
- $c_I \in C$ is the *initial control point*
- $c_F \in C$ is the *final control point*.

In general, δ is a partial function. If for a control point c and atomic transition tr, $\langle c, tr \rangle$ is in the domain of δ, we say that tr is *applicable* at c.

We are now in a position to define the execution of a process model. Let A be a process model as defined above. We first define a *state of execution* of A to be a pair $\langle u, c \rangle$, where [2] $c \in C$ and $u \in S^*$. We say that a state of execution

---

[2]S^* is the set of all finite sequences over S.

$e_1 = \langle us_1, c_1 \rangle$ *directly generates* a state of execution $e_2 = \langle us_1 s_2, c_2 \rangle$, denoted $e_1 \rhd_A e_2$, if either

1. $\exists tr . \delta(c_1, tr) = c_2$ and $\langle s_1, s_2 \rangle \in tr$, or
2. $c_1 = c_2$

In (1) we say that the transition is effected by the agent executing A, while in (2) we say that the transition is effected by the *environment*.

We now define a restriction on the relation $\rhd_A$. If, for e_1 and e_2 defined above, $e_1 \rhd_A e_2$ and $s_2 \in P(c_2)$, we say that e_1 *successfully* generates e_2, denoted $e_1 \Rightarrow_A e_2$. If $s_2 \notin P(c_2)$, execution is said to *fail*.

Let $\Rightarrow_A^*$ denote the reflexive transitive closure of the relation $\Rightarrow_A$. Then the action generated by A, denoted α_A, is defined to be

$$\alpha_A = \{b \mid \langle s, c_I \rangle \Rightarrow_A^* \langle b, c_F \rangle \text{ and } s \in P(c_I)\}$$

Each element of α_A is called a *behavior* or *act* of A. The action α itself is the set of all behaviors resulting from the execution of A.

Viewed intuitively, the device works as follows. If it is at control point c_1 and the world is in a state s_1 satisfying the correctness condition $P(c_1)$, the device can pass to control point c_2 and the world to state s_2 as long as there exists an applicable atomic transition tr between states s_1 and s_2 and $\delta(c_1, tr) = c_2$. *Alternatively*, the device can stay at control point c_1 and some transition or event occur in the world (perhaps resulting from the action of some other agent). In either case, for the execution to be successful (not to fail), the new world state must satisfy the correctness condition at c_2, i.e., s_2 must be an element of $P(c_2)$.

In performing the action α, the device starts at control point c_I. The action terminates when the device reaches c_F. Given an initial state of the world s, various sequences of world states can be generated by the process model as it passes from the initial to the final control point. The set of all such sequences constitute the action itself.

This is the same general view of action as presented by Allen [1] and McDermott [10]. However, our theory differs in that it allows us to distinguish between transitions effected by the agent and those effected by the external world. This is particularly important in the synthesis and verification of multiagent plans and concurrent programs (e.g., [3]).

Note that we do not require that a state satisfying the correctness condition at a control point be in the domain of some atomic transition applicable at that control point. Thus, it is possible for the agent to arrive at an intermediate control point and not to be able to immediately effect a further transition. In such cases, the environment must change before the action can progress. This could occur, for example, if an agent nailing two boards together expected another to help by holding the boards. Only when the "holder" (who is part of the environment) has provided the necessary assistance (and moved the state of the world into the domain of an applicable transition) can the "nailer" proceed with the action.

Neither do we require that an atomic transition performed by an agent always be successful i.e., the transition could sometimes leave the agent in a state that violated the current correctness condition. A process model that allowed such transitions could sometimes fail. In most cases, this is undesirable (though it may be unavoidable), and for the rest of the paper we will assume that this *cannot* happen. That is, we will assume that only the environment (or another agent) can cause an action to fail.

It should also be noted that the correctness conditions say nothing about termination — it may be that an action never reaches completion. This can be the case if the action is waiting for a condition to be satisfied by the environment (so that a transition can be effected), it loops forever, or the environment is *unfair* (i.e., does not give the action a chance to execute).

In many cases, we wish to model actions that proceed at an undetermined rate and fail if they are ever forced to suspend execution. For example, it is difficult to hit a golf ball if the environment is allowed to remove and replace the ball at arbitrary times during one's swing. Such uninterruptable actions require that, for any control point c, any state that satisfies the correctness condition at c also be in the domain of some atomic transition applicable at c.

4. Composition of Actions

A plan or program for an agent is a syntactic object consisting of primitive operations combined by constructions that represent sequencing, nondeterministic choice, iteration, forks and joins, etc. If we intend the denotations of such plans to be process models, we need some means of combining the latter in a way that reflects the composition operators in plans.

Of special interest, and indeed the motivation behind the model presented here, is the parallel-composition operator. We define this below.

Let $A_1 = \langle S, F_1, C_1, \delta_1, P_1, c_{I1}, c_{F1} \rangle$ and $A_2 = \langle S, F_2, C_2, \delta_2, P_2, c_{I2}, c_{F2} \rangle$ be two process models for actions α_1 and α_2, respectively. Then we define a process model representing the parallel composition of A_1 and A_2, denoted $A_1 \parallel A_2$, to be the process model $\langle S, F, C, \delta, P, c_I, c_F \rangle$, where

- $F = F_1 \cup F_2$

- $C = C_1 \times C_2$

- For all $c_1 \in C_1$, $c_2 \in C_2$ and tr in F_1,
  $\delta(\langle c_1, c_2 \rangle, tr) = \langle \delta_1(c_1, tr), c_2 \rangle$

- For all $c_1 \in C_1$, $c_2 \in C_2$ and tr in F_2,
  $\delta(\langle c_1, c_2 \rangle, tr) = \langle c_1, \delta_2(c_2, tr) \rangle$

- For all $c_1 \in C_1$ and $c_2 \in C_2$,
  $P(\langle c_1, c_2 \rangle) = P_1(c_1) \cap P_2(c_2)$

- $c_I = \langle c_{I1}, c_{I2} \rangle$

- $c_F = \langle c_{F1}, c_{F2} \rangle$

It is not difficult to show that the action α generated by $A_1 \parallel A_2$ is exactly $\{x \cap y \mid x \in \alpha_1 \text{ and } y \in \alpha_2\}$.

Note that the projection of δ onto C_1 and C_2 gives exactly the control function for the component process models. At any moment, each component is at one of its own control points; the pair of control points, taken together, represents the current control point of the parallel process.

Furthermore, the behaviors generated by these two processes running in parallel are also generated by each of them running separately. This means that any property of the behaviors of the independent processes can be used to determine the effect of the actions running in parallel. This is particularly important in providing a compositional logic for reasoning about such actions (see [3]).

The above model of parallel execution is an interleaving model. Such a model is adequate for representing almost all concurrent systems. The reason is that, in almost all cases, it is possible to decompose actions into more and more atomic transitions until the interleaving of transitions models the system's concurrency accurately. The nondeterministic form of the interleaving means that we make no assumption about the relative speeds of the actions. We can also define a parallel composition operator that is based on communication models of parallel action, in which communication acts are allowed to take place *simultaneously*. This, together with other composition operators, is described by me elsewhere [6].

5. Freedom from Interference

In plan synthesis and verification it is important to be able to determine whether or not concurrent actions interfere with one another. In the previous section we defined what it meant for two actions (strictly speaking, process models) to run in parallel. Now we have to determine whether execution of such a parallel process model could *fail* because of interaction between the two component processes.

Consider, then, two actions α and β generated by process models A and B, respectively. The process model corresponding to these actions being performed in parallel is $A \parallel B$. In analysing this model, however, we will view it in terms of its two component process models (i.e., A and B).

Assume that we are at control points c_1 in A and c_2 in B, and that tr is an atomic transition applicable at c_2. Clearly, if the process has not failed, the current world state must satisfy both $P(c_1)$ and $P(c_2)$. Now assume that process B continues by executing the atomic transition tr. This transition will take us to a new world state, while leaving us at the same control point within A. From A's point of view, this new state must still satisfy the condition $P(c_1)$. Thus, we can conclude that the transition tr executed at control point c_2 will not cause A to fail at c_1 if the following condition holds:

$$\forall s_1\, s_2 \,.\, s_1 \in P(c_1) \cap P(c_2) \text{ and } \langle s_1, s_2 \rangle \in tr \text{ implies } s_2 \in P(c_1)$$

We say that the transition tr at control point c_2 *does not interfere with* A if the above condition holds at all control points in A, i.e., for all correctness conditions associated with A.

We are now in a position to define freedom from interference. A set of process models $A_1, \ldots A_n$ is said to be *interference-free* [3] if the following holds for each process A_i: for all control points c in A_i and all transitions tr applicable at c and for all $j, j \neq i$, tr at c does not interfere with A_j.

Thus, if some set of actions is interference-free, none can be caused to fail because of interaction with the others. Of course, any of the actions could fail as a result of interaction with the environment.

From this it follows that, for ascertaining freedom from interference, it is sufficient to represent the functioning of a device by

1. A set of correctness conditions, and

2. A set of atomic transitions restricted to the correctness condition of the node from which they exit.

Knowledge of a process model's structure (i.e., the process control function), is unnecessary for this purpose. In a distributed system, this means that an agent need only make known the foregoing information to enable it to interact safely with other agents. We call such information a *reduced specification* of the action.

Let us consider the following example. Blocks A, B and C are currently on the floor. We wish to get blocks A and B on a table, and block C on a shelf, and have two agents, X and Y, for achieving this goal. Agent X has not got access to block B, but can place block A on the table and block C on the shelf. He therefore forms a plan for doing so. Agent Y cannot reach block A, but is happy to help with block B. Unfortunately, in doing so, he insists that the floor be clear of block C at the completion of his action.

The plans for agent X and Y are given below. The correctness conditions at each control point in the plans are shown in braces, "{" and "}". The "if" statement is assumed to be realized by two atomic transitions. The first of these is applicable when block C is on the floor, and results in block C being placed on the table. The second is applicable when block C is not on the floor, and does nothing (i.e., is a no-op). The process models corresponding to these plans should be self-evident.

Plan for agent X:

{(clear A) and (clear C)}
(puton A TABLE)
{(on A TABLE) and (clear C)}
(puton C SHELF)
{(on A TABLE) and (on C SHELF)}

Plan for agent Y:

{(clear B) and (clear C)}
(puton B TABLE)
{(on B TABLE) and (clear C)}
if (on C FLOOR) then
                 (puton C TABLE)
{(on B TABLE) and not (on C FLOOR)}

It is clear from the definition given above that these actions are interference-free. However, they interact in quite a complex manner. In some circumstances, agent Y *will* put block C on the table, which would seem to suggest interference. Nevertheless, interference freedom is assured because the only time that Y can do this is when it does not matter, i.e., before X has attempted to put C on the shelf. Note that if the test and action parts of the "if" statement were separate atomic transitions, rather than a single one, then the actions would not be free from interference.

6. General Reasoning about Actions

So far we have been interested solely in reasoning about possible interference among actions. For many applications, we may wish to reason more generally about actions. One way to do this is to construct a logic suitable for reasoning about process models and the behaviors they generate. That is, we let process models serve as interpretations for plans or programs in the logic. An interesting compositional temporal logic has been developed by Barringer et al [3]. Because it is compositional, process models provide a natural interpretation for the logic.

One may well ask what role process models play, given that the only observables are sequences of world states and that a suitable temporal logic, per se, is adequate for describing such sequences. However, in *planning* to achieve some goal, or *synthesizing* a program, we are required to do more than just describe an action in an arbitrary way — we must somehow form an object that allows us to choose our *next* action (or atomic transition) purely on the basis of the current execution state, without any need for further reasoning.

We could do this by producing a temporal assertion about the action from which, at any moment of time, we could directly ascertain the next operation to perform (e.g., a formula consisting of appropriately nested "next" operators). Thus, in a pure temporal logic formalism, plan synthesis would require finding an appropriately structured temporal formula from which it was possible to deduce satisfaction of the plan specification. However, instead of viewing planning syntactically (i.e., as finding temporal formulas with certain structural properties), it is preferable, and more intuitive, to have a model (such as a process model) that explicitly represents the denotation of a plan or program (see [6]).

Process models serve other purposes also. For example, interference freedom is easily determined, given a process model, but it is less clear how this could be achieved ef-

---

[3]This definition of the notion "interference-free" generalizes to arbitrary transitions that used by Owicki and Gries[11] for verifying concurrent programs. Synchronization primitives have not been included explicitly, but can be handled by conditional atomic transitions [8].

ficiently, given a general specification in a temporal logic. Even so, one would need to construct an appropriate process model first (or its syntactic equivalent in a temporal logic), as the implementation of the specifications might make it necessary to place additional constraints upon the plan.

In combination with a temporal logic such as suggested above, the proposed theory of action provides a semantic basis for commonsense reasoning and natural-language understanding. Process models are more general than previously proposed models (e.g., [7]), particularly in the way they allow parallel composition. They can represent most actions describable in English, including those that are problematic when actions are viewed as simple state-change operators, such as "walking to the store while juggling three balls" [1], "running around a track three times" [10], or "balancing a ball" (which requires a very complex process model despite the apparent simplicity of its temporal specification). The theory also allows one to make sense of such notions as "sameness" of actions, incomplete actions (like an interrupted painting of a picture) and other important issues in natural-language understanding and commonsense reasoning.

Process models are also suitable for representing most programming constructs, including sequencing, nondeterministic choice (including conditionals) and iteration. Parallelism can also be represented, using either an interleaving model, as described in section 4, or a communication model. The model used by Owicki and Gries [11] to describe the semantics of concurrent programs can be considered a special case of that proposed herein.

7. Conclusions

A nascent theory of action suitable for reasoning about interaction in multiagent or dynamically changing environments has been presented. More general than previous theories of action, this theory provides a semantics for action statements in both natural and programming languages.

The theory is based on a device called a process model, which is used to represent the observable behavior of an agent in performing an action. It was shown how this model can be utilized for reasoning about multiagent plans and concurrent programs. In particular, a parallel-composition operator was defined, and conditions for determining freedom from interference for concurrent actions were derived. The use of process models as interpretations of temporal logics suitable for reasoning about plans and programs was also indicated.

REFERENCES

[1]   Allen, J. F., "A General Model of Action and Time," Comp Sci Report TR 97, University of Rochester (1981).

[2]   Allen, J.F., "Maintaining Knowledge about Temporal Intervals," *Comm. ACM*, Vol 26, pp. 832-843 (1983).

[3]   Barringer, H., Kuiper, R., and Pnueli, A., "Now You May Compose Temporal Logic Specifications" (1984).

[4]   Fikes, R.E., Hart, P.E., and Nilsson, N.J., "STRIPS: A New Approach to the Application of Theorem Proving to Problem Solving," *Artificial Intelligence*, Vol 2, pp. 189-208 (1971).

[5]   Georgeff, M.P., "Communication and Interaction in Multiagent Planning," *Proc. AAAI-83*, pp. 125-129 (1983).

[6]   Georgeff, M.P., "A Theory of Plans and Actions," SRI AIC Technical Report, Menlo Park, California (1984).

[7]   Hendrix, G.G., "Modeling Simultaneous Actions and Continuous Processes," *Artificial Intelligence*, Vol 4 (1973).

[8]   Lamport, L., and Schneider, F.B., "The "Hoare Logic" of CSP, and All That", ACM Transactions on Programming Languages, Vol 6, pp 281-296 (1984).

[9]   McCarthy, J., "Programs with Common Sense," in *Semantic Information Processing* M. Minsky ed. (MIT Press, Cambridge, Massachusetts) (1968).

[10] McDermott, D., "A Temporal Logic for Reasoning about Plans and Processes," Comp. Sci. Research Report 196, Yale University (1981).

[11] Owicki, S. and Gries, D., "Verifying Properties of Parallel Programs: An Axiomatic Approach," *Comm. ACM*, Vol 19, pp 279-285 (1976).

THE REPRESENTATION OF EVENTS IN MULTIAGENT DOMAINS

Michael P. Georgeff *

Artificial Intelligence Center
SRI International
Menlo Park, California

Abstract

The purpose of this paper is to construct a model of actions
and events suited to reasoning about domains involving multiple
agents or dynamic environments. A model is constructed that
provides for simultaneous action, and the kind of facts necessary
for reasoning about such actions are described. A model-based
law of persistence is introduced to describe how actions affect the
world. No frame axioms or syntactic frame rules are involved
in the specification of any given action, thus allowing a proper
model-theoretic semantics for the representation. Some serious
deficiencies with existing approaches to reasoning about multiple
agents are also identified. Finally, it is shown how the law of
persistence, together with a notion of causality, makes it possible
to retain a simple model of action while avoiding most of the
difficulties associated with the frame problem.

1 Introduction

A notion of events and processes is essential for reasoning about
problem domains involving one or more agents situated in dynamic environments. While previous papers [3,4,5,6] discussed
the importance of the notion of *process*, herein we focus on the
representation of events and actions. As we will show, the approach avoids many of the difficulties associated with other models of events and actions.

2 Events

We assume that, at any given instant, the world is in a particular
world state. Each world state consists of a number of *objects* from
a given domain, together with various *relations* and *functions*
over those objects. A sequence of world states will be called a
world history.

A given world state has no duration; the only way the pas-
sage of time can be observed is through some change of state.
The world changes state by the occurrence of *events*. An event
(strictly, an *event type*) is a set of state sequences, representing
all possible occurrences of the event *in all possible situations* (see
also [1,12]).

In this paper, we will restrict our attention to *atomic events*.
Atomic events are those in which the state sequences are of length

---

* Also affiliated with the Center for the Study of Language and Information, Stanford University, Stanford, California.

This research has been made possible in part by a gift from the System
Development Foundation and by the Office of Naval Research under Contract N00014-85-C-0251.

two, and can be modeled as a transition relation on world states.
This transition relation must include all possible state transitions, *including those in which other events occur simultaneously
with the given event*. Consequently, the transition relation of an
atomic event places restrictions on those world relations that are
directly affected by the event, but leaves most others to vary
freely (depending upon what else is happening in the world).
This is in contrast to the classical approach, which views an
event as changing some world relations but leaving most others
unaltered.

For example, consider a domain consisting of blocks A and B
at possible locations 0 and 1. Assume a world relation that represents the location of each of the blocks, denoted loc. Consider
two events, $move(A, 1)$, which has the effect of moving block A
to location 1, and $move(B, 1)$, which has a similar effect on block
B. Then the classical approach (e.g., see reference [13]) would
model these events as follows:

$$move(A, 1) = \{\langle loc(A, 0), loc(B, 1)\rangle \rightarrow \langle loc(A, 1), loc(B, 1)\rangle$$
$$\langle loc(A, 0), loc(B, 0)\rangle \rightarrow \langle loc(A, 1), loc(B, 0)\rangle\}$$

and similarly for $move(B, 1)$.

Every instance (transition) of $move(A, 1)$ leaves the location of
B unchanged, and similarly every instance of $move(B, 1)$ leaves
the location of A unchanged. Consequently, it is impossible to
compose these two events to form one that represents the simultaneous performance of both $move(A, 1)$ and $move(B, 1)$, except
by using some interleaving approximation.

In contrast, our model of these events is:

$$move(A, 1) = \{\langle loc(A, 0), loc(B, 1)\rangle \rightarrow \langle loc(A, 1), loc(B, 1)\rangle$$
$$\langle loc(A, 0), loc(B, 1)\rangle \rightarrow \langle loc(A, 1), loc(B, 0)\rangle$$
$$\langle loc(A, 0), loc(B, 0)\rangle \rightarrow \langle loc(A, 1), loc(B, 1)\rangle$$
$$\langle loc(A, 0), loc(B, 0)\rangle \rightarrow \langle loc(A, 1), loc(B, 0)\rangle\}$$

and similarly for $move(B, 1)$.

This model represents all possible occurrences of the event,
including its simultaneous execution with other events. For example, if $move(A, 1)$ and $move(B, 1)$ are performed simultaneously, the resulting event will be the intersection of their possible
behaviors:

$$move(A, 1) \| move(B, 1) =$$
$$move(A, 1) \cap move(B, 1) =$$
$$\{\langle loc(A, 0), loc(B, 0)\rangle \rightarrow \langle loc(A, 1), loc(B, 1)\rangle\}$$

Thus, to say that an event has taken place is simply to put
constraints on some world relations, and leave most others to
vary freely.

Event e_1:

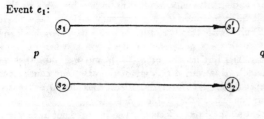

Event e_2:

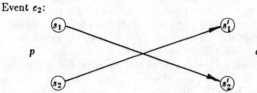

Figure 1: Two Incompatible Events

Of course, to specify events by explicitly listing all the possible transitions would, in general, be infeasible. We therefore need some formalism for describing events and world histories; herein, we will use something similar to situation calculus [11].

Essentially, there are two things we need to say about the possible occurrences of any given event. The first is needed to specify the effects of the event occurring in some given situation. The second is needed to specify under what conditions we consider the event to have occurred, and is essential if we are to reason about the possibility of events occurring simultaneously.

Let ϕ and ψ be conditions on world states (usually called *fluents* [11]), let $occurs(e)(s)$ represent the fact that the event e occurs in state s and, for a given world history w containing state s, let $succ(s)$ be the successor of s. Then we can describe the effects of an occurrence of e with axioms of the following form:[1]

$$\forall w, s \ . \ \phi(s) \wedge occurs(e)(s) \supset \psi(succ(s))$$

This statement is intended to mean that, in all possible world histories, if ϕ is true when the event e occurs, ψ will be true in the resulting state. It has essentially the same meaning as $\phi \supset [e]\psi$ in dynamic logic. Axioms such as these are essential for planning, allowing the determination of the strongest [provable] postconditions and weakest [provable] preconditions of events [15].

At first glance, it appears as if this is *all* we really need for planning and other forms of practical reasoning. For example, assume we have the following axioms describing events e_1 and e_2:

$$\forall w, s \ . \ \phi_1(s) \wedge occurs(e_1)(s) \supset \psi_1(succ(s))$$
$$\forall w, s \ . \ \phi_2(s) \wedge occurs(e_2)(s) \supset \psi_2(succ(s))$$

From this we can infer that

$$\forall w, s \ . \ (\phi_1 \wedge \phi_2)(s) \wedge ((occurs(e_1) \wedge occurs(e_2))(s)$$
$$\supset (\psi_1 \wedge \psi_2)(succ(s))$$

However, it would be unwise to take this as the basis for a plan to achieve $(\psi_1 \wedge \psi_2)$. The reason is that it may be impossible for the two events to occur simultaneously, even if $(\psi_1 \wedge \psi_2)(succ(s))$ is not provably false.

For example, consider the two events shown in Figure 1. Let's assume that p holds in states s_1 and s_2 and q holds in the successor states. (We have taken some liberties in naming states, but

---

[1]We will assume throughout that, in such axioms, s is an element of w.

that is not important for this example.) Events e_1 and e_2 satisfy the above axioms, where $\phi_1 = \phi_2 = p$ and $\psi_1 = \psi_2 = q$.

Given these axioms alone, it is quite consistent to assume that both events occur simultaneously, but there is no way to *prove* that they can so occur – in fact, given e_1 and e_2 as shown in Figure 1, such a statement is clearly false. (Given *sufficient* axioms about the effects of these events, we could, of course, prove that such events *could not* occur together.)

To describe what conditions constitute the occurrence of an event e, we need axioms of the form

$$\forall w, s \ . \ \phi(s) \wedge \psi(succ(s)) \supset occurs(e)(s)$$

This statement is intended to capture the fact that, for all world histories, we consider the event e to have occurred if ϕ holds at the beginning of the event and ψ holds afterwards. Facts such as these are critical for reasoning about whether two or more events can proceed simultaneously and *cannot* be inferred from statements of the former kind about the effects of events.

For example, consider that two events e_1 and e_2 both satisfy[2]

$$\forall w, s \ . \ p(s) \wedge q(succ(s)) \supset occurs(e_j)(s)$$

To prove that these events can occur simultaneously, all we need do is prove that, in some world history, p holds of one state and q holds of its successor.

Often, we may even be able to make stronger statements than these. For example, the event $move(A, 1)$ satisfies

$$\forall w, s \ . \ occurs(move(A, 1))(s) \equiv loc(A, 0)(s) \wedge loc(A, 1)(succ(s))$$

This specification completely characterizes the event $move(A, 1)$ – there is nothing more that can be said about the event. Thus, *at this point of the story*, the frame problem does not arise. Because the event, in and of itself, places no restrictions on the majority of world relations, we do not require (indeed, it would be false to require) a large number of frame axioms stating what relations the performance of the event leaves unchanged. In contrast to the classical approach, we therefore need not introduce any *frame rule* [7] or STRIPS-like assumption [2] regarding the *specification* of events.

3 Actions

When a process brings about an event we will say that the process performs an *action*. For now, we can consider an action and the event it brings about to be the same object – that is, a relation on world states. Later on, we shall have to distinguish the two.

If we are to form plans in multiagent worlds, one of the more important considerations is whether or not any two or more actions can be performed concurrently – it is of little use to form a plan that calls for the simultaneous performance of actions that simply cannot coexist. Thus, to guarantee the validity of a plan containing simultaneous actions, we need to prove that it is indeed possible to perform the actions simultaneously.

Consider two actions a_1 and a_2 that bring about events e_1 and e_2, respectively. In constructing a plan that involves the simultaneous performance of a_1 and a_2, it is not enough that it simply be *consistent* that e_1 and e_2 occur together. The example discussed in the preceding section is a case in point. Of course, this may be the best one can do given incomplete knowledge of the world but, in such cases, there is certainly no guarantee that the plan would ever succeed.

To guarantee the success of such a plan, we need to be able to *prove* that a_1 and a_2 can be performed simultaneously. To

---

[2]The events shown in Figure 1 do not satisfy this axiom!

do this, we need to prove that the intersection of the transition relations corresponding to e_1 and e_2 is nonempty and that its domain includes the states in which the actions a_1 and a_2 might be performed. For example, consider that we have

$$\forall w, s . \phi_1(s) \wedge \psi_1(succ(s)) \supset occurs(e_1)(s)$$

$$\forall w, s . \phi_2(s) \wedge \psi_2(succ(s)) \supset occurs(e_2)(s)$$

It is easy to see that, if we are in a state in which ϕ_1 and ϕ_2 hold, both events can occur together if there exists a world history containing a successor state in which ψ_1 and ψ_2 hold. Unfortunately, ascertaining this involves determining the *consistency* of $(\psi_1 \wedge \psi_2)$, which is undecidable in the nonpropositional case. Moreover, determining performability of actions on the basis of consistency arguments can lead to nonmonotonicity – addition of further axioms could invalidate any conclusions drawn.

In fact, a similar problem arises even for single-agent planning – it is not possible to infer from axioms describing the effects of actions that these effects are indeed satisfiable. To get around this problem, it is usual to assume that no action ever fails, i.e., that there is always a transition from any state satisfying the preconditions of the action to some subsequent state (e.g., [15]).

This option is not open to us in the multiagent domain – simultaneous actions are often not performable. What we need is some way to determine whether or not composite actions will fail on the basis of some property of the component actions. To do this, we introduce a notion of *action independence*.

The approach we adopt is to provide additional axioms specifying which relational tuples the action *directly affects*.[3] To do this, for every action a and n-ary predicate symbol P, we introduce a formula $\delta_P(a, \tilde{x})$, called a *direct-effects formula* ($\tilde{x}$ represents an n-tuple of free variables).

The meaning of this formula is that, for all $\tilde{x}$, if $\delta_P(a, \tilde{x})$ holds in some state s, *only* those relational tuples denoted by $P(\tilde{x})$ may be affected by the performance of action a; any relational tuple that is not a direct effect of action a is thus free to vary *independently* of the occurrence of a. Thus, $P(\tilde{x})$ may be *forced* to take on some particular truth value in any state resulting from the performance of a; conversely, all other atoms involving P are free to take on any truth value.

For example, $\delta_{loc}(move(A, 1), x, y) \equiv (x = A)$. This means that the action $move(A, 1)$ could affect any tuple denoted by $loc(A, y)$, for any y; on the other hand, it would not affect any other tuples in the relation denoted by loc. There are two important points to note here: (1) this does *not* mean that the other tuples of loc remain *unchanged* – some other action could occur simultaneously that affected these tuples also; and (2) if we wish to infer that $loc(B, y)$ does not change for some y, we need to know that A and B denote different objects.

Given such formulae, it follows that two actions a_1 and a_2 can occur simultaneously in a state s if s is in the domain of each action and, for each n-ary predicate P, $(\neg \exists \tilde{x}.(\delta_P(a_1, \tilde{x}) \wedge \delta_P(a_2, \tilde{x})))$ holds in s – that is, both actions don't directly affect the same relational tuple. For example, assuming unique names, we can infer that the location of B is unaffected by $move(A, 1)$ and that $move(A, 1)$ could be performed simultaneously with any action a' that changed the location of B, provided that, conversely, a' did not affect the location of A.

In the case that the same relational tuples *are* affected, it might

---

be that each relational tuple is changed by each action in the same way, and simultaneity would still be possible. But we then get forced back to considering consistency of formulae. There is no difficulty with this if consistency can be determined and does not involve any nonmonotonicity (such as when one condition (say, ψ_1) implies the other (ψ_2), and we know that ψ_1 is satisfiable). However, if this is not the case, any conclusions drawn must be subject to retraction and thus should be treated as *assumptions* about the problem domain.

Note that all the direct effects of an action need not be involved in any single occurrence of that action – they represent only *possible* effects. Also, the direct effects of an action do not define the possible state transitions – this is given, as before, by the state transition relation associated with the action.

There are some problems with this representation, not the least being that, in many cases of interest, we still have to check consistency of formulae. However, knowledge about the relational tuples that actions may affect, and reasoning about interactions on the basis of this knowledge, seems to be an important part of commonsense reasoning. As we will shortly see, such knowledge also plays an important role in determining the effects of actions performed in isolation.

4   The Law of Persistence

We have been viewing atomic actions or events as imposing certain constraints on the way the world changes while leaving other aspects of the situation free to vary as the environment chooses. That is, each action transition relation describes all the potential changes of world state that could take place during the performance of the action. Which transition actually occurs in a given situation depends, in part, on the actions and events that take place in the environment. However, if we cannot reason about what happens when some subset of all possible actions occurs – in particular, when only one action occurs – we could predict very little about the future and any useful planning would be impossible.

What we need is some notion of *persistence* that specifies that, in general, world relations only change when forced to [12]. For example, because the action $move(A, 1)$ defined in the previous section places no constraints on the location of B, we would not expect the location of B to change when $move(A, 1)$ was performed in isolation from other environmental actions.

One possibility is to introduce the following *law of persistence*:

$$\forall w, s, \tilde{x} . \phi_P(\tilde{x})(s) \wedge (\neg \exists a . (occurs(a) \wedge \delta_P(a, \tilde{x})))(s)$$
$$\supset \phi_P(\tilde{x})(succ(s))$$

where $\phi_P(\tilde{x})$ is either $P(\tilde{x})$ or $\neg P(\tilde{x})$.

This rule states that, provided no action occurs that directly affects the relational tuple denoted by $P(\tilde{x})$, the truth value of $P(\tilde{x})$ is preserved from one state to the next. It can be viewed as a generalization of the rule used by Pednault for describing the effects of actions in single-agent worlds [13]. For example, we could use this rule to infer that, if $move(A, 1)$ were the only action to occur in some state s, the location of B would be the same in the resulting state as it was in state s.

However, at this point we encounter a serious deficiency in the action model we have been using and, incidentally, in all others that represent actions and events as the set of all their possible behaviors (e.g., [1,12]). Consider, for example, a seesaw, with ends A and B and fulcrum F. We shall assume there are no other entities in the world, that the only possible locations for

---

[3]In the general case, we would also have to specify which functional values and constants were directly affected by the action. This is a straightforward extension of the described approach, and we will not consider it further (see reference [13]).

Location:

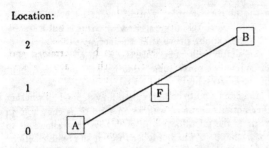

Figure 2: Possible Seesaw State after $move_F$

A, F, and B are 0, 1, and 2, and that these are always colinear. Assume that initially A, F, and B are at location 0, and consider an action $move_F$ that moves F to location 1 (see Figure 2), while allowing all possible movements of A and B, depending on what other actions are occurring at the same time (such as someone lifting B). Of course, the objects must always remain colinear.

The possible transitions for $move_F$ are to one of the states $\langle loc(A,1), loc(F,1), loc(B,1)\rangle$, $\langle loc(A,0), loc(F,1), loc(B,2)\rangle$, or $\langle loc(A,2), loc(F,1), loc(B,0)\rangle$. Furthermore, because the movement of F places constraints on both the locations of A and B, the direct affects of the action will include the locations of all objects:

$$\delta_{loc}(move_F, x, y) \equiv (x = A) \lor (x = F) \lor (x = B).$$

Thus, the effect of $move_F$, in addition to changing the location of F, will be to change either the location of A or the location of B or both. The question is, if no other action occurs simultaneously with $move_F$, *which* of the possible transitions can occur?

Let's assume that, because of the squareness of the fulcrum F, the action $move_F$ always moves A and B to location 1 at the same time, unless some parallel action forces either A or B to behave differently. Unfortunately, using our current action model there is simply no way to represent this. We cannot restrict the transition relation so that it always yields the state in which A, F, and B are all at location 1, because that would prevent A or B from being moved simultaneously with A. Furthermore, the constraint on locations is a contingent fact about the world, not an analytic one – thus, we cannot sensibly escape the dilemma by considering any of the relations *derived* from the others (as many philosphers have pointed out).

From a purely behavioral point of view this is how things should be. To an external observer, it would appear that $move(A,1)$ sometimes changed the location of A and not B (when some simultaneous action occurred that raised A to location 2), sometimes changed the location of B and not A (when some simultaneous action raised B), and sometimes affected the locations of both A and B. (Of course, the action would always change the location of F). As there is no *observation* that could allow the observer to detect whether or not another action was occurring simultaneously, there is no way the action $move_F$ could be distinguished from any other that had the same transition relation. For example, there would be no way to distinguish $move_F$ from an action $move'_F$ that exhibited the same set of possible behaviors but, when performed in isolation, left A where it was and moved B to location 2.

On the other hand, when reasoning about processes, we *do* want to be able to make this distinction. For example, there may be two different ways of moving F, one corresponding to $move_F$ and the other to $move'_F$. In other cases, while an action like

$move_F$ might be appropriate to seesaws, an action analogous to $move'_F$ might be needed for describing object movements in other situations. For example, consider the situation where, instead of being parts of a seesaw, A is a source of light and B is F's shadow.

We therefore make a distinction between actions and events – one that is critical for reasoning about processes and plans. That is, an event is simply identified with all its possible occurrences; in particular, two atomic events having the same transition relation are considered identical. However, actions with the same transition relation (such as $move_F$ and $move'_F$) are not necessarily identical – they may behave differently when performed in isolation and may play different causal roles in a theory of the world.

Clearly, therefore, we cannot determine which action we intend from knowledge (even complete knowledge) of all the possible state transitions (event occurrences) which constitute performance of the action. In particular, we *cannot use any general default rule or minimality criteria* to determine the intended effects of an action when performed in isolation. Indeed, in the case of $move_F$, note that we do *not* minimize the changes to world relations or maximize their persistence: both A and B change location along with F.

It appears, then, that the only thing we can do is to specify what happens when the action occurs in isolation *in addition to* specifying what happens when other actions occur in parallel. This is certainly possible, but the representation would be cumbersome and unnatural.

5 Causality

One way to solve this problem is by introducing a notion of causality. As used herein, if an action a_1 is stated to *cause* an action a_2, we require that a_1 always occur simultaneously with a_2. Thus, in this case, a_1 could never be performed in isolation – a_2 would always occur simultaneously with every occurrence of a_1.

For example, we might have a causal law to express the fact that whenever a block x is moved, any block on top of x and not somehow restrained (e.g., by a string tied to a door) will also move. We could write this as

$$\forall w, s, x, y, l \,.\, (occurs(move(x,l)) \land on(y,x) \land \neg restrained(y))(s)$$
$$\supset occurs(move(y,l))(s)$$

The notion of causality used by us is actually more general than that described above, and is fully described elsewhere [5]. We use the term in a purely technical sense, and while it has many similarities to commonsense useage, we don't propose it as a fully-fledged theory of causality. Essentially, we view causality as a relation between atomic actions that is conditional on the state of the world. We also relate causation to the temporal ordering of events, and assume that an action cannot cause another action that precedes it. However, we do allow an event to cause another that occurs simultaneously (as in this paper). This differs from most formal models of causality [8,12,16].

But how does this relate to the problem of persistence and the specification of the effects of actions performed in isolation? The answer is that we can thereby provide axioms that explicity describe how an action affects the world in the context of other actions either occurring *or not.*

For example, consider the action $move_F$ described in the previous section. We begin by modifying the definition of this action so that its only direct effect is the location of the fulcrum F itself. This means that the transition relation for $move_F$ will have to include world states in which A, F, and B are not colinear, but this is no problem from a technical point of view. Indeed, at least in this case, there is also an intuitive meaning to such worlds; namely, those in which the seesaw is broken. However, there is no problem with requiring all possible world histories (*not* all world states!) to satisfy the linearity constraint.

We then add causal laws which force the simultaneous movement of either A or B or both. For example, we might have the following causal law:

$$\forall w, s \, . \, occurs(move_F)(s) \wedge (\neg \exists a' \, . \, (occurs(a')$$
$$\wedge interferes(a', move(A, 1))))(s) \supset occurs(move(A, 1)(s)$$

where $interferes(a_1, a_2)(s)$ means that it is not possible to perform actions a_1 and a_2 simultaneously in state s (see Section 3).

The intended meaning of this causal law is that, if we perform the action $move_F$, $move(A, 1)$ is caused to occur simultaneously with $move_F$ unless another action occurs that forces A to occupy a location different from 1. A similar causal law would describe the movement of B. Both laws could be made conditional on the seesaw being intact, if that was desired.

There are a number of things to be observed about this approach. First, it would appear that we should add further causal laws requiring the movement of at least one of A or B in the case that both could not move to location 1. However, this is not necessary. For example, let us assume that, at the moment we perform $move_F$, some other action occurs simultaneously that moves B to location 2 (without directly affecting the location of A). As the direct effects of neither this action nor the action $move_F$ include the location of A, we might expect application of the above causal law to yield a resulting state in which A is at location 1. However, this is clearly inconsistent with the constraint that A, F, and B must remain colinear.

If we examine this more carefully, however, the impossibility of such a world state simply implies that the antecedent of the above causal law must, in this case, be false. That is, there must exist an action that occurs in state s and that cannot be performed simultaneously with $move(A, 1)$. Indeed, this is exactly the action that would have appeared in any causal laws that forced the colinearity constraint to be maintained. The point of this example is that in many cases we do not need to include causal laws to maintain invariant world conditions - we can, instead, use the constraints on world state to infer the existence of the appropriate actions.

Second, the application of causal laws need not yield a unique set of caused actions - it could be that one causal law requires the location of A to change and B not, while another requires the location of B to change and A not. Given only this knowledge of the world, the most we could infer would be that one but not both of the actions occurs - but *which* one would be unknown. (Interestingly, this bears a strong similarity to the different possible extensions of a theory under certain kinds of default rules [14].)

Third, actions are clearly distinct from events (cf. [1,12,16]). In particular, actions with the *same* transition relation - i.e., exhibiting the same set of possible behaviors - may play different causal roles. For example, with no outside interference, $move_F$ causes the movement of both A and B, whereas $move_F'$ causes the movement of A alone. This is *not* the same distinction that is made between actions and events in the philosophical literature, but it does have some similarities.

Finally, we may not be able to *prove* that no interference arises, which, in the above example, would prevent us from inferring that the action $move(A, 1)$ occurs. However, this is not a serious problem - if we cannot prove that the action either occurs or does not, we simply will not know the resulting location of A (unless, of course, we make some additional *assumptions* about what events are occurring).

Causal laws can be quite complex, and may depend on whether *or not* other actions occur as well as on conditions that hold in the world. It is the introduction of such laws that allows us to represent what happens when only a subset of all possible actions occur. We gain by having simpler descriptions of actions but, in return, require more complex causal laws. On the other hand, it is now easy to introduce other causal laws, such as ones that describe what happens when a block is moved with a cup on top of it, when the cup is stuck with glue, or tied with a string to a door, or when other blocks are in the path of the movement.

Some predicates are better considered as *defined* predicates, which avoids overpopulating the world with causal laws. For example, the distance between two objects may be considered a defined predicate. Instead of introducing various causal laws stating how this relation is altered by various move actions, we can simply work with the basic entities of the problem domain and infer the value of the predicate from its definiens when needed.

6   The Frame Problem

The frame problem, as Hayes [7] describes it, is dealt with in our approach by means of the law of persistence. This has a number of advantages. First, because this law is a property of our action model, and not of our action specification language, we avoid all of the semantic difficulties usually associated with the frame problem.

Second, we avoid the problem of having to state a vast number of uninteresting frame axioms by means of direct-effects formulae, which describe *all* those relational tuples (and, in the general case, functional values and constants) that can possibly change.

Third, we avoid having unduly complex direct-effects formulae and action representations by introducing causal laws that describe how actions bring about (cause) others. Of course, the causal laws can themselves be complex (just as is the physics of the real world), but the representation and specification of actions is thereby kept simple.

There are also important implementation considerations. The approach outlined here is at least tractable, as the relations and functions that can be affected by the occurrence of an action require, at most, provability of the formulae of interest. Interestingly, one of the most efficient action representations so far employed in AI planning systems - the STRIPS representation [2,10] - is essentially the special case in which (1) the transition relation for each action can be represented by a single precondition-postcondition pair; (2) the postcondition is a conjunction of literals; (3) the direct effects (which correspond to the elements in the delete list) include all the literals mentioned in the postcondition; and (4) no actions ever occur simultaneously with any other. The approach used by Pednault [13] can also be considered the special case in which there are no simultaneous actions.

Some researchers take a more general view of the frame problem, seeing it as the problem of reasoning about the effects of actions and events with *incomplete information* about what other actions or processes (usually the environment) may be occurring simultaneously. Unfortunately, this problem is often confused with the *representation* of actions, with the result that there is usually no clear model-theoretic semantics for the representation.

For example, one of the major problems in reasoning about actions and plans is in determining which actions and events can possibly occur at any given moment. Based on the relative infrequency of "relevant" actions or events, or that one would "know about" these if they occurred, it has been common to use various default rules (e.g., [12]) or minimal models (e.g., [9,16]) to constrain the set of possible action occurrences. However, there are many cases where this is unnecessary – where we can *prove*, on the basis of axioms such as those appearing in this paper, that no actions of interest occur. We may even have axioms that allow one to avoid consideration of whole classes of actions, such as when one knows that certain actions are external to a given process. Thus, in many cases, there is simply no need to use default rules or minimality principles – reasoning about plans and actions need not be nonmonotonic.

In the case that we *do* need to make assumptions about action occurrences, the use of default rules and circumscription can be very useful. For example, by minimizing the extension of the *occurs* predicate we can obtain a theory in which the only action occurrences are those that are *causally necessary*. However, there is no need to limit oneself to such default rules or minimality criteria. There may be domain-specific rules defining what assumptions are reasonable, or one may wish to use a more complicated approach based on information theory. We may be able to make reasonable assumptions about freedom from interference; to assume, for example, that a certain relational tuple will not be influenced by actions in other processes.

It is not our intention to consider herein the problem of making useful assumptions about actions and freedom from interference – it is, of course, not a simple problem. However, it is important to keep this problem separate from the issue of action representation. For example, it at first seems reasonable to assume that my car is still where I left it this morning, unless I have information that is inconsistent with that assumption. However, this assumption gets less and less reasonable as hours turn into days, weeks, months, years, and centuries. This puts the problem where it should be – in the area of making reasonable assumptions, not in the area of *defining* the effects of actions [2,7], the persistency of facts [12], or causal laws [16].

7   Conclusions

We have constructed a model of atomic actions and events that allows for simultaneity, and described the kind of facts required for reasoning about such actions. We introduced a *law of persistence* that allows the effects of actions to be determined and, most importantly, have shown how the representation of actions and their effects involves no frame axioms or syntactic frame rules. We also pointed out some deficiencies in existing approaches to reasoning about multiagent domains: for example, that consistency of predications over states or intervals cannot be taken as proof that actions can proceed concurrently, and that models that represent actions simply as the set of all their possible behaviors cannot make certain distinctions critical for planning in multiagent domains. Finally, we showed how the law of persistence, together with the notion of causation, makes it possible to retain a simple model of action while avoiding most of the difficulties associated with the frame problem.

Acknowledgments

I wish to thank especially Amy Lansky and Ed Pednault, both of whom helped greatly in clarifying many of the ideas presented in this paper.

References

[1]   Allen, J. F., "A General Model of Action and Time," Computer Science Report TR 97, University of Rochester, Rochester, New York (1981).

[2]   Fikes, R. E., and Nilsson, N. J., "STRIPS: A New Approach to the Application of Theorem Proving to Problem Solving," *Artificial Intelligence*, 2, pp. 189–208 (1971).

[3]   Georgeff, M. P., "A Theory of Action for Multiagent Planning," *Proc. AAAI-84*, Austin, Texas (1984).

[4]   Georgeff, M. P. "A Theory of Process" Workshop on Distributed AI, Sea Ranch, California (1985).

[5]   Georgeff, M. P. "Process, Action, and Causality," Workshop on Planning and Reasoning about Action, Timberline Lodge, Mount Hood, Oregon (1986).

[6]   Georgeff, M. P., and Lansky, A. L., "Procedural Knowledge," *Proc. IEEE*, Special Issue on Knowledge Representation (1986).

[7]   Hayes, P. J., "The Frame Problem and Related Problems in Artificial Intelligence," in *Artificial and Human Thinking*, A. Elithorn and D. Jones (eds.), Jossey-Bass (1973).

[8]   Lansky, A. L., "Behavioral Specification and Planning for Multiagent Domains," Tech. Note 360, Artificial Intelligence Center, SRI International, Menlo Park, California (1985).

[9]   Lifschitz, V. "Circumscription in the Blocks World," Computer Science Working Memo, Stanford University, Stanford, California (1985).

[10] Lifschitz, V. "On the Semantics of STRIPS," Workshop on Planning and Reasoning about Action, Timberline Lodge, Mount Hood, Oregon (1986).

[11] McCarthy, J., and Hayes, P. J., "Some Philosophical Problems from the Standpoint of Artificial Intelligence, in *Machine Intelligence 4*, pp. 463–502 (1969).

[12] McDermott, D., "A Temporal Logic for Reasoning about Processes and Plans," *Cognitive Science*, 6, pp. 101–155 (1982).

[13] Pednault, E. P. D., "Toward a Mathematical Theory of Plan Synthesis," Ph.D. thesis, Department of Electrical Engineering, Stanford University, Stanford, California (1986).

[14] Reiter, R., "A Logic for Default Reasoning," *Artificial Intelligence*, 13, pp. 81–132 (1980).

[15] Rosenschein, S. J., "Plan Synthesis: A Logical Perspective," *Proc. IJCAI-81*, Vancouver, British Columbia (1981).

[16] Shoham, Y. "Chronological Ignorance: Time, Knowledge, Nonmonotonicity, and Causation," Workshop on Planning and Reasoning about Action, Timberline Lodge, Mount Hood, Oregon (1986).

AN IMPLEMENTATION OF A
MULTI-AGENT PLAN SYNCHRONIZER

Christopher Stuart

Department of Computer Science
Monash University
Clayton 3168, Australia

ABSTRACT

A program is described which augments plans with synchronizing primitives to ensure appropriate conflict avoidance and co-operation. The plans are particularly suitable for describing the activity of multiple agents which may interfere with each other. The interpretation of a plan is given as a non deterministic finite automaton which exchanges messages with an environment for the commencement and conclusion of primitive actions which take place over a period of time. The synchronized plan allows any and all execution sequences of the original plan which guarantee correct interaction.

1. Introduction

All planning systems operate by combining actions or sub-plans in some way so that the total plan satisfies some constraint – usually to achieve a goal state. Knowledge of how actions interact with each other and the world is used to determine the appropriate combinations. In NOAH[5], for example, consideration of interactions between sub-plans is explicit in the planning process. A plan is a partial order of sub-plans. The planning technique is to expand sub-plans into partial orderings of lower level sub-plans, and then look for and resolve ensuing conflicts. The resolution may impose fixed orderings. This can be unnecessarily restrictive, as in the case where two sub-plans may execute in any order but not at the same time.

This paper considers the use of synchronizing primitives to resolve conflicts and produce a plan which is as unrestrictive as possible. The models of plan and action used are appropriate for simple agents or robots engaged in parallel and or repetitive tasks which may be described at a level not using sensory input to the agents. Use could be made of this technique, for example, in automated assembly lines. Georgeff[2] has also done related work on planning for multiple agents.

2. Underlying theory.

Here we give an informal summary of a fully formalized theory of action and the world, which is described in [6].

2.1. Actions

An agent changes the world by executing actions. When multiple agents are operating in parallel, it may be possible for two actions to be executing simultaneously, and so actions must have a beginning and an end. We consider an action to be decomposed into discrete transformations of the world, which are called *events*. An event also has an associated correctness condition, which must be true at the moment it is executed. An action will be a set of possible finite sequences of events.

2.2. The environment

The state of the *environment* in which an action executes consists of a world state, and a set of actions currently being executed. If an agent executes an action, one of the possible sequences of events for that action is selected non-deterministically and added to the environment state. The environment may at any time take a currently executing action, pop the next event from the event sequence, check for event failure, and change the world state according to that event.

The environment defines a set of symbols called *operators*, and gives each operator an interpretation as a set of event sequences (action). These operators are the means of interaction between an agent and the environment, and are exchanged as messages.

2.3. Agents

The execution of a plan corresponds to some sequence of messages between the environment and an agent. Let A be the set of operators. Then a sequence of messages will be denoted by a string over the alphabet $\{begin,end\} \times A$. For any $\alpha \in A$, (*begin* α) corresponds to the agent sending α to the environment to cause the associated action to be executed, and (*end* α) corresponds to the environment sending α to the agent to indicate that the associated action has completed. We refer simply to *strings* and assume them to be over this alphabet.

An *agent* is an acceptor for *strings*. The formal model for an agent is similar to a non-deterministic finite automaton. It has a set of nodes (agent states), and a set of arcs defining allowed state transitions with associated messages. An agent deadlocks if it is in a state from which there are no possible state transitions involving a (*begin* α) message, and the environment has finished executing all the operators sent by the agent.

An agent defines a set of possible strings, and for any string, an environment defines some set of possible world state sequences. The planning problem is to take information about the environment, and find an agent which has some desired effect on the world, such as the ultimate achieving of a goal world state, no matter what choices the environment makes. We say two agents are *equivalent* if in any environment they always induce the same set of possible sequences of world states.

An agent is *bounded* if there is a finite upper bound on the number of actions which the environment can be executing at a time. Thus a bounded agent will suffice to represent the activity of a finite number of concurrent multiple real world agents .

2.4.   Plans

Given three symbol sets A, M and S being *operators*, *memory states* and *signals* respectively, *plans* are defined recursively.

- For any $\alpha \in A$: α is a plan for executing an single action.

- For any $m \in M$, $s \in S$: (set m), (send s) and (guard m s) are synchronizing primitives.

- If p_1 and p_2 are two plans, then $p_1;p_2$ is the plan to execute them in sequence, $p_1 \| p_2$ is to execute them in parallel, $p_1 | p_2$ is to execute one or the other by non-deterministic selection, and p_1^* executes p_1 an arbitrary number of times.

The semantics for plans is given as a mapping from *plans* to *agents*, which is described in [6]. Intuitively, the agent for the simple plan α is an automaton accepting only the string *{(begin α),(end α)}*. The plan operators build automata in the conventional manner. The synchronizing primitives correspond to arcs in the automaton which have a side effect on plan execution without exchanging any messages with the environment. *Set* changes the *memory state* of the plan, and *guard* and *send* can only be executed simultaneously, and then only when the memory is in the specified state and the signals match. This particular form of primitive is an adaptation of synchronization in the parallel programming language CSP[3], which uses guards which may be a combination of an input/output operation and a normal conditional.

The following two results, given without proof, assert that there is a one to one correspondence between plans and bounded agents.

- Any agent which is given as the semantics of a plan is bounded.

- For any arbitrary bounded agent, there is a plan which has an interpretation equivalent to that agent.

3.   The interaction problem

The problem addressed here is that of ensuring that a plan does not deadlock, or allow any event to fail. Correctness conditions on events or actions can be used to represent many types of plan correctness. If a plan should achieve some goal state given some initial condition, this is ensured by beginning

the plan with an action that asserts the initial condition, and terminating it with an action that will always fail in the absence of the goal condition. A condition which must be maintained during a plan can be enforced with an action in parallel that will fail in the absence of the maintained condition.

A program has been developed which takes a plan and a description of an environment, and generates a revised plan which allows all and only the sequences of communication acts of the first plan that cannot cause failure, and also that will never deadlock.

3.1.   Preventing event failure

For this program we use a very simple form of event, corresponding to the operators of the STRIPS planner[1]. The world is modeled as a set of propositions. Events are constrained to add or delete propositions without reference to the current world state. Also, the correctness condition is a conjunction of propositions or negated propositions. Thus an event is four sets of propositions: a *require true* set, a *require false* set, an *add* set and a *delete* set.

It turns out in this case that to prevent event failure an action is completely defined by ten sets of propositions. The ten properties are defined by considering the execution of the action in isolation from other actions.

- A proposition (its negation) is *asserted* if it is inevitably true (false) after the execution.

- A proposition (its negation) is *retracted* if it could possibly become false (true) after the execution.

- The proposition (its negation) is *conflicted* if it could become false (true) at some stage during the execution.

- The proposition (its negation) is a *precondition* if it must be true (false) immediately before the action begins to ensure that no event will fail.

- The proposition (its negation) is a *during condition* if it must be true (false) for some event in the action.

The necessary and sufficient rules for ensuring no event failure are:

- An action which has a during condition may not run in parallel with an action that conflicts that during condition.

- An action α_1 which has a precondition may not begin until some action α_2 which asserts that condition has completed, and also no action α_3 which retracts that condition may be running from when α_2 begins until α_1 ends.

3.2.   Synchronizing Plans

We synchronize plans by inserting send operations, and running it in parallel with a *synchronization skeleton* consisting only of *guard* and *set* operations. The possible sequences of communication acts for the resulting plan is a subset of those for the original plan. Manna and Wolper describe an algorithm for generating such a skeleton from propositional temporal logic (PTL) formulae used to express constraints on execution sequences of a plan.[4]

PTL is a logic for reasoning about sequences of states. The interpretation of a PTL formula is a set of sequences for which it is *true*. Besides the usual temporal connectives of PTL (*always*, *eventually*, *until* and *next*) we use a *regular expression* operator equivalent in expressiveness to the grammar operators of Wolper.[8]

Given a plan, and for each primitive action the ten sets of propositions mentioned above, it is possible to generate PTL formula which are true for all and only those sequences of communication operations for which the environment cannot fail. These formulae correspond to the two correctness rules given above.

The propositions used in the PTL formula are *not* those manipulated by the agent, but instead correspond to the communication acts of the agent.

3.3. The algorithm

A program has been written which takes as input a plan and operator descriptions, and generates appropriate PTL formulae to express the constraint that sequences of communication acts do not allow the environment to fail. These formulae are given to a theorem prover similar to that described by Manna and Wolper[4], together with a regular expression representing the plan syntax. The regular expression is equivalent in power to the grammar temporal operators of Manna and Wolper, and is true for all and only those sequences of communication acts which may be executed by the plan.

The total set of PTL formulae is satisfied only by those sequences of communication acts which can be given by the initial plan, and which guarantee that no event will fail.

An advantage of using general logical techniques in this way is that theorem proving results may be used to make the process more efficient. Our theorem prover is extended in that it may replace formulae with equivalent but simpler formulae. The initial constraints are also simplified, so long as the conjunction of all the constraints remains equivalent. For example, if there is a constraint that two actions may not occur in parallel, and the syntax of the plan enforces that constraint already, then no extra constraint is generated.

The theorem prover produces a graph which is a model for the PTL formulae. This is converted into a plan equivalent to the CSP program generated by Manna and Wolper. The program is described in detail in [6].

The current version of the program only handles restricted classes of plans and actions (no loops, no selection, deterministic actions), but is being extended at the moment to include these.

4. An example

Consider the problem of three robots all trying to pickup a block and move it clockwise to a location which another robot will clear as it moves. The diagram shows the robots and blocks, and the initial and final positions.

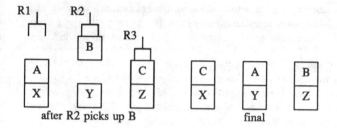

after R2 picks up B   final

The unsynchronized plan to achieve this is as follows:

```
( (START (R1 R2 R3) ((A X) (B Y) (C Z)))
  (PARALLEL ( (PICKUP R1 A X) (PUTDOWN R1 A Y))
            ( (PICKUP R2 B Y) (PUTDOWN R2 B Z))
            ( (PICKUP R3 C Z) (PUTDOWN R3 C X))))
```

The start action sets up the initial conditions, and then each robot in parallel executes a pickup and putdown. Clearly collisions might result.

The synchronized plan produced by the program is

```
( (PARALLEL
    ( (SEND (BEGIN 1))
      (START (R1 R2 R3) ((A X) (B Y) (C Z)))
      (PARALLEL
        ( (PICKUP R1 A X) (SEND (END 2 1 1))
          (SEND (BEGIN 2 1 2)) (PUTDOWN R1 A Y))
        ( (PICKUP R2 B Y) (SEND (END 2 2 1))
          (SEND (BEGIN 2 2 2)) (PUTDOWN R2 B Z))
        ( (PICKUP R3 C Z) (SEND (END 2 3 1))
          (SEND (BEGIN 2 3 2)) (PUTDOWN R3 C X))))

    ( (RECV (BEGIN 1))
      (SETQ N 2)
      (WHILE (NOT (EQ N 13))
        (SELECT-ONE-OF
          (IF (AND (EQ N 2) (RECV (END 2 3 1)))
              THEN (SETQ N 5))
          (IF (AND (EQ N 2) (RECV (END 2 2 1)))
              THEN (SETQ N 4))
      .......
          (IF (AND (EQ N 5) (RECV (END 2 1 1)))
              THEN (SETQ N 6)))))))
```

The syntax is close to CSP, and can be translated directly into plans as we have defined them. A large section of the synchronization skeleton has been removed in the example, since it contains 42 guarded commands – one for each arc in the model for the PTL formulae. The plan has the desired result of holding any putdown until the appropriate pickup has completed.

5. Conclusion and Future Work

There are still some improvements that can be made to the method. The above plan could have been synchronized with no reference to (BEGIN 1). It is worthy of investigation to consider how synchronization primitives could be inserted in the main plan without adding a whole new parallel branch with the synchronization skeleton, or how the synchronization skeleton could be made more modular.

The definition of actions and environments given here enables very strong properties to be given to the synchronized plans: in particular that *all and only* the correct executions of the initial plan are permitted. This is in contrast to previous means of synchronizing plans, such as in NOAH[5], which prohibit some execution sequences which might succeed.

By extending the definition of actions to include more general state transformations in events, a similar algorithm would generate a plan which is still less restrictive than that produced by previous plan modifying techniques, but would disallow certain correct executions. The action descriptions would be much more complex and not capture all the essential properties in the same way as can be done in the simple case with ten sets of propositions. The current version of the theorem prover makes the same assumption as Manna and Wolper: that only one proposition of the PTL formula is true at any moment. For extended actions, new propositions might need to be included which do not have this property.

There is also the problem of types of non-determinism. The current selection operator corresponds to the case where a plan may proceed in one of two directions, and the synchronizer is permitted to chose one over the other. This is *angelic* non-determinism. However, it may be the case for some plans that the choice is critical, but made at execution time, in which case the synchronizer must allow both cases or none at all. This is *demonic* non-determinism, and implies some additional structure to a plan which restricts the ways in which it may b synchronized. For added complexity, the decision may be based on the state of the world model, and so the synchronizer can determine the possible choices it must leave open, depending on the possible world models it derives for the moment of choice.

Loops typically display demonic non-determinism for choosing when to terminate. The synchronizer is not given total control over the number of times the loop will execute, but should always allow the loop to execute as often as necessary. Again, an explicit termination condition in terms of the world model adds further to the complexity.

Loops often have a termination condition which is a function of all the activity in the loop, and yet may not be derived from the given information. Such a termination condition could be specified if a plan segment were treated as a single hierarchical action, and could be given properties similar to those for individual actions. For example, one could specify that a loop would always assert some condition. Consider a loop of an action that removes a single item from a box until none are left. To represent this in the formalism given here, the entire loop would be given an assert condition that the box become empty. To guarantee termination, the entire loop could be given a during condition that no one places anything in the box. In this case, the plan synchronizer certainly does not have full control of the choice of when to terminate the loop.

A version of the program is being developed which will take as input an arbitrary plan as defined above, and also will handle both types of non-determinism, and properties of portions of the plan treated as hierarchical actions. The theoretical justification is being pursued concurrently.

Since this paper first appeared in IJCAI-85, the problem of types of non-determinism has been explored within the context of *branching time* temporal logic [7].

ACKNOWLEDGEMENTS

Much of this investigation was conducted at the AI center at SRI International. Thanks are due to the center and especially to Michael Georgeff for helpful discussion; and to Monash University for financial assistance, and where the work is proceeding.

REFERENCES

[1] Fikes, R.E., Nilsson, N.J. "STRIPS: A new approach to the application of theorem proving in problem solving." *Artificial Intelligence* 2 (1971), pp 189-208.

[2] Georgeff, M.P. "Communication and Interaction in Multi-Agent Planning." In *Proc. AAAI-83, pp 125-129.*

[3] Hoare, C.A.R. "Communicating Sequential Processes." In *Communications of the ACM* 21:8 (1978), pp 666-677.

[4] Manna, Z.; Wolper, P. "Synthesis of Communicating Processes from Temporal Logic Specifications." Report STAN-CS-81-872, Stanford University Computer Science Department. (September 1981)

[5] Sacerdoti, E.D. "A Structure for Plans and Behaviour." Tech Note 109, SRI AI Center, Melno Park, CA. (1975)

[6] Stuart, C.J. "An Implementation of a Multi-Agent Plan Synchronizer Using a Temporal Logic Theorem Prover." Tech Note 350, SRI AI Center, Menlo Park, CA. (1985)

[7] Stuart, C.J. "Branching Regular Expressions and Multi-Agent Plans." In *Reasoning about Actions and Plans,* Georgeff, M.P. and Lansky, A.L. (Eds), (Morgan Kaufmann 1986) pp 161-187.

[8] Wolper, P. "Temporal Logic Can Be More Expressive." In *Proc. of the 22nd Symposium on Foundations of Computer Science.* Nashville, TN. (1981)

COOPERATION WITHOUT COMMUNICATION

Michael R. Genesereth, Matthew L. Ginsberg, and Jeffrey S. Rosenschein*

Logic Group, Knowledge Systems Laboratory,
Computer Science Department, Stanford University,
Stanford, California 94305

ABSTRACT

Intelligent agents must be able to interact even without the benefit of communication. In this paper we examine various constraints on the actions of agents in such situations and discuss the effects of these constraints on their derived utility. In particular, we define and analyze *basic rationality*; we consider various assumptions about independence; and we demonstrate the advantages of extending the definition of rationality from individual actions to decision procedures.

I   Introduction

The affairs of individual intelligent agents can seldom be treated in isolation. Their actions often interact, sometimes for better, sometimes for worse. In this paper we discuss ways in which cooperation can take place in the face of such interaction.

A.   Previous work in Distributed AI

In recent years, a sub-area of artificial intelligence called distributed artificial intelligence (DAI) has arisen. Researchers have attempted to address the problems of interacting agents so as to increase efficiency (by harnessing multiple reasoners to solve problems in parallel [29]) or as necessitated by the distributed nature of the problem domain (e.g., distributed air traffic control [30]).

Smith and Davis' work on the contract net [6] produced a tentative approach to cooperation using a contract-bid metaphor to model the assignment of tasks to processors. Lesser and Corkill have made empirical analyses of distributed computation, trying to discover cooperation strategies that lead to efficient problem solutions for a network of nodes [3,4,7,21].

Georgeff has attacked the problem of assuring non-interference among distinct agents' plans [12,13]; he has made use of operating system techniques to identify and protect critical regions within plans, and has developed a general theory of action for these plans. Lansky has adapted her work on a formal, behavioral model of concurrent action towards the problems of planning in multi-agent domains [20].

These DAI efforts have made some headway in constructing cooperating systems; the field as a whole has also benefited from research into the formalisms necessary for one agent to reason about another's knowledge and beliefs. Of note are the efforts of Appelt [1], Moore [24], Konolige [19,18], Levesque [22], Halpern and Moses [8,16].

B.   Their assumptions

Previous DAI work has assumed for the most part that agents are mutually cooperative through their designer's fiat; there is built-in "agent benevolence." Work has focused on how agents can cooperatively achieve their goals when there are no conflicts of interest. The agents have identical or compatible goals and freely help one another. Issues to be addressed include those of synchronization, efficient communication, and (inadvertent) destructive interference.

C.   Overview of this paper

1.   True conflicts of interest

The research that this paper describes discards the benevolent agent assumption. We no longer assume that there is a single designer for all of the interacting agents, nor that they will necessarily help one another. Rather, we examine the question of how high-level, autonomous, independently-motivated agents ought to interact with each other so as to achieve their goals. In a world in which we get to design only our own intelligent agent, how should it interact with other intelligent agents?

---

*This research has been supported by the Office of Naval Research under grant number N00014-81-K-0004 and by DARPA under grant numbers N00039-83-C-0136 and N00039-86-C-0033.

There are a number of domains in which autonomous, independently-motivated agents may be expected to interact. Two examples are resource management applications (such as an automated secretary [15]), and military applications (such as an autonomous land vehicle). These agents must represent the desires of their designers in an environment that includes other intelligent agents with potentially conflicting goals.

Our model of agent interaction thus allows for true conflicts of interest. As special cases, it includes pure conflict (i.e., zero sum) and conflict-free (i.e., common goal) encounters. By allowing conflict of interest interactions, we can address the question of why rational agents would choose to cooperate with one another, and how they might coordinate their actions so as to bring about mutually preferred outcomes.

2.   No communication

Although communication is a powerful instrument for accomodating interaction (and has been examined in previous work [28]), in our analysis here we consider only situations in which communication between the agents is impossible. While this might seem overly restrictive, such situations do occur, e.g., as a result of commmunications equipment failure or in interactions between agents without a common communications protocol. Furthermore, the results are valuable in the analysis of cooperation with communication [28,27].

Despite the lack of communication, we make the strong assumption that sufficient sensory information is available for the agents to deduce at least partial information about each other's goals and rationality. For example, an autonomous land vehicle in the battlefield may perceive the actions of another autonomous land vehicle and use plan recognition techniques [9] to deduce its destination or target, even in the absence of communication.

3.   Study of constraints

In this paper we examine various constraints on the actions of agents in such situations and discuss the effects of these constraints on the utility derived by agents in an interaction. For example, we show that it can be beneficial for one agent to exploit information about the rationality of another agent with which it is interacting. We show that it can also be beneficial for an agent to exploit the similarity between itself and other agents, except in certain symmetric situations where such similarity leads to indeterminate or nonoptimal action.

The study of such constraints and their consequences is important for the design of intelligent, independently motivated agents expected to interact with other agents in unforeseeable circumstances. Without such an analysis, a designer might overlook powerful principles of coooperation or might unwittingly build in interaction techniques that are nonoptimal or even inconsistent.

Section 2 of this paper provides the basic framework for our analysis. The subsequent sections analyze progressively more complicated assumptions about interactions between agents. Section 3 discusses the consequences of acting rationally and exploiting the rationality of other agents in an interaction; section 4 analyzes dependence and independence in decision making; and section 5 explores the consequences of rationality across situations. The concluding section discusses the coverage of our analysis.

II   Framework

Throughout the paper we make the assumption that there are exactly two agents per interaction and exactly two actions available to each agent. This assumption substantially simplifies our analysis, while retaining the key aspects of the general case. Except where indicated to the contrary, all results hold in general [10,11,14,27].

The essence of interaction is the dependence of one agent's utility on the actions of another. We can characterize this dependence by defining the payoff for each agent i in an interaction s as a function p_i^s that maps every joint action into a real number designating the resulting utility for i. Assuming that M and N are the sets of possible moves for the two agents (respectively), we have

$$p_i^s : M \times N \to \mathbb{R}.$$

In describing specific interactions, we present the values of this function in the form of payoff matrices [23], like the one shown in figure 1. The number in the lower left hand corner of each box denotes the payoff to agent J if the agents perform the corresponding actions, and the number in the upper right hand corner denotes the payoff to K. For example, if agent J performs action a in this situation and agent K performs action c, the result will be 4 units of utility for J and 1 unit for K. Each agent is interested in maximizing its own utility.

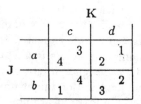

Figure 3: Column Dominance Problem

In dealing with another agent it is often reasonable to assume that the agent is also basically rational. The formalization of this assumption of *mutual rationality* is analogous to that for basic rationality.

$$\neg R_K^s(m) \;\Rightarrow\; W_K(s) \neq m$$

Using this assumption one can prove the optimality of a technique called *iterated dominance analysis*.

Theorem Basic rationality implies iterated dominance analysis.

Proof: For this proof, and those of several following theorems, see [10] and [11]. □

Iterated dominance analysis handles the column dominance problem in figure 3. Using the basic rationality of K, we can show that action d is irrational for K. Therefore, neither ad nor bd is a possible outcome, and J need not consider them.[2] Of the remaining two possible outcomes, ac dominates bc (from J's perspective), so action b is irrational for J.

IV Action Dependence

Unfortunately, there are situations that cannot be handled by the basic rationality assumptions alone. Their weakness is that they in no way account for dependencies between the actions of interacting agents. This section offers several different, but inconsistent, approaches to dealing with this deficiency.

The simplest case is complete independence. The independence assumption states that each agent's choice of action is independent of the other. In other words, each agent's reaction function yields the same value for every one of the other agent's actions. For all m, m', n, and n', we would then have

$$A_K^s(m) = A_K^s(m')$$
$$A_J^s(n) = A_J^s(n').$$

[2]We write mn to describe the situation where J has chosen action m, and K has chosen action n; we call this a *joint action*.

The main consequence of independence is a decision rule commonly known as *case analysis*. If for every "fixed move" of K, one of J's actions is superior to another, then the latter action is forbidden. The difference between case analysis and dominance analysis is that it allows J to compare two possible actions for each action by K without considering any "cross terms."

As an example, consider the payoff matrix in figure 4. Given independence of actions, a utility-maximizing agent J should perform action a: if K performs action c, then J gets 4 units of utility rather than 3, and if K performs action d, then J gets 2 units of utility rather than 1. Dominance analysis does not apply in this case, since the payoff (for J) of the outcome ad is less than the payoff of bc.

K

		c		d	
	a		2		4
J		4		2	
	b		3		1
		3		1	

Figure 4: Case Analysis Problem

Theorem Basic rationality and independence imply case analysis.

By combining the independence assumption with mutual rationality, we can also show the correctness of an iterated version of case analysis.

Theorem Mutual rationality and independence imply iterated case analysis.

As an example of iterated case analysis, consider the situation in figure 5. J cannot use dominance analysis, iterated dominance analysis, nor case analysis to select an action. However, using case analysis K can exclude action c. With this information and mutual rationality, J can exclude action a.

K

		c		d	
	a		3		4
J		3		2	
	b		1		2
		1		4	

Figure 5: Iterated Case Analysis Problem

Note that, if two decision procedures are not independent, the independence assumption can lead to nonoptimal results. As an example, consider the following well-known "paradox." An alien approaches you with two envelopes, one marked "$" and the other marked "¢". The first envelope contains some number of dollars, and the other contains the same number of cents. The alien is prepared to

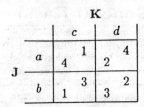

Figure 1: A payoff matrix

Although the utilities present in a payoff matrix can generally take on any value, we will only need the *ordering* of outcomes in our analysis. Therefore, we will only be using the numbers 1 through 4 to denote the utility of outcomes.

An agent's job in such a situation is to decide which action to perform. We characterize the *decision procedure* for agent i as a function W_i from situations (i.e., particular interactions) to actions. If S is the set of possible interactions, we have

$$W_i : S \to M.$$

In the remainder of the paper we take the viewpoint of agent J.

III   Basic Rationality

We begin our analysis by considering the consequences of constraining agent J so that it will not perform an action that is *basically irrational*. Let R_i^s denote a unary predicate over moves that is true if and only if its argument is rational for agent i in situation s. Then agent J is basically rational if its decision procedure does not generate irrational moves, i.e.,

$$\neg R_J^s(m) \Rightarrow W_J(s) \neq m.$$

W_J here is a function that designates the action performed by J in each situation, as described above. In order to use this definition to judge which actions are rational, however, we need to further define the rationality predicate R_J^s.

An action m' *dominates* an action m for agent J in situation s (written $D_J^s(m', m)$) if and only if the payoff to J of performing action m' is greater than the payoff of performing action m (the definition for agent K is analogous). The difficulty in selecting an action stems from lack of information about what the other agent will do. If such information were available, the agent could easily decide what action to perform. Let

the term $A_K^s(m)$ denote the action that agent K will perform in situation s if agent J performs action m:

$$W_K(s) = A_K^s(W_J(s)).$$

In what follows we call A_K^s the *reaction function* for K. Then the formal definition of dominance is

$$D_J^s(m', m) \iff p_J^s(m', A_K^s(m')) > p_J^s(m, A_K^s(m)).$$

We can now define the rationality predicate. An action is *basically irrational* if there is another action that dominates it.

$$(\exists m' \, D_J^s(m', m)) \Rightarrow \neg R_i^s(m)$$

Even if J knows nothing about K's decision procedure, this constraint guarantees the optimality of a decision rule known as *dominance analysis*. According to this rule, an action is forbidden if there is another action that yields a higher payoff for every action of the other agent, i.e.,

$$(\exists m' \forall n \forall n' \, p_J^s(m, n) < p_J^s(m', n')) \Rightarrow W_J(s) \neq m.$$

Theorem Basic rationality implies dominance analysis.

Proof: A straightforward application of the definition of rationality. $\Box$

As an example of dominance analysis, consider the payoff matrix in figure 2. In this case, it is clearly best for J to perform action a, no matter what K does (since 4 and 3 are both better than 2 and 1). There is no way that J can get a better payoff by performing action b.

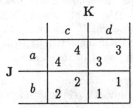

Figure 2: Row Dominance Problem

Of course, dominance analysis does not always apply. As an example, consider the payoff matrix in figure 3. In this situation, an intelligent agent J would probably select action a. However, the rationale for this decision requires an assumption about the rationality of the other agent in the interaction.

Figure 6: Omniscient Alien Problem

give you the contents of either envelope. The catch is that the alien, who is omniscient, is aware of the choice you will make. In an attempt to discourage greed on your part, he has decided to put one unit of currency in the envelopes if you pick the envelope marked \$ but one thousand units if you pick the envelope marked ¢. Bearing in mind that the alien has decided on the contents of the envelope before you pick one, which envelope should you select?

The payoff matrix for this situation is shown in figure 6. Since the payoff for \$ is greater that that for ¢ for **either of the alien's options, case analysis dictates choosing the \$ envelope.** Assuming that the alien's omniscience is accurate, this lead to a payoff of \$1.00. While selecting the envelope marked ¢ violates case analysis, it leads to a payoff of \$10.00.

We can easily solve this problem by describing the alien's reaction function and abandoning the independence constraint. The appropriate axioms are $A_K^s(\$) = 1$ and $A_K^s(¢) = 1000$.

These constraints limit J's attention to the lower left hand corner and the upper right hand corner of the matrix. Since the payoff for selecting the ¢ envelope is better than the payoff for selecting the \$ envelope, a rational agent will choose ¢. Although the example given here is whimsical, there are real-world encounters where the assumption of independence is unwarranted, and where the effect illustrated above must enter the rational agent's analysis.

Another interesting example of action dependence is *common behavior*. The definition requires that we consider not only the current situation s but also the permuted situation s' in which the positions of the interacting agents are reversed. An agent J and an agent K have *common behavior* if and only if the action of K in situation s is the same as that of agent J in the permuted situation s'.[3]

$$\forall s \; W_K(s) = W_J(s')$$

Common behavior is a strong constraint. While it may be insupportable in general, it is reasonable for interaction among artificial agents, especially those built from the same design. Unfortunately, it is not as strong as we would like, except when combined with general rationality.

---

[3]This constraint is similar to the *similar bargainers* assumption in [28,27].

V General Rationality

General rationality is a stronger version of basic rationality, the primary difference being that general rationality applies to decision procedures rather than to individual actions. We introduce a new set of relations and functions to define general rationality. Let $\mathcal{R}_i$ denote a unary predicate over procedures that is true if and only if its argument is rational for agent i. A *generally rational* agent can use a procedure only if it is rational.

$$\neg \mathcal{R}_J(P) \; \Rightarrow \; \exists s \; (W_J(s) \neq P(s)).$$

Recall that W_J here is a function that designates the action performed by J in each situation, as described above. In order to use this definition to judge which actions are rational, we of course need to define further the rationality predicate $\mathcal{R}_J$.

The definition of rationality for a decision procedure is analogous to that for individual actions. A procedure is irrational if there is another procedure that *dominates* it:

$$(\exists P' \; \mathcal{D}_J(P', P)) \; \Rightarrow \; \neg \mathcal{R}_J(P).$$

One procedure dominates another if and only if it yields as good a payoff in every game and a better payoff in at least one game. Let the term $A_K^s(P)$ denote the action that agent K will take in situation s if agent J uses procedure P. Then the formal definition of dominance is:

$$\mathcal{D}_J(P', P) \iff$$
$$\forall s \; p_J^s(P'(s), A_K^s(P')) \geq p_J^s(P(s), A_K^s(P))$$
$$\land \; \exists s \; p_J^s(P'(s), A_K^s(P')) > p_J^s(P(s), A_K^s(P)).$$

The advantage of general rationality is that, together with common behavior (defined in the last section), it allows us to eliminate joint actions that are dominated by other joint actions for all agents, a technique called *dominated case elimination*.

Theorem General rationality and common behavior imply dominated case elimination.

Proof: Let s be a situation with joint actions uv and xy such that $p_J^s(u, v) > p_J^s(x, y)$ and $p_K^s(u, v) > p_K^s(x, y)$, and let P be a decision procedure such that $P(s) = x$ and $P(s') = y$ (where s' is the permuted situation, where J and K's positions have been reversed). Let Q be a decision procedure that is identical to P except that $Q(s) = u$ and $Q(s') = v$. Under the common behavior assumption, Q dominates P for both J and K and, therefore, P is generally irrational. □

In other words, if a joint action is disadvantageous for both agents in an interaction, at least one will perform a different action. This conclusion has an analog in the informal arguments of [5] and [17].

No-conflict situations are handled as a special case of this result. The *best plan* rule states that, if there is a joint action that maximizes the payoff to all agents in an interaction, then it should be selected.

Corollary **General rationality and common behavior imply best plan.**

Proof: Apply dominated case elimination to each of the alternatives. □

As an example of best plan, consider the situation pictured in figure 7. None of the preceding techniques (e.g., dominance analysis, case analysis, iterated case analysis) applies. However, *ac* dominates all of the other joint actions, and so *J* will perform action *a* and *K* will perform action *c* (under the assumptions of general rationality and common behavior).

K

		c		d	
a		4		2	
	4		2		
b		1		3	
	1		3		

J

Figure 7: Best Plan

General rationality and common behavior also handle difficult situations like the prisoner's dilemma [2,5,25] pictured in figure 8. Since the situation is symmetric (i.e., $s = s'$, using our earlier notation), common behavior requires that they both perform the same action; general rationality eliminates the joint action *bd* since it is dominated by *ac*. The agents perform actions *a* and *c* respectively, and each receives 3 units of utility. By contrast, case analysis dictates that the agents perform actions *b* and *d*, leading to a payoff of only 2 units for each.

K

		c		d	
a		3		4	
	3		1		
b		1		2	
	4		2		

J

Figure 8: Prisoner's Dilemma

Unfortunately, general rationality and common behavior are not always consistent. As an example, consider the battle of the sexes problem in figure 9. Again the situation is symmetric, and common behavior dictates that both agents perform the same action. However, both joint actions on the *ac/bd* diagonal are forbidden by dominated case elimination.

This inconsistency can be eliminated by occasionally restricting the simultaneous use of general rationality and

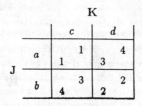

Figure 9: Battle of the Sexes

common behavior to non-symmetric situations. Nevertheless, in a no-communication situation, the resolution of a conflict such as that in figure 9 remains undetermined by the constraints we have introduced.

VI Conclusions

A. Coverage of this approach

There are 144 distinct interactions between two agents with two moves and no duplicated payoffs. Of these, the techniques presented here cover 117. The solutions to the remaining 27 cases are unclear, e.g., the situation in fig. 10.

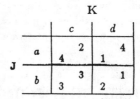

Figure 10: Anomalous situation

For a discussion of a variety of other techniques that can be used to handle these situations, as well as a discussion contrasting all of these approachs with those used in game theory, see [27].

B. Suitability of this approach

This paper's analysis of interactions presupposes a variety of strong assumptions. First, the agents are assumed to have common knowledge of the interaction matrix, including choices of actions and their outcomes. Second, there is no incompleteness in the matrix (i.e., there are no missing utilities). Third, the interaction is viewed in isolation (i.e., no consideration is given to future interactions and the effects current choices might have on them). Fourth, there must be effective simultaneity in the agents' actions (otherwise, there are issues concerning which agent moves first, and the new situation that then confronts the second agent).

Admittedly, these are serious assumptions, but there are some situations where they are satisfied. Consider as an example two ALVs approaching opposite ends of a narrow tunnel, each having the choice of using the tunnel or trying one of several alternate routes. It is not unreasonable to assume that they have common knowledge of one another's approach (e.g., through reconnaisance). Nor is it unreasonable to assume that the agents have some models of one another's utility functions. Finally, in the domain of route navigation, the choices are often few and well-defined. There might be no concern (in this case) over future encounters, and the decisions are effectively simultaneous. The types of analysis in this paper are an appropriate tool to use in deciding what action to take.

For most domains, of course, the assumptions listed above are far too limiting, and clearly more work needs to be done in developing this approach so that each of the most restrictive assumptions can be removed in turn. The work in [28,27] represents steps in that direction. Currently, research on the question of incomplete matrices is being pursued, so that the type of conflict analysis presented in this paper can be applied to interactions with incomplete information [26]. Future work will focus on issues arising from multiple encounters, such as retaliation and future compensation for present loss.

Intelligent agents will inevitably need to interact flexibly with other entities. The existence of conflicting goals will need to be handled by these automated agents, just as it is routinely handled by humans. The results in this paper and their extensions should be of use in the design of intelligent agents able to function successfully in the face of such conflict.

REFERENCES

[1] D. E. Appelt. *Planning Natural Language Utterances to Satisfy Multiple Goals*. PhD thesis, Stanford Univ., 1981.

[2] Robert Axelrod. *The Evolution of Cooperation*. Basic Books, Inc., New York, 1984.

[3] D. Corkill. *A Framework for Organizational Self-Design in Distributed Problem-Solving Networks*. PhD thesis, University of Massachusetts, Amherst, MA, 1982.

[4] Daniel D. Corkill and Victor R. Lesser. The use of meta-level control for coordination in a distributed problem solving network. IJCAI-83, pp. 748–756.

[5] L. Davis. Prisoners, paradox and rationality. *American Philosophical Quarterly*, 14, 1977.

[6] Randall Davis and Reid G. Smith. Negotiation as a metaphor for distributed problem solving. *Artificial Intelligence*, 20(1):63–109, 1983.

[7] Edmund H. Durfee, Victor R. Lesser, and Daniel D. Corkill. Increasing coherence in a distributed problem solving network. IJCAI-85, pp. 1025–1030.

[8] R. Fagin and J. Y. Halpern. Belief, awareness, and limited reasoning: preliminary report. IJCAI-85, pp. 491–501.

[9] Michael R. Genesereth. The role of plans in automated consultation. IJCAI-79, pp. 311–319.

[10] Michael R. Genesereth, Matthew L. Ginsberg, and Jeffrey S. Rosenschein. *Cooperation without Communication*.

HPP Report 84-36, Heuristic Programming Project, Computer Science Department, Stanford University, September 1984.

[11] Michael R. Genesereth, Matthew L. Ginsberg, and Jeffrey S. Rosenschein. *Solving the Prisoner's Dilemma*. Report No. STAN-CS-84-1032 (HPP-84-41), Computer Science Department, Stanford University, November 1984.

[12] Michael Georgeff. Communication and interaction in multi-agent planning. AAAI-83, pp. 125–129.

[13] Michael Georgeff. A theory of action for multi-agent planning. AAAI-84, pp. 121–125.

[14] M. L. Ginsberg. Decision procedures. In *Proceedings of the Distributed Artificial Intelligence Workshop*, pages 43–65, AAAI, Sea Ranch, CA, December 1985.

[15] Ira P. Goldstein. *Bargaining Between Goals*. A. I. Working Paper 102, Massachusetts Institute of Technology Artificial Intelligence Laboratory, 1975.

[16] Joseph Y. Halpern and Yoram Moses. *Knowledge and Common Knowledge in a Distributed Environment*. Research Report IBM RJ 4421, IBM Research Laboratory, San Jose, California, October 1984.

[17] D. R. Hofstadter. Metamagical themas—computer tournaments of the prisoner's dilemma suggest how cooperation evolves. *Scientific American*, 248(5):16–26, May 1983.

[18] Kurt Konolige. A computational theory of belief introspection. IJCAI-85, pp. 502–508.

[19] Kurt Konolige. *A Deduction Model of Belief and its Logics*. PhD thesis, Stanford University, 1984.

[20] A. L. Lansky. *Behavioral Specification and Planning for Multiagent Domains*. Technical Note 360, SRI International, Menlo Park, California, November 1985.

[21] V. Lesser and D. Corkill. The distributed vehicle monitoring testbed: a tool for investigating distributed problem solving networks. *AI Magazine*, 4(3):15–33, Fall 1983.

[22] Hector J. Levesque. A logic of implicit and explicit belief. AAAI-84, pp. 198–202.

[23] R. Duncan Luce and Howard Raiffa. *Games and Decisions, Introduction and Critical Survey*. John Wiley and Sons, New York, 1957.

[24] R. Moore. A formal theory of knowledge and action. In J. R. Hobbs and R. C. Moore, editors, *Formal Theories of the Commonsense World*, Ablex Publishing Co., 1985.

[25] D. Parfit. *Reasons and Persons*. Clarendon Press, Oxford, 1984.

[26] Jeffrey S. Rosenschein. *Cooperation in the Presence of Incomplete Information*. Technical Report, Knowledge Systems Laboratory, Computer Science Dept., Stanford Univ., 1986. In preparation.

[27] Jeffrey S. Rosenschein. *Rational Interaction: Cooperation Among Intelligent Agents*. PhD thesis, Stanford University, 1986. Also published as STAN-CS-85-1081 (KSL-85-40), Department of Computer Science, Stanford University, October 1985.

[28] Jeffrey S. Rosenschein and Michael R. Genesereth. Deals among rational agents. IJCAI-85, pp. 91–99.

[29] R. G. Smith. *A Framework for Problem Solving in a Distributed Processing Environment*. PhD thesis, Stanford University, 1978.

[30] R. Steeb, S. Cammarata, F. Hayes-Roth, and R. Wesson. *Distributed intelligence for air fleet control*. Technical Report WD-839-ARPA, The Rand Corporation, Dec. 1980.

Deals Among Rational Agents

Jeffrey S. Rosenschein
Michael R. Genesereth

Computer Science Department
Stanford University
Stanford, California 94305

Abstract

A formal framework is presented that models communication and promises in multi-agent interactions. This framework generalizes previous work on cooperation without communication, and shows the ability of communication to resolve conflicts among agents having disparate goals. Using a deal-making mechanism, agents are able to coordinate and cooperate more easily than in the communication-free model. In addition, there are certain types of interactions where communication makes possible mutually beneficial activity that is otherwise impossible to coordinate.

§1. Introduction

1.1 The Multi-Agent Paradigm and AI

Research in artificial intelligence has focused for many years on the problem of a single intelligent agent. This agent, usually operating in a relatively static domain, was designed to plan, navigate, or solve problems under certain simplifying assumptions, most notable of which was the absence of other intelligent entities.

The presence of multiple agents, however, is an unavoidable condition of the real world. People must plan actions taking into account the potential actions of others, which might be a help or a hindrance to their own activities. In order to reason about others' actions, a person must be able to model their beliefs and desires.

The artificial intelligence community has only lately come to address the problems inherent in multi-agent activity. A community of researchers, working on distributed artificial intelligence (DAI), has arisen. Even as they have begun their work, however, these researchers have added on a new set of simplifying assumptions that severely restrict the applicability of their results.

1.2 Benevolent Agents

Virtually all researchers in DAI have assumed that the agents in their domains have common or non-conflicting goals. Work has thus proceeded on the question of how these agents can best help one another in carrying out their common tasks [3, 4, 6, 7, 24], or how they can avoid

This research has been supported by DARPA under NAVELEX grant number N00039-83-C-0136.

interference while using common resources [10, 11]. Multiple agent interactions are studied so as to gain the benefits of increased system efficiency or increased capabilities.

Of course, when there is no conflict, there is no need to study the wide range of interactions that can occur among intelligent agents. All agents are fundamentally assumed to be helping one another, and will trade data and hypotheses as well as carry out tasks that are requested of them. We call this aspect of the paradigm the *benevolent agent assumption*.

1.3 Interactions of a More General Nature

In the real world, agents are not necessarily benevolent in their dealings with one another. Each agent has its own set of desires and goals, and will not necessarily help another agent with information or with actions. Of course, while conflict among agents exists, it is not total. There is often potential for compromise and mutually beneficial activity. Previous work in distributed artificial intelligence, bound to the benevolent agent assumption, has generally been incapable of handling these types of interactions.

Intelligent agents capable of interacting even when their goals are not identical would have many uses. For example, autonomous land vehicles (ALV's), operating in a combat environment, can be expected to encounter both friend and foe. In the latter case there need not be total conflict, and in the former there need not be an identity of interests. Other domains in which general interactions are prevalent are resource allocation and management tasks. An automated secretary [12], for example, may be required to coordinate a schedule with another automated (or human) secretary, while properly representing the desires of its owner. The ability to negotiate, to compromise and promise, would be desirable in these types of encounters.

Finally, even in situations where all agents in theory have a single goal, the complexity of interaction might be better handled by a framework that recognizes and resolves sub-goal conflict in a general manner. For example, robots involved in the construction of a space station are fundamentally motivated by the same goal; in the course of construction, however, there may be many minor conflicts caused by occurrences that cannot fully be predicted (e.g., fuel running low, drifting of objects in space). The building agents, each with a different task, could then negotiate with one another and resolve conflict.

1.4 Game Theory's Model and Extensions

In modeling the interaction of agents with potentially diverse goals, we borrow the simple construct of game theory, the payoff matrix. Consider the following matrix:

	c	d
a	3\1	2
b	2\5	0\1

The first player is assumed to choose one of the two rows, while the second simultaneously picks one of the two columns. The row-column outcome determines the payoff to each; for example, if the first player picks row b and the second player picks column c, the first player receives a payoff of 2 while the second receives a payoff of 5. If the choice results in an identical payoff for both players, a single number appears in the square (e.g., the $a \backslash d$ payoff above is 2 for both players). Payoffs designate utility to the players of a particular joint move [18].

Game theory addresses the issues of what moves a rational agent will make, given that other agents are also rational. We wish to remove the *a priori* assumption that other agents will necessarily be rational, while at the same time formalizing the concept of rationality in various ways.

Our model in this paper allows communication among the agents in the interaction, and allows them to make binding promises to one another. The agents are assumed to be making their decisions based only on the current encounter (e.g., they won't intentionally choose a lower utility in the hope of gaining more utility later on). The formalism handles the case of agents with disparate goals as well as the case of agents with common goals.

§2. Notation

We expand on the notation developed in [8]. For each game there is a set P of players and, for each player $i \in P$, a set M_i of possible moves for i. For $S \subset P$, we denote $P - S$ by $\bar{S}$, and write i instead of $\{i\}$ (so $\bar{i} = P - \{i\}$). We write M_S for $\prod_{i \in S} M_i$.

We denote by m_S an element of M_S; this is a joint move for the players in S. To $m_S \in M_S$ and $m_{\bar{S}} \in M_{\bar{S}}$ correspond an element $\vec{m}$ of M_P. The payoff function for a game is a function

$$p : P \times M_P \rightarrow \mathbb{R}$$

whose value at $(i, \vec{m})$ is the payoff for player i if move $\vec{m}$ is made.

Each agent is able to specify a set of joint moves (i.e., elements of M_P) that specify outcomes the agent is willing to accept; this set is called an *offer group*. If any move or moves offered by one agent are likewise offered by all other agents, this set of moves constitutes the *deal* (i.e., the deal is the intersection of all the agents' offer groups). In practice, a single element of the deal set will be selected by a fair arbiter, and the result of the selection communicated to all agents. At that point, the agents are all compelled to carry out their part of the move. Of course, if the deal set has only one member, no arbiter is needed.

We define a secondary payoff function $pay(i, m_i, D_i)$, the set of possible payoffs to i of making move m_i and suggesting offer group P_i:

$$pay(i, m_i, P_i) = \begin{cases} \{p(i, \vec{d}) : \vec{d} \in P_i \wedge \\ \quad \exists O_{\bar{i}}[O_{\bar{i}} \in allowed_o(i, P_i) \wedge \\ \quad \vec{d} \in O_{\bar{i}}]\}, \text{ if such a } \vec{d} \text{ exists;} \\ \{p(i, \vec{m}) : m_{\bar{i}} \in allowed_m(i, m_i)\}, \\ \quad\quad\quad\quad\quad\quad\quad \text{otherwise.} \end{cases}$$

We designate by $allowed_m(i, m_i)$ the set of moves that other agents might potentially make while i makes move m_i, and by $allowed_o(i, D_i)$ the set of offers that other agents might make while i suggests offer group D_i. Our formalism implicitly separates offer groups from moves (in other words, there will be no effect on moves by offer groups or vice versa). Intuitively, this reflects simultaneously revealing one's move and offer group, with one's eventual action determined by others' offer groups (that is, only if there is no agreement will you have to carry out your move). Future work might investigate the situation where offers are made before moves are chosen, and may thus affect them.

For nonempty sets $\{\alpha_i\}$ and $\{\beta_j\}$, we write $\{\alpha_i\} < \{\beta_j\}$ if $\alpha_i < \beta_j$ for all i, j (and say that $\{\beta_j\}$ *strictly dominates* $\{\alpha_i\}$). Likewise, we write $\{\alpha_i\} \leq \{\beta_j\}$ for nonempty sets $\{\alpha_i\}$ and $\{\beta_j\}$ if $\alpha_i \leq \beta_j$ for all i, j and the inequality is strict in at least one case. We then say that $\{\beta_j\}$ *dominates* $\{\alpha_j\}$.

Finally, we define $p(S, y_S)$ as $\{p(i, \vec{y}) : i \in S \wedge y_{\bar{S}} \in M_{\bar{S}}\}$. These are the possible payoffs to a group S of players of making move y_S.

2.1 Rational Moves

We will denote by $R_m(p, i)$ the set of rational moves for agent i in game p. We use the following definition to constrain what moves are elements of $R_m(p, i)$, that is, what moves are rational (we will follow the convention that free variables are considered universally quantified):

$$pay(i, y_i, \emptyset) < pay(i, x_i, \emptyset) \Rightarrow y_i \notin R_m(p, i). \quad (1)$$

In other words, if, when no binding agreement will be reached, every possible payoff to i of making move y_i is less than every possible payoff to i of making move x_i, then y_i is irrational for i. Of course, this does not imply that x_i *is* rational, since better moves may still be available.

In general, it will not be possible to fully specify the value of $pay(i, m_i, \emptyset)$ for all m_i, since there is not full information as to the moves that the other agents will make. Instead, we use (1) to show that some moves are *not* rational. Because the dominance relation is transitive but irreflexive (and there are a finite number of moves), it is impossible to show that all moves are irrational.

2.2 Rational Offer Groups

We define a *rational offer group* in a way analogous to how we defined a rational move above. We denote by $R_o(p, i)$ the set of rational offer groups for agent i in game p, and characterize a rational offer group by the following constraint on $R_o(p, i)$'s members:

$$\exists m_i[pay(i, m_i, P_i) < pay(i, m_i, O_i)] \Rightarrow P_i \notin R_o(p, i). \quad (2)$$

In other words, if for some move m_i every possible payoff resulting from offer group P_i is less than every possible payoff resulting from offer group O_i, then P_i is not a rational offer group.

There is one more constraint on members of $R_o(p, i)$: rational offer groups specify (through the function p) a continuous range of payoffs that are acceptable to an agent. Intuitively, a rational offer group must reflect the notion of "monotonic satisfaction"—if a rational agent is satisfied with a particular payoff, he will be satisfied with one of equal or greater value (this is a fundamental meaning of "utility"). Formally, we write

$$[p(i, \vec{r}) \leq p(i, \vec{s}) \wedge \vec{r} \in O_i] \Rightarrow \vec{s} \in O_i \qquad (3)$$

for all $O_i \in R_o(p, i)$ and moves $\vec{r}$ and $\vec{s}$. For a particular game and player, a rational offer group can thus be unambiguously specified by any of its members with the lowest payoff.

In general, there may be more than one rational offer group for an agent in a game. If full information were available to an agent about the offers others were going to make (along with their "backup moves"), it would be trivial to determine $R_o(p, i)$. In practice such information is not available, but a rational agent i may be able to discover *some* rational offer group, i.e., some offer group provably in $R_o(p, i)$.

2.3 Rational Moves and Offer Groups for a Set of Players

We also wish to define the rational moves and the rational offer groups available to a *set* of players. For $S \subset P$, we denote by $R_m(p, S)$ the rational moves for the group S in the game p. It follows that the members of $R_m(p, S)$ are elements of M_S. We assume that

$$R_m(p, S) \subset R_m(p, S') \times M_{S-S'} \text{ for } S' \subset S.$$

This states that no rational move for a set can require irrationality on the part of a subset. An obvious consequence of this assumption is that

$$R_m(p, S) \subset \prod_{i \in S} R_m(p, i).$$

A move that is rational for a group of players is thus rational for each player in the group.

Similarly, we denote by $R_o(p, S)$ the set of rational deals for S in the game p (that is, the members of $R_o(p, S)$ are sets of elements from M_P). It is the "crossproduct-intersection" of rational offer groups for the individual agents:

$$R_o(p, S) = \{O : O = \bigcap_{j \in S} O_j \wedge O_j \in R_o(p, j)\}.$$

2.4 Rationality Assumptions

The value of $pay(i, m_i, y_i)$ will depend, of course, on the values of $allowed_m(i, m_i)$ and $allowed_o(i, y_i)$ (i.e., the moves and the deals that other agents can make). In order to constrain the value of pay, we now define each of the $allowed$ functions ($allowed_n$ is defined as in [8]).

1. **Minimal move rationality:**
$allowed_m(i, m_i) = M_i$. Each player assumes that the others may be moving randomly.

2. **Separate move rationality:**
$allowed_m(i, m_i) \subset R_m(p, \bar{i})$. Each player assumes the others are moving rationally.

3. **Unique move rationality:**
For all m_i and m_i', $allowed_m(i, m_i) = allowed_m(i, m_i')$ and $|allowed_m(i, m_i)| = 1$. Each player assumes that the others' moves are fixed in advance. This may be combined with separate rationality.

The assumptions above do not fully specify what is or is not a rational move. Rather, they help constrain the set of rational moves by allowing us to prove that certain moves are not rational. We now define analogous assumptions regarding deals other agents might be making:

1. **Minimal deal rationality:**
$allowed_o(i, y_i) \subset \mathcal{P}(M_P)$, where $\mathcal{P}(M_P)$ denotes the power set of M_P. Each player assumes that the others may be making random deals.

2. **Separate deal rationality:**
$allowed_o(i, y_i) \subset R_o(p, \bar{i})$. Each player assumes that the others are making rational deals.

3. **Unique deal rationality:**
For all D_i and E_i, $allowed_o(i, D_i) = allowed_o(i, E_i)$ and $|allowed_o(i, D_i)| = 1$. Each player assumes that the others' offers are fixed in advance. This may be combined with separate deal rationality.

We refer to the combination of separate and unique move rationality as individual move rationality, and to the combination of separate and unique deal rationality as individual deal rationality. As in [8], any move that can be proven irrational under the assumption of minimal move rationality will be similarly irrational under the other move rationality assumptions. Analogously, any offer group that can be proven irrational under the assumption of minimal deal rationality will be irrational under the other deal rationality assumptions.

§3. Rational Deal Characteristics

With our notational conventions defined, we can now prove several characteristics of $R_o(p, i)$. We henceforth use $\vec{s}$ to denote any move that gives agent i his highest payoff.

Theorem 1 (Existence of a non-null rational offer group). $|R_o(p, i)| \geq 1$.

Proof. If $R_o(p, i)$ were empty then i would do best by making no offers and relying on his move to generate his payoff. But $pay(i, m_i, \vec{s})$ will be greater than or equal to $pay(i, m_i, \emptyset)$ for all m_i (since $\vec{s}$ will either be matched by other agents, increasing i's payoff, or will not be matched, and will therefore be harmless since it doesn't affect other's moves). Thus the offer group $\{\vec{s}\}$ would also be in $R_o(p, i)$, guaranteeing it to have at least one non-null member. □

It follows directly from the definition of a rational offer group (3) that all non-empty members of i's set of rational offer groups include $\vec{s}$. Together with Theorem 1, this implies that it is always rational for an agent to include in his offer group the move that gives him his highest payoff.

In addition, an agent can often restrict his offers to those whose payoffs are higher than that which he can get by making the null offer, relying on his move to give him this payoff.

Theorem 2 (Lower bound). *Assuming unique deal rationality, if for any move m_i and joint move $\vec{y} \neq \vec{s}$,*

$$p(i, \vec{y}) \leq pay(i, m_i, \emptyset),$$

$\exists O_i[O_i \in R_o(p,i) \land \vec{y} \notin O_i].$

Proof. There are two cases:

1. $p(i, \vec{y}) < pay(i, m_i, \emptyset)$: The only way for $\vec{y}$ to be in some rational offer group P_i is for the $\vec{y}$ deal not to be accepted (otherwise $pay(i, m_i, P_i)$ would be dominated by the offer group $pay(i, m_i, O_i)$ where $O_i = \{\vec{x} : p(i, \vec{x}) > p(i, \vec{y})\}$). But if $\vec{y}$ is not accepted, then it is equivalent to another offer group that includes only those moves with payoffs higher than $\vec{y}$. This smaller offer group will then also be in $R_o(p, i)$.

2. $p(i, \vec{y}) = pay(i, m_i, \emptyset)$: Assume that $\vec{y}$ is in some rational offer group P_i. If $\vec{y}$ is not accepted, or is accepted along with other offers, then $pay(i, m_i, O_i) > pay(i, m_i, P_i)$ where $O_i = \{\vec{x} : p(i, \vec{x}) > p(i, \vec{y})\}$, so there is another rational offer group without $\vec{y}$, namely the offer group O_i. If $\vec{y}$ is the only accepted offer, then $pay(i, m_i, \vec{s}) = pay(i, m_i, P_i)$ (where $\vec{s}$ is the move that gives i his highest payoff), since $\vec{s}$ will not be accepted anyway and therefore $pay(i, m_i, \vec{s}) = pay(i, m_i, \emptyset)$. Again, there is a rational offer group that does not include $\vec{y}$. □

Note that Theorem 2 will not hold for $\vec{s}$ (i.e., the joint move that gives i his highest payoff) since that would contradict Theorem 1 (Theorem 2's proof makes implicit use of the fact that $\vec{y} \neq \vec{s}$ in its construction of the dominating offer group O_i). Note also that Theorem 2 will *not* hold under minimal deal rationality. Imagine that a perverse opponent chooses his offer group as follows:

1. If you include in your offer group deals with low payoff (for you), he will accept the deal with your best payoff;

2. If you don't offer that low deal he will accept no deals and you will have to rely on your move to get a payoff.

Under these circumstances (fully consistent with minimal deal rationality), it might be to your advantage to offer a low-payoff deal, since that might be the only way to get your maximal payoff.

3.1 Restricted Case Analysis

The consequences of Theorem 2 will differ, of course, based on assumptions about $allowed_m$ since these will affect $pay(i, m_i, \emptyset)$ for any given m_i. Consider the following payoff matrix:

	c	d
a	1\4	0\5
b	3\2	2\7

It is shown in [8] that, assuming minimal move rationality (potentially random or even malevolent moves by other agents), the row agent can still use "restricted case analysis" to constrain his move to b. If unique deal rationality can be assumed then the offer group consisting solely of move $b\backslash c$ (i.e., bottom left corner) is *guaranteed* by Theorems 1 and 2 to be a rational offer group. Of course, there may be other rational offer groups, for example the offer $\{b\backslash d, b\backslash c\}$, depending on what deals the other player can offer.

We formalize part of the above discussion:

Corollary 3 (Restricted case analysis). *Assuming minimal move rationality and unique deal rationality, if for some x_i and y_i, for all $x_{\bar{i}}$ and $y_{\bar{i}}$,*

$$p(i, \vec{y}) < p(i, \vec{x}),$$

then there exists an $O_i \in R_o(p, i)$ such that no $\vec{y}$ is in O_i.

Proof. Follows from Lemma 3 in [8] and Theorem 2. □

3.2 Case Analysis and Iterated Case Analysis

There are restrictions on rational offer groups analogous to Corollary 3 that apply for case analysis and iterated case analysis under the assumptions of unique and individual move rationality, respectively. The case analysis situation is represented in the following payoff matrix, seen from the row player's perspective:

	c	d
a	4\1	2
b	3\5	0\1

The row player need only assume that the column player's move will not be affected by its own move (i.e., unique move rationality) to realize that making move a is in all circumstances superior to making move b. As long as unique deal rationality can also be assumed, there is a guaranteed rational offer group consisting only of move $a\backslash c$.

Corollary 4 (Case analysis). *Assuming unique move rationality and unique deal rationality, if for some x_i and y_i, for all $x_{\bar{i}}$ and $y_{\bar{i}}$ with $x_{\bar{i}} = y_{\bar{i}}$,*

$$p(i, \vec{y}) < p(i, \vec{x}),$$

then there exists an $O_i \in R_o(p, i)$ such that no $\vec{y}$ is in O_i.

Proof. Follows from Lemma 4 in [8] and Theorem 2. □

Similarly, if the column player can assume that the row player is rational and making moves independent of the column player's moves (i.e., individual move rationality), then he can prove that move d is optimal in the above matrix (since the row player will play a). With unique deal rationality, he has a guaranteed rational offer group of $\{a\backslash d, b\backslash c\}$ (the offer group $\{b\backslash c\}$ is also rational).

The effect of Theorems 1 and 2 is to show us that there is always a rational offer group that includes an agent's highest payoff outcome, and includes no outcomes below or equal to what he could achieve without deals. Below, we consider other constraints on an agent's rational offer groups.

§4. The Group Rationality Theorem

The work in [8] and [9] was concerned with the formalization of cooperative behavior, given certain constraints about the agents participating in an interaction. Using our notation, a desirable general result would have been

$$pay(P, \vec{y}, \emptyset) < pay(P, \vec{x}, \emptyset) \Rightarrow \vec{y} \notin R_m(p, P), \quad (4)$$

that is, if any joint move for all players is dominated by any other, then the dominated joint move is not rational for them. This result could not be proven, and the inability to do so stemmed directly from the lack of communication inherent in the model. Without at least minimal communication (e.g., self-identification), there is no way to coordinate on a universally perceived best move when several such moves exist.

We are now able to derive an important result about $R_o(p, P)$ very similar to the elusive non-communication result in (4).

Theorem 5 (Group offers). *Assuming individual deal rationality,*

$$p(P, \vec{y}) < p(P, \vec{x}) \Rightarrow \exists O_i [O_i \in R_o(p, i) \wedge \vec{y} \notin O_i]$$

for all $i \in P$.

Proof. There are two possible cases:

1. $\forall O_j [O_j \in R_o(p, \vec{i}) \Rightarrow \vec{y} \notin O_j]$: Since $\vec{y}$ will not be a consummated deal, if P_i is any offer group containing $\vec{y}$ then $pay(i, m_i, O_i) \geq pay(i, m_i, P_i)$ where $O_i = \{\vec{x} : p(i, \vec{x}) > p(i, \vec{y})\}$. Along with Theorem 1, this shows the existence of a non-null rational offer group without $\vec{y}$.

2. $\exists O_j [O_j \in R_o(p, \vec{i}) \wedge \vec{y} \in O_j]$: All other agents are rational (by assumption), and any rational offer group that includes $\vec{y}$ also includes $\vec{x}$ (3); thus, if P_i is any offer group containing $\vec{y}$, then $pay(i, m_i, O_i) > pay(i, m_i, P_i)$ where $O_i = \{\vec{x} : p(i, \vec{x}) > p(i, \vec{y})\}$. This, along with Theorem 1, shows the existence of a rational offer group without $\vec{y}$. □

Because of Theorem 5, a rational agent interacting with other rational agents knows that he need not offer a move that is dominated for all players—doing so cannot increase his payoff. If the other rational agents also know that all agents are rational, they too will realize that they can refrain from offering a move that is dominated for all players. Higher levels of knowledge [13], such as their knowing that all agents know that all agents are rational, are not needed. In addition, because of the definition of rational offer groups (3), the agents can refrain from offering any moves with smaller payoffs, since those groups would necessarily include the dominated move.

§5. Examples

We will now examine the consequences of our rational offer theorems in several additional types of games.

5.1 Best Plan

The best plan scenario is reflected in the following matrix:

	c	d
a	7	4
b	5	6

All agents recognize that there is a single best move; how will their offer groups reflect this? From Theorem 1, a rational agent knows that he can safely offer the move that gives him his best payoff (i.e., move $a\backslash c$), even assuming minimal deal rationality on the part of other players (though the theorem is noncommittal as to whether other

moves can or should be included with it). All players can also rule out move $a\backslash d$ using Theorem 2 if unique deal rationality holds (since $a\backslash d$ yields the lowest payoff). If there is an assumption of individual deal rationality, Theorem 5 can guarantee each agent that the offer group consisting solely of $a\backslash c$ is rational. Communication thus allows coordination on the best plan under more intuitive assumptions about the interaction than those used in [8].

5.2 Breaking Symmetries—Multiple Best Plan

Our rational offer group theorems allow us to solve the "Multiple Best Plans" case that could not be solved in [8]. The following matrix illustrates the scenario:

	c	d
a	-1	2
b	2	-1

Assuming minimal deal rationality, an agent can rationally offer $b\backslash c$ and $a\backslash d$. In addition, assuming unique deal rationality an agent knows that he can rationally not offer $a\backslash c$ and $b\backslash d$ (since they are lowest yield moves). This analysis can be done by both agents if they are rational and operating under the unique deal assumption. Their offer sets will overlap on the multiple best outcomes; selection of a single alternative from the multiple agreements then occurs.

5.3 Prisoner's Dilemma

The prisoner's dilemma is represented by the following matrix (we choose different names for our moves so as to conform to the literature):

	c	d
c	3	0\5
d	5\0	1

Each agent most desires to play d while the opponent plays c, then to play c along with the opponent, then to play d along with the opponent, and least of all to play c while the opponent plays d. The dilemma comes about because case analysis implies that it is always better to play d; both players choosing d, however, is less desirable *for both* than if they had chosen c. The dilemma has received much attention within the philosophy and game theory literature [2, 5, 22, 27]. In the usual presentation of the prisoner's dilemma, playing c is called "cooperating," and playing d is called "defecting." With the presence of binding promises, in fact, there is no dilemma:

Corollary 6 (Prisoner's Dilemma). *If all players know that all players are operating under the assumption of individual deal rationality, agents will cooperate in the prisoner's dilemma.*

Proof. The first player knows that it is rational to offer $d\backslash c$ (since it is rational even under minimal rationality, Theorem 1); he also knows it is irrational to offer $c\backslash d$ (from Theorem 2, since individual deal rationality includes unique deal rationality). By Theorem 5, there is a rational offer group without $d\backslash d$. Now he knows that the other agent will not offer $d\backslash c$ (since the other agent is assumed rational and operating under the assumption of unique deal rationality, Theorem 2). Since $d\backslash c$ will certainly not be met, $pay(i, d, \{d\backslash c\}) \leq pay(i, d, \{d\backslash c, c\backslash c\})$. Thus, the offer group $\{d\backslash c, c\backslash c\}$ is rational. The second agent will, if rational and working under the same assumptions, come to the same conclusion. The deal $c\backslash c$ will be struck, and the agents avoid the $d\backslash d$ trap. □

§6. Extending the Model

For certain types of interactions, the model presented above (i.e., the various assumptions and theorems about rational moves and deals) does not specify rational activity in sufficient detail. We can extend the model in a variety of ways to handle these cases, and at the same time capture a wider range of assumptions about the interaction. In this section, we briefly present some of the extensions that might be made to our original model.

6.1 Similar bargainers

Consider the following payoff matrix (equivalent to game 77 in Rapoport and Guyer's taxonomy [23])

	c	d
a	3	2
b	5\0	0\5

Assuming separate deal rationality, the first player can assume that $b\backslash c$ should be in a rational offer group of his, and that $b\backslash d$ should not be. What else can be said about what constitutes a rational offer group in this game? There are three choices, namely $\{b\backslash c\}$, $\{a\backslash c, b\backslash c\}$, and $\{a\backslash d, a\backslash c, b\backslash c\}$. In order to decide among the choices, we would like to make more assumptions about the "bargaining tendencies" of the other agent (since, in fact, some agents might be tougher deal-makers than others). We will ignore what value the agents might place on making a particular move in the absence of a deal, since the payoff is underdetermined.

Let us define two offer groups O_i and O_j to be *similar* if and only if they both have the same lower boundary for what deals are included or not included. It is true that $similar(O_i, O_j)$ if and only if

$$\exists n[p(i, \vec{y}) > n \Leftrightarrow \vec{y} \in O_i \ \land \ p(j, \vec{x}) > n \Leftrightarrow \vec{x} \in O_j]$$

for some number n. If we use the similar bargainers definition, we implicitly assume some meaningful measure for comparing inter-personal utility.

One assumption to use in deciding upon rational offer groups is now that the other agent will accept deals that you would accept; that is, $O_j \in R_o(p, j) \Leftrightarrow O_i \in R_o(p, i)$ where $similar(O_i, O_j)$.

Under this assumption, we can decide what deal is rational in the above game. Player 1 reasons that if he offers $\{b\backslash c\}$, player 2 (who is a similar bargainer) will offer only $\{b\backslash d\}$. There will be no match. In the same way, if it would be rational for player 1 to offer $\{a\backslash c, b\backslash c\}$ then player 2 will offer $\{a\backslash c, b\backslash d\}$, with an agreement on $a\backslash c$ and a payoff of $\{3\}$ for both. If player 1 offers $\{a\backslash d, a\backslash c, b\backslash c\}$ then player 2 will offer $\{a\backslash d, a\backslash c, b\backslash d\}$ and there will be agreement on $a\backslash d$ and on $a\backslash c$, with a payoff of $\{2, 3\}$ for both. Since $\{3\}$ dominates $\{2, 3\}$, agents who assume common knowledge

[13] of the similar bargainer assumption should choose the rational offer group that yields agreement on $a\backslash c$.

6.2 Stochastic Model—The Game of Chicken

Note, however, the following payoff matrix (commonly known as the game of chicken [23]):

	c	d
a	3	2\5
b	5\2	1

Two agents, even if they assume individual deal rationality and the similar bargainers assumption, will be faced with the following choices: a payoff of $\{3\}$ or a payoff of $\{2, 3, 5\}$. According to our definitions, neither of these sets dominates the other.

If, however, we extend the model to include a probabilistic choice from within the agreement set, it is clear that the latter agreement set dominates the former (with an expected value of 3.33 versus 3). A further stochastic extension to our model would allow moves themselves to be specified probabilistically (e.g., a with probability .5, and b with probability .5). In the game theory literature, this is the distinction between pure strategies and mixed strategies [18]. An analysis of this model is beyond the scope of the present discussion.

6.3 Conjunctive Offers—Battle of the Sexes

In the game of chicken example presented above, there was an added complexity that was temporarily ignored: the possibility of "defection." If one agent reasons that the other agent will accept all payoffs above 2, it is to the first agent's benefit to only offer moves of payoff 5 (this is analogous to the prisoner's dilemma, with the same potential that both players will use identical reasoning and no agreement will be reached). A similar problem can be seen in the so-called battle of the sexes matrix, seen below.

	c	d
a	-1	1\2
b	2\1	-1

One approach to solving this problem is to allow "composite" offers, for example, an offer consisting of a conjunct of several moves (the conjunct must be matched exactly in order for a deal to occur). Thus, the offer consisting of $a\backslash d \land b\backslash c$ can consistently be made by both agents without the potential of defection (and with an expected utility of 1.5 for each). This notion can be extended to general logical offers consisting of disjuncts, conjuncts and negations of joint moves. The battle of the sexes can thus be uniquely solved with the assumption of similarity in bargaining, if conjunctive offers are allowed.

§7. Previous Work

The subject of interacting rational agents has been addressed within the field of artificial intelligence as well as in the discipline of game theory. Here we will briefly review relevant contributions from these two areas, and contrast our present approach with previous efforts.

7.1 Work in Artificial Intelligence

As mentioned above, researchers in distributed artificial intelligence have begun to address the issues arising in multi-agent interactions. Lesser and Corkill [4] have performed empirical studies to determine cooperation strategies with positive characteristics (such as, for example, what types of data should be shared among distributed processors). They are solely concerned with groups of agents who share a common goal, but have acknowledged the benefit even under this assumption of having agents demonstrate "skepticism" (i.e., not being distracted by others' information).

Georgeff [10, 11] has developed a formal model to combine separate plans of independent agents. The primary concern is to avoid destructive interference caused by simultaneous access to a shared resource. The model used assumes that the agents have separate goals, but that these goals do not directly oppose one another. Cooperative action is neither required nor exploited, except insofar as it allows agents to keep out of each other's way.

Other notable efforts include Smith's work on the contract net [7], Malone's work extending the contract net model using economic theory [19], and the theoretical work on knowledge and belief of carried out by Appelt, Moore, Konolige, Halpern and Moses [1, 14, 15, 16, 17, 20, 21].

The current work extends these previous models of interaction by allowing a fuller range of goal disagreements among agents. By using a framework that captures total and partial goal conflicts, it allows investigation into compromise, promises and cooperative action.

This paper considers the communication scenario in ways similar to the manner in which previous work [8, 9] investigated cooperation among rational agents when no communication occurs. Below we briefly note the advantages that were gained when communication and promises were added to the interaction model.

The best plan interaction was handled in our framework by assuming individual deal rationality. Because in the no-communication case this scenario could not be solved using individual move rationality, other assumptions were introduced: *informed rationality* in [8] and *common rationality* in [9]. Informed rationality constrained $allowed_m$ in a way that assumed each player would respond in a rational way to the others' moves, whatever they might be.

It should be noted in passing that an assumption of common knowledge of rationality will also allow for a solution to the best plan case, though this has not previously been pursued in the literature.

To solve the prisoner's dilemma, even more assumptions had to be introduced. The interested reader is referred to [8] and [9] for full details; see also [25].

Even using a variety of assumptions, previous work could not handle the multiple best plan case, where there are several outcomes all equally recognized as best by all players. To break the symmetry, some communication is needed, though this communication can be as simple as self-identification and reliance on a common rule (e.g., agent with lowest name performs lowest ordered action).

7.2 Game Theory

Game theory has focused on a variety of interactions, and sought to characterize the types of actions that rational agents will take in each. Many of the same questions that come up in our work have been addressed by game theoreticians. Their approach, however, has left some important issues unexamined. Consider the following quote from the classic game theory text, [18]:

> Though it is not apparent from some writings, the term "rational" is far from precise, and it certainly means different things in the different theories that have been developed. Loosely, it seems to include any assumption one makes about the players maximizing something, and any about complete knowledge on the part of the player in a very complex situation... [*Games and Decisions*, p. 5]

As another example, consider the following best plan interaction:

	A_2	B_2
A_1	4	1/2
B_1	3/1	2/3

It was demonstrated above that the best plan case can only be solved under particular definitions of rationality. Rapoport and Guyer, however, writing in [23], put forward the following *assumption* regarding agents' behavior (citing the similarity with [26]):

> (A_3). If a game has a single Pareto equilibrium, the players will choose the strategy which contains it...
> Our assumption (A_3) says that $A_1 A_2$ is the natural outcome, which, of course, is dictated by common sense... we shall refer to this as a *prominent solution.* [*A Taxonomy of 2 × 2 Games*]

In short, game theory has sometimes been willing to take for granted certain types of behavior without carefully formalizing its definitions of rationality, or its assumptions of inter-agent knowledge.

These questions are particularly important in the field of artificial intelligence. We are not interested in characterizing game matrices: we want to characterize agent rationality and explore the consequences of various assumptions. The goal is to be able to implement intelligent agents whose strategies of behavior will be provably rational.

§8. Conclusion

Intelligent agents will inevitably need to interact flexibly in real world domains. Previous work has not modeled the full range and complexity of agents' varied goals. The benevolent agent assumption, which assumes that agents have identical or non-conflicting goals, has permeated previous approaches to distributed AI.

This paper has presented a framework for interaction that explicitly accounts for communication and promises, and allows multiple goals among agents. The model provides a unified solution to a wide range of problems, including the types of interactions discussed in [8] and [9].

Through the use of communication and binding promises, agents are able to coordinate their actions more effectively, and handle interactions that were previously problematical. By extending the communication model even further, a wider variety of interactions can be handled.

Acknowledgement

The authors wish to thank Matt Ginsberg, who has played an invaluable role in the development of our ideas on cooperation among rational agents.

References

[1] Appelt, D.E., Planning natural language utterances to satisfy multiple goals, Tech Note 259, SRI International, Menlo Park, California (1982).

[2] Axelrod, R., *The Evolution of Cooperation*, Basic Books, Inc., New York (1984).

[3] Cammarata, S., McArthur, D., and Steeb, R., Strategies of cooperation in distributed problem solving, *IJCAI-83*, Karlsruhe, West Germany (1983) 767–770.

[4] Corkill, D.D., and Lesser, V.R., The use of meta-level control for coordination in a distributed problem solving network, *IJCAI-83*, Karlsruhe, West Germany (1983) 748–756.

[5] Davis, L., Prisoners, paradox and rationality, *American Philosophical Quarterly* 14 (1977).

[6] Davis, R., A model for planning in a multi-agent environment: steps toward principles for teamwork, Working Paper 217, MIT AI Lab (1981).

[7] Davis, R., and Smith, R. G., Negotiation as a metaphor for distributed problem solving, *Artificial Intelligence* 20 (1983) 63–109.

[8] Genesereth, M. R., Ginsberg, M. L., and Rosenschein, J. S., Solving the prisoner's dilemma, HPP Report 84-41 (1984).

[9] Genesereth, M. R., Ginsberg, M. L., and Rosenschein, J. S., Cooperation without communication, HPP Report 84-36 (1984).

[10] Georgeff, M., Communication and interaction in multi-agent planning, *AAAI-83*, Washington, D.C. (1983) 125–129.

[11] Georgeff, M., A Theory of action for multi-agent planning, *AAAI-84*, Austin, Texas (1984) 121–125.

[12] Goldstein, I. P., Bargaining Between Goals, A.I. Working Paper 102, Massachusetts Institute of Technology Artificial Intelligence Laboratory (1975).

[13] Halpern, J. Y., and Moses, Y., Knowledge and common knowledge in a distributed environment, IBM Research Report IBM RJ 4421 (1984).

[14] Konolige, K., A first-order formalization of knowledge and action for a multi-agent planning system, Tech Note 232, SRI International, Menlo Park, California (1980).

[15] Konolige, K., Circumscriptive ignorance, *AAAI-82*, Pittsburgh, Pennsylvania (1982) 202–204.

[16] Konolige, K., A deductive model of belief, *IJCAI-83*, Karlsruhe, West Germany (1983) 377–381.

[17] Konolige, K., *A Deduction Model of Belief*, Ph.D. Thesis, Stanford University (1984).

[18] Luce, R.D., and Raiffa, H., *Games and Decisions, Introduction and Critical Survey*, John Wiley and Sons, New York (1957).

[19] Malone, T.W., Fikes, R.E., and Howard, M.T., Enterprise: a market-like task scheduler for distributed computing environments, Working paper, Cognitive and Instructional Sciences Group, Xerox Palo Alto Research Center (1983).

[20] Moore, R.C., Reasoning about knowledge and action, Tech Note 191, SRI International, Menlo Park, California (1980).

[21] Moore, R.C., A formal theory of knowledge and action, Tech Note 320, SRI International, Menlo Park, California (1984).

[22] Parfit, D., *Reasons and Persons*, Clarendon Press, Oxford (1984).

[23] Rapoport, A. and Guyer, M., A taxonomy of 2 x 2 games, *Yearbook of the Society for General Systems Research* XI (1966) 203–214.

[24] Rosenschein, J.S., and Genesereth, M.R., Communication and cooperation, HPP Report 84-5 (1984).

[25] Rosenschein, J.S., *Rational Interaction: Cooperation Among Intelligent Agents*, Ph.D. Thesis, Stanford University (1985).

[26] Schelling, T.C., *The Strategy of Conflict*, Oxford University Press, New York (1963).

[27] Sowden, L., That there is a dilemma in the prisoners' dilemma, *Synthese* 55 (1983) 347–352.

4.2 Reasoning about Collective Processes

In this section, we are concerned with research on coordination and coherence as it is developed collectively among sets of agents. Robert Tenney and Nils Sandell's paper gives a formal system-theoretic treatment of mechanisms for the real-time distributed coordination of complex distributed systems. They assume that in these systems the dynamics of one agent only depend upon the general characteristics of the other agents. They develop a formalism based upon the notion of a "domule," which is an independent decision agent that has well-defined interactions with other agents. Different system structures such as singly connected, doubly connected, acyclic, etc. are defined formally, and formal coordination strategies such as static, no communication, finite horizon, etc. are evaluated. The suitability of different system structures to different coordination strategies is examined. This paper provides a useful contrast to several of the papers in Chapter 4, Section 1, including those of Georgeff and of Genesereth, Ginsberg, and Rosenschein, who use different techniques for representing agents' models of other agents.

Bertram Bruce and Denis Newman have devised a representation scheme for beliefs, intentions and plans, which they use informally for a linguistic analysis of stories. Bruce and Newman develop the concept of *interacting plans*. Since agents take into account the actions of others, they must also determine and represent the predicted behavior and intentions of other agents, and hence also the beliefs held by other agents. A set of agents will together produce an interacting plan in which the beliefs and plans of every agent are embedded in the beliefs and plans of each agent.

Edmund Durfee, Victor Lesser and Daniel Corkill sum up a great deal of research on the Distributed Vehicle Monitoring Testbed (DVMT) in this key paper, as they describe a number of mechanisms that improve coherence in a network of problem solvers. *Network control* concerns overall allocation of tasks and responsibilities, as opposed to *local control*, which refers to the local decisions of each agent about what to do next. Coherence-improving mechanisms include (1) organizational structuring, using the notion of interest areas, which provides a long term framework to guide local control decisions, (2) local planning mechanisms that dynamically generate appropriate action sequences at each node, and (3) metalevel communication mechanisms that facilitate dynamic refinement of the organization. One of the strong points of this paper is the development and presentation of the results of experimental tests of these coordination mechanisms in the DVMT. It will be important to contrast this paper with the others in this book that treat the DVMT and its precursors, including those by Corkill, Durfee, Erman, Fennell, Hudlicka, and Lesser appearing in Chapter 3, Chapter 4, Section 4.2, and Chapter 6. We also suggest examining other DVMT papers listed in the Subject Index in Chapter 2, under the heading *DVMT*.

Edmund Durfee and Victor Lesser's paper introduces the important concept of a *partial global plan* (PGP). PGPs specify partial views of coordinated actions for groups of agents, and represents not only agents' intended actions, but their place in the overall problem solving framework, and the goals that motivate their actions. Individual agents in a group use PGPs as partial models of network activity and to generate individual node plans. The paper describes mechanisms and knowledge representations for generating and maintaining PGPs. Durfee and Lesser believe that PGPs provide a general and flexible mechanism that can model many styles of coordination and interaction, including negotiation. Other work on modeling interaction structures can be found in papers by Conry, Meyer, and Lesser, Davis and Smith, and Smith in Chapter 5.

Strategies for Distributed Decisionmaking

ROBERT R. TENNEY, MEMBER, IEEE, AND NILS R. SANDELL, JR., MEMBER, IEEE

Abstract—Several mechanisms which can be used in the real-time distributed coordination of large-scale dynamical systems which display a subsystem structure are derived. A spectrum of approaches using varying degrees of types of communication to reduce the uncertainty of each agent concerning the events controlled by others is presented. The organizational requirements of each coordination strategy in terms of constraints on the interagent relationships are derived, and it is shown that while any of the mechanisms discussed here work well in hierarchical organizational structures, many are adaptable to much larger classes of structures.

I. INTRODUCTION AND REVIEW

THE COORDINATED control of a complex system in real time is an important goal to be achieved in many engineering applications yet has been difficult to approach from a theoretical point of view (particularly in a stochastic setting). An earlier paper [1] suggested that this was a result of the fundamental formulation of stochastic optimal control problems using a centralized state-space model and posed an alternative formulation based on the concept of a *domule*. A domule is an independent decision agent with a model only of some subsystem on which it is an "expert," but which must communicate with other agents in order to achieve some desired overall performance. The domular

Manuscript received July 31, 1980; revised May 5, 1981. This work was supported in part by a National Science Foundation Graduate Fellowship and by the Office of Naval Research under Contract N00014-17-C-0532.
R. R. Tenney is with the Laboratory for Information and Decision Systems, Massachusetts Institute of Technology, Room 35-213, 77 Massachusetts Avenue, Cambridge, MA 02139.
N. R. Sandell, Jr., is with Alphatech, Inc., 3 New England Executive Park, Burlington, MA 01803.

formulation, an example of a physical system which could be described by it, and some theoretical properties of a domular structure were the subject of the earlier paper. Here we develop mechanisms, based on the underlying interactions between subsystems, to coordinate the making of decisions which are "best" in some system-wide sense. The three principal arguments supporting the direction taken here are as follows.

1) Past control theoretic technical approaches to decentralization based on a single, centralized state-space model have failed to produce a generally applicable theory of distributed decisionmaking which exhibits the characteristics desired of such a theory [2]–[4].

2) The alternative to a single, centralized state-space model is a distributed model [5] in which the dynamics of one element depend only on general characteristics of other models.

3) There exist many large-scale systems of interest which exhibit the structure required for the construction of a distributed model.

II. Notations and Definitions

The concept of a domule is based on a distributed system model. Each domule D_i, $i = 1, \cdots, N$, consists of the agent A_i and a subsystem model M_i with

Local state space X_i
Local output space Y_i
Local decision space U_i

Incoming interaction sets $Z_{1i}, \cdots, Z_{Ni}$

Produced interaction sets $Z_{i1}, \cdots, Z_{iN}$

Local dynamics $x_i(t+1) = f_i(x_i(t), z_{1i}(t),$
$$\cdots, z_{Ni}(t), u_i(t))$$
$$= f_i(x_i(t), \vec{z}_i(t), u_i(t))$$
(1)

Local output function $y_i(t) = h_i(x_i(t), \vec{z}_i(t))$ (2)

Aggregation function $z_{ij}(t) = g_{ij}(x_i(t)),$
$$j = 1, \cdots, N$$
(3)

Local cost function $c_i(x_i(t), x_i(t+1), \vec{z}_i, u_i).$ (4)

Subscripts denote the agent with which a variable is associated; superscripts refer to specific value of that variable. Variations of a particular variable x are

x^+	x at some future time
x^-	x at some previous time
x^*	optimal value of x
$\bar{x}$	upper bound on x
$\underline{x}$	lower bound on x
$\tilde{x}$	sequence of x's
$\hat{x}$	abstracted version of x [1, Sec. VII].

In addition, the following cost functions will appear.

$v_i(x_i, \vec{z}_i, t) =$ local cost to go (to some time T) when in x_i at t with interactions $\vec{z}_i(t)$

$w_i(\vec{z}_i; x_i, x_i^+, t) =$ minimal local cost of transferring from x_i to x_i^+ in t steps given incoming interaction sequences $\tilde{z}_{1i}, \cdots, \tilde{z}_{Ni}$ (computed using forward search [1, sec. VI]).

The structure of the system is defined by the pattern of interactions which are nontrivial. This structure can be represented as a graph with N nodes n_i representing the D_i and with links (n_i, n_j) indicating each nontrivial dynamical effect of the states of D_i on those of D_j. Structures of such a graph $\mathbf{G}$, with node set $\mathbf{N}$, are as follows.

Definition 1: $\mathbf{G}$ is *singly connected* if, for any n_i, n_k distinct nodes i, k in $\mathbf{N}$, there is exactly one ordered subset on $\mathbf{N}$, $(n_i, \cdots, n_k)$, such that

1) Either (n_i, n_{i+1}) or (n_{i+1}, n_i) is in G, for $i = 1, \cdots, k-1$
2) $n_i \neq n_j$ for any i, j.

This requires that there is exactly one path from each n_i to another n_k where the path can follow interactions in either

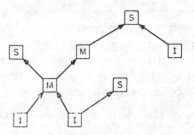
Fig. 1.   Singly connected topology.

direction. For such singly connected systems, the domules comprising it can be partitioned into three sets.

Definition 2: A domule n is a *superior* domule if there is no other n' such that (n, n') is an edge of $\mathbf{G}$.

Definition 3: A domule n is an *inferior* domule if there is no other n' such that (n', n) is in $\mathbf{G}$.

Definition 4: A domule n is a *middle* domule if it is neither superior nor inferior.

For example, superior, inferior, and middle domules are labelled S, I, and M, respectively, in the system of Fig. 1. These classes are of interest as the algorithms an agent uses will depend on its relation to the rest of the system as captured by the above definitions. Interactions flow from inferiors to superiors allowing the interpretation that the inferiors produce interactions to fill the needs of the superiors.

Another concept relevant to singly connected topologies is that of an *induction relation* which orders the nodes in some way.

Definition 5: An induction relation $\mathbb{H}$ on the nodes of a singly connected graph is one satisfying these two conditions.

1) If (n_i, n_j) is in $\mathbf{G}$, then either (n_i, n_j) or (n_j, n_i) is in $\mathbb{H}$, but never both.
2) For any n_i, there is at most one n_j such that (n_i, n_j) is in $\mathbb{H}$.

$\mathbb{H}$ provides a way of working through $\mathbf{G}$ in such a way that each link is traversed once. It is an immediate consequence of definition 1 and property 2 above that there is exactly one n_i such that no n_j exists for which (n_i, n_j) is in $\mathbb{H}$ (unless $\mathbf{G}$ separates into disconnected subsets).

Definition 6: A node n_i precedes n_j if (n_i, n_j) is in $\mathbb{H}$; it *succeeds* n_j if (n_j, n_i) is in $\mathbb{H}$. A node with no predecessor is an *initial* node; the one with no successor is the *terminal* node.

As will be seen in the next section, $\mathbb{H}$ can determine the "flow" of the coordination process. As there are N possible $\mathbb{H}$'s (one for each terminal node), this will imply that there are N possible flows.

Singly connected systems are particularly special structures involving no cycles or multiple paths between nodes which might cause complications in a coordinated strategy. Other classes of interest include the following.

Definition 7: A *hierarchical* system is one in which no agent affects more than one other: for each n_i, there is at most one n_j such that $(n_i, n_j) \in \mathbf{L}$. Thus it is singly connected.

Definition 8: A system is *doubly connected* if it contains a singly connected system and can be constructed from that system by adding only links (n_i, n_j) for (n_j, n_i) in that system. Thus if $\mathbb{L}_2$ is the interaction relation for a doubly connected system, then there exists $\mathbb{L}_1$ such that $\mathbb{L}_2 \supseteq \mathbb{L}_1$ and $\mathbb{L}_1$ describes a singly connected system, and

$$\mathbb{L}_2 \subseteq \{ (i, j) \mid (i, j) \in \mathbb{L}_1 \text{ or } (j, i) \in \mathbb{L}_1 \}. \quad (5)$$

A doubly connected system thus allows bidirectional flows of interactions between agents in what otherwise would be a singly connected system. It thus is useful for modeling systems structured around the exchange of interactions between agents (e.g., markets).

Definition 9: An *acyclic* system is one such that for each link (n_i, n_j) there is no sequence of links starting at n_j which leads back to n_i. Equivalently, there is no pair of distinct nodes n_i and n_j such that both (n_i, n_j) and (n_j, n_i) are elements of the transitive closure of $\mathbb{L}$. Finally, a generally structured system is one with no restriction on $\mathbb{G}$.

Thus there are five classes of system structure of interest, and it will be shown that each has particular properties of interest to the coordination mechanisms to be introduced in Section III. The above emphasis on singly connected systems is intended to support the analysis of Section III, which is limited to consideration of these systems. The other structures will be studied in Section IV.

The local cost functions defined for each domule in (4) are not enough to specify the objective of the collection of agents. The classic way to combine the local cost functions into a single, system-wide objective function is by viewing the controllers as a team [6] as in the following.

Definition 10: The team objective has each agent D_i working to

$$\min_{\tilde{u}_i} \max_{\gamma_i} \sum_{i=1}^{N} \sum_{t=0}^{T-1} c_i\big(x_i(t), x_i(t+1), \vec{z}_i(t), u_i(t)\big) \quad (6)$$

where γ_i is a set of uncertainties faced by D_i. The key points of this objective are that it is additively separable in time *and* space, optimizes long-term performance, and requires that decisions be made to achieve a single goal. The dynamics of the models relate the costs at one time to those at another.

The set γ_i reflects the fact that generally the individual agents must make decisions based on incomplete knowledge of the system structure. Since the principle of communication in terms of interaction variables usually prohibits complete elimination of γ_i as time proceeds, the global objective must be constructed to include this uncertainty. The exact set γ_i will depend on what is being communicated to the agent; Section III will illustrate this.

(Note that using uncertainty to model incomplete knowledge of the system model can be expected to lead to a conservative strategy as each agent plans for the worst case, which may never happen. The cost predicted by a strategy using uncertainty will thus be an upper bound on the cost actually incurred, which in turn may be greater than the global optimum.)

The antithesis of the team objective is the individual objective structure where each agent is interested only in minimizing his local cost. Between these two extremes lies a range of group objectives in which various groups of agents work together to achieve a common goal but each group has a different common objective. This may capture the notion of several organizations competing with one another.

Definition 11: The *individual objective* has each agent D_i striving to

$$\min_{\tilde{u}_i} \max_{\gamma_i} \sum_{t=0}^{T-1} c_i\big(x_i, x_i^+, \vec{z}_i, u_i\big) \quad (7)$$

where the maximum operation is again over all uncertainty not resolved by communication.

Definition 12: The group objective involves defining a partition $\mathbb{M}$ on the set of domules $\mathbb{N}$ with

$$|\mathbb{M}| = M \quad (8)$$

$$\cup \, m_i = \mathbb{N}, \qquad m_i \cap m_j = \varnothing \text{ if } i \neq j. \quad (9)$$

Then for each agent j in group m_i the objective is to

$$\min_{\tilde{u}_i} \max_{\gamma_i} \sum_{t=0}^{T-1} \sum_{k \in m_i} c_k\big(x_k, x_k^+, \vec{z}_k, u_k\big). \quad (10)$$

As in the team objective, the functional in (10) is expressed as a sum of local costs within the group.

III. Singly Connected Teams

The most highly structured problem is that of coordinating a team that is singly connected. Singly connected systems have the property that one agent's decisions can affect another agent's subsystem through only one series of domules. This section will describe six different coordination strategies for this type of problem, each reflecting the guidelines established in [1, sec. II].

By allowing various types of communication between interacting agents, several points on the trade-off curve of complexity versus optimality can be examined. Each strategy will reflect three unifying ideas which follow.

1) Coordination is done by selecting interaction sequences which yield good performance, then solving the resulting independent local problems to derive local control inputs.
2) Working *forward in time* only as far as is necessary or feasible.
3) Using *uncertainty* to gain local autonomy for agents when incomplete knowledge precludes perfect coordination.

As each agent can use its local model, at least to some extent, to predict the future consequences of its actions, certain bounds on system performance can be derived. As communication of various sorts improves each agent's ability to reduce its uncertainty about future events, these bounds can be expected to improve as communication increases. Note that this approach to communication as a *device to augment the local models*, rather than to adjust conditional probability densities on a state space, is crucial to this formulation.

The first of the six strategies considers a static or one-step problem. Introducing dynamics greatly increases the difficulty of the problem, so a decision strategy is first developed for the case of no interagent communication. One extension allows an agent only to predict to others interactions generated by it; a second allows full coordination but for only a finite future. By allowing only *a priori* communication, *abstraction* can be brought to bear to provide each agent with some information on the behavior of the subsystems external to that agent. Finally, by combining full coordination over a finite horizon with abstraction, a hybrid coordination mechanism can be developed. The concluding subsection discusses some implementation considerations of these mechanisms.

A. Static Teams

In a static situation, each agent can be viewed as making only one decision. In a domular setting care must be taken to formulate the problem in such a way that the decision of one agent can impact the situation of another or the need for communication vanishes. In a singly connected system the options for such impact are restricted and thus impose a constraint on the order in which decisions must be made by various agents if all possible interactions are to take place. The first decision must be made by an inferior agent, the last by a superior agent, and the decision times t_i of agent i is set to be

$$t_i = t_j + 1$$

for all j such that D_j affects D_i. (Such an ordering is clearly possible for any singly connected system.) With these t_j the static team decision problem is to

$$\min_{u_i(t_i)} \sum_{i=1}^{N} c_i(x_i(t_i), x_i(t_i + 1), \vec{z}_i(t_i), u_i(t_i)) \quad (11)$$

subject to

$$x_i(t_i + 1) = f_i(x_i(t_i), \vec{z}_i(t_i), u_i(t_i)) \quad (12)$$

$$z_{ij}(t_j) = g_{ij}(x_i(t_j)) \quad (13)$$

where (13) interconnects the domules so that coordination is necessary.

In order for an agent to make an optimal decision it must know the costs incurred by the rest of the system in *producing* or *responding to* interactions. If such costs were known, then an agent D_i could select

$$u_i^*, \vec{z}_i^*, {}_i\vec{z}^* = \arg\min \Big\{ c_i(x_i(t_i), x_i^+(t+1), \vec{z}_i(t), u_i)$$

$$+ \sum_j p_{ji}(z_{ji}(t_i)) + \sum_j r_{ij}(z_{ij}(t_1 + 1)) \Big\} \quad (14)$$

where

$\vec{z}_i$ set of interactions affecting $D_i = \{z_{ji}\}$

${}_i\vec{z}$ set of interactions produced by $D_i = \{z_{ij}\}$

$p_{ji}(z_{ji})$ the minimum cost of *producing* z_{ji} by D_j and agents affecting it

$r_{ij}(z_{ij})$ the minimum cost of *responding to* z_{ij} by D_j and the agents affected by it.

The reasoning behind (14) lies in the method for computing the $r_{ij}(\cdot)$ and $p_{ji}(\cdot)$. These cost functions are found by stepping through the system as ordered by an induction relation $\mathbb{H}$.

An algorithm which first inductively computes the $r_{ij}(\cdot)$ and $p_{ji}(\cdot)$ then uses them to achieve a coordinated selection of the u_i as follows.

Algorithm 1: Static team coordination.

Phase I: For any domule D_i, let D_k be its unique successor in $\mathbb{H}$. Assume that

1) for all predecessors D_j which *affect* D_i $p_{ji}(z_{ji})$ is known and has been communicated to D_i,
2) for all predecessors D_j which are *affected by* D_i $r_{ij}(z_{ij})$ has been communicated to D_i.

Then: a) if D_k affects D_i, pass to D_k the function

$$r_{ki}(z_{ki}) = \min_{\substack{u_i \ z_{ji} \\ j \neq k, i}} \min \Big\{ c_i(x_i, x_i^+, \vec{z}_i, u_i) + \sum_{\substack{\text{affectors} \\ \neq k}} p_{ji}(z_{ji})$$

$$+ \sum_{\text{affectees}} r_{ij}(z_{ij}) \Big\} \quad (15)$$

where the z_{ki} element of $\vec{z}_i$ is left as a free variable, or b) if D_k is affected by D_i, pass it the function

$$p_{ik}(z_{ik}) = \min_{u_i} \min_{z_{ji}} \Big\{ c_i(x_i, x_i^+, \vec{z}_i, u_i) + \sum_{\text{affectors}} p_{ji}(z_{ji})$$

$$+ \sum_{\substack{\text{affectees} \\ \neq k}} r_{ij}(z_{ij}) \Big\} \quad (16)$$

$$\text{subject to } g_{ik}(x_i^+) = z_{ik}. \quad (17)$$

Note that if D_i is an initial domule, it has no predecessors in $\mathbb{H}$ and hence the set of affectors and affectees outside of D_k is empty and $r_{ki}(\cdot)$ or $p_{ik}(\cdot)$ can be computed immediately. If D_i is the terminal domule a successor D_k does not exist and thus $r_{ki}(\cdot)$ or $p_{ik}(\cdot)$ need not be found.

Phase II: Again for any D_i, with D_k its unique successor in $\mathbb{H}$, assume that D_k has passed a value

$$\begin{cases} z_{ki}^*, & \text{if } D_k \text{ affects } D_i \\ z_{ik}^*, & \text{if } D_k \text{ is affected by } D_i \end{cases} \quad (18)$$

representing the optimal value of the interaction variables between D_i and D_k. Then D_i can

a) if D_k affects D_i, compute the minimizing arguments to (15), holding $z_{ki} = z_{ki}^*$.
b) if D_k is affected by D_i, compute the minimizing argument to (16) with the new constraint

$$g_{ik}(x_i^+) = z_{ik}^* \quad (19)$$

and pass the resulting z_{ij}^* or z_{ji}^* to the appropriate D_j. Note that if D_i is initial this step reduces to computing the optimal local u_i; if D_i is terminal, it reduces to solving (14). □

This is a variant of a spatial dynamic programming algorithm with Phase I being a forward sweep through the system to compute the cost functions $p_{ij}(\cdot)$ and $r_{ij}(\cdot)$ and a reverse sweep to actually compute the decisions. (Fig. 2 shows an example system and communicated quantities with D_4 as the terminal domule.)

Theorem 1: The controls computed by Algorithm 1 are globally optimal.

Proof: By induction, following ⊢. Each p_{ji} or r_{ij} gives the optimal costs to produce or respond to interactions, and (15), (16) assure that D_i computes a p_{ik} or r_{ki} with this property. (14) assures that the terminal domule selects globally optimal values which are then expanded by Phase II operations. It is thus straightforward manipulations of min operators in (14) which show that the decomposed optimization is equivalent to the desired global optimization. □

Algorithm 1 can be extended to handle *open-loop* dynamic problems by reformulating the one-step problem slightly. By replacing consideration of states, controls, and interactions with state sequences, control sequences, and interaction sequences over a time horizon $[0, T]$ and solving for open-loop optimal decisions, the problem structure remains the same. The $p_{ij}(\cdot)$ and $r_{ij}(\cdot)$ must be defined on z_{ij}^T and each of the minimizations modified to sum over time. (Note that the use of interaction sequences obviates the need for other subsystem models.) This suffers from the problem that a long time horizon leads to heavy communication requirements (exponential in T).

Static team problems can thus be solved in an optimal distributed fashion in the case of full communication. The next section will introduce a way of coordinating dynamical systems in the other extreme case, using uncertainty to overcome a total lack of communication capability.

B. Coordination with No Communication

This section addresses the question of making decisions in an environment where agents cannot communicate *at all*. Each can only seek to minimize its local contribution to total system cost, with no way of anticipating other agent's decisions or gauge its own effect on others. Because of the uncertainty as to interactions affecting it, each agent will adopt the minimum–maximum philosophy for making a decision.

Reflecting these considerations, the decision problem for D_i is given $x_i(t)$ and all $z_{ji}(t)$ (from the assumption of perfect knowledge of current interactions), find $u_i(t)$ to

$$\min_{u_i} \max_{\bar{z}_i} \min_{\tilde{u}_i} \sum_{\tau=t}^{T-1} c_i(x_i(\tau), x_i(\tau+1), z_i(\tau), u_i(\tau))$$

(20)

subject to local model dynamics. Note that the minimum–maximum over $\bar{z}_i$ and $\tilde{u}_i$ must be interlaced properly to

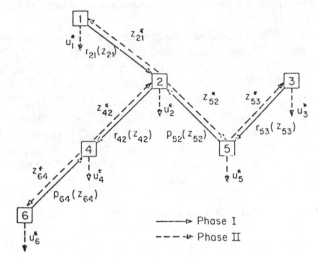

Fig. 2. Static coordination communication.

reflect the fact that each choice of $u_i(\tau)$ is made with knowledge of the current and past values of all $\bar{z}_i$.

The solution to these local problems can be obtained with dynamic programming as used in dynamic game theory. Let $\bar{v}_i(x_i, t)$ be the best guaranteed cost-to-go when the local system is in state x_i at time t just *before* knowledge of $z_i(t)$ is obtained. Then, at time $t - 1$, knowing $z_i(t-1)$, D_i will seek to

$$\min_{u_i} \{c_i(x_i(t-1), x_i(t), \bar{z}_i(t-1), u_i) + \bar{v}_i(x_i(t), t)\}$$

(21)

for the current state $x_i(t-1)$. Assuming all neighbors act in the most (locally) adverse manner, the $z_{ji}(t-1)$ which actually appear are those which

$$\max_{\bar{z}_i(t-1)} \min_{u_i} \{c_i(x_i(t-1), x_i(t), \bar{z}_i(t-1), u_i)$$

$$+ \bar{v}_i(x_i(t), t)\} \quad (22)$$

giving

$$\bar{v}_i(x_i, t-1)$$

$$= \max_{\bar{z}_i} \min_{u_i} \{c_i(x_i(t-1), x_i(t), \vec{z}_i, u_i) + \bar{v}_i(x_i(t), t)\}.$$

(23)

The solution $\bar{v}_i(x_i, t-1)$ approaches a form

$$\bar{v}_i(x_i, t) = \bar{v}_i(x_i) + \bar{g}_i t$$

(24)

(if the state space is reachable as $T \to \infty$).

The adversary assumption gives $\bar{v}_i(x_i, t)$ as an *upper bound* to the actual cost-to-go when in x_i at time t. A lower bound can be found assuming that neighbors are perfectly cooperative; that they will produce just those $\vec{z}_i$ needed to drive D_i optimally. The sequence

$$v_i(x_i, t-1) = \min_{z_i} \min_{u_i} \{c_i(x_i(t-1), x_i(t), \vec{z}_i, u_i)$$

$$+ v_i(x_i(t), t)\} \quad (25)$$

computes this lower bound and it converges to the form

$$v_i(x_i, t) = v_i(x_i) + g_i t. \qquad (26)$$

The value of (24) and (26) are twofold: they provide bounds on the actual average local cost incurred

$$\bar{g}_i \geqslant \lim_{T \to \infty} \frac{1}{T} \sum_{t=0}^{T-1} c_i(x_i(t), x_i(t+1), \vec{z}_i(t), u_i(t)) \geqslant g_i$$

$$(27)$$

and a decision strategy

$$u_i^*(t) = \arg\min_{u_i} \{ c_i(x_i(t), x(t+1), \vec{z}_i(t), u_i(t))$$

$$+ \bar{v}_i(x_i(t+1)) \}. \quad (28)$$

The tightness of the bounds $\bar{g}_i - g_i$ gives an indication of the need for communication to improve the local performance of D_i. The decision strategy can be implemented by precomputing $\bar{v}_i(x_i)$ and solving (28) as needed. Thus we have the following algorithm.

Algorithm 2: No communication. For each domule: Compute $\bar{v}_i(x_i, t)$ using (23) and (24). Choose $u_i(t)$ using (28). To evaluate the local effectiveness of this strategy, compute $\bar{g}_i - g_i$ using (23)–(26).

This strategy applies to systems where each agent knows nothing about the system outside of its local model, either *a priori* or in real time, requiring the use of uncertainty and minimum–maximum decisionmaking, which in turn, leads to suboptimality in the team sense. The next sections present ways to improve overall performance by reducing the uncertainty over which each agent must plan.

C. Coordination with Prediction Only

The first step to improving performance might be to allow communication *along* links of **G** in which each agent predicts future interactions generated by itself. As affected agents receive these predictions they can find a minimum cost response and thereby predict the interactions which will be generated to yet other agents. The bound on local cost incurred will be reduced as uncertainty about the incoming interactions is reduced; however the overall coordination is still teamwise suboptimal since no agent considers making a locally suboptimal decision in order to generate an interaction sequence which lowers the cost incurred in other parts of the system.

Note that the interaction predictions will be time-varying in general so the forward search algorithm of [1, sec. VI] must be used. If it converges in finite time a sequence of predictions need be made only for a finite period.

A crucial parameter in this strategy is thus the length of the predicted sequence of interactions T. For T infinite all forward search algorithms run by the agents will converge. If T is limited (e.g., by communications resources) then each D_i can only produce accurate predictions of interaction variables over a horizon $T - T_i$, where T_i is the time horizon required for forward search in D_i to converge. Of course D_i can always produce a prediction for one step

ahead as the present control is determined. Note that if predictions are not long enough to allow forward search to converge in the domule D_j receiving them, the forward search in D_j must be prematurely terminated. The way to do this, given by the philosophy of using uncertainty to replace modeling knowledge not available to an agent, is to assign a terminal cost $\bar{v}_i(x_i)$ as derived in (24) to the forward search computation after t_i steps

$$u_j^* = \min_{\substack{u_j \\ x_j^+}} w_j(\vec{z}_j; x_j, x_j^+, u_j, t_j) + \bar{v}_j(x_j^+) \quad (29)$$

where t_j is the minimum length of the predictions received by D_j. This is equivalent to assuming that incoming interactions will take on their predicted values over the horizon t_i and revert to worst-case values thereafter.

Algorithm 3: Coordination with prediction. *Inferior agents:* Solve for decisions locally as far into the future as possible, predict the interaction sequence which will result from those controls and send to the domules affected.

Middle agents: Each receives interaction prediction sequences from all others affecting it.

a) If forward search converges use it to determine as many controls, states, and resulting interactions as possible.

b) If forward search does not converge, use (29) to determine current control. Predict the next state, interaction (one-step prediction only).

Send interaction predictions to those affected.

Superior agents: Use middle algorithm, but only to determine current control. No predictions are needed.   □

This coordination method thus produces an improvement in performance bounds over using no communication as the predictions of interactions reduce the uncertainty faced by each local controller.

D. Limited-Horizon Coordination

In this section, a more effective form of coordination is discussed where communication is bidirectional and is done in terms of minimum costs to produce or to respond to possible sequences of interactions over a *finite period*. The approach is to select the best *overall* interaction for some fixed horizon T, given total uncertainty concerning interactions after T. This requires a way to compute the cost to produce or to respond to each interaction sequence by each part of the system (as ordered by **H**).

With the understanding that

a) each agent computes cost-to-produce or cost-to-respond functions based only on locally available information,

b) missing information is assumed to take its worst case value, and

c) each agent can update its plans at each time step to include new coordination information.

The finite-horizon coordination algorithm is an extension of the static Algorithm 1, where choices of z_{ij} are replaced by choices of sequences of z_{ij}, $\bar{z}_{ij}$, over the horizon T, and thus p_{ji} and r_{ij} are replaced by functions on Z_{ji}^T.

Algorithm 4: Limited-horizon coordination.

Phase 1: Each domule D_i receives $p_{ji}(\bar{z}_{ji})$ from predecessors affecting it, and $r_{ij}(\bar{z}_{ij})$ from those affected by it, and computes as follows.

a) If its successor D_k affects it,

$$r_{ki}(\bar{z}_{ki}) = \min_{\tilde{u}_i} \min_{\substack{\bar{z}_{ij} \\ \bar{z}_{ji}; j \neq k}} w_i(\bar{\bar{z}}_i; x_i, x_i^+, \tilde{u}_i, T) + \bar{v}_i(x_i^+)$$
$$+ \sum_{\substack{\text{affectors} \\ \neq k}} p_{ji}(\bar{z}_{ji}) + \sum_{\text{affectees}} r_{ij}(\bar{z}_i) \quad (30)$$

subject to the dynamical constraints of M_i, and with $\bar{z}_{ki}$ the free variable, or

b) if D_k is *affected by*

$$p_{ik}(\bar{z}_{ik}) = \min_{\tilde{u}_i} \min_{\substack{\bar{z}_{ij}; j \neq k \\ \bar{z}_{ji}}} w_i(\bar{\bar{z}}_i, x_i, x_i^+, \tilde{u}_i, T) + \bar{v}_i(x_i^+)$$
$$+ \sum_{\text{affectors}} p_{ji}(\bar{z}_{ji}) + \sum_{\substack{\text{affectees} \\ \neq k}} r_{ij}(\bar{z}_{ij}) \quad (31)$$

subject to M_i and

$$g_{ij}(\tilde{x}_i) = \bar{z}_{ij}. \quad (32)$$

Again initial domules only minimize over $\tilde{u}_i$; the terminal domule only accepts the communicated functions.

Phase II: Every D_i receives a $\bar{z}^*$ from its successor indicating the selected interaction sequence. It then finds the arguments which minimize (30) (or (31)) assuming the received $\bar{z}^*$ is produced (or is to be produced), sending the resulting $\bar{z}^*$'s to appropriate predecessors and applying the first element of $\tilde{u}_i^*$ as its control.

Initial domules merely solve for $\tilde{u}_i^*$ and apply $u_i^*(t)$; the terminal domule solves

$$\min_{\tilde{u}_i} \min_{\substack{. \quad \bar{z}_{ij} \\ \bar{z}_{ji}}} w_i(\bar{\bar{z}}_i; x_i, x_i^+, \tilde{u}_i, T) + \bar{v}_i(x_i^+) + \sum_{\text{affectors}} p_{ji}(\bar{z}_{ji})$$
$$+ \sum_{\text{affectees}} r_{ij}(\bar{z}_{ij}) \quad (33)$$

subject to its model constraints. $\qquad\square$

Since this algorithm allows the effects of one agent's decisions on his neighbors to be included, albeit for a finite horizon, it is to be expected that it leads to performance bounds better than those of the prediction-only strategy. This can be shown through the argument that the trajectory selected by the prediction strategy is always available for selection by the finite-horizon strategy, and another is selected only if it is known to be better, in a global sense, than that prediction.

There are two difficulties which can be encountered with the finite look-ahead strategy. They are

1) communication load grows exponentially with the length of the horizon (unless the system has special structure), and

2) horizons which are relatively short often do not give much improvement in performance, as the cost esti-

mates are more strongly affected by the static evaluator than the dynamic structure. (This suggests an improved evaluator will help the short horizon case greatly, as in Section F).

The first point above focuses on the practical use of this strategy in engineering the trade-off between communication capability and coordinated system performance. As the horizon T increases, so does communication, but

Theorem 2: As T increases, the performance of a system using finite-horizon coordination approaches the optimum.

Proof: As T increases the spaces over which interdomular coordination is performed, P_{ij}^T approach the spaces which would be used if the static coordination algorithm were used P_{ij}^∞. Since the latter generates the optimal interaction sequence, the sequence chosen using P_{ij}^T will approach this optimum.

E. Coordination with Abstraction

Turning from strategies which use increasing amounts of on-line communication to achieve improved performance, this section draws on the concept of abstraction to provide each agent with a simplified model of the external system which can be used to reduce the uncertainty either on the incoming interactions or on the way decisions may lead to increased or decreased costs in the other subsystems. To avoid convergence problems associated with techniques which identify such models on-line, the approach here will be to perform a single model building sweep through the system prior to actual decisionmaking.

The procedure embodied in this sweep through the structure will be to use the induction relation ⊞ to construct abstracted models of successively larger sections of the system until the terminal domule has a single, *simplified* model of the entire system. Each agent receives abstracted models from its predecessors, constructs a hybrid model by adding in its own state dynamics, and then passes an abstraction of the hybrid to its successor. Then, using no further communication, the abstraction can be used to reduce the uncertainty as to which interactions will be produced by inferiors thus improving performance bounds. Because interactions are similar to observations, abstraction in domules is more useful when a model of an inferior is constructed and passed to its superior than vice versa. Thus this strategy is most applicable to cases where ⊞ parallels 𝔾 as much as possible and is thus best suited to tree-structured systems (hierarchies).

The algorithm for the sweep along ⊞ which generates the abstractions follows.

Algorithm 5: Abstract model generation. Each D_i receives an abstract model $\hat{M}_j$ from all of its predecessors D_j. It can construct an intermediate model M_i' with state $x_i' = (x_i, \hat{x}_i, \cdots, \hat{x}_N)$.

State transition function:

$$f_i'(x_i', \bar{z}_i, u_i) = \big(f_i(x_i, \bar{z}_i, u_i), \hat{f}_1(\hat{x}_1, z_{1i});$$
$$\hat{f}_2(\hat{x}_2, z_{2i}), \cdots \big). \quad (34)$$

Cost function:

$$c_i'(x_i', \vec{z}_i, u_i) = c_i(x_i, x_i^+, \vec{z}_i, u_i) + \sum_{j=1}^{n} \hat{c}_j(\hat{x}_j, z_{ji}).$$

(35)

Aggregations:

$$g_{ij}'(x_i') = g_{ij}(x_i).$$

(36)

$\hat{M}_j$ can be constructed as an abstraction of this intermediate model and passed to the successor of D_i. If D_i is initial it forms an abstraction from its local model directly; if D_i is terminal, it constructs only the intermediate model M_i'. □

Recall that in (34)–(36) the abstracted state transition function $\hat{f}_j(\hat{x}_j, z_{ji})$ is a function of z_{ji} as the latter provides information on the state of M_j, and thus is used to track its evolution. The $\hat{c}_j(\cdots)$ are interval-valued as they are cost bounds; the sum in (35) is the usual set addition. The above assumes that the predecessors of D_i all affect D_i; for each that is affected by D_i, replace $\hat{f}_j(\hat{x}_j, z_{ji})$ with $\hat{f}_j(\hat{x}_j, z_{ij})$ and similarly for $\hat{c}_j$. Finally, if the successor to D_i affects D_i, there is no need for (36).

The development of abstraction showed that there are several ways to generate abstractions, from open-loop to closed-loop, depending on the degree to which the local control law can be determined *a priori*. If forward search shows a control option to be superfluous based on local information, it can be dropped from consideration (34)–(36).

These abstract models can be used with no further communication. Each agent uses the intermediate model created by combining his local model with the abstractions received. The local decision selects the input to minimize the worst possible costs incurred; since the abstractions will show that some interactions are infeasible, the set of possible worst cases is reduced, and hence performance bounds improve.

Algorithm 6: Decisionmaking with abstraction only. Each agent uses backwards dynamic programming on its intermediate model to derive the relative, worst-case cost-to-go functions

$$\bar{v}_i'(x_i') = \min_{u_i} \max_{z_{ij}} \max \left\{ \bar{v}_i'(x_i^+) + c_i'(x_i', \vec{z}_i, u_i) \right\} + \bar{g}_i$$

(37)

$$x_i^+ = f_i'(x_i', \vec{z}_i, u_i)$$

(38)

where z_{ij} is restricted to the set of those feasible given $\hat{D}_j$ is in state $\hat{x}_j$, and the second maximum in (37) is over the interval that follows. This can then be used in place of $\bar{v}_i(x_i)$ as a static evaluator for D_i

$$u_i^* = \operatorname*{argmin}_{u_i} \max \left\{ c_i'(x_i', \vec{z}_i, u_i) + \bar{v}_i'(x_i') \right\}$$

(39)

□

The abstraction thus has each D_i operating in a composite state space X_i' just as X was used in the case of no

communication. The resulting average cost $\bar{g}_i'$ and static evaluator $\bar{v}_i'(x_i')$ are used in the decision rule just as their counterparts were previously. Clearly $\bar{g}_i' \leqslant \bar{g}_i$ as the added structure of the dynamics of X_i' removes some possibilities of interaction sequences to be considered.

This strategy makes the control decision based on x_i', not x_i, as well as the z_{ji}. Thus each agent must use the observed z_{ji} to constantly update the states $\hat{x}_j$ occupied in each of the abstractions. Thus the processing required at each agent includes that required to generate the abstractions, to track the occupied state of the abstractions, and to implement the decision rule.

Abstraction thus allows communication of some (but *not complete*) knowledge of system structure to supplant real-time communications. The next section discusses a blend of this and a previous strategy to provide still better coordination.

F. Short-Term Coordination with Abstraction

By augmenting the finite-horizon coordination scheme with abstracted models and by using the static evaluator $\bar{v}_i'(x_i')$ rather than $\bar{v}_i(x_i)$ to terminate the forward search, improvement in system performance can be achieved. This improvement results from the reduction in uncertainty as to the possible interactions affecting a particular domule beyond a finite, detailed coordination horizon, just as abstraction alone reduced the uncertainty for an agent using no communication.

Algorithm 7: Finite-horizon coordination with abstraction.

Step I: Construct abstract models using Algorithm 5.

Step II: Apply the short-term coordination technique Algorithm 4, but operate each agent using D_j' rather than D_j, and specifically, $\bar{v}_j'(\cdot)$ rather than $\bar{v}_j(\cdot)$ as the termination of the cost along each $\tilde{x}_i$ in (12)–(33).

This hybrid algorithm uses the finite-horizon strategy to consider near-term (within T steps) interactions exactly and long-term (beyond T steps) interactions in a worst-case sense, with the latter limited by the additional knowledge of system structure supplied by the abstract models. (This limitation appears explicitly in the use of $\bar{v}_j'$.) Thus it is easy to show through the following.

Theorem 3: The bound on worst-case total system cost is at least as low for the hybrid algorithm as for finite horizon look-ahead.

Proof: The set of possible interactions to be considered by each agent as possible worst cases beyond the horizon T is at least as small for the hybrid as for finite look-ahead, so the worst-case bound is at least as low.

Theorem 4: The worst-case bound for the hybrid is at least as low as that for abstraction-only coordination.

Proof: Again, the hybrid has less uncertainty as the first T steps of interaction production (or response) costs are modeled exactly, where in the abstract algorithm they can only be bounded by computations based on $\hat{c}_j$.

G. Algorithm Evaluation

Although it is difficult to compare precisely these strategies in the absence of a specific problem, Table I summarizes some of their characteristics in a qualitative way. The entries are meant to convey the partial order on the performances and requirements of the strategies, assuming all other things (such as time horizon T) are equal. The performances reflect bounds established above; computational evaluations reflect reasonable assumptions on the cost of various operations.

In the context of a grain company's daily operations [1, sec. IV], more can be said. Clearly tight coordination is a necessity; this rules out the no communication (12) and prediction only (13) strategies, as they would have each agent moving grain out if its facilities as quickly as possible to minimize local storage costs.

The static strategy (11) can be eliminated from consideration for other reasons. Clearly generation and transmission of production/response cost functions would be prohibitively expensive for anything beyond a few days horizon due to the large number of possible delivery sequences that must be considered (each sequence describing the types, amounts, and qualities of grain delivered in each day).

The use of finite-horizon coordination with the interaction variables defined in [1] leads essentially to cost-to-produce/cost-to-respond functions which are defined over a set of loading or deliver schedules for the horizon of consideration. Each day, tentative schedules for the next T days are set up, assuming the (locally) worst possible behavior beyond then. The first day's plans are implemented, then a day later the plans are modified based on the possibilities of excluding that worst-case behavior on the $T + 1$st day.

The behavior of the system under the finite-horizon strategy is driven by the fact that the relative cost-to-go functions $\bar{v}_i$ would, for all storage facilities, penalize sequences of transactions which leave the facilities full at the end of a time horizon. This results from the fact that a possible influx of large amounts of grain, requiring outdoor storage and thus high losses, is the worst case behavior beyond time T. Thus each facility would favor reducing its stocks to a minimum at the end of the time horizon to the extent that such losses would not be offset by revenue gained by storing grain. As T increases, this latter term would dominate, and the various shipment options over the first days of the period start to impact the decision.

The main function of abstraction in this system would be to introduce knowledge of the seasonality which finite-horizon coordination lacks. In return, however, capacity for detailed planning of delivery schedules would be severely impaired.

Using both finite-horizon prediction and abstraction yields performance better than either alone. The abstraction modifies uncertainty as to worst-case events beyond the horizon, eliminating the possibility of a surge in supply

TABLE I
COMPARISON OF COORDINATION STRATEGIES

Algorithm	Performance	Communication		Processing	
		Initial	Real Time	Initial	Real Time
3.1	Best	Least	Most	Least	Most
3.2	Worst	Least	None	Some	Least
3.3	Poor	Some	Some	Moderate	Some
3.4	Fair	Some	Much	Some	Moderate
3.5/3.6	Fair	Much	None	Much	Some
3.5/3.7	Good	Most	Much	Much	Much

except during harvest time, allowing the system to consider decisions dominated by short-term opportunities.

This is best seen in the case of elevators. Given detailed predictions of the local supply model of the next one to four weeks production, plus the abstract model of later general seasonal effects, it can decide either to send remaining grain down the system to prepare for the new harvest, or to hold grain unless cost-to-respond data from a railroad indicates that shipment of a particular type and quality of wheat will generate revenue by supplying a certain customer's needs.

Thus the most suitable coordination mechanism for the automatic operations management of an integrated terminal is the hybrid strategy. This strategy can produce short term near-optimal decisions which take advantage of, or prepare for, longer term seasonal effects.

IV. MORE GENERAL STRUCTURES

The previous section dealt with the problem of coordinating the activities of a domular system with a singly connected topology, where the objective was the team goal: minimize the sum of the local costs incurred. This section will examine the six strategies proposed for applicability to wider classes of topology or objective, as defined in Section II.

A. Static Strategies

The static strategy can be extended with little difficulty to doubly connected systems and to acyclic topologies if the communication principles are relaxed somewhat. It will not work with general topologies as cycles preclude the use of an induction order. Since it provides perfect coordination between many agents, it is not useful for the individual objective structure. (The results of this section can be applied equally well to finite-horizon coordination by restricting attention to the T steps of the future and using uncertainty to model the remaining time).

The extension to doubly connected systems is made by substituting a more complicated expression for the cost-to-produce (or = respond) functions $p_{ij}(z_{ij})$ (or $r_{ji}(z_{ji})$) by conditioning them on a particular response (or production). Because of its structure, an induction ordering $\mathbf{H}$ can always be found exactly as in the singly connected case.

This is used to guide the propagation of the new forms of the cost functions through the system.

The modification of $p_{ik}(\tilde{z}_{ik})$ to be conditioned upon the concurrent reception of $\tilde{z}_{ki}$ is as follows. D_i computes

$$p_{ik}(\tilde{z}_{ik} \mid \tilde{z}_{ki}) = \min_{u_i} \min_{\substack{\tilde{z}_{ij}; j \neq k \\ \tilde{z}_{ji}; j \neq k}} w_i(\vec{z}_i; x_i, x_i^+, \tilde{u}_i, T) + \bar{v}_i(x_i^+)$$

$$+ \sum_{\text{affectors}} p_{ji}(\tilde{z}_{ji} \mid \tilde{z}_{ij}) + \sum_{\substack{\text{affectees} \\ \neq k}} r_{ij}(\tilde{z}_{ij} \mid \tilde{z}_{ji}) \quad (40)$$

subject to

$$g_{ik}(\tilde{z}_i) = \tilde{z}_{ik} \quad (41)$$

where D_k is the successor in $\mathbb{H}$ of D_i. (41) constraints the solution to (40) to produce the specified sequence of interactions $\tilde{z}_{ik}$ to D_k but the inclusion of $\tilde{z}_{ki}$ in (40) *as prespecified* (not available for minimization) leads to $p_{ik}(\tilde{z}_{ik} \mid \tilde{z}_{ki})$ being a function of two arguments. The response costs r_{ik} can be extended in an analogous manner; including these modified forms in the sum of (40) leads to a static strategy for doubly connected systems.

Acyclic topologies pose a more difficult problem. If D_1 affects D_4 through both D_2 and D_3, the cost to produce interactions z_{12} and z_{13} does not, in general, separate as

$$p_{1;2,3}(z_{12}, z_{13}) \neq p_{12}(z_{12}) + p_{13}(z_{13}). \quad (42)$$

Thus the costs to agents in such a structure depend in a nonseparable way on the interactions with each of their neighbors. This fact, plus the observation that one cannot define an induction order on the topology, leads to the conclusion that a typical acyclic topology cannot be coordinated using the static scheme. (However, the system can often be restructured, by combining agents, into a doubly or singly connected system.)

B. Coordination with No Communication

By virtue of the fact that the "no communication" strategy completely decomposes the coordination scheme into local searches for the controls and thus decisions are made by each agent completely independently of all others, it is applicable to all topologies and all objective structures. Objective structure is immaterial as teams, and thus groups, are reduced to acting on an individualistic basis when shorn of all capacity to communicate. This is the only strategy of the six applicable to the most general class of system structures.

C. Coordination with Prediction Only

This approach to coordination displays much the same behavior with respect to objective structure as the previous strategy, but it is suitable for acyclic topologies also. It is not applicable to cyclic structures because mutually conflicting objectives can lead to a gaming situation between agents.

That the prediction strategy works with an acyclic system under the team objective is easy to see. Each inferior domule can solve its local control problem, compute the interactions generated by applying the solution, and pass these predictions to the agents affected by the interactions. Other agents can use the predictions they receive to construct and send their own predictions. Repeating this process through the entire system eventually results in predictions arriving at all superior domules and the coordination is complete.

The reason that this scheme does not run into the separability problem of the static strategy is that each agent forms its predictions as an element of the Cartesian product of outgoing interaction sets, not as a function on that product set. The element is separable as each component can be sent to the agent it affects; a function may not be separable.

The strategy fails in double-connected or cyclic topologies. The predictions made by one agent may depend on those made by its neighbor, which in turn depends on those made by the one. As there is no guarantee that a mutually consistent pair of such predictions exists, this strategy cannot in general be used in any cyclic topology. Simple examples along the lines of zero sum games can easily be constructed to illustrate this.

D. Coordination with Abstraction

The construction and propagation of abstract models throughout a domular control system poses some difficulty, but flexibility is offered as abstracted models *are* separable and can be constructed in a cyclic topology.

Section III-E described a way to coordinate singly connected teams using abstract models. Such systems can also be coordinated using only production-cost models by replacing each with a less accurate, but separable, abstract models as follows. Each D_i can construct an abstract model of itself which bounds the set of possible (z_{ij}, z_{ik}) pairs producible (and the associated costs) given D_i occupies some abstracted state $\hat{x}_i$. This is the best possible model in the sense that the set of feasible (z_{ij}, z_{ik}) pairs is as small as possible.

A somewhat less precise model can be constructed by finding the smallest set of feasible (z_{ij}, z_{ik}) which *is* separable (and the smallest intervals which bound the cost of producing a pair which decompose as

$$\hat{c}_i(\hat{x}_i, z_{ij}, z_{ik}) = \hat{c}_{ij}(\hat{x}_i, z_{ij}) + \hat{c}_{ik}(\hat{x}_i, z_{ik}) \quad (43)$$

where intervals $\hat{c}_{ij}(\cdot, \cdot)$ and $\hat{c}_{ik}(\cdot, \cdot)$ are added in the usual set addition fashion). This model can be separated into the two sets which are the original set's projections onto P_{ij} and P_{ik} (Fig. 3), producing the tightest separable bound on the producible set and its costs. The separated bounds then comprise independent abstract models which can be sent to D_j and D_k.

For acyclic systems in general these models can be constructed in a single pass through the system. Inferior domules construct, separate, and communicate models to those they affect. Other agents repeat the process when they have received all appropriate models. Finally, the superior domules receive models and commence on-line coordination.

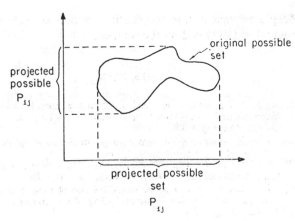

Fig. 3. Separation of possible interaction set.

TABLE II
SUMMARY OF APPLICABILITY OF COORDINATION STRATEGIES

	Static	No Comm.	Prediction	Finite Horizon	Abstraction	Hybrid
System Structure:						
Teams:						
Singly connected	x	x	x	x	x	x
Doubly Connected	x	x		x		
Acyclic		x	x		x	
General		x				
Individuals:						
All		x	x		x	

Abstraction is thus suited to acyclic topologies if the additional uncertainty introduced in the transition to separable models is tolerable. Cyclic topologies pose different, but not insurmountable, problems. Any agent can construct an abstract model of itself assuming all incoming interaction sequences are possible which can be separated and passed to neighboring agents. These agents repeat the process taking into account the constraints on possible incoming interactions which are implied by the received abstract models. Moreover, if a cycle exists, eventually models will arrive at the original agent which may limit the set of possible incoming sequences further than the constraints available for the original abstract model construction. A model, tighter (more precise) than the original, can then be built and the process iterated.

Turning to the effect of objective structure, the construction of abstract models is similar to the generation of predictions used in the prediction-only approach. Any agent can supply a model to another agent, provided incentives exist, so the model construction process can work exactly as with the team objective.

Finally, note that the combination of the finite horizon and abstraction techniques is feasible only in cases where each can be used alone.

E. Summary

Table II summarizes these conclusions. Singly connected systems are suited to the greatest variety of strategies, although hierarchies have an advantage when abstraction is used. Certain strategies are useful with either acyclic or doubly connected topologies but only one with no communication works well with both.

For individual objectives only three techniques apply as no agent is interested in global optimization. Note that technically for the prediction and abstraction strategies there must be an incentive for each agent to expend the efforts to produce the required information which benefits only those agents to which it is passed. Also, for system structures which contain several groups, each acting as a team of individual agents, the team coordination strategies can be used within groups and "individual" strategies between groups.

The most interesting conclusion to be drawn is that the most powerful technique—the hybrid one—applies only to systems with a singly connected team structure. When the advantage of cost-to-produce abstractions over cost-to-respond models is added, hierarchies fall out as the preferable organizational structure for the underlying system as they are most amenable to coordination. (It should be noted here that a hierarchy can always be found embedded in any system structure, and a coordination mechanism used which treats interactions not incorporated in the tree as unknown, i.e., taking worst-case values).

V. CONCLUSION

This concludes the development done to date on this approach to the study of distributed decision systems. The major contributions of this work are

1) the formulation of a distributed dynamic decision problem using only knowledge of the system structure local to each agent,
2) the use of uncertainty and the related best worst-case decision strategy to bridge the gaps in information provided from other agents about future capabilities,
3) the collection of several classes of coordination strategies including some which use "high level" abstracted models of a system external to a decision agent, and
4) an analysis of the system topologies for which each class is appropriate.

As is the case of other decision and control techniques, it is expected that the concepts explored here can be applied at a general level in some systems but that the addition of assumptions of special structure to the system models may generate far more practical algorithms for implementation. Obvious assumptions which may provide this advantage are linear dynamics, linear or quadratic cost functions, or Gaussian or Poisson stochastic processes driving the system. The goal of the study of these properties would be mainly to find ways to parameterize the cost-to-produce/cost-to-respond functions to reduce the communication required.

However, the most significant facet of this work is the new perspective it establishes on the issues of decentralized management of complex systems. It represents a significant departure from past approaches to this class of problems and promises better understanding of the interrelated roles of knowledge, communication, and decisionmaking under uncertainty.

ACKNOWLEDGMENT

Michael Athans provided much inspiration and conceptual guidance for this work; Alan Willsky and Marvin Minsky also offered insight and suggestions. The authors deeply appreciate this cooperation as well as the helpful suggestions provided by the referees.

REFERENCES

[1] R. R. Tenney and N. R. Sandell, "Structures for distributed decisionmaking," *IEEE Trans. Systems, Man, Cybernetics*, vol. 11, no. 8, pp. 517–527, Aug. 1981.

[2] H. S. Witsenhausen, "A counterexample in stochastic optimal control," *SIAM J. Contr.*, vol. 6, no. 1, 1968.

[3] P. Whittle and J. Rudge, "The optimal linear solution of a symmetric team control problem," *J. Appl. Probability*, vol. 11, 1974.

[4] N. R. Sandell, Jr. and M. Athans, "Solution of some nonclassical LQG stochastic decision problems," *IEEE Trans. Automat. Contr.*, vol. AC-19, Apr. 1974.

[5] D. P. Looze and H. Salhi, "Aggregation in hierarchical systems: Approximate decompositions," *Proc. 19th C.D.C.*, Albuquerque, NM, Dec. 1980.

[6] Y. C. Ho, "Team decision theory and information structures," *Proc. IEEE*, vol. 68, no. 6, June 1980.

Interacting Plans

BERTRAM BRUCE
Bolt Beranek and Newman

DENIS NEWMAN
University of California at San Diego

The paper explores certain phenomena which arise in stories, conversations, and human activity in general when the plans of two individuals are formed and carried out in an interactive situation. A notation system for representing interacting plans is introduced and applied in the analysis of a small portion of "Hansel and Gretel." The analysis illustrates how a single actor plan can be modified by the needs of cooperative interaction with others and how cooperative interactive episodes can be transformed and used deceptively by one party in achieving his or her own covert goals.

> Close to a large forest there lived a woodcutter and his wife and his two children. The boy was called Hansel and the girl Gretel. They were always very poor and had very little to live on. And at one time when there was a famine in the land, he could no longer procure daily bread.
>
> THE BROTHERS GRIMM

1. OVERVIEW

In the realms of stories, conversation, and human activity in general it is increasingly recognized that analysis proceeds in terms of actions connected through goals, effects, and enabling conditions. There has been extensive work to show just how goals and actions are connected but an important consequence of goal-based understanding of actions is often overlooked. If we can interpret an actor's behavior in terms of goals, then so can others who may be affected by that behavior. They may then act, not just in terms of their own goals, but in terms of their understandings of the actor's goals. This means that when two or more people inter-act, their plans can reach a level of complexity that is difficult to foresee from consideration of single actor plans.

The distinction between *single-actor plans* and *interacting plans* can be seen in the first episode of the fairy tale, "Hansel and Gretel" (Grimm, 1945). Hansel and Gretel are the children of a woodcutter who lives near a large forest with his children and his wife, their stepmother. The family is poor and with a famine in the land the stepmother is able to convince the kind but weak-willed father that they should abandon the children in the woods. The stepmother suggests that the next morning they take the children into the woods and leave them near a fire saying they will be back when they are finished cutting the wood. But Hansel overhears the parents' discussion of their plan and carries out a plan to foil it. He gathers pebbles and drops them along the trail. When the parents have left them, Hansel and Gretel are able to return home by following the pebbles in the moonlight.[1]

An analysis of this episode would show that Hansel has a goal—to be able to return home after being taken into the woods. To reach that goal he drops pebbles along the trail so that he and Gretel can retrace their steps. We could understand what Hansel does in terms of a plan in which dropping pebbles is an action appropriate to the goal. The plan would show how the actions of dropping pebbles and following the trail fit together, and how they produce desired outcomes for Hansel and Gretel.

But such a plan would be incomplete. Hansel and Gretel are being taken into the woods deliberately by their parents. Hansel knows that he should drop pebbles because he and Gretel have overheard their parents plotting against them. Thus, the children's plan is a response to their conception of their parents' plan. Hansel and Gretel are not just "returning home" but are "countering" the plan they perceive their parents to have. It would have been of little use for Hansel to drop pebbles on a familiar trail, and, if his parents were planning to kill the children outright, some other response would have been more effective. His action becomes meaningful only with respect to his perception of the structure of his parents' plan.

[1] The Grimm's version of this episode is given in the Appendix. For those readers who are trying to remember where the gingerbread house comes in, we provide the following synopsis of the rest of the story: The parents welcome them back home, but soon thereafter a similar episode occurs. This time, however, the door is locked when Hansel attempts to go out to gather pebbles. He resorts to an alternate plan of dropping bread crumbs. Unfortunately, birds eat the crumbs and Hansel and Gretel are lost in the woods. From there, they go on to find the wicked witch and the house "made of bread and roofed with cake." The witch captures the children and is going to eat Hansel, but Gretel manages to kill her. The children return home to their father with the witch's jewels. There, they find that their cruel stepmother has died in the interim.

This research was supported by the National Institute of Education under Contract No. MS-NIE-C-400-76-0116 and by a grant from the Carnegie Corporation to Michael Cole at Rockefeller University. Requests for reprints should be addressed to Bertram Bruce, Bolt Beranek and Newman Inc., 50 Moulton Street, Cambridge, Mass. 02138.

2. THE REPRESENTATION OF INTERACTING PLANS

2.1 The Problem

Most formal work on plans has been in artificial domains where the goal has been to produce or recognize a single actor plan. In such domains, the problem of independent actors with conflicting goals has not arisen. In ordinary human activity and especially in the activities found in stories, these situations are often of critical importance. For us, the essential problem can be stated as follows: How do we represent the plans that determine behavior in a way that explicates *interactions* among plans? In the course of analyzing and applying the representation to a range of texts, it became clear that the problem is not just to show how actions can be organized into plans. We need to do that, but we also need to show how cooperation takes place, how conflicts arise and are resolved, and how beliefs about plans determine actions, and how differing beliefs and intentions make a story.

We should emphasize that while we are proposing a formal method for representing the interactions between plans, we are not aiming for the level of precision which is presently realized with respect to artificial domains. More particularly, although our work builds on ideas developed in work on planning algorithms (Sacerdoti, 1975; Sussman, 1975; Tate, 1975), and on the use of plans in producing appropriate actions (Cohen, 1978; Perrault & Cohen, 1977) we are not proposing a new planning algorithm. Similarly, though plan recognition (Schmidt, Sridharan, & Goodson, 1978) is a necessary part of the process of engaging in interacting plans, we are not discussing plan recognition per se. We are concerned with knowing how a plan facilitates understanding of the actions of others (Bruce, 1975, 1977; Shank & Abelson, 1977). We hope, in particular, to explicate the forms that *interacting plans* can take through a notation system that incorporates ideas from work on single-actor plans, but focuses on plans in a social context.

2.2 Belief Spaces

The representation of interacting plans in our notation involves the use of a set of symbols within a space which represents one character's model of the interactive situation. The plans that are represented are those of the target character and those that the target character *believes* that the other character is carrying out or intending to carry out. Two separate models are required for representing the separate points of view of the two characters. Figure 1 shows three belief spaces (indicated by the double-lined rectangles) each containing

Our concern with interacting plans has been primarily directed to the analysis and representation of narrative text. An important aspect of narrative is that it recounts characters' plans. Most often, as in "Hansel and Gretel," more than one character is involved so that analyzing the plot structure of many stories requires taking interacting plans into account. Accordingly, we have been developing a system of notation that captures generalizations about plans and the common forms that interactions take. We have found that, as a basis for representing interaction, we have had to work out ways of representing single-actor plans and many of the details of the notation apply to these. But what we soon find in analyzing stories is that each of the characters is acting in a reality that includes perceptions of the other's plans. It also includes the knowledge that the other is assessing his or her plans and reacting accordingly. Thus a central aspect of representing interacting plans is showing how the beliefs and plans of one character are embedded in the beliefs and plans of the other.

Much of the complexity of stories in which characters interact arises because the story is about a *conflict* between the goals of two characters. A person in conflict with another may try to conceal the conflict or deceive the other into acting in a way that serves his or her own interest at the expense of the other. A character may thus construct a plan that is intended to be believed by the other, but is not actually carried out. The plan constitutes the character's "cover." As we shall see, such a *virtual plan* plays a central role in "Hansel and Gretel." The parents attempt to deceive the children into thinking that they are going on an ordinary wood fetching expedition, in order to conceal their real intent, which is to abandon the children. Where deception occurs it often mimics ordinary cooperative interaction. We have found that the representation of cooperative interaction is a prerequisite for representing the complexities introduced by conflict. "Hansel and Gretel" can serve to illustrate our concerns and findings because it contains single actor plans within interacting plans and cooperative plans within a situation of deception and differing beliefs. Deception and differing beliefs are a common feature of stories in which characters interact.

This paper is organized as follows: Section 2 presents a system for the representation of interacting plans. This notational system is a record of the generalizations we have discovered in analyzing stories, *Sesame Street* muppet skits, and natural conversations. Section 3 contains an analysis of the first part of "Hansel and Gretel." Through this analysis we illustrate a number of phenomena that appear to have a generality that goes well beyond this particular story, e.g., achieving multiple goals, social episodes, modifying scripts, and virtual plans. In Section 4 we discuss some of the limitations of our analysis. We conclude in Section 5 with a discussion of the complexities that remain to be explored.

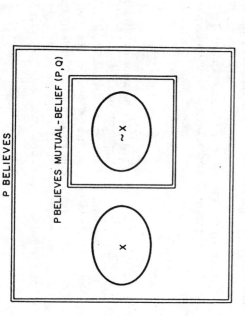

P BELIEVES

P BELIEVES MUTUAL - BELIEF (P,Q)

FIG. 2. A mutual belief space from P's point of view.

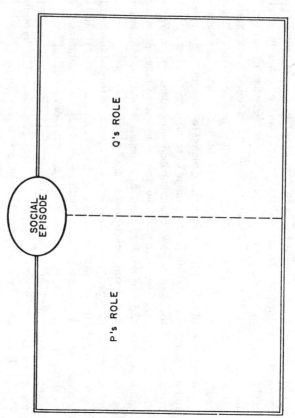

SOCIAL EPISODE

P's ROLE

Q's ROLE

FIG. 3. A social episode.

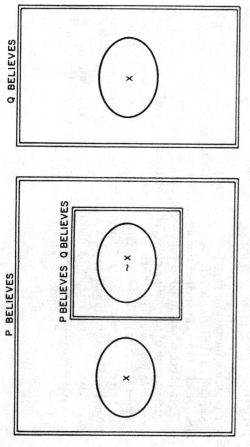

Q BELIEVES

P BELIEVES

P BELIEVES Q BELIEVES

FIG. 1. Belief spaces.

a state (the labeled ovals). This figure indicates that P's belief about Q's belief does not match Q's actual belief, though it does match P's actual belief.

Within one character's model of the situation there may be a *mutual belief space*. Any fact falling within this space is believed by the target character to be shared with the other character. That is, character P (whose space it is) believes Q believes P believes Q believes (etc.) the fact. The use of a mutual belief space within the character's model of the situation is intended to avoid the infinite regression of P's view of Q's view of P's view (etc.) of the situation. We discuss mutual belief spaces in more formal terms in the section of separate realities. Figure 2 shows a mutual belief space from P's point of view.

A mutual belief space is usually used in representing some cooperative interactive episode between two characters. Figure 3 illustrates the layout for representing a social episode. The episode is labeled in the state node at the top. In the space are included the intentions and actions which constitute the roles of the two characters. (The roles of the two characters are differentiated by a dashed line dividing the belief space.) By a character's *role* is meant the actions that the particular character (say, P) expects to perform, and which P believes that the other character expects P to perform. Role also includes the intentions that the other character could reasonably infer from the character's actions given the assumption that they are cooperating. In the representation of a story in which there are no conflicting intentions, both characters' models of the situation can be represented entirely within a mutual belief space. Where conflicting goals and deception are involved, part of at least one character's model of the situation will fall outside of the mutual belief space.

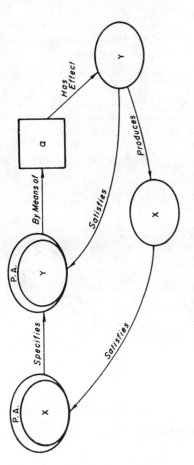

FIG. 4. Satisfaction of intentions.

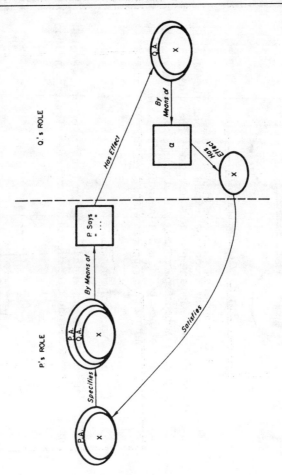

FIG. 5. The "request" configuration.

2.3 *Basic Elements of the Representation System*

The description of interacting plans ultimately rests upon two basic types of entities, *states* (represented by ovals) and *acts* (represented by rectangles). Each of these can be either *simple* or *complex* (internally structured). *Tags* are used to mark the temporal, or the real-hypothetical, status of the nodes, and there can be various *relations* between nodes (shown as labeled arrows). The basic elements that we use are the minimum that we have found necessary for representing plans and as such the set of elements expresses generalizations about plans. A full catalogue of the elements and other details of the notation system can be found in a longer version of this paper (Bruce & Newman, 1978).

It should be emphasized that acts and states are mental entities, that is, they are the target character's conception of aspects of his or her environment. The requirement that acts and states be mental entities and not absolute objective entities lays the foundation for different levels of characterization. People respond to their conception of another's actions. Mismatched conceptions may lead to conflicts or may be the result of deception.

While simple states and acts are represented as primitive we are not assuming that they would be primitive for an actor; rather we are choosing a convenient level of representation. It seems highly unlikely that there could be any set of "primitive" acts or states that would be universal across cultures, developmental levels, or situations. Instead, we can talk of particular characterizations that could be appropriately used in a given context.

2.4 *Common Configurations*

One of the findings of our interacting plans analysis is a set of configurations built out of the nodes and relations. Each configuration is a generalization taken from analyses of social interactions although often the general form of the configuration is found in both single actor plans and interacting plans. In this section we present a few of the most important configurations, each of which has at least one instantiation in the analysis of "Hansel and Gretel" that is to follow.

2.4.1 Satisfaction of Intentions

Figure 4 shows a simple configuration, the satisfaction of intentions. The double oval at the upper left represents an "Achieve" intention. It indicates that a person (P) intends to achieve(A) a state(X). This Achieve intention has specified another Achieve intention which is carried out by means of an act (α). (Throughout these configurations, Greek letters are used for acts and Roman letters for states.) States (as in this case, Y) may produce other states

without the activity of a person. A person may then cause Y in order to produce X. In this configuration, the effect (Y) of the act (α) satisfies the second Achieve intention and produces a state that satisfies the first intention.

2.4.2 Request

One frequently encountered configuration is the "request," as shown in Fig. 5. It occurs when a person attempts to achieve a goal by engaging another, and thus represents one of the simpler cases of interaction among plans. In the figure, person P has the intention to achieve X. This is indicated at the top left. Instead of acting directly to bring about X, P forms a new intention, to achieve the state of Q's having the intention to achieve X (shown in the triple oval). This new intention is achieved by means of a speech act, which has the effect of a new intention for Q (to achieve X).[2]

In general, the vertical dimension is used to indicate temporal sequence. Thus, the request is shown as preceding the act, α. It should also be pointed out that intentions, acts, and states do not necessarily exist contemporaneously. For example, the doing of the act that effects X brings X into existence (as a belief) but also eliminates the original intention to achieve X.[3]

2.4.3 Resolution of Conflict

Another common configuration is the "resolution of conflict," as shown in Figs. 6 and 7. This occurs in various forms, but typically originates as in Fig. 6, when a hypothetical side effect (shown in dotted outline) of an act (α) conflicts with some "Maintain" intention (and the actor, P knows that an act such as β could counter the side effect). The Maintain intention is represented by the double oval with "P.M." it is a sense awakened by the hypothetical state and induced to specify an Achieve intention (Fig. 7). The Achieve intention generates the act (β) which counters the hypothetical state.

The resolution of conflicts can occur within single actor plans (as in the two previous figures), but also plays an important role in interacting plans. For example, one way to resolve a conflict is to transfer the burden of responsibility to another person, e.g., to use a request to create in another a Maintain intention that will be awakened by the same hypothetical state. This strategy, when successful, will result in the other having to resolve the conflict at a later time. Examples of this occur at several points in "Hansel and Gretel" (see Section 3.4).

2.4.4 Initiation of a Social Episode

Another important configuration is the initiation of a social episode, as shown in Fig. 8. Often, to achieve certain goals one must engage others in an activity. The activity can be said to commence when the two (or more) participants each have the intention to maintain the activity. We say then that the activity is a social episode. Typically, an episode is initiated by means of a speech act, e.g., "Let's do....." When successful, the initiation produces a

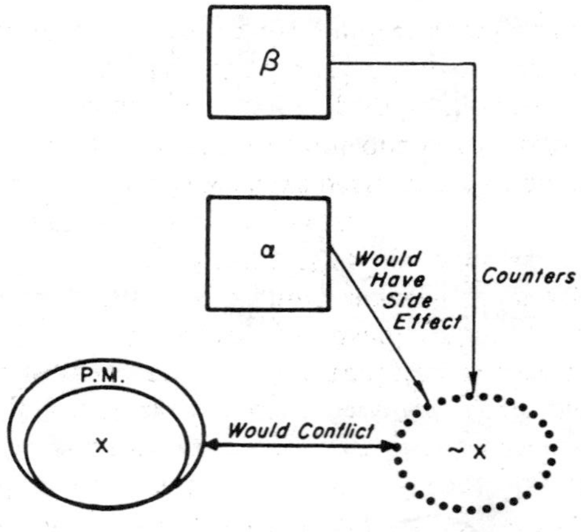

Maintain intention in the second participant. This, plus the Maintain intention of the first participant, produces the episode. The existence of the episode implies a new belief space, namely, a set of beliefs shared between the participants. One of these beliefs is that the initiation act is precisely that: an act to create the mutual belief space in which it resides.

2.4.5 Complex Act Configurations

The complex act representation is used when the effects of the "lower level" acts in combination produce the effect of the complex act. The representation

FIG. 6. Resolution of a conflict—I.

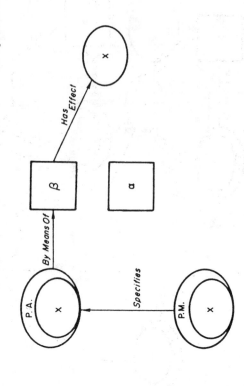

FIG. 7. Resolution of a conflict—II.

[2]We have deliberately left out any representation of the usual preconditions and outcomes of the request (see Bruce, 1975; Searle, 1969). We assume that these operate on the beliefs shown in the figure, but we are concerned here only with the transfer of intentions and the resulting plans.

[3]The reader should see Cohen (1978) for a formalism in which this process might be represented.

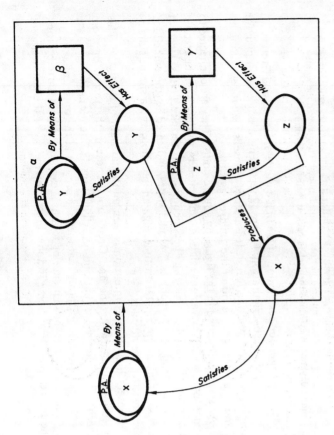

FIG. 9. Independent sub-acts in a complex act.

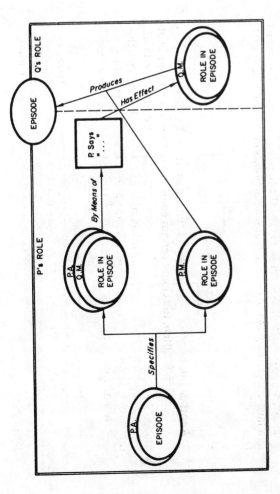

FIG. 8. Initiation of a social episode.

of an act as "complex," with its decomposition into "simple" acts, indicates that the effects (or preconditions or other aspects) of the component acts are relevant to representing interacting plans. Note that complex acts can be contained within complex acts (see the parent's plan in Fig. 21). The acts within a complex act can be related in many possible ways, two of which we identify here.

2.4.5.1 Independent Sub-Acts. In this kind of complex act, the temporal sequence is not a necessary order. for example, in "setting a table" (α), one could set glasses (β) before or after setting plates (γ).

2.4.5.2 Enabling Sub-Acts In "starting a fire" (α), one needs to gather combustible materials together (β) before lighting them (γ). The act of "gathering" has an effect (HasEffect)—the state of "materials together" (Y) which makes possible (Enables) the act of "lighting." Not all HasEffect—Enables chains need to be characterized as complex acts (e.g., Hansel's pebble gathering as shown in Fig. 12).

2.4.5.3 ByDoing This relation provides for abbreviating complex acts. While the complex act representation shows the intentional states which lead to doing the lower level acts, the ByDoing relation allows for a direct link between the higher level act and the lower level acts. Whenever this relation is used, it can be assumed to be expandable into one of the complex act representations.

3. AN INTERACTING PLANS ANALYSIS OF HANSEL AND GRETEL

3.1 A Guide to the Analysis

The examples to follow are all taken from "Hansel and Gretel." In this paper we consider only a small part of the story: the first attempt of the parents to get rid of the children. In fact, we focus on one aspect of the episode—the interactions between the plan of the parents to abandon the children and the plan of the children to block their parent's plan. The interactions occur in the context of a virtual plan, which the parents use to make the children believe that nothing unusual is about to happen when they go into the woods. In addition to its importance in this story, the virtual plan serves as a model for normal interactive episodes since its effectiveness depends upon its mimicking of real plans.

There are several restrictions we have been forced to place on the analysis. These are discussed in a later section, but one needs to be mentioned here. Though there are four characters in the episode, the father, the stepmother, Hansel, and Gretel, we will describe the episode as if there were only two: the parents and children. In describing the children's real plan, however, we will attribute it to Hansel, since he takes primary responsibility for formulating it and carrying it out.

For details of notation the reader should see Bruce and Newman (1978). Some general points are the following: In each diagram time is indicated by position on the page. Generally speaking, earlier states and acts appear near the top of the page, so that the episode can be "read" from the top of the diagram to the bottom. The parents' intentions and actions are always on the left side of the page, with higher level intentions farther to the left. The children's intentions and actions are always on the right side, with higher level intentions farther to the right.

3.2 Achieving a Goal with a Sequence of Actions

When the old people had gone to sleep, he got up, put on his little coat, opened the door, and slipped out. The moon was shining brightly and the white pebbles round the house shone like newly minted coins. Hansel stooped down and put as many into his pockets as they would hold.

Then he went back to Gretel and said, "Take comfort, little sister, and go to sleep. God won't forsake us." And then he went to bed again.

*   *   *

Then they all started for the forest.

When they had gone a little way. Hansel stopped and looked back at the cottage, and he did the same thing again and again. . . He had been dropping a pebble on the ground each time he stopped.

*   *   *

When the full moon rose, Hansel took his little sister's hand and they walked on, guided by the pebbles, which glittered like newly coined money. They walked the whole night, and at daybreak they found themselves back at their father's cottage.

We can begin our description of the first episode of Hansel and Gretel with a relatively simple configuration. Figure 12 represents a single-actor plan for finding one's way out of a forest. It is part of Hansel's plan for surviving his parents' attempts to be rid of the children.

Acts are represented in the figure by square nodes. They are connected to states (oval nodes) by various relations, indicated by the labels on the arrows. For example, the act "Hansel gathers pebbles," has the effect (HasEffect) of the state, "Hansel has pebbles." Modal states, indicated by the embedded ovals, contain some mental attitude, e.g., an intention, and a simple state as the object of the attitude.

Hansel's highest level intention is seen on the far right of the figure. This intention specifies that he and Gretel not be lost in the forest, or more specifically, that they get back home. All of Hansel's intentions in Fig. 12 are tagged with time t_s indicating that they are present at the outset of carrying out the plan. While the sequence of actions is carried out from top to bottom, the intention to be at home is done directly by means of the last action of

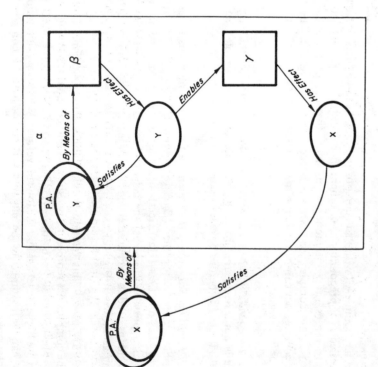

FIG. 10.   Enabling sub-acts in a complex act.

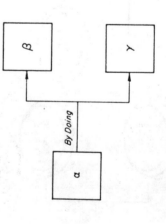

FIG. 11.   The ByDoing abbreviation.

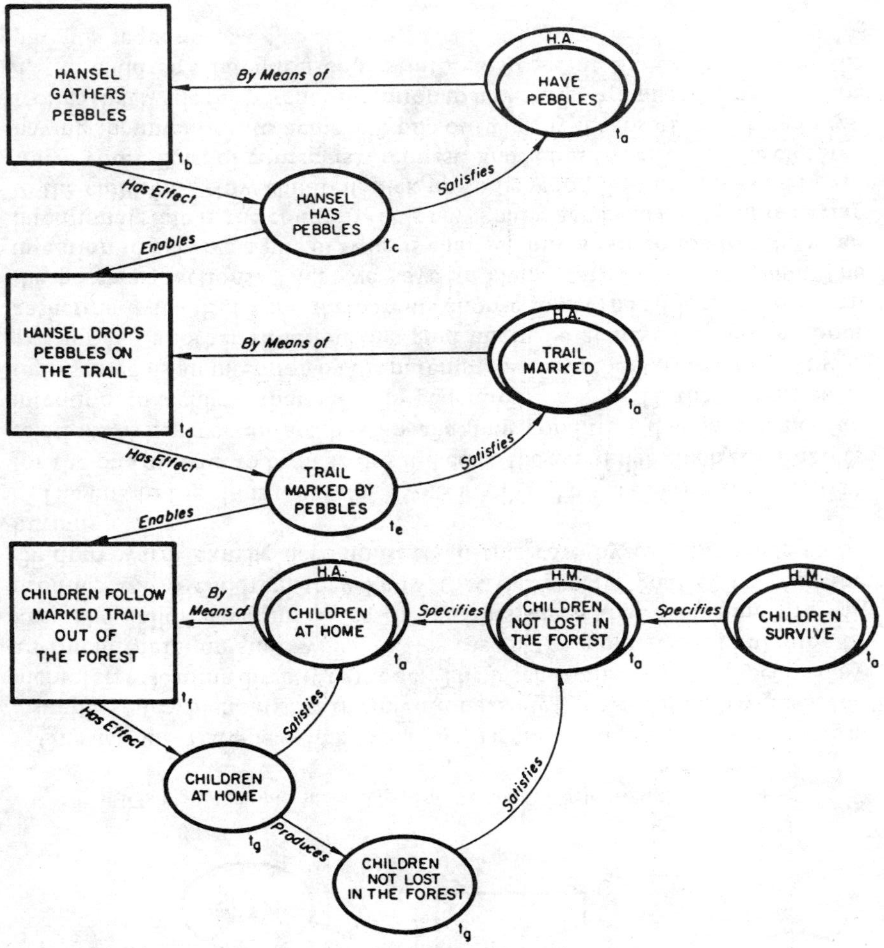

plans which we will attempt to represent. The parents' plan will be described in some detail before we return to show how Hansel's plan counteracts the effects of the parents' plan.

We will first show how to represent an *ordinary* wood fetching episode, which, we assume, is commonly carried out without any malevolent intent and is well known by the parents and children. Then, we will show how the parent's plan to get rid of the children is an attempt to use the children's cooperation in an ordinary episode.

3.3 A Simple Interacting Plan: A "Request"

> When they reached the middle of the forest, their father said, "Now, children, pick up some wood. I want to make a fire to warm you."
> Hansel and Gretel gathered the twigs together and soon made a huge pile. Then the pile was lighted...

The parents' plan is an interacting plan, since it is a plan to achieve goals in interaction with the children. The idea of an interacting plan can be illustrated with a simple example (see above) taken from their overall plan. Figures 13 and 14 represent the parents' plan to build a fire for the children once they are out in the forest. (For simplicity of presentation, this subplan will not be represented in the parents' full plan illustrated later on.)

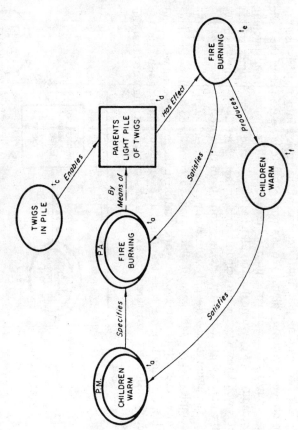

FIG. 13.   The parents' plan to keep the children warm.

FIG. 12.   Part of Hansel's plan for getting out of the forest.

following the trail. This action, however, requires that the trail be marked and this, in turn, requires that Hansel have a supply of pebbles with which to do the marking. Thus, the first two actions are done in order to establish the preconditions of the final action that gets the children home.

This plan, which is represented in isolation from the context of the interaction with the parents, is only a small part of what the reader would have to understand in order to follow the events of the story. The plan takes place over 24 hours to carry out. Concurrently, the parents are carrying out their plan to abandon the children in the forest. It is the interaction of these two

3.4 Achieving Multiple Goals

The fire building plan illustrates one of the basic configurations used to represent interacting plans. We can now begin to lay out some of the basic structures of the parent's plan to take the children on a wood fetching expedition. We assume that this plan has been carried out many times, so that it is well known to the participants, and, in fact, script-like. Figure 15 shows the parents' procedure for fetching wood from the forest.

The intent to have a supply of cut wood at home is achieved by means of the complex act of fetching wood which itself is accomplished by doing the three lower level acts of going to the work location in the forest, cutting wood, and then carrying it home. Note that this is an example of enabling sub-acts. We can consider the structure to be like a basic script for fetching wood that can

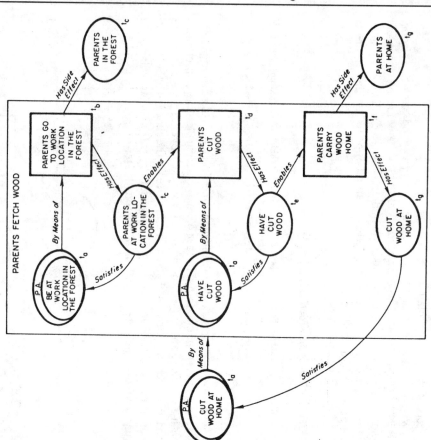

FIG. 15.   The parents' wood fetching plan.

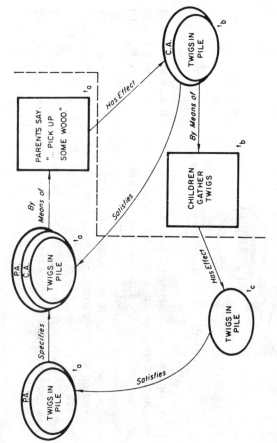

FIG. 14.   A simple interacting plan: Requesting help from the children.

One action ("Parents light pile of twigs") is shown in Fig. 13. Fire burning is a simple state which satisfies the intentional state (labeled "P.A.") which is the mental state leading directly to the act. The IntendAchieve state is specified by an IntendMaintain state which in this case is the more general intention to keep the children warm. Since the parents know that a burning fire will produce warm children, they know that the general goal of keeping the children warm can be accomplished in this case by causing a fire to be burning.

The link to Fig. 14 is the state "Twigs in pile." This is a necessary condition for the pile of twigs to be lit so it is linked to the act of lighting by an Enables relation. Whenever an act has an enabling condition that is not met, an intention to achieve that state is generated. In Fig. 14 that intention is represented as an intention by the parents to achieve the state of a pile of twigs existing. In another situation this goal might be achieved by going about gathering twins. But here, the parents choose to get the children to perform the necessary actions. Thus, we have an elementary *interacting plan*. The intention to achieve a pile of twigs is changed into an intention to achieve an intentional state in the children. This new goal is achieved by means of saying to the children, "Now children, pick up some wood. I want to make a fire to warm you." This, of course, is a request, and it has the effect of the children having the intention to achieve a pile ot twigs by means of gathering twigs. Notice that while the parent's intention to have twigs in a pile is present at time *a*, the children's intention comes into existence at time *b*, only after the parent's request.

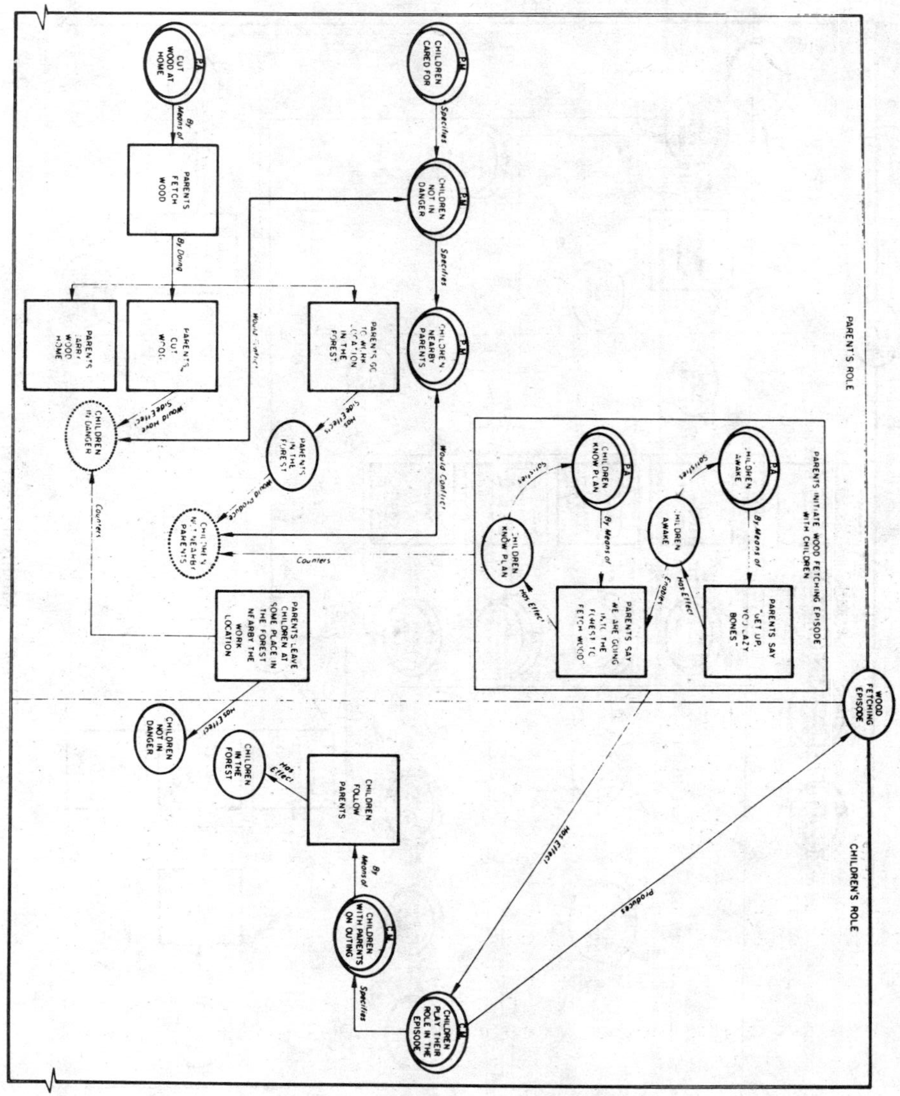

FIG. 16. Achieving multiple goals.

be carried out regardless of whether the children come along on the outing. (In subsequent diagrams, this basic structure is abbreviated using the ByDoing relation between the acts.) In the representation of the parent's plan, this script maintains its integrity since we assume that the parents know this procedure independently of its application on a particular occasion, when consideration must be given to particular contingencies that may arise.

The script itself affects other intentions the participants may have. For example, going to the work location has the side effect that the parents are in the forest. The belief that the work location is in the forest and not near home means that the parents will not be near the children when they go to work. If we turn now to Fig. 16, we can see that the state of being in the forest would produce the state of the children's not being near the parents which, in turn, would conflict with the intention to maintain nearness to the children.

Figure 16 illustrates an important configuration which arises when two intentions have to be coordinated (cf. Waldinger, 1975). Maintain intentions are often inactive as long as the state that is their goal is in existence and not threatened. When other plans are being formulated, however, the Maintain intentions may act as critics which survey the plan for conflicts. In the case of fetching wood, a possible conflict is found, and the Maintain nearness intention specifies a way to avoid the conflict, namely, to take the children on the outing. The state in the dotted oval (Children not nearby Parents) is a hypothetical state since it never actually occurs but is intended to be countered by an action which is consistent with the plan to fetch wood. As we see in the next section, the way in which the conflict is avoided is rather complex but follows the general pattern of the request illustrated in Fig. 14 (and in Fig. 5).

3.5 Initiation of a Social Episode

At daybreak, before the sun had risen, the woman came and said, "Get up, you lazybones! We are going into the forest to fetch wood."

The intention to maintain "nearness" leads to an action that counters the state of the children being left at home. The parents want to maintain a state of the children being along on the outing which is done by getting the children to have the intention to be on the outing. But the outing is not something the children can do on their own (like gathering twigs); it is essentially a shared undertaking, or social episode, in which the participants have recognized roles. Thus getting the children to have the intention of being on the outing is not done by a simple request but by initiating an episode. The children's following, which serves to maintain proximity to their parents, assures that they will be in the forest with the parents (and back home at the end of the episode.)

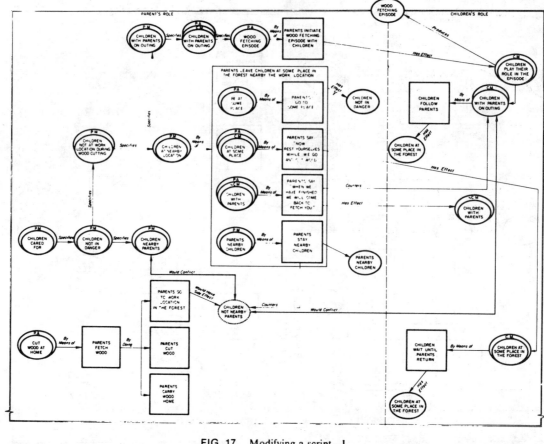

FIG. 17.   Modifying a script—I.

The parents' act of initiation is a complex act (near the top of Fig. 16) which contains two smaller acts. The first act is intended to wake the children up. The second act describes the plan: "We are going into the forest to fetch wood." The complex act has the effect that the children intend to maintain their role in the episode. Their intention (in combination with the fact that the parents intend there to be an episode) produces a state of mutual belief concerning a shared course of action. This state (the episode) is indicated at the top of Fig. 16 and by the large square that now surrounds the whole course of action. Placing the course of action in an episode means that it is mutually recognized or believed that the participants will perform their respective roles. The parent's announcement of the plan can produce this effect because going to fetch wood with the children along is an ordinary and commonly occurring event for which the participants know what each other will do. (Figures 16 and 17 are slightly abbreviated in that the parents' intention to maintain the episode is not shown.)

The children' role as indicated on Fig. 16 is clearly reactive to the parents' initiations. In addition, the role for the children mainly involves following into the forest. The other actions they perform are done in response to specific requests from their parents.

3.6   Modification of the Basic Script

... the woman said, "Now lie down by the fire and rest yourselves while we go and cut wood. When we have finished we will come back to fetch you."

As will be seen in Figs. 16 through 19, the basic script for fetching wood can be modified by the parents to integrate it with the intentions to care for the children. We have seen that a conflict between a side effect of fetching wood and the intention to remain near the children leads to an act that counters the undesirable state by initiating a social episode. This act can be seen at the top of Fig. 17 as specified directly by the intention to stay nearby. It becomes part of the ordinary sequence involved in going out to fetch wood when the children have to come along.

A second conflict can be seen in Fig. 16, namely, that between the intention to keep the children out of danger and the possible side effect of the children being in the immediate vicinity of the actual wood cutting (with swinging axes, falling trees, etc.). The parents can resolve this conflict by leaving the children at some place other than the work location (see Fig. 17). But now, leaving the children to go cut wood conflicts with being near them. So another action is added (within the complex act of leaving the children) that prevents the conflict. This act by the parents (Parents stay nearby Children) means that now the parents take over the responsibility for maintaining adequate proximity to the children.

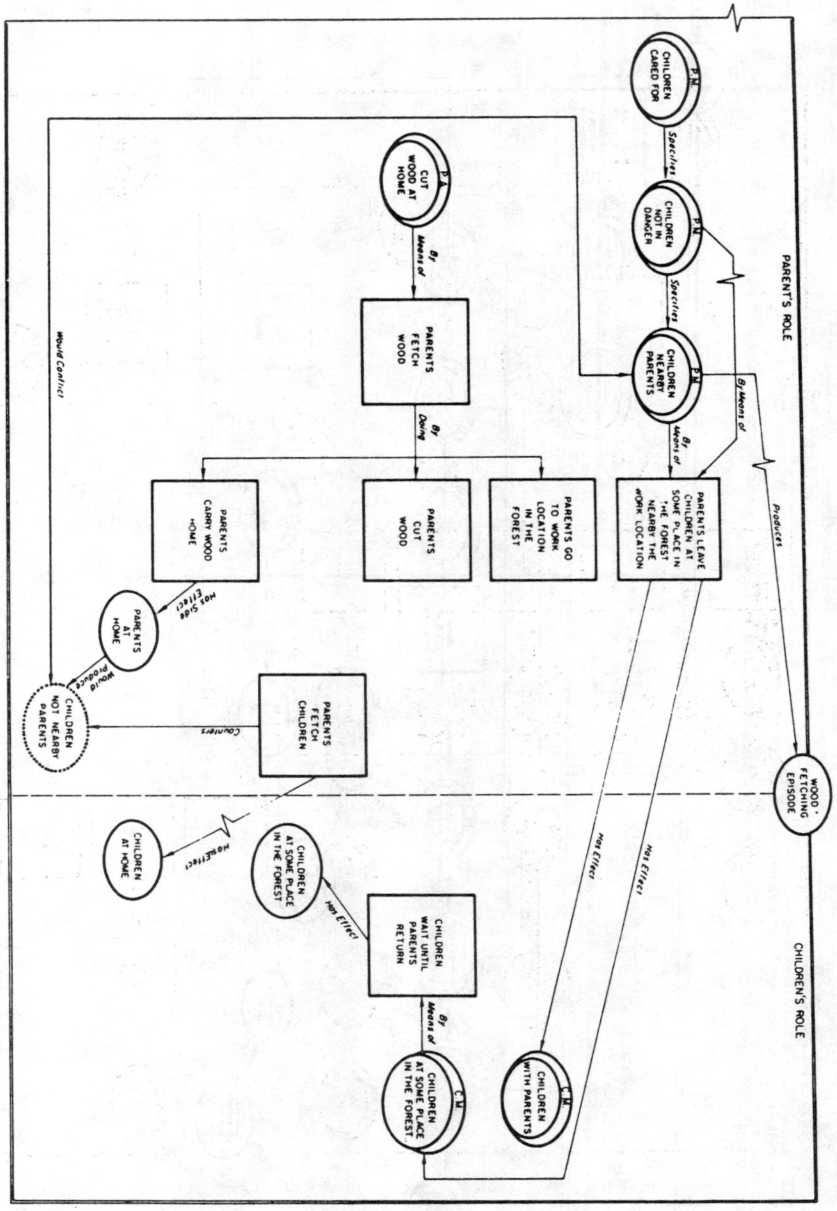

FIG. 18. Modifying a script—II.

The complex act of leaving the children is a set of actions, the outcomes of which, in combination, produce the effect of the children's being out of danger of swinging axes, etc. One of the actions within the complex act counters the children's intention to stay with the parents (which led to following) and another of the actions produces in the children a new intention to stay at the place where they are left.

All goes well with the ordinary wood fetching episode until, as seen on Fig. 18, the parents start to carry the cut wood back home. Since now the children are in the forest, this would conflict with the intention to stay near the children. Thus a new action is added in which the parents go back and fetch the children. As seen in Fig. 19, this action has the effect of turning off the children's intention to stay in the place where they were left and to reinstate the intention to stay with the parents. The children then follow the parents home and the ordinary episode is over.

The conflicts and the modifications to the basic script that are illustrated in Figs. 16 through 19 show how different goals can be coordinated, i.e., caring for the children and fetching wood. We assume that the full (ordinary) shared episode script would have been built up over time so that the final sequence is known as a unit by the participants. To understand the plan that the parents have to get rid of the children, however, it is necessary to see the basic wood fetching script in which the parents act alone as independent from the script for the ordinary wood fetching episode which includes a role for the children. The parents' deceptions involve only the latter, as we see when we now turn to the parents' real plan.

3.7. Embedding of the Virtual Plan

One night when he lay in bed worrying over his troubles, he sighed and said to his wife, "What is to become of us? How are we to feed our poor children when we have nothing for ourselves?"

"I'll tell you what, husband," answered the woman. "Tommorrow morning we will take the children out quite early into the thickest part of the forest. We will light a fire and give each of them a piece of bread. Then we will go to our work and leave them alone. They won't be able to find their way back, and so we shall be rid of them."

* * *

Hansel and Gretel sat by the fire, and when dinnertime came they each ate their little bit of bread, and they thought their father was quite near because they could hear the sound of an ax. It was no ax, however, but a branch which the man had tied to a dead tree, and which blew backwards and forwards against it. They sat there so long they got tired. Then their eyes began to close and they were soon fast asleep.

The interactive plan represented in Figs. 16 through 19 is never actually carried out in the story, at least not in full, and certainly not with the intentions indicated for the parents. The plan is actually a virtual plan that the parents want Hansel and Gretel to believe is being carried out. In order to

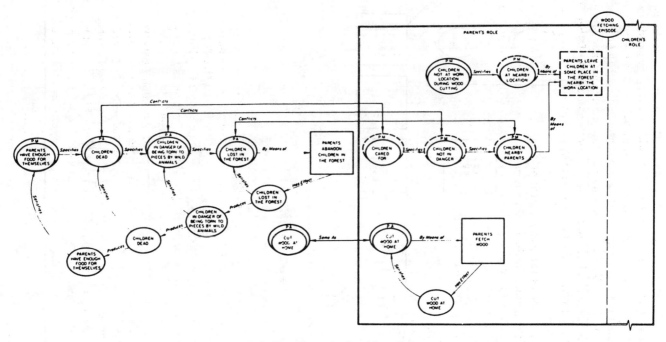

FIG. 20. The parents' real intentions.

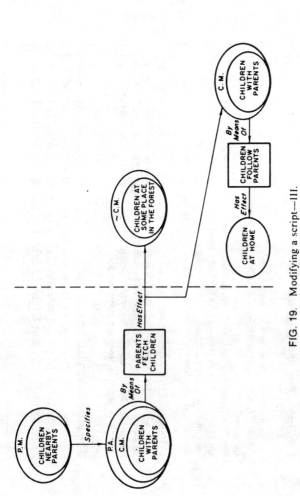

FIG. 19. Modifying a script—III.

represent the parents' actual view of the interactive situation, it is necessary to show how they intend to use the children's belief in this plan to achieve their real intention to get rid of the children by causing them to be lost in the forest.

The parents depend on the children's belief that it is an ordinary wood fetching episode to get the children to follow them into the forest. They also depend on the children's intention to wait in the nearby location so that the children do not follow them back out of the forest. In the actual plan, the critical lie occurs when the stepmother says to the children: "Now lie down by the fire and rest yourselves while we go and cut wood. When we have finished we will come back to fetch you." It is only by understanding what the ordinary sequence of events is in such a situation that it is possible to understand how the stepmother's statement produces the desired effect of leaving the children behind.

Figure 20 represents the basis of the parents' real plan as it relates to the episode that they want the children to believe is legitimately taking place. The parents' real intentions are represented on the far left. Basically they want to have enough food for themselves and this requires that they get rid of the children by leaving them in the forest where they would be eaten by wild animals, witches or other things that live there.

"Nay wife," said the man, "we won't do that. I could never find it in my heart to leave my children alone in the forest. The wild animals would soon tear them to pieces."
"What a fool you are!" she said. "Then we must all four die of hunger. You may as well plane the boards for our coffins at once."

The real action they perform is to abandon the children in the forest. Notice that each of their real intentions conflicts with one that the children could be expected to infer from their actions, given that the children are supposed to believe the actions to be taking place in a shared episode. Notice also that the intention to have a supply of cut wood at home is independent of the intention to get rid of the children. In fact, the stepmother says to the father "Then we will go to our work and leave them alone." The parents actually intend to do their work.

Figure 21 shows the parents' real plan in more detail. It can be seen that each of the actions in the episode is either real (indicated by solid lines) or virtual (indicated by dashed lines). Many of the actions within the episode (the virtual plan) are also specified by intentions in the real plan. These are marked by the SameAs relation. Going to a place in the forest (in the episode) is filled in (in the real plan) by going to the thickest part of the forest. The critical conflicts concern the parents' intention to stay nearby and to return to fetch the children. The complex act "Parents abandon Children in the forest, leaving them alone would give them no way of finding their way back. Thus the children would be lost.

3.8 Acting on an Interacting Plan

She gave him no peace till he consented. "But I grieve over the poor children all the same," said the man. The two children could not go to sleep for hunger either, and they heard what their stepmother said to their father.

Gretel wept bitterly and said, "All is over with us now."

"Be quiet, Gretel," said Hansel. "Don't cry! I will find some way out of it."

The parents are not the only ones who have concealed intentions, for the children are also carrying out a plan. Their plan is intended to block the effect of the parents' real plan by finding an alternative to following that would get them out of the forest. In Fig. 22, we attribute the children's plan to Hansel since he apparently has a richer understanding of both the virtual plan and its use in the real plan of the parents. It is he who gathers and drops the pebbles, and it is he who comforts the frightened Gretel.

The children also pretend to be participating in an ordinary wood fetching episode. Presumably it is necessary that they avoid direct confrontation with the parents for fear that the parents would otherwise take more drastic means to get rid of them. Hansel's method of blocking the parents' plan is so skillfully executed, in fact, that the parents never find out that he and Gretel know that the parents are plotting against them. Hansel, for example, tells Gretel: "Be quiet. Gretel" when she cries upon overhearing the plot. The intention to maintain secrecy is shown in the figure by the triple ovals with "P.B." indicating that Hansel intends for the parents not to believe certain facts. It is just as important for Hansel's plan as it is for the parents' plan that the ordinary episode be carried off as if it were the real plan.

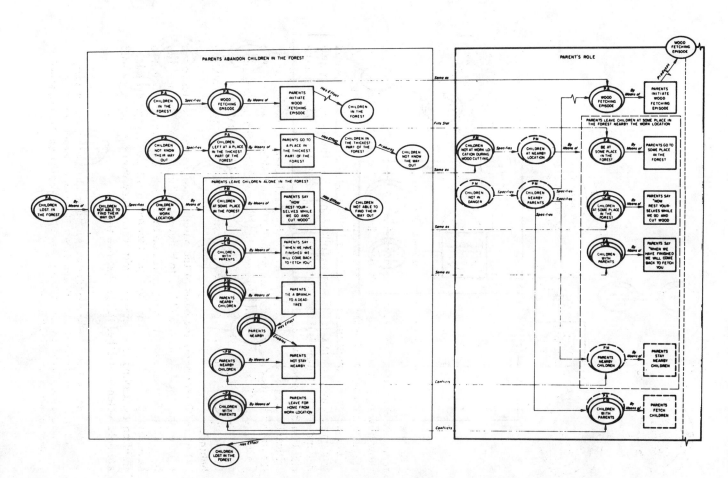

FIG. 21. The parents' real plan.

Figure 22 shows Hansel's real plan. His intention to survive specifies both that he find a way of getting out of the forest and that he avoid direct confrontation. Thus he plays a role in the episode, not because he is deceived into thinking that it is an ordinary episode, but in order to avoid a more direct showdown with the parents in which he might be the loser.

For both the children and the parents, the virtual plan is embedded in the real plan. For the parents it is a straightforward deception (or attempt at a deception). For Hansel, there is an additional embedding. His real plan contains a representation of the parents' real plan, which in turn includes their use of the virtual plan. As is evident from "Hansel and Gretel," deceptive plans often make use of ordinary plans. The representation of deception, then, becomes a special case which requires the representation of ordinary plans as a groundwork.

3.9 Separate Realities

One of the things that makes the first episode of "Hansel and Gretel" intriguing is that the characters have different views of what is happening. Each view (or view of a view) is a belief space, which can be categorized by who maintains the view. For example, there is the belief space that contains the parent's beliefs about the children's beliefs. Each diagram in the preceding analysis can be interpreted as being within a particular space, or spaces, since we are assuming no absolute facts, only beliefs.

We take advantage of the notation proposed by Cohen (1978) to indicate these representational spaces. For example, Figure 23 shows that state X is believed by P but that P believes Q believes the opposite.

One special representational space needs to be singled out. This is a *mutual belief space*, which indicates that from the point of view of the target character, states contained within it are believed, and are believed to be believed. For example, if P believes that both P and Q believe X, *and* that both P and Q believe that P and Q believe X, *and* that both P and Q believe that both P and Q believe that P and Q believe X, and so on, then we say that P believes that P and Q mutually believe X, or MB (P,Q). Cohen discusses mutual belief spaces further and gives a finite representation scheme for the indefinite recursion they imply. For our purposes, we will simply indicate when a space is a mutual belief space. Note that since no beliefs are necessarily shared, MB (P,Q) may not be the same as MB(Q,P), i.e., while P may believe that P and Q mutually believe X, Q may not believe it. We can symbolize the various belief spaces as follows:

PB   P believes that...

MB(P,Q)   P believes that P and Q have a mutual belief that... where P and Q indicate either the parents or the children.

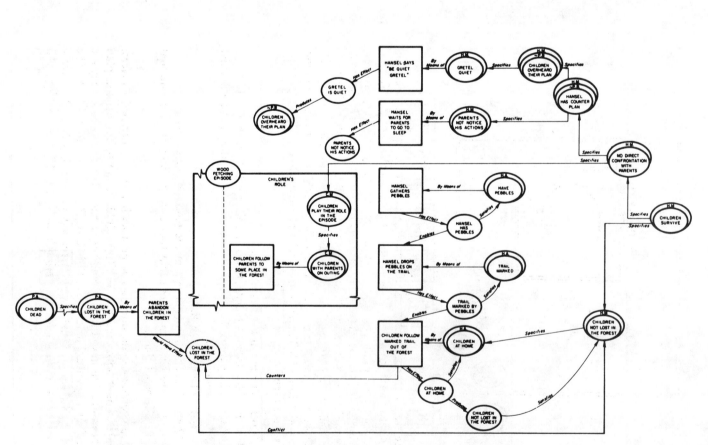

FIG. 22.   Hansel's real plan.

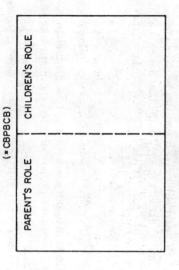

FIG. 24. The virtual plan.

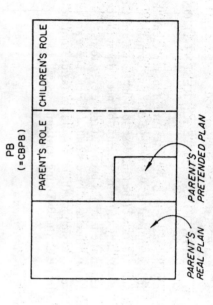

FIG. 25. The parents' beliefs.

(P,C), whereas more reality based facts such as being in the forest are in both PBMB (C,P) and MB(P,C). The children (i.e. Hansel) have their own plan, in CB. They believe only part of the virtual plan in MB (C,P).

This would get quite complicated were it not for the assumptions that, in overhearing his parent's plans, Hansel gains complete knowledge and that this knowledge matches that of the implied reader. Thus several of these belief spaces turn out to be congruent. In fact, there are only four distinct spaces as shown in Fig. 24 through 27. These spaces are the following:

1. The virtual plan (Fig. 24): This is what the parents think they have induced the children to believe. It is thus PBCB, and since the episode is supposed to be shared, PBMB (C,P). Since Hansel sees through the virtual plan it is also CBPBCB and CBPBMB (C,P).

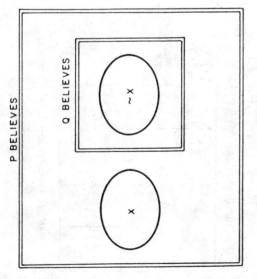

FIG. 23. Differing beliefs.

Since we are discussing the belief structures contained within stories, we also want to be able to represent the reader's beliefs which are often different from at least some of the characters'. Some stories may be written to give the reader initially a false belief (only later in the story does the reader realize that one character had been right all along.) We use RB to indicate the reader's beliefs. But to simplify matters let us assume that the reader has a "true" understanding of the first part of "Hansel and Gretel." Then we can omit the explicit indication of RB in front of every belief space. Some of the important belief spaces then become:

PB   The parents believe that...
PBCB   The parent's believe that the children believe that...
MB(P,C)   The parents believe that they and the children have a mutual belief that...
CB   The children believe that...
CBPB   The children believe that the parents believe that...
MB(C,P)   The children believe that they and the parents have a mutual belief that...

We can summarize the intrigues in the story in terms of such belief spaces: The parents have both a real plan to kill the children (in PB) and a virtual plan that they intend to have the children believe. Since they believe that they are succeeding, the virtual plan enters PBMB (C,P), and therefore, PBCB. The part of the virtual plan that is real for the parents goes into MB (P,C). Note that intentions of caring for the children are in PBMB (C,P) but not MB

participants. In ordinary cooperative interaction MB (X,Y) and MB (Y,X) would be congruent.[4]

4. LIMITATIONS OF THE REPRESENTATION

Undoubtedly the least controversial feature of the representation presented here is that it is complicated. We believe that this complexity is necessary because social interaction of the kind described in "Hansel and Gretel" is itself complex. The intricacy of the representation needed just to account for the story as related in the text has been a surprise even to us.

But what we have discussed here is only a sketch. There are several ways in which we have had to simplify the representation (aside from the trivial means of abbreviating, e.g., the ByDoing relation).

4.1 Combined Participants

As mentioned earlier, we combined the father and the stepmother into a single character called "the parents," and combined Hansel and Gretel into a character called "the children." This makes it impossible to represent important aspects of the episode. For example, our abbreviated representation does not allow us to distinguish between the father, who loves the children (but not enough), and the stepmother who sees them as additional drains on the family's limited resources. Their intentions are clearly differentiated in the story and could be represented formally with additional diagrams representing their initial conversation as a plan of the stepmother to convince the father. Our two-dimensional system, does not, however, allow us to represent more than two plans simultaneously.

4.2 Point of View

The diagrams show the wood fetching episode as equivalent from each point of view. A complete representation would require a view for each of the characters. For this particular case it may not be wrong to assume that wood fetching is a familiar activity to the family, familiar enough that most beliefs are *shared*. That is, the parents' view is of a shared plan that is not markedly different from the children's view.

4.3 Changes Over Time

We have also limited our discussion of how plans change while events are occurring. A complete representation of the plans discussed here would

---

[4]Our term "coinciding mutual belief" corresponds to Schiffer's (1972) term "mutual belief."

2. The parent's beliefs (Fig. 25): This includes the parent's real plan. Since Hansel knows their plan this space is both PB and CBPB.

3. The children's beliefs (Fig. 26): This includes the children's real plan. It is only CB since the parents do not know the children's real plan. Since the children do have all the facts this also is the same as RB (the reader's beliefs).

4. Coinciding mutual belief (Fig. 27): Items that are in the intersection of MB (P,C), MB (C,P), i.e., things which everyone accepts and everyone believes are mutually accepted. This is included in each of the above. Note that this space, under ordinary circumstances, would include the entire shared episode but is reduced in size here because of the deception engaged in by both

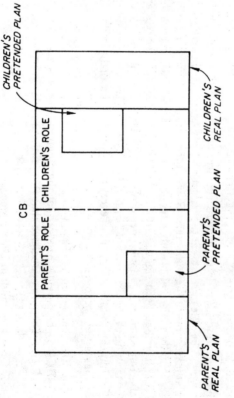

FIG. 26. The children's beliefs.

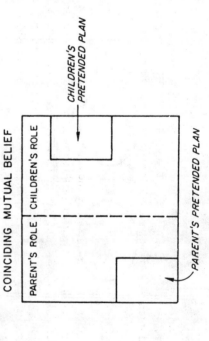

FIG. 27. Coinciding mutual beliefs.

require a complete set of diagrams for each time point in the episode. Attempting to represent all of the virtual plan at a single point forced us to adopt the simplifying assumption that the parent's intentions and the consequences of their actions are known in full to the parents at the time that they initiate the episode. A more reasonable assumption is that some of the detailed intentions and planned acts arise as events occur.

4.4 The Process of Planning

The diagrams here emphasize the end result of planning, i.e. a plan. We have limited our examples that would show how an interacting plan might be formulated. However it would be important to consider the process, since it is in planning that hypothetical solutions to conflicts are created and compared. The representation of this process would require considerably more apparatus than we have so far developed.

Plans are rarely formulated in advance. Instead, they typically consist of a goal and some loosely defined expectations about how the goal might be attained, but a full representation of such changing expectations would not be enough for our purposes where there is not one but a set of (interacting) plans, and the state of any plan is dependent upon the actions determined by the other plans. Furthermore, the re-actions based on the other plans may be quite unpredictable (since those actions depend as much upon the goals of those plans as upon external events). A plan must therefore incorporate knowledge of other plans, and our representation must reflect this interdependency.

But that is only the beginning of the problem. Each character, in order to react appropriately to the actions of other characters, may build a model of the other character's plan. As actions unfold, the model may have to be revised. A character, while formulating his or her plan during execution, is also reformulating models of the other plans. On top of that, he or she knows that the other characters have models of plans and that an effective way to achieve a goal is to affect the others' models. Eventually we would want to be able to represent an individual's process of planning and also the *social* process of formulating a shared plan in the course of interactions with others.

5. CONCLUSION

Our formal plans analysis demonstrates that even apparently simple stories may recount actions that derive from complex, interacting plans. The apparent simplicity vanishes when one begins to consider such things as the effect of an action is intended to have on the plans and actions of another character. Connections of this kind between actions and beliefs are difficult to explain without explicit representation of the interactions among plans.

Beyond the demonstration that interacting plans can be complex, our analysis shows several things. First, we believe we have identified a set of entities (acts, intentions, beliefs, states, etc.) and relations among these entities that are necessary and sufficient for the representation of interacting plans. Second, we have begun to collect a set of configurations, which are built from the basic elements and represent generalizations from specific interactions among plans. Third, we have shown that more complex notions, such as deception, can be represented using the configurations of basic elements. This type of analysis provides the basis for giving more precise meaning to terms such as "conflict" and "intention," familiar terms in traditional text analysis. Fourth, our analysis allows us to be more precise in measuring the relative complexity of texts along several dimensions. Whether differences along these dimensions make a difference for comprehension or recall is, of course, an empirical question.

In Bruce and Newman (1978) we discuss the complexity issue in some detail. Here we merely list a few of the dimensions that might make interacting plans complex:

1. Size of plan—A plan may involve a long sequence of acts or may be accomplished by a single act. The temporal duration of the plan may also be a factor.

2. Changes in plans—Plans in a story can remain fairly constant or may change in response to events occurring during the plan's execution. The number and magnitude of changes may be a source of difficulty.

3. Degrees of interaction—Hansel and Gretel's plans are tightly intertwined with their parents' plans. Each is trying to respond to the others and to get the others to do an act in a particular way. In other stories characters' plans may not interact as tightly or there may be only one character.

4. Conflicts—The number and types of conflicts among plans in a story may also be a source of complexity.

5. Embeddings—Interacting plans may contain multiple embeddings of beliefs within beliefs, e.g., A believes B believes A believes X. They may also contain embedded intentions.

6. Levels of characterization of the same action—The same act can be viewed at various levels or clumped together with other acts. Two characters may understand the same act in different ways or as part of different sequences. For example, the plan of Hansel and Gretel's parents (Fig. 21). their act of telling the children to wait is part of the complex act of leaving the children alone in the forest but in the sequences as it was supposed to be perceived by the children it is part of the complex act of having the children wait at a safe place.

7. Beliefs outside of the mutual belief space—In an ordinary cooperative episode most beliefs are held mutually by the characters. Often, though, there are beliefs outside of the mutual space, not necessarily conflicting beliefs, but beliefs that are not known to one or more characters.

8. Virtual plans—virtual plans are an important special case of beliefs outside of the mutual belief space. In a virtual plan, what A knows but B does not is that certain critical elements in what B believes is the mutual belief space are actually false. The mutual belief space is being used by A to cover over A's real intentions (that lie outside the space). Virtual plans work because by themselves they constitute a coherent course of action. The character is acting on the basis of a real plan (outside of the mutual belief space). but puts forward the virtual plan as an alternative explanation for his or her actions.

We have presented here a way of representing the interacting plans of characters in stories. In developing the system and in applying it to the analysis of "Hansel and Gretel" we have used our own commonsense knowledge and intuitions about social interaction. We assume that we share this knowledge and these intuitions with other (adult) readers of the story. We are not specialists in interpreting fairy tales although we have read this one rather closely. Rather, we were struck with how easy it was to view the characters as familiar and ordinary people who were engaged in a difficult conflict. That is, we found we could attribute our own knowledge and intuitions to the characters as though they were real.

It would be tempting, on this basis, to say that the system provides a way of representing actual social interaction. But while it seems reasonable that readers bring their ordinary knowledge to bear on stories, we have to keep in mind the intentions of the author to make the story be a story. The author's artfulness in constructing reasonable and informative dialogue, for examppe, may be covering over important processes that participants in conversations necessarily must engage in. We do not want to claim that our story analysis necessarily informs studies of social interaction. We do want to suggest, however, that this kind of story analysis is in a position to be informed by those studies. Readers find social interaction in stories, and we are attempting to represent what they find.

ACKNOWLEDGMENTS

We would like to thank Phil Cohen for his comments on an earlier draft of the paper and for discussions about mutual belief spaces. Also, Andee Rubin for comments on the paper and notation system; and, Maryl Gearhart for comments and for discussions on the study of social interactions.

APPENDIX: HANSEL AND GRETEL
(from Grimm, 1945)

Close to a large forest there lived a woodcutter with his wife and his two children. The boy was called Hansel and the girl Gretel. They were always very poor and had very little to live on. And at one time when there was famine in the land, he could no longer procure daily bread.

One night when he lay in bed worrying over his troubles, he sighed and said to his wife, "What is to become of us? How are we to feed our poor children when we have nothing for ourselves?"

"I'll tell you what, husband." answered the woman. "Tomorrow morning we will take the children out quite early into the thickest part of the forest. We will light a fire and give each of them a piece of bread. Then we will go to our work and leave them alone. They won't be able to find their way back. and so we shall be rid of them."

"Nay, wife." said the man. "we won't do that. I could never find it in my heart to leave my children alone in the forest. The wild animals would soon tear them to pieces."

"What a fool you are!" she said. "Then we must all four die of hunger. You may as well plane the boards for our coffins at once."

She gave him no peace till he consented. "But I grieve over the poor children all the same," said the man. The two children could not go to sleep for hunger either. and they heard what their stepmother said to their father.

Gretel wept bitterly and said. "All is over with us now."

"Be quiet, Gretel." said Hansel. "Don't cry! I will find some way out of it."

When the old people had gone to sleep. he got up. put on his little coat. opened the door. and slipped out. The moon was shining brightly and the white pebbles round the house shone like newly minted coins. Hansel stooped down and put as many into his pockets as they would hold.

Then he went back to Gretel and said. "Take comfort. little sister. and go to sleep. God won't forsake us." And then he went to bed again.

At daybreak. before the sun had risen, the woman came and said. "Get up. you lazybones! We are going into the forest to fetch wood."

Then she gave them each a piece of bread and said. "Here is something for your dinner. but don't eat it before then. for you'll get no more."

Gretel put the bread under her apron. for Hansel had the stones in his pockets. Then they all started for the forest.

When they had gone a little way. Hansel stopped and looked back at the cottage. and he did the same thing again and again.

His father said. "Hansel. what are you stopping to look back at? Take care and put your best foot foremost."

"Oh. father." said Hansel. "I am looking at my white cat. It is sitting on the roof. wanting to say good-by to me."

"Little fool. that's no cat! It's the morning sun shining on the chimney." said the mother. But Hansel had not been looking at the cat. He had been dropping a pebble on the ground each time he stopped.

When they reached the middle of the forest, their father said. "Now, children. pick up some wood. I want to make a fire to warm you."

Hansel and Gretel gathered the twigs together and soon made a huge pile. Then the pile was lighted. and when it blazed up the woman said. "Now lie down by the fire and rest yourselves while we go and cut wood. When we have finished we will come back to fetch you."

Hansel and Gretel sat by the fire. and when dinnertime came they each ate their little bit of bread. and they thought their father was quite near because they could hear the sound of an ax. It was no ax. however. but a branch which the man had tied to a dead tree. and which blew backwards and forwards against it. They sat there so long that they got tired. Then their eyes began to close and they were soon fast asleep.

When they woke it was dark night. Gretel began to cry. "How shall we ever get out of the wood?"

But Hansel comforted her and said. "Wait a little while till the moon rises. and then we will soon find our way."

When the full moon rose. Hansel took his little sister's hand and they walked on. guided by the pebbles. which glittered like newly coined money. They walked the whole night. and at daybreak they found themselves hack at their father's cottage.

They knocked at the door. and when the woman opened it and saw Hansel and Gretel she said. "You bad children. why did you sleep so long in the wood? We thought you did not mean to come back any more."

But their father was delighted. for it had gone to his heart to leave them behind alone.

REFERENCES

Bruce, B. C. Belief systems & language understanding. BBN Report No. 2973, Bolt Beranek & Newman Inc.. Cambridge, Mass.. 1975.

Bruce, B. C. Plans and social actions. In R. Spiro, B. Bruce. and W. Brewer (Eds.). *Theoretical issues in reading comprehension.* Hillsdale. N.J.: Lawrence Erlbaum Assoc.. 1978. in press. Also as Center for the Study of Reading Technical Report No. 34. University of Illinois at Urbana-Champaign. 1977.

Bruce, B. C. & Newman, D. Interacting plans. Center for the Study of Reading Technical Report No. 88. University of Illinois at Urbana-Champaign. 1978.

Cohen, P. R. On knowing what to say: Planning speech acts. Ph.D Thesis. Department of Computer Science. Univ. of Toronto. 1978.

Grimm, The Brothers. *Grimm's fairy tales.* (E.V. Lucas, L. Crane, & M. Edwards, trans.). New York: Grosset and Dunlap. 1945.

Perrault. C. R.. & Cohen. P. R. Planning speech acts. AI-Memo 77-1. Department of Computer Science. Univ. of Toronto. April 1977.

Sacerdoti, E. D. The nonlinear nature of plans. *Proceedings of the Fourth International Joint Conference on Artificial Intelligence,* Tbilisi, Georgia. USSR. 1975.

Schank, R. C.. & Abelson. R. P. *Scripts, plans, goals, and understanding.* Hillsdale. N.J.: Lawrence Erlbaum Assoc.. 1977.

Schiffer. S. R. *Meaning.* London: Oxford Univ. Press. 1972.

Schmidt. C. F.. Sridharan. N. S., & Goodson. J. L. The plan recognition problem: An intersection of artificial intelligence and psychology. *Artificial Intelligence,* 1978. in press.

Searle. J. R. *Speech acts: An essay in the philosophy of language.* Cambridge: Cambridge Univ. Press. 1969.

Sussman, G. *A computer model of skill acquisition.* New York: American Elsevier. 1975.

Tate, A. Interacting goals and their use. *Proceedings of the Fourth International Joint Conference on Artificial Intelligence,* Tbilisi, Georgia. U.S.S.R.. September 1975.

Waldinger. R. Achieving several goals simultaneously. Stanford Research Institute. Artificial Intelligence Group. Technical Note 107. 1975.

Coherent Cooperation Among Communicating Problem Solvers

EDMUND H. DURFEE, VICTOR R. LESSER, AND DANIEL D. CORKILL

Abstract—When two or more computing agents work on interacting tasks, their activities should be coordinated so that they cooperate coherently. Coherence is particularly problematic in domains where each agent has only a limited view of the overall task, where communication between agents is limited, and where there is no "controller" to coordinate the agents. Our approach to coherent cooperation in such domains is developed in the context of a distributed problem-solving network where agents cooperate to solve a single problem. The approach stresses the importance of sophisticated local control by which each problem-solving node integrates knowledge of the problem domain with (meta-level) knowledge about network coordination. This allows nodes to make rapid, intelligent local decisions based on changing problem characteristics with only a limited amount of intercommunication to coordinate these decisions.

We describe three mechanisms that improve network coherence: 1) an organizational structure that provides a long-term framework for network coordination to guide each node's local control decisions; 2) a planner at each node that develops sequences of problem-solving activities based on the current situation; and 3) meta-level communication about the current state of local problem solving that enables nodes to dynamically refine the organization. We present a variety of problem-solving situations to show the benefits and limitations of these mechanisms, and we provide simulation results showing the mechanisms to be particularly cost effective in more complex problem-solving situations. We also discuss how these mechanisms might be of more general use in other distributed computing applications.

Index Terms—Cooperative problem solving, distributed artificial intelligence, distributed control, intelligent communication, organizational design, planning.

I. INTRODUCTION

COOPERATION in a distributed computing environment requires two types of control decisions. One type is *network control*: tasks and responsibilities must be assigned to each computing agent. Typically, network control attempts to distribute the computing load among agents to maximize parallel computation. The other type is *local control*: each computing agent must choose a task to execute next from among its assigned tasks.

Much research in distributed computing systems has concentrated on network control algorithms that exchange tasks among agents based on protocols such as bidding [24], [27], [28]. These systems tend to have unsophisticated local control; a simple scheduling algorithm (for example, based on task reception times or on task deadlines) is used. Since tasks are usually assumed to be independent, the local control component of one agent can be unaware of the local control decisions being made elsewhere.

As distributed computation is used in more diverse applications, however, the task independence assumption becomes invalid. Examples of how interactions among tasks affect local control decisions include the following.

• If tasks have precedence constraints, the local control decisions of agents with succeeding tasks depend on the decisions of the agents with the preceding tasks.

• To improve reliability, equivalent tasks may be assigned to several agents. If one agent successfully executes a task, the other agents should avoid redundantly executing equivalent tasks.

• In a distributed programming environment, each agent may have pieces of several distributed programs. Because the pieces of a distributed program may need to synchronize or exchange information, the agents must consider how the timing of their local decisions will affect the activities of other agents.

These types of interactions are present in a *distributed problem-solving network*, where each computing agent is a semi-autonomous problem-solving *node* that can communicate with other nodes. Nodes work together to solve a single problem by individually solving interacting subproblems and integrating their subproblem solutions into an overall solution. These networks are typically used in applications such as distributed sensor networks [19], [27], distributed air traffic control [1], and distributed robot systems [13], where there is a natural spatial distribution of information but where each node has insufficient local information to completely and accurately solve its subproblems. To improve their local information, nodes must share subproblem solutions; cooperation thus requires intelligent local control decisions so that each node performs tasks which generate useful subproblem solutions. The use of a global "controller" to make these decisions for the nodes is not an option because it would be a severe communication and computational bottleneck and would make the network susceptible to complete collapse if it fails. Because nodes must make these decisions based only on their local information, well-coordinated or *coherent* cooperation is difficult to achieve [7], [20].

In the *functionally accurate, cooperative* (FA/C) ap-

Manuscript received October 17, 1985; revised October 3, 1986. This work was supported in part by the National Science Foundation under Grant MCS-8306327, by the National Science Foundation under Support and Maintenance Grant DCR-8318776, by the National Science Foundation under CER Grant DCR-8500332, and by the Defense Advanced Research Projects Agency (DOD), monitored by the Office of Naval Research under Contract NR049-041.

The authors are with the Department of Computer and Information Science, University of Massachusetts, Amherst, MA 01003.

IEEE Log Number 8716127.

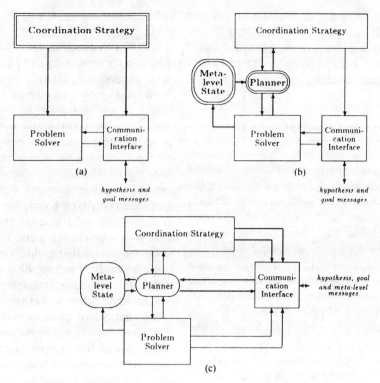

Fig. 1. Evolutionary phases of sophisticated local control. Initially, a node
has a problem solver and a communication interface for exchanging
hypotheses (partial problem solutions) and goals (intentions to form partial
problem solutions). In (a) a coordination strategy is added to guide problem
solving and communication decisions. In (b), a local planner and a meta-
level state representation are added to increase a node's problem solving
and coordination awareness. Finally, in (c), meta-level messages (high-
level views of node activities) can be exchanged through the communication
interface to increase network awareness.

proach to distributed problem solving [20], nodes cooperate by
generating and exchanging tentative, partial solutions based on
their local views. By iteratively exchanging their potentially
incomplete, inaccurate, and inconsistent partial solutions, the
nodes eventually converge on an overall network solution.
Coherent cooperation requires that, at any given time, each
node performs a sequence of tasks to generate a tentative
partial solution that is compatible with the solutions being
generated at other nodes. The nodes often have overlapping
views of the problem and alternative methods for forming
partial solutions to ensure both that problem solving can occur
despite errors in the local data and that network performance
will degrade gracefully if a subset of the nodes fails. Coherent
cooperation among these *overlapping nodes* is particularly
troublesome, since the nodes should work together to cover
the overlapping area without duplicating each other's work.

A distributed problem-solving network involves precedence
among tasks (smaller partial solutions must precede larger,
subsuming partial solutions), redundancy among tasks (overlapping nodes may redundantly generate identical partial
solutions), and timing of tasks (a timely generation and
exchange of certain partial solutions may guide nodes into
behaving more effectively). Sophisticated local control at each
node is thus paramount if nodes are to cooperate coherently. In
this paper, we examine important requirements for such
control and describe general approaches for meeting these

requirements. We implement and evaluate these approaches as
part of a simulated problem-solving network that performs a
vehicle monitoring task. The task has been abstracted both to
extend the set of cooperative problem-solving situations that
can be represented and to reduce the effort expended on
modeling the details of the task (since our goal is to investigate
general issues in distributed problem solving, *not* vehicle
monitoring).

In the next section, we present an overview of coherent
cooperation among problem solvers, and in Section III we
describe our experimental testbed. Section IV introduces the
first of three mechanisms to increase coherence through
improved local control—a coordination strategy that provides
each node with a general view of network responsibilities
(including its own) to guide its problem solving and communication decisions [Fig. 1(a)]. In Section V, the second
mechanism, a local planner, is described. The planner
increases the node's awareness of its local state and problem-
solving activities, and therefore allows it to make small,
dynamic refinements to its copy of the coordination strategy
[Fig. 1(b)]. Section VI outlines mechanisms that enable nodes
to make more informed communication decisions and that
allow nodes to exchange *meta-level information*—information specifically intended to increase coherence [Fig. 1(c)]. In
Section VII, we examine experimental results from more
complex environments (having as many as 13 problem-solving

nodes), citing the costs as well as the benefits of our mechanisms. Section VIII is devoted to a discussion of how our approach might be incorporated in other distributed computing systems. Finally, Section IX summarizes our current ideas about coherent cooperation and describes our plans for future research.

II. Problem Solving and Coherent Cooperation

Artificial intelligence researchers typically view problem solving as a search of the space of possible solutions to find the best one [29]. For example, given the problem of finding the shortest route between two cities, the problem solver searches the space of all possible routes for the shortest one. Solution spaces for nontrivial problems are extremely large and can neither be completely enumerated nor searched exhaustively. One way to make the search tractable is to transform the space of possible solutions into a space of partial solutions. A *partial solution* represents all complete solutions which contain it. Through the judicious selection of problem-solving tasks, an effective problem solver controls the incremental construction of alternate partial solutions so that one or more satisfactory complete solutions are found in a reasonable amount of time.

How search should be controlled depends on what constitutes a satisfactory solution and how long a reasonable time is. If only the best solution will do, the control must be conservative to avoid overlooking any potentially optimal portions of the space. If the control must find a solution quickly, it may limit the search to a small part of the space without the guarantee that the best (or any) solution is there. Therefore, a problem solver under time constraints must have sophisticated control to decide where to search. When control decisions must be based on potentially inaccurate or incomplete problem knowledge, their full ramifications cannot be predicted. This *control uncertainty* can be reduced only by giving the problem solver more accurate and complete information.

Control becomes more complex in a distributed environment because a problem solver must also consider how its local search complements that of other nodes. More effective problem solving can occur if nodes explore different parts of the space concurrently—the network more thoroughly searches the space and can find more satisfactory solutions within the same amount of time. Furthermore, a partial solution received from another node can supply new information that enables a node to form results that it previously had been incapable of developing, or to narrow the area it should search to find compatible partial solutions. This subtask interdependence means that effective distributed problem solving cannot be achieved without cooperation.

Achieving cooperation in a distributed problem-solving network is a difficult problem. Although the individual nodes are predisposed to work together toward network goals, they may compete or conflict with each other because each must locally interpret the network goals. Since the nodes may have different local views, incompatible local interpretations of network goals may be created. Even when nodes have compatible interpretations, however, network performance still depends on how coherently the nodes work together as a team.

Global coherence means that the activities of the nodes should make sense given overall network goals. Nodes should avoid unnecessarily duplicating the work of others, sitting idle while others are swamped with work, or transmitting information that will not improve overall network performance. Because network coordination must be decentralized to improve reliability and responsiveness, the amount of global coherence in the network depends on the degree to which each node makes coherent local decisions based on its local view of network problem solving. Full global coherence can be guaranteed only if each node has a complete and accurate view of the problem-solving activities and intentions of all nodes. In a network with changing characteristics and problem-solving situations, maintaining this view would require nodes to instantaneously broadcast all changes to their states. Because real-world communication channels have limited bandwidth and introduce delays and errors, there is no practical means to ensure full global coherence. The FA/C approach tolerates incorrect control decisions, so that network goals can be achieved with only partial global coherence. However, less than full coherence can waste resources and degrade performance. To use all computation and communication resources more effectively, our approach increases the coherence of local control decisions by reducing control uncertainty through sophisticated local processing and selective communication decisions. Our approach has been implemented and tested in a simulated problem-solving network.

III. The Distributed Vehicle Monitoring Testbed

By simulating a network of problem-solving nodes, the distributed vehicle monitoring testbed (DVMT) provides a framework where general approaches for distributed problem solving can be developed and evaluated [21], [22]. Each simulated node applies simplified signal processing knowledge to acoustically sensed data in an attempt to identify, locate, and track patterns of vehicles moving through a two-dimensional space. By varying parameters in the DVMT that specify the accuracy and range of the acoustic sensors, the acoustic signals that are to be grouped together to form patterns of vehicles, the power and distribution of knowledge among the nodes in the network, and the node and communication topology, a wide variety of cooperative distributed problem-solving situations can be modeled. Using simplified signal-processing knowledge reduces the processing complexity and knowledge engineering effort required in the DVMT without changing the fundamental network coordination characteristics of the distributed vehicle monitoring task.

A. The DVMT Nodes

Each problem-solving node has a blackboard-based, Hearsay-II architecture [12], with knowledge sources and levels of abstraction appropriate for vehicle monitoring. A *knowledge source* (KS) performs the basic problem-solving tasks of extending and refining *hypotheses* (partial solutions). A hypothesis is characterized by one or more *time locations* (where the vehicle was at certain times), by an *event class*

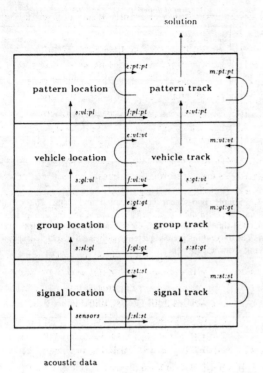

Fig. 2. Levels of abstraction and knowledge sources. KS's combine hypotheses to form more encompassing hypotheses on the same or higher levels. Synthesis (s:) KS's generate higher level hypotheses out of compatible lower level hypotheses. Formation (f:) KS's form a track hypothesis from two combinable location hypotheses. Extension (e:) KS's combine a track hypothesis with a compatible location hypothesis to extend the track. Merge (m:) KS's combine two shorter track hypotheses that are compatible into a single longer track. The sensors KS creates signal location hypotheses out of sensed data. Communication KS's are not shown.

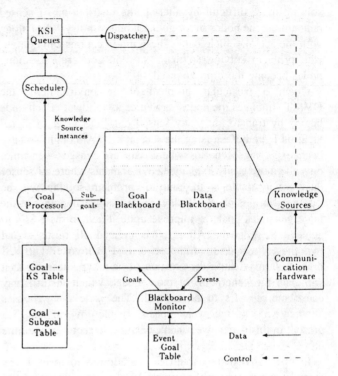

Fig. 3. DVMT node architecture. A KS forms hypotheses on the data blackboard, which in turn trigger the formation of goals on the goal blackboard. The goal processor forms KSI's to satisfy the goals, and the KSI's are scheduled. The dispatcher then invokes the KS for the best pending KSI and the cycle repeats.

(classifying the frequency or vehicle type), and by a *belief* (the confidence in the accuracy of the hypothesis).

The hypotheses are organized on a blackboard with four levels of abstraction: **signal** (for low-level analyses of the sensory data), **group** (for collections of harmonically related signals), **vehicle** (for collections of groups that correspond to given vehicle types), and **pattern** (for collections of spatially related vehicle types such as vehicles moving in a formation). Each of these levels is split into a level for location hypothesis (which have one time location) and a level for track hypotheses (which have a sequence of time locations). In total, nodes have eight blackboard levels and KS's for combining hypotheses on one level to generate more encompassing hypotheses on the same or on a higher level (Fig. 2).

A *knowledge source instantiation* (KSI) represents the potential application of a particular KS to specific hypotheses. Each node maintains a queue of pending KSI's and, at any given time, must rank the KSI's to decide which one to invoke next. To improve these decisions, we have extended the Hearsay-II architecture (Fig. 3) so that nodes can reason more fully about the *goals* of the KSI's [3], [4]. As explicit representations of the node's intentions to abstract and extend hypotheses, goals are stored on a separate goal blackboard and are given importance ratings. A goal-processing component recognizes interactions between goals and can adjust their ratings (for example, subgoals of an important goal might have their ratings boosted). The scheduler ranks a KSI based both

on the estimated beliefs of the hypotheses it may produce and on the ratings of the goals it is expected to satisfy. Goal processing can, therefore, alter KSI rankings to improve local control decisions.

A goal's rating may also be modified based on its source. Nodes have communication KS's and (simulated) communication hardware so that they can exchange hypotheses and goals (Fig. 3). Received hypotheses and goals trigger the same activities that locally generated hypotheses and goals do, so that a node is responsive both to internally generated information and to externally directed suggestions or requests for work received from other nodes. However, a node may modify the ratings of received goals or goals stimulated by received hypotheses: if the ratings of these goals are increased, the node is said to be *externally biased* and is essentially subservient to others; if the ratings of these goals are decreased, the node is *locally biased* and prefers its own activities over the suggestions of others; and if the ratings of these goals are not modified at all, the node is *unbiased*.

B. DVMT Problem-Solving Activity

A node that makes better local control decisions will invoke fewer KSI's since it searches the solution space more selectively. To evaluate an approach for improving local control decisions, therefore, we use the DVMT to simulate problem-solving environments and measure the number of local control decisions required to generate the solution. We explore the strengths and limitations of an approach by developing a set of environments that cover a range of problem-solving situations. For example, we might make problem solving more difficult by altering the distribution of sensed data among the nodes or by giving a node "noisy" data along with the actual vehicle data. These modifications can complicate problem solving so that issues in cooperation among nodes become more pronounced.

Given a particular problem-solving environment, the DVMT simulates the nodes' activities as follows.[1] Each node begins by transforming any sensed data into a set of signal location hypotheses (using the sensor KS). Although we have been exploring scenarios where data are sensed over time, only the more easily explained environments where all sensor data are available at the start of problem solving will be discussed in this paper. With each new signal hypothesis, the node generates goals to improve upon it and forms KSI's to achieve these goals. After it has created all of its signal hypotheses, a node then chooses a KSI to invoke. The KSI invocation may cause the creation of new hypotheses, which stimulate the generation of more goals, which in turn may cause more KSI's to be formed. The node then chooses another KSI and the cycle repeats. In the environments we present in this paper, we assume each cycle requires one time unit.

In these environments, nodes are allowed to form tracks from locations only at the vehicle level. Nodes thus perform both low-level problem-solving activities (creating group location and vehicle location hypotheses), and high-level activities (forming, extending, and merging vehicle track and pattern track hypotheses). Initially, the node will drive up its most promising data to form tracks and use the goals to extend these tracks to boost the importance of low-level processing that may eventually allow the tracks to be extended. This form of problem solving is called *island-driven* because it uses islands of high belief to guide further low-level processing, and is also *opportunistic* because nodes can react to highly rated new data (perhaps received from another node) to form alternative islands of high belief.

When *any* node generates, through its own uncertain decisions, a hypothesis that "matches" the correct (predefined) solution, the network has solved the problem.[2] Because nodes may have different knowledge and responsibilities, only a subset of the nodes may be capable of generating the solution. A node that finds the solution thus must broadcast its success to the other nodes before ceasing its activity, and the other nodes cease their activities when either they receive this message (which is subject to communication delays) or they generate the solution themselves, whichever is earlier. Network activity thus stops within a finite amount of time after any node first finds the solution.

In our environments, low-level processing requires a minimum of three time units to generate a fully supported

---

[1] More detailed descriptions can be found elsewhere [5], [21].

[2] The solution is thus specified before problem solving begins, but a node cannot use this information to guide its processing. Without the availability of such an "oracle," termination of problem solving is much more difficult, requiring nodes to determine whether further problem solving is likely to improve upon a possible solution which it has already generated or will cause it to generate another potentially better solution. In effect, the termination decision depends on the criteria for deciding whether network goals have been satisfied [5]. An effort is underway to address these issues [10].

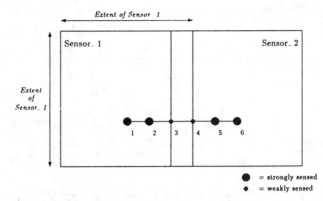

Fig. 4. Simple two-sensor configuration and data. The extents of the sensors' ranges in the two-dimensional space and the data points with their associated times are shown. Data at times 3 and 4 fall in the overlapping area. The data points are connected to indicate the vehicle track, the vehicle moving from left to right.

TABLE I
INITIAL MULTINODE EXPERIMENTS

Experiment	Nodes	Organization	Time
E1.1	1	–	29
E1.2	*optimal*(1)	–	24
E1.3	2	none	32
E1.4	2	unbiased	22
E1.5	2	loc-bias	17
E1.6	*optimal*(2)		14

	Legend
Nodes:	Number of nodes in network (*optimal*(*n*) = optimal solution time for *n* nodes)
Organization:	Bias of nodes
Time:	Earliest time at which a solution was found

vehicle location hypothesis (two KSI's to generate two group hypotheses and one KSI to combine these at the vehicle level). With *n* sequential vehicle locations, high-level processing requires a minimum of *n* time units to generate a pattern track hypothesis ($n - 1$ to generate the full vehicle track and one to synthesize it to the pattern track level). This analysis allows us to calculate a benchmark value for *optimal* performance: the minimum amount of time that the network would require if each node had no control uncertainty, and so, made only correct control decisions. Because nodes cannot always be expected to make only correct decisions, we have also developed a more subjective benchmark called *reasonable* performance. Given highly rated noise, a node should temporarily prefer to process it rather than less highly rated but true data. For environments with such noise, reasonable time is computed by adding to the calculation of optimal time an estimate of the amount of time needed to process and dismiss the noise. We refer to the optimal and reasonable performance benchmarks throughout this paper.

IV. INCREASING COHERENT COOPERATION USING ORGANIZATION

Consider the simple two-sensor and data configuration in Fig. 4. We might connect both sensors to a single problem-solving node and allow it to develop the entire solution. As is shown in Table I, the node (as simulated by the DVMT) requires 29 time units (hence, 29 KSI's) to generate the solution (E1.1), 5 more than optimal (E1.2). Despite having had all of the data, the node still had control uncertainty: it made five incorrect decisions to form pattern tracks out of short vehicle tracks rather than forming the complete vehicle track first. If we next connect the sensors to separate nodes that exchange *all* partial results with a communication delay of one time unit[3] (a node can perform one KSI in the time it takes to transmit a message), the performance (E1.3) is actually worse than the single node case! This is because the nodes were not *organized* to work together coherently. Not only did they completely duplicate each other's work, but each node also occasionally performed additional unnecessary KSI's because the partial results needed to continue developing the correct solution had not yet been received from the other node. These KSI's constructed less credible partial results along unlikely alternative solution paths.

Organization can improve performance by reducing the responsibilities of each node. In our simple case, we might make each node responsible for low-level processing only on data it gets from its own sensor[4] and insist that only high-level partial results, such as vehicle tracks, are exchanged. These modifications improve network performance significantly (E1.4) although it still is not optimal (E1.6)—the nodes still make incorrect local decisions. In addition, the organization reduces the number of communicated hypotheses from 172 in E1.3 to only four in E1.4.

Organization can also improve performance by making nodes externally biased, locally biased, or unbiased. In E1.4, each node first builds a short track based on its own highly sensed data and these tracks are then exchanged. Because the nodes are unbiased, each node tries to extend both its locally formed and its received track into the overlapping area. Hence, each node does low-level processing on both data points in the overlapping area, resulting in redundant work and less than completely coherent cooperation. If we modify the organization so that the nodes are more locally biased, then each will prefer extending its local track first. Since the extended tracks are also exchanged, each node can avoid the incorrect decisions to perform redundant low-level processing and performance is improved still further (E1.5).

Even with optimal coherent cooperation between nodes, two nodes cannot solve the problem in half the time it takes one node. In this environment, optimal solution time for one node is 24 (E1.2), for two nodes it is 14 (E1.6), and for three nodes it is 11 time units. Cooperating nodes incur processing overhead when they integrate their partial solutions. For

example, when one node is generating the overall network solution, either the other nodes are simultaneously generating the same solution (unnecessarily), or they are generating tentative partial solutions that cannot possibly be of use. In either case, we are only using *one-nth* of our *n-node* network *for that interval of time.* As the size of the network increases, the effective use of the network over this interval decreases,[5] the processing resources unused during integration being attributed to cooperation overhead.

Cooperation overhead and problem-solving parallelism must be balanced to achieve acceptable network performance. For a given problem, using too small a network can reduce parallelism (each node is overburdened), while using too large a network can incur excessive cooperation overhead. An effective problem-solving network, therefore, must have an appropriate number of nodes, and acceptable network performance depends on organizing these nodes to cooperate coherently.

A. Organizational Structuring

An **organizational structure** specifies a set of long-term responsibilities and interaction patterns for the nodes. This information guides the local control decisions of each node and increases the likelihood that the nodes will behave coherently by providing a global strategy for network problem solving. The construction and maintenance of the organizational structure is a network control problem, and we postpone its discussion until later in this paper. For the present, we assume that the organizational structure is established at network creation and is never altered [23].

The organizational structure is implemented in the DVMT as a set of data structures called **interest areas**. As implied by its name, an interest area specifies the node's interest (represented as a set of parameters) in a particular area of the partial solution space (characterized by blackboard levels, times, locations, and event classes). The scheduler uses the interest area to modify the ratings of goals; goals to generate hypotheses in desirable areas of the blackboard would have their ratings increased. Goals to transmit or receive information similarly have their ratings modified based on the interest areas of both the sending and receiving nodes. Since the goal rating is a factor in ranking KSI's, the interest areas can influence node activity; but because there are other factors in ranking KSI's (such as the expected beliefs of the output hypotheses), a node still preserves a certain level of flexibility in its local control decisions. The organizational structure thus provides guidance without dictating local decisions, and can be used to control the amount of overlap and problem solving redundancy among nodes, the problem-solving roles of the nodes (such as "integrator," "specialist," and "middle manager"), the authority relations between nodes, and the potential problem-solving paths in the network [6].

B. Further Experiments with Organizational Structuring

In this section, we briefly explore the effects of organizational structuring on some two-node environments based on

---

[3] This communication delay is used in all of the two-node networks in this paper. Simulating comparable time costs for computation and communication emphasizes the tradeoffs between waiting for a partial solution and deriving it locally. Consider a node that could begin to develop an important partial solution that it knows another node has already started to work on: if communication is comparatively very fast the node should always wait to receive the result; if communication is comparatively very slow the node should always derive the result locally; if communication and computation have comparable time costs, the decision requires more sophisticated reasoning.

[4] We assume in the environments in this paper that overlapping sensors senses the same data in the area of overlap: confidence in data is independent of the number of sensors which observe it. If two nodes independently derive the same partial solution based on independent observations, one of these derivations is redundant (unnecessary). Situations where independent derivation increases confidence are not addressed in this paper.

[5] This analysis holds for these distributed problem solving experiments because the network only develops a single solution and then stops. In *continuous* systems, this may not be the case.

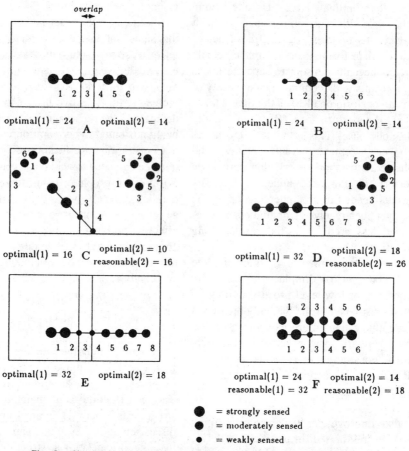

Fig. 5. Six simple two-sensor configurations. For each configuration, the optimal solution time for a one-node network [optimal (1)] and a two-node network [optimal (2)] is given. For cases where reasonable performance differs from optimal performance, reasonable solution time is also given. The sensed time is given near each data point. Note that noise in C and D cannot be correlated into tracks—data at sequential times are too far apart to be combined into a track.

simple two-sensor and data configurations (Fig. 5). Our intent is to show that overly specialized organizational structures allow effective network performance in particular problem-solving situations, but that no such organization is appropriate in all situations. We continue using two-node environments to keep the explanations uncomplicated. Experiments on larger network environments composed of up to 13 nodes are discussed later in this paper and elsewhere [5], [6].

Each of the six two-node environments (A–F) was devised to illustrate a specific problem-solving situation. Environment A (which we have previously studied) illustrates the situation where each node develops its own local hypothesis that guide-activity in the overlapping area. Environment B illustrates the situation where nodes will process data in the overlapping area first. Environment C illustrates the situation where one of the nodes (node 1, the left node) could potentially derive the solution alone. When the reception of information causes a node to shift its problem-solving focus, we say that the node is *distracted* [19]. In Environment D, we illustrate a situation with *positive* (beneficial) distraction: when node 1 sends a highly rated track hypothesis to node 2, node 2 will stop working on its moderately sensed noise and attempt to extend the track with its weakly sensed vehicle data. Environment E

illustrates *negative* (detrimental) distraction that causes redundant processing: when node 2 receives the strongly believed partial track from node 1, it may be tempted to work on the weakly sensed data in the overlapping area (work that node 1 is already doing), delaying important work on the moderate data. Finally, Environment F illustrates a complex problem-solving situation where a moderately sensed "ghost" track[6] now runs parallel to the true track. Intelligent local control decisions are crucial in this situation to avoid generating many unnecessary tracks that combine ghost data with true vehicle data.

The experimental results are summarized in Table II. The results from Environment A are included for completeness (E2.1–E2.4). Bias does not affect redundancy in Environment B since nodes process data in the overlapping area first. Splitting the overlapping area down the middle and assigning half to each node, however, does improve performance (E2.5, E2.6). In Environment C, such splitting degrades performance since node 1 cannot complete the solution track by itself and must try to distract node 2 into completing it instead (E2.7,

---

[6] Ghost tracks are sequences of noisy data points which mimic (and often parallel) an actual vehicle track.

TABLE II
EXPERIMENTS WITH ORGANIZATIONAL STRUCTURING

Experiment	Environment	Nodes	Organization	Overlap	Time
E2.1	A	1	–	–	29
E2.2	A	2	none	all	32
E2.3	A	2	unbiased	all	22
E2.4	A	2	loc-bias	all	17
E2.5	B	2	unbiased	all	26
E2.6	B	2	unbiased	split	20
E2.7	C	2	unbiased	all	21
E2.8	C	2	unbiased	split	25
E2.9	D	2	loc-bias	all	45
E2.10	D	2	unbiased	all	38
E2.11	E	2	unbiased	all	31
E2.12	E	2	loc-bias	all	28
E2.13	F	2	unbiased	all	75
E2.14	F	2	unbiased	split	71
E2.15	B	1	–	–	28
E2.16	C	1	–	–	33
E2.17	D	1	–	–	41
E2.18	E	1	–	–	34
E2.19	F	1	–	–	92

Legend

Environment:	Configuration from Figure 4
Nodes:	Number of nodes in network
Organization:	Bias of nodes
Overlap:	Whether each node is responsible for *all* of overlap or if overlap is *split* between them
Time:	Earliest time at which a solution was found

E2.8). Hence, the static division of responsibility in an overlapping area might backfire.

Similarly, altering the nodes' bias is more or less useful depending on the problem-solving situation. In situations with positive distraction (Environment D), making nodes locally biased decreases their responsiveness to received hypotheses and degrades network performance (E2.9, E2.10). However, in situations with negative distraction (Environment E), locally biased nodes perform better (E2.11, E2.12) because of their "skepticism" [5], [25]. Confusion caused by ghost data (Environment F) results in poor network performance regardless of organization (E2.13, E2.14). Mechanisms to help rectify this situation are presented in the next section. Finally, one-node or *centralized* experiments for Environments B–F (E2.15–E2.19) help to further illustrate how important the proper organization is in decentralized experiments, as again we see evidence that improper organizations can reduce (or completely negate) the performance improvements achievable through parallelism (for example, compare E2.17 to E2.9).

In summary, we have recognized the strengths and limitations of organizational structuring. An organization that assigns appropriate responsibilities (interest areas) and bias to nodes can result in acceptable network problem-solving behavior over the long term. However, an organization that is specialized for one short-term situation may be inappropriate for another. Because network reorganization may be costly and time consuming (see Section VIII), and since specific problem characteristics cannot be predicted beforehand, an organizational structure should thus be chosen which can achieve acceptable and consistent performance in the long term rather than being very good in a limited range of situations and very bad in others.

V. PLANNING AND DYNAMICALLY REFINING AN ORGANIZATION

To dynamically tailor an "all-purpose" organizational structure for specific network needs, we introduce the second mechanism to increase coherence: a planner. Our planner allows nodes to represent and reason about sequences of related actions. For example, given a highly rated hypothesis, a node typically executes a sequence of KSI's that drives up low-level data to extend the hypothesis. However, the entire sequence of KSI's is never on the queue at once because a KSI is only created when the hypotheses it will use have been created, which in turn require the execution of the previous KSI in the sequence. We have, therefore, developed a structure, called a *plan,* to explicitly represent a KSI sequence.

A plan, as a representation of some sequence of related (and sequential) activities, indicates the specific role that a node will be playing in the organization over a certain time interval. A node can use this additional information to improve its coordination knowledge by dynamically refining its interest areas. For example, consider a node that is responsible both for low-level synthesis activity in a small region and for integrating partial tracks over a much larger region. At a given time, the node might develop and begin to execute a plan to perform synthesis. Given this plan, the node could recognize that it is not integrating partial tracks, and therefore knows that any locally generated or received tracks should be forwarded to other nodes for integration. On the other hand, if the node were executing a plan to integrate partial tracks, it might decide that it should not transmit the larger tracks that it forms because this might occupy bandwidth that could better be used by other nodes to send additional partial tracks to it for integration.

A. Implementation of the Planner

Each *plan* represents a desire to achieve a high-level goal by performing a sequence of activities. To identify plans, the node needs to recognize these high-level goals. Inferring high-level goals based on pending KSI's is an inappropriate approach; it is like attempting to guess a chess opponent's strategy by observing isolated moves. Furthermore, the hypothesis and goal blackboards provide information at too detailed a level to efficiently infer these high-level goals. What is required is a structure similar to the blackboards where related hypotheses and goals are grouped together. We have developed a preliminary version of this structure which we call the *abstracted blackboard,* a structure reminiscent of the focus-of-control database first used in the Hearsay-II speech understanding system [12], [15]. Our implementation of the abstracted blackboard is incomplete because it does not adequately incorporate the information from the goal blackboard. However, for the type of processing performed in these environments, hypothesis abstraction is usually effective.

Hypotheses with similar level, time, and region characteristics are grouped together on the abstracted blackboard. This grouping acts as a smoothing operator, obscuring details about individual hypothesis interactions so that broader, long-term interactions between areas of the solution space can be discerned. By transforming the data blackboard into the

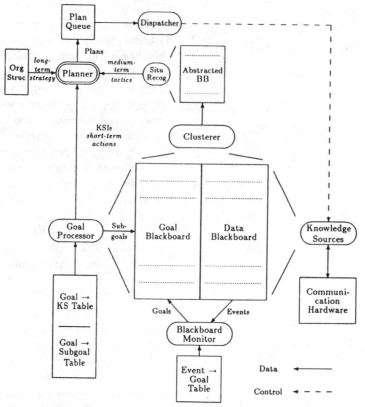

Fig. 6.   The modified problem-solving architecture of a node. The planner
integrates information about the KSI's, problem-solving situations, and
organizational structure to form plans. The dispatcher invokes the KS for
the best KSI of the best plan. Any new hypotheses that the KS forms trigger
changes to the goal and abstracted blackboards, generating new information
for the planner. The cycle then repeats.

abstracted blackboard, we explicitly generate a state representation that is uniquely appropriate for planning at a higher level
of abstraction.

The implementation, which is more completely outlined
elsewhere [9], clusters hypotheses and summarizes their
attributes into a set of values that are stored on the abstracted
blackboard. A *situation recognizer* scans the abstracted
blackboard to develop a higher level view of the problem
solving occurring at the node. Based on this view, it generates
higher level goals and passes them to the planner. A goal
might be to extend a highly believed portion of the blackboard
into a new area or to improve credibility in another area. The
planner in turn creates a plan to satisfy the higher level goal,
and associates with the plan a set of KSI's that represents
potential steps in the plan. This set is updated as the plan is
carried out and appropriate new KSI's are formed.

At any given time, a node will work on its most highly rated
plan; problem solving remains opportunistic because plans are
interruptable. The plan rating reflects the importance of
achieving the higher level goal, the expected performance of
the plan's KSI's (reflected by their ratings), and the interest
area specifications. We have, therefore, made important
modifications to the control structure of a node (Fig. 6). The
creation and ranking of plans requires the planner to integrate
the influences of the long-term strategy of the organizational
structure (the interest areas), the medium-term higher level

view of the current situation (the abstracted blackboard), and
the short-term KSI input indicating actions that can be
achieved immediately (the KSI queue). Hence, decisions in a
plan-based node are more informed than those in a KSI-based
node (a node without plans).

B. Experiments with Plan-Based Nodes

A planner increases a node's self-awareness and improves
its problem solving. We illustrate this improvement using
some simple one- and two-node environments, all based on the
configuration from Fig. 4. The results for these experiments
are summarized in Table III. In centralized environments, the
performance of plan-based nodes (E3.1–E3.6) is superior to
KSI-based nodes (Table II, E2.1 and E2.15–E2.19). Indeed,
in Experiments E3.1–E3.5, the centralized performance is
optimal (see Fig. 5 for optimal values). When there is
significant distraction due to the ghost track (Environment
F), distraction affects both types of nodes (neither finds the
solution in optimal time), but the high-level view of a plan-
based node helps it quickly recognize that the distracting data
will not satisfy the high-level goal which drives the plan. The
time spent deviating from the correct solution path is reduced,
and the plan-based node can generate the solution faster.

Having established that the problem-solving behavior of a
plan-based node is more effective than that of a KSI-based
node, we expect that a network of such nodes might have

TABLE III
EXPERIMENTS WITH THE PLANNER

Experiment	Environment	Nodes	Organization	Overlap	Time
E3.1	A	1	–	–	24
E3.2	B	1	–	–	24
E3.3	C	1	–	–	16
E3.4	D	1	–	–	32
E3.5	E	1	–	–	32
E3.6	F	1	–	–	32
E3.7	A	2	unbiased	all	14
E3.8	A	2	loc-bias	all	14
E3.9	B	2	unbiased	all	19
E3.10	B	2	unbiased	split	16
E3.11	C	2	unbiased	all	16
E3.12	C	2	unbiased	split	16
E3.13	D	2	loc-bias	all	35
E3.14	D	2	unbiased	all	27
E3.15	E	2	loc-bias	all	18
E3.16	E	2	unbiased	all	25
E3.17	F	2	unbiased	all	18
E3.18	F	2	unbiased	split	18

Legend

Environment:	Configuration from Figure 4
Nodes:	Number of nodes in network
Organization:	Bias of nodes
Overlap:	Whether each node is responsible for *all* of overlap or if overlap is *split* between them
Time:	Earliest time at which a solution was found

improved performance, not because they display better "teamwork" (their global knowledge does not increase), but rather because each is a better "player." These expectations were empirically verified on the environments. In Environment *A*, the solution is found at optimal time whether or not the plan-based nodes are locally biased (E3.7, E3.8). Each node will complete its plan to extend its locally created track before it begins extending the received track since the plan to extend the local hypothesis is formed first. In Environment B, dividing the overlapping area into separate regions of preference still has a positive effect, as would be expected (E3.9, E3.10). However, in Environment *C*, the division no longer has deleterious effects (E3.11, E3.12), because the new planner places greater emphasis on extending existing tracks rather than developing new tracks from signal data. Note that, since node 1 must generate the entire solution, performance in the two-node networks is the same as in the centralized experiment (E3.3).

A node's bias, and hence its susceptibility to distraction, still has important consequences in plan-based nodes. In Environment *D*, locally biased plan-based nodes, while performing better than their KSI-based counterparts, still perform far from optimally (E3.13). Unbiased plan-based nodes, on the other hand, have performance which is very nearly optimal (E3.14). Alternatively, in the environment with negative distraction (Environment *E*), the locally biased plan-based nodes give optimal performance (E3.15), while the unbiased nodes still display negative distraction (E3.16). These environments serve to illustrate that improving the planner of each node is not enough to ensure coherent cooperation—even though the nodes are better "players," dealing with distraction often requires nodes to have more knowledge about each other's activities.

The ghost track in Environment *F* can be more effectively handled by plan-based nodes, as we saw in the centralized case. Network performance is still not optimal—the node still requires time to examine and rule out the noisy data—but performance is reasonable (E3.17). Furthermore, note that division of the overlapping area does not make a difference (E3.18), for the same reasons that it did not affect Environment *C* with plan-based nodes.

In conclusion, the increased self-awareness afforded by the new planner significantly improves problem-solving performance. Similar results are found in experiments with the larger networks described later in the paper. The experiments emphasize the importance of sophisticated local control that recognizes and reacts appropriately to various problem-solving situations, and we are expanding the repertoire of situations that can be dealt with so that plans can be developed in more complex environments [11].

VI. Communicaton and Increasing Global Awareness

We have outlined two mechanisms that improve network coherence by increasing the knowledge available to nodes, both in terms of their general network responsibilities (organization) and their current states (plans). Unfortunately, even with this added sophistication, the nodes still may not always be completely coherent. Although the control uncertainty based on its own state has been reduced, a node will still be uncertain about the organizational role being played by each of the other nodes. The organizational structure limits the possibilities, but, to retain network flexibility, each node will not be overly limited. To dynamically refine their views of the roles being played by the other nodes, nodes must exchange information.

The exchange of hypotheses and goals can affect network coherence through distraction. Decisions about what information should be sent, to what nodes, and when they should be made intelligently, considering tradeoffs between the relevance, timeliness, and completeness of the hypotheses and goals [10]. We have developed three communication policies, called *send-all, locally complete,* and *first-and-last,* that are extensions to the ideas first developed by Lesser and Erman [19]. Each policy uses different criteria for selecting information to transmit and each affects network coherence and communication resource usage differently. Our experimental results indicate that a suitable communication policy can increase coherence and reduce communication in a given environment, but that no single static communication policy is appropriate for all problem-solving situations [10]. Therefore, selective communication of partial results decreases communication costs but does not represent a flexible approach to increasing coherent cooperation.

A. Meta-Level Communication

The information contained in hypothesis and goal messages is targeted toward improving the problem-solving activity of the nodes, not toward improving the coordination between them. To improve coordination, messages should contain less detailed information about specific actions and more general information about the current and planned problem-solving activities of the node. Hence, communication between nodes should not be limited to *domain-level* information (partial solutions) but should also include the exchange of *meta-level* information—information specifically intended to increase coherent cooperation in the network. Indeed, it is likely that information on any number of levels should be exchanged depending on the intended use of that information.

Abstracted blackboard entries summarize a node's hypotheses and provide a high-level view of where a node has searched. By exchanging portions of the abstracted blackboards, nodes can reason about each other's *past* activities. A node that knows the current plan of another node can also reason its *present* actions. Reasoning about the *future* actions of a node, however, is difficult because a node must not only estimate the duration and effects of a node's plans, but also must predict what further information the node may receive (from its sensors or another node) that could affect these estimations. We are currently developing mechanisms to generate such estimations and expectations [11].

Our current implementation assumes that a node can make completely accurate short-term predictions about future activity and we simulate this best case scenario by letting nodes access the abstracted blackboards and plan queues of other nodes. In Section VII, we briefly explore what happens when a node must work with out-of-date meta-level information because of channel delays. Eventually, nodes will have to reason more intelligently about transmitting meta-level information, considering the information's relevance, timeliness, and completeness.

When developing a plan, a node can use meta-level information to determine if the plan will redundantly derive information that another node has either generated (present in the abstracted blackboard) or is in the process of generating (the top plan). By avoiding redundant activity, solution generation rate can improve because less highly rated but potentially useful activities will be invoked earlier (rather than redundant invocation of highly rated activities). Meta-level information also allows nodes to better predict the effects a message will have on other nodes, thereby improving communication decisions.

B. Evaluating Meta-Level Communication Utility

We now examine network performance assuming that there are sufficient communication resources to accommodate both the exchange of hypotheses and the additional meta-level messages. The experimental results (Table IV) indicate that the distributed problem-solving networks with organizational structuring, plan-based nodes, and meta-level communication can often be completely coherent in their cooperation—they could not have acted better as a team. In Environment *A*, the solution is found in optimal time regardless of bias (E4.1, E4.2), as was the case without meta-level communication (Table III, E3.7, E3.8). Meta-level communication is advantageous in Environment *B* (E4.3, E4.4). Splitting the overlapping area among the two nodes no longer has an effect because now nodes can avoid redundancy dynamically. In essence, by communicating meta-level information, the nodes *are* splitting the overlapping area, but they are doing so dynamically rather

TABLE IV
EXPERIMENTS WITH META-LEVEL COMMUNICATION

Experiment	Environment	Nodes	Organization	Overlap	Time
E4.1	A	2	unbiased	all	14
E4.2	A	2	loc-bias	all	14
E4.3	B	2	unbiased	all	15
E4.4	B	2	unbiased	split	15
E4.5	D	2	loc-bias	all	36
E4.6	D	2	unbiased	all	26
E4.7	E	2	loc-bias	all	18
E4.8	E	2	unbiased	all	18
E4.9	F	2	unbiased	all	18
E4.10	F	2	unbiased	split	18

Legend
Environment: Configuration from Figure 4
Nodes: Number of nodes in network
Organization: Bias of nodes
Overlap: Whether each node is responsible for *all* of overlap or if overlap is *split* between them
Time: Earliest time at which a solution was found

than due to a static organizational decision.[7] The performance is slightly suboptimal because nodes unnecessarily exchange and integrate short hypotheses.

In Environment *D*, locally biased nodes still perform more poorly (E4.5, E4.6). In Environment *E*, however, it is no longer necessary to make nodes locally biased to prevent negative distraction because the exchange of meta-level information allows unbiased nodes to dynamically assign responsibility in the overlapping area (E4.7, E4.8). Meta-level communication does not improve performance in Environment *F* (compare E4.9 and E4.10 to Table III, E3.17 and E3.18) because the performance in these earlier experiments was already equal to what one could reasonably expect in a completely coherent network.

Based on these results, we can make several important conclusions. First, meta-level communication will sometimes not improve performance, particularly if that performance is already about as good as the network could reasonably achieve. The exchange of meta-level information can thus increase communication without improving performance. Second, statistically biasing nodes to counter negative distraction is unnecessary (E4.8) and may even be detrimental (E4.5) when nodes can use exchanged meta-level information to make informed decisions about how to react (if at all) to a received hypothesis. Finally, using meta-level information to dynamically divide responsibility in overlapping areas increases network coherence and flexibility. However, to completely organize the nodes dynamically using meta-level information would be infeasible due to the limited communication bandwidth, particularly in large, complex networks where each node must coordinate with many others. Our approach to coherent cooperation therefore stresses the use of both an organizational structure to act as a general, long-term framework for coordination and of meta-level communication to make small, short-term refinements to this framework based on the nodes' current problem-solving activities (plans).

---

[7] The first node to work on some part of the overlapping area essentially claims that part: the meta-level information reflects this work and causes other nodes to avoid redundantly working there. The overlapping area is thus split as a each node claims different portions of it.

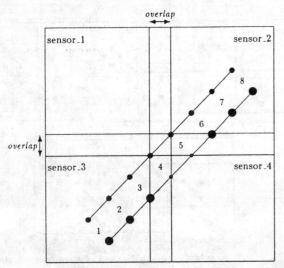

Fig. 7. Four-sensor configuration with sensed data. The sensors' ranges overlap. There are eight data points in the "ghost" track above the eight in the actual vehicle track. The size of the points reflects how strongly the data are sensed.

VII. Further Experiments in Coherent Cooperation

In this section, we attempt to show that the results obtained and conclusions drawn in the two-node environments are indicative of larger environments. We also determine when the improvements in network performance justify the additional computation and communication costs of our new mechanisms.

A. Experiments with Larger Problem-Solving Networks

As the size of distributed problem-solving networks increases, it becomes very difficult to describe (much less explain) network behavior. Therefore, all of our earlier discussions on experimental results were based on very simple one- or two-node environments. However, most of our research has been devoted to larger networks that display more interesting and complex behavior, and we now briefly indicate how increased node sophistication and meta-level communication can improve performance in these networks.

The larger networks we describe in this paper have a communication delay of two time units (a node can execute two KSI's in the time it takes to transmit a message) and are based on two different sensor and data configurations. The first of these has four sensors and 16 data points (Fig. 7), eight as part of the vehicle track and the other eight running parallel to it as a ghost track (recall Environment F, Fig. 4). Note that the vehicle data are strongly sensed at each end and are weakly sensed in the middle, while the ghost data are moderately sensed throughout. We base three networks on this configuration. The first is the centralized case, where one node receives data from all four sensors. The second is a four-node network where each node is attached to a different sensor. As in the two-node environments, the nodes are organized *laterally,* meaning that they exchange information among themselves and each attempts to form the network solution. The third network has five nodes: four are connected to their own sensors and they all communicate only with the fifth node (which receives no sensor data). In this *hierarchical* organization, the four "bottom-level" nodes perform low-level processing while the

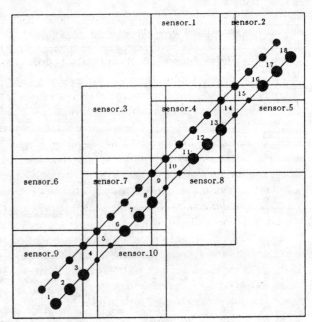

Fig. 8. Ten-sensor configuration with sensed data. The sensors' ranges overlap, there are 18 data points in both the actual (lower) and "ghost" (upper) tracks, and the size reflects how strongly sensed the data point is.

"top-level" node integrates the high-level hypotheses it receives into an overall solution.

In hierarchical organizations, bias is used to form authority relationships. For example, in the five-node network the top-level node can have a much more complete view of network problem solving than any of the bottom-level nodes. By making the bottom-level nodes externally biased and the top-level node locally biased, the top-level node can control network problem solving, and problem solving in hierarchical organizations can thus be more focused [6].

The second configuration has ten sensors and 36 data points (Fig. 8), with half of the data corresponding to the vehicle track and the other half to a parallel ghost track. The vehicle track has four sections of strongly sensed data surrounding three sections of weakly sensed data; the ghost track is moderately sensed throughout. Three networks are also based on this configuration: a centralized one-node network; a lateral ten-node network (where nodes with overlapping sensed areas may exchange information); and a 13-node hierarchical network. The hierarchical network has ten bottom-level nodes (one for each sensor), two intermediate-level nodes (each integrating data from five bottom-level nodes), and a top-level node to integrate the hypotheses from the intermediate-level nodes.

In Table V, we summarize the effects of the three mechanisms to improve local control. In the centralized cases (E5.1–E5.8), the planner enables nodes to achieve reasonable performance. Similarly, in both laterally and hierarchically organized networks, nodes also benefit from the planner, and meta-level communication allows performance that is generally as effective as is reasonable in a completely coherent network. This is true in the four-node (E5.9–E5.13), five-node (E5.14–E5.18), ten-node (E5.19–E5.23), and 13-node (E5.24–E5.28) networks. Finally, the experiments indicate that laterally organized nodes can be focused as hierarchically

TABLE V
EXPERIMENTS WITH LARGER CONFIGURATIONS

Experiment	Nodes	Sensors	OS	Planner	MLC	Other	Time
E5.1	1	4	–	no	–	–	102
E5.2	1	4	–	yes	–	–	40
E5.3	1	4	–	–	–	reasonable	40
E5.4	1	4	–	–	–	optimal	32
E5.5	1	10	–	no	–	–	262
E5.6	1	10	–	yes	–	–	96
E5.7	1	10	–	–	–	reasonable	96
E5.8	1	10	–	–	–	optimal	72
E5.9	4	4	yes	no	no	–	33
E5.10	4	4	yes	yes	no	–	26
E5.11	4	4	yes	yes	yes	–	15
E5.12	4	4	–	–	–	reasonable	15
E5.13	4	4	–	–	–	optimal	15
E5.14	5	4	yes	no	no	–	31
E5.15	5	4	yes	yes	no	–	28
E5.16	5	4	yes	yes	yes	–	17
E5.17	5	4	–	–	–	reasonable	16
E5.18	5	4	–	–	–	optimal	16
E5.19	10	10	yes	no	no	–	46
E5.20	10	10	yes	yes	no	–	28
E5.21	10	10	yes	yes	yes	–	18
E5.22	10	10	–	–	–	reasonable	18
E5.23	10	10	–	–	–	optimal	18
E5.24	13	10	yes	no	no	–	44
E5.25	13	10	yes	yes	no	–	36
E5.26	13	10	yes	yes	yes	–	23
E5.27	13	10	–	–	–	reasonable	20
E5.28	13	10	–	–	–	optimal	20

Legend

Nodes:	Number of nodes in network
Sensors:	Number of sensors in configuration
OS:	Use of organizational structuring
Planner:	Use of the planner
MLC:	Nodes exchange meta-level information
Other:	Indicates calculated time for reasonable or optimal performance
Time:	Earliest time at which a solution was found

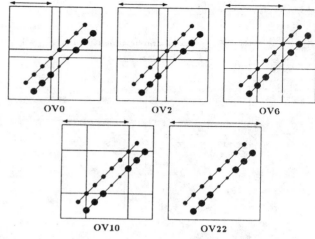

Fig. 9. Overlapping configuration. The range of a sensor is indicated, and the overlap between sensors varies from none (OV0) to complete (OV22).

organized nodes when they have increased self- and network-awareness (from the planner and meta-level communication).[8] Our mechanisms, therefore, improve performance in larger as well as smaller networks. In fact, the mechanisms become more important as network size increases. For example, since the number of potential hypothesis messages grows combinatorially with the network size and with the amount of data, nodes need to intelligently decide on which hypotheses to exchange. Our mechanisms improve communication decisions because a node can use its plans to predict whether a transmittable hypothesis may be further developed locally and it can use its meta-level knowledge to predict how the hypothesis may affect the activities of other nodes [10].

B. The Costs of Increasing Coherent Cooperation

Throughout this paper, our discussions have emphasized the issues in increasing coherent cooperation among overlapping nodes. By statically allocating different portions of the

---

[8] This requires *all* of the lateral nodes to be well informed, meaning that large amounts of meta-level communication must be exchanged compared to the hierarchical case where few nodes have the better view of network activity. Achieving more focused network activity may thus be more expensive in lateral organizations (although such lateral organizations may be more tolerant of node failures).

overlapping area to the nodes, we reduced unnecessary redundant processing in the area (recall that in this paper we assume independent derivation of a hypothesis does not increase confidence in that hypothesis), but risked delaying the timely coverage of the entire area. Through metal-level communication, overlapping nodes can dynamically assign responsibility in the overlapping area, and thus can cooperate more coherently. However, there are costs associated with these new capabilities of nodes.

We study the costs and benefits of our mechanisms on a set of environments with different amounts of overlap between nodes (Fig. 9). The environments are variations on the four-node laterally organized network described in Section VII-A. Again, each node receives data from one sensor, but we modify the amount of overlapping data nodes have by altering the sensitivity of each sensor so that it picks up more or less data. In all cases, each data point is received by at least one sensor; in Environment OV22, all data are received by all four sensors, so that each node has a complete view of the problem.

For each of these five environments, we ran three experiments. In the first, the nodes were given a lateral organization and were unbiased. In the second, the nodes were also given the planner. In the third, nodes could furthermore exchange meta-level information to avoid redundancy. Measurements for each experiment indicate network performance (as solution time) and the computation and communication requirements of the nodes. Without the planner, the computational cost is the network run time, while with the planner, we increase the run time by 50 percent—60 percent if meta-level communication is included as well. These increments are based on an estimate of the additional computation costs reflected by the DVMT. The communication requirements are indicated by the number of hypotheses and meta-level messages (where appropriate) exchanged, which are summed to indicate the total amount of communication. Finally, since meta-level messages abstract a number of hypotheses, statistics were accumulated to measure how many hypotheses would need to be exchanged to supply the equivalent information contained in the meta-level and hypothesis messages actually sent.

TABLE VI
EXPERIMENTS WITH OVERLAPPING CONFIGURATIONS

Experiment	Environment	Planner	MLC	Time	Comp.	Hyps	MLM	Comm.	Equiv
E6.1	OV0	no	no	26	26	8	0	8	8
E6.2	OV0	yes	no	15	23	10	0	10	10
E6.3	OV0	yes	yes	15	24	10	56	66	133
E6.4	OV2	no	no	33	33	18	0	18	18
E6.5	OV2	yes	no	26	39	25	0	25	25
E6.6	OV2	yes	yes	15	24	24	118	142	271
E6.7	OV6	no	no	51	51	27	0	27	27
E6.8	OV6	yes	no	25	38	30	0	30	30
E6.9	OV6	yes	yes	19	30	48	169	217	421
E6.10	OV10	no	no	116	116	51	0	51	51
E6.11	OV10	yes	no	34	51	40	0	40	40
E6.12	OV10	yes	yes	18	29	42	180	222	436
E6.13	OV22	no	no	212	212	336	0	336	336
E6.14	OV22	yes	no	42	63	48	0	48	48
E6.15	OV22	yes	yes	20	32	59	209	268	463

Legend

Environment:	Overlap environment tested
Planner:	Use of the planner
MLC:	Nodes exchange meta-level information
Time:	Earliest time at which a solution was found
Comp.:	Computational resources used for problem solving and planning
Hyps:	Number of hypotheses exchanged
MLM:	Number of meta-level messages
Comm.:	Communication resources used
Equiv:	Number of hypotheses which would need to be exchanged to equal amount of hypothesis and meta-level information

The experimental results are summarized in Table VI. In the environments with little or no overlap, the planner did not significantly alter the computation costs—although the nodes with the planner ran fewer tasks, their increased overhead for planning tended to balance this out. However, as overlap became much larger, planning became more advantageous. As a node becomes more uncertain about where to apply its computation resources, its *computational overhead* for planning (and meta-level communication) becomes increasingly acceptable. Deciding when the extra *communication overhead* of meta-level communication is acceptable is more difficult because meta-level communication always increases the communication resource usage. If bandwidth is extremely limited, then meta-level communication may be a luxury that cannot be afforded. Also, in environments with little or no overlap where meta-level communication has less effect, it might be done without whether or not bandwidth was tight. However, if the communication channels can handle the increased usage, meta-level communication can nearly halve the time necessary to generate the solution in highly overlapping environments (compare E6.11 to E6.12, E6.14 to E6.15). In applications where network performance is at a premium, the increased overhead of meta-level communication might be acceptable.

Overlap ensures reliable performance in distributed problem-solving networks by allowing them to derive solutions despite errorful data and node failures. Based on the empirical evidence, we conclude that our mechanisms are particularly efficacious in more highly overlapping, hence reliable, networks. By exchanging meta-level information, nodes use about half as much communication resources as they would have if they had exchanged enough hypotheses to convey the same information, and nodes save on computation resources since they exchange plans rather than inferring each others plans locally. In experiments where nodes receive obsolete meta-level information, however, the effects of the obsolescence become very dramatic. When nodes completely overlap (OV22), the exchange of obsolete meta-level information caused the network to find the solution in 54 time units—the network would have performed better if there had been no meta-level communication at all (E6.14)! In the future, we hope to provide nodes with the ability to make better predictions about each other's future activities based on the information they already have instead of constantly needing to update each other.

VIII. COHERENT COOPERATION IN DISTRIBUTED SYSTEMS

As the number of tasks a node may perform increases, choosing among them requires increasingly sophisticated local control, particularly if the tasks are highly interdependent. However, local control is not the whole story; any complete distributed computing system requires network control as well. When network responsibilities and processing load are poorly distributed, network control must reallocate organizational responsibilities and problem-solving tasks to ensure both that each node has a set of important tasks to perform and that all important tasks are assigned to one or more nodes.

One form of network control is task passing. A bidding

algorithm allows an overloaded node to make informed decisions about where it can send some of these tasks [7], [24]. Task passing using bidding protocols is an elegant mechanism for temporarily alleviating a poorly balanced situation. Unfortunately, its efficacy is highly dependent on the delay, bandwidth, and error rate of the communication channels.

• Bidding requires a sequence of message exchanges before a task is passed, and messages are subject to delays. If delays are substantially longer than task execution times, an overloaded node may execute its tasks faster locally than if it had passed them to idle nodes and waited for the results.[9]

• A task message specifies not only actions to execute but also a context (hypotheses, goals) for their execution. Channel bandwidth may limit the number of nodes that can obtain a task's context and might thus influence where a task is relocated [2].

• Since bidding requires mutual agreement among nodes, it may be inappropriate for environments with highly errorful channels [14].

Task passing overhead and delays may be reduced if nodes have sufficient network awareness to send tasks directly to one or more likely nodes using focused addressing [28]. Organizational knowledge and meta-level information can improve focused addressing decisions and lets nodes monitor network activity to detect whether a passed task is actually being performed. Even with these improvements, however, excessive amounts of task passing can burden communication resources and degrade network performance; task passing is generally effective only for remedying temporary, minor load imbalances.

The other form of network control makes long-term changes to node activities by modifying the organizational structure. Rather than passing an idle node a series of (possibly unrelated) tasks, it may be advantageous to change the role the node plays in the network. For example, the node may become responsible for integrating hypotheses from a number of other nodes. This change to the organization provides the node with a role that will keep it busy doing important tasks for an extended period of time—tasks that are related and likely to share context. Network control must also modify the organization to reallocate network responsibilities when nodes fail.

The complex problem of network reorganization is the topic of a parallel research effort. We have been developing a knowledge-based fault-diagnosis component to detect and locate inappropriate system behavior [16] and an organizational self-design component [5], [23]. The planner and meta-level communication, which increase a node's self- and network-awareness, are expected to prove useful in this research by helping to both detect when an organization is inappropriate and to determine how to improve it. We speculate that network reorganization will require some form of negotiation among nodes [7]. However, in domains where

communication is slow and uncertain, fully negotiated changes may be impractical, so that nodes may have different views of the organizational structure. Although this should be minimized to improve coherence, the FA/C approach allows network problem solving despite such inconsistencies.

Network control must be integrated with local control. Local control decisions affect network activity, and network control decisions influence what tasks a node has and how it ranks them. Coherent cooperation requires that both types of control be sophisticated to ensure that node activities and interactions contribute to overall network performance. In this paper, we have detailed mechanisms to improve local control decisions in the DVMT, and have considered approaches for network control. We believe, however, that our ideas are applicable in many other distributed computing systems.

Improving control decisions requires knowledge. Local control must know how a decision it makes will affect future activity both locally and at other nodes, and how decisions at other nodes may affect it; network control must know about the current and expected future activities of the nodes and how decisions to move tasks or responsibilities in the network will affect network performance. If tasks are nontrivial and interdependent, all this knowledge is difficult and time consuming to generate and, since it continuously changes, expensive to exchange. Our approach accepts that control decisions in realistic systems will not be made with complete knowledge and concentrates instead on generating and exchanging high-level views of activity that convey important knowledge without details.

The knowledge needed to make informed control decisions depends on the tasks and interactions in the network. In the DVMT, the important knowledge is about a node's search activities: organizational structuring constrains the possibilities, the planner predicts where a node will search in the near future, and meta-level communication exchanges these predictions. Details about specific KS's to run and goals to satisfy would not significantly improve control decisions. If a distributed system must provide real-time response, predictions about task results may be less important than task deadlines and estimated run times. In distributed systems with severe resource limitations, the expected resource needs of tasks is the important knowledge, while in systems where tasks on different nodes must synchronize, knowledge about the synchronization is crucial for smooth operation. In short, tasks may interact in any number of ways (cooperate to solve a problem, complete for limited resources, synchronize); the mechanisms that make control decisions and the knowledge used must be geared to the interactions in a particular application.

Once task interactions for an application are characterized, mechanisms like those in the DVMT can increase the coherence of cooperation. An organizational structure can broadly define network responsibilities—types of tasks a node may perform, resources assigned to a node, other nodes with which a node may need to synchronize. By planning task sequences, a node can predict what results it may generate, when it will be idle, what resources it needs, or exactly when it will be executing specific tasks. Meta-level communication

---

[9] In our larger environments, for example, a node may perform two local KSI's in the time it takes a message to be transmitted, so passing single KSI's would most likely be ineffective. Passing plans which represent extended sequences of KSI's might prove more useful, but by accepting longer tasks a node may significantly reduce its own responsiveness to local processing responsibilities.

enables these predictions to be exchanged, and network coherence improves as nodes work to generate compatible results, maximize the number of tasks which meet their deadlines, avoid resource conflicts, or synchronize task executions. We, therefore, believe that the approach outlined in this paper can be extended to many other distributed computing applications where tasks interact, and in fact have used the same approach in our distributed simulator for the DVMT [8].

IX. SUMMARY AND PERSPECTIVE

Coherent cooperation is a principal goal of distributed problem-solving network research. We have described an approach for achieving coherent cooperation that is responsive to changes in network activity as problem solving progresses. The approach stresses the importance of sophisticated local control that integrates knowledge of the problem domain with (meta-level) knowledge about network coordination. Such control allows nodes to make rapid, intelligent local decisions based on changing problem characteristics without the overhead of conferring with each other to coordinate these decisions. Instead, coordination is based on an organizational view of individual node activity, so nodes need not have detailed models of each other's problem-solving activities. Dynamic improvements to this organizational view may be achieved with the exchange of meta-level messages which briefly convey high-level coordination information. In short, the nodes initiate their own activities and take advantage of all available local and network knowledge to form the best "team" possible within the constraints of their environment.

This approach to distributed problem solving is based on the characteristics and performance criteria of a particular class of distributed applications. In contrast with others [18], we assume that the network contains only a limited number (tens to hundreds) of highly sophisticated, and loosely coupled, problem-solving nodes rather than thousands of relatively simple processing elements so we must coordinate our limited number of nodes to make the most effective team possible. Since we focus on domains where tasks are inherently distributed throughout the network and where communication between agents is potentially slow and unreliable, we regard coordination that requires mutual agreement on contracts before action [1], [7] to be insufficiently responsive to changing problem circumstances (indeed, mutual agreement might not even be possible [14]). To ensure reliability, we cannot accept centralized coordination [1]. The unpredictable nature of the problem-solving environment makes simple game theoretic models of agents unrealizable [26], while more complete models of agent beliefs [17] might require nodes to essentially duplicate each others reasoning.

In this paper we have focused on one particular aspect of our overall network coordination framework: modifications to the blackboard architecture of the individual nodes that enhance their ability to make predictions about their future activities. Network coherence is increased by allowing a node to refine its organizational role based on these predictions. Exchanging the predictions permits a node to refine its view of the organizational roles of the other nodes. We empirically established that each of these improvements enhanced the ability of nodes to cooperate coherently in a variety of problem-solving situations. Furthermore, we studied the costs and benefits of using these improvements, and established that they were particularly cost effective in more complex problem-solving situations. Finally, we outlined how our approach for improving local control decisions can be combined with network control, and discussed how our approach might be used in other distributed computing applications. Our current plans are to extend and improve these mechanisms in order to enlarge the range of distributed problem-solving situations where they can be applied to increase network coherence and improve cooperation.

ACKNOWLEDGMENT

We would like to thank J. Stankovic, R. Smith, K. Ramamritham, and L. Erman for their comments on earlier drafts of this paper.

REFERENCES

[1] S. Cammarata, D. McArthur, and R. Steeb, "Strategies of cooperation in distributed problem solving," in *Proc. Eighth Int. Conf. Artif. Intell.*, Aug. 1983, pp. 767–770.

[2] L. Casey and N. Shelness, "A domain structure for distributed computer systems," in *Proc. Sixth ACM Symp. Oper. Syst. Principles*, Nov. 1977, pp. 101–108.

[3] D. D. Corkill and V. R. Lesser, "A goal-directed Hearsay-II architecture: Unifying data and goal directed control," Tech. Rep. 81-15, Dep. Comput. Inform. Sci., Univ. Massachusetts, Amherst, MA, June 1981.

[4] D. D. Corkill, V. R. Lesser, and E. Hudlicka, "Unifying data-directed and goal-directed control: An example and experiments," in *Proc. Second Nat. Conf. Artif. Intell.*, Aug. 1982, pp. 143–147.

[5] D. D. Corkill, "A framework for organizational self-design in distributed problem solving networks," Ph.D. dissertation, Univ. Massachusetts, Feb. 1983. Available as Tech. Rep. 82-33, Dep. Comput. Inform. Sci., Univ. of Massachusetts, Amherst, MA, Dec. 1982.

[6] D. D. Corkill and V. R. Lesser, "The use of meta-level control for coordination in a distributed problem solving network," in *Proc. Eighth Int. Conf. Artif. Intell.*, Aug. 1983, pp. 748–756.

[7] R. Davis and R. G. Smith, "Negotiation as a metaphor for distributed problem solving," *Artif. Intell.*, vol. 20, pp. 63–109, 1983.

[8] E. H. Durfee, D. D. Corkill, and V. R. Lesser, "Distributing a distributed problem solving network simulator," in *Proc. Fifth Real-Time Syst. Symp.*, Dec. 1984, pp. 237–246.

[9] E. H. Durfee, V. R. Lesser, and D. D. Corkill, "Increasing coherence in distributed problem solving networks," in *Proc. Ninth Int. Conf. Artif. Intell.*, Aug. 1985, pp. 1025–1030.

[10] E. H. Durfee, V. R. Lesser, and D. D. Corkill, "Coherent cooperation among communicating problem solvers," Tech. Rep. 85-15, Dep. Comput. Inform. Sci., Univer. Massachusetts, Amherst, MA, Sept. 1985.

[11] E. H. Durfee and V. R. Lesser, "Incremental planning to control a blackboard-based problem solver," in *Proc. Fifth Nat. Conf. Artif. Intell.*, Aug. 1986, pp. 58–64.

[12] L. D. Erman, F. Hayes-Roth, V. R. Lesser, and D. R. Reddy, "The Hearsay-II speech understanding system: Integrating knowledge to resolve uncertainty," *Comput. Surveys*, vol. 12, pp. 213–253, June 1980.

[13] M. Fehling and L. Erman, "Report on the third annual workshop on distributed artificial intelligence," *SIGART Newsletter*, vol. 84, pp. 3–12, Apr. 1983.

[14] J. Y. Halpern and Y. Moses, "Knowledge and common knowledge in a distributed environment," in *Proc. Third ACM Symp. Principles Distributed Comput.*, 1984, pp. 50–61.

[15] F. Hayes-Roth and V. R. Lesser, "Focus of attention in the Hearsay-II speech understanding system," in *Proc. Fifth Int. Conf. Artif. Intell.*, Aug. 1977, pp. 27–35.

[16] E. Hudlicka and V. Lesser, "Design of a knowledge-based fault

detection and diagnosis system," in *Proc. Seventeenth Hawaii Int. Conf. Syst. Sci.*, Jan. 1984, pp. 224–230.

[17] K. Konolige, "A deductive model of belief," in *Proc. Eighth Int. Conf. Artif. Intell.*, Aug. 1983, pp. 377–381.

[18] W. A. Kornfeld and C. E. Hewitt, "The scientific community metaphor," *IEEE Trans. Syst., Man, Cybern.*, vol. SMC-11, pp. 24–33, Jan. 1981.

[19] V. R. Lesser and L. D. Erman, "An experiment in distributed interpretation," *IEEE Trans. Comput.*, vol. C-29, pp. 1144–1163, Dec. 1980.

[20] V. R. Lesser and D. D. Corkill, "Functionally accurate, cooperative distributed systems," *IEEE Trans. Syst., Man, Cybern.*, vol. SMC-11, pp. 81–96, Jan. 1981.

[21] V. Lesser, D. Corkill, J. Pavlin, L. Lefkowitz, E. Hudlicka, R. Brooks, and S. Reed, "A high-level simulation testbed for cooperative distributed problem solving," in *Proc. Third Int. Conf. Distributed Comput. Syst.*, Oct. 1982, pp. 341–349.

[22] V. R. Lesser and D. D. Corkill, "The distributed vehicle monitoring testbed: A tool for investigating distributed problem solving networks," *AI Magazine*, vol. 4, pp. 15–33, Fall 1983.

[23] H. E. Pattison, D. D. Corkill, and V. R. Lesser, "Instantiating descriptions of organizational structures," Tech. Rep. 85-45, Dep. Comput. Inform. Sci., Univ. Massachusetts, Amherst, MA. Nov. 1985.

[24] K. Ramamritham and J. A. Stankovic, "Dynamic task scheduling in hard real-time distributed systems," *IEEE Software*, pp. 65–75, July, 1984.

[25] S. Reed and V. R. Lesser, "Division of labor in honey bees and distributed focus of attention," Tech. Rep. 80-17, Dep. Comput. Inform. Sci., Univ. Massachusetts, Amherst, MA, Sept. 1981.

[26] J. S. Rosenschein and M. R. Genesereth, "Deals among rational agents," in *Proc. Ninth Int. Conf. Artif. Intell.*, Aug. 1985, pp. 91–99.

[27] R. G. Smith, "The contract-net protocol: High-level communication and control in a distributed problem solver," *IEEE Trans. Comput.*, vol. C-29, pp. 1104–1113, Dec. 1980.

[28] J. A. Stankovic, K. Ramamritham, and S. Cheng, "Evaluation of a flexible task scheduling algorithm for distributed hard real-time systems," *IEEE Trans. Comput.*, vol. C-34, pp. 1130–1143, Dec. 1985.

[29] P. H. Winston, *Artificial Intelligence.* Reading, MA: Addison-Wesley, 1977.

Victor R. Lesser received the B.A. degree in mathematics from Cornell University, Ithaca, NY, in 1966, and the M.S. and Ph.D. degrees in computer science from Stanford University, Stanford, CA, in 1969 and 1972, respectively. His Ph.D. thesis was in the area of computer architecture where he developed a design for microprogrammable multiprocessors that could be reconfigured so as to emulate a variety of parallel computer architecture.

After his Ph.D., he was a Research Computer Scientist in the Department of Computer Science, Carnegie-Mellon University, Pittsburgh, PA, from 1972 to 1977. At CMU, he was a principal in the Hearsay-II Speech Understanding System where he was responsible for the system architecture. While there he also was on the design team of CM*, and made contributions in the areas of the network operating systems and parallelism in artificial intelligence. Since arriving at the University of Massachusetts in 1977, where he is a Professor of Computer Science, he has lead research groups in the areas of Distributed Artificial Intelligence and Intelligent User Interfaces. He is also a principal investigator of the recently awarded Coordinated Experimental Research grant from the National Science Foundation for the study of issues in Distributed and Parallel Problem Solving.

Daniel D. Corkill received the B.S. and M.S. degrees in computer science from the University of Nebraska, Lincoln, in 1975 and 1976 and the Ph.D. degree in computer and information science from the University of Massachusetts, Amherst, in 1983. His Ph.D. research used organizational structuring as a framework for coordinating the activities in a distributed network of AI problem solving systems.

Since 1983 he has been a Research Computer Scientist in the Department of Computer and Information Science at the University of Massachusetts where he is continuing research on organizing and coordinating distributed problem solving networks. The long-term goal of this research is to develop networks of AI problem solvers that are able to organize and potentially reorganize their activities based on changing task and network conditions. In addition to his distributed AI research, he heads the Multiprocessor Lisp/AI Development Group as part of NSF/CER supported research in Cooperative Distributed and Parallel Processing. This work has led to the development of a generic blackboard implementation system (called GBB) and work on extensions to Common Lisp for supporting Lisp multiprocessing in a hybrid parallel/distributed multiprocessor. His other interests include planning and control in AI systems, advanced AI architectures, and the development of design and programming methodologies for constructing large AI systems.

Dr. Corkill is a member of the IEEE Computer Society, the Association for Computing Machinery, AAAI, and Upsilon Pi Epsilon.

Edmund H. Durfee received the A.B. degree in chemistry and physics from Harvard University, Cambridge, MA, in 1980, the M.S. degree in electrical and computer engineering and the Ph.D. degree in computer and information science from the University of Massachusetts, Amherst, MA, in 1984 and 1987, respectively.

He spent two years as a Polymer Chemist at the General Electric Corporate Research and Development Center. He is currently a Research Computer Scientist in the Department of Computer and Information Science at the University of Massachusetts, where his interests are in distributed computing and artificial intelligence.

Dr. Durfee is an IBM fellowship recipient and a member of the IEEE Computer Society, the Association for Computing Machinery, and AAAI.

Using Partial Global Plans to Coordinate Distributed Problem Solvers

Edmund H. Durfee and Victor R. Lesser
Department of Computer and Information Science
University of Massachusetts
Amherst, Massachusetts 01003

Abstract

Communicating problem solvers can cooperate in various ways, such as negotiating over task assignments, exchanging partial solutions to converge on global results, and planning interactions that help each other perform their tasks better. We introduce a new framework that supports different styles of cooperation by using *partial global plans* to specify effective, coordinated actions for groups of problem solvers. In this framework, problem solvers summarize their local plans into *node-plans* that they selectively exchange to dynamically model network activity and to develop partial global plans. However, because network and problem characteristics can change and communication channels have delays and limited capacity, problem solvers' models and partial global plans may be incomplete, out-of-date, and inconsistent. Our mechanisms allow problem solvers to agree on consistent partial global plans when possible, and to locally form partial global plans that lead to satisfactory cooperation even in rapidly changing environments where complete agreement is impossible. In this paper, we describe the mechanisms, knowledge representations, and algorithms that we have developed for generating and maintaining partial global plans in a distributed system. We use experiments to illustrate how these mechanisms improve and promote cooperation in a variety of styles.

I. Introduction

Communicating problem solvers can pool their resources and expertise, work in parallel on different parts of a problem to solve it faster, avoid harmful interactions such as resource conflicts or working at cross-purposes, and promote helpful interactions such as moving information to where it is most needed or tasks to where they can best be performed. The style in which the problem solving *nodes* should cooperate depends on problem domain

and environmental characteristics, and there are a variety of styles for which different mechanisms have been developed. Sometimes the nodes channel all of their information to coordinating nodes that generate and distribute multi-agent plans [Cammarata *et al.*, 1983, Corkill, 1979, Georgeff, 1983, Konolige, 1984, Steeb *et al.*, 1986]. When communication is very expensive, however, nodes should work relatively independently and selectively exchange their local solutions to converge on global solutions in a functionally-accurate/cooperative (FA/C) manner [Corkill, 1983, Lesser and Corkill, 1981]. Alternatively, they may negotiate in small groups to contract out tasks in the network [Davis and Smith, 1983, Smith, 1980].

The trouble with having different mechanisms for each style of cooperation is that some distributed problem solving situations call for several styles simultaneously. For example, consider a vehicle monitoring problem where nodes track vehicles moving through an area monitored by acoustic sensors. A sample problem situation (Figure 1) has four problem solving nodes, each connected to a different sensor (node i to sensor i) that supplies it with signal information at discrete times. A node tries to combine signals into tracks, which we represent as d_i–d_j where d_i is data for the track's first sensed time and d_j is data for its last. When all the data is present, then from a local perspective: node 1 plans to develop two tracks (d'_1–d'_5 and d_4–d_{12}); 2 plans for one track (d_{10}–d_{15}), but because its sensor is faulty it will need much time to filter out noisy data; 3 plans for one track (d_1–d_6); and 4 has no local plans. From a global perspective: node 1 should first work on track d_4–d_{12} since it has more global significance (joining the tracks of 2 and 3), and also should quickly generate and send a predictive result (like the short track d_8–d_9 which borders on node 2's view) to help 2 disambiguate its noisy data; 2 should expect this predictive information; 3 should take responsibility for the data that both it and 1 sense (d_4–d_6) since 1 has more data to process; and 4 should take on some tasks, either by getting data from other nodes, or by acting as network coordinator, or both. The nodes therefore need to negotiate about task assignments, exchange partial results to converge on global solutions, and plan interactions that will help each other perform their tasks better.

Instead of developing a hybrid system that uses different mechanisms for different styles of cooperation, we have constructed a unified framework that supports all these styles through the use of *partial global plans* that specify how sets of nodes will act and interact. Each basic style

This research was sponsored, in part, by the National Science Foundation under Grant MCS-8306327, by the National Science Foundation under Support and Maintenance Grant DCR-8318776, by the National Science Foundation under CER Grant DCR-8500332, and by the Defense Advanced Research Projects Agency (DOD), monitored by the Office of Naval Research under Contract NR049-041. Edmund Durfee was also supported by an IBM Graduate Fellowship.

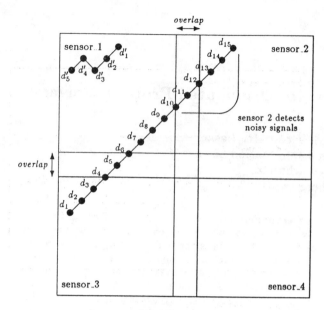

The four overlapping sensors detect signal data at discrete sensed times (the dots with associated times). Sensor_2 is faulty and not only generates signal data at the correct frequencies but also detects noisy signals at spurious frequencies.

Figure 1: Four-Sensor Configuration with Sensed Data.

of cooperation can be viewed as using partial global plans in some way. In the multi-agent planning style, the partial global plan is the multi-agent plan, while in the contracting style each contract is a partial global plan involving a pair of nodes. The FA/C style has an general, implicit partial global plan (in the form of an organizational structure) that predisposes nodes to exchange and integrate information. Within our new framework, nodes always use partial global plans to coordinate their behavior as best they can, and their style of cooperation depends on how they form, exchange, manipulate, and react to partial global plans. This framework lets nodes converge on common plans for network activity in a stable environment (where their plans do not change because of new data, failed actions, or unexpected effects of their actions). However, when network, data, and problem solving characteristics change and when communication channels have delay and limited capacity, the framework allows nodes to locally respond to new situations and to cooperate effectively even when they have inconsistent partial global plans.

Our approach to coordination emphasizes sophisticated local control: a problem solver uses its current local view of network activities to control its own actions. Therefore, although problem solvers selectively exchange information about local plans and partial global plans, each may use this information differently and asynchronously. Coordination is part of each problem solver's control activities and is interleaved with problem solving. This paper describes how this view of coordination through partial global plans has been implemented and shows how the new mechanisms allow nodes to coordinate in a vari-

ety of ways. In the next section, we briefly review how the problem solvers in our experimental domain plan their local activities. In section 3, we describe the implemented mechanisms for integrating local plans into partial global plans, covering such issues as how and where local plans are sent, which nodes develop partial global plans, what information about partial global plans is exchanged, and what happens if nodes have incomplete, obsolete, or inconsistent partial global plans. In Section 4, we use experimental results to evaluate the ability of the mechanisms to improve coordination and allow different styles of cooperation, and we discuss how network and problem characteristics affect how (and whether) nodes develop consistent views. Finally, we summarize our approach in Section 5, citing its strengths, weaknesses, and remaining open problems.

II. Distributed Vehicle Monitoring

The Distributed Vehicle Monitoring Testbed (DVMT) simulates a network of vehicle monitoring nodes, where each node is responsible for a portion of the sensed area and where the nodes develop partial tracks in parallel and exchange these to converge on a complete map of vehicle movements [Lesser and Corkill, 1983]. A node applies signal processing knowledge to correlate the data, attempting to recognize and eliminate errorful sensor data as it integrates the correct data into an answer map. Each problem solving node has a blackboard-based architecture [Erman et al., 1980], with knowledge sources (KSs) and blackboard levels of abstraction appropriate for vehicle monitoring.

Each node has a *planner* that uses an abstract view of the problem solving state to plan sequences of actions for resolving uncertainty about the potential solutions to develop and for developing them [Durfee and Lesser, 1986, Durfee and Lesser, 1987]. The abstract view is built by clustering related data into a hierarchy of abstractions, and it allows the planner to recognize long-term problem solving goals (to track some type of vehicle through a particular region). In the sample situation (Figure 1), for example, node 1 develops an abstract view indicating that two vehicles may have passed through its area and roughly where they were at each sensed time. The planner develops a plan to form a track satisfying each goal: it sketches out its long-term activities (the order it will process data); it builds predictions about how long each of these activities will take and about their likely results; and it details a sequence of short-term actions to process the next data. The planner adds detailed actions to the plan incrementally because how (and whether) it processes subsequent data can depend on the results of earlier actions and on unexpected changes to its data. Thus, the node interleaves plan execution with plan generation, monitoring, and repair so that it can respond to unexpected situations. Node 1's plan to form track d'_1–d'_5, for example, eventually fails because the KSs that know about allowed vehicle movements do not give credibility to hypotheses involving such sharp zigzagging.

To coordinate nodes whose plans may change at any time, we could force nodes to pursue their plans no matter what happens: nodes that commit to plans are much more predictable [Fikes, 1982]. Unfortunately, they are also unresponsive to changing circumstances. But nodes with the flexibility to respond to unexpected situations risk disrupting coordination when they take unpredictable actions that can lead them into interfering with each other or ignoring important tasks because they falsely assume other nodes are doing them. What we need are mechanisms that allow nodes to exchange useful information about their views and to use whatever local information they have to find the best balance between predictability and responsiveness.

III. Implementation

To model each other and modify their local plans based on their perceived opportunities for cooperation, nodes must integrate and reason about large amounts of information. Implementing the concept of coordination through partial global plans is thus a difficult task, and this section describes important issues and algorithms we have identified.

A. Network Models

To locally plan actions that help overall network problem solving, a node needs a dynamic model of network activity (Figure 2). The node has *local plans* based on its own knowledge and local view (from the clusters of its abstraction hierarchy). For example, node 1 in Figure 1 will have two local plans, and the one to form the track d_4–d_{12} is outlined in Figure 2. The node's planner summarizes each of its local plans into a *node-plan* that specifies the goals of the plan, the long-term order of the planned activities, and an estimate of how long each activity will take (based on the time costs of the plan's past and current activities). The planner uses this information to generate the node-plan's *activity-map*: a series of activities, where each activity has a predicted starting time, ending time, and result track. The node-plan for node 1's local plan to form track d_4–d_{12}, for example, is outlined in Figure 2. Since node-plans have much less detailed information than local plans and do not point to local data structures, nodes can cheaply exchange them and can reason about each other's node-plans as they can their own. Thus, nodes can communicate node-plans to build up models of each other [Corkill, 1979, Georgeff, 1984, Konolige, 1984].

A node's planner scans the model of the network to recognize *partial-global-goals* (PGGs). A PGG is global in the sense that it may (but does not necessarily) encompass the local goals of several nodes, and is partial in that only part of the network might participate in it. The planner identifies PGGs by comparing local goals and using simplified knowledge (in this domain, about allowable vehicle movements) to determine whether they are part of a larger goal (tracking the same vehicle). For each PGG, the planner forms a *partial-global-plan* (PGP) that represents the concurrent activities and intentions of all of the

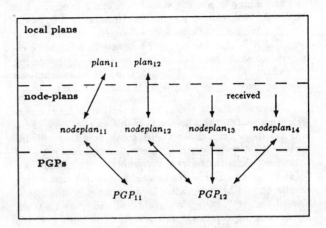

$plan_{12}$:
cluster information = $(cl_{11} \ldots cl_{1n})$
goal track = $((4\ region_4) \ldots (12\ region_{12}))$
goal vehicle types = $(1\ 2\ \ldots)$
long-term times order = $(4\ 5\ \ldots\ 12)$
long-term cost estimates = $((4\ c_4) \ldots (12\ c_{12}))$
past actions = $(4\ action_1 \ldots action_i)$
pending actions = $(4\ action_{i+1} \ldots action_n)$

$nodeplan_{12}$:
goal track = $((4\ region_4) \ldots (12\ region_{12}))$
goal vehicle types = $(1\ 2\ \ldots)$
long-term times order = $(4\ 5\ \ldots\ 12)$
long-term cost estimates = $((4\ c_4) \ldots (12\ c_{12}))$
activity-map = $((t_0, t_0 + c_4, d_4)$
$(t_0 + c_4, t_0 + c_4 + c_5, d_4$–$d_5) \ldots)$

PGP_{12}:
plan = $plan_{12}$
participants = $(plan_{12}\ plan_{21}\ plan_{31})$
goal track = $((1\ region_1) \ldots (15\ region_{15}))$
goal vehicle types = $(1\ 2\ \ldots)$
activity-map = $((t_0, t_0 + c_4, d_4)\ (t_0, t_0 + c_1, d_1) \ldots)$
s-c-graph = $(3\ d_1$–$d_3) + (1\ d_4$–$d_0) \rightarrow (1\ d_1$–$d_0) \ldots$
communication = $((3\ 1\ d_1$–$d_3)\ (1\ 2\ d_1$–$d_9) \ldots)$

The network model of node 1 from Figure 1 is graphically depicted along with simplified views of the data structures. A local plan has pointers to local data clusters, a goal track (a region for each sensed time) and vehicle types, the long-term order for processing data (data for sensed time i, then j, etc) and the estimated cost for each (time-cost pairs), and finally the specific KSs to process the next data. A node-plan has the local plan's goals and long-term information, and has an activity-map (each activity has a start-time, end-time, and result-track). A PGP points to participating plans, combines their goals, interleaves their node-plans' activity-maps, and has a solution-construction-graph and communication predictions (for example, node 3 forms d_1–d_3 and node 1 forms d_4–d_0 and node 1 combines them into d_1–d_0).

Figure 2: An Example of a Node's Network Model.

nodes that are working in parallel on different parts of the same problem (to potentially solve it faster). For example, the PGP to generate the overall track d_1–d_{15} (Figure 1) by combining the plans of nodes 1, 2, and 3 is outlined in Figure 2. The planner interleaves the participating node-plans' activity-maps to recognize the relative timing of the nodes' activities and to discover how activities might be re-ordered to avoid harmful interactions (such as performing redundant activities) and to promote helpful interactions (such as providing predictive information sooner).

Given a suitably ordered set of activities for the participating nodes, the planner uses this view of how nodes will act to develop expectations about how they will interact. It estimates when a node will complete a group of activities that together form a sharable result, and forms a *solution-construction-graph* that indicates how and where results should be integrated. For example, in the situation of Figure 1, node 3's track d_1–d_3 and node 1's track d_4–d_9 may be combined at node 1 to form track d_1–d_9 (Figure 2). The planner uses its network model to assign integration tasks to nodes with available computation resources or suitable expertise. Thus, while the activity-map provides details about how each node will form its own results, the solution-construction-graph provides a high-level view of how the nodes are pooling resources and working together. This view of node interactions helps nodes avoid wasting communication resources because they can better identify important communication actions (to send track d_1–d_3 from node 3 to node 1 as in Figure 2, for example).

To summarize, a network model has three types of information:

local plan: The representation of a plan maintained by a node that is pursuing the plan. Contains information about the plan's objective, the order of major plan steps, how long each is expected to take, and detailed actions (KSs) that have been taken or will be taken.

node-plan: The representation of a plan that nodes communicate about. Contains information about the plan's objective, the order of major plan steps, and how long each is expected to take. Details about short-term actions are not represented.

PGP: The representation of how several nodes are working toward a larger goal. Contains information about the larger goal, the major plan steps that are occurring concurrently, and how the partial solutions formed by the nodes should be integrated together.

A PGP can be formed for any number of nodes with compatible local goals. Initially, a node's PGPs correspond only to its local plans, but, as information from other nodes arrives, it builds larger, more encompassing PGPs. Because nodes build their network models asynchronously and over time, they may be incomplete or out-of-date and cooperating nodes may have inconsistent PGPs. The extent and quality of a node's network model and how it is formed depends on the *meta-level organization*: the communication topology, capacity, delay, and reliability; the

coordination responsibilities of different nodes; the credibility that a node has in coordination information from other nodes (which determines their authority relationships); and so on. The distributed problem solving network is therefore organized both in terms of problem solving responsibilities (the domain-level organization) [Corkill, 1983, Corkill and Lesser, 1983] and in terms of coordination responsibilities (the meta-level organization).

We assume in this paper that the meta-level organization is statically defined during network creation. A node sends its node-plans to those nodes specified in the organization, perhaps to a particular coordinator-node, or maybe to all other nodes so that they recognize PGPs individually (as in Figure 2 where node 1 receives node-plans from 2 and 3 and forms its own PGPs). When it coordinates other nodes, a node may send them PGPs to guide their actions, but two nodes with equal authority may also exchange PGPs to negotiate about (converge on) a consistent view of coordination. A node that receives a node-plan or PGP considers the sending node's credibility when deciding how (or whether) to incorporate the new information into its network model: it can follow a highly-rated PGP from a much trusted coordinator-node, but may disobey coordination requests if the credibility and ratings of its local information is superior. The meta-level organization therefore influences how nodes may converge on consistent views of network activity and how responsive they will be, allowing various levels of autocracy and democracy, obedience and insubordination.

Although they often convey similar information, node-plan and PGP messages serve different purposes. In some organizations, a node might not have authority to locally change a received PGP even if it believes the changes represent improvement. By sending its local view as a node-plan, it might persuade a node with more authority to change the PGP, or it could persuade other low-authority nodes that they should all change their PGPs together (in a kind of "grass-roots" movement). PGP messages say how nodes *are* working together, while node-plan messages provide context for deciding how nodes *might* cooperate. Finally, nodes could send only some of a PGP's information (leaving out the planned activities of some participants) so that recipient nodes have insufficient context to recognize and suggest improvements. This enforces consistent views and reduces computation at recipient nodes, since they blindly follow the PGP and cannot explore alternatives.

B. Group Activity

A PGP's activity-map interleaves the concurrent activities of the participating node-plans, and each activity has an estimation of when it begins, when it ends, what task (part of a track) it is working on, and what results (tracks) it will produce. The planner scans the activity-map to find activities that are more useful (such as activities that form important results to share) or less useful (such as activities that unnecessarily form redundant results). Each activity is rated based on attributes such as its expected time costs, its expected result quality, how it will be affected by preceding activities, and how it will affect later activities. The planner attempts to reorder activities to move more highly-rated ones earlier in the plan. For example, node 1 (Figure 1) has a plan to build track d_4–d_{12} and, since it locally has no reason to prefer certain activities over others, it chose (4 5 6 7 8 9 10 11 12) as the ordering (Figure 2). When the activities of nodes 2 and 3 are incorporated in the PGP, however, node 1's activities are no longer equally rated: because they provide node 2 with predictive information, the activities for generating tracks neighboring node 2 are more highly rated (for example, the partial track d_8–d_9), but because they may generate redundant results, the activities for times 4–6 and 10–12 have their ratings lowered. By rating activities in alternative orderings, the planner determines that node 1's activities should be reordered to (9 8 7 10 11 12 6 5 4).

To reduce planning overhead, the planner does not guarantee an optimal ordering (which would require a large search) but instead uses a less costly hill-climbing algorithm that generates a satisfactory ordering: it begins with the activity-map built from the node-plan activity-maps (which it expects each node to currently be following), and rates the activities. It then reorders the activities so that the most highly rated occur earlier, and then rates the activities in this new order. Because the ratings of activities depend on their relative ordering, reordering them may reduce ratings of some activities and raise ratings of others. The sum of the ratings before and after reordering are compared: if the original ordering has a higher total, then it is used; if the new order is better, then the process repeats until no better ordering can be found.

The planner uses the activity-map to form the solution-construction-graph. It first identifies the earliest times that different pieces of the overall solution will be generated and at what nodes, and then determines when and where they should be integrated into a single answer. For example, after reordering the activity-map as described above for the PGP to form track d_1–d_{15} (Figure 1), the planner makes a solution-construction-graph specifying that tracks d_1–d_6 from node 3 and d_7–d_{11} from node 1 should be combined at node 1, and the resulting track d_1–d_{11} should be combined at node 2 with that node's track d_{12}–d_{15}. Alternatively, in a slightly different network where node 4 has very good integration expertise (KSs), the solution-construction-graph has nodes 1, 2, and 3 send their tracks to 4 for integration. The planner builds the solution-construction-graph by: finding the pair of partial results that can be combined earliest (time both are at an integrating node plus an estimate of how long it will take, depending on its expertise, to combine them); adding the combination as a new partial result; and then repeating this process until a complete result is formed. This inexpensive, iterative algorithm generates a graph that is acceptable although possibly non-optimal.

The solution-construction-graph improves communication decisions since a node has a more global view of where results are needed than it has with a more local view [Durfee et al., 1985b, Durfee et al., 1987]. For example, it knows that track d_1–d_6 should be sent from node 3

to node 1. A node's planner can also make better local decisions by identifying whether it is or is not responsible for a particular result, and how much time it has to generate that result. In situations with multiple solutions, integration responsibilities for a solution are assigned to one node so that others can more quickly move on to other solutions. Also, since two partial results cannot be integrated until they are both at the integrating node, the planner may identify cases where the node has some time to spare: it predicts that n time-units are needed to form and send the result, but that the other result will not be ready for $n + i$ time-units. Our mechanisms allow the planner to work on important activities for other PGPs (perhaps generating predictive information) during the other i time-units, treating the $n + i$ time-units as a window in which the task to generate the result can be moved around [Vere, 1983].

C.   Planning Node Activities

The planner reasons about the concurrent actions of nodes and about their potential interactions to find the next problem solving action for the node to take, as shown in Figure 3. It first uses any received network information (node-plans and PGPs) to update the network model. It then finds the current-PGP: the PGP that specifies activities that the node should do at this time. The local plan that contributes to this PGP is updated and the next action is found. For example, if the PGP indicates that the local plan should develop data in a different order, the plan's long-term information is changed to reflect this and, if necessary, detailed short-term actions are found for the next data to process. When it is updated, the local plan may become inactive—it may not yet have data in the area where it is expected to work—so several PGPs may need to be tried before one with an active plan is chosen and node problem solving can continue (Figure 3, steps 2d–f). Finally, any highly-rated PGPs or node-plans that have been altered are sent to whatever other nodes should be informed (based on the meta-level organization). Sending only highly-rated information can reduce communication costs and the number of PGPs (combinations of node-plans), but may cause views to be inconsistent or important PGPs to be missed. A parameter decides how highly rated information must be to be sent. When more or less complete communication would improve planning, the experimenter (and in future implementations perhaps the node itself) may alter this parameter.

When finding the current-PGP, the planner first updates its set of local plans based on any new data from its sensors or other nodes (Figure 3, step 2a). The new data modifies the abstraction hierarchy, and the planner forms new plans for new potential solutions and modifies existing plans whose clustered information has changed. Node-plans are created for any new plans and the node-plans of modified plans are updated. The planner then updates the network model using new and updated node-plans either formed locally or received (Figure 3, step 2b). It updates the PGPs of any updated node-plans and uses new node-plans to either update existing PGPs (if com-

A node's planner will:

1. receive network information;
2. find the next problem solving action using network model:
   (a) update local abstract view with new data;
   (b) update network model, including PGPs, using changed local and received information (factoring in credibility based on source of information);
   (c) map through the PGPs whose local plans are active, for each:
      i. construct the activity-map, considering other PGPs;
      ii. find the best reordered activity-map for the PGP;
      iii. if permitted, update the PGP and its solution-construction-graph;
      iv. update the affected node-plans
   (d) find the current-PGP (this node's current activity);
   (e) find next action for node based on local plan of current-PGP;
   (f) if no next action (local plan inactive) then go to 2b (since local plans may have changed), else schedule the next action;
3. transmit any new and modified network information.

Figure 3: The Principal Planning Activities.

patible) or to generate new PGPs (if incompatible with all current PGPs). If any PGPs have been modified or created (as a result of changed node-plans or reception of credible PGPs), the planner then checks the set of PGPs, merging together any that are now compatible and separating any that are no longer compatible. For example, if the same vehicle passes through a node's area twice, then the node initially develops separate PGPs for the two potential tracks. If it later receives node-plans from other nodes indicating that its two potential tracks are connected, then it merges the PGPs into a single larger PGP.

Once the network model is updated, the planner proceeds to find the current-PGP. It first finds the PGPs to consider (leaving out PGPs that have already failed to generate useful actions because their local plans are inactive) and orders them. It also decides what nodes to plan for—usually just the current node, but if this node is also to coordinate others it should plan for them as well. The planner then steps through the PGPs from highest rated down (Figure 3, step 2c), updating their activity-maps and solution-construction-graphs, until all the desired nodes are planned for or no PGPs remain. For example, when the nodes it should plan for do not all participate in the same PGPs, the planner must update multiple PGPs until a current activity is found for each node.

When updating a PGP, the planner first generates a current activity-map by interleaving the activities of each of the participating plans (Figure 3, step 2ci). For the local plan, the planner uses the past and predicted steps straight from the plan data structure. For non-local plans, the planner can get the activities from two potential sources: from a received node-plan (if there is one) or from the

activity-map of the PGP (it may have been received from a node that had the node-plan). If the planner has information from both sources, it chooses between them using the information accompanying received node-plans and PGPs specifying how current and credible the model of the plan is. If the planner has neither source, it must have received the PGP (it could not have formed it locally without the node-plan) with the sending node intentionally holding back information so that this node could not generate its own (possibly better) activity-map but instead must blindly follow the activity-map supplied with the PGP.

If it forms one, the planner checks the activity-map against any PGPs that it has already planned for. A node that participates in this PGP may also be part of a previously formed PGP, and the activity-maps are compared to make sure the node is not expected to do two things at once. When there is a conflict, the node's activities in this (less highly-rated) PGP are moved to future, non-conflicting times. The planner then uses the hill-climbing algorithm previously described to reorder activities for better coordination (Figure 3, step 2cii). The sum of the activity ratings for the new activity-map is multiplied by the node's credibility in its own plans, and this value is compared with the value of the previous activity-map (if any).[1] If the value of the new activity-map is higher, the planner updates the PGP with the new activity-map (Figure 3, step 2ciii), forms the solution-construction-graph and communication expectations, and modifies its local plans and their node-plans based on the better activities (Figure 3, step 2civ). When the activity-map is improved but the credibility factors (authority relationships) do not allow the planner to change the PGP, the planner can transmit the node-plans that it believes should be modified: it assumes that if nodes with authority have the same view of these node-plans that it has, then those nodes will modify the PGP appropriately and the modified PGP will eventually be sent back to this node.

Once all of the PGPs have been updated and an action has been found for the node, the final step is to send out any important modified node-plans and PGPs, as described previously (Figure 3, step 3). To make problem solving decisions based on the best, most up-to-date view of network activities, a node invokes the entire series of activities—from modifying the network model, to developing PGP activity-maps, to sending out new information—each time it needs to choose an action to take. If the node wants to conserve computational resources, it can do these activities less often at the cost of possibly making poorer control decisions. Because nodes are asynchronously performing coordination activities and are interleaving these activities with problem solving, they must each balance the costs and benefits of these mechanisms.

---

[1] A PGP has a previous activity-map if it was received or previously formed locally, and its value is the sum of its activity ratings multiplied by the credibility of the node that generated it.

IV. Evaluation

To evaluate the planning mechanisms, we must consider their ability to improve coordination, their ability to permit cooperation in a variety of ways (depending on the organization), and their costs (computation and communication). We have implemented the mechanisms as described in the DVMT, and here we summarize some initial empirical findings. This discussion concentrates on how well the implementation meets the goals of improving coordination and allowing cooperation in a variety of styles, and only briefly addresses the costs of these mechanisms.

Using the situation in Figure 1 (which was constructed deliberately as a challenge to coordinate), we show how the new mechanisms improve network problem solving by considering three degrees of partial global planning: where no network information is exchanged (nodes have only local views); where network information is exchanged so that nodes can rate their plans based on global significance but *cannot* change local plans based on this view; and where nodes *can* change their local plans by reordering activities. In all the experiments, the domain-level organization lets nodes exchange hypotheses so any node can potentially form solutions. The first meta-level organization that we explore is broadcast—nodes broadcast their node-plans to each other (with a simulated communication delay) and individually form PGPs. Although all of the data is present at the start of problem solving, nodes can have inconsistent network models because their plans change over time (for example, when node 2 receives predictive information from node 1 it reduces the predicted time needs for processing its data). The results of the experiments are summarized in Table 1, experiments E1–E3. For each experiment we show the amount of time the network needed to find a solution (where each time unit corresponds to the execution of a KS) and the average plan-message traffic (node-plans and PGPs) in the network. The results show that the new mechanisms can substantially reduce the solution time at the cost of increasing communication (recall that a node currently transmits every highly-rated node-plan or PGP that it modifies without regard to the significance of the modification). We have found similar results in other problem situations.

A broadcast organization allows inconsistencies and uncoordinated behavior because a node's view of its own plans is more up-to-date than its view of other's plans. In one problem situation, for example, two nodes that had both planned to work on the same data assumed that the other would work there and changed their plans. The messages about the changed plans incurred communication delays, so time elapsed before the nodes recognized that the one of them involved in less highly-rated PGPs (as determined by their local models of network activity) should change its plan back again. In situations where their models are inconsistent, however, both or neither may change plans. A centralized meta-level organization can reduce such inconsistencies. In experiment E4, nodes 1-3 send node-plans to 4 which in turn sends PGP's back. Nodes 1–3 cannot locally modify the PGPs they get from 4, so that

Expt	Organization	Mechanisms	Time	AveMsgs
E1	broadcast	local only	139	0
E2	broadcast	PGPs, no reorder	46	3.4
E3	broadcast	all	27	4.6
E4	centralized	all	30	3.0
E5	ring	all	38	3.0

Legend	
Organization:	broadcast of node-plans, central coordinator, or node-plans passed around a ring
Mechanisms:	local only (no node-plan communication) PGP, no reorder (PGPs, no local changes) all (all mechanisms for forming PGPs)
Time:	Earliest time a solution was found (how many KSs each node ran)
AveMsgs:	Average number node-plan and PGP messages transmitted in the network at any time.

Table 1: Experiment Summary.

they are all following consistent (received) PGPs. This organization involves less communication than the broadcast but takes longer to respond to new situations (and to initially get multi-node PGPs to nodes 1–3) because of combined communication delays to and from node 4. It still performs fairly well because the nodes are following completely consistent views. This can be compared to a "ring" organization (experiment E5), where a node sends node-plans only to its clockwise neighbor. The ring organization also uses less communication than the broadcast, but performs worse than either of the other organizations. Delays in propagating network information around the ring cause nodes to have inconsistent views more often and for longer periods of time, impairing coordination.

Our experiments indicate, not surprisingly, that the quality of coordination depends substantially on how consistent the different nodes' network models are. Inconsistencies can have many causes such as communication delays and inaccurate estimates of when various pieces of the solution will be formed. When estimates are inaccurate, the communication and integration decisions may need to be modified and the changed plans communicated. So long as updated information is exchanged, nodes can in time recover from unexpected situations and once again coordinate their activities. The planner also can develop a more forgiving PGP by enlarging the duration estimates for activities, and thus providing some leeway in predicted interactions. The resulting PGP is less likely to need alteration, but also may have less crisp interactions between nodes. The balance between forming PGPs that anticipate incorrect predictions versus using communication to update PGPs depends on the communication resources and performance requirements.

Developing and maintaining PGPs involves computation and communication overhead. PGPs substantially reduced the number of KS executions needed to solve our complex experimental situations, but, for simpler cases where nodes have little uncertainty about how to coordinate, the new mechanisms may introduce unnecessary overhead. The tradeoffs in improving problem solving at the cost of increased planning overhead in a single node have been studied [Durfee and Lesser, 1986], but the evaluation becomes much more complex in a distributed system [Durfee *et al.*, 1985a] because of issues such as communication/computation tradeoffs, reliability, maintenance of consistent views, and assignment of planning responsibilities. For example, a broadcast is more costly than a centralized organization in both communication and computation (since each node forms similar PGPs) but can be much more responsive and reliable (since the network does not depend on a single coordinator).

Prescribing appropriate meta-level organizations and styles of cooperation for generic problem situations depends on the evaluation criteria considered, and is beyond the scope of this paper. What is important, however, is that our framework lets us explore different styles of cooperation using one set of mechanisms. We can have nodes pass around node-plans and plan for themselves, or send node-plans to a node that plans for everyone, in which case we can even force them to sit idle waiting for these PGPs by having them give no credibility to their locally developed PGPs. Or we could let nodes exchange PGPs so that they negotiate on a consistent global view by adopting the most highly-rated version of a PGP. Nodes can also use node-plans and PGPs to form contracts. A node with a particular task can generate a PGP activity-map that has the task being performed in the future at some remote nodes.[2] The PGP is sent to these nodes which locally develop node-plans representing these potential future tasks. These node-plans are modified and rerated to reflect the node's view of its own activities; for example, if it may form an activity-map for the node-plan indicating that the received tasks could not be performed until much later in the future. The nodes return these node-plans to the original node, which adopts the best one and follows it by sending task information (data) to the chosen node. In essence, one node requests bids for a cooperative plan and each of the others bids on how it expects it could cooperate. The node that likes the interaction most (or dislikes it least) is awarded the task. Moreover, because the returned node-plan conveys information about how the task fits into the bidding node's more global view, the originating node could use the node-plans it gets back to recognize that the task is unimportant and should not be awarded at all.

Depending on its relative credibility in received versus locally generated PGPs, a node could respond to an important local development by breaking its contract or disobeying a superior. The PGP-based framework for coordination permits different degrees of commitment for the various styles of cooperation. The nodes can be organized as predictable team-players or as locally responsive skeptics. In fact, a node with authority could elicit activity it desires from other nodes by misrepresenting itself or the network—changing its node-plans or PGPs based on some

local goal of how it wants the network to behave regardless of network goals. Our framework therefore not only allows nodes with common goals to work as a better team, but also lets nodes with competing goals satisfy their own goals by misrepresentation ("lying") and exerting authority ("threats") [Rosenschein and Genesereth, 1985].

V. Conclusion

A node in a distributed problem solving network must not only solve problems in its task domain but must also plan its activities to coordinate with others. However, planning is only important insofar as it improves domain problem solving: nodes should only plan as much or as little as they need to (or are able to) depending on the problem and network characteristics. The approach that we have described is therefore not strictly a distributed planning system because nodes may solve their domain problems without ever developing an overall network plan. Although our framework allows organizations where nodes can cooperatively develop and converge on a consistent distributed plan *before* domain problem solving begins, it emphasizes that planning usually occurs *during* problem solving and that nodes in an uncertain environment will build and modify their plans for network activity over time. When communication and computation resources are limited and when problem and network characteristics change rapidly, nodes simply may not be able to plan for optimal cooperation. Since the purpose of the network is to solve the domain problem, nodes need not cooperate optimally so long as they cooperate well enough to form acceptable solutions. What nodes need is the flexibility and local sophistication to use whatever information they have to decide how best to cooperate at a given time.

In this paper we introduced a new framework that uses partial global plans to promote many different styles of cooperation. Nodes build PGPs by exchanging short summaries of their local plans and recognizing when a group of nodes should work together. A node can hypothesize how the cooperating nodes could best interact and modify its local actions accordingly. We outlined important issues and algorithms in implementing these mechanisms, and showed experimentally how these mechanisms work.

Several avenues for further research remain. Nodes should be able to alter their meta-level organization: they need to exchange and reason about pertinent information to find a suitable style of cooperation for their current situation. Nodes also should use computation and communication resources effectively by selectively transmitting only plan information that will significantly impact network behavior and by selectively applying planning mechanisms to maximize the improvement in problem solving while minimizing the overhead costs. Finally, since nodes cooperate in so many different styles in this framework, we should try to develop some rules-of-thumb about how nodes should cooperate for generic problem situations.

---

[2]The node's planner thus not only reorders activities but also finds possible reassignments that move computational load from a bottleneck node to nodes that are not participating in highly-rated PGPs. Making such reassignments is a complex problem for which we as yet have only primitive mechanisms.

Although our mechanisms have been implemented in a specific problem domain, we believe that they are applicable to distributed problem solving systems in general. Our description has stressed the basic knowledge representations and reasoning that goes on, and though the decisions about how goals and activities interact and how they fit into this representation is domain dependent, the planning and communication algorithms are not. We expect to use these mechanisms for coordinating concurrently running KSs in a multiprocessor blackboard-based problem solver, and, through this paper, we hope to encourage their application in other distributed AI systems as well.

Acknowledgments

We would like to thank Reid Smith for many suggestions concerning the content and presentation of this paper.

References

[Cammarata et al., 1983] Stephanie Cammarata, David McArthur, and Randall Steeb. Strategies of cooperation in distributed problem solving. In *Proceedings of the Eighth International Joint Conference on Artificial Intelligence*, pages 767–770, August 1983.

[Corkill, 1979] Daniel D. Corkill. Hierarchical planning in a distributed environment. In *Proceedings of the Sixth International Joint Conference on Artificial Intelligence*, pages 168–175, August 1979.

[Corkill, 1983] Daniel David Corkill. *A Framework for Organizational Self-Design in Distributed Problem Solving Networks*. PhD thesis, University of Massachusetts, Amherst, Massachusetts 01003, February 1983. Available as Technical Report 82-33, Department of Computer and Information Science, University of Massachusetts, Amherst, Massachusetts 01003, December 1982.

[Corkill and Lesser, 1983] Daniel D. Corkill and Victor R. Lesser. The use of meta-level control for coordination in a distributed problem solving network. In *Proceedings of the Eighth International Joint Conference on Artificial Intelligence*, pages 748–756, August 1983.

[Davis and Smith, 1983] Randall Davis and Reid G. Smith. Negotiation as a metaphor for distributed problem solving. *Artificial Intelligence*, 20:63–109, 1983.

[Durfee and Lesser, 1986] Edmund H. Durfee and Victor R. Lesser. Incremental planning to control a blackboard-based problem solver. In *Proceedings of the Fifth National Conference on Artificial Intelligence*, pages 58–64, August 1986.

[Durfee and Lesser, 1987] Edmund H. Durfee and Victor R. Lesser. *Incremental planning to control a time-constrained, blackboard-based problem solver*. Technical Report 87-07, Department of Computer and Information Science, University of Massachusetts, Amherst, Massachusetts 01003, February 1987.

[Durfee et al., 1985a] Edmund H. Durfee, Victor R. Lesser, and Daniel D. Corkill. *Coherent Cooperation Among Communicating Problem Solvers*. Technical Report 85-15, Department of Computer and Information Science, University of Massachusetts, Amherst, Massachusetts 01003, April 1985. Also to appear in *IEEE Transactions on Computers*.

[Durfee et al., 1985b] Edmund H. Durfee, Victor R. Lesser, and Daniel D. Corkill. Increasing coherence in a distributed problem solving network. In *Proceedings of the Ninth International Joint Conference on Artificial Intelligence*, pages 1025–1030, August 1985.

[Durfee et al., 1987] Edmund H. Durfee, Victor R. Lesser, and Daniel D. Corkill. Cooperation through communication in a distributed problem solving network. In Michael N. Huhns, editor, *Distributed Artificial Intelligence*, Pitman, 1987. (In press. Also to appear as Chapter 7 in Scott P. Robertson, Wayne Zachary, and John Black, editors, *Cognition, Computing, and Cooperation: Collected works on cooperation in complex systems*, in press).

[Erman et al., 1980] Lee D. Erman, Frederick Hayes-Roth, Victor R. Lesser, and D. Raj Reddy. The Hearsay-II speech understanding system: integrating knowledge to resolve uncertainty. *Computing Surveys*, 12(2):213–253, June 1980.

[Fikes, 1982] R. E. Fikes. A commitment-based framework for describing informal cooperative work. *Cognitive Science*, 6:331–347, 1982.

[Georgeff, 1983] Michael Georgeff. Communication and interaction in multi-agent planning. In *Proceedings of the Eighth International Joint Conference on Artificial Intelligence*, pages 125–129, August 1983.

[Georgeff, 1984] Michael Georgeff. A theory of action for multiagent planning. In *Proceedings of the Fourth National Conference on Artificial Intelligence*, pages 121–125, August 1984.

[Konolige, 1984] Kurt Konolige. A deductive model of belief. In *Proceedings of the Eighth International Joint Conference on Artificial Intelligence*, pages 377–381, August 1984.

[Lesser and Corkill, 1981] Victor R. Lesser and Daniel D. Corkill. Functionally-accurate, cooperative distributed systems. *IEEE Transactions on Systems, Man, and Cybernetics*, SMC-11(1):81–96, January 1981.

[Lesser and Corkill, 1983] Victor R. Lesser and Daniel D. Corkill. The distributed vehicle monitoring testbed: a tool for investigating distributed problem solving networks. *AI Magazine*, 4(3):15–33, Fall 1983.

[Rosenschein and Genesereth, 1985] Jeffrey S. Rosenschein and Michael R. Genesereth. Deals among rational agents. In *Proceedings of the Ninth International Joint Conference on Artificial Intelligence*, pages 91–99, August 1985.

[Smith, 1980] Reid G. Smith. The contract-net protocol: high-level communication and control in a distributed problem solver. *IEEE Transactions on Computers*, C-29(12):1104–1113, December 1980.

[Steeb et al., 1986] Randall Steeb, Stephanie Cammarata, Sanjai Narain, Jeff Rothenberg, and William Giarla. *Cooperative Intelligence for Remotely Piloted Vehicle Fleet Control*. Technical Report R-3408-ARPA, Rand Corporation, October 1986.

[Vere, 1983] Steven A. Vere. Planning in time: windows and durations for activities and goals. *IEEE Transactions on Pattern Analysis and Machine Intelligence*, PAMI-5(3):246–267, May 1983.

4.3 Achieving Coherence by Resolving Disparities and Uncertainty

Conflict is endemic among agents that exist in dynamic worlds, and no realistic collection of agents can be expected to have precisely complete, consistent and compatible viewpoints at all times. Indeed, monolithic knowledge can be self-defeating, as authors of all three papers here point out. The synthesis of multiple prespectives and knowledge updating based on recurrent competition are key aspects of several of the papers presented here. Chapter 1, Section 6 also treats a number of mechanisms for resolution of disparities, some related to the ideas presented in this section.

Victor Lesser and Daniel Corkill make the distinction between conventional approaches to distributed system design and a new approach called *functionally accurate, cooperative systems* (FA/C systems) in their influential problem-raising paper. Conventional designs emphasize maintaining correctness of the distributed computation with consequent mechanisms and overhead for this purpose. By contrast, FA/C systems incorporate mechanisms that can deal with uncertainty and error as an integral part of the problem solving approach. FA/C systems consist of agents that work with, produce, and receive tentative data that may be incomplete, incorrect or inconsistent with the tentative data used by other agents. Agents can compute with this data, for example, by estimating values for missing data, and so on. Problem solving can also occur in the presence of both data uncertainty and control uncertainty — the discrepancy between local availability and local need for control information. Cooperation among agents is typically driven by the goal of eliminating errorful intermediate results to converge on a consistent solution. The functionally accurate, cooperative model is the framework used in the DVMT, and more details of mechanisms for conflict resolution in this system can be found in papers by Corkill, Durfee, Hudlicka, and Lesser in Chapter 4, Section 4.2, and Chapter 6.

William Kornfeld and Carl Hewitt propose a system design abstractly based upon the action of scientific communities, which they argue are highly parallel, redundant, pluralistic systems. The Ether system seeks to use a process of highly redundant conjecture and refutation. Processes also compete as well as cooperate. Many agents tackle the same or similar problems in parallel with different viewpoints, and results are broadcast to all interested agents. Some agents act mainly to criticize and refute proposals of others. Coherence in this system is a matter of both problem distribution and resource allocation, which is controlled by using *sponsors* to allocate resources. Kornfeld and Hewitt's ideas have influenced other systems, including the office work support system of Gerald Barber whose paper is included in Chapter 8.

In his continuing investigation into new techniques for *open systems* reasoning, Carl Hewitt gives a very clear and insightful discussion of the nature of office work as coping with conflicting, inconsistent and partial information. Organizations seek to generate sound, relevant and reliable information to support organizational decision making and action. According to Hewitt's model, organizational reasoning takes place within small coherent modules that he calls *microtheories*. These correspond to the viewpoints held by individuals or groups or departments in the organization (and in fact, even individuals may reason using multiple microtheories). In general microtheories will have some inconsistency with one another. Most office work will involve coping with these inconsistencies by collaboration, which involves negotiation among modules to deal with conflicts and inconsistencies between microtheories. Hewit sketches the beginnings of mechanisms for such conflict resolution and negotiation.

These three papers are primarily suggestive of a large collection of problems, rather than definitive approaches to their solution. Of the three, the FA/C concept of Lesser and Corkill has reached the most mature experimental development in the DVMT system. The investigation of reasoning under disparities among multiple agents is a deep and challenging area, deserving of wider research effort, and a review of these papers will suggest numerous avenues for approaching it.

Functionally Accurate, Cooperative Distributed Systems

VICTOR R. LESSER AND DANIEL D. CORKILL

Abstract—A new approach for structuring distributed processing systems, called functionally accurate, cooperative (FA/C), is proposed. The approach differs from conventional ones in its emphasis on handling distribution-caused uncertainty and errors as an integral part of the network problem-solving process. In this approach nodes cooperatively problem-solve by exchanging partial tentative results (at various levels of abstraction) within the context of common goals. The approach is especially suited to applications in which the data necessary to achieve a solution cannot be partitioned in such a way that a node can complete a task without seeing the intermediate state of task processing at other nodes. Much of the inspiration for the FA/C approach comes from the mechanisms used in knowledge-based artificial intelligence (AI) systems for resolving uncertainty caused by noisy input data and the use of approximate knowledge. The appropriateness of the FA/C approach is explored in three application domains: distributed interpretation, distributed network traffic-light control, and distributed planning. Additionally, the relationship between the approach and the structure of management organizations is developed. Finally, a number of current research directions necessary to more fully develop the FA/C approach are outlined. These research directions include distributed search, the integration of implicit and explicit forms of control, and distributed planning and organizational self-design.

I. INTRODUCTION

RECENT developments in microprocessor technology [55] and network technology [8], [33] have lowered the cost of processors and communication to a level where distributed processing is now practical. The potential advantages of a distributed processing approach over a centralized approach include [37]:

- *increased reliability and flexibility*—achieved through redundancy in communication paths and processing nodes and through the modularity of design (which permits incremental addition of new processing nodes and communication paths);
- *enhanced real-time response*—achieved through parallelism and through the placement of processing nodes near sensing devices and devices to be controlled;
- *lower communication costs*—achieved by abstracting (preprocessing) data for transmission (lowering communication bandwidth requirements) and by placing

processing nodes near the data (reducing the distance over which the data must be transmitted);

- *lower processing costs*—achieved through the use of cheaper less complex processors which can be mass produced and through load-sharing (allowing relatively idle processing nodes to handle some of the work of a busy processing node);
- *reduced software complexity*—achieved by decomposing the problem-solving task into subtasks, each more specialized than the overall task; the result of this decomposition is reduced software complexity at each processing node (which performs a small number of subtasks) as compared to software performing the complete task.

These potential advantages have yet to be exploited in a wide range of application areas. Only in the areas of process control [13], [30], [54] and distributed data bases [1], [45] have some of the promises of distributed processing been realized. Applications in these areas are characterized by task decompositions in which the data can be partitioned in such a way that each subtask can usually be performed *completely* by a single node—without the need for the node to see the intermediate states of processing at other nodes.

A number of additional applications which appear naturally suited to distributed implementation (such as sensor networks, automotive and air traffic control, power network grids, and tasks involving mobile robots) do not have the task decomposition characteristics of conventional distributed processing applications and therefore appear ill-suited to conventional approaches. In these applications the data necessary to achieve a solution *cannot* be partitioned in such a way that a node can complete a subtask without seeing the intermediate state of processing at other nodes.

An example of this type of application is distributed vehicle monitoring. Vehicle monitoring is the task of generating a dynamic area-wide map of vehicles moving through the monitored area. In one distributed version of this task [23], [34], [40], [58] processing nodes, with their associated acoustic sensors (of limited range and accuracy), are geographically distributed over the area to be monitored. Each processing node can communicate with other nearby nodes over a packet radio communication network [31]. Because acoustic sensors characteristically produce a significant amount of error, the purely localized processing of sensory

Manuscript received November 30, 1979; revised September 10, 1980. This work was supported in part by the National Science Foundation under Grant MCS78-04212, and in part by the Office of Naval Research under Grant N00014-79-C-0439. The views and conclusions contained in this document are the authors' and should not be interpreted as representing the official opinion or policy of the University of Massachusetts or any agency of the U.S. Government.

The authors are with the Computer and Information Science Department, University of Massachusetts, Amherst, MA 01003.

data would result in the "identification" of nonexistent vehicles, the missed detection of actual vehicles, and the incorrect location and identification of actual vehicles. In this application the amount of communication required to redistribute that raw sensory data necessary for correct localized processing would be significant.

An alternative approach for resolving these errors is for processing nodes to interact in a highly cooperative way, exchanging tentative partial results with one another. For example, each node's tentative vehicle identifications can be used to indicate to other nodes the areas in which vehicles are more likely to be found and the details (vehicle type, rough location, speed, etc.) of probable vehicles. In addition, consistencies between these tentative identifications serve to reinforce confidence in each node's identifications. Such cooperation is not only appropriate for vehicle identification, but it is also potentially useful in other stages of processing (identification of raw signals, groups of harmonically related signals, patterns of vehicles, etc.).

In order to perform this cooperative style of distributed processing, and thereby extend the range of applications to which distributed processing can be applied effectively, we have developed a new approach to distributed system design. We call this new approach *functionally accurate, cooperative* (FA/C). In the following section the FA/C approach is contrasted with conventional approaches to distributed system design. Section III discusses mechanisms used in knowledge-based artificial intelligence (AI) systems to resolve uncertainty and their appropriateness to the development of FA/C distributed systems. Section IV describes three preliminary investigations into the application of these knowledge-based AI techniques to FA/C distributed systems. Section V discusses a similar style of problem-solving exhibited by management organizations and illustrates how concepts from organizational theory may be used to analyze the effectiveness of FA/C distributed systems. Section VI describes current research directions toward an improved understanding of FA/C distributed systems.

II. FUNCTIONALLY ACCURATE, COOPERATIVE DISTRIBUTED SYSTEMS

Conventional approaches to distributed system design can be characterized by their emphasis on the maintenance of correctness in all aspects of the distributed computation. The distributed processing system is organized so that a processing node's local data base contains appropriate portions of the overall problem-solving data base needed by the node's algorithms [5], [45]. This type of approach suggests that a distributed system be viewed as a centralized system distributed over a network, with each piece (node) in the decomposition viewed as a part of the whole system.

In these conventional distributed systems a node rarely needs the assistance of another node in carrying out its problem-solving function. We call this type of distributed processing decomposition *completely accurate, nearly auton-*

omous (CA/NA), because each node's algorithms operate on complete and correct information ("completely accurate") and because each node usually has in its local data base the information it requires to complete its processing correctly ("nearly autonomous"). When such information is not locally available, a node requests another node to determine the required information, which is returned as a complete and correct result. In CA/NA distributed systems this form of node interaction is often implemented using asynchronous subroutine calls, in which one node is the master and the other is the slave.

The CA/NA approach, however, is not suitable for applications (such as the distributed vehicle monitoring example) in which algorithms and control structures cannot be replicated or partitioned effectively so as to match the natural distribution of data in the network. In this situation a CA/NA system is expensive to implement because of the high communication and synchronization costs required to guarantee completeness and consistency of the local data bases. We feel that the almost exclusive use of the CA/NA approach has restricted the types of applications which have been implemented in a distributed manner.[1]

There is an alternative and new approach to structuring distributed problem-solving systems which may be appropriate for applications in which the CA/NA approach is not suitable. In this new approach the distributed system is structured so that each node can perform useful processing using incomplete input data while simultaneously exchanging the intermediate results of its processing with other nodes to construct cooperatively a complete solution. The hope is that the amount of communication required to exchange these results is much less than the communication of raw data and processing results which would be required using the CA/NA approach.

One way to permit a node to perform useful processing on incomplete data is to loosen the requirement that it always produce a complete and correct result. Instead, a node produces tentative results which may be incomplete, incorrect, or inconsistent with the tentative results produced by other nodes. For example, a node may produce a set of alternative partial results based on reasonable expectations of what the missing data might be. This type of node processing requires a distributed problem-solving structure which produces acceptable answers in the face of incorrect and inconsistent intermediate results. We call a system with this problem-solving structure *functionally accurate* (FA) because it exhibits acceptable system input/output behavior but is distinct from *completely accurate* problem-solving structures, in which all intermediate results shared among subtasks are required to be correct and consistent.

In an FA problem-solving structure a node not only has to perform useful processing with incomplete input data, but also with the possibly incomplete, incorrect, and incon-

---

[1] When viewed from the perspective of the routing task alone, some algorithms used to determine message paths in a communication network work with incomplete and inconsistent views of the network [22], [61].

sistent tentative results received from other nodes. This leads to a style of problem-solving in which nodes cooperate to eliminate errorful intermediate results and to converge to a complete and consistent solution. One way this can be accomplished is through an *iterative coroutine* type of node interaction, in which nodes' tentative partial results are iteratively revised and extended through interaction with other nodes. This type of node interaction suggests that such a distributed system be viewed as a *cooperative* network of interrelated tasks [37]. Therefore, we call such FA systems *functionally accurate* and *cooperative* (FA/C).

The FA/C style of processing can be characterized as problem-solving in the presence of *uncertainty*. A node may be uncertain as to what input data it is missing, the missing values of the data, and the correctness, completeness, and consistency of the results of its processing and of the processing results received from other nodes. In order to resolve these *data uncertainties* a node must be able to

1) detect inconsistencies between its tentative partial results and those received from other nodes;
2) integrate into its local data base those portions of other nodes' results which are consistent with its results;
3) use the newly integrated results to make up for its missing input data so that its tentative partial results can be revised and extended.

Because consistency checking is such an important part of the FA/C approach, it is natural to think of dealing with distribution-caused uncertainty and errors as an *integral part* of the network problem-solving process. In fact, additional mechanisms required to handle hardware, communication, and processing errors may be unnecessary with the FA/C approach, since uncertainty resolving mechanisms are already a part of the distributed system's problem-solving structure [4], [17], [38].

In FA/C distributed systems it may be difficult to determine which alternative tasks are globally the most beneficial to perform without extensive internode communication. This *control uncertainty* is due to differences between the natural distribution of control information among the nodes in the network and the distribution of where the control decisions are made. The existence of data uncertainty (discussed above) and uncertainty as to whether information transmitted by a node is correctly received[2] further exacerbates this difficulty.

One way to allow the distributed system to make control decisions without complete control information is to have node activity be *self-directed*. Each node uses its local estimate of the state of network problem-solving to control its processing (i.e., what new information to generate) and its transmissions to other nodes [38]. The degree of self-

directed activity in an FA/C system is potentially quite large because a node is able to choose a processing direction for which all the necessary data may not be available or consistent with other nodes. For instance, if a node does not receive an appropriate partial result in a given amount of time, it has the option to continue processing, utilizing whatever data are available at that time, or to choose some other processing direction which appears to be more beneficial. This flexibility in node processing allows node interactions to be *asynchronous* and permits significant *decoupling* of node activity.

The self-directed control decisions made by each node may lead to unnecessary, redundant, or incorrect processing. The hope is that the system still produces acceptable answers (within allowable time constraints) and that the amount of additional communication resulting from incorrect local control decisions is less than the additional communication required to provide complete control information. This hope is not unreasonable, given that the additional data uncertainty caused by incorrect local control decisions may be resolvable by the same mechanisms used to resolve data uncertainties caused by incomplete local data bases. Self-directed control has the added benefit of increased system robustness in the face of communication and node failure and increased system responsiveness to unexpected events. Based on this form of node activity it is more appropriate to view an FA/C distributed system as being *synthesized* from individual local systems operating at each node as opposed to the decomposition viewpoint described above that is normally taken of a CA/NA system.

By focusing only on CA/NA and FA/C distributed systems we do not want to suggest that completely accurate, cooperative (CA/C) and functionally accurate, nearly autonomous (FA/NA) systems do not exist. In fact, most systems should be characterized somewhere between these four extremes. Where there exists uncertainty as to the data in the system, the use of a functionally accurate (FA) over a completely accurate (CA) approach seems appropriate (due to the FA approach's tolerance of data uncertainty). Likewise, where there exists uncertainty as to what nodes should be doing and what information they should exchange, the use of a cooperative (C) over a nearly autonomous (NA) approach seems appropriate (due to the additional processing flexibility provided by the C approach).

We believe the reason most distributed systems appear to be basically either CA/NA or FA/C is that data uncertainty and control uncertainty tend to go hand in hand. The presence of data uncertainty makes it difficult to determine the appropriate interaction patterns among nodes, and the presence of control uncertainty leads to increased incompleteness, inconsistency, and error in processing results. When these uncertainties are present the use of the FA/C approach is appropriate. Similarly, when there is little uncertainty about the completeness and consistency of data and task processing, there also tends to be little uncertainty as to the needed interactions among nodes. In this situation the more structured (and efficient) CA/NA approach is appropriate.

---

[2] In some distributed communication networks the usable capacity of the communications channel is significantly degraded if the correct reception of all messages needs to be verified. Therefore, systems that can function effectively without the acknowledgment of messages may be advantageous.

In the next section we show that the FA/C approach is well-suited to problems which can be represented as a *search process* requiring multiple (localized) partial decisions to arrive at a solution. These decisions should not be tightly ordered, but each decision should have some consistency relationship with other decisions. The existence of a number of alternative paths to an acceptable solution and a problem representation involving multiple levels of abstraction also facilitate the FA/C approach. AI researchers have been investigating problems with similar representation characteristics. Therefore it is not unreasonable that methodologies developed for these AI problems may be helpful in the development of FA/C distributed techniques. We now introduce this relationship.

III. KNOWLEDGE-BASED AI AND FUNCTIONALLY ACCURATE, COOPERATIVE DISTRIBUTED SYSTEMS

We feel that the key to the design of FA/C distributed systems is to incorporate mechanisms which can deal with uncertainty and error as an integral part of their problem-solving approach. Knowledge-based interpretation systems such as Hearsay-II [15], [16] and MSYS [3] are examples of systems that use algorithmic structures which can resolve uncertainty and error in this way. Problem-solving in these systems involves the examination of many alternative partial solutions in order to construct a complete and consistent overall solution. This style of problem-solving is required because of the uncertainty (incompleteness and noise) in input data and the use of incomplete, approximate, and inconsistent knowledge in these systems.

The exploration of alternative partial solutions takes the form of a search process in which a solution is constructed through the incremental piecing together of mutually constraining or reinforcing partial solutions.[3] These partial solutions arise both from the application of diverse knowledge to the same aspects of the problem and from the application of the same knowledge to diverse aspects of the problem. If sufficient constraints are available during this search process, incorrect partial solutions will naturally die out because it will not be possible to piece them together into more encompassing partial solutions. In this way, uncertainty is resolved as an integral part of the problem-solving process.

In many knowledge-based systems the number of possible partial solutions is large. In general, the more uncertainty that exists, the larger the number of alternatives that must be explored. If there exists a large amount of uncertainty in input data and knowledge, a significant amount of search can be required. Therefore, it is important to focus quickly on information which constrains the search space. Hence problem-solving in these systems is often asynchronous and opportunistic: there is no *a priori* order for decisionmaking, and decisions, if they look promising, are tentatively made with incomplete information and later reevaluated in light of new information. This type of

problem-solving, combined with diverse and overlapping sources of knowledge, allows a solution to be derived in many different ways (i.e., different ordering sequences of incrementally constructed partial solutions and possibly different partial solutions).

Another focusing technique used in some knowledge-based systems is to structure the search space into a loose hierarchy of increasingly more abstract representations of the problem. Using this structure a high-level partial solution developed bottom-up in an opportunistic way for one aspect of the problem can be used to constrain, in a top-down manner, the search for solutions to other aspects of the problem.

To illustrate these ideas, we briefly describe two knowledge-based systems, Hearsay-II [15] and MSYS [3], that exhibit this type of problem-solving. While Hearsay-II and MSYS were developed for speech understanding and vision understanding, respectively, their basic structures have general applicability and have been applied to such tasks as multisensor interpretation [44], protein-crystallographic analysis [14], and cryptography [46].

In the Hearsay-II speech understanding system, the understanding of spoken utterances is accomplished by combining partial solutions derived from acoustic, phonetic, syllabic, lexical, syntactic, and semantic knowledge applied to different portions of the utterance. Each area of knowledge is encapsulated in an independent module (*knowledge source*). The interaction of knowledge sources is based on an iterative data-directed form of the hypothesize-and-test paradigm. In this paradigm an iteration involves the creation of a hypothesis, which is one possible interpretation of some part of the data, followed by tests of the plausibility of the hypothesis. During both hypothesis creation and testing, knowledge sources use *a priori* knowledge about the problem and previously generated hypotheses to form a context for applying their knowledge. When a knowledge source creates a hypothesis from previously created hypotheses, the knowledge source extends the existing (partial) interpretation, thereby reducing the uncertainty of the overall interpretation. Processing terminates when a consistent hypothesis is generated which satisfies the requirements of a complete solution.

In the MSYS vision understanding system, each knowledge source processes a portion of the data in terms of its own limited knowledge. Each knowledge source attempts to explain what object(s) could potentially occur in a specific part of a segmented image.

> The consensus is achieved by a network of processes (representing independent knowledge sources) that communicate via shared global variables. Each process attempts to explain a fragment of the data (a region or a few regions in a segmented scene) in terms of its own limited knowledge. The confidence of an explanation is communicated to other processes attempting to explain overlapping fragments, and may cause them to reevaluate their own hypotheses. The confidence adjustment cycle continues until equilibrium is achieved [3, p. 3].

When this equilibrium is achieved, a coherent set of local views has been constructed. The MSYS problem-solving

---

[3]Similar uses of the aggregation of partial solutions arise in systems using the locus model [51], relaxation [50], [63], and the cooperating experts [2], [27], [36] paradigms.

technique is an example of a more general problem-solving paradigm, called *iterative refinement*, that is contained in different forms in many types of problem-solving systems [4], [50], [63], [64].

We feel that knowledge-based AI approaches to problem-solving provide a basis for the development of design methodologies for FA/C distributed systems. The mechanisms used in these problem-solving systems to resolve error from incorrect and incomplete data and knowledge can also be used to structure distributed algorithms so that they work effectively with incomplete and inconsistent local data bases. We next examine these mechanisms and their implications for FA/C distributed systems (mechanism/implication).

Asynchronous Nature of Information Gathering/Reduced Need for Synchronization: Problem-solving is viewed as an incremental, opportunistic, and asynchronous process. In this style of problem-solving a node does not have an *a priori* order for processing information and can exploit incomplete local information. Thus the processing order within nodes and the transmission of information among nodes do not need to be synchronized.

Use of Abstract Information/Reduced Internode Communication Bandwidth Requirements: The ability to use abstract information permits nodes to cooperate using messages which provide a high-level view of the system's processing without the need for detailed low-level data. This reduces the internode communication bandwidth needed for effective cooperation.

Resolution of Uncertainty Through Incremental Aggregation/Automatic Error Resolution: Uncertainty is implicitly resolved when partial results are aggregated and compared with alternative partial solutions. This incremental method of problem-solving allows a distributed system to detect and reduce the impact of incorrect decisions caused by incomplete and inconsistent local data bases and by hardware malfunction.

Problem-Solving as a Search Process/Internode Parallelism: Because many alternative partial solutions need to be examined, parallel search by different nodes is possible. Furthermore, the additional uncertainty caused by incomplete and inconsistent local data bases can be traded-off against more search. To the degree that this extra search can be performed in parallel, without proportionally more internode interaction, the communication bandwidth can be lowered without significant degradation in network processing time.

Multiple Paths to Solution/Self-Correcting Behavior: Because there are many paths to a solution, it is possible to leave uncorrected errors that would be considered fatal in a conventional distributed system. In addition, system reliability can be improved (at the cost of additional processing and internode communication) without modifying the basic problem-solving structure. This variability, which is achieved through the appropriate selection and focusing of local node activity, allows consideration of additional and/or redundant paths to a solution.

Knowledge-based systems use a number of additional mechanisms to implement uncertainty resolution. These mechanisms are also important in an FA/C distributed system and include the following.

1) An integrated representation of alternative partial solutions and the coordination of partial solutions among different problem representation levels permit the quick isolation of contradictory information.

2) Data-directed control structures allow processing to be sensitive to current relationships between alternative partial solutions and to new information.

3) Focus of attention strategies permits the dynamic allocation of resources among competing tasks through the evaluation of the importance of particular types of information to the problem-solving process.

4) Generator control structures (which incrementally generate credibility-ordered alternative hypotheses) reduce the possibility of combinatorial explosion during search.

5) Modular control structures (in which knowledge is structured into independent and anonymous processing modules) allow the dynamic routing of information to appropriate processing modules.

While AI paradigms provide techniques for resolving uncertainty, they have not dealt with all of the types of uncertainty that occur in a completely distributed system. Centralized global knowledge or global control has been used in these AI systems to coordinate various system modules. For example, the Hearsay-II paradigm relies on a centralized global data base (called the "blackboard") for the integration of local views generated by independent knowledge source modules, and for communication of these views to other knowledge sources. Scheduling is also centralized, based on the current hypotheses on the blackboard and a global agenda mechanism. Iterative refinement relies on either synchronization (lock-step iteration) or an explicit ordering relationship between modules in order to speed up or (in restricted cases) guarantee convergence. In addition, iterative refinement does not guarantee a consistent global solution, only a set of consistent local solutions.

It is important to reiterate, however, that even though the current formulations of these AI paradigms are not totally distributed, their ability to function with incomplete and incorrect knowledge makes them adaptable to distributed situations in which only partial and potentially inconsistent views of nonlocal information are available. The ease of this adaptability is shown in the next section in which the Hearsay-II architecture is applied to interpreting, in a distributed manner, data originating from spatially separated sensors, and the iterative refinement paradigm is applied to distributed network traffic-light control.

Other researchers have investigated different ideas for structuring unconventional distributed processing applications. The contract-net model for distributed processing [58], [59] provides mechanisms for decentralized task allocation in an uncertain environment. Even though this model takes a CA/NA view of the sharing of results among tasks, we feel that the contract mechanism they have developed may be useful in FA/C distributed systems to provide explicit high-level decentralized coordination among the self-directed nodes to ensure greater coherence in system-wide activity.

We also agree with Sacerdoti's suggestion [53] that natural language communication may provide a fruitful source of ideas for distributed interaction protocols which minimize communication. We are especially interested in the work on a goal-oriented model of human dialogue that is based on the concepts of dialogue games [43] and speech acts [9], and on model-based understanding (plan recognition) which is becoming an important part of natural language comprehension systems [7], [24], [28].

There is also an emerging body of literature on decentralized control theory [35], [62] that may eventually be relevant to the development of complex FA/C distributed systems. However, current work has mainly focused on distributed control algorithms that have a CA/NA character. This emphasis has resulted in distributed control algorithms that generally require some form of high-level control to sequentialize and order the aggregation of node results. Additionally, these algorithms are restricted to decompositions in which the results of a node's decisions affect the decisions of other nodes in the network in only highly constrained ways. Due to these characteristics, these algorithms need further development to apply to FA/C distributed systems.

Based on the initial inspiration of knowledge-based AI systems, we have developed a number of prototype FA/C systems. In the next section we discuss the design of these systems, the lessons we have learned about some of the key design issues in building FA/C systems, and the relevance of knowledge-based AI systems to these issues.

IV. Experiments in Functionally Accurate, Cooperative Distributed Processing

There have been two major thrusts to our research: to empirically evaluate the basic viability of the FA/C model of a distributed problem-solving system and to understand the strengths and weaknesses of knowledge-based AI mechanisms as a basis for FA/C distributed systems. We have pursued these objectives by modifying a number of the uncertainty resolving techniques developed for knowledge-based AI systems for use in FA/C distributed problem-solving systems:

1) incremental hypothesize-and-test in the style of Hearsay-II for use in distributed interpretation systems;
2) iterative refinement (successive approximation, relaxation) for use in distributed network traffic-light control;
3) partially ordered hierarchial planning for use in distributed planning systems.

We have been evaluating the effectiveness of the resulting FA/C system in each of these tasks.

A. An Experiment in Distributed Interpretation

The Hearsay-II architecture appears to be a good model for an FA/C system because it incorporates mechanisms for dealing with uncertainty and error as an integral part of the problem-solving approach. Further, the processing can be partitioned or replicated naturally among network nodes because it is already decomposed into independent and self-directed modules called *knowledge sources* (KS's) which interact anonymously and are limited in the scope of the data they need and produce. It was also our hypothesis that the control and data structures of Hearsay-II could be distributed effectively because there were already existing mechanisms within its problem-solving structure for resolving uncertainty caused by incomplete or incorrect input data and KS processing.

In order to test out these hypotheses we have been exploring the Hearsay-II architecture in distributed interpretation applications similar to the vehicle monitoring example (discussed in Section I). In these applications each processing node can be mobile, has a set of (possibly nonuniform) sensing devices, and interacts with nearby processors through a packet-radio communication network. Nodes communicate among themselves to generate a consistent interpretation of "what is happening" in the sensed environment.

Our approach to developing a distributed interpretation architecture based on the Hearsay-II model was to organize the network into nodes operating on partial and possibly inconsistent views of the current interpretation and system state. This has led to a distributed interpretation architecture structured as a network of Hearsay-II systems, in which each node in the network is an *architecturally complete* Hearsay-II system. "Architecturally complete" means that each node could function as a complete Hearsay-II system if it were given all of the sensory data and the required KS's. However, due to the distribution of sensory data and limited internode communication, each node has a limited view of the complete problem-solving data base and, in effect, a limited set of KS's. Within this basic framework we have introduced the following additional mechanisms to support effective internode cooperation in a dynamic environment without high communication bandwidth.

1) To limit internode communication, an *incremental transmission* mechanism (with processing at each step) has been developed in which only a limited subset of a node's information is transmitted to only a limited subset of nodes. A node acts as a *generator* which transmits only a few of the most credible pieces of information and which can subsequently respond to a lack of problem-solving progress by producing alternative information.
2) To increase network reliability, a knowledge-based mechanism called *murmuring* has been proposed. Here a node retransmits high-impact information if, during a specified time interval, it neither receives nor generates high-impact information. Murmuring can be used

to correct for lost communications due to intermittent channel or node failures and to bring new or moving nodes up to date.

3) To guarantee an appropriate communication connectivity among nodes, a decentralized mechanism for constructing a communication network has been developed. Using this mechanism, which relies on descriptions of the input/output (I/O) characteristics of each node, nodes act as store-and-forward message processors to provide additional connectivity. A similar mechanism can be used for the dynamic allocation of processing tasks among nodes.

4) To provide more sensitive implicit internode control while still retaining decentralization, each node may explicitly transmit its local control information (meta-information). Nodes can thus more directly determine the state of processing in other nodes.

Experiments were performed to determine how the problem-solving behavior of such a network of Hearsay-II systems compares to a centralized system. The aspects of behavior studied include the accuracy of the interpretation, time required, amount of internode communication, and robustness in the face of communication errors. These experiments were simulations only in part, since they used an actual interpretation system analyzing real data; i.e., the Hearsay-II speech understanding system [15].

Our goal was not to prove that one should design a distributed speech understanding system, but rather to point out some of the issues involved in designing a distributed interpretation system dealing with incomplete and inconsistent local data. We used the Hearsay-II speech understanding system because it has a structure that we felt was appropriate, and because it is a large knowledge-based interpretation system to which we had access.

In these experiments we modeled a spatial distribution of sensory data by having each node of the distributed speech understanding network sample one part (time-contiguous segment) of the speech signal. The nodes in the network exchanged only high-level intermediate results. These results consisted of hypotheses (and their associated belief values) about which phrases might have occurred in the utterance under interpretation. The control decisions about which KS to execute and what hypotheses to transmit to other nodes were made locally by each node. These local control decisions were based only on the node's local processing history and the intermediate results received from other nodes.

These network simulation experiments have shown that the Hearsay-II speech understanding system, with only minor changes involving the addition of some of the mechanisms described above, performs well as a cooperative distributed network even though each node has a limited view of the input data and exchanges only high-level partial results with other nodes. In an experiment with a three-node system, effective cooperation was achieved among the nodes with only 44 percent of the locally generated high-level hypotheses transmitted. This repre-

sents 77 percent of the number of high-level hypotheses created in the centralized runs. No low-level hypotheses nor raw speech data were exchanged. The three-node experiments showed an overall speedup of 60 percent over the centralized version.

In order to assess the robustness of the network system with respect to communication errors, experiments were run in which messages received by a node were randomly discarded with a specified probability. This served to model communication systems with good error detection but poor correction capabilities (such as a packet radio). Selection at the receiving end allowed for cases in which a broadcast message is received successfully by some nodes but not others.

In these experiments system performance degraded gracefully with as much as 50 percent of the messages lost. The system in many of these cases corrected for lost messages by either deriving the missing information in an alternative way or by constructing the solution in a different fashion. In summary, the system's performance with a faulty communication channel lends credence to our belief that by making uncertainty-resolving mechanisms an integral part of network problem-solving, the distributed system may be able to deal automatically with types of errors that were not anticipated during the initial design of the system. It also indicates that a trade-off can be established between the amount of processing and the reliability of communication.

These experimental results support our general model of FA/C distributed system design. They also indicate that the Hearsay-II architecture is a good one to use as a basis for this approach. A complete discussion of this work is contained in [38].

B. Distributed Network Traffic-Light Control

A second study concentrated on investigating the suitability of iterative refinement (IR) as the basis for an FA/C distributed approach to automotive traffic-light control. In our version of this task a processor, located at each intersection, decides the setting for the traffic lights at its intersection. In order to make these decisions, each processor uses data from sensors that measure the traffic flow entering the intersection. Processors can also directly communicate with processors at neighboring intersections.

A number of test programs were developed which simulate distributed iterative refinement algorithms for traffic control in which the knowledge applied at each node (intersection) is similar to that used in a standard centralized traffic control system called SIGOP-II [41]. This traffic control algorithm was chosen because it employs a serial version of the method of successive approximations and permits an easy spatial decomposition for parallel processing. Two classes of IR algorithms were studied: single-label IR (successive approximation) and multilabel IR (relaxation). In single-label IR each node considers only one possible setting (label) for its traffic lights during each decision iteration. This is in contrast to the multilabel IR, where all possible traffic-light settings (labels) are considered simultaneously during each iteration. Parallel successive approximation has been explored in previous work on asynchronous iterative methods [4], but not in applications involving nonlinear, discontinuous, and nonconvex cost functions. Parallel relaxation has been explored in previous work in image processing [25], [64], but not in distributed domains which have complex compatibility relationships between nodes and significant interactions between widely separated nodes in the network. Distributed network traffic-light control has all of these characteristics.

Experiments with these simulations on arterial traffic networks show that good, but not optimal, solutions can be generated [6]. The major difficulties with the single-label IR approach have been the need for significant synchronization, environmental updating,[4] coordination techniques to prevent oscillation of the algorithms, and the inability to guarantee convergence to reasonable solutions. The major difficulties with the multilabel IR approach have been the large number of labels (i.e., the size of the search space) needed for the technique, and the inability of nonlocal evidence to raise the rating of a key alternative due to *premature* reduction of the alternative's rating on the basis of nearby evidence.

In general we have found it difficult to reproduce the performance of the sequential SIGOP-II version without significant internode communication and synchronization. These problems are directly attributable to changes in the centralized SIGOP-II control structure caused by the introduction of a distributed control structure. In the centralized version a global node ordering for the refinements is precomputed using a maximal spanning tree based on the traffic volume at each node. We have found through numerous experiments that this ordering is essential in reducing the effects of nonneighboring interactions among nodes. A more detailed discussion of this research is contained in [6].

It appears that the power of the IR approach is limited because a node utilizes no global state information other than the traffic flow structures indicated by the node's immediate neighbors' traffic-light settings. Thus the amount and type of information used by a node to make decisions is severely limited. A single-label IR algorithm, for example, repeatedly makes a single decision using only information available locally or from its immediate neighbors. It does not consider alternatives or utilize a history of previous decisions. Although the multilabel IR algorithms do consider alternatives, they still do not utilize a history of previous decisions.

---

[4]Nonneighboring interactions among traffic-light settings are transmitted through an *environment*, the traffic flow structure, which is represented by auxiliary state variables in a formal description of the problem. This modeling permits a natural spatial decomposition of the problem involving direct interactions between neighboring signal controllers only. Unfortunately, environmental updating is often necessary because a change in control at one node often has nonlocal environmental effects which must be computed before searches by other nodes can be accurately performed.

Current research is aimed at introducing, in a distributed way, additional coordination between nodes to eliminate these problems. We are examining such techniques as multilevel relaxation [63] and distributed versions of the maximal spanning tree heuristics. In addition, we are looking into game theory [20], [47], [48] for new ideas. It is possible to view the distributed processors (signal controllers) solving the network traffic-light control problem as players of a game. The traffic-light control problem, in game theoretic terms, is an *n*-person nonzero-sum game. Already we have found that a game theory perspective of the problem leads to the use of similar coordination techniques that were utilized in our previous experiments with parallel single-label IR to control oscillation.

It is hoped that additional local processing might in some way substitute for explicit coordination between nodes. For example, in SIGOP-II the local solution at a node is a single label representing the hypothesized traffic-light setting for the node's intersection. Maintaining a history of the hypothesized labels at nodes may make it possible to eliminate some of the explicit nonlocal coordination. Similarly, introducing labels which represent not only a node's intersection setting, but also the settings of neighboring intersections (nonlocal partial solution), may also eliminate some explicit nonlocal coordination.

C. Distributed Planning

Experience with the two distributed interpretation applications has led us to understand that a distributed focus of attention is a crucial aspect of all FA/C distributed systems. Distributed focus of attention involves the dynamic allocation of processing power, memory, data, and communication resources within the distributed system. Focus of attention is a type of planning which is directed at a system's immediate internal processing. Thus we are investigating issues in a distributed focus of attention by working on the larger issue of distributed planning.

An initial investigation of distributed planning was made using Sacerdoti's NOAH planning system [52]. NOAH was selected as a suitable candidate for distribution for several reasons.

1) In NOAH, the determination of planned actions (plan development) is separate from the detection and elimination of interactions between the planned actions (plan criticism). This separation allows plan development to be performed locally, prior to the necessarily nonlocal analysis of interactions between actions planned by separate nodes.

2) Plans in NOAH are both partially ordered and hierarchical. The partial ordering of actions in NOAH eliminates the need to make action sequencing decisions until there exists a reason to make the decision. NOAH's hierarchical planning process, in which a high-level plan is developed before proceeding to increasing levels of detail, can help to generate a plan with less search than would be required if all details were considered from the outset. These techniques for reducing the combinatorial growth of planning also potentially lower the amount of interplanner communication required in a distributed setting.

3) Because the actions planned by NOAH remain partially ordered until increased sequencing is required, the plans are well-suited for parallel distributed execution without the need for additional processing to detect potential parallelism.

To complete the distribution of NOAH, its *world model* (the planner's simulation of the effects of planned actions on the environment) and plan criticism mechanisms had to be distributed. Each planner (node) is provided with a consistent initial world model which has enough detail to perform local plan development. As this world model is changed during local planning, the changes are communicated to other relevant planning nodes. When a planner receives world model changes from other nodes, it revises its own world model and determines whether any of its locally planned actions invalidate the received world model changes. If they do, an attempt is made to sequence its planned actions with the planned actions of the other node (i.e., to establish a timing relationship between the actions) so that the actions no longer interfere with each other. A set of interplanner protocols have been developed which accomplish this ordering and detect situations where a suitable ordering cannot be established.

Two important ideas were identified during this research. The first idea is the relationship between planned actions and the *resources* required to perform them. Actions interact through conflicts in resource allocation: actions may require the temporary use of particular resources (i.e., the resources are used during the action) or permanent use (the resources are required *in* the resulting world state itself). Actions may also free up resources that were previously in use. In a simple world of blocks lying on a table-top, the tops of blocks and the tabletop would be the modeled resources. A stacking action can result in all three types of resource changes. For example, if block A is moved from the top of block B to the top of block C, the top of A must be clear throughout the action (no blocks can be on top of A), the top of B is made clear as a result of the action, and the top of C is no longer clear as a result of the action. Resolving plan interactions is, in effect, *scheduling* resource usage in the developing plan. The identification of resource scheduling as an inherent component of the planning process suggests that distributed synchronization techniques may be applicable in the planning domain and vice versa.

The second idea is the role *spatial locality* plays in the distributed planning process. Since plan interactions occur via resource usage, and because resources (often) exist in physical space, the spatial knowledge of local resource requirements and their relationship with requirements of other planners can be used to reduce the amount of interplanner communication required to detect nonlocal resource conflicts. For example, a simple scheme is to announce at periodic intervals the smallest enclosing area of all current local resource usages. Only usages which overlap with another planner's announced area need be checked for possible plan interaction. Of course, if the announced area of another planner is enlarged, additional resource

usages may have to be checked. Such a simplistic scheme breaks down, however, in situations where the areas change dramatically (such as with mobile robots) or where resources have a wide spatial area (such as a broadcast channel). The determination of a balance between the acquisition of spatial resource usage information and the over-estimation of potential resource conflict areas is an important design issue in distributed planning applications. A more detailed presentation of this research is contained in [10].

The three experiments in distributing the hypothesize–test, iterative refinement, and nonlinear hierarchical planning paradigms discussed in this section indicate that knowledge-based AI techniques are potentially useful in FA/C distributed systems. However, much research needs to be done to understand why certain algorithms tolerate the various kinds of uncertainty present in distributed problem-solving systems better than others. In the next section we discuss a first step in this direction. Using concepts from organizational theory, we describe the characteristics of algorithms that relate to the differences in their ability to handle uncertainty. In Section VI we outline a number of research issues important in the development of a better understanding of FA/C distributed systems.

V. ORGANIZATIONAL THEORY AND FUNCTIONALLY ACCURATE, COOPERATIVE DISTRIBUTED SYSTEMS

In studying management organizations, organizational theorists have worried about how *decisionmaking under uncertainty* can be handled by various types of organizational structures. For example, Galbraith [21] has developed a set of paradigms for redesigning an organizational structure to cope with the increased communication caused by uncertainty (such as unexpected events and errorful information).

Galbraith draws upon Simon's work [56], [57] which recognized the limited information processing capabilities of humans. Called *bounded rationality*, this limitation applies to both the amount of environmental (sensory) information which can be effectively used to make decisions and the amount of control which can be effectively exercised. Bounded rationality has severe implications on the quality of decisionmaking when a large amount of uncertainty is present, for "the greater the task uncertainty, the greater the amount of information that must be processed...to achieve a given level of performance" [21, p. 4]. A motivation for variations in organizational structures (in terms of the type, frequency, and connectivity pattern of information flow) is to provide additional information processing capacity (to handle greater uncertainty) within the bounded rationality of the organization's individual members.

The concept of bounded rationality also applies to FA/C distributed computational structures and, in particular, can be used to analyze their ability to handle uncertainty.[5] We can characterize the rationality bounds of a node in a distributed system by looking at the scope of its local decisions (*control bounds*), the information that is used to update these decisions (*interpretation bounds*), and the updating process (*bounds on the nature of decisionmaking*). The specific attributes of these characteristics that are important in analyzing a node's rationality bounds include the following.

- *Control Bounds:* What is the range of the environment for which a node makes a decision? What is the amount of detail (level of abstraction) of this decision? What is its accuracy? Is the decision made explicitly or implicitly through the modification of other decisions?
- *Interpretation (Sensory) Bounds:* What is the range of the environment that can be used effectively by a node for decision-making? What is the detail of this environmental information? What is its accuracy? Is the information explicitly or implicitly available?
- *Bounds on the Nature of Decisionmaking:* How much information about the history and future goals of the decisionmaking process is available to a node? Is there only a single decision under consideration at a time or are alternatives considered simultaneously? What is the detail and accuracy of this information?

To illustrate these ideas we compare distributed Hearsay-II (DHS2) and distributed iterative refinement (DIR), two algorithmic structures used in the experiments discussed in Section IV. Assuming sufficient processing power and memory to execute both algorithms in a specified amount of time, we can characterize the DHS2 algorithm as having less bounded rationality (and therefore greater potential uncertainty resolving power). This more extensive rationality can be attributed to the following differences.

Control Differences: In DIR a node only makes a decision for its local environmental area. This decision is fully detailed and (hopefully) increasingly precise over the decision made during the previous iteration. In DHS2 a node makes decisions over varying ranges, levels of abstraction, and with varying accuracies, eventually making a decision which spans the entire environment. DHS2 therefore generates a globally coherent solution, while a DIR generates locally coherent solutions.

Interpretation Differences: In DIR only the local environment is explicitly available to a node. This information is fully detailed and as accurate as the sensors can provide. Additional environmental information *may* be implicitly available to the degree that decisions received from neighboring nodes are influenced by their local sensing (and their decisions influenced by their neighbors, and so on). DHS2 encompasses all the interpretation capabilities of DIR and, additionally, can explicitly incorporate nonlocal sensory information of varying range, abstraction, and accuracy.

---

[5]Fox [19] has also explored the effect of bounded rationality on computational structures. His focus, however, has emphasized the structure of communication between modules rather than the specifics of the internal processing of modules.

Nature of Decisionmaking Differences: In DIR the reasons for a particular decision are not remembered, but are only implicitly incorporated into the resultant decision. Only a single decision is under consideration by a node at a given time. This results in a *history-free* decisionmaking process which is Markovian in character. DHS2 provides for the explicit linkage of the decisions leading to a particular decision. Alternative competing decisions and their relationship to each other are also explicitly available.

From our experience with the network traffic-light control domain, the rationality bounds of the DIR algorithm were inadequate to handle the uncertainty caused by nonlocal interactions among nodes' decisions. On the other hand, the DHS2 experiment was effective in an environment with even stronger nonlocal interactions (which potentially span the entire network). By keeping explicit track of the partial solutions that make up larger partial solutions, nonlocal interactions among subproblems can be correctly handled by the DHS2 algorithm.

The design strategies used by an organization to handle the increased information processing requirements of decisionmaking (caused by uncertainty) are also relevant to FA/C distributed computational structures. Four design strategies are used by organizations [21].

- *Slack Resources:* An organization can reduce its need for information processing by decreasing its level of performance (using additional resources — time, equipment, personnel, etc.— or reducing the quality of performance).
- *Self-Containment:* An organization can reduce the need for information processing by choosing another decomposition in which tasks are more self-contained.
- *Vertical Information Processing:* An organization can increase its capacity to process information by collecting information at the points of origin and directing it to the appropriate places in the organization, and by the use of abstraction.
- *Lateral Relations:* An organization can increase its capacity to process information by placing in direct contact processors which share a common problem.

These strategies take the following forms in the internal processing structure of a node in an FA/C distributed system.

- *Slack Resources:* By using a search process in which partial alternative decisions are incrementally made over time, a node can avoid the need for enough information to make a timely, complete, and accurate decision. The search is performed at the expense of making additional (unnecessary and redundant) tentative decisions.
- *Self-Containment:* Decisionmaking at a node is self-directed. A node attempts to do the best that it can with the information it has.
- *Vertical Information Processing:* Decisionmaking at a node is opportunistic. The search space is structured into a loose hierarchy of increasingly more abstract

representations of the problem. Using this structure, a high-level partial solution developed in an opportunistic way for one aspect of the problem can be used to constrain the search for solutions to other aspects of the problem.

- *Lateral Relations:* A node can integrate decisions asynchronously received from any other node. These decisions can be at any level of abstraction.

We feel that through a study of the literature on organizational theory, and of successful organizational structures, ideas can be obtained for the design of FA/C distributed systems. This approach has already proved useful. The cooperating experts' paradigm used by Lenat [36] has as its basis a protocol analysis of a group of experts solving problems, and recent work by Fox [18] has shown the similarity between organizational theories and the design of complex knowledge-based AI systems. We also believe that ideas from the areas of organizational planning and group problem-solving [29], [32] may provide a source of techniques and metaphors for distributed planning.

Management organizations are only one example of natural systems that can be characterized as FA/C distributed systems. Theories describing other natural FA/C distributed systems may also be of benefit to the development of FA/C distributed processing systems. An example of one such system is a honey bee colony. Recent work by Reed and Lesser [49] has shown how the division of labor techniques used by the bees may provide insights into techniques for distributed focus of attention in FA/C distributed systems.

VI. Current Research Directions

Our research in the development of FA/C distributed problem-solving techniques has produced promising results. This work has highlighted many key issues that a general theory for FA/C distributed systems must address. These issues include the following.

- *Problem Decomposition:* How should the overall problem-solving task be broken into subtasks to minimize communication requirements, limit the complexity of any given subtask, and increase the reliability and performance of the overall system? Should the decomposition be static or evolve dynamically, based upon the current status of the system?
- *Obtaining Global Information:* What nonlocal aspects of the system need to be seen by individual nodes? What levels of abstraction are appropriate for representing this information? How can potentially inconsistent and errorful nonlocal information be aggregated to form a usable nonlocal view? How should nonlocal information be held—should a single complete copy be distributed throughout the system or should each node have the portion of this information which it requires? Do multiple copies of nonlocal information need to be completely consistent, or can the system perform without complete consistency as-

sumptions? How can dynamically changing data be represented?

- *Planning and Plan Execution:* How is planning and focus of attention performed in the system? Should planning and focusing be performed in an FA/C distributed fashion? How can the activity of nodes having overlapping information be coordinated in a decentralized and implicit way so as to control redundant computation? How can a node decide locally that it is performing unnecessary computation, selecting the aspect of the overall problem on which it should instead focus its attention?[6] How are plans executed in the system? What degree of synchronization between nodes is required during planning and plan execution in a given application?
- *Monitoring and Plan Modification:* How can the system monitor in a distributed way its success in achieving its goals? How can the system modify its current course of action in the event of an unexpected change in the environment or within the system itself? How can the system decide whether to modify its existing plan or generate a new plan based on the cost/benefit estimated for each?
- *Reliability:* What and how much uncertainty (error) can be handled using FA/C computational structures? What is the cost in processing and communication required to resolve various types of uncertainty? Is there the possibility that the system can get into a severely degraded state due to the failure of a single component [42]?
- *Task Characteristics and Selection of an Appropriate Network Configuration:* What characteristics of a task can be used to select a network configuration appropriate for it? When can implicit control and information flow structures be used? Similarly, when should flat, hierarchical, or matrix configurations, or mixtures of them, be used?[7]

We believe that answers to many of these issues will be found through the development of formal models for characterizing the uncertainty present in a task and system environment and the uncertainty-resolving power of algorithms in terms of the type and degree of uncertainty in data and control they can resolve. As a first step in this direction we are developing a formal model for Hearsay-II-like systems [39]. We also feel that research on new forms of adaptive decentralized control (which integrate both implicit and explicit forms of control) and techniques for distributed planning and organizational self-design are vital

---

[6] This is the problem of dynamic allocation of information and processing capabilities of the network. The issue is also related to the classical allocation problem in networks: how to decide if the cost of accessing a distant data base is too high and whether, instead, the processing should be moved closer to the data or the data moved closer to the processing.

[7] Candidate characteristics include the patterns of node interaction, the type, spatial distribution, and degree of uncertainty of information, interdependencies of partial solutions, size of the search space, desired reliability, accuracy, responsiveness and throughput, and available computing resources.

to the development of FA/C distributed system methodologies. The following sections outline some of our current research directions which begin to address these more generic research issues.

A. Distributed Search

Experiences with the distributed applications discussed in Section IV have led to the conjecture that all FA/C distributed problem-solving structures have at their heart distributed search. Therefore a crucial aspect of any FA/C distributed system model is a characterization of distributed search. Distributed search involves the integration of partial results emanating from multiple semi-independent loci of search control. An adequate model for describing and analyzing distributed search techniques has not been developed.

We feel that a model for distributed search must provide a common framework for addressing the following questions.

- *Structure of the Space of Possible Solutions:* What is the size of the space? What is the relationship (connectivity) between states in the space? What is the density and distribution of acceptable solution states in the space?
- *Representation of the Search Space:* How is the search space represented in the system: as a single-level space or as a multilevel space encompassing multiple levels of abstraction? If multilevel, what is the relationship between the levels?
- *Representation of Partial Results:* How is a partial result represented in the system? What is the relationship between the representation of a partial result and the representation of the search space? What are the levels of the search space and the number of states encompassed by a partial result? What is the relationship between partial results? How are partial results extended and merged together?
- *The Search Process:* How is the search space searched?[8] What is the overlap between the local searches? What is the interaction between choices made by the local searches? How are the local searches coordinated? Are the local searches performed synchronously or asynchronously of one another? What is the nature of the communication required between the local searches (level of abstraction and scope)? What types of uncertainty can the search process resolve? What are the criteria for search termination? How optimal is the search?

We hope this model will have a taxonomic character that will provide a framework in which new alternative search techniques become apparent. The model may also lead to the development of a small set of control primitives and data structures which are appropriate for all types of distributed search techniques and applications.

[8] Current characterizations of search using such terms as breadth-first and depth-first are inadequate even in centralized environments.

B. Explicit Versus Implicit Approaches to Control

In our model of FA/C distributed systems we have emphasized an "implicit" form of decentralized control. The degree of implicit versus explicit control in internode coordination can be characterized by the precision with which a node can specify the nature of the tasks that are to be executed by another node and the degree to which those tasks must be performed by the other node. From a communication perspective this control spectrum takes the form of the assumptions a node can make about who is going to receive its messages, how its messages are going to be processed, who is going to send it messages, the nature of the information contained in these messages, what processing is expected by the transmitters of these messages, and what responses they expect to receive.

We have emphasized implicit and decentralized control for FA/C distributed systems because in this type of control a node has fewer built-in assumptions about the nature of internode coordination. This permits nodes to be more adaptive and flexible in the face of data and control uncertainty. We have implemented this form of control by having *self-directed* nodes which are activated in a *data-directed* manner. In this control regime, nodes interact only through the transmission of data. When a node receives information, it must decide whether or not to accept the information, what credibility to associate with it, what processing results (*goals*) it should achieve in light of this information, and what processing *tasks* it should execute to accomplish these goals. Because these decisions are made locally, node processing is entirely self-directed. In a similar self-directed manner, a node decides what and when information should be transmitted, based on the state of its local processing and its perception of the state of problem-solving in the network.

This data-directed and self-directed approach to control can be contrasted with approaches where either goals or tasks are explicitly transmitted and with approaches where nodes are *externally directed*. By "externally directed" we mean that a node is required to perform some action in response to the receipt of a message. In these other approaches to control, nodes have less flexibility in their processing strategies. These alternative control regimes are illustrated in Table I. The more precise the message (i.e., tasks are more precise than goals and goals are more precise than data) and the more externally directed a node is, the more explicit the form of control.

In our experiments with the distributed Hearsay-II architecture described in Section IV-A, we have observed that the data-directed and self-directed control regime used in this architecture can potentially lead to redundant and unnecessary processing. It appears that this form of control may not always provide sufficient global coherence among the nodes. There are two approaches for obtaining increased global coherence. The first is to provide each node with a better view of the state of problem-solving in the network so that its data-directed and self-directed control decisions are more informed and consistent. This can be accomplished by having nodes exchange detailed meta-

TABLE I
IMPLICIT AND EXPLICIT FORMS OF CONTROL

	Data-directed	Goal-directed	Task-directed
Self-directed	* Receive data * Rate the data * Determine and rate goals based on the data * Determine and rate tasks based on the goals	* Receive goals * Rate the goals * Determine and rate tasks based on the goals	* Receive tasks * Rate the tasks
Externally directed	* Receive data and ratings * Determine and rate goals based on the data * Determine and rate tasks based on the goals	* Receive goals and ratings * Determine and rate tasks based on the goals	* Receive tasks and ratings

More explicit → (top) and *More explicit ↓* (right side)

information about the state of their local problem-solving and what they have learned about the states of other nodes. Another approach, which is compatible with the first, is to integrate more explicit forms of control into network problem-solving. These types of control can be used to institute more nonlocal and precise control over the activities of individual nodes.

One example of a more explicit approach to decentralized control is the work of Smith and Davis on the contract-net formalism [59]. In this approach nodes coordinate their activities through contracts to accomplish specific goals. These contracts are elaborated in a top-down manner; at each stage, a node decomposes its contracts into subcontracts to be accomplished by other nodes. This process uses a bidding protocol based on a two-way transfer of information to establish the nature of the subcontracts and which node will perform a particular subcontract. This elaboration procedure continues until a node can complete its contract without assistance. From an FA/C perspective the disadvantages of this approach are that it is difficult to quickly refocus the system to new events (because of the hierarchical nature of control) and that it does not really address the issue of coordinating the iterative coroutine exchange of partial and tentative intermediate results between nodes.

We believe that an integrated approach that incorporates the full range of implicit to explicit control may be required for effective problem-solving in some FA/C distributed systems. This integrated approach can provide the flexibility to handle control and data uncertainty while still maintaining a sufficient level of global coherence to guarantee that acceptable solutions will be generated within given resource constraints. One approach to an integrated control regime is to incorporate more explicit goal-directed behavior into our implicit data-directed control. The priority given to goals received from other nodes versus local data-directed activity determines the degree of explicit versus implicit control present in the system. Our approach is to permit both types of coordination, and to develop

adaptive mechanisms for the system that dynamically determine an appropriate combination [12]. An important part of the development of this approach will be empirical studies to understand the appropriate balance between data-directed and goal-directed activity.

C. FA/C Distributed Planning and Organizational Self-Design

Conventional planning systems generally require that plans be developed in a systematic fashion. For example, a major weakness in the current formulation of the distributed NOAH planning system (Section IV-C) is that it requires a systematic ordering of plan development and criticism. NOAH begins with a high-level representation of the plan (the goal) and expands that plan into a more detailed plan, which is analyzed for incompatible actions and possibly modified. The generation of the more detailed plan proceeds in the same order as the eventual execution of the actions (execution-time order). This expand–analyze cycle is repeated on the most-detailed (last-expanded) plan representation until the plan is sufficiently detailed for execution.

Each local planner considers only one possible local plan at a time. Because NOAH cannot simultaneously consider alternative partial plans, newly received planning decisions cannot be easily integrated into previously made planning decisions. Instead, when an incompatible planning decision (i.e., a conflict in resource usage) is received, a node must either ask the sending node to revise its decisions or the node must *backtrack* to a point where the received decision is no longer incompatible with its developing plan (and resume planning from that point). Backtracking may also involve cancelling planning decisions that were announced to other planners. This in turn can cause those planners to cancel their decisions and so on in a "domino" effect in which a number of planned actions are deleted. (This effect is directly related to the problems plaguing the single-label iterative refinement algorithm used in the distributed network traffic-light control domain of Section IV-B.) The requirement that a local planner make a *single* planning decision (without information about the decisions under consideration by other planners) can lead to much wasted planning effort and a corresponding cost in wasted communication. This style of processing does not foster a form of cooperation that can effectively deal with incomplete and inconsistent local planning data bases.

The Hayes–Roth cognitive model of planning [26] is an example of a style of planning in which a number of alternative, competing, partial plans are developed concurrently. Based on a Hearsay-II architecture [15], their planning model is hierarchical but not strictly limited to a top-down execution-time ordered planning sequence. Instead, planning proceeds *opportunistically*, with each new planning decision integrated into a subset of previously made decisions. New decisions may also produce independent, competing, partial plans at various levels of abstraction. As planning continues, some of these partial plans die out, and others are merged together into larger more complete plans. Planning terminates when an acceptable overall plan is developed.

In an environment where unpredictable external information is asynchronously received, an integrated representation of competing and cooperating partial plans allows the planner to retain relevant portions of previous planning results. This style of incremental plan modification allows better refocusing in light of new information than backtracking. It is also important in a distributed environment to attempt to quickly reduce the size of the planning (search) space, since additional search requires additional communication. The opportunistic behavior of the Hayes–Roth model allows greater flexibility in solving crucial aspects of the planning task before proceeding to less crucial aspects.

The success of distributing the Hearsay-II speech understanding system [38] suggests that the Hayes–Roth planning model can serve as a basis for the development of an FA/C distributed planning organization. However, a number of issues relating to the use of partial and inconsistent plans in such a framework remain to be resolved.

Planner interactions can also be reduced by the selection of action sequences which are applicable in a range of situations over alternative sequences which are less stable but perhaps more execution-time efficient. Most planners concentrate on finding optimal execution-cost or *solution-optimal* plans (after Sproull [60, p. 106]). Sproull's notion of *planning-optimal* plans, in which the cost of the planning *and* execution of the plan is optimized, is particularly apropos in the distributed planning environment. An FA/C style of planner would attempt to identify stable action sequences based on its expectations of the actions other planners might perform and on anticipated environmental changes. Understanding how portions of plans interact during planning and plan execution can provide measures of plan stability which can be used to evaluate alternative courses of action based on these expectations.

Given that the cost of communication is relatively expensive in comparison to the cost of processing in a distributed system, it is important to regard all aspects of the environmental spectrum as potential communications media. The typical distributed system viewpoint assumes that the message transfer channel is the sole conduit of information exchange in the system. However, observation of another planning system's executing plan can provide a variety of implicit information. Consider a room with a tall ladder and two repairmen with the task of replacing a ceiling light. If one repairman grabs the ladder to steady it, the other would probably assume it was his responsibility to climb up and replace the light—without any need for verbal communication. The application of planning (common sense reasoning) to the interpretation of another's actions is currently receiving attention from language researchers in the analysis of natural language utterances [7], [24], [28]. However, the interleaving of plan development and plan execution in a distributed environment leads to a number of unresolved technical questions.

An assumption made in the distributed NOAH planning system was the existence of a mechanism for allocating planning activity to individual nodes. Different allocations of planning activity (even for the same planning problem) produce significant differences in the complexity of the planning process. In fact, the allocation of planning activity is part of the larger issue of determining an appropriate organizational structure for the particular distributed problem-solving situation.

The *organizational structure* of a distributed system is the pattern of information and control relationships that exist between the nodes in the system and the distribution of problem-solving capabilities among the nodes in the system. Organizational structures include hierarchies, heterarchies or flat structures, matrix organizations, groups or teams, and market or price systems. *Organizational design* is the explicit planning of these internode relationships.

The organizational structure of a distributed system relates strongly to its effectiveness in a given problem-solving situation. This effectiveness is a multivalued measure incorporating such parameters as processing resources, communication requirements, timeliness of activity, accuracy of activity, etc. An organizational structure may lose effectiveness as the internal or external environment of the distributed system or the nature of the problem-solving task changes. In order to respond to such a change the distributed system must detect the decreased effectiveness of its organizational structure, determine plausible alternative structures, evaluate the cost of continuing with its current structure versus the cost of reorganizing itself into a more appropriate structure, and carry out such reorganization if appropriate.

Organizational design decisions are faced regularly in human organizations, especially those in the business community where pressures of efficiency are most severe. Theories of organizational design which attempt to explain the art of organizational structuring in these human organizations are highly relevant to the development of organizational design knowledge for distributed systems.

Research outlined in [11] bypasses further refinement of distributed planning techniques, such as those developed in distributing NOAH, in favor of the development of a framework which encompasses both planning and organizational self-design. Although many issues in distributed planning remain to be solved, the development of a technology for distributed organizational design seems the more salient research direction. A rephrasing of the programming adage "Don't optimize a bad algorithm—rewrite it" seems appropriate: "Don't work to improve plans within a bad organizational structure—*reorganize*."

VII. Conclusion

We feel that methodologies can be developed for functionally accurate, cooperative (FA/C) distributed systems in which the distributed algorithms and control structures function with both inconsistent and incomplete data. These methodologies are necessary in order to extend the range of applications that can be effectively implemented in distributed environments.

FA/C problem-solving structures are also important in the implementation of complex applications in centralized environments. These applications are often organized in the form of a collection of independent modules. In such a structure it can be conceptually difficult to develop, and expensive to maintain, a complete and consistent centralized problem-solving data base with which the modules interact. Techniques which permit the relaxation of completeness and consistency requirements would be a significant aid in the development and maintenance of these (logically distributed) systems.

There are two concepts that form the basis of FA/C distributed methodologies:

1) to view an FA/C distributed system as a network of cooperating systems which share common goals, where each system is able to perform significant local processing using incomplete and inconsistent data;
2) to handle the uncertainty in control, data, and algorithms introduced by distribution as an integral part of the network problem-solving process.

Techniques developed in the context of knowledge-based AI systems and organizational theory provide a basis for implementing both concepts.

Acknowledgment

The authors would like to acknowledge the research efforts of Lee Erman on distributed Hearsay-II and Richard Brooks on network traffic-light control which are discussed in this paper. We would also like to acknowledge discussions with the other members of the University of Massachusetts Cooperative Distributed Problem-Solving Research Group: Jasmina Pavlin, Scott Reed, and Ram Mukunda, Michael Arbib, Randy Davis, Lee Erman, and Reid Smith also provided helpful comments on early drafts of this paper.

References

[1] M. Adiba, T. C. Chupin, R. Demolombe, G. Gardavin, and J. LeBihan, "Issues in distributed database management systems: A technical overview," in *Proc. Fourth Int. Conf. on Very Large Data Bases*, 1978, pp. 89–110.

[2] M. A. Arbib, "Artificial intelligence and brain theory: Unities and diversities," *Ann. Biomedic. Eng.*, vol. 3, pp. 238–274, 1975.

[3] H. G. Barrow and J. M. Tenenbaum, "MSYS: A system for reasoning about scenes," SRI International, Menlo Park, CA, AI Center Tech. Note 121, 1976.

[4] G. M. Baudet, "Asynchronous iterative methods for multiprocessors," *J. Ass. Comput. Machinery*, vol. 25, no. 2, pp. 226–244, Apr. 1978.

[5] P. A. Bernstein, J. B. Rothnie, Jr., N. Goodman, and C. A. Papadimitriou, "The concurrency control mechanism of SDD-1: A system for distributed databases (The fully redundant case)," *IEEE Trans. Software Eng.*, vol. SE-4, no. 3, pp. 154–168, May 1978.

[6] R. S. Brooks and V. R. Lesser, "Distributed problem solving using iterative refinement," Dep. Comput. Inform. Sci., Univ. Massachusetts, Amherst, Tech. Rep. 79-14, May 1979.

[7] B. C. Bruce and D. Newman, "Interacting plans," *Cognitive Sci.*, vol. 2, no. 3, pp. 195–233, July 1978.

[8] W. W. Chu, *Advances in Computer Communications*. Dedham, MA: Artech House, 1977.

[9] P. R. Cohen and C. R. Perrault, "Elements of a plan-based theory of speech acts," *Cognitive Sci.*, vol. 3, no. 3, pp. 177–212, July 1979.

[10] D. D. Corkill, "Hierarchical planning in a distributed environment," in *Proc. Sixth Int. Joint Conf. on Artificial Intelligence*, Tokyo, Japan, Aug. 1979, pp. 168–175.

[11] ——, "An organizational approach to planning in distributed problem solving systems," Ph.D. thesis proposal, Dep. Comput. Inform. Sci., Univ. Massachusetts, Amherst, Tech. Rep. 80-13, May 1980.

[12] D. D. Corkill and V. R. Lesser, "A goal-directed Hearsay-II architecture," Dep. Comput. Inform. Sci., Univ. Massachusetts, Amherst, Tech. Rep., in preparation.

[13] D. G. Dimmler *et al.*, "Brookhaven reactor experiment control facility: A distributed function computer network," *IEEE Trans. Nucl. Sci.*, vol. NS-23, pp. 398–405, Feb. 1976.

[14] R. S. Englemore and H. P. Nii, "A knowledge-based system for the interpretation of protein X-ray crystallographic data," Comput. Sci. Dep., Stanford Univ., Stanford, CA, Tech. Rep. Stan-CS-77-589, Feb. 1977.

[15] L. D. Erman, F. Hayes-Roth, V. R. Lesser, and D. R. Reddy, "The Hearsay-II speech understanding system: Integrating knowledge to resolve uncertainty," *Comput. Surveys*, vol. 12, no. 2, pp. 213–253, June 1980.

[16] L. D. Erman and V. R. Lesser, "A multi-level organization for problem solving using many diverse, cooperating sources of knowledge," in *Advance Papers of the Fourth Int. Joint Conf. on Artifical Intelligence*, Tbilisi, Georgia, USSR, Sept. 1975, pp. 483–490.

[17] R. D. Fennell and V. R. Lesser, "Parallelism in AI problem-solving: A case study of Hearsay-II," *IEEE Trans. Comp.*, vol. C-26, no. 2, pp. 98–111, Feb. 1977.

[18] M. S. Fox, "An organizational view of distributed systems," in *Proc. Int. Conf. on Cybernetics and Society*, Denver, CO, Oct. 1979, pp. 354–359.

[19] ——, "Organization structuring: Designing large complex software," Dep. Comput. Sci., Carnegie-Mellon Univ., Pittsburgh, PA, Tech. Rep. CMU-CS-79-155, Dec. 1979.

[20] A. Friedman, *Differential Games*. New York: Wiley, 1971.

[21] J. Galbraith, *Designing Complex Organizations*. Reading, MA: Addison-Wesley, 1973.

[22] M. Gerla, "Deterministic and adaptive routing policies in packet-switched computer networks," in *Proc. Third IEEE Data Communications Symp.*, 1973, pp. 23–28.

[23] P. Green, Distributed Sensor Group, Lincoln Labs, Cambridge, MA, 1979, private communication.

[24] B. Grosz, "Utterance and objective: Issues in natural language communication," in *Proc. Sixth Int. Joint Conf. on Artificial Intelligence*, Tokyo, Japan, Aug. 1979, pp. 1067–1076.

[25] A. R. Hanson and E. M. Riseman, "Segmentation of natural scenes," in *Computer Vision Systems*, A. R. Hanson and E. M. Riseman, Eds. New York: Academic, 1978, pp. 129–163.

[26] B. Hayes-Roth and F. Hayes-Roth, "A cognitive model of planning," *Cognitive Sci.*, vol. 3, no. 4, pp. 275–310, Oct.–Dec. 1979.

[27] C. Hewitt, "Viewing control structures as patterns of passing messages," *Artificial Intelligence*, vol. 8, no. 3, pp. 323–364, Fall 1977.

[28] J. R. Hobbs, "Conversation as planned behavior," in *Proc. Sixth Int. Joint Conf. on Artificial Intelligence*, Tokyo, Japan, Aug. 1979, pp. 390–396.

[29] L. R. Hoffman, "Group problem solving," in *Advances in Experimental Social Psychology*, Vol. 2, L. Berkowitz, Ed. New York: Academic, 1965, pp. 99–132.

[30] T. G. Hoffman, "Upgrading gauge measurement with distributed computers," *Control Eng.*, vol. 22, pp. 39–41, 1975.

[31] R. E. Kahn, S. A. Gronemeyer, J. Burchfiel, and R. C. Kunzelman, "Advances in packet radio technology," *Proc. IEEE*, vol. 66, no. 11, pp. 1468–1496, Nov. 1978.

[32] H. H. Kelley and J. W. Thibaut, "Experimental studies of group problem solving and process," in *Handbook of Social Psychology*, G. Lindzey, Ed. Reading, MA: Addison-Wesley, 1954, pp. 735–785.

[33] S. R. Kimbleton and G. M. Schneider, "Computer communication networks: Approaches, objectives, and performance considerations," *Comput. Surveys*, vol. 7, no. 3, pp. 129–173, Sept. 1975.

[34] R. Lacoss and R. Walton, "Strawman design of a DSN to detect and track low flying aircraft," in *Proc. Distributed Sensor Nets Workshop*, Carnegie-Mellon Univ., Pittsburgh, PA, Dec. 1978, pp. 41–52.

[35] R. E. Larson, "A survey of distributed control techniques," in *Tutorial: Distributed Control*. New York: IEEE, Oct. 1979, ch. 5.

[36] D. B. Lenat, "Beings: Knowledge as interacting experts," in *Advance Papers of the Fourth Int. Joint Conf. on Artificial Intelligence*, Tbilisi, Georgia, USSR, Aug. 1975, pp. 126–133.

[37] V. R. Lesser and D. D. Corkill, "Cooperative distributed problem solving: A new approach for structuring distributed systems," Dep. Comput. Informat. Sci., Univ. Massachusetts, Amherst, Tech. Rep. 78-7, May 1978.

[38] V. R. Lesser and L. D. Erman, "Distributed interpretation: A model and an experiment," *IEEE Trans. Comput.*, Special Issue on Distributed Processing, vol. C-29, no. 12, pp. 1144–1163, Dec. 1980.

[39] V. R. Lesser, S. Reed, and J. Pavlin, "Quantifying and simulating the behavior of knowledge-based interpretation systems," in *Proc. First Nat. Conf. on Artificial Intelligence*, Stanford, CA, Aug. 1980, pp. 111–115.

[40] V. R. Lesser, J. Pavlin, and S. Reed, "A high-level simulation testbed for cooperative distributed problem-solving," Dep. Comput. Informat. Sci., Univ. Massachusetts, Amherst, Tech. Rep., 1981.

[41] E. D. Lieberman and J. L. Woo, "SIGOP II: A new computer program for calculating optimal signal timing patterns," *Trans. Res. Rec.*, Rep. 596, 1976.

[42] P. M. Merlin, "A methodology for the design and implementation of communication protocols," IBM Thomas J. Watson Res. Center, Yorktown Heights, NY, Tech. Rep., 1975.

[43] W. C. Mann, "Dialogue games," Informat. Sci. Inst., Marina del Ray, CA, Tech. Rep., 1979.

[44] H. P. Nii and E. A. Feigenbaum, "Rule-based understanding of signals," in *Pattern-Directed Inference Systems*, D. A. Waterman and F. Hayes-Roth, Eds. New York: Academic, 1978, pp. 483–502.

[45] R. Peebles and E. Manning, "System architecture for distributed data management," *Comput.*, vol. 11, no. 1, pp. 40–47, Jan. 1978.

[46] S. Peleg and A. Rosenfeld, "Breaking substitution ciphers using a relaxation algorithm," *Communic. ACM*, vol. 22, no. 11, pp. 598–605, Nov. 1979.

[47] A. Rapoport, *Two-Person Game Theory: The Essential Ideas*. Ann Arbor, MI: Univ. Michigan Press, 1966.

[48] ——, *N-Person Game Theory: Concepts and Applications*. Ann Arbor, MI: Univ. Michigan Press, 1970.

[49] S. Reed and V. R. Lesser, "Division of labor in honey bees and distributed focus of attention," Dep. Comput. Informat. Sci., Univ. Massachusetts, Amherst, Tech. Rep. 80-17, Sept. 1980.

[50] A. Rosenfeld, R. A. Hummel, and S. W. Zucker, "Scene labelling by relaxation operations," *IEEE Trans. Systems, Man, Cybernet.*, vol. SMC-6, no. 6, pp. 420–433, June 1976.

[51] S. Rubin and R. Reddy, "The locus model of search and its use in image interpretation," in *Proc. Fifth Int. Joint Conf. on Artificial Intelligence*, Boston, MA, Aug. 1977, pp. 590–595.

[52] E. D. Sacerdoti, *A Structure for Plans and Behavior*. New York: Elsevier North-Holland, 1977.

[53] ——, "What language understanding research suggests about distributed artificial intelligence," in *Proc. Distributed Sensor Nets Workshop*, Carnegie-Mellon Univ., Pittsburgh, PA, Dec. 1978, pp. 8–11.

[54] J. D. Schoeffl and C. W. Rose, "Distributed computer intelligence for data acquisition and control," *IEEE Trans. Nucl. Sci.*, vol. NS-23, pp. 32–54, Feb. 1976.

[55] *Scientific American*, Special Issue on Microelectronics, vol. 237, no. 3, Sept. 1977.

[56] H. A. Simon, *Models of Man*. New York: Wiley, 1957.

[57] ——, *The Sciences of The Artificial*. Cambridge, MA: MIT Press, 1969.

[58] R. G. Smith, "A framework for problem solving in a distributed processing environment," Ph.D. dissertation, Comput. Sci. Dep., Stanford Univ., Stanford, CA, Tech. Rep. STAN-CS-78-700, Dec. 1978.

[59] R. G. Smith and R. Davis, "Cooperation in distributed problem-solving," in *Proc. Int. Conf. on Cybernetics and Society*, Denver, CO, Oct. 1979, pp. 366–371.

[60] R. F. Sproull, "Strategy construction using a synthesis of heuristic and decision-theoretic methods," Ph.D. dissertation, Xerox Palo Alto Research Center, Palo Alto, CA, Tech. Rep. CSL-77-2, July 1977.

[61] W. D. Tajibnapis, "A correctness proof of a topology information maintenance protocol for a distributed computer network," *Communic. ACM*, vol. 20, no. 7, pp. 477–485, July 1977.

[62] R. R. Tenney, "Distributed decision making using a distributed model," Ph.D. dissertation, Lab. Informat. Decision Syst., Massachusetts Inst. Technol., Cambridge, Tech. Rep. LIDS-TH-938, Sept. 1979.

[63] S. W. Zucker, "Vertical and horizontal processes in low level vision," *Computer Vision Systems*, A. R. Hanson and E. M. Riseman, Eds. New York: Academic, 1978, pp. 187–195.

[64] S. W. Zucker, R. A. Hummel, and A. Rosenfeld, "An application of relaxation labelling to line and curve enhancement," *IEEE Trans. Comput.*, vol. C-26, no. 4, pp. 394–403, Apr. 1977.

The Scientific Community Metaphor

WILLIAM A. KORNFELD AND CARL E. HEWITT

Abstract—Scientific communities have proven to be extremely successful at solving problems. They are inherently parallel systems and their macroscopic nature makes them amenable to careful study. In this paper the character of scientific research is examined drawing on sources in the philosophy and history of science. We maintain that the success of scientific research depends critically on its concurrency and pluralism. A variant of the language Ether is developed that embodies notions of concurrency necessary to emulate some of the problem solving behavior of scientific communities. Capabilities of scientific communities are discussed in parallel with simplified models of these capabilities in this language.

I. Introduction

MUCH OF the present interest in parallel processing stems from a now well–documented technological trend—the declining cost of processing, storage, and communications. This is assuredly a valid motivation, but not the only one. Our research in artificial intelligence has led us to a very different reason for considering concurrent systems. We now feel parallelism is fundamental to the design and implementation of expert systems in many domains. In this paper we present a largely philosophical discussion of our motivations. A language called Ether has been designed to create highly parallel problem solving systems. The actual language differs in several details from the one described in this paper which has been created for pedagogical reasons. A discussion of the Ether language can be found in [11].

Engineers wishing to construct an artifact capable of implementing a process, such as problem solving, often study naturally occurring systems that already implement the process. This approach has led many researchers to investigate psychological models of human thought as a basis for constructing an artificial intelligence. Some of this research is reviewed later. Here we focus our attention on how scientific communities solve problems. That scientific communities are successful at generating and deciding between alternative explanations for phenomena is indisputable. Scientific progress, looked at globally and with a time scale of many decades, seems coherent and purposeful. Looked at locally, this is anything but true. At any one time many conflicting theories may purport to explain the same phenomenon. Scientists within a field often engage in highly charged arguments with one another. Occasionally what may ultimately turn out to be the wrong party to a dispute will gain temporary popularity; though the fields themselves seem to grow in depth and power over the long

haul. We believe the overall success of scientific research is due in large part to its tolerance of this diversity.

Scientific communities themselves can be the subject matter of scientific research. The nature of science has been a fertile topic in philosophy from the pre-Socratics through the present day. We hope to gain useful insights from this research that will aid us in the design of computer systems with some of the capabilities of scientific communities. We are particularly indebted to a number of philosophers and historians of science of this century, among them Popper, Lakatos, Kuhn, and Feyerabend. The observations expressed in the following sections owe a great deal to their work.

Our thesis is that the structure of problem solving in scientific communities can be used to justify many of the design decisions for parallelism and pluralism in Ether. We discuss the constructs of Ether in parallel with the characteristics of scientific communities that motivate them. We hope to glean useful ideas from the metaphor of scientific research that will aid in the future development of problem solving systems based on Ether.

We wish to warn the reader not to look for a direct correspondence between the components of Ether and analogous components in scientific communities. The relationship is one that can be seen only at a high level of abstraction. The most important aspects of this relationship are the high degree of concurrency and the nature of the concurrent activities with respect to the overall problem solving effort.

II. Communication

One of the most salient aspects of scientific communities is that they are *highly parallel systems*. Scientists work on problems concurrently with other scientists. They can work on the same problem or on quite different problems. They may or may not know of the work of other scientists. They may hold similar opinions to one another or quite divergent opinions. Popper and Lakatos have developed the thesis that this diversity is a *necessary* aspect of successful scientific research. One of our goals in the development of Ether is to facilitate the construction of systems with this kind of diversity.

Scientists do not, of course, work in a vacuum. They are able to communicate their ideas with one another. One scientist's results can sometimes have a profound effect on the nature of future work by other scientists. A principle goal in the design of the Ether language is making interaction between different parts of the system easy without

Manuscript received February 10, 1980; revised August 10, 1980.

The authors are with the Department of Computer Science, Massachusetts Institute of Technology, Cambridge, MA 02139.

many of the pitfalls that make current parallel processing systems, based on mechanisms like semaphores and shared memory, difficult to use.

Some of the communication in scientific communities concerns *resource control*. Research programs that seem more likely to lead to solutions of the goals of the system are allocated more resources than their less likely alternatives. Some of the activity of an Ether system is concerned with comparing competing methodologies and reallocating resources on the basis of relative merit.

All communication in Ether is done by *disseminating* messages. There are several kinds of communication that might take place. Scientists often communicate *results* of their own researches. We will refer to these kinds of messages as *assertions*. There are other kinds of messages that must be communicated. At any time the system has certain *goals*, either to demonstrate the validity of a proposition or to find a method for solving a given problem. The goals of one part of the system must be communicated to parts of the system embodying expertise that can help achieve the goal. This communication is done with messages.

Computation in Ether is done by computational elements known as *sprites*. For each sprite *s*, there is a set of messages called (INTERESTSET *s*) in which the sprite is potentially interested. Sprites can communicate with each other by disseminating messages. If a message *m* is disseminated which is an element of (INTERESTSET s_k), then s_k will receive the message *m*. The intent of dissemination is to achieve the effect of broadcasting a message without incurring all of the overhead of broadcasting.

As a result of receiving a message in which it is interested, a sprite can create new sprites and send more messages. A running Ether program contains a set of sprites and disseminated messages that interact with each other to produce more sprites and messages. Dissemination in Ether has important properties called *monotonicity, commutativity, parallelism,* and *pluralism* which are explained below.

Monotonicity: Once a message *m* is disseminated it cannot be "erased." It will remain available forever.

Commutativity: If a message *m* is an element of (INTERESTSET *s*) of a sprite *s*, then *s* will receive *m* regardless of whether the message was disseminated before or after the sprite was activated.

Parallelism: If a message *m* is disseminated which is in the interest set of sprites *s*1 and *s*2, then *s*1 and *s*2 will process the message concurrently. Similarly, if messages *m*1 and *m*2 are disseminated which are both in the interest set of a sprite *s*, then *s* will process the messages concurrently. More generally, if two Ether subsystems (collections of sprites and messages) *E*1 and *E*2 will produce larger collections of sprites and messages *E*1′ and *E*2′ when run in isolation from one another, then an Ether system consisting of $E1 \cup E2$ will produce a system *E* when run such that $E1' \cup E2' \subseteq E$.

Pluralism: Ether supports working on multiple and not necessarily compatible hypotheses at the same time.

The above properties are idealizations of certain characteristics of scientific communities. They allow computer programs to be written that emulate the way scientists work together in cooperation and competition.

We will now attempt to make more explicit the correspondence between the role played by these properties in Ether and their role in scientific communities.

Monotonicity: Scientists *publish* their results so they are available to all who are interested. Published work is collected and indexed in libraries. Scientists who change their mind can publish a later article contradicting the first. However, they are not allowed to go into the libraries and "erase" the old publication. Publications advocating obsolete and unpopular theories are stored along with currently popular theories.

Commutativity: It does not matter whether a scientist becomes interested in a publication before it is published or vice versa for it to be of use. Scientists who become interested in a scientific question make an effort to find out if the answer has already been published. In addition they attempt to keep abreast of further developments as they continue their work.

Parallelism: Scientists can work concurrently with one another without adverse effects.

Pluralism: There is no central arbiter of truth in scientific communities.

The properties of monotonicity and commutativity are goals of the scientific community which are only incompletely achieved in practice. For example, a publication can be lost or a scientist may not have read or understood an article important to his own research. Furthermore, in scientific communities the goals of commutativity and parallelism are tempered by resource constraints; it may be easier to perform an experiment than to determine if it has already be done. Ether has mechanisms for resource control that are intended to address some of these issues.

A. An Example in Ether

Sprites can communicate with other sprites by disseminating messages. A sprite consists of two parts, a *trigger pattern* and a *body*. The trigger pattern of a sprite *s* is a convenient way to express (INTERESTSET *s*), the set of messages in which the sprite is interested. When information has been disseminated that matches this template, the body of the sprite (Ether code) is executed in an environment supplied by the match. There may be code in the body to create new sprites or disseminate information to other sprites.

To make the concept of sprites more understandable it is useful to treat an example in detail. We will consider the problem of determining whether or not a path exists in a directed graph from one set of nodes called *origins* to another called *destinations*. Problems of this kind are common in problem solving and planning situations. The origins might represent the current situation or the hypotheses of the theorem to be proved. The destinations would represent the desired situation or the conclusions of the theorem.

The particular problem to be solved is posed to the system by disseminating a message of the form (GOAL (PATHEXISTS ORIGINS DESTINATION)). The goal is recorded as being achieved by disseminating a message of the form (ASSERTION (PATHEXISTS ORIGINS DESTINATIONS)).

The data base contains messages indicating patterns of local connectedness in the graph. A message of the form (IMMEDIATEPREDECESSOR $\langle N1 \rangle \langle N2 \rangle$) signifies that node $\langle N1 \rangle$ is known to be an immediate predecessor of node $\langle N2 \rangle$. Similarly, a message of the form (IMMEDIATESUCCESSOR $\langle N1 \rangle \langle N2 \rangle$) indicates $\langle N1 \rangle$ immediately succeeds $\langle N2 \rangle$.

An expression of the form

(WHEN $\langle$TRIGGER$\rangle \langle$COMMAND$_1 \rangle \cdots \langle$COMMAND$_j \rangle$)

is used to create a new sprite $\langle s \rangle$ with a trigger pattern $\langle$TRIGGER$\rangle$ and j commands. An expression of the form (ACTIVATE $\langle s \rangle$) can be used to activate the sprite $\langle s \rangle$. Thereafter, when messages which have been disseminated match the trigger, the commands are executed in an environment provided by the match. The commands are executed concurrently. These expressions are illustrated in the following definition of the procedure ALWAYSCHAIN-BOTHWAYS which has no parameters:

```
(DEFINE (ALWAYSCHAINBOTHWAYS)
  (ACTIVATE
    (WHEN (GOAL (PATHEXISTS = U = V))
      (CHAINFORWARD U V)
      (CHAINBACKWARD U V)))).
```

Suppose the expression (ALWAYSCHAINBOTHWAYS) has been executed (activating a sprite we will call s) and that the message

(GOAL (PATHEXISTS ORIGINS DESTINATIONS))

(which we will call m) has been disseminated. Then regardless of whether s is activated before or after m is disseminated, the sprite s will receive the message m and will bind the identifier U to ORIGINS and the identifier V to DESTINATIONS. The following two commands will then be executed concurrently:

(CHAINFORWARD ORIGINS DESTINATIONS)
(CHAINBACKWARD ORIGINS DESTINATIONS).

A command of the form (ALWAYSNOTICETRIVIALPATHS) will look to see if the sets $\langle X \rangle$ and $\langle Y \rangle$ have any nodes in common when a goal of the form (PATHEXISTS $\langle X \rangle \langle Y \rangle$) is disseminated. If this is the case an assertion to that effect will be disseminated. The following definition accomplishes the desired result:

```
(DEFINE (ALWAYSNOTICETRIVIALPATHS)
  (ACTIVATE (WHEN (GOAL (PATHEXISTS = X = Y))
    (IF ((X ∩ Y) ≠ φ)
      THEN (DISSEMINATE
        (ASSERTION (PATHEXISTS X Y))))))).
```

A command of the form (CHAINFORWARD $\langle X \rangle \langle Y \rangle$) will cause a subgoal for the form (PATHEXISTS $\langle s \rangle \langle Y \rangle$) to be disseminated for each successor $\langle s \rangle$ of $\langle X \rangle$. Furthermore, for each successor $\langle s \rangle$, a new sprite is created which disseminates the assertion that a path exists from $\langle X \rangle$ to $\langle Y \rangle$ if the subgoal is achieved.

```
(DEFINE (CHAINFORWARD = X = Y)
  (WHEN (IMMEDIATESUCCESSOR = s X)
    (DISSEMINATE (GOAL (PATHEXISTS {s} Y)))
    (ACTIVATE (WHEN (ASSERTION (PATHEXISTS {s} Y))
      (DISSEMINATE (ASSERTION (PATHEXISTS X Y)))))))).
```

Before continuing with this example, we would like to introduce some abbreviations which will reduce the bulk of the code without changing its meaning. Commands of the form (DISSEMINATE (ASSERTION $\langle x \rangle$)) are very common in the above code. We introduce the following definition so that we can use the abbreviation (ASSERT $\langle x \rangle$) instead.

```
(DEFINE (ASSERT = x)
  (DISSEMINATE (ASSERTION x))).
```

Additionally, command fragments of the form

```
(DISSEMINATE (GOAL ⟨g⟩))
(ACTIVATE (WHEN (ASSERTION ⟨g⟩)
  ⟨COMMAND₁⟩
  ...
  ⟨COMMANDₖ⟩))
```

will be abbreviated as follows:

```
(SHOW ⟨g⟩
  (WHENACHIEVED
    ⟨COMMAND₁⟩
    ...
    ⟨COMMANDₖ⟩)).
```

Using these abbreviations, the code for CHAINFORWARD appears as follows:

```
(DEFINE (CHAINFORWARD = X = Y)
  (WHEN (IMMEDIATESUCCESSOR = s X)
    (SHOW (PATHEXISTS {s} Y)
      (WHENACHIEVED
        (ASSERT (PATHEXISTS X Y)))))).
```

Commands of the form (CHAINBACKWARD $\langle X \rangle \langle Y \rangle$) are completely analogous to the ones for chaining forward. The corresponding definition is given below:

```
(DEFINE (CHAINBACKWARD = X = Y)
  (WHEN (IMMEDIATEPREDECESSOR = p Y)
    (SHOW (PATHEXISTS X {p})
      (WHENACHIEVED
        (ASSERT (PATHEXISTS X Y)))))).
```

This system is set in motion by executing the commands

(ALWAYSCHAINBOTHWAYS)

and

(ALWAYSNOTICETRIVIALPATHS).

In some examples introduced late in this paper we will find it useful to have a concise notation for a sprite which triggers on a set of messages which have been disseminated. We will use the notation

(WHEN {$\langle PAT_1 \rangle \langle PAT_2 \rangle$}
    $\langle COMMAND_1 \rangle$
    $\cdots$
    $\langle COMMAND_j \rangle$)

for a sprite which triggers on a set of messages which match $\langle PAT_1 \rangle$ and $\langle PAT_2 \rangle$. The above notation can be regarded as an abbreviation for the presence of either:

(WHEN $\langle PAT_1 \rangle$
    (ACTIVATE (WHEN $\langle PAT_2 \rangle$
        $\langle COMMAND_1 \rangle$
        $\cdots$
        $\langle COMMAND_j \rangle$)))
(WHEN $\langle PAT_2 \rangle$
    (ACTIVATE (WHEN $\langle PAT_1 \rangle$
        $\langle COMMAND_1 \rangle$
        $\cdots$
        $\langle COMMAND_j \rangle$))).

We reason that if messages M_1 and M_2 are disseminated and they match $\langle PAT_1 \rangle$ and $\langle PAT_2 \rangle$ respectively, then the commands $\langle COMMAND_1 \rangle, \cdots, \langle COMMAND_j \rangle$ will be executed with the same bindings in both cases.

III. Proposers

Scientific research consists of generating proposals to account for observations and processes for substantiating and refuting these theories. Popper has called the process *conjecture and refutation*. Theories evolve and become substantiated or rejected through an interplay of many processes. Three basic types are proposers, proponents, and skeptics. Proposals are new theories, goals, and techniques put forward for critical assessment and development. Proponent activities attempt to substantiate these proposals. Skeptical activities play the role of "devil's advocate" to test proposals using any techniques the system has at its disposal.

An important source of proposals are very general methods coming from "common sense" knowledge. For example, when trying to get from X to Z, it is often desirable to find another place Y such that Z is accessible from Y and Y is accessible from X. Of course these simple solutions will often not work without further elaboration. In this particular example it may be that it is better to overcome the obstacle which prevents direct access from X to Z than to try to find another route. For example suppose that X and Z are fields and there is a fence between them. It may be better to try to find a way through the fence than to find another field Y which is accessible to X and Z. We believe "common sense knowledge" is the source of many general proposal generators of this kind.

A somewhat more abstract way to generate new hypotheses is by metaphor. A situation may have several features in common with another situation for which a solution is known to be successful. Metaphor can be used to explain the origins of the two alternative theories of light debated early in the nineteenth century. Newton suggested that light consists of particles because it shares several features in common with particles. With no obstructions light moves in a straight line. If a mirror is placed in its path the light will be reflected at the same angle as would particles in an elastic collision with the surface of the mirror. Newton was very familiar with the concept of a particle. There were enough similarities between the theory of particle interaction and observed characters of light to put forward the theory that "light consists of particles."

Theories are proposed and then tested. We use the term "skeptics" for activities whose purpose is to reason about the implications of theories looking for *anomalies*. Anomalies are points where the implications of a theory differ from prediction. In many cases a theory is modified to account for the anomaly, but in a way that preserves the character and support structure of the original theory. This process is called *adjustment* (following Lakatos) and is discussed later in this paper.

IV. Proponent Activities

When new goals are proposed, sprites go to work attempting to establish these goals. Activities attempting to achieve a goal are collectively known as *proponents*. We have already presented an example of the efficacy of multiple proponents attempting to achieve a goal. When the message (GOAL (PathExists Origins Destinations)) is disseminated many sprites go to work trying to establish it. The activity of these sprites constitutes the proponent activity for the goal.

The most common kind of proponent we have studied thus far is what is sometimes known as *working backward from the goal* or *consequent reasoning*. The goal can be established by establishing one or more subgoals. The proponent functions by proposing these new goals.

A. Disjunctive Subgoals

For example, if we wanted to establish that someone (say "Joe") was a U.S. citizen, it would suffice to show he was either born in the U.S. or he was naturalized. To do this in Ether we create a sprite that watches for messages of the form

(GOAL (USCitizen $\langle PERSON \rangle$))

and then establishes new goals

(GOAL (NativeBorn $\langle PERSON \rangle$))

and

(GOAL (NaturalizedUSCitizen $\langle PERSON \rangle$)).

If either of the proponents working on these new goals succeeds, we are justified in asserting

(USCitizen $\langle PERSON \rangle$).

This can be said in Ether in the following way:

```
(WHEN (GOAL (USCITIZEN = PERSON))
  (SHOW (NATIVEBORN person)
    (WHENACHIEVED
      (ASSERT (USCITIZEN person))))
  (SHOW (NATURALIZEDUSCITIZEN person)
    (WHENACHIEVED
      (ASSERT (USCITIZEN person))))).
```

When a goal that matches (USCITIZEN = PERSON) is received by the above sprite it disseminates the two new subgoals

(NATIVEBORN person)

and

(NATURALIZEDUSCITIZEN person).

Additionally it activates sprites that watch for either of the two new goals to be achieved. If either is established the respective sprite asserts (USCITIZEN PERSON) to record that the goal (which triggered the whole sprite) has been achieved.

B. Conjunctive Subgoals

The previous example was of a situation where *any* of the subgoals could be achieved in order to achieve the initial goal. There is an analogous kind of proponent for which *all* subgoals must be achieved for the main goal to be achieved. To exemplify this, suppose we wish to establish that a person is capable of becoming naturalized as a U.S. Citizen. There are two conditions that must be shown; he must have lived in the U.S. for at least 5 years *and* has knowledge of U.S. government. We can implement this proponent activity with the following sprite:

```
(WHEN (GOAL (CANBENATURALIZED = PERSON))
  (SHOW {(>(YEARSRESIDENT person) 5)
    (KNOWLEDGEABLE person USGOVERNMENT)}
    (WHENACHIEVED
      (ASSERT (CANBENATURALIZED person)))))).
```

V. SKEPTICAL ACTIVITIES

Scientific knowledge is perpetually in a state of evolution. *All* scientific theories and beliefs are subject to overthrow. This realization is a relatively recent one in Western thought. The spectacular achievement of relativistic mechanics played a large role in changing our opinions of the significance of scientific knowledge. Newtonian mechanics had achieved the status of incontrovertible truth in the minds of most thinkers until the beginning of this century. The discovery that even this superbly justified theory could be ultimately found false left little room for complacency about the ultimate status of any beliefs.

Popper's philosophy of science begins with the observation that an asymmetry exists between the logical provability and refutability of scientific theories. Observation statements can never logically imply such theories but they *can* logically refute them. A simple example of this is the

hypothesis "All swans are white." No matter how many white swans we observe we can never deduce on logical grounds the truth of this theory. However, from an observation statement reporting just one black swan, we can logically conclude that "All swans are white." is false.

The simple theory implied by the white swan example is an obvious oversimplification. Its importance in the historical development of the philosophy of science is the beginning of the doctrine of *falsificationism*. The name Lakatos [14] gives for the most elementary doctrine, in which a single refuting "observation" would disallow the entire theory, is *naive falsificationism*. More sophisticated theories have emerged which will be discussed shortly. We call activities whose purpose is to discover anomalous implicants of theories *skeptics*.

The efforts of skeptics is then largely applied in attempts to discredit scientific conjectures. Popper proposed that it is essential to the progress of science that many scientists hold conflicting explanations of phenomena. Scientists spend must of their time deducing the implications of theories (theirs or others) and testing the agreement of these implications with observations. The acceptability of a theory or explanation is related to its ability to avoid being discredited. This is the idea of natural selection applied to theories. The polynomial is not equal to nondeterministic polynomial ($P \neq NP$) conjecture provides a convincing example from contemporary computer science. There is no *logical* reason for believing that no deterministic algorithms for NP-complete problems run in polynomial time. Yet people lay great faith in the truth of this statement. Why such certainty in a mere conjecture? It is commonly believed because *so many people have tried to disprove it and failed*.

Abandoning a theory whenever an anomaly appears would lead one to reject every scientific theory ever proposed. Few scientific theories of any worth are so pristine that they can be said to entail no anomalous implications. The anomalies engendered by a scientific theory must be weighed in the context of ongoing research on alternative theories. These anomalies will often lead to modifications of the theories in a process known as *adjustment* to be discussed shortly.

VI. SPONSORS

A fact about real computers as well as the society in which we live is that resources are finite and therefore must be allocated to what we consider to be the important tasks at hand. This is reflected in Ether through mechanisms to allocate the available computational resources to the activated sprites. The scientific community has several mechanisms for allocating effort. Two important ones are funding structures and peer review. Scientific research that is considered presently useful is more likely to get funded and thus pursued. Similarly, a scientist who investigates theories in current vogue is more likely to achieve the admiration of his peers, get university posts, etc., that will promote his further research.

To model this process in Ether, we must find some way of allocating computational effort to goals. We call an agent that provides computational effort a "sponsor." All work done happens under some sponsor; in particular, all sprites capable of triggering do so through the support of a sponsor. Trying to disprove the flat-earth theory is an example of a goal which may (or most likely, may not) be supported by a sponsor.

When the potential results of some proposed activity in support of a goal do not seem of sufficient value, the sponsor will not provide much (or any) resources. Conversely, computations which seem more promising to the sponsor are given greater resources. Often several competing approaches will be possible in a given situation. The system, not having enough knowledge to conclude categorically that one will succeed over another, will apportion resources to several. A good example of this in today's world is the search for a safe and abundant energy source. There are those who argue that nuclear power is the only viable near-term energy source, those who argue for solar power, and those who favor coal. While one of these groups of people may very well be right, the system as a whole supports activity working on all. Society as a whole has little alternative but to patiently wait for the results of one group to outstrip the others.

Goals are created with sponsors that support the activities (both proponents and skeptics). If the goal has been achieved, or if it is demonstrated that the goal cannot be achieved, all the activity can be halted by making a request to the sponsor. In Ether a command of the form (WITHHOLD $\langle s \rangle$ (WITH REASON $\langle r \rangle$)) can be used to request that the sponsor $\langle s \rangle$ withhold further support for the reason $\langle r \rangle$.

In a previous section we showed how to we could use sprites to begin work on a goal. In the example we had a goal of determining whether Joe could be naturalized. We will expand our treatment of this example to illustrate the use of sponsors.

To assign goals to sponsors we expand the message disseminated to be

(GOAL (CANBENATURALIZED JOE) (WITH SPONSOR $= s$)).

In addition to containing an indication of the goal

(CANBENATURALIZED JOE)

the message states that s will sponsor work aimed at achieving it. If it is determined that Joe has lived in the U.S. for less than five years then we must give up all hope of showing that he can be naturalized. This is one kind of skeptic for the goal (CANBENATURALIZED JOE) is shown in the following:

(WHEN {(ASSERTION (YEARSRESIDENT JOE $= n$))
   (ASSERTION ($\leqslant n$ 5))}
    (WITHHOLD s (WITH REASON
     {(ASSERTION (YEARSRESIDENT JOE $= n$))
     (ASSERTION ($\leqslant n$ 5))}))))).

If an assertion of the form (YEARSRESIDENT JOE 2) is present, it will cause the sponsor s to withhold support for the goal. A skeptic has succeeded in showing a goal, on which the system has been investing some of its resources, is unattainable. These resources can then be given to more promising ventures.

Another way sponsors are used in the system is to prevent resources from being wasted attempting to establish *results already known*. The example of a proponent to achieve the goal of showing that a person can be naturalized has been reformulated below to show the use of sponsors and skeptics:

(WHEN (GOAL (CANBENATURALIZED $=$ PERSON)
  (WITH SPONSOR $= s$))
   (SHOW {($>$ (YEARSRESIDENT PERSON) 5)
    (KNOWLEDGEABLE PERSON USGOVERNMENT)}
     (WHENACHIEVED
      (ASSERT (CANBENATURALIZED PERSON))
      (WITHHOLD s (WITH REASON
      (ESTABLISHED
       (CANBENATURALIZED PERSON))))))
   (SHOW (NOT ($>$ (YEARSRESIDENT PERSON) 5))
    (WHENACHIEVED
     (WITHHOLD s (WITH REASON
     (NOT ($>$ (YEARSRESIDENT PERSON) 5))))))
   (SHOW (NOT
    (KNOWLEDGEABLE PERSON USGOVERNMENT))
    (WHENACHIEVED
     (WITHHOLD s (WITH REASON
     (NOT (KNOWLEDGEABLE PERSON
     USGOVERNMENT)))))))).

The first *show* command disseminates two subgoals. If they are both achieved for some person then the sponsor is requested to withhold support for working on the goal for that person. The second *show* command disseminates a goal to establish that the person has been a resident in the U.S. less than five years; if established the sponsor s is asked to withhold support for the goal. The last *show* command creates a similar goal to show that the person is not knowledgeable about U.S. Government.

We believe that the construction of truly complex problem solving systems will require more precise mechanisms of control than solely the abilities to start and stop work on a goal; it should be possible to let activities use different amounts of resources in accordance with the system's assessments of how useful the results are likely to be. Sponsors are allowed to assign varying amounts of *processing power*, measured in units of cycles per second, to activities. Sponsors, when created, are allocated a certain quantity of processing power which they can in turn allocate to sponsors they create. A sponsor can redistribute any resources it has been allocated at any time as new knowledge is gained.

The statement of the properties of monotonicity, commutativity, and parallelism must be slightly rephrased in order to be valid in systems with a sponsor because a message m will cause the execution of the body of a sprite s only if s can obtain resources from a sponsor.

VII. ADJUSTMENT

Conjectures often develop by adjusting to anomalies discovered in their predecessors. Research programs are often manifest as producing a sequence of theories. Each one is an adjustment of its predecessor and is able to handle more cases than its predecessor. Lakatos [13] illustrates this through a historical development of the Euler formula for the relationship between the number of faces, vertices, and edges of a polyhedron. Euler's formula is $F + V = E + 2$. Lakatos then presents counterexamples such as an object which is a cube with a smaller cube glued to one of its sides as shown in Fig. 1. This object has 11 faces, 16 vertices, and 24 edges. When this anomaly was discovered, an examination of the proof of Euler's formula led to the discovery that the discrepancy between the proven theorem and the counterexample could be attributed to the ring-shaped face shown shaded in the diagram. The process lead to better understanding of the Euler's formula and the concept of "polyhedron." Lakatos analyzes some of the techniques by which mathematical hypotheses are modified in the face of such refutations.

When an anomaly is discovered in a theory, the outcome is often an adjustment of the theory rather than a total dismissal. This is because theories that have shown some success tend to develop a core of fundamental concepts that serve to motivate further work. The process of adjustment, then, is an effort to protect this core from being discredited. Kuhn has pointed out the ubiquity of these cores of successful research programs (that he calls *paradigms*) in the sciences. The significance of paradigms in the scientific communities is that they provide the framework of research programs to investigate promising ideas.

Only the most trivial kinds of theories can be proposed correctly the first time. Most theories that gain significant acceptance evolve through a continual interplay of proponents, skeptics, and adjustment. This aspect of the workings of a scientific community has not yet been modeled in an interesting way in Ether.

A. Adherence

We can make several important observations about the characterization of *adherence* to positions, theories, methods, etc. in scientific communities. We believe that these considerations have important implications in the design of programs for problem solving applications.

1) *Scientific communities are structured to support competition as well as cooperation.* A system must be able to support parts of itself working on related or unrelated problems concurrently.

2) *Current adherence does not imply adherence for all future time.* Messages must be labeled with their context (author, time, place, etc.).

3) *Adherence is a local rather than a global phenomenon.* We would like to support plurality of approaches within the system. Different approaches naturally require somewhat different belief sets. There is no

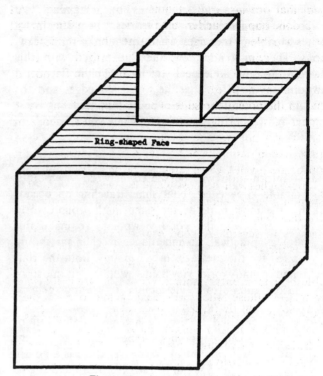

Fig. 1. Lakatos counterexample.

one who speaks for the scientific community as a whole.

Often opposing directions of research are found between schools of thought that do not closely interact. An example is schools of psychology. The Freudian and behaviorist schools explain human neuroses in very different ways. Neither has proved that its ideas are in all respects superior to its competitors. There is no good reason for the community as a whole to accept one theory over the other. In the absence of criterial experiments to discredit one theory or the other, these opposing ideas may coexist in the community for a long time. Evolution is often gradual, taking years or decades. On rare occasions it is quite rapid as the community reacts to a "breakthrough" that clearly decides an issue previously muddled.

Research effort in opposing directions is not only found between distinct schools of thought; it can often be found in the same research group or individual. A tradition of intercolleague criticism of ideas is found in many research centers.

VIII. VIEWPOINTS

The Ether examples of the previous sections did not involve any concept of *relativized belief*; in a sense, all assertions present were "believed" by the entire system. Relativized beliefs arise in accounting for the plurality of adherence in Ether. *Viewpoints* are a construct used in Ether to relativize messages as to assumptions, approaches, etc. From the sprites' point of view they represent *access points* to the messages in the system.

All thought happens in the context of certain assumptions. For example, we can distinguish between the *flat-*

world and *round-world* hypotheses by imagining two viewpoints, one for each of the theories. There are sprites that "watch for" messages which mention certain viewpoints. They may add new messages tagged with this viewpoint. We would expect statements in the flat-world viewpoint to the effect that the world has edges and the belief in the round-world viewpoint that traveling west long enough will bring you back to where you started.

A. Inheritance

Most information will be shared between viewpoints. For example knowledge about ships traveling on oceans will, for the most part, be the same in the round-world viewpoint as in the flat-world viewpoint. To make this methodology practical, an inheritance mechanism should be supplied for the messages in viewpoints. Both the flat-world and round-world viewpoints will inherit most of their information from viewpoints indicating general knowledge about the world.

Ether can be used to provide a simple definition of inheritance between viewpoints. Suppose that a viewpoint $v2$ inherits from viewpoint $v1$. Whenever there is a goal g with viewpoint $v2$ then it can be satisfied by attempting to show g with viewpoint $v1$. If g can be achieved with viewpoint $v1$ then it can be achieved with viewpoint $v2$. The following sprite shows how this procedure can be expressed very simply in Ether:

```
(WHEN (ASSERTION (INHERITSFROM = v2 = v1))
    (ACTIVATE (WHEN (GOAL = g (WITH VIEWPOINT v2))
        (SHOW (g (WITH VIEWPOINT v1))
        (WHENACHIEVED
            (ASSERT g (WITH VIEWPOINT v2)))))))).
```

In effect the above sprite gives viewpoint $v2$ a "virtual copy" of the information in $v1$.

We can illustrate the use of inheritance by showing how to implement conditional proof in logic. Suppose the goal is to prove that a formula p implies a formula q in some viewpoint v. This goal can be achieved by creating a new viewpoint v' which inherits from v, assuming p in v', and showing that q holds in v'. The following sprite expresses exactly this method:

```
(WHEN (GOAL (IMPLIES p q) (WITH VIEWPOINT = v))
(LET (v' BE (CreateNewViewpoint (WITH PARENT v)))
    (ASSERT (INHERITSFROM v' v))
    (ASSERT p (WITH VIEWPOINT v'))
    (SHOW q (WITH VIEWPOINT v')
    (WHENACHIEVED
        (ASSERT (IMPLIES p q) (WITH VIEWPOINT v)))))).
```

People rarely consider any belief totally false. Instead, it may be advisable to accept the utility of a proposition *with certain provisos*. Newtonian mechanics, although not "correct" is still quite useful. Newtonian mechanics is now believed to be valid asymptotically for small velocities. In fact many engineering disciplines find "relativistic effects" insignificant enough that they can be safely ignored. This kind of inheritance might be expressed schematically in Ether as follows:

```
(WHEN {((GOAL (FORMULA = E
  (WITH RELATIVEVELOCITY = v))
    (WITH VIEWPOINT RELATIVISTIC))
      (ASSERTION (= v {APPROXIMATELY} 0))}
    (SHOW (FORMULA E)
      (WITH VIEWPOINT NEWTONIAN)
      (WHENACHIEVED
        (ASSERT (FORMULA E)
          (WITH VIEWPOINT RELATIVISTIC)))))).
```

B. Translation

In many cases viewpoints although closely related do not inherit all information from one another. For example Newtonian mechanics is a special case of relativistic mechanics. However the frame transformations of Newtonian mechanics are not inherited from special relativity. The Newtonian frame transformations are *translations* of the relativistic ones. The following sprite translates all the relativistic transformations into their Newtonian counterparts:

```
(WHEN (ASSERTION (TRANSFORMATION = E (WITH RELA-
TIVEVELOCITY = v)) (WITH VIEWPOINT RELATIVISTIC))
    (ASSERT (TRANSFORMATION (LIMIT_{v→0} E)) (WITH VIEW-
POINT NEWTONIAN))).
```

Note that the above sprite does all the translation work in parallel and records all the results in the Newtonian point of view. This example differs from the previous ones illustrating inheritance in that all the translations are done on the grounds that they will prove to be generally useful instead of waiting for a problem in Newtonian mechanics that seems to need a transformation of a certain form. The style of reasoning illustrated above is often called "antecedent reasoning" or "reasoning forward from the data."

IX. FUTURE WORK

We have found the scientific community metaphor a useful one for stimulating the development of programing structures for artificial intelligence research. We plan to continue exploring this metaphor. We are now involved in the study of several application areas to be programmed in Ether using ideas developed in this paper. One of us (Kornfeld) is currently involved in research applying this problem solving approach to certain problems in program understanding and synthesis.

Pattern-directed invocation languages (such as Ether) pay dearly for their generality through lack of efficiency. We are now investigating a scheme known as *virtual collection of assertions* that we believe will make this class of system practical for much larger applications. Pattern-directed invocation languages have traditionally been implemented using methods that index messages in a uniform way. Sprites search this database for messages on which they can trigger. There are various schemes, such as discrimination nets and hash tables, that keep the speed of this search process from degenerating linearly with the number of messages. Knowledge can be stored and retrieved more readily when it is indexed in some *semantically* meaningful way. We propose to selectively augment the default indexing and retrieval methods. The new procedures say in effect "When you want to disseminate messages of a certain kind, what you *really* do is execute this procedure." The procedure will record the messages in a way that it can be efficiently retrieved. Correspondingly sprites which can trigger on messages or certain kinds perform compatible procedures. In this way we can gain the benefits of pattern-directed invocation without incurring all of the overhead.

The description system *Omega* [7] addresses issues involved in the construction and manipulation of semantic networks of structured descriptions. A description language has potential advantages over simple assertions as the medium for communication in Ether because semantic relationships we may want to talk about have already been encoded in the description language. The possibility exists for using Omega as the language by which communication in Ether happens. The efficient implementation of Ether involves the development of a solid basis in concepts of parallel communication. We hope to draw on the notions of message passing and serialization as developed in *Act 1* [9].

Although we have been talking about parallel *languages* we have not concerned ourselves with parallel *hardware*. We believe advantages of parallel processing languages for problem solving are substantial on a serial computer run in a time-sliced fashion. However, because of the inherent parallelism in Ether, parallel hardware could be effectively utilized. The *Apiary* [10], [21] is an architecture under construction at the Massachusetts Institute of Technology Artificial Intelligence Laboratory for implementing computer systems with large amounts of parallelism.

X. Conclusion

Our main point is that *scientific communities are highly parallel systems*. Many scientists are able to work concurrently on the same, similar, or quite different problems. At any one time, in a scientific community, alternative theories are expounded concurrently and argued. This diversity, rather than being superfluous to the growth of science, is essential to it.

We believe that these observations can supply important insights that will aid in the construction of problem solving systems. The Ether language has been designed to facilitate the construction of problem solvers with a high degree of concurrency and diversity. Ether programs do not begin to approach the complexity found in scientific communities; nevertheless, we believe the metaphor will prove fruitful in guiding the designs of future problem solvers.

XI. Related Work

Most of the ideas in the Ether system are not completely new. They are further developments of ideas in previous systems. This paper represents a further development of the scientific community metaphor for problem solving, which was proposed as an important topic for investigation in [6]. The motivation is that incorporating the problem solving mechanisms of scientific communities can be fruitful in the same way that incorporating the problem solving mechanisms of individual humans.

The *parallel pattern directed invocation* used in Ether is a descendant of a pattern-directed invocation developed for Planner-69 [4] which was implemented under the name Micro-Planner. In Planner when a goal was proposed an applicable *demon* was chosen to attempt to achieve the goal. If the *demon* concluded that it had failed then it would backtrack and another applicable demon would be chosen. The *parallel* pattern directed invocation of Ether differs in that all the applicable sprites which can get support will work on the goal concurrently. In addition there is the possibility of even more parallelism because there may be some skeptics which would like to demonstrate that the goal cannot be achieved. In view of these differences, Danny Hillis suggested the name *sprite* to replace the somewhat malevolent *demons* of Planner. The nested continuation control structure of Ether builds on similar constructs in [23], [5], [1].

Viewpoints are a means of relativizing messages according to different assumptions, authors, times, and theories. The intellectual roots for viewpoints come from several sources. McCarthy introduced the notion of a situation argument in predicates to relativize collections according to a situation where a situation was defined to be the entire state of the universe. In his system each situation represented the entire state of the universe at one time. In the development of the actor theory of computation, this notion of global state proved to be ineffective so a theory of local states was developed in its stead. In QA-4 Rulifson introduced a context mechanism to Planner-like systems. Contexts could be used to represent hypothetical assumptions. The QA-4 notion of context was limited by being tied to a control structure of "pushing" and "popping" contexts and by the way in which a particular notion of inheritance was wired into the interpreter. Providing inheritance and translation sprites provides a more powerful and useful mechanism for addressing issues of sharing knowledge between viewpoints. The inheritance in the natural deduction system used in Ether closely resembles the logical system developed by Kalish and Montague [24].

Turing was one of the first to develop the notion of an individual human metaphor for problem solving through the notion of his famous Turing Test. This paradigm was developed and deepened with the development of Artificial Intelligence as an identifiable field of research in the 1950's. Newell and Simon did notable work within this paradigm through their work in analyzing the protocols of individual human problem solving behavior on puzzles. More recently Minsky and Papert have attempted to develop the idea that the mind of an individual human is composed of a society of agents. The above research on *individual* human problem solving is complementary to our research on the scientific community metaphor.

It may well be the case that some of the problem solving mechanisms which we have explored in the context of scientific communities are also used by the human brain. Unfortunately the current state of the art in neurophysiology is too primitive to shed much light on the question. One of the most important benefits of studying scientific communities is that we have been able to find convincing examples of the problem solving techniques discussed in this paper. Moreover investigation of the structure of problem solving in scientific communities has greatly helped in the design and evolution of Ether.

ACKNOWLEDGMENT

The authors would like to thank Randy Davis, Fry, Ken Forbus, Ken Kahn, David Levitt, and Henry Lieberman for reading earlier drafts of this paper and supplying helpful comments. Conversations with Roger Duffey, Harold Goldberger, Pat Hays, Nils Nilsson, Allen Newell, John McCarthy, Jeff Rulifson, Luc Steels, Gerry Sussman, Sten-Ake Tarnlund, and Richard Weyhrauch have proved very useful in developing these ideas.

REFERENCES

[1] J. de Kleer, J. Doyle, C. Rich, G. Steele, and G. Sussman, "AMORD: A deductive procedure system," Massachusetts Inst. Technol., Cambridge, MA, Artificial Intelligence Lab., Memo 435, Jan 1978.
[2] S. Fahlman, "A system for representing and using real-world knowledge," Ph.D. dissertation, Dep. Elec. Eng. and Comput. Sci., Massachusetts Inst. Technol., Cambridge, MA, 1978.
[3] P. Feyerabend, "Against method," Minnesota Studies in Phil. of Sci., 1970.
[4] C. Hewitt, "PLANNER: A language for manipulating models and proving theorems in a robot," presented at the First Int. Joint Conf. on Artificial Intelligence, 1969, Washington D.C., Aug. 1969.
[5] ____, "How to use what you know," presented at the Fourth Int. Joint Conf. on Artificial Intelligence, Tblisi, U.S.S.R., Sept. 1975.
[6] ____, "Viewing control structures as patterns of passing messages," Artificial Intelligence J., vol. 8, pp. 323–364, June 1977.
[7] C. Hewitt, G. Attardi, and M. Simi, "Knowledge embedding in the description system OMEGA," in Proc. AAAI, Stanford, CA, Aug. 1980.
[8] C. Hewitt, G. Attardi, and H. Lieberman, "Specifying and proving properties of guardians for distributed systems," in Semantics of Concurrent Computations G. Kahn, Ed., Lecture Notes in Computer Science, No. 70. Berlin: Springer, 1976.
[9] ____, "Security and modularity in message passing," presented at the First Int. Conf. on Distributed Computing Systems, Huntsville, AL, Oct. 1979.
[10] C. Hewitt, "The Apiary network architecture for knowledgeable systems," in Proc. Lisp Conf., Stanford, CA, Aug. 1980.
[11] W. Kornfeld, "Using parallel processing for problem solving," Massachusetts Inst. Technol., Cambridge, MA, Artificial Intelligence Lab., Memo 561, 1979.
[12] T. S. Kuhn, The Structure of Scientific Revolutions, 2nd ed. Chicago, IL: University of Chicago, 1970.
[13] I. Lakatos, Proofs and Refutations. New York: Cambridge University, 1976.
[14] ____, "Falsification and the methodology of scientific research programmes," in Criticism and the Growth of Knowledge, Musgrave and Lakatos, Eds. New York: Cambridge University, 1970.
[15] V. R. Lesser, L. D. Erman, "A retrospective view of the Hearsay II architecture," presented at the Fifth Int. Joint Conf. on Artificial Intelligence, 1977.
[16] J. McCarthy, "Situations, actions, and causal laws," Stanford University, Stanford, CA, Stanford Artificial Intelligence Project, Memo 2, 1963.
[17] J. McCarthy and P. Hays, "Some philosophical problems from the standpoint of artificial intelligence," Stanford University, Stanford, CA, Stanford Artificial Intelligence Proj., Memo No. AI-73, Nov. 1968.
[18] K. R. Popper, Conjectures and Refutations. New York: Basic Books, 1962.
[19] ____, The Logic of Scientific Discovery. New York, Harper & Row, 1968.
[20] J. F. Rulifson, J. A. Derksen, R. J. Waldinger, "QA4: A procedural calculus for intuitive reasoning," Stanford University, Stanford, CA, Stanford Research Inst. Artificial Intelligence Center, Tech. Note 73.
[21] J. Schiller, "The design and implementation of APIARY-0," 1979.
[22] R. G. Smith and R. Davis, "Distributed problem solving: The contract net approach," in Proc. Second National Conf. of Canadian Soc. for Computational Studies of Intelligence, July 1978.
[23] M. B. Wilber, "A QLISP reference manual," Stanford University, Stanford, CA, Stanford Research Inst. Artificial Intelligence Center, Tech. Note 118, 1975.
[24] D. Kalish and R. Montague, Logic: Techniques of Formal Reasoning. New York: Harcourt Brace Jovanovich, 1964.

Offices Are Open Systems

CARL HEWITT
MIT Artificial Intelligence Laboratory

This paper is intended as a contribution to analysis of the implications of viewing offices as open systems. It takes a prescriptive stance on how to establish the information-processing foundations for taking action and making decisions in office work from an open systems perspective. We propose *due process* as a central activity in organizational information processing. Computer systems are beginning to play important roles in mediating the ongoing activities of organizations. We expect that these roles will gradually increase in importance as computer systems take on more of the authority and responsibility for ongoing activities. At the same time we expect computer systems to acquire more of the characteristics and structure of human organizations.

Categories and Subject Descriptors: D.1.3 [**Programming Techniques**]: Concurrent Programming; D.3.2 [**Programming Languages**]: Language Classifications—*very high-level languages*; D.4.5 [**Operating Systems**]: Reliability; I.2.4 [**Artificial Intelligence**]: Knowledge Representations Formalisms and Methods; I.2.8 [**Artificial Intelligence**]: Problem Solving, Control Methods and Search—*plan execution, formation, generation*

General Terms: Management

Additional Key Words and Phrases: Debate, decision making, due process, logic, microtheories, negotiation, offices, open systems

1. INTRODUCTION

In this paper we discuss the nature of office work from an open systems perspective. Coping with the conflicting, inconsistent, and partial information is one of the major challenges in office information systems. Due process is the organizational activity of human and computer systems for generating sound, relevant, and reliable information as a basis of action taking. Within due process logical reasoning takes place within relatively small coherent modules called microtheories. In general the microtheories will be inconsistent with one another. Due process makes use of debate and negotiation to deal with conflicts and inconsistencies between microtheories.

2. OFFICE WORK

We define an *office* as a place where *office work* is done, thus shifting the emphasis of our investigation from the nature of the locale to the nature of the activity performed. Office work can take place in an automobile with a mobile telephone,

in the anteroom of a lecture hall, or at a networked personal computer. Of course, the situation including place, time, and participants can materially affect the work. All office work takes place within a particular concrete situation. The point that we want to make here is that there is no *special* place where office work has to take place.

Later, we discuss how office work is situated in *particular concrete* space and time and how the situation provides an important part of the context in which the work is done.

We take *office work* to be information processing that is done to coordinate all the work that an organization does with the exception of direct manipulation of physical objects. The organizations in which office work takes place are "going concerns" in the sense of Everett Hughes [11]. For example, they include the processing of beliefs, goals, and mutual commitments as well as the development and management of responsibilities, policies, tasks, transactions, projects, and procedures. Office work is specialized by excluding *robotics*. Robotics involves information processing directly involved in the physical production, transformation, transportation, servicing, or consumption of physical objects.

Office work is situated social action in the sense that it is the action produced by participants at particular times and places. However, we need to extend the usual notion of situated social actions to encompass the social actions of computer systems in their interactions with other computer systems as well as the interactions of computer systems with human participants.

3. OPEN SYSTEMS

Offices are inherently open systems because of the requirement of communication with operational divisions as well as the external world in the task of coordinating the work of the organization. In all nontrivial cases the communication necessary for coordination takes place asynchronously. Unplanned dynamic adaptation and accommodation are required in organizational information systems to meet the unplanned changing needs of coordination since the execution of any plan requires articulation, change, and adjustment.

Open systems deal with large quantities of diverse information and exploit massive concurrency. They can be characterized by the following fundamental characteristics [9]:

(1) *Concurrency.* Open systems are composed of numerous components such as workstations, databases, and networks. To handle the simultaneous influx of information from many outside sources, these components must process information concurrently.

(2) *Asynchrony.* There are two sources of asynchrony in open systems. First, since the behavior of the environment is not necessarily predictable by the system itself, new information may enter the system at any time, requiring it to operate asynchronously with the outside world. Second, the components are physically separated distances prohibiting them from acting synchronously. Any attempt to clock all the components synchronously would result in an enormous performance degradation because the clocks would have to be slowed down by orders of magnitude in order to maintain synchronization.

The indeterminacy of concurrent computation is different from the usual nondeterministic computation studied in automata theory in which coin flipping is allowed as an elementary computational step. In general, it is not possible to know ahead of time that a concurrent system will make a decision by a certain time. Flipping a coin can be used as a method of forcing decisions to occur by making an arbitrary choice. Often as a matter of principle, however, due process refuses to invoke arbitrary random measures such as coin flipping to make a decision. For example, a jury might not return a verdict, and the judge might have to declare a mistrial.[1]

5. CONFLICTING INFORMATION AND CONTRADICTORY BELIEFS

Conflicting sources of information and inconsistent beliefs are a staple of life in organizational information systems. This partly results from dealing with differing external organizations that retain their own autonomy and belief structures.

Inconsistencies inevitably result from the measurements and observations made on complicated physical systems. Higher level abstractions are used to attempt to construct a consistent description of parts of the environment in which the organization operates. For example, a firm's earnings might be labeled "provisional" and then "subject to audit." But, even after being published in the annual report, they might later have to be "restated." In this case "provisional," "subject to audit," and "restated" are attempts to construct a consistent description from conflicting information about earnings.

Whatever consistency exists among the beliefs within an organization is *constructed* and *negotiated* by the participants. In the case of reported earnings, the chief executive officer, finance department, board of directors, and regulatory authorities play important roles in constructing and negotiating the financial reports.

Any belief concerning an organization or its environment is subject to internal and external challenges. Organizations must efficiently take action and make decisions in the face of conflicting information and contradictory beliefs. How they do so is a fundamental consideration in the foundations of organizational information systems.

Conflicting information and contradictory beliefs are engendered by the enormous interconnectivity and interdependence of knowledge that come from multiple sources and viewpoints. The interconnectivity makes it impossible to separate knowledge of the organization's affairs into independent modules. The knowledge of any physical aspect has extensive *spatiotemporal, causal, terminological, evidential,* and *communicative* connections with other aspects of the organization's affairs. The interconnectivity generates an enormous network of knowledge that is inherently inconsistent because of the multiple sources of knowledge making contributions at different times and places.

For example, suppose that in the middle of 1986 an organization undertakes to consider its knowledge of sales currently in progress for that year for the New England region. In such a situation, there is an enormous amount of information

---

[1] Agha [1] provides an excellent exposition of the nature of a mathematical model of concurrent computation and its differences with classical nondeterministic Turing-machine-based theories.

(3) *Decentralized control.* In an open system, a centralized decision maker would become a serious bottleneck. Furthermore, because of communications asynchrony and unreliability, a controlling agent could never have complete, up-to-date information on the state of the system. Therefore control must be distributed throughout the system so that local decisions can be made close to where they are needed.

(4) *Inconsistent information.* Information from outside the system or even from different parts of the same system may turn out to be inconsistent. Therefore decisions must be made by the components of an open system by considering whatever evidence is currently available.

(5) *Arm's-length relationships.* The components of an open system are at an *arm's-length relationship:* The internal operation, organization, and state of one computational agent may be unknown and unavailable to another agent for reasons of privacy or outage of communications. Information should be passed by explicit communication between agents to conserve energy and maintain security. This ensures that each component can be kept simple since it only needs to keep track of its own state and its interfaces to other agents.

(6) *Continuous operation.* Open systems must be reliable. They must be designed so that failures of individual components can be accommodated by the operating components while the failed components are repaired or replaced.

4. CONCURRENCY

The underlying concurrent basis of operation enables due process to react dynamically to asynchronous input and in many cases makes the results indeterminate.

4.1 Asynchronous Input

Concurrent systems differ from Turing machines in that they allow asynchronous communication from the external environment to affect ongoing operations. Organizations must efficiently take action and make decisions. Sequential systems deal with this problem as a kind of "interrupt" in which they "switch tasks." Organizational information systems rarely have all the material at hand needed to make an important decision. Information that is known in advance to be required arrives asynchronously as the decision making proceeds and is often incomplete. Unanticipated information can arrive at any time in the process and affect the outcome even though it arrives quite late. For instance, an unanticipated story in the *Wall Street Journal* on the morning of a corporate board meeting to give final approval to a merger has been known to kill or delay a deal.

4.2 Indeterminacy

Concurrent systems are inherently indeterminate. The indeterminacy of concurrent systems does not stem from invoking a random element such as flipping a coin. Instead it results from the indeterminate arrival order of inputs to system components. In general, complete knowledge of the state and structure of a concurrent system together with exact knowledge of the times and values of inputs does not determine the system's output. Concurrent systems are indeterminate for the same reason that other quantum devices are indeterminate.

about other pieces of information. The following considerations show a small part of the enormous interconnectivity of knowledge:

—*Spatiotemporal interconnectivity.* The organization has a great deal of knowledge about the history of sales in the New England region in the first few months of 1986, including how the sales were generated and recorded. In addition, it has sales projections of what will happen in the remainder of the year.

—*Causal interconnectivity.* The marketing department believes that increased advertising is causing sales to go up. On the other hand, the sales department believes that the increased sales commissions are the real reason for the increase in sales.

—*Terminological interconnectivity.* Some of the sales are really barter agreements with uncertain cash value. Do the barter agreements qualify as sales?

—*Evidential interconnectivity.* The accounting department fears that sales might really not be increasing because many of the products could be returned because of a new 30-day free trial offer. It does not believe that the evidence presented shows that sales are increasing.

—*Communicative interconnectivity.* The organization consists of a community of actors operating concurrently, asynchronously, and nondeterministically. The asynchronous communications engender interconnectivity, which defies any complete description of the global state of the organization at any particular point in time.

Conflicting information and contradictory beliefs are an inherent part of office work that must be explicitly addressed in any foundation for organizational information systems.

6. DUE PROCESS

Due process is the organizational activity of humans and computers for generating sound, relevant, and reliable information as a basis for decision and action within the constraints of allowable resources [4]. It provides an arena in which beliefs and proposals can be gathered, analyzed, and debated. Part of due process is to provide a record of the decision-making process that can later be referenced.

Due process is inherently reflective in that beliefs, goals, plans, requests, commitments, etc., exist as objects that can be explicitly mentioned and manipulated in the ongoing process.

Due process does not make decisions or take actions per se. Instead it is the process that informs the decision-making process. Each instance of due process begins with *preconceptions* handed down through traditions and culture that constitute the initial process but are open to future testing and evolution. Decision-making criteria such as preferences in predicted outcomes are included in this knowledge base. For example, increased profitability is preferable to decreased profitability. Also, increased market share is preferable to decreased market share. Conflicts between these preferences can be negotiated [18]. In addition preferences can arise as a result of conflict. Negotiating conflict can bring the negotiating process itself into question as part of the evaluative criteria

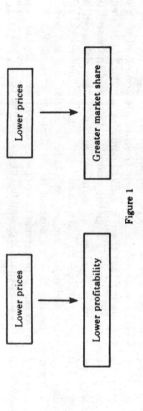

Figure 1

of how to proceed, which can itself change the quality of conflict among the participants [7, 7a].

Changing the price of a product can affect both its profitability and market share, as shown in Figure 1. Market research and internal cost analysis can help model the effects of lower prices on profitability and market share. The sales and financial divisions can have very different views on the subject. They need to organize their respective positions including counter-arguments to opposing views. The cost-effectiveness of generating new information by market research and new product development can be considered by using due process.

All this activity takes place within a context that sets the time frame for the decision-making process. Sometimes the time frames can be very short, and, at the same time, the decision could be very important to the organization. Consider the sudden appearance of a new product that is drastically undercutting prices and demands a quick decision as to whether or not to cut prices. It is extremely common for a "case" to occur in due process that has to be settled promptly but has implications for more general issues. A company may develop a general vacation policy because a request by a particular employee for certain vacation privileges has to be granted or refused [13]. Due process takes place within action-taking and decision-making situations. It occurs at a particular place and time within a community of actors (both human and computer) that communicate with one another in a historical context involving information gathering, discussion, and debate.

The communications involved in due process can be analyzed along the following dimensions:

Belief. The dimension of belief concerns the propositional content of a message. Belief is an integral part of organizational information gathering and analysis.

Commitment. The dimension of commitment concerns the plans of the actors as to their future actions. Commitment is an integral part of organizational planning. Organizations grant certain of their components the authority to commit the whole organization to certain future actions [2].

Request. The dimension of request concerns the attempt to influence the future actions of recipients of the message. Requests are used in organizational execution.

Declaration. The dimension of declaration concerns the ability to change the agreed state of affairs by the performance of the appropriate communicative act. Declarations are used in organizational rearrangements and confirmations.

Expression. The dimension of expression concerns the attitude of the actors (e.g., fear, anger, gratitude). Expressions are used in organizational resource adjustments.

An individual communicative act can involve several of the above dimensions. We take the meaning of each communicative act to be its subsequent effect on the participants whether they be human or computer. An important challenge in organizational information systems is to construct computer systems that can perform appropriately for the above kinds of communicative acts by making use of the information in the implications of communications in the wider context in which they take place.

6.1 Record Making

Due process produces a record of the decision-making and action-taking process, including which organization is responsible for dealing with problems, responses, and questions for the decision made or the action taken. This is the way in which responsibility is assessed for the decisions and actions taken.

The record also includes rationales for various courses of action such as

—*Predicted beneficial results.* Better targeted advertising will increase sales.
—*Policies guiding conduct.* Products may not be returned for credit more than 30 days after sale.
—*Reasons tied to specific institutional roles or processes.* A corporation may not be able to enter the computer business because of a consent decree that it has signed.
—*Precedent.* The organization might always have taken Patriots' Day as a holiday. Precedent may seem like a weak rationale. However, deciding according to precedent in the absence of strong alternatives has the consequences of predictability, stability, and improvement in the general coherence among decided cases.

Due process is an inherently self-reflective process in that the process by which information is gathered, organized, compared, and presented is subject to evaluation, debate, and evolution within the organization. Thus the debate is not just about whether to lower prices, but also about the beliefs used in the decision and the process used by the organization to decide whether to lower them.

6.2 Cooperation

Due process is not a magical way for an organization to make "correct" decisions. Instead it is concerned with the reasonableness with which information is gathered, organized, compared, and presented. It addresses the question, "How can the decision-making process be improved?" instead of the question, "What is the right decision?" Efforts to find the basis for "correct" decision making before the organization goes to work are fruitless. Attempting to critique a particular course of action chosen by an organization involves us in the very same activities that are embodied in due process.

In general due process involves cooperation among the participant actors in the organization. The participants' investment in the process of information gathering, evaluation, debate, and presentation helps to produce the consensus. Every participant knows that his or her views need to be put forth in order to be considered and balanced against the others. In general those actors whose authority and responsibility are most affected by the choice of action must at least give their passive cooperation. Preexisting organizational precedents and traditions are influential in the exact way that a choice of action is made. Even if the course of action taken is not the participant's first choice, the execution of the decision can be tailored to reflect the views and concerns that have been uncovered in due process. Also recompense can often be offered to disgruntled parties by making allowances in other concurrent decision making within the organization.

6.3 Task Performance Assessment

Assessing how well the task was performed or how the performance might be improved can be quite problematical. Each performance is unique. It must be assessed in terms of quality of analysis, planning, and execution, as well as the appropriate balance of these activities. Performance assessment is subject to severe limitations in available knowledge about realistic alternatives because of unknown interactions between details in a performance. For example, the timing of an advertising campaign can affect the results of sales.

7. MICROTHEORIES AS TOOLS IN DUE PROCESS

A *microtheory* is a relatively small, idealized, mathematical theory that embodies a model of some physical system. Prescriptively, a microtheory should be internally consistent and clearly demarcated. Any modification of a microtheory is a new microtheory. Special relativity, a spreadsheet model of a company's projected sales, and a Spice simulation of an integrated circuit are examples of microtheories. Microtheories are simple because they have simple axiomatizations. The physical system being modeled, however, may be enormously complicated. We expect that computer systems will require hundreds of thousands of microtheories in order to participate effectively in organizational work.

In general due process deals with *conflicting* microtheories that cannot always be measured against one another in a pointwise fashion. In due process, debate and negotiation takes place where rival microtheories are compared with one another without assuming that there is a fixed common standard of reference. We do not assume that there is a global axiomatic theory of the world that gradually becomes more complete as more microtheories are debugged and introduced. Instead we propose to deal with each problematical concrete situation by using negotiation and debate among the available overlapping and possibly conflicting microtheories that are adapted to the situation at hand. For many purposes in due process it is preferable to work with microtheories that are small and oversimplified, rather than large and full of caveats and conditions [17].

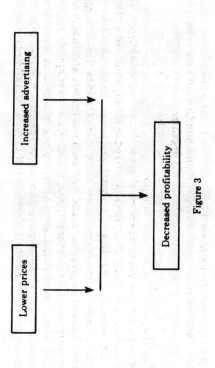

Figure 2

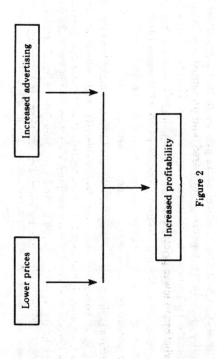

Figure 3

Logical deduction is a powerful tool for working *within* a microtheory. The strengths of logical deduction include

— *Well understood.* Logical deduction is a very well-understood and characterized process. Rigorous model theories exist for many logics including the predicate calculus, intuitionistic logics, and modal logics.

— *Validity locally decidable.* An important goal of logical proofs is that their correctness should be mechanically decidable from the proof inscription. In this way the situation of proof creation can be distinct from the subsequent situations of proof checking. In order to be algorithmic, the proof-checking process cannot require making any observations or consulting any external sources of information. Consequently all of the premises of each proof step as to place, time, objects, etc., must be explicit. In effect a *situational closure* must be taken for each deductive step. Proof checking proceeds in a closed world in which the axioms and rules of deductive inference have been laid out explicitly beforehand. Ray Reiter [16] has developed closure axioms that justify the default rules used in relational databases as logical deductions. Similarly the circumscription technique proposed by John McCarthy [14] is a closure operator on sets of axioms that results in stronger, more complete axiom sets.

— *Belief constraining.* Logical deductions deal with issues about logically entailed relationships among beliefs. If an actor believes P and (P implies Q), then it is constrained to believe Q. Similarly if an actor believes (P implies Q) and entertains the goal of believing Q, then it can entertain the goal of believing P. Examples below illustrate how both of these techniques can be valuable in evolving and managing belief structures.

Let us consider a simple concrete example to illustrate the use of logical deduction in organizational decision making. Commercial enterprises sometimes put their merchandise "on sale" to increase sales. Often this is done by cutting prices and increasing advertising. Consider the microtheory shown in Figure 2, which we shall call *profitable sale*.

We shall use the above deduction rule as a *microtheory* to explore how deduction can be used in organizational decision making. Microtheories are simply very

small partial logical theories. They are kept small and partial to avoid the problems of entanglement by interconnectivity, as discussed above.

We take a very general view of deduction: Deductive proofs are tree structures in which a computer can mechanically decide whether a step is valid just by inspecting the premises and conclusion of the deduction.

A microtheory should be internally consistent. Ideally there should even be good arguments for its consistency. If an inconsistency is discovered in a microtheory, then a repair can be attempted. Sometimes the repair attempt will fail in the face of well-justified contrary beliefs. This can be dealt with by splitting the microtheory into more specialized microtheories.

7.1 Contradictory Knowledge

Microtheories are often inconsistent with one another. The financial department might argue that lowering prices brings in less revenue, advertising increases expenses, and therefore profitability could very well decrease. We could express this model in the microtheory shown in Figure 3, which we shall call *unprofitable sale.*

Our second microtheory directly contradicts the first. Proofs are not convincing in a contradictory knowledge base in which we can prove both that the profitability will increase and that it will decrease. Therefore we confine logical deduction to within microtheories that are presumed to be consistent and use due process to mediate contradictory microtheories.

7.2 Counterarguments

The tree-structured, locally decidable character of logical deductive proof cannot take audiences into account. The *profitable-sale* microtheory cannot take into account the counterargument of the *unprofitable-sale* microtheory. We shall use extradeductive techniques such as negotiation and debate to deal with the inconsistencies and conflicts between microtheories.

A *metamicrotheory* has as part of its content axioms about other microtheories as in the work of Richard Weyhrauch [19]. Such metamicrotheories can be very useful. Due process reasoning often involves debate and negotiation between multiple conflicting metamicrotheories [20]. The metamicrotheories arise in the course of debate about the reasonableness and applicability of previously introduced microtheories. Often the metamicrotheories are also inconsistent with one another.

For example, the microtheory shown in Figure 4 takes into account the limited inventory as well as the decreased profitability and increased profitability microtheories to conclude that the sale would be of low profitability because of the limited inventory, whereas the metamicrotheory shown in Figure 5 concludes that desirable inventory clearance would take place as a result of the sale.

7.3 Context

The validity of a deductive proof is supposed to be timeless and acontextual. If it is valid at all, then it is supposed to be valid for all times and places. The timeless and acontextual character of logical deduction is a tremendous advantage in separating the proof-creation situation from the proof-checking context.

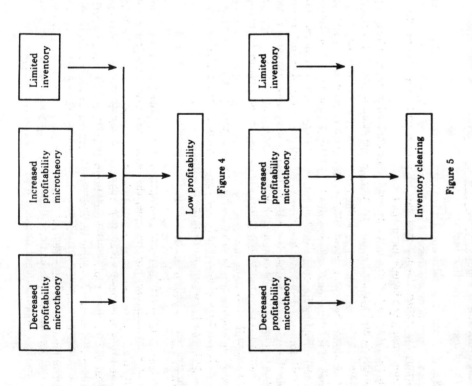

Figure 4

Figure 5

However, applicability of an empirical deductive rule such as the *profitable-sale* rule is problematic in many situations. For example, the rule might be challenged on the grounds that the conditions under which it worked in the past no longer hold because, for example, the market is saturated. To meet this constraint, we take the extradeductive step of dynamically adapting rules to the context at hand. Challenges to the applicability of the deductive rule may need to be entertained and debated [6]. For example, the *profitable-sale* rule might need to be further adapted by specifying that the increased advertising be presented to appeal to new customer needs that are not saturated. Operations like these contribute episodic precedents that are material for the synthesis of new microtheories.

7.4 Indeterminacy

Decisions need to be made on the basis of the arrival order of communications. The arrival order may not be determined by complete knowledge of system state, structure, and inputs. Consequently, the arrival order may not be able to be deduced. For example, decisions on whether to honor a withdrawal request for an account depend on the arrival order of withdrawals and deposits. The order of arrival of communications can drastically affect overall outcomes.

7.5 Description versus Action

Deduction can only *describe* possible actions and their possible effects; it cannot be used to take action [10]. Suppose that an organization wants to decide how to increase sales on March 1, 1986. The optimistic sales rule can be instantiated as shown in Figure 6. However, this deduction does not take any action. Instead it raises useful questions depending on the viewpoint from which it is considered. Considered from a viewpoint after March 1, 1986, it raises questions about the history of what happened. Logical deductions are useful in drawing further conclusions about the relationship of historical beliefs. On the other hand, when considered from a viewpoint before March 1, 1986, it raises questions about

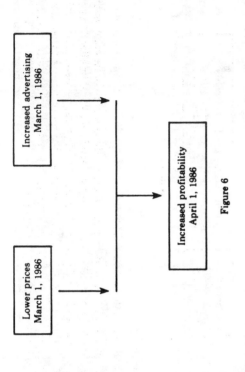

Figure 6

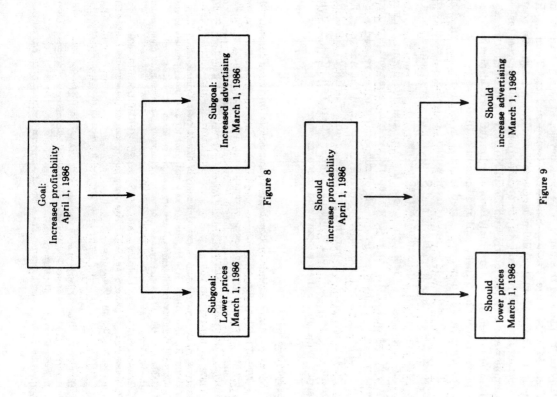

Figure 8

Figure 9

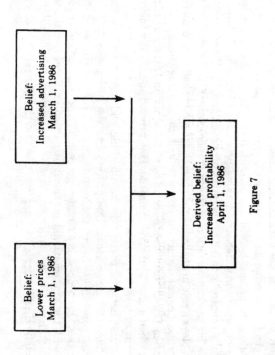

Figure 7

predicting the future. Deductions can be very useful in analyzing the logical relations among the beliefs about the future.

The validity of a deduction is supposed to be decided mechanically solely from the premises and conclusion. In this way the situation of proof checking can be separated from the situation of proof generation so that proof checking can be separated from the situation of proof generation and proof checking can take place in completely separate situations. In addition, the proof is supposed to be checkable solely from the text of the proof. In this way proofs can be checked by multiple actors at different times and places adding to the confidence in the deductions. The requirements of logical deduction preclude the possibility of introducing the term *now* into a deductive language. They mean that the validity of the deduction in Figure 6 is independent of whether it is made after March 1, 1986, and thus concerns the past or is made before March 1, 1986, and concerns the future.

Logical reasoning can be used before the happening to *predict* what might happen. It can be used after the happening to *analyze* what did happen. In either case logical proof does not control the action taken.

7.6 Constraints among Beliefs

Deduction is a powerful tool for propagating constraints among the beliefs and goals of a microtheory. For example, the belief that prices are lower and that advertising is increased on March 1, 1986, can be used to derive the belief that profitability is increased on April 1, 1986, as shown in Figure 7. Furthermore, the goal of increased profitability on March 1, 1986, can be used to derive the subgoals of lowering prices and increasing advertising, as shown in Figure 8.

New beliefs and subgoals derived by deduction in microtheories are useful to actor communities in conducting debates about the results and applicability of microtheories such as the *profitable-sale* and *unprofitable-sale* microtheories. Decisions then can be made on the basis of the results of the debates.

7.7 Recommendations and Policy

Deduction can be used to derive recommendations and to draw conclusions from policies (see Figure 9). However, the recommendations and implications of policy that are produced by deduction do not by themselves determine actions. In general, just as beliefs will be contradictory, recommendations for action will be in conflict (see Figure 10). The inconsistency among the microtheories results in inconsistent recommendations based on them.

8. CONCLUSIONS

Foundations for organizational information systems are still in a primitive state. The enterprise is inherently interdisciplinary, requiring contributions from anthropology, artificial intelligence, research on indicators and models, cognitive science, computer science, research on needs and organizational factors, economics, management science, philosophy of science, psychology, and sociology. Foundations are needed on which to describe their function, structure, and principles of operation that can serve as the basis for managing, evolving, and designing better organizational information systems.

The effort to find the basis for decisions before the organization goes to work is meaningless. Understanding decision making is not separable phenomena from understanding the process by which it arrived. It is to forget the very purpose for which the organizational decision-making processes have been fashioned. Due process plays a central role in the operation of organizational information systems and allows for the consideration of multiple inconsistent microtheories. Logical deduction plays a role in analyzing the constraints among beliefs and goals *within* microtheories. Logical deduction is not suited to deciding among conflicting microtheories. Due process is manifested by situated action at the particular time and place when a choice of action is made. Due process specifically includes the social actions of computer systems.

The contrast between correct decision making and the actual organizational processes does not make sense. Due process has a systematicity of its own. It serves to test constantly whether the organization has come to see new differences or similarities. Due process is a situated process: The outside sociophysical world interacts with the organizational processes at particular places and times of the process that result in a particular decision. In general the decision is not determined by these interactions, nor can it be said that the result of due process is too uncertain to obtain satisfactory choices in organizational course of action. The compulsion of adherence to due process is clear; any fundamental breakdown directly impairs the organization.

Due process is the only kind of system that will work when parts of the organization do not agree completely and represent different responsibilities. The meaning of the words in the rules, policies, and goals changes to them in due process.

Acknowledgments

Many of the ideas in this paper have been developed jointly with the members of the MIT Message Passing Semantics Group and the Tremont Research Institute. Fanya Montalvo, Elihu M. Gerson, and Susan Leigh Star contributed important ideas and helped with the organization. The due process task analysis example was developed jointly with David Kirsh. Tom Reinhardt greatly helped with the presentation. Our analysis of the limitations of deductive logic builds on previous work by Minsky [15] and the author [8, 9].

The ideas in this paper are related to previous work in distributed artificial intelligence. In particular we build on the work of Corkill and Lesser [3, 12]. The approach here differs from Davis and Smith [5] in that organizational mechanisms are emphasized instead of market mechanisms.

This paper describes research done at the Artificial Intelligence Laboratory of MIT. Major support for the research reported in this paper was provided by the System Development Foundation. Major support for other related work in the Artificial Intelligence Laboratory is provided, in part, by the Advanced Research Projects Agency of the Department of Defense under Office of Naval Research contract N0014-80-C-0505. I would like to thank Carl York, Charles Smith, and Patrick Winston for their support and encouragement.

REFERENCES

1. AGHA, G. *Actors: A Model of Concurrent Computation in Distributed Systems.* MIT Press, Cambridge, Mass., 1986.
2. BECKER, H. S. Notes on the concept of commitment. *Am. J. Sociol. 66* (July 1960), 32–40.
3. CORKILL, D. D. Hierarchical planning in a distributed environment. In *Proceedings of the 6th International Joint Conference on Artificial Intelligence* (Tokyo, Aug.). Kaufman, Los Altos, Calif., 1979, pp. 168–175.
4. DAVIS, K. C. *Discretionary Justice.* University of Illinois Press, Urbana, Ill., 1971.
5. DAVIS, R., AND SMITH, R. Negotiation as a metaphor for distributed problem solving. Memo 624, MIT Artificial Intelligence Laboratory, Cambridge, Mass., May 1981.
6. GASSER, L. G. The social dynamics of routine computer use in complex organizations. Ph.D. thesis, Computer Science Dept., Univ. of California at Irvine, 1984.
7. GERSON, E. M. On the quality of life. *Am. Sociol. Rev. 41* (Oct. 1976), 793–806.
7a. GERSON, E. M., AND STAR, S. L. Analyzing due process in the workplace. *ACM Trans. Off. Inf. Syst. 4,* 3 (July 1986).
8. HEWITT, C. PLANNER: A language for proving theorems in robots. In *Proceedings of ISCAI-69* (Washington, D.C., May). 1969.
9. HEWITT, C. The challenge of open systems. *BYTE* (Apr. 1985), 223–242.
10. HEWITT, C., AND DE JONG, P. Analyzing the roles of descriptions and actions in open systems. In *Proceedings of AAAI* (August). 1983.
11. HUGHES, E. C. Going concerns: The study of American institutions. In *The Sociological Eye.* Aldines, Chicago, Ill., 1971.

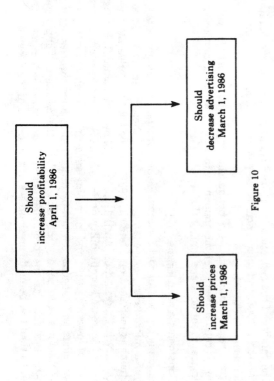

Should increase profitability April 1, 1986

Should decrease advertising March 1, 1986

Should increase prices March 1, 1986

Figure 10

12. LESSER, V., AND CORKILL, D. D. Functionally accurate, cooperative distributed systems. *IEEE Trans. Syst. Man Cybern. SMC-11*, 1 (Jan. 1981), 81–96.

13. MARCH, J. G., AND SIMON, H. A. *Organizations*. Wiley, New York, 1958.

14. McCARTHY, J. Applications of circumscription to formalizing common sense knowledge. In *Proceedings of the Non-Monotonic Reasoning Workshop* (New Paltz, N.Y.). 1984, pp. 295–324.

15. MINSKY, M. A framework for representing knowledge. In *The Psychology of Computer Vision*, P. Winston, Ed. McGraw-Hill, New York, 1975.

16. REITER, R. A logic for default reasoning. *Artif. Intell. 13*, 1, 2 (1980), 81–132.

17. STAR, S. L. Simplification in scientific work: An example from neuroscience research. *Soc. Stud. Sci. 13*, 2 (1983), 205–228.

18. STRAUSS, A. *Negotiations*. Jossey-Bass, San Francisco, Calif., 1978.

19. WEYHRAUCH, R. W. Prolegamena to a theory of mechanical formal reasoning. *Artif. Intell. 13*, 1, 2 (1980), 133–170.

20. WIMSATT, W. False models as means to truer theories. In *Systematics Symposium on Neutral Models in Biology* (Chicago, Ill.). 1985. To be published.

Chapter 5

Interaction Languages, Structures and Protocols

This section presents six important papers that give insight into the problems of interaction among agents of varying types, grain size, and capabilities. Randall Davis and Reid Smith's work on the Contract Net, reviewed in their key paper, introduced a simple form of negotiation as the basic form of node interaction. "Worker" and "manager" agents used highly coordinated dialogue interactions comprising the announcement, bidding, award and monitoring of contracts, to allocate problem solving tasks. This paper extends Davis and Smith's notions of task sharing and result sharing (see Chapter 3), and discusses a new control regime of *mutual selection* to solve problem of assigning a task to a worker—they termed this the *connection problem*. The application of the Contract Net to distributed sensing problems is described in this paper. Reid Smith's earlier paper on the Contract Net Protocol is a more detailed treatment of the interaction language and the behaviors it engenders, and it also explains the advance made over previous work in distributed computing.

Susan Conry, Robert Meyer, and Victor Lesser's paper introduces a more general multi-stage negotiation protocol that is useful for resolving resource allocation conflicts. The domain investigated was that of planning connection routes in a communication network under regional control of a number of autonomous route planning agents. The negotiation protocol makes it possible to detect and to resolve subgoal interactions, and also to detect over-constrained situations. It can be viewed as a generalization of the Contract Net Protocol to allow iterative exchanges in the negotiation of a contract award. Maintaining a global view can be prohibitively expensive, and multi-stage negotiation provides a mechanism for reaching an acceptable consensus among nodes that have conflicting goals and no global views.

James Levin and James Moore's very creative paper introduces *dialogue games*, which give a very powerful descriptive tool for representing interaction, and for distinguishing different types of interaction. Their work is oriented toward the study of natural language discourse by humans, and has not been not applied by them to the interaction of intelligent computer agents, but it provides a provocative model of dialogues that gives us insight into how more flexible dialogues can be designed for person-machine cooperation or interaction among automated agents. Related work has been pursued by Barbara Grosz and Candace Sidner [Grosz85; Grosz86; Grosz87], who have begun to integrate planning with discourse models.

Gul Agha and Carl Hewitt discuss communication, aggregation, and patterns of interaction among intelligent agents in terms of theoretical models that have sought to deal with the problems in general. The issue of dynamic reconfigurability means that their actor model must allow the creation of new actors in the evolution of the system. There must be a mechanism for communicating the existence of such new objects or processes to already existing ones. The actor model avoids the vicissitudes of synchronization of communication by using a mail system, which provides buffers, allows asynchrony, and provides referential transparency. Delivery of all communications is guaranteed. Local change is implemented by one actor specifying a replacement actor, and sometimes a continuation to handle interim results. Actor-to-actor interaction is highly coordinated and based on predefined behavioral scripts, but in Agha and Hewitt's view, aggregated communities of actors will provide much more flexible interaction patterns. Agha also provides a theoretical model of *composition* of a group of actors into a larger actor. An overview of actor languages can be found in [Agha86b].

Finally, Andrew Cromarty presents an approach to designing multiple coordinated expert systems wherein each expert system models the others as abstract remote data resource management agents. An agent then asynchronously negoti-ates access to these remote resources. Cromarty constructed his COP system in a hyperstar processing topology, which defines a particular model of distributed interaction. Agents in COP are large grained, there are no global shared data, and referential transparency and message routing are supported. A hypothesis management capability is also supported in COP. COP and the hyperstar network also provide an interesting contrast so some other interaction topologies and organizations described in papers in Chapters 1, 6, and 7.

Negotiation as a Metaphor for Distributed Problem Solving

Randall Davis
Artificial Intelligence Laboratory, Massachusetts Institute of Technology, Cambridge, MA 02139, U.S.A.

Reid G. Smith*
Defence Research Establishment Atlantic, Dartmouth, Nova Scotia B2Y 3Z7, Canada

Recommended by Lee Erman

ABSTRACT

We describe the concept of distributed problem solving and define it as the cooperative solution of problems by a decentralized and loosely coupled collection of problem solvers. This approach to problem solving offers the promise of increased performance and provides a useful medium for exploring and developing new problem-solving techniques.

We present a framework called the contract net that specifies communication and control in a distributed problem solver. Task distribution is viewed as an interactive process, a discussion carried on between a node with a task to be executed and a group of nodes that may be able to execute the task. We describe the kinds of information that must be passed between nodes during the discussion in order to obtain effective problem-solving behavior. This discussion is the origin of the negotiation metaphor: Task distribution is viewed as a form of contract negotiation.

We emphasize that protocols for distributed problem solving should help determine the content of the information transmitted, rather than simply provide a means of sending bits from one node to another.

The use of the contract net framework is demonstrated in the solution of a simulated problem in area surveillance, of the sort encountered in ship or air traffic control. We discuss the mode of operation of a distributed sensing system, a network of nodes extending throughout a relatively large geographic area, whose primary aim is the construction of a dynamic map of traffic in the area.

From the results of this preliminary study we abstract features of the framework applicable to problem solving in general, examining in particular transfer of control. Comparisons with PLANNER, CONNIVER, HEARSAY-II, and PUPs are used to demonstrate that negotiation—the two-way transfer of information—is a natural extension to the transfer of control mechanisms used in earlier problem-solving systems.

1. Introduction

Traditional work in problem solving has, for the most part, been set in the context of a single processor. Recent advances in processor fabrication techniques, however, combined with developments in communication technology, offer the chance to explore new ideas about problem solving employing multiple processors.

In this paper we describe the concept of *distributed problem solving*, characterizing it as the cooperative solution of problems by a decentralized, loosely coupled collection of problem solvers. We find it useful to view the process as occurring in four phases: problem decomposition, sub-problem distribution, sub-problem solution, and answer synthesis. We focus in this paper primarily on the second phase, exploring how negotiation can help in matching problem solvers to tasks.

We find three issues central to constructing frameworks for distributed problem solving: (i) the fundamental conflict between the complete knowledge needed to ensure coherence and the incomplete knowledge inherent in any distribution of problem solving effort, (ii) the need for a problem solving protocol, and (iii) the utility of negotiation as an organizing principle. We illustrate our approach to those issues in a framework called the contract net.

Section 2 describes our concept of distributed problem solving in more detail, contrasting it with the more widely known topic of distributed processing. Section 3 explores motivations, suggesting what we hope to gain from this work. In Section 4 we consider the three issues listed above, describing what we mean by each and documenting the importance of each to the problems at hand.

Section 5 describes how a group of human experts might cooperate in solving a problem and illustrates how this metaphor has proved useful in guiding our work. Section 6 then considers how a group of computers might cooperate to solve a problem and illustrates how this has contributed to our work.

Section 7 describes the contract net. We focus on its use as a framework for orchestrating the efforts of a number of loosely coupled problem solvers. More detailed issues of its implementation, as well the tradeoffs involved in its design, are covered elsewhere (see, e.g., [26, 27, 28]). Section 8 describes an application of the contract net. We consider a problem in distributed sensing and show how our approach permits a useful degree of self-organization.

Section 9 then takes a step back to consider the issue of transfer of control. We show how the perspective we have developed—notably the issue of negotiation—offers useful insights about the concept of control transfer. We review invocation techniques from a number of programming languages and illustrate that the whole range of them can be viewed as a progression from simple to increasingly more sophisticated information exchange. In these terms the negotiation technique used in the contract net becomes a natural next step.

* The author's current address is: Schlumberger–Doll Research, Ridgefield, CT 06877, U.S.A.

Sections 10 and 11 consider the sorts of problems for which our approach is well suited and describe the limitations and open problems in our work to date.

2. Distributed Problem Solving: Overview

In our view, some of the defining characteristics of distributed problem solving are that it is a *cooperative* activity of a group of *decentralized* and *loosely coupled* knowledge-sources (KSs). The KSs cooperate in the sense that no one of them has sufficient information to solve the entire problem: information must be shared to allow the group as a whole to produce an answer. By decentralized we mean that both control and data are logically and often geographically distributed; there is neither global control nor global data storage. Loosely coupled means that individual KSs spend most of their time in computation rather than communication.

Interest in such problem solvers arises from the promise of increased speed, reliability, and extensibility, as well as ability to handle applications with a natural spatial or functional distribution, and the potential for increased tolerance to uncertainty in data and knowledge.

Distributed problem solving differs in several fundamental respects from the more widely known topic of *distributed processing*. Perhaps the most important distinction arises from examining the origin of the system and the motivations for interconnecting machines.

Distributed processing systems often have their origin in the attempt to synthesize a network of machines capable of carrying out a number of widely disparate tasks. Typically, several distinct applications are envisioned, with each application concentrated at a single node of the network, as for example in a three-node system intended to do payroll, order entry, and process control. The aim is to find a way to reconcile any conflicts and disadvantages arising from the desire to carry out disparate tasks, in order to gain the benefits of using multiple machines (sharing of data bases, graceful degradation, etc.).

Unfortunately, the conflicts that arise are often not simply technical (e.g., word sizes, database formats, etc.) but include sociological and political problems as well (see, e.g., [6]). The attempt to synthesize a number of disparate tasks thus leads to a concern with issues such as access control and protection, and results in viewing cooperation as a form of *compromise* between potentially conflicting desires.

In distributed problem solving, on the other hand, there is a single task envisioned for the system and the resources to be applied have no other predefined roles to carry out. We are building up a system de novo and can as a result choose hardware, software, etc. with one aim in mind: the selection that will lead to the most effective environment for cooperative behavior. This also means we view cooperation in terms of benevolent problem solving behavior, i.e., how can systems that are perfectly willing to accommodate one another act

so as to be an effective team? Our concerns are thus with developing frameworks for *cooperative behavior between willing entities*, rather than frameworks for enforcing cooperation as a form of compromise between potentially incompatible entities.

A second important distinction arises from our focus on traditional issues of problem solving. We intend, for example, that the system itself should include as part of its basic task the partitioning and decomposition of a problem. Work in distributed processing, by comparison, has not taken problem solving as a primary focus. It has generally been assumed that a well-defined and a priori partitioned problem exists. The major concerns lie in an optimal static distribution of tasks, methods for interconnecting processor nodes, resource allocation, and prevention of deadlock. Complete knowledge of the problem has also been assumed (i.e., explicit knowledge of timing and precedence relations between tasks) and the major reason for distribution has been assumed to be load-balancing (e.g., [1, 2]). Since we do not make these assumptions, we cannot take advantage of this pre-planning of resources. As will become clear, this makes for significant differences in the issues which concern us and in the design of the system.

A final distinction results from the lack of substantial cooperation in most distributed processing systems. Typically, for instance, most of the processing is done at a central site and remote processors are limited to basic data collection (e.g., credit card verification). The word *distributed* is usually taken to mean spatial distribution of data—distribution of function or control is not generally considered.

One way to view the various research efforts is in terms of the three levels indicated in Fig. 1. At the lowest level the focus is the processor architecture. The main issues here are the design of the individual nodes and the interconnection mechanism. The components of an individual node must be selected (e.g., processors and memory), and appropriate low-level interconnection methods must be chosen (e.g., a single broadcast channel, complete interconnection, a regular lattice, etc.).

The middle level focuses on systems aspects. Among the concerns here are issues of guaranteeing message delivery, guaranteeing database consistency, and techniques for database recovery.

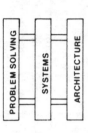

Fig. 1. A layered approach to distributed problem solving.

The focus at the top level is problem solving, where the concerns are internode control and knowledge organization; in particular how to achieve effective problem-solving behavior from a collection of asynchronous nodes. There is therefore a greater concern with the *content* of the information to be communicated between nodes than with the *form* in which the communication is effected.

All of these levels are important foci of research and each successive level depends on the ones below it for support. Our concern in this paper, however, lies primarily at the level of problem solving.

For the remainder of this paper we will assume that the hardware is a network of loosely coupled, asynchronous nodes. Each node has a local memory; no memory is shared by all nodes. Each node typically contains several distinct KSs. There is no central controller; each node makes its own choices about tasks to work on. The nodes are interconnected so that every node can communicate with every other by sending messages, perhaps over a broadcast channel. We also assume the existence of a low-level protocol to effect communication of bit streams between nodes.

3. Distributed Problem Solving: Motivation

A major motivation for this work lies in the potential it offers for making available more problem solving power, by applying a collection of processors to the solution of a single problem. It may, for example, prove much easier to coordinate the actions of twenty medium-sized machines than it is to build a single machine twenty (or even ten) times as large.

A distributed approach may also be well suited to problems that have either a spatial distribution or a large degree of functional specialization. Spatial distribution often occurs in problems involving interpretation of signal data from multiple sensors (e.g., [20]). Functional specialization may occur in problems like understanding continuous speech (e.g., [7]): information from many different knowledge-sources (e.g., signal processors, parsers, etc.) must be combined to solve the problem.

Distributed problem solving also offers a way to apply to problem solving the recent advances in both processor fabrication and communication technology. Low-cost, small-scale VLSI processors are now commonplace, with larger scale processors expected in the near future [21]. The synthesis of advanced computer and communication technology that has resulted in networks of resource-sharing computers (e.g., [13, 15]) offers a foundation for work on distributed architectures. With these two developments as foundations, work can begin focusing on techniques for effective use of networks of machines.

One reason for interest in distributed architectures in general is their capacity for reliable computation and graceful degradation. By placing problem solving in this environment, we have the chance to make it similarly reliable.

The use of an approach like the contract net, which distributes both control and data, also makes possible additional responses to component failure. In addition to the standard response of continuing to function as before (albeit more slowly), the option may exist of having the system reconfigure itself to take into account the hardware available.

Finally, and somewhat more speculatively, there is the issue of 'bounded rationality'. Some tasks appear difficult because of their size. They are 'too big' to contemplate all at once and are not easily broken into modular sub-problems (e.g., the working of the national economy, the operation of a large corporation). In such cases it may be difficult, both conceptually and practically, for a single problem solver to deal effectively with more than a small part of all of the data or knowledge required to solve the problem. Trying to scale up the hardware of a single problem solver may ease the practical problem but does not solve the conceptual difficulty. It may instead prove more effective to use multiple problem solvers, each of which handles some fraction of the total problem, and to provide techniques for dealing with the interaction between the sub-problems.

Recent work has explored a number of ideas relevant to accomplishing this goal. There is, for example, the original HEARSAY-II model of cooperating KSs ([7]), in which each KS had a sharply limited domain of expertise. It demonstrated the practicality of using a number of independent KSs to encode large amounts of knowledge about a domain. The work in [17] reports on an experiment that distributed knowledge and data, and to a limited degree, control. In Section 7 we describe an approach to distributing problem solving effort that dynamically distributes knowledge, data and control.

4. The Fundamental Issues

Our study of distributed problem solving to date has identified three issues that appear to be central to the undertaking: (i) the fundamental difficulty of ensuring global coordination of behavior when that behavior results from the aggregation of actions based on local *incomplete* knowledge, (ii) the necessity of a protocol dealing with *problem solving* rather than with *communication*, and (iii) the utility of *negotiation* as a fundamental mechanism for interaction. In this section we describe each of the issues briefly, Sections 5 and 6 then demonstrate how these issues arise from basic considerations of the task at hand.[1]

4.1. Global coherence and limited knowledge

One obvious problem that arises in employing multiple problem solvers is

[1] Other work on distributed problem solving is based on similar issues. Work described in [18], for example, also finds (i) and (ii) above to be central issues.

'coherence'. Any time we have more than one active agent in the system there is the possibility that their actions are in some fashion mutually interfering rather than mutually supportive. There are numerous ways in which this can happen. We may have conflict over resources, one agent may unknowingly undo the results of another, the same actions may be carried out redundantly, etc. In general terms, the collection of agents may somehow fail to act as a well-coordinated, purposeful team.

We believe that this problem is due to the fundamental difficulty of obtaining coordinated behavior when each agent has only a limited, local view. We could, of course, guarantee coordination if every agent 'knew everything', i.e., it had complete knowledge. If, for example, every problem solver had complete knowledge of the actions of all the others, it would be possible to avoid redundant or conflicting efforts.[2]

Yet any reasonable model of distribution appears to require incomplete, local views of the problem. Complete information is, for example, at least impractical. As we argue in Section 6, bandwidth limitations make it unreasonable to consider having every node constantly informed of all developments.

A limited local view also simplifies the problem conceptually. The problem becomes far more difficult to think about (and to program) if every problem solver has to keep track of everything. It also seems contrary to the basic notion of distribution; Part of the motivation is to allow a problem solver to focus on one part of the problem and ignore the rest.

For these reasons at least, then, any distribution of problem solving effort appears to imply incomplete, local knowledge.

And when we say "incomplete knowledge", we include in "knowledge" the information indicating "who needs to know what". That is, we do not assume that we start out with a map of subproblems and their interactions. Without such a map, there is the chance that necessary interactions are overlooked and hence we lose a guarantee of coordinated behavior.

As noted earlier, we consider problem decomposition—the creation of the map of subproblems—to be part of the system's task. Once the system creates its best guess at such a map, we can count on the locality of action and information to make distributed problem solving practical. By locality of action and information, we mean that the problems typically attacked in AI are generally decomposable into a set of subproblems in which the effects of the actions and the relevance of information is local. The actions taken to solve one subproblem generally affect only a few other subproblems; the

---

[2] This difficulty is not limited to distributed problem solving, it is only more painfully obvious there. The standard notion of problem decomposition in centralized systems results in limited, local knowledge, and the same difficulty manifests itself as the well-known problem of interacting subgoals.

---

information discovered in solving one subproblem is generally relevant to only a few other subproblems.[3] As a result, each problem solver will have to interact with at most a few others, making limited bandwidth a challenging but not fatal constraint.

To summarize: the conflict arises because distribution seems by its nature to require supplying each problem solver with only a limited, local view of the problem, yet we wish to accomplish a global effect—the solution of the problem at hand. It is not obvious how we can guarantee overall coordination from aggregations of actions based on local views with incomplete information. Thus, while the locality of action and information means that distributed problem solving is feasible, the necessity of incomplete knowledge means that guaranteeing coordinated activity is difficult.

One general answer is to provide something that extends across the network of nodes, something that can be used as a foundation for cooperation and organization. As will become clear, three elements of our framework help provide that foundation: (i) the concept of negotiation as a mechanism for interaction (Section 7.1), (ii) the network of tasks that results from decomposing a problem (Section 8.2), and (iii) a common language shared by all nodes (Section 7.3). The announcement—bid—award sequence of messages (Section 7.4) also offers some support. Even though each problem solver has only a limited view of the problem, these messages offer one way for a node to find out who else has relevant information. Together, all of these mechanisms provide an initial step toward a basis for achieving coordinated behavior.

4.2. The need for a problem solving protocol

In most work on protocols for distributed computation the emphasis has been on establishing reliable and efficient communication. Some degree of success has been achieved, at levels ranging from individual packets to atomic actions (see, e.g., [29]). But these protocols are only a prerequisite for distributed problem solving. In the same sense that communication among a group of entities needs a carefully constructed communication protocol, so problem solving by a group of entities requires a problem solving protocol. Cooperation cannot be established between nodes simply by indicating how they are to communicate; we must also indicate what they should say to each other.

The issue can also be viewed in the terms suggested by Fig. 1. At each level we need to give careful consideration to the basic architecture and we need the

---

[3] The first half of this observation—the locality of the effects of actions—is typically used to justify informal solutions to the frame problem. We can, for instance, account for the effects of an action with a list of consequences, because that list tends to be short and predictable.
Similarly, the impact of information tends to be local. If I, as one member of a team, am working on one part of a problem, most of what is discovered about the rest of the problem is irrelevant to me. Keeping me up to date on every detail will only prove to be a distraction.

For reasons discussed above, we assume that no one expert is in total control of the others, although one expert may be ultimately responsible for communicating the solution of the top-level problem to the customer outside the group.

One possible model for the interaction involves group members cooperating in the execution of individual tasks, a mode we have called 'task-sharing' [28]. In such a situation we might see each expert spending most of his time working alone on various subtasks, pausing only occasionally to interact with other members of the group. These interactions generally involve requests for assistance on subtasks or the exchange of results.

An expert (E1) may request assistance because he encounters either a task too large to handle alone, or a task for which he has no expertise. If the task is too large, he will first attempt to partition it into manageable subtasks and then attempt to find other experts who have the appropriate skills to handle the new tasks. If the original task is beyond his expertise, he attempts right away to find another, more appropriate expert to handle it.

In either case, E1's problem is now to find experts whose skills match the tasks that he wishes to distribute. If E1 knows which other experts have the necessary expertise, he can notify them directly. If he does not know anyone in particular who may be able to assist him (or if the tasks require no special expertise), he can simply describe the tasks to the entire group.

If another, available expert (E2) believes he is capable of carrying out the task that E1 announced, he informs E1 of his availability and perhaps indicates as well any especially relevant skills he may have. E1 may wind up with several such volunteers and can choose from among them. The chosen volunteer might then request additional details from E1 and the two will engage in further direct communication for the duration of the task.

In order to distribute the workload in a group of experts, then, those with tasks to be executed must find others capable of executing those tasks. At the same time, it is the job of idle experts to find suitable tasks on which to work. Those with tasks to be executed and those capable of executing the tasks thus engage in a form of *negotiation* to distribute the workload. They become linked together by agreements or informal contracts, forming subgroups of varying sizes that are created and broken up dynamically during the course of work.[5]

6. Observations and Implications

The metaphor of a group of human experts offered several suggestions about

[5]Subgroups of this type offer two advantages. First, communication among the members does not needlessly distract the entire group. This is important, because communication itself can be a major source of distraction and difficulty in a large group (see for example [9]). Thus one of the major purposes of organization is to reduce the amount of communication that is needed. Second, the subgroup members may be able to communicate with each other in a language that is more efficient for their purpose than the language in use by the entire group (for more on this see [27]).

appropriate protocols. In the same sense that we pay attention to hardware and systems architecture, so we need to consider a 'problem solving architecture'; as we have protocols that organize the communication of bits and files, so we need protocols to organize the problem solving activity.

As discussed in Section 7, the contract net takes a first step in this direction by providing a set of message types indicating the kind of information that nodes should exchange in order to effect one form of cooperation.

4.3. The utility of negotiation

The central element in our approach to a problem solving protocol is the concept of negotiation. By negotiation, we mean a discussion in which the interested parties exchange information and come to an agreement. For our purposes negotiation has three important components: (a) there is a two-way exchange of information, (b) each party to the negotiation evaluates the information from its own perspective, and (c) final agreement is achieved by mutual selection.

Negotiation appears to have multiple applications. In Section 7, for example, we explore its application to the problem of matching idle problem solvers to outstanding tasks. This matching is carried out by the system itself, since, as noted, we do not assume that the problem has already been decomposed and distributed.

In Section 9.2 we explore a second application of negotiation by considering its utility as a basis for transfer of control and as a way of viewing invocation as the matching of KSs to tasks. This view leads to a more powerful mechanism for control transfer, since it permits a more informed choice from among the alternative KSs which might be invoked. The view also leads to a novel perspective on the outcome of the interaction. In most previous systems, the notion of selecting what to do next typically involves taking the best choice from among those currently available. As will become clear, in the contract net either party has the option of deciding that none of the currently available options is good enough, and can decide instead to await further developments.

5. A Cooperating Experts Metaphor

A familiar metaphor for a problem solver operating in a distributed environment is a group of human experts experienced at working together, trying to complete a large task.[4] Of primary interest to us in examining the operation of a group of human experts are: (a) the way in which they interact to solve the overall problem, (b) the manner in which the workload is distributed among them, and (c) how results are integrated for communication outside the group.

[4]This metaphor has been used as a starting point by [11], [16] and [18], but has resulted in systems that differ from ours in several ways. The different systems are compared in Section 9.

We have argued above for loose coupling and based the argument on technological considerations. The point can be argued from two additional perspectives as well. First, the comments earlier concerning the locality of action and information suggest that, for the class of problems we wish to consider, tight coupling is unnecessary. The activities and results of any one problem solver are generally relevant to only a few others. More widespread dissemination of information will mostly likely only prove to be distracting.

A second argument, described in [18], takes a more emphatic position and argues for loose coupling even where it is known to produce temporary inconsistencies. They note that standard approaches to parallelism are typically designed to ensure that all processors always have mutually consistent views of the problem. Such complete consistency, and the tight coupling it requires, is, they claim, unnecessary. They suggest instead that distributed systems can be designed to be 'functionally accurate', i.e., the system will produce the correct answer eventually even though in an intermediate state some processors may have inconsistent views of the problem.

Thus we have arguments against tight coupling based on technological considerations (the communication/computation imbalance), pragmatic issues (the locality of action and information), and empirical results which suggest that it may be unnecessary.

Any unique node is a potential bottleneck.

Any node with unique characteristics is potentially a bottleneck that can slow down the system (Fig. 3). If those characteristics make the distinguished node useful to enough other nodes in the system, eventually those nodes may be forced to stand idle while they wait for service. This is equally true for a resource like data (for which the issue has been extensively studied) and a 'resource' like control (for which considerably less work has been done). If one node were in charge of directing the activities of all other nodes, requests for decisions about what to do next would eventually accumulate faster than they could be processed.[7]

What steps can we take to reduce the likelihood of bottlenecks due to centralized control? First, we can distribute it: Each node should have some

Any unique node is a potential bottleneck
- → distribute data
- → distribute control
- → organized behavior is hard to guarantee

FIG. 3. Further observations and implications.

[7]Such a node would also be an Achilles' heel in the system, since its failure would result in total failure of the system.

---

organizing problem solving effort. Here we consider how a group of computers might cooperate and examine what that can tell us about how to proceed. We approach this by comparing the use of multiple, distributed processors with the more traditional model of operation on a uniprocessor. We list several basic observations characterizing the fundamental differences and consider the implications that follow. While the list is not exhaustive, it deals with the differences we find most important.

Communication is slower than computation.

That is, bits can be created faster than they can be shipped over substantial distances.[6] With current technology, communication over such distances is in fact much slower than computation. Attempting to interconnect large numbers of high speed processors can easily lead to saturation of available bandwidth. Present trends indicate [23] that this imbalance in speed will not only continue, but that the disparity is likely to increase. It appears as well that the relative costs of communication and computation will follow a similar trend.

Several implications follow from this simple observation (Fig. 2). It means for example that we want problem decompositions that yield *loosely coupled* systems—systems in which processors spend the bulk of their time computing and only a small fraction of their time communicating with one another. The desire for loose coupling means in turn that we need to pay attention to the *efficiency* of the communication protocol: With a more efficient protocol, fewer bits need to be transmitted and less time is spent in communicating. It also means that we need to pay attention to both the *modularity* and *grain size* of the problems chosen. Problems should be decomposed into tasks that are both independent and large enough to be worth the overhead involved in task distribution. Non-independent tasks will require communication between processors, while for very small tasks (e.g., simple arithmetic) the effort involved in distributing them and reporting results would likely be greater than the work involved in solving the task itself.

Communication is slower than computation
- → loose-coupling
- → efficient protocol
- → modular problems
- → problems with large grain size

FIG. 2. Observations and implications.

[6]Over short distances, of course, permanent hardwired links can be very effective. Where distances are large or varying (e.g., mobile robots), bandwidth again becomes a limiting factor. Note also that we mean communicating all the bits involved in a computation, not just the final answer. Otherwise communicating, say, one bit to indicate the primality of a 100-digit number would surely be faster than doing the computation to determine the answer.

degree of autonomy in generating new tasks and in deciding which task to do next. By so dividing up and distributing the responsibility for control, we reduce the likely load on any one node. Second, we might distribute it redundantly: If more than one node is capable of making decisions about control, we further reduce the likelihood that any one node becomes saturated, and can ensure that no one node is unique. Finally, we can distribute control dynamically: We might provide a mechanism that allows dynamic redistribution in response to demands of the problem.

Organized behavior is difficult to guarantee if control is decentralized.

In a system with completely centralized control, one processor is responsible for directing the activities of all the others. It knows what all the other processors are doing at any given time, and, armed with this global view of the problem, can assign processors to tasks in a manner that assures organized behavior of the system as a whole. By 'organized', we mean that (among other things) all tasks will eventually be attended to, they will be dealt with in an order that reduces or eliminates the need for one processor to wait for results from another, processor power will be well matched to the tasks generated, etc. In more general terms, the set of processors will behave like a well-coordinated, purposeful team.

In the absence of a global overview, coordination and organization becomes much more difficult. When control is decentralized, no one node has a global view of all activities in the system; each node has a local view that includes information about only a subset of the tasks. The appropriate organization of a number of such subsets does not necessarily result in appropriate organization and behavior of the system as a whole.

In Section 4 we described the general problem of ensuring well-coordinated behavior; this is a specific instantiation of that problem with respect to control. We are trying to achieve a global effect (coherent behavior) from a collection of local decisions (nodes organizing subsets of tasks). We cannot centralize control for reasons noted above, yet it is not clear how to ensure coherent behavior when control is distributed.

7. A Framework for Distributed Problem Solving

7.1. A view of distributed problem solving

We view distributed problem solving as involving four central activities: problem decomposition, sub-problem distribution, solution of sub-problems, and synthesis of the overall solution. By decomposition we mean the standard notion of breaking a large problem into smaller, more manageable pieces; distribution involves the matching of sub-problems with problem solvers capable of handling them; the sub-problems are then solved; and finally those individual solutions may need to be synthesized into a single, overall solution.

Each of these can happen several times as a problem is decomposed into several levels of subproblems.

These four activities may occur individually and in the sequence noted, or may be combined or carried out in parallel. The point is simply that all of them can make important contributions to the problem solving process, so we need some mechanism for dealing with each.[8]

7.2. Task-sharing, negotiation and the connection problem

We have emphasized above the importance of having a protocol for organizing problem solving activity and proposed negotiation as a plausible basis for that protocol. But what shall we negotiate? Our work to date has followed the lead suggested by the cooperating experts metaphor and explored the distribution of tasks as an appropriate subject. Thus, in this paper we focus on application of the contract net to the distribution phase of distributed problem solving and show how negotiation appears to be an effective tool for accomplishing the matching of problem solvers and tasks.

To illustrate this, recall that the group of experts distributed a problem by decomposing it into ever smaller subtasks and distributing the subtasks among the group. We term this mode of operation 'task-sharing', because cooperation is based on the dynamic decomposition and distribution of subproblems.[9] But to enable distribution of the subproblems, there must be a way for experts with tasks to be executed to find idle experts capable of executing those tasks. We call this the 'connection problem'.

The contract net protocol supplies a mechanism to solve the connection problem: As we will see, nodes with tasks to be executed negotiate with idle nodes over the appropriate matching of tasks and nodes.

This approach is appropriate for a distributed problem solver because it requires neither global data storage nor global control. It also permits some degree of dynamic configuration and reconfiguration. A simple example of dynamic configuration is given in Section 8.3; reconfiguration is useful in the event of node failure or overloading. We have explored a number of simple mechanisms for detecting node failure and reconfiguring in response [26, 22], but the problem is not yet well studied.

A few words of terminology will be useful. The collection of nodes is referred to as a *contract net*. Each node in the net may take on the role of a *manager* or a *contractor*. A manager is responsible for monitoring the execu-

[8] For some problems the first or last activity may be trivial or unnecessary. Where a problem is geographically distributed, for example, the decomposition may be obvious (but see the discussion of the sensor net in Section 8). In problems of distributed control (e.g., traffic light control), there may be no need to synthesize an 'overall' answer.

[9] Task-sharing in its simplest form can be viewed as the distributed version of the traditional notion of problem decomposition. For a different approach to distribution, see [18].

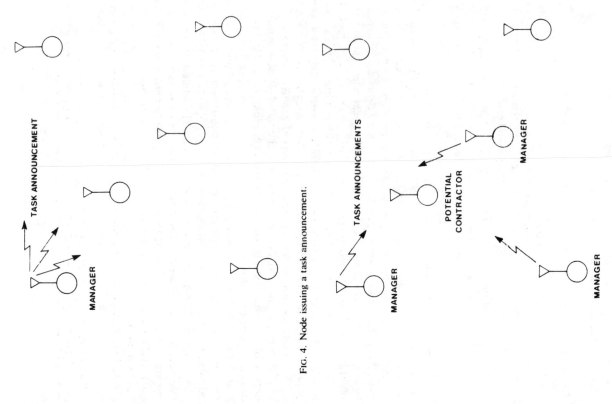

FIG. 4. Node issuing a task announcement.

FIG. 5. Idle node listening to task announcements.

tion of a task and processing the results of its execution. A contractor is responsible for the actual execution of the task.[10]

Individual nodes are not designated *a priori* as managers or contractors; these are only roles, and any node can take on either role dynamically during the course of problem solving. Typically a node will take on both roles, often simultaneously for different contracts. This has the advantage that individual nodes are not statically tied to a control hierarchy.

For the sake of exposition, we describe the protocol in successive layers of detail, describing first the *content* of the messages exchanged (Section 7.3), then their *format* (Section 7.4), and finally the details of the *language* in which they are written (Section 7.5).

7.3. Contract net protocol—message content

Message content is the heart of the issue, since it indicates what kinds of things nodes should say to one another and provides the basis for cooperation.

Negotiation is initiated by the generation of a new task. As suggested in the experts metaphor, this may occur when one problem solver decomposes a task into sub-tasks, or when it decides that it does not have the knowledge or data required to carry out the task. When this occurs, the node that generates the task advertises existence of the task with a *task announcement* message (Fig. 4). It then acts as the manager of that task for its duration. Many such announcements are made over the course of time as new tasks are generated.

Meanwhile, nodes in the net are listening to the task announcements (Fig. 5). They evaluate their own level of interest in each task with respect to their specialized resources (hardware and software), using *task evaluation procedures* specific to the problem at hand.[11]

When a task is found to be of sufficient interest, a node submits a bid (Fig. 6). A bid message indicates the capabilities of the bidder that are relevant to execution of the announced task.

A manager may receive several bids in response to a single task announcement (Fig. 7). Based on the information in the bids, it selects one or more nodes for execution of the task, using a task-specific *bid evaluation procedure*. The selection is communicated to the successful bidders through an *award* message (Fig. 8). The selected nodes assume responsibility for execution of the task, and each is called a contractor for that task.

A contractor will typically partition a task and enter into (sub)contracts with

[10]The basic idea of contracting is not new. For example, a rudimentary bidding scheme was used for resource allocation in the Distributed Computing System (DCS) [8]. The contract net takes a wider perspective and allows a broader range of descriptions to be used during negotiation. For a detailed discussion see [27].

[11]It is in general up to the user to supply this and other task-specific procedures, but useful defaults are available (see [26]).

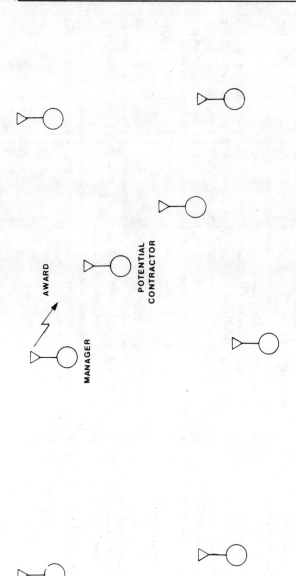

FIG. 8. Manager making an award.

other nodes. It is then the manager for those contracts. This leads to the hierarchical control structure that is typical of task-sharing.

A report is used by a contractor to inform its manager that a task has been partially executed (an *interim report*) or completed (a *final report*). The report contains a *result description* that specifies the results of the execution.[12]

The manager may terminate contracts with a *termination* message. The contractor receiving such a message terminates execution of the contract and all related outstanding subcontracts.

A contract is thus an explicit agreement between a node that generates a task (the manager) and a node that executes the task (the contractor, Fig. 9). Note that establishing a contract is a process of mutual selection. Available contractors evaluate task announcements until they find one of interest; the managers then evaluate the bids received from potential contractors and select the ones they determine to be most appropriate. Both parties to the agreement have evaluated the information supplied by the other and a mutual selection has been made.

We have dealt here with a simple example in order to focus on the issue of

[12]Interim reports are useful when generator-style control is desired. A node can be set to work on a task and instructed to issue interim reports whenever the next result is ready. It then pauses, awaiting a message that instructs it to continue and produce another result.

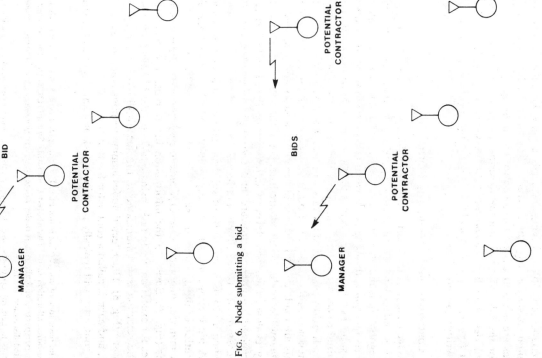

FIG. 6. Node submitting a bid.

FIG. 7. Manager listening to bids coming in.

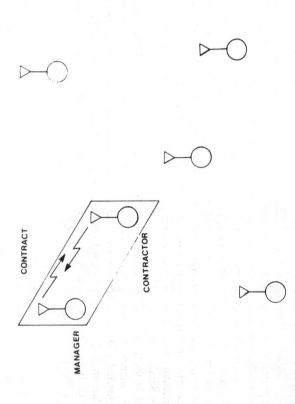

FIG. 9. A contract established.

cooperation. Additional complications which arise in implementing the protocol are discussed in detail in [26]; we note them briefly here for reference. *Focused addressing* is a more direct communication scheme used where the generality of broadcast is not required. *Directed contracts* are used when a manager knows which node is appropriate for a task. A *request-response* mechanism allows simple transfers of information without the overhead of contracting. And finally, a *node-available* message allows reversal of the normal negotiation process: When the computation load on the net is high, most task announcements will not be answered with bids because all nodes will already be busy. The node-available message allows an idle node to indicate that it is searching for a task to execute. The protocol is thus load-sensitive in response to changing demands of the task: When the load is low, the spawning of a task is the important event; when the load is high, the availability of a node is important.

7.4. Contract net protocol—message format

Each message is composed of a number of slots that specify the kind of information needed in that type of message. A task announcement message, for example, has four main slots (Fig. 10).[13] The *eligibility specification* is a list

[13] There are also slots that contain bookkeeping information.

of criteria that a node must meet to be eligible to submit a bid. The *task abstraction* is a brief description of the task to be executed. It enables a node to rank the announced task relative to other announced tasks. The *bid specification* is a description of the expected form of a bid. It gives a manager a chance to say, in effect, "Here's what I consider important about a node that wants to bid on this task." This provides a common basis for comparison of bids, and enables a node to include in a bid only the information about its capabilities that are relevant to the announced task. Finally, the *expiration time* is a deadline for receiving bids.

For any given application, the information that makes up the eligibility specification, etc., must be supplied by the user. Hence while the contract net protocol offers a framework specifying the types of information that are necessary, it remains the task of the user to supply the actual information appropriate to the domain at hand.

7.5. Contract net protocol—the common internode language

Finally, we need a language in which to specify the information in the slots of a message. For a number of reasons, it is useful to specify a single, relatively high level language in which all such information is expressed. We call this the *common internode language*. This language forms a common basis for communication among all the nodes.

As an example, consider a task announcement message that might be used in a system working on a signal processing task. Assume that one node attempting to analyze a signal determines that it would be useful to have a Fourier transform of that signal. Unwilling or unable to do the task itself (perhaps because of hardware limitations), it decides to announce the task in order to solicit assistance. It might issue a task announcement of the sort shown in Fig. 11.

The announcement is broadcast to all nodes within range ("To: *"), and indicates that there is a TASK of TYPE FOURIER-TRANSFORM to be done. In order to consider bidding on it a node must have an FFTBOX and a bid should specify estimated time to completion of the task.

The common internode language is currently built around a very simple *attribute, object, value* representation. There are a number of predefined

Main Task Announcement Slots

    Eligibility specification
    Task abstraction
    Bid specification
    Expiration time

FIG. 10. Task announcement format.

request for the transfer of any required information. If there were a number of distinct internode languages, then a new node entering the net could interact with only a limited subset of the nodes, those which spoke its language.[14] This would make addition of new nodes to the net less effective.

A common language also makes possible invocation schemes that are more flexible than standard procedure invocation, and this also facilitates addition of a new node to the net. For example, a common language makes it possible to use invocation based on describing tasks to be done,[15] rather than naming specific KSs (procedures) to invoke next. When this technique is used, new nodes can simply be added to the existing collection; they will find their own place in the scheme of things by listening to task announcements, issuing bids, etc. With more traditional invocation schemes (e.g., standard procedure calling), a new node would have to be linked explicitly to others in the network.

8. Example: Distributed Sensing

The protocol described above has been implemented in INTERLISP and used to solve several problems in a simulated multi-processor environment. The problems included search (e.g., the 8-queens problem) and signal interpretation (for details see [26]). In this section we describe use of the contract net on one such problem in signal interpretation: area surveillance of the sort encountered in air or ship traffic control. We explore the operation of a network of nodes, each having either sensing or processing capabilities and all spread throughout a relatively large geographic area. We refer to such a network as a distributed sensing system (DSS).

Although an operational DSS may have several functions, ranging from passive analysis to active control over vehicle courses and speeds, we focus here on the analysis function. The task involves detection, classification, and tracking of vehicles; the solution to the problem is a dynamic map of traffic in the area. Construction and maintenance of the map requires interpretation of the large quantity of sensory information received by the collection of sensor elements.

Since we want to produce a single map of the entire area, we may choose to have one processor node—which we will call the monitor node—carry out the final integration of information and transmit it to the appropriate destination. It is also useful to assign that node the responsibility for beginning the initialization of the DSS. Its total set of responsibilities therefore includes starting the initialization as the first step in net operation, integrating the overall

[14]Note that the extreme case (in which every pair of nodes communicates in its own private language) is precisely standard procedure invocation. To decode a procedure call, one must know the expected order, type, and number of arguments. This is information which is shared only by the caller and procedure involved, in effect a private language used for communication between them.

[15]As is also done in PLANNER and the other pattern-directed languages.

```
To:        *
From:      25
Type:      TASK ANNOUNCEMENT
Contract:  43-6

Eligibility Specification
    MUST-HAVE FFTBOX

Task Abstraction
    TASK TYPE FOURIER-TRANSFORM
    NUMBER-POINTS 1024
    NODE NAME 25
    POSITION LAT 64N LONG 10W

Bid Specification
    COMPLETION-TIME

Expiration Time
    29 1645Z NOV 1980
```

FIG. 11. Task announcement example.

(domain-independent) terms (like TYPE of TASK); these are supplemented with domain-specific terms (like FFTBOX). The domain-independent terms are part of the language offered to the user and help him organize and specify the information he has to supply. The domain-specific terms have to be added by the user as needed for the application at hand.

All of this information is stated in terms of something we here called a common internode language. The two important points here are that the information in messages is viewed as statements in a language, and that the language is common to all the nodes.

It is useful to view the messages as statements in a language because this sets the appropriate perspective on the character of the interaction we are trying to achieve. Viewing the message exchange as, say, pattern matching would lead to a much more restricted form of communication: A pattern either matches or fails; if it succeeds the only information available comes from the bindings of pattern variables. Viewing the messages as statements in a language offers the chance for a more interesting exchange of information, since the nodes are examining and responding to the messages, not simply matching patterns. In particular, we find the two-way exchange of information an important capability (see Section 9).

It is useful to identify a common 'core' language shared by all the nodes. This makes it much easier to add new nodes to the net. Any new node, preloaded with only the common internode language, can use that language to isolate the information it needs to begin to participate in solving the problem at hand. It can listen to and understand task announcements and express a

map as the last step in analysis, and then communicating the result to the appropriate agent. We will see that this monitor node does not, by the way, correspond to a central controller.

Since the emphasis in this work has been on organizing the problem solving activities of multiple problem solvers, work on the signal interpretation aspects did not include construction of low-level signal processing facilities. Instead it assumed the existence of appropriate signal processing modules and focused on the subsequent symbolic interpretation of that information.

8.1. Hardware

All communication in the DSS is assumed to take place over a broadcast channel (using for example packet radio techniques [14]). The nodes are assumed to be in fixed positions known to themselves but not known a priori to other nodes in the net. Each node has one of two capabilities: sensing or processing. The sensing capability includes low-level signal analysis and feature extraction. We assume that a variety of sensor types exists in the DSS, that the sensors are widely spaced, and that there is some overlap in sensor area coverage. Nodes with processing capability supply the computation power necessary to effect the high-level analysis and control in the net. They are not necessarily near the sensors whose data they process.

Fig. 12 is a schematic representation of a DSS.

In the example that follows, some assumptions about such things as node locations, what one node knows about another, etc., may seem to be carefully chosen rather than typically what one would expect to find. This is entirely true. We have combined a number of plausible but carefully chosen (and occasionally atypical) assumptions about hardware and software available in order to display a number of the capabilities of the contract net in a single, brief example.

8.2. Data and task hierarchy

The DSS must integrate a large quantity of data, reducing it and transforming it into a form meaningful to a human decision maker. We view this process as occurring in several stages, which together form a data hierarchy (Fig. 13).

As we have chosen to solve the problem for this illustration, at any given moment a particular node handles data at only one level of the data hierarchy, but may communicate with nodes at other levels. In addition, the only form of signal processing we consider is narrow band spectral analysis.[16]

At the bottom of the hierarchy we have audio signals, which are described in terms of several features: frequency, time of detection, strength, changes in strength, name and position of the detecting node, and name, type, and orientation of the detecting sensor.

Signals are formed into signal groups, collections of related signals. One common signal group is the harmonic set, a collection of signals in which the frequency of each signal is an integral multiple of the lowest frequency. In the current example, a signal group is described in terms of its fundamental frequency, time of formation, identity of the detecting node, and features of the detecting sensor.

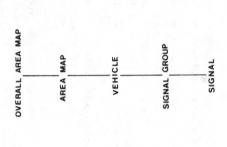

FIG. 13. Data hierarchy.

[16]Noise radiated by a vehicle typically contains narrow band signal components caused by rotating machinery. The frequencies of such signals are correlated with the type of rotating machine and its speed of rotation; hence they are indicators of the classification of the vehicle. Narrow band signals also undergo shifts in frequency due to Doppler effect or change in the speed of rotation of the associated machine; hence they also provide speed and directional information. (Unfortunately, alterations in signal strength occur both as a result of propagation conditions and variations in the distance between the vehicle and the sensor.)

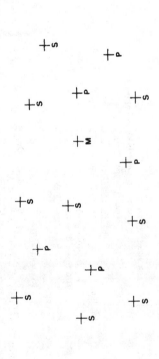

FIG. 12. A distributed sensing system. M: monitor node; P: processor node; S: sensor node.

transfer of control issues that form one focus of this paper. The operation phase is dealt with only briefly; for further discussion see [25].

The terminology in the discussion that follows highlights the fact that the nodes in the contract net play a dual role: They are simultaneously contractors obligated to carry out a task that they were awarded, and managers for any tasks which they in turn announce. For example, node number 2 in Fig. 15 is simultaneously (i) a *contractor* for the area task (and hence is charged with the duty of producing area maps from vehicle data), (ii) a *manager* for group formation tasks which it announces and contracts out, and (iii) a *manager* for any vehicle tasks which it contracts out. Nodes are thus simultaneously both workers and supervisors. (Compare Fig. 14 and Fig. 15.)

8.3.1. Initialization

The monitor node is responsible for initialization of the DSS and for formation of the overall map. It must first select nodes to be area contractors and

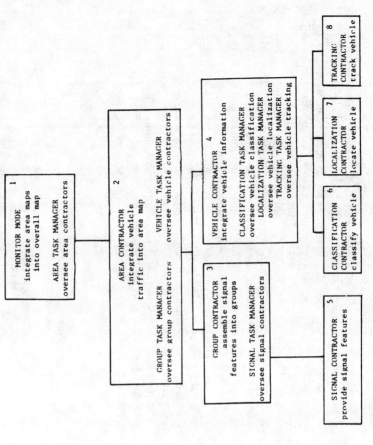

FIG. 15. Nodes and their roles.

The next level of the hierarchy is the description of the *vehicle*. It has one or more signal groups associated with it and is further specified by position, speed, course, and classification. Position can be established by triangulation, using matching groups detected by several sensors with different positions and orientations. Speed and course must generally be established over time by tracking.

The *area map* forms the next level of the data hierarchy. It contains information about the vehicle traffic in a given area. There will be several such maps for the DSS—together they span the total area of coverage of the system.

The final level is the complete or *overall area map*, produced in this example by the monitor, which integrates information in the individual area maps.

The hierarchy of tasks, Fig. 14, follows directly from the data hierarchy. The monitor node manages several *area* contractors. These contractors are responsible for the formation of traffic maps in their immediate areas. Each area contractor, in turn, manages several *group* contractors that provide it with signal groups for its area. Each group contractor integrates raw signal data from *signal* contractors that have sensing capabilities.

The area contractors also manage several *vehicle* contractors that are responsible for integrating information about individual vehicles. Each of these contractors manages a *classification* contractor that determines vehicle type, a *localization* contractor that determines vehicle position, and a *tracking* contractor that tracks the vehicle.

8.3. Contract net implementation

There are two phases to this problem: initialization of the net and operation. Although there are interesting aspects to both of these phases, our concern here is primarily with initialization, since this phase most easily illustrates the

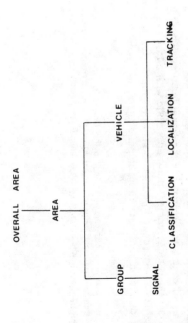

FIG. 14. Task hierarchy.

partition the system's span of coverage into areas based on the positions of the nodes selected. For purposes of illustration we assume that the monitor node knows the names of the nodes that are potential area contractors, but must establish their positions in order to do the partitioning.

It begins by announcing the task of area map formation. Because it knows the names of potential contractors, it can avoid using a general broadcast and instead uses focused addressing. The components of the announcement of interest here are the task abstraction, the eligibility specification, and the bid specification. The task abstraction is simply the task type. The eligibility specification is blank, since in this case the monitor node knows which nodes are potential contractors and can address them directly. The bid specification informs a prospective area contractor to respond with its position.

Recall that the purpose of a bid specification is to inform a node of how to bid so that a manager can select from all of the bidders the most appropriate one(s) to execute the task. In this case, node position is the relevant information. Potential area contractors respond with their positions, and, given that information, the monitor node can partition the overall span of coverage into approximately equal-sized areas. It then selects a subset of the bidders to be area contractors, informing each of its area of responsibility in an award message. The negotiation sequence thus makes available to the monitor node the positions of all of the potential area contractors, making possible a partitioning of the overall area of the DSS based on these positions. This in turn enables the DSS to adjust to a change in the number or position of potential area contractors.

Area contractors integrate vehicle data into area maps. They must first establish the existence of vehicles on the basis of group data. To do this, each area contractor solicits other nodes to provide that data. In the absence of any information about which nodes are suitable, each area contractor announces the task using a general broadcast. The task abstraction in this message is the type of task. The eligibility specification is the area for which the area contractor is responsible.[17] The bid specification is again node position. Potential group contractors respond with their respective positions, and based on this information the area contractors award contracts to nodes in their areas of responsibility.

The group contractors integrate signal features into groups, and start by finding a set of contractors to provide the signal features. Recall that we view node interaction as an agreement between a node with a task to be done and a node capable of performing that task. Sometimes the perspective on the ideal character of that agreement differs depending on the point of view of the

participant. For example, from the perspective of the signal task *managers*, the best set of contractors would have an adequate spatial distribution about the surrounding area and an adequate distribution of sensor types. From the point of view of the signal task *contractors*, on the other hand, the ideal match involves finding managers that are closest to them (in order to minimize potential communication problems).

The ability to express and deal with such disparate viewpoints is one advantage of the contract net framework. To see how the appropriate resolution is accomplished, consider the messages exchanged between the signal managers and potential signal contractors. Each signal manager announces its own signal task, using a message of the sort shown in Fig. 16. The task abstraction is the type of task, the position of the manager making the announcement, and a specification of its area of responsibility. This enables a potential contractor to determine the manager to which it should respond. The eligibility specification indicates that the only nodes that should bid on the task are those which (a) have sensing capabilities, and (b) are located in the same area as the manager that announced the task. The bid specification indicates that a bid should contain the position of the bidder and the number of each of its sensor types, information that a manager needs to select a suitable set of sensor nodes.

The potential signal contractors listen to the task announcements made by signal managers. They respond to the nearest manager with a bid (Fig. 17) that supplies their position and a description of their sensors. The managers use this

```
To:        *
From:      25
Type:      TASK ANNOUNCEMENT
Contract:  22-3-1

Eligibility Specification
           MUST-HAVE SENSOR
           MUST-HAVE POSITION AREA A

Task Abstraction:
           TASK TYPE SIGNAL
           POSITION LAT 47N LONG 17E
           AREA NAME A SPECIFICATION (...)

Bid Specification
           POSITION LAT LONG
           EVERY SENSOR NAME TYPE

Expiration Time
           28 1730Z FEB 1979
```

FIG. 16. Signal task announcement.

[17]This ensures that a node is eligible to bid on this task only if it is in the same area as the announcing area contractor and helps to prevent a case in which a group contractor is so far away from its manager that reliable communication is difficult to achieve.

the area maps are then passed to the monitor which forms the final traffic map.[18]

The initialization process reviewed above may appear at first glance to be somewhat more elaborate than is strictly necessary. We have purposely taken a fairly general approach to the problem to emphasize two aspects of contract net performance. First, as illustrated by the signal contract, contract negotiation is an interactive process involving (i) a *two-way transfor of information* (task announcements from managers to contractors, bids from contractors to managers), (ii) *local evaluation* (each party to the negotiation has its own local evaluation procedure), and (iii) *mutual selection* (bidders select from among task announcements, managers select from among bids).

Second, the contract negotiation process offers a useful degree of flexibility, making it well suited to AI problems whose decomposition is not known a priori and well suited to problems whose configuration is likely to change over time. To illustrate this, consider that exactly the same initialization process will work across a large variation in the number of and position of nodes available (indeed the description given never mentions how many nodes there are, where they are located, or how wide the total area of coverage is). There are clearly limits to this flexibility: If the area of coverage were large enough to require several thousand area contractors, it might prove useful to introduce another level of distribution in the hierarchy (Fig. 14) between the monitor node and the area contractor. But the current approach works with a wide range of available resources and needs no modification within that range. This can be useful when available hardware resources cannot be identified a priori with certainty, or when operating environments are hostile enough to make hardware failure a significant occurrence.

8.3.2. *Operation*

We now consider the activities of the system as it begins operation. For the sake of brevity the actions are described at the level of task announcements, bids, and contracts. For additional details and examples of messages sent, see [25].

When a signal is detected or when a change occurs in the features of a known signal, the detecting signal contractor reports this fact to its manager. This node, in turn, attempts either to integrate the information into an existing signal group or to form a new signal group (recall that the manager for the signal task is also a contractor for the task of group formation, Fig. 15).

[18] As noted, in this example one area contractor manages several group contractors and each group contractor in turn manages several signal contractors. It is possible, however, that a single group contractor could supply information to several area contractors, and a single signal contractor could supply information to several group contractors. It may be useful, for instance, to have a particular group contractor near an area boundary report to the area contractors on both sides of the boundary. This is easily accommodated within our framework.

```
To:         25
From:       42
Type:       BID
Contract:   22-3-1

Node Abstraction
LAT 62N LONG 9W
SENSOR NAME S1 TYPE S
SENSOR NAME S2 TYPE S
SENSOR NAME TI TYPE T
```

FIG. 17. Signal bid.

information to select a set of bidders that covers their area of responsibility with a suitable variety of sensors, and then award signal contracts on this basis (Fig. 18).

The signal contract is a good example of the negotiation process. It involves a mutual decision based on local processing by both the managers and the potential contractors. The potential contractors base their decision on a distance metric and respond to the closest manager. The managers use the number of sensors and distribution of sensor types observed in the bids to select a set of contractors that covers each area with a variety of sensors. Thus each party to the contract evaluates the proposals made by the other using its own distinct evaluation procedure.

To review the initialization process: we have a single monitor node that manages several area contractors. Each area contractor manages several group contractors, and each group contractor manages several signal contractors. The data initially flows from the bottom to the top of this hierarchy. The signal contractors supply signal features; each group contractor integrates the features from several signal contractors to form a signal group, and these groups are passed along to the area contractors, which eventually form area maps by integrating information based on the data from several group contractors. All

```
To:         42
From:       25
Type:       AWARD
Contract:   22-3-1

Task Specification
SENSOR NAME S1
SENSOR NAME S2
```

FIG. 18. Signal award.

9. A Progression in Mechanisms for Transfer of Control

9.1. The basic questions and fundamental differences

The contract net appears to offer a novel perspective on the traditional concepts of invocation and transfer of control. To illustrate this, we examine a range of invocation mechanisms that have been created since the earliest techniques were developed, and compare the perspective implicit in each to the perspective used in the contract net.

In doing this comparison, we consider the process of transfer of control from the perspective of both the caller and the respondent. We focus in particular on the issue of *selection* and consider what opportunities a calling process has for selecting an appropriate respondent and what opportunities a potential respondent has for selecting the task on which to work. In each case we con ider two basic questions that either the caller or the respondent might ask:

What is the character of the choice available? (i.e., at runtime, does the caller know about all potential respondents and can it choose from among them; similarly does each respondent know all the potential callers for whom it might work and can it choose from among them?)

On what kind of information is that choice based? (e.g., are potential respondents given, say, a pattern to match, or some more complex form of information? What information is the caller given about the potential respondents?)

The answers to these questions will demonstrate how our view of control transfer differs from that of the earlier formalisms with respect to:

Information transfer: The announcement-bid-award sequence means that there is the potential for more information, and more complex information, transferred in both directions (between caller and respondent) during the invocation process.

Local evaluation: The computation devoted to the selection process, based on the information transfer noted above, is more extensive and more complex than that used in traditional approaches. It is *local* in the sense that information is evaluated in a context associated with, and specific to, an individual KS (rather than embodied in a global evaluation function).

Mutual selection: The local selection process is symmetric, in the sense that the caller evaluates potential respondents from its perspective (via the bid evaluation procedure) and the respondents evaluate the available tasks from their perspective (via the task evaluation procedures).

Whenever a new group is detected, the contractor reports existence of the group to its manager (an area contractor). The area contractor attempts to find a node to execute a vehicle contract, which involves classifying, localizing, and tracking the vehicle. The area contractor must first determine whether the newly detected group is attributable to a known vehicle. To do this, it uses a request-response interchange to get from all current vehicle contractors an indication of their belief that the new group can in fact be attributed to one of the known vehicles.[19] Based on the responses, the area contractor either starts up a new vehicle contractor (if the group does not seem to fit an existing vehicle) or augments the current contract of the appropriate vehicle contractor, adding to it the task of making certain that the new group corresponds to a known vehicle. This may entail such things as gathering new data via the adjustment of sensors or the creation of contracts with new sensor nodes.

The vehicle contractor then makes two task announcements: vehicle classification and vehicle localization. A classification contractor may be able to classify directly, given the signal group information or it may require more data, in which case it can communicate directly with the appropriate sensor nodes.[20] The localization task is a simple triangulation which is awarded to the first bidder.

Once the vehicle has been localized, it must be tracked. This is handled by the vehicle contractor, which issues additional localization contracts from time to time and uses the results to update its vehicle description. Alternatively, the area contractor could award separate tracking contracts. The decision as to which method to use depends on loading and communication. If, for example, the area contractor is very busy with integration of data from many group contractors, it seems more appropriate to isolate it from the additional load of tracking contracts. If, on the other hand, the area contractor is not overly busy, we can let it handle updated vehicle contracts, taking advantage of the fact that it is in the best position to integrate the results and coordinate the efforts of multiple tracking contractors. In this example, we assume that the management load would be too large for the area contractor.

A variety of other issues have to be considered in the design and operation of a real distributed sensing system. Most of them, however, are quite specific to the DSS application and hence outside the main focus of this paper.

---

[19] In response to the request, the vehicle contractor has two options. It can compute the answer itself, or, if it decides that that would require more processing power than it can spare, it can issue a contract and have another node compute the answer.

[20] As this example illustrates, it is possible in the contract net for two contractors to communicate directly (i.e., horizontal communication across the hierarchy) as well as via the more traditional (vertical) communication between managers and contractors. This is accomplished with request-response exchanges. If the identity of the recipient of the request is not known by name, then the request can be sent out using the focused addressing scheme mentioned in Section 7.3.

PLANNER's [11] pattern-directed invocation provides a facility at the programming language level for nondeterministic KS retrieval, by matching goal specifications (patterns) against theorem patterns. In the simplest case, theorems are retrieved one by one and matched against the goal specification until a match is found. The order in which the theorems are tried is not defined by the language and is dependent on implementation decisions.

PLANNER does offer, in the *recommendation list*, a mechanism designed to allow the user to encode selection information. The *use* construct provides a way of specifying (by name) which theorems to try in which order. The *theorem base filter* construct offers a way of invoking a predicate function which takes one argument (the name of the next theorem whose pattern has matched the goal) and which can veto the use of that theorem.

Note that there is a degree of selection possible here, since the theorem base filter offers a way of choosing among the theorems that might possibly be used. The selection may involve a considerable amount of computation by the theorem base filter, and is local, in the sense that filters may be specific to a particular goal pattern. However, the selection is also limited in several ways. First, in the standard PLANNER invocation mechanism, the information available to the caller is at best the name of the next potential respondent. The caller does not receive any additional information (such as, for instance, exactly how the theorem matched the pattern), nor is there any easy way to provide for information transfer in that direction. Second, the choice is, as noted, a simple veto based on just that single KS. That is, since final judgment is passed on each potential KS in turn, it is not possible to make comparisons between potential KSs or to pass judgment on the whole group and choose the one that looks by some measure the best. Both of these shortcomings could be overcome if we were willing to create a superstructure on top of the existing invocation mechanism, but this would be functionally identical to the announcement-bid-award mechanism described above. The point is simply that the standard PLANNER invocation mechanism has no such facility, and the built-in depth-first search with backtracking makes it expensive to implement.

CONNIVER [19] represents a useful advance in nondeterministic invocation, since the result of a pattern-directed call is a 'possibilities list' containing *all* the KSs that match the pattern. While there is no explicit mechanism parallel to PLANNER's recommendation list, the possibilities list is accessible as a data structure and can be modified to reflect any judgments the caller might make concerning the relative utility of the KSs retrieved. Also, paired with each KS on the possibilities list is an association-list of pattern variables and bindings, which makes possible a determination of how the calling pattern was matched by each KS. This mechanism offers the caller some information about each respondent that can be useful in making the judgments noted above. CONNIVER does not, however, offer the respondent any opportunity to perform local processing or to select from among callers.

To put it another way, in the contract net the issue of *transfer of control* is more broadly viewed as a problem of connecting managers (and their tasks) with contractors (and their KSs). This view is inherently *symmetric* in that both the caller (manager) and respondents (bidders) have a selection to make. This symmetry in turn leads to the concept of establishing connection via *negotiation* between the interested parties. Then, if we are to have a fruitful discussion, the participants need to be able to 'say' interesting things to one another (i.e., they need the ability to transfer *complex information*). As the discussion below should made clear, previous models of invocation do not share these qualities. They view transfer of control as an essentially unidirectional process (from caller to respondent), offer minimal opportunity for selection at runtime, and provide restricted channels of communication between caller and respondent.

9.2. The comparison

In discussing the various approaches to invocation we often refer to 'standard' or 'traditional' forms of these approaches. Each of them could conceivably be modified in ways that would render our comments less relevant, but our point here is to examine the techniques as conceived and as typically used.

Standard subroutine (procedure) invocation represents, by our standard, a degenerate case. All the selection of routines to be invoked is done beforehand by the programmer and is hardwired into the code. The possible respondents are thus named explicitly in the source code, leaving no opportunity for choice or nondeterminism at runtime.

In traditional production rule systems, a degree of choice for the caller (in this case the interpreter) is available, since a number of rules may be retrieved at once. A range of selection criteria have been used (called *conflict resolution* schemes—see [5]), but these have typically been implemented with a single syntactic criterion hardwired into the interpreter. One standard scheme, for instance, is to assign a fixed priority to each rule and then from among those retrieved for possible invocation, simply select the rule with the highest priority. Selection is thus determined by a single procedure applied uniformly to every set of rules.

In this approach to invocation there is some choice available in selecting a KS to be invoked (since more than one rule may be retrieved), but the mechanism provided for making that choice allows for only a single, preselected procedure that is to be applied in all cases. In addition, all of the selection is done by the 'caller'; there is no mechanism that offers the rules any ability to select how they are to be invoked (e.g., if a rule can match the database in several ways, which of the possible matches will actually be used?). Finally, only minimal information is transferred from potential respondents back to the caller (at most a specification of what items in the database have been matched, and how).

The HEARSAY-II [7] system illustrates a number of similar facilities in a data-directed system. In particular, the focus of attention mechanism has a pointer to all the KSs that are ready to be invoked (i.e., those whose *stimulus frames* have been matched), as well as information (in the *response frame*) for estimating the potential contribution of each of the KSs. The system can effect some degree of selection regarding the KSs ready for invocation and has available to it a body of knowledge about each KS on which to base its selection. The response frame thus provides information transfer from respondent to caller that, while fixed in format, is more extensive than previous mechanisms. Considerable computation is also devoted to the selection process. Note, however, that the selection is not local, since there is a single, global strategy used for every selection.

The concept of meta-rules [3] offers a further advance in mechanisms to support more elaborate control schemes. It suggests that KS selection can be viewed as problem solving and can be effected using the same mechanism employed for pruning and reordering the applicable KSs and provides local selection by allowing meta-rules to be associated with specific goals.[21]

There are several things to note about the systems reviewed thus far. First, we see an increase in the amount and variety of information that is transferred from caller to respondent (e.g., from explicit naming in subroutines, to patterns in PLANNER) and from respondent to caller (e.g., from no response in subroutines to the response frames of HEARSAY-II). Note, however, that in no case do we have available a general information transmission mechanism. In all cases, the mechanisms have been designed to carry one particular sort of information and are not easily modified.

Second, we see a progression from the retrieval of a single KS to the retrieval of the entire set of potentially useful KSs, providing the opportunity for more complex varieties of selection.

Finally, note that all the selection so far is from one perspective; the selection of respondents by the caller. In none of these systems do the respondents have any choice in the matter.

To illustrate this last point, consider turning HEARSAY-II around and creating a system where respondents performed the selection: a 'task blackboard' system. The simplest form of such a system would have a central task blackboard that contains an unordered list of tasks that need to be performed. As a KS works on its current task, it may discover new (sub)tasks that require execution and add them to the blackboard. When a KS finishes its current task, it looks at the blackboard, evaluates the lists of tasks there, and decides which one it wants to execute.

[21]The concept of negotiation in the contract net grew, in part, from generalizing this perspective to make it 'bi-directional': Both managers and potential contractors can devote computational effort to selecting from the alternatives available to them.

Note that in this system the respondents would have all the selection capability. Rather than having a caller announce a task and evaluate the set of KSs that respond, we have the KSs examining the list of tasks and selecting the one they wish to work on. It is thus plausible to invert the standard situation, but we still have unidirectional selection—in this case, on the part of the respondent rather than the caller.

PUP6 [16], on the other hand, was the first system to suggest that transfer of control could be viewed as a *discussion* between the caller and potential respondents. In that system, if a KS receives more than one offer to execute a task, a special 'chooser' KS momentarily takes control and asks 'questions' of the respondents to determine which of them ought to be used. This is accomplished by querying the *parts* of the KS. Each KS is composed of a standard set of *parts*, each *part* designed to deal with a particular question about that KS. For example, the procedures in the WHEN and COMPLEXITY parts of a KS answer the questions "When should you take control?" and "How costly are you?" This interchange is highly stylized and not very flexible, but does represent an attempt to implement explicit two-way communication.

The contract net differs from these approaches in several ways. First, from the point of view of the caller (the manager), the standard task broadcast and response interchange has been improved by making possible a *more informative* response. That is, instead of the traditional tools that allow the caller to receive only a list of potential respondents, the contract net has available a mechanism that makes it possible for the caller to receive a description of potential utility from each respondent (the bidders). The caller also has available (as in other approaches) a list of respondents rather than a sequence of names presented one at a time.[22] Both of these make it possible to be more selective in making decisions about invocation.

Second, the contract net emphasizes *local evaluation*. An explicit place in the framework has been provided for mechanisms in which the caller can invest computational effort in selecting KSs for invocation (using its bid evaluation procedure) and the respondents can similarly invest effort in selecting tasks to work on (using their task evaluation procedures). These selection procedures are also local in the sense that they are associated with and written from the perspective of the individual KS (as opposed to, say, HEARSAY-II's global focus of attention procedure).

Third, while we have labeled this process *selection*, it might more appropriately be labeled *deliberation*. This would emphasize that its purpose for the caller is to decide in general *what to do* with the bids received and not merely *which of them to accept*. Note that one possible decision is that *none* of the bids is adequate and thus none of the potential respondents would be

[22]More precisely, the caller has available a list of all those that have responded by the expiration time of the contract.

invoked (instead, the task may be re-announced later).[23] This choice is not typically available in other problem solving systems and emphasizes the wider perspective taken by the contract net on the transfer of control issue.

Finally, there appears to be a novel symmetry in the transfer of control process. Recall that PLANNER, CONNIVER, and HEARSAY-II all offer the caller some ability to select from among the respondents, while a task blackboard system allows the respondents to select from among the tasks. The contract net (and PUPs), however, use an interactive, *mutual selection* process where task distribution is the result of a discussion between processors. As a result of the information exchanged in this discussion, the caller can select from among potential respondents while the KSs can select from among potential tasks.

10.   Suitable Applications

In this section we consider the sorts of problems for which the contract net is well suited.

The framework has, for instance, been designed to provide a more powerful mechanism for transfer of control than is available in current problem-solving systems. This mechanism will be useful when we do not know in advance which KS should be invoked or do not know which node should be given the task in question. In the first of these situations—not knowing in advance which KS to invoke—we require some machinery for making the decision. The contract net's negotiation and deliberation process is one such mechanism. It will prove most useful for problems in which we especially careful selection of KSs is important (i.e., problems for which we prefer the 'knowledge' end of the knowledge vs. search tradeoff).

The second situation—matching nodes and tasks—is inherent in a distributed architecture, since no one node has complete knowledge of either the capabilities of or the busy/idle state of every node in the network. We have labeled this the connection problem and have explored the negotiation and deliberation process as a way of solving it as well.

The framework is well-matched to problems that can be viewed in terms of a hierarchy of tasks (e.g., heuristic search), or levels of data abstraction (e.g.,

applications that deal with audio or video signals). Such problems lend themselves to decomposition into a set of relatively independent tasks with little need for global information or synchronization. Individual tasks can be assigned to separate processor nodes; these nodes can then execute the tasks with little need for communication with other nodes.

The manager-contractor structure provides a natural way to effect hierarchical control (in the distributed case, it's actually concurrent hierarchical control), and the managers at each level in the hierarchy are an appropriate place for data integration and abstraction.

Note, by the way, that these control hierarchies are not simple vertical hierarchies but are more complex generalized hierarchies. This is illustrated by the existence of communication links other than those between managers and contractors. Nodes are able to communicate horizontally with related contractors or with any other nodes in the net, as we saw in the DSS example, where classification contractors communicated directly with signal contractors using the request-response style of interaction.

The framework is also primarily applicable to domains where the subtasks are large and where it is worthwhile to expend a potentially nontrivial amount of computation and communication to invoke the best KS for each subtask. It would, for instance, make little sense to go through an extended mutual selection process to get some simple arithmetic done or to do a simple database access. While our approach can be abbreviated to an appropriately terse degree of interchange for simple problems (e.g., directed contacts and the request-response mechanism), other systems are already capable of supporting this variety of behavior. The primary contribution of our framework lies in applications to problems where the more complex interchange provides an efficient and effective basis for problem solving.

Finally, the contract net is also useful in problems where the primary concerns are in distributing control, achieving reliability, and avoiding bottlenecks, even if, in these problems, the more complex variety of information exchange described above is unnecessary. The contract net's negotiation mechanism offers a means for distributing control; sharing responsibility for tasks between managers and contractors offers a degree of reliability; and the careful design of the message types in the protocol helps avoid saturating the communication channel and causing bottlenecks.

11.   Limitations, Extensions, Open Problems

11.1.   The other stages

Earlier we noted that this paper focuses on application of the contract net to the distribution stage of distributed problem solving. The other stages—decomposition, sub-problem solution, and answer synthesis—are important foci for additional work. Problem decomposition, for example, is not a well-

---

[23]Similarly the potential bidders deliberate over task announcements received and may decide that none is worth submitting a bid. Note also that receiving bids but deciding that none is good enough is distinctly different from receiving no bids at all. In a system using pattern-directed inference, receiving no bids is analogous to finding no KSs with matching patterns; receiving bids but turning down all of them after due consideration has no precise analogy in existing languages. Agenda-based systems come close, in that KSs put on the agenda may have such a low ranking that they are effectively ignored. But this is not the same, for two reasons. First, if the queue ever does get sufficiently depleted, those KSs will in fact be run. Second, and more important, there is no explicit decision to ignore those KSs, simply an accident of the ordering, or perhaps the KS's own estimation of its individual utility. The contract net offers a mechanism for making the decision explicitly and based on an evaluation of all the candidates.

It would also be useful to develop a more advanced form of task-sharing. In our current formulation, task distribution results in the traditional form of "hand out a subtask and get back a result" interaction. We are currently exploring the possibility of expanding this to a more cooperative form of interaction in which "what is to be done" is negotiated as well as "who is to do it".

We are also exploring further development of the dynamic configuration capability which the contract net makes possible. As noted in Section 8.3, initialization of the DSS can take into account the resources available (number of sensors, etc.). We intend to extend this to dynamic reconfiguration: the negotiation technique should provide a mechanism that allows nodes which have become overloaded to shed some of their workload by distributing tasks to other available nodes.

11.4. Optimality of the negotiation process

As noted, a major goal of the contract net framework is to provide a mechanism for solving the connection problem—achieving an appropriate matching of tasks to processor nodes. Yet it is easily seen that the negotiation process described above does not guarantee an *optimal* matching of tasks and nodes.

There are two reasons why this may occur. First, there is the problem of timing. A node that becomes idle chooses a task to bid on from among the task announcements it has heard up to that time. Similarly, a manager chooses what to do on the basis of the bids it has received by the expiration time for its task announcement. But since the net operates asynchronously, new task announcements and new bids are made at unpredictable times. A better matching of nodes to tasks might be achieved if there were some way to know that it was appropriate for a node to wait just a little longer before bidding, or for a manager to wait a little longer before awarding a task.

Second, at any given instant in time, the complete matching of nodes and tasks results from a number of local decisions. Each idle node chooses the most interesting task to bid on, without reference to what other idle nodes may be choosing; each manager chooses the best bid(s) it has received without reference to what any other manager may be doing. The best global assignment does not necessarily result from the simple concatenation of all of the best local assignments.[24]

Consider for example a situation in which two managers (A and B) have both announced tasks, and two potential contractors (X and Y) have each responded by bidding on both tasks. Imagine further that from A's perspective, X's bid is rated 0.9 (on a 0 to 1 scale), while Y's is rated 0.8 (Fig. 19). Conversely, from B's perspective, X is rated 0.8 and Y is rated 0.2.

---

[24]This appears to be a variety of the 'prisoner's dilemma' problem (see e.g., [10, 30]).

understood process. It is easy to recognize when it is done well or badly, but there are relatively few principles that can be used prospectively to produce good decompositions. We address below the issue of sub-problem solution, noting that a more cooperative approach—one in which individual nodes share partial solutions as they work—can be useful in a variety of problems. Finally, as we have explored elsewhere [4], there are a number of approaches to synthesizing individual sub-problem results, each addressing a different anticipated level of problem interaction. In future work we intend to explore applications of the contract net and the negotiation metaphor to each of these topics.

12. Instantiating the framework

The framework we have proposed—the task announcement, bid, award sequence, the common internode language, etc.—offers some ideas about what kinds of information are useful for distributed problem solving and how that information can be organized. There is still a considerable problem involved in instantiating the framework in the context of a specific task domain. Our protocol provides a site for embedding particular types of information (e.g. an eligibility specification), but does not specify exactly what that information is for any specific problem.

In this sense the contract net protocol is similar to AI languages like PLANNER, CONNIVER, QLISP [24], etc., which supply a framework for problem solving (e.g., the notions of goal specifications, theorem patterns, etc.), but leave to the user the task of specifying the content of that framework for any given problem. We expect that further experience with our framework will lead to additional structure to help guide its use.

11.3. Alternate models of cooperation

We have emphasized task-sharing as a means of internode cooperation and have attempted to provide some mechanisms for the communication required to effect this mode of cooperation. We have not as yet, however, adequately studied *result-sharing* [28] as a means of cooperation. In what approach, nodes assist each other through sharing of partial results. This type of cooperation appears to be of use in dealing with several sorts of problems. For problems where erroneous data or knowledge lead to conflicting views at individual nodes, sharing results can help to resolve those inconsistencies (as for example in [17]). For some tasks, any individual subproblem is inherently ambiguous even when data and knowledge are complete and exact (e.g., the blocks world scene identification in [31]); here the sharing of intermediate results can be an effective means of reducing or removing ambiguity. It is our intention to examine the structure of communication for this mode of cooperation with a view to extending the contract net framework to incorporate it.

	A		B
X	0.9	X	0.8
Y	0.8	Y	0.2

Fig. 19. Managers rating bids from prospective contractors.

From a purely local perspective, both of the managers want X as their contractor; from a more global perspective it may make more sense to have A 'settle' for Y, and give X to B. Yet we cannot in general create the more global perspective without exchanging what may turn out to be extensive amounts of information.

The first of the two problems (timing) appears unavoidable given that we have chosen to deal with the kinds of problems typically attacked in AI, problems whose total decomposition is not known a priori. In a speech understanding problem, for instance, we cannot set up a fixed sequence of KS invocations beforehand because the utility of any given KS is not predictable in advance. Similarly, in a DSS, we have the same inability to predict KS utility, plus the added difficulty of new signals arriving at unpredictable moments.

If we do not know in advance which subtasks will arise and when, or exactly which KSs will be useful at each point, then we clearly cannot plan the *optimal* assignment of nodes to tasks for the entire duration of the problem. Some planning may be possible, however, even if we lack complete knowledge of a problem's eventual decomposition. We are currently studying ways to make use of partial information about tasks yet to be encountered or nodes that are soon going to be idle.

The second problem (local decisions) appears inherent in any decentralization of control and decision making. As noted earlier, we want to distribute control (for reasons of speed, problem-solving power, reliability, etc.). Given distributed control, however, globally *optimal* control decisions are possible only at the cost of transmitting extensive amounts of information between managers every time an award is about to be made. With that approach, inefficiencies due to suboptimal control decisions are traded for inefficiencies arising from transmission delays and channel saturation. We are currently studying this tradeoff and exploring ways of minimizing the difficulties that arise from this problem.

It appears then, that as a result of the unpredictability of the timing of subtasks and the necessity of making local decisions, precisely optimal matching of nodes to tasks is not possible. Note, however, that our stated goal is an *appropriate* assignment of nodes to tasks. Operation of the contract net is not predicated on optimal matching. In addition, the small set of experiments we have done so far (see [27]) indicate that overall performance is not seriously degraded by suboptimal matching.

11.5. Coherent behavior

We do not yet fully understand the more general problem of achieving globally coherent behavior in a system with distributed control. The fundamental difficulty was described earlier: We require distributed control in order to effect loose coupling, yet coherent behavior usually requires a global perspective.

Some aspects of the contract net protocol were motivated by attempts to overcome this problem. First, the task abstraction supplies information which enables a node to compare announcements and select the most appropriate. In a similar fashion, information in bids (the node abstraction) enables managers to compare bids from different nodes and select the most appropriate. Second, each node in a contract net maintains a list of the best recent task announcements it has seen—a kind of window on the tasks at hand for the net as a whole. This window enables the nodes to compare announcements over time, helping to avoid mistakes associated with too brief a view of the problem at hand.

We still have the problem that good local decisions do not necessarily add up to good global behavior, as the example in the previous section showed. However, the steps noted at least contribute to local decisions that are made on the basis of an extended (not snapshot) view of system performance and decisions that are based on extensive information about tasks and bids.

In the most general terms we see our efforts aimed at developing a problem solving protocol. The protocol should contain primitives appropriate for talking about and doing problem solving, and should structure the interaction between problem solvers in ways that contribute to coordinated behavior of the group. We have thus far taken an initial step in this direction with the development of the task announcement, bid, and award sequence.

12. Summary

The preceding discussion considered the contract net in a number of different contexts. In the most specific view, it was considered a mechanism for building a distributed sensing system. More generally, it offered an approach to distributed problem solving and a view of distributed processing. In the most general view, it was considered in the context of AI problem solving techniques. In the sections that follow we consider the advantages offered by the contract net in each of these contexts, reviewing in the process the central themes of the paper.

12.1. Contributions to distributed processing

A distributed processing approach to computation offers the potential for a number of benefits, including speed and the ability to handle applications that have a natural spatial distribution. The design of the contract net framework attempts to ensure that these potential benefits are indeed realized.

configuration would presumably require human intervention for its basic design (e.g., assigning nodes to tasks) and might require modifications to software as well.

Dynamic configuration also means that most nodes that must cooperate are able to communicate with one another directly. This reduces the amount of communication needed, since it reduces the need for either indirect routing of messages or the use of powerful transmitters.

The contract net also offers advantages in terms of increased reliability. By distributing both control and data, for instance, we ensure that there is no one node or even a subset of nodes whose loss would totally cripple the system. In addition, recovery from failure of a node is aided by the presence of explicit links between managers and their contractors. The failure of any contractor can be detected by its manager; the contract for which it was responsible can then be re-announced and awarded to another node. There is, in addition, the possibility of reliability arising from "load-sensitive redundancy". When load on the net is low, we might take advantage of idle processors by making redundant awards of the same contract. The system thus offers the opportunity to make resource allocation decisions opportunistically, taking advantage of idle resources to provide additional reliability.

The framework also makes it reasonably easy to add new nodes to the net at any time. This is useful for replacing nodes that have failed or adding new nodes in response to increased computational load on the net. Two elements of the framework provide the foundation for this capability. First, the contract negotiation process uses a form of "anonymous invocation": the KSs to be invoked are *described* rather than *named*. Second, there is a single language "spoken" by all the nodes.

The concept of describing rather than naming KSs has its roots in the goal-directed invocation of various AI languages and the notion of pattern-directed invocation generally (see, e.g. [32]), where it was motivated by the desire for more sophisticated forms of KS retrieval. It also however, turns out to offer an interesting and useful form of "substitutability", simply because where names are unique, descriptions are not, and a wide range of KSs may satisfy a single description. As a result, in a system with invocation by name, the addition of a new KS requires modification of the existing code to ensure that the new KS is indeed invoked. When invocation is by description, adding a new KS involves simply making it available to the existing collection of KSs; it will be invoked whenever its description is matched (in our case, whenever it chooses to bid on a task announcement). The contract net thus shares with other systems using anonymous invocation the ability to add new KSs by simply "throwing them into the pot".

Second, the use of a single language 'spoken' by all the nodes simplifies communication. If we are to add a new node, it must have some way of communicating with other nodes in the net. The contract net simplifies this issue by providing a very compact language: The basic protocol (task

---

In order to realize speed in distributed systems, we need to avoid bottlenecks. They can arise in two primary ways: by concentrating disproportionate amounts of computation or communication at central resources, and by saturating available communication channels so that nodes must remain idle while messages are transmitted.

To avoid bottlenecks we distribute control and data. In the DSS example, data is distributed dynamically as a result of the division of the net into areas during the initialization phase. Control is distributed dynamically through the use of a negotiation process to effect the connection of tasks with idle processors.

The contract net design also tries to avoid communication channel saturation by reducing the number and length of messages. The information in task announcements (like eligibility specifications), for instance, helps eliminate extra message traffic, thereby helping to minimize the amount of channel capacity consumed by communication overhead. Similarly, bid messages can be kept short and 'to the point' through the use of the bid specification mechanism.

Finally, the ability to handle applications with a natural spatial or functional distribution is facilitated by viewing task distribution as a connection problem and by having the processors themselves negotiate to solve the problem. This makes it possible for the collection of available processors to 'spread themselves' over the set of tasks to be done, distributing the workload dynamically.

12.2. Contributions to distributed problem solving

As we noted earlier (Section 6), a central issue in distributed problem solving is organization: How can we distribute control and yet maintain coherent behavior?

One way to accomplish this is by what we have called task-sharing, the distribution around the net of tasks relevant to solving the overall problem. As we have seen, the contract net views task-sharing in terms of connecting idle nodes with tasks yet to be done. It effects this matching by structuring interaction around negotiation as an organizing principle.

Negotiation in turn is implemented by focusing on what it is that processors should say to one another. The motivation for our protocol is thus to supply one idea on *what to say* rather than *how to communicate.*

As the example in Section 8 showed, use of the contract net makes it possible for the system to be configured dynamically, taking into account (in that example) such factors as the number of sensor and processor nodes available, their location, and the ease with which communication can be extablished. Such a configuration offers a number of improvements over a static, a priori configuration. It provides, for instance, a degree of simplicity: The same software is capable of initializing and running networks with a wide variation of available hardware. If the configuration were static, each new

protocol at the level of problem solving and provided a step toward indicating what kinds of information should be transferred between nodes.

The utility of negotiation as an interaction mechanism was demonstrated in two settings. First, our basic approach to cooperation relies on task-sharing, and negotiation is used to distribute tasks among the nodes of the net. This makes possible distribution based on mutual selection, yielding a good match of nodes and tasks. Second, negotiation was used to effect transfer of control. In that setting it offered a framework in which the matching of KSs to tasks was based on more information than is usually available (due to the transfer of information in both directions, and the transfer of more complex information). As a result, negotiation makes it possible to effect a finer degree of control and to be more selective in making decisions about invocation than is the case with previous mechanisms.

ACKNOWLEDGMENT

This work describes research done at the Artificial Intelligence Laboratory of the Massachusetts Institute of Technology and at the Defence Research Establishment Atlantic of the Department of National Defence, Research and Development Branch, Canada. Support for the Artificial Intelligence Lab is provided in part the Advanced Research Projects Agency of the Department of Defense under Office of Naval Research Contract N00014-80-C-505.

The assistance of Bruce Buchanan and Ed Feigenbaum in the original development of these ideas is greatly acknowledged. Carmen Bright, Joe Maksym, Lee Erman, Carl Hewitt, Patrick Winston, and Judy Zinnikas provided useful comments on earlier drafts of this paper.

REFERENCES

1. Baer, J.-L., A survey of some theoretical aspects of multiprocessing, *Compu. Surveys* **5** (1) (1973) 31–80.
2. Bowdon, E.K., Sr. and Barr, W.J., Cost effective priority assignment in network computers, in: *FJCC Proceedings* **41** (AFIPS, Montvale, NJ, 1972) 755–763.
3. Davis, R., Meta-rules: reasoning about control, *Artificial Intelligence* **15** (1980) 179–222.
4. Davis, R., Models of problem solving: Why cooperate?, *SIGART Newsletter* **70** (1980) 50–51.
5. Davis, R. and King, J., An overview of production systems, in: E.W. Elcock and D. Michie (Eds.), *Machine Intelligence* **8** (Wiley, New York, 1977) 300–332.
6. D'Olivera, C.R., An analysis of computer decentralization, Rept. LCS, TM90, MIT, Cambridge, MA, 1977.
7. Erman, L.D., Hayes-Roth, F., Lesser, V.R. and Reddy, D.R., The Hearsay-II speech-understanding system: Integrating knowledge to resolve uncertainty, *Comput. Surveys* **12** (1980) 213–253.
8. Farber, D.J. and Larson, K.C., The structure of the distributed computing system—Software, in: J. Fox (Ed.), *Proceedings of the Symposium on Computer-Communications Networks And Teletraffic* (Polytechnic Press, Brooklyn, NY, 1972) 539–545.
9. Galbraith, J.R., Organizational design—an information processing view, in: Kolb (Ed.), *Organizational Psychology* (Prentice Hall, Englewood Cliffs, NJ, 2nd. ed., 1974) 313–322.
10. Hamburger, H., N-person prisoner's dilemma, *J. Math. Sociology* **3** (1973) 27–48.
11. Hewitt, C., Description and theoretical analysis (using schemata) of PLANNER: A language for proving theorems and manipulating models in a robot, MIT AI TR 258, MIT, Cambridge, MA, 1972.

announcement, bid, award) provides the elementary 'syntax' for communication, while the common internode language provides the vocabulary used to express message content.

Thus, anonymous invocation means that it is possible for a new node to begin participating in the operation of the net by listening to the messages being exchanged. (If invocation were by name, listening to message traffic would do no good.) The use of a single language means that the node will understand the messages, and the use of a very simple language means that the task of initializing a node is easier.

12.3. Contributions to artificial intelligence

The contract net offers a novel view on the nature of the invocation process. As we have seen, it views task distribution as a problem of connecting tasks to KSs capable of executing those tasks, and it effects this connection via negotiation.

In Section 9 we used this perspective to examine existing models of invocation and evaluate them along several dimensions. This discussion showed, first, that in previous models connection is typically effected with a transfer of information that is unidirectional; hence the connection process is asymmetric. Control resides either with the tasks (goal-driven invocation) or with the KSs (data-driven invocation). In the contract net view, by contrast, the transfer is two-way, as each participant in the negotiation offers information about itself. This in turn means that control can be shared by both; the problem becomes one of mutual selection.

We then showed that the information transferred is typically limited in content. In the contract net, on the other hand, the information is not limited to a name or pattern, but is instead expanded to include statements expressible in the common internode language.

Third, the discussion showed that information about a more complete collection of candidate KSs is available before final selection is made. This makes possible a wider range of KS and task selection strategies than are possible if KSs and tasks must be selected or rejected as they are encountered.

Finally, we noted that this expanded view of invocation effects a true deliberation process, since one possible outcome of the negotiation is that none of the bids received is judged good enough, and hence none of the potential contractors will be selected. This appears to be a useful advance that has no precise analogy in previous programming languages and applications.

12.4. Conclusion: the major themes revisited

Two of the major themes of this paper are the notion of protocols aimed at problem solving rather than communication and the concept of negotiation as a basic mechanism for interaction. The first was illustrated by the use of message types like task announcement, bid, and award. This focused the contract net

12. Hewitt, C., Viewing control structures as patterns of passing messages, *Artificial Intelligence* **8** (1977) 323–364.

13. Kahn, R.E., Resource-sharing computer communications networks, *Proc. IEEE* **60** (11) (1972) 1397–1407.

14. Kahn, R.E., The organization of computer resources into a packet radio network, in: *NCC Proceedings* **44** (AFIPS, Montvale, NJ, 1975) 177–186.

15. Kimbleton, S.R. and Schneider, G.M., Computer communications networks: approaches, objectives, and performance considerations, *Comput. Surveys* **7** (3) (1975) 129–173.

16. Lenat, D.B., Beings: knowledge as interacting experts, *IJCA* **4** (1975) 126–133.

17. Lesser, V.R. and Erman, L.D., Distributed interpretation: a model and experiment, *IEEE Trans. Comput.* **29** (1980) 1144–1163.

18. Lesser, V.R. and Corkill, D.D., Functionally accurate cooperative distributed systems, *IEEE Trans. Systems Man Cybernet.* **11** (1) (1981) 81–96.

19. McDermott, D.V. and Sussman, G.J., The CONNIVER Reference Manual, AI Memo 259a, MIT, Cambridge, MA, 1974.

20. Nii, H.P. and Feigenbaum, E.A., Rule-based understanding of signals, in: D.A. Waterman and F. Hayes-Roth (Eds.), *Pattern-Directed Inference Systems* (Academic Press, New York, 1978) 483–501.

21. Noyce, R.N., From relays to MPU's, *Comput.* **9** (12) (1976) 26–29.

22. Prince, P.S., Recovery from failure in a contract net, B.S. Thesis, EECS Department, MIT, Cambridge, MA, 1980.

23. Roberts, L.G., Data by the packet, *IEEE Spectrum* **11** (2) (1974) 46–51.

24. Sacerdoti et al., QLISP—A language for the interactive development of complex systems, *Proc. NCC* **45** (1976) 349–356.

25. Smith, R.G. and Davis, R., Applications of the contract net framework: distributed sensing, *Proc. ARPA Distribued Sensor Net Symp.*, Pittsburgh, PA (1978) 12–20.

26. Smith, R.G., *A framework for distributed problem solving* (VMI Research Press, 1981); also: Stanford Memo STAN-CS-78-700, Stanford University Stanford, CA, 1978.

27. Smith, R.G., The contract net protocol: high level communication and control in a distributed problem solver, *IEEE Trans. Comput.* **29** (1980) 1104–1113.

28. Smith, R.G. and Davis, R., Frameworks for cooperation in a distributed problem solver, *IEEE Trans Systems Man Cybernet.* **11** (1981) 61–70.

29. Svodobova, L., Liskov, B. and Clark, D., Distributed computer systems: structure and semantics, MIT-LCS-TR-215, MIT, Cambridge, MA, 1979.

30. Tucker, A.W., A two-person dilemma, Mimeo, Stanford University, Stanford, CA, 1950.

31. Waltz, D., Understanding line drawings of scenes with shadows, in: Winston (Ed.), *The Psychology of Computer Vision* (McGraw-Hill, New York, 1975).

32. Waterman, D.A. and Hayes-Roth, F. (Eds.), *Pattern-Directed Inference Systems* (Academic Press, New York, 1978).

The Contract Net Protocol: High-Level Communication and Control in a Distributed Problem Solver

REID G. SMITH, MEMBER, IEEE

Abstract—The contract net protocol has been developed to specify problem-solving communication and control for nodes in a distributed problem solver. Task distribution is affected by a negotiation process, a discussion carried on between nodes with tasks to be executed and nodes that may be able to execute those tasks.

We present the specification of the protocol and demonstrate its use in the solution of a problem in distributed sensing.

The utility of negotiation as an interaction mechanism is discussed. It can be used to achieve different goals, such as distributing control and data to avoid bottlenecks and enabling a finer degree of control in making resource allocation and focus decisions than is possible with traditional mechanisms.

Index Terms—Artificial Intelligence (AI), connection, cooperation, distributed problem solving, focus, high-level protocols, negotiation, resource allocation, task-sharing.

I. INTRODUCTION

DISTRIBUTED *problem solving* is the cooperative solution of problems by a decentralized and loosely coupled collection of knowledge-sources (*KS*'s) (procedures, sets of production rules, etc.), located in a number of distinct processor nodes. The *KS*'s *cooperate* in the sense that no one of them has sufficient information to solve the entire problem; mutual sharing of information is necessary to allow the group, as a whole, to produce an answer. By *decentralized* we mean that both control and data are logically and often geographically distributed; there is neither global control nor global data storage. *Loosely coupled* means that individual *KS*'s spend most of their time in computation rather than communication.

Such problem solvers offer the promise of speed, reliability, extensibility, and the potential for increased tolerance to uncertain data and knowledge, as well as the ability to handle applications with a natural spatial distribution. There has been much recent interest in this type of problem solving in the Artificial Intelligence (AI) community. Its use has been con-

Manuscript received March 4, 1980; revised May 9, 1980. This work was supported in part by the Advanced Research Projects Agency under Contract MDA 903-77-C-0322, the National Science Foundation under Contract MCS 77-02712, and the National Institutes of Health under Grant RR-00785 on the SUMEX-AIM Computer Facility at Stanford University, Stanford, CA and by the Defence Research Establishment Atlantic of the Department of National Defence, Research and Development Branch, Dartmouth, N.S. Canada.

The author is with the Defence Research Establishment Atlantic, Dartmouth, N.S., Canada.

sidered in such applications as traffic-light control [5], distributed sensing [7], and heuristic search [10].

In this paper, we present the **contract net** protocol, a high-level protocol for communication among the nodes in a distributed problem solver. It facilitates distributed control of cooperative task execution (which we call *task-sharing* [9]) with efficient internode communication.

The role of a high-level protocol in a network such as the ARPANET has been discussed in previous papers (see, for example [11]). Traditional communication protocols form a low-level base for problem-solving communication. They enable reliable and efficient transmission of bit streams between nodes, but do not consider the semantics of the information being passed. A high-level protocol assigns interpretations to the bit streams. It offers a structure that assists the system designer in deciding *what* the nodes should say to each other, rather than *how* to say it.

We are not primarily concerned with the physical architecture of the problem solver. It is assumed to be a network of loosely coupled, asynchronous nodes. Each node contains a number of distinct *KS*'s. The nodes are interconnected so that each node can communicate with every other node by sending messages. No memory is shared by the nodes. We also assume the existence of a low-level communication protocol to support reliable and efficient communication of bit streams between nodes. A functional model of a node is shown in Appendix A.

II. CONNECTION AND CONTRACT NEGOTIATION

The key issue to be resolved in task-sharing is how tasks are to be distributed among the processor nodes. There must be a means whereby nodes with tasks to be executed can find the most appropriate idle nodes to execute those tasks. We call this the *connection problem*. Solving the connection problem is crucial to high performance in a distributed problem solver. It has two aspects: 1) *resource allocation* and 2) *focus*. Effective resource allocation is achieved by balancing the computational load among the nodes. It is essential if the maximum speedup possible from applying multiple nodes to a single overall problem is to be obtained.

Focus is achieved by effective selection of tasks for allocation to nodes and by effective selection of KS's for execution of tasks. It is essential for problems that do not have well-defined algorithms for their solutions (i.e., problems of the type most often considered in AI). For such problems, many tasks are typically generated during the search for solutions; and the execution of many of these tasks will not lead to a solution. In addition, the most appropriate *KS* to invoke for the execution of any given task generally cannot be identified *a priori*. The combination of many tasks and many applicable *KS*'s can lead to a *combinatorial explosion*. A problem solver must therefore maintain focus to achieve high performance in practical applications.

The connection problem can also be viewed from the perspective of an idle node. It must find another node with an appropriate task that is available for execution. In our approach, both nodes with tasks to be executed and nodes ready to execute tasks proceed simultaneously. They engage each other in discussions that resemble contract negotiation to solve the connection problem. It is this process that is the basis for the contract net protocol.

For our purposes, negotiation has four important components: 1) it is a local process that does not involve centralized control, 2) there is a two-way exchange of information, 3) each party to the negotiation evaluates the information from its own perspective, and 4) final agreement is achieved by mutual selection.

The collection of nodes is referred to as a contract net and the execution of a task is dealt with as a contract between two nodes. Each node in the net takes on one of two roles related to the execution of an individual task: manager or contractor. A **manager** is responsible for monitoring the execution of a task and processing the results of its execution. A **contractor** is responsible for the actual execution of the task. Individual nodes are not designated *a priori* as managers or contractors; these are only roles, and any node can take on either role dynamically during the course of problem solving. Typically, a node will take on both roles, often simultaneously for different contracts. As a result, nodes are not statically tied to a control hierarchy. This also leads to more efficient utilization of nodes, as compared, for example, to schemes that do not allow nodes that have contracted out tasks to take on other tasks while they are waiting for results.

A contract is established by a process of local mutual selection based on a two-way transfer of information. In brief, available contractors evaluate task announcements made by several managers and submit bids on those for which they are suited. The managers evaluate the bids and award contracts to the nodes they determine to be most appropriate. The negotiation process may then recur. A contractor may further partition a task and award contracts to other nodes. It is then the manager for those contracts. This leads to the hierarchical control structure that is typical of task-sharing. Control is distributed because processing and communication are not focused at particular nodes, but rather every node is capable of accepting and assigning tasks.

The basic idea of contracting is not new. A rudimentary bidding scheme, for example, was used for resource allocation in the distributed computing system (DCS) [2], [3]. We will note the similarities and differences between that scheme and the contract net protocol as we proceed.

Throughout the paper, reference is made to an experimental contract net system called CNET. It is a system of INTERLISP [12] functions that enables a user to simulate the solution of problems with a distributed processor.

III. EXAMPLE

This example is taken from a CNET simulation of a distributed sensing system (DSS) [7]. A DSS is a network of sensor and processor nodes spread throughout a relatively large geographic area. It attempts to construct and maintain a dynamic map of vehicle traffic in the area. Construction and maintenance of such a map requires the interpretation and integration of a large quantity of sensory information received by the collection of sensor elements.

Use of the contract net protocol in a DSS makes it possible for the sensor system to be configured dynamically, taking into account such factors as the number of sensor and processor nodes available, their locations, and the ease with which communication can be established.

We will examine the negotiation for one particular task, called the *signal* task, that arises during the initialization phase of DSS operation. The task involves gathering of sensed data and extraction of signal features. The managers for this task are nodes that do not have sensing capabilities, but do have extensive processing capabilities. They attempt to find a set of sensor nodes to provide them with signal features. The sensor nodes, on the other hand, have limited processing capabilities and attempt to find managers that can further process the signal features they extract from the raw sensed data.

Recall that we view node interaction as an agreement between a node with a task to be performed and a node capable of performing that task. Sometimes the perspective on the ideal character of that agreement differs depending on the point of view of the participant. For example, from the perspective of the *signal* task managers, the best set of contractors has an adequate spatial distribution about the surrounding area and an adequate distribution of sensor types. From the point of view of the *signal* task contractors, on the other hand, the best managers are those closest to them in order to minimize potential communication problems. The ability to express and deal with such disparate viewpoints is one advantage of the contract net protocol. To see how the appropriate resolution is accomplished, consider the messages exchanged between the *signal* managers and potential *signal* contractors. Each *signal* manager announces its own *signal* task, using a message of the sort shown in Fig. 1. Each message in the contract net protocol has a set of slots for the task-specific information in the message. The four slots of the task announcement are shown in the figure. The information that fills the slots is encoded in a simple language common to all nodes.

The task abstraction is the type of task and the position of the manager making the announcement. The position enables a potential contractor to determine the manager to which it should respond. The eligibility specification indicates that the only nodes that should bid on this task are those which 1) have sensing capabilities and 2) are located in the same area as the manager that announced the task. This helps to reduce extraneous message traffic and bid processing. The bid specifi-

To: * indicates a broadcast message.
From: 25
Type: TASK ANNOUNCEMENT
Contract: 22-3-1
Task Abstraction:
   TASK TYPE SIGNAL
   POSITION LAT 47N LONG 17E
Eligibility Specification:
   MUST-HAVE SENSOR
   MUST-HAVE POSITION AREA A
Bid Specification:
   POSITION LAT LONG
   EVERY SENSOR NAME TYPE
Expiration Time:
   28 1730Z FEB 1979

Fig. 1.   Signal task announcement.

To: 25
From: 42
Type: BID
Contract: 22-3-1
Node Abstraction:
   POSITION LAT 62N LONG 9W
   SENSOR NAME S1 TYPE S
   SENSOR NAME S2 TYPE S
   SENSOR NAME T1 TYPE T

Fig. 2.   Signal task bid.

To: 42
From: 25
Type: AWARD
Contract: 22-3-1
Task Specification:
   SENSOR NAME S1
   SENSOR NAME S2

Fig. 3.   Signal task award.

cation indicates the information that a manager needs to select a suitable set of sensor nodes–the position of the bidder and the name and type of each of its sensors. Finally, the expiration time is a deadline for receiving bids.

Each potential contractor listens to the task announcements made by *signal* managers. It ranks each announcement relative to the others thus far received, according to the distance to the manager. Just before the deadline for the task announcement associated with the perceived nearest manager, the node submits a bid (Fig. 2). The bid message supplies the position of the bidder and a description of its sensors. A manager uses this information to select a set of bidders that covers its area of responsibility with a suitable variety of sensors, and then awards a *signal* contract on this basis (Fig. 3). The award message specifies the sensors that a contractor must use to provide signal-feature data to its manager.

IV. THE CONTRACT NET PROTOCOL

We now describe the messages of the protocol and the encoding of information in their slots. We also describe the processing of each message. The BNF specification of the protocol is presented in Appendix B. The reader may find it helpful to refer to the specification while reading the following sections.

A. The Basic Messages

1) Task Announcements

A node that generates a task normally initiates contract negotiation by advertising existence of that task to the other nodes with a **task announcement** message. It then acts as the manager of the task. A task announcement can be addressed to all nodes in the net (*general broadcast*), to a subset of nodes (*limited broadcast*), or to a single node (*point-to-point*). The latter two modes of addressing, which we call *focused addressing,* reduce message processing overhead by allowing nonaddressed nodes to ignore task announcements after examining only the **addressee** slot. The saving is small, but is useful because it allows a node's communication processor alone to decide whether the rest of the message should be examined and further processed. It is also useful for reducing message traffic when the nodes of the problem solver are not interconnected with broadcast communication channels.

As shown in the example, a task announcement has four main slots. The **eligibility specification** is a list of criteria that a node must meet to be eligible to submit a bid. This slot re-

duces message traffic by pruning nodes whose bids would be clearly unacceptable. In a sense, it is an extension to the addressee slot. Focused addressing can be used to restrict the possible respondents only when the manager knows the *names* of appropriate nodes. The eligibility specification slot is used to further restrict the possible respondents when the manager is not certain of the names of appropriate nodes, but can write a *description* of such nodes.[1,2]

The **task abstraction** is a brief description of the task to be executed. It enables a node to rank the task relative to other announced tasks. An abstraction is used rather than a complete description in order to reduce the length of the message.[3]

The **bid specification** is a description of the expected form of a bid. It enables the manager to specify the kind of information that it considers important about a node that wants to execute the task. This provides a common basis for comparison of bids and enables a node to include in a bid only the information about its capabilities that is relevant to the task, rather than a complete description. This both simplifies the task of the manager in evaluating bids and further reduces message traffic.

The **expiration time** is a deadline for receiving bids. We assume global synchronization among the nodes. However, time is not critical in the negotiation process. For example, bids received after the expiration time of a task announcement are not catastrophic: at worst, they may result in a suboptimum selection of contractors.

a) The Common Internode Language

It is useful to encode slot information in a single high-level language understandable to all nodes We call this a *common internode language.* Such a language, along with a high-level programming language (for transfer of procedures between nodes), forms a common basis for communicating slot information among the nodes.

---

[1] Note that focused addressing is typically a heuristic process, since the information upon which it is based may not be exact (e.g., it may be inferred from prior responses to task announcements).

[2] We will see that *all* messages in the protocol that can be addressed to more than one node have an addressee slot and an eligibility specification slot to accommodate addressing by name and by description.

[3] A numerical *priority* measure is not, in general, sufficient to allow potential contractors to rank announced tasks. It assumes first, that all nodes agree on what constitutes an important task, and second, that the importance of a task can be captured in a one-dimensional quantity.

While the contract net protocol offers a framework that specifies the *type* of information that is to fill a message slot, it remains the difficult task of the user to specify the actual *content* of the slot for any particular problem domain. In this sense, the protocol is similar to AI problem-solving languages like PLANNER [4], which supply a framework for problem solving (e.g., the notions of goal specifications and theorem patterns), but leave to the user the task of specifying the content of that framework for any given problem.

CNET does, however, offer the user some additional assistance. It provides a very simple language, based on an *object, attribute, value* representation. The language includes a simple grammar, predefined for each slot, and a number of predefined domain-independent terms (e.g., TASK, TYPE, PROCEDURE, and NAME). The representation, the grammars, and the domain-independent terms are offered to the user to help him organize and specify the slot information. He must augment the language with domain-specific terms (e.g., SENSOR) as needed for the application at hand.

A message that does not have to be understood by many nodes (e.g., messages exchanged by a manager and contractor during execution of a contract) can be usefully encoded in a private language. This can reduce both the length of the messages and the overhead required to process them. In CNET, such "private" information is preceded by an "escape" character; this allows private information to be inserted in any message, even one that includes some public information encoded in the normal manner.

2) Task Announcement Processing

In CNET, all tasks are typed. For each type of task, a node maintains a rank-ordered list of announcements that have been received and have not yet expired. Each node checks the eligibility specifications of all task announcements that it receives. This involves ensuring that the conditions expressed in the specification are met by the node (e.g., MUST-HAVE SENSOR). If it is eligible to bid on a task, then the node ranks that task relative to others under consideration.

Ranking a task announcement is, in general, a task-specific operation. Many of the operations involved in processing other messages are similarly task-specific. CNET defines a *task template* for each type of task. This template enables a user to specify the procedures required to process that type of task. In Appendix E we describe the roles of the required procedures, together with the default actions taken by CNET when the user chooses to omit a procedure. In the following sections, whenever reference is made to task-specific actions, the reader may refer to Appendix E for further details.

3) Bidding

This announcement-ranking activity proceeds concurrently with task processing in a node until the task processor (see Appendix A) completes processing of its current task and becomes available for processing another task. At this point, the contract processor is enabled to submit bids on announced tasks. It checks its list of task announcements and selects a task on which to submit a bid. If there is only one type of task, the procedure is straightforward. If, on the other hand, there are a number of task types available, the node must select one of

them. The current version of CNET selects the most recently received task (older tasks are more likely to have been already awarded).

An idle node can submit a bid on the most attractive task when either of the following events occur: 1) the node receives a new task announcement or 2) the expiration time is reached for any task announcement that the node has received. At each opportunity, the node makes a (task-specific) decision whether to submit a bid or wait for further task announcements. (In the *signal* task, a potential contractor waits for further announcements in an attempt to find the closest manager.)

The **node abstraction** slot of a bid is filled with a brief specification of the capabilities of the node that are relevant to the announced task. It is written in the form indicated by the bid specification of the corresponding task announcement.

The node abstraction slot can also include a number of REQUIRE statements (e.g., REQUIRE PROCEDURE NAME FFT). Statements of this form are used by a bidder to indicate that it needs additional information if it is awarded the task. REQUIRE statements can be made if two conditions are met: 1) the required objects were not preceded by MUST-HAVE terms in the eligibility specification of the task announcement and 2) the objects are *transferable;* that is, they can be transferred by message. (A procedure falls into this class, but a hardware device does not.)

The task template is helpful here. If a node receives an announcement for a type of task with which it is not familiar (i.e., does not have the template), then it can request the template as a convenient shorthand for the entire set of procedures associated with that type of task.

4) Bid Processing

Contracts are queued locally by the manager that generated them until they can be awarded. The manager also maintains a rank-ordered list of bids that have been received for the task. When a bid is received, the manager ranks the bid relative to others under consideration. If, as a result, any of the bids are determined to be *satisfactory*, then the contract is awarded immediately to the associated bidder. (The definition of *satisfactory* is task-specific.) Otherwise, the manager waits for further bids.

Because a manager is not forced to always wait until the expiration time before awarding a contract, the average negotiation time for contracts is reduced over that of DCS [2].

If the expiration time is reached and the contract has not yet been awarded, several actions are possible. The appropriate action is task-specific, but the possibilities include: awarding the contract to the most acceptable bidder(s); transmitting another task announcement (if no bids have been received); or waiting for a time interval before transmitting another task announcement (if no acceptable bids have been received). This is in contrast to the traditional view of task allocation where the most appropriate node available at the time would be selected.

Successful bidders are informed that they are now contractors for a task through an **announced award** message. The **task specification** slot contains a specification of the data needed to begin execution of the task, together with any additional information requested by the bidder.

5) *Contract Processing, Reporting Results, and Termination*

Once a contract has been awarded to a node, it follows the state transition diagram shown in Appendix C. The data structures shown in Appendix D form a local context for communication between the contractor and manager (and other nodes) about the task being performed.

The **information message** is used for general communication between manager and contractor during the processing of a contract. (See Section IV-B.3 for further discussion of this message.)

The **report** is used by a contractor to inform the manager (and other report recipients, if any) that a task has been partially executed (an **interim report**) or completed (a **final report**). The **result description** slot contains the results of the execution. Final reports are the normal method of result communication. Interim reports, however, are useful when generator-style control is desired. A contractor can be set to work on a task and instructed to issue interim reports whenever the next result is ready. It then suspends the task until it is instructed by the manager to *continue* (with an information message) and produce another result.

The manager can also terminate contracts with a **termination** message. The contractor receiving such a message terminates execution of the contract indicated in the message and all of its outstanding subcontracts.

6) *Negotiation Tradeoffs*

In this section, we discuss choices made in the CNET implementation of the negotiation process. In the main, our concern has been with problem solving. We have been more interested in the types of information that must be passed between nodes than with these aspects of the negotiation process. As a result, the choices are only tentative and warrant further detailed analysis.

Because bids are binding and a node is allowed to have more than one bid outstanding at a time, a node may receive multiple awards. These are queued for processing in order of receipt. The cost is potentially slower overall system performance (the load may be less evenly balanced) than would be the case if multiple awards were prevented.

If nodes could refuse awards (as in DCS [3]), multiple awards could be prevented. However, the cost is at least one additional acknowledgment message per transaction. In some cases, it may be many additional messages (if an award is refused by several bidders).

Similarly, if a node could only have a single bid outstanding, multiple awards could be prevented. However, the cost would be significant delay. Nodes would be forced to remain idle until a task announcement had expired to find that their bids had been rejected, and have to start the process again. This could lower overall system performance.

The above delay could be reduced in some instances by explicitly informing unsuccessful bidders that their bids had been refused. The cost, however, would likely be a very large increase in message traffic, assuming that there are several

bidders per task. In addition, it would only lower the delay for contracts that were awarded before the expiration times of their task announcements were reached.

We have allowed a node to bid at intervals related to the receipt of task announcements rather than at fixed intervals. It is intuitively appealing, offers a reasonable compromise between message traffic and delay in allocating tasks, and has exhibited good performance in experience to date with CNET.

We have chosen to allow a node to submit, at most, a single bid at each opportunity. This reduces message traffic and the possibility that a single node could bid on far more tasks than it could process. For the same reasons, we allow only idle nodes to submit bids. Because of these choices, contracts are not centrally notarized as they were in DCS [2]. This further reduces message traffic and maintains the distributed nature of the negotiation process.

The current version of CNET uses a nonpreemptive scheduler in each node. It would appear to be useful, however, to allow preemptive scheduling instead of simply queueing contracts in order of receipt. This would help avoid the situation where time-critical tasks are not executed soon enough because less important tasks are queued ahead of them. The difficult question here is determining the criteria for preemption and providing a place for them in the common internode language. We are currently exploring this issue.

B. Complications and Extensions

In the following sections we consider some problems with the basic negotiation mechanism and present extensions to solve these problems. The extensions are evolving as we gain more experience with using the protocol in practical applications.

1) *Immediate Response Bids*

We have, thus far, discussed the negotiation process under the assumption that a node cannot submit a bid until it goes idle and is actually ready to process a new contract. This strategy can, however, lead to difficulty. For instance, a node that issues a task announcement may not receive any bids for one of several reasons: 1) there are no idle nodes; 2) some node is both idle and eligible, but ranks the task too low; or 3) no node is capable of working on the task even if it were idle (as may happen if the eligibility specification is too stringent or no node has the data necessary for executing the task). In the first two cases, the task announcement may be usefully reissued until a bid is obtained from an idle node; in the third case it would be pointless. Therefore, a node requires a way of determining what caused the lack of response.

A class of bids we call **immediate response** bids offers a mechanism for doing this. Three such bids have been identified, allowing a node to indicate that it is eligible but BUSY, that it is INELIGIBLE, or that it gave the task a LOW RANKING. A manager can specify that nodes are to respond in any of these cases or to respond in a subset of the cases (e.g., *respond if eligible, but busy*).

A node receiving a task announcement whose bid specification asks for an immediate response bid does not deal with the announcement in the usual way (ranking it immediately, but waiting until it is idle to submit a bid), but instead responds immediately with either a standard bid or the appropriate special form.

The immediate response mechanism permits a manager to take a more appropriate course of action if a task announcement elicits no bids. The normal procedure is to simply reissue the task announcement. If this continues to elicit no bids, then the manager can specify an immediate response bid. If the response is uniformly BUSY, then the manager can wait and reissue the task announcement later. If all nodes are INELIGIBLE, then the manager may loosen the eligibility specification. If all nodes gave the task a LOW RANKING, the manager can wait and reissue, in the hope that the more interesting tasks currently occupying the nodes will soon be done. The manager may also decide to execute the task itself when it becomes idle.

2) Directed Contracts

The normal contract negotiation process can be simplified in some instances, with a resulting enhancement in the efficiency of the protocol. If a manager knows exactly which node is appropriate for execution of a task, a **directed contract** can be awarded. No task announcement is made and no bids are submitted. Instead, a **directed award** message is sent to the selected node without negotiation.

In addition to the low-level acknowledgment used by an underlying communication protocol to ensure reliable communication, the contract net protocol uses a further high-level **acknowledgment** message for directed award messages. This allows a refusal or negative acknowledgment of the form, *I can't execute this contract because ...*, in addition to the low-level negative acknowledgment of the form, *I didn't receive your message correctly*.

If the node that receives a directed award either does not meet the eligibility specification or does not have a template for the task, then it transmits a **refusal** to the manager. Otherwise, the node uses task-specific criteria to determine whether to transmit an **acceptance** or **refusal** to the manager. The refusal message contains a **refusal justification** slot that specifies the reasons for the refusal (e.g., INELIGIBLE or NO TEMPLATE).

The action taken by a manager upon receipt of a refusal is also task-specific, in general.

3) Request and Information Messages

If a simple transfer of information is required, then a request-response sequence can be used without further embellishment. The **request** message is used to encode straightforward requests for information. The **information** message is used to respond to a request, and for manager/contractor communication during the execution of a contract (Section IV-A.5). This message is also used in *result-sharing* [9], a style of distributed problem solving in which nodes cooperate by sharing partial results.

If a node that receives a request message meets the eligibility specification and has the necessary information, then it responds with an information message. No task-specific decisions need to be made.

If a node that receives an information message meets the eligibility specification, then the action it takes is task-specific. If the contract named in the message is one that the node is processing, then the appropriate action is determined by a procedure associated with that contract. Otherwise, the node takes a default action. (The latter possibility arises in result-sharing because nodes communicate partial results to other nodes without being requested to do so, and without being explicitly linked by a contract.)

4) Node Available Messages

The protocol has been designed to allow a reversal of the normal negotiation process. When the processing load on a net is high, most task announcements will not be answered with bids because all nodes will be busy. Hence, the protocol includes a **node available** message. A node that transmits such a message is idle and searching for a task to execute. In this case, the **eligibility specification** is a list of criteria that the node will look for in a task. The **node abstraction** is a brief specification of the capabilities of the node and the **expiration time** is a deadline for receiving an award.

When a node receives a node available message, it tries to determine if it can match the node with a task that it has announced, but not yet awarded. First, it tries to match the eligibility specification in the node available message against the task abstractions of the tasks that it has waiting. A task for which this match succeeds is of interest to the volunteering node. The manager then tries to match the eligibility specification of the task against the node abstraction of the node available message. If this match succeeds, then the node is the sort which is required for the task. Hence, even in this case we have the mutual selection aspect, as the volunteering node selects a task and the task specifies the criteria necessary in a volunteer. If the two matches are successful, the manager sends a directed award message to the volunteer. If a node has several tasks for which both matches succeed, then CNET selects the oldest task (it is least likely to be awarded in the normal way).

In CNET, a node maintains a list of unexpired node available messages. Before it announces a new task, a node first tries to find a suitable volunteer in the list. If several volunteers are suitable, the newest volunteer is selected (it is least likely to have received an award).

A node can thus acquire a contract in one of two ways: it can wait for a suitable task announcement and submit a bid; or it can transmit a node available message and wait for a directed award. The decision as to which method to use is net-load dependent. If the net is not heavily loaded, then the use of the task announcement is warranted in all cases, since the availability of a task to be executed is the event of primary importance. If the net is heavily loaded, then unlimited use of task announcements serves only to saturate the available communication channels. In this case, the availability of an idle node is the event of primary importance and the use of node available messages is preferred.

In CNET, a node selects one of the two modes based on experience with its own task announcements. The scheme is rudimentary, however, and warrants further analysis.

V. Dynamic Distribution of Information

The contract net protocol enables dynamic distribution of information (i.e., procedures and data) via three methods. First, a node can transmit a request directly to another node for the transfer of the required information. The response is the information requested (e.g., the code for a procedure). Second, a node can broadcast a task announcement in which the task is a transfer of information. A bid on the task indicates that the bidder has the information and is willing to transmit it. Finally, a node can note, in its bid on a task, that it requires particular information in order to execute the task. The manager can then send the required information in the award message if the bid is accepted.

Dynamic distribution enables effective use of available computational resources: a node that is standing idle because it lacks information required to execute a previously announced task can acquire that information as indicated above. This also means that nodes do not have to be preloaded with extensive amounts of information which may or may not prove useful. Dynamic distribution also facilitates the addition of a new node to an existing net; the node can dynamically acquire the procedures and data necessary to allow it to participate in the operation of the net. This is especially useful in the distributed sensing application.

Dynamic distribution works, first, because all nodes know the syntax of the contract net protocol, which enables them to identify the slots that contain task-dependent information (e.g., the eligibility specification of a task announcement); second, because they know how to parse the common internode language, which enables them to identify the information in the slots that they do not possess; and third, because a negotiation process is used to effect task distribution, which makes it possible for a new node to begin participating in the operation of the net by listening to the messages being exchanged (specifically, task announcements) and submitting bids. This may be contrasted with more traditional task allocation schemes that explicitly assign tasks to nodes. In such schemes, new nodes must be explicitly linked to other nodes in the network.

VI. Discussion

We have presented a high-level protocol for distributed problem solving. The protocol facilitates distributed control of cooperative task execution with efficient internode communication. It has been designed to provide a more powerful mechanism for *connection* than is available in current problem-solving systems. The message types have been selected to capture the types of interactions that arise in a task-sharing approach to distributed problem solving. The message slots have been selected to capture the types of information that must be passed between nodes to make these interactions effective.

The connection of nodes with tasks to be executed and nodes that can execute those tasks is more general than load balancing. The difference can be illustrated by comparing the information placed in the slots of the task announcement with that used in DCS. In that system, a task announcement (*request for quotation*) contains only the name of the process to be executed and the amount of memory required. A bid is a measure of the excess memory available in a node. Note, however, that this is only one of the possible dimensions along which tasks and nodes can be evaluated. In general, such evaluation is task-dependent (as we saw in Section III) and may require a different form of information for each task. Recognizing this, the contract net protocol takes a wider perspective and allows a range of descriptions to be passed between the manager and bidders. In more general terms, since our concern is with problem solving, more attention is paid to the type of information that must be transferred between nodes to solve the connection problem. The connection that is effected with the contract net protocol is an extension to the *pattern-directed invocation* used in many AI programming languages (see [8] for a more in-depth discussion).

There are several reasons for adopting a distributed approach to problem solving. These include speed, reliability, extensibility, and the ability to handle applications that have a natural spatial distribution. The design of the contract net protocol attempts to ensure that these potential benefits are indeed realized.

In order to achieve high speed we wish to avoid bottlenecks. Such bottlenecks can arise in two primary ways: by concentrating disproportionate amounts of computation or communication at central resources and by saturating available communication channels so that nodes must remain idle while messages are transmitted.

To avoid bottlenecks we distribute control, data, and *KS*'s. Control is distributed through the use of negotiation to achieve connections for task distribution. Every node is capable of assigning and accepting tasks, and managers and contractors simultaneously seek each other out. Data and *KS*'s are also distributed dynamically as part of the negotiation process or with a request–response mechanism.

The contract net protocol includes several elements aimed at avoiding communication channel saturation. First, the information in task announcements (like eligibility specifications) helps eliminate extraneous message traffic. Similarly, bid messages can be kept short and "to the point" through the use of the bid specification mechanism. Second, specialized interactions, like directed contracts and requests, reduce communication for transactions that do not require the complexity of negotiation. Third, the protocol enables dynamic distribution of information on an as-required basis. Finally, it provides a very general form of guidance in determining appropriate partitioning of problems: the notion of tasks executed under contracts suggests relatively large task sizes. This is important if the speedup obtained from distribution is not to be outweighed by the effort required to effect that distribution.

Distribution of control also enhances reliability and permits graceful degradation of performance in the case of individual node failures. There are no nodes whose failure can completely block the contract negotiation process. In addition, recovery from the failure of a node is aided by the presence of explicit links between managers and their contractors. The failure of any contractor, for example, can be detected by its manager;

the contract for which it was responsible can then be reannounced and awarded to another node.

The use of a negotiation process for allocation of nodes to tasks facilitates the extension of an existing net to include new nodes. Such nodes can begin to participate in the operation of the net without first explicitly informing the other nodes of their presence. New node entry is also facilitated by the common internode language and dynamic distribution of information.

The ability to handle applications with a natural spatial distribution is facilitated by the local nature of negotiation. A net is able to configure itself dynamically according to the positions of the nodes and the ease with which they can establish communication.

The protocol is best suited to problems in which it is appropriate to define a hierarchy of tasks (e.g., heuristic search) and a hierarchy of levels of data abstraction (e.g., audio or video signal interpretation). Such problems lend themselves to decomposition into a set of relatively independent subtasks with little need for global information or synchronization. Individual subtasks can be assigned to separate processor nodes; these nodes can then execute the subtasks with little need for communication with other nodes.

VII. Conclusion

The main contribution of the contract net protocol is the mechanism it offers for structuring high-level interactions between nodes for cooperative task execution. It stresses the utility of negotiation as an interaction mechanism. Negotiation can be used at different levels of complexity. At one extreme, it is a means of achieving task distribution with distributed control and shared responsibility for tasks to maintain reliability and avoid bottlenecks. At the other extreme, the two-way transfer of information and mutual selection attributes of negotiation make possible a finer degree of control in making resource allocation and focus decisions than is possible with traditional mechanisms.

Appendix A

Contract Node Architecture

We view a node as having four major functional components (Fig. 4): a *local database,* a *communication processor* that handles low-level message traffic with other nodes, a *task processor* that carries out the computation associated with user tasks, and a *contract processor* that processes high-level protocol messages and manages node resources. It is assumed that the functions of the three processors are carried out concurrently.

Appendix B

Contract Net Protocol Specification

The BNF specification of the contract net protocol is shown in Fig. 5. Nonterminal symbols are enclosed by "⟨ ⟩," terminal symbols are written without delimiters, and nonterminals whose specific expansion is not germane to the discussion

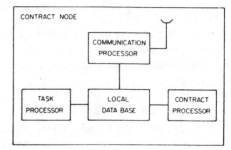

Fig. 4.   Contract node architecture.

⟨message⟩ ⟹ ⟨header⟩ ⟨addressee⟩ ⟨originator⟩ ⟨text⟩ ⟨trailer⟩
⟨header⟩ ⟹ [line-header] [identifier] [time] [acknowledge]
⟨trailer⟩ ⟹ [error-control] [line-trailer]
⟨addressee⟩ ⟹ [net-address] | [subnet-address] | [node-address]
⟨originator⟩ ⟹ [node-address]
⟨text⟩ ⟹ [cctext] | [pstext]
⟨pstext⟩ ⟹ ⟨task-announcement⟩ | ⟨bid⟩ | ⟨announced-award⟩ |
            ⟨directed-award⟩ | ⟨acknowledgment⟩ | ⟨report⟩ |
            ⟨termination⟩ | ⟨node-available-message⟩ |
            ⟨request-message⟩ | ⟨information-message⟩
⟨task-announcement⟩ ⟹ TASK-ANNOUNCEMENT [name]
                   {task-abstraction} {eligibility-specification}
                   {bid-specification} [expiration-time]
⟨bid⟩ ⟹ BID [name] {node-abstraction}
⟨announced-award⟩ ⟹ ANNOUNCED-AWARD [name] {task-specification}
⟨directed-award⟩ ⟹ DIRECTED-AWARD [name] {task-abstraction} *
            {eligibility-specification} {task-specification}
⟨acknowledgment⟩ ⟹ ACCEPTANCE [name] *
                ⟹ REFUSAL [name] {refusal-justification}
⟨report⟩ ⟹ INTERIM-REPORT [name] {result-description}
        ⟹ FINAL-REPORT [name] {result-description}
⟨termination⟩ ⟹ TERMINATION [name] *
⟨node-available-message⟩ ⟹ NODE-AVAILABLE {eligibility-specification} *
                {node-abstraction} [expiration-time]
⟨request-message⟩ ⟹ REQUEST [name] {eligibility-specification} *
                {request-specification}
⟨information-message⟩ ⟹ INFORMATION [name] {eligibility-specification} *
                {information-specification}

Fig. 5.   Contract net protocol specification.

are enclosed by "[   ]." Slots that are to be filled with information encoded in the common internode language are enclosed in "{   }." Message types that need not be included in a basic implementation are followed by "*."

One possible set of low-level message slots is shown for completeness. Other variations may be dictated by the specific communication architecture for which the protocol is implemented. Briefly: **line-header** delimits the beginning of a message; **identifier** is a unique identifier for the message; **time** specifies the time at which the message is transmitted; **acknowledge** is set only if acknowledgment of receipt of the message is required (this slot is included because delivery of some messages is not essential to the operation of the protocol (e.g., broadcast task announcements) and acknowledgments for such messages might greatly increase message traffic); **error-control** is used by an addressee to determine that the message has been correctly received; and **line-trailer** delimits the end of the message. Three forms of **addressee** slot are shown. These are used for general broadcast, limited broadcast, and point-to-point messages, respectively.

There are two forms of **text** slot. **cctext** (communication control text) indicates that the message is for checking net integrity, acknowledging receipt of messages, maintaining basic net communication data, such as routing tables, and so on. Messages of the form *Hello* and *I heard you*, exchanged periodically by IMP's in the ARPANET as status checks, fall into this category.

pstext (problem-solving text) indicates that the message is for high-level problem solving (see Section IV).

APPENDIX C

CONTRACT PROCESSING STATES

Contracts are processed according to the state transition diagram shown in Fig. 6, which uses the terminology of operating systems [1]. The contract processor of a node (Appendix A) is responsible for moving a contract through the states of the diagram. The standard progression through the states is shown by solid lines. Optional progressions are shown by dashed lines.

When a contract is awarded to a node (IN), it is placed in the READY state where it waits until the task processor is available. At that time, the contract is placed in the EXECUTING state and its processing is started. If subcontracts are generated, they are placed in the ANNOUNCED state. A subcontract may either be awarded to another node (OUT) or to this node (READY).

If execution cannot continue on the contract until some event occurs (e.g., receipt of a subcontract report), then the contract is placed in the SUSPENDED state; and another contract in the READY state is selected for processing. When the awaited event occurs, the contract is transferred back to the READY state where it awaits further processing.

When processing of the contract has been completed, it is placed in the TERMINATED state; and another contract in the READY state is selected for processing. Recently completed contracts are held in the TERMINATED state in order to facilitate recovery from the failure of a manager.

If a contract in the EXECUTING state is moved to either the SUSPENDED or TERMINATED state and if there are no contracts in the READY state, then the node attempts to acquire a new contract—either by making a bid on a recent task announcement or by transmitting a node available message (Section IV).

The scheduler used by a contract processor in the current version of CNET is nonpreemptive and gives priority to a contract whose execution can continue (e.g., due to receipt of a report) over a contract whose execution has not yet been started.

APPENDIX D

CONTRACT SPECIFICATION

A node maintains a structure of the form shown in Fig. 7 for each task for which it is the contractor. Such a structure forms a local context for the execution of a task.

name is a unique identifier for the contract. **manager** is the node that generated the task. **report recipients** are the nodes to which reports for the contract are to be sent. The default report recipient is the manager. **related contractors** are the nodes that are working on related contracts (e.g., subcontracts of the same contract).

The report recipients and related contractors slots facilitate more flexible communication and cooperation. They give a

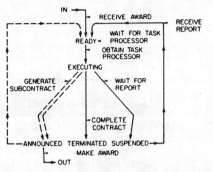

Fig. 6.   Contract processing states.

⟨contract⟩ ⟹ [name]
              [manager]
              [report-recipients]
              [related-contractors]
              (task)
              [results]
              (subcontract-list)

Fig. 7.   Contract structure.

node an explicit indication of other nodes in the net with which it may be useful to communicate (e.g., to enable use of focused addressing in task announcements) and help to reduce message traffic. Messages from one related contractor to another, for example, can be addressed directly and therefore do not have to follow the communication paths of the control hierarchy.

task is filled with a structure of the form shown in Fig. 8. The structure lists the type of the task, its specification, and the procedures that are required to handle the task in a contract net. These procedures are described in Appendix E.

results are the outcome of executing a task. They are transmitted to the report recipients of the contract. **subcontract-list** is the collection of subtasks generated from the initial contract. This slot is filled with a list of structures of the form shown in Fig. 9. Such structures contain the information held by a manager for a subtask.

name is a unique identifier for the subcontract. **contractor** is the name of the node responsible for its processing. **task** is the task structure (Fig. 8). **results** are the outcome of executing the subtask. **predecessors** are the names of subcontracts that are preconditions for the subcontract and **successors** are the names of subcontracts for which the subcontract is a precondition. Predecessors and successors are necessary for tasks that must be performed in a particular order, such as those that occur in planning applications [6]. A subcontract will not be announced (Section IV-A.1) until its predecessors have been completed.

APPENDIX E

TASK PROCESSING PROCEDURES

In this appendix, we discuss the task-specific procedures, the roles they play, and the default actions taken in CNET when no procedure is provided by the user. In the terms of the functional model of a node presented in Appendix A, the *execution procedure* runs in the task processor. The rest of the procedures run in the contract processor.

Announcement Procedure: Called each time a subtask is generated. Its role is to determine whether the task should be announced or awarded directly. In either case, it must determine the addressee. It must also compute the information re-

```
⟨task⟩ ⇒ [name]
         [type]
         [specification]
         [announcement-procedure]
         [announcement-ranking-procedure]
         [bid-procedure]
         [bid-ranking-procedure]
         [award-procedure]
         [acknowledgment-procedure]
         [refusal-processing-procedure]
         [report-acceptance-procedure]
         [termination-procedure]
         [information-acceptance-procedure]
         [execution-procedure]
```

Fig. 8.   Task structure.

```
⟨subcontract⟩ ⇒ [name]
                [contractor]
                ⟨task⟩
                [results]
                [predecessors]
                [successors]
```

Fig. 9.   Subcontract structure.

quired to fill the slots of a task announcement or directed award and indicate the names of any predecessor subcontracts. The default is to announce the task to all nodes with a task abstraction that states the task type and a default expiration time.

Announcement Ranking Procedure: Called when a task announcement is received. Its role is to rank the new announcement relative to others under consideration. The default is give the most recently received task announcement the highest ranking.

Bid Procedure: Called when a node has an opportunity to submit a bid. Its role is to decide whether or not to submit a bid and to add any common internode language statements to those called for in the bid specification of the associated task announcement. No default action is taken.

Bid Ranking Procedure: Called when a bid is received. Its role is to rank the new bid relative to others under consideration and determine whether the contract should be awarded to any of the current bidders. The default is to insert the new bid into the list of bids so that bids that REQUIRE the least information (Section IV-A.3) are ranked highest.

Award Procedure: Called when the expiration time for a task announcement is reached and the contract has not yet been awarded. Its role is to decide what action is to be taken. The default is to award the contract to the bidder that REQUIRE's the least additional information (or the first bidder in case of a tie) or to transmit another task announcement if no bids have been received.

Acknowledgment Procedure: Called when a node receives a directed contract for which it is eligible and has a task template. Its role is to decide whether to accept or reject the contract. The default is to accept.

Refusal Processing Procedure: Called when a refusal message is received. Its role is to determine what action is to be taken. The default is to transmit a task announcement.

Report Acceptance Procedure: Called when a report message is received. Its role is to determine what to do with the contents of the result description slot. The default is to add the contents of the slot to the results slot of the contract.

Termination Procedure: Called when a contract that has been terminated is about to be deleted from the local database.

(CNET maintains a list of the recently terminated contracts [Appendix C].) Its role is to take any specialized action that is required before the contract is deleted (e.g., storing contract slot information in the local database). No default action is taken.

Information Acceptance Procedure: Called when an information message is received. Its role is to determine what to do with the contents of the information specification slot. The default is to store the information in the local database.

Execution Procedure: Called when processing is started on the contract. Its role is to perform the computation required to execute the task.

ACKNOWLEDGMENT

Some aspects of this work are being pursued in collaboration with R. Davis at the Artificial Intelligence Laboratory of the Massachusetts Institute of Technology, Cambridge. The contributions of B. Buchanan and G. Wiederhold are also gratefully acknowledged.

REFERENCES

[1] P. Brinch Hansen, *Operating System Principles.*   Englewood Cliffs, NJ: Prentice-Hall, 1973.
[2] D. J. Farber and K. C. Larson, "The structure of the distributed computing system—Software," in *Proc. Symp. on Comput.-Commun. Networks and Teletraffic,* J. Fox, Ed.   Brooklyn, NY: Polytechnic Press, Polytechnic Inst. of Brooklyn, Apr. 1972, pp. 539–545.
[3] D. J. Farber, J. Feldman, F. R. Heinrich, M. D. Hopwood, K. C. Larson, D. C. Loomis, and L. A. Rowe, "The distributed computing system," *IEEE COMPCON Spring,* 1973, pp. 31–34.
[4] C. Hewitt, "Description and theoretical analysis (using schemata) of PLANNER: A language for proving theorems and manipulating models in a robot," Mass. Inst. Technol., Cambridge, MA, AI TR 258, Apr. 1972.
[5] V. R. Lesser, "Cooperative distributed processing," Dep. Comput. Inform. Sci., Univ. of Massachusetts, Amherst, MA, COINS TR 78-7, May 1978.
[6] E. D. Sacerdoti, "A structure for plans and behavior," SRI Int., Menlo Park, CA, AIC TN 109, Aug. 1975.
[7] R. G. Smith and R. Davis, "Applications of the contract net framework: Distributed sensing," in *Proc. ARPA Distributed Sensor Net Symp.,* Pittsburgh, PA, Dec. 1978, pp. 12+20.
[8] R. G. Smith, "A framework for problem solving in a distributed processing environment," Dep. Comput. Sci., Stanford, CA, STAN-CS-78-700 (HPP-78-28), Dec. 1978.
[9] R. G. Smith and R. Davis, "Cooperation in distributed problem solving," in *Proc. 1979 Int. Conf. Cybern. Soc.,* Oct. 1979, pp. 366–371.
[10] R. G. Smith, "Applications of the contract net framework: Search," in *Proc. 1980 Nat. Conf. Canadian Soc. for Computational Studies of Intell.,* May 1980, pp. 232–239.
[11] R. F. Sproul and D. Cohen, "High-level protocols," *Proc. IEEE,* vol. 66, pp. 1371–1386, Nov. 1978.
[12] W. Teitelman, *INTERLISP Reference Manual.*   Palo Alto, CA: Xerox Palo Alto Research Center, Dec. 1975.

Reid G. Smith (S'67–M'69–S'75–M'78) was born in Toronto, Ont., Canada, on October 4, 1946. He received the B.Eng. and M.Eng. degrees in electrical engineering from Carleton University, Ottawa, Ont., Canada in 1968 and 1969, respectively, and the Ph.D. degree in electrical engineering from Stanford University, Stanford, CA in 1979.

He has been associated with the Defence Research Establishment Atlantic in Dartmouth, N.S., Canada since 1969. He is currently engaged in research in artificial intelligence and distributed problem solving.

Multistage Negotiation
in Distributed Planning

Susan E. Conry
Robert A. Meyer
Victor R. Lesser

COINS Technical Report 86-67
December 1986

Department of Computer and Information Sciences
University of Massachusetts
Amherst, Massachusetts 01003

Abstract

In this paper we describe a multistage negotiation paradigm for planning in a distributed environment with decentralized control and limited interagent communication. The application domain of interest involves the monitoring and control of a complex communications system. In this domain planning for service restoral is performed in the context of incomplete and possibly invalid information which may be updated dynamically during the course of planning. In addition, the goal of the planning activity may not be achievable — the problem may be overconstrained. Through multistage negotiation, a planner is able to recognize when the problem is overconstrained and to find a solution to an acceptable related problem under these conditions. A key element in this process is the ability to detect subgoal interactions in a distributed environment and reason about their impact. Multistage negotiation provides a means by which an agent can acquire enough knowledge to reason about the impact of local activity on nonlocal state and modify its behavior accordingly.

*This work was supported, in part, by the Air Force Systems Command, Rome Air Development Center, Griffiss Air Force Base, New York 13441-5700, and the Air Force Office of Scientific Research, Bolling AFB, DC 20332 under Contract No. F30602-85-C-0008. This contract supports the Northeast Artificial Intelligence Consortium (NAIC). This work was also supported, in part, by the National Science Foundation under CER Grant DCR-8500332, and by the Defense Advanced Research Projects Agency (DOD), monitored by the Office of Naval Research under Contract NR049-041. This work was done while S. E. Conry and R. A. Meyer were on sabbatical at the University of Massachusetts.

1   INTRODUCTION

We present a multistage negotiation protocol that is useful for cooperatively resolving resource allocation conflicts which arise in a distributed network of semi-autonomous problem
solving nodes. The primary contributions of such a negotiation protocol are that it makes
it possible to detect and to resolve subgoal interactions in a distributed environment with
limited communication bandwidth and no single locus of control. Furthermore, it permits
a distributed problem solving system to detect when it is operating in an overconstrained
situation and act to remedy the situation by reaching a satisficing [1] solution.

Multistage negotiation is specifically *not* intended as a mechanism for goal decomposition in the system, though some goal decomposition is a natural result of negotiation in the
context of this paradigm. Our protocol may be viewed as a generalization of the contract
net protocol [2,3,4]. The contract net was devised as a mechanism for accomplishing task
distribution among agents in a distributed problem solving system. Task distribution takes
place through a negotiation process involving contractor task announcement followed by
bids from competing subcontractors and finally announcement of awards. Multistage negotiation generalizes this protocol by recognizing the need to iteratively exchange inferences
drawn by an agent about the impact of its own choice of what local tasks to perform in
satisfaction of *global goals*.

Multistage negotiation produces a cooperation strategy similar in character to the Functionally Accurate/Cooperative paradigm [5] in which agents iteratively exchange tentative
and high level partial results of their local subtasks. This strategy results in solutions
which are incrementally constructed to converge on a set of complete local solutions which
are globally consistent. Before describing multistage negotiation in detail, we first motivate
the need for a new cooperation paradigm.

2   MOTIVATION FOR MULTISTAGE NEGOTIATION

The distributed environment in which our negotiation takes place is a network of loosely
coupled problem solving agents in which no agent has a complete and accurate view of the
state of the network. Problem solving activity is initiated through the instantiation of one
or more top level goals at agents in the network. Each top level goal is instantiated locally
at an agent and is not necessarily known to other agents. Since the conditions which give
rise to goal instantiation may be observed at more than one place in the network, the same
goal may be instantiated by two or more agents independently. The desired solution to the
problem is any one that satisfies all of the top level goals.

In this type of distributed network, it is very expensive to provide a complete global view
to each agent in the system. Communication bandwidth is generally limited. Exchange
of enough information to permit each agent to construct and maintain its own accurate
global view would be prohibitively expensive. In addition, progress in problem solving
would be significantly slower due to a decrease in parallelism attributable to the need for
synchronization in building a complete view. Multistage negotiation has been devised as
a paradigm for cooperation among agents attempting to solve a planning problem in this
distributed environment. In the remainder of this section, we explain the contributions of

multistage negotiation in solving distributed planning problems.

One of the major difficulties which arises in planning systems is detecting the presence of subgoal interactions and determining the impact of those interactions. In distributed applications, the problem is exacerbated because no agent has complete knowledge concerning all goals and subgoals present in the problem solving system. For example, subgoals initiated by one node may interact with other subgoals initiated elsewhere, unknown to the first node. These interactions may become quite complex and may not be visible to any single node in the network. *A key objective of our multistage negotiation is to allow nodes to exchange sufficient information so that these interactions are detected and handled in a reasonable manner.* This objective is achieved by exchanging knowledge about the nonlocal impact of an agent's proposed local action without requiring the exchange of detailed local state information.

Another significant issue that arises in planning is recognizing when goals are not attainable. When satisfaction of a goal requires the commitment of resources, conflicts may arise among goals competing for limited resources. A planning problem is overconstrained if satisfaction of one top level goal precludes the satisfaction of others. Detection of an overconstrained situation in a distributed environment is, again, particularly difficult because no agent is aware of all goals, and each agent has only a limited view of the complete set of conflicts. *When a number of alternative choices for goal satisfaction are known, detection of an overconstrained situation is not possible without either multistage negotiation or a global view.*

In an overconstrained problem, a planning system must reformulate what it seeks as a satisfactory solution. Having several equally important top level goals, the planner must decide which ones should be sacrificed to permit satisfaction of others. Since the distributed network has no agent with sufficient knowledge to serve as an intelligent arbitrator, a consensus must be reached. *Multistage negotiation provides a mechanism for reaching a consensus among those nodes with conflicting goals concerning an acceptable satisficing solution.*

In the following sections, we first describe the problem in more detail, discussing the application domain itself as well as an example which illustrates the nature of the planning problem. We then discuss two models of problem solving relevant to this domain: one which is oriented from the perspective of a single goal and one which is node centered. In the fifth section we discuss a multistage negotiation protocol which utilizes these models and has been incorporated in a distributed planner for this problem. We illustrate this protocol with the aid of a simple example. Finally, we discuss ways in which this research extends existing work.

3   APPLICATION DOMAIN

The application domain of interest is the monitoring and control of a complex communications system. This system consists of a network of sites, each containing a variety of communications equipment, interconnected by links. These sites are partitioned into several geographic subregions with a single site in each subregion designated as a control facility. Each control facility has responsibility for communication system monitoring and control within its own subregion and corresponds to a single node in the distributed problem solving network. In order to distinguish between the communication network and the problem solving network, in this paper we reserve the term "site" to mean a physical location in the communication system. The term "node" will be used to refer to those sites at which processing and control reside.

The communication network considered here represents a long-haul, transmission "backbone" of a larger, more complex communications system. From this transmission oriented perspective, each user is provided with a dedicated set of resources (equipment and link bandwidth) which establishes a point-to-point connection, or **circuit** for a significant period of time. Any equipment failure or outage will cause an interruption of service to one or more users.

An overall knowledge-based system to perform the monitoring and control function would employ distributed problem solving agents involving data interpretation, situation assessment, fault diagnosis, and planning [6]. In this context planning is used to find restoral plans for user circuits which have been interrupted as a result of some failure or outage.

A restoral plan consists of a logical sequence of control actions which allocate scarce resources in order to restore end-to-end user connectivity (circuits). These actions allocate or reallocate equipment and link capacity along some route to specific circuits and are subject to a number of constraints. For example, a circuit is assigned to one of several priority categories. In attempting to restore service, resources belonging to circuits of a lower priority may be preempted. Depending upon the type of circuit, there may be special equipment needs which are not necessarily present at all sites. Available routes through the network may be constrained by lack of certain equipment items such as switches or multiplexers. Thus generation of a restoral plan for a single circuit uses conventional route finding algorithms [7] in combination with knowledge about circuit types and priority, needed equipment, network topology, and equipment configuration at all sites along the restoral path. For any specific circuit there will generally be many alternative restoral plans, so the planning system must then attempt to select a combination of alternatives which restores all circuits.

There are a number of features of this planning problem that make it interesting. There is implicit in this domain the assumption that the knowledge of each agent is incomplete. It may also be inaccurate and inconsistent with that of other agents. Restoral plans must be generated in a distributed fashion because no agent has a global view and reliability issues mitigate against delegating the responsibility for planning to a central node. The overall system goal is one of determining plans for restoral of all interrupted service. Although each agent implicitly knows this goal, it generally will not know all of the specific circuits which require restoral. The planning system need not satisfy the overall goal to be successful. In many instances, the overall goal may be infeasible, and thus a satisfactory plan will fall short of reaching this goal.

The distributed planning problem addressed in this paper and our approach to solving it can best be understood with the aid of an example. A simplified diagram of a small network is shown in Figure 1. In this phase of our work, we use a simplified model of a communications system which disregards any constraints arising from equipment configuration at a site. There are five subregions, labeled A, B, C, D, and E, shown. Each site is

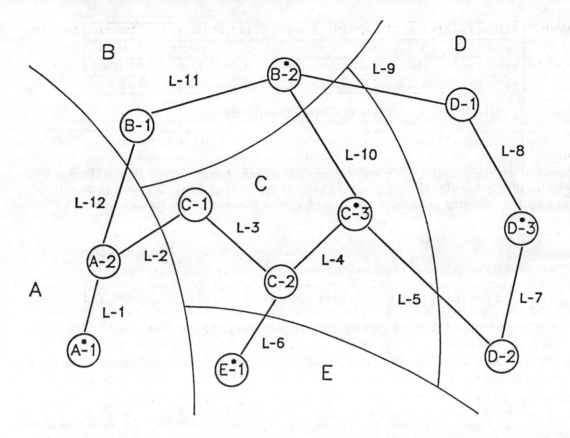

Figure 1: Example Network

designated by a letter-number pair, where the letter indicates the subregion in which the site is located. The communication network links are designated by L-number. The control facility for each subregion is located at the site marked with an "*". Each control facility has a planning agent to restore interrupted service. It should be noted that a separate communication network, of substantially lower bandwidth, is not shown, but is assumed to interconnect the control facilities for the purpose of exchanging messages among the agents.

For the purposes of describing the restoral problem, we assume that there is an equipment malfunction at station B-2 that fails all communication using link L-11. We also assume that each link can handle at most two circuits and that there are four circuits established at the time of the supposed failure. These are described in Table 1 by listing the sites and links along the route of each circuit. To simplify the presentation, these circuits all have the same restoration priority so that none of them should be preferred over the others for restoral in the event of service disruption.

As a result of the presumed failure, two circuits are disrupted, namely ckt-1 and ckt-2 (both use L-11 to get from B-1 to B-2). The planning activity is initiated when an agent observes disruption of a circuit terminating within its subregion and instantiates a restoral

ckt-1	(A-1	:L-1:	A-2	:L-12:	B-1	:L-11:	B-2)			
ckt-2	(B-1	:L-11:	B-2	:L-10:	C-3	:L-5:	D-2)			
ckt-3	(E-1	:L-6:	C-2	:L-4:	C-3	:L-5:	D-2	:L-7:	D-3)
ckt-4	(B-1	:L-12:	A-2	:L-2:	C-1	:L-3:	C-2)			

Table 1: Circuit Descriptions

goal. In this example, the restoral goals are autonomously instantiated in subregion A (for ckt-1), subregion B (for ckt-1 and ckt-2) and subregion D (for ckt-2). Each agent initially has only the following knowledge about *each circuit terminating in its subregion:*

- a circuit identifier that is unique within the network,

- a priority or degree of urgency for restoral,

- detailed routing of this circuit within this agent's area of responsibility, and

- the end stations of the circuit and the agents responsible for them.

In addition, each agent has detailed knowledge concerning the status of resources resident in its subregion.

The first phase of the planning process is plan generation, and since it uses only one stage of negotiation, as in contract nets [2,3,4], we shall not consider the details of plan generation here. When viewed from a global perspective, plan generation produces two alternative restoral plans for each circuit. Each plan is represented in Table 2 as a list of alternating sites and links, traversing the proposed restoral path. To clarify the example,

Plans for goal g1 to restore ckt-1:									
g1/p1	(A-1	:L-1:	A-2	:L-2:	C-1	:L-3:	C-2	:L-4:	C-3
	:L-5:	D-2	:L-7:	D-3	:L-8:	D-1	:L-9:	B-2)	
g1/p2	(A-1	:L-1:	A-2	:L-2:	C-1	:L-3:	C-2	:L-4:	C-3
	:L-10:	B-2)							
Plans for goal g2 to restore ckt-2:									
g2/p1	(B-1	:L-12:	A-2	:L-2:	C-1	:L-3:	C-2	:L-4:	C-3
	:L-10:	B-2	:L-9:	D-1	:L-8:	D-3	:L-7:	D-2)	
g2/p2	(B-1	:L-12:	A-2	:L-2:	C-1	:L-3:	C-2	:L-4:	C-3
	:L-5:	D-2)							

Table 2: Alternative Plans

we have adopted a naming convention for goals and alternative plans which incorporates the circuit name and plan number; thus the two alternative plans for restoring circuit ckt-1 are designated g1/p1 and g1/p2. It is essential to remember that these are global plans which have been generated in a distributed manner, and no single agent *necessarily* knows of all plans or any one complete plan.

As a result of plan generation, a node produces local alternative plan fragments which may be used to satisfy global goals. Each global plan listed in Table 2 is composed of several fragments distributed over a subset of the agents. This is illustrated in Table 3 which summarizes the knowledge each agent has about goals, alternative plan fragments,

Goal	Plan Frag.	Resources Used	Cost
g1	1A	L-1, L-2	9
g2	7A	L-2, L-12	9

Agent A

Goal	Plan Frag.	Resources Used	Cost
g1	2B	L-9	9
	5B	L-10	6
g2	8B	L-9, L-10, L-12	9
	11B	L-12	6

Agent B

Goal	Plan Frag.	Resources Used	Cost
g1	3C	L-2, L-3, L-4, L-5	9
	6C	L-2, L-3, L-4, L-10	6
g2	9C	L-2, L-3, L-4, L-10	9
	12C	L-2, L-3, L-4, L-5	6

Agent C

Goal	Plan Frag.	Resources Used	Cost
g1	4D	L-5, L-7, L-8, L-9	9
g2	10D	L-7, L-8, L-9	9
	13D	L-5	6

Agent D

Table 3: Local Knowledge About Plan Fragments

and local resources. Plan fragments are numbered and each is identified by a letter indicating the responsible agent. Note that agents are not *explicitly* aware of global alternative plans, but are only aware of local alternatives. For example, even though Agent A has resources needed by both g1/p1 and g1/p2, the local plan fragment is the same in both cases, and thus Agent A "sees" only one alternative plan for goal g1.

This example is considerably oversimplified in order to focus attention on the significant characteristics of this planning problem and to illustrate the cooperation strategy which results from multistage negotiation. The communication network has been simplified so that link capacity is the only resource, and thus there are no constraints arising from local equipment configurations. The number of circuits and link capacities are also much smaller than is typical. Since only two top level goals exist, the subgoal interactions are simple and can be recognized in only one step. In a more realistic problem, subgoal interactions often involve multiple dependencies and may require several steps of negotiation to detect and resolve.

The features of the planning problem which are important for the discussion of multistage negotiation in this paper are summarized below:

- Goals are autonomously generated at nodes in the system.

- The same system goal may be generated at more than one node, independently.

- Knowledge about local resource availability and potential goal interactions at each node differs from that at other nodes.

- Goal satisfaction in general requires nonlocal resources.

- The planning problem being addressed is, in general, overconstrained. A choice to satisfy some goals may preclude the satisfaction of others, so choice heuristics are necessary.

- Goals are prioritized, but this does not imply a total ordering with respect to priority.

4   MODEL OF PROBLEM SOLVING

The planning problem discussed in the previous section can be viewed in a broader context. In this section we characterize a problem solving model in which multistage negotiation is useful. The search space for a problem of this kind can be considered from two points of view: a task or goal centered perspective and a node centered perspective. Each of these ways of viewing the search space provides a different set of insights with respect to problem solving.

When viewed from the perspective of the system goal, the global problem appears as an AND-OR tree progressing from the system goal (at the root), down through goals and plans, to local plan fragments distributed among the agents. A goal centered view of our example problem is illustrated in Figure 2. Two goals have been instantiated, with four alternative plans and several local plan fragments. Of course, since this is a distributed environment, no single agent has a complete view of this tree. Observe that each agent is aware of both goals g1 and g2, but agent D is only aware of one plan fragment for g1, the one which is a component of g1/p1.

An agent may not simply satisfy a local goal by choosing any plan fragment, but must coordinate its choice so that it is compatible with those of other agents. Formulation of a plan as a conjunction of plan fragments induces a set of compatibility constraints on the local choices an agent makes in satisfaction of global goals. In Figure 2, we show the plan fragments interconnected by dashed lines. These dashed lines indicate the local knowledge an agent has about which other agents are involved in compatibility constraint relations with its own plan fragments. Observe that an agent generally does not have *complete* knowledge about these compatibility sets. In our application domain, these constraints involved shared resources between two agents.

From a node centered perspective, plan fragment selection is constrained by local resource availability. An agent cannot choose to execute a set of alternative plan fragments that require more local resources than are available. For example, agent B's local resources permit selection of any pair of its own plan fragments in satisfaction of g1 and g2, whereas

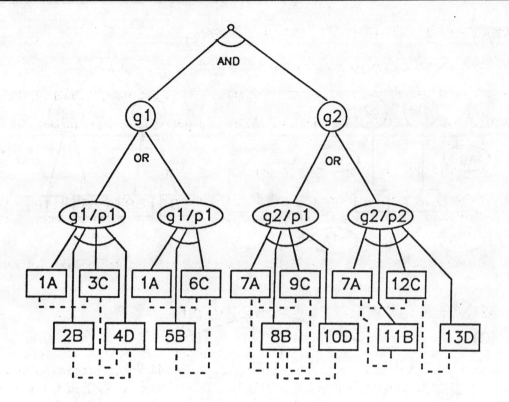

Figure 2: Global Search Space

agents A, C, and D each can select only one plan fragment. The resulting feasibility tree known to each agent is shown in Figure 3. In this figure, resource constraints associated with goals and plan fragments are enclosed by ovals and connected to the appropriate objects with dashed lines. Restoral goals initiated in a subregion are designated with an "*".

From each agent's perspective, the search is over a group of alternatives subject to a set of local resource constraints and a set of compatibility constraints imposed by actions of other agents. Multistage negotiation provides a mechanism by which agents coordinate their actions in selecting plans subject to both resource and compatibility constraints. As additional constraints are added to an agent's base of knowledge, its local feasibility tree is augmented to reflect what it has learned.

5   MULTISTAGE NEGOTIATION

In this section, we describe the multistage negotiation protocol we have developed and give an example of its application in the distributed planning problem which has been discussed. We first treat the protocol at a very high level, discussing the general strategy. We then provide more detail as to phases of planning and the role of negotiation in each. The section is concluded with a detailed trace of negotiation and reasoning in each agent pertinent to our simple example.

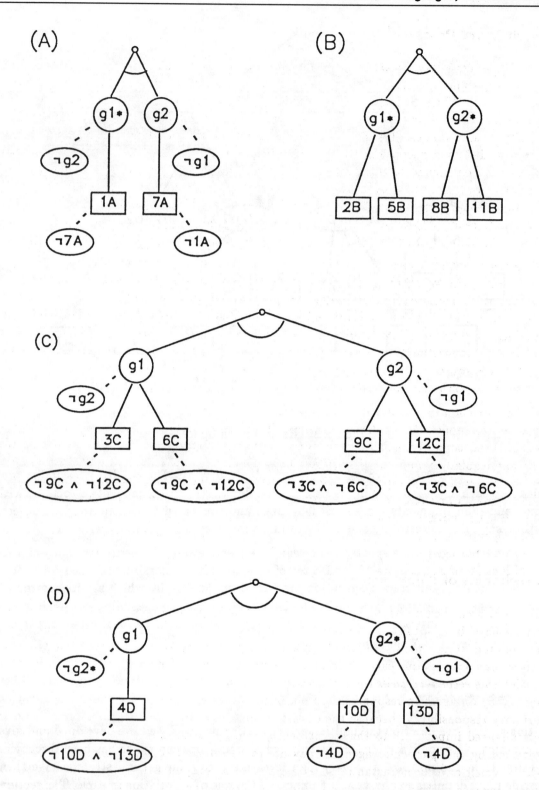

Figure 3: Local Feasibility Trees

High Level Protocol

Multistage negotiation provides a means by which an agent can acquire enough knowledge to reason about the impact of local activity on nonlocal state and modify its behavior accordingly. When problem solving activity is initiated, agents first engage in a phase of plan generation. Each agent ascertains what alternatives for partial goal satisfaction are locally possible and tenders contracts to appropriate agents for furthering satisfaction of the goals needed to complete these plans. On completion of this phase, a space of alternative plans has been constructed which is distributed among the agents, with each agent only having knowledge about its local plan fragments. An agent then examines the goals it instantiated and makes a tentative commitment to the highest rated feasible set of plan fragments relative to these goals. It subsequently issues requests for confirmation of that commitment to agents who hold the contracts for completion of these plan fragments.

Each agent may receive two kinds of communications from other agents: 1) requests for confirmation of other agents' tentative commitments, and 2) responses concerning the impact of its own proposed commitments on others. Impact of local actions is reported as confirmation that a tentative local choice is a good one or as negative information reflecting nonlocal resource conflict. The agent incorporates this new knowledge into its local feasibility tree. It rerates its own local goals using the new knowledge and possibly retracts its tentative resource commitment in order to make a more informed choice. This process of information exchange continues until a consistent set of choices can be confirmed.

Termination of the negotiation process can be done using system-wide criteria or it can be accomplished in a diffuse manner. If global termination criteria are desired in an application, some form of token passing mechanism [8,9,10] can be used to detect that the applicable termination criteria have been met. When synchronized global termination is not required in an application, the negotiation can be terminated by an "irrevocable" commitment of resources. A node initiates plan execution in accordance with its negotiated tentative commitment at some time after it has no pending activities and no work to do for other agents.

Mechanics of Negotiation

When a node begins its planning activity, it has knowledge of a set of top level goals which have been locally instantiated. A space of plans to satisfy each of these goals is formulated during plan generation without regard for any subgoal interaction problems. After plan generation, each node is aware of two kinds of goals: *primary goals* (or p-goals) and *secondary goals* (or s-goals). In our application, p-goals are those instantiated locally by an agent in response to an observed outage of a circuit for which the agent has primary responsibility (because the circuit terminates in the agent's subregion). These are of enhanced importance to this agent because they relate to system goals which *must* be satisfied by this particular agent if they are to be satisfied at all. An agent's s-goals are those which have been instantiated as a result of a contract with some other agent. An agent regards each of its s-goals as a possible alternative to be utilized in satisfaction of some other agent's p-goal.

A plan commitment phase involving multistage negotiation is initiated next. As this phase begins, each node has knowledge about all of the p-goals and s-goals it has instantiated. Relative to each of its goals, it knows a number of alternatives for goal satisfaction. An alternative is comprised of a local plan fragment, points of interaction with other agents (relative to that plan fragment), and a measure of the cost of the alternative (to be used in making heuristic decisions). Negotiation leading to a commitment proceeds along the following lines.

1. Each node examines its own p-goals, making a tentative commitment to the highest rated set of locally feasible plan fragments for p-goals (s-goals are not considered at this point because some other agent has corresponding p-goals).

2. Each node requests that other agents attempt to confirm a plan choice consistent with its commitment. Note that an agent need only communicate with agents who can provide input relevant to this tentative commitment.

3. A node examines its incoming message queue for communications from other nodes. Requests for confirmation of other agents' tentative commitments are handled by adding the relevant s-goals to a set of active goals. Responses to this agent's own requests are incorporated in the local feasibility tree and used as additional knowledge in making revisions to its tentative commitment.

4. The set of **active goals** consists of all the local p-goals together with those s-goals that have been added (in step 3). The agent rates the alternatives associated with active goals based on their cost, any confirming evidence that the alternative is a good choice, any negative evidence in the form of nonlocal conflict information, and the importance of the goal (p-goal, s-goal, etc.). A revised tentative commitment is made to a highest rated set of locally consistent alternatives for active goals. In general, this may involve decisions to *add* plan fragments to the tentative commitment and to *delete* plan fragments from the old tentative commitment. Messages reflecting any changes in the tentative commitment and perceived conflicts with that commitment are transmitted to the appropriate agents.

5. The incoming message queue is examined again and activity proceeds as described above (from step 3). The process of aggregating knowledge about nonlocal conflicts continues until a node is aware of all conflicts in which its plan fragments are a contributing factor.

Two issues need clarification at this point. One deals with the question of termination and the other is concerned with the quality of the result obtained through negotiation (relative to optimality).

Negotiation in this framework continues as long as there are any pending activities in an agent. The only way a situation leading to nontermination could arise involves an agent's making a tentative commitment and subsequently entering a cycle of retracting and remaking that commitment indefinitely. It is not reasonable to expect that an agent should never retract a tentative commitment. It is also not reasonable to expect that an agent would never decide, based on new knowledge, to recommit to an alternative it had previously rejected. An agent's local reasoning must be able to detect when it is making a tentative commitment it has previously made with no new knowledge. Negotiation activity in an agent terminates either when it has no pending activity and no incoming communications or if an attempt is made to return to a previous commitment with no new knowledge from other agents. Endless loops of commitment and decommitment are prevented through this mechanism.

The other issue of importance at this point is related to the quality of the result obtained through negotiation. In the initial negotiation stage, each agent examines only its p-goals and makes a tentative commitment to a locally feasible set of plan fragments in partial satisfaction of those goals. Since each agent is considering just its p-goals at this stage, the only reason for an agent's electing not to attempt satisfaction of some top level goal is that two or more of these goals are locally known to be infeasible. (This corresponds to an overconstrained problem.)

In subsequent stages of negotiation, both p-goals and relevent s-goals are considered in making new tentative commitments. The reasoning strategy employed at each agent will only decide to forego commitment to one of its p-goals if it has learned that satisfaction of this p-goal precludes the satisfaction of one or more other p-goals elsewhere in the system. *If the system goal of satisfying all of the p-goals instantiated by agents in the network is feasible, no agent will ever be forced to forego satisfaction of one of its p-goals (because no agent will ever learn that its p-goal precludes others), and a desired solution will be found.* If, on the other hand, the problem is overconstrained, some set of p-goals cannot be satisfied and the system tries to satisfy as many as it can. While there is no guarantee of optimality, the heuristics employed should ensure that a reasonably thorough search is made.

To make these concepts concrete, multistage negotiation is applied to the simplified planning problem discussed in the previous sections.

Example

We return to our example of planning activity, assuming that each agent has the knowledge depicted in the appropriate part of Figure 3. A summary of the transactions that occur during negotiation to achieve plan selection is shown in Table 4. This table is segmented by agent and by "time slice" to convey a sense of progress in problem solving through negotiation. The notational conventions are relatively simple. Tentative commitment to a locally known activity and the associated communication issued to an appropriate agent is denoted in the form (plan fragment name; message → agent). Exchange of conflict information is indicated in the form (conflict; type of conflict → agent). To make the trace easier to follow, each received message is noted in the form (source agent → message).

As is evident in Table 4, negotiation begins with tentative commitments to alternatives in agents A, B, and D. Though the problem is overconstrained (it is not possible to restore both ckt-1 and ckt-2), no agent is yet aware of that fact. In response to the initial tentative commitments, there is activity in agents A and C. Agent A knows that it cannot act to satisfy both g1 and g2, but it does *not* know if this precludes satisfaction of g2 (since g2 is an s-goal, there might exist another global plan not requiring any action by A). Since A recognizes the need to *attempt* satisfaction of its own p-goal first, agent A informs agent B there is a conflict between what B requested and satisfaction of one of A's p-goals. Thus A has given B the knowledge that the plan fragment B selected would force A to forego one

A	B	C	D
1A; OK? → C	11B; OK? → A 5B; OK? → C		13D; OK? → C
B → OK? 11B conflict; (11B AND ¬ p-goal g1) → B		A → OK? 1A B → OK? 5B D → OK? 13D match 6C with 1A and 5B 1A is OK → A 5B is OK → B conflict; (13D AND ¬ g1 via C) → D	
C → 1A is OK	A → (11B AND ¬ p-goal g1) C → 5B is OK 8B; OK? → A		C → (13D AND ¬ g1 via C) 10D; OK? → B
B → OK? 8B conflict; (8B AND ¬ p-goal g1) → B	D → OK? 10D 8B; OK? → C		
	A → (8B AND ¬ p-goal g1) B knows g1 and g2 not both possible (not both g1 and g2) → D	B → OK? 8B conflict; (8B AND ¬ g1 via C) → B	
	C → (8B AND ¬ g1 via C)		B → (not both g1 and g2)

Table 4: Summary of transactions during negotiation

of its p-goals.

Agent C has now received three communications requesting that plan fragments be extended. It observes that it can effect a plan completion for g1, satisfying both the request from A and the request from B. It also observes that it cannot satisfy both g1 and g2 with use of its locally known plan fragments due to local resource constraints. Since it has the opportunity to complete a plan for ckt-1 and not for ckt-2, it elects to tentatively commit its resources to plan fragment 6C. Messages reflecting this commitment are formulated and transmitted to A and B, while a message indicating the conflict in C is sent to D.

As a result of this second round of communications, activity in subregions B and D is concerned with exploring the remaining alternatives they have for restoral of ckt-2. An acceptable plan for ckt-1 is already reflected in tentative commitments. Agent B elects to try plan fragment 8B and agent D elects to try 10D. Agent B learns that an attempt to satisfy g2 via 8B also fails in A, so it now knows that the problem is overconstrained. Based on the fact that a way of satisfying g1 has already been located, B elects to forego satisfaction of g2 and advises D that it should also give up on g2. Negotiation terminates with tentative commitments reflecting a plan choice for g1.

In concluding this section we summarize, by "time slice", changes to the local feasibility trees that take place during the negotiation illustrated in Table 4.

Slice 1:

- No changes.

Slice 2:

- No changes in constraints by A.
- 6C is tentatively committed to a *complete* plan by C.

Slice 3:

- 1A is marked as tentatively satisfying g1 by A.
- 5B is marked as tentatively satisfying g1 by B.
- Agent B adds the constraint ($\neg$ g1) to 11B.
- Agent D adds the constraint ($\neg$ g1 via C) to 13D. (Note that in this example, the new constraint on 13D is, in fact, redundant. In other examples, with a more complex set of goals, new constraints propagated in this way often provide additional information.)

Slice 4:

- No changes.

Slice 5:

- Agent B adds the constraint ($\neg$ g1) to 8B.
- Agent B propagates the constraint ($\neg$ g1) on 8B and 11B to their parent, g2. *Agent B now knows the problem is overconstrained.*

Slice 6:

- Agent D modifies the constraint ($\neg$ g1) on goal g2* to ($\neg$ g1*). *Agent D now knows the problem is overconstrained.*

This example illustrates ways in which knowledge is integrated into the local feasibility tree as it is acquired through negotiation. It shows how knowledge aggregated at the level of plan segments can be propagated in drawing inferences concerning interactions at the goal level. It also shows how the network of agents can become aware that it has an overconstrained problem.

6   CONCLUDING REMARKS

In this paper, we have presented a new paradigm for cooperation in distributed problem solving systems. This paradigm incorporates features found in two cooperation strategies treated in the literature: the contract net protocol [2,3,4] and the FA/C paradigm [5]. It has been devised to permit an agent in a distributed problem solving system to acquire enough knowledge to reason about the impact of local activity on nonlocal state and to modify its behavior accordingly.

Three characteristics of distributed planning problems motivate development of a more general cooperation paradigm. First, subgoal interaction problems that arise in the context of a distributed planning system in which agents do not have a global view are very difficult to detect and even more difficult to handle in a reasonable way. Second, many application domains embody planning problems that are overconstrained. When these planning problems are addressed by a network of planning agents, it is essential that the system be able to determine whether or not the problem is overconstrained. Third, when the planning problem is overconstrained, it is necessary for the agents involved to arrive at an agreement as to a set of goals whose satisfaction is regarded as an acceptable solution to the problem at hand. None of these issues can be resolved in the context of the previously proposed cooperation paradigms without the exchange of sufficient knowledge as to permit each agent to construct a global view.

Another factor motivating formulation of a more general cooperation paradigm is the observation that many application domains have characteristics that distinguish them from other multi-agent planning problems which have been investigated. The strategies suggested by Lansky [11] and Georgoff [12] dealing with planning for a multiple agent domain by a centralized planner are not applicable in situations where there is no central planner. In addition, the agents in our networks are not motivated purely by self interest. They are interested in cooperating to achieve some goals pertinent to system performance. For this reason, the metaphor proposed by Genesereth and others [13] does not represent the domain characteristics. It should be noted, however, that our metaphor can be adapted for use in networks of agents which are selfish (as long as they do not lie a great deal).

The mechanisms presented in this paper are related to the techniques that have been utilized in conventional planning systems. Each agent in our system builds a data structure analogous to the Table of Multiple Effects used by NOAH [14] and NONLIN [15] in detecting subgoal interactions. This structure is incrementally built using knowledge gleaned through negotiation. In detecting and resolving conflicts, a form of criticism analogous to that performed by NOAH's Resolve Conflicts critic is employed. Criticism is necessary in our distributed problem solving systems for the same reason it was needed in NOAH - decisions are made initially based on local criteria, whereas nonlocal conditions affect the viability of those decisions. Unlike NOAH (and like NONLIN), alternatives are not discarded after they have been rejected. Backtracking in the form of revised tentative commitment is a feature of the protocol.

In many planning problems, the constraints arising from resource availability are very important in determining a satisfactory solution to the planning problem. We have found that resource constraints play a crucial role in our system as well. The ability to reason about resources is critical in determining adequate solutions. This was recognized in the design of SIPE [16]. Since we have no central planner, the mechanisms for reasoning about resources are somewhat different from those employed in SIPE, but resources as a factor in problem solving are just as important to multistage negotiation as they were in SIPE.

The distributed planning system discussed in this paper is currently in the final stages of implementation on an existing distributed system simulation facility [17].

References

[1] J. G. March and H. A. Simon, **Organizations**, Wiley, 1958.

[2] Reid G. Smith "The Contract Net Protocol: High Level Communication and Control in a Distributed Problem Solver," **IEEE Transactions on Systems, Man, and Cybernetics, vol. SMC-10, no. 12**, December 1980.

[3] R. G. Smith and R. Davis "Frameworks for Cooperation in Distributed Problem Solving," **IEEE Transactions on Systems, Man, and Cybernetics, vol. SMC-11, no. 1**, January 1981, pp. 61-70.

[4] R. Davis, and R. G. Smith "Negotiation as a Metaphor for Distributed Problem Solving," **Artificial Intelligence, vol. 20, no. 1**, January 1983, pp. 63-109.

[5] V. R. Lesser and D. D. Corkill "Functionally Accurate, Cooperative Distributed Systems," **IEEE Transactions on Systems, Man, and Cybernetics, vol. SMC-11, no. 1**, January 1981, pp. 81-96.

[6] S. E. Conry, R. A. Meyer, and J. E. Searleman "A Shared Knowledge Base for Independent Problem Solving Agents," **Proceedings of the Expert Systems in Government Symposium**, IEEE Computer Society, McLean, Virginia, October 1985.

[7] A. S. Tanenbaum, **Computer Networks**, Prentice-Hall, 1981.

[8] S. Vinter, K. Ramamritham, and D. Stemple "Recoverable Communicating Actions in Gutemberg," **Proceedings of the International Conference on Distributed Computing Systems**, May 1986.

[9] E. W. Dijkstra and C. S. Scholten "Termination Detection for Diffusing Computations," **Information Processing Letters, vol. 11, no. 1**, August 1980, pp. 1-4.

[10] N. Francez "Distributed Termination," **ACM Transactions on Programming Languages and Systems, vol. 2, no. 1**, January 1980, pp. 42-55.

[11] A. L. Lansky "Behavioral Specification and Planning for Multiagent Domains," Technical Note 360, Artificial Intelligence Center, SRI International, Menlo Park, California, November 1985.

[12] M. Georgeoff, "Communication and Interaction in Multi-Agent Planning," **Proceedings of the National Conference on Artificial Intelligence (AAAI-84)**, August 1984, pp. 125-129.

[13] M. R. Genesereth, M. L. Ginsberg, and J. S. Rosenschein "Cooperation Without Communication," **Proceedings of the National Conference on Artificial Intelligence (AAAI-86)**, August 1986, pp. 51-57.

[14] E. D. Sacerdoti **A Structure for Plans and Behavior**, Elsevier-North Holland, New York, 1977.

[15] A. Tate "Project Plannig using a Hierarchic Non-Linear Planner," Research Report No. 25, Department of Artificial Intelligence, University of Edinburgh, August 1976.

[16] D. E. Wilkins, "Domain-Independent Planning: Representation and Plan Generation," **Artificial Intelligence, vol 22**, pp. 269-301.

[17] D. J. MacIntosh and S. E. Conry, "SIMULACT: A Generic Tool for Simulating Distributed Systems" to appear in the **Proceedings of the Eastern Simulation Conference**, April 1987.

Dialogue-Games: Metacommunication Structures for Natural Language Interaction

JAMES A. LEVIN
JAMES A. MOORE

USC Information Sciences Institute

INTRODUCTION

A pervasive aspect of natural language is the wealth of implicit communication accompanying even simple dialogues:

Person 1: Do you have a match?
Person 2: Sorry, I don't smoke.

Our studies of naturally occurring human dialogue have led to the recognition of a class of regularities which characterize important aspects of communication. People appear to interact according to established patterns which span several turns in a dialogue and which recur frequently. These patterns appear to be organized around the goals which the dialogue serves for each participant. Many things which are said later in a dialogue can only be interpreted as pursuit of these goals, established by earlier dialogue.

These patterns have been represented by a set of knowledge structures called *Dialogue-Games*, capturing shared, conventional knowledge that people have about communication and how it can be used to achieve goals. A Dialogue-Game has *Parameters*, which represent those elements that vary across instances of a particular pattern—the particular dialogue participants and the content topic. The states of the world which must be in effect for a particular Dialogue-Game to be employed successfully are represented by *Specifications* of these Parameters. Finally, the expected sequence of intermediate states that occur during instances of a particular conventional pattern are represented by the *Components* of the corresponding Dialogue-Game.

Representations for several Dialogue-Games are presented here, based on our analyses of different kinds of naturally occurring dialogue. A process model is discussed, showing Dialogue-Game identification, pursuit, and termination as part of the comprehension of dialogue utterances. This Dialogue-Game model captures some of the important functional aspects of language, especially indirect uses to achieve implicit communication.

This simple dialogue demonstrates that an immense amount of shared information is necessary for the communication to be effective. This example requires "world knowledge" of the following sort:

1. One is likely to possess matches if and only if one smokes.
2. The word "have" as used here is not simply ownership but also immediate access.
3. A match really is not required: anything that can perform the *function* of a match is satisfactory, such as a lighter, a lighted cigarette, or any flame.

The example also requires knowledge of conventional reasons for certain behaviors:

Assuming X is relatively inexpensive:

1. If I want you to give me X, I may ask you if you have X.
2. If you do not provide X, you convey your apologies (even though there is no formal requirement for you to have X, or to give it to me even if you have it).
3. A negative reply probably terminates the interaction, since the initiating request has been denied.

It also relies on conventional knowledge of what response each can reasonably expect of the other:
Assuming Z is relatively inexpensive:

If you know I want Z, and if you have it, you may give it to me.

We have developed a model of dialogue comprehension, the Dialogue-Games model, that represents knowledge that people have about language and how it can be used to achieve their goals through interaction with other people. The model specifies the processes by which this knowledge is used to comprehend the utterances of another person. This processing infers what goals the other person could have for generating his utterance.

After looking at the current state of language comprehension research, we will present a detailed description of the Dialogue-Games model, covering both the representations for particular kinds of interactions, and the processes for using these knowledge structures in comprehension. Afterward, we will discuss how this model addresses some of the important problems of language comprehension modeling.

PAST RESEARCH ON LANGUAGE COMPREHENSION

Most of the research into language comprehension has focused on the comprehension of single sentences or fragments of sentences. However, some research has indicated the importance of the context created by surrounding sentences on the comprehension of an individual sentence. Much of this research has

some recent researchers have started using dialogues between people as their primary source of language to study.

To account for the conduct and comprehension of dialogues, multisentential knowledge units have also been proposed by linguists and sociolinguists to explain certain kinds of regularities observed in naturally occurring dialogues. These regularities have been called ''rules'' by Labov and Fanshel (1974) and ''sequences'' by Sacks, Schegloff, and Jefferson (1974).

Once these multisentential knowledge units are evoked, they serve as a basis for comprehending the successive inputs. This is achieved by generating expectations and by providing a framework for integrating the comprehension of an utterance with that of its predecessors. Recently, we proposed (Levin & Moore, 1976) multisentential knowledge units that are specified primarily by the speaker's and hearer's goals. These differ from the other proposed multisentential units, some of which are specified only by co-occurrence properties, others by causal characteristics. These goal-oriented units which we call *Dialogue-Games*,[1] specify the kinds of language interactions in which people engage, rather than the specific content of these interactions. People use language primarily to communicate with other people, in pursuit of their own goals. The Dialogue-Game multisentential structures were developed to represent this knowledge about language and how it can be used to achieve goals.

An important problem facing researchers in language comprehension is posed by sentences with which the speaker performs what philosophers of language have called ''indirect speech acts'' (Searle, 1969). The direct comprehension of these sentences fails to derive the main communicative effect. For example, declarative sentences can be used to seek information (''I need to know your Social Security number.''); questions can be used to convey information (''Did you know that John and Harriet got married?'') or to request an action (''Could you pass the salt?''). These kinds of utterances, which have been extensively analyzed by philosophers of language (Austin, 1962; Grice, 1975; Searle, 1969; 1975), are not handled satisfactorily by any of the current theories of the direct comprehension of language. However, these indirect language usages are widespread in naturally occurring language—even two-year-old children can comprehend indirect requests for action almost as well as direct requests (Shatz, 1975).

One theory proposed to account for these indirect uses of language is based on the concept of ''conversational postulates'' (Gordon & Lakoff, 1971; Grice, 1975). If the direct comprehension of an utterance is implausible, then the

[1]The term ''Dialogue-Game'' was adopted by analogy from Wittgenstein's term ''language game'' (Wittgenstein, 1958). However, Dialogue-Games represent knowledge people have about language as used to pursue goals, rather than Wittgenstein's more general use. Although there are also similarities with other notions of ''game,'' the properties of Dialogue-Games are only those described here. For example, they are not necessarily competitive, consciously pursued, or zero-sum.

studied the comprehension of stories, starting with Bartlett (1932), who found that a story influences the ability of subjects to recall the individual utterances within that story. In particular, he found that some sentences that did not make sense within the rest of the story were replaced in the recalls by other sentences that were similar in some ways, but differed so that they fit the story.

A similar result was found by Bransford and Johnson (1973), using ''ambiguous stories.'' They generated stories, each of which could be interpreted in two widely different ways, and influenced the interpretations derived by subjects by giving each story one of two titles. For example, one story was entitled either ''Watching a peace march from the fortieth floor'' or ''A space trip to an inhabited planet.'' Most of the sentences in the story could be interpreted either way, but one sentence made sense only within one of these two interpretations. Subjects given one title were able to recall this sentence well, but those given the other title (with the incompatible interpretations) were not. Generally, these results indicate that knowledge spanning multiple sentences is involved in comprehending each individual sentence of a story. This multisentential knowledge is used to tie the comprehension of each sentence together, and any sentence which does not fit into this knowledge is not easily assimilated or remembered.

A specific model for the form of this multisentential knowledge is the ''story schema,'' organized within a story grammar (Rumelhart, 1975). This model has been supported by the results of story recalls (Rumelhart, 1977). Other similar kinds of theoretical constructs for organizing multiple sentences of stories have been proposed called: ''frames'' (Charniak, 1975; Minsky, 1975), ''scripts'' (Schank & Abelson, 1975), and ''commonsense algorithms'' (Rieger, 1975a).

Stories have been studied because they are well structured, especially in comparison to naturally occurring oral language. Sentences are usually grammatical in written stories, and some of the topic structuring is explicitly marked by paragraphing. However, there are a number of problems with using stories for studying language comprehension. A speaker's motivations play an important role in structuring what he says. These motivations are particularly obscure for the ''speaker'' of a story. Another problem is that a writer generally reworks his ''utterances,'' a number of times before they are communicated to his audience.

A good writer tailors his sentences to serve multiple purposes—this makes for good literature, but also for a difficult subject for the study of language comprehension. Third, a number of recent studies have shown that speakers modify their speech to fit their hearers. Not only do adults modify their speech based on their knowledge of the person they are talking to, but even four-year-old children use different language when talking with two-year-olds than when talking with adults (Shatz & Gelman, 1973). It is more difficult to investigate how people modify their language use depending on knowledge of the hearer in stories, because the hearer of a story is an entire audience of readers. For these reasons, indirect meaning is derived using these postulates. Clark and Lucy (1975) formalized and tested this model, and found support for a three-stage model (deriving the literal meaning, check its plausibility, and if implausible, deriving the "intended meaning" from conversational rules).

In general, this approach to indirect speech acts is inference-based, depending on the application of conversational rules to infer the indirect meaning from the direct meaning and the context. A different approach has been proposed by Labov and Fanshel (1974) and by Levin and Moore (1976). Multisentential knowledge, organizing a segment of language interaction, can form the basis for deriving the indirect effect of utterance within the segment. For example, a multisentential structure for an information-seeking interaction can supply the appropriate context for interpreting the subsequent utterances to seek and then supply information. The inference-based approach requires one set of conversational rules for information requests, a different set of rules for answers to these requests, and a way to tie these two rule sets together. The Dialogue-Game model postulates that there is but one knowledge structure for this kind of interaction, and leads to a model of three sets of cooperating processes for: (1) using this knowledge recognizing when this kind of interaction is proposed, (2) using this knowledge to comprehend utterances within its scope, and (3) identifying when the interaction is to be terminated.

3. *Information-seeking*: Person 1 wants to know some specific information, and interacts with Person 2 in order to learn it.

4. *Information-probing*: Person 1 wants to know whether Person 2 knows some particular information, and interacts with him to find out.

5. *Instructing*: Person 1 wants Person 2 to know some information, and interacts with him to impart the information.

6. *Griping*: Person 1 is unhappy about some state of affairs, and interacts with Person 2 to convey that unhappiness.

This classification is certainly not a complete classification of all systematic types of interaction dialogues. Rather, it is an initial attempt to delineate the nature of these stereotypical interactions. One point that is evident from this description is the importance of the goals of the participants in determining the type of interaction. In all of these interactions, one participant wants something, and initiates the dialogue in an attempt to achieve that goal. Furthermore, it appears to be the case that the other person cooperates with the dialogue only if he holds goals which will be served by such cooperation. The Dialogue-Games model has been built to account for these and similar regularities about language elements of dialogue, and contains the following generalizations about language comprehension:

1. Part of the comprehension of any utterance is to associate particular functions with it, inferring that the speaker is using the utterance as a means to accomplish one or more particular identified goals which he holds.

2. The speaker ordinarily holds multiple goals, and these are related in highly constrained ways.

3. The goals held by the two participants of a dialogue are not independent but rather are closely related in ways which strongly and systematically constrain co-occurrence of goals.

4. These related sets of participants' goals underlie a significant amount of dialogue behavior and the knowledge of these recurrent goal patterns is essential for language comprehension.

5. People use their knowledge of goal structures in dialogue to effect implicit communication of various kinds, including the performance of indirect speech acts and the implicit communication of assumptions about each other.

Concerning particular communication structures, we also hold that:

6. Changes of "topic" in dialogue are directly dependent upon changes in the participants' goal structures, and are accomplished as side effects of goal structure changes.

7. Indirect communication, including indirect questions and requests, arises out of the part of language comprehension which associates functions with utterances.

THE DIALOGUE-GAME MODEL

This section describes our Diaglogue-Games model at its current state of development. In particular, we attempt to answer the following questions:

1. What is the knowledge we are representing within the definition of a particular Dialogue-Game?

2. How is this knowledge used to model the receptive acts of dialogue participants?

3. What sort of machinery does it take to support this model?

An Overview of Dialogue-Games

In our studies of naturally occurring dialogues, we have concentrated upon those regularities relating to the *function* of the dialogue for the participants, as distinct from its *topic*. In our studies of a number of different types of naturally occurring dialogues, we have identified the following types of systematic interaction.

1. *Helping*: Person 1 wants to solve a problem, and interacts with Person 2 in an attempt to arrive at a solution.

2. *Action-seeking*: Person 1 wants some action performed and interacts with Person 2 to get him to perform it.

to be of the same nature as those of the voice dialogue and face-to-face interactions we have examined.

What's in a Game?

A Dialogue-Game consists of three parts: a set of *Parameters*, the collection of *Specifications* that apply to these Parameters throughout the conduct of the DG (Dialogue-Game), and a partially ordered set of *Components* characterizing the dynamic aspects of the DG.

For the balance of this section, we will elaborate on these three parts and exemplify these with an example of the HELPING DG. Bidding and Acceptance are operations which people use to enter Dialogue-Games. Bidding accomplishes:

1. Identification of the DG.
2. Establishment of the bidder's interest in pursuing the DG.
3. Identification of the Parameter configuration intended.

It is performed many different ways, often very briefly. It is typically the source of a great deal of implicit communication. Acceptance is one of the typical responses to a Bid, and only acceptance leads to pursuit of the DG. Acceptance accomplishes:

1. Recognition that a bid has been made.
2. Satisfactory recognition of the particular DG and Parameter values bid.
3. Agreement to pursue the DG.
4. Assumption of the acceptor's role in the DG.

Acceptance is often implicit, especially in relatively informal dialogue. It can be indicated by agreement or approval, or by beginning to pursue the DG (i.e., attempts to satisfy the goals). Alternatives to acceptance include rejecting, negotiating, and ignoring.

Bidding and acceptance appear to be part of DG entry and termination for the Dialogue-Games of ordinary adult dialogue. In the case of termination, there are three other alternatives: interruption and spontaneous termination, either by goal satisfaction or unconditional goal failure.

Parameters. Dialogue-Games are intended to capture a certain collection of information, common across many dialogues. However, the particular individuals involved, and the subject of the dialogue may vary freely over dialogues described by the same Dialogue-Game. To represent this, each Dialogue-Game has a set of Parameters that take on specific values for each particular dialogue.

The dialogue types we have represented so far as Dialogue-Games have required only three Parameters: the two participants involved (called "Roles"), and the subject of the dialogue (called "Topic").

Dialogue Sources

There are several approaches one can take to studying the comprehension of dialogue. For example, one can collect dialogues conducted within an artificial environment. This is the approach taken by Chapanis (1975) and by Deutsch (1974), for example, who gave their subjects tasks to perform, and collected dialogues conducted while they were pursuing these tasks. The problem with this kind of dialogue for our purposes stems from the central importance of speaker goals in our studies. One of the general problems with an experimental situation is that subjects are asked to adopt artificial goals. Normally this is not an important problem, but it does become critical in cases where the nature of the subject's goal is a central point of interest. In a situation where a person is asked to adopt a certain goal solely because he is a subject in a scientific experiment, there are problems with insuring that he has in fact adopted that goal in the same way as a person who has that goal naturally. The literature on experimenter effects (e.g., Rosenthal, 1974) shows the difficulty with precisely controlling the motivations of subjects. For this reason, we have decided to study naturally occurring dialogues.

In our previous work, we have analyzed a wide variety of dialogues, including transcripts of the Apollo 13 lunar mission, radio talk shows, and teaching interactions. However, the data we have relied upon most heavily are interactions between the users of the TENEX computer system and the system's operators. The TENEX system contains a mechanism (called the "LINK") through which two users of the system can directly communicate by typing on their terminals. Once a "LINK" is established, that which either participant types appears on both computer terminals. We have focused our research on these LINK sources, because they are:

Natural. These dialogues are spontaneous, not part of an experiment. They are initiated by the participants for their own reasons.

Unbiased. These dialogues are completely unaffected by the goals of our research; most of them were conducted before the research started.

Without nonverbal cues. The participants of these dialogues interacted only through typing on their respective computer terminals, and saw only what was typed by the other. Thus, no nonverbal cues were available, even though the conversations were clearly successfully conducted.

Self-transcribed. The difficulty of transcribing voice interactions is avoided (capturing tone and stress patterns and problems in legibility), since these LINK transcripts are typed by the participants themselves in the course of conducting the dialogue.

We have a collection of over 1000 transcripts available to us. We have examined approximately 60 in some detail, and have found that they are sufficiently varied and complex to be of interest. Their goal pursuit methods and structures appear

Parameter Specifications. One of the major aspects distinguishing various types of dialogues is the set of goals held by the participants. Another such aspect is the individual knowledge states of the participants. We have found that for each type of dialogue there is a corresponding set of descriptions which must hold for the goal and knowledge states of the participants, vis-a-vis each other and the subject. Within the formalism of the Dialogue-Game, these are called the Parameter Specifications, and are represented by a collection of predications on the Parameters.

We claim that these Specifications are known to the participants of the dialogue, and the requirement that they be satisfied during the conduct of a DG is used by the participants to signal what DGs they wish to conduct, to recognize what DG is being bid, to decide how to respond to a bid, to conduct the DG once the bid is accepted, and to terminate the DG when appropriate. These Specifications also provide the means with which to explain certain kinds of implicit communication.

Components. The Parameter Specifications represent those aspects of a dialogue type that remain constant throughout the course of a dialogue of that type. We have also found that certain aspects change in systematic ways; these are represented in Dialogue-Games as Components. In the Dialogue-Games we have developed so far, the Components have been represented as a set of participants' subgoals, partially ordered in time.

Once a DG has been bid and accepted, the two participants each pursue the subgoals specified for their role by the Components of this DG. These subgoals are complementary—each set facilitating the other. Furthermore, by the time the termination stage has been reached, pursuit of the Component-specified subgoals will have assured satisfaction of the higher-level goals of the participants, for which the DG was initiated in the first place.

An Example Dialogue-Game: HELPING

In this section, we will introduce our representational formalism by discussing in detail a representation of the helping interaction, in which one person helps another accomplish some task. First we will present the HELPING Dialogue-Game as it would be entered into our semantic network implementation, and then we will describe in detail both this Dialogue-Game (DG) and the underlying representational format. In the following discussion, the formal statements made to the system are in *ITALICIZED CAPITALS*. The messages printed by the computer system are *italicized*, and the annotated descriptions of each part are in **boldface type**.

DEFINEDG (HELPING)

The Parameters are:

>*HELPEE HELPER TASK*

These are just arbitrary names, given meaning only by what follows.
The Parameter Specifications are:

>*(HELPEE ISA PERSON)*
>*(HELPEE WANTS (HELPEE PERFORMS TASK))*
>*((HELPEE ABLE (HELPEE PERFORMS TASK)) NOT)*
>*(HELPEE PERMITTED (HELPEE PERFORMS TASK))*
>*(HELPER ISA PERSON)*
>*(HELPER WILLING (HELPER ENABLE (HELPEE PERFORMS TASK)))*
>*(HELPER ABLE (HELPER ENABLE (HELPEE PERFORMS TASK)))*

According to these Specifications, a helpee is a person who wants to perform a task that he is permitted to do, but is unable to do so. A helper is a person who is both able and willing to enable the helpee do his task.

The Components are:

>*DS1: (HELPEE WANTS (HELPER KNOWS (HELPEE PERCEIVES EVENT/EXPECTED-1 PAST)))*
>*DS2: (HELPEE WANTS (HELPER KNOWS ((HELPEE PERCEIVES EVENT/EXPECTED-2 PAST) NOT)))*
>*TS: ((HELPER WANTS (HELPEE KNOWS ACTION/3)) AND ((HELPEE PERFORMS ACTION/3 FUTURE) CAUSES EVENT/ EXPECTED-2 FUTURE))*
>*((DS1 AND DS2) THEN TS)]*

These Components specify two stages of the HELPING DG pursuit, a diagnosis (of the problem) stage and a treatment stage. During the first stage, the helpee wants the helper to know about a context of normal events that occurred, and a violation of that context when an expected event did not occur. Then, the helper wants the helpee to know some action he can take in the future to cause the expected event to occur.

These statements are taken in by the DEFINEDG function and stored in a semantic network, using the ELINOR semantic network representation format (Norman, Rumelhart, & the LNR Research Group, 1975). This network consists of a set of nodes, interconnected by relations. Each of the Parameters is stored as a node, each with a relation connecting it to the node for helping, as shown graphically here:

```
HELPING
        ├── parameter → HELPEE
        ├── parameter → HELPER
        └── parameter → TASK
```

The Components of a DG specify a set of subgoals that, if achieved, usually lead to the achievement of the higher-level goals of the participants given in the Parameter Specifications. In the HELPING DG, there are three Components, two of which are pursued together before the third is pursued. This captures the two-stage nature of the helping interactions present in the dialogues that we have studied: an initial "diagnosis" stage focusing on identifying what the problem is, and a "treatment" stage during which the helper provides the required assistance. We found this two-stage nature in all the helping dialogues in which the request for help was not immediately rejected.

The two Components of the first stage specify a "context→violation" pattern we have found in our analysis of helping interactions. In this pattern, the help-seeking participant lays out a completely normal set of actions taken and results observed, and then describes some violation of expectation that occurred. A violation can be either some expected result which did not occur, or some unexpected result which did occur.

In an analysis of fourteen helping dialogues, we found a simple Context→Violation sequence in five cases, the Context→Violation→More Context sequence in three cases, and a compound Context→Violation→More Context→Another Violation sequence in two cases. In one case, the use described a context setting only, after which the operator asked him what his problem was. This "failure" to follow the Context→Violation pattern in fact is evidence for the pattern, since the Helper in this case guided the course of the dialogue back to the pattern. (There were, however, two cases that deviated from the Context→Violation pattern in a more serious manner—both described a desired end state, rather than a puzzling violation of expectation.)

Overview of Dialogue-Game Processing. For an overview of how this representation of regularities of the helping interaction is involved in the comprehension of a dialogue, let us quickly run through a hand simulation of how it is used in comprehending a particular helping dialogue.[2]

1.1 L: Are you there? Go ahead.

2.1 O: Yep, what's up?

[2]Technical terms used in the dialogue

TELNET: A program for communicating with remote computers.

SUBSYS: system program

TYPESCRIPT: A file containing a record of a user's interactions with a program

"BUSY": part of an error message when one tries to read a file that is open

RESET: a command that clears the system, closing any open files

EXP: a command, which deletes temporary files

DISCONNECT: a command that terminates one's connection to a remote computer

DIVERT.OUTPUT.STREAM.TO.FILE: a command which diverts the output stream of the program to a file

TTY: A computer terminal

HELPING Parameter Specifications. The Parameter Specifications are a set of predications on the Parameters. In our input formalism, the second element of an input clause is the name of the predicate for that clause, and all the other elements are arguments of that predicate. Thus, the clause (*HELPEE PERFORMS TASK*) is stored as a particular instance of the predicate PERFORMS, with HELPEE and TASK as arguments:

```
A0004
      ┌── pred→PERFORMS
      ├── agent→HELPEE
      └── object→TASK
```

An element of a clause may simply be a name of a node, or it may be an entire predicate itself. Some predicates take propositional arguments. For example, the clause *HELPEE WANTS (HELPEE PERFORMS TASK)* causes the following structure to be stored:

```
A0005
      ┌── pred→WANTS
      ├── agent→HELPEE
      └── prop→A0004
```

The Parameter Specification predicates create an interrelated structure with the Parameter nodes as central elements. This structure represents conventional knowledge about the participants and the topic of helping interaction. The goal of the person seeking help is expressed by the WANTS clause. Other clauses specify the participants' abilities (or inabilities) with respect to the task, and other properties of the participants. As we shall see later, this knowledge about the Parameters is used in several ways—to select a particular DG, to initiate a DG, to generate expectations, and to terminate a DG. The set of Parameter Specifications represents the state of the world that has to hold throughout the course of a particular kind of interaction.

HELPING Components. Components represent those aspects of a kind of interaction which systematically change during the course of the interaction. Each Component clause creates a predicate structure that is tied to the DG node with a "component" relation. The Components are often ordered in time, as is the case in the HELPING DG.

In the DEFINEDG function, names ending with a "." are interpreted as the explicit name of the structure created. So part of the structure created by the Component clauses of the HELPING DG is:

```
HELPING
      ┌── component→DS1
      ├── component→DS2
      └── component→TS
```

DEFINEDG (INFO-SEEK)

The Parameters are:

>*SEEKER SOURCE INFO*

The Parameter Specifications are:

>(S11:(SEEKER KNOWS INFO) NOT)
>(SOURCE KNOWS INFO)
>S3:(SEEKER WANTS S11)
>S4:(SOURCE WILLING S11)]

The Components are:

>((SOURCE WANTS (SEEKER AWARE INFO))
THEN
(SEEKER WANTS (SOURCE AWARE (SEEKER OBLIGATED-TO SOURCE))))]

In the previous dialogue, one Dialogue-Game (INFO-SEEK) is being used to initiate another Dialogue-Game (HELPING). This represents a phenomena described by sociologists as "pre-sequences" (Schegloff, 1968; Terasaki, 1976).

The importance of the Parameter Specifications is brought out by comparing the INFO-SEEK DG with a different kind of interaction we call INFO-PROBE. In this interaction, a person requests information of another person which the first person already knows, in order to test the other's knowledge.

DEFINEDG (INFO-PROBE)

The Parameters are:

>*PROBER PROBEE INFO*

The Parameter Specifications are:

>S1:(PROBER KNOWS INFO)
>S2:(PROBER WANTS S21:(PROBER KNOWS S211:((PROBEE KNOWS INFO) WHETHER)))
>S3:(PROBEE WILLING S21)]

The Components are:

>((PROBEE WANTS (PROBER AWARE S211))
THEN
(PROBER WANTS (PROBEE AWARE (PROBER ASSESSMENT-OF S211))))]

Both of these DGs can be initiated by a simple question, and in that case must be distinguished from each other on the basis of their Parameter Specifications. We

---

3.1 L: Know anything about the TELNET SUBSYS? Go ahead.

4.1 O: Try me.

5.1 L: I just connected to [computer site name 1] via TELNET,
5.2 and tried the DIVERT.OUTPUT.STREAM.TO.FILE command.
5.3 Strange things happened. Esp., my TELNET typescript is
5.4 "busy". Go ahead.

6.1 O: TELNET.TYPESCRIPT will always be busy until you do a RESET,
6.2 but when you do that, be careful not to EXP, since that
6.3 is a temporary file. Go ahead.

7.1 L: I see . . . it's not enough for me just to do a DISCONNECT?
7.2 Go ahead.

8.1 O: Correct, is that the only problem?

9.1 L: No. Does the DIVERT.OUTPUT.STREAM.TO.FILE work?
Must the file exist
9.2 before I divert to it? Will the output also come to my TTY?
9.3 Go ahead.

[eight more turns occur in this interaction]

After this dialogue is opened in turns 1 and 2, the question in turn 3 is interpreted by the Dialogue-Game model as a bid to engage in the HELPING DG, since it can be seen as an attempt to establish the Operator as fitting the HELPER role in relation to the TASK of using the TELNET SUBSYS. In this case, the Linker is probing for the Operator's knowledge, to see whether he fits that specification of the HELPER role. Once this DG bid is accepted (turn 4), the Linker pursues in turn 5 the goals specified in the first two Components of the DG, first setting up a context in 5.1 and 5.2, then describing in 5.3 a violation of his expectations. Once these Component goals are achieved, the Operator pursues in turn 6 the goal specified in the third Component of the DG. Finally the Operator bids a termination to the overall HELPING DG in turn 8, which in this dialogue is rejected by L, since he seeks additional help pursued in the remainder of the dialogue not shown here.

Although this has been a very sketchy view of how the HELPING Dialogue-Game is involved in comprehension, we will present a more detailed view later. However, even at this level of detail, there are several points of interest.

First, notice that there is an interaction involved, turns 3 and 4, just to get the HELPING DG going. These two turns constitute themselves a simpler Dialogue-Game, called INFO-SEEKing:

The Parameter Specifications are:

>(*DELIVERER KNOWS NEWS*)
>(*S21:(RECIPIENT KNOWS NEWS) NOT*)
>(*RECIPIENT WANTS S21*)
>(*DELIVERER WANTS (DELIVERER KNOWS S411:(RECIPIENT ASSESSMENT-OF NEWS))*)]

The Components are:

>((*DELIVERER WANTS (RECIPIENT AWARE NEWS*))
  THEN
  (*RECIPIENT WANTS (DELIVERER AWARE S411*)))]

Thus, Announcements are distinguished here from the simple delivery of news because of the second "assessment" Component. A simple example of this kind of announcement is given by Terasaki (1976):

    1 D: Guess what-I haven't had a drink for eight days now.
    2 R: Fan-tas-tic!

The first turn delivers the report of the news, and the second consists of R's assessment of it.

Terasaki also found extensive uses of preannouncement sequences, similar to the "pre" sequences mentioned previously. A small example of such a "pre" occurs in the example above: "Guess what." "Many "pre" sequences are more extensive, often spanning several turns. But most of the examples given in her analysis can be seen as Dialogue-Games used to initiate the ANNOUNCING DG.

None of the instances of announcements given in the appendix of Terasaki's paper deal with task-oriented interaction, in which the participants are consciously involved in solving some problem. Yet she has found regularities in these interactions that fit directly into the Dialogue-Games model. This is evidence that Dialogue-Games are characteristic of language use in general, rather than artifacts of specialized task-oriented interaction.

Dialogue-Game Processing

In this section we describe the five stages of dialogue assimilation by the Dialogue-Game model and detail the involvement of Dialogue-Games with each stage: (1) nomination, (2) recognition, (3) instantiation, (4) conduct, and (5) termination. Our description of the model should be viewed as representing the changing cognitive state of one of the participants, throughout the course of the dialogue. The Dialogue-Game model consists of a long-term memory (LTM), a workspace (WS), and a set of Processors that modify the contents of WS, contingent upon the contents of LTM and WS. LTM contains a representation of the knowledge that the particular dialogue participant being modeled brings to

can tell whether a question is a "probe" question or a real question if we know or can infer that the asker already knows the information being asked about. The comprehension of such a question within the Dialogue-Game model uses the Parameter Specifications to determine which of these Dialogue-Games to evoke.

Each Dialogue-Game can be seen as a problem-solving operator, selected to accomplish some given high-level goal (represented in the Parameter Specifications), and then specifying (through its Components) a set of subgoals to pursue. Given that human problem solving is often top-down and depth-first in its pursuit of goals (Newell & Simon, 1972), we would expect to see nested Dialogue-Games. And since the topic content is a Parameter of Dialogue-Games, we would expect to see topics to be themselves nested. This topic structure occurs in most of the dialogues we have analyzed for topic (Mann, Carlisle, Moore, & Levin, 1977), and has been found by others analyzing dialogues (Deutsch, 1974).

However, the Dialogue-Game model by no means *requires* strict nesting. The Processors of the Dialogue-Game model run concurrently and semiautonomously, so that multiple peer goals can be pursued simultaneously if they do not conflict. And in fact, in some dialogues that we have analyzed, strict nesting is violated, with the dialogue participants switching among several independent topics. For example, in one section of the Apollo-13 air-to-ground voice transcript, the Lunar Module Pilot discusses with the Capsule Communicator on the ground his meal, while discussions of the availability of water and an ongoing report of an instrument's reading were suspended, being resumed afterward without reintroduction. The topic of "water availability" started before the discussion of the instrument's reading, and also stopped before it stopped, thus giving a nonnesting topic structure.

Dialogue-Games in Non-Task-Oriented Dialogues

So far, most of the naturally occurring dialogues we have studied have been task oriented, with the participants consciously involved in solving some problem. Are the Dialogue-Game structures, with the associated goal oriented view of language, restricted to this special use of language?

Terasaki (1976) has analyzed a body of non-task-oriented dialogues, within the sociolinguistic viewpoint (cf. Sacks, Schegloff, & Jefferson, 1974). Focusing on the ways in which people announce news to other people, Terasaki found regularities very similar to those represented by the Dialogue-Games model. Although phrased in different terms, much of the structure she found can be represented as an ANNOUNCING Dialogue-Game:

DEFINEDG (ANNOUNCING)

The Parameters are:

>*DELIVERER RECIPIENT NEWS*

the dialogue before it starts. This includes knowledge about the world, relevant objects, processes, concepts, the cognitive state of his partner in dialogue, rules of inference and evidence, words and their semantic representation, case frames for verbs and predicates and, of course, the multrum language structures, the Dialogue-Games.

WS is the volatile short-term memory of the model, containing all the partial and temporary results of processing. The contents of WS at any moment represent the model's state of comprehension and focus at that point. The Processors are autonomous specialists, operating independently and in parallel, to modify the entities in WS (called "activations"). These Processors are also influenced by the contents of WS, as well as by the knowledge in LTM. Thus, WS is the place in which these concurrently operating Processors interact with each other. This anarchistic control structure resembles that of the HEARSAY system (Erman, Fennell, Lesser, & Reddy, 1973).

Nomination. When dialogue participants propose a new type of interaction, they do not consistently use any single word or phrase to name the desired type of interaction. Thus we cannot determine which Dialogue-Game(s) represent the dialogue type, through a simple invocation by name (or any other preknown collection of words or phrases). Instead the type of dialogue is communicated by attempts to establish various entities as the values of the Parameters of the desired Dialogue-Game. Thus, an utterance which is comprehended as associating an entity (a person or a concept) with a Parameter of a Dialogue-Game suggests that Dialogue-Game as a possibility for nomination.

The Dialogue-Game model has two ways in which these nominations of new Dialogue-Games occur. One of the Processors of the model is a "spreading activation" (Collins & Loftus, 1975) system called Proteus (Levin, 1976). Proteus generates new activations in WS on the basis of relations in LTM of concepts that are already "active" (have associated activations in WS). Proteus brings into focus concepts related to those already active. A collection of activations in WS may lead to focusing on some aspect of a particular Dialogue-Game, in this sense "nominating" it as a possible new Dialogue-Game.

Match and Deduce are two of the model's Processors which operate in conjunction to generate new activations from existing ones, by means of finding and applying rule-like transformations. They operate through partial match and plausible inference techniques, and if they activate Parameters, then the Dialogue-Game that contains those Parameters becomes nominated as a candidate Dialogue-Game. Match and Deduce operate together as a kind of production system (cf. Newell, 1973).

For example, from the input utterance:

"L: I tried to send a message to P at S and it didn't go."

the following two sequences of associations and inferences would result:

(1a) L tried to X.
(2a) L wanted to X.
(3a) L wants to X.
(4a) HELPEE wants to do TASK.

(1b) It didn't go.
(2b) What L tried to do didn't work.
(3b) X didn't work.
(4b) L can't X.
(5b) L didn't know how to X.
(6b) HELPEE doesn't know how to do TASK.

(Where: L = HELPEE and X = do TASK = send a message to P at S.) At this point, (4a) and (6b), since they are both Parameter Specifications for the HELP-ING DG, cause the model to activate this Dialogue-Game, nominating it as an organizing structure for the dialogue being initiated.

Recognition. The Processors described so far are reasonably unselective and may activate a number of possible Dialogue-Games, some of which may be mutually incompatible or otherwise inappropriate. There is a Processor called the Dialogue-Game Processor, which investigates each of the nominated Dialogue-Games, verifying inferences based on the Parameter Specifications and eliminating those Dialogue-Games for which one or more Specifications are contradicted.

A second mechanism (part of Proteus) identifies those activations which are incompatible and sets about accumulating evidence in support of a decision to accept one and delete the rest from the WS.

For example, suppose the utterance:

How do I get RUNOFF to work?

leads to the nomination of two DGs:

INFO-SEEK DG (person asking question wants to know answer)

and

INFO-PROBE DG (person asking question wants to know if other knows answer)

These two Dialogue-Games have a lot in common but differ in one crucial aspect: In the INFO-SEEK DG, the questioner *does not* know the answer to the question, while in the INFO-PROBE DG he *does*. These two predicates are represented in the Parameter Specifications of the two Dialogue-Games, and upon the nomination of these Dialogue-Games, are discovered to be contradictory. Proteus represents this discovery with a structure which has the effect of eliminating from WS the conflicting Dialogue-Game for which there is the least

the goals described in the Parameter Specifications which were held by the participants prior to the evocation of the Dialogue-Game.

In the case of the HELPING DG, the goals in the "diagnostic" phase are that the HELPEE describe a sequence of related, unexceptional events leading up to a failure of his expectations. These model the state of the HELPER as he assimilates this initial part of the dialogue, both in that he knows how the HELPEE is attempting to describe his problem, and also that the HELPER knows when this phase is past, and the time has come (the "treatment" phase) for him to provide the help which has been implicitly requested.

Termination. The processes described above model the identification and pursuit of Dialogue-Games. How, then, are they terminated? As we said previously, the Parameter Specifications represent those aspects of dialogues that are constant over that particular type of dialogue. The Dialogue-Game model pushes this a step further in representing that the dialogue type continues *only as long as* the Parameter Specifications are perceived to hold by both participants. Whenever any predicate in the Specification ceases to hold, then the model predicts the impending termination of this Dialogue-Game.

For example, if the HELPEE no longer wants to perform the TASK (either by accomplishing it or by abandoning that goal), then the HELPING DG terminates. If the HELPER becomes unwilling to give help, or discovers that he is unable, then the HELPING DG also terminates.

DIALOGUE-GAMES AND COMPREHENSION ISSUES

Now that we've introduced the Dialogue-Game model, with representations for several Dialogue-Games and a description of the Processors for using them in comprehension, let us consider again some of the issues addressed by this model.

What are the functions served by these multisentential structures? In some ways, adding levels of structure just seems to complicate the comprehension process. However, the Dialogue-Game structures add a number of important characteristics to a comprehension model. Given that a particular Dialogue-Game has been identified, the number of utterances that have to be generated to successfully communicate is reduced—thus Dialogue-Games allow for more abbreviated communication. Conversely, a fewer number of utterances have to be comprehended to understand sufficiently what is being communicated, thus giving the comprehension model the ability to function when given "noisy" input, as is the case of most naturally occurring dialogue. In general, multisentential structures such as Dialogue-Games allow the comprehension processes to generate expectation of what will occur, which can be used by lower-level comprehension processes to resolve ambiguities. Some of the earlier comprehension models had a problem with the unlimited, undirected inferences that the model could make. For example, the inference part (Rieger, 1975b) of the

supporting evidence. Such support might be, for example, either the knowledge that the speaker is the hearer's teacher or that he is a novice programmer (which would lend support for the choice of the INFO-PROBE DG or INFO-SEEK DG, respectively). Through these processes, the number of candidate Dialogue-Games is reduced until those remaining are compatible with each other and the knowledge currently in WS.

Instantiation. Once a proposed Dialogue-Game has successfully survived the filtering processes described above, it is then instantiated by the Dialogue-Game Processor. Those Parameter Specifications not previously known (represented in the WS) are established in the WS as new inferred knowledge about the Parameters. It is through these instantiation processes that a large part of the implicit communication between participants of the dialogue is modeled.

To illustrate this, suppose that the following are represented in WS (i.e., known):

SPEAKER does not know how to do a TASK.
SPEAKER wants to know how to do that TASK.
SPEAKER wants to do the TASK.

This would, presumably, be adequate to nominate the HELPING DG. In the process of instantiating this Dialogue-Game, the following predicates, derived from the Parameter Specifications, would be added to WS:

SPEAKER believes HEARER knows how to do TASK.
SPEAKER believes HEARER is able to tell him how to do TASK.
SPEAKER believes HEARER is willing to tell him how to do TASK.
SPEAKER wants HEARER to tell him how to do TASK.
SPEAKER expects HEARER to tell him how to do TASK.

The model predicts that these predicates are implicitly communicated by an utterance which succeeds in instantiating the HELPING DG. This would correspond to a dialogue in which "I can't get this thing to work" is taken to be a request for help (which on the surface it is not).

Conduct. Once a Dialogue-Game is instantiated, the Dialogue-Games Processor is guided by its Components in comprehending the rest of the dialogue. For the speaker, these goals guide what he is next to say; for the hearer, these provide expectations for the functions to be served by the speaker's next utterances.

As we will see in more detail later, these "tactical" goals are central to our theory of language: an utterance is not deemed to be comprehended until some consequence of it is seen as serving a goal imputed to the speaker. Furthermore, although the goals specified in the Components are active only within the conduct of a particular DG, they are so constituted that their achievement satisfies

MARGIE system (Schank, Goldman, Rieger, & Riesbeck, 1975) was faced with this problem. The Dialogue-Game model uses the satisfaction of these expectations as a way of stopping the otherwise unlimited amount of inference processing.

The Dialogue-Game structures provide a basis for directing inferences in a particular direction. As a part of the larger theoretical view of language as a problem solving mechanism (Moore, Levin, & Mann, 1977), Dialogue-Games provide the knowledge to focus the comprehension process in the direction of determining what goals the speaker is pursuing by saying each utterance.

A Goal-Oriented View of Language

The usual approaches to language comprehension treat the problem as one of decoding the words of the given utterances, building some abstract representation that encompasses the surface words. Current language comprehension systems build a representation of what has been called the "propositional" content of the utterances processed. Recently, philosophers of language (Austin, 1962; Searle, 1969; Grice, 1975) have focused on the functional aspects of language. People use language not merely to convey information, but also to make promises, to give orders, to do things beyond the scope of the propositional content of what they say.

Our approach to language builds upon this functional view. When attempting to understand people's behavior, it has been fruitful to view them as goal pursuing organisms. This approach dominates the studies of human problem solving (Newell & Simon, 1972). We have extended this view to the study of human language behavior. In this view, people use language as a way of pursuing goals that they currently hold. When a person generates an utterance, the choice of what to say and who to say it to is primarily determined by how likely the utterance is to further goals of the speaker if directed toward the particular other person.

Inherent in the Dialogue-Game model is a Meta-goal of comprehension: *To comprehend an utterance, find some previously known goal of the speaker which this utterance can be seen as furthering.* This Comprehension Meta-goal is used in the model in two different ways to handle the problem that language comprehension systems have with the explosion of possible inferences. Given a powerful inference mechanism and a large database, a language comprehension system can make an unbounded set of inferences about a given utterance.

The first way in which the new goal-oriented view of language helps solve this problem is that it suggests a "Stopping Rule" for Comprehension: *Continue processing an utterance until the system infers that the utterance serves a goal that is known to be held by the speaker.*[3] In some cases, this Stopping Rule will

be satisfied relatively soon, so only a minimal amount of processing will have to be spent in comprehending the given utterance. In other cases, if a goal for the utterance is not immediately obvious, then processing will continue until one is found, serving as some more indirect use of language.

The Meta-goal of comprehension also helps limit the explosion of inferences by providing a focus for comprehension processing, favoring inferences which look for possible goals over other inferences. This focusing of effort is built into the Dialogue-Games model, since the Dialogue-Games themselves serve to concentrate processing on goal-oriented aspects. Knowledge of participant goals is a central part of the Dialogue-Games, and the processing flows through these goals, activating other goals in turn. These multiutterance knowledge structures serve as a systematic basis for generating likely goals and subgoals for the speaker. Given the context of an interconnected set of goals (many of which were generated by Dialogue-Games), then it is much easier to find a goal that a given utterance can be inferred as serving.

Indirect Uses of Language

As has been pointed out by the philosophers of language (Austin, 1962; Searle, 1969, 1975), not only do people do things with words, but they also do things with words *indirectly*. People make requests with declarative statements, give orders with interrogative statements, make promises with assertions, etc. For example, in one of our Link dialogues, the following interaction occurs:

L: Do you know the system clock is an hour fast?
O: Thanks. I didn't reset it.

Although phrased as a question, the Linker's utterance is functioning instead as an announcement to the Operator. If the Operator were to comprehend only the direct usage of the Linker's statement, the Linker would be surprised and either upset, or perhaps amused ("O: Could you hum a few bars?"). Similarly, in another Link dialogue:

L: We would like to unarchive tapes 1120 and 1121. . . .
O: OK but you'll have to give me those names again. . . .

the declarative statement by L is interpreted as a request for action by the Operator, rather than simply as a direct assertion by the Linker of his likes or dislikes.

Currently, the best model of how these indirect uses of language function is Speech Act Theory (Searle, 1969; Grice, 1975). Within this theory, utterances are seen as having both a propositional component and a speech act component. The propositional part encompasses the reference and predication aspects that theories of language have concentrated on in the past. The speech act component of an utterance specifies how the utterance is being *used* by the speaker—to declare, to inquire, to promise, to order, to suggest, etc. Speech acts have felicity conditions, which must hold for the act to be performed sincerely. The indirect

---

[3]This "Stopping Rule" for comprehension was originated by William C. Mann, and further developed in our discussions with him.

However, Speech Acts are unilateral actions, **while Dialogue-Games are bilateral.** A Dialogue-Game by definition involves an interaction between two people, and encompasses multiple utterances and turns of a dialogue. Speech acts generally refer to a single utterance. Much of the complexity of existing Speech Act theory, with its proliferation of types of Speech Acts, can be simplified by reconceptualizing Speech Acts as very simple and few in number, operating within the framework of multiutterance structures such as Dialogue-Games. This modified view of Speech Act theory is described by Heringer (1977).

SUMMARY

We have presented here a model for Dialogue-Games—knowledge structures spanning multiple utterances, capturing common knowledge about language and how it is used to achieve goals. A number of representations for particular types of interaction have been described, based on our analyses of naturally occurring dialogues. These structures, along with the set of processes outlined here for using them in comprehension, have proven valuable for dealing with some previously puzzling problems in studies of human language use, including ways in which language can be used indirectly. The Dialogue-Games model illustrates the utility of a goal-oriented view of language, a promising new approach to the study of language.

ACKNOWLEDGMENT

We would like to thank William C. Mann for his many contributions to the ideas described here.

REFERENCES

Austin, J. L., *How to do things with words*. Cambridge, Mass.: Harvard University Press, 1962.
Bartlett, F. C. *Remembering*. Cambridge, England: Cambridge University Press, 1932.
Bransford, J. D., & Johnson, M. K. Considerations of some problems of comprehension. In W. G. Chase (Ed.), *Visual information processing*. New York: Academic Press, 1973.
Chapanis, A. Interactive human communication. *Scientific American*, 1975, **232**, 36–42.
Charniak, E. Organization and inference in a frame-like system of common sense knowledge. In R. Schank & B. L. Nash-Webber (Eds.), *Theoretical issues in natural language processing*. Cambridge, Mass.: Bolt Beranek and Newman. 1975.
Clark, H. H., & Lucy, P. Understanding what is meant from what is said: A study in conversationally conveyed requests. *Journal of Verbal Learning and Verbal Behavior*, 1975, **14**, 56–72.
Collins, A. M., & Loftus, E. F. A spreading-activation theory of semantic processing. *Psychological Review*, 1975, **82**, 407–428.
Deutsch, B. G. The structure of task oriented dialogs. *Proceedings of IEEE Speech Symposium*. Pittsburgh, Pa.: Carnegie-Mellon University, 1974.
Erman, L. D., Fennell, R. D., Lesser, V. R., & Reddy, D. R. System organizations for speech understanding. *Proceedings of the third international joint conference on artificial intelligence*. Palo Alto, Calif.: Stanford University, 1973.

uses of language described previously are called "indirect speech acts" (Searle, 1975).

The Dialogue-Game model deals with these indirect uses of language in several ways. The most common case is the use of one Dialogue-Game interaction in order to initiate another DG. The example given at the very beginning by "Do you have a match?" is a case of this "initiation indirect speech." These indirect uses have the function of establishing the Parameters of the second DG. Examples of indirect requests for information are:

Assertions of the speaker's own lack of knowledge
Questions about the other person's knowledge
Assertions about the speaker's own desires for the information
Questions about the other person's willingness to supply the information

Any utterance which will serve to establish the Parameters of the Info-seek DG can serve as an indirect request.

A second indirect use of language is that intended to terminate an ongoing Dialogue-Game. A Dialogue-Game can continue only as long as its Parameter Specifications are known to hold. So any utterance which establishes that some Parameter Specification of an ongoing DG no longer holds will have the indirect function of terminating that Dialogue-Game. So a statement in a Link dialogue:

L: Thank you for solving my problem. . . .

not only serves as a thanks-giving statement, but also as a bid for termination of the ongoing HELPING DG, since it makes it clear to the Operator that the Linker has become *able* to do the Task. These "termination indirect speech" utterances are often used to break off an interaction—for instance, the traditional "Its getting late and we really must go" serves not only as an assertion of fact and obligation, but also indirectly as a bid for terminating a visit.

A third, and somewhat less obvious, indirect use of language encompassed by the Dialogue-Game model is the set of "pursuit indirect speech" utterances. These are utterances which fulfill one Component goal of an ongoing Dialogue-Game, thus generating an expectation that the next Component will be pursued. For example, in the HELPING DG, an utterance which accomplishes the first stage of diagnosing the problem will generate the expectation that the Helper communicate to the Helpee a solution for the problem. Thus, the utterance serves indirectly as a request for the needed information.

Dialogue-Games and Speech Acts

There are a number of similarities between Dialogue-Games and Speech Acts as they are currently conceived. They both specify ways of interpreting individual utterances, depending both on the words of the utterance and on the context in which the utterance occurs. They both depend on knowledge of the dialogue participants, especially in relation to the content topic of the interaction.

Shatz, M., & Gelman, R. The development of communication skills: Modifications in the speech of young children as a function of listener. *Monographs of the Society for Research in Child Development*, 1973, **9**, 77–110.

Terasaki, A. K. Pre-announcement sequences in conversation (Tech. Rep. 99). Irvine, Calif.: School of Social Sciences, University of California, 1976.

Thorndyke, P. W. Cognitive structures in comprehension and memory of narrative discourse. *Cognitive Psychology*, 1977, **9**, 77–110.

Wittgenstein, L. *Philosophical investigations* (3rd ed.). New York: Macmillan, 1958.

Gordon, D., & Lakoff, G. Conversational postulates. *Papers from the Seventh Regional Meeting*. Chicago Linguistic Society, 1971.

Grice, H. P. Logic and conversation. In P. Cole & J. L. Morgan (Eds.), *Syntax and semantics*. New York: Academic Press, 1975.

Heringer, J. T. Felicity conditions as discourse constraints. Paper in preparation, Marina del Rey, Calif.: Information Sciences Institute, 1977.

Labov, W., & Fanshel, D. *Therapeutic discourse: Psychotherapy as conversation*. Draft copy, 1974.

Levin, J. A. Proteus: An activation framework for cognitive process models. Unpublished doctoral dissertation, University of Calif., San Diego, 1976.

Levin, J. A., & Moore, J. A. Dialogue-Games: A process model of natural language interaction. *Proceedings of the AISB Summer Conference*. Edinburgh, Scotland: University of Edinburgh, 1976.

Mann, W. C., Carlisle, J. H., Moore, J. A., & Levin, J. A. An assessment of reliability of dialogue annotation instructions (ISI/RR-77-54). Marina del Rey, Calif.: Information Sciences Institute, 1977.

Mann, W. C., Moore, J. A., Levin, J. A., & Carlisle, J. H. Observation methods for human dialogue (ISI/RR-75-33). Marina del Rey, Calif.: Information Sciences Institute, 1975.

Minsky, M. A framework for representing knowledge. In P. H. Winston (Ed.), *The psychology of computer vision*. New York: McGraw-Hill, 1975.

Moore, J. A., Levin, J. A., & Mann, W. C. A goal-oriented model of natural language interaction (ISI/RR-77-52). Marina del Rey, Calif.: Information Sciences Institute, 1977.

Newell, A. Production systems: Models of control structures. In W. G. Chase (Ed.), *Visual information processing*. New York: Academic Press, 1973.

Newell, A., & Simon, H. A. *Human problem solving*. Englewood Cliffs, N.J.: Prentice-Hall, 1972.

Norman, D. A., Rumelhart, D. E., & the LNR Research Group. *Explorations in cognition*. San Francisco: Freeman, 1975.

Rieger, C. The commonsense algorithm as a basis for computer models of human memory, inference, belief and contextual language comprehension. In R. Schank & B. L. Nash-Webber (Eds.), *Theoretical issues in natural language processing*. Cambridge, Mass.: Bolt Beranek and Newman, 1975. (a)

Rieger, C. Conceptual memory. In R. Schank (Ed.), *Conceptual information processing*. Amsterdam: North-Holland, 1975. (b)

Rosenthal, R. *The volunteer subject*. New York: Wiley, 1974.

Rumelhart, D. E. Notes on a schema for stories. In D. G. Bobrow & A. Collins (Eds.), *Representation and understanding: Studies in cognitive science*. New York: Academic Press, 1975.

Sacks, H., Schegloff, E. A., & Jefferson, G. A simplest systematics for the organization of turn-taking for conversation. *Language*, 1974, **50**, 696–735.

Schank, R. C., & Abelson, R. P. Scripts, plans and knowledge. *Proceedings of the fourth international joint conference on artificial intelligence*. Tbilisi, USSR, 1975.

Schank, R. C., Goldman, N. M., Rieger, C. J., & Riesbeck, C. K. Inference and paraphrase by computer. *Journal of the Association for Computing Machinery*, 1975, **22**, 309–328.

Schegloff, E. Sequencing in conversational openings. *American Anthropologist*, 1968, **70**, 1075–1095.

Searle, J. R. *Speech acts: An essay in the philosophy of language*. Cambridge, England: Cambridge University Press, 1969.

Searle, J. R. Indirect speech acts. In P. Cole & J. L. Morgan (Eds.), *Syntax and semantics*. New York: Academic Press, 1975.

Shatz, M. How young children respond to language: Procedures for answering. *Papers and reports on child language development*. Palo Alto, Calif.: Stanford University, 1975.

Concurrent Programming Using Actors: Exploiting Large-Scale Parallelism

Gul Agha
Carl Hewitt

The Artificial Intelligence Laboratory
Massachusetts Institute of Technology
Cambridge, Massachusetts 02139

June 8, 1986

Abstract

We argue that the ability to model shared objects with changing local states, dynamic reconfigurability, and inherent parallelism are desirable properties of any model of concurrency. The *actor model* addresses these issues in a uniform framework. This paper briefly describes the concurrent programming language *Act3* and the principles that have guided its development. *Act3* advances the state of the art in programming languages by combining the advantages of object-oriented programming with those of functional programming. We also discuss considerations relevant to large-scale parallelism in the context of *open systems*, and define an abstract model which establishes the equivalence of systems defined by actor programs.

The report describes research done at the Artificial Intelligence Laboratory of the Massachusetts Institute of Technology. Support for the laboratory's artificial intelligence research is provided in part by the the System Development Foundation and in part by the Advanced Research Projects Agency of the Department of Defense under Office of Naval Research contract N00014-80-C-0505. The authors acknowledge helpful comments from Fanya Montalvo, Carl Manning and Tom Reinhardt.

1 Background

The theory of concurrent programming languages has been an exciting area of research in the last decade. Although no consensus has emerged on a single model of concurrency, many advances have been made in the development of various contending models. There have also been some consistent paradigm shifts in the approach to concurrency; an interesting discussion of such paradigm shifts may be found in [Pratt 83].

The actor model of computation has developed contemporaneously in the last decade along with other models based on Petri Nets, the λ-calculus, and communicating sequential processes. There has been a great deal of useful cross fertilization between the various schools of thought in addressing the very difficult issues of concurrent systems. Over the years Hoare, Kahn, MacQueen, Milner, Petri, Plotkin, and Pratt, have provided fruitful interaction on the development of the actor model.

Landin [65] first showed how *Algol 60* programs could be represented in applicative-order λ-calculus. Kahn and MacQueen [77] developed this area further by expanding on the construct of *streams* which captured functional systems. Brock and Ackerman [77] extended the Kahn-MacQueen model with the addition of inter-stream ordering information in order to make it more suitable for concurrent computation. Pratt [82] generalized the functional model by developing a theory of processes in terms of sets of partially ordered multisets (*pomsets*) of events. Each pomset in Pratt's *Process Model* represents a *trace* of events. Pratt's model satisfies several properties desirable in any model of concurrent computation. For example, the model does not assume the existence of global states: a trace is only a partial order of events. Thus the model is compatible with the laws of parallel processing formulated in [Hewitt and Baker 77] and shown to be consistent in [Clinger 81].

On the practical side, McCarthy [59] first made functional programming available by developing LISP. The standard dialect of LISP now incorporates lexical scoping and closures which makes the semantics simpler and programming modular [Steele, *et al* 84]. *Act3* generalizes the lexical scoping and upward closures of LISP in the context of parallel systems.

Hoare [78] proposed a language for concurrency, called *CSP*, based on sequential processes. *CSP*, like *Act3*, enhances modularity by not permitting any shared variable between processes; instead, communication is the primitive by which processes may affect each other. At a more theoretical level, Milner [80] has proposed the *Calculus of Concurrent Systems (CCS)*.

One of the nice properties of *CCS* is its elegant algebraic operations. In both *CSP* and *CCS*, communication is synchronous and resembles a handshake. In contradistinction, the actor model postulates the existence of a mail system which buffers communication.

The plan of this paper is as follows: the first section outlines the actor model. The second section describes the *Act3* language. The final section discusses the general principles of open systems and there relation to the actor model.

2 The Actor Model

In this section we motivate the primitives of the actor model. We will outline the basic issues and describe a set of minimal constructs necessary for an actor language.

2.1 Foundational Issues

A number of difficult open problems and foundational issues in the design of programming languages for concurrent systems merit attention. We consider the following three significant:

1. **Shared Resources.** The programming model must deal with the problem of shared resources which may change their internal state. A simple example of such an object in a concurrent environment is a shared bank account. Purely functional systems, unlike object-based systems, are incapable of implementing such objects [Hewitt, *et al* 84].

2. **Dynamic Reconfigurability.** The programming model must deal with the creation of new objects in the evolution of the system. In particular, to accommodate the creation of new objects, there must be a mechanism for communicating the existence of such new objects (or processes) to already existing ones. Thus when a bank creates a new account, it should be able to inform its book-keeping process of the existence of such an account. Since the interconnection topology of processes is static in systems such as *CSP* and *dataflow* [Brock 83], this requirement is necessarily violated these systems.

3. **Inherent Parallelism.** The programming model should exhibit inherent parallelism in the sense that the amount of available concurrency should be clear from the structure of programs. It should not

be necessary to do extensive reasoning to uncover implicit parallelism that is hidden by inappropriate language constructs. In particular, the assignment command is a bottleneck inherited from the von Neumann architecture. Assignment commands tie the statements in the body of a code in such a way that only through flow analysis is it possible to determine which statements can be executed concurrently. Functional Programming has the advantage of being inherently parallel because it allows the possibility of concurrent execution of all subexpressions in a program [Backus 78].

The object-based and functional, λ-calculus-based languages represent two of the most important schools of thought in programming language theory today. As the above discussion suggests, both have certain advantages. *Act3* attempts to integrate both in a manner that preserves some of their attractive features.

2.2 Basic Constructs

The actor abstraction has been developed to exploit message-passing as a basis for concurrent computation [Hewitt 77; Hewitt and Baker 77]. The actor construct has been formalized by providing a mathematical definition for the behavior of an actor system [Agha 85]. Essentially, an actor is a computational agent which carries out its actions in response to processing a communication. The actions it may perform are:

- Send communications to itself or to other actors.

- Create more actors.

- Specify the *replacement behavior.*

In order to send a communication, the sender must specify a mail address, called the *target.* The *mail system* buffers the communication until it can be delivered to the target. However, the order in which the communications are delivered is nondeterministic. The buffering of communications has the consequence that actor languages support recursion. In languages relying on synchronous communication, any recursive procedure immediately leads to *deadlock* [Hewitt, *et al* 1984] [Agha 1985].

All actors have their own (unique) mail addresses which may be communicated to other actors just as any other value. Thus mail addresses provide a simple mechanism for *dynamically reconfiguring* a system of actors. The only way to affect the behavior of an actor is to send it a communication. When an actor accepts a communication, it carries out the actions specified by its behavior; one of these actions is to specify a *replacement actor* which will then accept the next communication received at the mail address.

Two important observations need to be made about replacement. First, replacement implements local state change while preserving *referential transparency* of the identifiers used in a program. An identifier for an object always denotes that object although the behavior associated with the object may be subject to change. In particular, the code for an actor does <u>not</u> contain spurious variables to which different values are assigned (see [Stoy 77] for a thorough discussion of referential transparency). Second, since the computation of a replacement actor is an action which may be carried out concurrently with other actions performed by an actor, the replacement process is intrinsically concurrent. The replacement actor <u>cannot</u> affect the behavior of the replaced actor.

The net result of these properties of replacement actors is that computation in actor systems can be speeded-up by *pipelining* the actions to be performed. As soon as the replacement actor has been computed, the next communication can be processed even as other actions implied by the current communication are still being carried out. In actor-based architectures, the only constraints on the speed of execution stem from the logical dependencies in the computation and the limitations imposed by the hardware resources. In von Neumann architectures, the data dependencies caused by assignments to a global store restrict the degree of pipelining (in the form of instruction pre-fetching) that can be realized [Hwang and Briggs 84].

All actors in a system carry out their actions concurrently. In particular, this has the implication that message-passing can be used to spawn concurrency: An actor, in response to a communication, may send several communications to other actors. The creation of new actors also increases the amount of parallelism feasible in a system. Specifically, *continuations* can be incorporated as first-class objects. The dynamic creation of *customers* in actor systems (discussed later) provides a parallel analogue to such continuations.

2.3 Transitions on Configurations

To describe an actor system, we need to specify several components. In particular, we must specify the behaviors associated with the mail addresses internal to the system. This is done by specifying a *local states function* which basically gives us the behavior of each mail address (i.e., its response to the next communication it receives). We must also specify the unprocessed communications together with their targets. The communication and target pairs are referred to as *tasks*. A *configuration* is an instantaneous snapshot of an actor system from some viewpoint. Each configuration has the following parts:

- A *local states function* which basically gives us the behavior of a mail address. The actors whose behaviors are specified by the local states function are elements of the *population*.

- A set of *unprocessed tasks* for communications which have been sent but not yet accepted.

- A subset of the population, called *receptionist* actors, which may receive communications from actors outside the configuration. The set of receptionists can not be mechanically determined from the local states function of a configuration: it must be specified using knowledge about the larger environment.

- A set of *external actors* whose behavior is not specified by the local states function, but to whom communications may be sent.

A fundamental transition relation on configurations can be defined by applying the behavior function of the target of some unprocessed task to the communication contained in that task (see the definition below). Given the nondeterminism in the *arrival order* of communications, this transition relation represents the different possible paths a computation may take. The processing of communications may, of course, overlap in time. We represent only the acceptance of a communication as an event. Different transition paths may be observed by different viewpoints, provided that these paths are consistent with each other (i.e. do not violate constraints such as causality).

Definition 1 Possible Transition. *Let c_1 and c_2 be two configurations. c_1 is said to have a possible transition to c_2 by processing a task τ, symbolically, $c_1 \xrightarrow{\tau} c_2$ if $\tau \in tasks(c_1)$, and furthermore, if α is the target of the task then the tasks in c_2 are*

$$tasks(c_2) = (tasks(c_1) - \{\tau\}) \cup T$$

where T is the set of tasks created by α in response to τ, and the actors in c_2 are

$$actors(c_2) = (actors(c_1) - \{\alpha\}) \cup A \cup \{\alpha'\}$$

where A are the actors created by α in response to τ and α' is the replacement specified by α. Note that α and α' have the same mail address.

In the actor model, the delivery of all communications is guaranteed. This form of fairness can be expressed by defining a second transition relation which is based on processing finite sets of tasks until a particular task is processed, instead of simply processing a single task [Agha 84]. A denotational semantics for actors can be defined in terms of the transition relations; this semantics maps actor programs into the initial configuration they define [Agha 85].

3 The Act3 Language

Act3 is an actor-based programming language which has been implemented on the *Apiary architecture*. The Apiary is a parallel architecture based on a network of Lisp machines and supports features such as dynamic load balancing, real-time garbage collection, and the mail system abstraction [Hewitt 80]. *Act3* is a descendant of *Act2* [Theriault 83] and is written in a LISP-based interface language called *Scripter*.

A program in *Act3* is a collection of behavior definitions and commands to create actors and send communications to them. A behavior definition consists of an identifier (by which the actor may be known), a list of the names of acquaintances, and a script (which defines the behavior of the actor in response to the communication it accepts). When an actor is created its acquaintances must be specified. For example, a bank-account actor may have an acquaintance representing its current balance.

When a communication is accepted by an actor, an environment is defined in which the script of the actor is to be executed. The commands in the script of an actor can be executed in parallel. Thus *Act3* differs fundamentally from programming languages based on communicating sequential processes since the commands in the body of such processes must be executed sequentially.

We will first provide the syntax for a kernel language, *Act*, and use it to explain the basic concepts of message-passing. We then discuss some extensions to *Act* which are provided in *Act3*. Finally, we illustrate these extensions by means of examples.

3.1 The Kernel Language Act

The language *Act* is a sufficient kernel for the *Act3* language: all constructs in the *Act3* language can be translated into *Act* [Agha 85]. Since there are so few constructs in *Act*, it will be easier to understand the primitives involved by studying *Act*. The acquaintance list in *Act* is specified by using identifiers which match a pattern. The pattern provides for freedom from *positional* correspondence when new actors are created. Patterns are used in pattern matching to bind identifiers, and authenticate and extract information from data structures. The simplest pattern is a *bind pattern* which literally binds the value of an identifier to the value of an expression in the current environment. We will not concern ourselves with other patterns here.

When an actor accepts a communication it is *pattern-matched* with the *communication handlers* in the actor's code and dispatched to the handler of the pattern it satisfies. The bindings for the communication list are extracted by the pattern matching as well. The syntax of behavior definitions in *Act* programs is given below.

```
⟨act program⟩ ::=
    ⟨behavior definition⟩* (⟨command⟩)*
⟨behavior definition⟩ ::=
    (define (id {(with identifier ⟨pattern⟩) }*)
        ⟨communication handler⟩*)
⟨communication handler⟩ ::=
    (Is-Communication ⟨pattern⟩ do ⟨command⟩*)
```

The syntax of commands to create actors and send communications is the same in actor definitions as their syntax at the program level. There are four kinds of commands; we describe these in turn. *send commands* are used to send communications. The syntax of the *send command* is the keyword *send* followed by two expressions: The two expressions are evaluated; the first expression must evaluate to a mail address while the second may have an arbitrary value. The result of the send command is to send the value of the second expression to the target specified by the first expression. *let commands* bind expressions to identifiers in the body of commands nested within their scope. In particular, *let commands* are used to bind the mail addresses of newly created actors. *new expressions* create new actors and return their mail address. A *new expression* is given by the keyword *new* followed by an identifier representing a behavior definition, and a list of acquaintances.

The *conditional command* provides a mechanism for branching, and the *become command* specifies the replacement actor. The expression in the *become command* may be a *new expression* in which case the actor becomes a forwarding actor to the actor created by the *new expression*; in this case the two actors are equivalent in a very strong sense. The expression can also be the mail address of an existing actor, in which case all communications sent to the replaced actor are forwarded to the existing actor.

```
⟨command⟩ ::= ⟨let command⟩ | ⟨conditional command⟩ |
              ⟨send command⟩ | ⟨become command⟩

⟨let command⟩ (let (⟨let binding⟩*) do ⟨command⟩*)

⟨conditional command⟩ ::= (if ⟨expression⟩
                              then do ⟨command⟩*)
                              else do ⟨command⟩*))

⟨send command⟩ ::= (send ⟨expression⟩ ⟨expression⟩)

⟨become command⟩ ::= (become ⟨expression⟩)
```

A Recursive Factorial. We first provide a simple factorial example to illustrate the use of message-passing in actors to implement control structures. The code makes the low level detail in the execution of an actor language explicit. We will subsequently provide some higher-level constructs which will make the expression of programs easier. The factorial actor creates *customers*, called FactCust, whose behavior is also given below. Note that the behavior of a factorial is *unserialized*, i.e, it is not history sensitive.

```
(define (Factorial())
  (Is-Communication (a doit (with customer ≡m)
                            (with number ≡n)) do
    (if (= n 0))
        (then (send m 1))
        (else (let (x = (new FactCust (with customer m)
                                      (with number n)))
                (send Factorial (a do (with customer x)
                                      (with number n-1)))))))))
```

```
(define (FactCust (with customer ≡m)
                  (with number ≡n))
  (Is-Communication (a number k) do
    (send m n*k)))
```

The acceptance of a communication containing an integer by Factorial causes n to be bound to the integer and concurrently for factorial to become "itself" so that it can immediately process another integer without any interaction with the processing of the integer it has just received. When the factorial actor processes a communication with a non-zero integer, *n*, it will:

- Create an actor whose behavior will be to multiply *n* with an integer it receives and send the reply to the mail address to which the factorial of *n* was to be sent.

- Send itself the "request" to evaluate the factorial of *n* − 1 and send the value to the customer it created.

The customer created by the factorial actor is also an independent actor. The work done to compute a factorial is conceptually distributed by the creation of the customer. In particular, this implies that computation can be speeded-up if several factorials are to be evaluated concurrently. In the case of the factorial, the same result can be obtained by multiple activations of a given function. However, the solution using multiple activations does not work if the behavior of an actor is serialized.

3.2   Functional Constructs

In this section we will develop some notation for representing expressions at a higher-level. *Act3* provides many such constructs which make *Act3* far more expressive than *Act*, although the two languages have the same expressive power. To allow functional programming without forcing the programmer to explicitly create the customers, *Act3* provides *call expressions* which automatically create a customer and include its mail address in the communication sent; the value of the *expression* is returned (in a message) to the customer created at the time of the call. The code below specifies a factorial actor in expressional terms. By comparing the code to that in the previous section, one can see how it is executed in an actor-based environment.

```
(define (call Factorial (with number ≡n))
  (if (= n 0)
    (then 1)
    (else (* n (call Factorial (with number n-1))))))
```

Parallel control structures can also be specified quite easily. For example, a parallel algorithm for evaluating the factorial function of *n* is by recursively subdividing the problem of computing the range product from 1 to *n*. We define an actor, RangeProduct, for recursively computing the range product in the above manner. The code for Rangeproduct is given below. Note that the One-Of construct provides a generalized conditional command: it dispatches on the value of the expressions (cf. the guarded command [Dijkstra 76]).

```
(define (call RangeProduct (with low ≡lo)
                           (with High ≡hi))
  (One-Of
    (if (= lo hi) lo)
    (if (> lo hi) 1)
    (if (< lo hi)
      (Let ((mid = (/ (+ lo hi) 2)))
        (* (call Rangeproduct (with low lo)
                              (with high mid))
           (call Rangeproduct (with low (+ mid 1))
                              (with high hi)))))))
```

The pipelining of the replacement actors implies that two calls to the RangeProduct actor are in fact equivalent to creating two actors which function concurrently. This equivalence follows from the unserialized nature of the behavior: In case the behavior is unserialized, the behavior of the replacement is known immediately and thus its computation is immediate; in particular, it can be computed even before a communication is received.

Act3 provides a number of other expressional constructs, such as delayed expressions and allows one to require *lazy* or *eager* evaluation strategies for expressions. Such evaluation strategies have been used in extensions of pure functional programming to model *history-sensitive* behavior [Henderson 80]. However, because these systems lack a mail address abstraction, the interconnection network topology of processes is entirely static.

3.3 Modelling Local-State Change

A problem with functional programming is the difficulty of dealing with shared objects which have changing local states. Some constructs, such as *delayed expressions* have been defined to model changing local states. However, the problem with these techniques is that they create expressional forms totally local to the caller and thus can not be used to represent shared objects. Actors permit a graceful implementation of shared objects with a changing local state. The example below shows the implementation of a bank account in *Act3*. A bank account is a canonical example of a shared object with a changing local state.

We use the keyword Is-Request to indicate a request communication is expected. A *request* communication comes with the mail address of the *customer* to which the *reply* is to be sent. The customer is used as the target of the reply. A *request* also specifies a mail address to which a *complaint* can be sent, should the request be unsuccessful. From a software point of view, providing independent targets for the complaint messages is extremely useful because it allows the error-handling to be separated from successfully completed transactions.

```
(define (Account (with Balance ≡b))
  (Is-Request (a Balance) do (reply b))
  (Is-Request (a Deposit (with Amount ≡a)) do
    (become (Account (with Balance (+ b a))))
    (reply (a Deposit-Receipt (with Amount a))))
  (Is-Request (a Withdrawal (with Amount ≡a)) do
    (if (> a b)
      (then do (complain (an Overdraft)))
      (else do
        (become (Account (with Balance (- b a))))
        (reply (a Withdrawal-Receipt (with Amount a)))))))
```

Note that the become command is pipelined so that a replacement is available as soon as the *become command* is executed. The commands for other actions are executed concurrently and do not affect the replacement actor which will be free to accept further communications.

3.4 Transactional Constructs

Analyzing the behavior of a typical program in terms of all the transitions it makes is not very feasible. In particular, the development of *debugging tools* and *resource management* techniques requires us to preserve the abstractions in the source programs. Because *actors* may represent shared objects, it is often critical that transitions relevant to independent computations be kept separate. For example, if the factorial actor we defined is asked to evaluate the factorial of −1, it will create an "infinite loop." Two observations should be made about such potentially infinite computations. First, any other requests to the factorial will not be affected because the guarantee of delivery means that communications related to those requests will be interleaved with the "infinite loop" generated by the −1 message. Second, in order to keep the performance of the system from degrading, we must assess costs for each "computation" independently; we can then cut-off those computations that we do not want to support indefinitely.

To formalize the notion of a "computation," we define the concept of *transactions*. Transactions are delineated using two specific kinds of communications, namely, *requests* and *replies*. A request, r_1, may trigger another request, say r_2; if the reply to r_2 also precedes the reply to r_1, then the second transaction is said to be *nested* within the first. Proper nesting of transactions allows simpler resource management schemes since resources can be allocated dynamically for the sub-transaction directly from the triggering transaction.

Transactions also permit the development of *debugging* tools that allow one to examine a computation at different levels of granularity [Manning 84]. Various constructs in *Act3* permit proper nesting of transactions; for example, requests may be buffered while simultaneously preserving the current state of a server using a construct called *enqueue*. The request is subsequently processed, when the server is free to do so, using a *dequeue* operation. Enqueue and dequeue are useful for programming servers such as those controlling a hard copy device; they guarantee continuous availability [Hewitt *et al* 1984].

Independent transactions may affect each other; requests may be sent to the same actor whose behavior is history-sensitive thus creating events which are shared between different transactions. Such intersection of events creates interesting problems for the dynamic allocation of resources and for debugging tools. Dynamic transaction delimitation remains an exciting area of research in the actor paradigm.

4 Open Systems

It is reasonable to expect that large-scale parallel systems will be composed of independently developed and maintained modules. Such systems will be open-ended and continually undergoing change [Hewitt and de Jong 85]. Actor languages are intended to provide linguistic support for such *open systems*. We will briefly outline some characteristics of open systems and describe how the actor model is relevant to the problem of open systems.

4.1 Characteristics of Open Systems

We list three important considerations which are relevant to any architecture supporting large-scale parallelism in open systems [Hewitt 85]. These considerations have model theoretic implications for an algebra used to characterize the behavior of actors:

- *Continuous Availability.* A system may receive communications from the external environment at any point in time. There is no closed-world hypothesis.

- *Modularity.* The inner workings of one subsystem are not available to the any other system; there is an arms-length relationship between subsystems. The behavior of a system must be characterized only in terms of its interaction with the outside.

- *Extensibility.* It is possible for a system to grow. In particular, it is possible to compose different systems in order to define larger systems.

Actors provide an ideal means of realizing open systems. In the section below, we outline a model which realizes the above characteristics and, at the same time, abstracts the internal events in an actor system. We thus address the problem of abstraction in the context of open system modelling.

4.2 A Calculus of Configurations

We have described two transition relations on configurations (see §2.3). These relations are, however, operational rather than extensional in nature. The requirements of modularity imply that an abstract characterization of the behavior of an actor system must be in terms of communications received from outside the system and those sent to the external actors. All communications sent by actors within a population, to other actors also within the population, are not observable from the outside.

In the denotational semantics of sequential programming languages, it is sufficient to represent a program by its input-output behavior, or more completely, as a map from an initial state to a final state (the so-called *history relation*). However, in any program involving concurrency and nondeterminism, the history relation is not a sufficient characterization. Specifically, when two systems with identical history relations are each composed with an identical system, the two resulting systems have different history relations [Brock and Ackerman 81]. The reason for this anomaly is the closed-world assumption inherent in the history relation: It ignores the possible interactions of the output with the input [Agha 85].

Instead, we represent the behavior of a system taking into account the fact that communications may be accepted from the outside at any point. There are three kinds of derivations from a configuration:

1. A configuration c is said to have a derivation to c' given an *input task* τ, symbolically, $c \xrightarrow{+\tau} c'$, if

$$states(c') = states(c)$$
$$tasks(c') = tasks(c) \cup \tau \wedge target(\tau) \in population(c)$$

where *states* represents the local states function (see §2.3), and *tasks* represents the tasks in a configuration. The receptionists remain the same but the external actors may now include any actors whose mail addresses have been communicated by the communication accepted.

2. A configuration c is said to have a derivation to c' producing an *output task* τ, symbolically, $c \xrightarrow{-\tau} c'$, if

$$states(c') = states(c)$$
$$tasks(c') = tasks(c) - \tau \wedge target(\tau) \notin population(c)$$

where the *states* and the *tasks* are as above, and "−" represents set theoretic difference. The external actors of c' are the same as those of c. The receptionists may now include all actors whose mail addresses have been communicated to the outside.

3. A configuration c has a *internal* or silent derivation to a configuration c', symbolically, $c \xrightarrow{\varrho} c'$, if it has a possible transition to c' for some task τ in c.

We can now build a calculus of configurations by defining operations such as composition, relabeling (which changes the mail addresses), restriction (which removes a receptionist), etc. We give the axioms of compositionality to illustrate the calculus of configurations.

Definition 2 Composition. *Let $c_1 \parallel c_2$ represent the (concurrent) composition of c_1 and c_2. Then we have the following rules of derivation about the composition:*

1. (a) *Let τ be a task whose target is in c_1, then*

$$\frac{c_1 \xrightarrow{+\tau} c_1', \; c_2 \xrightarrow{-\tau} c_2'}{c_1 \parallel c_2 \xrightarrow{\varrho} c_1' \parallel c_2'}$$

(b) *Let λ be any derivation (input, output, or internal), provided that if λ is an input or output derivation then its sender or target, respectively, is not an actor in c_1, then*

$$\frac{c_1 \xrightarrow{\lambda} c_1'}{c_1 \parallel c_2 \xrightarrow{\lambda} c_1' \parallel c_2}$$

2. *The above rules hold, mutatis mutandis, for $c_2 \parallel c_1$.*

The only behavior that can be observed in a system is represented by the "labels" on the derivations from its configurations. These represent the communications between a system and its external environment. Following Milner [80] we can define an *observation equivalence* relation on configurations. The definition relies on equality of all possible finite sequences of communications sent to or received from the external environment (ignoring all internal derivations). One way of formalizing observation equivalence is inductively:

Definition 3 Observation Equivalence. *Let c_1 and c_2 be any two tasks, μ be either an input or an output task, ϱ represent any arbitrary (finite) number of internal transitions, and $\xrightarrow{\varrho'\mu}$ represent a sequence of internal transitions followed by a μ transition, and furthermore $\approx_k$ be defined inductively as:*

1. $c_1 \approx_0 c_2$
2. $c_1 \approx_{k+1} c_2$ *if*

(a) $\forall \mu (if\ c_1 \overset{e'\mu}{\Longrightarrow} c'_1\ then\ \exists c'_2 (c_2 \overset{e'\mu}{\Longrightarrow} c'_2)\ \land\ c'_1 \approx_k c'_2)$

(b) $\forall \mu (if\ c_2 \overset{e'\mu}{\Longrightarrow} c'_2\ then\ \exists c'_1 (c_1 \overset{e'\mu}{\Longrightarrow} c'_1)\ \land\ c'_1 \approx_k c'_2)$

Now c_1 is said to be observationally equivalent to c_2, symbolically, $c_1 \approx c_2$, if $\forall k(c_1 \approx_k c_2)$.

The notion of observation equivalence allows one to distinguish between systems which behave differently in response to new tasks after they have sent some communication to an external actor. On the one hand, observation equivalence creates fewer equivalence classes than a history ordering on all events; such a relation retains too much information. On the other, observation equivalence distinguishes between more configurations than the history relation between inputs and outputs, which has been shown to not retain enough information about the behavior of the system.

We can characterize actor programs by the equivalence classes of initial configurations they define. Properties of actor system can be established in a framework not relying on a closed-world assumption, while at the same time providing an abstract representation of actor systems that does not rely on the internal details of a system's behavior.

5 Conclusions

Actor languages uniformly use message-passing to spawn concurrency and are inherently parallel. The mail system abstraction permits a high-level mechanism for achieving dynamic reconfigurability. The problem of shared resources with changing local state is dealt with by providing an object-oriented environment without the sequential bottle-neck caused by assignment commands. The behavior of an actor is defined in *Act3* by a script which can be abstractly represented as a mathematical function. It is our claim that *Act3* has the major advantages of object-based programming languages together with those of functional and applicative programming languages.

An actor language also provides a suitable basis for large-scale parallelism. Besides the ability to distribute the work required in the course of a computation, actor systems can be composed simply by passing messages between them. The internal workings of an actor system are not available to any other system. A suitable model to support the composition of different systems is obtained by composing the configurations they may be in.

References

[Agha 84] Agha, G. Semantic Considerations in the Actor Paradigm of Concurrent Computation. Proceedings of the NSF/SERC Seminar on Concurrency Springer-Verlag. 1984. Forthcoming

[Agha 85] Agha, G. Actors: A Model of Concurrent Computation in Distributed Systems. A.I. Tech Report 844. MIT. 1985.

[Backus 78] Backus, J. Can Programming be Liberated from the von Neumann Style? A Functional Style and Its Algebra of Programs. *Communications of the ACM 21*. 8 (August 1978). 613-641.

[Brock 83] Brock, J.D. A Formal Model of Non-determinate Dataflow Computation. LCS Tech Report 309. MIT. Aug. 1983.

[Brock and Ackerman 81] Brock J.D. and Ackerman, W.B. Scenarios: A Model of Non-Determinate Computation. In *107: Formalization of Programming Concepts*, Springer-Verlag. 1981, pp. 252-259.

[Clinger 81] Clinger, W. D. Foundations of Actor Semantics. AI-TR- 633, MIT Artificial Intelligence Laboratory, May. 1981.

[Dijkstra 77] Dijkstra, E. W. *A Discipline of Programming.* Prentice-Hall. 1977.

[Henderson 80] Henderson, P. *Functional Programming: Applications and Implementation.* Prentice-Hall International, 1980.

[Hewitt 77] Hewitt, C.E. Viewing Control Structures as Patterns of Passing Messages. *Journal of Artificial Intelligence 8-3* (June 1977), 323-364.

[Hewitt 80] Hewitt, C.E. Apiary Multiprocessor Architecture Knowledge System. Proceedings of the Joint SRC/University of Newcastle upon Tyne Workshop on VLSI, Machine Architecture, and Very High Level Languages, University of Newcastle upon Tyne Computing Laboratory Technical Report, October, 1980, pp. 67-69.

[Hewitt 85] Hewitt, C. The Challenge of Open Systems. *Byte 10*, 4 (April 1985). 223-242.

[Hewitt and Baker 77] Hewitt, C. and Baker, H. Laws for Communicating Parallel Processes. 1977 IFIP Congress Proceedings, IFIP, August. 1977. pp. 987-992.

[Hewitt and de Jong 82] Hewitt, C. de Jong. P. Open Systems. A.I. Memo 692. MIT Artificial Intelligence Laboratory, 1982.

[Hewitt, et al 84] Hewitt, C., Reinhardt, T., Agha, G. and Attardi, G. Proceedings of the NSF/SERC Seminar on Concurrency. A.I. Memo 781, Massachusetts Institute of Technology, 1984.

[Hoare 78] Hoare, C. A. R. Communicating Sequential Processes. *CACM 21*, 8 (August 1978), 666-677.

[Hwang and Briggs 84] Hwang, K. and Briggs, F. *Computer Architecture and Parallel Processing.* McGraw Hill, 1984.

[Kahn and MacQueen 78] Kahn, K. and MacQueen, D. Coroutines and Networks of Parallel Processes. Information Processing 77: Proceedings of the IFIP Congress. IFIP, Academic Press, 1978, pp. 993-998.

[Landin 65] Landin, P. A Correspondence Between ALGOL 60 and Church's Lambda Notation. *Communication of the ACM 8, 2* (February 1965).

[Manning 85] Manning, C. A Debugging System for the Apiary. M.I.T. Message-Passing Semantics Group Memo, January, 1985.

[McCarthy 59] McCarthy, John. Recursive Functions of Symbolic Expressions and their Computation by Machine. Memo 8, MIT, March, 1959.

[Milner 80] Milner, R. *Lecture Notes in Computer Science. Vol. 92: A Calculus of Communicating Systems.* Springer-Verlag, 1980.

[Pratt 82] Pratt, V. R. On the Composition of Processes. Proceedings of the Ninth Annual ACM Conf. on Principles of Programming Languages, 1982.

[Pratt 83] Pratt, V. R. Five Paradigm Shifts in Programming Language Design and their Realization in Viron, a Dataflow Programming Environment. Proceedings of the Tenth Annual ACM Conf. on Principles of Programming Languages, 1983.

[Steele, Fahlman, Gabriel, Moon, Weinreb 84] Steele Jr., Guy L.. *Common Lisp Reference Manual.* Mary Poppins Edition edition, Department of Computer Science, Carnegie-Mellon University, Pittsburgh, Pa, 1984.

[Stoy 77] Stoy, Joseph E. *Denotational Semantics: The Scott-Strachey Approach to Programming Language Theory.* The MIT Press, Cambridge, MA, 1977.

[Theriault 83] Theriault, D. Issues in the Design and Implementation of Act2. Technical Report 728, MIT Artificial Intelligence Laboratory, June, 1983.

Control of Processes by Communication over Ports
as a Paradigm for
Distributed Knowledge-Based System Design

Andrew S. Cromarty
Advanced Decision Systems

Expert Database Systems: Larry Kerschberg, Editor. Copyright 1987 by The Benjamin/Cummings Publishing Company, Inc.

Abstract

There are two fundamental prerequisites to the effective design and construction of distributed knowledge-based systems. First, there must be a supply of *tools* available that directly support the design and implementation task at as high a conceptual level as is possible. Second, there must be a *design metaphor* that motivates and directs the productive use of those tools. Unfortunately, the demand for working distributed expert systems currently far outstrips the supply of cleanly designed tools to support their construction, and existing design paradigms for both expert systems and distributed systems are taxed to, or even beyond, their limits in the service of distributed knowledge-based system construction. What is needed, therefore, is a set of tools that permit the smooth integration of technology from both knowledge-based and distributed systems design, and a model of how to use them.

We present an approach to designing multiple coordinated expert systems wherein each expert system models the others as *abstract remote data resource management agents*. Agents negotiate access to remote resources (including data) by asynchronously passing messages to the manager of the desired resources. The agents are embedded in a *HyperStar* topology that offers the benefits of a hierarchical star but permits special-purpose interagent communications links (*HyperLinks*) to be established to meet performance criteria such as timely data transfer or use of special data communications protocols.

This approach has been implemented in the form of LISP-compatible language extensions that supply agenda-based message receipt processing, referentially transparent interagent message routing, resource allocation based on cost/benefit analysis, and database primitives that are specialized for managing hypotheses in both local and remote databases. It has been used in the design or implementation of several demonstrated, working distributed knowledge-based systems. We discuss at length the specific language extensions that support two important aspects of this model: management of remote resources and management of distributed hypothesis databases.

1 Introduction

As knowledge-based systems technology matures, and particularly as distributed artificial intelligence (AI) systems are developed, AI researchers are increasingly finding themselves faced with many of the same concerns that confront designers of distributed database systems. For example:

- *Communications costs:* The costs of gaining access to data and other resources in complex distributed knowledge-based systems are no longer uniform, nor are they negligible. In order to ensure the delivery of timely, high-quality results, distributed expert systems must take into account such factors as the costs of communicating data or preempting other users of resources, as well as the value of those data and resources, when they formulate a data query, request exclusive or immediate access to some shared resource, or update a remote or shared data space.

- *Fault tolerance:* In a complex system, partial failures are a fact of life. Such failures may cause loss of data in transit, damage to an agent's processing state, or temporary lockup in a data access synchronization mechanism. To be useful and effective, distributed knowledge-based systems must be able to provide services to users even though some of their components may be dysfunctional or inaccessible at any given time; techniques that support recovery from faults must be provided, including mechanisms for reconstitution of the distributed system when some parts fail.

- *Database consistency:* Consistency must be maintained (or, alternatively, inconsistency must be managed) for multiple diverse databases. A data space being updated by multiple agents may come to contain stale or conflicting data if it those agents use different data sources or if they apply different processing approaches to the same data. It may not be possible to guarantee the consistency and timeliness of data under all circumstances in systems that must contend with nonzero communication and synchronization costs, partial subsystem failures, and different views among different agents as to which data need to be shared. At a minimum, techniques for recording the sources of information – including the results of computation (e.g. hypotheses) as well as initial data – must be employed to permit the system to reason about the probable integrity of its data.

- *Multiple data views:* Different parts of a distributed system may have quite different views of shared data and other resources upon which they wish to operate. Attempts to take advantage of context during reasoning exacerbate the problem of multiple disparate views. Especially vexing are problems involving allocation of shared resources in the absence of guarantees that the agents negotiating for those resources have identical views of the resource under contention; this can be quite problematic if the resource is mutable, such as a shared data space. Techniques for enforcing abstractions of shared resources are desirable in order to ensure some reasonable degree of resource integrity in the presence of conflicting views of those resources.

Despite these challenges, distribution of both processing and data will be an ineluctable characteristic of future AI systems. Data are inherently distributed in many problem domains, such as distributed sensor nets for weather or seismic analysis and multiple point-of-entry data processing systems; use of on-site knowledge-based systems can substantially improve processing performance by reducing large volumes of raw data at the collection site to compact observations, hypotheses, and reports that are then communicated to other processing sites. In addition, distributed processing systems, and particularly distributed AI systems, will become increasingly common as MIMD (multiple data multiple instruction) parallel processing machines reach the market. Several such machines are commercially available now and many more are under development.

There are further reasons to expect and welcome the advent of distributed knowledge-based systems. For example, a distributed system approach can be effective in promoting good system design, by enforcing strong separation of functionality through modularization and "information hiding" techniques [44]. These design techniques are especially important for large, complex knowledge-based systems that are designed and implemented by teams rather than individuals.

It is thus becoming increasingly clear that we need to carefully integrate existing technology from both the expert systems and distributed database disciplines in order to support the effective design and construction of distributed knowledge-based systems. However, despite the general trend towards the integration of software techniques into hardware [5,43] and the integration of database techniques into both operating systems [10,37,47,48,49] and logic programming languages [8,23], specific attempts to integrate knowledge-based system design techniques with distributed systems technology are still relatively immature. In fact, we still lack consensus as to what constitutes a good paradigm for providing such distributed processing support for knowledge-based systems.

The remainder of this report commences with a review of some important approaches to distributed computation, discussing at length some of the critical design tradeoffs we must make when constructing new tools to support intelligent distributed processing. We then examine a specific approach to distributed knowledge-based computation for large-grained independent agents, and a system that implements that approach. Finally, we focus in detail on some specific, practical constructs and mechanisms for supporting resource and knowledge management in a distributed knowledge-based system.

2   Current approaches to distributed processing

There are three principal metaphors for distributed computation today. *Distributed processing/operating systems* (including, for our purposes, distributed database systems) apply operating system design principles to the distributed computation problem, frequently by augmenting a conventional operating system with primitive operations that, e.g., ensure synchronized access to shared resources, a problem of special interest to the operating systems community. *Blackboard systems* are a class of AI programs that share a common architectural approach in which knowledge is distributed to subroutine-like "knowledge sources" that frequently are described as independent "agents." *Programming language parallelism* represents an attempt to provide a model of parallel or distributed processing by directly embedding it in the programming language.

2.1   Distributed operating systems

The distributed operating systems approach provides some of the important functionality that will be required in knowledge-based systems. The resource management perspective to which such systems generally subscribe, for example, can be so implemented as to permit distributed agents to be treated as providers of "services rather than servers" [16]. The distributed operating systems community has also identified some important techniques for reliably managing distributed data resources in the face of hardware and software faults and temporary disruption of computing or communications services.

The operating systems metaphor provides the needed functionality at a relatively low level of abstraction, however. It provides little or no support for many concepts central to knowledge-based systems, such as treatment of the *hypothesis* as a primitive datum, the use of uncertain reasoning techniques for the interpretation of multisource data or the determination of the flow of control, and orchestration of multiple interacting computational tasks *within* a single operating system process.

2.2 Distributed-knowledge designs

The blackboard [29] approach, based on the Hearsay [18] speech understanding system, does provide many of the abstractions and tools appropriate to the task of constructing distributed knowledge-based systems. For example, it provides a database that is structured so as to permit interpretation of database entries as hypotheses in a two-dimensional hypothesis space. A model of control for distributed intelligent agents is provided in the form of multiple *knowledge sources* (KS's) that embody expertise in some problem solving subdomain. The KS's are capable of performing database management operations such as entering, updating, deleting, or supporting hypotheses in the shared global "blackboard" database; they are made eligible for execution ("triggered") by the presence of specific database entries that satisfy the KS's "preconditions." Agenda-based control is typically employed to manage eligible KS's.

Although blackboard systems provide a *distributed knowledge* paradigm by virtue of their packaging of knowledge into discrete agent-like KS's, existing blackboard systems are not true distributed processing systems (see, for example, Enslow [16]) because the data resources they manipulate are centralized rather than physically distributed and there is not "comparative autonomy" of the KS's.[1] This is attributable to the tightly-coupled design of such systems: even if the KS's were executable on different processors, the shared blackboard database implicitly serializes access to the key resource that drives the system's computational behavior, and under the blackboard model agents need frequent, high-bandwidth access to the shared data space to perform their computations. The design and implementation of blackboard systems that are truly distributed is a topic of current research.

2.3 Distributed programming languages

We shall be concerned with a third approach to providing support for the construction of knowledge based distributed systems, that of embedding constructs that support distributed knowledge-based system directly in the programming language as a set of compatible language extensions. Making distributed processing constructs a part

---

[1]There is often ambiguity in the use of the terms *parallel* and *distributed*. We shall use *parallel* to refer to systems in which more than one "computation" occurs simultaneously, where a computation is at level of the granularity of elemental operations controllable by a programmer. *Distributed knowledge* systems are those that separate knowledge into different abstract "agents" or "modules" that are modeled as being capable, at least in principle, of independent computation. Systems in which distributed-knowledge agents actually do execute in parallel are *distributed processing* systems; these are the systems of interest to us in this paper, and hence we are interested in both distributed knowledge and parallel processing systems.

---

of the programming language can have important implications for the AI system builder's model of the design task: it can raise the level of abstraction of both the treatment of distributed processing, on the one hand, and the tools that comprise the programming language, on the other. It also makes the new tools available in a coherently designed, well-integrated, and familiar software development environment, and requires that an efficient, effective, and debugged distributed processing scheme be designed and implemented just once by a language designer, rather than requiring the distributed system builder to design, construct, debug, and document new problem-specific tools each time a new system is contemplated.

Several approaches to providing parallel processing support within programming languages already exist, and it is reasonable to try to understand why they do not suffice as languages for constructing distributed knowledge-based system. Ideally, such an understanding would be achieved through the succinct and informed delineation of their strengths and weaknesses as judged against well-understood and generally accepted evaluation criteria. Unfortunately, although parallel processing certainly is not even a new idea in computing, there is not yet a consensus on what constitutes an appropriate taxonomic characterization of parallelism. Perhaps the most common categorization scheme for parallelism, due to Flynn [21], separates computing systems according to whether parallelism applies to the data stream (SIMD), the processing (MISD), or both data and processing (MIMD). A taxonomic scheme that adopts a stronger software perspective is that of Wand and Wellings [51], who have identified four classes of concurrent processing: *coroutines*, *fork and join*, *Cobegin/Parbegin*, and *process declarations*. The Wand and Wellings taxonomy does not cover some important cases, however, and it somewhat arbitrarily splits process-oriented distributed computing approaches into two classes. For our purposes, we shall instead employ a taxonomic scheme that admits three variants of parallel or distributed programming languages: *agent-based*, *data flow*, and *SIMD-parallel*[2] models.

A detailed discussion of data flow [1,2,3,27] and SIMD-parallel [4,11,30,32] programming approaches is beyond the scope of this paper. For present purposes, it suffices to say that although such techniques are not incompatible with a distributed processing approach, neither SIMD parallelism nor data flow qualifies as a technique of interest for the introduction of distributed processing, as we have defined it, into languages that support knowledge-based system design, principally because the granularity of parallelism that they support is much finer than that of the communicating, cooperating expert systems for which we wish to achieve "comparative autonomy."

This is not true of agent-based language designs. Agent-based languages include "object-oriented" languages such

---

[2] SIMD is Flynn's abbreviation for "Single Instruction Multiple Data" parallelism.

as Smalltalk [24] and LISP Flavors [52], the task-based languages such as Ada [15,31], Mesa [41], and occam [39], and arguably, languages that provide parallelism through explicit demarcation of block structure (e.g. Edison [6], Argus [38], Multilisp [28], and Qlambda [22]) or coroutines (Simula [14], Modula-2 [53], and Icon [26]). Agent-based programming languages offer a style of programming in which data (especially including data that would be referred to as "knowledge" in an AI system) are distributed to abstract computational entities modeled as being capable of autonomous computation and, most frequently, interagent communication achieved by passing messages between agents. Although most existing implementations of agent-based languages either lack true parallelism or support only relatively low-level distributed operating systems primitives, as a class they seem to hold the most potential for providing a useful model of communicating expert systems that must collectively manage and process data.

This model of computation corresponds closely to the intuitive model of communicating expert systems as a system of intelligent agents that undertake to cooperatively solve some problem of mutual interest. In particular, it is a model of distributed processing in which we can continue to employ existing AI programming techniques within nodes in a distributed system, providing each node with a viewpoint according to which other nodes are seen as distant agents capable of engaging in service-oriented transactions, that is, of providing services or making requests for services that other agents can provide.

A wide variety of topological alternatives have been identified in the distributed systems literature (see, for example, Feng [19]), and a thorough analysis of appropriate topologies is well beyond the scope of this discussion. In summary, we have elected to employ an architecture we call the *HyperStar*, which can be thought of as a logical extension of a hierarchical star topology. A star topology has the potential for faster interagent communications than a tree network if interagent traffic is relative infrequent; a hierarchical star improves on the star by decentralizing control and communications to some extent, and hence improving reliability and reducing the extent of communications and processing bottlenecks, at the cost of introducing an increase in the time-cost of interagent communications from finite-time to logarithmic in the number of agents (for a lightly-loaded communications network).[3]

Unlike the static star and tree topological families, however, the HyperStar is explicitly designed to support dynamic reconfiguration of the network of distributed agents. The nominal topological design is similar to a hierarchical star network, but special-access links that "step outside the dimensionality of the star network" are permitted between nodes to provide special (e.g. private) communication protocols, rapid data paths, or shortcuts through the hierarchical graph structure. Because there is a cost associated with such links, they are not routinely provided upon demand; rather, they are treated as a *formal resource,* and resource allocation techniques embedded in each local "controller" node are employed to determine whether a given pair of

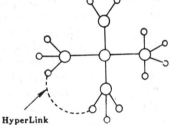

HyperLink

Figure 1: The HyperStar architecture

2.4   Connecting the agents together

Ideally, in order to maximize our ability to capitalize on existing AI system development technology, this service-oriented viewpoint would be implemented in a LISP-like environment – in particular, a LISP-like environment that has been compatibly augmented with a small set of language constructs that satisfy our need to communicate with other agents about services and resources, without requiring the local node to have any special knowledge of such details as how to route messages to other nodes or what those messages look like. The language thus must make some assumptions about the appropriate distributed architecture (that is, topology) in which the nodes are embedded, but we do not want the topology to limit either performance or flexibility, since we wish to support real-time computing and dynamic changes in the network.

nodes qualify for a special *HyperLink* that traverses the baseline hierarchical architecture. The cost measure for such a link attempts to take into account the possible loss of integrity that may occur when a "controller" node cannot inspect and validate internode message traffic as well as the obvious cost of tying up an agent's communications ports.

In addition to increasing message delivery performance, use of HyperLinks can enhance robustness and survivability. All nodes are given the latent ability to assume the responsibilities of a local "controller" if the present controller

---

[3] The HyperStar bears some resemblance to the *Hypertree* of Goodman and Sequin [25], which was a tree architecture with internode links that laterally traversed each tree layer. The Hypertree links did not cross layer boundaries, however, and the Hypertree as described by its authors was restricted to a tree topology rather than the more general hierarchical star topology. In fact, a Hypertree can be trivially implemented using a HyperStar, although the reverse is not true.

disappears from the network or is damaged or destroyed; a HyperLink can then be used to patch across failed nodes in the connectivity graph.

The HyperStar thus provides a topologically regular minimal spanning tree for the graph in which the agents are embedded, guaranteeing the availability of a well-known route and a well-known upper cost bound for interagent communications.[4]

3   The HyperStar as a model of distributed agent interaction

We now turn to a more detailed analysis of some specific language constructs that support knowledge-based distributed processing. We shall introduce the approach with a description of COP, a research prototype that has been constructed to provide a HyperStar-based distributed processing environment for cooperating expert systems. We then focus more closely on the constructs that the prototype employs to manage abstract resources and distributed hypothesis databases.

3.1   Implementation overview

A distributed system testbed named COP[5] has been developed for experimentation and prototyping of language features that support distributed reasoning, communication, and control applications. COP employs the HyperStar loosely-coupled architecture described in the previous section. The COP testbed is implemented in several dialects of LISP and works on VAX/UNIX, SUN, Pyramid, and Symbolics 3600 LISP machine systems. It consists of wholly LISP-compatible language extensions[6] representing some seven thousand lines of LISP code. COP has been employed as both a design model and a distributed communications and control substrate in several large working distributed AI system designs, including applications in image understanding, consultation expert systems, and intelligent distributed database systems. (See Cromarty et al. [12] for a brief description of one such design.)

As a loosely-coupled distributed system, COP distributes processing (both knowledge and computation) across different agents, and data sharing is achieved through message passing. There are several important characteristics of such a loosely-coupled system:

- *Minimization of data bottlenecks:* There are no globally shared data in the COP model. This eliminates shared-access synchronization operations, which are very expensive in a distributed system because they result in serialization of multiple agents whenever data access occurs. Synchronization is eliminated at the cost of increased requirements for duplication of data, however; specifically, message passing costs replace synchronization costs and multiple update messages can be required under some conditions. Because there are no collisions between different agents trying to obtain high-bandwidth and frequent access to a single common global database, however, there is no a priori data-sharing bottleneck.

  Note that this is workable only if agents are fairly large-grained expert systems that have a low ratio of external communications to internal computation[7] and the high degree of computational independence this implies; even lowering the communications cost cannot prevent serialization if an agent finds itself blocked waiting for another agent to complete a lengthy transaction involving a shared resource. Fortunately, these large-grained independent expert systems are the kind we currently know how to build best.[8]

- *Minimal restrictions on programming style:* Because COP agents are loosely coupled, COP can afford to be agnostic on the issue of the programming style adopted within an agent. Existing distributed system implementations that employ COP freely mix pure LISP, procedural programming languages, object-based programming, and logic programming software written using expert system tools. Since COP provides distributed processing primitives as a set of features rather than as part of a complete new language or programming environment, few prior style constraints are imposed.

- *Parallel execution of cooperating expert systems:* COP can provide true parallel execution by mapping its component expert systems into agents executing on multiple processors, and the existing COP implementation supports both multitasking and multiprocessing. Interestingly, a decision to support networked multiprocessing essentially forces loose coupling (no shared global data) upon us. Networking does require implementation of special mechanisms for both

---

[4] It is interesting to note that the Connection Machine, a massively parallel SIMD processor, implements an analogous strategy in hardware: a mesh-connected grid spans the dynamic n-cube connectivity graph of its 65,000 processors.

[5] This is a double acronym emphasizing the two most important design decisions in the model: *Communication Over Ports* and *Control Of Processes.*

[6] A minimal extension of the Berkeley UNIX 4.2bsd and the Symbolics operating system software environment was also necessary to support the multiple processor version of COP. These extensions permit LISP processes to converse directly with a TCP/IP server that provides network access to LISP processes on other processors.

[7] Fishburn [20] recently has reported the same conclusion on the basis of empirical studies of distributed system performance. He observes that good distributed system design dictates that "each message should invoke, or be a summary of, a large computation."

[8] In addition, simulation studies by Enslow and Saponas [17] have shown that the communications costs of control operations are lower than would be expected for a fairly wide range of fully distributed decentralized-control systems.

remote data access and interagent synchronization, however.[9]

• *Referential transparency and message routing:* Implementation of a structured topological model on top of a multiple processor network where processors are in general located in an arbitrary graph structure introduces a message routing problem. COP effects *referential transparency* by maintaining its own internal routing tables to provide Enslow's "services, not servers" model of distributed computation, obviating the need for the application programmer to know or care where in the network other agents are located or how to reach them. This is all accomplished transparently from the viewpoint of the programmer, much as contemporary programming languages transparently provide such mundane operations as managing I/O buffers and mapping multidimensional array indices into a linear memory address space.

COP operations start when an initial "controller" agent "creates the world."[10] The controller does not rigidly step the thread of control at each node. Instead, it is responsible for creating processes, issuing tasking commands, and allocating shared resources (including active arbitration between client tasks). In a full HyperStar network, there are multiple such controllers and these control decisions are distributed as much as possible; this not only ensures survivability and reliability through distribution of responsibility and authority, but also reduces network bandwidth requirements compared to a more conventional star-like hierarchical control architecture.

Each child node in the HyperStar contains an agenda-based system that is used for message processing and dispatch, providing the capability of priority-based message receipt and thus preventing critical messages from being ignored because of prior processing demands. Use of the agenda mechanism for message handling as well as task management within a node helps to ensure real-time dispatch of messages (in the formal sense of real-time, that is, response after a provably fixed time has elapsed – see O'Reilly and Cromarty [42]).

Control regime flexibility is another asset of this loosely-coupled approach. While Hearsay-like architectures permit a variety of control regimes to be employed, the centralization of control in such systems results in only one such control regime being active (i.e. possible) at a given moment. Tightly-coupled centralized-control systems thus suffer from serialization of control regimes, as well as serialization of processing during database (blackboard) contention. Conversely, the total separation of agents in a COP-like architecture permits different control regimes to be employed by each agent to solve different subproblems; in fact, not only the *control policies* but even the *control mechanisms* can be different in different simultaneously executing agents.[11]

In the accompanying table, we illustrate some of the design tradeoffs in selecting a COP-like loosely-coupled system as contrasted with the characteristics of a tightly coupled system, specifically a tightly-coupled contemporary Hearsay-III-derived distributed knowledge architecture augmented to support the object-oriented (inheritance-based) style of programming now being introduced into a number of research prototype and commercially available expert system tools.[12]

3.2   Managing shared resources in a hyperstar network

The defining feature of a *process,* according to the conventional operating systems model, is that it acts as a *consumer of resources.* Thus the adoption of the process as the level of granularity of agents in our distributed system approach carries with it a significant responsibility to provide appropriate language mechanisms for managing the resources with which those agents are concerned.

Jensen [34] has proposed a definition of "resource" in a computational context as corresponding to an instance of an abstract datatype. This definition affords us the insight that data instances, which are the fundamental quantity at which language operators direct their computation, are a commodity to which access should be restricted. This appeals to the intuitive, economic sense of "resource" with which we are familiar: it is a potentially scarce entity to which some form of access is desired. The definition seems incomplete, however, in that it does not seem to directly capture our intuitions about *physical* resources[13] (disks, printers, etc.) to which access is desired, instead forcing us to wrap around them the computational abstraction of a datatype with associated operators.

---

[9] We discuss remote data access later. For a discussion of interagent synchronization techniques, see Jefferson [33], Lamport [35], Reed [45], and Schneider [46].

[10] "Creating the world" involves creating processes, assigning to child processes the initial tasking orders that imbue them with "agenthood," and entering into the controller's database the relevant information specifying the roles (user interface, resource manager, etc.) recognized for each new child node, the port(s) through which that agent can be reached, and routing table information that identifies the preferred path to the child agent.

[11] We emphasize that COP is intended to provide a set of *mechanisms* from which designers of distributed AI applications can select to forge policies appropriate to their problem domain. For example, a designer might use this software as a substrate upon which to implement techniques for interagent negotiation over sharable resources. Specific interagent negotiation *policies* tend to be domain-dependent; in all cases, however, they rely upon a primitive set of resource management *mechanisms* such as are described here. In this respect, COP is "lower level" than much contemporary work in distributed AI, where problem domain, policy, and mechanism are routinely commingled.

[12] This strawman Hearsay-clone architecture actually represents a collage of several expert system tools under commercial development that are known to the author. An example of a system that is quite similar to this strawman system is described in Cunningham *et al.* [13].

[13] Called "real" resources by Wand [50], in contrast with "abstract" resources such as files or directories.

Table 1: Distributed architecture characteristics: Hearsay-clone vs. COP

Feature	Hearsay clone	COP
Coupling model	Tightly coupled	Loosely coupled
How distributed	Knowledge	Processing
Programming style	Object-based	Agnostic (any)
Data mgmt paradigm	Blackboard	Distributed DBMS
Speed of inter-agent communication	Very fast	Moderate to slow (networked)
Speed of intra-agent communication	Very fast	Very fast
Frequency of inter-agent communication	Very often	Moderate or infrequent
Level of inter-agent communication	Low-level (function calls)	High-level (tasking, status)
Model of message receipt processing	Function call	Agenda task or function call
Granularity of modularization	Medium to fine-grained	Large-grained preferred
Style of interagent communication	Function calls as "message sends"	Message passing with dispatch
Means of data sharing	Global shared data, function parameters	Message passing and distributed DBMS access
Price of sharing data among multiple agents	Synchronization primitives reduce degree of parallelism.	Duplication of data and consistency msgs are necessary.
Control model	Centralized	Decentralized
Freedom of inter-agent side effects	Very poor	Very good
Multiple control regimes possible?	Yes	Yes
Multiple control regime constraints	One for entire system (serial)	One for each node (parallel)

We choose to adopt a more liberal sense of "resource": for the purposes of COP, a resource is simply any entity over which interagent deliberation is required before access is permitted. COP selectively provides a small set of operations to permit this deliberation and access-granting (or denial) procedure to any agent declared to be a *resource manager*, and provides a resource-requesting function to all agents. The primitive resource management functions COP exports to such agents include:

(**request-resource** *resource amount expected-benefit*)
(**valid-resource-status?** *status*)
(**valid-resource-type?** *type*)
(**process-resource-request** *requestor resource why amount expected-benefit*)
(**allocate-resource** *resource recipient amount*)
(**permit-resource-request** *requestor resource amount . info*)
(**deny-resource-request** *requestor resource*)

The standard mechanism for signifying that a resource is required is to execute **request-resource**, which is a primitive made available by the communications slave to all agents. **request-resource** sends a message to the resource's managing agent requesting *amount* amount of resource *resource*, with expected benefit *expected-benefit* (in the present implementation, this is expected to be a value in the range [0.0,1.0]).

An improper resource request will result in error message traffic, which is expensive compared to checking the validity of putative resource arguments before using them. **valid-resource-type?** is a predicate that permits the AI system developer to ensure the propriety of a suspected name for a resource before it is used in a resource request. Similarly, **valid-resource-status?** is a predicate that ensures that a suspected resource "status" is legitimate. For the purposes of the resource management system, there are four valid mutually exclusive values of *status* that a resource may hold:

- Resources that are **'available** can be allocated without further decision-making.

- Resources that are **'busy** will result in refusal of access.

- Resources that are **'preemptible** are currently in use but may be reallocated before becoming **'available** under some circumstances.

- A resource that **'requires-cb-analysis** may be available or busy and, like **'preemptible** resources, may be reallocated if need be.

The **'preemptible** and **'requires-cb-analysis** states differ in that the former indicates that the resource is already busy but that we can justify interrupting its current use if need be, whereas the latter means that the resource may be available (i.e. not in use at the moment) but we only grant access to it if the requestor passes muster according to a cost-benefit model. Preemptible status is an important status class because some resources can maintain their state across usages by multiple consumers at a very low cost, while others may have a high startup cost and may be "non-reentrant." For example, processes executing on a processor with rapid context switching capabilities are normally **'preemptible**, since they can resume processing after a more important, e.g. higher priority, consumer (process) takes and then relinquishes control of the resource (processor).

process-resource-request is the handler for resource requests provided to each resource manager. The *expected-benefit* and reason for the request (*why*) are taken into account in the decision-making process insofar as is possible, trading off the gravity of this request against both the priority assigned to other requests for the same resource and – in cases where the information is available, such as when a controller node is also the resource manager – the system's plans and expectations for usage of that resource in the future. In addition, the AI system designer can provide the resource manager with a qualitative model of the resource and any constraints that apply to its use, allowing the system to take advantage of semantics associated with different *why* values to reason about the probable outcomes of competing requests.

allocate-resource is a primitive employed by the resource manager to allocate *amount* amount of *resource* to *recipient*. In essence, a capability for access to the resource is granted to the requestor and a record is made of the new status of the resource. The **permit-resource-request** primitive is then invoked to communicate that capability to the requestor, including explicit specification of the *resource* (since several requests may be outstanding) and the *amount* (since the amount granted may not be identical to the amount requested). In the case of a denied request, **deny-resource-request** is employed to communicate that denial to the requestor.

One case of resource management deserves special mention. COP considers *roles* to be an allocatable resource. Thus the resource management functions can be used to permit a node to request, or be instructed to assume, a control role relative to another agent or a resource manager role for some shared resource. This capacity is an important component in COP's set of fault tolerance mechanisms, especially for reconstitution after partial network failure.

3.3 Distributed hypothesis database management

In addition to primitives for communications, control, and resource management, COP provides a special *hypothesis management capability*. That is, a database management system is built into COP for managing a structured multiple-hypothesis database such as might be employed in a blackboard system or as the "knowledge base" provided as part of a rule-based expert system. Consistent with COP's decentralized, MIMD, large-grained approach to distributed intelligent computation, however, the COP hypothesis management subsystem implementation is structured as a package of optional database-like functions and messages that can be employed by any agent either to access a remote database or to support intraagent hypothesis management activities. It is thus possible to construct one or more "database agents" or "blackboard manager agents," and these databases may be either internal to the agents that access them or distinct remote information management agents.

The database is explicitly constructed to manage *hypotheses*, that is, predicate relations corresponding to assertions about the computational world or domain of expertise of the expert agents. It provides for a simple uncertainty representation wherein each database assertion, or hypothesis, carries with it a degree of support (in whatever the preferred degree-of-belief space is, although all existing implementations have used real numbers in the range [0.0, 1.0]). Also provided is a weak form of *endorsement* construct (in the sense of Cohen and Grinberg [9]) that associates with each hypothesis the identity of the agent that asserted it into the hypothesis database. The current implementation of the hypothesis database subsystem has additional explicit knowledge about two-dimensional geographic location of objects, to support simple spatial reasoning such as occurs in computer vision systems and some robotics and planning problems.

A mechanism for defining a simple taxonomic inheritance network within each database is built into the hypothesis management package. Taxonomic relations can be applied to the *type* slot of any hypothesis in a hypothesis database. When a **lookup-hyp** message subsequently is received by a database manager agent, if no literal match is found then *is-a* relations optionally specified by the AI system developer will be used, if present, to find matches that satisfy the database query according to taxonomic inheritance rules. The developer specifies these *is-a* relations in a simple tabular format during system construction; they are then installed into dynamic data structures that can be altered at execution time, if desired. In addition, each hypothesis can have "parent" and "child" fields that correspond approximately to *has-as-parts* relations.

The hypothesis structures induced by hypotheses subject to those inheritance and parent-child relations are arbitrary graph structures, but individual competing hypothesis-based interpretations can be represented as *overlapping trees* that span portions of the graph. Where the trees have no intersection, they are deemed *consistent,* and where they share common elements, they are deemed to *conflict.*

In databases of hypotheses that are being used by multiple agents to represent alternative interpretations of some sensory world, such as frequently occurs in AI applications to problems in sensor fusion, computer vision, and signal understanding, an especially important database operation is identifying the *maximally supported consistent hypothesis.* Selecting the "best" such structured hypothesis tree in this representational system then consists in the following two-step procedure:

1. Identify all sets of non-conflicting interpretations of the hypothesis data, by identifying the mutually non-conflicting hypothesis trees in the hypothesis database whose root nodes are at the desired level of abstraction in the hypothesis space.

2. Select the maximal hypothesis tree from this set (that is, the one containing the largest number of component observation hypotehses) that has the highest degree of support associated with it.

Selection of the best hypothesis tree is an atomic primitive database operation that COP provides to all database manager agents.

The accompanying figure illustrates the use of this technique to extract the maximally supported consistent interpretation of a set of phonemes (primitive speech sounds) as a sequence of words. The trees containing subtrees that share common elements represent self-inconsistent interpretations (assignments of meaning) of the observation set. After trees containing inconsistent subtrees are eliminated, the subtrees with greatest support are selected, and

of those, the one that accounts for the greatest number of phoneme-level observations (A, in the example) is deemed "best."

The "best" hypothesis will be the one that accounts for the greatest amount of both our certainty and our observations without requiring any region simultaneously to be part of two separate shrubs.

Because the queries most likely to be put to the database system cannot always be predicted in advance in a typical knowledge-based application, COP's hypothesis database implementation provides for optional declarations to specify that the access paths to select database relations are to be stored redundantly using database "inversion" (in the conventional database sense). By requesting that the database be redundantly indexed in inverted form, it is possible for the AI system developer to obtain quite rapid associative lookup and update performance at the cost of some extra space and slightly higher costs for hypothesis insertion and deletion.

In order to provide these hypothesis management functions, the following operators and messages are defined. When executed internally as functions by a database manager agent, they operate on the local database; when sent as messages to another agent, they act on the database of the recipient, which is normally a database manager agent.

- (**create-hyp** *type endorsers degrees-of-support location orientation children*) – Creates a new hypothesis in the database.

- (**extend-hyp** *hyp-ID . pairs*) – Extends a new hypothesis in the database. *pairs* are property-list-like frame-slot pairs of values to add to existing values for this hypothesis. (This permits an agent to contribute its support to a hypothesis already asserted by another agent, for example, or to extend the set of hypothesized "child" objects for some object in a hypothesis database.)

- (**lookup-hyp** *area qualifiers contents*) – The recipient looks in the hypothesis database for the first candidate hypothesis in *area.* If *qualifier-pairs* are supplied, they are used to create a predicate against which each candidate encountered is tested until one matches. For example, consider a hypothesis database for a image understanding system which classifies ve-

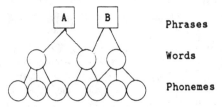

Figure 2: Selecting the maximally supported consistent hypothesis

hicles such as trucks and tanks; the message (lookup-hyp 'area '(1 2 3 4) '(type tank)) will find the first object of type **tank** in the region whose lower-left and upper-right corners are (1,2) and (3,4). If the lookup succeeds, the value is returned using the **hyp-reports** message; if it fails, **empty-region** is sent back instead. If more than one qualifier is to be tested, they are listified, as in (**type tank endorsers (vc)**), which asks for all hypotheses in the specified area that are tanks endorsed (only) by the "vc" agent. Note that the **type** subqualifier is a special case: if, for example, (**type tank**) is requested, any object that *is-a* tank (e.g., any of **T-62-tank**, **T-72-tank**, or **tank**) will suffice. The returned message will contain whatever fields appear in *contents*. For instance, if *contents* is (**type endorsers**) then the response might be (**hyp-ID hyp27 type (T-72-tank) endorsers (vc)**).

- (lookup-hyps *area qualifiers contents*) – This is identical to **lookup-hyp** except that it collects and returns *all* hypotheses in the specified area that satisfy *qualifiers*, rather than the first one. Answers are returned via the **hyp-reports** message.

- (report-best-hyp-tree *type area*) – This message provides a top-level goal to a database manager agent. The agent is instructed to send a **best-hyp-tree** message identifying the best hypothesis of type *type* within the area *area*.

- (hyp-report *area qualifiers hyp*) – This is the proper successful response to a **lookup-hyp** request. The *area* and *qualifiers* args are echoed back from the request to remind the recipient which query is being answered. *hyp* is *(hyp-ID key₁ key₂ ...))*, where *hyp-ID* is the hypothesis ID and *key_n* are the keys that appeared in the *contents* field of the original **lookup-hyp** message, in the same order. As with all other such messages, *keyn* refers to the key-value pair, i.e. ... type (tank) endorsers (vc) ....

- (hyp-reports *area qualifiers hyps*) – This is the equivalent of **hyp-report** for the multiple lookup case, i.e. the response to **lookup-hyps** messages. Its format is identical except that each hypothesis in the response is now a list. The keyword *hyps* appears in the message as the key for the list of hypotheses; the structure of hypotheses is ((*hyp-ID key₁ key₂ ...*) (*hyp-ID key_i key_j ...*) ...), where the *key_n* indicate attribute-value pairs in a frame-structured (property-list) form.

- (display-area *area*) – Valid only when issued by a recognized user interface agent, this message provides a top-level goal to the database manager agent. The database manager is instructed to search the hypothesis database for all objects in region *area*. The parameters of any objects in *area* are sent to the user

interface agent to be displayed.

- (display-hyp *hyp-ID type location support*) – Sent in response to a **display-area** or **display-unit** request, this message identifies for a user interface agent an object at *location* of type *type* (a list) having hypothesis ID *hyp-ID* with maximal degree of support *support*.

- (display-unit *type area*) – This message may be received only from designated user interface agent; it provides a top-level goal to a database manager agent. The database manager agent is instructed to search the hypothesis database for an object of type *type* in hypothesis region *area*. It is an error for the hypothesis database manager agent to fail to find the requested object *type* in *area*. The parameters of the object of type *type* in *area* are sent to the user interface agent to be displayed.

- (empty-region *area [type]*) – When a display-area request cannot be serviced because there are no objects within the specified area, this message is sent by the controller to notify the requestor of the search failure. This message is also sent when a *display-unit* request fails, in which case the optional *type* argument is also specified.

- (best-hyp-tree *type area root-hyp-ID tree*) – This message from a database manager agent provides a bona fide user interface agent with a full description of the best hypothesis tree rooted in an object of type *type* within area *area*. It is sent in response to a **report-best-hyp-tree** request. If there was no such tree within that region, the *root-hyp-ID* and *tree* are nil. Otherwise *root-hyp-ID* is the unique hypothesis ID for the hypothesis at the root of the tree of interest and *tree* is a list of the hypotheses that are the root's descendants.

- (no-more-hyps *area*) – This message is queued at the end of the user interface agent's agenda after all **display-hyp** commands have been issued in response to a **display-area** request. The *area* argument is identically whatever was provided in the original **display-area** request. (This message class is employed to resynchronize the database and user interface agents after a multiple-message data transfer.)

4   Conclusions

The language extensions we have described provide a set of tools for specifying communications and control relations between cooperating, communicating agents that perform problem-solving activities in a distributed system. The expert systems are embedded as nodes in a loosely-coupled HyperStar distributed system topology; the language extensions provide each expert system with primitives sufficient to permit it to view the other expert systems as providers of services (principally sharable resources, data, and computations). This approach has served as an effective design model or implementation vehicle for several practical distributed expert systems, including several multiple agent consulting expert systems and two large distributed computer vision systems [7,12,36,40].

Among the important features of the system are its direct support for databases not merely of anonymous, structured data values but of *hypotheses*. These hypotheses incorporate degrees of belief, endorsement tagging to identify the agent that made the database entry, and implicit relations to other database entries according to their place in parent-child (*a-part-of*) and taxonomic (*is-a*) graphs. Tools are provided for extracting from the database the "best" (that is, best-supported maximal consistent) hypothesis; for gaining access to both local and remote databases of such hypotheses; and for negotiating access to other non-data resources.

Also provided is a mechanism for patching around failed subsystems to promote fault-tolerant distributed system behavior, as well as explicit mechanisms for enforcing a fairly high-level abstract treatment of shared resources and for determining how distributed agents should be permitted to communicate (specifically, whether they should be permitted private communications links) as judged on the basis of the costs and benefits that will accrue.

Tightly-coupled knowledge-based paradigms, and especially blackboard-based systems, have enjoyed considerable popularity within the AI community as a putative model of distributed knowledge based system design. We nonetheless expect loosely-coupled distributed systems approaches like the one described here to make significant contributions to the development of effective and practical distributed knowledge-based systems, especially as true parallelism, physically distributed processing, increased modularity, and access to heterogeneous shared resources (including foreign communications networks and existing remote databases) come to be regarded as desirable and, ultimately, necessary characteristics of distributed knowledge-based system design.

References

[1] W. B. Ackerman. Dataflow languages. *IEEE Computer*, 15(2):15, February 1982.

[2] W. B. Ackerman and J. B. Dennis. *VAL - A value-oriented algorithmic language (Preliminary reference manual)*. Technical Report 218, MIT Laboratory for Computer Science, June 1979.

[3] P. Arvind, K. Gostelow and W. Plouffe. *An asynchronous programming language and computing machine*. Technical Report TR114a, Department of Information and Computer Science, University of California at Irvine, December 1978.

[4] G. Barnes *et al.* The ILLIAC IV computer. *IEEE Transactions on Computers*, C-17:746, 1968.

[5] J. Batali *et al.* The Scheme-81 architecture – System and chip. In Jr. Paul Penfield, editor, *Proceedings of the MIT Conference on Advanced Research in VLSI*, Artech House, Dedham, MA, 1982.

[6] P. Brinch-Hansen. Edison: A multiprocessor language. *Software Practice and Experience*, 11(4):325-361, April 1981.

[7] R. Chestek *et al.* Knowledge based terrain analysis. In J. Gilmore, editor, *Applications of Artificial Intelligence (SPIE Proc. 548)*, pages 46-56, 1985.

[8] W. Clocksin and C. Mellish. *Programming in Prolog*. Springer-Verlag, New York, 1981.

[9] P. Cohen and M. Grinberg. A theory of heuristic reasoning about uncertainty. *AI Magazine*, 4(2):17-24, 1983.

[10] R. Cook and J. Brandon. The Pick operating system, Part I: Information management. *Byte*, 9(11):177-198, October 1984.

[11] Thinking Machines Corporation. *The Connection Machine supercomputer: A natural fit to applications needs*. (Product description document publicly available from Thinking Machines Corporation.), Thinking Machines Corp., 245 First St., Cambridge, Mass., July 1985.

[12] A. Cromarty *et al.* Distributed database considerations in an expert system for radar analysis. In L. Kerschberg, editor, *Expert Database Systems*, Benjamin Cummings, Palo Alto, Ca., 1985.

[13] J. Cunningham *et al.* Modelling an EW system using an object-oriented approach. In *Proceedings of the Symposium on Expert Systems in Government*, IEEE Computer Society, October 1985.

[14] B. Dahl, O. Myhrhaug and K. Nygaard. *SIMULA-67 Common Base Language*. Technical Report S-2, Norwegian Computing Centre, Oslo, 1968.

[15] V. Downes and S. Goldsack. The use of the Ada language for programming in a distributed system. In V. Hasse, editor, *Real Time Programming*, Pergamon Press, 1980.

[16] P. Enslow. What is a "distributed" data processing system? *Computer*, 11:13-21, January 1978.

[17] P. Enslow and T. Saponas. *Performance of distributed and decentralized control models for fully distributed processing systems: Initial simulation studies*. Technical Report RADC-TR-82-105, Rome Air Development Center, 1982.

[18] L. Erman *et al.* The Hearsay-II speech-understanding system: Integrating knowledge to resolve uncertainty. *ACM Computing Surveys*, 12(2), June 1980.

[19] T.-y. Feng. A survey of interconnection networks. *Computer*, 14:12-27, 1981.

[20] J. Fishburn. *Analysis of Speedup in Distributed Algorithms.* UMI Research Press, Ann Arbor, Mich., 1984.

[21] M. Flynn. Some computer organisations and their effectiveness. *IEEE Transactions on Computers*, C-21(9):948-960, September 1972.

[22] R. Gabriel and J. McCarthy. *Queue-based multiprocessing LISP.* Technical Report STAN-CS-84-1007, Stanford University, June 1984.

[23] M. Genesereth. An overview of meta-level architecture. In *Proceedings of the 1983 National Conference on AI*, pages 119-124, 1983.

[24] A. Goldberg and D. Robson. *SmallTalk-80: The Language and its Implementation.* Addison-Wesley, Reading, MA, 1983.

[25] J. Goodman and C. Sequin. Hypertree: A multiprocessor interconnection strategy. *IEEE Transactions on Computers*, :932-933, December 1981.

[26] R. Griswold and D. Hanson. *Reference manual for the Icon programming language.* Technical Report TR 79-1, Department of Computer Science, University of Arizona, January 1979.

[27] A. J. Gurd. Fundamentals of dataflow. In F. Chambers, D. Duce and G. Jones, editors, *Distributed computing*, chapter 1, pages 3-19, Academic Press, 1984.

[28] R. Halstead. Multilisp: A language for concurrent symbolic computation. *ACM Transactions on Programming Languages and Systems*, 7(4):501-538, October 1985.

[29] B. Hayes-Roth. *The blackboard architecture: A general framework for problem solving?* Technical Report HPP-83-30, Heuristic Programming Project, Computer Science Department, Stanford University, 1983.

[30] W. D. Hillis. The Connection Machine: A computer architecture based on cellular automata. *Physica*, 10D:213-228, 1984.

[31] J. Ichbiah *et al.* Preliminary Ada Reference Manual. *ACM SIGPLAN Notices*, 14(6A), June 1979.

[32] K. Iverson. *A Programming Language.* Wiley, New York, N.Y., 1962.

[33] D. Jefferson. Virtual time. *ACM Transactions on Programming Languages and Systems*, 7(3):404-425, July 1985.

[34] E. D. Jensen. Distributed control. In *Distributed Systems: Architecture and implementation*, pages 175-190, Springer-Verlag, 1981.

[35] L. Lamport. Time, clocks, and the ordering of events in a distributed system. *Communications of the ACM*, 21(7):558-565, July 1978.

[36] T. Levitt *et al.* A model-based system for force structure analysis. In J. Gilmore, editor, *Applications of Artificial Intelligence (SPIE Proc. 548)*, pages 169-175, 1985.

[37] H. Levy. *Capability-based Computer Systems.* Digital Equipment Corporation (pub.), 1984.

[38] B. Liskov and R. Scheifler. Guardians and Actions: Linguistic support for robust, distributed programs. *ACM Transactions on Programming Languages and Systems*, 5(3):381-404, July 1983.

[39] D. May. occam. *ACM SIGPlan Notices*, 18(4):69-79, April 1983.

[40] T. Miltonberger *et al.* Preliminary results on a model-based image understanding system for detecting space object anomalies from inverse synthetic aperture radar (isar) images. In *Proc. Fifth Phoenix Conference on Computers and Communications*, IEEE, 1986.

[41] W. Mitchell, J. Maybury and R. Sweet. *Mesa Language Manual Version 5.0.* Xerox Palo Alto Research Center, Palo Alto, CA., April 1979.

[42] C. O'Reilly and A. Cromarty. "Fast" is not "real-time": Designing effective real-time AI systems. In J. Gilmore, editor, *Applications of Artificial Intelligence (SPIE Proc. 548)*, 1985.

[43] E. Organick. *A Programmer's View of the Intel 432 System.* McGraw-Hill, NY, 1983.

[44] D. Parnas. Information distribution aspects of design methodology. In *Proceedings of the IFIP Congress*, pages 26-30, IFIP, 1971. Booklet TA-3.

[45] D. Reed. Implementing atomic actions on decentralized data. *ACM Transactions on Computer Systems*, 1(1):3-23, February 1983.

[46] F. Schneider. Synchronization in distributed programs. *ACM Transactions on Programming Languages and Systems*, 4(2):179-195, April 1982.

[47] D. Spooner. *The logical object concept in the unified model.* Technical Report, Department of Computer Science, Penn. State University, 1979.

[48] D. Spooner. *A unified security model for data base and operating systems.* Technical Report, Department of Computer Science, Penn. State University, 1980.

[49] E. Spooner, D. Gudes and J. Spirn. *Security aspects of the unified model.* Technical Report CS-80-17, Department of Computer Science, Penn. State University, 1980.

[50] I. Wand. Architectures. In F. Chambers, D. Duce and G. Jones, editors, *Distributed computing*, chapter 9, pages 141-146, Academic Press, 1984.

[51] I. Wand and A. Wellings. Programming languages. In F. Chambers, D. Duce and G. Jones, editors, *Distributed computing*, chapter 14, pages 201-215, Academic Press, 1984.

[52] D. Weinreb and D. Moon. *LISP Machine Manual.* MIT AI Lab, Cambridge, MA, fourth edition, 1981.

[53] N. Wirth. *Modula-2.* Technical Report, Institut for Informatic, ETH, Zurich, Switzerland, December 1978.

Part III

Implementation Frameworks and DAI Applications

Chapter 6

Implementation Languages and Systems

This section contains papers on three integrative systems, called MACE, ABE and AGORA, and two distributed object-oriented systems — an integrated procedural- and logic-based language called ORIENT84/K and an actor-derived language called ABCL/1. Both the integrative systems and the distributed languages offer great flexibility in problem-solving styles and inter-node or inter-agent organization. A paper on the important area of description and diagnostic mechanisms for DAI systems is also included. Taken together, these ideas provide a wide range of implementation frameworks and ideas for DAI systems.

Mario Tokoro and Yutaka Ishikawa's ORIENT84/K system supplies a language for programming using concurrent objects. The objects consist of a behavior part, containing procedural methods, a knowledge part containing rules and facts, and a monitor part that monitors and controls the object. The system is an attempt to unify concepts of procedural- and logic-based programming, and has been influenced by message passing in SMALLTALK and by predicate logic rules in PROLOG. It bears some practical resemblance to another less widely publicized language called OIL, designed for programming the FAIM1 concurrent AI machine [Cohen85].

Akinori Yonezawa, Jean-Pierre Briot and Etsuya Shibayama's ABCL/1 uses "objects" that are derived from actors, but that are larger-grained processes with a local persistent memory or state. The "large-grain actors" approach is an attempt to limit the amount of process spawning in the actor model, with its associated overhead of maintaining addresses and process management. It provides a good contrast with Agha and Hewitt's paper in Chapter 5.

Les Gasser, Carl Braganza and Nava Herman's MACE is a generic testbed allowing the integrated representation of problem solving and communication structures of different grain size and interaction style. MACE "agents" are concurrent objects, consisting of a user-definable procedural part called an *engine*, along with a collection of databases. MACE agents provide multi-agent composition into *organizations*, and special deductive database facilities for modeling other agents, representing them by their roles, skills, goals, plans, or other user-definable attributes. Designed for experimentation, and implemented in a heterogeneous multicomputer environment, the MACE system includes user-controlled tracing and monitoring facilities.

The AGORA environment, under construction by Roberto Bisiani and his associates, has been designed as part of a large speech recognition project. It allows the integration of multiple languages and highly parallel computations, with a view to integrating a heterogeneous collection of hardware systems. A primary feature of AGORA is the invisibility (to the programmer) of its underlying hardware.

The ABE architecture of Frederick Hayes-Roth, Lee Erman, Scott Fouse, Jay Lark, and James Davidson supports the integration of collections of independent cooperating problem solving components of several different grain sizes and problem-solving styles. It was developed at Teknowledge as an environment for the development of practical intelligent systems. ABE also supplies capabilities for composing components or modules into large collections hierarchically, and for allowing modules to be members of several hierarchies using a concept of *meshing*. ABE processes can manage resources locally, because resources are passed with control flow among modules. The control structure of ABE is *nearly hierarchical,* and the hierarchical structure is an explicit choice to provide some constraint on module interaction.

These architectures and languages indicate three trends in flexible implementation frameworks for DAI: a trend toward language and system mechanisms for *encapsulation, isolation, and local control,* a trend toward *heterogeneous, multigrain problem-solving frameworks,* and a trend toward language and system support for *flexible organization and interaction structures* (see Chapter 1, Sections 4, 5, and 7).

Finally, Eva Hudlicka and Victor Lesser describe the *diagnosis module* (DM), which was developed for monitoring and identifying inappropriate behavior in the DVMT system. The DM uses a causal model of the problem solving system to reason about the system's expected behavior, and to identify faults at a problem-solving (versus programming) level. This research is one of the few efforts at hand to use knowledge based approaches to understanding, modeling, and diagnosing the behavior of distributed AI systems. It will be a foundation for organizational self design, because a problem-solving system must be endowed with the capacity to recognize its own failings to know when to reconfigure itself. It also provides another approach to modeling organization and interaction in a DAI system. Indeed, it is one of just a few research attempts at distributed diagnosis, another promising research focus in DAI. (For related ideas, see also Chapter 1, Sections 3 and 5, the papers on organization in Chapter 3, and other papers on the DVMT system by Corkill, Durfee, Hudlicka, and Lesser in this book.)

AN OBJECT-ORIENTED APPROACH TO KNOWLEDGE SYSTEMS

Mario Tokoro and Yutaka Ishikawa

Department of Electrical Engineering
Keio University
3-14-1 Hiyoshi, Yokohama 223 JAPAN

ABSTRACT

A method for an object oriented modeling of knowledge systems called DKOM (Distributed Knowledge Object Modeling) is proposed. In this modeling method, a knowledge system consists of cooperative knowledge objects, where each knowledge object consists of a behavior part, a knowledge part, and a monitor part. An object oriented language called ORIENT84/K has been designed based on the DKOM. The behavior part of an object contains methods like those in Smalltalk; the knowledge part contains rules and facts like those in Prolog; and the monitor part monitors and controls the object. The relation between class and object, the relation between the behavior part and knowledge part, inference from knowledge, addition and deletion of knowledge, addition and deletion of methods, and access control of objects are described. An expert system is built using ORIENT84/K and the performance of ORIENT84/K is compared with some other programming languages/systems.

1. INTRODUCTION

Various knowledge-based systems have been built to understand intellectual processes in the fields of expert systems, robotics, natural language understanding, learning systems and so forth [Barr and Feigenbaum 1981]. In the development of most of these systems, first tailored software tools had to be produced to build individual objective systems [Hayes-Roth et al. 1983], and most of the systems were programmed in Lisp, which is considered to be a low level language for knowledge system implementation. Thus, demands for generalized programming languages/systems have arisen.

There have been several programming languages/systems proposed to support the building of knowledge systems. For example, KRL [Bobrow and Winograd 1976] and FRL [Goldstein and Roberts 1977] are based on **frames** and are implemented on Lisp. OPS-5 [Forgy 1981] is based on the **production system** and is implemented on Lisp. PIE [Goldstein and Bobrow 1981] is based on

frames and is implemented on Smalltalk. LOOPS [Bobrow 1982] combined an **object-oriented paradigm** and a production-based **rule-oriented paradigm** on Lisp. LOOKS [Mizoguchi et al. 1984] and Mandala [Furukawa et al. 1984] have adopted **logic programming paradigm** approaches.

In order to build large knowledge systems, we need a programming language/system with (i) a wider application area, (ii) a higher descriptivity and maintainability, and (iii) a higher execution efficiency. With this in mind, we propose a new modeling method, called **Distributed Knowledge Object Modeling** (DKOM), for representing knowledge systems. In DKOM, a knowledge system is composed of distributed **Knowledge Objects** (KO), each of which consists of a **behavior part**, a **knowledge-base part**, and a **monitor part**. Knowledge objects run in parallel, and communicate with each other by message passing. A knowledge object makes decisions according to its knowledge in responding to a request message. It may send messages to other objects to ask their help in making a decision. It can acquire knowledge using inquiry messages and can generalize its knowledge. The monitor part monitors and controls all the activities of the object.

An object oriented language called ORIENT84/K has been designed based on the DKOM. This language provides the capability of describing the behavior of an object as the Smalltalk-80 [Goldberg and Robson 1983] system. It provides the capability of describing rules and facts as Prolog. A prototype of ORIENT84/K has been implemented on Franz Lisp. The final version will be implemented on an object oriented architecture which is being built [Ishikawa and Tokoro 1984]. It will provide capabilities for the execution of a knowledge system in a distributed multiprocessor environment.

In the next section, we discuss issues in generalized programming languages/systems for building knowledge systems and propose the Distributed Knowledge Object Modeling (DKOM). In section three, we describe an object oriented language ORIENT84/K with examples. In section four, we describe a knowledge system programmed in ORIENT84/K and the descriptive capability of ORIENT84/K is discussed in comparison with other programming languages/systems. In the last section, we conclude with remarks on the DKOM and ORIENT84/K and future plans.

2. DISTRIBUTED KNOWLEDGE OBJECT MODEL

2.1. Principal Objective

Let us first consider the intellectual behavior of a human being. We have acceptors such as eyes and ears to receive data, memory to record information, and actuators such as hands and vocal chords to output data. The process of our behavior could be simplified and described as follows:

(1) On accepting data through acceptors, we interpret the data in order to recognize them as information.

(2) We then infer from knowledge in our memory to make a decision. We may initiate actions through actuators to obtain further knowledge for making decisions. Or we may hypothesize and prove, and we generalize rules in making decisions.

(3) By using the decision made in (2), we initiate final actions that are usually irreversible.

(4) We monitor the effect of the actions made in (3) as feed-back for future decision making. We also monitor the process of inference in (2) to improve our decision making process.

There have been various discussions about knowledge systems and their description languages/systems, but mainly from the viewpoint of process (2). Since process (2) is the process of simulating the real world in a knowledge system, modeling from the viewpoint of process (2) is appropriate for most knowledge systems, especially for expert systems. In other areas of knowledge systems such as robotics, knowledge systems include all the above processes.

Our principal objective is to devise a new modeling scheme and programming language/system based on the modeling scheme for describing large knowledge systems: the programming language/system can simulate all of the four processes listed above. In the following subsections, we discuss some important issues in achieving our principal objective.

2.2. Execution Mechanisms

Representing a program in either a **declarative manner** or a **procedural manner** is an old yet important issue [Winograd 1975]. Writing a program in a declarative manner is usually very easy for knowledge systems in a well-defined area. On the other hand, it usually gives us less efficiency than a procedural representation. In addition, when we would like to control the execution of programs, programs become very complicated.

Representing a program in a procedural manner is suitable for describing behavior of an object. A procedural language can easily manipulate arbitrary data structures. However, it is not always appropriate to describe rules and facts. Therefore, we would like to utilize both representations and their execution mechanisms in our programming language/system.

2.3. Modularization Mechanisms

In representing knowledge systems, there are two levels of modularization:

(1) the **rule/fact level modularization** in which modular programming is achieved at the granularity of a rule or a fact, and

(2) the **object level modularization** in which modular programming is achieved at the granularity of an object.

The rule/fact level modularization premises that a knowledge system consists of a collection of knowledge fragments. Production system-based languages such as OPS-5 and predicate logic-based languages such as Prolog are examples of this modularization. Since each knowledge fragment can be treated independently from others, it is easy to append knowledge to and delete knowledge from a knowledge system. On the other hand, it is difficult to find relations among rules and facts. In addition, for a large knowledge system, conditions for each rule or fact tends to be complex.

The object level modularization premises that knowledge relating to an object should be contained in the object and that a knowledge system consists of a collection of such objects. Such modularization is favorable from the viewpoint of execution efficiency. However, it is sometimes difficult to represent general rules or interrelations among objects.

We would like to utilize both of the modularization. That is to say, we would like to describe a knowledge system as a collection of objects, where knowledge in each object is represented at the level of a rule or a fact.

2.4. Predicate Logic Approach and Object Oriented Approach

Prolog can be considered to be a predicate logic-based declarative language (rather than procedural language) with the rule/fact level modularization. The Smalltalk-80 system can be considered as a procedural language (rather than declarative language) with the object level modularization.

Although these languages appear in quite different manners, there is a duality relation between them. In predicate logic, predicate "m is Q to n" is described as

$$Q(m, n).$$

Thus, predicate Q knows and holds all the pairs of

X and Y which make this predicate true. In object orientation, object m provides the following method of implementing an equivalent effect:

```
Q: x | |
    x isNil ifTrue:[ ↑ n ]
    ↑ x == n.
```

The unification function of Prolog can also be described in the object oriented manner by using broadcast messages. For example, a Prolog clause

C(X, Y) :- P(X, Z), Q(Z, Y).

for a given x for X can be described in an object-oriented manner as follows:

```
C: y | z answer |
    answer ← OrderedCollection new.
    z ← nil.
    z ← self P: z.
    (z isEmpty) whileFalse:[
        (((z removeLast) Q: y) isNil)
            ifFalse:[ answer addLast: y]
    ]
    ↑ answer.
```

In predicate logic, it is natural to represent relations among concepts (objects) and it is powerful for deriving new relations from a given relation among concepts. It is, however, impossible to represent history sensitive characteristics, or states, of concepts. Thus, we need lists of characters to be passed between predicates in Prolog. In this sense, Prolog is used as a list processing language whose syntax is predicate logic oriented.

In object orientation, the abstraction of concepts is easily achieved by using class definitions and the instantiation of the object. Hierarchical abstraction is also achieved by using the notion of class inheritance. Thus, object orientation is suitable for representing the characteristics or properties of objects, including the time-varying states of objects. In object orientation, however, it is really difficult to represent relations among objects as we saw in the above example.

2.5. Proposal of Distributed Knowledge Object Modeling

In concluding the above discussions, we propose a method of **Distributed Knowledge Object Modeling** (DKOM) for knowledge systems. In order to represent a large knowledge system in a simple and natural way, we consider that it should be composed of small knowledge systems, each of which can simulates all the processes described in subsection 2.1. Thus, in DKOM, a knowledge system consists of distributed **Knowledge Objects** (KO's). A knowledge object consists of **behavior part,** **knowledge-base part,** and **monitor part** (Fig. 1). It is created by its class. A class can have multiple super classes.

Knowledge objects run in parallel, and communicate with each other by message passing. A knowledge object makes decisions based upon its knowledge in responding to a request message. It may send messages to other objects to ask for their help in making decisions. It can acquire knowledge by inquiry messages and can generalize knowledge.

The behavior part is described in a procedural manner. It contains methods defined in its class and that inherited from its super classes. A method can be considered to be a procedure that describes an action of the object or as an attribute of the object. A method sends messages and manipulates its own variables in this object. There are some predefined methods (which are defined in class Object) for accessing the knowledge-base part. There are a few predefined methods for inferring from the knowledge in the knowledge-base part.

The knowledge-base part of an object is described in a declarative manner. It is the local knowledge-base of the object, containing rules and facts defined in its class, inherited from its super classes, and acquired through inquiry message to other objects. This part could be thought of as own variables of the object, except that there are predefined methods to infer from the knowledge in this part.

The monitor part is the demon for the object. It controls incoming messages, monitors the object's behavior and inferences, and improves the behavior and the knowledge-base of this object by using gathered statistics.

The following section describes an object-oriented language called ORIENT84/K, which is based on DKOM.

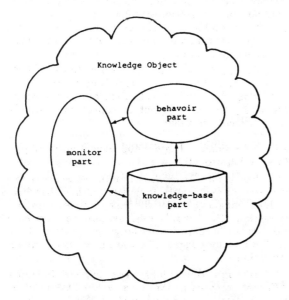

Fig. 1 The components of a Knowledge Object

3. ORIENT84/K

In this section, an outline of the language is described with examples.

3.1. General Structure

The syntax and semantics of ORIENT84/K owe much to and are extended from Smalltalk-80. It has the **metaclass-class-instance** hierarchy, and the **multiple inheritance** from multiple super classes. All the objects run in parallel.

A class describes the common attributes and local knowledge-base of the instances of this class. Such an instance is called a knowledge object of the class. Knowledge objects communicate with each other by message passing.

The syntax and semantics of the knowledge-base part owe much to Prolog. We extended the kind of terms and modified the syntax in defining the interface with the behavior part. The capability of list processing is omitted, since list processing can be naturally described in the behavior part.

In the following subsection, the syntax and semantics of ORIENT84/K is described with using a modified BNF notation, where / is used for selection instead of usual | , {a} is optional, both {a}... and a... represent aaa..., and a{b}... represents aba...ba.

3.2. Class

A class definition consists of two sections: a **class section** and an **instance section**. The class section defines the class's **monitor part, behavior part,** and **knowledge-base part.** The instance section defines the instance's **monitor part, behavior part,** and **knowledge-base part.**

<class definition> ::=   **CLASS** <class name>
  INHERIT FROM <class name>...
  CLASS SECTION <section body>
  INSTANCE SECTION <section body>
<section body> ::=
  OWN VARIABLES <own variable definition>...
  MONITOR PART <monitor part>
  BEHAVIOR PART <behavior part>
  KNOWLEDGE-BASE PART
    <knowledge-base part>
<own variable definition> ::=
  <own variable>{ \ <class name> }
<own variable> ::= <variable name>

The declaration **INHERIT FROM** specifies the super classes of this class. Variables can optionally be **typed** by classes. The default type for a variable is **any.**

3.3. Monitor Part

The monitor part has the following functions: access control, prioritorized message handling, and statistics gathering. The specification of this part is not fixed, since this part largely relates to a system description language of the same ORIENT84/K language family.

<monitor part> ::=
  ACCESSIBLE FROM <access permission list>...
  PRIORITY <methods priority>...
<access permission list> ::= <object name>
  :<message pattern definition>...
<methods priority> ::= <priority level>
  :<message pattern definition>...

The declaration **ACCESSIBLE FROM** specifies to whom an instance shows which subset of methods of the instance. An access permission list can be added/deleted in the execution of the object by the **add_permission** <access permission list> and **delete_permission** <access permission list> predefined methods of class Object.

Arrival of a message with a higher priority method suspends the execution of any lower priority method which might be executing. The declaration of **active values** would be specified in the monitor part. A statistic gathering function should be provided in the monitor part so that the method part can utilize the statistical information for reorganizing methods and knowledge.

3.4. Behavior Part

The behavior part contains methods. Methods are the attributes of the instance which are seen by others. A method is executed by receiving a corresponding message, and may or may not return an answer to the caller. The execution of a message may change the state of the object.

<behavior part> ::= <method definition>...
<method definition> ::=
  <message pattern definition>
  |{ <temporary variable definition>... }|
  <statement>...
<temporary variable definition> ::=
  <temporary variable>{ \ <class name> }
<message pattern definition> ::= <unary selector>/
  <binary selector> <formal variable definition> /
  { <keyword> <formal variable definition> }...
<formal variable definition> ::=
  <formal variable>{ \ <class name>}
<temporary variable> ::= <variable name>
<formal variable> ::= <variable name>

In order to add and delete methods to and from the object, we have the following predefined methods: **add_method** <method definition> and **delete_method** <message pattern definition>.

3.5. Knowledge-Base Part

The knowledge-base part is the local knowledge base of the object. It contains the facts of the object, facts of other objects, and rules obtaining among objects which are defined in its class, inherited from super classes, and/or acquired by message passing. It can be considered to be the object's special own variables which contain rules and facts. Unlike in Smalltalk-80, the rules and facts defined in a class and acquired by message passing, together with inherited rules and facts, can be used by methods defined in the class and super classes. That is to say, the visibility of rules and facts through the super chains is equivalent to that of methods in Smalltalk-80.

<knowledge-base part> ::= <clause>...
<clause> ::= <fact definition> / <rule definition>
<fact definition> ::= <left hand formula> .
<rule definition> ::= <left hand formula>
      |{ <temporary variable definition>... }|
        <right hand formula>{,}... .

<left hand formula> ::=
    <predicate> (<L-term>{,}...)
<right hand formula>::=<atomic formula> /
    self <message pattern>
<atomic formula> ::= <predicate>(<R-term>{,}...)
<L-term> ::= <string constant> / <own variable> /
    <K-formal variable definition>
<R-term> ::= <string constant> / <own variable>
    / <K-formal variable>
    / <temporary variable> / !
<string constant> ::= '<characters>'
<K-formal variable definition> ::=
    <K-formal variable>{ \ <class name>}
<K-formal variable> ::= ? <variable name>

Four kinds of terms are used in the knowledge-base part: a string constant, an own variable, a K-formal variable, and a temporary variable. As shown in Table 1, string constants correspond to constants in Prolog. K-formal variables corresponds to variables in Prolog and are used to pass information between the behavior part and the knowledge part. There are no correspondents of own variables in Prolog. Own variables are used to pass information from the behavior part to the knowledge part. When unified, an own variable acts as a constant in Prolog, since it has been bound to an object. In the clause of brother(?x, ?y), f declares a temporary variable as in the method part. Thus, temporary variables correspond to variables in Prolog.

A mechanism to call a method of an object from inside the knowledge-base part of the object is provided. By using this mechanism, preserving all the backtrack information, a rule can call a method for more information, and then continue inferences.

The contents of the knowledge-base part can be changed at any time by the execution of the predefined methods **addKB** (<clause>) **appendKB** (<clause>) and **deleteKB** (<clause>). The **addKB** and **appendKB** methods correspond to **asserta** and **assertz** of Prolog, respectively.

3.6. Interaction between Behavior and Knowledge-Base Part

As in Conniver [Sussman and McDermott 1972], a method can initiate inference by using the predefined methods **unify** and **foreach_unify**. Information is passed between the behavior part and the knowledge-base part through L-formal variables and own variables. Symbol ? is used to show that ?<variable name> returns a unified result from the knowledge-base part and this result is accessed by the <variable name> in the behavior part. The unify method returns one set of unified results for the L-formal variables. The foreach_unify returns all sets of unified results for the L-formal variables. It sends **value** for each set of unified result to the **block** that follows.

For example, a method which sends mail to all the brothers of somebody m is described in this model as follows:

INSTANCE VARIABLES
    john tom mike andy peter henry robert
BEHAVIOR PART
    sendToBrothersOf: m mail: mess1 | x |
      foreach_unify(brother(m, ?x))
        do:[:x| → x sendMail: mess1].
KNOWLEDGE-BASE PART
    "RULE"
      brother(?x, ?y) | f |
        father(?x, f), father(?y, f).
    "FACT"
      father(john, henry).
      father(tom, robert).
      father(mike, henry).
      father(andy, robert).
      father(peter, robert).

The following is an example of changing the content of the knowledge base part. In order to acquire the facts of the mother-child relation, the following expression, which yields broadcasting, is executed:

    askMother | m x |
      foreach_unify(name(?x))
        do:[:x | m ← x mother.
        appendKB(mother(x, m))].

Table 1 Correspondence between ORIENT84/K variables and Prolog variables

ORIENT84/K	Prolog
father(?x, 'y').	father(X, y).
father(x, y).	none

brotner(?x, ?y) | f |
   father(?x, f), father(?y, f).
	brother(X, Y) :-
	   father(X, F), father(Y, F).

3.7. Synchronization

In Smalltalk, objects are not executed concurrently. Thus, a message is sent and the object blocks until the receiver returns the results. In contrast, objects are executed concurrently in DKOM. In order to maximaly utilize the capability of this modeling, we added a syntax for the non-blocking message send that does not need the result to be returned. Thus, <expression> can be in the form:

→ <object name> <message pattern>.

The non-blocking message send is effectively used to send a broadcast message as shown in one of the previous examples.

4. BUILDING AN EXPERT SYSTEM

4.1. Program

In order to examine the descriptive capability of ORIENT84/K, a well-known expert system problem, the building of an expert system for the emergency management of inland oil and hazardous chemical spills at the Oak Ridge National Laboratory ORNL, was chosen. This expert system was described in EMYCIN, KAS, EXPERT, OPS-5, ROSIE, RLL, and others, in order to compare their descriptive capability [Hayes-Roth et al. 1983].

This problem is classified as a crisis-management problem. When a discovery of spills of oil, hazardous chemical, or base is reported, the expert system locates the source of the spill, identifies the spilled material, estimates the quantity of the spill flow, evaluates the hazards, notifies inhabitants, designates countermeasures for the spill flow, and reports to responsible authorities.

The expert system possesses knowledge of geographical information, quantities and kinds of materials in storages, characteristics of the materials, countermeasures, regulations concerning the hazards of chemical materials, and so forth. In order to pursue these tasks, the expert system infers from this knowledge, asks the reporter, and frees men for getting more information.

We built a simplified version of this expert system with using ORIENT84/K. The program for this expert system consists of five classes: class Problem defines an object which receives the discovery of spills, class ORNL defines an object which advises about the way to find the source of a spill and to identify the material, class Building defines the storage of materials and countermeasures, class OSC defines the inference method for finding the source, and class Material defines the characteristics of materials. The hierarchical relation among these classes is shown in Fig. 2.

In execution, a user sends messages to class Problem to create an instance problem1, which contains the information about the discovery of a spill. Then, the user sends instance problem1 to the instance ornl of the class ORNL. The instance ornl analyzes the information and advises the user for locating the source of the spill. According to the advices, the user gets more information, and reports back to the instance ornl. When the sources are determined, the instance ornl sends messages to an instance bldgXXXX, which is an instance of class Building to perform countermeasures. Then, the instance ornl sends the user advice for locating other sources of spills. Fig: 3 shows the relation of objects in execution. Fig. 4 shows a part of the class definitions.

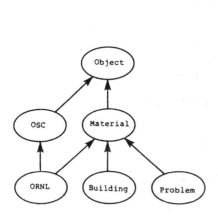

An arrow indicates the superclass-subclass relation

Fig. 2 The hierarchical relation
among the class

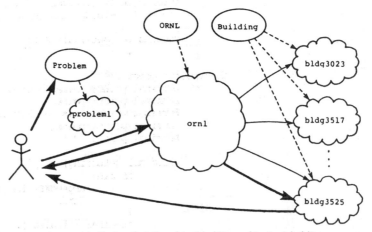

An arrow indicates that the object holds an object. A boldface arrow indicates that the object sends a message to an instance or a class. A dotted arrow indicates that the object is created by the class.

Fig. 3 The relation among objects in execution

```
CLASS                    OSC
   INHERIT FROM          Object
   CLASS SECTION
                             .
                             .
                             .
   INSTANCE SECTION
                             .
                             .
      KNOWLEDGE-BASE PART
                             .
                             .
      findSource(?bldg, ?source, ?smat) | loc tbldg |
            flow_loc(loc), find(?source, loc),
                source(tbldg, ?source),
                storage(?smat, ?source), obj(?bldg, tbldg).

      find(?source, ?dest) | yy |
            arc(yy, ?dest), findl(?source, yy).
      find(?source, ?dest) | mat |
            posmat(mat), storage(mat, ?source),
                !, self checkpoint: ?dest.

      findl(?source, ?dest) | tt |
            merge(?dest), !, arc(tt, ?dest), fss(tt),
                !, self checkpoint: ?dest, find(?source, ?dest).
      findl(?source, ?dest) | |
            fss(?dest), find(?source, ?dest).
                             .
                             .

CLASS                    ORNL
   INHERIT FROM          OSC Material
   CLASS SECTION
                             .
                             .
   INSTANCE SECTION
      BEHAVIOR PART
                             .
                             .
      call: problem | bldg loc mat |
                             .
                             .
            foreach_unify(findSource(?bldg, ?loc, ?mat)) do: [
             :bldg |    ->bldg countermeasure: loc.
            ]
            problem set_material: mat.
                             .

      checkpoint: point | |
            Terminal print: 'Please inspect '.
            Terminal print: point.
            Terminal print: ' Is the liquid flowing in '.
            Terminal print: point.
            Terminal print: '? '.

            (Terminal getstring) = 'y'
                    ifTrue: [
                            appendKB(flow(point)).
                            ↑true.
                    ]
                    ifFalse: [ ↑false ].
                             .
                             .
```

Fig. 4 The description of an expert system in ORIENT84/K

4.2. Discussion

As we see the part of the program of this expert system in Fig. 4, ORIENT84/K naturally describes the problem in both the object-oriented paradigm with message passing and the predicate logic-based paradigm.

The same expert system has been programmed using Prolog. The structure of the part of the program for inference was the same as that in the class ORNL. Since Prolog does not support the object-oriented paradigm, we used a file for each instance in the ORIENT84/K program and reconsulted the files as the program proceeded. One of the weak points in Prolog is the difficulty of naming predicates uniquely. In the other words, there is no visibility control in Prolog. Thus, even though we store clauses in different files, all of the clauses are flat at the time of execution. This caused program bugs. On contrary, ORIENT84/K provides a knowledge-base for each object. Therefore, it was easier to write this expert system in ORIENT84/K. ORIENT84/K also surpassed Prolog in writing parts other than unification.

We also described the same expert system in LISP. In the LISP program, we stored the geography of the drain flows in a list and searched the possible sources of the spill on the list. It seems to be difficult to change the list when new buildings, new drains, or new materials were added.

When we would implement the same expert system in Smalltalk, we should define a class which provides methods of inference and the structure to retain knowledge. The program would look similar to that written in ORIENT84/K. The essential difference, however, is that the inference mechanism and the knowledge-base are defined together in a class in Smalltalk, while they are contained in an object or distributed in multiple objects in ORIENT84/K.

5. Conclusion

In this paper we proposed the method for the Distributed Knowledge Object Modeling (DKOM) and described the outline of an object oriented language called ORIENT84/K as a realization of this modeling method.

The modeling method views a knowledge system as the composition of cooperative knowledge objects, where each object holds its knowledge-base and communicates with other objects by message passing in order to acquire knowledge. These features coincide with the human activities of communicating, acquiring knowledge, making decisions, and doing actions.

The language provides the rule/fact level modularization and the object level modularization. Thus, we can build knowledge systems in the object-oriented manner and the predicate logic-based rule-oriented manner. Each knowledge object consists of the monitor part, the behavior part, and the knowledge-base part. The behavior part can be considered as a meta function to the knowledge-base part, and the monitor part that interfaces other objects (or worlds) as a meta function to the behavior part. With a little experience in writing programs in ORIENT84/K, we believe such a combination facilitates building large knowledge systems in various fields.

The prototype of the ORIENT84/K system is implemented in Franz Lisp and running on the Unix† operating system. The specification of the language is not complete, especially for the monitor part. This is partially because we would still like to improve the language through the feedback of writing programs. The other reason is because ORIENT84/K is a member of the ORIENT84 family of languages which run on a distributed object-oriented architecture [Ishikawa and Tokoro 1984], and we need to keep coherence throughout the family languages.

The distributed object oriented architecture has been designed and its software simulator is running also on the Unix operating system. Implementation of the ORIENT84/K system on this architecture is about to start, besides the design of some other family languages and the modification of the architecture to execute ORIENT84/K programs efficiently before siliconization planned in 1986.

ACKNOWLEDGEMENT

The authors are indebted to Motoo Kawamura and Takeo Maruichi for their help in the implementation of ORIENT84/K as well as for their valuable comments. The authors are also grateful to the members of ICOT WG2; the discussion with the members on wide spectrum of topics in knowledge representation, languages, and systems inspired this work.

REFERENCES

Barr, A. and Feigenbaum, E.A., "The Handbook of Artificial Intelligence", Volume 1, 2, and 3, William Kaufmann, Inc., 1981, 1982, 1982.

Bobrow, D.G. and Winograd, T., "An Overview of KRL, a Knowledge Representation Language," CSL-76-4, Xerox PARC, July 1976.

Bobrow, D.G., "The LOOPS Manual," Palo Alto Research Center Xerox PARC, KB-VLSI-81-13, 1982

Forgy, C., "The OPS-5 User's Manual," Technical Rept. CMU-CS-81-135, Computer Science Dept., Carnegie-Mellon Univ., 1981.

Furukawa, K. Takeuchi, Yasukawa, H, and Kunifuji, S., "Mandala : A Logic Based Knowledge Programming System," FGCS '84, ICOT, 1984.

Goldberg, I. and Robson, D, "Smalltalk-80: The Language and its Implementation," Addison-Wesley Publishing Co., 1983.

---

† Unix is a trademark of the Bell Laboratories.

Goldstein, I.P. and Roberts, R.B., "NUDGE: A Knowledge-Based Scheduling Program", IJCAI 5, 1977.

Goldstein, I.P. and Bobrow, D., "An Experimental Description-Based Programming Environment: Four Papers," CSL-81-3, Xerox Palo Alto Research Center, 1981.

Hayes-Roth, F., Waterman, D.A., and Lenat, D.B., "Building Expert Systems," Addison-Wesley Publishing Co., 1983.

Ishikawa, Y. and Tokoro, M., "The design of an object oriented architecture," Proc. of the 11th Int'l Symp. on Computer Architecture, Jun 1984.

Mizoguchi, F. Katayama, Y., and Owada, H., "LOOKS: Knowledge Representation System for Designing Expert System in the Framework of Logic Programming," FGCS '84, ICOT, 1984.

Sussmann, G.J. and McDermott, D.V., "From PLANNER to CONNIVER: A genetic approach," AFIPS, 1972.

Winograd, T., "Frame representations and the declarative/procedural controversy," in Representation and Understanding studies in Cognitive Science, Bobrow, D.G. and Colins, A., eds., Academic Press, 1975.

Object-Oriented Concurrent Programming in ABCL/1

Akinori Yonezawa Jean-Pierre Briot and Etsuya Shibayama

Department of Information Science
Tokyo Institute of Technology
Ookayama, Meguro-ku, Tokyo 152
(03)-726-1111 ext. 3209

Abstract

An object-oriented computation model is presented which is designed for modelling and describing a wide variety of concurrent systems. In this model, three types of message passing are incorporated. An overview of a programming language called ABCL/1, whose semantics faithfully reflects this computation model, is also presented. Using ABCL/1, a simple scheme of distributed problem solving is illustrated. Furthermore, we discuss the reply destination mechanism and its applications. A distributed "same fringe" algorithm is presented as an illustration of both the reply destination mechanism and the future type message passing which is one of the three message passing types in our computation model.

1. Introduction

Parallelism is ubiquitous in our problem domains. The behavior of computer systems, human information processing systems, corporative organizations, scientific societies, etc. is the result of highly concurrent (independent, cooperative, or contentious) activities of their components. We like to model such systems, and design AI and software systems by using various metaphors found in such systems [Smith 1985] [Special Issue 1981] [Yonezawa and Tokoro 1986] [Brodie et al. 1984]. Our approach is to represent the components of such a system as a collection of *objects* [Stefik and Bobrow 1986] and their interactions as *concurrent* message passing among such objects. The problem domains to which we apply our framework include distributed problem solving and planning in AI, modelling human cognitive processes, designing real-time systems and operating systems, and designing and constructing office information systems [Tschritzis 1985].

This paper first presents an object-based model for parallel computation and an overview of a programming language, called ABCL/1 [Yonezawa et al. 1986] [Shibayama and Yonezawa 1986a], which is based on the computation model. Then, schemes of distributed problem solving are illustrated using ABCL/1. Though our computation model has evolved from the Actor model [Hewitt 77] [Hewitt and Baker 1977], the notion of *objects* in our model is different from that of *actors*.

2. Objects

Each *object* in our computation model has its own (autonomous) processing power and it may have its local persistent memory, the contents of which represent its *state*. An object is always in one of three modes: *dormant*, *active*, or *waiting*. An object is initially dormant. It becomes active when it receives a message that satisfies one of the specified patterns and constraints. Each object has a description called *script* (or a set of methods) which specifies its behavior: what messages it accepts and what actions it performs when it receives such messages.

When an active object completes the sequence of actions that are performed in response to an accepted message, if no subsequent messages have arrived, it becomes dormant again. An object in the active mode sometimes needs to stop its current activity in order to wait for a message with specified patterns to arrive. In such a case, an active object changes into the waiting mode. An object in the waiting mode becomes active again when it receives a required message. For instance, suppose a buffer object accepts two kinds of messages: a [:get] message from a consumer object requesting the delivery of one of the stored products, and a [:put <product>] message from a producer object requesting that a product (information) be stored in the buffer. When the buffer object receives a [:get] message from a consumer object and finds that its storage, namely the buffer, is empty, it must wait for a [:put <product>] message to arrive. In such a case the buffer object in the active mode changes into the waiting mode.

An active object can perform usual symbolic and numerical computations, make decisions, send messages to objects (including itself), create new objects and update the contents of its local memory. An object with local memory cannot be activated by more than one message at the same time. Thus, the activation of such an object takes place one at a time.

As mentioned above, each dormant object has a fixed set of patterns and constraints for messages that it can accept and by which it can be activated. To define the behavior of an object, we must specify what computations or actions the object performs for each message pattern and constraint. To write a definition of an object in our language ABCL/1, we use the notation in Figure 1. Figure 2 shows a skeletal definition of an object.

```
[object object-name                      [object Buffer
  (state representation-of-local-memory )   (state ... )
  (script                                   (script
    (=> message-pattern where constraint      (=> [:put ... ]  ...  )
       ...action... )
        .                                     (=> [:get]  ...  ) )]
        .
        .
    (=> message-pattern where constraint
       ...action... ) )]
```

Figure 1. Object Definition   Figure 2. Buffer

(state ...) declares the variables which represent the local persistent memory (we call such variables *state* variables) and specifies their initialization. *object-name* and the construct "where *constraint*" are optional. If a message sent to an object defined in the notation above satisfies more than one pattern-constraint pair, the first pair (from the top of the script) is chosen and the corresponding sequence of actions is performed.

An object changes into the waiting mode when it performs a special action. In ABCL/1, this action (i.e., the transition of an object from the active mode to the waiting mode) is expressed by a *select*-construct. A select construct also specifies the patterns and constraints of messages that are able to reactivate the object. We call this a *selective message receipt*.

```
(select
  (=> message-pattern where constraint     ... action ...)
        .
        .
  (=> message-pattern where constraint     ... action ...))
```

Figure 3. Select Construct

As an example of the use of this construct, we give, in Figure 4, a skeleton of the definition of an object which behaves as a buffer of a bounded size.

```
[object Buffer
  (state declare-the-storage-for-buffer )
  (script
    (=> [:put aProduct]        ; aProduct is a pattern variable.
       (if the-storage-is-full
         then (select          ; then waits for a [:get] message.
                (=> [:get]
                   remove-a-product-from-the-storage-and-return-it )))
         store-aProduct   )

    (=> [:get]
       (if the-storage-is-empty
         then (select          ; then waits for a [:put ...] message.
                (=> [:put aProduct]
                   send-aProduct-to-the-object-which-sent-[:get]-message ))
         else remove-a-product-from-the-storage-and-return-it )) )]
```

Figure 4. An Example of the Use of Select Constructs

Suppose a [:put <product>] arrives at the object Buffer. When the storage in the object Buffer is found to be full, Buffer waits for a [:get] message to arrive. When a [:get] message arrives, Buffer accepts it and returns one of the stored products. If a [:put] message arrives in *this* waiting mode, it will not be accepted (and put into the *message queue* for Buffer, which

will be explained in §3). Then, Buffer continues to wait for a [:get] message to arrive. A more precise explanation will be given in the next section.

As the notation for a select construct suggests, more than one message pattern (and constraint) can be specified, but the ABCL/1 program for the buffer example in Figure 4 contains only one message pattern for each select construct.

3. Message Passing

An object can send a message to any object as long as it knows the name of the target object. The "knows" relation is dynamic: if the name of an object T comes to be known to an object O and as long as O remembers the name of T, O can send a message to T. If an object does not know or forgets the name of a target object, it cannot at least directly send a message to the target object. Thus message passing takes place in a point-to-point (object-to-object) fashion. No message can be broadcast.

All the message transmissions in our computation model are asynchronous in the sense that an object can send a message whenever it likes, irrespective of the current state or mode of the target object. Though message passing in a system of objects may take place concurrently, we assume message arrivals at an object be linearly ordered. No two messages can arrive at the same object simultaneously. Furthermore we make the following (standard) assumption on message arrival:

[Assumption for Preservation of Transmission Ordering]
> When two messages are sent to an object T by the same object O, the temporal ordering of the two message transmissions (according to O's clock) must be preserved in the temporal ordering of the two message arrivals (according to T's clock).

This assumption was not made in the Actor model of computation. Without this, however, it is difficult to model even simple things as objects. For example, a computer terminal or displaying device is difficult to model as an object without this assumption because the order of text lines which are sent by a terminal handling program (in an operating system) must be preserved when they are received. Furthermore, descriptions of distributed algorithms would become very complicated without this assumption.

In modelling various types of interactions and information exchange which take place among physical or conceptual components that comprise parallel or real-time systems, it is often necessary to have two distinct modes of message passing: *ordinary* and *express*. Correspondingly, for each object T, we assume two message queues: one for messages sent to T in the ordinary mode and the other for messages sent in the express mode. Messages are enqueued in arrival order.

[*Ordinary* Mode Message Passing]
> Suppose a message M sent in the ordinary mode arrives at an object T when the message queue associated with T is empty. If T is in the dormant mode, M is checked as to whether or not it is acceptable according to T's script. When M is acceptable, T becomes active and starts performing the actions specified for it. When M is not acceptable, it is discarded. If T is in the active mode, M is put at the end of the *ordinary* message queue associated with T.

If T is in the waiting mode, M is checked to see if it satisfies one of the pattern-and-constraint pairs that T accepts in *this* waiting mode. When M is acceptable, T is reactivated and starts performing the specified actions. When M is not acceptable, it is put at the end of the message queue.

In general, upon the completion of the specified actions of an object, if the ordinary message queue associated with the object is empty, the object becomes dormant. If the queue is not empty, then the first message in the queue is removed and checked as to whether or not it is acceptable to the object according to its script. When it is acceptable, the object stays in the active mode and starts performing the actions specified for the message. If it is not acceptable, the message is discarded and some appropriate default action is taken (for instance, the message is simply discarded, or a default failure message is sent to the sender of the message). Then if the queue is not empty, the new first message in the queue is removed and checked. This process is repeated until the queue becomes empty. When an object changes into the waiting mode, if the ordinary message queue is not empty, then it is searched from its head and the first message that matches one of the required pattern-and-constraint pairs is removed from the queue. Then the removed message reactivates the object. If no such message is found or the queue itself is empty, the object stays in the waiting mode and keeps waiting for such a message to arrive. Note that the waiting mode does not imply "busy wait".

[*Express* Mode Message Passing]

Suppose a message M sent in the *express* mode arrives at an object T. If T has been previously activated by a message which was also sent to T in the *express* mode, M is put at the end of the *express* message queue associated with T. Otherwise, M is checked to see if it satisfies one of the pattern-and-constraint pairs that T accepts. If M is acceptable, T starts performing the actions specified for M even if T has been previously activated by a message sent to T in the *ordinary* mode. The actions specified for the previous message are suspended until the actions specified for M are completed. If so specified, the suspended actions are aborted. But, in default, they are resumed.

An object cannot accept an *ordinary* mode message as long as it stays in the active mode. Thus, without the express mode message passing, no request would be responded to by an object in the active mode. For example, consider an object which models a problem solver working hard to solve a given problem (cf. §7). If the given problem is too hard and very little progress can be made, we would have no means to stop him or make him give up. Thus without the express mode, we cannot monitor the state of an object (process) which is continuously in operation and also cannot change the course of its operation. More discussion about the express mode will be found in §5.3, §10.2, and §10.3.

As was discussed above, objects are autonomous information processing agents and interact with other objects only through message passing. In modelling interactions among such autonomous objects, the convention of message passing should incorporate a *natural* model of synchronization among interacting objects. In our computation model, we distinguish

three types of message passing: *past*, *now*, and *future*. In what follows, we discuss each of them in turn. The following discussions are valid, irrespective of whether messages are sent in the ordinary or express mode.

[*Past* Type Message Passing] (send and no wait)

Suppose an object O has been activated and it sends a message M to an object T. Then O does not wait for M to be received by T. It just continues its computation after the transmission of M (if the transmission of M is not the last action of the current activity of O).

We call this type of message passing *past* type because sending a message finishes before it causes the intended effects to the message receiving object. Let us denote a past type message passing in the ordinary and the express modes by:

$$[T <\text{-} M] \quad \text{and} \quad [T <<\text{-} M],$$

respectively. The past type corresponds to a situation where one requests or commands someone to do some task and simultaneously he proceeds his own task without waiting for the requested task to be completed. This type of message passing substantially increases the concurrency of activities within a system.

[*Now* Type Message Passing] (send and wait)

When an object O sends a message M to an object T, O waits for not only M to be received by T, but also waits for T to send some information back to O.

This is similar to ordinary function/procedure calls, but it differs in that T's activation does not have to end with sending some information back to O. T may continue its computation after sending back some information to O. A now type message passing in the ordinary and express modes are denoted by:

$$[T <\text{==} M] \quad \text{and} \quad [T <<\text{==} M],$$

respectively. Returning information from T to O may serve as an acknowledgement of receiving the message (or request) as well as reporting the result of a requested task. Thus the message sending object O is able to know for certain that his message was received by the object T though he may waste time waiting. The returned information (certain values or signals) is denoted by the same notation as that of a now type message passing. That is, the above notation denotes not merely an action of sending M to T by a now type message passing, but also denotes the information returned by T. This convention is useful in expressing the assignment of the returned value to a variable. For example, $[x := [T <\text{==} M]]$.

Now type message passing provides a convenient means to synchronize concurrent activities performed by independent objects when it is used together with the parallel construct. This construct will not be discussed in this paper. It should be noted that recursive *now* type message passing causes a local deadlock.

[*Future* Type Message Passing] (reply to me later)

Suppose an object O sends a message M to an object T expecting a certain requested result to be returned from T. But O does not need the result immediately. In this situation, after the transmission of M, O does not have to wait for T to return the result. It continues its computation immediately. Later on when O needs that result, it checks its special *private* object called *future object* that was specified at the time of the transmission of M. If the result has been stored in the future object, it can be used.

Of course, O can check whether or not the result is available before the result is actually used. A future type message passing in the ordinary and express modes are denoted by:

$$[T <= M \$ x] \quad \text{and} \quad [T <<= M \$ x],$$

respectively, where x stands for a special variable called *future variable* which binds a future object. We assume that a future object behaves like a queue. The contents of the queue can be checked or removed *solely* by the object O which performed the future type message passing. Using a special expression "(ready? x)", O can check to see if the queue is empty. O could access to the first element of the queue with a special expression "(next-value x)", or to all the elements with "(all-values x)". If the queue is empty in such cases, O has to wait. (Its precise behavior will be given in §6.2.).

A system's concurrency is increased by the use of future type message passing. If the now type is used instead of the future type, O has to waste time waiting for the currently unnecessary result to be produced. Message passing of a somewhat similar vein has been adopted in previous object-oriented programming languages. Act1, an actor-based language developed by H. Lieberman [1981] has a language feature called "future," but it is different from ours. The three types of message passing are illustrated in Figure 5.

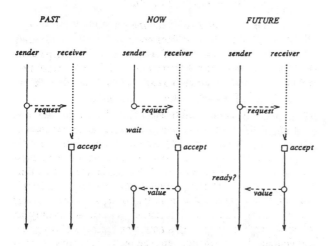

Figure 5. The Three Message Passing Types

Though our computation model for object-oriented concurrent programming is a descendant of the Actor computation model which has been proposed and studied by C. Hewitt and his group at MIT [Hewitt 1977] [Hewitt and Baker 1977] [Yonezawa and Hewitt 1979] [Lieberman 1981], it differs from the Actor computation model in many respects. For example, in our computation model, an object in the waiting mode can accept a message which is not at the head of the message queue, whereas, in the actor computation model, a (serialized) actor can only accept a message that is placed at the head of the message queue. Furthermore, now type and future type message passing are not allowed in the Actor computation model. Therefore, an actor A which sends a message to a target actor T and expects a response from T must terminate its current activity and receive the response as just one of any incoming messages. To discriminate T's response from other incoming

messages arriving at A, some provision must be made before the message is sent to T. Also the necessity of the termination of A's current activity to receive T's response causes unnatural breaking down of A's task into small pieces.

4. Messages

We will consider what information a message may contain. A message is composed of a singleton or a sequence of *tags*, *parameters*, and/or *names of objects*. Tags are used to distinguish message patterns. (In the buffer example mentioned in Figure 4, :get and :put are tags, and "aProduct" denotes a parameter in the [:put ...] message.) Object names contained in a message can be used for various purposes. For example, when an object O sends a message M to an object T requesting T to do some task, and O wishes T to send the result of the requested task to a specified object C1, O can include the name of C1 in the message M. Objects used in this way correspond to "continuation" (or customer) in the Actor computation model. Also, when O requests T to do some task in cooperation with a specified object C2, O must let T know the name of C2 by including it in the message M.

Besides the information contained in a message itself, we assume two other kinds of information can be transmitted in message passing. One is the *sender name* and the other is the *reply destination*. When a message sent from an object O is received by an object T, it is assumed that the name of the sender object O becomes known to the receiver object T. (We denote the sender name by "&sender" in ABCL/1.) This assumption considerably strengthens the expressive power of the model and it is easy to realize in the implementation of our computation model. A receiver object can decide whether it accepts or rejects an incoming message on the basis of who (or what object) sent the message.

When an object T receives a message sent in a now or future type message passing, T is required to reply to the message or return the result of the requested task (or just an acknowledgement). Since the destination to which the result should be returned is known at the time of the message transmission, we assume that such information about the destination is available to the receiver object T (and this information can be passed around among objects). We call such information the *reply destination*. To specify the object to which the result should be returned, the *reply destination* mechanism provides a more uniform way than simply including the name of the object in the request message. This mechanism is compatible with the three types of message passing, and enables us to use both explicit reply destinations in case of past type message as well as implicit ones in case of now or future type messages (cf. §6 and §9). Furthermore, the availability of the reply destination allows us to specify continuations and implement various *delegation* mechanisms [Lieberman 1986] uniformly. This will be discussed in the §8.

The fact that sender names and reply destinations can be known to message receiving objects not only makes the computation model powerful, but also makes it possible that the three different types of message passing: *past*, *now*, and *future*, be reduced to just one type of message passing, namely the *past* type message passing. In fact, a now type message passing in an object T can be expressed in terms of past type message passing together with the transition into the waiting mode in the execution of the script of the object T. And a future type message passing can be expressed in terms of past and now type message passing, which are in turn reduced to past type message passing. These reductions can be actually demonstrated, but to do so, we need a formal language. Since the programming language ABCL/1 to be introduced in the subsequent sections can also serve this purpose, we will give an actual demonstration after the explanation of ABCL/1 (cf. §6). The reply destination mechanism plays an important role in the demonstration.

5. An Overview of the Language ABCL/1

5.1. Design Principles

The primary design principles of our language, ABCL/1, are:

[1] [Clear Semantics of Message Passing] The semantics of message passing among objects should be transparent and faithful to the underlying computation model.

[2] [Practicality] Intentionally, we do not pursue the approach in which every single concept in computation should be represented purely in terms of objects and message passing. In describing the object's behavior, basic values, data structures (such as numbers, strings, lists), and invocations of operations manipulating them may be assumed to exist as they are, not necessarily as objects or message passing. Control structures (such as *if-then-else* and looping) used in the description of the behavior of an object are not necessarily based upon message passing (though they can of course be interpreted in terms of message passing).

Thus in ABCL/1, *inter*-object message passing is entirely based on the underlying object-oriented computation model, but the representation of the behavior (script) of an object may contain conventional *applicative* and *imperative* features, which we believe makes ABCL/1 programs easier to read and write from the viewpoint of *conventional* programmers. Since we are trying to grasp and exploit a complicated phenomenon, namely parallelism, a rather conservative approach is taken in describing the internal behavior of individual objects. Various applicative and imperative features in the current version of ABCL/1 are expressed in terms of Lisp-like parenthesized prefix notations, but that is not essential at all; such features may be written in other notations employed in various languages such as C or Fortran.

5.2. Creating Objects and Returning Messages

In our computation model, objects can be dynamically created. Usually, when an object A needs a new object B, A sends, in a now or future type message passing, some initial information to a certain object which *creates* B. Then B is returned as the value (or result) of the now/future type message passing. This way of creating an object is often described in ABCL/1 as follows:

```
[object CreateSomething
  (script
    (=> pattern-for-initial-info  ![object ... ] ) )]
```

where [object ....] is the definition of an object newly created by the object CreateSomething. The CreateAlarmClock object defined in Figure 6 creates and returns an alarm clock object when it receives a [:new ...] message containing the person (object) to wake. The time to ring is set by sending a [:wake-me-at ...] message to the alarm clock object. It is supposed to keep receiving [:tick ...] messages from a clock object (called the Ticker and which will be defined in the next subsection). When the time contained in a [:tick ...] message is equal to the time to ring, the alarm clock object sends a [:time-is-up] message to the person to wake in the express mode.

```
[object CreateAlarmClock
  (script
    (=> [:new Person-to-wake]

    ![object
      (state [time-to-ring := nil])
      (script
        (=> [:tick Time]
          (if (= Time time-to-ring)
            then [Person-to-wake <<= [:time-is-up]]))

        (=> [:wake-me-at T]
          [time-to-ring := T]) )] ) ) )]
```

Figure 6. Definition of CreateAlarmClock Object

Note that the "Person-to-wake" variable in the script of the alarm clock object to be created is a free variable (it is not a state variable nor a message parameter). It will be "closured" when creating this object, which implies that the scope rule of ABCL/1 is lexical. The notation using ! is often used in ABCL/1 to express an event of returning or sending back a value in response to a request which is sent in a now or future type message passing. In the following fragment of a script:

(=> *pattern-for-request*   ... !*expression* ...   ),

where is the value of *expression* returned? In fact, this notation is an abbreviated form of a more explicit description which uses the reply destination. An equivalent and more explicit form is:

(=> *pattern-for-request* @ *destination*   ... [*destination* <= *expression*] ...)

where *destination* is a pattern variable which is bound to the reply destination for a message that matches *pattern-for-request*. When a message is sent in a past type message passing, if we need to specify the reply destination, it can be expressed as:

[T <= *request* @ *reply-destination*].

Note that *reply-destination* denotes an object. In the case of now or future type message passing, pattern variables for reply destination are matched with certain objects that the semantics of now/future type message passing defines. (See §6.) Thus the programmer is not allowed to explicitly specify reply destinations in now or future type message passing. So the following expressions [*target* <== *message* @ *reply-destination*], and [*target* <= *message* @ *reply-destination* $ x] are illegal.

There is another way to create an object. That is, an object can be obtained by copying some object. We can use the copy instantiation model [Briot 1984] after defining a prototype [Lieberman 1986], rather than defining a generator object (analog to a class). Each object can invoke a primitive function "self-copy" whose returning value is a copy of the object itself (Me), which will be exemplified in §9.

5.3. Ordinary Mode and Express Mode in Message Passing

The difference between the ordinary mode and express mode in
message passing was explained in §3. The notational distinction between the two modes in message transmission is made
by the number of "<", one for the ordinary mode and two for
the express mode (namely <= and <==, vs. <<= and <<==).
The same distinction should be made in message reception
because a message sent in the ordinary mode should not be
interpreted as one sent in the express mode. To make the distinction explicit, we use the following notation for expressing
the reception of a message sent in the express mode.

(=>> *message-pattern* where *constraint*   ... *action* ...),

The reception of a message sent in the *ordinary* mode is
expressed by the following notation as explained above:

(=> *message-pattern* where *constraint*   ... *action* ...)

This notational distinction protects an object from unwanted
express mode messages because the object accepts only messages that satisfy the patterns and constraints declared after the
notation "(=>>". Express mode messages which do not satisfy
such patterns and constraints are simply discarded.

Suppose a message sent in the express mode arrives at an
object which has been currently activated by an ordinary mode
message. If the script of the object contains the pattern and
constraint that the message satisfies, the current actions are
temporarily terminated (or suspended) and the actions
requested by the express mode message are performed. If the
object is accessing its local persistent memory when the
express mode message arrives, the current actions will not be
terminated until the current access to its local memory is completed. Also, if the object is performing the actions whose
script is enclosed by "(atomic" and ")" in the following
manner:

(atomic   ... *action* ...),

they will not be terminated (or suspended) until they are completed. And if the actions specified by the express mode message are completed and no express mode messages have
arrived yet at that time, the temporarily terminated actions are
resumed by default. But, if the actions specified by the express
mode message contains the "non-resume" command, denoted
by:

(non-resume),

the temporarily terminated actions are aborted and will not be
performed any more.

Note that, in the above explanation, the actions temporarily terminated by an express mode message are the ones
that are activated (specified) by an ordinary mode message.
When an object is currently performing the actions specified by
an express mode message, no message (even in the express
mode) can terminate (or suspend) the current actions.

To illustrate the use of express mode, we give the
definition of the behavior of a clock object Ticker which sends
[:tick ...] messages to all the alarm clocks he knows about (the
value of its state variable "alarm-clocks-list"). The definition
of the Ticker object is given in Figure 7. The two state variables of Ticker, "time" and "alarm-clocks-list", respectively
contain the current time and a list of alarm clocks to be
"ticked". When Ticker receives a [:start] message, it starts
ticking and updating the contents of "time".

[alarm-clocks-list <= [:tick...]]

means sending [:tick ...] messages to each member of "alarm-
clocks-list" simultaneously. We call this way of sending messages *multicast*. When Ticker receives a [:stop] message sent in
the express mode, it stops ticking by the effect of (non-
resume). This message must be sent in the express mode
because Ticker always stays in the active mode to keep ticking
(in the while loop). An [:add ...] message appends new alarm
clock object to the "alarm-clocks-list" in Ticker. This message
also should be sent in the express mode for the same reason.

```
[object Ticker
  (state [time := 0] [alarm-clocks-list := nil])
  (script
   (=> [:start]
    (while t do
      (if alarm-clocks-list
       then [alarm-clocks-list <= [:tick time]])
      [time := (1+ time)]))
   (=>> [:add AlarmClock]
    [alarm-clocks-list := (cons AlarmClock alarm-clocks-list)])
   (=>> [:stop] (non-resume)) )]
```

Figure 7. Definition of Ticker Object

The definition of the CreateAlarmObject (which appeared in
Figure 6) should be slightly changed in order for a newly
created alarm clock object to be known by Ticker. The description of an alarm clock object is the same as in Figure 6, but
when created it will now be bound to a temporary variable
"AlarmClock". Then, after the created object is sent to Ticker
to be appended to Ticker's "alarm-clocks-list", it is returned to
the sender of the [:new ...] message as in the case of Figure 6.

```
[object CreateAlarmClock
  (script
   (=> [:new Person-to-wake]
    (temporary
     [AlarmClock := [object   description of an alarm clock object ]])
    [Ticker <<= [:add AlarmClock]]
    !AlarmClock) )]
```

Figure 8. New Definition of CreateAlarmClock Object

6. A Minimal Computation Model

Below we will demonstrate that

[1] A now type message passing can be reduced to a combination of past type message passing and a selective message
reception in the waiting mode, and
[2] A future type message passing can also be reduced to a
combination of past type message passing and now type
message passing.

Thus both kinds of message passing can be expressed in terms
of past type message passing and selective message reception
in the waiting mode, which means that now type message passing and future type message passing are derived concepts in
our computation model. (The rest of this section could be
skipped if one is not interested in the precise semantics of
"now" and "future" types message passing.)

6.1. Reducing Now Type

Suppose the script of an object A contains a now type message
passing in which a message M is sent to an object T. Let the
object T accept the message M and return the response (i.e.,
send the response to the reply destination for M). This situa-

tion is described by the following definitions for A and T written in ABCL/1.

```
[object A
  ...
  (script
    ...
    (=> message-pattern          ... [T <== M] ...        ) ... )]

[object T
  ...
  (script
    ...
    (=> pattern-for-M @ R    ... [R <= expression ] ...    ) ... )]
```

** Note that the script of T can be abbreviated as:
```
           (=> pattern-for-M    ... !expression ...)
```

We introduce a new object "New-object" which just passes any received message to A, and also introduce a *select*-construct which receives only a message that is sent from "New-object". The behavior of the object A can be redefined without using now type message passing as follows:

```
[object A
 (script
   ...
   (=> message-pattern
   (temporary  [New-object := [object (script (=> any   [A <= any]))] ])
     ...
   [T <= M @ New-object]
   (select
     (=> value where (= &sender New-object)
       ... value ... ))    ... ) ... )]
```

Note that the message M is sent by a past type message passing with the reply destination being the newly created "New-object." Immediately after this message transmission, the object A changes into the waiting mode and waits for a message that is passed by the "New-object". The constraint
                "where (= &sender New-object)"
in the select-construct means that the messages sent by New-Object can only be accepted. "New-object" serves as a unique identifier for the message transmission from A to T in past type: [T <= M @ New-object].

6.2. Reducing Future Type

Suppose the script of an object A contains a future type message passing as follows:

```
[object A
  (state ... )
  (future ... x ... )          ; declaration of a future variable x.
  (script
    ...
    (=> message-pattern
      ... [T <= M $ x] ...
      ... (ready? x) ... (next-value x) ... (all-values x) ... ) ... )]
```

Then we consider the future variable x in A to be a state variable binding a special object created by an object CreateFutureObject. (In general, such a object, namely a future object, is created for each future variable if more than one future variable is declared.) Also we rewrite the accesses to x by now type message passing to x as follows:

```
[object A
  (state ... [x := [CreateFutureObject <== [:new Me]]] ... )
  (script
    ...
    (=> message-pattern
      ... [T <= M @ x] ... [x <== [:ready?]] ...
      ... [x <== [:next-value]] ... [x <== [:all-values]] ... ) ... )]
```

Note that the future type message passing [T <= M $ x] is replaced by a past type message passing [T <= M @ x] with the reply destination being x. Thus, the future type message passing is eliminated. The behavior of the future object is defined in Figure 9. As mentioned before, it is essentially a queue object, but it only accepts message satisfying special pattern-and-constraint pairs. A queue object created by CreateQ accepts four kinds of messages: [:empty?], [:enqueue...], [:dequeue], and [:all-elements].

```
[object CreateFutureObject
 (script
   (=> [:new Creator]
   ![object
     (state [box := [CreateQ <== [:new]]])
     (script
       (=> [:ready?] where (= &sender Creator)      ; if [:ready?] is sent
         !(not [box <== [:empty?]]))  ; by the Creator,
                                 ; and if the box is non-empty, t is returned.
       (=> [:next-value] @ R where (= &sender Creator)
         (if [box <== [:empty?]]
           then (select  ; waits for a message to come, not sent by the
                  (=> message where (not (= &sender Creator))  ; Creator.
                     [R <= message]))              ; it is returned
                                   ; to the reply destination for a [:next-value] message.
           else  ![box <= [:dequeue]]))
         ; removes the first element in the queue and returns it.
       (=> [:all-values] @ R where (= &sender Creator)
         (if [box <== [:empty?]]
           then (select  ; waits for a message to come, not sent by the
                  (=> message where (not (= &sender Creator))  ; Creator.
                     [R <= [message]]))            ; sends a singleton list.
           else  ![box <== [:all-elements]]))
         ; removes all the elements in the queue and returns the list of them.
       (=> returned-value
         [box <= [:enqueue returned-value]]) )] ) )]
```

Figure 9. Definition of Future Object

Note the fact that the contents of the queue object stored in "box" can be checked or removed *solely* by the object which is bound to the pattern variable "Creator". Furthermore, if the queue is empty, the object which sends messages [:next-value] or [:all-values] has to wait for some value to arrive.

7. Project Team: A Scheme of Distributed Problem Solving

In this section, we present a simple scheme of distributed problem solving described in ABCL/1. In doing so, we would like to show the adequacy of ABCL/1 as a modelling and programming language in the concurrent object-oriented paradigm.

Suppose a manager is requested to create a project team to solve a certain problem by a certain deadline. He first creates a project team comprised of the project leader and multiple problem solvers, each having a different problem solving strategy. The project leader dispatches the same problem to each problem solver. For the sake of simplicity, the problem solvers are assumed to work independently in parallel. When a problem solver has solved the problem, it sends the solution to the project leader immediately. We assume the project leader also tries to solve the problem himself by his own strategy. When either the project leader or some problem solvers, or both, have solved the problem, the project leader selects the best solution and sends the success report to the manager. Then he sends a *stop* message to all the problem solvers. If nobody has solved the problem by the deadline, the project leader asks the manager to extend the deadline. If no solution has been found by the extended deadline, the project leader sends the failure report to the manager and commits suicide. This problem solving scheme is easily modeled and described in ABCL/1 without any structural distortions. (See Figure 10.)

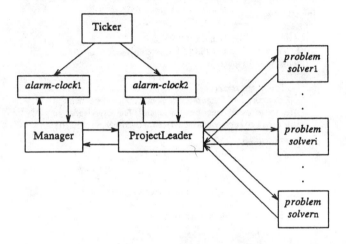

Figure 10. A Scheme for Distributed Problem Solving

The definition of the project leader object is given in Figure 11. Initially it creates an alarm clock object which will wake the project leader, and keeps it in a state variable "time-keeper". "Me" is a reserved symbol in ABCL/1 which denotes the innermost object whose definition contains the occurrence of "Me". We assume that the Ticker defined in Figure 7 is now ticking. When the project leader object receives a [:solve...] message from the manager object, it requests its alarm clock (time-keeper) to wake itself at certain time. Then, the project leader object *multicasts* to the project team members a message that contains the problem description. Note that dispatching the problem to each problem solver is expressed as a *multicast* of the problem specifications and also the message passing is of *future* type. If a problem solver finds a solution, it sends the solution to the future object bound to "Solutions" of the project leader object. While the project leader engages himself in the problem solving, he periodically checks the variable by executing "(ready? Solutions)" as to if it may contain solutions obtained by problem solvers. Note that there is a fair chance that more than one problem solver sends their solutions to the future object bound to "Solutions". As defined in the previous section, solutions sent by problem solvers are put in the queue representing the future object in the order of arrival. "(all-values Solutions)" evaluates to the list of all the elements in the queue. Note that the sequence of actions from selecting the best solutions to terminating the team members' tasks is enclosed by "(atomic" and ")" in Figure 11. Thus, the sequence of actions is not terminated (or suspended) by an express mode message.

```
[object ProjectLeader
  (state [team-members := nil] [bestSolution := nil]
    [time-keeper := [CreateAlarmClock <== [:new Me]]])
  (future Solutions)
  (script
    (=> [:add-a-team-member M]
      [team-members := (cons M team-members)])

    (=> [:solve SPEC :by TIME]
      (temporary [mySolution := nil]) ; temporary variable

      [time-keeper <= [:wake-me-at (- TIME 20)]]
      [team-members <= [:solve SPEC] $ Solutions]
                            ; multicast in future type
      (while (and (not (ready? Solutions)) (null mySolution))
        do ... try to solve the problem by his own
               strategy and store his solution in mySolution ...)
      (atomic
        [bestSolution := (choose-best mySolution (all-values Solutions))]
        [Manager <<= [:found bestSolution]]
        [team-members <<= [:stop-your-task]]))

    (=>> [:time-is-up] where (= &sender time-keeper)
      (temporary new-deadline)

      (if (null bestSolution)
        then
          [new-deadline := [Manager <<== [:can-extend-deadline?]]]
          (if (null new-deadline)
            then [team-members <<= [:stop-your-task]] (suicide)
            else [time-keeper <= [:wake-me-at new-deadline]])))

    (=>> [:you-are-too-late] where (= &sender Manager)
      (if (null bestSolution)
        then [team-members <<= [:stop-your-task]] (suicide))) )]
```

Figure 11. Definition of ProjectLeader Object

If no solution is found within the time limit the project leader himself has set, a [:time-is-up] message is sent by his time keeper (an alarm clock object) in the *express* mode. Then, the project leader asks the manager about the possibility of extending the deadline. If the manager answers "no" (i.e., answers "nil"), it sends a message to stop all the problem solvers and commits suicide.

Though the definition of the manager object (denoted by "Manager" in Figure 11) and problems solvers are easily written in ABCL/1, we omit them here.

8. Delegation

The *reply destination* mechanism explained in §4 and used in §6 is the basic tool to provide various delegation strategies [Lieberman 1986]. The explicit use of pattern variables for reply destinations enables us to write the script of an object which delegates the responsibility of returning a requested result to another object.

Below we define an object A, and an object B which will delegate all unknown messages to A. The pattern variable "any" will match any message not matched by the other patterns in the script of B (this is analog to the last clause with predicate t in a Lisp cond construct). The variable R will match the reply destination. So any kind of message, namely past type with or without reply destination, or now type, or future type message, will be matched and fully delegated to the object A, which could in turn, also delegate it to another object.

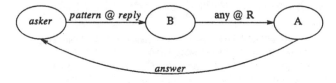

```
[object A                        [object B
  (state ... )                     (state ... )
  (script                          (script
    (=> patternA1                    (=> patternB1
       ... )                           ... )
    ...                              ...
    (=> patternAn                    (=> patternBp
       ... ) )]                        ... )
                                     (=> any @ R   [A <= any @ R]) )]
```

This is illustrated by Figure 12, showing an answer is delivered directly to the asker without coming back through B.

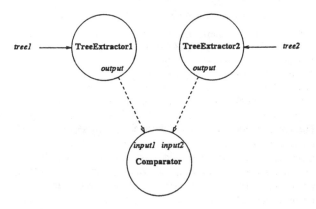

Figure 12. Illustration of Basic Delegation

9. A Distributed Algorithm for the Same Fringe Problem

The same fringe problem is to compare the fringes of two trees (Lisp lists). We will present a solution of the same fringe problem in ABCL/1, which will permit us to illustrate the use of both *future* type messages and *reply destinations*.

Our approach to the problem is similar to the one proposed by B. Serpette in [Serpette 1984]. Basically, there are three objects in this model:

- two tree extractors, extracting recursively the fringe of each tree,
- one comparator, comparing the successive elements of the two fringes.

These three objects will work in parallel. (See Figure 13.)

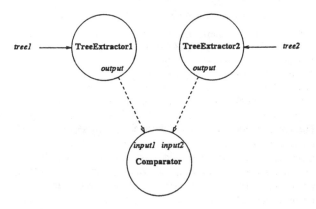

Figure 13. The Same Fringe: Tree Extractors and Comparator

The two tree extractors are linked to the comparator through two dashed arrows. Each one represents the data-flow of the successive elements of the fringe extracted by each tree extractor.

The Comparator object, defined in Figure 14, owns two state variables: "Extractor1" and "Extractor2" binding the two tree extractors, and two *future* variables "input1" and "input2"

which are used for receiving the fringes from these two extractors. "Extractor1" will be bound to the object TreeExtractor defined in Figure 15, the second extractor ("Extractor2") will be created by requesting TreeExtractor to copy itself. When the Comparator object receives the [tree1 :and tree2] message, it will send a future type message [:fringe tree] to each TreeExtractor in order to request it to compute the fringe of each of the trees. Comparator assumes that Extractor1 and Extractor2 will reply the successive elements of the fringes, which will be enqueued in the future objects bound to input1 and input2, respectively.

```
[object Comparator
  (state
    [Extractor1 := TreeExtractor]
    [Extractor2 := [TreeExtractor <== [:copy]]])
  (future  input1 input2)
  (script
    (=> [tree1 :and tree2]
       [Extractor1 <= [:fringe tree1] $ input1] ; future type message
       [Extractor2 <= [:fringe tree2] $ input2] ; future type message
       [Me <= [:eq (next-value input1) :with (next-value input2)]])

    (=> [:eq atom1 :with atom2]
       (if (eq atom1 atom2)
          then (if (eq atom1 'EOT)
                  then (print "same fringe")
                  else [Me <= [:eq (next-value input1)
                                 :with (next-value input2)]])
          else (print "fringes differ"))) )]
```

Figure 14. The Same Fringe Comparator

When two values from the two extractors become available to Comparator through input1 and input2, Comparator sends an [:eq (next-value input1) :with (next-value input2)] message to itself. Note that if one of the two queues (i.e., the future objects bound to variables input1 and input2) is empty, Comparator has to wait until both queues become non-empty. (See the definition of a future object in §6.2.) If the two elements are equal, Comparator will compare next elements unless they were equal to the special atom EOT (as End Of Tree), which indicates the end of the extraction. If both are EOT, the two fringes are declared to be the same. On the other hand, if the two elements differ, Comparator will declare the two fringes to be different.

We could have defined a CreateTreeExtractor object, as generator of the tree extractors, but (to show a different way of creating objects) we will rather define the prototype object TreeExtractor, and later copy it to create the second tree extractor we need. The TreeExtractor object, defined in Figure 15, owns a single state variable "output" to remember the reply destination to which it has to send the successive elements of the fringe during the extraction.

The script [:copy] will return a copy of itself. This will be a *pure* (exact copy of the original object) copy of TreeExtractor. The [:fringe tree] script will bind the reply destination to the variable "Pipe". This reply destination is a future object which was bound to the future variable "input1" or "input2" of Comparator. It will be assigned to the state variable "output", thus connecting† its "output" with one "input" of the Comparator (like in the Figure 13). Then it will send to itself the message [:extract tree] with itself being the reply destination.

---

† like the communication pipes in the ObjPive model [Serpette 1984], inspired by the Un*x pipes. In contrast, these "pipes" are virtual (no assumption of shared memory).

```
[object TreeExtractor
 (state output)
 (script
  (=> [:copy]   !(self-copy))

  (=> [:fringe tree] @ Pipe
   [output := Pipe]
   [Me <= [:extract tree] @ Me])

  (=> [:extract tree] @ C
   (cond
    ((null tree)  [C <= [:continue]])
    ((atom tree)  [output <= tree] [C <= [:continue]])
    (t   [Me <= [:extract (car tree)]]
          @ [object
              (state [Extractor := Me])
              (script
               (=> [:continue]
                   [Extractor <= [:extract (cdr tree)] @ C])] ])  ))

  (=> [:continue]  [output <= 'EOT]) )]
```

Figure 15. The Same Fringe TreeExtractor

To extract the fringe of a tree, the continuation-based programming style is adopted, which is in contrast to iterative or recursive ones. This model was initiated by Carl Hewitt [Hewitt et al. 1974], who gave a solution of the same fringe problem using continuations in a coroutine style. In contrast, our algorithm is fully parallel. The "[:extract tree] @ C" message script will bind the variable C to the reply destination, which represents the continuation, i.e., the object which will do the following:

- If the tree is null, the tree extractor just activates the continuation C, by sending it the message [:continue].
- If the tree is atomic, then this element is sent to the output, (so the corresponding "input1/2" of Comparator will receive a new element) and the continuation will be activated.
- The last case means that the tree is a node (a Lisp cons). We have to extract its left son (car), and then its right son (cdr). This second part to be performed later is specified in a dynamically created object (a new continuation), which will request the tree extractor to extract the cdr of the tree, when receiving the [:continue] message. The bindings of variables "tree" and "C" are memorized in the new continuation because of the lexical scoping of ABCL/1.

When the tree extractor receives the [:continue] message, that means the end of the extraction. So it will send EOT to the output, and stop there.

Note that in this algorithm if the two fringes are found to be different, the two extraction processes go on. Comparator could then send a *stop* message to either "freeze" or kill them. To deal with such a situation, we could devise various strategies which are related to the issues of objects' "capability" and garbage collection. This will be a subject for further study.

10. Concluding Remarks

10.1. Importance of the Waiting Mode

The computation model presented in this paper has evolved from the Actor computation model. One of the important differences is the introduction of the waiting mode in our computation model. As noted at the end of §3, without now type (and/or future type) message passing, module decomposition in terms of a collection of objects tends to become unnatural. Thus the now type message passing is essential in structuring solution programs. In our computation model, the now type message passing is derived from the waiting mode and the past type message passing in a simple manner as demonstrated in §6.1. In contrast, the realization of a now type message passing in the Actor computation model forces the unnatural decomposition of actors and requires rather cumbersome procedures for identifying a message that corresponds to the return (reply) value of now type message passing.

10.2. Express Mode Message Passing

We admit that the introduction of the express mode message passing in a high-level programming language is rather unusual. The main reason of introducing the express mode is to provide a language facility for *natural* modelling. Without this mode, the script of an object whose activity needs to be interrupted would become very complicated. When an object is continuously working or active, if no express mode message passing is allowed, there is no way of interrupting the object's activity or monitoring its state. One can only hope that the object terminates or suspends its activity itself and gives an interrupting message a chance to be accepted by the object. But this would make the structure of the script of the object unnatural and complicated. It should also be noted that the express mode message passing is useful for debugging because it can monitor the states of active objects.

10.3. Interrupt vs. Non-Interrupt

Our notion of *express* mode message passing is based on a very simple *interrupt* scheme. Even in this simple scheme, we must sometime protect the activity of an object from unwanted interruptions by using the "(atomic ...)" construct. (See the script of ProjectLeader in Figure 11.) Appropriate uses of this construct sometimes requires skills.

An alternative scheme might be what we call the *mail priority* model. In this model, objects are not interrupted during their activities. An express mode message sent to an object arrives at the express queue without interrupting the object. When the object is ready to check its message queues, it always first consult its express queue (with first priority), and consult its ordinary queue only when there is no (more) message in the express queue. Now there is no fear of *bad* interruptions that the programmer has to take care of. But, on the other hand, as noted in the previous subsection, the activity of an object cannot be stopped or monitored when it is in progress. To alleviate this situation, we can introduce a built-in primitive, say "(check-express)", with which an object can check to see whether an express mode message has arrived while the object is carrying out its actions. "(check-express)" can be placed in the script of an object and it is invoked as one of the actions performed by the object. When it is invoked, if a message is in the express queue and it satisfies one of the pattern-and-constraint pairs in the script, the execution of the actions specified for the message pattern intervenes.

Since both schemes have various advantages and disadvantages and they depend on the application areas of our language, we need more experiments to draw a firm conclusion.

10.4. Parallelism and Synchronization

Let us review the basic types of parallelism provided in ABCL/1:

[1] Concurrent activations of independent objects.

[2] Parallelism caused by past type and future type message passing.

[3] Parallelism caused by the *parallel* constructs [Yonezawa et al. 1986] (we did not explain in this paper) and *multicasting* (cf. §5.3 and §7).

Furthermore, ABCL/1 provides the following four basic mechanisms for synchronization:

[1] Object: the activation of an object takes place one at a time and a single first-come-first-served message queue for ordinary messages is associated with each object.

[2] Now type message passing: a message passing of the now type does not end until the result is returned.

[3] Select construct: when an object executes a select construct, it changes into the waiting mode and waits only for messages satisfying specified pattern-and-constraint pairs.

[4] Parallel construct: see [Yonezawa et al. 1986].

10.5. Relation to Other Work

Our present work is related to a number of previous research activities. To distinguish our work from them, we will give a brief summary of ABCL/1. Unlike CSP [Hoare 1978] or other languages, ABCL/1 has characteristics of *dynamic* nature: objects can be created dynamically, message transmission is asynchronous, and the "knows"-relation among objects (i.e., network topology) changes dynamically. An object in our computation model cannot be activated by more than one message at the same time. This "one-at-a-time" nature is similar to that of Monitors [Hoare 1974], but the basic mode of communication in programming with monitors is the call/return bilateral communication, whereas it is unilateral in ABCL/1.

10.6. Other Program Examples

A wide variety of example programs have been written in ABCL/1 and we are convinced that the essential part of ABCL/1 is robust enough to be used in the intended areas. The examples we have written include parallel discrete simulation [Yonezawa et al. 1984] [Shibayama and Yonezawa 1986], inventory control systems [Kerridge and Simpson 1984] [Shibayama et al. 1985] à la Jackson's example [Jackson 1983], robot arm control, mill speed control [Yonezawa and Matsumoto 1985], concurrent access to 2-3 trees and distributed quick sort [Shibayama and Yonezawa 1986].

Acknowledgements

We would like to thank Y. Honda and T. Takada for their implementation efforts on Vax/11s, Sun workstations, and a Symbolics.

References

[Briot 1984] Briot, J-P., *Instanciation et Héritage dans les Langages Objets*, (thèse de 3ème cycle), LITP Research Report, No 85-21, LITP - Université Paris-VI, Paris, 15 December 1984.

[Brodie et al. 1984] Brodie, M., J. Mylopoulos, J. Schmidt (Eds.), On Conceptual Modelling, Springer, 1984.

[Hewitt et al. 1974] Hewitt, C., et al., *Behavioral Semantics of Nonrecursive Control Structures*, Proc. Colloque sur la Programmation, Paris, April, 1974.

[Hewitt 1977] Hewitt, C., *Viewing Control Structures as Patterns of Passing Messages*, Journal of Artificial Intelligence, Vol. 8, No. 3 (1977), pp.323-364.

[Hewitt and Baker 1977] Hewitt, C., H. Baker, *Laws for Parallel Communicating Processes*, Proc. IFIP-77, Toronto, 1977.

[Hoare 1974] Hoare, C.A.R., *Monitors: An Operating System Structuring Concept*, Communications of the ACM, Vol. 17, No. 10 (1974), pp.549-558.

[Hoare 1978] Hoare, C.A.R., *Communicating Sequential Processes*, Communications of the ACM, Vol. 21 No. 8 (1978), pp.666-677.

[Jackson 1983] Jackson, M., System Development, Prentice Hall, 1983.

[Kerridge and Simpson 1984] Kerridge, J. M., D. Simpson, *Three Solutions for a Robot Arm Controller Using Pascal-Plus, Occam and Edison*, Software - Practice and Experience - Vol. 14, (1984), pp.3-15.

[Lieberman 1981] Lieberman, H., *A Preview of Act-1*, AI-Memo 625, Artificial Intelligence Laboratory, MIT, 1981.

[Lieberman 1986] Lieberman, H., *Delegation and Inheritance: Two Mechanisms for Sharing Knowledge in Object-Oriented Systems*, Proc. of 3rd Workshop on Object-Oriented Languages, Bigre+Globule, No. 48, Paris, January 1986.

[Serpette 1984] Serpette, B., *Contextes, Processus, Objets, Séquenceurs: FORMES*, (thèse de 3ème cycle), LITP Research Report, No. 85-5, LITP - Université Paris-VI, Paris, 30 October 1984.

[Shibayama et al. 1985] Shibayama, E., M. Matsuda, A. Yonezawa, *A Description of an Inventory Control System Based on an Object-Oriented Concurrent Programming Methodology*, Jouhou-Shori, Vol. 26, No. 5 (1985), pp.460-468. (in Japanese)

[Shibayama and Yonezawa 1986] Shibayama, E., A. Yonezawa, *Distributed Computing in ABCL/1*, in "Object-Oriented Concurrent Programming" edited by A. Yonezawa and M. Tokoro, MIT Press, 1986.

[Shibayama and Yonezawa 1986a] Shibayama, E., A. Yonezawa, *ABCL/1 User's Manual*, Internal Memo, 1986.

[Smith 1985] Smith, R. G., *Report on the 1984 Distributed Artificial Intelligence Workshop*, The AI Magazine Fall, 1985.

[Special Issue 1981] Special Issue on Distributed Problem Solving, IEEE Trans. on Systems, Man, and Cybernetics, Vol. SMC-11, No.1, 1981.

[Special Issue 1982] Special Issue on Rapid Prototyping, ACM SIG Software Engineering Notes Vol. 7, No. 5, December 1982.

[Stefik and Bobrow 1986] Stefik, M. K., D. G. Bobrow, *Object-Oriented Programming: Themes and Variation*, The AI Magazine, 1986

[Tschritzis 1985] Tschritzis, D. (Ed.), *Office Automation*, Springer, 1985.

[Yonezawa and Hewitt 1979] Yonezawa, A., C. Hewitt, *Modelling Distributed Systems*, Machine Intelligence, Vol. 9 (1979), pp.41-50.

[Yonezawa et al. 1984] Yonezawa, A., H. Matsuda, E. Shibayama, *Discrete Event Simulation Based on an Object-Oriented Parallel Computation Model*, Research Report C-64, Dept. of Information Science, Tokyo Institute of Technology, November 1984.

[Yonezawa et al. 1985] Yonezawa, A., Y. Matsumoto, *Object-Oriented Concurrent Programming and Industrial Software Production*, Lecture Notes in Computer Science, No.186, Springer-Verlag, 1985.

[Yonezawa et al. 1986] Yonezawa, A., E. Shibayama, T. Takada, Y. Honda, *Modelling and Programming in an Object-Oriented Concurrent Language ABCL/1*, in "Object-Oriented Concurrent Programming" edited by A. Yonezawa and M. Tokoro, MIT Press, 1986.

[Yonezawa and Tokoro 1986] Yonezawa, A., M. Tokoro (Eds.), Object-Oriented Concurrent Programming, MIT Press 1986 (in press).

Implementing Distributed AI Systems Using MACE

Les Gasser   Carl Braganza   Nava Herman

Distributed Artificial Intelligence Group, Computer Science Department,
University of Southern California, Los Angeles 90089-0782

Abstract: *This paper describes the experimental DAI development system MACE (Multi-Agent Computing Environment) using the implementation of a distributed blackboard system as an example. MACE is an instrumented testbed for building DAI systems at different levels of granularity. MACE agents run in parallel, and communicate via messages. They have have facilities for knowledge representation (e.g., models of other agents) and reasoning. The MACE environment maps agents to processors, handles inter-agent communication, and provides a language for describing agents, tracing and instrumentation, a facility for remote demons, and a collection of system-agents which construct user-agents from descriptions, monitor execution, handle errors, and interface to a user. MACE is implemented on a 16-node INTEL SYM-1 large-memory hypercube and in a Lisp machine environment. We have used MACE to model lower-level parallelism (several distributed production rule systems) and to build higher-level distributed problem-solving architectures (distributed blackboard and contract-net schemes).*

1 Introduction

Distributed Artificial Intelligence (DAI) is a subfield of AI concerned with the problems of describing and constructing multiple "intelligent" systems which interact. MACE (for Multi-Agent Computing Environment) is a language, environment, and testbed for experimenting with a variety of DAI systems. While other experimental testbeds have been built for DAI research (E.g., [8,9,11]), these have generally encompassed only a single problem-solving architecture or domain. The MACE approach is to provide high-level support for DAI experiments with components of varying granularity and in multiple problem domains.

The MACE system is a collection of components, including:

- A collection of **agents**: Agents are the basic computational units of the MACE system.

- A community of **system agents**: The pre-defined system agents provide MACE command interpretation, interfaces to users and other machines, agent-constructors, agent/processor allocation, error handling, tracing, execution monitoring, etc.

- A collection of **facilities** which all agents may use: These include a pattern matcher, a simulator, several standard

agent engines, handlers for standard errors, and standard messages understood by all agents.

- **A description database:** Agent descriptions are maintained in a description database by a system-agent cluster which constructs new descriptions, verifies descriptions, and constructs executable agents from descriptions.

- A collection of **kernels:** MACE kernels on each processor collectively handle message routing, perform I/O to terminals, files, or other devices, and schedule agents for execution.

MACE is designed to be a testbed for DAI experiments. Most MACE agents know about some other agents in their environment; they expect to draw upon and coordinate with the expertise of others they know about. They may need to know the identity and location of their acquaintances, something about their capabilities, etc. MACE agents represent this information in the form of "models of other agents in the world." In addition, agents may be organized into sub-units or coalitions which act in response to particular problems. In this sense they respond as organized groups or composites. The MACE agent description language includes facilities for describing organized clusters of agents.

MACE experiments can be instrumented to allow for measurements of the characteristics of problem-solvers. Message traffic, queue and database sizes, work done by an agent, and load on a processor node are common measurements. MACE incorporates extensive pattern-matching facilities for interpreting messages, for pattern-directed invocation of asynchronous events (e.g., demons and other event-monitors), and for associative database access within agents. Versions of MACE have been implemented on an Intel Hypercube and on TI Explorer Lisp machines, networked together.

2 An Example: A Distributed Blackboard System

We will describe MACE and its uses by showing part of an implementation of a simple distributed blackboard (DBB) system in a multi-processor, distributed-memory environment. The blackboard architecture has been a mainstay of AI since its inception in the HEARSAY system [1,2,7,10]. The BB architecture embodies a particular communication structure: a centralized repository of information to which many knowledge sources

(KS's) have access. In typical blackboard systems access and updating is synchronous and controlled by a *scheduler*. The BB model is inherently a shared-memory concept, and the synchronous nature of most KS invocation and the requirement for consistency among KS's restrict the parallelism available [3]. Another problem of distributing a blackboard-based problem-solver results from the need to keep the passive data structure from having to know about which KS's need access, so that new KS's can be easily added.

Our DBB example is a simple blackboard-based arithmetic calculator. (The example is intended only for illustration of MACE, and not for a demonstration of arithmetic problem-solving.) The calculator contains two BB levels: HIGH-BB and LOW-BB. HIGH-BB holds complex arithmetic expressions which must be reduced to simpler ones before they can be evaluated, while LOW-BB contains simple expressions whose results can immediately be calculated.

The BB system contains several arithmetic knowledge sources, each representing an arithmetic operator (e.g., PLUS-KS adds numbers, TIMES-KS multiplies them, etc.) Here we focus only on the PLUS-KS knowledge source. PLUS-KS is a MACE *organization* made up of 3 MACE agents: an *organization-manager agent* and two *organization-members*. One member (SIMPLE-PLUS) calculates simple expressions by referencing the LOW-BB, while the other (DECOMPOSE-EXPRESSION) reduces complex addition expressions from the HIGH-BB into subexpressions. It places still-complex subexpressions back on the HIGH-BB and simple expressions onto the LOW-BB. Other KS's compose partial solutions into more complete solutions; they are not represented here. We are concerned with the representation and interaction of the HIGH-BB, PLUS-KS, and SIMPLE-PLUS agents.

We will trace the description of these agents and their operation through the paper. MACE code for these agents is shown in Table 1.

3   What is an Agent?

MACE agents are self-contained, active *objects* which communicate using messages. Agents exist in an *environment*. They *contain knowledge*, they *sense their environment*, and they *take actions*.

Agents have *attributes* which are the repositories of their procedural and declarative knowledge. Attributes are not directly visible to any other agent, but the contents of attributes may be sent in messages to other agents, as a way of transferring knowledge. The PLUS-KS contains three attributes: a world model called **acquaintances**, an procedural part called **engine**, and an initialization part called **init-code**.

The environment of an agent comprises the MACE system, other agents, and the world outside MACE. Agents can sense other agents and the outside world by receiving messages. Events in the kernel environment and internal to the agents themselves (e.g., alarm timers) can be sensed directly by the agent via its *engine-shell*.

Each agent has an **engine** which defines the agent's activities and how it interprets messages. The engine manipulates the knowledge stored by the agent's attributes in response to messages received by the agent. Agents can take 3 kinds of action:

- They can change their internal state by manipulating their attributes;

- They can send messages to other agents;

- They can send *monitoring requests* to the MACE kernel to monitor kernel-level events (e.g., timers), events elsewhere in the system, and their own internal state changes.

To carry out these actions, agents may contain locally-defined functions. Since these functions may give an agent specific skills, they may be sent in messages as a way of transferring skills to other agents (like other attributes).

4   What Agents Know

While the agent description framework is general, MACE provides facilities for representing particular kinds of knowledge. Frameworks for organizational and interactional knowledge are the primary higher-level knowledge structures built into MACE. This knowledge is built into an attribute called **acquaintances**. **Acquaintances** is an associative database which provides an environmental model using explicit models of other agents in the world. This might be knowledge of the *roles, skills, location,* etc. of other agents. A world model has representations of other agents in terms of the following qualifiers:

name The name of the agent being modeled.

class The name of the modeled agent's class.

address The location of the modeled agent. This address is used in communicating with the agent.

role The *relationship(s)* the modeled agent bears to this agent. Currently, the role has four predefined values:

self The model is of the agent itself.

creator The model is of the agent's creator.

org-member The model is of a member of the organization which this agent defines (see below).

member-of The model is the abstraction part of a parent organization.

This list of values may include additional user-declared roles.

skills Skills are what this agent knows to be the capabilities of the modeled agent. Skills are pairs consisting of patterns which match goals the skill will achieve, and a set of alternative procedures for achieving the goals. The format of procedures is left to the programmer, but there are generally two types of methods: *explicit procedures* can be directly invoked by the agent's engine, and their structure depends on the engine definition. USE in the DBB example names an explicit procedure. *References* are the names

Table 1: **PLUS Knowledge Source in MACE**

```
; PLUS-KS is a MACE organization with 2 members:

((NAME PLUS-KS)
 (IMPORT ENGINE FROM DBB-DEF)
 (ACQUAINTANCES
  (PLUS-KS
   [ROLE (SELF)]
   [GOALS ((TASK ? (ADD $ $)))]
   [SKILLS (((TASK ?ID (ADD (R! ?X NUMBERP) (R! ?Y NUMBERP)))
             (REF (AN ACQUAINTANCE WITH
               ([GOAL ((?ID ADD (R! ?P NUMBERP) (R! ?Q NUMBERP)))]
                [ROLE ORG-MEMBER]))
             (BY-SENDING (?ID (?X + ?Y))))) ...
  (SIMPLE-PLUS
   [ROLE (ORG-MEMBER)]
   [GOALS ((?ID ADD (R! ?S NUMBERP) (R! ?T NUMBERP)))])]

  (DECOMPOSE-EXPRESSION ...

  (INIT-CODE (DEMON (RMSG LOW-BB (TASK (?ID ADD $X $Y))
                    (TASK ?ID (ADD ?X ?Y))) ...

; SIMPLE-PLUS is a member of the PLUS-KS organization:

((NAME SIMPLE-PLUS) ...
 (ACQUAINTANCES
  (SIMPLE-PLUS
    [ROLE (SELF)]
    [GOALS ((?ID ADD (R! ?X NUMBERP) (R! ?Y NUMBERP)))]
    [SKILLS (((?ID ADD (R! ?X NUMBERP) (R! ?Y NUMBERP))
             (USE [(SEND-TO-AGENT @(ADDRESS LOW-BB)
                                  (RESULT ?ID (+ ?X ?Y)))] ))) ])
  (PLUS-KS [ROLE (MEMBER-OF)])
  (LOW-BB)
))
```

---

of known agents which can possibly achieve the goals. For example, PLUS-KS uses the REF reference to look up another agent with matching goals and send it a message.

goals Goals are what this agent understands the modeled agent wants to achieve. The overall goal of an agent is to get other agents (or possibly itself) to send it certain messages - that is, to get its environment to behave in a certain way.

plans Plans are this agent's view of the way the modeled agent will achieve its goals. Plans are represented by a partially ordered collection of skills.

The MACE system provides *selectors* to fetch information on acquaintances. Selectors are pattern-directed associative retrieval functions. Selections can be made on the basis of name, name and class, class, role, skills, goals, or plans. Selectors allow the agent to abbreviate and reference the address of an acquaintance in a meaningful way. In the SIMPLE-PLUS agent, the selector

@(ADDRESS LOW-BB) is used to extract the address of the LOW-BB from SIMPLE-PLUS's world-model.

Agents may also have specialized local knowledge, represented in user-defined attributes.

5 How Agents Sense Their World

Agents sense their world by receiving messages and by being forcibly notified of internal and system-level events. Some sensing is active sensing in the form of requests for notification of events. Two kinds of events can be actively monitored by agents in MACE:

- Events which are effects of the visible actions of some agent, including sending or receiving specific messages, status changes, and the creation or destruction of agents.

These events are monitored by *Demons* which are mappings from event descriptions to messages. When an event matching the demon's event-description occurs, and it issues the message to the monitoring agent.

In the DBB, PLUS-KS is initialized with two demons under its control (only one is shown). The demons monitor the HIGH-BB and LOW-BB for postings of relevant information. Receipt of a message matching the event template (a message template) triggers the demon to send a corresponding message to PLUS-KS.

- Events which are the result of kernel actions or state-changes in the agent doing the monitoring. These events are monitored by *imps*. Imps are predicate-action pairs. Imp predicates test internal attributes or certain predefined kernel events (e.g., alarms). *Pattern-Triggers* are special imps specified by a message template and an action. They trigger on receipt of a message which matches the template. Pattern-triggers can be used to implement standard or guarded methods-like behaviors.

6   How Agents Act: Engines

MACE agents take actions when the kernel evaluates the **engine** of the agent. An agent's engine is the only executable part of the agent, apart from its initialization code. The engine and its associated attributes (e.g., local variable or function attributes) provide the procedural knowledge incorporated in the agent.

The MACE system provides several simple engines; two are simple production systems, and a third is a basic user-interface engine. The user can define engines as well. In the DBB, the user has defined another engine which he has placed in another agent class description (DBB-DEF) and imported.

The MACE system wraps the agent's engine in an *engine shell*. The engine shell provides standard error handling facilities, protects the MACE system from engine errors, prioritizes messages, and handles standard messages which all agents understand (e.g., certain debugging and examination messages).

Sending messages is a type of action. Messages can be addressed to individual agents, to groups of agents, or to all agents of a particular class. Messages can be addressed to agents on MACE systems on other machines, as long as a communication link exists. Every agent in the MACE system has a unique address. This address is comprised of the agent's name, its class, the node on which it resides, and the machine on which the agent is running. A message always contains a return-address.

7   Organizations

To save resources and attention when they act collectively, agents organize their activities. Organizing saves resources by providing a basis for expectations of how others will behave. We view an organization as a structure of expectations and commitments. The actions of organizational participants are patterned, governed by routines and commitments, and based on expectations of others. Thus an organization never really exists, except indirectly in the commitments and expectations of its members. In MACE, the term *organization* refers to the abstraction which allows agents to treat a collection of activities as being part of a known concerted effort.

MACE represent an organization as an abstraction represented by a communication agent called a *manager*. The communication agent is named for the organization, and its only function is to disseminate messages sent to the organization to the appropriate members of the organization - that is, to allocate work. Work is allocated on the basis of known goals of organization members. Each organizational member is represented with an *org-member* role entry.

In the DBB, PLUS-KS is an organization comprising two members: SIMPLE-PLUS and DECOMPOSE-EXPRESSION. DE-COMPOSE-EXPRESSION may be a member of several organizations, since a TIMES KS will have to decompose complex expressions as well. Incoming messages arriving from a demon attached to a blackboard level are matched against PLUS-KS's skills. The skills contain knowledge about how to achieve the goals represented in the arriving messages. PLUS-KS, as an organization manager, has but one type of skill: referring work to other agents, using the REF command. In the example, an incoming simple expression will be allocated to an org-member agent whose goals match the goal-description in the REF command. The SIMPLE-PLUS KS will be selected because both its goals and its role (as modeled in PLUS-KS's world model) match.

8   Describing Agents

Programmers would like to describe MACE agents which have attributes in common with other MACE agents (e.g., engines, local functions, behavioral rules, etc.). Hierarchical classification and attribute inheritance are the schemes commonly used for related descriptions in object-oriented languages. In MACE, we may want to selectively import some but not all attributes of related agent-descriptions. Moreover, a distributed-memory parallel environment presents difficulties for inheritance-based schemes at execution time [4,5]. For the moment, we consider execution-time inheritance unworkable. Each executable MACE agent is a self-contained object which inherits nothing from other agents at run time.

MACE provides a language called the *MACE Agent Description Language* or *ADL* for describing agents. The ADL is a procedural language for describing the database operations necessary to construct a new agent description. New descriptions of agents are built using queries and assertions into the description database (e.g. *NEW* or *IMPORT* - the engine is an imported feature of the PLUS-KS and SIMPLE-PLUS in the DBB). The ADL is also used to specify initialization procedures for the agent. This code is executed upon the instantiation of an agent, in the processor environment where the agent has been loaded. Agent descriptions are stored in a database which is used by an agent cluster which constructs both new executable agents and new descriptions. MACE differentiates the description of an agent from its executable form. Table 2 provides a grammar to specify the ADL.

Table 2: Agent Description Language Grammar

CLASS-DESCR	⇒	(CLASS-NAME DESCR-BODY)
CLASS-NAME	⇒	(name <*class-name*>)
	⇒	
DESCR-BODY	⇒	(copy-of <*class-name*>) DESCR
	⇒	DESCR
DESCR	⇒	(import IFEATURE from <*class-name*>) DESCR
	⇒	(new FEATURE) DESCR
	⇒	(delete IFEATURE) DESCR
	⇒	INIT-CODE
	⇒	
IFEATURE	⇒	IMPORTABLE-F
	⇒	FNAME
FEATURE	⇒	IMPORTABLE-F VALUE
	⇒	FNAME <*function definition*>
	⇒	acquaintances ACQ-DESCR
IMPORTABLE-F	⇒	engine
	⇒	attribute <*attribute-name*>
	⇒	acquaintance <*acquaintance-name*>
FNAME	⇒	function <*function name*>
	⇒	engine
ACQ-DESCR	⇒	(<*acquaintance-name*> ACQ-BODY) ACQ-DESCR
	⇒	
ACQ-BODY	⇒	ACQ-QUAL ACQ-BODY
	⇒	
ACQ-QUAL	⇒	[plans <*Skills-List*>]
	⇒	[goals <*Pattern-Descriptors-List*>]
	⇒	[roles <*Predefined-Roles-List*>]
	⇒	[skills <*Goal-Method-Descriptors-List*>]
INIT-CODE	⇒	(init-code <*Lisp Code*>)

The init-code attribute can contain arbitrary code that will be executed when an agent of this class is instantiated. The code forms no part of the agent, and cannot be referenced within the agent. In the DBB, the initialization code starts the PLUS-KS with demons attached to the HIGH-BB and LOW-BB.

The MACE Class Description Database of stored class descriptions can be used in the creation of new class descriptions. Class descriptions are created and modified by issuing *design orders* to the MACE system's *builder agent*, which is responsible for accepting commands to add, delete and modify class descriptions into or from the class database. Design orders are messages, and they may be issued by any MACE agent. Typically they are issued by the user via a user-interface agent tied to the builder agent.

9 Experiences with MACE

In addition to the distributed blackboard, the MACE concept has been proven by building several communities of interacting agents, based on existing Distributed AI paradigms. We have implemented a version of Reid Smith's contract net problem-solver [5,11] in Mace, and applied it (as did Smith) to the N-queens problem. Each contract net node is composed of four MACE agents, including a communication manager, a contract manager, a work processor, and a knowledge base.

We have built three simple distributed production systems, based on the Rule-Agents concept [6] - a dataflow-like approach to production systems. Under this approach, each rule is an agent, and there is no global database or inference engine. Rules fire in parallel and send tokens to other rule-agents, Rule agents themselves may query a user via the system user-interface and monitor agent for messages which are not produced by other rules.

In the future, we expect to apply MACE to problems of modeling how agents form alliances and routinize interaction for coordinated problem-solving. We are working toward using MACE for robotics problems, including parts-passing and distributed planning/task allocation.

10 Acknowledgements

We thank Janet Coates, Gary Doney, Lunze Liu, and Fernando Tenorio for implementation work and/or comments on earlier drafts. We also thank the Intel Corporation and Prof. Kai Hwang for their support. Part of this research was funded under Lawrence Livermore Laboratory contract number 9094505.

References

[1] Daniel D. Corkill, Kevin Q. Gallagher, and Kelly E. Murray. GBB: A Generic Blackboard Development System. *Proceedings AAAI-86*.

[2] L.Erman, R. Hayes-Roth, V. Lesser, and R. Reddy. The HEARSAY-II Speech Understanding System: Integrating Knowledge to Resolve Uncertainty. *ACM Computing Surveys*, June, 1980.

[3] R. Fennel and V. Lesser. Parallelism in AI Problem-Solving. *IEEE Trans. Computers* 1978.

[4] L. Gasser, C. Braganza, and N. Herman. MACE: Experimental DAI Research on the Intel Hypercube. *Proceedings 2nd Conference on Hypercube Multiprocessors*. Knoxville, TN, Sept. 1986.

[5] L. Gasser, C. Braganza, and N. Herman. MACE: A Flexible Testbed for Distributed AI Research. in M. Huhns, Ed. *Distributed Artificial Intelligence*, Pitman, 1987.

[6] L. Gasser and M.F. Tenorio. *Rule-Agents: A Distributed, Object-Oriented Approach to Production Systems Using MACE*. Technical Report, Dept. of Computer Science, USC,1986.

[7] Barbara Hayes-Roth. A Blackboard Architecture for Control. *Artificial Intelligence*, 26(2): 251-321, March 1985.

[8] Victor R. Lesser and Daniel D. Corkill. The Distributed Vehicle Monitoring Testbed: A Tool for Investigating Distributed Problem Solving Networks. *AI Magazine*, pp. 15-33, 1983.

[9] David McArthur and Philip Klahr. *The Ross Language Manual*. Rand, 1982.

[10] H. Penny Nii. CAGE and POLIGON: Two Frameworks for Blackboard-based Concurrent Problem Solving. Report No. KSL 86-41, Knowledge Systems Laboratory, Computer Science Department, Stanford University, Stanford, April 1986.

[11] Reid G. Smith. *A Framework for Distributed Problem Solving*. UMI Research Press, Ann Arbor, Michigan, 1981.

A Software and Hardware Environment for Developing AI Applications on Parallel Processors

R. Bisiani

Computer Science Dept.
Carnegie Mellon University
Pittsburgh, PA 15213
[412] 268-3072

Abstract

This paper describes and reports on the use of an environment, called **Agora**, that supports the construction of large, computationally expensive and loosely-structured systems, e.g. knowledge-based systems for speech and vision understanding. **Agora** can be customized to support the programming model that is more suitable for a given application. **Agora** has been designed explicitly to support multiple languages and highly parallel computations. Systems built with **Agora** can be executed on a number of general purpose and custom multiprocessor architectures.

1. Introduction

Our long-term goal is to develop a software environment that meets the need of application specialists to build and evaluate certain kinds of heterogeneous AI applications quickly and efficiently. To this effect we are developing a set of tools, methodologies and architectures called **Agora** (marketplace) that can be used to implement custom programming environments.

The kinds of systems for which **Agora** is useful have these characteristics:

- *they are heterogeneous* - no single programming model, language or machine architecture can be used;
- *they are in rapid evolution* - the algorithms change often while part of the system remains constant, e.g. research systems;
- *they are computationally expensive* - no single processor is enough to obtain the desired performance.

Speech and vision systems are typical of this kind of AI applications. In these systems, *knowledge-intensive* and conventional programming techniques must be integrated while observing real time constraints and preserving ease of programming.

State-of-the-art AI environments solve some but not all of the problems raised by the systems we are interested in. For example, these environments provide multiple programming models but fall short of supporting "non-AI" languages and multiprocessing. Some of these environments are also based on Lisp and are therefore more suitable (although not necessarily limited) to shared memory architectures.

For example, some programming environments provide abstractions tailored to the incremental design and implementation of large systems (e.g. LOOPS [14], STROBE [16]) but have little support for parallelism. Other environments support general purpose parallel processing (e.g. QLAMBDA [11], Multilisp [13], LINDA [7]) but do not tackle incremental design (Linda) or non-shared memory computer

architectures (QLAMBDA, Multilisp). ABE [10] and AF [12] are the only environments we are aware of that have goals similar to **Agora**'s goals. ABE has, in fact, broader goals than **Agora** since it also supports *knowledge engineering*.

Agora supports heterogeneous systems by providing a *virtual machine* that is independent of any language, allows a number of different programming models and can be efficiently mapped into a number of different computer architectures. Rapid evolution is supported by providing similar *incremental programming* capabilities as Lisp environments. Programs that run on the parallel virtual machine can be added to the environment and share the same data with programs that were designed independently. This makes it possible to provide an unlimited set of *custom* environments that are tailored to the needs of a user, including environments in which parallel processing has been *hidden* from the end user. Finally, parallelism is strongly encouraged since systems are always specified as parallel computations even if they will be run on a single processor.

Agora is not an "environment in search of an application" but is "driven" by the requirement coming from the design and implementation of the CMU distributed speech recognition system [5]. During the past year, we designed and implemented an initial version of **Agora** and successfully used it to build two prototype speech-recognition systems. Our experience with this initial version of **Agora** convinced us that, when building parallel systems, the effort invested in obtaining a quality software environment pays off manyfold in productivity. **Agora** has reduced the time to assemble a complex parallel system and run it on a multiprocessor from more than a six man-months to about one man-month. The main reason for this lies in the fact that the details of communication and control have been taken care of by **Agora**. Application research, however, calls for still greater improvement. Significant progress in evaluating parallel task decompositions, in CMU's continuous speech project, for example, will ultimately require that a single person assemble and run a complete system within one day.

This paper is an introduction to some of the ideas underlying **Agora** and a description of the result of using **Agora** to build a large speech recognition system. The current structure of **Agora** is the outcome of the experience acquired with two designs and implementations carried out during 1985. One of these implementations is currently used for a prototype speech recognition system that runs on a network of Perqs and MICROVAXES. This implementation will be extended to support a shared memory multiprocessor, Sun's and IBM RT-PC's by the end of the second quarter of 1986.

2. Agora's Structure

Agora's structure can be explained by using a "layered" model, see Figure 2-1 starting from the bottom.

[1]Many individuals have contributed to the research presented is this paper, please refer to the Acknowledgements section for a list of each contribution. This research is sponsored by the Defense Advanced Research Projects Agency, DoD, through ARPA Order 5167, and monitored by the Space and Naval Warfare Systems Command under contract N00039-85-C-0163. Views and conclusions contained in this document are those of the authors and should not be interpreted as representing official policies, either expressed or implied, of the Defense Advanced Research Projects Agency or of the United States Government.

[2]Unix is a Trademark of AT&T

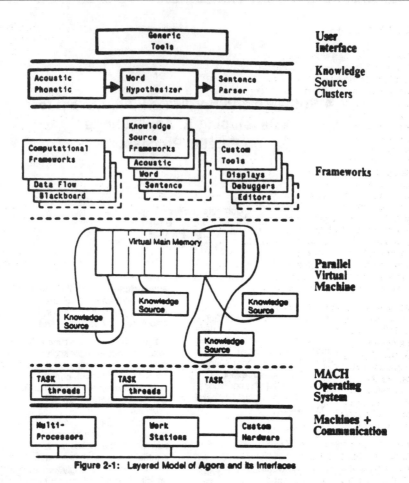

Figure 2-1: Layered Model of Agora and its Interfaces

-The first layer is a network of heterogeneous processors: single processors, shared memory multiprocessors, loosely-connected multiprocessors and custom hardware accelerators. The Mach operating system provides the basic software to execute computations on all these machines and Agora provides tools to map Mach abstractions into real machines. Mach is a Unix-compatible[2] operating system that runs on multiprocessors, see [2].

-The Mach layer provides three major abstractions: message passing, shared memory and threads. *Message passing* is the main communication mechanism: all Agora implementations can run on machines that provide message passing as the only communication mechanism. *Shared memory* (when available in the underlying computer system) is used to improve performance. *Threads* (processes that share the address space with other processes) are used to support the fast creation of new computations (a useful but not always vital characteristic).

-*The parallel virtual machine layer* represents the "assembly language level" of Agora. Computations are expressed as independent procedures that exchange data by using Agora's primitives and are activated by means of a pattern matching mechanism. Computations can be programmed in either C or Common Lisp. It is in this layer that the most suitable Mach primitives are selected, the code is compiled and linked, tasks assigned to machines, etc. Computations expressed at this level are machine independent. Although systems can be fully described at this level, the virtual machine level is best used to describe *frameworks* rather than program user computations.

-*The framework layer* is the level at which most of the application researchers program. A framework is like a specialized environment built to interact with the user in familiar terms. The description, assembly, debugging and production run of an application system are all performed through its associated framework(s). Frameworks, as used in Agora, are very similar to ABE's frameworks, see [10].

First, *application engineers* program one or more "frameworks" that implement the programming environments that an application requires. A framework provides all the tools to generate and maintain a given kind of program. For example, a framework could contain virtual machine code to implement data-flow and remote-procedure-call communication mechanisms and a tool to merge user-supplied code with the existing virtual machine code. Such a framework could also contain a *structured* graphical editor that allows the user to deal with programs in terms of data-flow graphs.

Researchers can then use frameworks to create framework instantiations, i.e. frameworks that contain user provided code and data. Components of a framework instantiation can themselves be instantiations of some other framework. A framework instantiation can then be integrated with other framework instantiations to generate more complex frameworks. In the speech system, for example, the word hypothesizer is described by using a framework that embodies the asynchronous control necessary to run the word hypothesizer in parallel and code to display the data processed: a user need only be familiar with the algorithms and the language in which they are written in order to be able to experiment with different word hypothesization algorithms. A word hypothesizer generated in this way can be merged with an acoustic-phonetic framework instantiation by using, for example, a data-flow framework. Tools from all the original frameworks are made available in the combined framework.

We cannot describe frameworks in detail in this paper. Currently, we have implemented a "Unix-like" framework which lets users build parallel programs that communicate by using streams. We are implementing a data-flow framework that will let a user program through a graphic editor and a number of very specialized frameworks like the word hypothesizer framework described later.

3. The Agora Virtual Machine

The **Agora** virtual machine has been designed with two goals in mind: first, to be able to efficiently execute different programming models. Second, to avoid restricting the possible implementations to certain computer architectures. **Agora** is centered around representing data as sets of *elements* of the same type (elements can be regarded as variable-size records). Elements are stored in global structures called *cliques*. Each clique has a name that completely identifies it and a type (from a set of globally-defined types). **Agora** forces the user to split a computation into separate components, called Knowledge Sources (KS), that execute concurrently. Knowledge Sources exchange data through cliques and are activated when certain patterns of elements are generated. Any KS that knows the name of a clique can perform operations on it since **Agora** "registers" the name of each clique when it is created. Since "names" are global, the only requirement for sharing a clique between KSs is that a clique be first "created" by a KS and then declared "shared" by another KS. In a speech recognition system, for example, an element could be a phoneme, word, sentence or some other meaningful intermediate representation of speech; a clique could contain all the phonemes generated by a KS and a KS could be the function that scores phonetic hypotheses.

Element types are described *within the KS code* by using the syntax of the language that is used to program the KSs, with some additional information. The additional information is stripped from the source code by **Agora** before the code is handed to the compiler or interpreter. This means that users need not learn a different language. This is in contrast with other language-independent data transport mechanisms, like the mechanism described in [4], that use a separate language to define the data. The type declarations can contain extra information for scheduling and debugging purposes, e.g. the expected number of accesses per second, the legal values that elements can assume, display procedures, etc.

KSs can refer to sets of elements by using *capabilities*. Capabilities are manipulated by **Agora** functions and can be used to "copy" from a clique into the address space of a KS and viceversa (often no real copy will be necessary). There are two "modes" of access: *Read-only* and *Add-element*. Elements cannot be modified or deleted after they are written but Knowledge Sources can signal that they are not interested anymore in a given Element Clique.

Each KSs contains one or more user functions. KS functions are completely independent of the system they are used in and must only be able to deal with the types of element they use. KSs are created by calling an **Agora** primitive, each call to this function can generate multiple instances of the same KS. When a KS instance is created, a pattern can be specified: once the pattern is satisfied the KS function is activated. The pattern is expressed in terms of "arrival events" (the fact that an element has entered a clique) and in terms of the values of the data stored in the elements. For example, one can specify a pattern that is matched every time a new element enters the clique or that only matches if a field in the element has a specific value. More than one clique can be mentioned in the same pattern but no variables are permitted in the pattern (i.e. there is no

binding). It is also possible to specify if an event must be considered "consumed" by a successful match or if it can be used by other patterns (this can be very useful to "demultiplex" the contents of a clique into different KSs or to guarantee mutual exclusion when needed).

A KS can contain any statement of the language that is being used and any of the **Agora** primitives, expressed in a way that is compatible with the language used. The Agora primitives are similar to the typical functions that an operating system would provide to start new processes (create new KS's in **Agora**), manipulate files (create, share and copy cliques) and schedule processes (i.e. change the amount of computation allocated to a KS).

KS's are mapped into Mach [2] primitives. In this mapping a KS can be clustered with other KS's that can benefit from sharing computer resources. For example, a cluster could contain KSs that access the same clique or KSs that should be scheduled (i.e. executed) together. Although clusters could also be implemented as Mach tasks, sharing the address space between "random" tasks can be very dangerous. Clusters can be implemented (in decreasing order of efficiency) as multiple processes that share memory or as multiple processes communicating by messages. Multiple instances of the *same* KS have a very effective and simple implementation on the Mach operating system [2] as a single process (task, in Mach terminology) in which multiple "threads" of computation implement the KSs.

Currently, the composition of clusters must be fully specified by the user, but **Agora** maintains information on which KSs are runnable and on how much of the cluster computation power each KS should be receiving. The computation power associated with a KS can be controlled by any KS in a cluster by using **Agora** primitives.

In conclusion, the **Agora** virtual machine provides mechanisms to statically and dynamically control multiprocessing: KSs can be clustered in different ways and executed on different processor configurations. Clusters can be used to dynamically control the allocation of processors. Therefore, **Agora** provides all the components necessary to implement focus-of-attention policies within a system, but the responsibility of designing the control procedures remains with the user.

4. Example of a System Built with Agora

We will illustrate how **Agora** can be used by describing the design of the CMU speech recognition system, ANGEL [5]. ANGEL uses more computation than a single processor could provide (more than 1,000 MIPS), is programmed in two languages (currently, the system comprises more than 100,000 lines of C and CommonLisp code), uses many different styles of computation, and is in continuous evolution since more than 15 researchers are working on it. Figure 4-1 shows the top level organization of the system. Arrows indicate transfer of both data and control. At the top level most of the components communicate using a data-flow paradigm, with the exception of a few modules that use a remote-procedure-call) paradigm. Eventually, a blackboard model will be used at the top

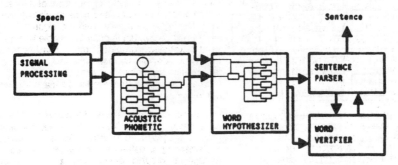

Figure 4-1:   Structure of the ANGEL Speech Recognition System:
Top-level and Internal Structure of the
Acoustic-phonetic and Word-hypothesizer Modules

level. In Figure 4-1, two components contain a sketch of the structure of their subcomponents. For example, the acoustic phonetic component uses both data-flow and blackboard paradigms. It is important to note that Figure 4-1 shows the *current* structure and that part of the work being done on the system concerns expanding the number of modules and evaluating new ways of interconnecting them.

Frameworks are used to provide each component with the environment that is best suited to its development. At the top level there is a framework that provides a graphic editor to program data-flow and remote-procedure-call computations. Each subcomponent of the top level framework is developed using a different framework. We will use the word hypothesizer subcomponent as an example. The word hypothesizer generates word hypotheses by applying a beam search algorithm at selected times in the utterance. The inputs of the search are the phonetic hypotheses and the vocabulary. The times are indicated by a marker, called *anchor* that is computed elsewhere. The word hypothesizer must be able to receive anchors and phonemes in any order and perform a search around each anchor after having checked that all the acoustic-phonetic hypotheses within *delta* time units from the anchor are available. Phonetic hypotheses arrive at unpredictable times and in any order.

The word hypothesizer requires two functions: *the matching function* (**match()**) that hypothesizes words from phonemes and *the condition function* (**enough_phonemes()**) that checks if there are enough phonemes within a time interval from the anchor. The "editor" of the word-hypothesizer framework lets a researcher specify these two functions and binds them with the virtual machine level description. This description, that has been programmed by an application engineer, provides the parallel implementation. The framework also contains a display function that can be altered by a user.

The stylized code in Figure 4-2 describes the virtual machine level description used within the word hypothesizer framework. A speech researcher does not need to be aware of this description but only of the external specification of the two functions **match()** and **enough-phonemes()**. This description could be written in any language supported by **Agora** (currently C and Common Lisp).

```
Type declarations for cliques

KS setup
    Initialization: Create word and phoneme lattice clique
        Instantiate a few copies of KS word-hypothesize
        to be activated at the arrival of each new anchor
KS word-hypothesize
    Initialization: Declare the word, phoneme lattice and
        anchor cliques as shared
    Entry point: if enough_phonemes() then execute
        match() else instantiate KS wait to be
        activated at  each new phoneme
KS wait
    Initialization: Declare the word, phoneme lattice and
        anchor cliques as shared
    Entry point: if there are enough phonemes then match()
```

Figure 4-2: The Virtual Machine Level Implementation of the Word Hypothesizer

There are three Knowledge Sources: KS **setup** creates instantiations of KS **word-hypothesize** that are activated when "anchors" arrive. When any of these KSs receives an "anchor", it checks if there are enough phonetic hypotheses and, if so, executes **match()**. If not enough hypotheses are available, it creates an instantiation of KS **wait** that waits for all the necessary phonemes before executing **match()**.

The KS *word-hypothesize* can be compiled into a task if the target machine does not have shared memory. A parameter of the KS creation procedure indicates to **Agora** how many copies of the KS the framework designer believes can be efficiently used. If the machine has shared memory, then threads can be used and the parameter becomes irrelevant since new threads can be generated without incurring in too much cost. **Agora** can also be instructed to generate the **wait** KSs as threads of the same task. This is possible if KS **wait** and the functions it calls do not use any global data.

5. Custom Hardware for the Agora Virtual Machine

In a parallel system, the duration of an atomic computation (granularity) must be substantially bigger than the overhead required

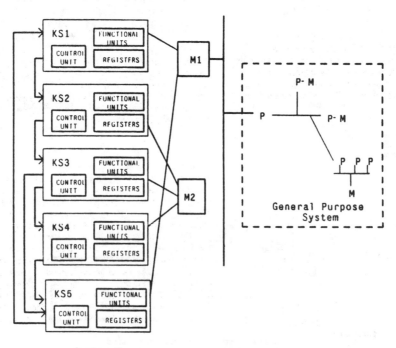

Custom Processor

Figure 5-1: A custom hardware architecture for search

to start and terminate it. This overhead can be very large when using (conventional) general purpose architectures. **Agora** shares this characteristic with many other languages and environments. For example, Multilisp [13] cannot be used to efficiently implement computations at a very small granularity level unless some special hardware is provided to speed-up the implementation of futures. The effect of the overhead can be seen in the performance curves for the *quicksort* program presented in [13], Figure 5: the parallel version of the algorithm requires three times more processing power than the sequential version in order to run as fast (although it can run faster if more processing power is available). Therefore, hardware support *tailored to the style of parallelism provided by a language or an environment* is necessary. A proposal for an architecture that supports small granularity in concurrent Smalltalk can be found in [9].

The **Agora** virtual machine efficiently supports computations with a granularity larger than 500 ms when implemented on general purpose machines connected by a local area network. In the case of shared memory architectures, the limiting factor is the operating system overhead. Most of the current parallel environments, such as the Cosmic Cube [15] and Butterfly [3] environments, provide only minimal operating system functionality: typically, only the basic functions required to use the hardware. In these systems, granularity could be as small as a few hundred microseconds. **Agora** supports systems that are too large and complex to be implemented without a full operating system environment and must pay the price of operating system overhead. Therefore, the minimum granularity of an **Agora**'s KS on shared memory systems and Mach is about 10ms.

There is no single set of hardware which can lower the KS granularity independently of the computation being performed since each different style of computation poses different requirements on the virtual machine primitives. Therefore, our strategy is to develop architectures tailored to specific computations. So far, we have designed an architecture that supports computations that can be pipelined but are data-dependent and cannot be easily vectorized. For example, pipelines can be generated every time an algorithm executes a large number of iterations of the same loop. The architecture exploits the fact that data-flow control can be implemented very efficiently by direct connections between processors and the fact that a hardware semaphore associated with each element of a clique can speed-up concurrent access to elements. The architecture is *custom* because a set of KS's has to be explicitly decomposed and the architecture *configured* for that particular decomposition. This process is convenient when an algorithm is reasonably stable.

Figure 5-1 shows the structure of the architecture and how it interfaces with the rest of the system. Each KS is executed in a separate processor. Processors communicate through shared memory as well as through dedicated links. Dedicated links take care of data-flow while shared memories serve two functions: input/output and synchronized access to shared data to resolve data-

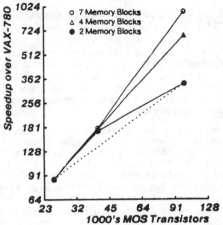

Figure 5-3: Speedup vs. transistors

dependencies.

Each processor contains: a simple hardwired control unit that executes a fixed program, functional units as required by the KS function, and register storage. An instruction can specify which data to read from local storage, what operations to perform on them, and where to store the result. A typical instruction can perform an addition or multiplication or access the shared memory. The architecture can be implemented as a fully-dedicated VLSI device or device set that communicates with the rest of the system through shared memory. Therefore, each processor can have different functional units and be wired directly to the processor(s) that follow it. A more expensive implementation with off-the-shelf components is also possible.

We evaluated the architecture by decomposing the *match* procedure used in the word hypothesizer described in the previous section. The match function uses a "best match, beam search" algorithm though other, more sophisticated search algorithms are already being planned. The current algorithm requires about 20 to 40 million instructions per second of speech with a 200-word vocabulary when executed in C on a VAX-11/780, depending on how much knowledge can be applied to constrain the search. A 5000-word vocabulary will require 500 to 1000 million instructions per second of speech.

We have simulated the custom architecture instruction-by-instruction while it executes the beam search algorithm with real data. The simulation assumed performance figures typical of a CMOS VLSI design that has not been heavily optimized (and therefore might be generated semiautomatically using standard cell design techniques). See [1] for details. The presence of 1, 2, 4, or 7 physical memory blocks was simulated to evaluate memory access bottlenecks. Figure 5-2 shows our simulation results as speedup relative to the performance of a VAX-11/780.

With five KS's and one physical memory we see a speedup of 170. This configuration could be implemented on a single custom chip by using a conservative fabrication technology (memories would still be implemented with off-the-shelf RAM's). With 28 KS's and seven memories, we can obtain speedups of three orders of magnitude, enough to cope with a 5,000 word vocabulary in real time. Moreover, each of the 28 processors is much smaller (in terms of hardware) than the original single processor and all 28 processors could share the same VLSI device by using the best available fabrication technology. This fact is illustrated graphically in Figure 5-3 which plots the speed-up against the transistor count of the design. The transistor count was obtained by adding the number of transistors in actual layouts of the various functional units and

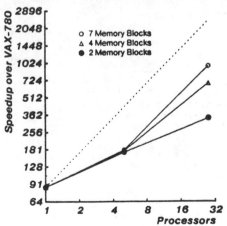

Figure 5-2: Speedup vs. processors

registers, and is a crude estimate of the amount of silicon area required in a VLSI design.

6. Conclusions

Agora has a number of characteristics that make it particularly suitable for the development of complex systems in a multiprocessor environment. These include:

- the complexity of parallel processing can be hidden by building "reusable" custom environments that guide a user in describing, debugging and running an application without getting involved in parallel programming;
- computations can be expressed in different languages;
- the structure of a system can be modified while the system is running;
- KSs are activated by patterns computed on the data generated by other KS's;
- KSs are described in a way that allows **Agora** to match the available architecture and its resources with the requirements of the computation;
- custom architectures can easily be integrated with components running on general purpose systems.

Acknowledgements

The parallel virtual machine has been designed with Alessandro Forin [6, 8]. Fil Alleva, Rick Lerner and Mike Bauer have participated in the design and implementation of Agora. The custom architecture has been designed with Thomas Anantharaman and is described in detail in [1]. The project has also benefited from the constructive criticism and support of Raj Reddy, Duane Adams and Renato De Mori.

References

1. Ananthamaran, T. and Bisiani,R. Custom Search Accelerators for Speech Recognition. Proceedings of the 13th International Symposium on Computer Architecture, IEEE, June, 1986.

2. Baron, R., Rashid, R., Siegel, E., Tevanian, A., and Young, M. "Mach-1: An Operating System Environment for Large Scale Multiprocessor Applications". *IEEE Software Special Issue* (July 1985).

3. anon. *The Uniform System Approach to Programming the Butterfly(TM) Parallel Processor.* BBN Laboratories Inc., November 1985.

4. Birrel, A.D. and Nelson,B.J. "Implementing Remote Procedure Calls". *Trans. Computer Systems 2*, 1 (February 1984), 39-59.

5. Adams, D.A., Bisiani, R. The CMU Distributed Speech Recognition System. Eleventh DARPA Strategic Systems Symposium, Naval Postgraduate School, Monterey, CA, October, 1985.

6. Bisiani, R. et. al. Building Parallel Speech Recognition Systems with the Agora Environment. DARPA Strategic Computing Speech Workshop, Palo Alto, CA, February, 1986.

7. Carriero,N. and Gielernter,D. The S/Net's Linda Kernel. Proceedings of the Tenth ACM Symposium on Operating Systems Principles, December, 1985.

8. Bisiani,R. et.al. Agora, An Environment for Building Problem Solvers on Distributed Computer Systems. Proceedings of the 1985 Distributed Artificial Intelligence Workshop, Sea Ranch, California.

9. Dally, W.J. *A VLSI Architecture for Concurrent Data Structures.* Ph.D. Th., California Institute of Technology, March 1986.

10. Erman,L. et.al. ABE: Architectural Overview. Proceedings of the 1985 Distributed Artificial Intelligence Workshop, Sea Ranch, California.

11. Gabriel,R.P. and McCarthy,J. Queue-based multiprocessing Lisp. Symp. Lisp and Functional Programming, August, 1984.

12. Green,P.E. AF: A Framework for Real-time Distributed Cooperative Problem Solving. Proceedings of the 1985 Distributed Artificial Intelligence Workshop, Sea Ranch, California.

13. Halstead, H. "Multilisp: A Language for Concurrent Symbolic Computation". *ACM Trans. on Programming Languages and Systems 7*, 4 (Octber 1985), 501-538.

14. Bobrow,D.G. and Stefik,M.J. A Virtual Machine for Experiments in Knowledge Representation. Xerox Palo Alto Research Center, April, 1982.

15. Seitz, C. L. "The Cosmic Cube". *Comm. ACM 28*, 1 (January 1985), 22-33.

16. Smith,R.G. Strobe: Support for Structured Object Knowledge Representation. Proceedings of the Eighth International Joint Conference on Artificial Intelligence, August, 1983.

ABE:
A COOPERATIVE OPERATING SYSTEM
AND DEVELOPMENT ENVIRONMENT*

Frederick Hayes-Roth
Lee D. Erman
Scott Fouse**
Jay S. Lark
James Davidson

*Teknowledge, Inc.
Palo Alto, CA 94303*

---

* Reprinted from *AI Tools and Techniques*, M. Richer (ed.), Ablex Publishing, Norwood, NJ, 1988.

This is an early description of in-progress research. The ideas described here require experimental testing and will likely change. This does not constitute a commitment by Teknowledge to any product or service. ABE is a trademark of Teknowledge, Inc.

This research is partially sponsored by the Air Force Systems Command, Rome Air Development Center, Griffiss Air Force Base, NY 13441-5700 and the Defense Advanced Research Projects Agency, 1400 Wilson Blvd., Arlington, VA 22209, under contract F30602-85-C-0135.

** Teknowledge Federal Systems, Inc.

Table of Contents

INTRODUCTION   458
TECHNICAL DESCRIPTION: A COOPERATIVE OPERATING SYSTEM   459
    AND ENVIRONMENT
    Composition and Computational Metaphor   460
    Frameworks   461
    Distribution   464
    Reuse   465
EXAMPLE APPLICATION   468
INTELLIGENT SYSTEMS REVISITED   476
    Combining Knowledge and Data Processing   476
    Exploratory Development   477
    Handling Complexity   477
    High Performance   478
    Reusability   479
    Heterogeneous Software and Hardware   479
    Next-Generation Operating Environments   479
RELATIONSHIP TO OTHER SYSTEMS   480
PROTOTYPE SYSTEM STATUS   483
RESEARCH AND ENGINEERING ISSUES   483
CONCLUSION: FROM KNOWLEDGE SYSTEMS TO INTELLIGENT   484
    SYSTEMS ENGINEERING
ACKNOWLEDGMENTS   485
References   486

INTRODUCTION

As we have learned more about the usefulness of artificial intelligence (AI) techniques for commercial and military applications, we have discovered the need for a higher degree of integration with conventional computing and a higher degree of modularity in knowledge processing functions. These two needs go hand in hand. Many early AI tools implicitly assumed that the task they addressed was building systems that would stand alone on high-powered and high-priced workstations, usually LISP machines. However, it has become clear that most applications impose many constraints on their delivery environments. These constraints include user interface packages, size and performance requirements, and integration standards ranging from subroutine calling conventions to network communication protocols.

Teknowledge's ABE™ system addresses the problem of combining conventional computing functions with knowledge processing capabilities. It enables the development of cooperative application systems that can exploit new-generation multiprocessing and distributed hardware. We call these new-generation applications *intelligent systems*, and we believe that ABE embodies excellent methods for engineering these systems.

ABE is intended for system architects and application developers. It supports the exploratory and evolutionary development of applications that must integrate both conventional and knowledge processing capabilities. It provides several high-level graphical design and development environments, which we call *frameworks*. It encourages a high degree of modularity and facilitates radical reorganization of software components and the mapping of those components onto the hardware used to deploy them. ABE, in essence, provides an environment and operating system for intelligent systems.

At present, Teknowledge offers the ABE software system as a prototype to a limited number of advanced users. These users typically face the problem of developing applications that must combine several software subsystems into an effective whole. These subsystems may employ conventional or AI capabilities. Developers typically create a near-solution, then modify it incrementally, extending the system in numerous directions. For one-person programs built on a single workstation, modern programming environments supplied as part of systems such as Smalltalk [Goldberg and Robson 83], Symbolics Genera [Walker, Moon, Weinreb, and McMahon 87], or KEE IntelliCorp 86] would seem appropriate. We think of that kind of problem as "programming in the small." Evolutionary programming "in the large," on the other hand, requires methods and tools that span multiple system architectures and organizations, machines, languages, and tool packages. ABE provides these methods and tools.

ABE views knowledge processing as merely one facility within a larger computing application. Moreover, ABE projects the benefits of evolutionary programming, which we have so long associated with AI tools, from AI programming in the small to commercial and military programming in the large. We believe that ABE's approach will succeed because it separates the essential benefits of early AI tools from the accidental ones [Brooks 87] and repackages those benefits in forms more directly useful for industry.

This article describes the motivations behind ABE, provides an overview of ABE, and relates ABE's characteristics to those motivations. We present an example application to illustrate these points. A more detailed description of ABE's architecture is presented in [Erman, Lark, and Hayes-Roth 88].

TECHNICAL DESCRIPTION: A COOPERATIVE OPERATING SYSTEM AND ENVIRONMENT

Our strategy in designing ABE has been to conceive of a next-generation operating system that would provide an excellent environment for building intelligent systems. These systems would combine conventional and knowledge processing functions into cooperative and synergistic applications, all running on a variety of networked and multiprocessing computers. For these reasons, we call ABE a *cooperative operating system* and a *development environment* for intelligent systems.

From our perspective, the principal features of an operating system are its computational metaphor and composition methodology. Systems such as OS/360 and Unix present to the developer a view of system design and computation consisting principally of concepts about program parts, assemblies of composite structures, and interconnections. System developers study and employ operating systems from this perspective. We call ABE's computational metaphor and composition methodology MOP (Module-Oriented Programming).

Composition and Computational Metaphor

Operating systems succeed or fail, in part, based on the usefulness of the tools they provide for assembling applications from parts. We believe that this will become increasingly true as people attempt to build systems that span diverse technologies, languages, machines, multiprocessing architectures, and distribution alternatives.

In the context of these diverse alternatives, ABE provides a common and unifying environment for building application systems. As an operating system, we can usefully compare MOP to UNIX. Where UNIX provides byte streams, pipes, and filters for assembling systems from components, MOP provides abstract datatypes (ADTs), ports, and modules. All modules consume and produce instances of ADTs. One module can connect to another module if the first produces through an output port an instance of an ADT that is compatible with the ADT expected by the second module in an input port. In contrast to UNIX's low-level byte-stream datatype, ABE's ADTs are typically high-level structures such as *plans*, *assumptions*, or *queries*. ABE encourages users to think in terms of meaningful structures, to reuse ADTs from the catalog, and to reuse modules that process the types of ADTs needed. In these ways, ABE follows the successful style of UNIX but attempts to elevate the connectivity concerns from byte streams to a higher level of abstraction.

MOP's computational model differs substantially from that of UNIX. Instead of a series of filters with relatively straightforward, data-directed control, MOP defines modules as distributed objects that can asynchronously communicate data with each other along flexible communication paths. Modules are persistent (i.e., they retain state between invocations) and can operate concurrently. Modules explicitly supply other modules with the *computational resources* needed to carry out their tasks.

MOP uses *events* as a primitive means for communication between concurrent modules with each other. Events can signal that another module has finished executing, that external data has arrived, or that another module wants to change the computational resources that it has at its disposal. (See [Forrest and Lark 88] for more details on the multiprocessing aspects of the MOP model.)

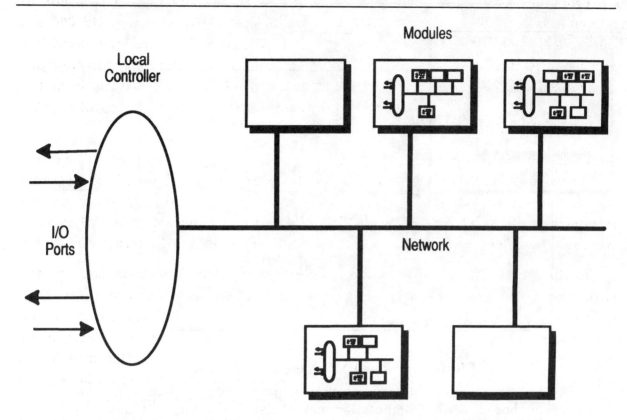

Figure 1: MOP: ABE's underlying computational model

The Module-Oriented Programming (MOP) computational model provides each composite module with a network for connecting a set of interacting component modules. The local controller determines the behavior of the composite system by managing control and communication among the component modules and between the network and the external world. The figure also shows that any module can recursively embed another module. Although not shown in the figure, MOP also supports nonhierarchical composition, called *meshing*, by allowing one module to be included in more than one composite module simultaneously.

Frameworks

MOP also introduces a second kind of higher-level concept in lieu of the connectivity model provided by UNIX pipes and shell scripts. In MOP, designers may compose a system from any number of modules according to any arbitrary communication and control topology. MOP provides a computational model for expressing these compositions, which Figure 1 outlines. ABE supplies a virtual machine, called *Kiosk*, for executing MOP-composed systems.

MOP was designed as a general computational model, to allow for a wide variety of structure and behavior descriptions and to support their implementation on a variety of computing systems. That generality makes MOP unsuitable for expressing most

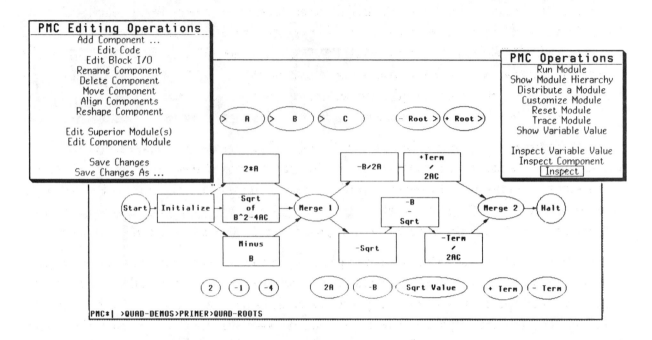

Figure 2: The PMC (procedural) framework

ABE provides a variety of frameworks for constructing composite modules. Each framework embodies its own computation metaphor and provides a language of symbols for expressing programs (i.e., compositions of modules). This figure shows an example of a composite module built in the PMC (Procedural Module Control) framework. PMC allows a system designer to directly express the control flow through a system of modules, much as conventional programming languages express control of subroutines. Within a composite PMC module, component modules can run concurrently.

This PMC program calculates solutions to the quadratic equation, $AX^2+BX+C=0$. The program contains several component modules (Initialize, Minus B, etc.), input variables (A, B, C), output variables (+root, -root), internal variables (2A, -B, +term, etc.), merge nodes (merge 1, merge 2) for synchronizing parallel execution streams, and unique start and halt nodes. The node labeled "Sqrt of B^2-4AC" is itself a composite module, built in the DF (Dataflow) framework; this is an example of one composite module embedded in another.

Each framework provides a graphical interface for viewing and editing the program. Typically, rectangles depict component modules, ovals depict data objects (for PMC, variables), and arrows show movement of control and data appropriate to the framework (for PMC, control flow). The menus in the figure show some of the operations available to the user while developing a PMC module.

ABE's MOP model supports building modules with a wide range of granularities, but it emphasizes large-sized modules. This figure uses a very simple example, to convey ABE's constructs clearly. Typically, ABE modules embody more complex functionalities -- for example "replan in the face of the failure of the current plan," rather than "multiply two numbers."

applications perspicuously. Therefore, ABE supplies a variety of more conventional and restricted *frameworks* for users to design and develop problem-solving compositions. Each framework supports compositions of a particular sort, such as dataflow (DF), blackboard (BBD), transaction processing (TX), and procedural control (PMC). Figure 2 shows an example of the PMC framework; others are presented later. Within each framework, ABE provides graphically-oriented development tools; the figure also indicates some features of those tools.

ABE enforces an extreme form of uniformity that enables the radical evolution of application systems: every system composed of ABE modules using any of ABE's frameworks becomes an ABE module, and all ABE modules can be composed with other modules in any of ABE's frameworks. We call this property *uniform composability* of ABE modules, and we refer to modules composed in this way as *composite modules*.

To build systems in ABE, one composes modular subsystems from new or pre-existing modules. Modular composition can embed modules hierarchically, as shown in Figure 1. Modules may also be composed by nonhierarchical *meshing*, permitting the same module instance to participate in--be shared by--more than one composite module. ABE's uniform composability, diversity of composition frameworks, and composition by embedding and meshing provide a solution to the problems of managing complexity.

Modules that are not composed of other modules are called *primitive*. Such primitive modules are considered *black boxes* because ABE has no visibility into their internal structure. Developers specify the behavior of such modules by coding them in some convenient programming language. The BBOX framework (see Figure 3) supports the creation of primitive modules. ABE will provide hooks to several programming languages so that developers can create these primitive modules. BBOX ensures that these modules meet the input-output requirements for ABE modules -- they consume and produce instances of ADTs and respond to the standard Kiosk control operations.

The developer of a typical application will want to import many modules. That is, the developer will have the desired function in a pre-existing computer program and will want to provide its function through the BBOX "wrapper" that encodes and decodes ADT instances and channels them to the appropriate entry points. Importing an alien capability into the ABE catalog requires a one-time engineering effort to identify the key functionality and code the wrapper; in our experience, complex modules require on the order of one person-week to import. Thereafter, the ABE developer views this module no differently than any other primitive module.

If developers want to connect and control modules using some metaphor not provided by one of ABE's supplied frameworks, they can create a customized composite module by creating a custom controller. The code in the custom controller makes direct calls to Kiosk functions to control embedded component modules. Externally, this custom module looks like any other ABE module. ABE's KSK framework, a

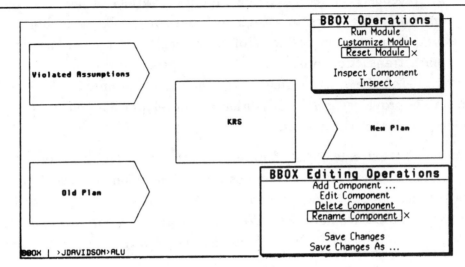

Figure 3:   The BBOX (black box) framework

This figure shows an example of a module in the BBOX (Black Box) framework. The application developer uses the BBOX framework to create modules, both from scratch, by programming them in some convenient language, and by importing existing functions. In either case the input and output ports are defined (in this figure: Old Plan, Violated Assumptions, and New Plan) and the basic operation is created (KRS). The basic operation either accesses an existing function (here: the Knobs Replanning System [Dawson, Brown, Kalish, and Goldkind 87]), or contains arbitrary code defining a new function.

generalization of BBOX, supports building these custom composite modules.

Distribution

ABE provides a third extension to the computational model of UNIX, namely the notion that modules may run on distributed or multiprocessing computing facilities. When developers originally describe a system, ABE assumes nothing special about the location of the component modules. ABE finds these modules in its catalog and uses its underlying Kiosk operating system to assure that the modules intercommunicate correctly according to the module composition specifications. At the lowest level, this generally means assuring that messages are sent to the right places, received and interpreted correctly, and delivered at an appropriate time or in an appropriate sequential order, and that modules are invoked at the right times. Over time, as the developer wants to change the physical allocation of modules to processors, ABE facilitates this. The developer simply specifies which modules are to run on which machines. Thus, developers can work out problems of architecture, function, and distribution at a logical level, and easily change the mapping to the underlying computing facilities in response to changes in logical structure, physical resources, and experience with system operation.

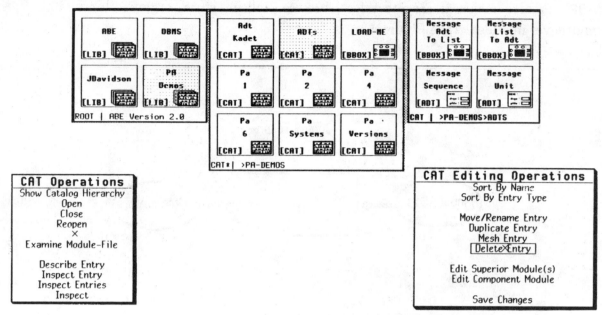

Figure 4: The CAT (catalog) framework

The ABE catalog facility is used to select, browse, collect, organize, and document modules. CAT supports a mostly hierarchical structure of subcatalogs, with ABE modules appearing at the leaves of the hierarchy. CAT's structure approximates that of the UNIX file system, and provides these features: hierarchical structure, a single distinguished root, pathnames for referring to catalogs, shared pointers for nonhierarchical structures (i.e., multiple pointers to the same catalog or module from different catalogs, using different names), and separately-mountable libraries (independent subtrees of catalogs). The figure shows a simple example with three catalogs. The root catalog is on the left. PA-DEMOS, in the center, is one of its next-level subcatalogs, and the entry for it is shaded in the root. Similarly, ADTS, on the right, is an entry in PA-DEMOS. The menus in the figure show some of the CAT operations available to the user.

CAT provides facilities for organizing modules according to a particular metaphor. Thus, it is an ABE framework -- each catalog is a composite module, with components that are other catalogs, standard ABE modules, and ADTs. Rather than providing for the execution of its component modules, CAT's purpose is to allow for their examination and selection. In addition to unifying the implementation, treating CAT as a framework has been useful for understanding and refining the notions of "module" and "framework."

Reuse

ABE embodies a philosophy of system design and development that emphasizes the reuse of software components. It has always been desirable for developers to reuse code, but this has proved difficult for many reasons. ABE provides tools that address these problems. First, ABE's uniform composability and diversity of frameworks help fabricate new solutions to complex problems by assembling primitive modules into composite modules, modules into subsystems, and subsystems into applications. Second, ABE's catalog makes it easy to select, browse, collect, store, organize, and reuse these multilevel modules. (See Figure 4.)

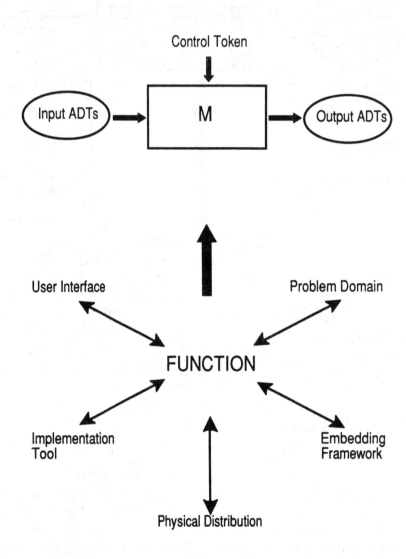

Figure 5: High-dimensional modularity in ABE

Third, ABE's emphasis on uniformity and reusability encourages a kind of program structuring that we call *high-dimensional* (HD) modularity. HD modular parts perform functions on ADTs, produce ADT instances, and can be combined freely with other modules that have consistent ADT requirements. (See Figure 5.) HD modules do not

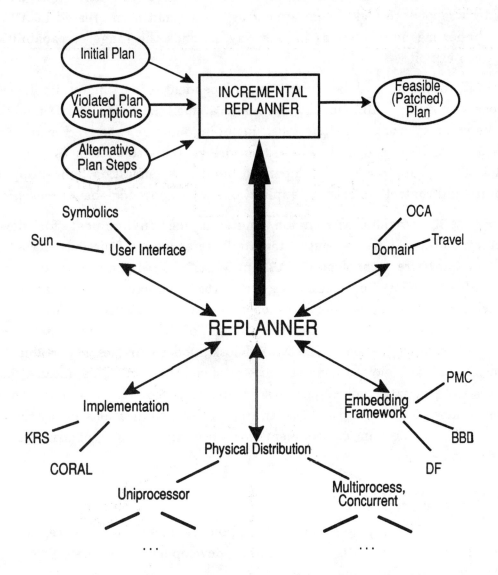

Figure 6:   An example of high-dimensional modularity

This figure shows a replanning function as an example of high-dimensional modularity. We have built replanning modules of this functionality with different tool languages (KRS, CORAL), for different machines (Symbolics, Sun), used within different frameworks (PMC, BBD, DF), distributed to remote machines, and applied to different domains (Offensive Counter Air Mission Planning, Travel Planning).

restrict developers to use any particular user interface, language, or framework for developing the rest of their application, or any particular hardware or underlying communication networks. In this way, HD modules support a high degree of reusability. (See Figure 6.)

As previously stated, the ABE catalog contains alien functions that have been imported by wrappers to make them appear as if they had been created in ABE as HD modules. Importing new functions in this way expands the range of capabilities ABE developers can exploit.

We want to make modular functions independent of as many implementation assumptions as possible. ABE currently provides a small collection of HD modules that perform knowledge processing functions, including storage and retrieval of logical formulae, plan analysis, and assumption monitoring. This collection, as it grows with increased ABE use, should allow developers to build new-generation hybrid applications that organize and control pre-existing applications with knowledge-based reasoning.

In sum, ABE provides a common and unifying environment for developing intelligent systems. These systems integrate heterogeneous functions across diverse software and hardware technologies. ABE provides a virtual machine and operating system called MOP/Kiosk for module-oriented programming. Using MOP, developers define intelligent systems as assemblies of modular subsystems. Below the virtual machine layer, ABE keeps separate the details of hardware, processors, resource allocation, and communication. The MOP/Kiosk model provides a portable basis so that applications can move among a variety of platforms. This means that ABE applications can tolerate radical changes in delivery requirements and can exploit revolutionary new ideas in hardware, software, and communications infrastructure. In this way, ABE provides an environment for entering the age of cooperative and intelligent systems.

EXAMPLE APPLICATION

We now describe a representative application development sequence, to illustrate the basic capability that ABE provides for developing systems. The particular application used is the Pilot's Associate.

The Pilot's Associate project is a prototype of an expert pilot aid. It has access to a variety of sensors and data channels which allow it to determine a view of the current situation and to make decisions accordingly. Lockheed Aeronautical Systems Co. (LASC) and McDonnell Aircraft are developing separate versions of the Pilot's Associate; the system presented here was influenced by the work of LASC [Smith and Broadwell 88].

We present a sequence of stages in the development of our system which serves as a time-lapse record of system evolution. Each stage represents a runnable system. At each stage, problems and issues appear which motivate the transition to the next stage. We show each version using ABE's graphical interface, in which viewers can be opened onto individual modules. Viewers provide a basis for examining, editing, and monitoring modules.

We intend this example to illustrate the basic system development methodology which has motivated the design of ABE. The methodology assumes that designers of intelligent systems cannot specify a complete and correct design on the first iteration. Rather, the system will need to evolve, possibly radically. There are two basic reasons for the need to change designs. The first is the classical need to adapt to changing requirements. This is amplified with intelligent systems, since the requirements themselves are often hard to specify and certainly not commonly understood. The second reason for evolving designs is the fact that the designs for many of the component functions of intelligent systems are not well understood. The conventional approach requires a designer to freeze a general system organization, encapsulating all uncertainty in isolated components. This approach breaks down when the components, as they are elaborated, no longer fit into the original functional organization.

ABE promotes a system development methodology that is based on experimental design. There is no set of analysis tools for intelligent systems that will allow us to determine if a design is correct or even adequate, so we must provide an environment that will allow us to discover attributes of an architecture and then easily modify that architecture in response to the lessons learned.

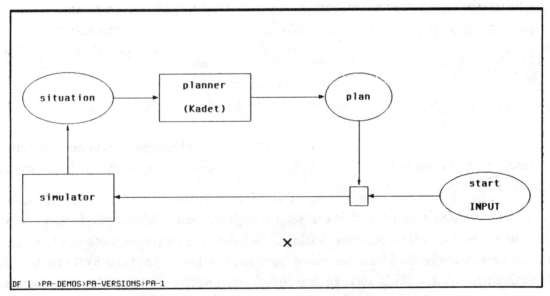

Figure 7:   Pilot's associate, initial version

The initial version of our Pilot's Associate system is constructed by lashing together two components, in a simple loop, as shown in Figure 7. The Planner and Simulator are existing components, both written using the KADET planning system Edwards and Hoffman 87, which was developed for the Lockheed Pilot's

Associate program. The Simulator models the behavior of friendly and enemy planes, producing as output a situation description. This is fed to the Planner, which plans the activity of the friendly plane. The plan produced is then used by the simulator to update its model, and the cycle continues. The Planner and Simulator were developed before ABE was available, and so were not created as ABE modules; the first task for building this initial version was to import them into ABE as modules.

The system is built as a composite module using ABE's DF (Dataflow) framework. The composite module consists of two *nodes* (Planner, Simulator), each of which is a component module, and two *places* (Plans, Situations), which can hold data tokens, represented as instances of ADTs. The nodes and places are connected by *links*. The links define the flow of input data from places to nodes, and the flow of output data from nodes to places. DF also provides constructs for reading and writing exogenous data (in this case, a single input place), and for splitting and joining data streams (in this case, a single join in lower right). The Planner and Simulator are BBOX modules embedded in the composite DF module.

In DF, a node can run whenever it has input data available on each of the input places. Within a composite DF module, nodes can run concurrently, reflecting the natural concurrency of dataflow models.

This system uses ADTs corresponding to the message traffic of the Pilot's Associate system, in particular plans and situations. These ADTs are structured objects, with slots for source, destination, time, type, and body.

This initial system runs, but suffers from performance problems because the planner executes on every cycle, even if the situation has not changed in ways that require replanning. A remedy is to add knowledge in the form of a situation monitor which compares the previous plan to the current situation, checking for potential plan reusability. Such a component has been created as an ABE BBOX module, and is added to the system, in Figure 8.

The revised system is shown in the left of the figure. The Situation Monitor (also shown at upper right) outputs a set of violated constraints, producing an empty set if the previous plan remains valid. Besides the addition of the Situation Monitor, the planner itself has required revision, in order to deal with the additional constraints input. This change has been accomplished by wrapping the original planner inside a layer of functionality that serves to store situations in those cases where replanning is not required and that outputs these buffered situations to the planner when planning is required. The Buffered Planner, built in ABE's KSK framework, is shown in the lower right. KSK provides LISP-level calls to other ABE modules; note that the KADET Planner module itself has not changed. This system executes in the same manner as the previous one, except that in some cycles the call to the KADET planner is bypassed, based on the decision made by the situation monitor.

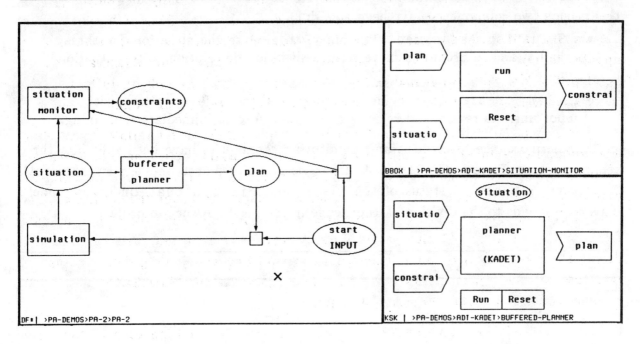

Figure 8:   Pilot's associate, with situation monitor

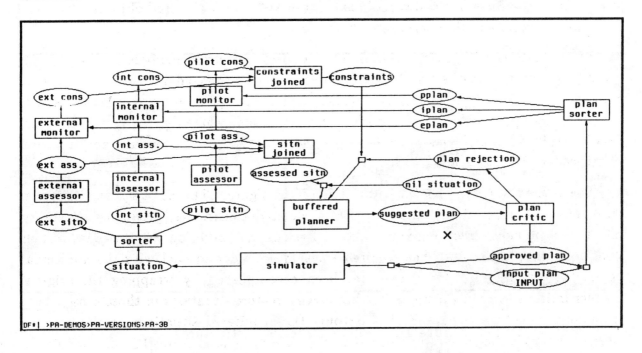

Figure 9:   Pilot's associate, with situation assessor and plan critic

The performance problem has been addressed, but the system still lacks certain required functionality. Some of this is added in the next version, shown in Figure 9. In this version two components have been added:

- a Situation Assessment capability, to analyze the situation for threat lethality, and to provide a more refined situation description to the situation monitor;

- a Plan Critic, to provide the user (in the role of pilot) with an opportunity to review and reject a given plan, forcing immediate replanning.

Furthermore, the assessment and monitoring capabilities have been split into three separate tracks: External Situation (status of other planes and the environment), Internal Situation (status of this plane), and Pilot Situation (pilot model). This corresponds to the division of knowledge in the Pilot's Associate project.

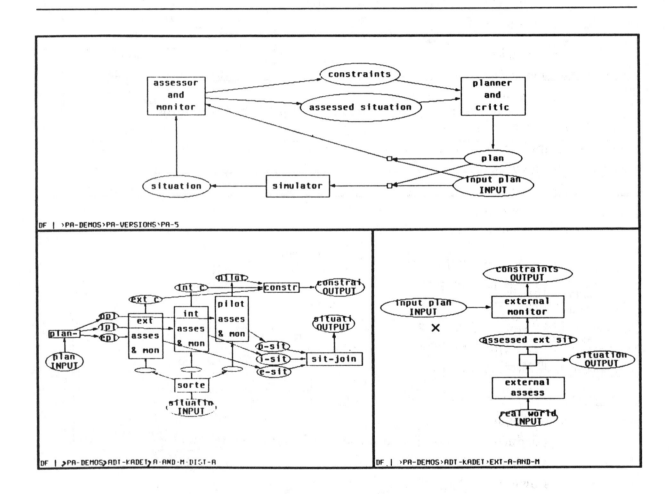

Figure 10: Pilot's associate, restructured

The system now provides the required functionality, but has become very complex. To facilitate further development, the complexity can be reduced by reorganizing the system, in particular by restructuring the modules and connections and introducing more levels. The result is shown in Figure 10.

The top level (shown at the top of the figure) is once again a simple loop. We have merged the Planner and Plan Critic into a single module. The Assessor and Monitor (with a viewer at lower left) contains three embedded modules, corresponding to the three tracks of domain expertise. A viewer has been opened onto the External Assessor and Monitor, and appears at lower right, showing the separate assessment and monitoring capabilities. Each of these three modules was built using the DF framework.

This system has the same functionality as the previous one, but a simpler organization, reminiscent of the first version. ABE's composition capabilities enable the system developer to deal with complexity by partitioning and hiding it, and by uncovering portions selectively.

The three tracks of the Assessor and Monitor module execute in parallel. To exploit the parallelism, we can use ABE's distribution facilities to move one or more of these modules to remote processors. This is shown in Figure 11.

ABE separates the specification of system functionality from the assignment of modules to individual processors, allowing either to be changed independently. This figure shows how the logical structure of an ABE application can be mapped onto a particular hardware configuration. The hardware configuration has two Symbolics computers and one Sun computer connected by an Ethernet. Symbolics 1 is the machine designated local -- it is where the user/developer is working.

The figure shows the mapping of modules to particular machines. The three Assessor and Monitor component modules operate in parallel, so the developer has chosen to distribute two of them to remote machines. Within External Assessment and Monitoring, the External Monitor module has been redistributed back to Symbolics 1. This provides a form of pipelining, in that assessment of a situation could begin before monitoring is completed for the previous situation.

To this point, the main modules of the system--the Simulator and Planner--have been executing sequentially. In an actual sensor-interpretation application, sensor data (in this case produced by the simulator) will arrive at a rate independent of the system's ability to deal with it. Thus the system must be reconfigured to allow the simulator to execute at its own rate. This change is made in Figure 12.

This version contains three top-level components. The Pilot's Associate module (with a viewer opened in lower left) contains the original Planner and Assessor and Monitor, connected in a new loop. The Simulator is now in its own top-level module (not opened in the figure).

ABE Application Logical Structure

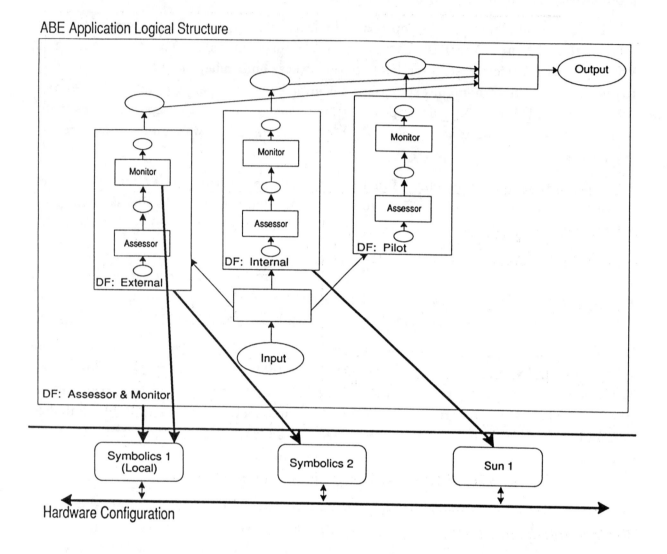

Figure 11:   Pilot's associate, distributed

These two subsystems communicate via two global LISP databases--one each for plans and for situations. These databases, shown in the viewer at right, use ABE's TX framework. TX implements a transaction model of processing, providing subroutine-like communications and control between one or more clients and one or more servers. The database module consists of two servers (the actual databases) and four clients. Each of these client modules is also a component module inside either the Pilot's Associate or Simulator module.

In this version, the top level module merely starts the three component subsystems, in parallel. This top-level module is constructed using the PMC (Procedural Module

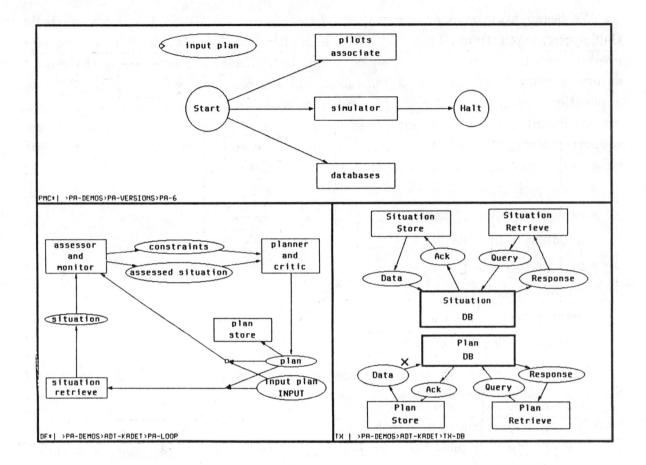

Figure 12:   Pilot's associate, with asynchronous communication

Control) framework.

When this system is run, the Pilot's Associate module retrieves the current situation from the database, performs assessment and planning, and writes the new plan into the plan database. The Simulator executes in a similar fashion, retrieving plans and writing situations. It runs asynchronously at a rate independent of the Pilot's Associate module, which was the objective of this change.

This sequence has shown the use of ABE to evolve a running application and to carry out experimentation at the system level. The changes in the system have been motivated by needs to address performance problems, add functionality, and meet additional requirements. These are typical of the problems that arise in developing large systems. ABE supports experimentation with software architectures, while reusing individual components.

INTELLIGENT SYSTEMS REVISITED

We began work on ABE as a response to needs evident within DARPA's Strategic Computing applications [Davis 85]. These applications include the Pilot's Associate project described in the previous section, and Battle Management systems that could automate many functions of situation assessment and planning. We recognized in these applications needs that had also appeared in many of the ambitious plans we had seen for intelligent factory management systems and next-generation professional office-support systems. In all these areas, developers expressed the desire for intelligent systems engineering, with the following primary requirements:

- the combination of knowledge and data processing;

- exploratory development;

- handling complexity;

- high performance;

- reusability;

- heterogeneous software and hardware; and

- next-generation operating environments.

We will elaborate on each of these requirements and describe the tools and techniques that ABE supplies to satisfy them.

Combining Knowledge and Data Processing

While trying to exploit the recent advances in knowledge processing, application developers find that they need to combine symbolic reasoning capabilities with in-place capabilities such as database, display, transaction processing, analysis, and reporting systems. Some knowledge engineering tools are starting to address the problem of integration with conventional capabilities, but the techniques they use are limited in two ways. First, they utilize current conventions for software system integration, namely conventional subroutine calls. This requires some amount of low-level programming to work out interface conventions for each new hybrid application. Second, although there are many paradigms for knowledge processing, any single product provides only a few of these. In the long-run, application developers will need to select and combine specialized knowledge processing functions, preferably from off-the-shelf products. This capability will require more modularity and technological refinement than is available for today's commercial knowledge engineering tools.

In designing ABE, we wanted a flexible way of connecting together software components, and we particularly wanted to accelerate the modularization of functions to perform knowledge processing tasks. We wanted system developers to make use of pre-existing tools and subsystems and to be able to redesign and restructure their systems easily when new and improved components came along. ABE provides such tools for defining interfaces to such capabilities and for cataloging the resulting modules, and we have begun building interfaces to certain standard capabilities, for example, SQL relational databases.

Exploratory Development

Government and commercial application developers have perceived a need for exploratory development "in the large" for the ambitious system they are considering. Although the so-called "waterfall" method of software development [Royce 70] has been used for decades, developers have generally found that they cannot get desirable results in new areas when they must specify the systems formally at the outset. Rather, developers have learned to appreciate the higher quality results that are obtained from incremental and evolutionary development. At the same time, major system contractors have begun bidding to build systems like the Pilot's Associate, in which system performance depends critically on uncertain factors such as the amount and quality of know-how extracted from pilots, the amount, quality, and accuracy of data, and the trade-offs between risk aversion and ambitiousness in decision-making. These determinants of system behavior can have a critical impact on the size, complexity, organization, and speed of the overall system. As a result, experimentation and evolutionary development become critical.

In designing ABE, we wanted to support system developers in formulating overall system architectures using very high-level tools so that they could defer low-level implementation concerns until an appropriate time. In addition, we wanted to provide methods and tools for radical restructuring of applications, which inevitably occurs as developers learn more about a problem domain, the computational performance, and the critical trade-offs. The example Pilot's Associate system illustrates many of the changes a complex intelligent system will undergo in its evolution from requirements to fielding and demonstrates some of ABE's capabilities that support those changes.

Handling Complexity

Several kinds of complexities confront those who wish to exploit the power of evolutionary development environments and knowledge processing to help manage the complexity of system development projects. First, they lack good tools for expressing what they want systems to do and how they want them to do it. They have found that implementation languages such as LISP or Ada are too low-level, and they have found that nonexecutable design languages such as SADT [Ross 77] cannot predict performance, assure skeptics that the designed system will actually work, or continue to be used as the implementation evolves. Second, developers want to talk about combining capabilities from existing and proposed new subsystems but they lack suitable languages or conventions. Commercial products and standards such as IBM SAA [IBM 87] or ISO's OSI [Voelcker 86] provide either extremely low-level protocols or vague high-level notions for describing how to interconnect subsystems. They do not help developers formulate and specify how a collection of entities cooperate to solve a problem. Finally, many developers see a need to combat complexity by organizing islands of stability -- subsystems that attack parts of the overall problem, and that can ultimately knit together in some effective way. Although some AI paradigms such as the blackboard architecture [Erman, Hayes-Roth, Lesser, and Reddy 80] have suggested ways of combining independent specialists into cooperative integrated systems, no general and practical concepts have emerged to help people formulate system architecture strategies for defeating complexity by some divide-and-conquer approach.

In designing ABE, we wanted to meet all three challenges. We wanted to provide executable high-level design languages, abstract high-level tools for describing system interconnections, and practical techniques for easily composing complex systems from subsystems. The ABE features of multiple diverse frameworks, uniform composability of modules, and hierarchical and meshed module organizations all work to control system complexity.

High Performance

Most application developers want systems that can perform quickly, even when dealing with great complexity. In some applications, such as Pilot's Associate, slow performance can prove fatal. AI systems, on the other hand, have generally proven slow relative to conventional systems. Several related requirements emerge from this situation. First, we want modular implementations of knowledge processing functions that will permit the application developer to tune the software, the hardware, and the mapping from software to hardware to achieve a suitable performance level for key functions. Second, these applications should be able to use existing high-performance software and hardware components where appropriate. Third, we want to exploit the natural concurrency in applications on networked and multiprocessing platforms. Finally, we want special high-level tools for formulating and assuring real-time performance requirements.

ABE supports modularity of knowledge processing functions in ways that do not depend on the underlying implementation machine or language. Second, ABE assumes that most functions will be performed by existing systems and helps system designers use these capabilities and combine them with other native or imported ABE functions. Third, ABE allows application developers to exploit the concurrency in their applications; the MOP computational model supports the natural expression of concurrency in applications, and Kiosk executes modules concurrently on networked workstations. Finally, we are developing a set of high-level tools for defining, designing, and implementing systems that meet stressing time requirements in the face of limited computing resources.

Reusability

Everyone wishes that software could be bought or reused, in contrast to the tendency to build each new system from scratch. This has been a major problem within conventional computing for years, but the situation within AI has been even worse. AI developers face a major roadblock created by the monolithic nature of most knowledge engineering tools. Each such tool provides a complete problem-solving paradigm and an associated programming language and environment intended for all aspects of the application system. The tool and application become combined in a monolithic fashion.

Developers aspire to reuse several different things: data structures for common kinds of tasks, domain-specific knowledge bases, inference engines and other knowledge processing functions, overall architectures for specific kinds of solution systems and, last but not least, conventional application libraries and databases. In ABE, we seek to provide effective support for each of these reusability concerns. We have adopted a methodology to support reuse and have embedded that in the ABE system.

Heterogeneous Software and Hardware

As alluded to several times above, many developers look to AI to add value to existing computing systems. This means they need knowledge processing functions that can work with conventional functions. They increasingly require a way to access and combine functionalities that run on different hardware using different and often immiscible languages, such as Common LISP and COBOL or Ada. They reject the notion of recreating conventional capabilities such as data collection and analysis, simulation, and statistics within the monolithic LISP machine workstation environment.

In designing ABE, we aimed to make it easy for system architects to compose integrated systems from heterogeneous parts using a high-level view of functionalities and their interactive combination. We thought that ABE should simplify the integration task by hiding the details of heterogeneous-systems plumbing from the applications developer.

Next-Generation Operating Environments

The most advanced developers already perceive the outlines of a new generation of information systems. These next-generation systems will combine heterogeneous hardware and software into distributed applications under intelligent control. Functions that were previously centralized will move to workstations. Assumptions of locality will give way to requirements for location-independence. Stable monolithic environments will become highly dynamic, disaggregated, and decentralized. Although end-users will carry some of the burdens for coping with the changes, stresses, and opportunities these new environments provide, application developers will face an increasing demand for systems that effectively coordinate far-flung components. This converts what had been simple applications development tasks into major systems programming tasks. In this context, application developers will want an environment that simplifies re-allocation and redistribution of resources and functionalities.

We have designed ABE to simplify the task of building applications atop distributed and reconfigurable computing infrastructures. We have tried to create a next-generation operating system and system development environment to shield the application developer from what otherwise would become great systems programming requirements.

RELATIONSHIP TO OTHER SYSTEMS

To place ABE in the context of other next-generation system development environments, we first describe a set of abstraction levels for those environments. From lowest to highest these are:

- hardware: memories, processors, and networks;
- virtual machines;
- programming language systems;
- modular functions and abstract datatypes (ADTs);
- system design and development frameworks;
- skeletal systems; and
- applications.

We do not propose this set of levels as a prescription for building systems, but intend it for noting and relating abstractions of particular interest to each of the various development environments, as shown in Figure 13.

The lowest abstraction level deals with the realization and distribution of a system on *hardware*. At this level, a systems programmer must deal with *processors*, real and virtual *memory*, and *networks* of distributed hosts.

Several hardware vendors have produced products which focus on the network part of the hardware level, for example, Apollo's NCS [Apollo 87], and Sun's NFS [Sandberg 86] and NeWS [Sun 86]. Carnegie Mellon University's MACH [Rashid 86] also fits into this class. ABE attempts no advance in this area; we are currently using facilities supplied by the Symbolics environment and are also beginning to make use of UNIX and MACH.

At the next level up, the *virtual machine* makes specific commitments on how data and control are passed among computational agents, and provides a buffer between the language developers and the hardware. See, for example, Carnegie Mellon's Agora system. [Bisiani and Forin 87] ABE's MOP virtual machine is loosely-coupled, without either a shared memory model or a shared namespace. ABE's computational model explicitly supports specialization of the local controller for each system. Also, ABE's model allows recursive (and nonhierarchical) embedding of ABE systems. These last two

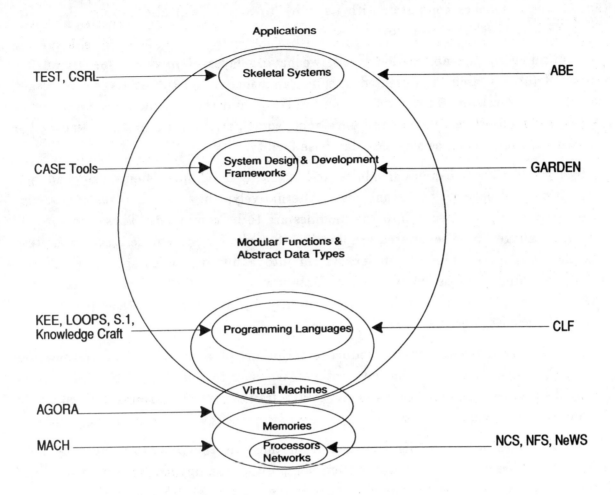

Figure 13: Abstraction layers for next-generation systems environments, with associated development efforts

features together support deeply composed and heterogeneous systems.

A *programming language* is implemented on (i.e., its compilers produce code for) a virtual machine. Each language implements a particular programming metaphor, such as procedures, frames, objects, or rules. Most language systems come with tailored development environments.

No single language is best for all programming tasks; the programmer should be able to select a language appropriate for the task at hand. Some systems provide several programming languages integrated at this level. These include, for example, LOOPS [Stefik, Bobrow, Mittal, and Conway 83], KEE [IntelliCorp 86], and Knowledge Craft [Carnegie Group 85], S.1 [Erman, London, and Scott 84], and CLF [Balzer 86].

ABE allows the development of modules in several existing languages, such as C and Common LISP. ABE also supports modules implemented in various other tools, such as KEE, on the Symbolics computer; with its move to Sun, it will also support S.1, with others, such as FORTRAN, to follow.

Continuing up the abstraction levels, we have a layer of *modular functions and abstract datatypes*, each implemented in some language. FORTRAN statistical packages exemplify this level. ABE supports the accumulation and reuse of modular components via its catalog structure. We are also developing some particular examples of knowledge processing modules, such as a generic database facility.

System developers can use modules and ADTs to build up systems using ad hoc composition and integration techniques. Alternatively, they can use *system design frameworks* (SDFs) to specify how the modules are to be combined. These are special-purpose languages, often expressed graphically, that allow a system designer to express both the decomposition of a complex system into a number of components and the interactions among those components. Dataflow graphs and structure charts are examples of SDF languages, which are exemplified by a number of CASE (Computer-Aided Software Engineering) tools [Suydam 87].

In addition to the ability to produce descriptions of a system, some frameworks provide the means to execute that description. We refer to this class of tools as *system design and development frameworks*. ABE's frameworks fall into this class, as do those provided by Garden [Reiss 87].

As languages, SDFs are distinguished from those at the *programming languages* level by their design and intent for system composition, as opposed to construction of individual modules. ABE supplies modifiable graphical representations of its frameworks.

ABE supplies several frameworks, including ones built on paradigms of dataflow, procedures, blackboards, and transactions. Although ABE allows access to the framework implementations, it does not currently provide much support for creating or modifying frameworks. ABE does support building arbitrary, ad hoc compositions of modules by direct use of its underlying MOP/Kiosk virtual machine.

At the highest level, next-generation systems are built on top of *skeletal systems*. Skeletal systems provide a high level of abstraction to the system developer, reducing the development task to one of "filling in the blanks." Examples of these are TEST [Kahn, Kepner, and Pepper 87] and CSRL [Bylander and Mittal 86]. ABE treats skeletal systems as modules, and thus makes use of the same facilities to support their accumulation and reuse.

PROTOTYPE SYSTEM STATUS

Teknowledge first made ABE (Version 1) available in February 1987 for a small number of advanced users. Demonstration Version 1 was replaced in early 1988 by Version 2. During 1988, Teknowledge plans to distribute a dozen or so copies of this research product to selected advanced user groups with appropriate requirements and qualifications. These advance licensees will help apply, test, refine, and extend ABE, leading to Version 3, planned for completion in 1989.

Version 2.0 includes the following capabilities:

- the MOP/Kiosk virtual machine, supporting modules, composition techniques, and abstract data types;
- desktop user interface;
- design and development frameworks (including procedural, dataflow, blackboard, transaction, blackbox, native Kiosk, and catalog), each with its specialized graphical development interface;
- a catalog of functionalities, including a selection of ADTs, native modules, imported modules, and skeletal systems;
- interfaces to several commercial tools, such as KEE and the Informix relational database system;
- support for multiprocessing and distribution;
- operation on Symbolics and Sun computers; and
- several demonstration systems.

RESEARCH AND ENGINEERING ISSUES

We believe that ABE represents the first of a new generation of operating systems and development environments that addresses the task of building heterogeneous, cooperative, intelligent systems. Although ABE is already useful in this arena, we expect to continue its evolution as we learn more about several issues, including those described below.

Modular Knowledge Processing Functions: As we gain greater experience with the usefulness of knowledge processing, we will want to precipitate modules to perform the key functions. This work will continue indefinitely.

HD-Modularity and Abstract Data Types: At present we have identified several dimensions of separation (see Figure 5), but we have as yet few modules that possess all these degrees of freedom. Creating more HD-modules will require continued effort. One aspect of HD-modularity derives from the use of high-level abstract data types for inputs and outputs. Although we have collected a few dozen of these, we expect mature application-specific catalogs to contain hundreds of appropriate ADTs that simplify the task of new system development.

Design and Development Frameworks: ABE provides a handfull of design and development frameworks based on previous experience. ABE enables us to extend this framework set and to preserve uniform composability. This should make it desirable for tool designers to create new frameworks that effectively address particular kinds of subproblems. Thus, we expect to see a proliferation of frameworks and, ultimately, tools for creating new frameworks.

Importation: To date, we have imported a few dozen modules. However, we anticipate that importation will continue indefinitely. Over time, we expect a great number of capabilities to enter industry-specific ABE catalogs.

Skeletal Systems and Customization: We have demonstrated with ABE the value of storing and reusing nearly-complete applications that capture a somewhat general problem-solving structure and that can be easily customized for different application domains. This work is at an early stage, and much remains to be done. The modularization of existing solution systems and the assembly of generic skeletal systems is a challenging task that should attract great interest.

Integrating Interfaces: At present, ABE employs emerging window management standards as ways of enforcing a separation of HD-modules from the user interface and of integrating into a single interface the user-oriented communications of multiple cooperating modules. We expect that this metaphor for integrating interfaces will prove limited, and new research will be needed to provide more flexible and customizable tools for merging user-interface communications.

Real-Time Operation: We have an experimental version of a run-time framework for ABE called RT. RT helps system developers create programs that can complete their functions in a timely fashion even when computing resources are limited. We will fully integrate this framework into ABE Version 3.0. This system is being tested by a limited number of users during 1988.

Parallelism and Compilation: During 1988 we will enhance ABE's performance by making better use of parallelism and software compilation. We have designed ABE from the outset for high performance, but Version 2 does not include implementations of our best current ideas. However, we expect to pursue research in this area for several years to exploit the best emerging platforms.

CONCLUSION: FROM KNOWLEDGE SYSTEMS TO INTELLIGENT SYSTEMS ENGINEERING

Teknowledge focuses on the use of knowledge processing to add value to commercial and governmental operations. Since our first area of business was expert systems, we offered expert system shells on a wide variety of platforms, then reimplemented them in C, and finally consolidated and redesigned them for embedding in mainstream computing applications.

The ABE research product, however, addresses a broader and more ambitious set of objectives that have arisen out of application developers' attempts to envision the next generation of computing applications. These applications will need to combine conventional and knowledge processing functions to achieve higher levels of synergy than previously possible. Although obviously more complex than earlier applications, these systems will need to be assembled primarily from existing parts, at considerably less expense than previously incurred. In addition, these systems will need to withstand frequent and often radical environmental changes that will come with new technology and economies.

In this next generation, the concept "AI tool" will disappear. In its place we anticipate two new kinds of capabilities will appear: specialized knowledge processing functions, implemented either in software or custom hardware, and intelligent integration capabilities to make it easier for system developers to assemble solutions by connecting together parts and customizing them as needed. For such a vision to come true, we require a flexible and powerful environment for evolutionary development. This environment will need to sit atop a new operating system that both isolates application developers from low-level infrastructure details and allows them to exploit some of the revolutionary advances that will occur at that level. We are aiming ABE to fill that role.

ACKNOWLEDGMENTS

A number of people have contributed substantially to ABE. Sergio Antoy, Terry Barnes, Stephanie Forrest, Alan Garvey, and Pean Lim have contributed to the design and implementation. Bruce Bullock and Neil Jacobstein have provided significant technical guidance and other support. Michael Fehling was instrumental in the early conception and design of the MOP model of computation. Stephanie Forrest and several anonymous reviewers provided helpful suggestions for this paper.

ABE, Module-Oriented Programming, MOP, CORAL, and S.1 are trademarks of Teknowledge, Inc. UNIX is a trademark of AT&T. Knowledge Craft is a trademark of Carnegie Group Inc. KEE is a trademark of IntelliCorp, Inc. Sun is a trademark of Sun Microsystems, Inc. Symbolics and Genera are trademarks of Symbolics, Inc. Ada is a trademark of the Department of Defense, Ada Joint Program Office. VAX and VMS are trademarks of Digital Equipment Corp. Informix is a trademark of Informix Software, Inc. OS/360 is a trademark of IBM.

References

[Apollo 87]

>   Apollo Computer Inc. *Network computing system: A technical overview.*
>   Apollo Computer Inc., Chelmsford, MA, 1987.

[Balzer 86]

>   Balzer, R. M. Living in the next-generation operating system. In H. J. Kugler
>   (editor), *Information Processing 86.* North-Holland, Amsterdam, 1986.
>   Reprinted in *IEEE Software,* 4(6), November, 1987, 77-85.

[Bisiani and Forin 87]

>   Bisiani, R. and Forin, A. Architectural support for multilanguage parallel
>   programming on heterogeneous systems. In *Inter. Conf. on Architectural
>   Support for Programming Languages and Operating Systems (ASPLOS-II).*
>   October, 1987.

[Brooks 87]

>   Brooks, F. P., Jr. No silver bullet: Essence and accidents of software
>   engineering. *IEEE Computer* 20(4):10-19, April, 1987.

[Bylander and Mittal 86]

>   Bylander, T. and Mittal, S. CSRL: A language for classificatory problem
>   solving and uncertainty handling. *AI Magazine* 7(3):66-77, August, 1986.

[Carnegie Group 85]

>   Carnegie Group Inc. *Knowledge Craft manual guide.* Carnegie Group Inc.,
>   Pittsburgh, PA, 1985.

[Davis 85]

>   Davis, D. B. Assessing the strategic computing initiative. *High Technology*
>   :41-49, April, 1985.

[Dawson, Brown, Kalish, and Goldkind 87]

>   Dawson, B. C., Brown, R. H., Kalish, C. E., and Goldkind, S.
>   *Knowledge-based replanning system.* Technical Report RADC-TR-87-60,
>   Rome Air Development Center, Griffiss Air Force Base, NY, May, 1987.

[Edwards and Hoffman 87]

>   Edwards, G. R., and Hoffman, M. A. The KADET planning framework. In
>   *Presented at DARPA Knowledge-Based Planning Workshop.* Austin, Texas,
>   December, 1987.

[Erman, Hayes-Roth, Lesser, and Reddy 80]

>   Erman, L. D., Hayes-Roth, F., Lesser, V. R., and Reddy, D. R. The Hearsay-II
>   Speech-Understanding System: Integrating Knowledge to Resolve Uncertainty.
>   *Computing Surveys* 12(2):213-253, June, 1980.

[Erman, Lark, and Hayes-Roth 88]

> Erman, L. D., Lark, J. S., and Hayes-Roth, F. ABE: An environment for
> engineering intelligent systems. *IEEE Transactions on Software Engineering*
> Special issue on AI, 1988. In press. Also: Teknowledge, Inc., Tech. Rep. TTR-
> ISE-87-106, Nov., 1987.

[Erman, London, and Scott 84]

> Erman, L. D., P. E. London, and A. C. Scott. Separating and integrating
> control in a rule-based tool. In *Proc. IEEE Workshop on Principles of
> Knowledge-Based Systems*, pages 37-43. Denver, CO, December, 1984. 37-43.

[Forrest and Lark 88]

> Forrest, S. and Lark, J. S. *Parallel and distributed processing in ABE*.
> Technical Report TTR-ISE-88-101, Teknowledge, Inc., Palo Alto, CA, January,
> 1988.

[Goldberg and Robson 83]

> Goldberg, A., and Robson, D. A. *Smalltalk-80: The language and its
> implementation*. Addison-Wesley, 1983.

[IBM 87] IBM. SAA: An overview. IBM order number GC26-4341. 1987

[IntelliCorp 86]

> IntelliCorp, Inc. *KEE software development system user's manual*.
> Intellicorp, Inc., Mt. View, CA, 1986.

[Kahn, Kepner, and Pepper 87]

> Kahn, G. S., Kepner, A., and Pepper, J. TEST: A model-driven application
> shell. In *Proc. National Conf. on Artificial Intelligence*, pages 814-818.
> Seattle, July, 1987. 814-818.

[Rashid 86]

> Rashid, R. F. Threads of a new system. *UNIX Review* :37-49, August, 1986.

[Reiss 87]

> Reiss, S. P. Working in the garden environment for conceptual programming.
> *IEEE Software* 4(6):16-27, November, 1987.

[Ross 77] Ross, D. Structured analysis (SA): A language for communicating ideas.
> *IEEE Transactions on Software Engineering* 3(1):16-34, 1977.

[Royce 70]

> Royce, W. W. Managing the development of large software systems: Concepts
> and techniques. In *Proc. Wescon*. August, 1970. Also available in *Proc.
> ICSE9*, IEEE Computer Society Press, 1987.

[Sandberg 86]

Sandberg, R. *The Sun Network File System: Design, Implementation and Experience.* Technical Report, Sun Microsystems, Inc., Mt. View, CA, 1986.

[Smith and Broadwell 88]

Smith, D. and Broadwell, M. The Pilot's Associate -- an overview. In *SAE Aerotech Conference.* Los Angeles, CA, May, 1988.

[Stefik, Bobrow, Mittal, and Conway 83]

Stefik, M., Bobrow, D. G., Mittal, S., and Conway, L. Knowledge programming in LOOPS. *AI Magazine.* 4(3):3-13, Fall, 1983.

[Sun 86] Sun Microsystems, Inc. *NeWS: A definitive approach to window systems.* Sun Microsystems, Inc., Mt. View, CA, 1986.

[Suydam 87]

Suydam, W. CASE makes strides toward automated software development. *Computer Design* , Jan. 1, 1987.

[Voelcker 86]

Voelcker, J. Helping computers communicate. *IEEE Spectrum* 23(3):61-70, March, 1986.

[Walker, Moon, Weinreb, and McMahon 87]

Walker, J. H., Moon, D. A., Weinreb, D. L., and McMahon, Mike. The Symbolics Genera programming environment. *IEEE Software* 4(6):36-45, November, 1987.

List of Figures

Figure 1:   MOP: ABE's underlying computational model

Figure 2:   The PMC (procedural) framework

Figure 3:   The BBOX (black box) framework

Figure 4:   The CAT (catalog) framework

Figure 5:   High-dimensional modularity in ABE

Figure 6:   An example of high-dimensional modularity

Figure 7:   Pilot's associate, initial version

Figure 8:   Pilot's associate, with situation monitor

Figure 9:   Pilot's associate, with situation assessor and plan critic

Figure 10:   Pilot's associate, restructured

Figure 11:   Pilot's associate, distributed

Figure 12:   Pilot's associate, with asynchronous communication

Figure 13:   Abstraction layers for next-generation systems environments, with associated development efforts

Modeling and Diagnosing Problem-Solving System Behavior

EVA HUDLICKÁ AND VICTOR LESSER

Abstract —A new component of a problem-solving system, called the diagnosis module (DM), that enables the system to reason about its own behavior is described. The aim of the diagnosis is to identify inappropriate control parameter settings or faulty hardware components as the causes of observed misbehavior. The problem-solving system being diagnosed is a distributed interpretation system, the distributed vehicle monitoring testbed (DVMT), which is based on a blackboard problem-solving architecture. The diagnosis module uses a causal model of the expected behavior of the DVMT to guide the diagnosis. Causal-model-based diagnosis is not new in AI. What is different is the application of this technique to the diagnosis of problem-solving system behavior. Problem-solving systems are characterized by the availability of the intermediate problem-solving state, the large amounts of data to process, and in some cases, the lack of absolute standards for behavior. New diagnostic techniques that exploit the availability of the intermediate problem-solving state and address the combinatorial problem arising from the large amount of data to analyze are described. A technique has also been developed, called comparative reasoning, for dealing with cases where no absolute standard for correct behavior is available. In such cases the diagnosis system selects its own "correct behavior criteria" from objects within the problem-solving system which did achieve some desired situation. The diagnosis module for the DVMT has been implemented and successfully identifies faults.

I. Introduction

THE COMPLEXITY of man-made systems is rapidly increasing to the point where it is becoming difficult for us to understand and maintain the systems we build. Artificial intelligence (AI) problem-solving systems are particularly susceptible to this information overload problem due to their often *ad hoc* design, large knowledge bases, and decentralized control mechanisms. This has recently resulted in a trend toward more autonomous systems: systems that can explain their behavior, aid the developers with debugging, and monitor and adapt their behavior to changing requirements. Central to all these functions is the ability of the problem-solving system to reason about its own behavior.

In this paper we describe a component of a problem-solving system, the diagnosis module (DM), that reasons

Manuscript received January 15, 1986; revised November 8, 1986. This work was supported in part by the National Science Foundation under Grants NSF DCR-8500332 and NSF DCR-8318776 and by the Defense Advanced Research Projects Agency (DOD) monitored by the Office of Naval Research under Contract N00014-79-C-0439, P00009.

E. Hudlická was with the Computer and Information Science Department, University of Massachusetts, Amherst, MA 01003. She is now with the Advanced Systems and Tools Group at DEC, HL2-3/C10, 77 Reed Road, Hudson, MA 01749.

V. Lesser is with the Computer and Information Science Department, University of Massachusetts, Amherst, MA 01003.

IEEE Log Number 8714383.

about a problem-solving system's behavior to diagnose the faults responsible for inappropriate system behavior. The DM has been implemented and successfully diagnoses faults in a distributed problem-solving system, the distributed vehicle monitoring testbed (DVMT) [11]. The faults diagnosed may be either hardware failures (e.g., a failed sensor) or inappropriate parameter settings, which we call *problem-solving control errors* (e.g., the confidence factor assigned to a sensor's output). The DM consists of about 5000 lines of Lisp code and runs on a VAX under the VMS operating system.

The Diagnosis Module

By way of an example, let us motivate the use of a diagnosis module in a problem-solving system. Suppose that a problem-solving system fails to generate the desired result. In our case the DVMT-distributed interpretation system fails to track a vehicle in some part of the sensed environment. Knowing the general characteristics of the desired result, the DM traces back through the history of problem solving guided by the model of correct processing. The DM determines what intermediate results would have had to be produced to achieve the desired results. In this way the cause of the failure to generate a desired result can be traced back to the lack of low-level data; this problem could then possibly be traced further to a failed sensor or an incorrect setting of the control parameter that specifies the confidence factor associated with the sensor's output. In the latter case diagnosis involves understanding that data from the sensor were available but not processed because they were below an acceptable confidence threshold.

Characteristics of Diagnosis of Problem-Solving System Behavior

Diagnosis is not a new problem for AI. Many systems exist for medical diagnosis [14], [16], diagnosing digital circuits [4], [6], [9], electrical devices [12], and large systems such as nuclear reactors [13]. We have found that diagnosis of problem-solving system behavior is different from the techniques used in these domains. While some diagnostic techniques are generally applicable across all domains,[1]

[1] For example, given a symptom, go back through the events that led up to it until the cause is found.

aspects of problem-solving system behavior require new diagnostic techniques.

Problem-solving systems are characterized by:

- complete knowledge of the internal system structure;
- availability of the intermediate problem-solving state;
- large amount of data to process during diagnosis;
- in many cases, lack of absolute standards for correct behavior.

Since the structure of the system is known, we can use a causal model of the system in which problem-solving behavior is modeled as a series of states. These states are linked by causal relationships to represent the sequence of events required for a desired result to be produced. Diagnosis then consists of determining why some expected state was not reached by exploring the appropriate part of the causal model of the system.

Since the internal system state is available (by directly examining the system data structures), we need not address the problem of determining the internal state from the inputs and outputs.[2] However, we introduce a correspondingly difficult combinatorially explosive problem: the states of the causal model must be mapped onto the record of system behavior. In many cases a number of possible intermediate results from this record could be used in diagnosis. For example, the problem-solving system may have partially explored a number of alternative paths in attempting to generate a solution. All of these are stored in the system as part of the intermediate state record. In a multilevel blackboard system such as the DVMT, the intermediate state includes the many possible hypotheses on the blackboard which *could* have been on the path to a solution. The crucial question is, does diagnosis require an exhaustive analysis of all the search paths explored by problem-solving system search or is there a way for diagnosis to limit its analysis?

Much of the work reported here was devoted to developing techniques for avoiding the potential combinatorial explosion of diagnostic paths to analyze by choosing which particular piece of data to use in diagnosis and how to group related diagnostic paths. For example, the formalism for modeling the problem-solving system allows the representation of a *class of objects* so that during diagnosis, the DM can reason about classes of situations rather than individual cases.

Dealing with Lack of Absolute Standards for Behavior

Causal model diagnostic techniques work as long as a model of the expected behavior is available. Such a model requires the existence of absolute criteria for system behavior. In most cases we can provide such criteria when dealing with problem-solving systems. For example, an expected sequence of events in the DVMT system behavior is the creation of a hypothesis, followed by the creation of a goal, and then followed by the scheduling of a knowledge source. Cases exist, however, where no absolute criteria exist and a fixed model for correct system behavior cannot be constructed *a priori*. Instead, we need to compare the behavior of the faulty object to a similar object that seems to behave correctly. In understanding why these objects differ, we often uncover a fault. This lack of absolute criteria for system behavior led to the development of a diagnostic technique we call *comparative reasoning* (CR). When using CR, the diagnosis module examines similar cases within the system and from these chooses a standard with which to compare the suspect situation; this comparison is accomplished using a simple form of qualitative reasoning [3]. A model is thus dynamically constructed where both causal analysis and qualitative reasoning are used to analyze the factors responsible for the suspected situation.

Let us look at a simple example of this type of reasoning in the DVMT, which is an agenda-based problem-solving system. The agenda contains a list of knowledge source (KS) processes that could be executed. They are ordered by their rating, which is a function of a number of parameters. Suppose that the DM traces some symptom to a KS that did not execute because its rating was too low. The next step is to discover which of the parameters influencing the rating is responsible for the low overall rating of the KS. However, no absolute standards exist for any of these parameters. The comparative reasoning analysis involves first selecting a similar KS; this can be accomplished by choosing one that is at the top of the agenda and thus likely to execute or one that has already executed. The next step involves the pairwise comparison of the parameters influencing the KS rating for the low-rated KS and the high-rated KS. Suppose the low-rated KS that did not execute (i.e., the problem KS) has two parameters, A-problem KS and B-problem KS, and the high-rated KS that is used for comparison (i.e., the model KS) has the same parameters, A-model KS and B-model KS. Further, suppose the comparison of parameter values reveals A-problem KS = A-model KS, but B-problem KS ≪ B-model KS. The diagnostic module's analysis can then conclude that the B parameter was responsible for the low rating of the problem KS. This intermediate result in the diagnosis can be traced further; for example, the B parameter could be low because it was based on the belief associated with the KS's input data. This low belief could then be traced further to the low setting of the parameter controlling the confidence level that the system associates with the sensor generating the data.

Comparative reasoning brings up many interesting problems. The choice of a good object to use as a model for the object of interest is a nontrivial task, as is the matching of the parallel states in the two instantiated models.

---

[2] Many other diagnostic systems have dealt with the type of reasoning necessary given a blackbox view of the system (Genesereth's DART [6] and Davis's digital circuit analyzer [4] systems deal mainly with the problems associated with this view), and our modeling formalism supports this type of reasoning. What the availability of the intermediate states allows us to do is to get beyond these reasoning mechanisms and explore other interesting problems associated with diagnosing the behavior of complex systems.

The rest of the paper is organized as follows. Section II briefly describes the distributed vehicle monitoring testbed (DVMT). Sections III and IV discuss the modeling formalism and provide a more detailed description of the diagnostic reasoning techniques. An indepth description of a diagnostic session is developed through an example in Section V. The example illustrates the use of the comparative reasoning technique. Section VI discusses the methods we have developed for reducing the combinatorics explosion resulting from the large amounts of data to diagnose. Section VII summarizes the work and outlines some directions for future research.

II. CONTEXT: THE DVMT

The problem-solving system we model and diagnose is called the DVMT, a distributed problem-solving system in which a number of processors cooperate to interpret acoustic signals. The goal of the system is to construct a high-level map of vehicle movement in the sensed environment. Raw data are sensed at discrete time locations at the signal level. The final answer is a pattern track describing the path of vehicles, moving as a unit in some fixed pattern formation. To derive the final pattern track from the individual signal locations, the data undergo two types of transformation: the individual locations must be aggregated to form longer tracks, and both the tracks and the locations must be driven up several levels of abstraction, from the signal level, through the group and vehicle levels, up to the pattern level (see Fig. 1).

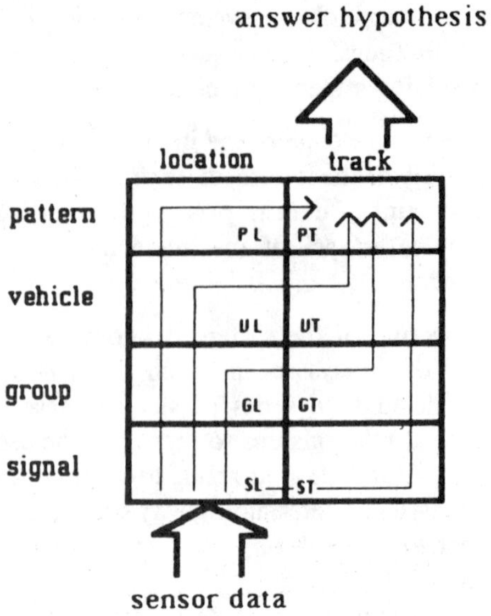

Each processor in the DVMT system is based on an extended Hearsay-II architecture where data-directed and goal-directed control are integrated [1]. The problem-solving cycle at each processor begins with the creation of a hypothesis that represents the position of a vehicle. Hypotheses then generate goals that represent predictions about how these hypotheses can be extended by incorporating more of the sensed data. Finally, a hypothesis together with a goal triggers the scheduling of a knowledge source (knowledge source instantiation) whose execution will satisfy the goal by producing a more encompassing hypothesis (one which includes more information about the vehicle motion). This cycle begins with the input data and repeats until a complete map of the environment is generated. Fig. 2 illustrates the processing structure at each node.

III. STRUCTURE OF THE SYSTEM BEHAVIOR MODEL

This section describes the modeling formalism used to represent the possible behaviors of the DVMT system. By representing the internal structure of the DVMT (i.e., the causal relationships among DVMT events), we generate the system behavior model (SBM) that supports not only diagnosis, but also simulation of the system behavior. Unlike some other causal models, such as CASNET [16], which represent causal relationships among pathological states, the SBM represents the normal system behavior. The errors are represented as deviations from the expected

Fig. 1. Levels of abstraction in DVMT data transformations. Data blackboard has eight levels of abstraction. Input data, acoustic signals representing vehicle positions at discrete time intervals, come in at signal level (sl). Final answer, at pattern track level, is integrated picture of "raw" sl data representing how vehicles move through environment.

situations that were not achieved by the system. The model can thus reason both about the causal sequences of expected events (thereby simulating the correct system behavior) and about the sequences of abnormal events (thereby diagnosing faulty system behavior). The work of Genesereth [6] and Davis [4] is similar in that it uses the violated expectations approach to diagnosis.

The system behavior in the DVMT is modeled by a set of causally related states corresponding to a series of events in the system. Each event results in the creation of an object (e.g., hypothesis, goal, or knowledge source instantiation) or the modification of the attributes of some existing object. *The states in the model represent the results of such events in the DVMT system.* Depending on what we want to model, a state may represent simply whether some event has occurred, or it may represent some finer aspect of the event's outcome.[3]

The SBM formalism consists of three major components: *hierarchical state transition diagrams* which represent the possible system behaviors at various levels of detail; *abstracted objects* which represent individual objects (i.e., data structures) or classes of objects in the DVMT system; and *constraint expressions* among the different attributes of the abstracted objects which represent the relationships among the objects. We can view the model as two parallel networks (see Fig. 4).[4] At the higher level is the state transition diagram, consisting of states and directed state transition arcs. At the lower level is the network consisting of the abstracted objects whose attri-

---

[3] There are two types of states in the model. *Predicate states*, which represent whether an event has occurred or not, and *relationship states*, which represent the relationship among two objects in the DVMT. The relationship states are used in comparative reasoning.

[4] Fig. 3 contains the legend for the figures in this paper.

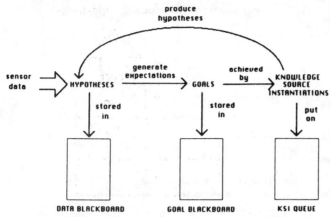

Fig. 2. Structure of processing at each node in DVMT system. DVMT begins its interpretation task with arrival of sensed data. All data are represented by hypotheses and stored on data blackboard. Arrival of hypothesis stimulates creation of goal, which represents prediction of how hypothesis might be extended in future. Hypothesis together with goal stimulate instantiation of knowledge source (KSI). Each such instantiation is rated and if rating is high enough, KSI is inserted onto scheduling queue. At beginning of each system cycle highest rated KSI executes and produces additional hypotheses. Cycle repeats until final answer is derived or until there are no more data to process.

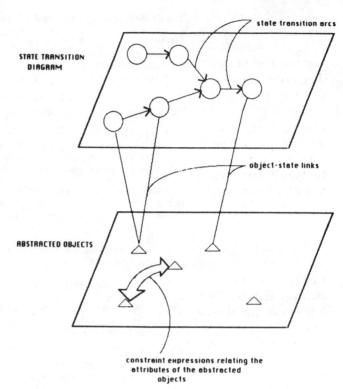

Fig. 4. High-level view of modeling formalism. SBM modeling formalism consists of three major components: state transition diagram clusters representing expected sequences of events in DVMT, abstracted objects representing DVMT objects such as hypotheses or goals, and constraint expressions representing relationships among attributes of neighboring abstracted objects. SBM can thus be viewed as two parallel networks: one containing state transition diagrams, other containing abstracted objects and constraint expressions.

LEGEND

○	STATE (uninstantiated)	●	TRUE STATE
◎	UNDERCONSTRAINED STATE	Ⓟ	PRIMITIVE STATE
△	UNDERCONSTRAINED ABSTRACTED OBJECT	Ⓒ	COMPARATIVE STATE
△	ABSTRACTED OBJECT	Ⓜ	MERGED STATE
→	STATE TRANSITION ARC	◍	FALSE STATE
⊗	NON EXPANDABLE STATE	Ⓢ	SYMPTOM STATE

RELATIONSHIP STATES

▷ GREATER-THAN its parallel state

◁ LESS-THAN its parallel state

⊜ EQUAL to its parallel state

(in cases where there are multiple parallel states these signs may be associated with the arcs linking the parallel states)

Fig. 3. Legend for figures in paper.

butes are linked by the constraint expressions that capture the relationships among the object attributes. The constraint expressions relating the attributes of two abstracted objects are shown in Fig. 5. The two networks are connected by state–object links.

States are linked to other states to form an AND/OR graph. If an event is influenced independently by a number of preceding events, then the states representing these events will be ORed. That is, any one of the preceding events determines the outcome of the event in the same manner. If the outcome of an event is influenced by a number of preceding events acting together, then the states representing these events will be ANDed. Fig. 6 shows a part of the system model.

The states are linked to the abstracted objects which describe characteristics of objects in the problem-solving

system record. Abstract objects are represented as frames. If all attribute slots of a frame have fixed values, the abstracted object corresponds to a specific instance of an object in the system. When some abstract object attributes are not specified precisely, the abstracted object is *underconstrained* and represents a whole class of objects. For example, an underconstrained hypothesis object could have a list of levels in its level attribute and thus represent the entire class of hypotheses at any of those blackboard levels. If objects exist in the DVMT that match the characteristics of an abstracted object, then the desired event that is specified by the state/object has occurred. The objects are represented as separate entities from the states for efficiency reasons to avoid the duplicate representation of similar sets of object attributes since several states may refer to the same object.

The state transition diagram representing the system behavior is organized into small clusters for manageability (see Fig. 7). These clusters are then organized into a hierarchy corresponding to increasingly detailed views of the system. Thus a high-level cluster represents selected events as contiguous states while a more detailed cluster represents other events which occur in between these states. Such a hierarchical representation allows reasoning at different levels of abstraction. This is useful during diagnosis because it allows the system to focus quickly on the problem by postponing a more detailed analysis until it is

This attribute points to objects that exist in the DVMT. If no such objects exist, it is false.

```
((vmt-ids (f      find-track-hyps
   (path self time-location-list)
   (path self event-class)
   (path self node)
   pt))
```

This attribute represents the path of the vehicle.

```
(time-location-list
     (((pt message-ob) (path x1 tll/trl))
      ((pt vt-hyp-ob) (path x1 time-location-list))
      ((pt pl-hyp-ob) (path x1 time-location-list))
```

This attribute represents a creation of shorter pt segments that could produce the desired segment. The function *create-trace-segments* looks for existing shorter segments and then chooses the longest non-overlapping ones for instantiation.

```
      ((pt pt-hyp-ob) (f create-track-segments
       (path x1 time-location-list)
       (path x1 event-class)
       pt
       (path x1 node)))))
```

This attribute represents the specific type of signal. The function phd:higher-level-event-classes determines the event classes for the pattern level from the vehicle level according to the system signal grammar.

```
(event-class   (((pt message-ob) (path x1 event-classes))
                 ((pt vt-hyp-ob)
   (f      higher-level-event-classes
           vt
                   (path x1 event-class)))
   ((pt pt-hyp-ob) (path x1 event-class))
   ((pt pl-hyp-ob) (path x1 event-class))))
(level          pt)
(node   (path x1 node)))
```

Fig. 5. Constraint expressions among abstracted objects. Constraint expressions linking abstracted object attributes allow DM to determine attribute values of one object based on attribute values of any of its neighboring objects. Figure shows relationship among attributes of object representing pattern track hypothesis and its neighboring objects: shorter pattern tracks (pt-hyp-ob), pattern location hypotheses (pl-hyp-ob), vehicle track hypotheses (vt-hyp-ob), and received pattern tracks (message-ob). First part of each constraint expression specifies context: current state and neighbor whose values are to be used. For example, (pt message-ob) means that current state is pt and object whose values are to be used is neighboring message object. Second part of expression specifies which of object's attribute values should be used. For example, (path x1 tll/trl) specifies tll/trl (time-location-list/time-region-list) attribute of neighboring object (represented by variable x1 which always refers to neighbor object that was instantiated most recently and whose values are to be used).

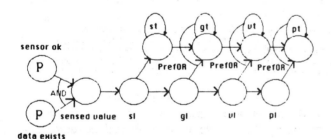

Fig. 6. Answer derivation model. Model cluster represents data transformation DVMT is expected to perform; that is, to produce pattern track (pt) hypotheses from incoming sensor data at signal level (sl). Arrival of initial data depends on sensor functioning (SENSOR-OK state) and data's existence (DATA-EXISTS state). SENSED-VALUE state represents separate sensed signal for each sensor.

necessary. For example, consider the case when the DM tries to determine why some hypothesis was not constructed. Rather than looking for the knowledge source instantiation that could have produced that kind of hypothesis, the DM first looks for the necessary supporting data, and only if these data exist does it investigate the knowledge source instantiations to see whether they were

scheduled and if so, why they did not run. This means that the diagnosis is first done using the answer derivation cluster and only later using the KSI scheduling cluster[5] (see Fig. 7). A subset of the states, designated as primitive, represents reportable faults during diagnosis.

The SBM thus represents a generalized description of selected aspects of the DVMT system behavior. Fig. 7 shows the set of model clusters we have constructed.

IV. Use of SBM in Reasoning about DVMT Behavior

Reasoning about DVMT behavior consists of instantiating the part of the SBM that represents the system behavior relevant to the situation being analyzed. The aim of all the different reasoning strategies is to explore the causes, or the effects, of an initial situation provided as input to the DM.[6] This situation is represented by an instantiated

---

[5] The KSI scheduling cluster represents the events that occur in between each pair of states in the answer derivation cluster.

[6] Currently, this is done by hand. In a fully fault-tolerant system the input would come from a detection component.

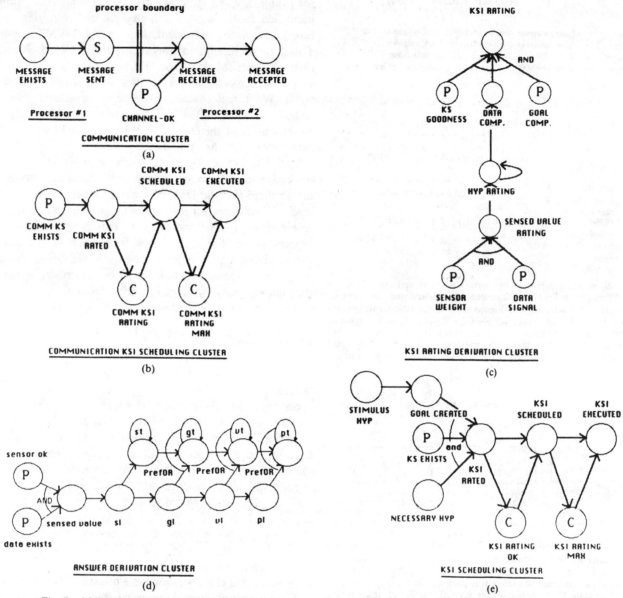

Fig. 7. Model clusters representing DVMT behavior. Figure shows diagrams of all five model clusters used in diagnosis. At highest level are answer derivation cluster and communication cluster. KSI scheduling and Comm KSI scheduling clusters represent events that take place in between each pair of states at higher level models. KSI rating derivation cluster represents additional knowledge about value relationships among rating components of various objects. (a) Communication cluster. (b) Communication KSI scheduling cluster. (c) KSI rating derivation cluster. (d) Answer derivation cluster. (e) KSI scheduling cluster.

state and its abstracted object, that is, a state and object whose attributes have been evaluated (see Fig. 8). The DM propagates these known values through the SBM using the constraint expressions among the abstracted objects and thereby instantiates a sequence of states causally related to the initial situation. We call such a sequence a *causal pathway.*

When the initial situation represents some desirable event in the DVMT that never occurred, we call it a *symptom.* A symptom represents an object that was never created by the DVMT, usually a hypothesis.[7] Upon receiving a symtpom, the DM traces back through the SBM to

find out at which point the DVMT stopped working "correctly." This is done by comparing the behavior necessary for the desired situation to occur, as represented by the instantiated model, with what actually did occur in the problem-solving system, as determined from the DVMT data structures. The aim is to construct a path from the symptom state to some false primitive states which caused it and thus explain, in terms of these primitive causes, why the DVMT system did not behave as expected. This type of diagnostic reasoning thus consists of backward chaining through the SBM. Since it constructs a causal pathway linking the initial symptom to the faults that caused it, we call this type of reasoning *backward causal tracing* (BCT). Fig. 9 shows a BCT-constructed causal pathway.

The BCT search stops when all possible pathways relevant to the situation being analyzed have been explored.

---

[7]A symptom could also represent a class of objects, such as all hypotheses at some blackboard level. This would be done using underconstrained objects.

State MESSAGE-SENT0111

f-n	(p:or (message-received0110))	; front neighbor
b-n	(p:or (message-exists0217)))	; back neighbor
value	F	; state is false
object-ptrs	message-ob0071	; abstracted object

Abstracted Object MESSAGE-OB0071

vmt-ids	F
from-node	2
message-type	hyp-ob
till/trl	((5 (14 10)) (6 (16 12)) (7 (18 14)) (8 (20 16)))
event-classes	1
level	vt
node	2
to-node	3

Fig. 8. Symptom represented by instantiated state and abstracted object. Situation in DVMT is represented by instantiated state and its associated abstracted object. Figure shows instantiated MESSAGE-SENT state and its object MESSAGE-OBJECT. Object represents hypothesis at vehicle track (vt) level that was to be sent from Node 2 to Node 3. That this hypothesis was never sent is represented by value attribute of the state, which is f (false). Only subset of attributes is shown.

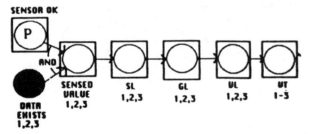

Fig. 9. BCT-constructed causal pathways. Instantiated answer derivation cluster where BCT traced lack of vehicle track (vt) 1–3 hypothesis to failed sensor, represented by false SENSOR-OK state. Instantiated model shows intermediate states that form causal pathway from false symptom state VT to primitive false state SENSOR-OK. Intermediate states are VL state representing three necessary locations and, similarly, GL and SL states, and SENSED-VALUE state, representing signals sensed by individual sensors (in this case only one sensor exists and therefore only one sensed value).

For example, to determine why some hypothesis was not constructed, the DM must examine all possible ways in which it could have been generated: that is, via several pathways within a node, from locally available data, or from data received from other nodes. Within the instantiated model the analysis is done exhaustively by a depth-first search. An exhaustive search is feasible here because the search space has already been reduced by the methods to be discussed in Section VI: for example, grouping together objects that behave similarly, using underconstrained objects to reason about a class of objects rather than the individual cases, and using existing data to constrain the search.

In addition to symptoms, initial situations may represent arbitrary events in the DVMT whose effect on the DVMT behavior needs to be simulated. This is the case,

for example, when the DM needs to see what effects some identified fault, such as a faulty parameter setting or a failed hardware component, has on the DVMT system. This type of simulation thus consists of forward chaining through the SBM. Here the DM constructs a causal pathway which links the initial situation to all situations caused by it. We therefore call this type of reasoning *forward causal tracing* (FCT). FCT uses underconstrained objects to reason about the class of problems caused by the fault, rather than just the individual cases.

Both BCT and FCT are more complex than simple backward and forward chaining because the model is hierarchical and the DM must decide when to change the level of resolution, for instance, when to reason at different levels of abstraction and when to reason about classes of objects. In addition to BCT and FCT, we have also found the need for a new type of diagnostic reasoning we call *comparative reasoning*, which will be described in detail through an example in the following section.

V. DIAGNOSTIC SESSION USING COMPARATIVE REASONING

This section describes a DM diagnostic session of a failure scenario where the use of comparative reasoning is necessary to handle situations in which no absolute criteria for correctness exist. CR works by selecting a situation from the DVMT which can be used as a model with which to compare a problematic situation. CR then compares these two situations in the DVMT system and tries to explain why they are different. This is done by systematically tracing the development of both situations and comparing them at each step. This type of reasoning is necessary because we cannot always understand the system behavior by looking at an isolated object in the system and comparing that object to some fixed standard, as is done with backward causal reasoning.

The following example illustrates the use of comparative reasoning to track the low rating of a knowledge source instantiation (KSI) to a low-rated hypothesis at an early point in the data transformation. The diagnosis begins with a missing high-level hypothesis at the pattern track (pt) level.[8] The diagnosis module reconstructs, based on a causal model of processing in the DVMT, the internal events and intermediate results that would be required to generate the desired data. As a result of this backward trace, it discovers that the desired hypothesis was not derived because lower level location hypotheses were never produced. Specifically, while hypotheses did exist at the group location (gl) level, they were never driven up to the next level, the vehicle location (vl). The diagnosis module further determines that this was due to the fact that the

---

[8]We will be following the convention of representing both symptoms and faults (i.e., any undesirable situations) by false states in the case of predicate states and by the qualitative relationships lower-than or greater-than in the case of relationship states. For example, a lack of some hypothesis at the vehicle track (vt) level will thus be represented by a false state VT, with its associated abstracted object representing the specific vt hypothesis.

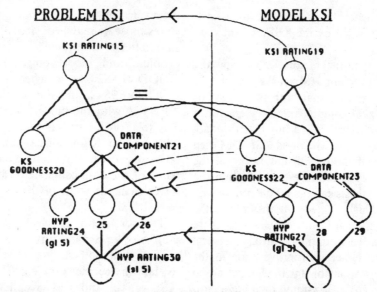

Fig. 10.   Instantiated SBM for fault scenario 2. Instantiated SBM for diagnosis of low KSI rating by comparative reasoning. Comparative reasoning works by instantiating two copies of model cluster, in this case KSI rating derivation cluster, and comparing "problem object rating" with "model object rating." "Model object" is chosen by diagnosis module based on selection criteria contained in SBM. Here low KSI-RATING15 is traced to low HYP-RATING30 of sl hypothesis.

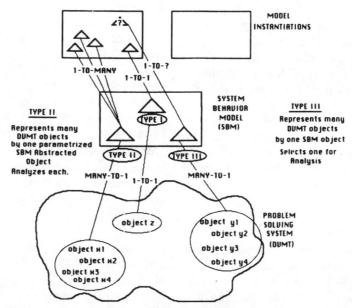

Fig. 11.   Types of abstractions used in model construction and reasoning. Figure shows types of abstractions necessary to represent complex system. Bottom part of figure represents DVMT. Middle part represents uninstantiated SBM, and upper part represents two instantiations of SBM.

KSI that would have created the desired vl hypotheses never executed because its rating was too low. Recall that it is always the highest rated KSI on the scheduling queue that executes. It is thus possible for a KSI with a low rating to remain on the queue for a long time. The diagnosis up to this point is done via backward causal tracing. The low-rated KSI is represented by the state KSI RAT-ING15 in Fig. 10.[9]

The point of the diagnosis here is to determine what caused the KSI rating to be low. The DM now switches to comparative reasoning and to a cluster representing the

derivation of the KSI rating, the KSI rating cluster. Let us call the low-rated KSI the *problem KSI* and the maximally rated KSI on the queue (with the appropriate characteristics) the *model KSI*. Before CR can continue, a model object must be found for the low-rated KSI. Such an object must be of the same type of the problem object and it must, of course, be rated higher than the problem object. In this case we are looking for a "successful" KSI (i.e., a high-rated KSI which is about to run) that takes a hypothesis at the gl level and produces a corresponding hypothesis at the vl level. The model KSI is represented by the state KSI-RATING19 in Fig. 10. The DM has a model of how a KSI rating is derived from its components: a KS

[9] This is a relationship state whose value is "lower-than."

parameter called KS-goodness, the goal that is to be satisfied by the hypotheses produced by the KSI, and the data the KSI is to use.

In this case, CR examines the factors influencing the KSI rating for both the problem KSI and a model KSI selected from the queue. It notes that both the KS-goodness parameters and the goal components are identical in both the problem and the model KSI's but that the data component rating is lower for the low-rated KSI. This then is identified as the cause of the overall low rating of the problem KSI. The next step is to trace back through the derivation of this low hypothesis rating and determine why *it* is rated low. Again, the highly rated hypothesis from the model KSI is used as a standard with which to compare the low-rated hypothesis. This continues through several levels of abstraction until either a primitive node in the model is reached which is responsible for the low rating (in this case, a low sensor weight or low-rated data are identified) or if the search is unsuccessful, until the causal pathway can no longer be extended.

Notice that there are now two parallel instantiations of the KSI rating cluster: one for the problem KSI and one for the model KSI. The two clusters will be instantiated one state at a time and compared in an attempt to find an explanation for the low rating of the problem KSI. The search through the model (i.e., which neighbors will be expanded next) is now determined by the type of relationship found among the problem state and the model state (i.e., <, =, or >), rather than the state value (true or false), as was the case with predicate states. CR continues to expand back neighbors as long as they can explain the current state's relative value with respect to the parallel state. A state's relative value is explained by its predecessor states" values if they have the same relationship. For example, a < state is explained by its preceding < states, but not by > or by = states.

The value for state KSI-RATING15 is, of course, < (this is guaranteed by the process selecting the model object; if no appropriate model exists, no object will be instantiated, the problem state will not have a parallel state, and diagnosis will stop). To understand why KSI-RATING15 is low,[10] the DM expands its back neighbors to see if any of them are abnormally low. Since a KSI rating is a function of the KS goodness (a parameter which determines the quality of a knowledge source) and the data component (the ratings of the hypotheses the KSI is working with), the back neighbors of the state KSI-RATING are KS-GOODNESS and DATA-COMPONENT. These are instantiated, and their values are determined from the values of their corresponding objects in the DVMT system. The resulting states are KS-GOODNESS20 and DATA-COMPONENT21.

Similarly, the back neighbors of the model KSI rating state KSI-RATING19 must be expanded so that the comparisons can continue. This expansion produces the states KS-GOODNESS22 and DATA-COMPONENT23. Before

the values of these states can be determined, the parallel states must be matched. (Recall that the value of relationship states is determined by comparing the ratings of the problem and model objects.) The problem state KS-GOODNESS20 is matched with the model state KS-GOODNESS22, and the problem state DATA-COMPONENT21 with the model state DATA-COMPONENT23. The relationship of = is found for the KS-goodness states, because the KS-goodness values are identical. The relationship of the data-component states is <, because the value of the data-component rating of the problem KSI is lower than the value of the data-component rating of the model KSI.

The next step is to select a subset of the expanded back neighbors to expand further. As in backward causal tracing, we want to continue expanding only those states that explain the current problem. The current problem is a low KSI rating, and we have determined that one of the components influencing this rating is normal (KS goodness) and one is below normal (data component), where "normal" means "same as the parallel state." Clearly, the normal value could not have caused the KSI rating to be low. The KS-GOODNESS20 state is, therefore, a dead end as far as the diagnosis is concerned because this state is not causally related to the KSI-RATING15 state. The low DATA-COMPONENT21 state, however, is responsible for the low KSI-RATING15, and we therefore follow this state backward by expanding its back neighbors.

The value of the data component of a KSI is a function of the data (i.e., the stimulus and the necessary hypotheses). In this case there were three gl hypotheses, one for each event class, whose rating determined the rating of the data component. (Knowledge sources that transform lower level hypotheses into higher level ones often combine several low-level hypotheses of different event classes into one higher level one.) The back neighbor of data-component, hyp-rating, is therefore instantiated into three states, one for each of the three hypotheses of the problem KSI. These states are HYP-RATING24, HYP-RATING25, and HYP-RATING26. Their associated abstracted objects are objects representing group location hypotheses, GL-HYP-OB's.

The state matching is more difficult here than before because there are three parallel states to choose from on the model side; each problem hyp-rating state has to select one of the model hyp-rating states. In this case a heuristic is used to select the appropriate model state: the DM looks for a model state that minimizes the difference between the ratings of the two objects while maintaining the constraint that the model rating must be higher than the problem rating. (This is discussed in more detail in [8].) In the current example, this difference minimization results in the following state pairs: HYP-RATING24 and HYP-RATING29, HYP-RATING25 and HYP-RATING27, and HYP-RATING26 and HYP-RATING28. The values of these states are < since all the hypotheses ratings are lower than the model hypotheses ratings. Diagnosis, therefore, continues with the expansion of the back neighbors

---

[10] Low here really means "lower than the model object" since there is no such thing as absolutely low or high.

of these states. We begin with the state HYP-RATING24 and expand its back neighbors. The back neighbor of this state is another hyp-rating state, representing the rating of the hypothesis at the sl level from which the gl hypothesis referred to by the state HYP-RATING24 was derived. The resulting state is HYP-RATING30. We also expand the back neighbor of the parallel state which results in the instantiation of the state HYP-RATING31. The state matching is trivial here since there is only one model state to choose from. The two states are matched, the value of state HYP-RATING30 is determined to be lower than its parallel state HYP-RATING31, and diagnosis continues by expanding the back neighbors of this state. Thus the low rating of a KSI at the vl level has been traced to a low-rated hypothesis at the sl level. We will end the diagnosis here, although it normally continues all the way to the sensor-weight and data-signal states, which represent the primitive causes that are ultimately responsible for the hypotheses ratings. See [8] where this example is discussed in more detail.

VI. REDUCING THE COMBINATORIAL PROBLEMS IN DIAGNOSIS

In a typical run the DVMT creates hundreds of objects in each of its processing nodes. To diagnose a given situation, a subset of these objects has to be represented in the instantiated SBM; the model then has to be searched in an attempt to find the causes for the situation. This section describes the methods for dealing with the potential combinatorial explosion resulting from the large amount of data stored in the problem-solving system record (see Fig. 11). The following is a list of these methods:

1) parametrizing a group of objects to represent the entire group by one parametrized abstracted object (occurs during model construction);
2) parametrizing groups of states to represent them by one state in the model (occurs during model construction);
3) allowing the existing data to constrain the search during diagnosis (occurs during model instantiation);
4) selecting a representative from a group of related objects and reasoning about it (occurs during model instantiation);
5) grouping similar objects together and reasoning about them as a group to reduce the search (occurs during model instantiation);
6) abstracting the common characteristics of a group of objects to represent and reason about the group by one abstracted object, usually an underconstrained object (occurs during model instantiation).

This rest of this section motivates and describes methods 3–6. The first two are discussed in detail in [8, ch. 6].

Constraining the Search by Existing Data

In some cases the number of possible ways that a DVMT object could have been derived is too large to be able to explore each possible derivation path. One way of constraining the search without eliminating the diagnosis of a possible fault is to use the existing data generated by the DVMT to rule out certain paths. This situation occurs, for example, in track hypotheses elongation, where a number of shorter track segments hypotheses or individual location hypotheses are combined to form a longer track hypothesis.

Suppose we are trying to analyze why a track consisting of eight locations was not created. We could consider all the possible combinations of shorter track segments and locations and analyze why they were not created. In these cases not only would the combinatorics be prohibitive, but it would not even be useful to explore all the possible derivation paths since the system would not explore all of them either, being constrained by the data it has. We can reduce the number of pathways to explore by allowing the existing data to constrain the search during diagnosis. Rather than exploring all the possible ways of deriving some longer track, we consider only the track segments that have already been derived by the system and analyze why they were not extended further.

Selecting a Representative Object from a Class of Objects

Another use of abstraction involves the selection of a representative object from a group of objects and analyzing its behavior rather than the behavior of each of the individual objects. For this strategy to be effective we must guarantee that the set of faults diagnosed when analyzing the representative object is the same as the set of faults diagnosed if each of the objects was analyzed separately. As for the foregoing method, track elongation best illustrates the use of this technique. To create a longer track hypothesis, the DVMT system will aggregate shorter track segment and location hypotheses. Therefore, at any time a number of shorter track segments will exist. In this case we choose the longest segment and analyze why it was not extended further. This does not reduce the number of faults we can identify because the undiagnosed shorter track segments fall into one of two categories. In one case the shorter undiagnosed segments were later extended into a longer segment and no fault exists. In the other case, the reason they were not extended is the same as the reason the longest track of the group was not extended. This fault will be identified by analyzing why the longest track segment was not extended, thus bypassing identical (redundant) diagnosis for the shorter track segments.

Grouping Together Similarly Behaving Objects

In cases where a single object in the model is expanded into a number of objects in the instantiated model, it may be possible to group some of these objects together and diagnose each group as a unit. This is more efficient than creating a separate state for each of the objects and then repeating identical diagnostic paths with each of the states. In the initial stages of this project every object created in the instantiated SBM had its corresponding state created and attached. During diagnosis then, each of these state–object pairs would be processed. This led to a combinatorics problem, even in relatively simple cases. Consider the diagnosis of the following situation. A pattern track hypothesis ranging from time 1 through time 8 is missing. To diagnose it, the system instantiates the SBM and traces the problem to the lack of the necessary data for this hypothesis. Because the hypothesis has eight time locations, eight locations are missing. Thus there are eight pathways to follow during diagnosis. Notice also that they all reduce to the same problem; missing data. It would be much more efficient if we could recognize that all these objects behave similarly and, therefore, require the same diagnosis and can be grouped and diagnosed together. In other words, all the objects behaving similarly can be grouped under one state. This state is then the only one that needs to be followed during diagnosis because the predicate or value it represents is the same for all its associated objects. There is, therefore, only one diagnostic path to follow through the model.

Currently, the grouping is performed by applying a function to some combination of the state or object attributes. The result of this function determines the number of equivalence classes for the objects. A separate state is then created for each of those equivalence classes, and all the objects in that class are attached to that state. This object grouping greatly reduces the number of paths that need to be examined during diagnosis without sacrificing the completeness of the diagnosis. As soon as the object behavior changes and requires a different diagnostic pathway, the system creates a separate state for it as specified in the grouping criteria. An example of a criterion for grouping objects is the existence of a corresponding object in the DVMT. All the abstracted objects which do not have a corresponding object in the DVMT are grouped together under one state (which is false), and all those that do are grouped under another (which is true).

Underconstrained Objects

Another way of using abstraction when reasoning about the system is to group together a number of objects and represent the whole class as one abstracted object in the instantiated model. This is done by underconstraining some of the attribute values of the abstracted object. Underconstrained objects are useful when it is known that a group of objects will behave identically and we can, therefore, save time by reasoning about the group as a whole. A situation where this is useful is the simulation of the effects of an identified fault. Suppose the system has identified a bad sensor in the DVMT system. It would be useful to propagate the effects of this sensor forward through the model and thereby not only explain any pending symptoms, which were caused by the same fault, but also account for future symptoms. In this case the simulation involves reasoning about the class of hypotheses generated from data in the area covered by the failed sensor. Clearly, it is more efficient to represent this whole class as one object rather than reasoning about all the possible hypotheses. Examples where this occurs are found during the forward simulation of an identified fault.

The following example illustrates the use of underconstrained objects to represent and reason about a class of objects. This capability is then applied to simulating the effects of an identified fault on system behavior. Suppose a problem-solving system is configured such that four communicating nodes exist, each working on its part of the overall problem. Each node has different parameters that control various aspects of its processing. For example, a set of parameters controls the internode communication (i.e., who should talk to whom and about what). If these parameters are set incorrectly, then the entire system will fail in its problem solving because the different parts of the overall solution cannot be integrated.

The lack of an overall solution will result in each node having a set of symptoms to diagnose relating to missing solution parts due to lack of communication. The DM will begin with one of these symptoms, for example, the lack of a specific piece of data, and will trace it to a failure: an incorrect communication parameter setting. Once this fault is identified, its effects will be propagated through the system. As an example, consider what would happen if two nodes were expected to exchange data in a certain area, but the communication parameters were wrong and no messages were sent. This would be discovered by the DM when it is determined that a particular piece of data is missing from one of the nodes. When the fault is identified, it is generalized to reflect that no data in the entire affected region will be communicated. In this way all symptoms representing missing data in that region will be accounted for when the effects of the fault are simulated.

To summarize, due to the complexity of a problem-solving system, as compared to other systems to which causal model diagnosis has been applied, we have utilized a number of techniques to handle the combinatorial problems. In this section we have highlighted the types of abstractions necessary to make problem-solving system modeling and diagnosis feasible.

VII. SUMMARY AND FUTURE RESEARCH

This paper discussed our work in the area of *problem-solving system diagnosis*. Our approach integrates a number of known techniques (diagnosis, simulation, qualitative reasoning, and constraint networks) and describes two new ones (comparative reasoning and the use of underconstrained abstracted objects) in an attempt to solve the problems encountered in representing and reasoning about problem-solving system behavior.

We have implemented a component of a problem-solving system, the diagnosis module, that diagnoses faults in the problem-solving system behavior by using a causal model of the system. The faults can be either hardware failures or inappropriate control parameter settings, which we call *problem-solving control errors*.

Our approach to diagnosis has been determined by the following characteristics of the DVMT problem-solving system.

- The system maintains a number of data structures (blackboards, queues) that contain its recent history. We exploit this availability of the system's intermediate states in constructing an instantiation of the system model to represent how a particular situation was reached.
- For many events in the DVMT system no absolute criteria exist for behavior. This means that in many cases we cannot determine whether an event is appropriate simply by comparing it to some fixed ideal event. We must instead take a more global view and examine the event's relationship with other events in the system. The lack of absolute standards for system behavior necessitates a new type of diagnostic reasoning we call comparative reasoning.
- Because of the complexity of the DVMT system, we could not represent every aspect of the system in the model. The problem of devising a concise representation of a large set of possible system behaviors led to various types of abstractions, both in the model construction and in the use of the instantiated model. These abstractions allow us to represent and reason about classes of objects rather than individual cases.

To perform diagnosis with these constraints, we have built upon a number of techniques developed elsewhere. We use causal networks similar to CASNET [16], except that we model correct rather than faulty behavior. We have also added the explicit representation of objects in the diagnosed system, in addition to representing the sequence of expected states. The mapping between these abstracted objects in the model and the data structures in the system is not always straightforward; we cannot just represent each object in the problem-solving system by a corresponding abstracted object due to the large number of system objects. We have developed techniques for reducing these combinatorial problems. We have parametrized abstracted objects and underconstrained objects to represent classes of situations in the problem-solving system. We have also developed techniques for dynamically selecting a specific system object to represent, which will capture the necessary characteristics of the situation that needs to be diagnosed. We have exploited the techniques developed by Genesereth [6] and Davis [5] in forward and backward reasoning from first principles. Again, however, we have had to extend these techniques to handle the increased complexity of a problem-solving system as compared with simple digital circuits. Our use of fault simulation represents synthesis of both techniques to understand what symptoms can be explained as a result of an identified fault. Finally, the work on comparative reasoning represents a new technique built on the basic backward/forward causal reasoning and qualitative analysis technique developed elsewhere. The diagnosis module is currently being used to help explain the DVMT system behavior, and we are planning to integrate it into the DVMT to provide more sophisticated metalevel control [7].

Although this work was done with a specific system in mind, we believe that the modeling formalism as well as the diagnostic techniques we have developed are equally applicable to other systems, problem-solving or otherwise, that have knowledge of the internal system structure and access to the system's history. The techniques we developed help alleviate problems associated with the diagnosis of a large number of cases (underconstrained objects) and make possible the diagnosis of some cases where no absolute criteria exist for system behavior (comparative reasoning). Although we have only used underconstrained objects in simulating the effects of a fault, it is extendable to generalizing over a group of symptoms and thus combining many diagnostic paths into one. Comparative reasoning was used to compare why two ratings of knowledge sources differed. It could easily be extended to comparing other quantities, such as the length of tracks or length of derivation paths. We see many possibilities for further research in this area based on our initial experience.

1) The abstracted objects could be extended to represent object components and composite objects and reasoning techniques could be devised for these new object types. Such an object hierarchy could be used to represent both low-level domain and system knowledge and high-level expectations about the system behavior. We have already begun work in this area.

2) The model could be extended to represent not only what the system should do but the assumptions underlying the reasons for doing it. This would permit a much deeper analysis of the system behavior.

3) The issues could be formalized in comparative reasoning, and comparative reasoning extended to be able to compare several system runs with different parameter settings and understand why they differ.

4) Our approach relies on the availability of the intermediate problem-solving states to reconstruct the actual system behavior. In large systems this becomes a problem as the system would quickly become flooded with information. Another area of future research would attempt to develop techniques for reducing the amount of information kept by the system and yet maintain enough so that past behavior can be reconstructed.

The work described here is a first pass at this large problem. Diagnosis is a pervasive activity in problem-solving system development and use; it plays a role in debugging, in metalevel control, and in explaining system behavior. We believe we have demonstrated that causal-model-based diagnosis of problem-solving system behavior is feasible and that while our work deals with a specific problem-solving system, the techniques described here are applicable to other systems.

ACKNOWLEDGMENT

We would like to thank our colleagues Paul Cohen, Susan Conry, and Daniel Corkill, as well as the reviewers, for their careful reading of this article and their thoughtful suggestions for modification.

REFERENCES

[1] D. D. Corkill, V. R. Lesser, and E. Hudličká, "Unifying data-directed and goal-directed control: An example and experiments," in *Proc. 2nd Nat. Conf. Artificial Intelligence*, Aug. 1982, pp. 143–147.

[2] D. D. Corkill, "A framework for organizational self-design in distributed problem-solving networks," Ph.D. dissertation, Dept. Computer and Information Science, Univ. Massachusetts, Amherst, Feb. 1983.

[3] S. E. Cross, "An approach to plan justification using sensitivity analysis," *Sigart*, vol. 93, pp. 48–55, July 1985.

[4] R. Davis *et al.*, "Diagnosis based on descriptions of structure and function," in *Proc. 2nd Nat. Conf. Artificial Intelligence*, Aug. 1982, pp. 137–142.

[5] R. Davis, "Diagnostic reasoning based on structure and behavior," *Artificial Intelligence*, vol. 24, pp. 347–410, 1985.

[6] M. Genesereth, "Diagnosis using hierarchial design models," in *Proc. Nat. Conf. Artificial Intelligence*, Aug. 1982, pp. 278–283.

[7] E. Hudličká and V. Lesser, "Meta-level control through fault detection and diagnosis," in *Proc. Nat. Conf. Artificial Intelligence*, Aug. 1984, pp. 153–161.

[8] E. Hudličká, "Diagnosing problem-solving system behavior," Ph.D. dissertation, Dept. Computer and Information Science, Univ. Massachusetts, Amherst, Feb. 1986.

[9] V. E. Kelly and L. I. Steinberg, "The CRITTER system: Analyzing digital circuits by propagating behaviors and specifications," in *Proc. Nat. Conf. Artificial Intelligence*, 1982, pp. 284–289.

[10] V. R. Lesser and L. D. Erman, "Distributed interpretation: A model and an experiment," *IEEE Trans. Comput.*, Special Issue on Distributed Processing Systems, Vol. C-29, pp. 1144–1162, Dec. 1980.

[11] V. Lesser and D. D. Corkill, "The distributed vehicle monitoring testbed: A tool for investigating distributed problem solving networks," *AI Mag.*, vol. 4, pp. 15–33, Fall 1983.

[12] D. McDermott and R. Brooks, "ARBY: Diagnosis with shallow causal models," in *Proc. Nat. Conf. Artificial Intelligence*, 1982, pp. 370–372.

[13] W. R. Nelson, "REACTOR: An expert system for diagnosis and treatment of nuclear reactor accidents," in *Proc. Nat. Conf. Artificial Intelligence*, Aug. 1982, pp. 296–301.

[14] R. S. Patil, P. Szolovits, and W. B. Schwartz, "Causal understanding of patient illness in medical diagnosis," in *Proc. 7th Int. Joint Conf. Artificial Intelligence*, vol. 2, 1981, pp. 893–899.

[15] C. Reiger and M. Grinberg, "The declarative representation and procedural simulation of causality in physical mechanisms," in *Proc. 5th Joint Conf. Artificial Intelligence*, vol. 1, Aug. 1977.

[16] S. M. Weiss, C. A. Kulikowski, S. Amarel, and A. Safir, "A model-based method for computer-aided medical decision making," *Artificial Intelligence*, vol. 11, pp. 145–172, 1978.

Eva Hudličká received the B.S. degree in biochemistry from the Virginia Polytechnic Institute and State University, Blacksburg, the M.S. in computer science from The Ohio State University, Columbus, and the Ph.D. degree in computer science from the University of Massachusetts, Amherst, in 1986.

She has recently joined the Advanced Systems and Tools Group at DEC after spending a year as a Visiting Assistant Professor at the University of Massachusetts. Her research interests include knowledge-based diagnosis, causal models, and model-based development environments for AI software.

Dr. Hudličká is a member of ACM and AAAI.

Victor Lesser, for a photograph and biography please see page 379 of this TRANSACTIONS.

Chapter 7

Blackboard Structures

Conventional blackboard architectures incorporate a shared common data area or *blackboard* as the common medium for memory and interaction among a collection of *knowledge sources*. Control in typical blackboard systems is sequential and organized by a centralized scheduler, but the knowledge sources work with semantically disparate rules or procedures. The conception behind the blackboard architecture is "cooperative interaction of communicating knowledge sources." The blackboard architecture concept has been a mainstay of many projects in DAI, as the primary local structure of individual problem-solving nodes that cooperate (as in numerous distributed interpretation experiments and the DVMT — see papers by Corkill, Durfee, Erman, Hudlicka, Lesser, and Yang et al. in Chapter 3, Chapter 4, Sections 4.2 and 4.3, and Chapters 6 and 8). Under the influence of the trend to distribution, blackboard architectures have evolved from HEARSAY-II (the "classical" blackboard system [Erman80]) through HASP, with its control blackboard with control metalevels, to new distributed blackboard architectures.

In her paper, Barbara Hayes-Roth introduces the "blackboard control architecture," which is realized in the OPM system. This work has to some extent explicated and provided mechanisms for solving control problems such as the independent generation of desirable and feasible actions and their reconciliation, the prioritization of action, and the dynamical planning of useful sequences of actions. The blackboard control architecture system can represent for example HEARSAY-II's scheduler and HASP's solution-based focusing.

While Hayes-Roth's article doesn't explicitly treat distribution of control, its thorough conceptualization of the control problem lays the groundwork for further research, especially when combined with the approaches that add concurrency to blackboard regimes, described in the other papers of Ensor and Gabbe (Chapter 7), Fennell and Lesser (Chapter 3), and Gasser et al. (Chapter 6).

Daniel Corkill, Kevin Gallagher and Philip Johnson describe the generic (domain-independent) blackboard system GBB, which is an interesting attempt to provide both flexibility and efficiency. These are achieved by the use of abstraction techniques to provide a good relationship between the representation of the application area and the blackboard implementation. While the paper included here discusses the basic structures of GBB, Corkill et al.'s ultimate aim is to incorporate parallelism both within and among blackboard-based problem solvers.

With Luiz Leao and Sarosh Talukdar's COPS system, we move to a blackboard architecture designed for the distributed environment of a network of heterogeneous computers. Each blackboard process is rule-based, and internally sequential. Distributed processes exchange messages by writing onto each other's blackboards. They can become notified of remote events on each other's blackboards using "ambassadors," which are simply local rules that represent the interests of remote processes. The COPS framework provides a very clear and simple mechanism for controlling interaction among multiple blackboard-based problem solvers. However, the price of this simplicity is less runtime flexibility; most of the interaction protocol must be designed into the ambassadors, rather than being planned at runtime by problem solvers.

Robert Ensor and John Gabbe tackle the thorny problem of true concurrency of execution of knowledge sources sharing the same blackboard. This requires additional new mechanisms for scheduling knowledge source activities, synchronizing knowledge source interactions, and accessing shared data, which are achieved using the concept of a "transaction manager." Ensor and Gabbe see distribution of blackboard access essentially as a distributed database problem. The transaction manager receives blackboard update requests, groups them into transactions, schedules them for activation in the black-

board, and maintains consistency using locks. In this respect, their system uses techniques related to those of Fennell and Lesser (See Chapter 3), and the two papers make an interesting comparison.

As blackboard systems become more prevalent, especially in concurrent and heterogeneous environments, more collaboration will take place between researchers in databases and those in knowledge based systems, to solve the problems of distributing access and data. The commonality and data consistency provided by shared blackboard data structures for multiagent interaction will give way to more sophisticated techniques for increasing concurrency while maintaining control.

A Blackboard Architecture for Control

Barbara Hayes-Roth
*Heuristic Programming Project, Stanford University,
Stanford, CA 94305, U.S.A.*

ABSTRACT

The control problem—which of its potential actions should an AI system perform at each point in the problem-solving process?—is fundamental to all cognitive processes. This paper proposes eight behavioral goals for intelligent control and a 'blackboard control architecture' to achieve them. The architecture distinguishes domain and control problems, knowledge, and behavior. It enables AI systems to operate upon their own knowledge and behavior and to adapt to unanticipated problem-solving situations. The paper shows how OPM, a blackboard control system for multiple-task planning, exploits these capabilities. It also shows how the architecture would replicate the control behavior of HEARSAY-II and HASP. The paper contrasts the blackboard control architecture with three alternatives and shows how it continues an evolutionary progression of control architectures. The paper concludes with a summary of the blackboard control architecture's strengths and weaknesses.

1. The Control Problem

In attempting to solve a domain problem, an AI system performs a series of problem-solving actions. Each action is triggered by data or previously generated solution elements, applies some knowledge source from the problem domain, and generates or modifies a solution element. At each point in the problem-solving process, several such actions may be possible. The control problem is: *which of its potential actions should an AI system perform at each point in the problem-solving process?*

The control problem is fundamental to all cognitive processes and intelligent systems. In solving the control problem, a system decides, either implicitly or explicitly, what problems it will attempt to solve, what knowledge it will bring to bear, and what problem-solving methods and strategies it will apply. It decides how it will evaluate alternative problem solutions, how it will know when specific problems are solved, and under what circumstances it will interrupt its attention to selected problems or sub-problems. Thus, *in solving the control problem, a system determines its own cognitive behavior.*

other control issues. For example, the planner might have two feasible actions: (a) a domain action that would generate an abstract plan encompassing three of the requested tasks: the health club, the florist, and the vet; and (b) a control action that would adopt a heuristic favoring actions whose knowledge sources are reliable. If, for example, the planner has an operative heuristic favoring actions that generate abstract partial plans, it performs the domain action first. Alternatively, if it has an operative heuristic favoring control actions, it performs the control action first. If the planner has both heuristics, it performs the action favored by the heuristic it considers more important.

3. The Blackboard Control Architecture

The blackboard control architecture extends and elaborates the standard blackboard architecture [7] in order to achieve the behavioral goals set forth in Section 2. Section 3.1 below summarizes the basic assumptions of the standard architecture and the blackboard control architecture's extension of them. Sections 3.2–3.4 examine the blackboard control architecture in more detail: its approach to domain problem-solving, its approach to control problem-solving, and its basic scheduling mechanism. These sections use the multiple-task planning domain introduced in Section 2 for illustration. Because both control and multiple-task planning are planning domains, the discussion distinguishes the 'control plan' and the 'domain plan' where necessary. Section 3.5 summarizes the blackboard control architecture's important features: explicit representation of domain and control problems, knowledge, and solutions; integration of domain and control problem-solving in a single basic control loop; interpretation and modification of a system's own knowledge and behavior; adaptation of knowledge and behavior to dynamic problem-solving situations; and uniform treatment of domain and control problem-solving as incremental, opportunistic processes. The blackboard control architecture is implemented as BB1 [14], a domain-independent system-building environment.

3.1. From the blackboard architecture to the blackboard control architecture

The blackboard architecture is a problem-solving framework developed for the HEARSAY-II speech-understanding system [7], used in a variety of other problem domains [11, 15, 21, 23, 26, 30], and abstracted in several system-building environments [8, 14, 25]. It treats problem-solving as an incremental, opportunistic process of assembling a satisfactory configuration of solution elements. For example, it treats multiple-task planning as a process of assembling a satisfactory configuration of decisions about what tasks to perform, when to perform them, and so forth. It entails three basic assumptions:

(1) *All solution elements generated during problem-solving are recorded in a structured, global database called the blackboard.*
The blackboard structure organizes solution elements along two axes, solu-

tion intervals and levels of abstraction. Different solution intervals represent different regions of the solution on some problem-specific dimension(s). For example, for the multiple-task planning domain, solution intervals represent the plan execution time intervals. Different levels of abstraction represent the solution in different amounts of detail. For example, for the multiple-task planning domain, one level of abstraction represents a planned sequence of tasks, while a lower level also elaborates the details of performing individual tasks and the routes for travelling between successive tasks.

(2) *Solution elements are generated and recorded on the blackboard by independent processes called knowledge sources.*

Knowledge sources have a condition-action format. The condition describes situations in which the knowledge source can contribute to the problem-solving process. Ordinarily, it requires a particular configuration of solution elements on the blackboard. The action specifies the knowledge source's behavior. Ordinarily, it entails the creation or modification of solution elements on the blackboard. Only knowledge sources whose conditions are satisfied can perform their actions.

Although implementations vary, in most blackboard systems knowledge-source activity is event-driven. Each change to the blackboard constitutes an event that, in the presence of specific other information on the blackboard, can trigger (satisfy the condition of) one or more knowledge sources. Each such triggering produces a unique knowledge-source activation record (KSAR). A KSAR is similar to an item on a task agenda. It represents a unique triggering of a particular knowledge source by a particular blackboard event. When a KSAR is chosen by the scheduling mechanism discussed below, its knowledge source's action executes in the context of its triggering information, typically producing new blackboard events.

Knowledge sources are independent in that they do not invoke one another and ordinarily have no knowledge of each other's expertise, behavior, or existence. They are cooperative in that they contribute solution elements to a shared problem. The blackboard architecture achieves simultaneous independence and cooperation among knowledge sources by permitting them to influence one another's problem-solving behavior only indirectly, by anonymously responding to and modifying information recorded on the blackboard.

(3) *On each problem-solving cycle, a scheduling mechanism chooses a single KSAR to execute its action.*

Because several KSARs may compete to execute their actions, a scheduling mechanism determines which KSARs execute their actions and in what order. The most common mechanism is a 'sophisticated scheduler' that uses a variety of criteria (e.g., knowledge-source reliability, triggering information credibility, expected value of the knowledge source's action) to choose a KSAR for execution on each problem-solving cycle. The sophisticated scheduler is discussed in more detail in Section 5.

Despite increasing sophistication in problem-solving knowledge and heuristics, most AI systems employ relatively simple control programs. In contrast, people do not rely upon pre-determined control programs to guide all of their problem-solving efforts. Instead, they draw upon a repertoire of control knowledge that includes proven control programs and heuristics for dynamically constructing, modifying, and executing control programs during efforts to solve particular domain problems.

This adaptability in the control of one's own problem-solving behavior is the hallmark of human intelligence. Because of it, people do not simply solve a problem. They often know something about how they solve the problem, how they have solved similar problems in the past, why they perform one problem-solving action rather than another, what problem-solving actions they are likely to perform in the future, and so forth. They use this knowledge to adapt their behavior to the demands of the problem-solving situation, to explain their behavior, to cope with new problems, to improve their approaches to familiar problems, and to transfer problem-solving knowledge to other people and to computers. Truly intelligent AI systems must do no less.

Accordingly, this paper suggests that AI systems should approach the control problem as a real-time planning problem. It operationalizes *intelligent* control problem-solving as achievement of (at least) the following behavioral goals:

(1) Make explicit control decisions that solve the control problem.

(2) Decide what actions to perform by reconciling independent decisions about what actions are desirable and what actions are feasible.

(3) Adopt variable grain-size control heuristics.

(4) Adopt control heuristics that focus on whatever action attributes are useful in the current problem-solving situation.

(5) Adopt, retain, and discard individual control heuristics in response to dynamic problem-solving situations.

(6) Decide how to integrate multiple control heuristics of varying importance.

(7) Dynamically plan strategic sequences of actions.

(8) Reason about the relative priorities of domain and control actions.

Section 2 discusses and justifies each of these goals.

A 'blackboard control architecture' is proposed to achieve the goals. It has several important features, some of them previously suggested by other researchers. First, the architecture explicitly represents domain and control problems, knowledge, and solutions [2, 4, 5, 9, 11, 15, 16, 18, 20, 21, 24, 26]. Second, the architecture integrates domain and control problem-solving in a single basic control loop. Third, the architecture articulates, interprets, and modifies representations of its own knowledge and behavior [5, 8, 23, 27]. Fourth, the architecture adapts its problem-solving knowledge, its application of that knowledge, and its basic control loop to dynamic problem-solving situations. Finally, the architecture incorporates these features in a uniform

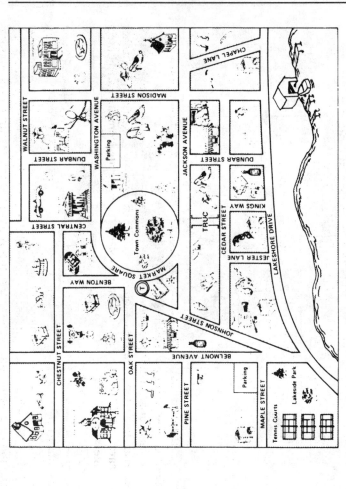

FIG. 1. Town map used for multiple-task planning.

blackboard architecture in which domain and control problem-solving behaviors are characteristically incremental and opportunistic [1, 3, 7, 13]. Section 3 describes the blackboard control architecture. Section 4 shows how it achieves each of the behavioral goals enumerated above. Appendix A provides a more detailed illustration with problem-solving traces from OPM [14], a blackboard control system for multiple-task planning.

Section 5 contrasts the blackboard control architecture with three alternatives: the basic blackboard architecture with a sophisticated scheduler, the basic blackboard architecture with solution-based focusing, and meta-level architecture. Although each of these alternatives has valuable features, none achieves all of the behavioral goals enumerated above. In addition, Appendix B shows how the blackboard control architecture could replicate the control behaviors of HEARSAY-II's sophisticated scheduler [6] and HASP's solution-based focusing [22].

Despite the blackboard control architecture's behavioral innovations, it does not depart radically from previous architectures. The second part of Section 5 shows how the blackboard control architecture continues an evolutionary progression of control architectures.

Section 6 summarizes the blackboard control architecture's strengths and weaknesses.

2. The Semantics of Control

What kinds of control behaviors should an AI system exhibit?

This section sets forth eight behavioral goals for an AI architecture. Each goal rests upon assumptions about effective problem-solving and the nature of intelligence. Thus, the goals are claimed to be necessary (but not sufficient) behaviors for an intelligent system. Although some readers may disagree with this analysis, at least it exposes the goals and assumptions underlying the blackboard control architecture to examination and criticism. It also provides criteria against which to evaluate the architecture and its alternatives.

2.1. An illustrative problem domain: multiple-task planning

The behavioral goals are illustrated with examples from a hypothetical intelligent planner that solves the following problem:

You have just finished working out at the health club (see Fig. 1). It is 11:00 and you can plan the rest of your day as you like. However, you must pick up your car from the Maple Street parking garage by 5:30 and then head home. You would also like to see a movie today, if possible. Show times at both movie theaters are 1:00, 3:00, and 5:00. Both movies are on your 'must see' list, but go to whichever one most conveniently fits into your plan. Your

other errands are as follows:
– Pick up medicine for your dog at the vet.
– Buy a fan belt for your refrigerator at the appliance store.
– Tour two of the three luxury apartments.
– Meet a friend for lunch at the restaurant of your choice.
– Buy a toy for your dog at the pet store.
– Pick up your watch at the watch repair.
– Special-order a book at the book store.
– Buy fresh vegetables at the grocery.
– Buy a gardening magazine at the newsstand.
– Go to the florist to send flowers to a friend in the hospital.

Develop a plan that:
  (a) specifies which tasks to perform, the ordering of tasks, and the routes to travel between successive tasks;
  (b) accomplishes as many tasks as possible, accomplishes high-priority tasks rather than low-priority tasks, honors time constraints, and provides efficient routes.

2.2. Behavioral goals for intelligent control

(1) *Make explicit control decisions that solve the control problem*

To solve a problem, a system performs a subset of its potential problem-solving actions in a particular order. Intelligent problem-solving entails explicitly solving the control problem—*deciding* which actions to perform and when to perform them—as well as performing selected actions. For example, given several possible next actions, the hypothetical planner explicitly decides to perform the action that locates the vet on the town map.

(2) *Decide what actions to perform by reconciling independent decisions about what actions are desirable and what actions are feasible.*

Intelligent control reasoning recognizes both the desirability and the feasibility of potential actions. An intelligent system decides what kinds of actions it should perform, thereby establishing its operative control heuristics. It decides what actions it can perform, thereby identifying its currently executable knowledge sources. The system reconciles these two kinds of decisions in order to decide what actions to perform. For example, the planner might decide that it should perform actions involving high-priority tasks. It might also decide that, in the current problem-solving situation, it can execute several knowledge sources, including one whose action would locate the vet, a high-priority task. Reconciling its task-priority heuristic and its executable knowledge sources, the planner decides to locate the vet.

Although an intelligent system does not allow either the desirability or the feasibility of potential actions to dominate control problem-solving, it drives the problem-solving process in either direction under appropriate circumstances.

Suppose the system decides that it should perform actions having a particular attribute, but discovers that it cannot perform any such actions. In other words, the specified actions are desirable, but not feasible. In that situation, an intelligent system performs actions that *enable* it to perform the desired actions. For example, the planner might decide that it should perform actions that generate abstract partial plans, but discovers that it cannot perform any such actions. In that situation, the planner examines its knowledge sources that produce abstract plans, determines that it needs task-location information in order to apply them, and adopts a control heuristic favoring actions that generate task-location information.

Conversely, suppose the system has decided that it can perform several pending actions that share an 'interesting' attribute, but notices that it has not yet decided that it should perform such actions. In other words, the specified actions are feasible, but not explicitly desirable. In that situation, an intelligent system performs actions that *incline* it to perform the feasible actions. For example, the planner might decide that it can perform several actions sharing the attribute 'triggered by time constraints', which is interesting because the

problem instructions include a requirement to honor time constraints. However, it also might notice that it has not yet decided that it should perform such actions. In that situation, the planner adopts a control heuristic favoring actions triggered by time constraints.

(3) *Adopt variable grain-size control heuristics.*

In some problem-solving situations, the most useful control heuristics prescribe classes of actions, while in others, the most useful heuristics prescribe specific actions. Similarly, in some situations, the most useful heuristics prescribe actions to be performed at any time during a relatively long problem-solving time interval, while in others, the most useful heuristics target actions for specific problem-solving 'cycles'. An intelligent system adopts control heuristics whose grain-size is appropriate for the problem-solving situation.

For example, the planner might generate two credible partial plans, PP-NW and PP-SE (see Fig. 2). In that situation, any actions that extend either partial plan or connect the two plans would advance the problem-solving process. Therefore, the planner adopts a relatively large-grain control heuristic favoring actions whose triggering information includes an unconnected end-point of either of the plans or whose solution context is the spatial-temporal region

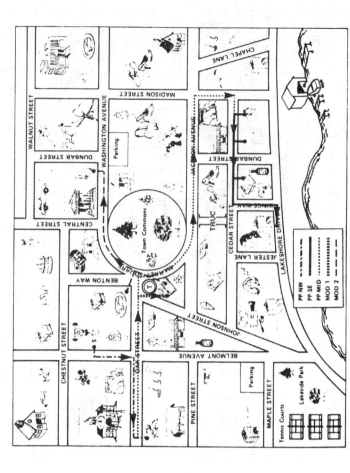

FIG. 2. Illustration of partial plans.

between the two plans. The heuristic prescribes performance of such actions during the problem-solving time interval beginning immediately and continuing until the two partial plans are connected.

Once the planner has connected the two partial plans, for example with PP-MID (see Fig. 2), the only remaining problem-solving objective is to connect the integrated plan with its termination point. In that situation, the planner adopts a smaller-grain control heuristic favoring actions whose knowledge source is Extend-Route and solution interval is '5:30 Maple Street Parking Garage'. The heuristic prescribes performance of those actions on the few remaining problem-solving cycles.

(4) *Adopt control heuristics that focus on whatever action attributes are useful in the current problem-solving situation.*

Attributes of a problem-solving action's triggering information, knowledge source, or solution context may affect its utility in different problem-solving situations. An intelligent system adopts control heuristics that focus on whatever attributes are useful in the current problem-solving situation. For example, if a planning problem specifies tasks that vary widely in priority, the planning system adopts a heuristic favoring actions triggered by high-priority tasks. If problem-solving time is at a premium, it adopts a heuristic favoring actions whose knowledge sources are efficient and reliable. If the planning system has already generated two credible partial plans, it adopts a heuristic favoring actions whose solution contexts represent the interval between those plans.

(5) *Adopt, retain, and discard individual control heuristics in response to dynamic problem-solving situations.*

Different control heuristics are useful in different problem-solving situations and the problem-solving situation can change repeatedly during the problem-solving process. An intelligent system adopts, retains, and discards control heuristics in response to dynamic problem-solving situations. For example, the planner might determine early in the problem-solving process that the requested tasks vary widely in priority and that the allowable plan execution time is insufficient for performing all of them. It immediately adopts a heuristic favoring actions triggered by high-priority tasks. Ordinarily, it would retain that heuristic for the duration of the problem-solving process. However, if the planner subsequently develops a partial plan that includes all of the high-priority tasks but does not exhaust the allowable execution time, it abandons the heuristic. For another example, sometime in the middle of the problem-solving process, the planner might generate the partial plans, PP-NW and PP-SE (see Fig. 2). At that point, it adopts a heuristic favoring actions that connect those plans. However, once the planner has completely connected PP-NW and PP-SE (for example, with PP-MID in Fig. 2), that heuristic is no longer useful and the planner abandons it.

(6) *Decide how to integrate multiple control heuristics of varying importance.*

Several operative control heuristics (those the system has adopted and not yet abandoned) may bear simultaneously, but differentially, on a particular problem-solving situation. An intelligent system integrates all operative heuristics in deciding which specific action to perform next. For example, the planner might decide that: (a) it is very important to generate abstract partial plans until there are at least three high-credibility partial plans; (b) it is always moderately important to perform actions whose knowledge sources are reliable; and (c) it is always moderately important to perform actions whose triggering information is credible. Until decision (a)'s criterion is met, the planner uses all three heuristics to decide which actions to perform. After (a)'s criterion is met, the planner abandons it and uses only the remaining two heuristics.

On a given problem-solving cycle, several potential actions may have different ratings against different subsets of the operative control heuristics. An intelligent system decides how to integrate each action's ratings and by what rule to choose a single action to perform next. For example, early in the problem-solving process, the planner might decide simply to choose the potential action that has the highest sum of ratings, weighted by importance, against all operative control heuristics. Later, as problem-solving time becomes more precious, it might decide to identify the subset of its potential actions that rate high on knowledge source speed and reliability and to choose from that set the single action that has the highest weighted sum of ratings against the remaining control heuristics.

(7) *Dynamically plan strategic sequences of actions.*

Strategic sequences of actions sometimes provide problem-solving power not achievable through independently chosen actions. An intelligent system plans strategic sequences of actions under appropriate circumstances. For example, the successive-refinement strategy reduces the combinatorics of search for multiple-task planning problems that specify a large number of tasks. The hypothetical planner uses that strategy to plan a sequence of: (a) actions that generate abstract partial plans; followed by (b) actions that refine, extend, and connect the most credible partial plans.

Strategic plans are complex control heuristics. Rather than prescribing a single kind of action, they prescribe a sequence of different kinds of actions. Therefore, an intelligent system deals with strategic plans just as it deals with simpler heuristics. It adopts variable grain-size strategic plans that focus on whatever action attributes are useful in the current problem-solving situation. It adopts, retains, and abandons strategic plans in response to dynamic problem-solving situation. It integrates strategic plans with its other control heuristics in deciding which specific action to perform next.

Dynamic planning also entails a readiness to interrupt, resume, or re-plan

The architectural features summarized above interact to produce a problem-solving style that is characteristically incremental and opportunistic. Executed KSARs apply various inference methods (e.g., goal-driven, data-driven) to generate solution elements, one at a time, in different blackboard locations. They extend the most promising solution elements and eventually merge them with others to form the complete solution. The relative orderliness with which the solution develops depends largely upon the scheduler's behavior. At one extreme, it can follow a rigorous procedure, scheduling a planned sequence of KSARs that monotonically assemble compatible solution elements. At the other extreme, it can apply a variety of conflicting criteria, opportunistically scheduling KSARs that assemble disparate, competing solution elements out of which a complete solution emerges only gradually.

Briefly, the blackboard control architecture extends and elaborates the three standard assumptions as follows:

(1) *The blackboard control architecture defines explicit domain and control blackboards.*

The domain blackboard records solution elements for the current domain problem. Its solution intervals, levels of abstraction, and vocabulary are domain-specific and determined by the designer of an application system. The control blackboard records solution elements for the control problem. These solution elements are decisions about a system's own desirable, feasible, and actual behavior. The control blackboard's solution intervals, levels of abstraction, and vocabulary are domain-independent and defined by the architecture.

(2) *The blackboard control architecture defines explicit domain and control knowledge sources.*

Domain knowledge sources operate primarily on the domain blackboard. They are domain-specific and determined by the application system designer. Control knowledge sources operate primarily on the control blackboard. They articulate, interpret, and modify representations of the system's own knowledge and behavior. Some control knowledge sources are domain-specific; others are domain-independent. All knowledge sources are represented as data structures that are, themselves, available for interpretation and modification.

(3) *The blackboard control architecture defines a simple, adaptive scheduling mechanism to manage both domain and control KSARs.*

Three 'basic' control knowledge sources iterate a three-step problem-solving cycle: (1) enumerate pending KSARs; (2) choose one KSAR; (3) execute the action of the chosen KSAR. The basic control knowledge sources have no specific control knowledge, but simply adapt to dynamic solution state information recorded on the domain and control blackboards. Because they manage both domain and control KSARs, the basic control knowledge sources indirectly influence their own behavior.

performance of a strategic sequence of actions in response to dynamic problem-solving situations, as discussed below.

Some actions that do not conform to an adopted plan have other desirable attributes. An intelligent system interrupts its execution of strategic plans to perform such actions. For example, the planner might: (a) adopt the successive-refinement strategy; (b) begin performing a sequence of actions that, if completed, would generate PP-MID, connecting PP-NW with PP-SE (see Fig. 2); and (c) complete actions plotting the route segments beginning at the vet and ending at the intersection of Oak Street and Johnson Street. At this point, the planner can perform either of two actions, one that would continue the strategic action sequence and one that would interrupt it. The strategic action would plot a route segment from the intersection of Oak Street and Johnson Street to the next intersection on the way to PP-SE. The non-strategic action would modify PP-NW to include the newsstand, a task previously excluded from consideration for being low-priority, but now worth incorporating in the plan because it is very convenient to the plotted route. In this situation, the planner interrupts its strategic route-plotting actions to perform the action that incorporates the newsstand in the plan (MOD1 in Fig. 2).

Some interruptions do not affect a strategic plan's utility. On completing non-interfering interruptions, an intelligent system resumes plan execution. For example, inclusion of the newsstand makes only a minor modification to PP-NW. The planner subsequently resumes its strategic route-plotting actions to complete PP-MID.

On the other hand, some interruptions obviate pending strategic actions. On completing interfering interruptions, an intelligent system adapts its execution of the strategic plan to the new problem-solving situation. For example, following incorporation of the newsstand, the planner might perform additional interrupting actions, further extending PP-NW to include lunch at the Oak Street Restaurant followed by a stop at the Washington Avenue Pet Store (MOD2 in Fig. 2). Given this substantial extension of PP-NW, a route from the vet to the watch repair no longer makes sense. Therefore, the planner does not resume its efforts to plot that route. Instead, it 'backs up' in its strategic plan, first plotting routes within the extended PP-NW and then plotting a route connecting it to PP-SE—this time a route from the pet store to the watch repair.

(8) *Reason about the relative priorities of domain and control actions.*

Just as an intelligent system performs domain actions to generate solution elements for a domain problem, it performs control actions to generate solution elements for the control problem, namely control decisions. Because there is no *a priori* reason to presume that either type of action is more productive on any particular problem-solving cycle, the system reasons about the relative priorities of domain and control actions just as it reasons about

3.2. Domain problem-solving

The blackboard control architecture solves domain problems with the same methods used in standard blackboard systems. Domain knowledge sources respond to, generate, and modify solution elements on a domain blackboard, under the control of a scheduling mechanism. This section presents an illustrative domain blackboard and knowledge sources. The architecture does not specifically include these components. It defines them to be domain-specific and determined by the application system designer, requiring only that they satisfy the architectural constraints given above. In the present case, the domain blackboard and knowledge sources were derived from thinking-aloud protocols produced by people while working on multiple-task planning problems [15]. They illustrate the kind of blackboard structure and knowledge sources assumed by the architecture and provide a context in which to discuss its other components.

3.2.1. A *domain blackboard for multiple-task planning*

Solution elements for the multiple-task planning problem are decisions about which tasks to perform, in what order to perform tasks, and by what routes to travel between successive task locations. Each decision is represented as a data structure with attributes and values. Because these attributes are incidental to the multiple-task planning domain and not intrinsic to the blackboard control architecture, this discussion ignores them and gives only the gist of domain decisions.

A related set of decisions on the domain blackboard constitutes a partial domain plan. For example, the partial plan in Fig. 3 specifies:

> Perform a set of tasks including the health club, the pharmacy, the vet, etc. First perform tasks in the northwest part of town, in this order: health club, florist, vet.... Go from the florist to the vet by travelling south on Belmont to Oak and west on Oak to the vet. . . .

As the example illustrates, partial plans may encompass variable-size segments of an evolving complete plan. At any point in the problem-solving process, the domain blackboard may contain several complementary or alternative partial plans. The multiple-task planning problem is solved when the system has generated and merged one or more partial plans to form a complete and satisfactory plan at the lowest level of the domain blackboard.

Different solution intervals on the multiple-task planning blackboard represent different temporal intervals in the plan execution sequence. Decisions toward the left side of the blackboard designate tasks or travel planned to occur early in the plan execution sequence, while those on the right side designate tasks or travel planned to occur later in the sequence.

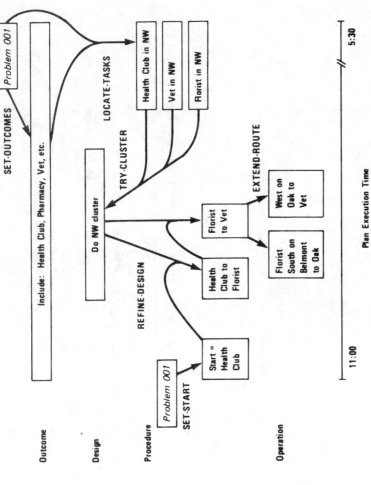

FIG. 3. Partial multiple-task plan.

Outcome Level
Definition: Tasks included in or excluded from the plan
Example: Include: health club, pharmacy, vet, etc.

Design Level
Definition: General temporal layout of the plan
Example: Do tasks in the northwest cluster first

Procedure Level
Definition: Sequence of individual tasks
Example: Do the vet after the florist

Operation Level
Definition: Details of task performance and travel between tasks
Example: Go from the florist south on Belmont Ave. to Oak St.

FIG. 4. Levels of abstraction for the multiple-task planning blackboard.

The multiple-task planning blackboard has four levels of abstraction. Fig. 4 defines and provides an example decision for each level.

3.2.2. Domain knowledge sources for multiple-task planning

Domain knowledge sources solve the multiple-task planning problem by creating and modifying decisions on the domain blackboard. The blackboard control architecture represents all knowledge sources as data structures with the attributes defined in Table 1. Knowledge sources reside in a system's 'permanent' memory, as opposed to the 'working' memory embodied in blackboard structures.

For example, Fig. 5 describes the knowledge source Refine-Design. As indicated by its Problem-Domain, Refine-Design is useful for multiple-task planning problems. As indicated by its Description, it refines a Design decision as a series of Procedure decisions. Refine-Design's Trigger indicates that it is potentially useful in situations in which a blackboard event creates a new Procedure decision that sequences two tasks. Its Pre-Condition indicates that it cannot actually execute its Action unless: (a) there is a decision about the general Design of the plan that constrains extension of the triggering Procedure; and (b) there are decisions establishing the locations and orientations (directions and distances) of unplanned tasks with respect to the second task in the triggering Procedure. Refine-Design's Condition-Vars specify that the values of P and D that satisfy its Condition predicates should be bound and used to perform its Action. Its Scheduling-Vars provide values (or functions for computing values) for the variables: Trigger-Weight, Action-Level, Action-Interval, KS-Efficiency, KS-Credibility, and KS-Importance, to be recorded in any KSAR generated for Refine-Design and available for use in scheduling. Finally, its Action, when executed, creates a new Procedure decision that extends the triggering Procedure in accordance with the specified Design. Because Refine-Design can be triggered by the events it creates, ordinarily it is

---

```
Name = 'Refine-Design'
Problem-Domain = (Multiple-Task Planning)
Description = 'Refines a Design decision as a series of
               Procedure decisions'
Condition =
  Trigger =
    An Event creates a new Procedure, P
    P's Type is 'sequence'
  Pre-Condition =
    There is a Design, D, whose specification
      encompasses P's Task2
    For each unplanned task, there is a Procedure whose Type
      is 'location' and Orientation-List includes P's Task2
Condition-Vars = (P, D)
Scheduling-Vars =
  Trigger-Weight = P's Weight
  Action-Level = 'Procedure'
  Action-Interval = >P
  KS-Efficiency = 0.5
  KS-Credibility = 0.9
  KS-Importance = 0.9
Action =
  Let Candidates be the set of unplanned tasks whose Orientation
    to P's Task2 satisfies D
  Let Next-Task be the member of Candidates that is closest to
    P's Task2
  Create a Procedure whose Type is 'sequence'
  Let its Task1 be P's Task2
  Let its Task2 be Next-Task
```

Fig. 5. Multiple-task planning knowledge source: Refine-Design.

TABLE 2. Attributes of knowledge source activation records (KSARs)

Attribute	Definition
Name	Identifying number
KS	Name of the triggered knowledge source
Triggering-Cycle	Cycle on which the knowledge source was triggered
Triggering-Event	Event that triggered the knowledge source
Triggering-Decision	Decision where the Triggering-Event occurred
Pre-Condition-Values	Pre-Conditions and current bindings
Condition-Values	Bindings of Condition-Vars to be used in Action
Scheduling-Values	Bindings of Scheduling-Vars to be used in scheduling
Ratings	Ratings on operative heuristics
Priority	Expected (numerical) value of action

TABLE 1. Attributes of knowledge sources

Attribute	Definition
Name	Identifying label
Problem-Domain	Domain(s) of application
Description	Characteristic behavior
Condition	Situation of interest: Trigger and Pre-Condition
Trigger	Event-based predicates for triggering
Pre-Condition	State-based predicates required for execution
Condition-Vars	Specification of variables used in Condition
Scheduling-Vars	Specification of variables to be used in scheduling
Action	Program of blackboard changes

triggered repeatedly to refine a single Design as a connected series of Procedures.

The blackboard control architecture represents knowledge sources as data structures with the attributes in Table 2. It records them at the To-Do-Set level of the control blackboard (discussed below) to represent domain actions the problem-solving system can perform. For example, when triggered by event E-40 on cycle 31, Refine-Design generates KSAR-103, shown in Fig. 6.

KSAR-103 indicates that the knowledge source Refine-Design is triggered on cycle 31 by event E-40 at decision Procedure5. Its Pre-Condition-Values indicate that its first Pre-Condition is satisfied by Design1, but that its second Pre-Condition is not yet satisfied, implying that KSAR-103 cannot actually execute its Action yet. Its Condition-Values indicate that KSAR-103 should use Procedure5 and Design1 to execute its Action. Its Scheduling-Values indicate that the system's confidence in KSAR-103's triggering information is 0.8, that its Action would produce a new event at the Procedure level in the solution interval beginning at 11:20, that Refine-Design's efficiency is 0.5, that it operates on the domain blackboard, and that it would produce a very important decision. (The Ratings and Priority attributes of KSARs are discussed in Section 3.4.1 below.)

3.2.3. An example of multiple-task planning

Fig. 3 shows how several multiple-task planning knowledge sources might interact to produce a partial plan incrementally:

(1) Set-Outcomes, triggered by a Problem decision on the control blackboard (discussed below), creates an Outcome decision to include the health club, the pharmacy, the vet, etc., in the plan.

(2) Set-Start, also triggered by the Problem decision, creates a Procedure decision to start at the health club.

(3) Locate-Tasks, also triggered by the Problem decision, begins creating Procedure decisions locating each task.

(4) Notice-Cluster, triggered by creation of three Procedure decisions locating the health club, the vet, and the florist in the northwest part of town, creates a Design decision to perform those tasks first.

(5) Refine-Design, triggered previously by creation of the Procedure decision to start at the health club, now has its Pre-Conditions satisfied by creation of the Design decision and by the Procedure decisions locating tasks. It creates a Procedure decision to go from the health club to the florist.

(6) Refine-Design, triggered by the Procedure decision to go from the health club to the florist, and constrained by the Design decision, creates a Procedure decision to go from florist to the vet.

(7) Extend-Route, triggered by the Procedure decision to go from the florist to the vet, creates an Operation decision to travel from the florist, south on Belmont, to Oak.

(8) Extend-Route, triggered by the Operation decision to travel from the florist to Oak, creates an Operation decision to travel west on Oak to the vet.

This example abstracts a cooperative interaction among selected KSARs out of a larger problem-solving context. In practice, other KSARs would compete with those discussed above, possibly assisting in the development of the partial plan in Fig. 3, possibly interrupting or even terminating its development. Appendix A discusses some of these other behavior patterns. Section 4 presents program traces from OPM, a blackboard system for multiple-task planning, to illustrate some of these other behavior patterns in detail.

3.3. Control problem-solving

The blackboard control architecture solves the control problem with the same methods it uses for domain problems. Control knowledge sources respond to, generate, and modify solution elements on a control blackboard, under the control of a scheduling mechanism. They dynamically compose a prescriptive control plan out of modular control heuristics. A simple scheduler adapts to the current control plan to select potential actions for execution. The architecture defines specific solution intervals and levels of abstraction for a domain-independent control blackboard. It defines the attributes and values of decisions that occur at each level. It entails several generic control knowledge sources, but permits additional domain-specific control knowledge sources.

3.3.1. The control blackboard

Solution elements for the control problem are decisions about what actions are desirable, feasible, and actually performed at each point in the problem-solving

```
KSAR-103
KS = 'Refine-Design'
Triggering-Cycle = 31
Triggering-Event = E-40
Triggering-Decision = Procedure5
Pre-Condition-Values =
  ((There is a Design, D, whose specification encompasses P's
    Task2) ('Design-001's specification encompasses 'florist'))
  ((For each unplanned task, there is a Procedure whose Type is location
    and Orientation-List includes 'vet'))
Condition-Values = ((P Procedure5) (D Design1))
Scheduling-Values = ((Trigger-Weight 0.8) (Action-Level 'Procedure')
  (Action-Interval > 11:20) (KS-Efficiency 0.5) (KS-Credibility 0.9)
  (Action-Blackboard 'Domain') (KS-Importance 0.9))
Ratings = Nil
Priority = 0
```

Fig. 6. An example KSAR.

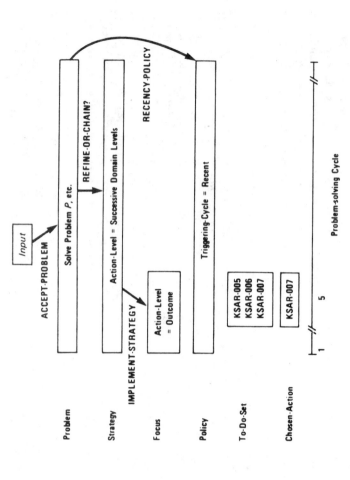

FIG. 7. Partial control plan.

process. Each control decision is represented as a data structure with the attributes defined in Table 3. These attributes are instantiated for decisions at each level of abstraction below.

A related set of decisions on the control blackboard constitutes a partial control plan. For example, the partial plan in Fig. 7 specifies:

> Solve Problem *P*, etc. Prefer KSARs whose Actions occur at successive domain levels. Begin with KSARs whose Actions occur at the Outcome level.... Also prefer KSARs triggered on recent problem-solving cycles.... On cycle 005, these KSARs are feasible: KSAR-005, KSAR-006, KSAR-007. On cycle 005, perform KSAR-007....

As the example illustrates, partial control plans may encompass variable-size segments of an evolving control plan. At any point in the problem-solving process, the control blackboard may contain several complementary or competing partial plans. As discussed below, the control problem is solved when the Problem's Criterion is met and its Status is changed to 'solved'.

Different solution intervals on the control blackboard represent different problem-solving time intervals in terms of problem-solving cycles. Control decisions toward the left side of the control blackboard refer to problem-solving actions planned for early problem-solving cycles, while those on the right side refer to actions planned for later problem-solving cycles.

The control blackboard's levels of abstraction represent different categories of control decisions. Decisions at the *Problem*, *Strategy*, *Focus*, and *Policy* levels describe desirable actions, thereby determining which of the system's control heuristics operate during particular problem-solving time intervals. As explained below, heuristics at these different levels differ in scope. Decisions at the To-Do-Set level describe feasible actions, identifying all KSARs eligible for execution on each problem-solving cycle. Decisions at the Chosen-Action level describe actions scheduled for execution on each problem-solving cycle. In general, the architecture uses heuristics at the Problem, Strategy, Focus, and Policy levels to evaluate pending KSARs at the To-Do-Set level in order to schedule KSARs for execution at the Chosen-Action level.

Fig. 8 defines and gives examples of decisions at each level of the control blackboard. Each decision in Fig. 8 corresponds to one of the decisions in the partial control plan in Fig. 7. For brevity, the example decisions in Fig. 8 include only Goal and Criterion attributes. The following sections discuss all the attributes of each decision (see Table 3) in detail.

3.3.1.1. *Problem decisions*

A single Problem decision represents the problem a system has decided to solve and guides the entire problem-solving episode. Creating a Problem decision on the blackboard initiates problem-solving by triggering at least one domain or control knowledge source. The Problem's attributes may subsequently trigger or constrain the behavior of other knowledge sources. Changing the Problem's Status to 'solved' terminates problem-solving activities.

TABLE 3. Basic attributes of control decisions

Attribute	Definition
Name	Identifying level and number
Goal	Prescribed action (predicate or function of KSAR attributes)
Criterion	Expiration condition (predicate)
Weight	Goal importance (0–1)
Rationale	Reason for Goal
Creator	KSAR that created the decision
Source	Triggering decision (or Input)
Type	Role in control plan (e.g., Strategic, Solution-Based)
Status	Function in control plan (e.g., Operative, Inoperative)
First-Cycle	First operative cycle
Last-Cycle	Last operative cycle

The Criterion in this example refers to several attributes that occur only at the Problem level: Levels of abstraction for the problem domain ('Outcome, Design, Procedure, Operation'), the Problem's Requested-Tasks ('health club, vet, etc.'), and the Problem's Constraints ('(start 1100), (finish 1730), etc.'). Two other level-specific attributes indicate that the Problem-Domain is 'multiple-task planning' and that the available Problem-Solving-Time is '10 minutes''.

The Problem's Weight indicates the importance of solving the Problem, ordinarily 1, the highest possible value. Its Rationale is either task-specific and provided by the system designer, for example 'to demonstrate planning under uncertainty', or the default 'to cooperate with the system designer'.

Ordinarily, a Problem's Source is 'input', its Type is 'requested by system designer', and its Creator is 'KSAR-001', the first KSAR created and executed. Its Status is 'operative' until some knowledge source determines that its Criterion has been met and changes its Status to 'inoperative'. Assuming the system can solve only one problem at a time, the Problem's First-Cycle is 1. The knowledge source that changes the Problem's Status to 'inoperative' also records the current cycle number as its Last-Cycle.

The discussion above assumes that a system can solve only problems posed by the system designer (or other user). If a system posed problems to itself, the Source might be 'KS 555', the Type might be 'self-imposed', and the Rationale might be 'experiment with a new Strategy knowledge source'.

3.1.2. Strategy decisions

Strategy decisions establish general sequential plans for problem-solving. Ideally, a single Strategy decision created early in the problem-solving process guides the remainder of the process. However, Strategy decisions may occur at any point in the process and span arbitrary intervals of the remaining problem-solving time. Under some circumstances, conflicting or complementary Strategies may replace one another or operate simultaneously.

Functionally, a Strategy provides parameters for a generic control knowledge source, Implement-Strategy, that generates more specific decisions implementing the Strategy at the lower Focus level.[1] As discussed below, Focus decisions, but not Strategy decisions, are used to rate and schedule KSARs. Thus, Strategy decisions do not directly influence scheduling decisions; they influence them indirectly through the Focus decisions that implement them.

A Strategy's Goal describes a prescribed sequence of actions as a predicate on one or more KSAR attribute-description pairs. The attributes must be legal values. The descriptions must entail sequences of legal values.

[1] For complex strategic plans, the architecture permits additional levels to intervene between Strategy and Focus levels. For example, representing HEARSAY-II's Strategy on the control blackboard requires an intervening Tactic level (see Appendix B). In that case, Strategy decisions function as generators for Tactic decisions, which function as generators for Focus decisions. Thus, any intermediate levels expand the aggregation hierarchy defined for Strategy and Focus levels.

Problem
Definition: Problem the system has decided to solve
Example:
Goal = (KS Problem-Domain = multiple-task-planning)
Criterion =
((complete solution at lowest domain Level)
(all Requested-Tasks planned)
(all Constraints met)
(route efficient))

Strategy
Definition: General sequential plan for solving the problem
Example:
Goal = (Action-Level = successive domain Levels)
Criterion = complete solution spanning all domain Levels

Focus
Definition: Local (temporary) problem-solving goals
Example:
Goal = (Action-Level = Outcome)
Criterion = complete solution at Outcome Level

Policy
Definition: Global (permanent) scheduling criteria
Example:
Goal = (Triggering-Cycle = recent)

To-Do-Set
Definition: Sets of pending KSARs
Example:
Goal = ((Triggered-List = (KSAR-008, KSAR-009))
(Invocable-List = (KSAR-005, KSAR-006, KSAR-007)))

Chosen-Action
Definition: KSARs chosen to execute
Example:
Goal = KSAR-007

FIG. 8. Levels of abstraction for the control blackboard.

A Problem's Goal prescribes actions whose knowledge sources apply to its domain, for example 'KS Problem-Domain = multiple-task-planning'. Its Criterion characterizes an acceptable solution. opm's Problem Criterion includes four requirements: 'complete solution at lowest domain Level, all Requested-Tasks planned, all Constraints met, planned route efficient'. For some domains, including multiple-task planning, solving the Problem entails modifying or elaborating the initial Criterion or Constraints. For example, if there is not enough time to perform all Requested-Tasks, the Criterion predicate 'all Requested-Tasks planned' can be changed to 'all important Requested-Tasks planned'.

For example, 'Action-level = successive domain Levels' prescribes a sequence of actions that add or modify solution elements at successive Levels of the domain blackboard. A Strategy's Criterion characterizes the desired result of applying the Strategy, for example 'complete solution spanning all domain Levels'. Its Weight (0–1) indicates the expected utility of applying the Strategy, for example 0.9. Its Rationale is the reason for recommending the Strategy, such as 'insufficient time to perform all Requested-Tasks'.

Four attributes specific to the Strategy level provide parameters for implementing the Strategy's Goal as a series of more specific Goals at the Focus level. Consider implementation of the Goal 'Action-Level = successive domain Levels'. The Strategy's Focus1 describes the first Focus Goal it prescribes as a predicate or function on one or more KSAR attribute-description pairs. The attributes must be legal KSAR attributes. The descriptions must evaluate to legal values. The Focus1 'Action-Level = highest domain level' evaluates to 'Action-Level = Outcome'. The Strategy's Refocus-Criterion is a predicate that, when true, indicates that the Strategy prescribes a new Focus, for example 'complete and satisfactory solution in Focus'. The Strategy's Refocus-Increment is a function that, when applied to the current Focus Goal, generates the Goal of the next prescribed Focus. Applying the Refocus-Increment 'level below' to the Goal 'Action-Level = Outcome' generates the Goal 'Action-Level = Design'. The Strategy's FocusN describes the last Focus Goal it prescribes, for example 'Action-Level = lowest domain level', which, for multiple-task planning, evaluates to 'Action-Level = Operation'. Thus, the Strategy Goal 'Action-Level = successive domains Levels' prescribes a series of Focus decisions whose Goals are 'Action-Level = Outcome', 'Action-Level = Design', 'Action-Level = Procedure', and 'Action-Level = Operation'. It further prescribes that each Focus should remain operative until a complete and satisfactory solution exists at the level currently in the strategic Focus.

Ordinarily, a Strategy's Source is 'Problem1' and its Type is 'problem-appropriate', indicating that it is a known Strategy for handling the current Problem. However, a Strategy might be induced from experience or transferred from another problem domain. In that case, its Source would be the triggering information, its Type would be 'induced' or 'transferred', and its Rationale might be 'apparent solution improvement' or 'useful for analogous problem domain: spatial planning'.

A Strategy's Creator is the KSAR that created it, for example 'KSAR-002'. A Strategy's Status is 'operative' until some knowledge source determines either that its Criterion has been met or that it is no longer productive and changes its Status to 'inoperative'. Its First-Cycle is the cycle after it is created and its Last-Cycle is the cycle on which it becomes inoperative.

3.3.1.3. *Focus decisions*

Focus decisions establish local problem-solving objectives to execute KSARs with particular attributes and values. Sometimes a sequence of Focus decisions implements a previously created Strategy decision. Other Focus decisions operate independently of one another and of prior Strategy decisions. Focus decisions are explicitly temporary and operate during restricted problem-solving time intervals. Several complementary or competing Focus decisions may operate simultaneously.

Focus decisions are used to rate KSARs. As a consequence, they can influence scheduling decisions. However, a given Focus decision actually influences scheduling decisions only if: (a) the current To-Do-Set contains KSARs with the attributes and values it prescribes; and (b) the current integration and scheduling rules (discussed in Section 3.4 below) incorporate the Focus decision.

A Focus decision's Goal is a predicate or function on one or more KSAR attri-bute-value pairs.[2] For example, the Goal 'Action-Level = Outcome' prescribes execution of KSARs whose Actions occur at the Outcome Level. Its Criterion is a predicate that, when true, indicates that the Goal is no longer useful, for example 'complete solution at the Outcome Level'. Its Weight indicates the expected utility of the prescribed actions.

A Focus decision's Rationale, Source, and Type depend upon its etiology. If the Focus implements a previously generated Strategy, its Rationale describes its role within the Strategy, for example 'implements Strategy's Focus1', its Source is the Strategy, for example 'Strategy1', and its Type is 'strategic'. If it simply prescribes feasible problem-solving actions—that is, an identified subset of those appearing in recent To-Do-Sets—its Rationale is 'is feasible'. Its Source is the set of To-Do-Sets, for example 'To-Do-Set15, To-Do-Set25', and its Type is 'inferred'. If it prescribes actions in a blackboard region where progress would be especially useful, its Rationale might be 'unsatisfactory partial solution' or 'contiguous to a credible partial solution', its Source is the blackboard region, for example 'domain interval 10', and its Type is 'solution-based'.

A Focus decision's Creator is the KSAR that created it, for example 'KSAR-003'. Its Status is 'operative' until some control knowledge source notices that its Criterion has been met and changes its Status to 'inoperative'. Its First-Cycle and Last-Cycle are the first and last cycles on which it is operative.

3.3.1.4. *Policy decisions*

Policy decisions establish global scheduling criteria favoring KSARs with particular attributes and values. In contrast to Focus decisions, Policy decisions ordinarily remain operative from the time they are created until the end of the

---

[2] Focus Goals can be predicates whose true/false values indicate satisfaction/non-satisfaction of the Goal or functions whose numerical values indicate degree of satisfaction. An example of a Goal function appears in the discussion of Policy decisions (Section 3.3.1.4).

problem-solving episode. They carry no internal expiration Criteria. The only exception occurs when some knowledge source independently determines that a Policy should become inoperative. Ordinarily, several Policy decisions operate simultaneously.

Like Focus decisions, Policy decisions are used to rate KSARs and they can influence scheduling decisions. Again, however, a given Policy decision actually influences scheduling decisions only if: (a) the current To-Do-Set contains KSARs with the attributes and values it prescribes; and (b) the current integration and scheduling rules incorporate the Policy decision.

A Policy decision's Goal is a predicate or function on one or more KSAR attribute-value pairs. For example, the Goal 'Triggering-Cycle = recent' prescribes execution of KSARs triggered on the last few problem-solving cycles.[3] A Policy's Weight is the expected value of its prescribed actions.

A Policy's Rationale, Source, and Type depend upon its etiology. If a Policy decision establishes scheduling criteria known to be useful for the current Problem, its Rationale might be 'useful for multiple-task planning problems', its Source is 'Problem1', and its Type is 'Problem-appropriate'. If a Policy establishes scheduling criteria in response to a particular problem-solving state, its Rationale characterizes the state, for example 'problem-solving time is running out', its Source is 'problem-solving state on cycle c', and its Type is 'solution-based'.

A Policy's Creator is the KSAR that created it. Its Status remains 'operative' until either the problem-solving process terminates or a domain-specific control knowledge source changes its Status to 'inoperative'. Its First-Cycle and Last-Cycle are the first and last cycles on which it is operative.

3.3.1.5. To-Do-Set decisions

To-Do-Set decisions identify all pending KSARs on each problem-solving cycle. They record a cycle-by-cycle history of all problem-solving actions the system can perform. Because knowledge source Triggers are event-based while Pre-Conditions are state-based and possibly transient, a To-Do-Set's Goal distinguishes a Triggered-List and an Invocable-List of pending KSARs. Update-To-Do-Set, a basic control knowledge source defined in the Section 3.4, places newly triggered KSARs on the Triggered-List. When their Pre-Conditions become true (after an arbitrary problem-solving time interval), it moves them to the Invocable-List. If any of their Pre-Conditions subsequently become false, it moves them back to the Triggered-List. KSARs can move back and forth between the two lists. However, only KSARs on the Invocable-List can be scheduled for execution. A To-Do-Set's Only-Cycle is the only problem-solving cycle on which it is operative.

3.3.1.6. Chosen-Action decisions

Chosen-Action decisions identify KSARs scheduled to execute on each problem-solving cycle. Thus, they record a cycle-by-cycle history of all problem-solving actions the system actually does perform. A Chosen-Action's Goal is the scheduled KSAR, for example 'KSAR-005'. Its Rationale lists the Focus and Policy decisions that lead to its selection, for example 'Focus1, Policy1'. Its Consequences list the blackboard events produced by executing the KSAR's Action. Its Status is 'scheduled' at the time it is created and changes to 'executed' after it executes. Its Only-Cycle is the only cycle on which it is operative.

3.3.2. Higher-level control knowledge sources

Control knowledge sources solve the control problem by creating, modifying, and interpreting decisions on the control blackboard. Higher-level control knowledge sources, discussed in this section, determine what kinds of problem-solving actions are desirable. Thus, they determine which of the system's control heuristics operate during particular problem-solving time intervals. Three basic control knowledge sources, discussed in Section 3.4 below, identify feasible actions and, based on the operative control heuristics, determine which of the feasible actions is executed on each problem-solving cycle.

Higher-level control knowledge sources are represented as data structures with the attributes defined in Table 1. A few of them (for example, the knowledge source Implement-Strategy mentioned below) are generic; most are domain-specific.

Figure 9 shows the illustrative control knowledge source, Refine-or-Chain? As indicated by its Problem-Domain, Refine-or-Chain? is a domain-specific control knowledge source appropriate for multiple-task planning problems. However, notice that Refine-or-Chain?'s other attributes are expressed in domain-independent terms. Thus, its knowledge is, in principle, general over multiple domains and its Problem-Domain potentially expandable to include other domains.

Refine-or-Chain? decides which of two problem-solving strategies the system should use. Its Trigger specifies the creation of a new Problem decision. It has no additional Pre-Condition. Its Condition-Vars bind the value of P, the triggering Problem decision, for use in carrying out its Action. Its Scheduling-Vars bind the values of several potentially useful scheduling variables. Its Action examines the triggering Problem's attributes to evaluate the feasibility of performing all of the Requested-Tasks in the available plan execution time. If performing all of the Requested-Tasks is not feasible, Refine-or-Chain? changes the Problem's Criterion 'all Requested-Tasks planned' to 'all important Requested-Tasks planned' and creates the successive-refinement Strategy decision discussed above. It gives the Strategy a high Weight, 0.9, and records its Rationale, 'insufficient time for all Requested-Tasks'. On the other hand, if performing all of the Requested-Tasks is clearly feasible, Refine-or-

[3] A more sophisticated form of the same Goal might, for example, specify the function 'Prefer-Recent Triggering-Cycle' to return the numerical values 100, 90, 50, 0 for Triggering-Cycle = the current cycle, the preceding cycle, 2–5 cycles ago, 6 or more cycles ago.

Chain? creates a simpler temporal-chaining Strategy decision: Generate a plan by incorporating tasks in the order in which they will be executed. Because this is not an especially powerful strategy, Refine-or-Chain? gives it an intermediate Weight, 0.7, and records its Rationale, 'more than sufficient time for all Requested-Tasks'. In either case, Refine-or-Chain? records the Strategy's Source, 'Problem1', and its Type, 'Problem-appropriate'. When triggered, Refine-or-Chain? generates a KSAR with the attributes defined in Table 2.

3.3.3. An example of control planning

Fig. 7 shows how four illustrative control knowledge sources might interact to develop a partial control plan incrementally:

(1) Accept-Problem, triggered by input requesting solution of a problem, P, creates a corresponding Problem decision.

(2) Refine-or-Chain?, triggered by creation of the Problem decision, determines that it is not feasible to perform all of the Requested-Tasks in the available plan execution time. It changes the Problem decision's Criterion 'all Requested-Tasks planned' to 'all important Requested-Tasks planned' and creates a Strategy decision representing the successive-refinement Strategy.

(3) Implement-Strategy, triggered by creation of the successive-refine Strategy, creates a Focus decision that implements the Strategy's Focus1, favoring actions at the Outcome Level.

(4) Recency-Policy, triggered by creation of the Problem decision, creates a Policy decision favoring actions triggered by recent blackboard events.

This example abstracts a simple, cooperative interaction among selected control KSARs out of a larger problem-solving context. In practice, other KSARs would compete with those discussed above, possibly assisting in the development of the partial control plan in Fig. 7, possibly interrupting or even terminating its development. Section 4 discusses some of these other behavior patterns. Appendix A presents program traces from OPM to illustrate some of these other behavioral patterns in detail.

3.4. Scheduling mechanism: basic control knowledge sources

The blackboard control architecture's scheduling mechanism comprises three domain-independent, basic control knowledge sources: Update-To-Do-Set, Choose-KSAR, and Interpret-KSAR. These knowledge sources operate at the To-Do-Set and Chosen-KSAR levels of the control blackboard, determining and documenting all of a system's feasible and actual problem-solving actions.

Because these three knowledge sources execute the basic control loop that runs a problem-solving system, they do not generate KSARs that compete with other domain and control KSARs for scheduling priority. Instead, they are invoked directly whenever their Conditions are satisfied. The specification of 'new' or 'changed' decisions in the Conditions of these knowledge sources

```
Name = 'Refine-or-Chain?'
Problem-Domain = (Multiple-Task Planning)
Description = 'Creates a successive-refinement strategy if plan execution time is inadequate;
               otherwise creates a temporal-chaining strategy'

Condition =
  Trigger =
    An Event creates a new Problem, P
  Pre-Condition = T
  Condition-Vars = (P)
Scheduling-Vars =
  Trigger-Weight = P's Weight
Action-Blackboard = 'Control'
Action-Level = 'Strategy'
KS-Efficiency = 0.7
KS-Credibility = 0.8
KS-Importance = 1
Action =
  Create a Strategy
  If P's Execution-time not ≥
     time required for all of P's Requested-Tasks
  Then change P's Criterion 'all Requested-Tasks planned'
     to 'all important Requested-Tasks planned'
  Let the new Strategy's Goal be
     'Action-Level = successive domain Levels'
  Let its Criterion be
     'complete plan spanning all domain Levels'
  Let its Weight be 0.9
  Let its Rationale be
     'insufficient time for all requested tasks'
  Let its Focus1 be 'highest domain Level'
  Let its Refocus-Criterion be
     'complete solution in focus'
  Let its Refocus-Increment be 'Level below'
  Let its FocusN be 'lowest domain Level'
  Otherwise let its Goal be
     'Action-Level = successive time intervals'
  Let its Criterion be
     'complete plan at lowest domain Level'
  Let its Weight be 0.7
  Let its Rationale be
     'more than sufficient time for all requested tasks'
  Let its Focus1 be
     'task interval that begins at P's start'
  Let its Refocus-Criterion be
     'complete solution in Focus at the lowest domain Level'
  Let its Refocus-Increment be
     'first-empty-time-unit-after'
  Let its FocusN be
     'task interval that ends at P's finish'
  Let its Source be 'P'.
  Let its Type be problem appropriate
```

Fig. 9. Control knowledge source: Refine-or-Chain?

(discussed below) insures that each one will be invoked exactly once for any Condition-satisfying change to the blackboard. The three knowledge sources are coordinated so that Update-To-Do-Set's Action produces a blackboard modification that satisfies Choose-KSAR's Condition, Choose-KSAR's Action produces a blackboard modification that satisfies Interpret-KSAR's Condition, and Interpret-KSAR's Action produces a blackboard modification that satisfies Update-To-Do-Set's Condition. The three basic control knowledge sources are described below.

3.4.1. Basic control knowledge source: Update-To-Do-Set

Update-To-Do-Set (see Fig. 10) is invoked when the Status of the most recently created Chosen-Action changes to 'executed'. Its Action increments the problem-solving cycle and creates a new To-Do-Set, as follow.[4] Update-To-Do-Set sets the new To-Do-Set's Only-Cycle to the current cycle. It initially sets the To-Do-Set's Goal to the Goal of the most recent prior To-Do-Set, removing the executed KSAR from its Invocable-List. It then examines all domain and control knowledge sources that specify the current Problem's Problem-Domain (or 'Any') and all blackboard events listed as the Chosen-Action's Consequences. For every unique pairing of a knowledge source and an event that satisfies the knowledge source's Trigger, Update-To-Do-Set creates a new KSAR and gives it the attributes defined in Table 2. Update-To-Do-Set adds each new KSAR to the new To-Do-Set's Triggered-List. It then evaluates the Pre-Conditions of KSARs on the Triggered-List and moves those whose Pre-Conditions are true to the Invocable-List. (The other KSARs simply remain on the Triggered-List.) Thus, Update-To-Do-Set evaluates the feasibility of all of the system's own potential actions except those of the basic control knowledge sources.

Update-To-Do-Set also computes and records each KSAR's Ratings against operative Focus and Policy decisions and its Priority. It computes a KSAR's Ratings by evaluating each operative Focus and Policy decision's Goal against the KSAR's Scheduling-Vals. It computes a KSAR's Priority by applying an integration rule (always recorded in Policy1) to the KSAR's Ratings. Because control knowledge sources can change Focus decisions, Policy decisions, and the integration rule, a KSAR's Ratings and Priority can also change from cycle to cycle.[5] The following examples illustrate the computation of Ratings and Priorities for the KSARs in Fig. 11.

Suppose that Policy1 contains the integration rule 'number of positive ratings on operative Focus and Policy decisions' and that the control blackboard contains one operative Policy decision—Policy2, whose Goal is 'KS-Importance ≥ 0.8'. KSAR-052's KS-Importance is only 0.7, so its Rating on Policy2 is 0 and its Priority is 0. KSAR-051's KS-Importance is 0.9, so its Rating on Policy2 is 100 and its Priority is 1.

Now suppose a control knowledge source records a new Policy decision—Policy3, whose Goal is 'Action-Blackboard = Control'. KSAR-052 satisfies Policy3, but not Policy2, so its new Priority is 1. KSAR-051 satisfies Policy2, but not Policy3, so its new Priority is 1.

Finally, suppose a control knowledge source changes Policy1's integration rule to 'sum of weighted ratings on operative Focus and Policy decisions'. Assume also that Policy2's Weight is 5 and Policy3's Weight is 10. KSAR-052's new Priority is $0 + (10 * 100) = 1000$. KSAR-051's new Priority is $(5 * 100) + 0 = 500$.

Update-To-Do-Set records each KSAR's Ratings and Priority on the control

```
Name = 'Update-To-Do-Set'
Problem-Domain = (Any)
Description = 'Maintains To-Do-Sets of pending Actions'
Condition =
    The Status of the most recent Chosen-Action, K,
        changes to 'executed'
Condition-Vars = K
Action =
    Increment the current cycle by 1
    Create a To-Do-Set
    Let its Only-Cycle be the current cycle
    Let its Goal be the Goal of the most recent prior To-Do-Set
    Remove K from the new Goal's Invocable-List
    If K has Consequences
        Then for each knowledge source, KS, whose
            Problem-Domain = Problem1's Problem-Domain or 'Any'
            For each Event (one of K's Consequences)
                If KS's Trigger is true
                    Then create a KSAR and add it to the Triggered-List
    For each KSAR on the Triggered-List
        For each KSAR Pre-Condition that is true
            Bind the variables in the Pre-Condition
        If all of the Pre-Conditions are true
            Then move the KSAR from the Triggered-List
                to the Invocable-List
    For each KSAR on the Triggered-List or the Invocable-List
        Compute and record the KSAR's Ratings against all operative
            Focus and Policy Goals
        Compute and record the KSAR's Priority by applying the
            Integration-Rule in Policy1 to the KSAR's Ratings
```

FIG. 10. Basic control knowledge source: Update-To-Do-Set.

[4] In practice, creating a new To-Do-Set on each cycle is not necessary for the architecture to function and it inefficiently consumes space. For this reason, both OPM and BB1 use a version of Update-To-Do-Set that simply updates a single To-Do-Set.

[5] For efficiency, the version of Update-To-Do-Set used in OPM and BB1 does not recompute each KSAR's Ratings and Priority on each cycle, but simply updates its Ratings against changed Focus and Policy decisions and, if necessary, updates its Priority.

KSAR-052
KS = 'Implement-Strategy'
Triggering-Event = E-035
Triggering-Cycle = 046
Triggering-Decision = Problem-001
Condition-Values =
  P = Problem-001
Scheduling-Values =
  Action-Blackboard = 'Control'
  Action-Level = 'Focus'
  Trigger-Weight = 0.9
  KS-Importance = 0.7
  KS-Efficiency = 0.7
  KS-Credibility = 1.0

KSAR-051
KS = 'Insert-Outcome'
Triggering-Event = E-032
Triggering-Cycle 044
Triggering-Decision = Outcome-001
Condition-Value =
  t = 'vet'
Scheduling-Values =
  Action-Blackboard = 'Domain'
  Action-Level = 'Outcome'
  Trigger-Weight = 0.9
  KS-Importance = 0.9
  KS-Efficiency = 0.7
  KS-Credibility = 0.8

FIG. 11. Example To-Do-Set Invocable-List.

blackboard. As discussed below, Choose-KSAR uses this information to make scheduling decisions. In addition, higher-level control knowledge sources can inspect and reason about the implications of KSAR Ratings and Priorities.

3.4.2. Basic control knowledge source: Choose-KSAR

Choose-KSAR (see Fig. 12) is triggered by the creation of a new To-Do-Set. Its Action-Action schedules a KSAR according to the current scheduling rule (always recorded in Policy1).[6] Following the examples above, given the integration rule, 'number of positive ratings on operative Focus and Policy decisions', and Policy2, 'KS-Importance ≥ 0.8', KSAR-052's Priority is 0 and KSAR-051's Priority is 100. Choose-KSAR schedules KSAR-051. Given the addition of Policy3, 'Action-Blackboard = Control', both KSARs have Priority 100. Choose-KSAR must schedule one of them arbitrarily. Finally, given the new integration rule, 'sum of weighted ratings on operative Focus and Policy

[6]OPM uses a different, probabilistic scheduling rule, discussed in Appendix A.

Name = 'Choose-KSAR'
Description = 'Decides which pending action to perform next'
Problem-Domain = (Any)
Condition =
  There is a new To-Do-Set, A
  Conditions-Vars = (A)
Action =
  Choose the KSAR, K, from A's Goal's Invocable-List
    that satisfies the Scheduling-Rule in Policy1
  If any of K's Pre-Conditions is not true
    Then unbind the variables in the Pre-Condition
      Move K from the Invocable-List to the Triggered-List
      Choose another KSAR
  Create a new Chosen-Action
  Let its Goal be K
  Let its Status be 'Scheduled'
  Let its Rationale be the Foci and Policies that favor it
  Let its Only-Cycle be the current cycle

FIG. 12. Basic control knowledge source: Choose-KSAR.

---

decisions', KSAR-052's Priority is 1000 and KSAR-051's Priority is 500. Choose-KSAR schedules KSAR-052.

Since Pre-Conditions specify potentially transient state information, a KSAR's Pre-Conditions may be invalidated by blackboard modifications occurring after Update-To-Do-Set moves it to the Invocable-List. Therefore, after making its choice, Choose-KSAR reevaluates the chosen KSAR's Pre-Conditions. If any of them is no longer true, Choose-KSAR unbinds the Pre-Condition variables, moves the KSAR back to the Triggered-List and chooses another KSAR. When it finds a KSAR whose Pre-Conditions are true, it creates a Chosen-Action whose Goal is the chosen KSAR, Rationale is the list of Foci and Policies that favor it, Status is 'Scheduled', and Only-Cycle is the current problem-solving cycle. Thus, Choose-KSAR schedules all of the system's actions except those of the three basic control knowledge sources.

3.4.3. Basic control knowledge source: Interpret-KSAR

Interpret-KSAR (see Fig. 13) is triggered by the creation of a new Chosen-

---

Name = 'Interpret-KSAR'
Description = 'Performs a chosen action'
Problem-Domain = 'Any'
Condition =
  There is a new Chosen-Action, K
  Condition-Vars = (K)
Action =
  Interpret and execute K's Goal's Action
  Let K's Consequences be all resulting blackboard events
  Change K's Status to 'executed'

FIG. 13. Basic control knowledge source: Interpret-KSAR.

Action. Its Action interprets and executes the Action of the KSAR recorded as the Chosen-Action's Goal. It also records the Chosen-Action's Consequences (resulting blackboard events) and changes its Status to 'Executed'. Thus, it executes all of the system's actions execpt those of the three basic control knowledge sources.

3.4.4. Character of the basic control loop

As the example above illustrates, the blackboard control architecture's basic control loop is explicit and modifiable. Choose-KSAR has no *a priori* scheduling priorities for KSARs representing domain or control actions, actions at different levels of abstraction, or actions having any other specific attributes. Any KSAR attributes may or may not be recorded in KSARs for a given knowledge source and may or may not appear in the Goals of operative Foci and Policies on a given problem-solving cycle. Even the rule for integrating ratings against multiple heuristics is recorded (and modifiable) in Policy1. Update-To-Do-Set computes and records each KSAR's Ratings and Priority based on this dynamic state information recorded on the control blackboard. Choose-KSAR adapts its scheduling behavior to the current KSAR Ratings and Priorities and the current scheduling rule, which is itself recorded (and modifiable) in Policy1. Interpret-KSAR. executes whatever KSAR Action is scheduled.

3.5. Important features of blackboard control architecture

(1) *The blackboard control architecture explicitly represents domain and control problems, knowledge, and solutions.*
The architecture accommodates domain problems posed by a system user or by the problem-solving system itself. It defines the control problem as a real-time planning problem whose solution determines what domain and control actions the problem-solving system should, can, and does perform at each point in the problem-solving process. The architecture specifies explicit domain and control knowledge sources to solve their respective problems on explicit domain and control blackboards. It accommodates domain blackboard structures specified by an application system designer. It specifies the structure of the control blackboard and a vocabulary for expressing control decisions and the relationships among them. Finally, it permits variable—arbitrarily large—grain-size heuristics at different levels of abstraction, but requires small grain-size KSAR actions for actual execution.

(2) *The blackboard control architecture integrates domain and control problem-solving in a single basic control loop.*
The architecture's three basic control knowledge sources (Update-To-Do-Set, Choose-KSAR, and Interpret-KSAR) manage the triggering, scheduling, and interpreting of all problem-solving actions, including both domain and control actions, in a uniform manner and with no *a priori* control biases.

(3) *The blackboard control architecture articulates, interprets, and modifies representations of its own knowledge and behavior.*
The architecture represents all domain and control knowledge sources, all solution elements generated for a domain problem, and all solution elements generated for the control problem as data structures, available for interpretation and modification. Its control knowledge sources operate directly on these representations.

(4) *The blackboard control architecture adapts its problem-solving knowledge, its application of that knowledge, and its basic control loop to dynamic problem-solving situations.*
The architecture requires only the three basic control knowledge sources: Update-To-Do-Set, Choose-KSAR, and Interpret-KSAR. These knowledge sources have no specific control knowledge of their own, but adapt to whatever control decisions are recorded by higher-level control knowledge sources on the control blackboard. Thus, their behavior and the system's overall problem-solving behavior are determined entirely by dynamic interactions among domain and control knowledge sources and the simultaneously evolving solutions to domain and control problems.

(5) *The blackboard control architecture realizes these features in a uniform mechanism.*
The architecture achieves all domain and control problem-solving with condition-action knowledge sources that respond to, generate, and modify solution elements in a global blackboard structure under the management of a single scheduling mechanism. Both domain and control problem-solving are characteristically incremental and opportunistic, entailing fortuitous, synergistic interactions among independently generated solution elements.

4. Behavioral Goals Revisited

This section shows how blackboard control systems (AI systems developed within the blackboard control architecture) achieve the behavioral goals set forth in Section 2. Each goal is illustrated with examples from the behavior of OPM [16], a blackboard system that performs multiple-task planning. Appendix A presents and analyzes detailed traces of OPM's problem-solving behavior. As indicated in the discussion, the current OPM system performs most, but not all of the example behaviors. However, all of the example behaviors could be implemented in BB1 [14], a domain-independent implementation of the blackboard control architecture.

(1) *A blackboard control system makes explicit control decisions that solve the control problem.*
The basic knowledge source Choose-KSAR decides which KSARs execute on each problem-solving cycle. Choose-KSAR bases its decisions on other

control decisions, made by other control knowledge sources, that characterize KSARs the system should and can execute during variable-length problem-solving time intervals. The traces in Appendix A contain many examples of control decision-making.

(2) *A blackboard control system decides what actions to perform by reconciling independent decisions about what actions are desirable and what actions are feasible.*

Higher-level control knowledge sources make Problem, Strategy, Focus, and Policy decisions about actions the system should perform, thereby establishing its operative control heuristics. The basic knowledge source Update-To-Do-Set makes To-Do-Set decisions about actions the system can perform, thereby identifying triggered knowledge sources. The basic knowledge source Choose-KSAR makes Chosen-Action decisions, taking into account prior decisions at all higher levels of the control blackboard, to determine what actions the system does perform. The traces in Appendix A provide many examples of all three kinds of decisions and their interactions.

As implemented, OPM balances the desirability and feasibility of potential actions. However, it could drive the problem-solving process in either direction by introducing appropriate control knowledge sources.

Suppose OPM has created a Strategic Focus on the Design level, but its current To-Do-Set contains no invocable KSARs whose actions occur at that level. In other words, Design level actions are desirable, but not feasible. In that situation, OPM needs to perform actions that enable it to execute Design level KSARs. Specifically, it needs to perform actions whose blackboard modifications satisfy the Triggers and Pre-Conditions of knowledge sources whose Actions occur at the Design level. A control knowledge source, Enable-KS-Focus, could create a new Focus decision favoring such actions. In the present example, Enable-KS-Focus would be triggered by the creation of a highly weighted Focus decision favoring KSARs at the Design level in the context of a To-Do-Set containing no invocable KSARs at the Design level. Enable-KS-Focus would examine OPM's knowledge sources whose Actions occur at the Design level and determine that task-location information is necessary to satisfy their Pre-Conditions. Enable-KS-Focus would then create a new Focus decision favoring KSARs whose Actions generate task-location information. Obviously, this enabling process could regress further.

Alternatively, suppose OPM's recent To-Do-Sets contain several KSARs triggered by time constraints, which is interesting because the Problem's Criterion requires OPM to honor time constraints, but that it has not decided that it should perform such actions. In other words, these actions are interesting and feasible, but not explicitly desirable. In that situation, OPM needs to perform actions that incline it to execute KSARs triggered by time constraints. Specifically, it needs to perform an action that establishes a Focus decision

favoring the desired actions. A control knowledge source, Exploit-Feasibility, could perform this function. In the present example, Exploit-Feasibility would be triggered by the creation of To-Do-Sets containing many KSARs triggered by time constraints (an interesting attribute) in the context of no Focus (or Policy) decision favoring such actions. Exploit-Feasibility would create a new Focus decision favoring KSARs triggered by time constraints. Exploit-Feasibility could be parameterized to assess different degrees of interestingness and create Focus decisions with correspondingly different Weights.

(3) *A blackboard control system adopts variable grain-size control heuristics.*

Control knowledge sources operate at different levels of abstraction, establishing operative control heuristics of different grain-sizes. Problem decisions have the largest grain-size. They prescribe any actions appropriate for the problem domain and they remain operative for the duration of the problem-solving process. For example, OPM's Problem decisions prescribe any actions appropriate for the multiple-task planning domain. Decisions in the Strategy-Focus hierarchy have successively smaller grain-sizes. Strategy decisions prescribe sequences of different kinds of problem-solving actions and they remain operative for relatively long problem-solving time intervals. Focus decisions prescribe particular kinds of actions and they remain operative for relatively short problem-solving time intervals. For example, the successive-refinement Strategy used by OPM prescribes actions at successive domain levels and remains operative until the Problem is solved. One of the Focus decisions that implements that Strategy prescribes actions at the Design level and remains operative only until the Design level plan is complete. In contrast to the Strategy-Focus hierarchy, Policy decisions prescribe particular kinds of actions, but they usually remain operative for long problem-solving time intervals. For example, OPM usually records a Policy favoring recently triggered KSARs early in the problem-solving process and that Policy usually remains operative for the duration of the problem-solving process. To-Do-Set and Chosen-Action decisions have the smallest grain-size, identifying specific KSARs whose actions can be and are performed on specific problem-solving cycles. The OPM trace in Appendix A contains many examples of decisions of different grain-sizes.

(4) *A blackboard control system adopts control heuristics that focus on whatever action attributes are useful in the current problem-solving situation.*

Different control heuristics may refer to attributes of a KSAR's knowledge source, triggering information, or solution context. For example, as discussed in Appendix A, OPM creates Policies favoring KSARs with reliable, important, and efficient knowledge sources. It creates Policies favoring KSARs with recent triggering events. It creates Focus decisions favoring KSARs whose Actions occur at specific blackboard levels and in specific plan intervals.

(5) *A blackboard control system adopts, retains, and discards individual control heuristics in response to dynamic problem-solving situations.*

Because a blackboard control system treats control as a real-time planning problem, it naturally adapts its operative control heuristics to dynamic problem-solving situations. Higher-level control knowledge sources may, in principle, create or modify control heuristics at any point in the problem-solving process—namely, whenever (a) their Conditions are satisfied and (b) Choose-KSAR schedules them. In practice, some knowledge sources may be triggered by events that occur a predictable number of times or at predictable points in the problem-solving process. For example, OPM's control knowledge sources, defined in Appendix A, include some that are triggered exactly once on predictable problem-solving cycles, some that are triggered exactly once on unpredictable problem-solving cycles, and some that can be triggered repeatedly on unpredictable problem-solving cycles.

As illustrated in Appendix A, OPM's current control knowledge sources dynamically establish operative control heuristics and change each one's Status to 'inoperative' when its Criterion is satisfied. In addition, control knowledge sources could modify control heuristics in other situations. For example, a control knowledge source, Reject-Heuristic, could be triggered by situations in which an operative control heuristic influences Choose-KSAR's behavior with no corresponding improvement in the problem solution. Reject-Heuristic would change the ineffective heuristic's status to 'inoperative'.

(6) *A blackboard control system decides how to integrate multiple control heuristics of varying importance.*

Independent control knowledge sources create and assign different Weights to simultaneously operative, conflicting or complementary, heuristics on the control blackboard. The trace in Appendix A contains numerous examples of simultaneously operative control heuristics. The basic control knowledge sources (Update-To-Do-Set, Choose-KSAR, and Interpret-KSAR) integrate simultaneously operative heuristics at the Focus and Policy levels to make scheduling decisions. The 'integration rule' and 'scheduling rule' they use are, themselves, recorded and modified by control knowledge sources on the control blackboard. For example, OPM's knowledge source Planning-Policies records a probabilistic scheduling rule. Under this rule, the probability that Choose-KSAR schedules any particular pending action on a particular cycle is proportional to the action's Weighted ratings on operative Focus and Policy decisions (discussed in Appendix A). By contrast, corresponding knowledge sources for HEARSAY-II and HASP record a deterministic scheduling rule under which Choose-KSAR always schedules the pending action with the highest Priority, determined by the recorded integration rule to be the sum of weighted ratings on operative Focus and Policy decisions (discussed in Appendix B).

(7) *A blackboard control system dynamically plans useful sequences of actions.*

A blackboard control system plans strategic sequences of actions with control knowledge sources that create Strategy decisions and then implement them as prescribed series of Focus decisions. The generic knowledge source Implement-Strategy incrementally implements successive strategic Focus decisions in response to dynamic problem-solving situations. Each Focus decision influences Choose-KSAR's scheduling decisions on subsequent problem-solving cycles. For example, the discussion of OPM's 'Strategic Top-Down Domain Planning' in Appendix A shows in detail how two control knowledge sources, Refine-Or-Chain? and Implement-Strategy, cooperate to create and implement the successive-refinement strategy.

A blackboard control system also interrupts, resumes, and terminates strategic action sequences in response to dynamic problem-solving situations, as discussed below.

A blackboard control system interrupts strategic action sequences in two ways. First, it interrupts its adherence to a strategic Focus when Choose-KSAR, adapting to conflicting Focus and Policy decisions, schedules a KSAR that does not match the strategic Focus. For example, in the discussion of OPM's 'Opportunistic Bottom-Up Domain Planning' in Appendix A, Choose-KSAR interrupts a strategic sequence of actions whose current Focus is at the Operation level to schedule Outcome and Procedure level actions that satisfy an 'Action-Importance' Policy. Second, a blackboard control system interrupts its transition between successive strategic Focus decisions when Choose-KSAR schedules competing KSARs in favor of those that update the strategic Focus. For example, Choose-KSAR might not decide to schedule a pending Implement-Strategy KSAR. In either case, OPM interrupts a planned strategic sequence to perform one or more non-strategic actions that have other desirable attributes.

A blackboard control system resumes interrupted strategic sequences whenever Choose-KSAR decides that pending strategic actions are preferable to non-strategic alternatives. The blackboard representation of an evolving control plan supports strategy resumption by preserving strategic context—the original Strategy decision, all previously implemented strategic Focus decisions, and the To-Do-Set of pending KSARs. The discussion of 'Opportunistic Bottom-Up Domain Planning' in Appendix A shows how OPM resumes its strategic Operation level actions following completion of the interrupting Outcome and Procedure level actions mentioned above.

Of course, with Strategy interruption, intervening events might obviate pending strategic actions. A blackboard control system can respond appropriately to this kind of situation. For example, suppose Choose-KSAR interrupts its successive-refinement Strategy just before Implement-Strategy creates the Design level Focus. Suppose also that the interrupting actions create a complete Design level plan. Subsequently resuming the successive-refinement Strategy, Choose-KSAR schedules the pending Implement-Strategy KSAR, which creates the unnecessary Design Focus. However, the Design Focus's Criterion is satisfied as soon as it is created, immediately re-triggering Implement-Strategy. When Choose-KSAR schedules the new Implement-Strategy KSAR, it declares the Design Focus 'inoperative' and creates the subsequent Procedure level Focus. If it is very important for Strategic Focus decisions to be implemented promptly and accurately, Implement-Strategy can be given a KS-Importance value that is substantially higher than those of other knowledge sources or the integration rule or scheduling rule can explicitly favor it. OPM has a moderately weighted Policy favoring all control knowledge sources.

Sometimes intervening events change the results of previous strategic actions, requiring the system to back up and redo parts of a strategic plan. For example, suppose OPM interrupts strategic actions at the Operation level to perform actions that substantially revise its Outcome level plan. It should not resume the interrupted actions to continue refining the superseded Outcome level plan at the Operation level. It should back up to the Design level and begin refining the revised Outcome level plan. It could achieve this behavior through the actions of additional control knowledge sources that revise the state of the control plan. To illustrate, the knowledge source Back-Up might be triggered by substantial changes to partial solutions that satisfied the Criteria of preceding strategic Focus decisions. In the present example, Back-Up would be triggered by changes to the Outcome level solution because it satisfied the Criterion of the preceding strategic Focus on the Outcome level. Back-Up's action would declare the current strategic Focus 'inoperative' and create an intermediate Strategic Focus corresponding to the earliest strategic Focus whose Criterial partial solution changed. In the present example, Back-Up would declare the Operation level Focus 'inoperative' and create a new version of the Outcome Focus Criterion. Implement-Strategy would be triggered immediately by satisfaction of the Outcome Focus Criterion and create a new Design level Focus.[7]

Finally, some intervening events obviate the interrupted Strategy itself. For example, OPM might adopt a temporal-chaining strategy and subsequently decide that there is insufficient time to perform all Requested-Tasks. It should abandon that strategy (but preserve the domain plan generated so far) in favor of a new strategy. OPM could achieve this behavior with a new control knowledge source, Reject-Strategy, that notices when an operative Strategy's

Rationale is invalidated and declares both the Strategy and all of the Focus decisions that implement it 'inoperative'. If the To-Do-List contains pending Implement-Strategy KSARs for the abandoned Strategy and Choose-KSAR subsequently schedules them, they will fail Choose-KSAR's final validation of the Pre-Condition requiring that the triggering Strategy be operative (see Section 3.4.2).

Once a control heuristic has been tried and abandoned, the system ordinarily should not try it again without making an explicit decision that the heuristic is, after all, worthwhile. In other words, it should not make the same mistake twice. The control blackboard's preservation of inoperative (formerly operative) heuristics supports this kind of behavior. Any knowledge source that creates new heuristics can make its action contingent upon there being no redundant heuristic, operative or inoperative, on the blackboard. For a more sophisticated approach, the knowledge sources that declare heuristics 'inoperative' could also declare their Post-Mortems, justifying the change in Status. Knowledge sources that considered creating redundant heuristics could use that information in deciding whether or not to do so.

(8) *A blackboard control system reasons about the relative priorities of domain and control actions.*

Event-driven, condition-action knowledge sources operate on a structured blackboard to generate solution elements for both domain and control problems. Reasoning about the relative priorities of different domain actions, different control actions, and domain versus control actions is uniform. Thus, Update-To-Do-Set integrates pending domain and control KSARs in a single To-Do-Set. Choose-KSAR schedules KSARs from the To-Do-Set based on operative Foci and Policies. Because the architecture has no *a priori* biases regarding the relative priorities of domain and control actions, operative Foci and Policies may or may not include heuristics that distinguish domain and control KSARs. Further, all operative heuristics are, themselves, established through the actions of previously executed control KSARs. Finally, Interpret-KSAR executes the actions of all scheduled domain and control KSARs. The OPM trace in Appendix A includes several illustrations of the architecture's uniform treatment of domain and control actions.

5. Relationship to Other Work

The first section below compares the blackboard control architecture with three alternative control architectures. The second section places it in an evolutionary progression of control architectures.

5.1. Comparison with alternative architectures

This section compares the blackboard control architecture with three alternatives: the standard blackboard architecture with a sophisticated scheduler,

---

[7] Although OPM currently does not include the control knowledge source, Back-Up, its Policy favoring recently triggered KSARs *incidentally* achieves the same objective. Choose-KSAR schedules KSARs that refine a recently created Outcome decision in favor of those that refine a previously created Outcome decision.

the standard blackboard architecture with solution-based focusing, and meta-level architecture. Each of these alternatives shares certain features with the blackboard control architecture and achieves some of the behavioral goals set forth in Section 2. However, as summarized in Table 4, only the blackboard control architecture achieves all of the behavioral goals.

Three caveats are in order.

First, it is important to distinguish between an architecture's theoretical entailments and its computational sufficiency. For example, the blackboard control architecture explicitly entails dynamic control heuristics (goal 5). Thus, the architecture is not only computationally sufficient to achieve goal 5; it does so in a theoretically natural and computationally elegant manner. In contrast, meta-level architecture entails a fixed repertoire of control heuristics. Although some implementations are computationally sufficient to achieve goal 5, they do so in a theoretically anomalous and computationally awkward manner. The discussion below ignores computational sufficiency, focusing instead upon each architecture's theoretical entailments.

Second, other scientists may question the set of behavioral goals used to evaluate alternative architectures. Section 2 presents arguments for the necessity, but not the sufficiency, of these goals for intelligent systems. The alter-native architectures discussed below may surpass the blackboard control architecture. Each of these alternatives shares certain features with the blackboard control architecture in their achievement of other important goals not considered in this paper.

Third, the discussion below omits important research efforts that address related issues, but do not propose specific AI architectures. Notable examples are Smith's and Riviere's work on reflection in 3-LISP [28] and Wilensky's work on meta-planning [33].

5.1.1. The sophisticated scheduler

Many basic blackboard systems attack the control problem with a sophisticated scheduler [4, 7, 18, 21]. Like the basic control knowledge source Choose-KSAR, the sophisticated scheduler selects one of a set of pending KSARs on each problem-solving cycle. Unlike Choose-KSAR, which has no specific control knowledge and simply adapts to operative control decisions on the control blackboard, the sophisticated scheduler is a complex program embodying all of a system's control knowledge. For example, the HEARSAY-II scheduler [7] incorporates control heuristics favoring KSARs with efficient and reliable knowledge sources, credible triggering information, and credible solution contexts. On each problem-solving cycle, the scheduler chooses the pending KSAR that has the highest combined ratings against all of these heuristics. (Appendix B discusses HEARSAY-II and its control behavior in more detail.)

The sophisticated scheduler is an innovative and powerful mechanism for achieving considerable flexibility and opportunism in complex problem-solving processes. However, as indicated in the first column in Table 4, the sophisticated scheduler achieves only behavioral goals 1 and 4. It fails to achieve goal 2 because it cannot pursue recursive sub-goals of its control heuristics and it cannot generate new heuristics favoring feasible actions. It fails to achieve goal 3 because all of its heuristics prescribe actions of a fixed grain-size, namely individual KSARs. It fails to achieve goal 5 because its scheduling heuristics are implicit and not modifiable. It fails to achieve goal 6 because its integration rule (sum of weighted ratings) and its scheduling rule (highest-priority KSAR) are also implicit and not modifiable. It fails to achieve goal 7 because it makes only instantaneous scheduling decisions, cannot plan sequences of actions, and has no mechanism for maintaining, modifying, and incorporating strategic context over extended problem-solving intervals. It fails to achieve goal 8 because it does not reason about or even perform control actions.

Responding to some of the same behavioral limitations described above, other researchers have introduced improvements to the sophisticated scheduler, as discussed below.

Lesser and Corkill [21] integrated the sophisticated scheduler with a planning component to coordinate sequences of KSARs that satisfy high-priority problem-solving goals. Although they considered implementing the planning component, itself, as a blackboard system, they did not actually do so. Instead, their planning component embodies specific strategic heuristics. By

TABLE 4. Achievement of behavioral goals by alternative architectures

Behavioral goals	Alternative control architectures and representative systems			
	Sophisticated scheduler HEARSAY-II	Solution-based focusing HASP	Meta-level architecture MOLGEN	Blackboard control architecture OPM
(1) Make explicit decisions that solve the control problem.	+	+	+	+
(2) Reconcile desirability and feasibility of actions.	-	-	-	+
(3) Adopt variable grain-size control heuristics.	-	-	-	+
(4) Adopt heuristics that focus on useful action attributes.	+	-	+	+
(5) Dynamically adopt, retain, and discard control heuristics.	-	-	-	+
(6) Decide how to integrate multiple control heuristics.	-	-	-	+
(7) Dynamically plan strategic action sequences.	-	-	-	+
(8) Reason about control vs. domain actions.	-	-	-	+

contrast, the blackboard control architecture implements dynamic planning capabilities within a larger, uniform blackboard architecture for domain and control problem-solving.

Hudlicka and Lesser [18] propose the fault detection/diagnosis (FDD) method to modify deficient strategies during problem-solving. The FDD method detects suspicious or undesirable situations, diagnoses which scheduling parameters produced the undesirable situation, and modifies those parameters to improve problem-solving performance. In the context of the blackboard control architecture, the FDD method defines a class of extremely sophisticated control knowledge sources for analyzing the impact of operative control decision and modifying those decisions when necessary. These knowledge sources would operate along with other control knowledge sources on the control blackboard.

Erman, London, and Fickas [8] developed HEARSAY-III, a uniform blackboard environment with separate domain and control blackboards and a default low-level scheduler that simply schedules any pending KSAR. Although these researchers intended HEARSAY-III to support general control problem-solving, it provides no theory of effective control problem-solving and no specific mechanism for implementing it. The blackboard control architecture is complementary to HEARSAY-III. It provides a theory of effective control behavior (the behavioral goals that motivate it) and a mechanism (its blackboard structure and vocabulary, higher-level control knowledge sources, and three basic control knowledge sources). The blackboard control architecture could be implemented in HEARSAY-III.

Appendix B shows how the blackboard control architecture replicates the behavior of the prototypical sophisticated scheduler used in HEARSAY-II. The architecture explicates important control reasoning done by HEARSAY-II's system builders, but not explicit in the system they built. It produces a control plan that is easy to comprehend, analyze, and compare to other control plans. It illuminates control heuristics that are potentially useful in other problem domains.

5.1.2. Solution-based focusing

Many basic blackboard systems attack the control problem with solution-based focusing [25, 26, 30]. Like the sophisticated scheduler, solution-based focusing relies upon a complex program that embodies all of a system's control knowledge. Unlike the sophisticated scheduler (and the blackboard control architecture), solution-based focusing does not identify or select among pending KSARs. Instead, it sequentially selects specific blackboard events and executes knowledge sources triggered by each one. In some implementations, all triggered knowledge sources execute in a pre-determined sequence; in others, the focusing program uses other aspects of the current solution to determine which subset of triggered knowledge sources execute and in what order. For example, the HASP control program [26] operates as follows:

1. For each currently due clock event, selected in last-in-first-out order, execute the pre-determined sequence of triggered knowledge sources associated with the event's type.
2. For each expected event whose specified blackboard events have occurred, selected in last-in-first-out order, execute the pre-determined sequence of triggered knowledge sources associated with the event's type.
3. For the most recent simple event, execute the pre-determined sequence of triggered knowledge sources associated with the event's type.
4. Repeat 2 and 3 until all expected events and simple events are processed.
5. Repeat 1–4.

(Appendix B discusses HASP and its behavior in more detail.)

Solution-based focusing is an efficient mechanism for achieving a moderate amount of flexibility in complex problem-solving processes. However, as indicated in the second column in Table 4, solution-based focusing achieves only behavioral goal 1. It fails to achieve goal 2 because it cannot pursue recursive sub-goals of its control heuristics and it cannot generate new control heuristics favoring feasible actions. It fails to achieve goal 3 because all of its heuristics prescribe actions of a fixed grain-size, namely pre-specified sets of knowledge sources. It fails to achieve goal 4 because its heuristics prescribe actions according to attributes of their triggering events, but disregard attributes of their knowledge sources and solution contexts. It fails to achieve goal 5 because its operative scheduling heuristics are implicit and not modifiable. It fails to achieve goal 6 because its integration rule (sum of weighted ratings) and its scheduling rule (highest-priority KSAR) are also implicit and not modifiable. It fails to achieve goal 7 because it executes a pre-determined control plan (sometimes with local tuning), rather than dynamically constructing and modifying a control plan in the course of problem-solving. It fails to achieve goal 8 because it does not reason about or even perform control actions.

Appendix B shows how the blackboard control architecture replicates the prototypical solution-based focusing procedure in HASP. The architecture explicates important control reasoning obscured in HASP's control program. It produces a control plan that is easy to comprehend, analyze, and compare to other control plans. It illuminates control heuristics that are potentially useful in other problem domains.

5.1.3. Meta-level architecture

Meta-level architecture [2, 3, 5, 6, 10, 19, 20, 29, 32] distinguishes domain actions and meta-level actions, which select among or otherwise operate on domain actions. Similarly, meta-rules perform meta-level actions. Continuing the progression, meta-meta-level actions operate on meta-level actions, and so forth. In addressing the control problem, meta-level architectures execute all actions at a given meta-level to identify the ideal action to execute at the next lower level. Thus, the basic control loop is: (a) execute all meta-level actions; (b) execute the ideal domain action. With additional meta-levels of knowledge, the loop expands recursively, for example: (a) execute all meta-meta-level actions as follows: (a1) execute all meta-meta-level actions; (a2) execute the ideal meta-level action; (b) execute the ideal domain action.

Because of the use of common terms and the resulting potential for confusion, it is important to distinguish between: (a) meta-rules and decisions versus control knowledge sources and decisions; and (b) meta-level versus levels of the control blackboard.

First, because control knowledge sources make decisions that refer to pending KSARs, all of them operate at one or more meta-levels. Control knowledge sources whose decisions refer exclusively to domain KSARs operate at the lowest meta-level. For example, Identify-Gaps-To-Fill (see Appendix A) makes a meta-level decision to favor domain KSARs whose Action-Interval (or Action-Level) is a selected region on the domain blackboard. However, some control knowledge sources make decisions that refer to control KSARs or to both domain and control KSARs. For example, Planning-Policies (see Appendix A) establishes general scheduling criteria (e.g., KS-Efficiency = high) that refer to all domain and control KSARs. When applied to domain KSARs, its decision operates at the lowest meta-level. When applied to some control KSARs, such as a pending KSAR for Identify-Gaps-To-Fill, its decision operates at the meta-meta-level. When applied to control KSARs whose own effects are at meta-meta or higher levels, its decision operates at still higher meta-levels. Thus, *many control knowledge sources make decisions whose meta-levels are functions of their current applications* (see also [20]). In general, all control knowledge sources and decisions operate at *some* meta-level(s), there is no fixed mapping of meta-levels onto control knowledge sources.

Second, meta-level and level of the control blackboard are orthogonal. For example, a Focus decision might prescribe domain KSARs whose Action-Level is Outcome, while a Policy decision might prescribe domain KSARs whose Triggering-Decisions are credible. Although both are meta-level decisions, their difference in scope (temporary versus permanent) places them at different blackboard levels. Conversely, decisions whose effects occur at different meta-levels may appear at a single blackboard level. For example, a meta-meta-level decision favoring KSARs that refer to the Action-Intervals of domain KSARs might also appear at the Policy level. In fact, as illustrated above with Planning-Policies and its decisions, a single decision at a single blackboard level may have effects at multiple meta-levels. Thus, for the blackboard control architecture, *meta-level is not a defining theoretical construct, but simply another* potentially useful attribute of KSARs and the decisions they generate, available for consideration during scheduling.

Meta-level reasoning architectures provide a perspicuous mechanism for explicitly representing control (meta-level) knowledge and its application during problem-solving. However, as indicated in the third column of Table 4, meta-level reasoning achieves only behavioral goals 1 and 4. It fails to achieve goal 2 because it cannot pursue recursive sub-goals of its control heuristics (but see [19]) and it cannot generate new heuristics favoring feasible actions. It fails to achieve goal 3 because all its heuristics prescribe actions of a fixed grain-size, namely individual rules. It fails to achieve goal 5 because it applies its entire repertoire of meta-level rules on every pass through the basic control loop. It fails to achieve goal 6 because, although it can differentially weight rules within a meta-level, its basic control loop embodies a priority system favoring rules at higher meta-levels. It fails to achieve goal 7 because it has no mechanism for maintaining, modifying, and incorporating strategic context over extended problem-solving intervals. It fails to achieve goal 8 because it does not reason about domain versus control actions; its basic control loop simply alternates sets of control (meta-level) actions with single domain actions.

The blackboard control architecture can replicate the control behavior of meta-level systems. For example, NEOMYCIN's meta-level reasoning [12] implements a procedure represented as an aggregation hierarchy of actions planned to occur at sequential stages of the problem-solving process. Its organization mirrors the Strategy-Focus hierarchy on the control blackboard. The blackboard control architecture could incorporate control knowledge sources to establish and implement NEOMYCIN's procedure.

5.2. Evolutionary perspective

Despite its behavioral innovations, the blackboard control architecture is not a radical departure from previous control architectures. Rather, it represents a stage in the evolution of control architectures, each of which instantiates a simple three-step process:

1. Identify the set of permissible next computations.
2. Select the next computation from among the permissible computations.
3. Execute the selected computation.

As discussed below, successive architectures, including the von Neumann architecture, the production system architecture, the basic blackboard architecture with a sophisticated scheduler, and the blackboard control architecture, elaborate on their predecessors by introducing additional knowledge and intelligence into each of the three steps in the control process. First consider the classic von Neumann architecture:

1. Advance (load, then increment) the instruction counter.
2. Fetch the next instruction.
3. Execute the fetched instruction.

In Step 1, the von Neumann architecture identifies a set of exactly one permissible next computation with a two-part operation, advance the instruction counter: (a) load the current contents of the instruction counter (an address); and (b) increment the instruction counter. In Step 2, it selects the next computation by fetching the contents of the loaded address. In Step 3, it executes the selected computation, a single instruction. These steps define a sequential programming environment with branching whenever an executed instruction modifies the contents of the instruction counter.

Next consider the production system architecture:

1. Form the conflict set.
2. Resolve the conflict and select a rule.
3. Execute the selected rule.

In Step 1, the production system identifies a set of n permissible next computations as the set of productions whose left-hand sides evaluate to true. In order to identify this set, the system uses knowledge of the rules in the system's repertoire and the semantics of simple pattern matching. In Step 2, it selects the next computation by resolving the conflict among rules in the set and selecting one of them. In order to perform this selection, the system uses knowledge of the priorities of individual rules and sometimes additional data in working memory. In Step 3, it executes the selected computation, the right-hand side of a production rule, which ordinarily comprises a program of instructions. These innovations define a pattern-directed programming environment.

Now consider the basic blackboard architecture with a sophisticated scheduler:

1. Update the To-Do-Set.
2. Schedule a Pending KSAR.
3. Execute the Scheduled KSAR.

In Step 1, the sophisticated scheduler identifies a set of n permissible computations as the set of pending knowledge source activations: unique combinations of knowledge sources and triggering conditions. The triggering of knowledge sources can entail arbitrary computations, complex pattern matching, and the binding of contextural variables for incorporation into the resulting KSARs. In Step 2, the scheduler selects the next computation by scheduling one of the pending KSARs. In making these decisions, it uses knowledge of triggering event characteristics, knowledge source characteristics, problem characteristics, scheduling heuristics, and solution state. In Step 3, it executes the next computation, a knowledge source action, which ordinarily has the

computational power of a program of production rules. These innovations permit programs comprising variable-sized chunks of knowledge and increased potential for variability and fine-tuning in the application of knowledge. In particular, they permit multiple, possibly conflicting scheduling criteria and intelligent flexibility in program performance.

Finally, consider the blackboard control architecture. It uses the same three steps as the sophisticated scheduler, but introduces several innovations. In Step 1, it generates an expanded To-Do-Set of permissible computations, including both triggered and invocable domain and control KSARs, and records it on the control blackboard. In Step 2, it adapts to dynamic scheduling criteria, recorded on the control blackboard, in order to select one of the pending KSARs and it records the selected KSAR on the control blackboard. In Step 3, it executes the next computation, which may be either a domain action or a control action whose consequences reflexively influence Step 2, and again it records the consequences on the control blackboard. These innovations provide a flexible environment for explicit, dynamic control planning; a perspicuous, interpretable representation of the actual control plan; and a uniform mechanism for integrating domain and control problem-solving.

6. Strengths and weaknesses of the blackboard control architecture

The blackboard control architecture provides extreme flexibility in system behavior. Blackboard control systems can follow rigorous procedural strategies. They can coordinate implementation of successive strategic phases with problem-specific situations. They can interrupt, resume, or terminate adopted strategies. They can adopt variable subsets of simultaneously applicable strategic and non-strategic heuristics. They can use variable rules for integrating adopted heuristics and choosing among pending problem-solving actions. In sum, blackboard control systems adapt to complex control plans whose operative strategies, heuristics, and integration and scheduling rules can change repeatedly in the course of problem-solving.

Further, the blackboard control architecture places all of the parameters governing system behavior under system control. Blackboard control systems determine what strategies to follow. They determine when to implement successive strategic phases. They determine which heuristics apply in the current problem-solving situation and which ones to adopt. They determine the rule by which to integrate simultaneously applicable heuristics and the rule by which to schedule pending problem-solving actions. In sum, they determine the strategies, heuristics, and integration and scheduling rules that define their own control plans.

Thus, blackboard control systems do not specify 'complete' control procedures or 'correct' combinations of control heuristics. They do not attempt to enumerate (a necessarily small number of) important problem-solving contingencies. Instead, they dynamically construct and modify situation-specific control plans out of modular control heuristics, adapting their problem-solving behavior to a wide range of unanticipated problem-solving situations.

The blackboard control architecture's greatest weakness is its high overhead, combining computational and storage costs. Given today's hardware and operating systems, if one's goal is to build high-performance application systems, the blackboard control architecture is probably inappropriate. Such systems may benefit from intelligent control mechanisms, but they are bound by severe computational and storage constraints. Because the blackboard control architecture exacerbates, rather than ameliorates these problems, it would ordinarily be too inefficient for a final application system.

On the other hand, the blackboard control architecture offers an extremely flexible and modular environment for experimental development of application systems prior to reimplementation in a high-performance environment. The architecture permits system builders to introduce, modify, and remove control knowledge sources independently. It permits them to exploit previous system development efforts by transferring and combining control knowledge sources from different application systems. If the control knowledge sources configured for an application system entail a relatively simple control plan that is effective for all of the specific problems the application system must solve, the system builder can compile them in a more efficient, run-time control procedure.

Returning to the motivations set forth in the introduction to this paper, the blackboard control architecture provides a framework and mechanism for intelligent control behavior. Blackboard control systems do not simply solve problems. They know something about how they solve problems, why they perform one problem-solving action rather than another, and what problem-solving actions they are likely to perform in the future. They use this knowledge to adapt their behavior to the demands of dynamic problem-solving situations. Research in progress exploits this knowledge to produce intelligent explanation and learning behaviors.

ACKNOWLEDGMENT

This work was supported by a DARPA grant to the Heuristic Programming Project at Stanford University and by an ONR contract to the Rand Corporation. Lee Erman, Frederick Hayes-Roth, Perry Thorndyke, and an anonymous reviewer provided helpful comments on an earlier version of the manuscript. Special thanks to Mark Stefik for editorial assistance and to Edward Feigenbaum for sponsoring the work.

REFERENCES

1. Barnett, J.A. and Erman, L.D., Making control decisions in an expert system is a problem-solving task, Tech. Rept., USC/Information Sciences Institute, 1982.

2. Clancey, W.J., The advantages of abstract control knowledge in expert system design, Tech. Rep. HPP-83-17, Stanford University, Stanford, CA, 1983.

3. Clancey, W.J., Acquiring, representing, and evaluating a competence model of diagnostic strategy, Tech. Rept. HPP-84-2, Stanford University, Stanford, CA, 1984.

4. Corkill, D.D. and Lesser, V.R., A goal-directed Hearsay-II architecture: Unifying data-directed and goal-directed control, in: Proceedings National Conference on Artificial Intelligence, Pittsburgh, PA, 1982.

5. Davis, R., Applications of meta level knowledge to the construction, maintenance, and use of large knowledge bases, Tech. Rept. Memo AIM-283, Stanford University, Artificial Intelligence Laboratory, Stanford, CA, 1976.

6. Doyle, J., A truth maintenance system, Artificial Intelligence 15 (1980) 179–222.

7. Erman, L.D., Hayes-Roth, F., Lesser, V.R. and Reddy, D.R., The Hearsay-II speech-understanding system: Integrating knowledge to resolve uncertainty. Computing Surveys 12 (1980) 213–253.

8. Erman, L.D., London, P.E. and Fickas, S.F., The design and an example use of Hearsay-III, in: Proceedings Seventh International Joint Conference on Artificial Intelligence, Vancouver, BC (1981) 409–415.

9. Genesereth, M.R. and Lenat, D.B., Self-description and -modification in a knowledge representation language, Tech. Rept. HPP-80-10, Stanford University, Stanford, CA, 1980.

10. Genesereth, M.R. and Smith, D.E., Meta-level architecture, Tech. Rept. HPP-81-6, Stanford University, Stanford, CA, 1982.

11. Hanson, A. and Riseman, E., VISIONS: A computer system for interpreting scenes, in: A. Hanson and E. Riseman (Eds.), Computer Vision Systems (Academic Press, New York, 1978).

12. Hasling, D.W., Clancey, W.J. and Rennels, G., Strategic explanations for a diagnostic consultation system, Tech. Rept. STAN-CS-83-996, Stanford University, Stanford, CA, 1983.

13. Hayes-Roth, B, Flexibility in executive processes, Tech. Rept. N-1170-ONR, Rand Corporation, Santa Monica, CA, 1980.

14. Hayes-Roth, B., BB1: An architecture for blackboard systems that control, explain, and learn about their own behavior, Tech. Rept. HPP-84-16, Stanford University, Stanford, CA, 1984.

15. Hayes-Roth, B. and Hayes-Roth, F., A cognitive model of planning, Cognitive Sci. 3 (1979) 275–310.

16. Hayes-Roth, B., Hayes-Roth, F., Rosenschein, S. and Cammarata, S., Modelling planning as an incremental, opportunistic process, in: Proceedings Sixth International Joint Conference on Artificial Intelligence, Tokyo, Japan (1979) 375–383.

17. Hayes-Roth, F. and Lesser, V.R., Focus of attention in the Hearsay-II speech understanding system, in: Proceedings Fifth International Joint Conference on Artificial Intelligence, Cambridge, MA (1977) 27–35.

18. Hudlicka, E. and Lesser, V.R., Meta-level control through fault detection and diagnosis, Tech. Rept., University of Massachusetts, Amherst, MA, 1984.

19. Laird, J.E., Universal subgoaling, Tech. Rept., Carnegie-Mellon University, Pittsburgh, PA, 1984.

20. Lenat, D.B., Davis, R., Doyle, J., Genesereth, M., Goldstein, I. and Schrobe, H., Reasoning about reasoning, in: F. Hayes-Roth, D.A. Waterman and D.B. Lenat, (Eds.), Building Expert Systems (Addison-Wesley, Reading, MA, 1983).

21. Lesser, V.R. and Corkill, D., Functionally accurate cooperative distributed systems, IEEE Trans. Systems, Man, Cybernetics 1 (1981) 81–96.

22. McCarthy, J., Programs with common sense, in: Proceedings Teddington Conference on the Mechanization of Thought Processes, 1960.

23. Nagao, M., Matsuyama, T. and Mori, H., Structured analysis of complex photographs, in: Proceedings Sixth International Joint Conference on Artificial Intelligence, Tokyo, Japan (1979) 610–616.

24. Newell, A.. Shaw, J.C. and Simon, H.A., Report on a general problem-solving program, in: Proceedings International Conference on Information Processing, 1959.

25. Nii, H.P. and Aiello, N., AGE (attempt to generalize): A knowledge-based program for building knowledge-based programs, in: *Proceedings Sixth International Joint Conference on Artificial Intelligence*, Toyko, Japan (1979) 645–655.
26. Nii, H.P., Feigenbaum, E.A., Anton, J.J. and Rockmore, A.J., Signal-to-symbol transformation: HASP/SIAP case study. *AI Magazine* 3 (1982) 23–35.
27. Smith, B., Reflection and semantics in a procedural language, Tech. Rept. MIT-TR-272, Cambridge, MA, 1982.
28. Smith, B. and Rivieres J.D., Interim 3-LISP Reference Manual. Tech. Rept., XEROX PARC, Palo Alto, CA, 1984.
29. Stefik, M., Planning and meta-planning (MOLGEN: Part 2), *Artificial Intelligence* **16** (1981) 141–169.
30. Terry, A., Hierarchical control of production systems, Ph.D. Thesis, University of California, Irvine, CA, 1983.
31. Van Melle, W., A domain-independent production-rule system for consultation programs, in: *Proceedings Sixth International Joint Conference on Artificial Intelligence*, Tokyo, Japan (1979) 923–925.
32. Weyrauch, R.W., Prolegomena to a theory of mechanized formal reasoning, *Artificial Intelligence* **13** (1980) 133–170.
33. Wilensky, R., *Planning and Understanding* (Addison-Wesley, Reading, MA, 1983).

Appendix A. OPM: A Blackboard Control System for Multiple-Task Planning

OPM [16] is a blackboard control system that solves multiple-task planning problems like the one described in Section 2. This appendix presents excerpts from one of OPM's problem-solving traces to illustrate some of the possible behaviors of a blackboard control system and its achievement of the behavioral goals set forth in section 2.

OPM includes the following higher-level control knowledge sources:

- Accept-Problem is triggered by user input and creates a corresponding Problem decision.
- Modify-Criterion is triggered by a new Problem decision and, if necessary, refines the Problem Criterion. When there is insufficient time to perform all requested tasks, it changes the predicate 'all Requested-Tasks planned' to 'all important Requested-Tasks planned'.
- Planning-Policies is triggered by a new Problem decision. It recommends general scheduling Policies favoring recently triggered KSARs, KSARs with general control knowledge sources, and KSARs with efficient, reliable, and important knowledge sources. It also recommends the scheduling rule: let the probability of scheduling a KSAR be proportional to the sum of its weighted ratings on all operative Foci and Policies.
- Refine-or-Chain? is triggered by a new Problem decision. It records either a successive-refinement Strategy decision or a temporal-chaining Strategy decision, as explained in Section 3.
- Implement-Strategy is triggered by either a new Strategy decision or satisfaction of a strategic Focus decision's Criterion. It implements an adopted Strategy as a series of Focus decisions, as explained in Section 3.

- Identify-Gaps-To-Fill is triggered by situations in which some blackboard regions contain fewer or less reliable solution elements than others. It creates Focus decisions favoring actions in those regions.
- Conserve-Resources is triggered when problem-solving time is 75% depleted. It recommends increasing the Weights of Policies favoring KSARs with efficient and reliable knowledge sources.
- Detect-Solution is triggered by the emergence of a plan that satisfies the Problem decision's Criterion. It changes the Problem's Status to 'solved'.

OPM uses these basic control knowledge sources:

- Update-To-Do-Set is invoked by execution of a Chosen-Action. It maintains a single To-Do-Set.
- Choose-KSAR is invoked by updating of the To-Do-Set. It chooses a KSAR from the To-Do-Set's Invocable-List, validates its Pre-Conditions, and records it as a Chosen-Action.
- Interpret-KSAR is invoked by creation of a Chosen-Action, which it executes.

These knowledge sources correspond to control heuristics derived from thinking-aloud protocols produced by people as they performed the multiple-task planning task. They control a version of OPM containing approximately fifty domain knowledge sources. They operate on the control blackboard defined in Fig. 8. In the trace below, they produce the control plan abstracted in the top panel of Fig. A.1.

A.1. Character of the problem-solving process

Fig. A.1 abstracts a protocol of OPM's problem-solving behavior for a single planning problem. Each number in Fig. A.1 represents a decision generated on a particular problem-solving cycle. Thus, the number 1 represents the decision made on cycle 1, the number 2 represents the decision made on cycle 2, and so forth. An ordered pair of numbers represents an ordered series of decisions. Thus, 140–143 represents the series 140, 141, 142, 143, while 88–84 represents the reverse series 88, 87, 86, 85, 84.

Placement of a number reflects three factors. First, placement on the upper or lower blackboard indicates whether the decision was a control or problem decision. Second, vertical placement within a blackboard indicates the decision's level of abstraction. For simplicity, control decisions at To-Do-Set and Chosen-Action levels do not appear in Fig. A.1. However, it should be understood that decisions at these two levels precede each decision that does appear. Third, horizontal span within a blackboard level designates the solution interval encompassed by a decision. For the control blackboard, solution interval refers to the sub-sequence of problem-solving cycles encompassed by a decision. For the domain blackboard, solution interval refers to the sub-sequence of Operation-level plan elements encompassed by a decision.

Decisions on the control blackboard reflect OPM's orderly generation of a simple, well-defined control plan for this problem:

(1) Accept-Problem, triggered by input of the user's problem, creates decision 1, which describes the problem to be solved and remains operative for the entire problem-solving process.

(2) Planning-Policies, triggered by creation of the Problem, creates decision 2, which establishes general scheduling Policies that apply throughout the problem-solving process.

(3) Modify-Criterion, also triggered by creation of the Problem, creates decision 3, which changes the original Criterion predicate, 'all Requested-Tasks planned' to 'all important Requested-Tasks planned'.

(4) Refine-or-Chain?, also triggered by creation of the Problem, creates decision 4, the successive-refinement Strategy that remains opeative for the duration of the problem-solving process.

(5) Implement-Strategy, triggered by creation of the Strategy, creates decision 5, an Outcome level plan.

(6) Domain KSARs execute and develop a complete Outcome level plan.

(7) Implement-Strategy, triggered by completeion of the Outcome level plan, creates decision 20, the Design level Focus.

(8) Domain KSARs execute, some of which develop a complete Design level plan.

(9) Implement-Strategy, triggered by completion of the Design level plan, creates decision 45, the Procedure level Focus.

(10) Domain KSARs execute.

(11) Identify-Gaps-To-Fill, triggered by a solution gap in the interval 2:00–4:00, creates decision 52, a Focus on that interval.

(12) Domain KSARs execute, some of which develop a complete Procedure level plan.

(13) Implement-Strategy, triggered by completion of the Procedure level plan, creates decision 89, the Operation level Focus.

(14) Domain KSARs execute.

(15) Conserve-Resources, triggered by depletion of 75% of the allowable problem-solving time, creates decision 111, which increases the Weights on Policies favoring KSARs with efficient and reliable knowledge sources to 0.9.

(16) Domain KSARs execute, some of which complete the Operation level plan.

(17) Detect-Solution, triggered by its determination that the current plan on the domain blackboard meets the Problem's Criterion, creates decision 144, changing the Problem's Status to 'solved'.

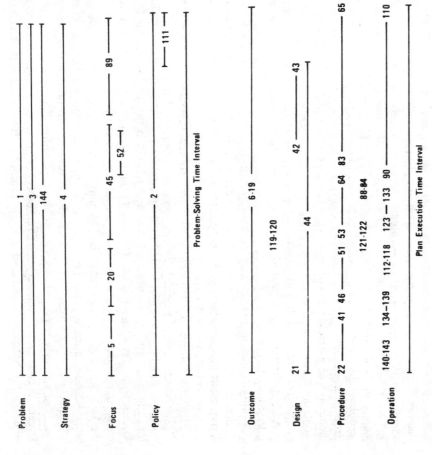

FIG. A.1. Abstracted OPM protocol.

The simplicity of the control plan and the orderliness with which it is generated reflect the small number of control knowledge sources in the system and their excellent fit to this particular problem.

By contrast, decisions on the domain blackboard show the highly opportunistic generation of solution elements that is characteristic of blackboard systems. Decisions generated on successive problem-solving cycles may be at higher or lower levels of abstraction than their predecessors. They may encompass larger or smaller, overlapping or non-overlapping, earlier or later plan intervals. However, let us consider the generation of plan elements separately for the two blackboard dimensions.

A.2. Planning at different levels of abstraction

Fig. A.2 ignores solution interval and plots the level of abstraction for domain decisions as a function of cycle in the problem-solving process. Again, an ordered pair of numbers represents an ordered sequence of decisions. Each 'F' represents a control decision to focus on KSARs at the designated level of abstraction.

As Fig. A.2 shows, domain decisions conform roughly to the series of Focus

by combining its name and triggering event number. Thus, the first KSAR on this To-Do-Set is Try-Cluster-042.

The example begins on problem-solving cycle 43. On previous cycles, OPM adopted a highly Weighted (0.9) successive-refinement Strategy and the following Policies and Weights: Trigger-Recency = high, 0.9; Trigger-Weight = high, 0.5; KS-Efficiency = high, 0.3; KS-Credibility = high, 0.5; Action-Blackboard = 'Control', 0.9; and KS-Importance = high, 0.9. OPM has completed a satisfactory Outcome level plan. Its current Strategic Focus (Weight = 0.9) is on KSARs whose actions occur at the Design level. It has begun making decisions at that level.

Cycle 43:
Focus = Design

To-Do-Set =

Try-Cluster	E-042	Domain	Design
Notice-Proximity	E-041	Domain	Procedure
Try-Beeline	E-034	Domain	Operation
Try-Artery	E-034	Domain	Operation
Set-Start-Or-End	E-033	Domain	Procedure
Try-Cluster	E-011	Domain	Design
Try-Loop	E-011	Domain	Design
Try-Sweep	E-011	Domain	Design
Try-Forward	E-011	Domain	Procedure

Chosen-Action = Try-Cluster-042

Event 43—Design Decision:
Organize the plan around the cluster of errands in the southeast part of town.

On cycle 43, the To-Do-Set contains nine domain KSARs. Try-Cluster-042 is the most recent and its Action is in the Design Focus. None of the other KSARs is both recent and in Focus. None has any other highly weighted scheduling attributes. Therefore, under OPM's probabilistic scheduling rule, Choose-KSAR is most likely to schedule Try-Cluster-042 and, as indicated below the To-Do-Set, it does. Choose-KSAR creates a new Design decision to organize the plan around a previously identified cluster of errands.

Cycle 44:
Focus = Design

To-Do-Set =

Use-Cluster-C	E-043	Domain	Design
Notice-Proximity	E-041	Domain	Procedure
Try-Beeline	E-034	Domain	Procedure
Try-Artery	E-034	Domain	Procedure
Set-Start-Or-End	E-033	Domain	Procedure
Try-Cluster	E-011	Domain	Design
Try-Loop	E-011	Domain	Design
Try-Sweep	E-011	Domain	Design
Try-Forward	E-011	Domain	Procedure

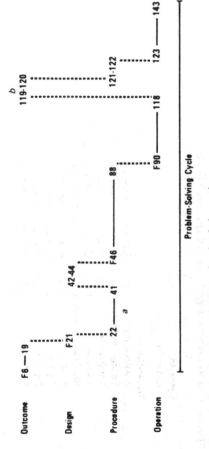

FIG. A.2. Strategic opportunism over levels of abstraction.

decisions prescribed by the successive-refinement Strategy decision. An initial series of Outcome decisions leads to series of Design decisions, Procedure decisions, and Operation decisions. This progression reflects Choose-KSAR's adaptation to heavily weighted strategic Focus decisions. It uses less heavily weighted, non-strategic Policy and Focus decisions mainly to discriminate among alternative KSARs in the current strategic Focus. However, there are two deviations from the top-down pattern, marked as 'a' and 'b' in Fig. A.2. First, a preliminary series of Procedure decisions intervenes early in the Design series. Second, pairs of Outcome and Procedure decisions intervene in the Operation series. These deviations reflect Choose-KSAR's potential to adapt to non-strategic Policies and Foci in favor of even a heavily weighted strategic Focus under the probabilistic scheduling rule. The following discussion illustrates the control decisions underlying both the strategic top-down progression and the opportunistic deviations illustrated in Fig. A.2.

A.2.1. *Strategic top-down domain planning*

First, let us examine the control decisions underlying the top-down progression from Design to Procedure levels.

In the discussion below, To-Do-Sets are condensed for brevity and stylized for comprehensibility. To illustrate, the first KSAR in the To-Do-Set for Cycle 43, below, is 'Try-Cluster E-042 Domain Design'. It represents the triggering of knowledge source 'Try-Cluster' by event 42. The next two words indicate that the KSAR's Action-Blackboard is 'Domain' and its Action-Level is 'Design'. Some KSARs in subsequent To-Do-Sets also indicate that their KS-Importance is 'Important'. The To-Do-Set lists KSARs in reverse chronological order, with the most recently triggered KSARs at the top. Other KSAR attributes (e.g., Trigger-Weight, KS-Efficiency, KS-Credibility) are omitted because they do not influence the behavior illustrated in these examples. Each KSAR is referred to

Chosen-Action = Use-Cluster-C-043

Event 44—Design Decision:
Travel from the florist to the southeast cluster and then to the final destination, doing errands on the way.

The new To-Do-Set on cycle 44 contains a new KSAR, Use-Cluster-C-043. It also contains the unexecuted KSARs remaining from the previous To-Do-Set. Again, because Use-Cluster-C-043 is the only KSAR that is both very recent and in Focus, Choose-KSAR schedules it. Choose-KSAR creates a new Design decision encompassing the entire plan.

Cycle 45:
Focus = Design

To-Do-Set =

Implement-Strategy	E-044	Control	Focus
Try-Forward	E-044	Domain	Procedure
Notice-Proximity	E-041	Domain	Procedure
Try-Beeline	E-034	Domain	Operation
Try-Artery	E-034	Domain	Operation
Set-Start-Or-End	E-033	Domain	Procedure
Try-Cluster	E-011	Domain	Design
Try-Loop	E-011	Domain	Design
Try-Sweep	E-011	Domain	Design
Try-Forward	E-011	Domain	Procedure

Chosen-Action = Implement-Strategy-044

Event 45—Focus Decision:
Prefer KSARs that operate at the Procedure level.

On cycle 45, the To-Do-Set contains two new KSARs, Implement-Strategy-044 and Try-Forward-044, along with all of the previously unexecuted KSARs. Implement-Strategy is a control knowledge source, triggered by completion of the Design level plan, whose action is at the Focus level. It is also one of the two most recently triggered knowledge sources. Choose-KSAR schedules it. Implement-Strategy changes the Status of the Design level Focus to 'inoperative' and creates a new Procedure level Focus.

Cycle 46:
Focus = Procedure

To-Do-Set =

Try-Forward	E-044	Domain	Procedure
Notice-Proximity	E-041	Domain	Procedure
Try-Beeline	E-034	Domain	Operation
Try-Artery	E-034	Domain	Operation
Set-Start-Or-End	E-033	Domain	Procedure
Try-Cluster	E-011	Domain	Design
Try-Loop	E-011	Domain	Design
Try-Sweep	E-011	Domain	Design
Try-Forward	E-011	Domain	Procedure

Chosen-Action = Notice-Proximity-041

Event 46—Procedure Decision:
The movie is on Cedar Street, which is too far from the florist and in the wrong direction.

On cycle 46, there are no new KSARs. However, notice the changes in which KSARs are in Focus. Where Try-Cluster-011, Try-Loop-011, and Try-Sweep-011 were in the Design Focus on cycle 45, they are not in the new Procedure Focus on cycle 46. Conversely, the previously unfocused KSARs Try-Forward-044, Notice-Proximity-041, Set-Start-Or-End-033, and Try-Forward-011 are in the new Procedure Focus.

This cycle also illustrates the impact of Choose-KSAR's probabilistic scheduling rule. Because KSAR Try-Forward-044 is the most recent KSAR and in Focus, Choose-KSAR is most likely to schedule it, but in this case it does not. Instead, it schedules Notice-Proximity-041, which is also in Focus, but slightly less recent and, therefore, slightly less likely to be scheduled. Notice-Proximity-041 produces the first decision in the newly Focused Procedure level series.

In summary, this excerpt of OPM's behavior shows how it incrementally and dynamically implements the planned sequence of problem-solving activities prescribed by the successive-refinement Strategy: (a) Choose-KSAR adapts to an operative Strategic Focus, scheduling domain actions at the Design level; (b) the scheduled domain actions produce a Design level solution, which triggers Implement-Strategy; (c) Choose-KSAR, adapting to an operative Policy favoring control knowledge sources, schedules Implement-Strategy, which changes the Strategic Focus to the Procedure level; and (d) Choose-KSAR adapts to the new Strategic Focus, scheduling actions at the Procedure level. The result is top-down development of the domain plan.

A.2.2. Opportunistic bottom-up domain planning

Now let us examine the control decisions underlying the opportunistic deviation marked 'b' in Fig. A.2. The example begins on cycle 118. OPM has developed a complete plan at Outcome, Design, and Procedure levels. Its current Strategic Focus is on KSARs whose Action-Level is 'Operation'. OPM has begun making decisions at that level and is in the process of plotting a route from the vet to the watch repair store.

Cycle 118:
Focus = Operation

To-Do-Set =

Try-Artery	E-117	Domain	Operation
Extend-Route	E-117	Domain	Operation
[Rest of To-Do-Set]			

Scheduled-Action = Extend-Route-117

Event 118—Operation Decision:
Continue east on Oak Street toward the watch repair store

On cycle 118, the To-Do-Set contains two new KSARs, Try-Artery-117 and Extend-Route-117, both in the Operation Focus. Choose-KSAR is equally likely to schedule either of the two KSARs. (Other KSARs on the To-Do-Set have lower scheduling probabilities and are omitted for brevity.) It schedules Extend-Route-117, which creates the decision to continue east on Oak Street toward the watch repair store.

Cycle 119:
Focus = Operation

To-Do-Set =

Notice-Other-Tasks	E-118	Domain	Outcome	Important
Extend-Route	E-118	Domain	Operation	
Try-Artery	E-117	Domain	Operation	
[Rest of To-Do-Set]				

Scheduled-Action = Notice-Other-Tasks-118

Event 119—Outcome Decision:
The newsstand is very convenient to the route from the vet to the watch repair

On cycle 119, there are two new KSARs. Extend-Rule-118 is in the Operation Focus, while Notice-Other-Tasks-118 is not. However, Notice-Other-Tasks is a very important knowledge source. It notices when tasks previously excluded from the plan turn out to be very convenient, given the detailed specification of the plan. Thus, Notice-Other-Tasks is a bottom-up knowledge source that generates Outcome decisions on the basis of prior Operation decisions. Because the Operation level Focus and the KS-Importance Policy have equal Weights, Choose-KSAR is equally likely to schedule either KSAR. It schedules Notice-Other-Tasks-118, producing the observation that the newsstand, a previously excluded task, is convenient to the planned route from the vet to the watch repair.

Cycle 120:
Focus = Operation

To-Do-Set =

Insert-New-Outcome	E-119	Domain	Outcome	Important
Extend-Route	E-118	Domain	Operation	
Try-Artery	E-117	Domain	Operation	
[Rest of To-Do-Set]				

Scheduled-Action = Insert-New-Outcome-119

Event 120—Outcome Decision:
Include the newsstand in the plan

On cycle 120, the To-Do-Set contains a new KSAR, Insert-New-Outcome-119. Insert-New-Outcome is also an important knowledge source that incorporates a convenient task in the Outcome level plan. Because it is also the most recent KSAR in the To-Do-Set, Choose-KSAR schedules it, adding the newsstand to the Outcome level plan.

Cycle 121:
Focus = Operation

To-Do-Set =

Patch-Procedure	E-120	Domain	Procedure	Important
Refine-Design	E-120	Domain	Procedure	Important
Extend-Route	E-118	Domain	Operation	
Try-Artery	E-117	Domain	Operation	
[Rest of To-Do-Set]				

Scheduled-Action = Patch-Procedure-120

Event 121—Procedure Decision:
Go from the vet to the newsstand

On cycle 121, there are two new KSARs, Patch-Procedure-120 and Refine-Design-120. Neither is in the Operation level Focus, but because they concern insertion of the new Outcome level task in a previously specified Procedure, they are both important. Choose-KSAR schedules Patch-Procedure-120, producing the Procedure level decision to do the newly planned task, the newsstand, after the vet.

Cycle 122:
Focus = Outcome

To-Do-Set =

Terminate-Route	E-121	Domain	Operation	
Refine-Design	E-120	Domain	Procedure	Important
Extend-Route	E-118	Domain	Operation	
Try-Artery	E-117	Domain	Operation	
[Rest of To-Do-Set]				

Scheduled-Action = Refine-Design-120

Event 122—Procedure Decision:
Go from the newsstand to the watch repair

On cycle 122, there is one new KSAR, Terminate-Route-121, which is in the Operation Focus. Being most recent and in Focus, Terminate-Route-121 has the highest probability of being scheduled. However, because Refine-Design-120 is important and relatively recent, it also has a relatively high probability of being scheduled. Again demonstrating the effects of its probabilistic scheduling rule, Choose-KSAR schedules Refine-Design-120, even though it does not have the highest scheduling probability. It produces the Procedure level decision to go to the watch repair after the newly planned task, the vet.

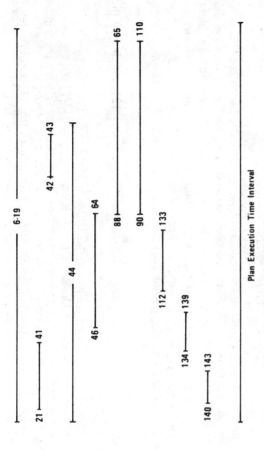

Fig. A.3. No pattern over plan execution intervals.

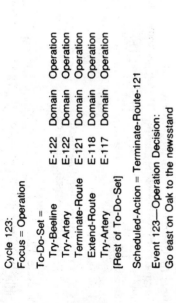

Cycle 123:
Focus = Operation

To-Do-Set =
Try-Beeline   E-122 Domain Operation
Try-Artery   E-122 Domain Operation
Terminate-Route E-121 Domain Operation
Extend-Route   E-118 Domain Operation
Try-Artery   E-117 Domain Operation
[Rest of To-Do-Set]

Scheduled-Action = Terminate-Route-121

Event 123—Operation Decision:
Go east on Oak to the newsstand

On cycle 123, there are two new KSARs, both of which are in the Operation level Focus and, therefore, most likely to be scheduled. In fact, all of the most recent five KSARs on the To-Do-Set are in Focus. Choose-KSAR schedules KSAR Terminate-Route-121. It resumes the Operation level decision series with a decision to go east on Oak Street to the newsstand.

In summary, this excerpt shows how OPM dynamically implements, interrupts, and resumes a planned series of problem-solving activities: (a) Choose-KSAR adapts to an operative Strategic Focus, scheduling actions at the Operation level; (b) Choose-KSAR adapts to an operative Policy favoring important KSARs, interrupting the planned series of Operation level actions by scheduling important Outcome and Procedure level actions; and (c) having scheduled all pending important actions, Choose-KSAR resumes scheduling the planned Operation level actions. The result is strategic opportunism.

A.3. Planning for different plan intervals

Fig. A.3 ignores level of abstraction and shows the progression of plan intervals encompassed by successive decision sequences. A decision sequence is a series of decisions referring to contiguous plan intervals. The set of plan intervals encompassed by a sequence is indicated by a horizontal line in Fig. A.3. For example, the first sequence, at the top of Fig. A.3, comprises decisions 6–19 and encompasses the entire plan. The last sequence, at the bottom of Fig. A.3, comprises decisions 140–143 and encompasses a short, early plan interval including the initial task.

If there were a strong relationship between decision sequence and temporal interval in the plan, Fig. A.3 would show a small number of long decision sequences, all of which proceeded either forward or backward over plan intervals. By contrast, Fig. A.3 displays numerous irregularities in the relationship between decision sequences and temporal interval in the plan. The ten decision sequences in Fig. A.3 include some that are unordered with respect to plan interval (e.g., —6–19—), some that move forward over plan intervals (e.g., 21–41), and some that move backward over plan intervals (e.g., 88—65). Successive decision sequences may reflect overlapping, but not identical plan intervals (e.g., —6-19— to 21–41), forward discontinuity (e.g., 21–41 to 42–43), backward discontinuity (e.g., 112—133 to 134—139), temporal reversal (e.g., 88—65 to 90—111), or some combination of these transitions (e.g., 46—64 to 88—65).

These irregularities reflect the absence of any Strategic Focus on plan interval or specific Policy that systematically discriminates among plan intervals. Any apparent local regularity in Choose-KSAR's scheduling of KSARs encompassing different plan intervals is an artifact of Focus and Policy decisions that really have nothing at all to do with plan interval. For example, a Focus decision that promotes decisions at a given level of abstraction may coincidentally lead to decisions at contiguous plan intervals. A Policy to favor KSARs with recent triggering events may do the same thing. However, because there is no Strategic Focus or Policy that explicitly discriminates among plan intervals, plan generation shows no global pattern with respect to plan interval.

A.4. General comments

The protocol abstracted in Fig. A.1 and analyzed in Figs. A.2 and A.3 represents OPM's performance under the successive-refinement strategy. This strategy was adopted and implemented dynamically during the effort to solve a particular planning problem. Other problems benefit from Refine-or-Chain?'s alternative temporal-chaining strategy: incorporate plan elements in the order in which they would execute in the world. For such problems, OPM adopts the temporal-chaining strategy and produces the opposite results: little or no order in the scheduling of KSARs with respect to levels of abstraction, but roughly sequential scheduling of KSARs for successive plan intervals. These patterns of problem-solving behavior are quite similar to those produced by people solving the same problems with the same strategies.

The analysis in this section shows how the blackboard control architecture combines strategy and opportunism in problem-solving behavior. First, its control knowledge sources generate OPM's several kinds of control heuristics: Strategy decisions to define sequential plans for problem-solving actions; solution-based Focus decisions to emphasize actions appropriate for dynamic problem-solving situations; Policy decisions to impose general scheduling criteria throughout the problem-solving process. Its control blackboard preserves the distinctions among these heuristics in its different levels of abstraction. The blackboard control architecture's three basic knowledge sources (Update-To-Do-Set, Choose-KSAR, and Interpret-KSAR) provide a uniform scheduling mechanism to control OPM's generation of domain and control decisions and to integrate and adapt to the prescriptions of all operative control decisions. The result is the apparently complex problem-solving behavior illustrated in Figs. A.1. However, the decomposition of potential control factors in Figs. A.2 and A.3 reveals the orderly flow of Strategic behavior, overlaid with opportunistic interruptions and resumptions induced by non-strategic Focus and Policy decisions.

Appendix B. Replication of HEARSAY-II and HASP Control Behavior

This section shows how the blackboard control architecture would replicate the idiosyncratic, knowledge-intensive control behaviors of HEARSAY-II and HASP.

B.1. Replication HEARSAY-II's control behavior

HEARSAY-II interprets a subset of spoken English approximately in real time. Beginning with a parameterized representation of the speech signal, HEARSAY-II attempts to identify the data base query it represents. In so doing, it generates intermediate hypotheses regarding the Segments, Syllables, Words, Word Sequences, and Phrases the signal represents. These seven kinds of hypotheses appear at different levels of abstraction on the HEARSAY-II blackboard. The blackboard's solution intervals represent different temporal loci in the speech signal.

HEARSAY-II uses an implicit two-phase control strategy. During phase 1, it operates bottom-up, exhaustively scheduling all KSARs that produce hypotheses at the Parameter level, then the Segment level, then the Syllable level, and finally the Word level. During phase 2, it operates opportunistically, scheduling KSARs that have the highest ratings on several criteria: knowledge

source efficiency, knowledge source reliability, credibility of the triggering hypothesis, credibility of related hypotheses on the blackboard, need for hypotheses in targeted areas of the blackboard. The two-phase strategy was developed through extensive experimentation with a variety of methods and chosen because, of those tried, it worked the best. In particular, it compensates for the uncertainty of HEARSAY-II's low-level signal-processing knowledge sources. Opportunistic scheduling at higher levels of abstraction is effective only after establishing lower-level hypotheses up to the word level with relatively high confidence.

HEARSAY-II's strategy is implicit because the scheduler, which is the only 'official' repository of control knowledge, has no knowledge of it and does not explicitly implement it. In fact, the scheduler has knowledge only of the opportunistic scheduling criteria defined for its phase 2 processing. On each problem-solving cycle, regardless of strategic phase, the scheduler evaluates pending KSARs against its criteria and chooses the one with the highest weighted sum of ratings.

HEARSAY-II achieves bottom-up processing in phase 1 through careful engineering of four knowledge sources (one each for Parameter, Segment, Syllable, and Word levels) to insure: (a) that the appropriate one is triggered on each of the first four problem-solving cycles; and (b) that their actions generate all possible hypotheses at the associated levels in a single execution. In effect, while the scheduler has no knowledge of the bottom-up phase, it has no alternative but to select these knowledge sources in the desired bottom-up sequence. It is only after all four initial KSARs have executed that multiple KSARs are triggered simultaneously and the scheduler exerts any real influence over problem-solving activities. Thus, although HEARSAY-II's speech-understanding behavior follows an implicit control plan, its scheduler does not explicitly execute that plan.

HEARSAY-II implements another scheduling factor independent of the scheduler. A few special knowledge sources monitor the developing solution and create 'shadow hypotheses' to identify blackboard regions where little problem-solving progress has been made. These shadow hypotheses directly trigger relevant knowledge sources (which otherwise would not be triggered), combining triggering and attentional focusing functions in a mechanism entirely outside of the scheduler.

Although this account of HEARSAY-II's scheduler and other control mechanisms omits a few details, it is substantially correct (Lee Erman, personal communication).

Under the blackboard control architecture, eight control knowledge sources, in addition to Update-To-Do-Set, Choose-KSAR, and Interpret-KSAR, would operate as follows to produce the prototypical HEARSAY-II control plan illustrated in Fig. B.1.

(1) Accept-Problem accepts a user-specified problem description and

creates a corresponding Problem decision, thereby initiating problem-solving activity.

(2) Scheduling-Rule, triggered by the Problem, creates Policy1, whose Goal specifies 'maximize the sum of ratings on all operative Foci and Policies'.

(3) Try-Two-Phase-Strategy, also triggered by the Problem, creates a Strategy decision representing the two-phase strategy described above.

(4) Implement-Strategy-As-Tactics, triggered by the appearance of the Strategy, creates a Tactic decision representing the bottom-up phase of the strategy described above.[8]

(5) Implement-Tactic-As-Foci, triggered initially by the appearance of the bottom-up Tactic, creates a Focus whose Goal is 'Action-Level = "Parameter" and Criterion specifies that no Parameter-level KSARs remain in the To-Do-Set.

(6) Domain KSARs whose Action-Level = 'Parameter' execute in an arbitrary order.

(7) Implement-Tactic-As-Foci, triggered by the absence of Parameter-level KSARs in the To-Do-List, creates a Focus whose Goal is 'Action-Level = "Segment" and Criterion specifies that no Segment-level KSARs remain in the To-Do-Set.

(8) Domain KSARs whose Action-Level = 'Segment' execute in an arbitrary order.

(9) Implement-Tactic-As-Foci, triggered by the absence of Segment-level KSARs in the To-Do-List, creates a Focus whose Goal is 'Action-Level = "Syllable" and Criterion specifies that no Syllable-level KSARs remain in the To-Do-Set.

(10) Domain KSARs whose Action-Level = 'Syllable' execute in an arbitrary order.

(11) Implement-Tactic-As-Foci, triggered by the absence of Syllable-level KSARs in the To-Do-List, creates a Focus whose Goal is 'Action-Level = "Word" and Criterion specifies that no Word-level KSARs remain in the To-Do-Set.

(12) Domain KSARs whose Action-Level is 'Word' execute in an arbitrary order.

(13) Implement-Strategy-As-Tactics, triggered by the absence of Word-level KSARs in the To-Do-List, creates the opportunistic Tactic, 'Action = "Opportunistic".

(14) Implement-Tactic-As-Foci, triggered by creation of the opportunistic Tactic, creates a Focus whose Goal is 'All KSARs'.

(15) Opportunistic-Criteria, also triggered by creation of the opportunistic Tactic, creates Policy decisions whose Goals favor KSARs with efficient and

[8] Because HEARSAY-II's two-phase strategy is more complex than either of OPM's strategies, the control blackboard has a Tactic level to permit an intermediate level of Strategy refinement before the Focus level refinement.

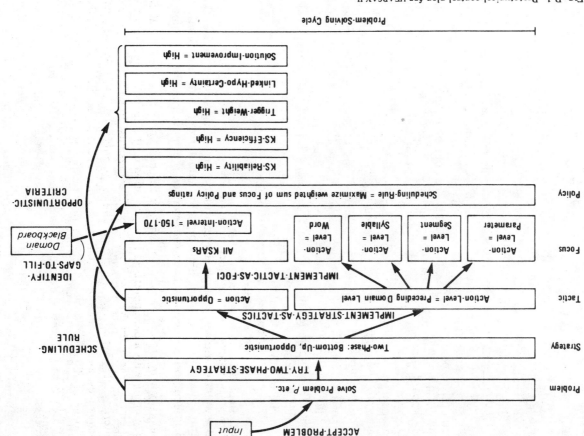

Fig. B.1. Prototypical control plan for HEARSAY-II.

reliable knowledge sources, whose triggering information is credible, that create credible new hypotheses, that link new hypotheses to credible existing hypotheses, and that improve the solution.

(16) Domain KSARs execute in an order determined by the sum of their ratings against these Policies.

(17) Identify-Gaps-To-Fill, triggered by the comparative emptiness of solution interval '150–170', creats a Focus whose Goal is 'Action-Interval = 150–170'.

(18) Domain KSARs operate in this blackboard region and then in other regions.

(19) Detect-Solution monitors the developing solution and, when it detects a solution that meets the Problem decision's Criterion, changes the Problem's status to 'solved' and terminates problem-solving activities.

As the example illustrates, the blackboard control architecture can replicate HEARSAY-II's control behavior while providing several additional advantages. First, as discussed in Section 4, it achieves the behavioral goals set forth in Section 2. Second, it explicates important control reasoning done by HEARSAY-II's system builders, including some that is obscured in the scheduling program and some that is achieved implicitly with other mechanisms. Third, it illuminates control heuristics applicable to different problem domains. For example both HEARSAY-II and OPM use the control knowledge sources Accept-Problem and Identify-Gaps-To-Fill. HEARSAY-II's Implement-Strategy-As-Tactics and Implement-Tactic-As-Foci are computationally equivalent to OPM's Implement-Strategy-As-Tactics and Implement-Strategy-As-Foci. Fourth, it produces a control plan that is easy to comprehend, analyze, and compare to other control plans.

B.2. Replication of HASP's control behavior

HASP interprets sonar signals in real time. Beginning with a coded 'Line' representation of the signal, it attempts to characterize a 'Situation Board' that identifies, locates, groups, and characterizes the movement of all ships and other platforms in a circumscribed area of the ocean. In so doing, HASP generates intermediate hypotheses about the Harmonics in the signal, Sources of harmonics such as propellers or engines, and Vessels such as submarines or aircraft carriers. These five kinds of hypotheses appear at different levels of abstraction on the HASP blackboard. Its solution intervals represents different intervals in the signal.

HASP uses an iterative control strategy based on three event categories: Clock events must be processed before specified target times. Expected events can be processed when specified other blackboard events occur. Simple events can be processed at any time. Within each category, particular types of events trigger pre-determined sequences of knowledge sources. HASP's control program operates on three lists of unprocessed clock, expected, and simple events and a table of event types and associated knowledge source sequences to implement the following procedure:

1. For each currently due clock event, selected in last-in-first-out order, execute the prescribed sequence of triggered knowledge sources associated with the event's type.

2. For each expected event whose specified blackboard events have occurred, selected in last-in-first-out order, execute the prescribed sequence of triggered knowledge sources associated with the event's type.

3. For the most recent simple event, execute the prescribed sequence of triggered knowledge sources associated with the event's type.

4. Repeat 2 and 3 until all expected events and simple events are processed.

5. Repeat 1–4.

Although this account of HASP's control behavior and mechanism omits some details, it is substantially correct (H. Penny Nii, personal communication).

Under the blackboard control architecture, six control knowledge sources, in addition to Update-To-Do-Set, Choose-KSAR, and Interpret-KSAR, would operate as follows to produce the prototypical HASP control plan illustrated in Fig. B.2.

(1) Accept-Problem accepts a user-specified problem description and creates a corresponding Problem decision.

(2) Scheduling-Policies, triggered by creation of the Problem, creates Policy1, whose Goal specifies 'maximize the sum of ratings on all operative Foci and Policies'. It also creates a Policy decision whose Goal is 'Action-Blackboard = Control' and Weight is high and a Policy decision whose Goal is 'KS-Priority = High' and Weight is low. These Policies and their Weights insure that HASP's procedural strategy executes invariably and that, within a specific Focus (selected event), triggered knowledge sources execute in the prescribed order.

(3) Try-Iterative-Strategy, also triggered by the Problem, creates a Strategy decision representing the iterative strategy described above.

(4) Iterate-Strategy-As-Tactics, triggered initially by creation of the Strategy, creates a Tactic whose Goal is 'Triggering-Event-Category = "clock"'.

(5) Iterate-Tactic-As-Step, triggered by creation of the clock-event Tactic, creates a Step whose Goal is 'Triggering-Event-Category = "clock"'.[9]

(6) Iterate-Step-As-Foci, triggered by creation of the clock Step, creates a Focus whose Goal is 'Triggering-Event = E-005 (that is, the most recently generated clock event)'.

(7) All pending domain KSARs with that Triggering-Event execute in descending order of KS-Priority.

[9] HASP's Strategy requires an additional Step level intervening between Tactic and Focus levels.

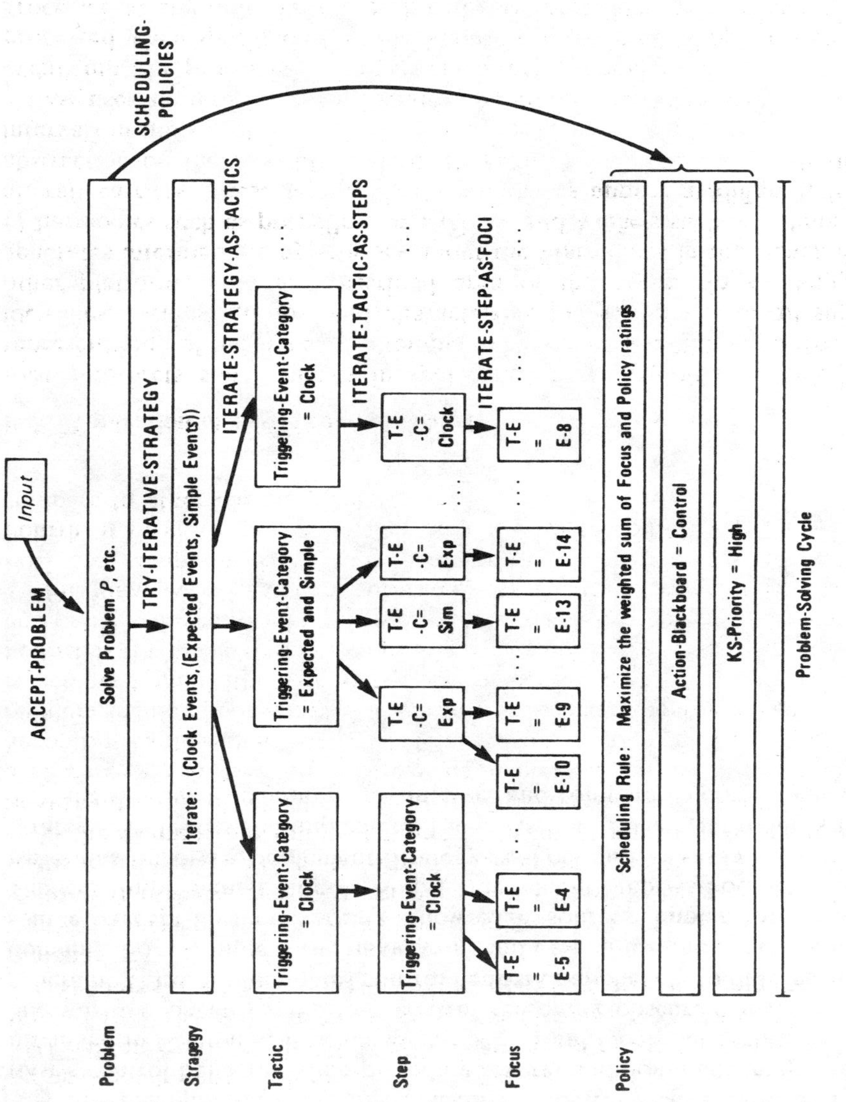

(8) Iterate-Step-As-Foci, triggered repeatedly by the absence of KSARs with the currently Focused Triggering-Event from the To-Do-Set, creates a series of Focus decisions whose Goals specify previously generated clock events.

(9) For each Focus decision, all pending domain KSARs with the Focused Triggering-Event execute in descending order of KS-Priority.

(10) Iterate-Strategy-As-Tactics, triggered by the absence of clock-event KSARs from the current To-Do-Set, creates a Tactic whose Goal is 'Event-Category = "expected and simple"'.

(11) Iterate-Tactic-As-Steps, triggered initially by creation of the new Tactic, creates a Step whose Goal is 'Triggering-Event-Category = "expected"'.

(12) Iterate-Step-As-Foci, triggered by creation of the expected-event Step, creates a Focus whose Goal is 'Triggering-Event = E-010 (that is, the most recently generated expected event)'.

(13) All pending domain KSARs with that Triggering-Event execute in descending order of KS-Priority.

(14) Iterate-Step-As-Foci, triggered repeatedly by the absence of KSARs with the currently Focused Triggering-Event from the To-Do-Set, creates a series of Focus decisions whose Goals specify previously generated expected events.

(15) For each Focus decision, all pending domain KSARs with the Focused Triggering-Event execute in descending order of KS-Priority.

(16) Iterate-Tactic-As-Steps, triggered by the absence of expected-event KSARs from the current To-Do-Set, creates a Step whose Goal is 'Triggering-Event-Type = "simple"'.

(17) Iterate-Step-As-Foci, triggered by creation of the simple-event Step, creates a Focus whose Goal is 'Triggering-Event = E-013 (the most recently generated simple event)'.

(18) All pending domain KSARs with that Triggering-Event execute in descending order of KS-Priority.

(19) If the executed domain KSARs generate new expected events, Iterate-Tactic-As-Steps is triggered again to create another expected-event Step. It is followed by multiple triggerings of Iterate-Step-As-Foci, creating a series of Foci on expected events, effectively reverting to item (12) above.

(20) For each Focus, all pending domain KSARs with that Triggering-Event execute in descending order of KS-Priority.

(21) If there are pending simple events, Iterate-Tactic-As-Steps is triggered again to create another simple-event Step. It is followed by a triggering of Iterate-Step-As-Foci, creating a Focus on the most recent simple event, effectively reverting to item (17) above.

(22) All pending domain KSARs with that Triggering-Event execute in descending order of KS-Priority.

(23) Iterate-Strategy-As-Tactics, triggered by the absence of expected-event

Fig. B.2. Prototypical control plan for HASP.

and simple-event KSARs in the To-Do-Set, updates the Clocktime and creates a new clock-event Tactic, effectively reverting to item (4) above. It continues creating new iterations of the Strategy in this fashion indefinitely.

As the example illustrates, the blackboard control architecture can replicate HASP's control behavior while providing several additional advantages. First, as discussed in Section 4, it achieves the behavioral Goals set forth in Section 2. Second, it explicates important control reasoning obscured in HASP's control program. Third, it illuminates control heuristics applicable to different problem domains. For example HASP, HEARSAY-II, and OPM all use the control knowledge source Accept-Problem. HASP's knowledge sources Implement-Strategy-As-Tactics, Implement-Tactic-As-Steps, Implement-Step-As-Foci are iterative variations on OPM's Implement-Strategy-As-Foci and HEARSAY-II's Implement-Strategy-As-Tactics and Implement-Tactic-As-Foci. Fourth, it produces a control plan that is easy to comprehend, analyze, and compare to other control plans.

Achieving Flexibility, Efficiency, and Generality in Blackboard Architectures

Daniel D. Corkill, Kevin Q. Gallagher, and Philip M. Johnson

Department of Computer and Information Science
University of Massachusetts
Amherst, Massachusetts 01003

Abstract

Achieving flexibility and efficiency in blackboard-based AI applications are often conflicting goals. Flexibility, the ability to easily change the blackboard representation and retrieval machinery, can be achieved by using a general purpose blackboard database implementation, at the cost of efficient performance for a particular application. Conversely, a customized blackboard database implementation, while efficient, leads to strong interdependencies between the application code (knowledge sources) and the blackboard database implementation. Both flexibility and efficiency can be achieved by maintaining a sufficient level of data abstraction between the application code and the blackboard implementation. The abstraction techniques we present are a crucial aspect of the generic blackboard development system GBB. Applied in concert, these techniques simultaneously provide flexibility, efficiency, and sufficient generality to make GBB an appropriate blackboard development tool for a wide range of applications.

I.   Introduction

Blackboard architectures, first introduced in the Hearsay-II speech understanding system from 1971 to 1976 [Erman *et al.*, 1980], have become popular for knowledge-based applications. The interest in the generic blackboard control architecture of BB1 [Hayes-Roth, 1985] is but one example of the increasing popularity of blackboard architectures. The blackboard paradigm, while relatively simple to describe, is deceptively difficult to implement effectively for a particular application. As noted by Nii [Nii, 1986], the blackboard model with its knowledge sources (KSs), global blackboard database, and control components does *not* specify a methodology for designing and implementing a blackboard system for a particular application.

Historically, most blackboard-based systems have been built from scratch, implementing the blackboard model according to the criteria that appeared most appropriate for the particular application. Some implementations were built for execution *efficiency*, with considerable effort placed on providing fast insertion and retrieval

of objects on the blackboard. The KSs and control components in these implementations were so tied to the underlying blackboard database that making modifications to the blackboard structure or insertion/retrieval strategies was difficult. Other implementations were designed with *flexibility* in mind. These applications were built on top of a general-purpose blackboard database retrieval facility (for example, a relational database system [Erman *et al.*, 1981]). While these implementations could be restructured relatively easily, their inefficiency in accessing objects on the blackboard made them slow. Finally, a few implementations were simply built in a hurry, with little effort toward achieving either flexibility or efficiency.

In this paper, we concentrate on the two conflicting issues of flexibility and efficiency of blackboard systems. We show that by appropriately hiding information between three phases of blackboard system development—blackboard database specification, application coding (KSs and control components), and blackboard database implementation—it is possible to achieve both flexibility *and* efficiency. This principle of blackboard data abstraction is an integral design principle of the generic blackboard development system GBB [Corkill *et al.*, 1986]. Abstraction also makes GBB sufficiently general for use in a wide range of applications. Although we describe the benefits of blackboard abstraction in the context of GBB, these abstractions are appropriate for any blackboard development environment.

II.   On Flexibility and Efficiency

Flexibility in a blackboard system is the ability to change the blackboard database implementation, the insertion/retrieval strategies, and the representation of blackboard objects without modifying KS or control code and vice-versa. Flexibility is important for two reasons. First, the application writer's understanding of the insertion/retrieval characteristics and the representation of blackboard objects may be uncertain and therefore subject to change as the application is developed. Second, even after a prototype of the application has been completed, the number and placement of blackboard objects as the application is used may differ from the prototype. This again requires changes to the blackboard representation in order to achieve the desired level of performance. Therefore, it is important that the blackboard implementation provides enough flexibility to allow these changes without significant changes to the KSs, the control code,

This research was sponsored in part by the National Science Foundation under CER Grant DCR-8500332, by a donation from Texas Instruments, Inc., by the Defense Advanced Research Projects Agency, monitored by the Office of Naval Research under Contract NR049-041, and by the National Science Foundation under Support and Maintenance Grant DCR-8318776.

or to the blackboard database implementation machinery. With sufficient flexibility it is possible to actually "tune" the blackboard representation to the specific characteristics of the application.

Efficiency in the insertion and retrieval of blackboard objects is an equally important design goal. Typically, improving the execution efficiency of blackboard systems is achieved through improvements to the quality and capability of the control components. Reducing the number of "inappropriate" KSs that are executed (by making more informed scheduling decisions) can significantly reduce the time required to arrive at a solution. Making appropriate control decisions should never be neglected in the development of an application. In this paper, however, we assume that a high-quality control component and high-quality KSs will be written by the application implementer. We will focus on the remaining source of execution inefficiency—the cost of inserting and retrieving objects from the blackboard.

A. The Need For Blackboard Database Efficiency

Why are we placing such an emphasis on the efficiency of the blackboard database? In addition to inserting new hypotheses on the blackboard, KSs perform *associative retrieval* to locate relevant hypotheses that have been placed on the blackboard by other KSs. This need for KSs to *locate* appropriate information on the blackboard is often overlooked in casual discussions of blackboard-based systems. A KS is typically invoked by one or more triggering *stimulus* objects. The KS then looks on the blackboard to find other objects that are "appropriately related" to the stimulus object. Each KS thus spends its time:

1. retrieving objects from the blackboard based on their "location" on the blackboard;

2. performing computations using existing objects (to determine new blackboard objects to create);

3. creating and placing these new objects onto the blackboard.

The ratio of items 1 and 3 over item 2 defines the amount of time the KS spends interacting with the blackboard versus the amount of time the KS spends performing computations. The larger this *interaction/computation ratio* is, the more that blackboard efficiency issues will dominate performance. The ratio of item 1 over item 3 defines the *read/write ratio* of blackboard interactions for the KS. This ratio can be used to aid the selection blackboard implementation and retrieval strategies.

Note that associative retrieval is central to the blackboard paradigm. Associative retrieval is used to provide *anonymous communication* among KSs by allowing KSs to look for relevant information on the blackboard rather than receiving the information via direct invocation by other KSs. Yet the blackboard provides more than this anonymous communication channel among KSs. Objects on the blackboard often have significant *latency* between the time they are placed on the blackboard and the time they are retrieved and used by another KS. If it were not for this latency, the blackboard could be "compiled away"

into direct calls among KSs by a configuration-time compiler. This latency in blackboard objects indicates that the blackboard also serves as a global *memory* for the KSs. Objects are held on the blackboard to be used when and if they are needed by the KSs. Without the blackboard each KS module would have to maintain its own copy of objects received from other modules. Whether the memory is globally shared (on the blackboard) or private, an efficient means of scanning the remembered objects is still required.

The amount of time a KS spends creating and scanning for objects versus performing other computations (the interaction/computation ratio) varies greatly between different applications and even between different KSs in a single application. Of course, the greater this ratio the more significant the efficiency of the blackboard implementation becomes. Experience with the Hearsay-II speech understanding system [Erman *et al.*, 1980] and the Distributed Vehicle Monitoring Testbed (DVMT) [Lesser and Corkill, 1983] demonstrates that blackboard performance has a significant effect on system performance in these applications.

If the underlying hardware provided true associative retrieval, these efficiency issues would become irrelevant and the implementer would only need to write the application KSs and control code. However, the present hardware situation requires that the associative retrieval of blackboard objects be simulated in software by appropriate retrieval strategies on the blackboard database.

B. Basic Blackboard Operations

Before we continue, it is useful to describe in more detail the blackboard operations that are typically required to support an application.

Insertion: When a blackboard object is created, it must be placed onto the blackboard. Placement onto the blackboard involves creating one or more *locators*, pointers that are used to retrieve the object. In the simplest situation where blackboard objects are merely pushed onto a list, the single locator is the list pointer. With retrieval strategies supporting efficient retrieval of objects based on complex criteria, multiple locators are used. These locators are determined based on attribute values of the object.

Merging: When placing an object onto the blackboard, it can be important to determine if an "identical" object already exists on the blackboard. The semantics of identity depend on the application, but an example is two hypotheses created by different KSs that differ only in their belief attribute. Often it is desirable that hypotheses on the blackboard be unique; that is, no identical hypotheses be created on the blackboard. Instead, the two hypotheses should be merged into a single blackboard object that reflects the two by merging their belief attributes into a single attribute value in the existing hypothesis.

Merging can be handled in two ways. One approach is to have all KSs avoid creating identical hypotheses by checking for an existing hypothesis before creating a new one. If an existing hypothesis is found, its attributes are updated by the KS. The second approach builds an application-specific merging capability into the basic blackboard object insertion machinery.

Retrieval: Retrieval involves searching the blackboard for objects that satisfy a set of constraints specified in a retrieval pattern. Retrieval can be broken down into two steps. The first step determines a set of locators (based on the retrieval pattern) that contain pointers to potentially desirable objects. The second step eliminates those candidates from the first step that do not satisfy the constraints of the retrieval pattern. Since this elimination process can be computationally expensive, an efficient retrieval strategy is one where the first step substantially reduces the number of candidates. In order to implement an efficient, yet flexible, retrieval strategy the constraints must be expressed declaratively so that they may be examined by the blackboard implementation machinery to determine the appropriate set of locators to use in the retrieval.

Deletion: Deleting an object from the blackboard requires removing it from the locators which point to it. Since other blackboard objects may contain *links* pointing to the deleted object, these links must also be found and eliminated. For example, if links are maintained as bidirectional pointers (as is the case in GBB), deleting these links is simply a matter of traversing all links from the deleted object and then eliminating the inverse links.

Repositioning: If the attributes that determine the object's locators (such attributes are termed *indexing attributes*) are modified, the locators may also need to be changed (deleting some and adding others) to maintain consistency in the blackboard database. In many applications, all indexing attributes are static—only the values of the other attributes (such as belief) are allowed to change. Domains involving objects that move over time, however, are examples of situations where the positioning of objects may need to be modified during the course of problem solving.

III. Past Practice

In this section, we characterize approaches that have been used to implement associative retrieval in blackboard systems.

A. The Unstructured Blackboard

A simplistic approach to building a blackboard application is to represent each blackboard level as an unstructured list of the objects residing on that level. KSs add a new object to the blackboard by simply pushing it onto the appropriate list. Retrieval is performed by having the KS scan the list for objects of interest.

This approach only appears to be simple, as there is no work to implementing the blackboard implementation machinery (global variables serve quite nicely). Actually, all the effort has been shifted into the KSs. Each KS must worry about the entire retrieval process, and since each object on the blackboard level must be tested for appropriateness, the KS must perform this test as efficiently as possible. Each KS may also need to worry about merging blackboard objects; avoiding the creation of a blackboard object that is semantically equivalent to an existing object. If merging is not performed, KSs must consider the possibility that semantically equivalent objects may be retrieved

from the blackboard. Insertion, deletion, and repositioning of blackboard objects must also be directly handled by the KSs as well.

B. The General-Purpose Kernel

In this approach, a general-purpose blackboard database facility is provided to the KS and control component implementers. The facility supports blackboard object retrieval based on the attributes of the objects. In its most general form, all attributes of the objects may be used as retrieval keys (for example, blackboard objects may be stored in a relational database). The application implementers retrieve objects by writing queries in the retrieval language. This approach provides a very flexible development environment, but the unused generality of the blackboard database implementation poses severe time/space performance penalties.

C. The Customized Kernel

As noted above, the use of a general-purpose retrieval strategy for all blackboard applications is a source of inefficiency. Retrieval of blackboard objects in a particular application may be made significantly faster using a specialized retrieval mechanism. Furthermore, retrieval of different classes of blackboard objects within a single application may be best achieved using different retrieval strategies. One solution is to custom-code the appropriate retrieval strategy for each situation. In this approach an insertion/retrieval kernel is written that is tailored to the situations that arise in a particular application. When a KS needs to locate blackboard objects, it invokes kernel functions to perform an initial retrieval from the blackboard and then uses procedural "filters" to identify which returned objects are actually of interest. This approach is significantly more efficient then the general-purpose approach when the kernel functions significantly prune the number of blackboard objects that need to be filtered by the KS. However, it poses a number of disadvantages:

- A new customized kernel must be written to suit the different insertion/retrieval characteristics of each application.

- If the kernel is found to be inappropriate to the application, due to incorrect intuition during the initial design or to changing application characteristics, it must be rewritten.

- The KS code is directly coupled to the particular kernel. The code must be written with the knowledge of which attributes are matched by the kernel code and which attributes must be filtered by the KS. Changing the kernel attributes requires rewriting the KSs.

- The kernel code is tied to the blackboard representation. Changes to the blackboard representation require modifications to the kernel code.

- The KS and kernel code is tied to the structure of blackboard objects. Changes to the representation of attributes require code modifications.

In short, although the custom-coded kernel approach can provide efficient insertion and retrieval of blackboard objects, that efficiency comes at the cost of inflexibility to changes in the KS and control code and to changes in the blackboard and object representation.

IV. Blackboard Database Abstraction in GBB

By appropriately combining a number of blackboard data abstraction techniques, it is possible to "have your cake and eat it too" with respect to flexibility and efficiency. The generic blackboard development system GBB [Johnson *et al.*, 1987] provides the application implementer and blackboard database administrator with distinct, abstract views of the blackboard. Developing an application using GBB involves three separate, but interrelated phases:

blackboard & blackboard object specification:
This phase involves describing the blackboard structure (the blackboard hierarchy), the structure of each blackboard level, the attributes associated with each class of blackboard objects (called *units* in GBB), and the mapping of units onto blackboard levels (called *spaces* in GBB).

application coding: This phase involves writing KSs and control code in terms of the blackboard and blackboard object specifications. Application code deals with the creation, deletion, retrieval, and updating of units. Retrieval is specified by patterns based on the structure of the relevant blackboard space(s).

blackboard database implementation specification:
This phase involves specifying the blackboard database implementation and retrieval strategies. The locator data structures appropriate for the particular characteristics of the application are specified in this phase. These specifications are also made in terms of the blackboard structure and unit specifications.

By maintaining an abstracted view of the blackboard, the details of decisions made in each of the three phases can be hidden until they are combined in GBB's code generation facility.

A. Abstracting the Blackboard

In GBB, each blackboard space is a highly structured n-dimensional volume. Space dimensionality provides a *metric* for positioning units onto the blackboard in terms that are natural to the application domain. Units are viewed as occupying some n-dimensional extent within the space's dimensionality.

For example, in a speech understanding system, one of the dimensions of a blackboard space could be *utterance time*. In the domain of vehicle tracking, a space might contain the dimensions *sighting time*, *x-position*, and *y-position*. In GBB, such dimensions are termed *ordered*. Ordered dimensions use numeric ranges which support the concept of one unit being "nearby" another unit along that dimension. In the speech understanding domain, this allows a KS to extend a phrase by retrieving words that begin "close in time" to the phrase's end time.

GBB also supports *enumerated* dimensions. An enumerated dimension consists of a fixed set of labeled categories. For example, in the vehicle tracking domain a space might also have the enumerated dimension "classification" corresponding to a set of vehicle types.

Space dimensionality is a key means of abstracting the blackboard database. It provides information hiding by allowing the application code to create and retrieve units according to the dimensions of spaces, without regard to the underlying implementation of the blackboard structure. Dimensional references, however, contain enough information when combined with information about the structure of the blackboard to allow efficient retrieval code to be generated.

Here is an example of the space definitions from the DVMT application that specifies the *time*, *x-position*, *y-position*, dimensions discussed above (as well as a sensory event classification dimension):

```
(define-spaces (PT PL VT VL GT GL ST SL)
  :UNITS (hyp)
  :DIMENSIONS
    ((time       :ORDERED *bb-time-range*)
     (x          :ORDERED *bb-x-range*)
     (y          :ORDERED *bb-y-range*)
     (event-class :ORDERED *bb-event-class-range*))).
```

B. Abstracting Unit Insertion

When a unit is created in GBB, it is inserted on the blackboard based on the unit's attributes. There are two decisions to be made when inserting a unit on the blackboard. The first is what space or spaces to store the unit on and the second is the location of the unit within the n-dimensional volume of each space. The definition of each unit includes the information required to make these two decisions based on the values of the unit's attributes. This insulates the KS code from the details of the blackboard structure. For example, the KS code does not need to know which attributes and dimensions are actually used to create locators for the unit. Thus changes in the blackboard structure do not necessitate changing KS code.

Here is an example of the hypothesis unit class definition from the DVMT application:

```
(define-unit (HYP (:NAME-FUNCTION generate-hyp-name)
                  (:INCLUDE basic-hyp-unit))
  :SLOTS
  ((belief            0   :TYPE belief)
   (event-class       0   :TYPE event-class)
   (level             nil :TYPE symbol)
   (node              0   :TYPE node-index)
   (time-location-list () :TYPE time-location-list))
  :LINKS
  ((supported-hyps (hyp supporting-hyps)
      :UPDATE-EVENTS (supported-hyp-event))
   (supporting-hyps (hyp supported-hyps)
      :UPDATE-EVENTS (supporting-hyp-event)))
  :DIMENSIONAL-INDEXES
  ((time          time-location-list)
   (x             time-location-list)
   (y             time-location-list)
   (event-class event-class))
  :PATH-INDEXES
  ((node node :TYPE :label)
   (level level :TYPE :label))
  :PATHS
  ((t ('node-blackboards node 'hyp level)))).
```

The *dimensional indexes* define how attributes semantically specify the positioning of hypothesis units onto the dimensionality of a space. (The details of which attributes are actually used in locator construction are specified in the unit-space mapping discussed in Section E.) These specifications include the information required for destructuring when highly structured attribute values are used for unit positioning. Path indexes specify the space(s) on which created units are to reside. A unit is simply created by supplying its attributes:

```
(make-hyp :NODE              *current-node-number*
          :LEVEL             bb-level
          :TIME-LOCATION-LIST time-location-list
          :EVENT-CLASS       event-class
          :BELIEF            computed-belief).
```

C.   Abstracting Unit Retrieval

GBB's basic unit retrieval function, find-units, permits a complex retrieval to be specified in its pattern language. This declarative pattern language provides an abstraction over the blackboard database. A find-units pattern consists of an n-dimensional retrieval specification for particular classes of units on a blackboard space. This means that the KS code need only specify the desired classes of units, the spaces on which to look, and the values for the dimensions.

We will present an example of unit retrieval shortly.

D.   Abstracting the Blackboard Path

Specifying a blackboard space in KS and control code is another area where data abstraction is important. In GBB, the *blackboard* is a hierarchical structure composed of atomic blackboard pieces called *spaces*. In addition to being composed of spaces, a blackboard can also be composed of other blackboards (themselves eventually composed of spaces). This hierarchy is a tree where the leaves are spaces and the interior and root nodes are blackboards. Units are always stored on spaces; GBB's blackboards simply allow the implementer to organize the set of spaces in the system. At a conceptual level, the space upon which to store the unit is specified by the sequence of nodes traversed from a root blackboard node through all intermediate blackboard nodes to the leaf space node. This sequence, which unambiguously specifies a space, is called the *blackboard/space path*. In addition, blackboards and spaces can be *replicated*, which creates multiple copies of blackboard subtrees. These copies of the blackboard structure are disambiguated by qualifying the replicated blackboard or space with a index.

In the original design of GBB, the blackboard path was directly specified in find-units. Even here, the lack of abstraction caused difficulty in modifying the blackboard structure without modifying the application code. For example, consider the DVMT application where the basic data blackboard consists of eight spaces (the abstraction levels SL, GL, VL, PL, ST, GT, VT, and PT). Using a very simple control shell for initial prototyping of the KSs, the blackboard structure might consist of a single blackboard containing the eight levels and another blackboard containing the scheduling queues. Later on, however, a more complicated control shell might be desired which contains a separate *goal blackboard* on which goal processing

activities are performed. The goal blackboard mirrors the structure of the data blackboard, and contains eight corresponding spaces. Specifying complete blackboard/space paths makes such a transition cumbersome, because each call to find-units must be changed to reflect the new blackboard-space paths.

To eliminate this problem, GBB now provides an abstract path specification mechanism which allows blackboard/space paths to be specified relative to other paths, to another space instance, or to the spaces on which a unit instance resides. For example, the path to a stimulus hypothesis's space is coded as:

```
(make-paths :UNIT-INSTANCES stimulus-hyp).
```

The path to the ST level of a hyp in the DVMT application can be coded as: r

```
(change-paths
  (make-paths :UNIT-INSTANCES stimulus-hyp)
  '(:CHANGE-RELATIVE :UP st))
```

where :UP indicates to move up one level in the blackboard/space hierarchy and st indicates to move back down to the ST space.

The path to a corresponding goal space given a hypothesis unit in the DVMT application would be coded as:

```
(change-paths
  (make-paths :UNIT-INSTANCES stimulus-hyp)
  '(:CHANGE-SUBPATH hyp goal)).
```

The following call to find-units illustrates the use of abstraction in unit retrieval:

```
(find-units 'hyp
  ;; We look on the same space as the 'stimulus-hyp' ::
  (make-paths :UNIT-INSTANCES stimulus-hyp)
  '(:AND
     ;; Check for adjacent (in time) hypotheses within
     ;; the maximum velocity range of vehicle movement ::
     (:PATTERN-OBJECT
       (:INDEX-TYPE    time-location-list
        :INDEX-OBJECT ,(hyp$time-location-list stimulus-hyp)
        :DISPLACE      ((time 1))
        :DELTA         ((x ,*max-velocity*)
                        (y ,*max-velocity*)))
       :ELEMENT-MATCH :within)
     ;; Check event class for frequency within
     ;; *max-frequency-shift* of stimulus-hyp ::
     (:PATTERN-OBJECT
       (:INDEX-TYPE    event-class
        :INDEX-OBJECT ,(hyp$event-class stimulus-hyp)
        :DELTA         ((event-class ,*max-frequency-shift*))
       :ELEMENT-MATCH :within))))
```

E.   Specifying the Implementation Machinery

Specifying how locators are to be constructed from unit attribute values is made by defining a mapping for each unit class onto each blackboard space. The mapping is specified in terms of the dimensionality of the space. For example, here is a simple implementation of the levels in the DVMT application where only the *time* dimension is used for locator construction (the other dimensions are checked during the filtering step of the retrieval process):

```
(define-unit-mapping (hyp) (pt pl vt vl gt gl st sl)
  :INDEXES (time)
  :INDEX-STRUCTURE
    ((time :SUBRANGES (:START :END (:WIDTH 1))))).
```

To add in other dimensions into the locator structure, only the mapping declaration need be changed. Here is the same definition implementing a locator strategy for *time* and *x-y-position*:

```
(define-unit-mapping (hyp) (pt pl vt vl gt gl st sl)
  :INDEXES (time (x y))
  :INDEX-STRUCTURE
    ((time :SUBRANGES (:START :END (:WIDTH 1)))
     (x    :SUBRANGES (:START :END (:WIDTH 10)))
     (y    :SUBRANGES (:START :END (:WIDTH 15)))))).
```

The parentheses in the :INDEXES value in the above example indicates that the locators for the *time* dimension are to be implemented as a single vector and the locators for the *x* and *y* dimensions are to be grouped into a two-dimensional array. Without the extra level of parentheses, three vectors of locator structures would be implemented.

F. Abstracting the Control Interface

In GBB, the control interface is separated from the blackboard database implementation by viewing changes to the blackboard as a series of *blackboard events*. Control components are then defined to be triggered on particular events.

An important capability for constructing generic control shells is the definition of basic units (such as basic-hyp) that can be included in the definition of application units. GBB's unit inclusion mechanism (see the definition of the HYP unit in Section B) allows event handling to be appropriately inherited to the including unit's definition. The application implementer does not need to know the details of the event handling machinery in specifying blackboard units, and different control shells can be substituted without changing the unit definitions.

V. Summary

Blackboard database abstraction is an appropriate implementation goal for all the reasons typically associated with data abstraction. In this paper, we have described how information hiding abstractions can be combined to permit a blackboard implementation system to simultaneously provide flexibility, efficiency, and generality. These abstractions are:

1. Viewing blackboard levels (*spaces*) as *structured* n-dimensional volumes, blackboard objects (*units*) as occupying some extent within a space's n dimensions, and retrieval patterns as constrained volumes within a space's dimensions.

2. Extracting the information determining a unit's dimensional extent and the space(s) on which the unit is to be placed (the *blackboard path*) directly from the values of the unit's attributes and from the general (class) definition of the unit.

3. Specifying the constraints of a retrieval pattern relative to the attribute values of another (*stimulus*) unit.

4. Specifying the blackboard path for unit retrieval relative to the path of another (*stimulus*) unit or relative to a particular space instance.

5. Separating control machinery from the blackboard database implementation via the use of *blackboard events* to trigger control activities.

6. Separating the three phases of blackboard system development (blackboard and unit definition, application and control coding, and blackboard implementation specification), but combining the product of each phase in a code generation facility to produce an efficient, customized implementation.

These abstractions are implemented in the current release of GBB, and our initial experience using these information hiding abstractions indicate that they work well at providing flexibility, efficiency, and generality in the development of blackboard-based AI applications.

References

[Corkill *et al.*, 1986] Daniel D. Corkill, Kevin Q. Gallagher, and Kelly E. Murray. GBB: A generic blackboard development system. In *Proceedings of the National Conference on Artificial Intelligence*, pages 1008–1014, Philadelphia, Pennsylvania, August 1986. (Also to appear in *Blackboard Systems*, Robert S. Engelmore and Anthony Morgan, editors, Addison-Wesley, in press, 1987).

[Erman *et al.*, 1981] Lee D. Erman, Philip E. London, and Stephen F. Fickas. The design and an example use of Hearsay-III. In *Proceedings of the Seventh International Joint Conference on Artificial Intelligence*, pages 409–415, Tokyo, Japan, August 1981.

[Erman *et al.*, 1980] Lee D. Erman, Frederick Hayes-Roth, Victor R. Lesser, and D. Raj Reddy. The Hearsay-II speech-understanding system: Integrating knowledge to resolve uncertainty. *Computing Surveys*, 12(2):213–253, June 1980.

[Hayes-Roth, 1985] Barbara Hayes-Roth. A blackboard architecture for control. *Artificial Intelligence*, 26(3):251–321, July 1985.

[Johnson *et al.*, 1987] Philip M. Johnson, Kevin Q. Gallagher, and Daniel D. Corkill. *GBB Reference Manual*. Department of Computer and Information Science, University of Massachusetts, Amherst, Massachusetts 01003, GBB Version 1.00 edition, March 1987.

[Lesser and Corkill, 1983] Victor R. Lesser and Daniel D. Corkill. The Distributed Vehicle Monitoring Testbed: A tool for investigating distributed problem solving networks. *AI Magazine*, 4(3):15–33, Fall 1983. (Also to appear in *Blackboard Systems*, Robert S. Engelmore and Anthony Morgan, editors, Addison-Wesley, in press, 1987 and in *Readings from AI Magazine 1980–1985*, in press, 1987).

[Nii, 1986] H. Penny Nii. Blackboard systems: The blackboard model of problem solving and the evolution of blackboard architectures. *AI Magazine*, 7(2):38–53, Summer 1986.

COPS: A System For Constructing Multiple Blackboards

Luiz V. Leao   Sarosh N. Talukdar
Engineering Design Research Center
Carnegie-Mellon University
Pittsburgh, PA 15213

ABSTRACT

COPS is an environment for distributed problem solving. It provides facilities for distributing blackboards and problem-solving processes over networks of heterogenous computers. Sets of rules, called ambassadors, can be placed at each blackboard, to handle matters of interest to remote processes.

1. INTRODUCTION

COPS was developed in 1986 as a general purpose environment for large engineering tasks. These tasks often require multiple blackboards distributed over a network of computers. For instance, consider the process of designing an artifact. The result of such a process is a set of "aspects," each aspect being a view, or model, of the artifact being designed 7. Sets of specifications, sketches, blueprints, circuit diagrams, and sets of equations are all examples of aspects. The task of the designer is to select aspects and instantiate them so they are consistent, each with every other. A good way to do this is with a network of processes and blackboards, each blackboard being designated to contain one aspect.

In the succeeding material we will describe the facilities that COPS makes available for constructing networks of processes and blackboards.

2. AMBASSADORS

Processes in COPS can coexist in a single machine or can occupy several, networked machines. Each process is treated as a production system and is provided by COPS with a *production memory*, a *working memory.* and an *inference engine.* The user designates some processes to act as blackboards. Other processes can read from and write in the working memories of these processes(Fig.2.1). This "remote writing" is done directly by facilities provided by COPS. However, "remote reading" from a blackboard requires the user to construct an "ambassador."

An ambassador is a group of rules that is placed in the production memory of a blackboard processs. An ambassador represents`the interests of a remote processes and transmit information back to it, allowing knowledge sources to be fragmented and distributed .

Ambassadors are activated by rule-demons that *steal inference engine cycles* on the blackboard process. These triggering demons usually set-up new, temporary lines of reasoning that allow the ambassadors to intervene and exchange working memory elements with their associated processes to report and update their states.

Typical tasks for an ambassador are: to react to patterns of data on a blackboard, to be aware of the state of its remote process, to transfer data this process, to move data from conceptually isolated areas of the working memory (independent variable spaces, separated just by naming conventions, in the implementation) to the blackboard, to interlock with other ambassadors on critical sections of the code or, in summary, to control, modify and move information in the blackboard.

An ambassador can simultaneously represent more than one process . An interesting application is to use an ambassador to allocate work among different clones of the same process. When this is done, we can conceptually abstract the ambassador and the process it represents as a single knowledge source. The performance of this fragmented knowledge source is then a function of the number of clones of the same process in execution.

In this way, the trade-off between performance and resource utilization of the knowledge source can be dynamically adjusted. This control does not have to be part of the knowledge source itself. In act, it is very desirable to avoid that. A more global resource control mechanism can then be implemented, designed to observe the problem solving process in execution and, from a more global point of view, to adjust its resource utilization and performance.

blackboard process

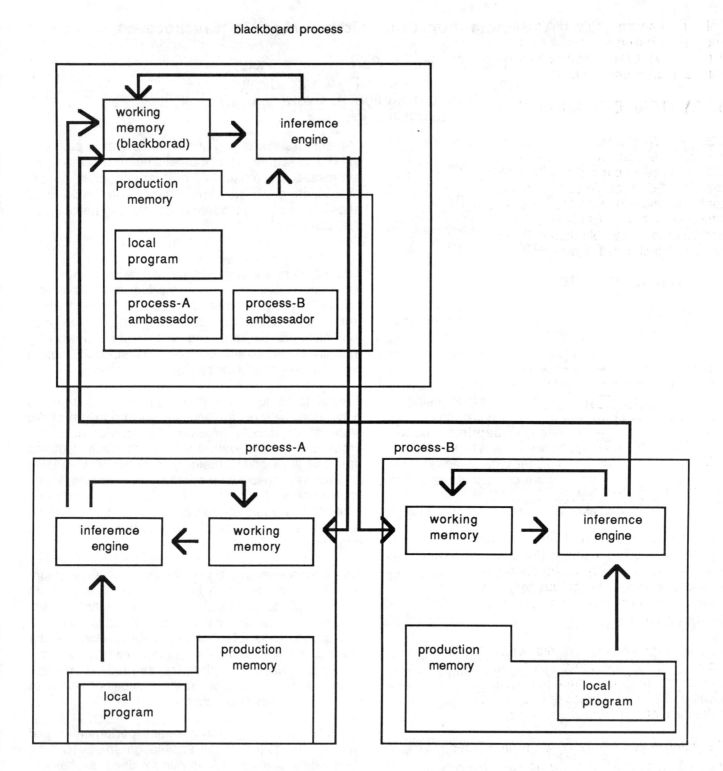

Figure 2-1: Ambassadors allow a rule-based process to work as a *blackboard* .

This mechanism could be itself implemented as a knowledge based system, able to collaborate with the other systems concurrently sharing the computational environment.

3. SYSTEM ORGANIZATION

COPS distributed systems are built by the interconnnection of different kinds of processes. COPS processes are the basic building blocks. They can be used as blackboards, providing the means for control of and communication among the process attached to them. Those blackboard systems can be attached to other blackboards, forming multi-level multiple blackboard structures (Fig. 3.1).

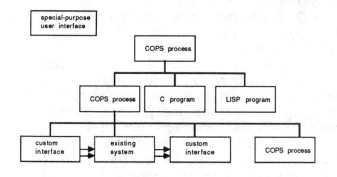

Figure 3: COPS systems can accommodate processes written in other languages by connecting them via pipes to custom interfaces to the message system.

Numerical programs and other nonrule-based code can be included by using a message interface. The usual way is to provide ambassadors that attach them to a blackboard. The ambassadors will perform the integration between the blackboard and the numerical process.

This mechanism only works when the input and output of those programs can be re-programmed to access the message interface routines. There are cases when this is not desirable to even possible, as in the case of commercial packages.

The solution is to write separate interfaces for input and output, connected to the package by **pipes**. The input interface can usually be made very simple while the output interface is usually complex. **Lex** and **yacc**[5] are good options for implementing output interfaces.

Although hierarchial organizations are not enforced, they come naturally from the COPS structure. The mechanism for the creation of process is intrinsically hierarchial, leading to a hierarchial management of the created processes. Accessing an existing process, though, is much more natural in nonhierarchial way.

4. IMPLEMENTATION

4.1 Introduction
We decided to build COPS as an extension of the OPS5 language because OPS5 is well known, widely accepted and readily available.

In COPS, knowledge is represented in the form of productions that are separated into different sets, according to organizations devised during the application system design level. Each set of productions runs in an independent COPS environment as a single process.

A single COPS environment is upwardly compatible with an OPS5 environment. Any existing OPS5 program should be able to run unmodified in a COPS environment. The COPS environment extends the OPS5 environment by allowing productions to write to nonlocal working memories, by providing network-wide process management functions and by also providing a series of inter-process handshaking operations. The COPS inference engine has an execution cycle that differs from the OPS5 inference engine execution cycle, as shown in Figs. 4-1 and 4-2.

In a COPS environment, the working memory can be modified at any moment due to the arrival of a message, corresponding to a write from another process. Those messages arrive asynchronously to the execution cycle of the receiving process. The execution cycle is the fundamental and indivisible execution unit. This means that the contents of the working memory remain undisturbed, from the outside, during the execution of a rule; external writes received during rule execution are delayed until its end.

The concept of *end of execution* when no rule is valid is not true in a COPS environment. At some moment in the future of a process with an empty conflect-set, an external write can result in a nonempty conflect-set, implying therefore that the rule-firing should resume. As a consequence, in a COPS environment, a program only finishes execution when a production explicitly executes a **halt** action.

> *while not halt*
> *match*
> *if conflict-set is empty*
> *then halt*
> *else select*
> *execute*

Fig 4-1:   OPS5 inference engine execution cycle

> *while not halt*
> *accept pending messages*
> *match*
> *if conflict-set is empty*
> *then wait*
> *else select*
> *execute*

Fig 4-2:   COPS inference engine execution cycle. In the case of an empty conflict-set, the interpreter enters a **wait** state, where the working memory is updated at message arrival. The interpreter will continue rule-firing upon a nonempty conflict-set condition.

In a COPS environment, a production can **create** new elements in the working memories of other COPS environments which, of course, may be running remote machines. This is accomplished by the sequential delivery of messages. The two processes involved execute asynchronously. The process which sends the element does not have to wait for its delivery. The sending process has no way of knowing what the state of the receiving process will be when the message arrives, unless the two processes were deliberately synchronized beforehand.

In order to write a remote process, a process must have access rights to it, corresponding to the possession of a valid descriptor for that process. This is usually handled by the process management functions. A process, when creating a new remote process or trying to connect to an already existent one, will receive access rights when it reports back its creation or connection.

The sending and receiving processes do not have to be COPS environments, as long as they use the same communications interface. This way, a nonrule-based program can write and receive information from a COPS process.

An executing COPS environment can optionally assign a remote process as its **blackboard**. From an operational point of view, for the assigning environment, the only consequences are in the process management handshaking and in allowing the use of **post-cops** instead of **send-cops** to write to this remote process.

4.2 Overview of the language

The COPS language is a superset of the OPS5 language. It was part of the effort of this implementation to minimize the number of extensions to the OPS5 language itself, in order to increase compatibility and make it easier to upgrade existing applications to the new environment. For this and other reasons, the process management functions were not included in the language itself, but are a collection of rules that inhabit the production memory with the rule-based application at run time.

The extensions were limited to three new RHS actions (Fig. 4-3):

- **post-cops**, that results in the creation of a new working memory element in the remote recognizes as its blackboard;
- **send-cops**, a generalized *post-cops*, that results in the creation of an element in the working memory of any process to which the executing process has access rights; and
- **wait-cops**, that results in the executingprocess entering a *wait-state*, and staying in this state until an element arrives from a remote process.

Other than some new reserved names, there are no restrictions to the execution of any OPS5 programs in the COPS environment.

4.3 Process management functions

Process management is used here to refer to the functions used to handle multiple processes in a distributed environment. Those functions were implemented in COPS without further extensions to the OPS language itself. There were specific reasons

- to allow the process management control variables to be handled by rules and maintained in the working memory itself, resulting in data thatcanbematched by conditions in rules; this way we can use rules to manage the process resources.

Process management is thus implemented by means of a run time package of rules. Those rules are included in the production memory of every COPS process and, by reacting to the appropriate working memory elements, they execute the necessary functions and communicate with the process management routines. This results in a very flexible mechanism, easily overridden and readapted to special purposes. It allows for the implementation of complex functions without overloading the language. The interface to those functions becomes also somewhat simpler and less rigid than it would be if implemented as new actions in the language itself.

The COPS run-time rule package contains two distinct groups of rules: the service-request rules and the inter-process handshake rules.

Service request rules provide access to the process management functions. By creating an appropriate reserved working memory element type, the running process can perform the corresponding process management function.

There are seven process management service-request working memory element types (Fig. 4-4):

- **cops-name**, names the running process allowing remote processes to create working memory elements in its memory;

- **cops-blackboard**, assigns an existing remote process as its blackboard, also reporting back to that remote reprocess its existence;

- **cops-create**, creates a process on the desired host;

- **cops-kill**, terminates a process on the desired host;

- **cops-connect**, connects to an existing remote process;

```
( p   forward-matcher-out
  ( matcher-out  ↑id <id>   result <result>)
  ( simulation-running ↑id <id>   )

  →

  ( remove1 )
  ( remove2 )
( post-cops matcher-out ↑result <result>) )

...

( p begin-simulation
( diagnostic id <id> )
( cops-token    ↑kind  power-systems-csim
                ↑descriptor <csim> )

  →

  ( remove 1)
  ( send-cops <csim> diagnostic ↑id <id>) )

...

( p wait-point
  ( goal ↑context wait-point)

  →

  (modify 1 ↑context wait-point)
  (wait-cops))
```

Figure 4-3: Examples of post-cops, send-cops and wait-cops (from the TOAST[3] system).

- to keep to a minimum the amount of extensions to the OPS5 language;

- to allow some of the inter-process handshaking operations to be substantially transparenttotheexecutingrule-based application; and

- **cops-disconnect**, disconnects from an existing remote process without terminating it; and
- **cops-error**, handles error conditions.

```
( p  init-csim
  ( start-csim
➔
  ( remove 1)
  ( make post-ready)
  ( makes cops-create
        host h
        command "cops.r sim sim#cops-id# #cops-name#")
  ( make cops-create
        host ius2
        command "cops.r sim sim#cops-id# #cops-name#")
  ( makes cops-create
        host k
        command "cops.r sim sim#cops-id# #cops-name#") )


  ...

( p  quit-kill-local
  ( quit)
  ( cops-process host <host> pid<pid>)

➔

  ( remove2)
  ( make cops-kill host<host> pid<pid> )
```

Figure 4-4:

    Examples of service-request elements: cops-create and cops-kill; the first production will create three different copies of the same simulator (sim) by executing the command line on the appropriate host; the second production will terminate the process <pid> on <host>, originally created by a cops-create (from the TOAST[3] system).

Inter-process handshake rules react to working memory elements usually created by remote processes in the working memory of the running process.

The COPS run-time package essentially consists of rule-demons. Demons are rules that do not have goals or contexts as first conditions (Fig.4-5). They are designed to redirect the attention of the system to some special events, represented by the creation of specific working memory element types.

Demons allow us to perform *cycle stealing* from the current line of reasoning of a running environment

to be changed, allowing for the execution of the desired function.

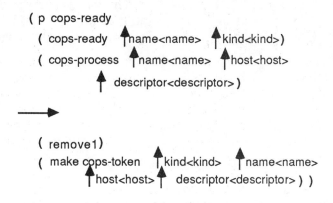

Figure 4-5:

    An inter-process handshake demon: when a cops-ready element is received from another process a cops-token is created (from the COPS run-time rule package).

4.4 Cycle stealing

Because demons can shift the attention of the COPS environment, they are particularly suited to react to arriving working memory elements.

An arriving working memory element is more recent than any other element modified or created in the last rule-firing, even a newly created goal or context. A demon that matches this element as a first condition will fire in the next cycle. By creating a new temporary context it can induce the beginning of another sequence of rule-firing in a different line of reasoning. If, at the end of this line of reasoning, the resulting garbage working memory elements are properly removed and the rule-firings did not interfere with the activities that were being performed, the system should resume execution, unperturbed by the cycles that were stolen from it to perform the different task.

This *interruption* mechanism works at any level of depth. A newly arriving working memory element can fire another demon in the next cycle, changing again the focus of attention. More than one simultaneously arriving element can select multiple demons for firing, resulting in the execution of the demon associated with the working memory element that arrived last. If the application was properly designed, the subsequent demons will fire in order until all situations are treated.

The use of this technique is the key to building robust intellectually manageable distributed systems using COPS. It allows us to conceptually associate tasks with groups of rules. The tasks related to arriving working memory elements will be triggered by demons, interrupting whatever is executing. After the tasks finish, the former chain of rule-firing resumes. Those tasks will eventually synchronize on well defined points, usually on working memory elements that are associated with the global condition of the system. By reasoning with those conditions we can build one more level of abstraction, isolating ourselves from the tasks that create the conditions. Because those tasks are usually asynchronous to the main problem solving line, it becomes much easier to understand and implement the whole application.

5. SYNCHRONIZATION

In COPS, synchronization among concurrent tasks is accomplished by the use of working memory elements to represent events. Waiting for an event is nothing more than having a production that reacts to that particular event (Fig. 5-1).

```
( p  wait-point
   ( goal  ↑  context wait-point )

   ⟶

   ( modify 1  ↑ context wait-point )
   ( call wait-cops) )


( p begin-diagnosys
   ( goal  ↑  context wait-point )
   ( all-open-breakers-known )

   ⟶

   ( modify 1  ↑ context start-diag) )
```

Figure 5-1:

Example of event synchronization: when in wait-point, the event all-open-breakers-known (sent from a remote process) will fire the begin-diagnosys rule (from the TOAST[3] system).

The most basic wait state is a null conflict-set. Only when at least one rule is satisfied, will the system resume execution. This is not a very useful waiting point, except when the environment is almost totally demon triggered.

One can wait for events at waiting-points (Fig. 5-1) or be interrupted when the desired event happens, by having a demon that reacts to it (Fig. 5-2).

Multiple events can be easily synchronized by coding the desired pattern of events as rule conditions. Very complex even combinations can be represented by such rules. Simultaneous waiting for multiple patterns of evens can be obtained by a group of rules, each rule reacting to one of the desired patterns.

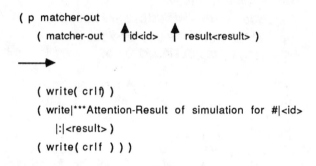

```
( p matcher-out
   ( matcher-out  ↑id<id>  ↑ result<result> )

   ⟶

   ( write( crlf) )
   ( write|***Attention-Result of simulation for #|<id>
      |:|<result> )
   ( write( crlf ) ) )
```

Figure 5-2:

Example of event triggering a demon: whatever is the current line of reasoning, a matcher-out element, created from another process, will trigger the demon and be printed (from the TOAST[3] system).

The production model provides very powerful indivisible read/modify operations, in the form of rules, simplifying tremendously the locking schemes. A rule execution is indivisible, keeping the contents of the working memory stable for the whole execution cycle. This way, all actions in the right-hand-side are guaranteed to be executed together, permitting locking procedures almost as elaborate as desired.

In general, productions are very appropriate to succinctly represent event patterns. They also seem good for mapping our synchronization abstractions into reliable code.

6. AN EXAMPLE

We will use the system Fig. 6-1, a hypothetical blackboard based system, to better illustrate COPS. A couple of different traces of its execution, considered from the point of view of the blackboard process, will be discussed in some detail.

In our example we have a blackboard that creates three processes. The blackboard is a COPS process with different groups of rules in its production memory:

- a **resource-manager**, that controls process creation and termination;

- **ambassadors**, for the created process;

- the **run-time COPS rule package**, that is always loaded in the COPS environment; and

- the **local rule-basedprogram**,that interfaces with the user and does whatever it was designed to do.

We will concentrate on a small portion of the execution, from activation to just after the end of initialization. It is a characteristic of our hypothetical system that at a fixed moment during initialization there is a task for process-A to execute. We will not further detail the functions of this hypothetical blackboard based system in order to keep the example as clear as possible.

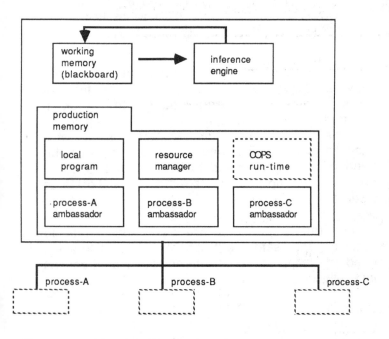

Figure 6-1: A hypothetical blackboard based system, used to illustrate COPS.

One of the possible execution paths is shown in Fig. 6-2. Let's examine it in detail, from the blackboard process point of view.

After the first initialization rule is executed, the resource-manager is activated, possibly triggered by some element created by the first initialization rule. The resource-manager rule that is executed asks for the creation of processes A, B and C. In fact, this rule creates three **cops-create** working memory elements. A COPS run-time demon reacts to those elements and fires, once for each element. Each firing will generate a request for the creation of a process. While they are being created, the blackboard process continues execution; two more rules of the initialization sequence fire. At this point there is already, a task for process-A.

During the execution of the last inference engine cycle an external message arrived, containing a new working memory element that announces that process-B is active. When the execution cycle ends, this new element is added to the working memory. Because it is the most recent element, it shifts the attention of the system. A **cops-active** demon reacts to it and executes, doing the necessary bookkeeping and making a **cops-process** working memory element that informs the system that a process-B is active (and gives the process kind, host, identification number, etc.) At this point a rule in the ambassador positively acknowledges the new process, which will possibly stay in a wait state till there is some task for it to perform.

Initialization continues for one more cycle, when another **cops-active** element arrives. Once more, two cycles are stolen for bookkeeping and acknowledgement after which the local initialization resumes rule-firing. Two more cycles ahead initialization is complete and there is nothing else to do: the conflict-set is empty (the local program is possibly waiting for whatever results it will get from process-A). This causes the blackboard process to enter a **wait-state**.

At the moment when the process-A active element arrives, it is added to the working memory and conflict-set is re-evaluated. This time it is not null: the **cops-active** demon is ready to execute.

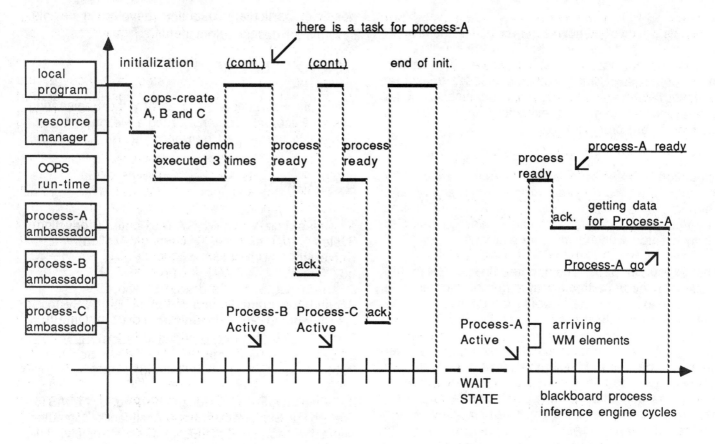

Figure 6-2:   One possible execution path for our hypothetical blackboard based system.

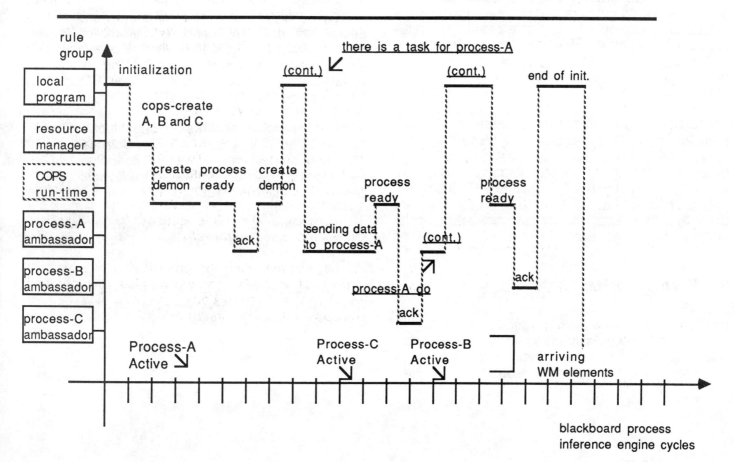

After this positive acknowledgement, the ambassador for process-A finds out that there is a task for process-A and that process-A is active. This results in a sequence of firings by ambassador rules that retrieves the necessary data for process-A. After this, process-A continues executing, in parallel with the blackboard process.

At this point we will abandon the analysis of this execution path. This example detailed how, by inhabiting the cam same production memory and sharing the same inference engine, different groups of rules steal inference engine cycles to react to newly created working memory elements.

The execution path is not deterministic. Had the processes been activated at different moments in time, the execution path would be different, as the one in Fig. 6-3 illustrates.

Here process-A reports itself active much earlier than in the former example (actually with the **cops-active** demon interrupting the sequence of executions of the **cops-create** demon). This way, as soon as there is a task for process-A, its ambassador recognizes it and reacts, obtaining the data much earlier. The ambassador for process-A is itself interrupted when process-C becomes active, but resumes firing rules as soon as process-C's ambassador acknowledges. As a result, process-A begins working on its task much earlier than in the first case, actually resulting in no **wait-state** in the blackboard process before the end of its initialization.

These variations on execution are essentially hidden from the application designer. By reasoning at a rule/condition level, the particular execution path becomes irrelevant. The programmer can be sure that only the appropriate conditions will trigger one particular task. As long as the interactions are controlled, the tasks will execute properly in spite of the particular sequence of events.

7. FINAL COMMENTS

Ambassadors seem to provide a good way for building collaborative mechanisms among knowledge sources distributed over a network of computers. We have found them, and the multiple blackboards they make

possible, particularly useful in developing flexible systems for design automation [7].

ACKNOWLEDEMENTS

This work was supported in part by the Engineering Design Research Center, Carnegie-Mellon University, and in part by Banco Itau S. S. of Brasil.

REFERENCES

1.   Leao, Luiz V. "COPS: A Distributed Production System", Master's thesis, Carnegie-Mellon University, April 1986.

2.   Talukdar, S. N., Cardozo, E., Leao, L. V., Banares-Alcantara, R. and Joobbani, R. "A System for Distributed Problem Solving", Part 1, <u>Coupling Symbolic and Numeric Computing in Expert Systems</u>, J. S. Kowalik (ed.), pp. 59-67, Elsevier Science Publishers, B. V. (North-Holland), 1986.

3.   Talukdar, S. N., Cardozo, E., Leao, L., "TOAST: The Power System Operator's Assistant", Computer Magazine, pp. 53-67, IEEE Computer Society, July, 1986.

4.   Rychener, M., Banares-Alcantara, R. and Subrahmanian, E., "A Rule-based Blackboard Kernel System; Some Principles in Design", *Proceedings of the Workshop on Principles of Knowledge-based Systems*, IEEE Computer Society, Denver, CO, pp. 59-64, December 1984.

5.   Computer Science Division, Department of Electrical Engineering and Computer Science, University of California, "*UNIX Programmer's Manual, 4.2 Berkeley Software Distribution*, Berkeley, California, 1983.

6.   Brownston, L., Farrell, R., Kant, E. and Martin, N., *Programming Expert Systems in OPS5*, Addison-Wesley, 1985.

7.   Talukdar, S. N., Papanikolopoulos, N., Elfes, A. "The TAO of Design", AAAI Workshop on Design, Minneapolis, August, 1988.

TRANSACTIONAL BLACKBOARDS

J. Robert Ensor and John D. Gabbe
AT&T Bell Laboratories
Holmdel, NJ 07733

ABSTRACT

The blackboard architecture is a popular structuring framework for expert systems. With this structure, an expert system is built as a collection of knowledge sources which are scheduled by a controller and communicate through a shared data region, called a blackboard. The performance of such a system may be significantly enhanced by the concurrent execution of the knowledge sources. However, introduction of concurrent execution into blackboard systems requires extension of the architecture with new mechanisms for scheduling knowledge source activities, synchronizing knowledge source interactions, and accessing shared data. This paper describes our design for transaction-based facilities supporting parallel execution of knowledge sources in a blackboard system.

I. INTRODUCTION

The blackboard architecture is an important structural framework for expert systems. In this architecture, an expert system consists of a shared data region (called the blackboard), a set of knowledge sources, and a control mechanism. The blackboard is a data base which is shared by the knowledge sources as their communication medium. Containing rules and hypotheses which express the domain expertise of the system, the knowledge sources respond to each other through observed changes in the blackboard. The control mechanism schedules execution of the knowledge sources according to information from its goal queues and the blackboard.

Several expert systems have been built according to the blackboard architecture. Examples include a speech-understanding system (Erman et al, 1980), a sonar interpretation system (Nii and Feigenbaum, 1978), a vehicular tracking system (Lesser and Corkill, 1978), and a protein crystallography interpretation system (Terry, 1983). Although these systems are founded on the blackboard architecture, they vary significantly within the framework, demonstrating the utility and flexibility of the paradigm. Experience suggests that this architecture is particularly suitable for systems representing multiple areas of expertise and systems solving problems with complex information interdependences.

Multiprocessor computing environments should be capable of increasing the scope and utility of expert systems and successfully addressing problems beyond the reach of most uniprocessors, such as real time speech recognition or robot control. The domain and control knowledge of an expert system may be distributed onto several processors. The interactions of modular knowledge sources may simulate their modeled events, with both communication paths and timing of interactions. Thus multiprocessor configurations have the potential to support the construction and execution of expert systems with new and useful properties.

Multiprocessor computers are often difficult to use. While the processors can execute in parallel, the exchange of data, code, and results among these processors can often make the overall system slow. Therefore, a balance must be reached among the costs of loading code, accessing data, and communicating requests and responses. Two extreme approaches have received most attention by researchers. At one extreme are systems in which processing nodes frequently exchange small sets of data and do small computations with each data set (e.g., Dennis, 1980). At the other extreme are systems that place a large, autonomous program on each processing node. In these systems, the nodes exchange data infrequently and spend most of their time performing "local" computations (e.g., Lesser, 1978). The work described in this paper focuses on supporting systems closer to the latter extreme. We present mechanisms for constructing expert systems as collections of knowledge sources communicating through a shared data medium. These are systems in which knowledge sources executing on different processors perform moderate to large computations between communications.

The integrity of data that is accessed asynchronously by several clients must be maintained. Providing transactional access to shared data bases is a common solution to this problem. A sequence of operations on one or more data elements, beginning with a start-transaction request and ending with either a commit- or an abort-transaction request, a *transaction* is a unit of activity with three properties: atomicity, consistency preservation, and permanence. Atomicity means that, in net effect and even when failures occur, either all operations in the unit happen (the transaction commits) or none of them happens (it aborts). Consistency preservation means that a transaction moves data from one consistent state to another. Permanence means that the effect of a committed transaction persists, surviving any noncatastrophic failures, until the next transaction involving that data is committed.

We extend the blackboard architecture to support systems executing in multiprocessor environments by providing transactional access to the blackboard. Our extensions are novel in their ease of use and in the richness of structure that they support. Two mechanisms are provided for safe access to the blackboard data. Knowledge sources can communicate by accessing shared data in separate transactions. Furthermore, several knowledge sources can participate in a common transaction if they need to see a common, consistent view of shared data.

II. SYSTEM STRUCTURE

Figure 1 illustrates a system that we designed to understand the use of the blackboard. We term the control and knowledge sources *agents* because they are both modular units of activity. The agents are distributed on various processors and may execute concurrently. Knowledge source activities on each node are controlled by the control sources on that node. (The collection of control sources is the controller mentioned in the blackboard architecture description.) In our present implementation, the distribution of agents is subject to restrictions. The initial distribution is specified by the system designer, and we provide no mechanism to support agent migration among processors. Although the blackboard resides on a single machine, it could be distributed without changing its interface.

A. The Blackboard

The blackboard is a repository of data; each datum holds an arbitrary Lisp s-expression. Because agents may share data and reference them in an interleaved fashion, some mechanism is needed to maintain consistency of the blackboard. We associate a transaction manager with this data base, and require that any reference to the blackboard be part of a transaction.

The blackboard transaction manager controls asynchronous references to shared data via locks. There are two types of locks: write and read. The holder of a write-lock has exclusive access to the locked datum and may modify the datum. Holders of read-locks may read the datum concurrently. No writer may access a datum while a read-lock for that datum is held. When a client first references a datum, the transaction manager attempts to obtain the appropriate lock. All locks are held to the end of the transaction in which they were obtained. Thus the transaction manager preserves data consistency by preserving serializability (Eswaran, 1976).

When trying to obtain a lock, the transaction manager might find that it is not available. The transaction that needs the unavailable lock is suspended until the lock can be obtained. Sometimes more than one transaction may be waiting to obtain a lock, and this introduces the potential for deadlock among the waiting transactions. For example, transaction A might wait for a lock held by transaction B, while transaction B waits for some other lock held by transaction A. The transaction manager detects deadlocks and resolves them by aborting a suspended transaction. This abortion is simply reported to the agents participating in the transaction; these agents must then decide what action is appropriate.

Data consistency among agents interacting within a transaction is maintained by time stamps. If serializability among agents within a transaction is violated,

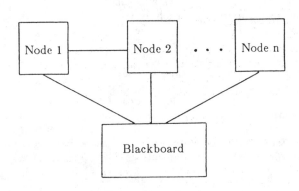

Figure 1a
Network of Processing Nodes

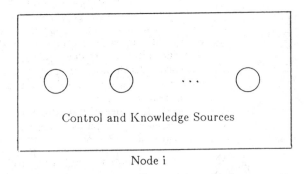

Figure 1b
Agents Within a Node

the blackboard transaction manager aborts the transaction. This abortion is reported to the agents participating in the transaction, as with deadlock detection.

Computation based on the transactional blackboard is not data driven; that is, accessing values in the blackboard does not automatically trigger agent activity. This seems appropriate in a distributed environment because the blackboard might not be able to schedule activities on remote sites. This is in contrast to the centralized case supported in previous proposals (e.g., the Hearsay III approach of Balzer et al, 1980).

B. The Agents

Each knowledge source contains some of the system's domain specific knowledge. This knowledge is expressed in terms of the data visible to the agent – that portion of the blackboard accessible to the agent plus those data sent as message parameters by other agents. As a knowledge source executes, it examines the visible system state. If the system state matches a condition known to the knowledge source, the agent takes specified actions. These actions include requesting that the controller schedule a knowledge source activity by placing an entry on the controller goal queue, performing some operations on the blackboard, and/or sending a message to another knowledge source.

C. Inter-agent Communication

The multiprocessor environment fosters a richness of system structure. Each processor can support a community of agents – complexes of control sources and groups of knowledge sources working closely together – and these communities can interact with communities on other processors. Agents executing on the same machine can communicate with efficiency and facility, for they may directly access common data and may include arbitrary references as parameters in the messages that they send to each other. Since the cost of message transmission between machines is higher than a few memory references on a single one, agents executing on separate machines cannot communicate so cheaply. Further, these agents may include only values in their message parameters, and the conversion of local data to transmittable data values may be expensive. Each node in our system then contains procedures to convert the value of arbitrary s-expressions to transmittable data values. In addition, each communicating agent needs access to procedures to reference these transmitted data values once they have been received.

Agents may also communicate through the blackboard, and two mechanisms are provided for this interaction. Agents can interact by accessing shared data in separate transactions, or several agents can participate in a common transaction. This latter mechanism is often useful; for example, the controller might start a transaction to check the precondition of a goal-queue entry. The knowledge source that the controller then activates might need to access the data mentioned in the goal-queue entry. Because the knowledge source should see these data in the same state as the controller, it continues the same transaction. To include a second agent in a transaction, the first agent merely passes its transaction identifier and status to the second. The transaction status indicates whether the transaction is to be committed, aborted, or continued.

D. Scheduling and Transaction Protocols

The controller maintains one or more goal queues, each comprised of entries generated by knowledge sources. A goal-queue entry has three parts: an expression (called the precondition), an action to be taken if that precondition is true, and a status indicator which may contain a transaction identifier if the action is to continue an on-going transaction.

Scheduling activity by selecting entries from its goal queue, the controller proceeds down the goal queue evaluating entry preconditions. If the precondition is false, its action can not be selected, and the goal is deferred. If the precondition holds, the corresponding action is executed. In evaluating a precondition, the controller might need to access data in the blackboard. If there is no transaction identifier associated with the queue entry, the controller begins a new transaction. If an identifier is already associated with the queue entry, the controller continues this transaction. At the end of the decision process, the controller aborts the newly-started transactions associated with deferred goals. If an agent is activated as a result of the queue entry selection, that agent is given any associated transaction identifier.

In addition to scheduling, the control agents are responsible for the initiation and termination of transactions. These activities are based on the contents of the goal queues. As mentioned above, the controller begins a transaction or continues an existing one when it schedules a knowledge source for activity. When an agent finishes executing, it notifies the controller. The controller now checks the goal queue for entries with the transaction identifier of the knowledge source just completed. If the queue has no entries with this transaction identifier, the controller terminates the transaction according to the transaction status. If other entries contain this identifier, the associated actions will presumably continue this transaction.

III. IMPLEMENTATION

Our initial implementation of an expert system using the transactional blackboard is designed to execute on a network of three Symbolics Lisp Machines connected via an Ethernet. Zetalisp flavors (Weinreb, 1981), the blackboard and knowledge and control sources communicate with each other via messages, the parameterized invocations of flavor methods. The message parameter restrictions discussed above are enforced at run-time by the execution environment. The blackboard transaction manager, which reads or writes objects on behalf of agent requests, and its associated data base reside on a single machine.

A. Data

Lisp s-expressions are the unit of storage and retrieval in the blackboard, and a blackboard datum is indexed by a Lisp name. Because the blackboard has no knowledge of the internal structure of the data it stores, the storage and retrieval support functions available to an agent are responsible for constructing transmittable data for storage and reconstructing the representations on retrieval. Generally, these functions need access to the definitions of the data in order to reconstruct their representations.

B. Transactions

Access to the blackboard data is allowed only within transactions. The transaction manager associated with the blackboard receives requests from agents, executes on their behalf, and packages responses. With each request to the blackboard, an agent presents a unique agent identifier and a transaction identifier. The transaction identifier is returned to an agent when it begins a transaction as a return value of the *start-transaction* command.

The blackboard transaction manager supports five transaction states and state-changing messages. Figure 2 illustrates these states and the messages that cause state transitions. Starting in the ground state, a transaction moves with the *start-transaction* message into the active state where read and write messages are handled. *Commit-* and *abort-transaction* messages terminate a transaction by moving it to the committed and ground states respectively. The straddle and precommitted states provide for the implementation of two- and three-phase commit protocols (Skeen, 1981), which are a means of coordinating transactions involving more than one transactional server.

1. Atomicity. Atomicity ensures that at the end of a transaction all the write actions associated with the transaction have taken place (the transaction commit-

ted), or all the data referenced by the transaction are restored to the state that existed when the transaction began (the transaction aborted). In each transaction, an existing datum is copied before it is first written. (If there is no existing datum, the "copy" so indicates.) This copy then serves to save the state of the datum that existed before the transaction began. If the transaction commits, the copy is discarded; if the transaction aborts, the copy replaces the current version of the datum.

2. Consistency. Our transactional blackboard has two broad consistency tasks: first, to maintain data consistency among several transactions (inter-transactional consistency), and second, to preserve a consistent view of data for those agents within an individual transaction (intra-transactional consistency).

Inter-transactional consistency of blackboard data is maintained with locks. The write locks are exclusive and guarantee that no activity can interfere with the writer while it is modifying data. Read locks are shared, and many agents may concurrently read a datum. Since the datum is not modified during this time, consistency is maintained. All locks are held to the end of the transaction, and requests made to locked data are queued until release of locks.

The transaction manager checks for deadlock whenever it queues a read or write request. In the present implementation, the blackboard retries queued requests referencing a particular datum in the order in which they are received. If a deadlock exists, the manager calls a deadlock handler to abort one of the transactions. Although the transaction manager contains a default handler, a preferred deadlock handler may be specified by an agent when it initiates a transaction to allow deadlock resolution to be based on domain knowledge.

Intra-transactional consistency is maintained through the use of time-stamps. The time stamps are used to enforce serialization through a basic time-ordered scheduling algorithm (Bernstein, 1981). When an agent first participates in a transaction, it is assigned a time-stamp, called the agent time for that agent. The write time-stamp for each blackboard datum is the agent time of the write request being executed on that datum. The read time-stamp for each datum is the later of the datum's current read time-stamp and the agent time of the read request being executed on that datum. A datum maintains a separate read time-stamp for each transaction holding a read-lock. A read request for a datum is rejected if the agent time is earlier that the datum's write time-stamp. A write request is rejected if the agent time is earlier than either the read or write time stamp of the datum. The establishment of a serializable intra-transaction schedule and concomitant coordination of the participating agents is the responsibility of the agent controlling the transaction. The blackboard regards an intra-transaction time-order violation as a

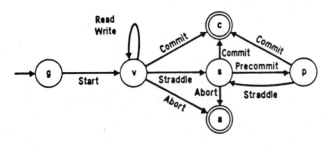

Figure 2
Transaction States

fatal error and aborts the offending transaction. The blackboard's transaction manager checks for possible time-order violations before queuing a store or retrieve request, so the errors are detected immediately.

3. Persistence. Persistence ensures that the results of committed (and straddled and precommitted) transactions will survive system crashes. To implement persistence, copies of data are kept on devices with independent failure modes and recovery protocols are supported. We use a straightforward logging and checkpoint scheme to preserve copies on independent devices. The implementation might be expensive in both space and time. It is not practical to encumber all agents with this overhead, and thus logging can be deactivated for any transaction. If a transaction is not logged, crash recovery returns its data to some previous (archived) consistent state, instead of the most recent consistent state. The recovery protocols are not expensive to implement because they are driven by external agents, not the blackboard itself.

IV. CONCLUSIONS

Our transactional blackboard architecture supports the construction of expert systems for multiprocessor environments. The transactional interface allows asynchronous requests to be safely issued to the shared data of the blackboard. Clients of this transactional service must specify the boundaries of each transaction, and they must deal with aborted transactions. We feel that this marginal cost over a serial system is small and should not interfere with the business of building expert systems.

More importantly, we provide mechanisms to make use of this shared data in an intelligent way. Control decisions are based on domain knowledge and communication costs. The controller presumably tries to utilize the processors of the computing facility to effect good system performance or to model some system of interest. The controller remains knowledge-based and does not use scheduling to protect shared data. Knowledge sources are not required to provide explicit synchronization or protect the consistency of shared data. If several agents wish, they may participate in common transactions. To do so, they only need to pass transaction identifiers among themselves.

We are using this architecture to build some expert systems. Our experience indicates that this architecture is very helpful for large, multi-author projects, where each designer works rather independently to implement a small area of expertise. In addition to reaffirming the advantages of modularity in program structure, we would like to report on the performance advantages realized by executing our expert systems on multiprocessor computers. Unfortunately, we have not yet performed the necessary experiments.

REFERENCES

Balzer, R., Erman, L. D., London, P., and Williams, C., "Hearsay III: A Domain-Independent Framework for Expert Systems," in *Proc. 1st National Conference on Artificial Intelligence*, pp. 108-110, Stanford, CA., August 1980.

Bernstein, P. A., and Goodman, N., "Concurrency Control in Distributed Database Systems", *ACM Computing Surveys*, 13:2, pp 185-221, (June 1981).

Dennis, J. B., "Data-flow Supercomputers," *Computer*, 13:11, (November 1980), pp. 48-56.

Erman, L. D., F. Hayes-Roth, V. Lesser, and D. Reddy, "The HEARSAY-II speech-understanding system: intergrating knowledge to solve uncertainty", *ACM Computing Surveys*, 12 (2), pp. 213-253, (June 1980).

Eswaran, K. P., et alia "The Notions of Consistency and Predicate Locks in a Database System", *Comm. ACM*, 19:11, pp. 624-633, (November 1976).

Lesser, V. R. and Corkill, D. D., "Cooperative distributed problem solving a new approach for structuring distributed systems", TR 78-7, Department of Computer and Information Science, Univ. of Massachusetts, Amherst, MA, 1978.

Nii, H. P., and Feigenbaum, E. A., "Rule-based Understanding of Signals," in *Pattern-Directed Inference Systems*, D. A. Waterman and R. Hayes-Roth (eds.), Academic Press, 1978.

Skeen, D., "Nonblocking Commit Protocols", Proceedings of ACM-SIGMOD International Conference on Management of Data, pp. 133-142 (April 1981).

Terry, A., "The CRYSALIS Project: Hierarchical Control of Production Systems," Stanford Heuristic Programming Project Memo HPP-83-19, Computer Science Department, Stanford University, Stanford, CA, 1983.

Weinreb, D., and Moon, D., *Lisp Machine Manual*, Symbolics Inc. Cambridge, MA, 1981.

Chapter 8

Example Applications of DAI

DAI systems have been built in a wide range of domains, as illustrated by a number of the subject headings in Chapter 2. In this chapter, we present papers from several classical DAI domains. Of course, many papers in other chapters also provide insight into particular domain-dependent DAI techniques. One of the most studied groups of DAI application domains is distributed interpretation, distributed sensing, and situation assessment. Since distributed sensing systems have been well represented in other chapters, we refer the reader to those papers (especially papers by Corkill, Davis, Durfee, Erman, Hudlicka, Lesser, Smith, and Wesson et al. in Chapter 3, Chapter 4, Sections 4.2, 4.3, and Chapters 5 and 6). Other application areas represented elsewhere in this book are air traffic control (ATC) in papers by Steeb, Cammarata, and associates (Chapter 1), complex task planning in the paper by Hayes-Roth (Chapter 7), organizational information systems in the paper by Hewitt (Chapter 4, Section 4.3), VLSI design in the paper by Ensor and Gabbe (Chapter 7) and automatic program construction in Lenat's paper (Chapter 4, Section 4.1). Numerous other areas are being studied by DAI researchers, but in some cases results are as yet tentative. Examples include work in intelligent CAD/CAM, in cooperative systems of robots and teleoperation, etc. We refer the reader to the Subject Index in Chapter 2 for further references.

The first four papers in this chapter are concerned with using DAI in office information systems. Office information systems are particularly interesting as a DAI application domain because they involve the coordinated activity of both people and automated agents, in dynamic and open worlds. Many organizational environments are characterized by rapid local change, disparate and conflicting viewpoints and goals,

and numerous reasonably routine procedures that nonetheless need local adaptations to remain effective. The systems described in this section all attempt in one way or another to cope with this flexibility, procedural capability, and representational complexity. In particular, all of these systems include interesting ways of modeling and representing the activities of other agents and the organizations under which they interact (see Chapter 1, Section 5, and Chapter 3) and of resolving disparities (see Chapter 1, Section 6, and Chapter 4, Section 4.3).

Uttam Mukhopadyay and coworkers describe the Multiple Intelligent Node Document Servers (MINDS) system, which uses learning techniques in a distributed knowledge-based query domain. MINDS searches remote knowledge bases for documents, with individual nodes collaborating with others to locate the requested materials. At one level the use of each knowledge-base is learned, and at a second level of organization, document distribution patterns, including user interests and preferences are also learned.

Gerald Barber describes an approach to supporting office work and organizational problem solving by representing the goals and problem solving activities of workers and the structure of the organizational environment. His conception of office work is that it is evolutionary and prone to contradiction. A main focus of Barber's work is the issue of the disparate viewpoints that occur in organizations, and the resolution of conflicts and contradictions that arise in dealing with knowledge in the workplace (for context, see also the discussions of resolving disparities in Chapter 1, Section 6). Barber also recognizes the role of *reflection* in problem-solving, and that a system must reason about its own behavior as a partner in the work process. He also gives explicit attention to the role of resource allocation using sponsors, and builds upon the idea originated in the work of William Kornfeld and Carl Hewitt (Chapter 4, Section 4.3).

Sergei Nirenberg and Victor Lesser's OFFICE system also provides intelligent assistance in office environments. They argue that three different perspectives — task-centered, agent-centered and cognition-oriented — are needed for effective office problem solving. OFFICE provides combined support for these multiple perspectives. Nirenberg and Lesser draw on earlier work in the POISE system, which focused on planning and plan recognition. They also suggest that agents in a helpful office support environment must be able to model knowledge of the other agents whose work they are supporting They also note that knowledge of relationships in the environment, such as authority relationships, must be modeled, illustrating one domain-specific situation in which *agent and organizational modeling* play important roles.

Bruce Croft and Lawrence Lefkowitz's POLYMER system, another successor to POISE, is based on a network of knowledge-based workstations. Multiagent activities and planning techniques are represented and supported, as well as negotiation processes to resolve conflicts arising during the execution of multiagent plans. POLYMER represents explicit contracts among agents within and outside the system for doing work, and provides ways of tracking those contracts and replanning when contracts are not fulfilled. From this perspective, POLYMER provides a somewhat more sophisticated model of contracting and negotiation for organizing problem solving than the Contract Net system of Davis and Smith (see their papers in Chapters 3 and 5 for contrast).

The final two papers in this chapter concern digital system design and air-traffic control, respectively. J-Y. Yang, Michael Huhns and Larry Stephens's DAI system supports the design of digital logic systems using a distributed set of specialized experts. Individual experts include those in circuit design, gate design, register level design, instruction sets, architecture and fabrication technology. The problems of finding an optimal design cannot be solved alone by one expert and conversely need the cooperation of all experts for success. Each node maintains knowldege about its own expertise and the expertise of all of the other nodes with which it coordinates — again, particular examples of agents modeling others with which they coordinate. The system supports iterative refinement of the design using a dynamic planning ability, focused control mechanisms and an internode question-and-answer mechanism.

Nicholas Findler and Ron Lo take up anew the air-traffic control problem, extending the work of Steeb, Cammarata, and associates (see Chapter 1). They describe a scheme for cooperative planning with planning activity performed by all aircraft in a spatial cluster. Conflict resolution is done using a negotiation mechanism that uses globally agreed conflict resolution principles. They experiment with two approaches to information exchange: a *centralized scratch pad*, which functions like a temporary blackboard for handling particular conflicts among a set of participating planes, and a *distributed scratch pad*, which attempts to spread the work of predictive simulation necessary for conflict resolution hierarchically among participant planes. Their approach has certain similarities to other research using multiple blackboard systems (see Chapter 7).

An Intelligent System for Document Retrieval in Distributed Office Environments*

Uttam Mukhopadhyay,† Larry M. Stephens, Michael N. Huhns,‡ and
Ronald D. Bonnell
*Center for Machine Intelligence, University of South Carolina,
Columbia, SC 29208*

MINDS (Multiple Intelligent Node Document Servers) is a distributed system of knowledge-based query engines for efficiently retrieving multimedia documents in an office environment of distributed workstations. By learning document distribution patterns, as well as user interests and preferences during system usage, it customizes document retrievals for each user. A two-layer learning system has been implemented for MINDS. The knowledge base used by the query engine is learned at the lower level with the help of heuristics for assigning credit and recommending adjustments; these heuristics are incrementally refined at the upper level.

1. Introduction

Documents are used in computerized office environments to store a variety of information. This information is often difficult to utilize, especially in large offices with distributed workstations, because users do not have perfect knowledge of the documents in the system or of the organization for their storage. The goal of the MINDS project is to develop a distributed system of intelligent servers that (1) learn dynamically about document storage patterns throughout the system, and (2) learn interests and preferences of users so that searches are efficient and produce relevant documents [1,2]. The strategy adopted for evaluating a set of learning heuristics that are applicable to this goal is presented. In particular, this paper describes the heuristic evaluation testbed, distance measures for metaknowledge, document migration heuristics, evidence assimilation techniques, and results of a system simulation.

*This research was supported in part by NCR Corporation.

†New address: Computer Science Department, General Motors Research Laboratories, Warren, MI 48090.

‡New address: Artificial Intelligence Department, Microelectronics and Computer Technology Corporation, 9430 Research Boulevard, Austin, TX 78759.

Received June 17, 1985; accepted August 30, 1985.

2. Distributed Workstation Environment

A. Organization of Documents

Queries regarding documents are frequently based on the contents of the documents. Automatic text-understanding systems could conceivably process these queries by reading the documents, but would be expensive to develop and use. The names of documents provide clues to their contents, but names are not descriptive enough for reliable processing of content-based queries. However, a set of keywords may be used to describe document contents: the retrieval of documents can then be predicated on these keywords as well as on other document attributes, such as author, creation date, and location. Complex qualifiers, which are conjunctions or disjunctions of predicates on these attributes, may also be used. Each document is thus represented by a surrogate containing its attributes. The document and its surrogate are subsequently updated or deleted as dictated by system usage. Surrogates occupy only a fraction of the storage space required by the documents, but usually contain enough information for users to determine whether a document is useful.

The presumed office environment consists of a network of single-user workstations. Each user may query the system about his own locally-stored documents or about those stored at other workstations. These documents are not permanently located but may migrate to other workstations. Multiple copies of documents are allowed, but documents stored at one location must have unique names.

B. The User's Perspective

In typical distributed document management systems, document directories are either centralized or distributed, with or without redundancy [3]. However, the directory information is consistent throughout the system; information is stored redundantly only to reduce directory access time. The algorithm for document retrieval consists of matching predicates for retrieval with the document properties stored in the directory. The documents for which the match is successful are then retrieved from the indicated storage addresses. Since the directory information is consistent throughout the system, the response to a query is the same without regard to the identity of the query originator.

In a large system, the response to a user's query may consist of many documents, only a few of which may be relevant to that user. Also, the set of documents relevant to a second user may be quite different from that to the first, even though their queries are identical. The problem appears to originate from a lack of specificity in formulating the query. A judicious choice of predicates would apparently cause all the documents that are irrelevant to the query originator to be rejected. However, this would require a sophisticated query language, rich enough to allow the expression of a user's short-term and long-term goals, plans, and interests. A comprehensive framework for document surrogates would also be required. Formulating queries would be extremely cumbersome and the increased power of the system would be offset by the additional effort demanded from the user.

In the absence of any information about the user, whether explicitly stated in the query or embedded in the system knowledge base, a response will necessarily consist of a superset of the sets of relevant documents described by the query from the perspective of each user. User-transparency in a large multiple-user environment may thus cause a query response to contain a large number of irrelevant documents. It is our view that systems of the future need to maintain models of their users in a background mode in order to make document searches more efficient and productive without burdening the user.

MINDS is a distributed document server with some special characteristics that allow personalized document retrieval. Additional information, in the form of personalized document metaknowledge, is stored at each workstation to allow the system to scan the document bases of all system users in a best-first fashion from the viewpoint of the query originator. MINDS maintains (at each workstation) models of both the current system state and the local user's document preferences.

3. Query Processing

A. Workstation Interactions

The MINDS system shares tasks, knowledge, and metaknowledge for cooperation among the workstations. A complex query is processed by first decomposing it into simpler subtasks, with the help of locally-stored metaknowledge, such that the search space for a subtask is limited to the documents owned by one user. Subtasks are

then transmitted to the respective workstations where they are processed. Responses to the subqueries are transmitted back to the workstation that initiated the subqueries, where the results are synthesized and ranked in decreasing order of relevance as estimated by the metaknowledge. If the subquery is content-based, relevant metaknowledge is also sent to the query originator along with the documents and surrogates constituting the response to the subquery. The transmitted metaknowledge may be used for updating the metaknowledge of the receiver in accordance with the learning strategy. Other activities, such as creating, deleting, and copying documents, require cooperation among the workstations. Again, metaknowledge may be modified as a side-effect of these activities.

B. Metaknowledge

The relevance of a keyword to a particular document is assumed to be either zero or one, in accordance with traditional (Boolean) indexing. Further, query-term weights are also assumed to be either zero or one. (See Bartschi [4] or Kraft and Buell [5] for a survey of fuzzy and generalized information retrieval techniques.) These assumptions are made to simplify the query processing at each workstation so that the distributed aspects of our research would be emphasized: metaknowledge is used for finding the best locations for the query processing to take place. Each metaknowledge element (Fig. 1) is a four-tuple with fields for two users, a keyword, and a certainty factor in the closed interval [0,1]. The metaknowledge element, (Smith, Jones, compiler, 0.8), represents the following:

Smith's past experience suggests that the possibility of finding relevant documents on compilers among those owned by Jones is high (8 on a scale of 10).

Formally, given U, the set of all users, and K, the set of all keywords, the metaknowledge function, M, is the mapping

$$M : U \times U \times K \rightarrow [0,1].$$

The metaknowledge is partitioned among the workstations such that if Ui is the subset of users at workstation i, then only the metaknowledge for $Ui \times U \times K$ is stored at that workstation.

A certainty factor [6] provides a basis for ordering the search for documents. It reflects (1) the breadth of information at a workstation pertaining to a specific keyword, (2) how useful documents concerning this keyword have proven to be in the past, and (3) how recently the workstation has acquired its information. The metaknowledge is first initialized with default values of certainty factors. A set of heuristic learning rules defines the constraints for modifying these values during system usage.

If a user had metaknowledge for each document rather than for each user of the system, the knowledge would be precise. However, the disadvantages of this approach are (1) for an average of n documents per user, the meta-

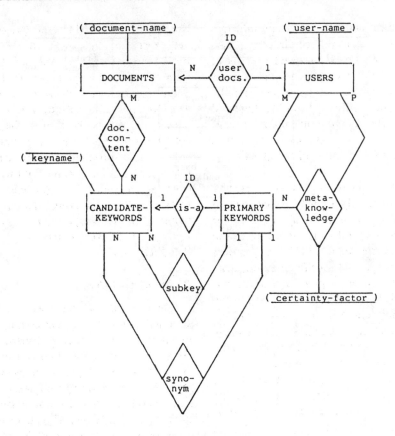

Note: Most non-key attributes have been removed for clarity.

FIG. 1.   Entity-relationship diagram for the metaknowledge of the system.

knowledge overhead would be n times as much, and (2) for new documents, no prediction of relevance can be made. On the other hand, there are positive correlations among the documents owned by a particular user, so that conceptual-level properties may be assigned to correlated clusters of these documents. Future additions to a cluster would have properties similar to the cluster prototype. For example, the metaknowledge stored by Smith associating the document base of Jones with the keyword *compiler* is a conceptual-level property of Jones' document base. This property can be exploited by Smith to facilitate document searches and is therefore stored at Smith's workstation.

4. The Learning Testbed

A. The Learning Cycle

MINDS is being developed for operation in a wide range of office environments. The state of an environment at any instant of time is given by the content and configuration of the metaknowledge and document bases of the system. Commands issued by users comprise the system inputs, and retrieved documents and surrogates constitute the outputs. The state of the system changes as a result of executing a command [7]. These system dynamics are shown in Figure 2.

A testbed has been implemented to develop a robust body of learning heuristics for MINDS. A strategy for this development, outlined in Figure 3, is based on simulating the performance of different versions of MINDS, each implemented with a different set of learning heuristics. Each simulation is run on a representation of a specific office environment, consisting of an initial database of documents and their locations, the initial metaknowledge of the users, and a command sequence representing plausible document transactions. The performance of the set of heuristics is measured periodically during the simulation. This set is then tested on other simulated environments. Based on the evaluations of each simulation, heuristics are discarded, added, or modified; the simulations are then repeated. Good heuristic refinement rules (metaheuristics) expedite the search for an optimal set.

B. Domain Modeling and Knowledge Representation

The practical value of the heuristics developed in the testbed depends on the validity of the office models used in the simulations. An office is modeled by aggregate descriptors such as the number of users and the relative frequencies of certain commands. These descriptors are used to generate a distributed document base, metaknowledge for each user, and a command sequence.

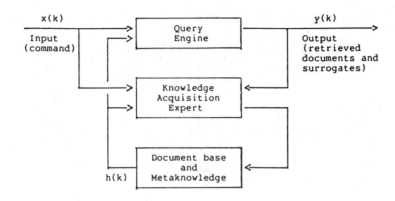

Output function: $y(k) = q(x(k), h(k))$

State function: $h(k+1) = a(x(k), h(k))$

FIG. 2. Block diagram of system dynamics.

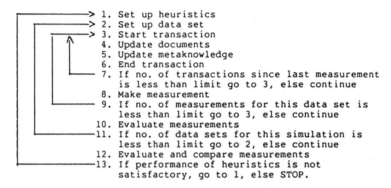

FIG. 3. The heuristics refinement cycle.

Although document retrievals may be based on several types of predicates such as authorship and location, only content-based (keyword) retrievals are considered in the simulations since other types of retrievals do not modify the metaknowledge. Commands which do not affect the system state, and thus are not important for learning, are also not simulated.

Each document is given a name and several descriptive keywords. A READ operation with a keyword-based predicate is a retrieval that culminates in the reading of one or more documents from the set returned. In an actual system, a user would then provide a relevance factor on a [0,1] scale for each document read. If the documents were to be retrieved and read by another user, the relevance factors would probably be different. Also, if the same user evaluated the same documents in terms of some other keyword, the relevance factors would probably be different. In the simulations, the contents of each document are not stored, only the relevance factor it would be accorded by each user in terms of each descriptive keyword.

If documents are distributed uniformly such that there is no preferred sequence of workstations to search, the metaknowledge will not prove helpful. However, instead of employing an exhaustive search strategy, people in offices (computerized or otherwise) always seem to rely on past experiences to order their searches in a best-first fashion. This suggests that the distribution of knowledge in offices is not uniform.

The correlation among the documents owned by a particular user is modeled in the testbed by biasing the relevance factors associated with the documents. For example, if Jones' documents on compilers are biased from Smith's viewpoint by 0.2, then the relevance factors associating Smith with compilers in documents owned by Jones will have a uniform distribution between 0.2 and 1.0. A bias of -0.4 would cause a distribution between 0 and 0.6. The bias is mutual in that:

$$\text{BIAS (Smith, Jones, compiler)} = \text{BIAS (Jones, Smith, compiler).}$$

A typical document base is shown in Figure 4.

Metaknowledge is stored as shown in the example of Figure 5. Each user has metaknowledge which captures his personal view of the dispersion of relevant documents and consists of certainty factors for all combinations of

```
((user1
  (doc27 (key13 (obj_user1 0.0)(obj_user2 0.1)(obj_user3 0.3))
         (key7  (obj_user1 0.7)(obj_user2 0.2)(obj_user3 0.5))
         (key5  (obj_user1 0.7)(obj_user2 1.0)(obj_user3 0.4)))
  (doc28 (key0  (obj_user1 0.1)(obj_user2 0.4)(obj_user3 0.3))
         (key11 (obj_user1 0.2)(obj_user2 0.1)(obj_user3 0.0))))
        .
        .
        .
  (user3
  (doc37 (key10 (obj_user1 0.6)(obj_user2 0.5)(obj_user3 0.7))
         (key14 (obj_user1 0.6)(obj_user2 0.3)(obj_user3 0.4))))))
```

FIG. 4.   Document base representation in the testbed.

```
((user1 (key0 (obj_user1 0.4) (obj_user2 0.4) (obj_user3 0.4))
        (key1 (obj_user1 0.9) (obj_user2 0.7) (obj_user3 0.7))
                        .
                        .
                        .
        (key9 (obj_user1 0.2) (obj_user2 0.2) (obj_user3 0.5)))
              .
              .
              .
 (user3 (key0 (obj_user1 0.1) (obj_user2 0.6) (obj_user3 0.4))
                .
                .
                .
        (key9 (obj_user1 0.9) (obj_user2 0.0) (obj_user3 0.4))))
```

FIG. 5.   Metaknowledge representation in the testbed.

users and keywords, including his view of his own documents. A system of n users and m keywords would result in n times m certainty factors in each of the n metaknowledge sets.

Two choices were considered for initializing the metaknowledge at the start of the experiment. The first, an unbiased assignment of certainty factors (say 0.5), would result in ties for determining the best locations to search; if the conflict-resolution strategy is to choose the first location to appear in the list, then the system would tend to learn about users placed at the top of the list earlier than those placed near the end. The second initialization strategy would be to randomly allocate certainty factors, possibly with a uniform distribution, to ensure that the learning progresses in an unbiased fashion. The second strategy was adopted for the simulations reported in this paper.

C. Metaknowledge Update Heuristics

The heuristics for updating metaknowledge are based on the paradigm of an intelligent office-worker who conducts an ordered search for documents based on past experiences in the office environment. When Smith asks Jones for documents on compilers and Jones provides one or more documents that are relevant to him, Smith learns that Jones' document base is likely to continue having useful documents on compilers. If Jones has no documents on compilers, or if none of the documents on compilers are relevant to him, Smith will learn that this may not be a

good place to search for documents on compilers in the future. In either case, Jones may assume that Smith will continue searching other locations and acquire documents on compilers from some other user. Consequently, Jones will increase his belief in Smith's ability to provide documents on compilers in the future. This increase in belief will be modest since Smith's newly acquired knowledge on compilers may not be of the type relevant to Jones.

(1) Initial Set of Heuristics. Move and copy commands do not explicitly appear in the command sequence for this set of simulations. They do appear, however, in some of the learning heuristics for document migration. The results described in Section 4.D were generated by the following set of heuristics:

Heuristic 1. (also applicable for the DELETE part of MOVE)
    IF   a document is deleted
    THEN no metaknowledge is changed

Heuristic 2.
    IF   a document is created by user1
    THEN metaknowledge of user1 about user1 regarding each keyword of the document is increased to 1.0 (the maximum relevance).

Heuristic 3.
    IF   a retrieve command predicated on keyword1 is issued by user1
    AND at least one user2 surrogate contains keyword1

THEN (a) user1 metaknowledge about user2 regarding keyword1 is increased (weight 0.1)

(b) user2 metaknowledge about user1 regarding keyword1 is increased (weight 0.1)

Heuristic 4.

IF   a retrieve command predicated on keyword1 is issued by user1

AND   no user2 surrogate contains keyword1

THEN (a) user1 metaknowledge about user2 regarding keyword1 is decreased to zero

(b) user2 metaknowledge about user1 regarding keyword1 is increased (weight 0.1)

Heuristic 5.

IF   a read command predicated on keyword1 is issued by user1

AND   no user2 document contains keyword1

THEN (a) user1 metaknowledge about user2 regarding keyword1 is decreased to zero

(b) user2 metaknowledge about user1 regarding keyword1 is increased (weight 0.1)

Heuristic 6.

IF   a read command predicated on keyword1 is issued by user1

AND   at least one user2 document contains keyword1

THEN (a) user1 metaknowledge about user2 regarding keyword1 is changed, based on the highest relevance of all user2 documents regarding keyword1.

(b) user2 metaknowledge about user1 regarding keyword1 is increased (weight 0.1)

Heuristic 7.

IF   a read command predicated on keyword1 is issued by user1

AND   document1 owned by user2 contains keyword1

AND   the relevance of document1 to user1 by way of keyword1 exceeds the move-copy threshold

AND   user1 does not have document1

THEN (a) user1 copies document1 from user2

(b) metaknowledge of user1 about user1 regarding keyword1 of the document is increased to 1.0

Heuristic 8.

IF   a read command predicated on keyword1 is issued by user1

AND   user1 has copied document1 from user2

AND   the maximum relevance of document1 to user2 by way of any keyword is less than the delete threshold

THEN document1 is deleted from the document base of user2

These heuristics have also been written in first-order logic and as OPS5 rules for implementation purposes.

(2) Assimilation of Evidence. The learning heuristics shown above enable the metaknowledge to be changed on the basis of new evidence which typically consists of the relevance rating of a document, the observation of a document being copied, etc. The metaknowledge updating scheme should be able to take into account

(a) Temporal Precedence—the system is dynamic and therefore recently acquired evidence is more indicative of the current state of the system than evidence acquired earlier. If $f1$ is the mapping function for a downward revision of the certainty factor (contradiction) and $f2$ is the mapping function for an upward revision (confirmation), then $f2(f1(x)) \geq f1(f2(x))$, for all $0 \leq x \leq 1$. This is illustrated in the bottom graph of Figure 6 for linear functions of $f1$ and $f2$. The choice of linear functions is arbitrary; any monotonically increasing function which maps a given certainty factor into one having a greater (smaller) value can be used for confirmation (contradiction).

(b) Reliability of Evidence—some types of evidence are more reliable than others. If a surrogate with a desired keyword is successfully retrieved by Jones from Smith, this action by itself does not completely support the proposition that Smith's documents on compilers are going to prove relevant to Jones in the future, since the relevance of this document to Jones is not known. However, if this document is read by Jones, then the relevance value assigned by him constitutes reliable evidence. The reliability of the source is also important for evaluating the metaknowledge sent by a user. When Smith offers metaknowledge to Jones about documents on compilers, Jones will pay heed to it only if he has found Smith to be a reliable source of documents on compilers in the past.

(c) Degree of Support—the degree of support for a proposition may vary. When a user is asked if the document he has read is relevant to him, his answer does not have to be limited to "yes" or "no," but may be a value in the range $[0,1]$.

(d) Saturation Characteristics—when the initial certainty factor for a metaknowledge element is high, additional confirmatory evidence will not change (increase) it substantially. However, if the evidence were to be contradictory, the change (decrease) in confidence factor would be large. The situation is exactly reversed when the initial certainty factor is low.

The metaknowledge updating scheme presented here has all these features and is based on two linear functions that map the current certainty factor to a new one (Fig. 6). The choice of linear functions is arbitrary as discussed previously. The first function deals with confirmatory evidence that causes upward revision while the second one deals with contradictory evidence that causes downward revision. When a surrogate with a keyword is retrieved successfully, the revised certainty factor is given by $(1-r) * f1(x) + r * f2(x)$, where $f1$ and $f2$ are the functions dealing with downward and upward revision, x is the original certainty factor, and r is the reliability of this type of information (typically 0.1). For example, if the evidence supports a proposition to a degree of $r = 0.7$, the mapping function is the weighted average of the two original functions (see Fig. 7).

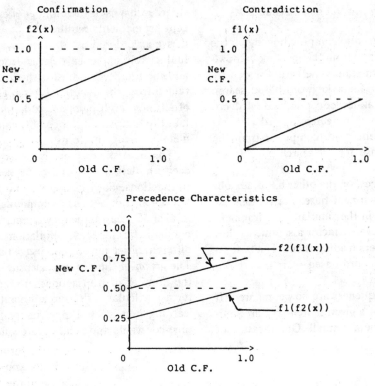

FIG. 6. Update functions for metaknowledge certainty factor and temporal precedence characteristics.

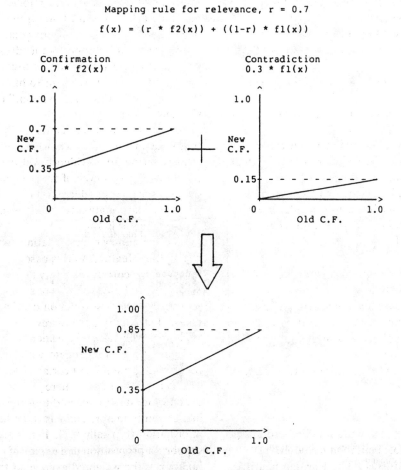

FIG. 7.   Updating scheme for metaknowledge certainty factors.

D. *Learning by Decreasing the Heuristic Distance*

A heuristic function is used to compute how much the current metaknowledge differs from the ideal metaknowledge for a particular system state. The actual search sequence adopted by a user for a keyword-based search would depend on his metaknowledge; individual document bases would be scanned in decreasing order of certainty factors. These sequences are computed from the current metaknowledge base for all search-pairs (user, keyword).

The ideal search sequences, on the other hand, are obtained from the current document base. For reasons explained earlier, documents in the simulated environment are augmented with the relevance factor assignments they would have elicited from users reading them. The best sequences for conducting keyword-based searches are obtained from this information.

The two sets of search sequences are now compared. If the two search sequences for a given search-pair are similar, the distance between them is small. One measure of disorder in a list is the number of exchanges between adjacent list elements required by a bubble-sort procedure to derive an ordered list. In this case the initial list is an actual search sequence derived from the metaknowledge, and the final ordered list is the ideal search sequence obtained from the document base. The measure of disorder of all the search-pairs are added together in order to obtain the heuristic distance between the current and ideal metaknowledge patterns.

This heuristic distance is measured at the beginning of each simulation and after each measurement cycle of ten transactions. For the simulation results shown in Figures 8–11, 450 transactions (commands) were executed and a total of 46 measurements were made. Although the learning heuristics for these simulations were kept unchanged, different office models and usage patterns were employed. The graph of the distance measurements as a function of the number of transactions produces the learning curve for a particular office environment and particular set of learning heuristics. Properties of these graphs, such as time-constants and steady-state values, are being used to

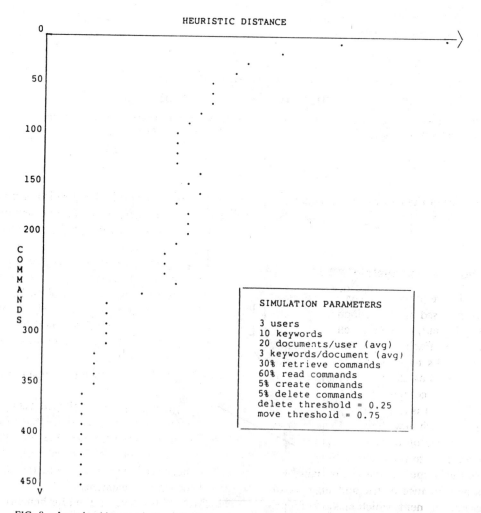

FIG. 8. Learning (decrease in heuristic distance) as metaknowledge is accumulated while processing document commands.

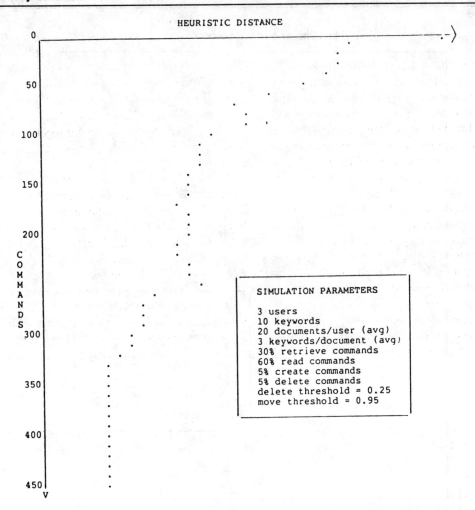

FIG. 9. Learning (decrease in heuristic distance) as metaknowledge is accumulated while processing document commands.

evaluate the performance of the heuristics in order to derive metaheuristics.

5. The Multilayered Learning System Model

Buchanan et al. [8] have proposed a general model for a learning system (LS) based on four functional components, a performance element, a learning element, a critic, and an instance selector. Each component has bidirectional communication links to a blackboard containing the knowledge base as well as all temporary information used by the learning system components.

The performance element is responsible for generating an output in response to each new stimulus. The instance selector draws suitable training instances from the environment and presents them to the performance element. The critic evaluates the output of the performance element in terms of a performance metric and suggests adjustments to the learning element, which makes appropriate changes to the knowledge base. The LS operates within

the constraints of a world model which is the conceptual framework of the system, containing assumptions and methods for domain activity and domain-specific heuristics [9].

The world model can not be modified by the LS that uses it, but it may be altered by a higher-level system based on the observed performance of the LS. This system may itself be a learning system. Incremental refinement of the world model can thus be accomplished in a higher-level learning system (LS2) whose performance element is the learning system at the lower level (LS1). Several well-known LSs have been characterized using this multilevel framework [8,10].

Dietterich et al. [11] have developed a simple model for learning systems that incorporates feedback from the performance element to the learning element. The included knowledge base is not specified as a blackboard. This model has been used to examine the factors that affect the design of the learning element.

The MINDS two-level testbed for heuristic refinement has been mapped into an integrated framework, combin-

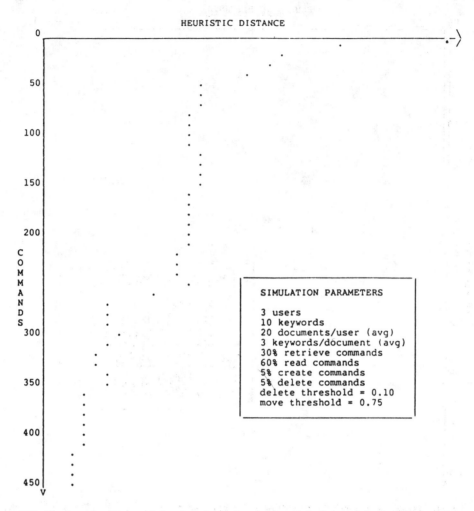

FIG. 10.   Learning (decrease in heuristic distance) as metaknowledge is accumulated while processing document commands.

ing features of both of the above general models. This framework is shown below:

The User Layer

Goal: Learn to customize document searches for individual users in a dynamic setting.

The Upper Layer (LS2, Fig. 12)

Purpose: Improve the performance of LS1 by selecting a good set of learning heuristics.

Environment: All command sequences, initial metaknowledge configurations and initial document distributions that comprise the training set.

Instance Selector: Chooses an interesting environment (a combination of command sequence, metaknowledge configuration, and document distribution) with help from the critic.

Critic: *Evaluation.* Uses metaheuristics (presently sup-

plied by the authors) to analyze learning curves for LS1 with the current set of learning heuristics.

Diagnosis. Singles out heuristics that are not useful.

Therapy. Selects new heuristics to replace useless ones or suggests modifications for existing ones. Also suggests interesting environments for testing a new set of heuristics.

Learning Element: Redefines the current set of heuristics as recommended by the critic.

World Model: The LS1 world model along with the set of metaheuristics for updating the LS1 heuristics, the method for evaluating the performance of LS1, and the scheme for heuristic updating.

The Lower Layer (LS1, Fig. 13)

Purpose: For each user learn a good set of confidence factors to predict the outcomes of all keyword-based searches of individually-owned document bases.

Environment: Set of all possible combinations of document distributions and user commands.

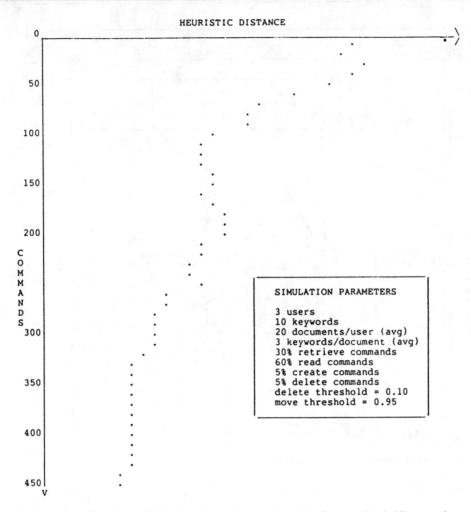

FIG. 11. Learning (decrease in heuristic distance) as metaknowledge is accumulated while processing document commands.

Performance Element: Uses the document metaknowledge (set of confidence factors) to plan a document base search sequence for a user. Also executes other commands which may change the document distribution pattern.

Instance Selector: The next command is read from a predefined sequence of commands. The document distribution pattern chosen to be part of the environment for the execution of a command is simply the document configuration arrived at after execution of the last command.

Critic: *Evaluation.* Examines the result of searching a target document base with the help of the learning heuristics.

Diagnosis. Determines that the document bases be searched in the order that would have proved most fruitful as determined from the results.

Therapy. Recommends increases and/or decreases of certainty factors.

Learning Element: Adjusts the certainty factors in the metaknowledge according to the critic's recommendation.

World Model: Representations of the document base, knowledge base and commands, the metaknowledge updating scheme, and the learning heuristics for the evaluation of results and recommendation of therapies.

6. Conclusions and Plans

The testbed has provided a useful tool for developing the heuristics needed for learning the document storage patterns of individuals using distributed workstations. Environments of this type are modeled by higher-level descriptions which are used to generate a document base, metaknowledge, and a plausible transaction sequence for each user.

Simulations are run for these environments and the resulting learning curves are used to identify a better set of heuristics. A search strategy is required for rapid convergence to an optimal set of heuristics for a given office environment. Part of the current research effort is to identify metaheuristics that would help refine existing heuristics, as well as discover new ones.

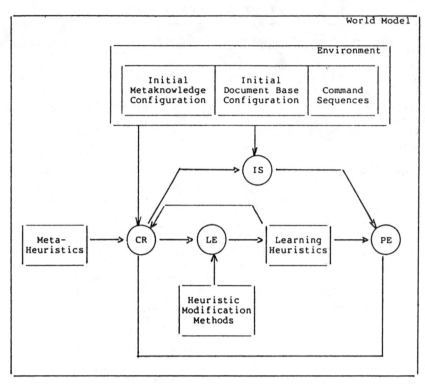

CR - Critic
LE - Learning Element
PE - Performance Element
IS - Instance Selector

FIG. 12.   Learning system LS2 (upper layer).

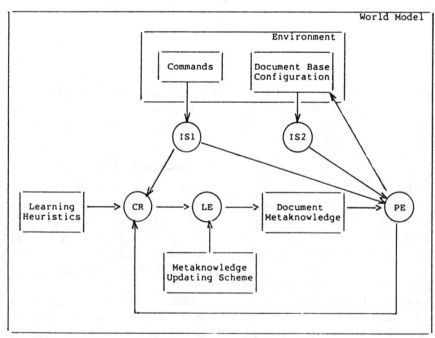

CR - Critic
LE - Learning Element
PE - Performance Element
IS1 - Instance Selector for commands
IS2 - Instance Selector for document base configuration

FIG. 13.   Learning system LS1 (lower layer).

References

1. Bonnell, R. D.; Huhns, M. N.; Stephens, L. M.; Mukhopadhyay, U. "MINDS: Multiple Intelligent Node Document Servers," *Proceedings IEEE First International Conference on Office Automation*, December 1984, 125–136.
2. Bonnell, R. D.; Huhns, M. N.; Stephens, L. M.; Mukhopadhyay, U. "A Distributed Expert System Approach to the Intelligent Filing System," *USCMI Technical Report 84-17*. Columbia, SC: University of South Carolina; November 1984.
3. Rothnie, J. B.; Goodman, N. "A Survey of Research and Development in Distributed Database Management," *Proceedings IEEE Third International Conference on Very Large Data Bases*. 1977, 30–44.
4. Bartschi, M. "An Overview of Information Retrieval Subjects." *IEEE Computer*. 18(5):67–84; 1985.
5. Kraft, D. H.; Buell, D. A. "Fuzzy Sets and Generalized Boolean Retrieval Systems." *Int. J. Man-Machine Studies*. 19:45–56; 1983.
6. Buchanan, B. G.; Shortliffe, E. H. "Reasoning Under Uncertainty," *Rule-Based Expert Systems*. Reading, MA: Addison-Wesley; 1984.
7. Lenat, D. B.; Hayes-Roth, F.; Klahr, P. "Cognitive Economy In a Fluid Task Environment," In: R. S. Michalski, Ed., *Proceedings of the International Machine Learning Workshop*. Urbana, IL: University of Illinois, Dept. of Computer Science; 1983.
8. Buchanan, B.; Mitchell, T.; Smith, R.; Johnson, Jr., C. "Models of Learning Systems," In: J. Belzer et al., Eds., *Encyclopedia of Computer Science and Technology*, Vol. 11. New York: Marcel Dekker; 1977:24–51.
9. Winston, P. H. "Learning Structural Descriptions from Examples," *The Psychology of Computer Vision*. New York: McGraw-Hill; 1975:157–210.
10. Rendell, L. A. "Conceptual Knowledge Acquisition in Search," In: L. Bolc, Ed., *Knowledge Based Learning Systems*. New York: Springer-Verlag; 1985.
11. Dietterich, T. G.; London, B.; Clarkson, K.; Dromey, G. "Learning and Inductive Inference," In: P. R. Cohen, E. A. Feigenbaum, Eds., *The Handbook of Artificial Intelligence, Volume 3*. Los Altos, CA: William Kaufmann, Inc.; 1982:323–511.
12. Michalski, R. S.; Carbonell, J. G.; Mitchell, T. M., Eds. *Machine Learning: An Artificial Intelligence Approach*. Palo Alto, CA: Tioga Publishing Co.; 1983.
13. Dietterich, T.; Michalski, R. "Learning and Generalization of Characteristic Descriptions: Evaluation Criteria and Comparative Review of Selected Methods," *Proc. Sixth Int. Joint Conf. on Artificial Intelligence*, 1979, 223–231.

Supporting Organizational Problem Solving with a Work Station

GERALD BARBER
Massachusetts Institute of Technology

An approach to supporting work in the office is described. Using and extending ideas from the field of artificial intelligence (AI) we describe office work as a problem-solving activity. A knowledge-embedding language called OMEGA is used to embed knowledge of the organization into an office worker's work station in order to support the office worker in problem solving. A particular approach to reasoning about change and contradiction is discussed. This approach uses OMEGA's viewpoint mechanism, which is a general contradiction-handling facility. Unlike other knowledge representation systems, when a contradiction is reached the reasons for the contradiction can be analyzed by the deduction mechanism without having to resort to search mechanisms such as a backtracking.

The viewpoint mechanism is the heart of the problem-solving support paradigm, a paradigm which supplements the classical AI view of problem solving.

An example is presented in which OMEGA's facilities are used to support an office worker's problem-solving activities. The example illustrates the use of viewpoints and of OMEGA's capabilities to reason about its own reasoning processes.

Categories and Subject Descriptors: H.3.4 [**Information Storage and Retrieval**]: Systems and Software—*information networks*; H.4.1 [**Information Systems Applications**]: Office Automation; I.2.1 [**Artificial Intelligence**]: Applications and Expert Systems—*office automation*; I.2.4 [**Artificial Intelligence**]: Knowledge Representation Formalisms and Methods—*semantic networks*

General Terms: Design, Languages

1. INTRODUCTION

This paper describes an approach to supporting work in the office. Using and extending ideas from the field of artificial intelligence (AI) we describe office work as a problem-solving activity. A knowledge-embedding language called OMEGA is used to embed knowledge of the organization into an office worker's workstation in order to support the office worker in problem solving. OMEGA's viewpoint mechanism is used to reason about change and contradiction.

In the following section we introduce our abstract characterization of organizations under the name of *office semantics*. In Section 3 we discuss the character of the knowledge used in organizational work and the problem-solving characteristics of office work. Section 4 considers the problem of describing office work and how this is best done in terms of the goals of the organization and the actions of its members. Section 5 concerns the AI problem-solving paradigms applied to

office work. We discuss how the classical AI view of problem solving is not appropriate and propose to supplement it with the problem-solving support paradigm. In Section 6, the notion of supporting office workers in their problem-solving activities is introduced. Sections 7 and 8 concern viewpoints and contradiction handling in OMEGA. Sections 9 and 10 present an extended example of the notion of supporting problem solving in office work with viewpoints. Section 11 contains the conclusion.

2. OFFICE SEMANTICS

Office semantics is the study of information-intensive organizational work. Its name reflects the concern with *the intent behind the act.* Office semantics is concerned with understanding the reasons behind the physical tasks that are performed in organizational work. To understand organizational behavior a distinction is made between the *application structure* of the organization and its *organizational structure*, as illustrated in Figure 1.

We make the distinction between the application and organizational structures because they are bodies of knowledge that often react to different forces of change and because of their differing functions in the organization. The organizational structure responds to forces such as work force mobility and change in the formal structure of the organization. The application structure responds to changes in laws governing aspects of the application, for example tax laws. Changes in product and service requirements also affect the application structure. The organizational structure realizes the problem-solving strategies necessary to fulfill the requirements of the application structure. For this reason the application and organizational structures are interdependent in the task of achieving the organization's goals. The distinction between the application and organizational structures does not imply that one is more relevant to organizational work than the other. Organizational work must conform to the constraints and rules derived from both the organizational and application structures.

3. OFFICE WORK AS PROBLEM SOLVING

A fundamental premise is that problem solving is basic to office work. Office work has four fundamental characteristics (Figure 2).

3.1 Open-ended Knowledge World

In contrast to some knowledge domains investigated by AI researchers, such as the Blocks World [17], the world of organizational knowledge is not closed. Fikes,

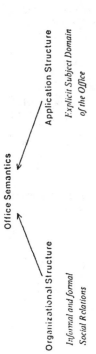

Fig. 1. Office semantics: Application and organizational domains.

Office Semantics

Organizational Structure
Informal and formal Social Relations

Application Structure
Explicit Subject Domain of the Office

3.4. Describing Cognitive Processes

In order to discuss cognitive processes they must be describable. In the general case it is not possible to describe all mental activity involved when a person is thinking through a problem. Further, describing all mental activity involved is not desirable since much of it may be irrelevant to the problem at hand and idiosyncratic to the particular individual. The goal of describing cognitive processes is not to develop a psychological theory of the individual in an organizational setting but to describe the individual's task-relevant knowledge and thought processes in a way that—taken in aggregate—explains organizational behavior.

The premise is that there is a way to describe an *organizational person* in terms of application and organizational knowledge. In adopting this premise an assumption is made that an organization works in such a way as to factor out the individual idiosyncrasies of its members. This can be seen by the fact that as organizations grow in size their members have less of an impact on the organization's characteristics. The reason for making this assumption is that many organizations have similar behaviors but are made up of diverse personalities.

4. DESCRIBING OFFICE WORK

The purpose of describing office work is not only to make a record of the activities involved in the performance of office tasks but to uncover the implicit assumptions of the work. The work description includes the mental and physical activities that an office worker engages in and the reasons for these activities. An approach to characterizing work in the office is to consider it as organized in procedures in a fashion similar to the computer science notion of procedure. In this way office work would be described as a sequence of steps with decision points to manage flow of control.

4.1 Pitfalls of a Procedural Description Methodology

A procedural characterization is problematic for several reasons. Even routine tasks in offices encounter unexpected obstacles. In a procedural approach it is necessary to foresee the possible alternative courses of action when a procedural step cannot be performed. Determining what the alternatives are is part of what office work is; all alternatives cannot be determined in advance. As a result, a procedural approach is not a very useful style of work description because it needs to be augmented by the procedure's goal structure. When a procedure is augmented in this way, one can examine the procedure's goal structure in order to generate alternative steps when a step cannot be performed. Interesting studies along these lines are contained in [5, 14].

4.2 Explicit Representation of Goals and Actions

A description of office work in terms of goals and actions is a direct way of characterizing office work. A procedural description of an order-entry task, for example, succinctly characterizes the important points of the task. But precisely because of its succinctness a procedural description suffers from two defects: first, it glosses over minor details that may be problematic or critical in practice; second, the reasons for the actions specified by a procedural description must be

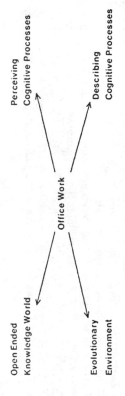

Perceiving
Cognitive Processes

Open Ended
Knowledge World

Office Work

Describing
Cognitive Processes

Evolutionary
Environment

Fig. 2.   Characteristics of office work.

Henderson, and Suchman at the XEROX Palo Alto Research Center have described in detail the open-ended characteristic of the organizational world [5, 14]. The complete set of actions relevant to the organizational world is unknown and unknowable. The set of all possible states are unknowable as are all possible alternatives for achieving a goal. The result is that unforeseen situations are a common occurrence. This is as much a property of the perceiver of the world as it is of the world itself since it is our assumption that the perceiver is of limited cognitive capabilities.

The open-ended character of the organizational knowledge world places demands on the kind of description system used to describe organizational knowledge. In particular, the description system must be able to assimilate new information about actions, situations, and alternatives to achieving goals in an incremental fashion. The description system must be able to reason with partial information about problem-solving states.

3.2 An Evolutionary Environment

Organizations are continuously changing. Any attempt to understand and describe organizational behavior must cope with the problem of trying to describe a dynamic, evolving system. This is a central problem both in talking about organizations and in doing work within organizations. A description system must be able to describe an organization that is continuously changing. A description system must also furnish tools to manage change so office workers may use it in performing their tasks. The OMEGA description system provides the viewpoint mechanism to describe and reason about change.

3.3 Perception of Cognitive Processes from Overt Physical Actions

Understanding what task someone is doing and the reasons for each action performed in carrying out a task by watching the person perform the task is in general not possible. Information used in performing the task is not manifest in the physical actions the task entails. Additionally, interview and observation give at best partial and often apparently contradictory information. From this characteristic, two observations can be made: first, the quality of information gathered by observation or interview is limited; second, and hence, more effective methodologies are desirable. Partly because of this problem the approach we take is to *support* problem solving rather than replace the individuals in an organization doing the problem solving.

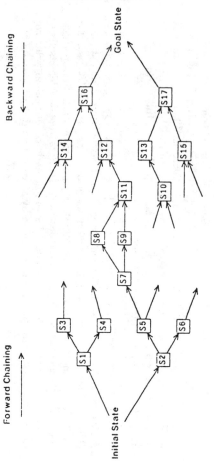

Fig. 3. The classical AI problem-solving paradigm.

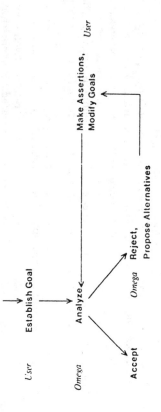

Fig. 4. The problem-solving support paradigm.

inferred. Thus if it is impossible to fulfill a requirement in the procedural description, such as obtaining the delivery address for an order, the office worker must rely on intuition and experience to select an alternative action. The more desirable approach is to state explicitly the reasons the action achieves.

The explicit representation of goals and actions provides a recourse to handle unexpected contingencies. Office workers are able to handle unexpected contingencies in their daily work because they know the goals of the office work and because they know what actions are needed to achieve the goals of the office work. These goals and actions are often implicit in the work and in the office worker's knowledge of their work. If a particular action cannot be performed, the computer system can possibly suggest an alternative action. Failing this the office worker can use the computer system to examine the goals an alternative action must inherit from the action that cannot be performed. Together, the office worker and computer system can construct a new plan of action that maintains the necessary constraints and makes progress toward achieving the goals in question.

To support the problem-solving activity in office work, knowledge about the goals and constraints of the office work is explicitly represented. This builds a teleological structure of the office work within the computer. Actions that would be performed during the course of the office work are linked to the reasons they are performed and to the constraints that they are required to maintain. Explicit representation of the goals and actions exposes hidden assumptions and implicit goals about the office work. In addition, explicit representation makes the actions performed by an office worker more understandable by machine or by another individual.

Added coherence between different functional elements of a system has the benefit that the user's actions and the goals of the office procedure can be understood in terms of each other. It is useful for the system to understand the goals in order to interpret the user's requests and suggest problem-solving tools for achieving the goals. In turn, the user's actions suggest what the current goals are and narrows the variety of problem-solving methods and size of the solution space. Discussion about characterizing office work in terms of goals is contained in [1, 6].

5. PROBLEM-SOLVING PARADIGMS

A classical problem-solving paradigm in AI is depicted in Figure 3. However, this paradigm is difficult to apply in the organizational world. The organizational world differs from traditional AI worlds such as cryptarithmetic or the Blocks World in that it is distributed and parallel; thus there is more than one individual working on the problem. Also, it is open-ended in the sense that all actions and consequences of actions are not known.

In the view of problem solving shown in Figure 3, the problem solver is given a well-defined initial state, for example the configuration of a chess board, a well-defined final state, for example to win the game, and a finite collection of actions or state transformers. The characterization of problem solving is as a search for the sequence of actions that will achieve the goal state. The test to see if the goal state has been achieved is objective and two valued, either the goal is achieved or not. The problem solver is assumed to be a single individual, for example a single chess player playing an opponent, as opposed to a team of chess players playing an opponent. Thus there are no problems with synchronization or conflict with other problem solvers. When more than one problem solver is cooperating on a problem, as in an organization, a global state description of the problem and the problem solver is no longer practical.

This is a seductive paradigm but it is hard to apply in the organizational setting. The reason for this is that in using this paradigm one determines a possible means to achieve a goal by examination of the current and goal states. But in many cases in office work the goal is vague and how much information is relevant to achieving the goal is not clear; this makes an assessment of the current state difficult. This problem is suggested by the case studies in [18] and has been pointed out by [14].

In addition, the purpose of this paradigm is to support problem solving. Our approach is to support problem solving with the *problem-solving support paradigm* shown in Figure 4.

In the problem-solving support paradigm, the office worker establishes a goal, for example to send a message or to complete a step in an office procedure. Based on what OMEGA knows about the goal, it either tries to establish the goal or to refute the goal. If it is not possible for OMEGA to establish the goal, it notifies the office worker that the goal cannot be established or that contradictory information has been discovered during the attempt to establish the goal. At this point the office worker can either modify the goal or make further assertions, possibly supplying necessary information to establish the goal. OMEGA then attempts to establish the goal again. This cycle continues until the goal is established. The analysis is accomplished using OMEGA's viewpoint mechanism.

6. SUPPORTING OFFICE WORK

OMEGA provides a uniform framework within which to implement tools to support an office worker's problem solving. This has the benefit that different tools may cooperate easily in achieving the goals of particular office tasks.

Knowledge is embedded in the form of descriptions about objects in the system and the relationships between these objects. Office Talk, OBE, and other systems [4, 16, 19] have adopted forms as the basic element of the system; they attempt to represent everything in the system using forms. In contrast to the forms model, we adopt a model in which descriptions are the basic element of the system. Since the knowledge base is represented using OMEGA's description lattice, data do not have to be cast in a rigid form as they do in traditional data processing applications. The consequence is that office tasks may be reasoned about more on an individual basis.

Among some of the functions that a forms model provides are

storage of information as in records,

transfer of information as in messages,

display of information in an abstracted and structured manner,

accumulation and modification of information as the form is used by individuals in the accomplishment of their tasks.

However, descriptions provide much greater functionality than a forms model. Descriptions are a very general facility; not only do they provide the functions that forms-based systems have as shown above but they also are the basis for OMEGA's reasoning machinery. Descriptions provide

a means for error checking of information in an office system,

a basis for retrieval and deduction based on stored information,

a means by which the *structure of office activity and problem-solving processes* are described,

a means by which the *structure of the application and organizational domains* of an organization are specified,

viewpoints by which change and inconsistent states may be reasoned about.

A central part of OMEGA's reasoning capabilities is realized using the viewpoint mechanism. This is described below, followed by an example of the use of OMEGA in supporting an office worker.

7. VIEWPOINTS

Viewpoints may be thought of as repositories for descriptions and thus statements. Viewpoints are reminiscent of McCarthy's situational calculus [11] and the contexts of QA4 [12] and Conniver [15]. The most notable difference between viewpoints and these systems is that viewpoints are objects within the system that may be reasoned about and described just as any other description in the system. Viewpoints are not restricted to being organized into a tree structure as are the contexts of Conniver and QA4.

A key property of viewpoints is that information is only added to them and is never changed. Consider, for example, a description of an invoice. The description is in a viewpoint and may be further described in the viewpoint increasing its specificity. There may be rules that maintain constraints between attributes of descriptions, so that as information is added to a viewpoint further information may be deduced. For example, a rule for invoice descriptions may state that the subtotal plus sales tax must equal the total; thus when any two of the attributes is known the third may be calculated. Should a description in an attribute be changed in a particular viewpoint, for example the subtotal change from \$5 to \$10, then the following scenario might occur:

1. A new viewpoint is created and described as being a successor to the old viewpoint.
2. All descriptions that were not derived from the changed description are inherited by the new viewpoint.
3. The new description is added in the new viewpoint, and any deductions resulting from this new information are made.
4. The descriptions in the new viewpoint describe the changed state of the invoice.

In this case the new viewpoint inherits all but the changed description and the descriptions deduced from the changed description from the old viewpoint. What actions are taken when information in a viewpoint is changed is controlled via sprites [10]. Sprites are procedures that fire when a condition they are watching for arises in the knowledge base. Sprites typically fire when assertions are made or goals are posted. In the example above, a simple action is specified: all information not derived from the changed information is inherited by the new viewpoint. Other actions would be to disallow change, in the case of protected information, or to signal a contradiction and allow the user to help resolve it.

7.1 Handling Change

Many approaches have been developed to manage change; we begin with the most simple and proceed to the more sophisticated. In some cases the approach to keeping track of changing information has been via updates to data structures. Systems based on property lists or records, such as in LISP or PASCAL, have used *put* and *get* types of operations to update and read database information. These are low level operations and have the disadvantage that they provide no support for propagating changes. Thus, deductions based on updated information must be handled explicitly, leading to excessive complexity and modularity problems. Languages like FRL [7] solve this problem by using triggers on data

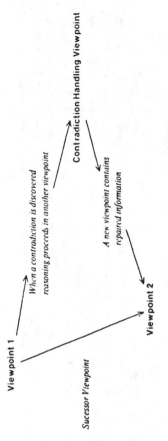

Viewpoint 1

When a contradiction is discovered reasoning proceeds in another viewpoint

Contradiction Handling Viewpoint

A new viewpoint contains repaired information

Viewpoint 2

Successor Viewpoint

Fig. 5.   Handling contradictions with viewpoints.

structure slots (actually the slots of frames) to help propagate changes. The problem with this approach is that there is little support for keeping track of what was deduced and why.

The language KRL has been used to implement a knowledge-based personal assistant called ODYSSEY [6]. ODYSSEY aids a user planning travel itineraries by keeping track of what cities a traveler will visit, how the traveler will get to the cities, and where the traveler will stay in the cities. In this system, *pushers* and *pullers* are used to propagate deductions as a result of updates and to make deductions on reads. A simple dependency mechanism is used to record information dependencies. The problem is that there is a transition period from the time when a value is changed to the time that all changes are propagated. During this transition period the database is in an inconsistent state and rules may fire making deductions based on inconsistent information. In both KRL and FRL, it is necessary to be very careful about the order in which triggers fire for as updates are made there is both new and old information in the database making it difficult to prevent anomalous results due to inconsistencies.

The AMORD system attempts to maintain a globally consistent database at all times. A Truth Maintenance System [3] maintains the status of all facts; when a fact becomes *outed*, or disbelieved, the status of all facts that depend on the original fact is also set to out. During the period of time that facts are being outed or reinstated, the database is unavailable for the firing of rules. Thus when the rules do fire, they always see a consistent database. This system reduces considerably the possibility of making erroneous conclusions at the expense of a global notion of truth and efficiency.

Steele has developed a constraint-based programming language [13]. In this system, a network of nodes and connections is used to build a constraint network. Values deduced by rules at the nodes propagate through the network, creating a flow of information through the net from input and constant values to deduced values. Like AMORD, Steele's system enforces a global notion of truth. Like KRL, rules can fire on an inconsistent database signaling contradictions. These rules represent false alarms because once the propagation caused by the original change is done the database is consistent and the fired rules are no longer relevant. Partially because of the false alarm problem, Steele has devised a system of prioritized queues that defers the processing of fired rules that are likely due to false alarms until rules that are likely to bring the database into a consistent state have fired. Because of the global truth requirement, false alarms will not cause inconsistent results; as is the case with the KRL system, they will just lead to inefficiency.

A characteristic shared by all these systems is that they are nonmonotonic. Information is lost when, for example, values of slots are changed in FRL, or when inputs are changed in Steele's constraint system. This is a fundamental limitation because it means that the systems are constrained in their history-keeping capabilities. If a value of some parameter in one of these systems is changed from A to B, causing the implications of B to be deduced, and then it is changed back to A, there is no way for the system to know the parameter's value was A at a previous time. One might object that this is not the case in AMORD, that when the parameter is changed back to A the status of the relevant facts is simply changed from *out* to *in*, and no recomputation is necessary. This may be

true, but this behavior is implemented by a mechanism beyond the reach of the system's deduction machinery. There is no way for AMORD to reason about the fact that the parameter's value was A.

8. CONTRADICTION HANDLING WITH VIEWPOINTS

The systems described above cannot reason directly about contradictions because they are based on logics where truth is a global characteristic of a statement. Since these systems enforce a global notion of truth, when a contradiction exists, anything can be derived by their inference rules. Thus when a contradiction is detected, the systems deduction machinery is useless. The approach taken by AMORD and Steele's constraint system, for example, is to use a mechanism outside the logic to reestablish consistency. Once the world in consistent, the deduction mechanism can operate normally. The viewpoint mechanism provides a method to quarantine inconsistency to within a viewpoint so that reasoning can still be done outside of the inconsistent viewpoint and thus valid conclusions can still be made.

The ability to limit the effect of contradictions to within viewpoints is done by explicitly keeping track of what is believed to be true, that is, *assertions*, and why they are believed to be true, *justifications*. This information is expressed in the OMEGA language so it is within reach of the deduction mechanism. It has been stated that a programming language is not general purpose if an implementation for the language cannot be written in the language itself [13]. We agree and recast this statement: a language is not knowledge-embedding if it cannot represent and reason about why it believes what it does believe. Given any statement, OMEGA can answer whether the statement is believed to be true and why, whether the statement is believed to be false and why, or whether OMEGA does not know.

Contradiction handling in using viewpoints proceeds as indicated in Figure 5. In this example, reasoning in viewpoint 1 has discovered a contradiction. This causes activity to cease in that viewpoint and to switch to the contradiction-handling viewpoint. In the contradiction-handling viewpoint, the justifications for the assertions that are in contradiction are analyzed. The assertions are filtered, depending on the source of the contradiction, and moved to viewpoint 2. The relationship between the two viewpoints is described and reasoning proceeds in viewpoint 2 where it left off in viewpoint 1.

The Goal:

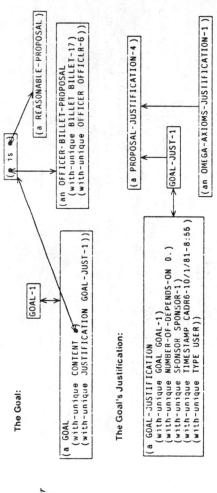

(a GOAL
  (with-unique CONTENT)
  (with-unique JUSTIFICATION GOAL-JUST-1))

(an OFFICER-BILLET-PROPOSAL
  (with-unique BILLET BILLET-17)
  (with-unique OFFICER OFFICR-6))

(a REASONABLE-PROPOSAL)

The Goal's Justification:

(a PROPOSAL-JUSTIFICATION-4)

GOAL-JUST-1

(an OMEGA-AXIOMS-JUSTIFICATION-1)

(a GOAL-JUSTIFICATION
  (with-unique GOAL GOAL-1)
  (with-unique NUMBER-OF-DEPENDS-ON 0.)
  (with-unique SPONSOR SPONSOR-1)
  (with-unique TIMESTAMP CADR6-10/1/81-8:55)
  (with-unique TYPE USER))

Fig. 7. The assignment proposal goal.

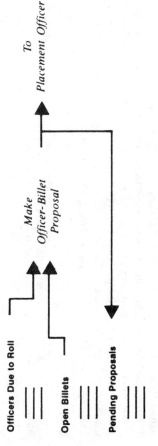

Fig. 6. The assignment officer role.

9. AN EXAMPLE

This section consists of an example of the ideas that have been developed in earlier sections. The main ideas we will address are the following:

Problem-Solving Support. Use of the problem-solving support paradigm in helping office workers in their tasks.

Goals. Use of goals to describe office work. How these goal descriptions can help office workers in the performance of their tasks.

Contradiction Handling. Examples of OMEGA's contradiction-handling capabilities in dealing with real work knowledge.

The example is taken from an office in the Defense Department that is part of the *officer transfer process.* This process is the method by which Navy officers are reassigned to tours of duty, or *billets,*[1] when their present billet assignments expire. The *assignment officer* fills the role depicted in Figure 6.

Conceptually, the assignment officer's role is simple: he or she has a list of officers that are *due to roll*[2] and a list of open billets. The assignment officer chooses an officer-billet pairing and passes this proposal on to the *placement officer* for acceptance, keeping a record of the proposal. The placement officer accepts or rejects the proposal. The assignment officer represents the interests of the officers that are due to roll. Thus in each officer-billet proposal the assignment officer chooses a billet that will help attain the career objectives of the officer due to roll.

As an example, we show how part of the officer transfer process can be described in terms of goals and how this description can help assignment officers in their work. The following description focuses on the internal mechanism that OMEGA uses to reason about a particular domain. We do not describe the user interface with which the user would make assertions or post goals or the way that OMEGA would present the results of its reasoning processes to the user. Our goal is first to get the underlying mechanism working right and then to work on a user interface for those mechanisms.

9.1 Posting a Goal

Shown in Figure 7 is the top-level goal for a particular assignment proposal. The goal is to show that OFFICER-6 and BILLET-17 form a reasonable assignment proposal. This goal may have been posted by the assignment officer because he or she wanted to establish that the officer-billet pair formed a reasonable proposal or the goal may be part of a query that is trying to determine all the reasonable proposals for a particular group of officers and billets.

The goal is represented within OMEGA's description structure. The boxes in the diagram represent descriptions. A single-headed arrow indicates that the description at the tail of the arrow is related to the description at the head of the arrow by the inheritance or *is* relation. A double-headed arrow indicates two descriptions that are *same,* or inherit from each other. Arrows that point inside a box indicate components of the description represented by the box. Viewpoints are collections of goals and assertions. In Figure 7 GOAL-JUST-1 is depicted as being in viewpoint PROPOSAL-JUSTIFICATION-4 by the inheritance relation.

As can be seen, the goal has two parts: a content and a justification. The content is the logical statement of the goal and the justification is the reason the goal was posted. In this case, the goal is that a particular officer-billet proposal is reasonable. Various information is registered in the justification, including the goal type, USER, which means that this is a top-level goal entered by the user; the goal time stamp, when and where the goal was posted; and the sponsor. The sponsor allocates computational resources toward establishing the goal. A sponsor is given certain quanta of resources with which to establish a goal. If the sponsor runs out of quanta before establishing the goal it must ask for more quanta before it can proceed. If the goal is achieved or if it is shown to be unachievable then the sponsor may be *stifled.* When a sponsor is stifled, no further processing can proceed to establish the goal under the auspices of the sponsor. The use of sponsors in OMEGA is based on the work of Kornfeld as described in [9].

---

[1] Billets are jobs. An officer is usually assigned to a billet for three years.

[2] An officer is due to roll when his or her current billet assignment will expire in six months.

The Subgoals:

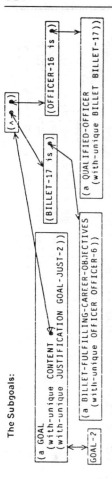

```
(a GOAL
  (with-unique CONTENT ◇
  (with-unique JUSTIFICATION GOAL-JUST-2))

GOAL-2

(a BILLET-FULFILLING-CAREER-OBJECTIVES
  (with-unique OFFICER OFFICER-6))
```

(OFFICER-16 is ?)

(BILLET-17 is ?)

```
(a QUALIFIED-OFFICER
  (with-unique BILLET BILLET-17))
```

(a PROPOSAL-JUSTIFICATION-4)

GOAL-JUST-2

The Subgoals' Justification:

```
(a GOAL-JUSTIFICATION
  (with DEPENDS-ON GOAL-JUST-1)
  (with DEPENDS-ON PROPOSAL-REASONABLE-SPRITE-JUST-1)
  (with-unique GOAL GOAL-2)
  (with-unique NUMBER-OF-DEPENDS-ON 2.)
  (with-unique SPONSOR SPONSOR-2)
  (with-unique TIMESTAMP CADR6-10/1/81-9:01)
  (with-unique TYPE COMPOUND))
```

Fig. 8. The assignment proposal subgoals.

```
(an OFFICER
  (with NUMBER-OF-PAST-BILLETS 2.)
  (with NUMBER-OF-SCHOOLING 2.)
  (with PAST-BILLET DESK-JOB)
  (with PAST-BILLET SAILOR)
  (with SCHOOLING ADMINISTRATION)
  (with SCHOOLING LIFE-AT-SEA)
  (with-unique NAME Juan Diaz)
  (with-unique ULTIMATE-CAREER-OBJECTIVE PILOT))
```

OFFICER-6

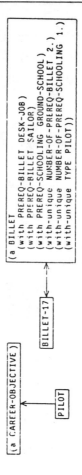

```
(a BILLET
  (with PREREQ-BILLET DESK-JOB)
  (with PREREQ-BILLET SAILOR)
  (with PREREQ-SCHOOLING GROUND-SCHOOL)
  (with-unique NUMBER-OF-PREREQ-BILLET 2.)
  (with-unique NUMBER-OF-PREREQ-SCHOOLING 1.)
  (with-unique TYPE PILOT))
```

BILLET-17

(a CAREER-OBJECTIVE)

PILOT

Fig. 9. Some officer and billet knowledge.

Now suppose that OMEGA has been told the following about what constitutes a reasonable proposal.

$$(\Rightarrow (\wedge \equiv B \text{ is (a Billet-Fulfilling-Career-Objectives}$$
$$\text{(with-unique Officer} \equiv O))$$
$$\equiv O \text{ is (a Qualified-Officer}$$
$$\text{(with unique Billet} \equiv B)))$$
$$\text{(is (an Officer-Billet-Proposal}$$
$$\text{(with unique Billet} \equiv B)$$
$$\text{(with unique Officer} \equiv O))$$
$$\text{(a Reasonable-Proposal)))}$$

In the above implication, the $\equiv$ symbol is used to mark universally quantified variables. Thus this implication states that an officer-billet proposal is reasonable if the officer is a qualified officer for the particular billet and if the billet fits in with the officer's career objectives. OMEGA decides that a particular assignment is reasonable only according to the definition OMEGA has concerning what it takes to be a reasonable proposal. The above goal would be used as a filter to pick out the most obvious characteristics of the proposed assignment. The assignment officer may look at a proposal that OMEGA has judged reasonable and reject it because of some criteria that OMEGA does not know about.

9.2 Posting of Subgoals

The assertion of the above rule creates several sprites,[3] one of which looks for a goal that matches the consequent of the implication. If the sprite fires, it posts the antecedent of the implication as a goal. The sprite then creates a second sprite that watches to see if the antecedent is asserted. When the antecedent is asserted, the second sprite fires and asserts the consequent. Thus as a result of the above implication and the goal in Figure 7, the subgoals shown in Figure 8 are posted.

Notice that the justification for this subgoal contains a new sponsor, SPONSOR-2. The sprite that created the new subgoal also created a new sponsor for the processing that attempts to establish the subgoal. The reason for this is so that when the subgoal is achieved (or shown to be unachievable), the subgoal can be stifled without affecting the processing of the supergoal. In addition, the sprite also linked the subgoal to the goal by setting up the following is relation.

GOAL-JUST-1 is a Goal-Justification
    (with Depended-on-by GOAL-JUST-2)

This enables analysis of the reasoning when, for example, a goal cannot be achieved or is shown to be unachievable because of the failure of some subgoal. It is also useful when OMEGA explains how it has achieved a goal.

A conjunctive goal, as in Figure 8, is handled in the following fashion. A sprite notices that there is a conjunctive goal. The sprite fires and posts the two conjuncts as goals. In addition, the sprite creates additional sprites that watch for the assertion of each of the conjuncts or negation of either conjunct. When both conjuncts are asserted, the conjunction is asserted; if either conjunct is negated the negation of the conjunction is asserted.

Suppose the following knowledge is stored in the description lattice with relevance to the goal shown in Figure 8. Note that for brevity we do not include the assertions and justifications in Figure 9, we just illustrate the is relations directly. Note also that the officer fulfills the billet prerequisites for past billets but not those for schooling. In the following paragraphs, we describe how OMEGA discovers this.

In this discussion, we concern ourselves with how OMEGA shows that OFFICER-6 is a qualified officer. The method used to show that BILLET-17 fulfills

---

[3] A sprite watches for the assertion of an implication. When the sprite fires on such an assertion it creates four sprites corresponding to the four ways the implication can be used. These correspond to the antecedent and consequent reasoning of the implication and its contrapositive.

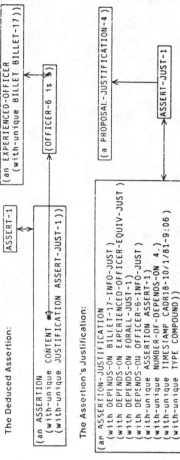

The Deduced Assertion:

```
ASSERT-1
(an ASSERTION
    (with-unique CONTENT o)
    (with-unique JUSTIFICATION ASSERT-JUST-1))

(an EXPERIENCED-OFFICER
    (with-unique BILLET BILLET-17))
(OFFICER-6 is S)
```

The Assertion's Justification:

```
ASSERT-JUST-1
(an ASSERTION-JUSTIFICATION
    (with DEPENDS-ON BILLET-17-INFO-JUST)
    (with DEPENDS-ON EXPERIENCED-OFFICER-EQUIV-JUST)
    (with DEPENDS-ON FORALL-JUST-1)
    (with DEPENDS-ON OFFICER-6-INFO-JUST)
    (with-unique ASSERTION ASSERT-1)
    (with-unique NUMBER-OF-DEPENDS-ON 4.)
    (with-unique TIMESTAMP CADR18-10/1/81-9:06)
    (with-unique TYPE COMPOUND))
(a PROPOSAL-JUSTIFICATION-4)
```

Fig. 11. The experienced officer assertion.

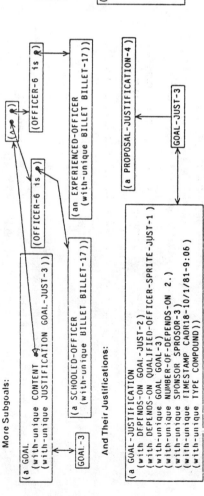

More Subgoals:

```
GOAL-3
(a GOAL
    (with-unique CONTENT o)
    (with-unique JUSTIFICATION GOAL-JUST-3))
(OFFICER-6 is P)
(a SCHOOLED-OFFICER
    (with-unique BILLET BILLET-17))
(an EXPERIENCED-OFFICER
    (with-unique BILLET BILLET-17))
```

And Their Justifications:

```
(a GOAL-JUSTIFICATION
    (with DEPENDS-ON GOAL-JUST-2)
    (with DEPENDS-ON QUALIFIED-OFFICER-SPRITE-JUST-1)
    (with-unique GOAL GOAL-3)
    (with-unique NUMBER-OF-DEPENDS-ON 2.)
    (with-unique SPONSOR SPONSOR-3)
    (with-unique TIMESTAMP CADR18-10/1/81-9:06)
    (with-unique TYPE COMPOUND))
(a PROPOSAL-JUSTIFICATION-4)
GOAL-JUST-3
```

Fig. 10. Subgoals to establish qualified officer status.

the officer's career objectives follows a similar course. OMEGA has been given the following equivalence concerning qualified officers.

$$(\Leftrightarrow /\!\!\backslash \equiv O \text{ is (an Experienced-Officer}$$
$$\text{(with unique Billet} \equiv B))$$
$$\equiv O \text{ is (a Schooled-Officer}$$
$$\text{(with unique Billet} \equiv B)))$$
$$\text{(is} \equiv O \text{ (a Qualified-Officer}$$
$$\text{(with unique Billet} \equiv B))))$$

As in the previous implication, when this equivalence is asserted sprites are created that watch for goals that match either the left or right halves of the equivalence. When a sprite fires after matching one half of the equivalence as a goal, it posts the other half as a goal. In addition, sprites are created that watch for the assertion or negation of either side of the equivalence. Thus when an assertion or negation of one side is made, the assertion or negation of the other side is made. Thus we have subgoals shown in Figure 10 posted with a new sponsor.

OMEGA has been told the following concerning what it takes to be an *experienced officer*.

$$(\Leftrightarrow \text{(for all} \equiv P$$
$$(\Rightarrow \equiv B \text{ is (a Billet}$$
$$\text{(with unique Prereq-Billet} \equiv P))$$
$$\equiv O \text{ is (an Officer}$$
$$\text{(with unique Past-Billet} \equiv P))))$$
$$\text{(is} \equiv O \text{ (an Experienced-Officer}$$
$$\text{(with unique Billet} \equiv B))))$$

This goal is more difficult to achieve. This rule states that if it is true that for every prerequisite of a billet, the prerequisite is a past billet for an officer, then the officer is an experienced officer for the billet and vice versa. As with the previous equivalence, the right half of the statement will be posted as a goal when

the left half is posted as a goal. Since this new goal involves a universal quantification, some knowledge of the domain over which the variable ranges is necessary. This is the purpose of the NUMBER-OF-PREREQ-BILLETS and the NUMBER-OF-PAST-BILLETS attribute descriptions.

9.3 A Subgoal is Established

The method used to prove the universally quantified statement is first to retrieve the number of prerequisite billets and the number of past billets via sprites. The general approach is to insure that all the prerequisites are past billets; this means we must retrieve all the prerequisite billets. We know when we have retrieved them all by the NUMBER-OF-PREREQ-BILLETS attribute. Once they are all retrieved, we check to see that each is a past billet. If each is a past billet, then the universally quantified statement is asserted. If one prerequisite is not a past billet (which we can know since we know how many there are), then the negation of the statement is asserted. If there is not enough information to determine the truth or falsity of the statement, the sprites remain waiting for additional information. Once the necessary information is known, if the sponsor of the sprites is still active, the statement or its negation will be asserted.

The reason that the NUMBER-OF-PAST-BILLETS attribute is necessary is so that OMEGA can know when to stop looking for billets. Without the number stated explicitly, OMEGA cannot conclude that an officer has two past billets only because that is all the information that is stored explicitly in the description system. For example, it may be possible to prove the existence of more billets than are explicitly known about. Without explicitly stating the number of past billets, the question of whether all billets are known or not is undecidable. This is an example of how OMEGA's goals of monotonicity and assimilation of new information affect its reasoning processes.

In our example the sprites, using the information that appears in Figure 9, will conclude that the officer is an experienced officer and will make the assertion shown in Figure 11. Notice that this assertion depends on four different sources: BILLET-17-INFO-JUST, OFFICER-6-INFO-JUST (Figure 9), FORALL-JUST-

1 (the justification for the universally quantified statement), and EXPERI-ENCED-OFFICER-EQUIV-JUST (the justification for the equivalence statement). In particular, it does not depend on any of the goals that were posted in the process of achieving the goal; as pointed out in [2], this would be a mistake since we do not want the truth or falsity of an assertion to depend on interest (as indicated by posted goals) in achieving the assertion. As with goals, this assertion is placed in PROPOSAL-JUSTIFICATION-4 by the inheritance relation shown in the bottom right hand corner of Figure 11. Thus we have one of the conjuncts of Figure 10 established.

9.4 A Subgoal is Refuted

The attempt to establish the truth of the second conjunct follows in a similar manner. In this case, the following rule is used to try to establish that an officer is a *schooled officer* for a particular billet:

```
(⇐ (for all ≡S
      (⇒≡B is (a Billet
          (with unique Prereq-Schooling ≡S))
      ≡O is (an Officer
          (with Schooling ≡S))))
(is ≡O (a Schooled-Officer
      (with unique Billet ≡B))))
```

The difference is that in this case the outcome is the negation of the posted goal. In this case, OMEGA will assert that

```
¬(OFFICER-6 is (a Schooled-Officer
      (with unique Billet BILLET-17)))
```

The failure to establish this fact implies the failure to establish the conjunctive goal in the rule for establishing that an officer is qualified, and hence the negation of the conjunction will be asserted. This results in the negation of the second half of the equivalence:

```
¬(OFFICER-6 is (a Qualified-Officer
      (with unique Billet BILLET-17)))
```

We have been able to propagate back the fact that OFFICER-6 was not a *schooled officer* because we had been using equivalences in our reasoning. When we get to our original implication, shown again below, we can go no further.

```
(⇐ (∧ ≡B is (a Billet-Fulfilling-Career-Objectives
          (with unique Officer ≡O))
      ≡O is (a Qualified-Officer
          (with unique Billet ≡B)))
(is (an Officer-Billet-Proposal
      (with unique Billet ≡B)
      (with unique Officer ≡O))
      (a Reasonable-Proposal)))
```

This rule is only one way that a proposal can be shown to be reasonable. There may be other rules that can possibly achieve the goal.

At this point the question is how can we know when a goal cannot be achieved and how do we notify the user. One approach is the following. Suppose there are only three conditions under which a proposal may be judged reasonable. The following rule could be used.

```
(⇐ (∨ r1 r2 r3)
    (is (an Officer-Billet-Proposal
        (with unique Billet ≡ B)
        (with unique Officer ≡ O))
        (a Reasonable-Proposal)))
```

Thus OMEGA can know that when all of r1, r2, and r3 fail, then the goal cannot be established. This approach has two undesirable consequences. First, if the assignment officer asserts that a particular proposal is reasonable then OMEGA can conclude that one of r1, r2, or r3 is true, which in fact may not be the case. There may be some other criterion that the assignment officer has used to judge a proposal as reasonable. The second problem is what to do when another criterion for judging a proposal reasonable is to be told to OMEGA. This would mean that the above rule would have to be contradicted and a new viewpoint would have to be constructed with a new equivalence rule having four criteria for judging a proposal reasonable.

9.5 Using Sponsors to Reason About Reasoning

A superior approach is to use information concerning the sponsor of a particular goal. As described before, a sponsor is given quanta with which to accomplish a goal. When the sponsor uses all of its quanta, it must ask for more to proceed. If a sponsor has quanta but can do no more work (i.e., it is quiescent), then it waits for additional work. The sponsor informs OMEGA about these events by making assertions. In our case the assertions will be simply the total quanta the sponsor has used. These assertions are made at two times: when the quanta allotted to the sponsor are exhausted or when the sponsor is quiescent.

Thus when a user posts a goal he or she will also specify the amount of quanta to be allocated for achieving the goal. When the quanta are used, or no more can be used at a particular time, then an assertion is made as to how much has been used. Note that if the assertion is made because the sponsor is quiescent at a particular time, this does not mean that no more can be used in the future. A new assertion, made from other sponsored activity, may once again enable work to be done on a particular goal. Thus, in the case above, when no more work can be done for a particular sponsor, the following is asserted.

```
Sponsor-1 is (a Quiescent-Sponsor
        (with Exhausted-Quanta 4.3))
```

Note that this assertion is monotonically compatible with past assertions of this type. The assertion will trigger a sprite that was created at the time the sponsor was given its quanta for the particular goal. Again, at the time the sprite actually fires, it may well be that the sponsor is no longer quiescent. The sprite may well check to see if the sponsor is quiescent or if the sponsor's goal has been established. If the sponsor is not quiescent or the goal has been established the sprite may take no further action. If the sponsor is quiescent then it can examine the progress toward the goal. The progress toward the goal is analyzed by examining the DEPEND-ON-BY attributes in the goal's justifications.

In this way OMEGA can determine what subgoals were posted for a goal and whether the goal or its negation was asserted. In our case, it is determined that

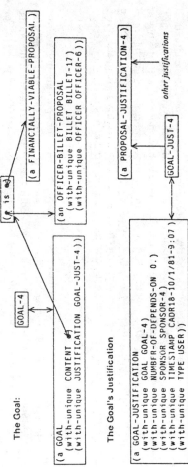

OFFICER-16 is not a Qualified Officer

OFFICER-16 is not Schooled and Experienced   An officer is Qualified if and only if
                                                   he is Schooled and Experienced

                    and

OFFICER-16 is not Schooled

$A \leftarrow B$ means A depends on B

Fig. 12.   Why the officer is not qualified.

OFFICER-6 was determined not to be a qualified officer. The information shown in Figure 12 can be extracted from OMEGA's descriptions and presented to the user through a suitable user interface.

Thus the user can see that the reason OMEGA has concluded that the officer is not qualified is because the officer is not schooled. At this point, the assignment officer may add the following assertion.

```
(⇒ (∧ =O is (an Experienced-Officer
              (with unique Billet =B))
       =O is (a Schooled-or-Enrolled-Officer
              (with unique Billet =B))
       =B is (a Billet-Fulfilling-Career-Objectives
              (with unique Officer =O)))
   (is (an Officer-Billet-Proposal
          (with unique Billet =B)
          (with unique Officer =O))
       (a Reasonable-Proposal)))
```

This assertion says that if an officer is experienced (i.e., the officer is schooled or enrolled in school), and if the billet satisfies the officer's career objectives, then the proposal is a reasonable proposal. The assignment officer would then go on to describe to OMEGA what it means for an officer to be schooled or enrolled in school for a particular billet.

10. REASONING ABOUT CONTRADICTIONS

In the previous section, we described how a user might interact with OMEGA when he or she is trying to achieve some goal and the goal cannot be achieved. The sponsors of a computation communicate with OMEGA and thus allow it to reason in a limited but useful fashion about the progress in achieving a particular goal. In this section, we describe how contradictions are handled when they arise in the course of achieving some goal. For example, contradictions can arise when a user makes an assumption that violates a system constraint.

In the following example, we continue the scenario from the previous section. Now the assignment officer has judged a proposal as reasonable and must calculate travel expenses for the proposed reassignment. The contradiction will arise when the assignment officer assumes there is enough money in the current quarter's expense account to cover the reassignment. To begin the calculation of travel expenses, the assignment officer posts the goal that the proposal be financially viable (Figure 13).

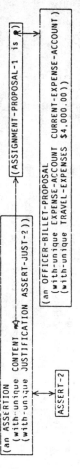

The Goal:

GOAL-4

```
(a GOAL
   (with-unique CONTENT ●)
   (with-unique JUSTIFICATION GOAL-JUST-4))
```

(a FINANCIALLY-VIABLE-PROPOSAL.)

(an OFFICER-BILLET-PROPOSAL
   (with-unique BILLET BILLET-17)
   (with-unique OFFICER OFFICER-6))

The Goal's Justification

GOAL-JUST-4

```
(a GOAL-JUSTIFICATION
   (with-unique GOAL GOAL-4)
   (with-unique NUMBER-OF-DEPENDS-ON 0.)
   (with-unique SPONSOR SPONSOR-4)
   (with-unique TIMESTAMP CADR18-10/1/81-9:07)
   (with-unique TYPE USER))
```

(a PROPOSAL-JUSTIFICATION-4)

other justifications

Fig. 13.   Representation of the goal for financial viability.

The Assertion:

ASSERT-2

```
(an ASSERTION
   (with-unique CONTENT ●)
   (with-unique JUSTIFICATION ASSERT-JUST-2))
```

(ASSIGNMENT-PROPOSAL-1 is ●)

(an OFFICER-BILLET-PROPOSAL
   (with-unique EXPENSE-ACCOUNT CURRENT-EXPENSE-ACCOUNT)
   (with-unique TRAVEL-EXPENSES $4,000.00))

The Assertion's Justification:

ASSERT-JUST-2

```
(an ASSERTION-JUSTIFICATION
   (with DEPENDS-ON REASONABLE-GOAL-JUST)
   (with DEPENDS-ON TRAVEL-EXPENSE-CALC-SPRITE-1)
   (with-unique ASSERTION ASSERT-2)
   (with-unique NUMBER-OF-DEPENDS-ON 2.)
   (with-unique TIMESTAMP CADR18-10/1/81-9:12)
   (with-unique TYPE COMPOUND))
```

(a PROPOSAL-JUSTIFICATION-4)

Other Justifications

Fig. 14.   Travel expense assertion.

A sprite exists within OMEGA that watches for a goal of this sort. When the sprite fires on the goal, it calculates the travel expenses for the proposed assignment and asserts this information. An abbreviated description of the sprite is shown below.

```
(when-goal Calc-Sprite-2 Travel-Expense-Sprite-Just-1
  (is (an 'Officer-Billet-Proposal      ;Goal to match
        (with unique 'Officer =O)
        (with unique 'Billet =B))
      (a 'Financially-Viable-Proposal))
  =G-JUST =VP =SPONSOR      ;Goal elements
  1. Calculate travel expenses,
  2. Use current expense amount,
  3. Assert the travel expenses and expense account.)
```

The assertion the sprite makes with its justification is shown in Figure 14.

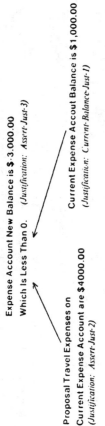

Expense Account New Balance is $-3,000.00
Which Is Less Than 0.   *(Justification: Assert-Just-3)*

Current Expense Accout Balance is $1,000.00
(Justification: Current-Balance-Just-1)

Proposal Travel Expenses on
Current Expense Accout Account are $4000.00
(Justification: Assert-Just-2)

The Assertion of Contradiction: *(Justification: Assert-Just-3)*

Fig. 16.   Contradiction dependencies.

In Figure 15, we have assumed that the assertion which calculated the NEW-BALANCE has the justification ASSERT-JUST-3. A sprite will fire when the contradiction is asserted. The sprite will retrieve the justifications for the offending assertions. The sprite will analyze the assertions, retrieving the descriptions in the NEW-BALANCE attributions, and present to the user the information shown in Figure 16. When this information is presented, the user can immediately see the cause of the contradiction and can take corrective actions, for example, by using the next quarter's expense account.

11. CONCLUSION

We have presented the OMEGA knowledge system along with some simple examples. OMEGA's problem-solving and viewpoint capabilities are useful for describing and reasoning about objects whose properties vary with time and for handling contradictions that arise during reasoning processes. Simple examples have been chosen to illustrate OMEGA's functionality. They do not reflect the level of complexity that OMEGA can handle. In the first example, OMEGA performed part of an office procedure after an office worker posted the goal of the procedure. In actual application, OMEGA could perform many complicated tasks relating to any particular goal that an office worker might post. In the second example, OMEGA discovered and illustrated a problem in an attempt to establish a goal. In actual application, this would be very useful as obstacles in the performance of complicated tasks could easily be found with OMEGA's aid.

The viewpoint mechanism presented here is related to that in ETHER [9] and to the layers of the PIE system [8]. Viewpoints are a powerful unifying mechanism which combine aspects of McCarthy's situational tags [11] and the contexts of QA4 [12]. They serve as a replacement for update and pusher-puller mechanisms.

Office work is a problem-solving activity that can be supported with the use of knowledge-embedding languages. A problem solving support paradigm has been presented as a framework within which to develop support tools for the office worker. The OMEGA viewpoint mechanism provides a facility to help the office worker achieve his or her goals, and to analyze contradictions when they arise.

ACKNOWLEDGMENTS

I would like to thank Carl Hewitt, my research advisor, for sparking my interest in this field. He has been an invaluable source of inspiration and insightful questions. Almost all of the work presented in this paper is based on his ideas. This research has been influenced by conversation with many people. For

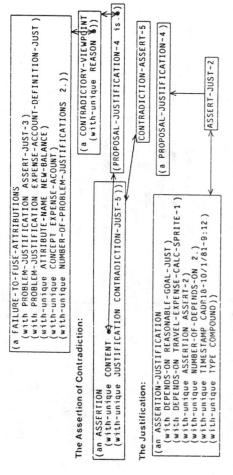

```
(a FAILURE-TO-FUSE-ATTRIBUTIONS
  (with PROBLEM-JUSTIFICATION ASSERT-JUST-3)
  (with PROBLEM-JUSTIFICATION EXPENSE-ACCOUNT-DEFINITION-JUST)
  (with-unique ATTRIBUTE-NAME NEW-BALANCE)
  (with-unique CONCEPT EXPENSE-ACCOUNT)
  (with-unique NUMBER-OF-PROBLEM-JUSTIFICATIONS 2.))
```

```
(a CONTRADICTORY-VIEWPOINT
  (with-unique REASON ●))
```

The Assertion of Contradiction:

```
(an ASSERTION CONTENT
  (with-unique JUSTIFICATION CONTRADICTION-JUST-5)))
```

(PROPOSAL-JUSTIFICATION-4 is .)

CONTRADICTION-ASSERT-5

(a PROPOSAL-JUSTIFICATION-4)

ASSERT-JUST-2

The Justification:

```
(an ASSERTION-JUSTIFICATION
  (with DEPENDS-ON REASONABLE-GOAL-JUST)
  (with DEPENDS-ON TRAVEL-EXPENSE-CALC-SPRITE-1)
  (with-unique ASSERTION ASSERT-2)
  (with-unique NUMBER-OF-DEPENDS-ON 2.)
  (with-unique TIMESTAMP CADP:18-10/1/81-9:12)
  (with-unique TYPE COMPOUND))
```

Fig. 15.   Assertion of the contradiction.

For brevity, the assignment proposal has been asserted to be same with the description for ASSIGNMENT-PROPOSAL-1. The assertion in Figure 14 states that the assignment proposal will incur a cost of $4000 from the current expense account for travel expenses. Now OMEGA uses the following rule to calculate the new balance on the expense account.

```
⇒ (is ≡P
    (an Officer-Billet-Proposal
      (with unique Travel-Expenses ≡TE)
      (with unique Expense-Account
        (an Expense-Account
          (with unique Account-# ≡AN)
          (with unique Balance ≡B)))))
    (is (an Expense-Account (with unique Account-# ≡AN))
      an Expense-Account
      (with unique New-Balance (− ≡B ≡TE)))))[4]
```

Assume that the expense account has a balance of $1000 and that the description of an expense account includes the following.

```
(an Expense-Account) is (an Expense-Account
    (with every Balance (>= 0))
        (with every New-Balance (>= 0)))
```

Here we use the abbreviation (>= 0) for the description
(a Dollar-Amount (with Lesser-or-Equal-Amount 0)).
This describes an amount of dollars with the constraint that 0 is less than or equal to the amount.

When the rule that calculates the new balance fires, it will assert that the new balance is −$3000. This will be fused with the constraint that every balance and new balance be greater than or equal to 0. The attempt to fuse will fail, signaling a contradiction by making the assertion shown in Figure 15.

---

[4] Note that we have used the abbreviation (− A B) for the description (a Difference (of Minuend A)(of Subtrahend B)).

listening to and commenting on the work, I would like to thank Giuseppe Attardi, Mike Brady, Marilyn Brockman, Gene Ciccarelli, Stan Curtis, Bill Kornfeld, Henry Lieberman, Maria Simi, and John Teeter. The diagrams in this paper were made with the OMEGA Presenter on M.I.T.'s LISP Machine. The presenter was developed by Gene Ciccarelli in conjunction with myself.

I would also like to acknowledge the assistance of IBM, the Advanced Research Projects Agency, and the Office of Naval Research.

REFERENCES

1. Barber, G.R. Office semantics. Ph.D. dissertation, Massachusetts Institute of Technology, Cambridge, Mass., 1982.
2. de Kleer, J., Doyle, J., Steele, G.L., and Sussman, G.J. AMORD: Explicit control of reasoning. In *Proceedings of the Symposium on Artificial Intelligence and Programming Languages* (Rochester, N.Y., August 15–17), 1977, ACM, New York, pp. 116–125.
3. Doyle, J. Truth maintenance systems for problem solving. Tech. Rep. AI-TR 419, Artificial Intelligence Lab, Massachusetts Institute of Technology, Cambridge, Mass., May, 1977.
4. Ellis, C.A. and Nutt, G.J. Office information systems and computer science. *ACM Comput. Surv.* 12, 1 (March 1980), 27–60.
5. Fikes, R.E. and Henderson, D.A. On supporting the use of procedures in office work. In *Proceedings of the 1st Annual AAAI Conference.* American Association for Artificial Intelligence, Aug. 1980.
6. Fikes, R.E. Odyssey: A knowledge-based assistant. *Artif. Intell.*, 16, 3 (July 1981), 331–362.
7. Goldstein, I.P. and Roberts, R.B. NUDGE, a knowledge-based scheduling program. In *Proceedings of the 5th International Joint Conference on Artificial Intelligence.*
8. Goldstein, I. PIE: A network-based personal information environment. In *Proceedings of the 1st Annual AAAI Conference.* American Association for Artificial Intelligence. Aug. 1980.
9. Kornfeld, W. Using parallel processing for problem solving. A.I. Memo 561, Massachusetts Institute of Technology, Cambridge, Mass., December, 1979.
10. Kornfeld, W. Concepts in parallel problem solving. Ph.D. dissertation, Massachusetts Institute of Technology, Cambridge, Mass. 1982.
11. McCarthy, J. and Hayes, P.J. Some philosophical problems from the standpoint of artificial intelligence. *Machine Intelligence 4*, Edinburgh University Press, Edinburgh, Scotland, 1969, pp. 463–502.
12. Rulifson, J., Derksen, J., and Waldinger, R. QA4: A procedural calculus for intuitive reasoning. Tech. Note 73, Artificial Intelligence Center, Stanford Research Institute, Stanford, Calif., Nov. 1972.
13. Steele, G.L. The definition and implementation of a computer programming language based on constraints. Tech. Rep. AI-TR 595, Artificial Intelligence Lab, Massachusetts Institute of Technology, Cambridge, Mass., August, 1980.
14. Suchman, L. Office procedures as practical action: A case study. Tech. Rep., XEROX PARC, Palo Alto, Calif. Sept. 1979.
15. Sussman, G.J. From PLANNER to CONNIVER—A genetic approach. In *Proceedings of the AFIPS Fall Joint Computer Conference*, vol. 41, AFIPS Press, Arlington, Va., 1972, pp. 1171–1179.
16. Tsichritzis, D. A form manipulation system. In *Proceedings of the NYU Symposium on Automated Office Systems*, New York Univ., New York, N.Y., 1979.
17. Winograd, T. Procedures as a representation for data in a computer program for understanding natural language. MAC-TR 83, Massachusetts Institute of Technology, Cambridge, Mass, 1971.
18. Wynn, E. Office conversation as an information medium. Ph.D. dissertation, Dep. of Anthropology, Univ. of California, Berkeley, Calif., 1979.
19. Zloof, M.M. A language for office and business automation. Res. Rep. 35086, IBM, Yorktown Heights, N.Y., Jan. 1980.

Received January 1982; revised August 1982; accepted August 1982

PROVIDING INTELLIGENT ASSISTANCE
IN DISTRIBUTED OFFICE ENVIRONMENTS[1]

Sergei Nirenburg   *Victor Lesser*

Colgate University   University of Massachusetts

Abstract. We argue that a task-centered, an
agent-centered and a cognition-oriented perspective are all needed for providing intelligent assistance in distributed office environments. We
present the architecture for a system called
OFFICE that combines these three perspectives.
We illustrate this architecture through an example.

1. Introduction.

In this paper we describe OFFICE, a system that provides
intelligent assistance in the office environment. A
schematic diagram of the type of system we are proposing
is shown in Figure 1.

In this diagram the office worker operating together with
his/her workstation constitute one node in the office
problem solving network. The initiative in such a
problem-solving environment is mixed: it can be originated by the office worker performing a low-level task
or specifying a high-level goal to be accomplished or the
office system OFFICE requesting the worker to perform a
task. Thus, we see OFFICE as an intelligent assistant to
the office worker.

We argue that a task-centered, an agent-centered and a
cognition-oriented perspective are all needed for
providing intelligent assistance in distributed office
environments. We need knowledge from each of these
perspectives in order to support not only effective local
interaction between OFFICE and the office worker, but
also to coordinate cooperative problem solving among the
nodes in the system. Coordinating problem solving is an
especially difficult task, given the semi-autonomous
nature of processing at each node; the bandwidth of the
communication channel (which makes it not feasible for
nodes to have a complete global view of problem solving
in the network); the diversity of the types of knowledge
necessary for coordinating and scheduling office activities; and the necessity to provide guidance to the office
worker about how to prioritize his own tasks so that they
are coherent with the goals of the whole system.

We see the coordination problem as breaking down into a
number of subproblems, which include managing
resources; equalizing workload distribution; managing
goal conflicts; maintaining a proper level of redundancy
in task execution and especially in information flow;
analyzing dependencies in the sets of goals, plans and
events, etc. Automation of any of the above tasks clearly
involves manipulation of many types of knowledge, both
domain and control.

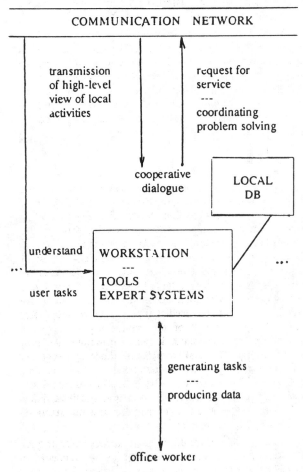

Figure 1. A node in a network of cooperative office
workstations.

[1] This work was supported by the Air Force Systems Command,
Rome Air Development Center, Griffiss Air Force Base, NY
13441-5700, and the Air Force Office of Scientific Research, Bolling Air Force Base, D.C. 20332 under contract number F30602-

To illustrate the problem of local scheduling that takes into account global coherence, consider an office consisting of an executive, E, and his/her secretary, S. Suppose, E is dictating letters to S, and the telephone rings. S answers, and the call appears to be about a very important shipment, and S is asked to provide some information about it. The scheduling choice here is between continuing with the letters (task T1) and performing the request that came over the phone (task T2). We want our system to consider a number of factors here, including the relative importance of the tasks (say, a number of people may be idle in the company because of the lack of raw materials that are to be shipped), the time limitations (suppose, the information is needed before the end of the business day, and it's already 4 p.m.; also, the estimated time of finding the requested information), personal characteristics of S and E, etc. If the secretary were scheduling purely locally, he/she may prefer to schedule T2, but knowing that E will be detained by her doing so, S may prefer T1 based on global coherence considerations. S's knowledge about personal characteristics of E can also be a factor: if E is very conscious of his/her status and importance, then the decision of scheduling T1 is even more strengthened; if not, and if S has the characteristic of being assertive, T2 may be preferred, after an explanation to E.

In what follows we, first, trace the project's genesis from three research projects in connected fields and discuss its functionality. Second, we describe how an office can be modelled in a distributed computer system such as OFFICE and describe its architecture and the basic processing cycle. Finally, we give an example of OFFICE operation where we concentrate on its reasoning capabilities.

The Task-Oriented Perspective.

Our initial effort in developing an expert system in the office domain is the task support system POISE (Croft et al., 1983). POISE has been designed to support office workers in their problem solving activities through the use of plan recognition and planning. In the plan recognition mode the system obtains messages about certain atomic events (such as tool invocations) and tries to determine into which of typical tasks known to the system this event fits. In this manner POISE is able to monitor the activities in an office, predict future activity and detect errors. If, as a result of the monitoring, the system understands the user's task, it can in principle take over its completion. This task completion mode is integrated with the planning mode of operation. In the planning mode POISE is supplied with a typical tasks and its parameters and tries to execute as much of it as possible, based on its knowledge of the task structure and the status of domain objects in a semantic database.

POISE's knowledge takes the form of an hierarchy of typical tasks. Each task is represented by a precondition statement that defines the necessary conditions for its execution; a goal statement that specifies the intended effect of the task; the sequence of subtasks needed to be performed in order to accomplish the task and the con-

straints among the parameters of the subtasks and those of the task. See Figure 2 for an example.

```
PROC    Purchase-items (Purchasing Amount Items Vendor)
DESC    Procedure for purchasing items with non-state funds.
IS      Receive-purchase-request
        ! (Process-purchase-order | Process-purchase-requisition)
        ! Complete-purchase
```

COND

Process-purchase-order.Amount OR	= Receive-purchase-request.Amount
Process-purchase-requisition.Amount	= Receive-purchase-request.Amount
Process-purchase-order.Items OR	= Receive-purchase-request.Items
Process-purchase-requisition.Items	= Receive-purchase-request.Items
Process-purchase-order.Vendor OR	= Receive-purchase-request.Vendor
Process-purchase-requisition.Vendor	= Receive-purchase-request.Vendor
Process-purchase-order.Amount OR	= Complete-purchase.Amount
Process-purchase-requisition.Amount	= Complete-purchase.Amount
Process-purchase-order.Items OR	= Complete-purchase.Items
Process-purchase-requisition.Items	= Complete-purchase.Items
Process-purchase-order.Vendor OR	= Complete-purchase.Vendor
Process-purchase-requisition.Vendor	= Complete-purchase.Vendor

WITH	Purchaser	= Receive-purchase-request.Purchaser
	Amount	= Receive-purchase-request.Amount
	Items	= Receive-purchase-request.Items
	Vendor	= Receive-purchase-request.Vendor

Figure 2. A plan in POISE

POISE plans are structured so that they in principle allow concurrent execution of subtasks of a task. Straightforward transformation of POISE into a distributed system cannot, however, be performed. Since POISE does not have a developed agent-oriented perspective, there is no way in it to express a fact such as 'requests made by the manager of the office have priority over those made by other workers' or the fact that even though certain workers are better at doing certain types of jobs, if they are not available to do a job of this type, then other workers have to be assigned this responsibility. There is also no way of talking about seemingly independent tasks being actually parts of a cooperative problem solving situation. this includes the considerations of arbitration of competing claims for limited resources.

POISE does not distinguish or reason about the agents' roles and the objects in plans. Thus, for instance, it does not have the possibility to understand that an unusual event happened if it gets the message that the president of a company typed a letter (and not a secretary). Therefore it cannot infer that the secretary may have a day off or that a goal must be instantiated of changing workload distribution among the employees.

Another deficiency of POISE is that the plan recognition and planning architectures are not designed for being

distributed and assume a global blackboard and a single locus of control. POISE gives us some ideas about what an intelligent assistant could be but its architecture is not appropriate for use in a distributed environment and it lacks a distributed agent-oriented perspective.

The Distributed Agent-Oriented Perspective.

One of the research areas where we can look for ideas of how to implement the distributed agent-oriented perspective is the field of distributed AI. One of the current approaches there is the study of functionally accurate, cooperative (FA/C) distributed problem solving (Lesser and Corkill, 1983; Corkill, 1982; Durfee et al., 1984, 1985). With this approach, a problem is solved in cooperation by a set of semi-autonomous processing nodes (agents) that may have inconsistent and incomplete local databases. each node independently generates tentative partial solutions, communicates them through a network to other nodes, receives messages (partial solutions, goals, plans and facts) from other nodes, and modifies its processing in accordance with new input. The experience of this work has shown that the control problem is difficult; that the network communication is both difficult and computationally expensive; most importantly, it was found that the key to global coherence is having sophisticated agents who can reason about their own view of processing as well as the views of other agents. They have developed a system in which each node is guided by a high-level strategic plan for cooperation among the nodes in the network. This plan, which is a form of metalevel control, is represented as a network organizational structure that specifies in a general way the information and control relationships among the nodes. Examples of this information include static priorities among local tasks, to whom and what information to communicate and how to prioritize tasks that have been requested by other nodes versus those that were locally generated.

Other work by Smith and Davis (1981) has focused on the knowledge and the protocols necessary for nodes to decide in a distributed way how to allocate subtasks to other nodes. This involves a two-way bidding protocol in which the contractors (taking on the task perspective) and bidders (taking on an agent perspective) communicate to determine the best task allocation.

The work by Lesser et al. focuses on how to do local scheduling given a static task allocation that may redundantly allocate tasks among nodes, while Smith and Davis focus on dynamic task allocation. The office domain requires an integration of both approaches together with augmenting the knowledge used by both approaches for scheduling. The office domain also presents challenges to both approaches because of the tighter and more complex interactions among agents that exists in this domain, compared to the distributed interpretation domain from which both of the above approaches evolved.

The Cognition-Oriented Perspective.

The distributed problem solving approaches described above concentrated on the architecture of the network and the nodes, with the view of organizing the control structure. The types of knowledge necessary for control and communication in OFFICE are studied in the field of cognitive agency research (e.g. Georgeff, 1984, Moore, 1985, but mainly Nirenburg et al., 1985, 1986). The view of the world in this field is that cognitive agents are immersed in a world which is non-monotonic, in the sense that changes in the world can be introduced not only because of the activities of a single agent but also through uncontrolled external events. Agents are capable of a variety of cognitive tasks. They can perceive objects and events in the world. They possess a set of goal types and means of achieving goals of these types: plans. They perform goal and plan generation, selection and execution in complex situations in which many goals and plans coexist and compete for the attention of the agent's conscious processor.

The study of the knowledge that underlies the reasons for particular choices of goals and plans by an agent (in other words, reasons for scheduling and communication decisions) is the central theme of this approach. This knowledge is claimed to involve such factors as personality traits, and physical and mental states of the agent, in addition to the knowledge about the domain situation and the typical tasks and goals. Our approach is to use all the types of knowledge discussed in the cognitive agency approach within the architectural framework inspired by the distributed AI research.

2. An Architecture for a Distributed Office System.

We present here, through an example, an architecture for an intelligent assistance system that integrates the task-, agent- and cognition-oriented perspectives.

2.1. Representing an office.

An office is modelled as a network whose nodes are interpreted as office workers and edges, as communication channels. Every node in the network is a complete problem solver that consists of an office worker and his/her workstation. Following POISE, OFFICE deals with typical activities in a university-based research project (RP), namely: purchasing equipment, hiring and travel. The types of agents in the RP office include Principal Investigator (PI), Research Associate (RA), Graduate Student (GS), Secretary (S), Vendor (V) and Accountant (A). A typical instance of a project may involve 1 PI, 2 RA's, 6 GS's, 1 S, 3 V's (e.g., DEC, Symbolics and TI) and and 2 A's (say, one in Accounts Receivable and one in Personnel).

Figure 3 shows the communication channels for the RP office.

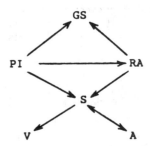

Figure 3. The network of processing nodes in a model of an RP office. The arrows illustrate authority relationships (see below).

Every node in the office network is aware of its responsibilities to carry out parts of certain plans. They also know who or where from they can and should seek information that is necessary for them to perform their tasks (recall that information about the typical agents for all types of tasks is among the knowledge that every agent possesses).

At any moment t each agent in OFFICE has an agenda of current goals or, more precisely, of current goal instances, as illustrated in (1),

$$\left\{ PU^5_{\sigma_1}, PU^6_{\sigma_1}, HI^1_{\sigma_3}, TR^2_{\sigma_4} \right\}_t \qquad (1)$$

where PU^i, HI^j and TR^k stand for instances of goal types *Purchase, Hire* and *Travel*, and σ_i designate subsets of network nodes that are working cooperatively on particular goals. Intuitively, at any given moment the office workers are pursuing a number of goals, working in teams. Note that some such goals can be in conflict or can compete for resources. Therefore, the agents must have means of resolving these conflicts.

The architecture of an agent in OFFICE is illustrated in Figure 4. A frame-based representation is used for objects, goals, plans and actions, including messages. Plans are represented in extended EDL (cf. Nirenburg et al., 1985). An agent has knowledge about the goals it is typically responsible for as well as about plans that are typically used to accomplish these goals. (If node A has a goal G on its agenda, then A is *responsible* for achieving G.) It also has the knowledge about the current state of its goal agenda, as well as a subset of the contents of other agents' agendas. Scheduling knowledge used by the agent to select goals and plans for processing is represented as a set of condition-action rules. The agent also is aware of the authority relationships in the office, illustrated in Figure 3, that are part of the agent's scheduling knowledge.

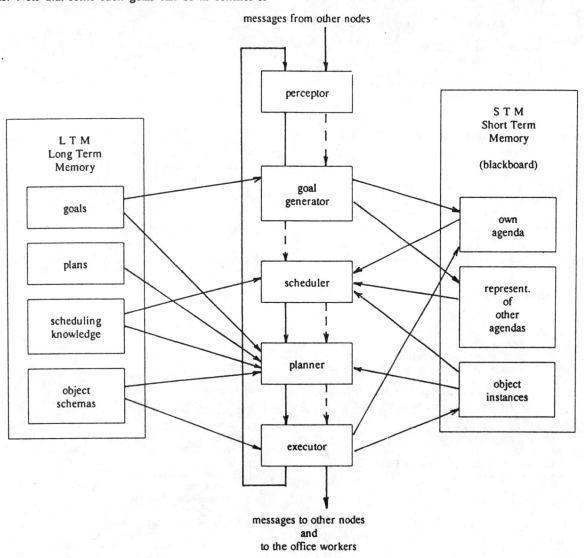

Figure 4. Node Architecture.
⟶ flow of data
- - - -> flow of control

Representations of two top-level goal types in OFFICE are given in Figure 5. A number of OFFICE plans are illustrated in Figure 6.

```
(goal HIRE-PERSON
  (Typical-Responsible-Agents RP PI)
  (Typical-Plan Hire-plan)
  (time-scale days)
  (importance 2)
  (beneficiary Research-Project)
  (Supergoals  Conformity-between-Workers-and-Work-Amount
               Use-All-Resources-Available)
  (Trigger (or (sum of expenditures is less than available funds)
               (there are less workers than needed to do work)))
)

(goal PURCHASE
  (Typical-Responsible-Agents  PI)
  (Typical-Plan Purchase-plan)
  (time-scale days)
  (importance 1)
  (beneficiary (PI S RA GS))                    ;any member of RP
  (Supergoals  Get-Equipment
               Use-All-Resources-Available)
  (Trigger  (and (there are funds available)
                 (the beneficiary's resources are incomplete,
                  compared to the typical resources allocated
                  to this role-holder)))
)
```

Figure 5. The goals HIRE-PERSON and PURCHASE.

```
(Purchase-plan
  (icon PU)
  (With ((Agent RP.member)
         (Object POBJ) ;is not specified at the moment of
                       ;plan instantiation
         (Amount int)  ; - " -
         (  ...))
  (is ((specify-item-to-buy (agent = RP.member
                             object = item
                             approx-price = int))
       (make-document (agent = RP.member
                       doc-type = purchase-request
                       object = item))
       (communicate (agent = RP.member
                     destination = Secretary
                     object = purshase-request))
       (plan-selector ((process-purchase-order (agent = Secretary
                                                object = item))
                       (process-purchase-requisition (agent = Secretary
                                                      object = item)))
          ;both plans are compound
       (complete-purchase (agent = Secretary
                           object = item))
    )
  (preconditions  (Agent has money. Vendor has Object))
  (effects (Agent has less money.
            Vendor has more money.
            Agent has Object))
  )

(Process-Purchase-Order
  (with (agent = secretary
         object = item
         destination = vendor
         price = int))
```

```
  (preconditions (approx-price < $250 ))
  (is (make-document (agent = secretary
                      doc-type = purchase-order
                      object = (item vendor)))
      (communicate (agent = secretary
                    object = purchase-order
                    destination = vendor)))
)

(Complete-Purchase
  (with (agent = secretary
         object = item
         source = vendor))
  (is (# (communicate (agent = vendor
                       destination = secretary
                       object = item))
         (communicate (agent = vendor
                       destination = secretary
                       object = bill)))
      (check-goods (agent = secretary
                    object = item))
      (plan-selector ((pay-for-goods (agent = secretary
                                      destination = vendor
                                      object = item
                                      amount = bill.amount)
                       (cancel-goods (agent = secretary
                                      destination = vendor
                                      object = item
                                      amount = bill.amount))))
)

(make-document                ;a primitive plan
  (with (agent = person
         doc-type = purchase-request | bid-request | purchase-order |
                    disbursement-form | item-rejection-form | cv | offer ...
         destination = person | organization
         object = (item, price ...)  ;parameters that are mentioned in
                                     ;the document
  )
  (is primitive)
  (effects   ) ;the document exists
)

(check-goods
  (with (agent = person
         object = item))
  (is primitive)
)

(Communicate
  (with (agent = person
         destination = person
         object = message
         type = assertion | question | order
         instrument = medium))
              ;medium is a list of phone, mail, csnet, etc.
  (is primitive)
  (action-for-primitive))

(Get-Info
  (with (agent = person
         object = message
         was-invoked-by = person3
         instrument medium))
  (is (plan-selector (ask-track (agent = person1
                                 destination = person2
                                 was-invoked-by = person3
                                 instrument = medium))
                      find-track (agent = person
                                  object = message)))
```

```
(effects (communicate (agent = person1
              destination person3
              object = message
              instrument = medium) ))
)
```

Figure 6. A sample of OFFICE plans.

Local and Global Scheduling Knowledge

A special part of the knowledge in OFFICE is the knowledge about scheduling and prioritizing activities by the nodes in the network. A part of the scheduling knowledge is static, that is, is considered true irrespective of the circumstances in which the scheduling takes place. The other portion of the scheduling knowledge is dynamic in that it takes into account the presence of other goals on the node's agenda and the suggests the ways of dealing with goal conflict.

The static part of an agent's scheduling knowledge includes the authority and responsibility structure of the office and the profiles of actual workers in specific roles within the organization. The latter includes both the workers' stated attitudes and preferences with respect to the types of jobs they are performing and their personality profiles, as understood by the current agent, on the basis of which the above attitudes and preferences can be inferred.

The dynamic part of this knowledge includes a snapshot of problem solving activities from the current agent's perspective; a representation of time and other resources; and a set of operational rules that contribute to the task of scheduling. In this paper we will present these rules as a set of scheduling heuristics, bypassing, for the sake of clarity and understandability the actual formalism in which they are expressed. The scheduling heuristics are as follows:

1. Static priorities are stated for all the types of top-level goals. The instances of goals with higher static priorities will be preferred. Thus, for instance, *Purchasing* can be declared more important than *Hiring*.

2. The more time a goal spends on the agenda, the higher the priority it acquires.

3. The less time the accomplishment of a goal will take (as estimated by an agent), the higher the priority it acquires.

4. The smaller the effort needed for the accomplishment of a goal (as estimated by an agent), the higher the priority it acquires. This rule measures effort in terms of both the amount of energy exertion on the part of the agents and the number of intermediate steps (plans) still estimated as needed to accomplish the goal.

5. If a precondition for a plan selected to achieve a goal is false, the goal's priority goes down; however, for specific types of preconditions and nodes a new goal of satisfying this precondition can be established.

6. The higher the authority of the node responsible for a goal, the higher the priority it acquires.

7. Beliefs about the agendas of other network nodes weigh less in the decision process than the contents of own agenda. For example, if the level of authority responsible for a goal G is *inferred* by a node then it will increase the priority of G to a lesser degree than in the case when the authority level was explicitly obtained as input.

8. If the accomplishment of a goal satisfies preconditions for the execution of a plan (or a number of plans) leading to the achievement of other goals (on any of the goal agendas in the network), the priority of the goal is considered higher.

The influence of prioritizing rules based on the above scheduling heuristics is calibrated to produce a general dynamic priority for every goal on a node's agenda.

2.2. How Do the Agents Operate?

A cycle of processing by each agent involves a consecutive invocation of the perceptor, the goal generator, the scheduler, the planner and the executor (cf. Figure 4).

The perceptor

obtains as input (either through the network or from the office worker) *messages* about changes in the world that were received since the previous time cycle (changes are various new states, including results of actions performed by agents in the system).

Input messages are classified according to their *speech act* character. Messages can be either assertions or requests. Assertions can be definitions, opinions, facts, promises, threats and advice. Requests can be questions (request-info) or commands (request-action). Commands are orders, suggestions or pleas. This classification is needed to improve the understanding capabilities of the system (as compared, e.g., with POISE). Also, it allows a clear way of setting goals for the nodes in the network.

Next, the perceptor 'understands' these actions in terms of *plans* they are parts of and, correspondingly, in terms of what was the *goal* that the agent of that action pursued. This step embodies the *plan recognition* activity of the system, since, in the general case, it must understand plans of others in order to perform its own plan production.

The goal generator

updates the agenda of the node's goals due to new inputs. Thus, the arrival of the following input:

```
(message-14
  (instance-of message)
  (speech-act order)
  (sender PI-1)
  (receiver Secretary-33)
  (proposition (communicate Secretary-33
                Vendor-101
                'what is the price of desk-22?'
                Phone))
```

will lead to the generation of the low-level goal instance 'Get-Info-34' that will be fulfilled when the secretary knows the price of the desk. The plan selection for reaching this goal also is specified in the message: using the telephone. 'Get-Info-34' is added to secretary's agenda of goals to accomplish.

There are thus two kinds of sources of goals for every node. One source is the state of the (office) world (if there are more workers than workstations, the goal of purchasing equipment will be generated and put on the office head's agenda). The other source, as in the above example, is messages (requests and orders) from other nodes.

The scheduler

selects a goal to pursue from among a number of candidate goals on the agenda. It applies condition-action rules designed on the basis of the above scheduling heuristics and evaluates the current local state of problem solving from the current agent's perspective. After the scheduler finishes operation, one goal from the node's agenda is selected for processing, and control is passed to the planner.

The planner

has the task of providing a plan for the achievement of the goal scheduled by the scheduler. If the agent knows of a *canned plan* that typically leads from the current state to the goal state, the planner simply passes the plan to the executor (see below). If more than one plan can be used to achieve a given goal, the planner selects one of them, based on the scheduling rules. The same heuristics that are used for scheduling goals are also used for plan selection. This is in itself a scheduling heuristic.

The knowledge needed by the planner includes the list of plan types, the list of plans that are believed by the node to be instrumental in achieving the goal selected by the scheduler, and the for competing plans.

The executor

is called after the planner selects a plan for achieving the current goal.[1] It performs the following sequence of steps:

a) creates an instance of the chosen plan (if such an instance does not already exist) and lists it under the corresponding goal on the agenda.

b) checks preconditions of the plan; if preconditions do not hold (the plan is not immediately applicable) then sets precondition states to be (sub)goal states; puts them on the goal agenda (note that one of preconditions is 'to have values for all non-optional parameters') else expands the agenda tree by substituting the current plan by the sequence of its component plans.

c) if the first subplan in this sequence has the current node as its agent, it is processed by the executor; if another role in the office is the agent of a subplan, the execution of the current plan is interrupted and a value of its 'status' slot is set to 'suspended' and a corresponding message is issued to the agent of the next subplan.

---

[1] This is a simplification. In reality, planning and execution steps can be interleaved.

d) if the plan is 'primitive' the actions specified in it are performed. Then the executor checks whether the plan is completed; if yes, the executor reports this, through the communication channels, to the node responsible for supergoal of the goal which the current plan helped achieve. In this way responsibility relationships are both statically and dynamically introduced into the system.

3. An Example Run of OFFICE.

We will consider 2 top-level goals: Purchase and Hiring. The processing will be traced from the standpoint of one specific network node, that of Secretary (S). At the beginning of the run S already has a *nonempty* agenda of plans and goals. It also has a representation of agendas of other nodes in the network. This representation may contain mistakes, because it is mainly a result of plan understanding activities of the node. The contents of S's agenda and S's belief about the agendas of a sample of other nodes at the beginning of our manual trace are given in Figure 7.

```
                        ------------------
                        S's own agenda:
                        ------------------


AGENDA ITEM 1:
  Purchase-plan3 (object = terminal)
    communicate (agent = S, destination = PI, object =
                  [communicate (agent = V1, object = terminal,
                                destination = S)
                   communicate (agent = V1, object = bill,
                                destination = S)])
    check-goods (agent = PI, object = terminal16)
    plan-selector (agent = S, object =

                  [pay-for-goods (agent = S, destination = V1,
                                  object = bill)
                   cancel-goods (agent = S, destination = V1,
                                 object = (terminal16 bill)])


AGENDA ITEM 2:
  process-purchase-order5 (object = book)
    make-document (agent = S, document-type = purchase-order,
                   object = book, destination = V2)
    communicate (agent = S, object = purchase-order, destination = V2)


              --------------------------------------
              Secretary's beliefs about PI's agenda:
              --------------------------------------


AGENDA ITEM 1:
  Purchase-plan3 (object = terminal16)
    complete-purchase (agent = PI, object = terminal16)


AGENDA ITEM 2:
  Hiring-plan2 (RA)
    evaluate (agent = PI, object = candidate3)
    make-document (agent = S, object = offer, destination = candidates)
    communicate (agent = S, object = offer, destination = candidates)
    select (agent = candidate, object = accept/rej)
    make-doc (agent = candidate, object = accept/rej)
    communicate (agent = candidate, object = accept/rej)
    plan-selector (agent = S, object =
                  [acceptance-track rejection-track])
```

```
          -----------------------------------
                S's representation of RA1's agenda:
          -----------------------------------
```

AGENDA ITEM 1:
   PU1 (object = book11)
      process-purchase-order (agent = S, object = book11)
      complete-purchase (agent = S, object = book11)

An agenda item consists of the name of a goal and the names of those of the plans selected for its accomplishment that are not yet (completely) executed, with the bindings for their parameters. Plan names are printed in **bold**. Plan names with numbers appended represent plan instances. The above agendas say that the secretary has the plans to facilitate the purchase of a terminal and to facilitate purchasing of a book asked for by a research associate (Purchase-plan1); S believes PI has plans to hire a research associate (Hiring-plan2) and to facilitate the purchase of a terminal (Purchase-plan3). S also believes that RA1 has the plan of purchasing a book (Purchase-plan1). PI is responsible for both g on its agenda; S is co-responsible for the Purchase-plan3. In contrast, S is responsible only for a subplan of the top-level plan Purchase-plan1. RA1 is responsible for Purchase-plan1.

Figure 7. Sample Contents of the Agendas of an Agent.

Now let us trace the operation of OFFICE through a number of time slices starting with the above state, observing the decision S makes and the changes to its agenda due to new inputs.

------ time slice 1 ------

Suppose, there is a message posted on the secretary S's blackboard : message19 from research associate RA2, of type *order*, that asks to get a price for a desk from vendor V by phone. This message is received by S and a new goal, GET-INFO11, is generated and put on its agenda. S also updates its representation of RA2's agenda by adding there the (inferred) plan of buying a desk. Note that the inferred Purchasing goal is not on S's agenda; therefore, S is not responsible for it.

Next, the scheduler must choose one of the 3 goals on the agenda (PU3 P-P-O5 and GET-INFO11) for immediate processing.

In our example the Get-Information goal will be chosen. This happens because the Purchasing goal is out of contention since it is in the stage of waiting for ordered goods (terminal) to come (Scheduling Heuristic 5). The choice is, therefore, between the Process-Purchase-Order and the Get-Information. P-P-O has, of course, been on agenda for a longer time (Scheduling Heuristic 2), but GET-INFO can be performed by just placing a phone call, while P-P-O requires typing out a form (Scheduling Heuristic 4). There is no rush on the book order, so the goal that can potentially be achieved sooner (Scheduling Heuristic 3) is selected (Scheduling Heuristics 2 and 3 prevail in this case over Scheduling Heuristic 4).

Next, a plan **get-info** is found for achieving the chosen goal; this plan is instantiated and the executor runs its

first subplan: **communicate15** (agent = S, object = message34, proposition = message19.proposition, destination = V2, type = question, instrument = phone). As a result of that subplan, the vendor is informed about the question.

------ time slice 2 -----

New inputs: a) Message20: a terminal and a bill arrived from vendor V1 b) Message 21: the price for the book arrived from V2.

The messages are perceived and understood as the execution of specific plans traced on S's agenda: a) refers to the two *communicate* plans that are objects of the next component of the plan chosen for the Purchase3 goal instance; b) is the response to message19 above.

The above messages do not lead to the generation of any new goals. The scheduler now has the following choice: PU3, P-P-O5 and GET-INFO11. P-P-O5 has the same status as at the previous cycle. PU3 is now at a point where the PI must be told that preconditions are met for the execution of the *check-goods* plan (because the terminal arrived). Only one action remains to be performed in GET-INFO11, and that is to relay the information obtained from V2 to RA2.

At this point GET-INFO11 is chosen for the following reasons. S knows that PI is currently in a meeting with a candidate for hiring. Even though the importance of the *check-goods* plan is relatively high (Scheduling Heuristic 1), it cannot be performed at this point (the presence of PI is necessary) and is therefore rated low. GET-INFO11 is closer to completion than the other goals. In accordance with Scheduling Heuristic 3, it is selected, and S sends the plan (**communicate** agent= S, Destination = RA2, Object = Message21.proposition) to the executor.

After this plan is executed, the entire tree for GET-INFO11 is deleted from the agenda.

4. Summary and Status.

We hope we have shown that in order to provide assistance in distributed office environments we need to integrate the agent-centered, the task-centered and the cognition-oriented perspectives. It is important to carefully choose the task and delineate the world corresponding to it. It is equally important to provide an architecture that can support sophisticated scheduling activities by nodes in a distributed problem solving network. At the same time one should try to explore the sources of real-world knowledge that is used as the basis for scheduling. In addition to the observable world situation the scheduling algorithm must have access to the knowledge about the internal states of the processors, or, in other words, the 'personality profile' of the agents to whom the system provides assistance.

The node-level knowledge and processors have been implemented in Zetalisp on a Symbolics 3600 Lisp Machine. We are currently developing the network level of the system.

References

Corkill, D.D., 1982. A Framework for Organizational Self-Design in Distributed Problem Solving Networks. Ph.D. Dissertation, University of Massachusetts, Amherst. (Available as COINS Technical Report 82-33.)

Corkill, D.D. and V.R. Lesser, 1983. The use of meta-level control for coordination in a distributed problem solving network. Proceedings of 8th IJCAI, 748 - 756.

Croft, B.W., L.S.Lefkowitz, V.R. Lesser and K.E. Huff, 1983. POISE: an intelligent interface for profession-based systems. Proceedings of the Conference on Artificial Intelligence, Oakland University, Rochester, MI.

Durfee, E.H., D.D. Corkill and V.R. Lesser, 1984. Distributing a distributed problem solving network simulator. COINS Internal Memo, University of Massachusetts.

Durfee, E.H., D.D. Corkill and V.R. Lesser, 1985. Increasing coherence in a distributed problem solving network. Proceedings of Ninth IJCAI, Los Angeles, August 1985, 1025 - 1030.

Georgeff, M., 1984. A theory of action for multiagent planning. Proceedings of AAAI-84, 121 - 125.

Lesser, V.R., D.D.Corkill, 1981. Functionally accurate, cooperative distributive systems. *IEEE Transactions on Man, Systems and Cybernetics*, SMC-11, 81-96.

Lesser, V.R., D.D.Corkill, 1983. The distributive vehicle monitoring testbed: a tool for investigating distributed problem solving networks. *AI Magazine*, 4, 15-33.

Nirenburg, I., S. Nirenburg and J. Reynolds, 1985. POPLAR: Toward a Testbed for Cognitive Modelling. Technical Report COSC7, Colgate University.

Nirenburg, S., I.Nirenburg and J. Reynolds, 1986. Studying the Cognitive Agent. Technical Report COSC9, Colgate University.

Smith, R.G. and R. Davis, 1981. Frameworks for cooperation in distributed problem solving. *IEEE Transactions on Systems, Man and Cybernetics*, SMC-11, 61-70.

Knowledge-Based Support of Cooperative Activities

W.B. Croft

L.S. Lefkowitz

Department of Computer and Information Science

University of Massachusetts, Amherst, MA. 01003

Abstract

In many environments people cooperate to perform activities. These activities involve actions such as making decisions, communicating, and creating, updating and retrieving information. A system that is designed to support these activities and the decision making that is part of them must contain knowledge about the activities, the objects they create and manipulate, and the people or "agents" who are responsible for their execution. We describe such a system, POLYMER, which emphasizes the use of planning techniques for flexible activity execution and exception handling. The representation of multi-agent activities is described in detail and examples are given of how a "negotiation" process is used to resolve inconsistencies that arise during activity execution.

1 Introduction

Making decisions is an important part of the problem-solving process in many environments. In an office, for example, people make decisions as part of accomplishing office activities or goals. Decision support in these cases can consist of providing the system users with information about the context of their decisions, suggesting actions that may provide this information, and showing the implications of particular decisions [1,2]. Many activities involve cooperation between people. Responsibility for making decisions and achieving goals is shared between groups of people with different roles (or talents). From this point of view, group decision support means supporting the activity that the group is trying to perform, including keeping track of responsibilities and assisting with negotiation between members of the group if those responsibilities change.

The POLYMER system [3] has been designed to support activities such as those in an office. The characteristics of these activities are that they are loosely structured, can have many exceptions, change frequently, and involve both user actions (such as decisions) and actions with system tools. To address the problems that arise from these characteristics, POLYMER uses an integrated representation of activities and other objects in the environment, and provides flexible execution of activities with an interactive planner. The planner is interactive in the sense that planning decisions are made in consultation with the user and new situations can be introduced by unexpected user actions. An important class of exceptions occurs when the responsibility for achieving the goals of a plan is shared between several agents. If one of these agents does something unexpected that causes a problem in the plan, the system may initiate negotiation between the agents in order to resolve the problem. The process of negotiation, which has been described before in the context of office work [4], is formalized in the sense that the goal of negotiation is a consistent plan and the basis of the negotiation is the set of activity (or plan) descriptions.

The aim of this paper is to describe how cooperative activities are supported by a system such as POLYMER. The main parts of this support are:

1. Maintaining a representation of the environment that is shared by problem solvers or agents.

2. Assisting in the execution of activities by formulating and executing plans.

3. Initiating negotiation between agents when actions cause plan failure.

4. Assisting in negotiation that is initiated by agents.

In the rest of the paper, we will describe in more detail how this support is provided in POLYMER. This description will be done using an example of an office procedure that has been used in previous research [5]. The *journal editing* activity consists of selecting reviewers for a paper, getting the reviews, and making a decision on the paper. This example is typical of some types of office work in that, despite its apparent simplicity, it is quite difficult to capture the many variations of the activity in procedural languages. It can also be regarded as a cooperative activity involving the editor, the author, and the reviewers. We shall use this example in the description of the plan formalism and the negotiation process.

2 The POLYMER System Architecture

The basic POLYMER architecture is shown in Figure 1. The "kernel" of the system consists of the Object Management System (OMS) and the Task Manager. The OMS implements the representation language that is used to describe and manipulate the entities in POLYMER and the specific environment being modeled. Two important types

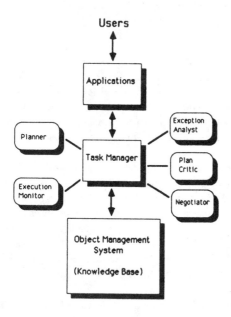

Figure 1: The POLYMER Architecture

of entity are the activities and the agents who can carry out activities. The OMS is object-oriented in the sense that methods or operations are attached to entities and are inherited through abstraction hierarchies. The connection of activity descriptions to other entities such as forms can be regarded as an extension of this modeling approach [6]. The representation language will be described more in the next section. The Task Manager supports activities that are started by users. It controls the planning and execution of activities, and the associated exception handling and negotiation. Office applications are built using this kernel and provide the interface for the users. Examples of applications are a form handler and a project manager.

The basic cycle of the POLYMER system for a single user is as follows:

1. The user (through an application) posts a goal.

2. The planner generates a plan to achieve the goal. The hierarchical planning techniques used are essentially the same as those in NONLIN [7] or SIPE [8]. The result of planning is a procedural net that specifies the sequence of actions required to achieve the goal. Many of the plans in our environment depend heavily on constraints provided by user actions. For example, filling out a form provides information about the values of object attributes. Since these constraints may be necessary for planning decisions, it follows that the plans generated will, in general, be partial. The minimal requirement for the planner is to generate, possibly through interaction with the user, a set of expectations for the next step in the plan.

3. The execution monitor selects an action for execution and either sends a message to the appropriate object in the OMS or sends a message to the user (via the application).

4. The execution monitor compares the actual action taken (and its result) with the expected action. If there are no differences, the system returns to step 2, otherwise it classifies the type of exception that has occurred [9].

If an exception does arise, the basic exception handling cycle proceeds as follows;

1. The plan critic determines the effect of the exception on the plan.

2. The exception analyst attempts to find an explanation for the exception using the current plan and entity descriptions stored in the OMS.

3. The negotiator uses the information supplied by the exception analyst to determine, through interaction with the user, whether the explanation found is valid or what information is missing from the OMS. The goal is to produce a consistent plan (verified by the plan critic). Note that the "negotiation" here involves a person and the planner. An informal description of the flavor of the negotiation is "if you are going to break the rules, tell me why this is valid". The knowledge acquired during this dialogue is added to the OMS.

The environment we are more concerned with in this paper is one with multiple users (agents), some of whom are at POLYMER sites and others out in the "real" world. Our model of distribution is that agents have responsibilities for specific goals and, in carrying out these goals, may use their own knowledge base or a global knowledge base. The *primary* agent for a particular activity may use "contracting" agents to achieve subgoals. No distinction is made at this

will attempt to coordinate the activities of all agents involved in a particular activity. This means that the planner will be used to develop a single plan using the activity descriptions for all the involved agents. The assumption with actions is that the plans which are used to carry these out

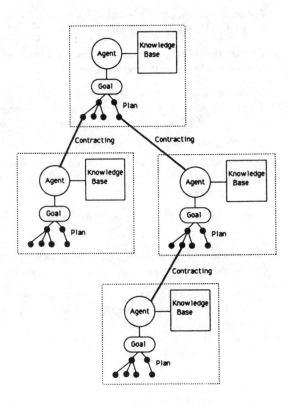

Figure 2: Primary and Contracting Agents

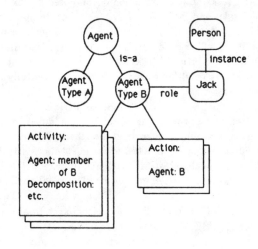

Figure 3: Activities, Actions and Agents

level between agents using POLYMER and those in the real world (Figure 2). If more than one agent could achieve a subgoal, we assume that a particular agent will be chosen either by the primary agent or by some default rule.

At a given POLYMER site, the planner will have access to objects representing the contracting agents. The agent objects connect activity descriptions, action descriptions and "people" objects (Figure 3). People objects can be connected to multiple agent objects to represent the different roles a person can play in an organization. Agents can perform activities or actions. The main difference between these two is that activities are used for planning, whereas actions are "primitive". That is, an action is carried out by sending a message to the agent. Actions can represent tool operations as well as actions carried out by agents at the same POLYMER site but off-line (for example, decision making), agents at a different POLYMER site, and agents who are in the real world. In all cases, a message is sent containing the appropriate objects as parameters and the system waits for a reply. The form of the message will differ according to the agent type as specified in the OMS. For example, a message to a remote POLYMER user could be electronic, whereas to a real world agent it will probably be via U.S. Mail.

Two more points relating to planning should be made. First, at a particular POLYMER site, the Task Manager

(which are not known) will not interfere with the known plan. The second point is that there is also a class of agents which are not represented in the OMS. These unknown agents can be responsible for changes in the state of the world (i.e., the OMS) that will affect the plan. For example, a particular item may be found to be out of stock due to unrecorded transfers. These types of exceptions may be handled using replanning algorithms similar to those described by Wilkins [8].

The basic cycle of planning/execution for a given agent in this distributed environment does not change significantly compared to the single user case. The major difference is that a new class of exceptions may occur where an agent fails to satisfy a goal for which they are responsible, either by returning an incorrect result or by explicitly indicating that the goal cannot be satisfied. Whether the system detects a plan inconsistency or the agent sends a message, a cycle of negotiation and plan criticism is initiated between the affected agents. The exception analyst and plan critic are used to detect similarities between the achieved and expected goals and to detect problems in the current plan. The negotiation between agents can take place via mail on the system or a completely different media (such as the telephone), but the result of the negotiation must be communicated to the Task Manager and this information must produce a consistent plan. We will give an example of negotiation in section 4.

3   Representing Activities

The knowledge representation scheme used in POLYMER draws heavily on three earlier systems developed at the University of Massachusetts. POISE [2] was a planning and plan recognition system using a script-like model of the user's tasks. Each description decomposed a task into simpler tasks and permitted a fairly elaborate specification of the ordering of these subtasks. The objectives and preconditions of tasks could also be specified, providing a goal-based perspective of tasks intended to complement the script-based view, although this facility was never fully developed.

GRAPPLE [10], a successor to POISE, is a plan recognition system containing representation language that decomposes tasks into subgoals, rather than into subtasks. These subgoals may be matched to the goals of other tasks, thereby dynamically creating a task hierarchy. POLYMER permits tasks to be expressed in terms of both subgoals and subtasks.

K^n_{AC} [11], a knowledge acquisition system also derived from POISE, advocates a more uniform, frame-based representation of *activities*, *objects* and *relations*. Similarly, POLYMER uses the KEE™ system as the basis for such a uniform representation of its domain knowledge.

The KEE™ system is built on frame structures called *units*. KEE™ units may be arranged in generalization and part-of hierarchies and their attributes (e.g., slots) may be defined by the user. The basic POLYMER knowledge structures, *activities*, *objects* and *relations*, are defined as such *units*. Domain knowledge is then encoded in terms of these basic knowledge types. Finally, these domain knowledge structures are instantiated during the running of the POLYMER system.

Each activity has the following attributes:

Goal - the state of part of the world model upon completion of that activity. Objects used by the plan are specified as variables (such as *?paper*).

KEE™	Unit
POLYMER	Activity Object Relation
Application	Fill.Out.Form Mail.Message
Runtime	Mail.Message<096>

Figure 4: Levels of knowledge representation in POLYMER

- *Preconditions* - a set of conditions that must be true in order for the activity to be applicable.

- *Effects* - side-effects or secondary effects that may set, add, or delete states in the world model.

- *Decomposition* - the decomposition of an activity into the steps that must be performed in order to accomplish its goal. Each step may be either a goal, an activity, or an action.

- *Control and Plan Rationale* - temporal and causal constraints used for planning to determine correct step orderings.

- *Agents* - agents that can be responsible for the activity.

- *Constraints* - additional constraints on potential plans. Can be used to specify constraints on agents for steps.

In the remainder of this section, we present an example of POLYMER activity descriptions in the journal editing environment. The object descriptions associated with these activities will not be described in order to save space. These descriptions are very similar to those found in any powerful semantic data model.

The process of reviewing a paper submitted for publication can be described as follows. Upon receiving the paper from its author, the editor of the journal must obtain reviewers for the paper, consider their reviews, and decide whether to accept the paper as is, request modifications, or reject the paper outright. The author must be informed of the decision and, if the paper is re-submitted, the new version must be re-reviewed. This cycle may continue until the paper is either accepted or rejected.

The top-level activity description (*accept-or-reject*) reflects the potential cyclic nature of this task. It attempts to achieve the goal of having reached a decision on the paper and having this decision being either "accepted" or "rejected". If the decision is anything else, the task will continue.

ACTIVITY: ACCEPT-OR-REJECT.WAY1

```
            Goal:  refereed(?paper)
   Preconditions:  member(?paper, papers)
  Decomposition:  GOAL decision-reached = known(status(?paper))
        Control:  repeat decision-reached until
                      or(status(?paper, "accepted"),
                         status(?paper, "rejected"))

         Agents:  ?editor = member(?editor, editors)
```

For each cycle, the journal editor must obtain reviews of the paper, make a decision based on these reviews, and inform the author of this decision.

ACTIVITY: DECIDE-ON-PAPER.WAY 1

Goal: known(status(?paper))
Preconditions: has(?editor, ?paper)
member(?paper, papers)
written-by(?paper, ?author)
Decomposition: GOAL *paper-reviewed* = reviewed(?paper)
GOAL *decision-reached* = decision(?paper, ?decision)
GOAL *author-notified* = has(?author, ?decision)
Constraints: member(?decision, {"accepted" "rejected" "accepted-with-modifications"})
Rationale: paper-reviewed **enables** decision-reached
decision-reached **enables** author-notified
Agents: ?editor = member(?editor, editors)

To obtain the needed reviews of the paper, the editor must first select each reviewer and ask if each is willing to review the paper. If a reviewer agrees to review the paper, the editor sends a copy of the paper to that reviewer and awaits a review.

ACTIVITY: REVIEW-PAPER.WAY 1

Goal: reviewed(?paper)
Preconditions: member(?paper, papers)
member(?journal, journals)
edits(?editor, ?journal)
Decomposition: GOAL *reviewers-selected* = and(
reviewers(?paper, ?reviewers),
sufficient-reviewers(?journal, ?reviewers))
GOAL *paper-distributed* = has(?reviewer, copy-of(?paper))
GOAL *have-reviews* = has(?editor, review(?reviewer))
Control: **before** reviewers-selected paper-distributed have-reviews
repeat (paper-distributed **to** have-reviews) **for** ?reviewer **in** ?reviewers
Agents: ?editor = member(?editor, editors)

In order to model the process of obtaining the reviewers in a realistic manner, a somewhat novel control structure was required. A simple, iterative model of the task would have the editor select a reviewer, send the reviewer a request, await a reply, and then, if there were still an insufficient number of reviewers for the paper, repeat the whole process. Unfortunately, this does not capture the parallelism normally found in such tasks. Even formalisms that permit specifying that multiple instantiations of the task may be carried out in parallel, do not permit the activity description writer to specify that a new reviewer needs to be selected and invited whenever the editor realizes that there will not be sufficient reviewers for the paper.

Consider a specific example. If a journal requires 3 reviewers for each submitted paper, the editor may select and send out requests to 3 reviewers, simultaneously. Upon receiving a negative reply from any one of these re-

viewers (i.e., if any reviewer declines), the editor will realize that no matter how the two outstanding reviewers reply, at least one more reviewer will still be needed. Thus, there is no need for all the replies to be received before additional requests may have to be sent out.

To handle such situations, POLYMER contains a generic looping structure that, in addition to a termination condition, permits the specification of when a new iteration should begin. The iteration condition, in this example, would be that the additional number of reviewers needed for a paper (i.e., the total number required less the number who have already accepted) is greater than the total number of outstanding reviewers (i.e., reviewers who have been invited to review the paper but have not yet replied). The "too-few-reviewers" predicate in the following activity description performs this check.

ACTIVITY: GET-REVIEWERS.WAY 1

Goal: and(reviewers(?paper, ?reviewers),
sufficient-reviewers(?journal, ?reviewers))
Decomposition: GOAL *reviewer-designated* = reviewer(?paper, ?reviewer)
Control: **repeat** reviewer-designated **until** sufficient-reviewers(?journal, ?reviewers)
iterate-when too-few-reviewers(?paper)
Agents: ?editor = member(?editor, editors)

The ability of activities to depend on states of the world caused by *unknown* agents is shown in the following task. In designating reviewers, the editor may want to prompt the invited reviewer for a reply if none has been received within a specified time period. In order to trigger this reply, the current world time must be referred to (via the *time-is(time)* kb-wff). If the specified time is reached before a reply is received, then the goal for the "timely-reply-received" step will be satisfied. The repeat structure (in the control clause) assures that the steps repeat until a reply is received.

ACTIVITY: DESIGNATE-REVIEWER.WAY 1

Goal: reviewer(?paper, ?reviewer)
Decomposition: GOAL *reviewer-asked* = has(?reviewer, ?request)
GOAL *timely-reply-received* = or(
has(?editor, ?reply),
time-is(
+(finish-time(
reviewer-asked),
?reminder-delay)))
Rationale: reviewer-asked **enables** timely-reply-received
Constraints: member(?reminder-delay, delta-times)
value(?reminder-delay, "2 weeks")
Control: **repeat** reviewer-asked **to**
timely-reply-received **until** exists(?reply)
Agents: ?editor = member(?editor, editors)

In the following activities, the decomposition consists of *actions* as well as *activities*. These *action* steps are performed by sending a message to the agent responsible for that step (or the agent responsible for the whole activity, by default). Thus, in the following task, the editor is sent a message to select a reviewer from a set of possible reviewers.

ACTIVITY: INVITE-REVIEW.WAY 1

> **Goal:** has(?reviewer, ?request)
> **Decomposition:** ACTION *reviewer-chosen* = select(?reviewer, ?reviewers)
> GOAL *reviewer-asked* = sent(?reviewer, ?request)
> **Agents:** *?editor* = member(?editor, editors)

The final activity description for the journal editing task is an activity to be performed by the reviewer, rather than by the editor. Thus, when the *decide-to-review* action is performed, the planner asks the current reviewer for a decision, rather than asking the editor, as above.

ACTIVITY: AGREE-TO-REVIEW.WAY 1

> **Goal:** has(?editor, ?reply)
> **Decomposition:** ACTION *decide-to-review* = decide(?question, ?reply)
> GOAL *respond-to-editor* = sent(?editor, ?reply)
> **Agents:** *?reviewer* = member(?reviewer, people)

4   The Negotiation Process

Negotiation takes place in two cases:

1. It may be initiated by the system when an exception results in an inconsistent plan. If the primary agent causes the exception, the negotiation is between the agent and the Task Manager. If a contracting agent causes the exception, the negotiation is between agents and the Task Manager. That is, informal negotiation takes place between the agents (perhaps by electronic mail or telephone) and the results of this part of the negotiation must be checked with the Task Manager.

2. It may be initiated by agents in order to change the current plan. Once the negotiation has been started, this is handled in the same way as the agent-agent negotiation in the first case.

Whenever a change to the plan is communicated to the Task Manager by an agent, the plan critic checks consistency and indicates if other agents will be affected. Any part of an activity description or plan is open to negotiation and part of the negotiator's task is to identify if a change is permanent (i.e., the activity descriptions should be changed) or applies only to the current plan.

The first example of negotiation in the journal editing environment is caused by the editor making a decision on a paper before the *paper-reviewed* subgoal is achieved. This is entered as a predicate by the editor and causes an exception of the type "step-out-of-order". The most likely inference in this case is that there is a short-cut that is not specified in the system. Negotiation between the Task Manager and the editor is initiated on this basis. The plan can be made consistent if the constraint on having a sufficient number of reviewers reports is relaxed. If the editor confirms this inference, the system will create a "policy" that the editor can change the *sufficient-reviewers* constraint for a particular review.

An example of agent-agent negotiation initiated by the system occurs when a reviewer fails to provide the review within the specified time limit. This causes a plan violation and the system informs the editor. The editor communicates with the reviewer and gets a promise of the review in another week. The editor then changes the constraint on the plan to include the new date. This is not specified as a general rule, but as a change to an instance of a plan.

An example of agent-initiated negotiation could occur when an author contacts an editor after receiving a rejection. The editor agrees to get another review and must communicate this decision to the Task Manager. By changing the plan instance to increase the required number of reviewers, an inconsistency is created and the plan critic will indicate that the *paper-reviewed* goal must be re-achieved. The previous reviews will be taken into account in generating the new plan.

It must be emphasized that the incentive for the agents to communicate decisions to the Task Manager is that, in the normal course of events, much of the routine work can be handled by the system. In the case of the last example, once a new plan had been generated, the system would take care of notifying the new reviewer and waiting for the review. The system is maintaining a record of the status of many parallel tasks and recording the history of each task. The major problem that remains to be solved is the design of a user interface for the display of activity descriptions and the current plan. The same issue arises in designing a plan specification interface and research is underway in this area.

The status of the POLYMER system is that the kernel is mostly implemented. The two example applications mentioned (form handler, project manager) will be built as a test of the kernel. This initial version has very simple exception analyst and negotiator modules. The implementation of the exception analyst is proceeding in a separate project and our aim is to integrate this facility, together with the negotiator, in the next version.

Acknowledgments

The POLYMER system was designed in cooperation with Carol Broverman. This research was supported in part by Ing. C. Olivetti & C.

References

[1] W. B. Croft and L.S. Lefkowitz, "Decision support using office procedures", Proceedings of the 17th Hawaii International Conference on System Sciences, 609-615 (1984). Also published in IEEE tutorial for Office Automation.

[2] W. B. Croft and L.S. Lefkowitz, "Task Support in an Office System", *ACM Transactions on Office Information Systems*, 2, 197-212, (1984).

[3] L.S. Lefkowitz and W. B. Croft, "An interim report on the POLYMER planning system", COINS Technical Report, University of Massachusetts, (1987).

[4] R.E. Fikes, "A commitment-based framework for describing informal cooperative work", *Cognitive Science*, 6, 331-347, (1982).

[5] M.D. Zisman, "Representation, specification and automation of office procedures", Ph.D. dissertation, Wharton School, Univ. of Pennsylvania, (1977).

[6] W. B. Croft, "Task management for an intelligent interface", *IEEE Bulletin on Database Engineering*, 8, 8-13, (1986).

[7] A. Tate, "Generating project networks", Proceedings IJCAI-77, 888-893, (1977).

[8] D. E. Wilkins, "Recovering from execution errors in SIPE", SRI Technical Report 346, (1985).

[9] C. Broverman and W. B. Croft, "Reasoning about exceptions during plan execution monitoring", Proceedings AAAI-87, 190-195 (1987).

[10] C. Broverman, K. Huff, V. Lesser, "The role of plan recognition in design of an intelligent user interface", Proceedings of IEEE Conference on Man, Machine and Cybernetics, 863-868, (1986).

[11] L.S. Lefkowitz and V. Lesser, "Knowledge Acquisition as Knowledge Assimilation", Proceedings of the 2nd AAAI Knowledge Acquisition for Knowledge-Based Systems Workshop, (to appear).

An Architecture for Control and Communications in Distributed Artificial Intelligence Systems

JU-YUAN DAVID YANG, MEMBER, IEEE, MICHAEL N. HUHNS, MEMBER, IEEE,
AND LARRY M. STEPHENS, MEMBER, IEEE

Abstract—This paper presents an architecture and implementation for a distributed artificial intelligence (DAI) system, focusing on the control and communication aspects. Problem solving by this system occurs as an iterative refinement of several mechanisms, including problem decomposition, kernel-subproblem solving, and result synthesis. In order for all related nodes to make optimum use of the information obtained from these problem-solving mechanisms, the system dynamically reconfigures itself, thereby improving its performance during operation. This approach offers the possibilities of increased real-time response, improved reliability and flexibility, and lower processing costs. A major component in the node architecture is a database of metaknowledge about the expertise of a node's own expert systems and those of the other processing nodes. This information is gradually accumulated during problem solving. Each node also has a dynamic-planning ability, which guides the problem-solving process in the most promising direction; a focus-control mechanism, which restricts the size of the explored solution space at the task level while reducing the communication bandwidths required; and a question-and-answer mechanism, which handles internode communications. Examples in the domain of digital-logic design are given to demonstrate the operation of the system. The results obtained show a significant reduction in the numbers of tasks executed and messages communicated in the system.

I. INTRODUCTION

A DISTRIBUTED artificial intelligence (DAI) system consists of multiple physically-separated processing nodes, each having at least one expert system. Such a DAI system is characterized by the completeness and exactness of the knowledge sources (KS) constituting its expert systems, and by the completeness and correctness of the input data at each processing node. In distributed sensor networks [1]–[5], distributed air traffic control systems [6]–[9], and multiple agent planning systems [10], [11], each processing node sees only a small part of the problem environment and has complete but possibly inexact knowledge sources. A DAI system for engineering design differs from these examples in that the knowledge sources are distributed among the processing nodes, and no one node has sufficient knowledge sources to solve an entire problem. Furthermore, the input data and the design con-

Manuscript received March 21, 1984; revised December 17, 1984.
J. Y. D. Yang is with Advanced Product Development, Burroughs Corporation, Paoli, PA 19301, USA.
M. N. Huhns and L. M. Stephens are with the Department of Electrical and Computer Engineering, University of South Carolina, Columbia, SC 29208, USA.

straints are usually exact and available to all nodes. Very large scale integrated (VLSI) design is an example of this type of engineering design [14].

VLSI design is a hierarchical process requiring knowledge at the circuit, gate, register, instruction set, architecture, and fabrication technology levels. This knowledge could be distributed among multiple nodes which would operate in parallel. Desired behavior descriptions and performance specifications would serve as input data to these nodes. Due to the incompleteness of these knowledge sources and the partial view that each node has of the problem environment, coordination among the nodes would be necessary during the design process.

A distributed problem-solving approach offers the possibilities of increased real-time response, reliability, flexibility, and lower processing costs. Before these advantages can be realized, a theory for the construction of DAI systems must be developed. In developing such theories, artificial intelligence researchers have observed several relevant metaphors in human societies and have extracted a number of features which should be an integral part of a DAI system. Moreover, several DAI systems and one testbed have been implemented to test those theories.

A functionally accurate, cooperative (FA/C) distributed system has been proposed and implemented by Lesser and Corkill [1]–[5]. In this approach each processing node is semiautonomous, has a partial and inconsistent view of the problem environment, and has complete knowledge sources. A unifying data- and goal-directed control is used to guide its problem-solving processes and extend the partial views to a global solution. In addition, a high-level simulation testbed has been implemented to study how different control and communication policies perform under varying distributions of uncertainties and errors in the intermediate states of the processing.

Thorndyke *et al.* [6]–[9] focus on the development of a theory of cooperation and teamwork. They approach the theory of cooperation as an empirical investigation. The task of air traffic control serves as the domain for these DAI experiments.

In multiagent planning for robot environments [10]–[13], models of distributed action are investigated as a theoretical foundation for DAI. The approaches include developing formalisms adequate for representing the effects of actions on the cognitive state of other agents, looking at ways of modifying the classical AI paradigms (e.g., STRIPS and situation calculus) to accommodate multiple agents, and studying alternative ways a planner might reason about how another agent will act.

Teamwork in multiagent planning is also studied in [10]. This work focuses on the planning act itself, and considers the nature and style of planning appropriate to a world in which more than one active agent is present. Several results have been obtained, one of which is that plans should be robust and cautious. Smith and Davis proposed a contract-net [15]–[19] with a negotiation mechanism to structure node interactions and solve the connection problem in a task-sharing system.

As mentioned above, each processing node has either a partial view of the problem environment, or incomplete domain knowledge, or both. Moreover, both data and domain knowledge could be incomplete and inexact. Usually a number of plausible hypotheses may be generated in this kind of situation. In turn, this may lead to the generation of a large number of subtasks for the system to communicate and solve.

The use of DAI should reduce the communication bandwidth needed in a distributed processing system, because the nodes will communicate only higher-level, more accurate information. Also, the costs of communications are expensive compared to the costs of computing elements at present. Furthermore, when the arrival rate of incoming messages approaches the service rate of a communication channel in a computer network, the system performance is significantly degraded [20]. Thus communications cannot be neglected in the design of DAI systems.

A large amount of research, which addresses the issue of efficient utilization of resources, has been done on multicomputer architectures [21]. However, the difficulty in using these architectures is that there is no general mapping of problems onto computers, i.e., the software-partitioning problem [22]. This paper augments that research by presenting an architecture which is self-partitioning and, through learning, achieves maximum speed-up due to parallelism.

In summary, the major issues involved in the construction of a DAI system are 1) the appropriate distribution of subproblems among the processing nodes; 2) the choice of control mechanisms which maintain global coherence during problem solving, utilize knowledge sources efficiently, and achieve optimum performance; and 3) the specification of communication policies so that the processing nodes can interact. The processing nodes must cooperate when no one of them has sufficient information to solve the entire problem. This sharing of information is necessary to allow the system as a whole to produce a consistent answer.

This paper addresses these issues through the architectural design of a DAI system, focusing on the control and communication aspects. The system presented is dynamically self-organized and can improve its performance dur-

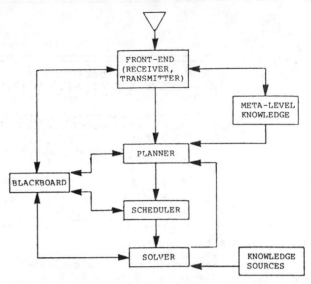

Fig. 1.   Node organization.

ing operation by making optimum use at all related nodes of the information obtained from the problem-solving process. A detailed description of the architecture is given in Section II. A logic design example is given in Section III to demonstrate its operation. Two sets of experimental measurements—the number of tasks executed and the number of messages transmitted among the system nodes—are used to evaluate its performance.

II.   System Architecture

In general, the optimum system structure will vary from problem to problem. One method for organizing this structure is to do it dynamically, during problem solving. Problem solving using this method is then an iterative refinement of problem decomposition, kernel-subproblem solving, and result synthesis. Problem decomposition is an adjustable planning process based on the information currently available in the system [23], [24]. This information is derived during problem decomposition and the solving of kernel subproblems which iteratively interact. Establishing a problem-solving hierarchy in a distributed environment requires that planning and problem solving be combined with internode communications.

The processing node requires the following capabilities for problem solving: 1) a dynamic planning ability which adjusts the problem-solving plan and guides it, by either actual calculations or estimations, in the most promising direction based on the latest problem-solving status; 2) an intranode communication facility that allows different processes at the same processing node to share information; 3) an internode communication facility that permits the different processing nodes to share tasks and results; 4) a problem-deduction ability that solves tasks by invoking required knowledge sources; and 5) a learning ability that enables the system to change its organization and improve its performance as more problem-solving experience is obtained. In this architecture all processing nodes have the identical organization shown in Fig. 1. Each node consists

TABLE I
THE FORMAT OF A METAKNOWLEDGE FRAME

```
PROBLEM    : a brief description of the problem.
RS-PROCESS : a result synthesis process or function.
DECOMP     : a decomposition mechanism.
CANDIDATES : a list of processing nodes which might solve the
             problem (if it is not solvable by this node).
CONFIDENCE : an actual or estimated measure of the quality of
             the solution.
```

TABLE II
THE FORMAT OF A TASK FRAME ON THE BLACKBOARD

```
NAME       : a task identifier.
PROBLEM    : a brief description of a problem.
ORIGINATOR : the identification of the node
             requesting a problem solution
DATA       : associated input data.
RESULT     : a result.
PROCESS    : a result synthesis process.
PLAN       : a problem-solving plan.
TIME-OUT   : a deadline for returning a result.
CONFIDENCE : the quality of the result.
```

of a front-end processor, planner, scheduler, solver, blackboard, metalevel knowledge, and knowledge sources. Detailed descriptions of each component are presented in the rest of this section.

A. Metalevel Knowledge

In the area of expert systems, researchers suggest several reasons for emphasizing knowledge itself rather than formal reasoning methods [25]. Reasoning about internode communications and dynamic planning are suitable activities for expert systems. To exhibit good performance, each activity requires adequate knowledge about the types of problems a node can attempt to solve and how well it will succeed. This is knowledge about the problem domain and is called metalevel knowledge or metaknowledge.

Two types of knowledge are needed for reasoning about communications. One type consists of the kinds of problems the node is interested in solving, as well as the corresponding problem-decomposition and result-synthesis mechanisms which its expert systems provide. The other type consists of its estimates of the knowledge and capabilities of other processing nodes. This knowledge indicates how well a processing node can solve a particular type of problem. A system may be initialized such that each processing node has no knowledge about other nodes. In this case the system can learn both kinds of knowledge as information is exchanged during problem solving.

Each type of metaknowledge is organized according to the frame-like structure shown in Table I. The frame has five slots, the first of which provides a brief description of the problem to which this metaknowledge can be applied. A node may or may not know how to solve a given problem. For a problem known to be solvable, the next two slots store the name of the corresponding result-synthesis process or function and the name of the corre-

sponding problem-decomposition mechanism. For a problem not known to be solvable, the fourth slot stores a list of identifiers for other processing nodes which are believed to have knowledge about this problem. This slot is initially empty but is gradually filled as information accumulates during problem solving. The final slot is a confidence value indicating how well either the local node (if the problem is known to be solvable) or the other processing nodes (if the problem is not known to be solvable) are expected to succeed in solving this type of problem.

B. Blackboard Communication Mechanism

In the proposed DAI system internode communications are achieved by the use of a blackboard. A blackboard, an active data structure located at each processing node, allows information sharing among the nodes by storing tasks, plans, and partial results and transmitting them at the appropriate time in the problem-solving process. In addition, the blackboard provides a means for sharing information about the different problem-solving processes within the node, such as the dynamic-planning and problem-deduction processes.

The blackboard is organized according to a task-oriented and frame-like structure, as shown in Table II. Each frame contains information about a locally-generated task or a task received from another node. The information stored in each frame includes a task identifier, a brief description of the task, the address of the originating node, any associated data, results (if any), result-synthesis functions (if the task is solvable), a confidence value which indicates the quality of the result, and a problem-solving plan.

In addition, after an unsolved task is transmitted to other nodes for solution, a time-out slot is filled with a deadline by which the other processing nodes must return their results. This is done because it is possible that the other processing nodes will assign a low priority to the task; thus there may be a long delay before this task is executed. The time-out provides a way for the task-originating node to detect this delay so that it may take other action to obtain a solution.

C. Front-End Processor

A fundamental DAI system requirement is to allow processing nodes to share tasks and tentative results. This enables the nodes to cooperate in solving a complex problem. In the architecture described in this paper, this requirement is achieved by a front-end processor.

TABLE III
THE BNF SPECIFICATION OF THE PROTOCOL

```
<MESSAGE>         :== <ADDRESSEE> <ORIGINATOR> <TEXT>;
<ADDRESSEE>       :== <ADDRESS>;
<ORIGINATOR>      :== <ADDRESS>;
<ADDRESS>         :== <NET-ADDRESS> <SUBNET-ADDRESS>
                      <NODE-ADDRESS>;
<NET-ADDRESS>     :== COMMON-LANGUAGE-ELEMENT;
<SUBNET-ADDRESS>  :== COMMON-LANGUAGE-ELEMENT;
<NODE-ADDRESS>    :== COMMON-LANGUAGE-ELEMENT;
<TEXT>            :== <TEXT-TYPE> <TEXT-NAME>
                      <TASK-ABSTRACTION> <ATTRIBUTE-LIST>;
<TEXT-TYPE>       :== QUESTION | ANSWER;
<TEXT-NAME>       :== COMMON-LANGUAGE-ELEMENT;
<TASK-ABSTRACTION> :== COMMON-LANGUAGE-ELEMENT;
<ATTRIBUTE-LIST>  :== <ATTRIBUTE-NAME ATTRIBUTE-VALUE>
                      <ATTRIBUTE-LIST>;
<ATTRIBUTE-NAME>  :== INPUT | OUTPUT | IMPORTANCE |
                      CONFIDENCE | COST (problem dependent);
<ATTRIBUTE-VALUE> :== QUALITATIVE | QUANTITATIVE;
```

A common language is required to allow processing nodes to communicate their intentions and share information with each other. This parallels how people communicate in human organizations. The common language is, of course, problem-dependent. Hence, the architecture described herein provides only a framework; the actual implementation is the responsibility of the user. Embedding the common language into a system is accomplished by capturing and representing the expertise needed for problem decomposition and by incorporating the knowledge sources needed to solve tasks in the problem domain.

A protocol is also required for correct communications. The protocol is a set of rules which specifies how to synthesize meaningful and correct messages. Elements of the common language serve as do words in a natural language such as English. The protocol has the same function as grammar in a natural language. The protocol used in this architecture is a phrase-structure grammar. A Backus–Naur (BNF) specification of this protocol is given in Table III. Basically, there are two types of messages communicated among processing nodes: a question-type and an answer-type. In general, all requests are expressed as question-type messages and all responses are expressed as answer-type messages.

Broadcast transmissions and directed transmissions are the most frequently used means of communications in human organizations. Examples of broadcast transmissions are newspapers, radio broadcasts, and television broadcasts. The telephone system, telegrams, and postal mail are good examples of directed transmissions. For the architecture described in this paper, both broadcast and directed transmissions are chosen to provide the greatest flexibility.

For a given situation, the selection of the appropriate mechanisms is based on the intentions of the processing node and its knowledge about the capabilities of other processing nodes. When the capabilities of the other processing nodes are well understood, the node can select the processing node with the best match and use a directed transmission mechanism. Otherwise, a broadcast mechanism is used. Broadcast communications also serve as a method to collect information about other processing nodes.

When a question is sent out by broadcast, there is usually more than one response. On the other hand, in the directed transmission case, there is no more than one response. Thus, to minimize the number of messages transmitted within the system, directed transmissions are chosen whenever possible.

An incoming message is accepted only when it is a system-wide broadcast transmission or a correctly addressed, directed transmission. Incorrectly addressed messages are rejected by the receiver, which then takes no further action. If the accepted message is answer-type, the associated data are placed into the corresponding frame on the blackboard. These data are also used to update the metaknowledge database. Otherwise the data are discarded when they are no longer required by any unsolved tasks.

For an accepted question-type message, the contents of the meta knowledge database are used to decide whether the question is within the areas of the node's expertise. If it is not, the message is discarded without notifying the processing node which originated it. For a question within the areas of the node's expertise, a task is generated to address the question. A task frame is formulated and written on the blackboard to save the information associated with the question. The task is then sent to the planner as an unplanned task.

For unsolved subtasks that are not yet transmitted but are in the current solution plan (described in the next section), the front-end processor first determines a transmission mechanism and a destination, based on the information stored in the metaknowledge database. This procedure is also applied to any results awaiting transmission. A corresponding message is then formulated according to the protocol and sent through a message channel.

It is desirable and important to develop a learning method for accumulating information which can improve the future performance of the system. Messages transmitted among processing nodes during the problem-solving process provide a rich source for this knowledge acquisition. The knowledge accumulated is that which is relevant to internode communication reasoning and dynamic planning. Based on newly received information, all related

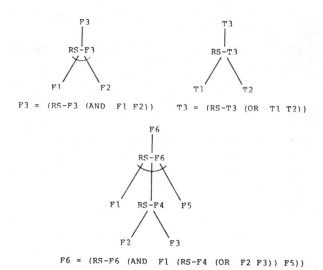

F3 = (RS-F3 (AND F1 F2))   T3 = (RS-T3 (OR T1 T2))

F6 = (RS-F6 (AND F1 (RS-F4 (OR F2 F3)) F5))

Fig. 2.   Examples of problem-solving plans.

existing metaknowledge is updated. The updated meta-knowledge then provides a basis for improving the communication and planning performance of the system.

D. Task Planner

The planner is invoked when there are tasks whose solutions need initial planning or replanning. The planner searches the metaknowledge database for a suitable problem-decomposition mechanism and then generates a problem-solving plan. This plan consists of not only the essential subtasks for problem solving, but also the alternatives to those subtasks if the original problem can be solved by more than one method. Any results, and the information about whether a subtask is solvable, solved, or unsolved, are also contained in the plan. Thus the plan contains all the relevant task-level problem-solving information.

The problem-solving plan is represented by a modified AND/OR graph as shown in Fig. 2. The modification to the standard AND/OR graph is that the result-synthesis functions (RS-F3, RS-F4 and RS-F6 in Fig. 2) are explicitly rather than implicitly specified at every nonleaf node. An equation-like format represents the modified AND/OR graph for programming purposes. This equation-like expression is similar to the ASSIGN statement in a formal programming language. The left-hand side is the ancestor task and the right-hand side is a list composed of a result-synthesis function and its argument. This argument is a list composed of an operator, indicating the graph-type (either an AND or an OR), and the names of all the descendant subproblems (preconditions) in the graph. For those modified AND/OR graphs with more than two levels, the expression is generated by recursively applying this format to all of the two-level subgraphs from the root node to the leaf nodes.

E. Current Solution Plan

In general, most tasks or problems may be solved by several different methods. For example, there are several kinds of integrated circuits (IC's) which can be used to implement a sequential machine. These include small-scale IC's (SSI), such as NAND and NOR gates; medium-scale IC's (MSI), such as flip-flops and counters; and large-scale IC's (LSI), such as programmable-logic arrays (PLA's), read-only memories (ROM's), and microprocessors. The verification of a digital system design is another task which can be solved by several methods, such as simulation or prototype testing.

Communications have been identified as being likely to cause a bottleneck in a distributed-processing system. One way to overcome this bottleneck is to reduce the number of tasks explored during the problem-solving process. A focus-control mechanism similar to that in GODDESS [26] is introduced to achieve this reduction. Based on the current status of the system, the knowledge accumulated about other processing nodes, and the experience derived from past problem-solving efforts, the focus-control mechanism identifies the most promising path for problem solving and identifies the subtasks along this path. Only one plan, called the current solution plan, is chosen for those subtasks which have more than one solution path. The current solution plan is represented by marking the subtasks along the chosen path as being ready for problem solving.

Before the focus-control mechanism can be applied, a set of parameters and two functions have to be defined. The set of parameters is used for calculating a cost for each task. One of the two functions calculates the cost, and the other, a focus function, determines the best subtask. At an OR node, this focus function selects the best subtask from its descendants; there is no selection involved at an AND node.

The focus-control mechanism works in a bottom-up fashion. It starts by calculating the costs of all leaf tasks; then it backs up one level to calculate the cost for its ancestor task. For an AND-node task the cost is generated by adding up the costs of its descendant subtasks; the list of selected tasks is then formed by concatenating the lists of selected tasks of its subtasks with these subtasks themselves. For an OR-node task the cost is the lowest among those of its descendant subtasks; the list of selected tasks is then formed by concatenating the subtask itself with the list of selected tasks of the subtask having the lowest cost. This process is repeated until the root task at the top of the tree is reached. The selected subtasks and their corresponding result-synthesis functions form the current solution plan. An example is shown in Fig. 3. The equation-like expression consists of only those selected subtasks and their result-synthesis processes.

This mechanism differs from the A^* algorithm [27] in the way it searches for the best solution path. The A^* algorithm uses a top-down search and requires an estimation of the effort needed to reach a goal from its current position for every visited node. The focus-control mechanism uses a bottom-up search and needs an estimation for only leaf nodes (subtasks). The advantage of this mechanism is that the solution space at the task level is usually much smaller than that at the problem domain level.

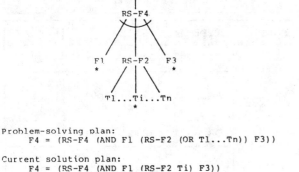

```
Problem-solving plan:
    F4 = (RS-F4 (AND F1 (RS-F2 (OR T1...Tn)) F3))

Current solution plan:
    F4 = (RS-F4 (AND F1 (RS-F2 Ti) F3))

Focus function:   Ti = Focusfunc(C1,...,Cn)

Cost function:    Ci = Costfunc(Pi1,...,Pim)
```
where the Pij's are parameters used to calculate the cost
of precondition Ti.

Fig. 3.   Procedure for focus-control mechanism.

The focus-control mechanism not only restrictively selects subtasks but also exploits all the parallel subtasks involved in the current problem solving. The system then makes the necessary transmissions to distribute unsolved subtasks among processing nodes in the system. This aspect of the focus-control mechanism enhances system response.

The data-driven control mechanism developed for the Hearsay-II speech understanding system [28], [29] is regarded as an effective mechanism for problem domains in which each processing node has only a partial view of the problem and receives erroneous data. After a problem-decomposition phase, a focus-control mechanism is iteratively applied to direct the solving process along the most promising path. This is a bottom-up data-driven process. The information used is knowledge about the capabilities of processing nodes instead of input data. The information may be actual or estimated. Hence, an additional function of the focus-control mechanism is to mitigate and eliminate the error caused by inaccurate estimations of the capabilities of other processing nodes.

As in STRIPS and ABSTRIPS [27], the goal-directed problem-decomposition mechanism for planning is efficient for maintaining global coherence in problem solving. Metalevel control is achieved through problem decomposition, dynamic planning (i.e., iteratively applying the focus-control mechanism), and the hierarchical system-wide problem solving. This hierarchy is arranged through inter-node communications and is designed to maintain global coherence and ameliorate errors caused by the distributed approach. Rosenschein [13] states that in his multiagent planning system a plan is constructed by a single agent and then distributed to the other agents. In our architecture, however, the planning process is distributed and dynamically adapted during the problem-solving process.

F. Solver

After a problem is received and its solving plan created, the appropriate knowledge sources are initiated to solve it

task by task. To insure that the problem solving remains on the most promising path (estimated by the focus-control mechanism), the solution of one task in the plan depends not only on the availability of the results of its descendant subtasks, but also on their qualities. For a subtask with many solution approaches, the one selected by the focus-control mechanism should have the best result before this portion of the problem-solving plan can be deduced. Otherwise it indicates that there is an error during application of the focus-control mechanism, probably caused by an inaccurate estimation. This error should be corrected during the next focus-control process by selecting another alternative.

The operation of the solver starts by searching for deducible subplans within the current solution plan. There are two kinds of deducible subplans, i.e., AND-deducible subplans and OR-deducible subplans. An AND-deducible subplan is a two-level modified AND graph that has all of its descendant subtasks in the current solution plan and which has results available for all of these subtasks. An OR-deducible subplan is a two-level modified OR graph which has one of its descendant subtasks in the current solution plan; the result for this one subtask is the best among the results of all descendant subtasks. Since only one of the subtasks of an OR plan is explored at any one time, some of the needed results will not be available at the time of making the comparison. One method for handling this difficulty is to judge the quality of a result by a cost instead of by the result itself. This cost may be calculated from the result or just estimated.

When deducible subplans are found, they are executed one-by-one by applying the corresponding result-synthesis function to the available subtask results. Then the problem-solving plan is also deduced. These two steps are repeated until there are no more deducible subplans or the entire problem is solved. If it is solved, a final result is inserted into the corresponding task frame on the blackboard. Otherwise, an intermediate result is saved on the blackboard and the problem-solving plan of the corresponding task is updated. The unsolved problem is then returned to the planner to make further plan adjustments. Two examples are given in Fig. 4.

G. Scheduler

The efficient utilization of system resources is an important issue in the design of a DAI system. This is especially true in a system that has only limited software and hardware resources and a large number of tasks to solve. Many approaches have been taken to solve this problem. While most are based on a statistical point of view, a different view is taken in this paper, based on the assignment of priorities to tasks as a function of several factors [30]. These factors include 1) the importance of the task in the whole problem-solving process; 2) the difficulty of the process needed to solve this task (this may be measured in terms of estimates for needed processing time, communication bandwidth, and other system resources);

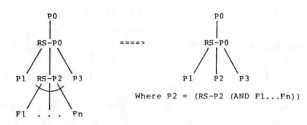

IF preconditions Fl through Fn
(1) are in the current solution plan, and
(2) their results are available.
THEN
the left-hand-side problem-solving plan can be transformed
by deduction to the right-hand-side problem-solving plan.

(a)

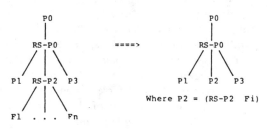

IF precondition Fi
(1) is in the current solution plan, and
(2) its result is the best at the current stage.
THEN
the left-hand-side problem-solving plan can be transformed
by deduction to the right-hand-side problem-solving plan.

(b)

Fig. 4.   Deducible problem-solving plans. (a) Deducible AND-subplan. (b)   Deducible OR-subplan.

and 3) the availabilities of and confidences in the results of its subtasks. The scheduling process is repeated during problem solving each time a new task is added to the queue. Tasks are executed one-by-one according to their priorities. An investigation of the scheduler is not the primary concern of this paper. In order to make the system complete, however, a scheduler has been implemented as a first-in, first-out (FIFO) buffer.

III.   EXAMPLES, RESULTS, AND PERFORMANCE EVALUATION

This section contains an example (implemented in Franz Lisp on a VAX 11/780) that demonstrates the operation of the system, as well as some results that show the major features of the architecture.

A. Application of DAI Architecture to Logic Design

The design of digital-logic circuits is chosen as an environment in which salient aspects of the architecture for a DAI system can be elucidated. An optimum design strategy is one in which all possible design approaches are explored and the best is chosen according to some criterion. An optimum computer-aided implementation of this strategy is one in which resources are used the most efficiently—these resources are processing time at a node and internode communications. In digital logic, a complex design problem can often be decomposed into a set of interrelated subproblems, each of which is to design a simple logic

TABLE IV
DEVICES AVAILABLE AT EACH PROCESSING NODE

NODE	TYPE	GATE	DELAY
NODE-AOIX	NOT	7404	10
	AND	7408 (2-input)	15
		7411 (3-input)	12
		7421 (4-input)	15
	OR	7432 (2-input)	12
	XOR	7406 (2-input)	15
		74135 (3-input)	15
NODE-NAND	NAND	7400 (2-input)	11
		7410 (3-input)	11
		7420 (4-input)	12
		7430 (8-input)	10
		74133 (13-input)	3
NODE-NOR	NOR	7402 (2-input)	10
		7427 (3-input)	8.5
		7425 (4-input)	10.5
		74260 (5-input)	4

function. These subproblems can be worked on in parallel in a distributed system, if intermediate results are exchanged. In addition, several different approaches are often available for implementing a particular logic function. A variety of expertise, which can also be distributed, is then needed to consider these different approaches. Thus, digital-logic design provides an appropriate application for a DAI system.

The DAI system is organized so that each processing node has only a partial view of the problem and knowledge sources are distributed among the processing nodes. Furthermore, there are alternatives for solving parts of the problem. The design of carry-look-ahead adders is chosen as a specific example. The DAI system consists of three processing nodes, where each node uses different kinds of gates to implement logic circuits. The first processing node, NODE-AOIX, uses AND, OR, INVERTER, and XOR gates. The second processing node, NODE-NAND, uses NAND gates, and the third processing node, NODE-NOR, uses NOR gates. Table IV shows the gates, with their associated propagation delays, that are available at each processing node.

A problem-decomposition mechanism is shown in Fig. 5. The problem of designing an n-bit carry-look-ahead adder is first decomposed into three subtasks: 1) synthesize carry generation and propagation signals for each bit; 2) generate the most-significant-bit carry signal. and 3) implement the n-bit sum signal. There are two alternatives for the second and third subtasks. One is for a node to solve the task by using its own expertise. The other is for a node to request assistance from other processing nodes. If a processing node decides to use its own expertise, then the subtask of designing the n-bit sum signal is further decomposed into n subtasks. Each subtask is to implement one bit of the sum signal. As was true for its ancestor task, there are two alternatives for a node: either to use its own

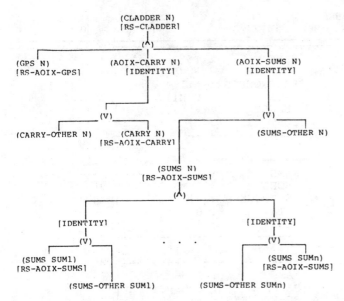

Note: `^` indicates an AND-node and `v` indicates an OR-node.

Fig. 5. Decompositon mechanism for carry-look-ahead adder design problems, at NODE-AOIX.

expertise or to transmit the problem to other processing nodes. For simplicity, the problem-decomposition mechanisms available at all three processing nodes are the same. The only difference among them is that only processing node NODE-AOIX has the expertise needed to solve the first subtask, the synthesis of carry generation and propagation signals.

The system performance is judged by two measurements. These are the number of tasks executed at each processing node and the number of messages transmitted through the system communication channel. A successful system is one which minimizes execution time and minimizes the message traffic.

B. System Demonstration

The task of designing the 2-bit sum signals of a carry-look-ahead adder is given to the system as a question-type message with the node identification of NODE-AOIX as its addressee. After the check of addressee, this message is accepted only by NODE-AOIX and rejected by other processing nodes. A task frame, shown as Table V, is generated and written on the blackboard to maintain the information associated with this problem.

Problem decomposition occurs according to the mechanism stored in the metaknowledge database of NODE-AOIX. A problem-solving plan,

$$(\text{RS-AOIX-SUMS } (\text{AND } (\text{IDENTITY } (\text{OR } T1 \ T2)) \\ (\text{IDENTITY } (\text{OR } T3 \ T4))))$$

is then generated. The (IDENTITY (OR T1 T2)) subplan is for the design of the first bit of the sum signal. This notation indicates that there are two alternatives: subtask T1, which uses this node's own expertise, or subtask T2, which attempts to seek assistance from other processing nodes. The

result-synthesis function for this subplan is IDENTITY, which simply passes the result of its descendant subtask to its ancestor task. The (IDENTITY (OR T3 T4)) subplan is for the implementation of the second bit of the sum signal. As in the design of the first bit of the sum signal, subtask T3 uses its own expertise and subtask T4 looks for assistance from other nodes. RS-AOIX-SUMS is another result-synthesis function which generates the final implementation for this design problem.

In this example, propagation delay is the only parameter used to judge the quality of the implementations. Initially, the system is built in such a way that each processing node assumes that the expertise of other processing nodes is better than its own. Thus during the focus-control process, NODE-AOIX determines that subtasks T2 and T4 are better than subtasks T1 and T3, respectively. The current solution plan is chosen to be

$$(\text{RS-AOIX-SUMS } (\text{AND } (\text{IDENTITY } T2) \ (\text{IDENTITY } T4))).$$

Since subtasks T2 and T4 are unsolvable, NODE-AOIX forms two question-type messages according to the communication protocol and broadcasts them through the system channel. The reason for choosing the broadcast transmission mechanism is that there is no knowledge about the capabilities of the other processing nodes at the beginning of the problem-solving process.

After making the necessary checks, NODE-NAND and NODE-NOR independently accept both subtasks T2 and T4. Since these are completely solvable tasks to the two processing nodes, the required knowledge sources are invoked, the tasks are solved, and the generated results are returned to NODE-AOIX as answer-type messages. After the results to subtasks T2 and T4 are received by NODE-AOIX, they are inserted into the corresponding task frames on the blackboard. Since the subplan, (IDENTITY (OR T3 T4)), is a deducible OR-subplan, it is deduced by applying the result-synthesis function IDENTITY to the result of subtask T4. In contrast to this, the subplan (IDENTITY (OR T1 T2)) is a nondeducible OR-subplan, because the implementation of subtask T2 has a propagation delay (19 ns) worse than that (15 ns) estimated for subtask T1. This is due to an overly optimistic estimate for the cost of subtask T2.

During the second iteration, the current solution plan is adjusted to

$$(\text{RS-AOIX-SUMS } (\text{AND } (\text{IDENTITY } T1) \ T5))$$

to reflect the effect of the newly received information. The subtask T5 is generated by the deduction of subplan (IDENTITY (OR T3 T4)), whose result is already available. Since subtask T1 is a solvable task to NODE-AOIX, the required knowledge sources are invoked. Then the final result is generated by applying the result-synthesis function RS-AOIX-SUMS to the results of subtasks T1 and T5. A message-flow diagram, together with problem-solving plans and intermediate results, is shown in Fig. 6.

This DAI system can be compared to a centralized system, i.e., one with all problem-solving expertise located at one node, by using the number of subtasks which must

TABLE V
TASK FRAMES

NAME	: T	NAME	: T5
PROBLEM	: SUMS	PROBLEM	: SUMS
RS-PROCESS	: RS-AOIX-SUMS	RS-PROCESS	: nil
DATA	: 2	DATA	: SUM1
PLAN	:	RESULT	:
COST	: nil	COST	: 22

NAME	: T1	NAME	: T2
PROBLEM	: SUMS	PROBLEM	: SUMS-OTHER
RS-PROCESS	: RS-AOIX-SUMS	RS-PROCESS	: nil
DATA	: SUM0	DATA	: SUM0
COST	: 15	COST	: 1

NAME	: T3	NAME	: T4
PROBLEM	: SUMS	PROBLEM	: SUMS-OTHER
RS-PROCESS	: RS-AOIX-SUMS	RS-PROCESS	: nil
DATA	: SUM1	DATA	: SUM1
COST	: 42	COST	: 1

```
(RS-AOIX-SUMS (AND (IDENTITY (OR T1 T2)) (IDENTITY (OR T3 T4))))
(RS-AOIX-SUMS (AND (IDENTITY T2) (IDENTITY T4)))
(RS-AOIX-SUMS (AND (IDENTITY T1) T5))
```

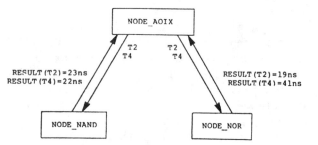

Fig. 6. Message-flow diagram of 2-bit sum signals in a carry-look-ahead adder design problem.

be executed in each case. For simplification, we assume that the execution times required for subtask communications, result communications, result synthesis, and result comparisons are negligible. The problem chosen has two design subproblems, each of which can be solved by three approaches. Hence, there are six subtasks to be solved, and these could be completed by a centralized system (having no metaknowledge) in six time units. The use of initial metaknowledge about the expected value of the results reduces the number of subtasks which must be solved to five. The centralized system solves these in five time units while the DAI system solves these in two time units as described above. After additional metaknowledge is accumulated, the systems need to solve only two subtasks which can be calculated in one time unit and two time units for the distributed and centralized systems, respectively. Table VI summarizes these results.

Learning in this system occurs by the accumulation of metaknowledge. In the digital-logic design example, all subproblem designs are judged on the basis of propagation delays; the metaknowledge is in the form of underestimates for these delays. (As in the A^* algorithm, underestimates are used to prevent the system from choosing a suboptimal design alternative.) As the system operates, these underestimates are adjusted to more accurately reflect the actual propagation delays. The adjustments consist of a weighted average of the old and new delay values.

C. Results

For clarity, only a simple example has been described. Next, two more complicated examples—the designs of 2-bit and 3-bit carry-look-ahead adders—are presented to illustrate the major features of the architecture, including the focus-control mechanism and the self-improvement ability. These two examples are given to the system at four different times: $t0$, $t1$, $t2$, and $t2'$. Time $t0$ is the moment at which the system is set up and has no experience about solving this kind of problem. Time $t1$ is some time later, when the system has solved ten examples of this kind of problem. Time $t2$ is even later, when the system has even more experience about solving this type of problem. The communication mechanism used in problem solving at time $t2'$ is directed transmission, instead of the broadcast mechanism used at times $t0$, $t1$, and $t2$.

Without using a focus-control mechanism, in the worst case, the system explores all the alternatives. The total number of tasks created and executed is 22 for the design of a 2-bit carry-look-ahead adder and 31 for the 3-bit adder. When making use of the focus-control mechanism, the number of tasks created is significantly reduced. At time $t0$, only 16 tasks are executed in the 2-bit design case and 18 tasks in the 3-bit case, without sacrificing the quality of the design.

As described above, the planning mechanism dynamically makes adjustments in the problem-solving plan based on the current status of problem solving, and attempts to execute as few tasks as possible. The number of tasks executed at each processing node at the four time instances is shown in Table VII. The number of tasks executed

TABLE VI
COMPARISON OF CENTRALIZED AND DISTRIBUTED AI SYSTEMS

PROCESSING ARCHITECTURE	NO META-KNOWLEDGE	INITIAL META-KNOWLEDGE	COMPLETE META-KNOWLEDGE
Centralized AI System	6 / 6	5 / 5	2 / 2
Distributed AI System	6 / 2	5 / 2	2 / 1

Subtasks_Solved / Time_Units_Elapsed

TABLE VII
NUMBER OF TASKS EXECUTED BY EACH NODE

PROBLEM	NODE	NUMBER OF TASKS EXECUTED			
		t0	t1	t2	t2´
DESIGN1	NODE1	5	4	4	2
	NODE2	6	4	4	1
	NODE3	5	2	2	1
DESIGN2	NODE1	7	6	5	2
	NODE2	6	6	6	2
	NODE3	5	4	2	1

Note: DESIGN1 -- 2-bit carry-look-ahead adder.
      DESIGN2 -- 3-bit carry-look-ahead adder.

TABLE VIII
NUMBER OF MESSAGES TRANSMITTED BY EACH NODE

PROBLEM	NODE	NUMBER OF MESSAGES			
		t0	t1	t2	t2´
DESIGN1	NODE1	9	6	6	4
	NODE2	8	4	4	2
	NODE3	8	5	5	1
DESIGN2	NODE1	9	8	7	4
	NODE2	8	7	5	2
	NODE3	8	7	6	5

Note: DESIGN1 -- 2-bit carry-look-ahead adder design.
      DESIGN2 -- 3-bit carry-look-ahead adder design.

decreases from time $t0$ to time $t2$. This trend is the same for all three processing nodes and both design problems. The time saved by not exploring extra tasks at time $t2$ ranges from 14 to 60 percent compared to time $t0$.

Table VIII shows the number of messages transmitted from each processing node at the four time instances during the solution of the two logic design problems. The decrease in communications at time $t2$ compared to time $t0$ ranges from 22 to 50 percent. The decrease in communications is even greater in the case of using directed transmissions, ranging from 27 to 87 percent. The measure-

ments of processing time and communication bandwidth reflect the benefit of using a problem-solving history and the importance of equipping a system with a learning ability.

IV.   CONCLUSION

An architecture for a distributed artificial intelligence system, with a particular focus on the control and communication aspects, has been presented. Problem solving has been viewed as an iterative refinement of several phases, including a dynamic planning process, a distribution of kernel subproblems (which results in a problem-solving hierarchy), and a solving of kernel subproblems. Internode communications among the individual planning processes in the distributed environment creates this hierarchy. These communications may be either broadcast or directed, unlike the distributed Hearsay-II architecture which uses a shared-memory (broadcast) mechanism; using directed communications reduces the message traffic in a system. Also, in contrast to our architecture, Hearsay-II does not make use of any hierarchy which might be available in a problem-solving domain and has no learning mechanism for accumulating problem-solving experience.

The system presented herein is a general architecture for distributed problem solving which can be adapted to many types of problems in a variety of domains. It is composed of three knowledge-based systems: 1) a problem-dependent collection of knowledge sources, 2) a communication reasoning system in the form of metaknowledge about problem decomposition and result synthesis, and 3) a mechanism for the accumulation of metaknowledge.

The goal-directed problem-decomposition component of the processing node architecture maintains global coherence during problem solving. Reductions both in the size of the explored solution space at the task level and in the required communication bandwidths are achieved by a focus-control mechanism. Errors, which sometimes arise during focus control, are reduced by a search process of deducible subplans and the iterative behavior of the problem solving. In addition, a learning ability utilizes problem-solving experience to improve system performance.

Examples in the domain of digital-logic design demonstrate the operation of the DAI system. The results show a significant reduction in the number of tasks executed and the number of messages communicated within the system.

REFERENCES

[1] V. R. Lesser and D. D. Corkill, "Functionally accurate, cooperative distributed systems," *IEEE Trans. Syst., Man, Cybernet.*, vol. SMC-11, no. 1, pp. 81–96, Jan. 1981.

[2] D. D. Corkill, V. R. Lesser, and E. Hudlicka, "Unifying data-directed and goal-directed control: An example and experiments," in *Proc. Second Nat. Conf. on Artificial Intelligence*, Aug. 1982, pp. 143–147.

[3] V. Lesser *et al.*, "A high-level simulation testbed for cooperative distributed problem solving," in *Proc. Third Int. Conf. on Distributed Computing Systems*, Miami, FL, Oct. 1982, pp. 341–350.

[4] D. D. Corkill, "A framework for organizational self-design in distributed problem solving networks," Ph.D thesis, Dep. Computer and Inform. Sci., Univ. Massachusetts, Amherst, February 1983.

[5] D. D. Corkill and V. R. Lesser, "The use of meta-level control for coordination in a distributed problem solving network," in *Proc. Eighth Int. Joint Conf. on Artificial Intelligence*, Karlsruhe, West Germany, vol. 2, Aug. 1983, pp. 748–756.

[6] D. McArthur, R. Steeb, and S. Cammarata, "A framework for distributed problem solving," in *Proc. AAAI-82*, 1982, pp. 181–184.

[7] _____, "Strategies of cooperation in distributed problem solving," in *Proc. Eighth Int. Joint Conf. on Artificial Intelligence*, Karlsruhe, West Germany, vol. 2, Aug. 1983, pp. 767–770.

[8] P. Thorndyke, D. McArthur, S. Cammarata, and R. Steeb, "Distributed problem solving in air traffic control," *Rep. Second Workshop on Distributed AI*, pp. 17–18, June 1981.

[9] _____, "AUTOPILOT: A distributed planner for air fleet control," in *Proc. IJCAI-1981*, Aug. 1981, pp. 171–177.

[10] R. Davis, D. Brotsky, and J. Zinnikas, "Teamwork in multi-agent planning; Distributed AI as an approach to complexity," *Rep. Second Workshop on Distributed AI*, pp. 15–16, June 1981.

[11] K. Konolige and N. J. Nilsson, "Multiple-agent planning systems," in *Proc. First Annual Nat. Conf. on Artificial Intelligence*, Aug. 1980, pp. 138–142.

[12] D. E. Appelt, "A planner for reasoning about knowledge and action," in *Proc. First Ann. Nat. Conf. on Artificial Intelligence*, Aug. 1980, pp. 131–133.

[13] J. S. Rosenschein, "Synchronization of multi-agent plans," in *Proc. Nat. Conf. on Artificial Intelligence AAAI-82*, Pittsburgh, Aug. 1982, pp. 115–119.

[14] M. Stefik and L. Conway, "Toward the principled engineering of knowlege," *Artificial Intelligence Mag.*, vol. 3, no. 3, pp. 4–16, summer 1982.

[15] R. G. Smith, "A framework for problem solving in a distributed processing environment," Dept. Computer Sci., Stanford Univ., Stanford, CA, STAN-CS-78-700 (HPP-78-28) Dec. 1978.

[16] _____, "The contract net protocol: High-level communication and control in a distributed problem solver," *IEEE Trans. Comput.*, vol. C-29, pp. 1104–1113, Dec. 1980.

[17] R. G. Smith and R. Davis, "Frameworks for cooperation in distributed problem solving," *IEEE Trans. Syst., Man, Cybernet.*, vol. SMC-11, no. 1, pp. 61–70, Jan. 1981.

[18] R. G. Smith, "A framework for distributed problem solving," Ann Arbor, MI: UMI Press, 1981.

[19] R. G. Smith and R. Davis, "Negotiation as a metaphor for distributed problem solving," *Artificial Intelligence*, vol. 20, no. 1, pp. 63–109, Jan. 1983.

[20] L. Kleinrock, *Queueing Systems, Volume 2: Computer Applications.* New York: Wiley, 1976, ch. I.

[21] *Proc. 1984 Int. Conf. on Parallel Processing*, IEEE Computer Society Press, Silver Spring, MD, 1984.

[22] C. E. Houstis, R. D. Bonnell, and R. M. Stevens, "Software partitioning in a distributed environment," in *Proc. INFOCON 83*, San Diego, CA, April 1983.

[23] J. D. Yang, M. N. Huhns, and L. M. Stephens, "Dynamic planning for the control of distributed problem solving," USCMI Dep. Elect. Computer Eng., Univ. South Carolina, Columbia, USCMI Technical Report 83-10, June 1983.

[24] J. D. Yang, "An architecture for control and communications in distributed artificial intelligence systems," Ph.D. dissertation, Dep. Elect. Computer Eng., Univ. South Carolina, Columbia, Dec. 1983.

[25] F. Hayes-Roth, D. A. Waterman, and D. B. Lenat, *Building Expert Systems.* Reading, MA: Addison-Wesley, 1983, ch. I.

[26] J. Pearl, A. Leal, and J. Saleh, "GODDESS: A goal-directed decision structuring system," *IEEE Trans. Pattern Anal. Machine Intel.*, vol. PAMI-4, no. 3, pp. 250–262, May 1982.

[27] N. Nilsson, *Principles of Artificial Intelligence*, Palo Alto, CA: Tioga, 1980.

[28] L. D. Erman, F. Hayes-Roth, V. R. Lesser, and D. R. Reddy, "The Hearsay-II speech understanding system: Integrating knowledge to resolve uncertainty," *Computing Surv.*, vol. 12, no. 2, pp. 213–253, June 1975.

[29] L. D. Erman and V. Lesser, "A multi-level organization for problem solving using many, diverse, cooperating sources of knowledge," in *Proc. Fourth Int. Joint Conf. on Artificial Intelligence*, USSR, Sept. 1975, pp. 483–490.

[30] M. N. Huhns, L. M. Stephens, and R. D. Bonnell, "Control and cooperation in distributed expert systems," in *Proc. IEEE Southeastcon*, April 1983.

An Examination of Distributed Planning in the World of Air Traffic Control

NICHOLAS V. FINDLER AND RON LO

Artificial Intelligence Laboratory and Computer Science Department, Arizona State University, Tempe, Arizona 85287

Received October 10, 1984

A *Distributed Planning System* is a network whose nodes represent distinct processors, each cooperating with a selected set of others to achieve a common set of goals. We address two important issues in this paper: (i) How individual processors should be interconnected so that their capacities are fully utilized and their goals can be accomplished effectively and efficiently. (ii) What kind of planning activity the individual processors should engage in. We have chosen the Air Traffic Control (ATC) environment, an intellectually challenging domain of much practical importance, to study different ideas in distributed planning systems. Here we show the results obtained with one type of possible organizational architecture, *Location-Centered Cooperative* mode of operation. We describe and demonstrate algorithmically a simulation-based planning process based on this architecture. The work described in this paper is part of our continuing effort in examining ways in which greater responsibilities can be delegated to computers in ATC. © 1986 Academic Press, Inc.

1. INTRODUCTION

There are problem-solving tasks whose size and certain other characteristics do not allow them to be processed effectively by using a single computer system. Such tasks involve spatially distributed input/output, extensive communication over a long distance, and, possibly, time-stressed demands for solution. Under such conditions, a distributed system of cooperating, semi-autonomous processors can be more effective than a centralized system [1]. Formal, analytical techniques for solving such problems have not yet been developed [2]. It is, therefore, necessary to define a simulated environment that can then be used to gain empirical experience with different methodologies.

Distributed Planning is an indispensable part of Distributed Problem Solving, which is the cooperative solution of problems by a decentralized and loosely coupled collection of problem solvers, each of which may reside on its own distinct processor [20]. Our objective is to derive an effective strategy for distributed problem solving in utilizing the reliable and low-cost computing power obtained through Distributed Computer Systems [21] research. The two major issues are:

• how individual processors should be interconnected so that their capabilities are fully utilized and their goals can be accomplished effectively and efficiently;

• what kind of planning activities the individual processors should engage in.

In this paper, we discuss the design and implementation of a distributed planning system for empirical studies of one possible organizational architecture—the *Location-Centered, Cooperative (LCC) mode of group planning*. Section 2 describes our view of the interrelationship between planning and decision making. The discussion on the planning process should contribute to the understanding of the problem-solving strategy proposed. The task of Air Traffic Control (ATC) is presented in Section 3. Section 4 touches upon a variety of different architectures and modes of operations in the domain of Distributed Air Traffic Control (DATC). Section 5 proposes the kernel design of the processors in our simulated environment and defines some DATC terminology. Section 6 specifies certain rules in formalizing the negotiation process. Section 7 discusses the knowledge base representation and the concept of simulation-based planning. Various algorithms contributing to the planning and decision-making process are provided. Section 8 integrates the ideas presented in the previous sections, and discusses the pros and cons of using the Centralized Scratch Pad (CSP) as a device for interprocess communication and synchronization in Distributed Planning. Finally, Section 9 presents a generalized methodology for supporting communication and control, Distributed Scratched Pads (DSP). The algorithm of a distributed planner, used in the LCC mode of planning, is also included. A description of current activity concludes the paper.

2. ON DECISION MAKING AND PLANNING

We are concerned with planning activity which in general precedes decision making. It is in order here to review some basic concepts in this context.

Decision making, in general, represents a time sequence of choices which constitute the basis of action. Viewed in this way, decision making may be considered a response mechanism operating in a task environment and guided by a problem-solving strategy. The consequences of a decision may in ad-as good as that of any other choice—in other words, he is capable of making consistently optimum decisions.

Simon [3] has replaced the above, idealized and abstract actor with the "satisficing man." This individual's environment is complicated, vague, and uncertain. Instead of optimizing, he is content if his current level of aspiration is met ("satisficed"). This model considers incomplete and inconsistent information, conflicts, limited information processing ability, limited perceptions, and desires. He is, however, able to learn and to modify both the structure and the contents of his goals. Such "bounded rationality" is realistic at the level of both individual and organizational decision making.

Students of planning and decision making include researchers in artificial intelligence, management science, operations research, statistics, psychology, economics, human engineering, and some "fringe" areas of other disciplines. The motivation comes from one or several of the following aims: to understand, explain, predict, and improve human judgmental processes; and to enhance and replace them, partially or fully, with computer systems.

Considerable effort has been spent by researchers in Artificial Intelligence to understand and to automate the *planning process*—at least in relatively small and well-defined universes [4–8]. Without going into the details of the work in this area, it can be safely said that much research needs to be done before computer-based planning systems can be made responsible for large-scale, real-life activities.

vance be understood completely, partially, or not at all, and in a deterministic or probabilistic manner.

The goals of decision making may be positive (to attain certain objectives) or negative (to avoid certain events). These goals may be of the short-range or long-range type. In the latter case particularly, a *planning* process precedes the actual decision making, which contrasts and, in some sense, tries out alternative methods of attack in a coarse-grained way. Planning applies a (crude) model to a task, consisting of the current and the desired situation, to compute a sequence of (major) action steps for achieving the goal, i.e., to reach the desired situation.

Plans are in general continually refined and incrementally modified. A part of the plan may take care of the *resource allocation* among three activities: gathering more information if necessary, refining and modifying the plan if necessary, and making progress in carrying out the plan. The modification of the plan makes economic sense as long as the cost involved is less than the expected increase in the utility of the modified plan. This simple and plausible statement implies that there are many indispensable pieces of information available for the human or computer analyst performing the operation, such as

- measures on the cost and complexity of planning;
- reliability values of alternate plans;
- utilities of individual goal achievement;
- probabilities of achieving goals as the consequence of an ordered sequence of actions;
- trade-off among alternate subgoals; etc.

However, this type of information is rarely available and even if it is, its reliability is rather low. The difficulty is aggravated by changing environments and goals, and the lack of heuristic guidance in combating *combinatorially explosive search domains*.

Returning to the problem of decision making, we can distinguish between *situations of conflict*, in which different decision-making strategies compete to accomplish some mutually exclusive goals, and situations in which no antagonistic confrontation occurs and decisions are made, say, vis-a-vis nature. If the goal is a multidimensional objective, its (vector) components need not be orthogonal (for example, one component may be minimum deviation from given flight schedules and another the adherence to predetermined flight paths). In fact, there may be constraints with and partial conflict between such components.

In real-life situations, the conditions for "rational" decision making do not prevail. Namely, a "rational" decision maker is assumed to be fully aware of (1) the set of alternatives open to choice, (2) the relationships between the outcomes (payoffs) and his choice, (3) the preference ordering among outcomes; and his choice. He can, therefore, make a choice the consequence of which is at least

3. ON THE AIR TRAFFIC CONTROL TASK ENVIRONMENT

The ATC task domain satisfies certain important criteria that made it appropriate for "applied" Artificial Intelligence studies:

- it is complex enough to be challenging for humans;
- one can identify problem areas of different sizes that could be attacked successively;
- one can define plausible metrics along several dimensions to measure the performance of a proposed system;
- until a subsystem is fully developed and tested, it can operate in a realistic, simulated world;
- a successful automated ATC system would share with systems working in other fundamentally important environments the capabilities of planning, problem solving, and decision making under dynamically changing conditions while satisfying hierarchies of constraints.

Furthermore, in favor of selecting ATC as a vehicle of our studies are the facts that ATC is a relatively small universe with well-defined boundaries; it covers a limited set of distinct situations and actions; and, most importantly, the results of the work can be verified and used in conjunction with partial

ment means that each member processor of a spatially clustered group participates and collaborates in the plan generation, and engages in a formalized negotiation process with the others.

In the following, we discuss the kernel design of the processors, define some DATC terminology, and identify the rules of negotiation. Finally, we describe the data structures and algorithms used in implementing the method proposed.

5.   A KERNEL DESIGN OF PROCESSORS AND OTHER ISSUES

The following characteristic features of the DATC task environment are noted:

•   availability of multiple processors;
•   widely dispersed data gathering/sensing;
•   limited and at times noisy communication channels;
•   time-stressed demands on decision making;
•   natural clustering of activities, both spatially and functionally.

The objectives of planning are

•   error-free and on-time routing;
•   reduction of uncertainties which potentially lead to unresolvable conflicts;
•   adherence to predetermined constraints, such as horizontal and vertical separation;
•   conservation of resources (fuel, airport facilities, etc.).

In our first approximation, we may assume that all (commercial) aircraft are functionally identical. Figure 1 shows the kernel design of a processor participating in the LCC mode of planning.

We also assume a constant and limited bandwidth communication between aircraft. Broadcasting aimed at each member of the group simultaneously is also possible. The messages are received error free in our simulation but we may include "murmuring" [19] at a later time.

Information is obtained by an aircraft both by *communication* from others and by *sensing* (radar). Each aircraft has a limited sensory horizon. Its knowledge of the world is restricted, uncertain, and changing as it and other aircraft move through air space. The *Plan Generation Unit* of each processor performs certain "width" (involving a number of aircraft) and "depth" (time span) of planning assigned to the processor. The *Look-Ahead Unit* performs the simulation of future events, calculates the extrapolated trajectories, and consults with the *Incident Detector*. The latter, relying on the safety rules in its Knowledge Base, identifies and reports the type, participants, time, and location of any incident that may occur. In such cases, the Look-Ahead Unit directs the Plan Generation Unit to modify the current plan. Such modi-

human control and in an economically and technologically important domain. A number of individuals and institutions have made significant contributions to the ultimate computerization of ATC [9–12].

The major goal of a computer system in the ATC task environment is to direct and guide all aircraft within its jurisdiction through its phases of flight: takeoff, ascent, cruising, descent, and landing. In addition to the primary objective of safety, there are a number of secondary measures of quality, such as adherence to time schedules and flight paths, fuel consumption, sudden changes in flight parameters, the number of violations of statutory restrictions (for example, minimum vertical and horizontal separation between aircraft).

We have been engaged in constructing a number of large, domain-free programming systems with the idea of customizing them for ATC-related task [13–18]. The work described in this paper is part of our continuing effort in examining ways in which greater responsibilities can be delegated to computers in ATC.

4.   ON DISTRIBUTED AIR TRAFFIC CONTROL

Distributed Air Traffic Control (DATC) is the domain in which we study Distributed Planning Systems (DPSs). A DPS consists of a group of agents, a network of processors, each cooperating with a selected set of others to achieve a common set of objectives. The following basic questions need to be addressed:

(i)   How should individual processors be interconnected so that their capabilities are fully utilized and their goals can be accomplished effectively and efficiently?
(ii)   What kind of planning activity should the individual processors be engaged in?

System reliability and communication limitations make it impractical to have a single control processor direct all the others' activities. A variety of different architectures have been proposed [10] for the organization of a DATC environment:

•   Individual planning by each processor, either autonomously or cooperatively;
•   Group planning in either a location-centered or a function-centered mode;
•   Global planning divided into segments of some type or with a hierarchy of responsibilities.

After some initial studies on the effectiveness, flexibility, and resource demands of these architectures, we have decided to examine the *Location-Centered, Cooperative (LCC) mode of group planning* first. Such an arrange-

All aircraft involved in a specific conflict or violation define the *incident space*. It is

$$S(I_j) = \bigcup_{\forall A_j \text{ in } I_j} R(A_i),$$

where I_j is the jth incident. An *incident subset* consists of all incidents that are within a certain locality. The *adjacent incident space* of an incident subset I_k^* is defined as

$$S(I_k^*) = \bigcup_{\forall I_j \text{ in } I_k^*} \bigcup_{\forall A_i \text{ in } I_j} R(A_i).$$

Note that the aircraft in an Adjacent Incident Space are the ones to be considered with the planning process in the LCC mode.

Next, the *incident criticality factor*, F, of an incident is the sum of the priority factors, f (described later), of all aircraft involved in the given incident. That is,

$$F(I_j) = \sum_{\forall A_i \text{ in } I_j} f(A_i).$$

6. NEGOTIATION RULES

In order to resolve conflicts, one or more aircraft must change some flight parameters. The questions are: Which one(s) should effect the changes and in what chronological order? We have formulated four rules the combined effect of which is to formalize the priority ranking process.

Rule 1. The most important selection criterion is that that aircraft should replan/change its course first which would be involved in a conflict within the shortest period of time, considering all its conflict groups. The *urgency factor* of aircraft A_i, U_i, is defined as (-1) times the shortest time period in minutes after which a conflict would arise—for reasons to be seen later.

Rule 2. The second most important consideration is given to the *status*, S, of an aircraft. It is defined as the sum of the emergency level on board (critically ill person, hijacking attempt, etc.), E, and a measure of the amount of fuel yet available, $S = E + G$, where both E and G can assume the values 2, 1, and 0 (normal).

Rule 3. Next, we have to devise a measure that takes into account the

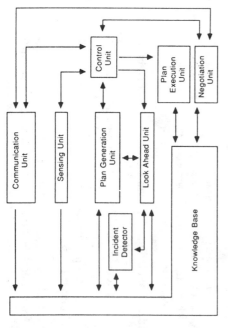

FIG. 1. Kernel design for the process control structure in each aircraft, using the LCC architecture.

fication may also be necessary if the updates from the *Sensing Unit* are at variance with the representation of the world in the Plan Generation Unit. The *Negotiation Unit* distributes work load among the affected aircraft and reaches conflict resolution with them if necessary. Finally, the *Control Unit* coordinates and controls the above processes.

Some *definitions* follow. Let the *radar range* of aircraft A_i be $R(A_i)$. All other aircraft within that range constitute the *surrounding aircraft* of A_i. The identifications of these aircraft are on the *surrounding aircraft list* (SAL) of A_i.

An *incident* is either a conflict or a violation. A *conflict* is a situation in which two or more aircraft get too close to each other. The aircraft involved in the same conflict form a *conflict group*, represented as a list. Note that if there are three or more aircraft in a conflict group then each aircraft is in (pairwise) conflict with every other member of the group. Appropriate commands must be issued so that all conflicts are resolved in time. A *conflict list*, associated with an aircraft, contains as sublists the conflict groups to which the given aircraft belongs. For example, the conflict list of aircraft A may be $((B\ C)(D))$. This means that there is conflict between A and B, A and C, B and C, and A and D, but not between B and D, and C and D.

A *violation*, in contrast, involves only one aircraft that violates some predefined flight parameter. There are two types. *Type I violation* is shown in the simulation at a future time point. It must be resolved before it could occur in real life. (Such is, for example, the "Final Approach Altitude Violation.") These are more severe if uncorrected than *Type II violations*. The latter are resolved preceding, concurrently with, or subsequent to the violation. (Such is, for example, the "Unheeded Request Violation.")

(weighted number of) incidents the aircraft are involved in within their respective adjacent incident space. This leads to a measure

$$W_i = V_i + \sum_{k=1}^{C_i} n_{i,k},$$

where V_i is the number of violations A_i is involved in and $n_{i,k}$ is the number of aircraft involved in the kth conflict of aircraft A_i, $k = 1, \ldots, C_i$; C_i being the total number of conflicts of A_i.

Rule 4. Finally, if the above rules led to a tie, another selection criterion assigns the replanning task to the aircraft that is surrounded by the least number of other aircraft (the least number of aircraft within its radar range).

The arguments in favor of these heuristics are threefold:

(i) the aircraft so identified has the most degrees of freedom;
(ii) this aircraft will need the least number of subsequent messages about later course changes;
(iii) the number of aircraft affected by this command is the smallest.

The number of aircraft surrounding A_i is N_i.

Let us look at the situation in Fig. 2. The conflict location among aircraft A, B, and C is marked with " * ", and between aircraft A and D with " + ". The individual aircraft and their conflict lists, therefore, are

A: ((B C)(D))
B: ((A C))
C: ((A B))
D: ((A)).

The participants in the conflict group (A B C) have an earlier incident to resolve than those in (A D)—Rule 1. Assume that the status of the aircraft A, B, and C are the same—Rule 2. Since aircraft A is involved in a higher number of incidents than B and C, it must do the replanning (i.e., changing its flight parameters) first—Rule 3.

The example in Fig. 3 shows three conflict locations: one among aircraft A, B, and C: " * ", one between A and D: " + ", and one between B and E: "⊙." The conflict lists of the individual aircraft are

A: ((B C)(D))
B: ((A C)(E))
C: ((A B))
D: ((A))
E: ((B)).

Here the urgency factor (Rule 1) makes us select aircraft B or E. Rule 3 now identifies aircraft B as the one to change its course first.

In order to minimize the need for intercomputer communication and for arithmetic computations, we propose the formula

$$f(A_i) = 8 * U_i + 4 * S_i + 2 * W_i - N_i,$$

where

$f(A_i)$ is the priority factor of the ith aircraft,
U_i is its urgency factor,
S_i is its status,
W_i is the weighted number of incidents in which it is involved,
N_i is the number of aircraft by which it is surrounded.

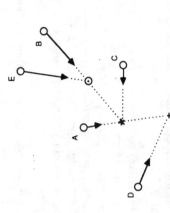

FIG. 3. Three expected conflict locations: " * " among aircraft (A B C), " + " between aircraft (A D), and "⊙" between aircraft (B E).

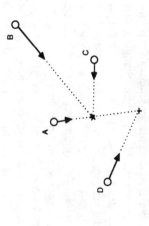

FIG. 2. Two expected conflict locations: " * " among aircraft (A B C), and " + " between aircraft (A D).

As can be seen, each rule through its numerical evaluation contributes appropriately to the priority factor. The higher its value, the more critical the situation of the aircraft. Also, a higher value of the priority factor is a measure of higher productivity (effectiveness) in changing that aircraft's course to eliminate *all* incidents. The values of the variables can be transmitted through radar signals in the sensing stage. The computation is based on simple table look-ups, shifting, and addition. Thus the whole negotiation process needed for the LCC architecture need not involve the Communication Unit, and the cycle for request-response can be eliminated.

The above formalism leads to an ordered list of the aircraft to be considered in resolving a *given incident*. The question now is in which order the *incidents* should be resolved. We have defined for this purpose the incident criticality factor in Section 5 as

$$F(I_j) = \sum_{\forall A_i \text{ in } I_j} f(A_i).$$

The incidents to be considered for resolving are ordered according to decreasing values of F.

7. PROBLEM SOLVING WITH SIMULATION IN ATC

We discuss the knowledge base necessary, how planning is combined with simulation, and the different algorithms to be used.

Wesson [9] developed a problem-solving method that uses a rule-based knowledge representation, and combines planning and simulation. The following ideas and algorithms start from and enhance his work. We introduce, however, significantly novel concepts for the DATC environment in the next section.

The knowledge base of a planner includes *directives* aimed at avoiding incidents. For example, the following seven directives are available to resolve a *two-aircraft separation conflict*:

(1) Climb (1000 feet each time) until an unoccupied level is found.
(2) Descend (1000 feet each time) until an unoccupied level is found.
(3) Turn (vector) right.
(4) Turn (vector) left.
(5) Slow down.
(6) Accelerate.
(7) Hold.

The various incidents possible are associated with the appropriate directives in the knowledge base. The planner's task is to compute

(i) which directives to use;
(ii) when they should be used; and
(iii) what parametric values should be applied in the directives chosen, and for which aircraft.

A directive with (tentative) parametric values becomes a *command*. The knowledge base also contains location- and aircraft-specific information, such as airway maps, flight plans, aircraft performance data, and current aircraft data (position, direction, speed, acceleration, immediate plans, etc.). *Simulation-based planning* uses snapshots of the real world (every navigation-related detail within given boundaries of the airspace) and the knowledge base to predict

(i) the behavior of the aircraft within its jurisdiction as time progresses,
(ii) the consequences of the commands issued.

The planner can thus identify impending trouble spots and, in general, receives information feedback about planned actions. As a safety measure, sensory information updates the image of the real world at regular times. If this deviates from the expected image by more than a permitted extent (due to, for example, adverse weather conditions or less than satisfactory pilot adherence to the commands), a replanning process must be initiated.

Next, we discuss the simulation-based planning algorithms which are used in centralized ATC.

(1) Plan-Ahead

Input: A snapshot of the real world, and a value specifying the time period for simulation.
Output: A plan for commands.

procedure PLAN-AHEAD (snapshot-of-the-real-world, ST)
(* ST: Simulation Time *).
begin
repeat
  Detect incidents and put them on an incident-list
  if incident-list is not empty then
  begin
    Divide incident-list into spatially disjoint incident-subsets.

    (* The possibility of interactions among these incident subsets is near zero. *)

    for each incident-subset
    begin

Select the incident with the highest incident criticality factor and resolve this level-zero incident.

(* Resolving one incident at a time in this order may also resolve other, less critical incidents and cause others. *)

(* The algorithm RESOLVE, defined later, resolves a given incident and returns a single response command. *)

Post-process the plan

(* Place the command, returned by RESOLVE, in the plan. Scan plan, eliminating redundant or counterproductive commands associated with this incident location, aircraft, etc. This is done by comparing new and previously issued commands. *)

end
Select time of earliest command.
if this command time < current simulation time then
    Backdate to it

(* Backdating means changing the world model back to one prevailing at an earlier time point. *)

end
Issue commands in plan.
Update world model in event-driven time steps
until ST time units have elapsed.

(* 20 minutes is a reasonable value of ST in most cases *)

end (* PLAN-AHEAD *)

(2) Resolve

Input: A copy of the world model and the level number.
Output: If called by PLAN-AHEAD then return a single command.
        If called by TRY-COMMAND then return the best command's value.

function RESOLVE (copy-of-world-model, level number)
begin
for each possible directive responding to the given incident
    begin
        Compute specific parameters of the directive

TRY-COMMAND on a copy of the given world model at the given level.

(* TRY-COMMAND, defined later, is used to try out a command in world model. *)

(* Looking ahead one level means updating world model to an incident, resolving the incident, updating to the next incident, and evaluating the world. *)

end
if called by PLAN-AHEAD
then return the best command
else return the best command's value

(* Command's value is defined as the result of evaluating the world model at a specific time. The evaluation is based on the number of currently active aircraft, distances they are from their goals, delays, deviations from flight paths, etc. *)

end

(3) Try-Command

Input: A copy of the world model and the level number.
Output: The evaluation of the world model.
procedure TRY-COMMAND (copy-of-world-model, level number)
begin
if command has not been tried in current world model before
then
    begin
        Backdate or update world model as needed for executing the command.
        Update to next incident.
        Increase level number.
        if level = terminal level
        then evaluate the world and return the numerical result
        else RESOLVE this new incident at the current level.
    end

(* Search tree levels are explained in text below *)

end
end

Let us now summarize the behavior of the **PLAN-AHEAD**. It accepts a ''snapshot'' of the real world, i.e., an image of its relevant features. It updates this world model, extrapolating over time, step by step far enough (at present *up to* 20 minutes). It checks with each update for incidents and issues commands, if any, as specified in the current plan. All incidents must be resolved. If there is no incident foreseen, the world model is compared continually with the real one and, if necessary, corrected. A new cycle of simulation starts again. Two possible concerns arise. First, some incidents may be responded to by several directives. Therefore, to find the best, **RESOLVE** calls **TRY-COMMAND** which returns the result of the directives' evaluation. This may involve the second concern; namely a given command may cause new incidents to occur at a later time for which **RESOLVE** is called again. The question is, How far into the future should this process go? We do not employ a fixed length of time in this method but, instead, use the concept of *node levels* on the search tree. A *node* represents the most severe incident expected at a specific time point. **TRY-COMMAND** is designed to perform its task over a variable number of levels up to the terminal level (set at two at present). Looking ahead one level consists of the following steps:

(i) Issue an already planned or newly generated command to resolve the current incident.

(ii) Update the world image to the next incident (even if it occurs beyond ST).

An exemplary sequence of events is shown in Fig. 4. The numbers in the left-hand column are minutes elapsed after current real time. Incidents are indicated by '' × .'' The evaluation results are in parentheses at the terminal nodes. The initial plan involving no command (vertical line starting at 0 minutes) leads to a conflict. **TRY-COMMAND** backs up time and issues two alternative commands, responses 1 and 2, one after the other. The longest

incident-free course of action (and best evaluation result) is marked with asterisks (*) as the solution path.

There are several issues that need to be discussed. First, all aircraft whose behavior may affect the resolution of a given incident are found in the *adjacent incident space*. These aircraft are the ones considered by the Plan-Generation Unit and which participate in the simulation by the **TRY-COMMAND** procedure.

The Plan Generation Unit has the task of doing the simulation-based planning. The Plan Execution Unit controls the aircraft in the real world according to the plan. The former activity, of course, must produce satisfactory sequences of commands much faster than the time needed for the execution of the (preceding) plan, under all conditions. If planning, in general, takes much less time than plan execution, we would not have to limit the depth of the search tree to two levels; longer and, in principle, better plans could be generated. However, we must bear in mind that, even at the start of the simulation, the knowledge of the world by the Planning Unit may be incomplete and, to a degree, uncertain. This problem becomes gradually more serious as time passes for reasons already discussed.

We have stated before that resolving one incident may resolve others as well and may also cause other, later incidents. In order to find the most productive incident resolution, we have defined the *incident criticality factor* associated with an incident as the sum of the priority factors of all the aircraft involved in the incident. Incidents are then ordered (dynamically) according to their incident criticality factors. The most critical one has the highest incident criticality factor value and that has to be resolved first.

8. ISSUES IN DISTRIBUTED AIR TRAFFIC CONTROL

In a sequence of ''conceptual refinement,'' we have first solved the problem of a single aircraft resolving violations and two-aircraft conflicts. In the latter case, the tasks of planning and constructing the search tree are evenly distributed between the two aircraft. The better of the two locally optimum commands is then selected and broadcast to all aircraft in the adjacent incident space. This is called the *effective command*—it is derived from the appropriate resolution directive by computing for it a set of parametric values and is assigned to a specific aircraft.

We have then considered distributing the planning task in multiaircraft incidents to several units in the adjacent incident space, rather than letting them only wait and check their message boxes at regular times. We have first established the concept of a *Centralized Scratch Pad*, which is attached to an aircraft designated on the basis of its highest priority factor in an incident. The available branches of the search tree to be developed are *posted* on it by the Plan Generating Unit of this and other participating aircraft. During the

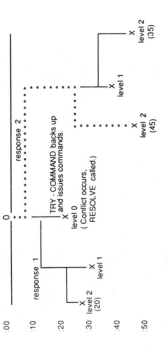

FIG. 4. An exemplary search tree used by the procedure **TRY-COMMAND**. * * * , solution path; (× × ×), numerical result of world model evaluation, × × × .

course of planning, each participating aircraft will put the world model evaluations at different levels into the corresponding slot of the scratch pad. Eventually, the halting condition will be satisfied (all simulations are completed) and the best solution path is selected by the aircraft in charge of the Scratch Pad. This plan is then broadcast to all aircraft involved.

The Centralized Scratch Pad, used for interprocess communication and as a synchronization mechanism, has two major drawbacks. Messages may not be timely in leaving or arriving because of the limited communication channel capacities. Also, one single processor storing all the control information is not a good idea from the systems point of view. We shall present an alternative approach that remedies these problems.

The search trees in the DATC context, like the one shown in Fig. 4, are similar to a state-space tree. A *state* is now represented by the current world, in which one or more incidents occur, and the result of its evaluation. The *operators* are the effective commands to resolve incidents. The initial state is associated with the node representing the level 0 incident, and the goal state is associated with the terminal node that has the best evaluation result. Whereas game trees describe moves of two opposing players and state-space trees contain the steps of a single problem solver, DATC search trees are characterized by the actions of several cooperating problem solvers. These can be in charge of the independent simulation of different branches of the search tree and, thus, all participate in the planning process. This idea gives rise to the notion of a hierarchy of distributed scratch pads at different levels.

9. DISTRIBUTED SCRATCH PADS

Let us consider the following sequence of events. All aircraft look ahead up to the next incident they would get involved in. The aircraft with the largest priority factor among those in the first incident provides the *top-level* scratch pad. The processor on this aircraft posts the possible solution directives on it and broadcasts the need for simulation to all aircraft in the adjacent incident space. Available processors develop the different branches of the search tree, by computing the respective effective commands, up to the next level of incidents. These aircraft in turn provide level 1 scratch pads with the necessary information and broadcast the need for further simulations. Once computed, the images of the extrapolated world are evaluated and the best ones level by level are filtered back to the top-level scratch pad.

Finally, the top-level processor makes its selection for the commands to be used on the solution path and broadcasts its decision.

The algorithms below represent these ideas and are used in the LCC mode of group planning.

---

(1) **Distributed-planner**

Input: A snapshot of the real world, aircraft executing the algorithm (aircraft A), and a value specifying the time period for simulation.

Output: A plan of commands.

procedure **DISTRIBUTED-PLANNER** (snapshot-of-the-real-world, aircraft A, ST)

(* See definitions of all terms in Section 5 *)

begin
repeat
  Detect incidents among surrounding aircraft and put them on an incident list.
  Select the incident with the highest incident criticality factor.
  Find the aircraft in the adjacent-incident-space of this incident.
  if aircraft A is the one with the highest priority factor
  then
    begin
      Collect all information about the aircraft in the adjacent-incident-space to form the world model
      (* Information includes navigation information, flight plan, etc. *)
      Resolve this level-zero incident.
    end
  else
    begin
      PROCESS-RESOLUTION-DIRECTIVES if possible.
      repeat
        Check message box.
      until the resolution command is obtained
    end
  Post-process the plan.
  Select time of earliest command.
  if this command time < current simulation time then
    Backdate it
  Issue commands in plan.
  Update world model in event-driven time steps.
until ST time units have elapsed.
end (* DISTRIBUTED-PLANNER *)

(2) **Resolve**

Input: A copy of the world model and the level number.

Output: If called by **DISTRIBUTED-PLANNER** then return a single command.
    If called by **TRY-COMMAND** then return the best command's value.

function **RESOLVE** (copy-of-world-model, level number)
begin
    Create a scratch pad at the given level.
    Broadcast the existence of the scratch pad at the given level to the aircraft in the adjacent-incident-space.
    PROCESS-RESOLUTION-DIRECTIVES if possible
    Wait until all simulations are complete.
    if called by **DISTRIBUTED-PLANNER**
    then return the best command
    else return the best command's value.
end (* RESOLVE *)

(3) **Process-Resolution-Directives**

Input: aircraft in adjacent-incident-space.
Output: none.

begin
while there exist in any scratch pad resolution directives to be simulated
begin
    Take the first resolution directive, compute the directive parameters.
    TRY-COMMAND on a copy of the world model.

(* **TRY-COMMAND** invoked here is identical to the one described in Section 7 *)

Update the corresponding scratch pad information.
end (* **PROCESS-RESOLUTION-DIRECTIVES** *)

We do not discuss here a few simple algorithms, such as the one that

- updates the adjacent incident space for the simulation,
- updates the "intention" (timed route to destination or to the boundary of own radar range) of the aircraft considered,
- updates conflict lists, etc.

Further, a detailed specification of the information of the scratch pad and its processing, and of the simulation and selection of commands, is beyond the scope of this paper. These also comprise error detection and recovery facilities through a measured degree of redundancy in the information stored and in its processing.

10. CURRENT ACTIVITY

We are in the process of studying the above idea empirically, using a flexible programming system for the testbed. We shall shortly consider also other possible architectures for Distributed Planning Systems.

ACKNOWLEDGMENTS

Part of this work was supported by the U.S. Department of Transportation under Contract DTRS-5863-C-00001. We are indebted to the other members of our Group for Computer Studies of Strategies, particularly Neal Mazur. The word processing of this text was done by Qing Ge.

REFERENCES

1. Corkill, D. D. A framework for organizational self-design in distributed problem solving networks. Ph.D. Dissertation, Department of Computer and Information Science, University of Massachusetts, Amherst, 1982.
2. Lesser, U. R., and Corkill, D. D. A distributed vehicle monitoring testbed: A tool for investigating distributed problem solving networks. AI Magazine 4 (1983), 15–33.
3. Simon, H. A. Models of Man. Wiley, New York, 1957.
4. Sacerdoti, E. D. A Structure for Planning and Behavior. Elsevier/North-Holland, Amsterdam, 1977.
5. Schank, R. C., and Abelson, R. P. Scripts, Plans, Goals, and Understanding. Erlbaum, Hillside, N.J., 1977.
6. McDermott, D. Planning and acting. Cognitive Sci. 2 (1978), 79–109.
7. Konolige, K., and Nilsson, N. J. Multiple-agent planning systems. Proc. First AAAI Nat. Conf., 1980, pp. 138–142.
8. Stefik, M. Planning with constraints (MOLGEN: Parts 1, 2). Artificial Intelligence 16 (1981), 111–139, 141–169.
9. Wesson, R. Problem-solving with simulation in the world of an air traffic controller. Ph.D. dissertation, Department of Computer Science, University of Texas, Austin, 1977.
10. Steeb, R. S. Cammarata, Hayes-Roth, F. A., Thorndyke, P. W., and Wesson, R. B. Distributed intelligence for fleet control. RAND Corp. Rep. R-2728-ARPA, 1981.
11. Swetram, G. F., Jr. A preliminary characterization of the AERA man–machine interface for ATC computer replacement. MITRE Working Paper, WP-81W00135, 1981.
12. Chien, R. T. Artificial intelligence and human error prevention study in ATC systems. Final Report to the Department of Transportation and the Federal Aviation Administration, 1982.
13. Findler, N. V., Sicherman, G., and Feuerstein, S. Teaching strategies to an Advice Taker/Inquirer system. Proc. EuroIFIP79 Conf., London, 1979, pp. 457–467.
14. Findler, N. V., Brown, J. E., Lo, R., and You, H. Y. A module to estimate numerical values of hidden variables for expert systems. Internat. J. Man-Machine Systems 18 (1983), 323–335.
15. Findler, N. V., and Lo, R. A note on the functional estimation of values of hidden variables—An extended module for expert systems. Internat. J. Man-Machine Systems 18 (1983) 555–565.

16. Findler, N. V. An overview of the Quasi-Optimizer system. *Large-Scale Systems* **5** (1983), 123–130.

17. Findler, N. V. Some artificial intelligence contributions to air traffic control. *Proc. Jerusalem Conf. on Information Technology*, Jerusalem, 1984, pp. 470–475.

18. Findler, N. V., Bickmore, T. W., and Cromp, R. F. A general-purpose man–machine environment with special reference to air traffic control. *Internat. J. Man-Machine Studies*, **23** (1985) 587–603.

19. Lesser, V. R., Reed, S., and Pavlin, J. Quantifying and simulating the behavior of knowledge-based interpretation systems. *Proc. First AAAI Nat. Conf.*, 1980, pp. 111–115.

20. Smith, R. G. A framework for distributed problem solving. *Proc. IJCAI-79*, 1979, pp. 836–841.

21. Stankovic, J. A. A perspective on distributed computer systems. *IEEE Trans. Comput.* C-33 12 (Dec. 1984).

Index

A

ABCL/1, 34, 434
ABE, 33, 451, 457
Abelson, R. P., 249, 386
abstract information, use of, 299
abstract model for problem solving, 107
abstract model generation, 242
abstracted
    blackboard, 275
    information, 97
    objects, in DVMT diagnosis, 492
abstraction, 24, 239
    of common frameworks, 31
    techniques for blackboards, 544
abstraction level, 12, 74, 80, 97
abstraction level, data, 64
ABSTRIPS, 611
acceptance, in dialogue games, 388
achieve intention, 251
achievement of common knowledge, 31
Ackerman, W. B., 398
acknowledged communication, information distribution policy, 103
acquaintance, 8, 401
    databases, 29
    list in ACT3, 401
ACT, 34
    behavior definitions in, 401
    kernel language, 401
ACT1, 34
ACT3, 34, 398
    acquaintance list in, 401
    calculus of configurations, 405
    development of, 398
    factorial example, 402
    functional constructs, 402
    language, 401
    modeling local state changes, 403
    resource management techniques, 404
    transactional constructs, 404
action
    composition of, 207
    conflict, 202
    dependence, 223

description, levels of characterization, 265
enabling conditions, 248
in the world, 9
incompatible, 11
independence, 212
knowledge, 27
representation of, 215
seeking, dialogue game, 387
simultaneous, 207
theory of, 205, 211
activity
    map, 287, 289
    map of PGP, 288
    representation, 599, 602
actor, 7, 33, 152, 164, 398, 434, 437
    BEING, 163
    construct, formalization, 399
    definition, 399
    language, 34, 406
    message passing in, 402
    model, 398–399, 434
    model, basic constructs, 399
    model, basic issues, 399
    model, communication in, 399
    model, development of, 398
    model, mail system, 399
    model, set of minimal constructs, 399
adaptability, 8
    organizational, 157
adaptation, 25, 521
    in organizations, 148
    of environmental changes, 73
adaptive decentralized control, 305
adherence to positions, theories, methods in scientific communities, 317
adjustment, 317
    of theories, 314
ADL agent description language, 448
advantages of distributed processing, 295
AF, 451
agenda, 593
agenda-based problem solving, 491
agent, 3, 446, 600
    agent-centered perspective, 590

agent-oriented perspective, 592
    benevolence, 220
    capabilities, knowledge of, 26
    describing, 448
    formal description of, 216
    knowledge, 446
    modeling, rationales for, 26
    organization manager, 446
    rational, 227
    resources and demands, knowledge of, 26
    self knowledge, 446
    sponsor, 16
aggregate (Cluster) planning, 91
aggregated information, 97
aggregation versus knowledge tradeoff, 68
Agha, Gul, 7, 11, 29, 33–34, 398–399
AGORA, 33, 451
    virtual machine, 453
air-traffic control, 18, 90, 102–103, 606, 617
    distributed, 619
    task environment, 618
algorithm uncertainty, 144
Allen, James F., 185, 194, 200, 205–206
allocation of resources, 15, 315
allocation of tasks, 10
alternative
    architectures, comparison of, 525
    coordination structures, 152
    hypotheses, 126
    organizations, comparison of, 72
    partial solutions, 299
    plans, 372
    representations, development, 32
ambassadors (in COPS), 547
AMORD system, 582
analysis of system topologies, 246
analytic communication dimensions, 323
anarchic committee (AC), 74
ANGEL speech recognition system, 453
announced award, in Contract Net, 360
announcing, dialogue game, 392
anonymous communication, 542
anonymous invocation of KSs, 354
answer synthesis, 63, 606
APIARY, 319
    architecture, 401
Appelt, Douglas, 233
application domains, communications system, 369
application structure of an organization, 578
applications, suitable for Contract Net, 351
approach, distributed operating systems, 409
appropriate differences, 30
appropriateness of task assignment, 353
approximate knowledge, 295
arbitrator, 101
architectural transitions, 99–100
architectures
    blackboard-based, 286
    comparison of alternative, 525

distributed air-traffic control, 619
    distributed planning, 91
    distributed problem solving, 90
area contractor, 346
arm's length relationships, 322
ARPANET, 357
articulation work, 14, 19
assessment, task performance, 324
assumption surfacing, 31
assumptions, 459
asynchronous
    cooperative planning, 93
    data-directed control, 124
    information gathering, 299
    input, 322
    interactions, 297
    iterative methods, 302
    problem solving, 122, 298
    requests on blackboard, 561
asynchrony, 321, 435
atomicity of transaction, 557, 561
Austin, J. L., 169, 173, 199, 386, 395
authority, 9, 72, 78, 292
    and knowledgeable mediation, 31
    and responsibility structure, 595
    protocols, 77
    relationships, 593
automatic error detection, 137
automatic programming, 161
autonomous systems, 490
autonomy, 9
availability of coordination, 12
award in Contract Net, 341, 360

B

backward causal tracing (BCT), 495
Baker, Henry, 399, 434, 437
Barber, Gerald, 578
bargainers, similar, 224
basic control loop, in blackboard architecture, 521
basic problems of distributed AI, 10
basic rationality, 220, 222
basis of commonality, 16
battle of the sexes, 232
BB1, 33–34, 509, 521, 541
BBOX, 462
behavior, coherent, 353
behavior definitions, 401
    in ACT3 programs, 401
behavior, distributed system, fault tolerant, 418
behavioral uncertainty, 144, 148
BEING, 20, 161
    internal details of, 164
    systems, pure, theory of, 165
belief, 171, 264
    about other nodes, 595
    communication, 323

contradictory, 322
embedding, 171
knowledge, 27
of other agents, 187
relativized, 317
space, 30, 249
space, mutiple, 31
space, mutual, 30
system, representing and predicting, 72
benevolence of agents, 220
benevolent agent assumption, 233
bias
external, 271
local, 271
of node, 271
bid, 7, 153, 268, 282, 340–341, 358, 360
requests, 155
specification, 342
specification, in Contract Net, 66, 359
bidding, in dialogue games, 388
Bisiani, Roberto, 33, 451
blackboard, 33, 80, 110, 299, 462, 509, 608
abstracted, 275
architecture, 505, 541, 557
architecture, transactional, 561
asynchronous requests on, 561
-based architecture, 286
control architecture, 510
control architecture features, 521
control architecture, strengths and weaknesses, 528
customized, 541
data abstraction, 541
database abstraction, 544
efficiency, 541–542
events, 510, 546
flexibility, 541
generic, 541
global, 591
handler, 110
kernel, 543
kernel, customized, 543
-like shared data facility, 118
monitoring mechanism, 110
object, 544
operations, 542
scheduler, 110
specification, 544
system, distributed, 445
system, multilevel, 491
systems, 5, 34
transactional, 557
blocks world, 66, 217
Bonnell, Ronald D., 566
bottleneck avoidance, 14
bounded rationality, 141, 143, 145, 303
Braganza, Carl, 445
Briot, Jean-Pierre, 434, 438
broadcast communication, information distribution policy, 103
broadcast organization, 291

Brock, J. D., 398
broker, 154
Brooks, Richard, 309
Bruce, Bertram, 22, 30, 184–185, 248–249
Burge, John W., 71

C

CA/C, 297
CADRE, 559
calculus of configurations, in ACT3, 405
Cammarata, Stephanie, 102, 285
capability, 19
in AGORA, 453
modeling of other agents', 188
CASNET, 492, 501
causality
causal-model-based diagnosis, 490
CAUSE-TO-WANT, 188
formal models of, 213
interconnectivity of knowledge, 323
model, 490
necessity, 215
pathway, 495
causality group, 210, 213
caveats for cooperation, 63
ccordination
availability, 12
centralized
global knowledge, 121
market, 151, 153
metalevel organization, 291
organization, 20
scratch pad, 617, 624
tasks, selection policy, least spatially constrained, 104
tasks, selection policy, most knowledgeable, least committed agent, 104
tasks, selection policy, shared convention, 104
versus network organization, 132
certainty, degrees of, 67
Chandrasekaran, B., 10, 20, 23
Chapanis, A., 388
Chapman, David, 192
Charniak, Eugene, 386
choice of architectures, 99
Chomsky, Noam, 170
Choose-KSAR, 518, 520
CHOOSER, (a BEING), 164
CHRYSALIS, 121
classification of dialogue games, 387
CLF, 480
Clinger, William, 7
closely coupled multiprocessor environment, 118
CNET, 358
coarse grain parallelism, 547
Coffman, E. G., 109
cognition-oriented perspective, 590, 592
cognitive agency research, 592

Cohen, D., 148
Cohen, Philip, 18, 169, 171, 185, 188, 415
coherence, 8, 19
    global, 102
    global and limited knowledge, 335
    network, 268, 283
coherent
    behavior, 353
    cooperation, 269–270, 281
    cooperation, increased through organization, 272
Collins, A. M., 393
collision avoidance in air-traffic control, 102
combinatorial explosion, avoiding, 491
combinatorial problems, of diagnosis, 499
commitment
    and communication, 323
    degrees of, 292
    mutual, 321
    plan, 377
common internode language, 342, 609
common internode language, Contract Net, 359
common knowledge, 31
commonsense algorithms, 386
commonsense knowledge, 314
communication
    act, 194
    act, meaning of, 324
    among nodes, 127, 606
    analytic dimensions of, 323
    and control topology, 460
    anonymous, 542
    by messages, 547
    conservation heuristics, 88
    constraints, 99–100
    Contract Net protocol, 357
    cost, 93, 133, 408
    device to augment local models, 238
    DVMT, empirical results in, 278
    errors in, 130, 134
    explicit internode communication, 126
    generating paths for, 130
    in actor model, 399
    interagent, 558
    metacommunication structure, 385
    need for, 83
    network structure, 73
    overhead in hierarchical architectures, 97
    paths, 103
    policy, 79, 277, 607
    policy, dynamic thresholding, 131
    policy, first and last, 277
    policy, full transmission, 131
    policy, incremental transmission, 128
    policy, locally complete, 129, 132, 277
    policy, murmuring, 129
    policy, send external time-varying information, 83
    policy, send internal time-varying information, 83
    policy, send-all, 277
    primitives, 187–188

    procedures, 93
    protocol, based on phrase-structure grammar, 609
    protocols, 29, 77
    routine, 83
    scheduling heuristics, 88
    slower than computation, 338
    system, application domain, 369
communicative interconnectivity of knowledge, 323
community of interacting agents, 449
comparative reasoning, 490–491, 496
comparison
    alternative architectures, 525
    alternative organizations, 72
    Contract Net with conventional mechanisms, 349
competence theory, 170
competing hypotheses, 126
competing results, 62
competitive problem solving, 122
completely accurate, cooperative (CA/C) systems, 297
completely accurate, nearly autonomous (CA/NA) systems, 296
complex acts, 192
complexity, 141, 144, 149
    coordination, 146
    informational, 145
    interaction, 227
    organization, 151
    reduction techniques, 145
    shift, in organizations, 147
    system composing, 477
    task, 145
composing complex systems, 477
composite modules, 462
composition, 459
composition by embedding and meshing, 462
composition of actions, 207
compositional adequacy, 169, 180
compositional adequacy of speech acts, 178
comprehension, meta-goal of, 395
compromise, 227, 334
computation cost, 9
computation in ETHER, 312
concept formation, 161–162
conceptual distance, 8
concurrency, 321
    approaches to, 398
    paradigms shifts in, 398
    programming language, 398
    systems, calculus of, 398
confidence inconsistent, 29
configuration
    common, in interacting plans, 251
    dynamic, 354
    experiments with large, 280
    experiments with overlapping, 281
    initiation of social episode, 252
    overlapping, 280
    request, 251
    resolution of conflict, 252
    satisfaction of intentions, 251

conflict
    among goals, 233, 595
    avoidance, 216
    interagent disparities, 29
    of action, 202
conflicting
    information, 322
    microtheories, 324
    theories, 311
CONGEN, 63
conjecture and refutation, 314
conjunctive subgoals, 315
connection of processors, 617
connection problem, 64, 339, 357
connectionism, 5
connectivity, 19
Conry, Susan, 367
consensus, 298, 324, 369
consequent reasoning, 314
consistency, 561
    global, 368
    guaranteed, database, 334
    inter-transactional, 561
    of database, 408
    preservation of transaction, 557
consistent hypothesis, maximally supported, 416
constraint
    among beliefs, 327
    -based programming language, 582
    expressions, 492
    overconstrained situation, 369
    propagation, 67
    resolution, 32
context, 326
context acts, 17
context, local, 108–109
contingency theory, 144, 147
contingency theory design strategies, 144
continuations, 400
continuous operation, attribute of open systems, 322
contract, 7
    directed, 342
    negotiation, 358
    node architecture, in Contract Net, 364
    processing states, in Contract Net, 365
    specification, in Contract Net, 365
Contract Net, 7, 18, 26, 35, 64, 78, 127, 299, 307, 333, 339, 445, 607
    announced award, 360
    bidding, 360
    comparison with conventional mechanisms, 349
    contract node architecture, 364
    contract processing states, 365
    contract specificatione, 365
    directed award, 362
    directed contracts, 362
    example of, 346
    extensions, 351
    implementation of, 345
    information transfer, 348

    limitations, 351
    local evaluation, 348
    mutual selection, 348
    node abstraction, 360
    node-available messages, 362
    open problems, 351
    protocol, 7, 18, 340, 342, 357
    protocol, specification, 364
    request and information message, 362
    suitable applications for, 351
    task processing procedures, 365
    task specification, 360
    time-constrained decisions, 360
contract-bid, 220
contracting, 600
    in organizations, 146
contractor, 339
    area, 346
    group, 346
    in Contract Net, 358
    signal, 346
contradiction
    beliefs, 322
    handling facility, in OMEGA, 578
    handling in OMEGA, 583
    handling, with viewpoints, 582
    knowledge, 325
    reasoning about, 587
control
    asynchronous data-directed, 124
    behavior, of HASP, 538
    behavior, of HEARSAY-II, 536
    blackboard, 513
    decentralized, 322, 339
    decisions, attributes of, 514
    decisions, explicit, 507
    dependencies, 12
    errors, diagnosing, 490
    errors in, 120
    errors, in problem solving, 490, 500
    heuristics, 507–508, 522
    heuristics, dynamic, 525
    heuristics, multiple, 523
    hierarchies, 72
    knowledge, 517
    knowledge, representation, 28
    knowledge sources, 518
    loop, basic, in blackboard architecture, 521
    planning, 518
    plans, 509
    problem, 505
    problem solving, 513
    procedural, 462
    PUP6, 164
    semantics, 506
    strategy, sufficiency of, 122
    structures, data-directed, 299
    structures, generators, 299
    structures, modular, 299

topology and communication, 460
    uncertainty, 270, 297
convergence, 69
conversational postulates, 185, 386
CONVINCE, 188
convince speech act, 184
cooperating
    expert systems, 412
    expert systems metaphor, 337
    experts, 62, 74, 80
    intelligent agents, 187
cooperation, 19, 62, 216, 287, 324, 357
    activity, 599
    by mutual aggregation of results, 68
    by mutual restriction, 68
    caveats for, 63
    coherent, 269–270, 281
    coherent, increased through organization, 272
    cost of increasing coherent, 280
    experiments in coherent, 279
    frameworks, 61
    heuristics for, 72
    paradigm, 382
    synergistic, 163
    without communication, 220
cooperative
    action, 233
    application systems, 457
    behavior among willing entities, 62, 334
    interaction, 200
    interactive episodes, 248
    knowledge objects, 425
    office workstations, 590
    operating system, 458
    paradigm, 368
    planning, 90
    problem solving, 71, 99, 120, 122, 295
    strategy, 102, 105
coordination, 19, 257, 286, 601
    complexity, 146
    control, 236
    costs, 151
    modeling, 151
    of partial solutions, 299
    partial global plan framework, 292
    personal-machine, 4
    problem solving, 590
    processes, 151
    strategies, organizational requirements of, 236
    structure, 152
    structures, alternative, 152
    structures, alternative, definitions of, 154
    structures, comparisons of, 154
    structures, generic, 151
    task, 141
    through partial global plans, 287
    with abstraction, 242, 245
    with abstraction, short term, 243
    with prediction only, 241, 245

without communication, 240, 245
COP, 412, 415
COPS, 547
Corkill, Daniel D., 6, 19, 25, 34, 220, 233, 268, 285–286, 295, 525, 541, 592, 606
correctness, in distributed computation, 296
cost, 8
    communication, 408
    increasing coherent cooperation, 280
counterarguments, 325
coverage, 19
coverage problem, 130
credibility, 9
    hypothesis, 286
    information, 123
    sufficiency of, 122
critic, plan, 604
critical data set, 110
Croft, W. Bruce, 591, 599
Cromarty, Andrew S., 408, 413
CSP, 218, 398, 444
CSP primitives, 203
CSRL, 481
custom architecture, 455
custom hardware for AGORA virtual machine, 454
customized blackboard, 541
customized blackboard kernel, 543

D

natural language and DAI, 300
data
    abstraction on blackboard, 541
    access characteristics in HEARSAY-II, 117
    bottlenecks, 412
    dependencies, 12
    distribution, need for, 101
    inaccuracies, 93
    integrity, 109
    partitioning, 12
    pooling for uncertainty reduction, 99
    set, critical, 110
    uncertainties, resolving, 297
database abstraction on blackboard, 544
database consistency, 408
data-directed control structures, 299
dataflow, 462
Davis, Randall, 7, 32, 61, 78, 136, 220, 285, 307, 333, 501, 592, 607
DCS distributed computing system, 340, 358
deadlock, 561
deal-making mechanism, 227
deals, 227
debate, 321
decentralized
    control, 300, 322, 339, 367
    control, adaptive, 305
    market, 153
deception, 248

decision
    basis, 11
    making, 321
    procedure for agent, 222
declaration, as communication, 324
decomposed distributed system, 125, 297
decomposition, 10–11, 63, 77, 121, 606–607
    configuration for particular, 455
    dimensions of, 123–124
    hierarchical, 63
    problem, 63
decoupling node activity, 297
deductive distance, 10
degree of clustering, 99
DeKleer, Johan, 31
delayed expressions, in ACT3, 403
delegation, 441
dependency of actions, 223
des Rivieres, James, 525
descheduling, 116
description, 10–11
    agents, 448
    versus action, 326
design metaphor, 408
design of distributed systems, 145
design strategies in contingency theory, 144
design, VLSI, 559
Deutsch, B. G., 388
development, 9
    alternative representations, 32
diagnosis, 490, 526, 575
    module (DM), 490
    problem solving system behavior, 490
diagnosticity, of information, 123
dialogue, 127
    function of, 387
    interaction, 18
    sources, 388
dialogue game, 18, 32, 385–386, 388
    acceptance, 388
    action seeking, 387
    announcing, 392
    bidding, 388
    classification, 387
    example, 389
    griping, 387
    helping, 387, 389
    information probing, 387
    information seeking, 387
    instructing, 387
    model, 385
    nomination, 393
    overview, 387
    processing, 390
    processing, overview, 390
different perspectives, 61
dimensions of decomposition, 124
dimensions of distribution, 123
direct effects formula, 212

directed award, in Contract Net, 362
directed contracts, in Contract Net, 362
disparity
    goals, 227
    recognising, 30
    reconciling, 31
    representing, 30
distraction, 62, 134, 274
    negative, 274
    positive, 274
distributed
    agent, model of interaction, 412
    air-traffic control, 90, 606, 619
    air-traffic control, architectures for, 619
    architecture, characteristics, 414
    artificial intelligence, 84, 120, 187, 606
    authority, 78
    computation, correctness in, 296
    control, 357
    coordination, 236
    decisionmaking, 236
    decomposition, 121, 124
    Distributed Knowledge Object Modeling (DKOM), 425–426
    distributed-knowledge designs, 410
    focus of attention, 302
    focus of control, 137
    HEARSAY-II, 68, 123
    HEARSAY-II architecture, 121
    hypothesis database management, 415
    interpretation, 120, 295, 490
    network traffic light control, 295, 300–301
    object-oriented languages, 33–34
    office environments, 566, 590
    office system architecture, 592
    operating systems approach, 409
    organization, 547
    planning, 22, 90, 295, 302, 367, 611, 617
    planning architectures, 91
    planning problem, 370, 382
    problem solver, 102, 285
    problem solving, 3, 61, 103, 121, 187, 296, 333, 354, 357, 434, 492, 547, 592, 606
    problem solving architectures, 90
    problem solving network, 268
    problem solving, phases, 63
    processing, 120
    processing, advantages of, 295
    scratch pad, 617, 625
    search, 306
    sensing, 61, 65, 343–344, 357
    sensor network, 71, 83, 606
    simulation, 33
    situation assessment, 71
    situation assessment, heuristics, 85
    speech recognition, 451
    system design, theory of, 149
    workstations, 566
distributed artificial intelligence, 33
distribution, 10

control as dimension of distribution, 124
distribution-caused uncertainty, 120, 295, 297
information as dimension of distribution, 123
methods, 90
processing as dimension of distribution, 124
division of labor, 145
document retrieval, 566
domain plans, 509
dominance analysis, 222
dominated case elimination, 224
domination relationship for actions, 222
domule, 236
DOO languages, 34
Doyle, Jon, 31
due process, 8, 35, 321, 323
Durfee, Edmund H., 6, 23, 25, 29, 268, 285, 592
DVMT, 6, 30, 34, 270, 285–286, 367, 490, 492, 542
behavior, reasoning about, 494
modified node architecture, 276
dynamic
allocation, 302
communications addressing, 99
configuration, 354
control heuristics, 525
distribution of information, 363
hierarchical cone (DHC), 74
information, 125
planning, 508, 526, 606–607, 611
problem solving, 521
problem solving situations, 508, 523
reconfigurability, 398–399
reconfiguration, 606
reconfiguring, 400

E

economic theory, 233
economics, 84
EDL, 593
efficiency, 9
blackboard, 541
problem solving, 118
EFIGE, 29
eligibility specification, 342, 359
in Contract Net, 66
ELINOR semantic network representation, 389
embedding, by compositon, 462
embedding of plans, 265
empirical evaluation
in communication in DVMT, 278
of air-traffic control, 104
of HEARSAY-II multiprocssing, 112
of organizational structuring, 275
of partial global plans, 291
of planner in DVMT, 277
EMYCIN, 430
enabling sub-acts in interacting plans, 253
encapsulation, 145

endorsement construct, 415
engineering-science perspective, 4
Ensor, J. Robert, 557
environment, 216
evolutionary, 579
environmental
constraints, 99
dynamics, 99
influences, 99
uncertainty, 99, 144
equivalence of systems, 398
Erman, Lee, 67, 99, 120, 286, 309, 526, 541
Ernst, George, 192
error detection, automatic, 137
error-resolution mechanisms, 299
errors in control, 120
ETHER, 24, 34, 311, 319
events, 210
blackboard, 546
incompatible, 211
reasoning about, 205
representation, 210
simultaneous, 210
specification of, 211
evidential reasoning and argumentation, 32
evolutionary development of applications, 457
evolutionary environment, 579
example of
blackboard use, 559
Contract Net, 346
dialogue game, 389
network model, 287
exceptions, 599
excess resources, 78
exchanging metalevel information, 6
execution interference analysis, 116
expectation, 78
experiment, 130
in coherent cooperation, 279
with humans, 75
with large configurations, 280
with organizational structure, 273
with overlapping configurations, 281
experimental
design, 468
method, 122
testbeds, 33–34
experimenter effects, 388
exploratory development, 476
express message passing, 436, 443
expression, as communication, 324
external actors, 400
externally-directed nodes, 306

F

FA/C, 295
system, 268, 285–286

approach and search, 298
model, and organization design, 304
falsificationism, 315
FA/NA, 297
Fanshel, D., 386
fault detection, 526
fault tolerance, 408
fault tolerant distributed system behavior, 418
faulty communication channel, 301
feasibility trees, 376
Feigenbaum, Edward, 425
Fennell, Richard D., 106
Fickas, Steven, 526
Fikes, Richard, 173, 192, 287, 578
final report, in Contract Net, 341, 361
Findler, Nicholas V., 617
first and last communication policy, 277
first-mover opportunity, 147
fit to specification, 14
fixed interaction languages, 17
flat network structure, 127
flexibility
    achieving, 541
    organization structure, 157
focus of attention, 9
    strategies, 299
focus-control, 610
focused addressing, 19, 128, 342, 359
formal theory, 200, 205, 210, 220
    definition of process model, 206
    models of causality, 213
forward causal tracing (FCT), 496
Fox, Mark, 20, 25, 136, 140, 304–305
frame, 386
frame problem, 173, 214
frame rule, 211
frame-based representation, 602
framework, 452, 454, 458
FRL language, 581
function of dialogue, 387
functional aspects of language, 395
functional decomposition, 100
functional decomposition, in organizations, 146
functional hierarchy, 151, 153
functionally-accurate
    cognitive model, 137
    cooperative (FA/C) systems, 6, 285, 295, 297, 592, 606
    cooperative paradigm, 368
    nearly autonomous (FA/NA) systems, 297
functional/product division, 12
function-centered architectures, 90, 96

G

Gabbe, John D., 557
Galbraith, Jay, 144, 151, 157, 303
Gallagher, Kevin Q., 541
game of chicken, 232

game theory, 228, 233, 302
Gasser, Les, 11, 27, 29, 33, 445
GBB, 33–34, 541, 544
generating hypotheses by metaphor, 314
generator control structures, 299
generic blackboard development system, 541
Genesereth, Michael, 220, 227, 292, 501
Georgeff, Michael, 200, 205, 210, 216, 220, 233, 285
Gerson, Elihu, 19, 30, 328
Ginsberg, Matthew L., 220
global
    blackboard, 591
    centralized node organization, 81
    coherence, 102, 591, 607
    coherence with local control, 69
    control, 121
    perspective, 78
    planning, 91
    view, need for, 101
goal, 152
    conflict, 233, 595
    conflict, managing, 590
    disagreements, 233
    induction, 17
    intelligent control, 507
    interactions, knowledge about, 374
    knowledge, 27
    multiple, 249
    oriented view of language, 395
    other agents, 187
    priority conventions, 32
GODDESS, 610
going concerns, 321
Gordon, D., 174, 185, 386
GPS, 192
grain size, 507, 522
    and modularity, 338
granularity, 193
    levels of, 445
    of tasks, 11
graph, directed, 106
GRAPPLE, 602
Grice, H. P., 169, 386, 395
Grinberg, M., 415
griping, dialogue game, 387
Grosz, Barbara, 17
group
    activity, 288
    contractors, 346
    decision support, 599
    organization, 149
    planning, 617
    rational offer, 228
    rationality theorem, 230
guaranteed database consistency, 334
guaranteed message delivery, 334
Guyer, M., 233

H

HACKER, 166
Halpern, Joseph, 233
handling change, in office work, 581
handoffs, 94
Hansel and Gretel, 248, 253, 266
hardware environment, 117
hardware, heterogeneous, 478
harmful interaction, 200
HARPY, 121
HASP, 80, 505, 523, 536
    control behavior of, 538
    control program, 526
Hayes, Patrick, 173, 192, 194
Hayes-Roth, Barbara, 34, 308, 505, 541
Hayes-Roth, Frederick, 71, 99, 308, 425
HEARSAY-II, 59, 64, 67, 74, 80, 99, 106, 121, 141, 298–299, 304, 335, 505, 523, 536, 542, 611
    control behavior of, 536
    local contexts in, 109
    measurements on, 118
    multiprocessing mechanisms, 108
    organization, 107
    simplified organization, 108
HEARSAY-III, 526
helping, dialogue game, 387, 389
Henderson, D. A., 579
Heringer, J. T., 396
Herman, Nava, 445
heterarchical strcture, 149
heterogeneous processors, network of, 452
heterogeneous software and hardware, 478
heuristics of cooperation, 72
Hewitt, Carl, 7, 24, 29, 33, 311, 321, 398–399, 434, 437
hierarchical
    architecture, 90, 97
    architecture, communication overhead, 97
    decomposition, 63
    organization, 20, 71, 74, 279
    planning, 13
    planning, partially ordered, 300
    problem solving, 611
    state transition diagrams, 492
    structure, 122, 127, 236
hierarchy, 591
    data, 344
    multidivision, in organizations, 147
    simple, 147
    task, 345
    uniform, 147
high-dimensional (HD) modularity, 465
high-level protocol, 357
Hintikka, J., 171
historical basis, 9
history, of problem solving, 517
Hoare, C. A. R., 203, 398
Huberman, Bernardo A., 34
Hudlicka, Eva, 29, 490, 526

Huhns, Michael, 25, 566, 606
human organization, 140, 151
human organization, analyzing, 151
human-based network experiments, 75
human-computer interaction, 4
hypercube, 33, 445
Hyperlinks, 408
Hyperstar
    architecture, 411
    distributed system topology, 417
    network, 413
    topology, 408
hypothesis, 415, 418
    credibility, 286
    database management, 415
    management capability, 415
    maximally supported consistent, 416
    structure, 416
    test, 122

I

ICE, 29
illocutionary speech acts, 173
impactedness of information, 147
implementation of Contract Net, 345
implementation on multiprocessor, 118
incident
    criticality factor, 620
    in air-traffic control, 620
    space, 620
incompatible, 29
    actions, 11
    events, 211
incomplete, 29
    data, 121
    information, 133, 214
    knowledge, 333
    local views, 124
    meta-information, 133
inconsistent, 599, 604
    data, 121
    information, 322
    local views, 124
    microtheories, 325
increased local capability, 21
increased localization, 21
increasing contextual awareness, 22
incremental
    aggregation, 135, 137, 299
    aggregation of partial solutions, 121
    communication strategy, 129
    hypothesize-and-test, 300
    transmission strategy, 128
independently motivated agents, 221
indeterminacy, 326
indeterminacy, in open systems, 322
indirect speech acts, 386

indirect uses of language, 395
individual planning, 91
industrial control, 72
INFORM, 188
inform, speech act, 176, 184–185
information
    complexity, 145
    distribution policy, 102
    hierarchy, 80
    impact, 68, 123
    impactedness, 147
    level, 157–158
    level, of blackboard, 125
    probing, dialogue game, 387
    seeking, dialogue game, 387
    transfer in Contract Net, 348
information-distribution policy, 103
informed rationality in common rationality, 233
inherent parallelism, 398
inherently decomposable, 13
inheritance between multiple viewpoints, 318
initiation of social episode, 257
initiation of social episode, configuration, 252
instructing, dialogue game, 387
integrating interfaces, 483
integration, 77, 523
integration without conflict, 32
integrative systems, 33, 451
integrity, data, 109
intelligent control, 505
intelligent control, goals for, 507
intentions, 251
interacting
    experts, 161
    plan, simple example - request, 255
    plans, 22, 248
    plans, example of analysis, 253
interaction, 16
    among plans, 265
    analysis, 201
    complexity, 227
    cooperative, 200
    dialogues, 18
    harmful, 200
    human-computer, 4
    levels, 12
    model of distributed agent, 412
    multi-agent, 227
    of agents modeling, 228
    problem, 217
    protocols, 18
    resolution, 203
    set, 202
interagent actions, 194
interagent disparities
    conflict, 29
    uncertainty, 29
interconnectivity of knowledge
    communicative, terminological, causal, spatiotemporal, 323

INTERESET, 312
interest area, 273
interest area, of node, 125
interference analysis, execution, 116
interference, destructive, inadvertent, 220
interference, freedom from, 207
interference-free processes, 208
interim report in Contract Net, 341
internode
    communication, 606
    communication mechanism, 127
    communication, minimizing, 125
    language, common, 342
    parallelism, 299
interpretations, 9
Interpret-KSAR, 518, 520
interval dependent actions, 193
introspection, 193
invocation, pattern-directed, 66
irrationality, basic, 222
Ishikawa, Yukata, 425
isolation, 9
iterative
    approximation, 151
    coroutine interaction, 297
    local planning, 93
    methods, asynchronous, 302
    refinement, 67, 299–300, 606

J

Jefferson, G., 386
Jensen, E. D., 413
Johnson, Philip M., 541
journal editing task, 599

K

KADET, 468
Kahn, Kenneth, 398
Kalish, D., 319
KEE, 458, 480, 602
Kiosk, 460
KNAC, 602
knowledge, 9
    about local resource availability, 374
    about potential goal interactions, 374
    achievement of common knowledge, 31
    actions, 27
    agent capabilities, 26
    agent resources and demands, 26
    beliefs, 27
    communicating, 27
    craft, 480
    dependency, 14
    embedding language, OMEGA, 578
    goals, 27

limited and global coherence, 335
organizational, 6, 28
plans, 27
responsibilities, 27
solution progress, 27
sufficiency of, 122
units, multisentential, 386
knowledge preconditions problem, 192
knowledge source, 61, 80, 107, 122, 271, 298, 357, 453, 510
attributes of, 512
control, 518
high level control, 517
instance (KSI), 496
knowledge source Activation Record (KSAR), 510
modeling, 512
knowledge-based interpretation systems, 120
Konolige, Kurt, 187–188, 233, 285
Kornfeld, Kurt, 24
Kornfeld, William, 7, 30, 311
KRL language, 582
KSAR's, attributes of, 512
Kuhn, Thomas, 317

L

Labov, W., 386
Lakatos, Imre, 311, 314–315, 317
Lakoff, G., 174, 185, 386
language
actor, 34
comprehension, 385
comprehension system, 395
fixed interaction, 17
functional aspects of, 395
goal-oriented view of, 395
indirect uses of, 395
problem solving mechanism, 395
Lansky, A. L., 220
lateral organization, 279
lateral relations, as organization design strategy, 304
law of persistence, 210
Leao, Luiz V., 547
learning, 566, 606–607
by accumulation of metaknowledge, 614
heuristics, 567
multilayered model, 573
least spatially constrained, selection policy for centralized tasks, 104
Leftkowitz, L. S., 599
Lenat, Douglas, 20, 161, 305
Lesser, Victor, 6, 19, 25, 30, 67, 106, 120, 220, 233, 268, 285, 295, 305, 367, 490, 525–526, 542, 590, 592, 606
levels of abstraction, 64, 97, 125, 157, 510, 512
control blackboard, 514–515
information, 80
reasoning at different, 496
Levin, James A., 18, 32, 385, 393, 395
Lieberman, Henry, 437–438
limited horizon coordination, 241

lisp machine, 445
Lo, Ron, 617
load balancing, 13, 78, 590
locality
capability, increased, 21
local consistency, 30
local contexts, 108–109
local contexts in Hearsay-II, 109
local control, 268
local control, evolutionary phases of, 269
local evaluation, 347
local evaluation in Contract Net, 348
local feasibility trees, 376
local knowledge, 373
local knowledge of relevance, 128
local plan, 287–288
local resource, knowledge about availability, 374
local states, changing, 398
local states function, 400
locally complete communication policy, 129, 277
location dimension, of knowledge, 125
location-centered cooperation, 617
lock
handler, 110
super, 109
locking, 109
node, 109
region, 109
locutionary speech acts, 173
Loftus, E. F., 393
logic, 321
logical, 10
deduction, 325
inconsistency, 29
omniscience, 15
London, P. E., 526
LOOPS, 480
lying, 292

M

MACE, 29, 33–34, 445
MACE agent description language, 448
MACH operating system, 452, 480
MacQueen, D., 398
maintaining shared representation, 599
Malone, Thomas, 20, 151, 233
management, 9
manager, 7, 339
manager, in Contract Net, 341, 358
manager, transaction, 558
managing communication, 23
manning resource use, 23
manning uncertainty, 23
Mann, W. C., 395
Mantalvo, Fanya, 328
March, James G., 151, 157
market, 148, 151

centralized, 153
decentralized, 153
marketlike organization, 20
mechanisms, 15
Marschak, J., 151
matrix structure, 127
McArthur, David, 102
McCarthy, John, 173, 192, 194, 319, 325
McDermott, Drew, 194, 200, 205–206
meaning, of communicative acts, 324
measurements on HEARSAY-II, 118
mediating acts, 175
merging, 542
meshing, by composition, 462
message delivery guaranteed, 334
message passing, 425, 434–435
message puzzle task (MPT), 72–73
message routing, 413
metalevel
    exchanging information, 6
    metacommunication structure, 385
    metadescription, 193
    metagoal of comprehension, 395
    metainformation, 125, 129
    metainformation, incomplete, 133
    metaknowledge, 566–567, 606
    metaknowledge certainty factors, 571
    metaknowledge update heuristics, in MINDS, 569
    metalevel architecture, 506, 526
    metalevel communication, 268, 277
    metalevel control, 611
    metalevel information, 24, 269
    metalevel knowledge, 608
    metalevel organization, 288
    metalevel organization, centralized, 291
    metamicrotheories, 325
metaphor, generating hypotheses by, 314
methods, solving decomposition problems, 13
Meyer, Robert, 367
MICRO-PLANNER, 319
microtheories, 321, 324
microtheories, conflicting, 324–325
Milner, Robin, 398, 405
MINDS, (Multiple Intelligent Node Document Servers), 566
minimal deal rationality, 229
minimal move rationality, 229
minimally connected subgraphs, 13
minimizing internode communication, 125
Minsky, Marvin, 319, 328, 386
misrepresentation, 292
model
    interaction of agents, 228
    of other agents, 22, 25
    of other organized activity, 25
    production-lattice, 29
modeling
    coordination, 151
    intentions of others, 91
    knowledge sources, 512

of other agents, 187
of plans, 172
other agents, 84, 161, 171, 238, 446
other agents' capabilities, 188
other agents' goals, 93
other agents' planning activities, 93
other agents' world model, 93
problem solving system behavior, 490–491
shared objects, 398
model-theoretic semantics, 215
modular control structures, 299
modular knowledge processing functions, 482
modularity and grain size, 338
modularization mechanisms, in ORIENT84/K, 426
monotonicity of knowledge, 312
Montague, R., 319
Moore, James, 18, 32, 385, 395
Moore, Robert, 185, 192, 233
MOP (Module-Oriented Programming), 459
Morgan, J., 185
Morgenstern, Leora, 192
Moses, Yoram, 233
most knowledgeable, least committed agent, selection policy for centralized tasks, 104
motivation, independent, of agents, 221
MSYS, 67, 121, 298
Mukhopadhyay, Uttam, 566
multiagent, 194
    activities, 599
    formalism, 187
    interaction, 227
    plan, 187, 192, 194, 197, 200–201, 205, 216, 606
    plan synthesizer, 204
    planning, 15, 21
    synchrony, 189
    system, 3
multidivision hierarchy, 149
multilayered learning system model, 573
multilevel blackboard system, 491
multilevel relaxation, 302
multiparty speech acts, 181
multiparty speech acts, plans for, 181
multiple
    belief spaces, 31
    best plan, 231
    control heuristics, 523
    control heuristics, integrating, 508
    data views, 409
    goals, 249, 256
    hypotheses, 126, 312
    languages, 451
    multiple-task planning, 505
    paths to solution, 299
    problem solvers, 344
    problem solvers, in ABCL/1, 440
    task planning, 513
    viewpoints, 317
    viewpoints, inheritance between, 318
    viewpoints, translation among, 318

multiple-task planning, 506, 511
multiprocessing
    environment, 561
    environment, closely coupled, 118
    implementation, 118
    knowledge based, 106
    problem-solving organization, 107
multisentential knowledge, 386
multistage negotiation, 367, 375
murmuring, 129, 137, 300
    communication, information distribution policy, 103
mutual
    aggregation of results, 68
    belief, 264
    belief space, 30, 250, 262
    commitment, 7, 321
    constraining partial solutions, 298
    plan construction, 22
    rationality, 223
    reinforcing partial solutions, 298
    restriction, 68
    selection, 347, 355, 358
    selection in Contract Net, 348

N

naive falsificationism, 315
natural systems approach, 4
naturalness, 9
NCS, 480
need for data distribution, 101
need for global view, 101
need for redundancy, 13
negotiation, 7, 32, 62, 64, 130, 227, 321, 333, 335, 339, 355, 357, 367, 375, 377, 380, 599, 607, 620
    an organizing principle, 333
    optimality of, 352
    policy, 413
    protocol, 368
    tradeoffs, 361
    unit, 620
    utility as interaction mechanism, 355
    utility of, 337, 357
NEOMYCIN, 527
network
    awareness, 25
    coherence, 268, 283
    configuration, 126
    configuration, selection, 137–138
    control, 268
    HEARSAY-II systems, 125
    HEARSAY-II systems, simulation, 131
    model, 287, 290
    model, example, 287
    problem solving, 120, 295
    responsibilities, 277
    versus centralized organization, 132
    views, 22

Newell, Allen, 107, 192, 319, 393
Newman, Denis, 22, 30, 185, 248
NeWS, 480
Newton, Isaac, 314
NFS, 480
Nii, Penny, 541
Nilsson, Nils, 173, 187–188, 192, 201
Nirenburg, Sergei, 590
NOAH, 192, 216, 302, 307, 309
    multiagent planning, 197
    world model of, 303
node
    abstraction, in Contract Net, 360
    architecture in DVMT, modified, 276
    available messages, in Contract Net, 362
    examining, 109
    plan, 285, 287–288
nomination, in dialogue games, 393
non-conflicting goals, 227
non-hierarchical organization, 73
NONLIN, 192, 600
nonlocal interaction, 68
Norman, Donald, 389

O

object-centered
    autonomous architectures, 90–91
    cooperative architectures, 90, 93
object-oriented
    modeling of knowledge systems, 425
    programming, 434
    systems, 425, 434
obtaining global information, 305
ODYSSEY system, 582
OFFICE, 590
office, 599
    representing an, 592
    semantics, 578
    support for, 581
    work, 321, 599
    work as problem solving, 578
    work, characteristics of, 579
    work, description, 578–579
    worker problem-solving, 578
offices, 321, 566, 590
OIL, 34
OMEGA, 319
    a knowledge embedding language, 578
    contradiction handling in, 583
    knowledge system, 588
omniscient alien problem, 224
OMS, 601
on-demand communication, information distribution policy, 103
open problems, 35
open system, 3, 7, 33, 321, 404
    characteristics, 321, 404
    composition in, 405

continuous availability, 404
extensibility, 404
modularity, 404
observation equivalence, 405–406
OPM, 505, 518, 521, 529
opportunistic
connection, 7
information gathering, 136
planning, 533
problem solving, 122, 298
opportunity, first-mover, 147
OPS-5, 430, 548
option multiplicity, 99–100
O'Reilly C., 413
organization, 6, 20, 151, 448
anarchic committee, 71
application structure of, 578
as a community with rules of behavior, 20
authority structure, 20
broadcast, 291
centralized, 20
centralized metalevel, 291
centralized versus network, 132
changes, 73
complexity of, 151
contracting, 146
design, 151
design, and FA/C model, 304
design strategies, 304
design, theory of, 149
dynamic hierarchical cone (DHC), 74
flat, 73
functional decomposition, 146
global centralized node, 81
HEARSAY-II, 107
hierarchical, 20, 71, 279
human, 140, 151
increases coherent cooperation, 272
lateral, 279
location-centered cooperative, 617
manager, 448
manager agent, 446
marketlike, 20
multiprocessing problem solving, 107
non-hierarchical, 73
of distributed systems, 120
person in, 579
problem solving, 117
product decomposition, 146
refinement of, 275
self-design, 6, 25, 99, 305, 307
structure, 149, 308
structure and flexibility, 157
structure, flat, 127
structure, hierarchical, 127
structure, matrix, 127
structure, selection, 137
structure, size of, 156
theory, 74, 84, 136, 140, 149, 303

unilevel network of communicating nodes, 81
unilevel network of noncommunicating nodes, 81
organizational
adaptability, 25
analysis, 141
architecture, 617
behavior, 84
goals, 578
information systems, foundations for, 328
knowledge, 6, 28
knowledge, representation, 28
policies, 105
policies in air-traffic control, 104
policy, 102–104
problem solving, 578
roles, 15
self design, 295
structure, 148, 268, 273, 286
structure, experiments with, 273
structuring, 103
structuring, empirical results for, 275
view of distributed systems, 140
ORIENT84/K, 34, 425
modularization mechanisms, 426
structure of, 428
OSI, 476
overconstrained problems, 367
overconstrained situation, 368–369
overlapping
configurations, 280
configurations, experiments with, 281
hierarchical structure, 127
nodes, 269
roles, 14

P

Papert, Seymour, 319
paradigm-specific shells, 33
parallel
AI, 3
execution of cooperating expert systems, 412
hardware environment, 106
process model, 207
processors, 451
relaxation, 302
successive approximation, 302
virtual machine, 452, 456
parallelism
effective, 113
in artificial intelligence, 106
inherent, 399
large-scale, 398
partial control plan, 514
partial global plan, 6, 22, 29–30, 285, 288
framework for coordination, 292
goals (PGGs), 287
implicit, 286

principal planning activities, 290
partial interpretations, 122
partial solution, 270
  alternative, 299
  coordination of, 299
  mutually constraining, 298
  mutually reinforcing, 298
partially ordered hierarchical planning, 300
Parunak, Van Dyke, 7, 35
pattern-directed invocation, 66, 319, 363, 434
Pavlin, Jasmina, 29
payoff function, 151
payoff matrix, 221–222, 228
people, 599
perception, 9
performance analysis of HEARSAY-II multiprocessing, 110
performance measures for air-traffic control, 105
performatives, 173
perlocutionary speech acts, 173
permanence of transaction, 557
Perrault, C. Raymond, 18, 169, 185, 188
persistence, 212, 561
persistence, law of, 212
person, organizational, 579
personality profile (of assisted agents), 597
person-machine
  cooperation, 190, 590
  coordination, 4
  experiments, 72
  interaction, 166
phrase-structure grammar-based communication protocol, 609
Pilot's Associate, 467
plan
  alternative, 372
  based theory of speech acts, 169
  centered architectures, 90, 96
  commitment, 377
  critic, 604
  formal description of, 216
  fragment, 373–374
  hierarchical, 600
  in POISE, 591
  interacting, 22, 248
  knowledge, 27
  models of, 172
  modification, 265
  node, 285
  partial global, 285
  restoral, 370
PLANNER, 5, 319, 349, 360
  recommendation list, 349
  theorem base filter construct, 349
planning, 21
  activities, principal in PGPs, 290
  algorithm, 249
  communication act, 188
  communications, 18
  hierarchical, 13
  simulation based, 622

PLASMA, 34
pluralism, 24, 311
PMC (Procedural Module Control), 473
point of view principle, 183
point of view principle, for defining speech acts, 180
POISE, 591, 602
policy
  information distribution, 102
  negotiation, 413
  organizational, 102
POLYMER, 599
  knowledge structures, 604
  system architecture, 600–601
Popper, Karl, 311, 314–315
possible plans, in speech acts, 170
possible worlds, 187, 192
Pratt, V. R., 398
Pratt's process model, 398
precedent, 324
predictions, 78
preemptible state, 415
price, 148
price-system, 149
prioritizing tasks, 15
prisoner's dilemma, 225, 231
problem decomposition, 63, 305, 606–607, 611
Problem solution graph, 29
problem solving, 321
  agenda-based, 491
  as search process, 299
  behavior of scientific communities, 311
  control errors, 490, 500
  graph, 610
  mechanism, language as, 395
  networks, larger, 279
  process knowledge, 27
  support paradigm, in office work, 580
  with simulation in air-traffic control, 622
problems, overconstrained, 367
procedural control, 462
procedural description methodology, in office work, 579
procedural net, 600
process
  concept, 210
  control function, 206
  knowledge, problem solving, 27
  model, 205–206, 209, 385
  model, formal definition, 206
  model, parallel, 207
  model, Pratt's, 398
Process Assembly Network (PAN), 72, 80, 82
processor utilization, 113
procrastination, 165
product
  decomposition, in organizations, 146
  hierarchy, 151–152
production costs, 151
production system, 5, 393, 547
  architecture, 528

production-lattice models, 29
programming languages for concurrent systems, 399
project team, 440
PROLOG, 425
proponent, 30, 314
proposer, 30, 314
Proteus, 393
protocol
    Contract Net, 7, 18, 26, 340, 342
    high level, 377
    negotiation, 368
    transaction, 558
PUP6, 161
    control in, 164

Q

QA-4, 319
qualitative reasoning, 491

R

Radner, R., 151
Ramamritham, K., 7, 35
range restriction, 67
Rapoport, A., 233
rationales, agent modeling, 26
rationales for Distributed AI, 8
rationality
    action, 16
    agents, 227
    basic, 220, 222
    bounded, 141, 143
    deal characteristics, 229
    decision making, 618
    general, 224
    minimal deal, 229
    minimal move, 229
    mutual, 223
    offer groups, 228
    separate deal, 229
    separate move, 229
    unique deal, 229
    unique move, 229
reaction function, 222
real-time communication, 243
real-time operation, 483
real-time planning, 523
reasoning about
    action, 192, 367
    communication, 608
    contradiction, 587
    DVMT behavior, 494
    events, 205
    plans, 192
    reasoning, 586
receptionist actor, 400

recognizing disparities, 30
recommendation list in PLANNER, 349
reconciling disparities, 31
reconciling independent decisions, 507, 522
record keeping, 165
record making, 324
recursive allocation, 15
reduced internode communication bandwidth, 137
reduced specification of an action, 208
redundancy, 83, 93, 133
    need for, 13
    proper levels of, 590
Reed, Scott, 305
referential transparency, 400, 413
refinement of organization, 275
reflection, 78, 193, 297, 306, 324, 521, 607
refuting theories, 314
region examining, 109
Reiter, Raymond, 325
relativized belief, 317
relaxation, 67, 300
    multilevel, 302
    paradigm, 128
    parallel, 302
reliability, 9, 14, 305
repeated transmission communication, information distribution policy, 103
replacement actor, 400
report in Contract Net, 341
representation
    frame-based, 602
    of actions, 215
    of actions as sequences of states, 200
    of beliefs and goals of others, 187
    of capabilities of others, 187
    of control knowledge, 28
    of disparities, 30
    of events, 210
    of organizational knowledge, 28
representation of activities, 599
representing activities, 602
REQUEST, 188
request
    and information messages, in Contract Net, 362
    as communication, 323
    configuration, 251
    definition of speech act, 175
    inform, 169
    request, 169
    response mechanism, 342
    speech act, 184–185
request-response activity, 127
requires-cb-analysis state, 415
resolution
    conflict, configuration, 252
    data uncertainties, 297
    mechanisms, for error, 299
    uncertainty, 295

resource
    allocation, 14–15, 304, 315, 357, 441
    constraints, 140
    consumption, 14
    control, in scientific communities, 312
    definition, 413
    limitations, 9
    management, 590
    management techniques, in ACT3, 404
    manager, 414
    minimization, 13
    shared, 11
resources, 9
resources, slack, 146
responsibility and authority structure, 595
restoral plan, 370
result
    description in Contract Net, 341
    sharing, 61, 66, 352
    synthesis, 606
reusability, 478
reuse of software components, 464
Rieger, C., 386
Robert Wesson, 59
robot planning, 606
robustness, 130
role, 7, 29, 33, 103, 250, 258, 446
    of agents (POISE), 591
    organizational, 15
Rosenschein, Jeffrey, 18, 187, 220, 227, 292, 611
Rosenthal, R., 388
routine
    communication, 83
    interaction, 16
rule agents, 449
rule-based blackboards, 547
rules, for dialogues, 386
Rulifson, Jeff, 319
Rumelhart, D. E., 386, 389

S

S.1, 480
SAA, 476
Sacerdoti, Earl, 192, 300, 302
Sacks, H., 386
SADT, 476
safety analysis, 202
Sandell, Nils R., 236
satisfaction of intentions, configuration, 251
satisficing man, 618
satisficing solutions, 368
DVMT, 6
HEARSAY-II, 275
Schank, Roger, 249, 386
scheduling
    knowledge, dynamic, 595
    knowledge, local and global, 595
    mechanism, 518

    mechanism, in blackboard architecture, 510
Schegloff, E. A., 386
scientific community, 7, 30
scientific community metaphor, 24, 311
scope, of information, 123
scratch pad, 617
    centralized, 617, 624
    distributed, 617, 625
script, 8, 249, 386, 401
    modification, 249, 258, 260
search, and FA/C approach, 298
Searle, J., 169, 386, 395
selection
    and focusing of KS's, 125
    in communication, information distribution policy, 103
    mutual, 347
    policy for centralized tasks, least spatially constrained, 104
    policy for centralized tasks, most knowledgeable, least committed agent, 104
    policy for centralized tasks, shared convention, 104
self
    containment, 157
    correction, 137
    monitoring, 78
    partitioning, 607
    reference, 324, 521
    self-containment, as organization design strategy, 304
    self-correcting behavior, 299
    self-directed node activity, 297
    self-directed nodes, 306
semantic distance, 10
semantics of control, 506
send-all communication policy, 277
separate deal rationality, 229
separate move rationality, 229
separate realities, 262
sequence
    for dialogues, 386
    of states, representing actions as, 200
sequencing operators, 187
serializability, 558
shared
    blackboard-like data facility, 118
    convention, selection policy for centralized tasks, 104
    memory environment, 117
    objects, models of, 398
    resources, 11, 399
    resources, management, 413
shared responsibilities, 599
Shibayama, Etsuya, 434
short-term coordination with abstraction, 243
SIAP, 121
SIGOP-II, 301
similar bargainers assumption, 224
Simon, Herbert, 141, 151, 157, 303, 319
simple hierarchy, 149
simulation, 71, 91
    based planning, 617, 622
    distributed system, 383

event driven, 130
    HEARSAY-II, 110
    model, 110
    problem solving with, in air-traffic control, 622
    system behavior, 492
simultaneous
    action, 194, 207, 210
    events, 210
single-transmission communication, information distribution policy, 103
singly connected teams, 238
SIPE, 600
situated process, 328
situated social action, 321
situation assessment, 71
situational complexity, 99, 101
size of organization structure, 156
skeletal systems, 481
skeptic, 30, 314
skill, 33, 446
slack resources, 78, 146
    organization design strategy, 304
SMALLTALK, 425, 458
Smith, Brian C., 525
Smith, James, 7
Smith, Reid, 29, 32, 61, 78, 136, 148, 220, 233, 285, 307, 333, 357, 434, 592, 607
social
    action, situated, 321
    actions, of computer systems, 321
    episode, 249, 257
    episode, initiation, 257
    protocols, 197
sociology, 84
software, heterogeneous, 478
solution
    -based focusing, 526
    construction graph, 288–289
    intervals, 510
    partial, 270
    space density, 99, 101
sophisticated scheduler, 525
space-centered architectures, 90, 94
span of control problem, 72, 77
spatial distance, 9
spatiotemporal interconnectivity of knowledge, 323
specialization, 9, 100, 157
speech act, 17, 169–170, 173, 188, 199, 323–324, 396
    competence theory, 170
    convince, 184
    indirect, 174
    inform, 176, 184–185
    modeling, 169
    multiparty, 181
    request, 175, 184–185
    Searle's, 174
    theory, 395–396
speech recognition, 453
speed, 9

sponsor agents, 16
sponsors, 161, 315, 586
spreading activation, 128, 393
sprite, 312, 581, 587
Sproull, R. F., 148
stagnation measures, 130
standard structure of agents, 161
standardization, 33
standards for behavior, no absolute, 491
Star, Leigh, 328
Stasz, Cathleen, 71
state matching, 498
state, preemptible, 415
state, requires-cb-analysis, 415
state transition diagrams, hierarchical, 492
static teams, 239
Steeb, Randall, 18, 20, 23, 102, 285
Steele, Guy L., 582
Stephens, Larry, 566, 606
stochastic optimal control problems, 236
stopping rule for comprehension, 395
story
    analysis, 253
    comprehension, 248
    recalls, 386
    schema, 386
Stoy, Joseph E., 400
strategy
    cooperation, 102
    decisions, 515
    incremental communication, 129
    planning, 532
streams, 398
STRIPS, 173, 188, 192, 200, 611
    assumption, 201, 211
    representation, 214
    assumption, 204
Stuart, Christopher, 216
subcontract, 340
subgroups, 62
substantiating theories, 314
subtask aggregation, 13
successive approximation, 300
successive approximation, parallel, 302
Suchman, L., 579
sufficiency
    control strategy, 122
    credibility evaluation, 122
    knowledge, 122
Sunshine, Carl A., 71
supervisory nodes, 97
Symbolics Genera, 458
synchronization, 187, 200, 220
    plans, 216–217
    reduced need, 299
    techniques, interagent, 413
    in COPS, 553
synergistic cooperation, 163
synthesized distributed system, 125, 297

system behavior model (SBM), 492
system design frameworks (SDFs), 481
system topologies, analysis of, 246

T

Talukdar, Sarosh N., 547
task
    abstraction, 342
    abstraction, in Contract Net, 66, 359
    allocation, 7, 14, 151
    allocation heuristics, 89
    announcement, 7, 340, 343, 359
    assignment, appropriate, 353
    assignment, optimal, 102–103
    centralization, 104
    complexity, 140, 145
    coordination, 141
    coordination problems, 102
    coverage, 102
    decomposition, 7, 77, 103, 121, 304
    distribution, 32, 333, 357
    environment, air-traffic control, 618
    hierarchy, 345
    message, 282
    performance assessment, 324
    processing procedures, in Contract Net, 365
    sharing, 339, 355
    sharing policy, 104
    specification, in Contract Net, 360
task-allocation decisions, 14
task-centered perspective, 590
tasking protocols, 77
task-oriented perspective, 591
task-sharing, 61, 64, 357
Tate, Austin, 192
taxonomy of how organizational types, 20
team
    singly connected, 238
    static, 239
    theory, 151
temporal chaining strategy, 524
temporal distance, 9
temporal representation, 193
Tenney, Robert R., 236
Terasaki, A. K., 392
termination message in Contract Net, 341
terminological interconnectivity of knowledge, 323
TEST, 481
theorem base filter construct in PLANNER, 349
theory of action, 192–193, 205, 211, 216
Thorndyke, Perry, 606
threats, 292
time constraint, 99–100, 507
time-constrained decisions, in Contract Net, 360
timeliness, of information, 123
Tokoro, Mario, 34, 425
tool to build experty systems, 547

tools for DAI, 33
topic of dialogue, 387
traffic control, 72, 295, 300–301
transaction, 557–558, 560
    analysis, 141, 144, 147
    manager, 558, 561
    transactional blackboard, 557
    transactional blackboard architecture, 561
    transactional constructs, in ACT3, 404
transactions in negotiation, 380
translation among multiple viewpoints, 318
truth maintenance system, 31, 582
Turing, Alan, 319
TWEAK, 192
types of speech act, 173

U

unacknowledged communication, information distribution policy, 103
uncertainty, 13, 67, 140–141, 144, 149
    algorithmic, 144
    avoidance, 14
    behavioral, 144, 148
    control, 270, 297
    distribution-caused, 297
    environmental, 144
    informational, 147
    interagent disparities, 29
    organization structure, 304
    problem-solving, 297
    reduction, data pooling, 99
    reduction techniques, 147
    resolution of, 299
    resolving, in data, 297
    using it to gain local autonomy, 238
uniform composability, 462
unilevel network of communicating nodes, 81
unilevel network of noncommunicating nodes, 81
unique deal rationality, 229
unique move rationality, 229
unique node, 338
uniqueness avoidance, 13
units, goal oriented, 386
UNIX, 459
unsolicited communication, information distribution policy, 103
Update-To-Do-Set, 518–519
urgency, 14
utility function, 221
utility of negotiation, 357

V

value, 9
variable grain-size control heuristics, 507, 522
vertical information processing, as organization design strategy, 304
vertical integration, 148

viewpoint, 19, 317, 319, 581
    contradiction handling with, 582
    mechanism, in OMEGA, 588
virtual machine, 451
virtual plan, 249, 259, 263, 266
    embedding of, 259
VISIONS, 121
VLSI design, 606
voting, 15
VULCAN, 34
vulnerability
    cost, 151
    organization, 157

W

Wand, I., 413

WANT, 172, 185
Wesson, Robert, 20, 29, 71
Weyhrauch, Richard, 325
Wilensky, Robert, 525
Wilkins, D. E., 200, 601
willing entities, cooperative behavior among, 334
Winston, Patrick H., 163
work, 9
worker, 7
world model, 84, 92, 575
    NOAH, 303

Y

Yang, Ju-Yuan David, 606
yes/no questions, planning, 180
Yonezawa, Akinori, 34, 434